THE GRUMMAN AMPHIBIANS

– GOOSE, WIDGEON & MALLARD –

FRED J.KNIGHT

with COLIN R.SMITH

Air-Britain

Published in the United Kingdom by

Air-Britain (Historians) Ltd

Regd Office:
Victoria House, Stanbridge Park,
Staplefield Lane, Staplefield,
West Sussex RH17 6AS, England

Sales Dept:
41 Penshurst Road, Leigh,
Tonbridge, Kent TN11 8HL, England

Membership Enquiries:
Barry J. Collman,
1 Rose Cottages, 179 Penn Road,
Hazlemere, Bucks. HP15 7NE, England

Correspondence regarding this book to:
Fred J. Knight
Email: fredjknight@tiscali.co.uk

ISBN 978-0-85130-440-3

Printed in the UK
by Henry Ling Limited
at The Dorset Press
Dorchester
DT1 1HD

Origination by Howard Marks
Cover origination by Sue Bushell

Front Cover:

*John Kimberley's fine shot of the MacMillan-Bloedel Goose
aircraft, C-FIOL, "Dryad" and C-FHUZ, "Dryad II", during high-
speed taxying for a company photo shoot in British Columbia,
in August 1994.*

Back Cover:

*Top: The Texas Company's Mallard N2948, c/n J-11, showing the
aircraft's sleek lines.* *(Harold G Martin)*

*Bottom: Halter Yachts Inc's G-44A, N86627, c/n 1453, taxying on
Clear Lake, California in October 1985.* *(John Wegg)*

CONTENTS

Leroy Randle Grumman 1895 – 1982.

(Grumman photo)

Introduction

When Leroy Grumman and the board of the Grumman Aircraft Engineering Corporation took the decision to start production of the G-21 Grey Goose in 1937, little could they have known that this would lead to the production of four twin-engined amphibian models with a total production of almost 1,200 aircraft, extending over nearly twenty five years. They certainly could not have imagined that seventy five years later many of these aircraft would still be flying.

The majority of the 345 Gooses built were delivered to the military, but many were sold on as surplus at the end of WWII and enjoyed long careers, providing local airline service and personal transport for business executives and sportsmen, this latter use being precisely what the aircraft was initially designed for.

The G-44 Widgeon was designed in 1940, as a smaller version of the Goose, to suit small businesses, hunters and fishermen, but it also found favour with the military and saw service throughout WWII. The improved G-44A Widgeon was built solely for the post-war civilian market, but even a handful of these saw some military use.

In 1944 Grumman initiated the design of a much larger amphibian for the US Navy as a replacement for the JRF Goose. The G-64 Albatross was to remain in production until 1960, with some 464 aircraft being delivered to military customers worldwide, and this robust warplane will be the subject of a second volume in this series.

In 1946, Grumman decided that a scaled-up Goose would make a suitable third-level airliner for the post-war recovery that the industry felt was sure to come. However, with so many war-surplus twin-engined aircraft available at a lower cost, the G-73 Mallard did not attract too many customers. With the onset of the Korean War and with substantial Albatross contracts to fulfil, Grumman decided to close the Mallard production line in May 1951, because of poor sales and a general reluctance to use scarce aluminium to build luxury air yachts. Thus only 59 Mallards were built, nearly all of which were for wealthy businessmen and sportsmen. Eventually though, Leroy Grumman's dream of Mallards in airline service was realised, if only temporarily.

Given the romance of, and fascination with, water-borne aircraft it is perhaps surprising that Grumman's amphibian twins have previously received relatively little attention from aviation authors. In this volume we have endeavoured to fully document the history of each of the 721 Goose, Widgeon and Mallard airframes produced between 1937 and 1951, after licence production of the G-44 had ceased at the SCAN factory in France, and the Mallard production line had closed at Bethpage, on Long Island. Because, for various reasons, not all the official documentation is available it is recognised that some questions remain unanswered.

Inevitably, facts, photographs and explanations will surface after publication, but this volume should nevertheless provide all Grumman enthusiasts with a detailed history of these fine aircraft, surpassing anything published hitherto.

Acknowledgements

This book would not have been possible without the help of many individuals. My particular thanks go to my co-author, Colin R Smith, who added much to the story of the military use of the Grumman amphibians, and to Peter J Marson, who has done a sterling job as my editor.

The staff at the Grumman History Center, now the Northrop Grumman History Center, have provided willing assistance over the years. My special thanks go to "Schoney" Schonenberg, Lois Lovisolo and Larry Feliu.

My thanks also to David H Marion, of Antilles Seaplanes, who provided access to the archives of McKinnon Enterprises Inc, allowing a valuable insight into the complicated history of the turbine Goose conversions.

The excellent drawings were provided by Mike Zoeller, to whom my special thanks.

The many others, from around the world, who have provided help in varying measures are listed below: Will Alcott, Tony Arbon, Bill ("Mr Widgeon") Bailey, Fred Ball, Peter Berry, Martin Best, John Bradley, Dennis Buehn, Mick Burrow, Phil Butler, Chris Chatfield, Jacques Chillon, Noel Collier, Barry Collman, Capt James Cothron, Alan Cowdrey, Mark R Cranston (aerofotoworld), Stephen Darke, John M Davis, David Daw, Raymond Deerness, Guy Denton, Nigel Dingley, Wade Dorsey, Tony Doyle, Jean-Pierre Dubois, Carlos Dufriche, Ron Durand, Graham C Evans, Malcolm P Fillmore, Edwin E Forsberg, Ken Freeze, J P Fu, Peter Gerhardt, José Luis González Serrano, Jennifer Gradidge, Duncan Grant, John Gregory, Kay Hagby, Dan Hagedorn, William Haines, Steven T Hamilton, William Harrison, Owen Harnish, Noam Hartoch, Steve Harvey, John Havers, Karl Hayes, Leif Hellström, Patrick-Xavier Henry, Coen van den Heuvel, Peter Hillman, Lee Howard, Hagel Jarlevik, Petur P Johnson, Terry Judge, Phillippe Jung, Leon Kaplan, Henk C Kavelaars, George Kernahan, John Kimberley, Ingvar Klett, Marc Koelich, Steve Krauss, Art Kreiger, William T Larkins, Dr Joe Leeker, Fred Lynn, Andy Marden, Timothy R Martin, Ian MacDonald, Jack McNulty, Andrew Merrifield, Ken Molson, John Mounce, Terry Murphy, Sid Nansen, David Neufeld, Michael Ody, Paul Oelkrug, Jorge Nunez Padin, Dave Parker (British Columbia Museum), Robert Parmerter, Marco Pennings, Philip Perry, Brian Pickering (Military Aircraft Photos [MAP]), Mervyn Prime, Johan Ragay, Ragnar J Ragnarsson, Eino Ritaranta, Matthew E Rodina Jr, Álvaro Romero, Douglas Rough, Capt Dick Sanders, Tony Sapienza, Paul Silbermann (Smithsonian Institute), Tom Singfield, Colin M Smith, Russ Smith, Timothy Smith, Vic Smith, Charles H Spurgeon, Carlton A Stidsen (NE Air Museum), Baldur Sveinsson, Luis Tavares, Barrie Towey, Capt Archie Vanhee, Peter Vercruijsse, Jerry Vernon, Patrick Vinot-Préfontaine, Aad van der Voet, David Vornholt, Andrew Wade, Paul Wakefield, John Wegg, Ann Whyte (Pan American Airways), Dave Wilton, John Woods, Philip Yeadon.

Lastly, but not least, I must thank my long-suffering wife, Anne, who has endured many years of my talking nothing but Grummans!

Fred J. Knight
October, 2013

First flown on 24th April 1933 as the XJF-1 (Grumman Design number G-7) for the United States Navy, the single-engined Grumman Duck amphibian was the biplane predecessor of Grumman's successful twin-engined monoplane amphibians, the Goose, Widgeon, Mallard and Albatross and confirmed Grumman's reputation in this field. First delivered as the JF-1 and JF-2 to the US Navy and US Coast Guard respectively (Grumman Designs G-9), further development and upgrading resulted in the J2F-1 to J2F-6, production of the latter being resumed under licence by the Columbia Aircraft Corporation from 1942 to 1945.

Illustrations show: (top left) the prototype XJF-1 Duck BuAer 9218 and (top right) a JF-1 BuAer 9436 for the United States Navy and (centre) the last of a batch of 80 J2F-6s licence-built by Columbia, former BuAer 33614 survived to see several civilian owners post-war and was photographed at Leticia, Colombia in January 1977 as N55S. Bottom: This unique formation of three of Grumman's twin-engined amphibians, G-44A Widgeon NC86635, an unidentified US Navy JRF Goose and G-73 Mallard probably NC2948 was set up circa 1947 by Grumman's Publicity Department (for a further view of this unique formation, see page 80). (Top: both DM Hannah Collection. Middle: Stephen Piercey. Bottom: Harold G Martin)

The Grumman 'A' float was the company's first aircraft-related product, seen here fitted to a Vought O2U-4 Corsair in 1930.   (Grumman photo 585)

CHAPTER 1: ORIGINS

THE GRUMMAN AIRCRAFT ENGINEER-ING CORPORATION was formed on 5th December, 1929. The Chairman of the Board was Leroy (later known as Roy) Randle Grumman who had been born in Huntingdon, New York on 4th January, 1895. His father George, of a Scots-Irish family who emigrated to America in the mid-seventeenth century, was a carriage builder and no doubt inspired the young Grumman to an interest in things mechanical. Indeed, after graduating from Long Island High School, Grumman received a Bachelor of Science degree in Mechanical Engineering from Cornell University in 1916.

After the United States of America entered World War I, Roy Grumman enlisted in the US Navy Reserve in June 1917. After spells at Columbia University, the Massachusetts Institute of Technology (MIT) (for ground training) and then at Miami and Pensacola in Florida (learning to fly), he graduated in September 1918, as Naval Aviator No.1216, and was commissioned as Ensign, and later as a pilot instructor, at the Naval Air Training School, Pensacola.

In 1919, after an aeronautical engineering course at MIT, Grumman was transferred to the League Island Naval Yard, on the Delaware River near Philadelphia, where he was the acceptance test-pilot for flying boats built by the Curtiss Aeroplane Company, and also for those built by the Navy. At the same time Grumman acted as Project Engineer for the Loening M-8 monoplanes which were also being built in the Navy yard. The M-8 was the result of a request to design a two-seat fighter that would better the British-built Bristol Fighter. The resultant monoplane was considered a daring innovation in a world of biplanes. Its designer, Grover C Loening, was guided by a strong belief in the inherent speed advantages and simplicity of construction of a monoplane as opposed to a biplane. The United States Navy, after ordering 47 M-8s, ordered six aircraft designated M-8-1S to be con-figured as twin-float seaplanes, and at least one of these was fitted with amphibious floats featuring retractable wheels – the shape of things to come!

Grover Loening frequently visited the Navy yard with his brother, Albert, and they became interested in the progress Roy Grumman was making as an engineer, and in his ability as a test-pilot. They offered him a job and in October 1920 Grumman resigned his naval commission and joined the Loening Aeronautical Engineering Corporation in New York as a test-pilot on amphibian types, including the OL-, OA- and the Air Yacht. He soon became General Manager of the company which was headquartered on the East River at 31st Street.

Because of the lull in aviation activity after the Armistice of 1918, financial institutions were tiring of aeronautical stocks by the early 1920s and were seeking ways of making more profit. One solution was to merge small companies to produce larger more efficient, and hopefully more profitable, ones. Lindbergh's transatlantic flight in May 1927 provided a further spur, and thus in 1928 the Loening Company was bought by the banking firm of Hayden, Stone & Company, which already had a financial interest in the Curtiss Wright Company. Part of the deal was that Loening would be absorbed by the Keystone Aircraft Company and move from New York to the Keystone plant in Bristol, Pennsylvania. Another condition of the deal was that the Loening brothers could not form another company in competition with their old one.

Move to Pennsylvania or face unemployment: that was the choice, and Roy Grumman decided that neither was what he wanted. He had a young family and a nice home on Long Island, where he could enjoy his favourite pastime of sailing. Nor did he want to become a "nonentity" in a large corporation. So after discussions with Leon A "Jake" Swirbul, the factory manager, and William T "Bill" Schwendler, the assistant plant manager, they decided to form their own aircraft company. Roy Grumman mortgaged his house, Jake Swirbul persuaded his mother to borrow $6,000, and although the Loening brothers were not permitted to participate in the new company they did decide to help finance it. Edmund Poor, Loening Aircraft's assistant treasurer also agreed to invest in, and work for, the fledgling enterprise. EC "Clint" Towl, a boyhood friend of Ed Poor who had studied engineering at Cornell University and later had experience in the world of stock-broking also agreed to invest on the condition that he was also given a job. On 5th December 1929 the six investors in the new company, Leroy Grumman, Albert & Grover Loening, Ed Poor, Leon Swirbul and Clinton Towl signed a subscription agreement affirming two classes of stock: a 7% preferred at $100 par value, and a $25 par value common stock. On the following day, the Grumman Aircraft Engineering Corporation was incorporated and set up at Baldwin, on Long Island, New York.

The company's first premises were uninspiring – a rented building of 11,465 square feet that had been used previously by the Cox-Klemin Aircraft Company, situated on Railroad Avenue, Baldwin. More recently used as a car garage/showroom, it was now semi-derelict with broken windows and piles of oak leaves on the floor. One of those who helped sweep up the leaves was young Clint Towl who could not possibly have dreamt that one day he would become Chairman of the Board of the Grumman Corporation.

The company's most precious asset was its personnel, and they were of the best. During the 1920s aircraft design and construction slowly changed from an art to a technology. Immigrant artisans who fled Europe before and after World War I plied their trades in the aircraft shops of the eastern United States of America, and the Loening Company employed its fair share of them. Some of Loening's skilled workers decided to remain nearer to New York on Long Island, and work for Grumman rather than move south to Pennsylvania with Loening/ Keystone.

The first of these was Joseph A Stamm, who was appointed purchasing agent and company secretary in December 1929 (the latter post held by him until 1966) and by 2nd January 1930 a work force of 15 began aircraft repair activities using spares

that were also acquired from the old Loening plant.

A Loening Air Yacht repair and a Loening Commuter rebuild, the latter producing a good profit, were among the first contracts, but were not enough to keep the team fully employed, so it was decided that non-aviation activities would fill the gaps. Using their metal-working skills the Grumman team built aluminium truck bodies and trailers for the Motor Haulage Corporation, a diversification that became an important part of the business for the rest of the century.

Grumman's first aviation product was an amphibious float to be fitted to the United States Navy's Vought O2U-4 Corsair observation biplanes. This was the Grumman Model A float of 1930, of which eight were delivered. So successful was it that in 1931 the Navy ordered the slimmer Model B floats for the Vought O3U-1 Corsair observation biplanes. 15 Model B floats were delivered in 1932. The Model A and B floats were later re-designated as Design G-1 and G-2, respectively. A fuller explanation of Grumman Design Numbers is given in Appendix 9.

Design No.3 was a 1930 proposal for a parasol monoplane amphibian for the United States Coast Guard, with twin engines and tail fins. It remained only a proposal however, and was not built.

The first aircraft designed and built by Grumman was the XFF-1 (Design G-5) two-seat biplane fighter. Ordered by the US Navy in March 1931, it flew on 29th December that year. A further contract was awarded for a reconnaissance version, designated XSF-1 (Design G-6). These orders, with the hope of a production contract to follow, highlighted the need for bigger premises, preferably on an airport site. The temporary solution was a move to

a factory at Valley Stream on Long Island, adjacent to Curtiss Field. These facilities were only leased and by the end of 1932 the Grumman Aircraft Engineering Corporation had moved again - this time to Farmingdale on Long Island. The company had also won a contract for the XJF-1 (Design G-7) amphibian biplane, their third aircraft type; and an order for twenty-seven FF-1 fighters.

By the end of 1935 JF-1 and JF-2 (Design G-9) amphibians were being delivered to the US Navy and US Coast Guard, respectively. The F2F-1 (Design G-8) biplane fighter was in production and the XF3F-1 (Design G-11) biplane fighter prototype had flown.

In 1936, having received an order for eight (Design G-20) Duck amphibians from the Argentine government (their first export contract), and with F3F-1 fighters and J2F-1 (Design G-15) amphibians being delivered to the US Navy, Grumman bought 120 acres of land in Bethpage. The site, alongside the Long Island Railroad, provided room for future expansion, and an aerodrome. The first phase was the building of Plant No.1 which was completed in April 1937 with a floor area of almost 65,000 square feet.

In the meantime, work had begun on Design No.21 – Grumman's first twin-engined aircraft, and on 29th May 1937 the G-21 Goose amphibian became the first new aircraft to fly at Bethpage. It was also the first Grumman monoplane to fly, beating Design G-18, the XF4F-2 Wildcat, by a little over three months, and the first in a line of twin-engined amphibian aircraft built by Grumman, mainly to military contracts, but also for civil use, all of which served with distinction in many parts of the world. Their story is described in the following pages.

Grumman's Design No.3 proposal for the US Coast Guard in 1930, which was not built.   *(Grumman photo)*

A busy scene at Bethpage showing the initial stages of the G-21 Goose hull construction, circa July 1937. (Grumman photo)

Chapter 2:
G-21 Goose Development

As we have seen, the G-21 story began in the 1920s when Leroy Grumman was working for Grover Loening at the Loening Aeronautical Engineering Corporation in New York. It was during his time there that Grumman developed his penchant for amphibious aircraft, and his JF-1 Duck design of 1933 owed much to the earlier Loening XO2L-2. The Grumman-Loening partnership suffered a temporary set-back when Loening, having sold his own company and put his money into the new Grumman company, decided to take Leroy Grumman to court for patent infringements relating to his ingenious retracting landing gear design. Loening did very well out of this action for he settled out of court for $25,000 and was also awarded a three-year contract as a Grumman consultant. In Grumman's favour, however, was the fact that he had free access to Loening's expertise in amphibian design.

The stage was set, and from that point on the G-21 Goose was a product of circumstance, or perhaps even an engineered meeting of circumstance. On the one hand was an aircraft manufacturer who up to that time had only produced military aircraft but had an eye on the civil market; while on the other hand was a growing number of wealthy businessmen and sportsmen wanting a versatile personal transport aircraft in which to commute from their homes to their places of work. In some cases this meant from a Long Island estate to a waterfront Wall Street office on New York's East River.

Some of these people, who had previously operated Loening Air Yachts or similar aircraft to perform that task, now formed a syndicate and hired Grover Loening to suggest a suitable replacement aircraft for their needs. Loening agreed to design such an aircraft and soon arrived at a specification for the syndicate's commuter - a high-wing monoplane amphibian featuring a fully retractable undercarriage and twin engines to give ample power reserves. Of course, he advised the syndicate, led by Wilton Lloyd Smith, the New York financier, that the Grumman Aircraft Engineering Corporation should build the aircraft. Thus it was that the military plane-maker met his future civil customers and was assured of an order for three aircraft that would later increase to twelve.

Early design work to Loening's specification was carried out by Leroy Grumman and his chief engineer, William T "Bill" Schwendler. The detail was added by Ralston Stalb, a naval architect and hydrodynamicist who specialised in hull design. He had been chief engineer at Loening Aircraft, had joined Grumman prior to the move to Bethpage, and having contributed greatly to the design of the G-21 hull, was, as we shall see, to leave the mark of his genius on all the Grumman hulls that followed.

The deep all-metal, two-step semi-monocoque hull consisted of a 24ST frame covered with smooth 24ST "Alclad" sheet. It was divided by bulkheads into six water-tight compartments: the bow compartment, the anchor compartment, the pilot's cockpit, main cabin, baggage compartment/lavatory and the tail compartment. Each of these could be sealed quickly in an emergency by closing their communicating doors against rubber gaskets. The anchor compartment had a top-side hatch which gave entry to stowage for the anchor and mooring tackle. Part of the radio installation was also situated here, and there was even room for excess baggage.

The next compartment aft was the pilot's cockpit, access to which was provided either from the anchor compartment through a door underneath the windscreen, or from the main cabin. The crew of two sat side-by-side behind dual wheel control yokes and a full instrument panel. There was also an overhead control panel whilst the fuel management, vacuum system and ventilation controls were mounted on the rear bulkhead. Cockpit windows were of toughened shatter-proof glass and were large enough to provide good visibility.

Behind the cockpit was the main cabin which was entered either from the cockpit or from outside, through a large door in the port side of the hull unobstructed by the wing and far enough above the waterline to prevent water being shipped in a rough sea. The passenger cabin, cockpit ventilation and heating systems and sound proofing were all provided by the Sperry Gyroscope Company, creating a comfortable environment for passengers and crew. Standard seating consisted of four adjustable armchairs and two fixed seats nearer the cockpit, all of which offered good views through the large windows. Whilst most military versions of the Goose were only sparsely fitted out, in later variants and conversions customised interiors were fitted to order.

Aft of the main cabin was a large

In photo, **PILOT'S PANEL**, top row, l to r: **Air speed indicator, Turn and Bank indicator, Rate-of-Climb indicator. Middle row: Artificial horizon, Landing Gear unsafe warning light, Directional Gyro combined with a turn needle and skid ball. Bottom: Radio Receiver band selector, tuner with knob below, Microphone plug-in with switch. CENTER PANEL, l to r: Altimeter, Magnetic compass, Clock, Engine fire extinguisher selector and discharge handle. COPILOT'S PANEL: Vacuum gauge with Venturi selector below it. Switch panel below copilot's control wheel: Battery, Generator, Running lights, Anchor lights, Passing lights, rheostats for instrument and spotlights. Gauge is ammeter/voltmeter. OVERHEAD PANEL, top to bottom, rows l to r; 1st row: Two Prop pitch levers with 2 Carburetor Heat levers adjacent, Flap Control (UP-30-60), Mixtures, Throttles. 2nd row: Carburetor Air Temp gauge (Lt Eng), Engine Gauge Unit (Lt Eng = oil temp, oil press, fuel press), Cylinder head Temp selector (L or R), Starter switches. 3rd row: Carb Air Temp (Rt Eng), Engine Gauge Unit (Rt Eng), Ambient Air Temp gauge, Cylinder Head Temp gauge (0-600 degrees F), Mag switches. Small panel under Mag sws has 2 tachometers, top, with 2 Manifold Pressure gauges below.**

G-21 Goose cockpit showing the basic instrumentation typical of the era. The opening between the control yokes allowed access to the bow compartment. Above is the guide to the cockpit published with the original photo.　　　　　　　　　　　　　*(Grumman photo 6095)*

connected to the wings by three hinges. Both the flaps and the ailerons were of fabric-covered metal frame construction. The flaps were vacuum operated with an actuating cylinder and return spring situated just outboard of the wing centre section under the rear gap plate. The ailerons were statically and dynamically balanced. Control of stability in the water was achieved by adding a float to each wing. The all-metal floats were of 760 pounds displacement each and were attached to the outer wing panel by two fixed vertical struts. Incidence and transverse bracing were achieved with streamline tie-rods.

The all-metal (24ST) tail-plane assembly consisted of six units: The vertical fin was an integral part of the fuselage; the left and right stabilisers, which were braced to the fuselage by streamline struts; the left and right elevators, and the rudder of fabric covered aluminium alloy and fitted with trim tabs, were statically and dynamically balanced.

The main landing gear consisted of Hayes wheels fitted with Goodrich tyres and could be retracted into wheel wells in the side of the hull. Retraction or extension was achieved by use of a selective ratchet-type hand crank located between the seats in the cockpit. Forty one turns of the crank handle were required to raise or lower the gear. The success or otherwise of this operation could be checked by looking through the small windows provided for this purpose behind the cockpit seats. The tail wheel assembly was of the self-aligning full swivel type fitted with a Hayes aluminium alloy wheel complete with a Goodrich self-earthing pneumatic tyre. Retraction, into a well behind the second step, was achieved by means of a cable linkage to the main gear retraction mechanism. Although the Goose was of rugged construction it also showed graceful lines which were not compromised by the clever design of the retractable landing gear. This was Grover Loening's design, which is often wrongly attributed to Roy Grumman, and was the subject of the proposed court action referred to above. Landings on surfaces other than water were smoothed by the Bendix combined pneumatic/hydraulic ("pneudraulic") type struts. The hull was claimed to be strong enough to withstand a wheels-up landing even on the roughest of terrain, and was thoroughly proofed against corrosion to help provide a long airframe life with low maintenance costs.

Among the safety factors highlighted in early advertising for the Goose was the use of "proven & dependable" Pratt & Whitney engines of 400hp each. This rating was based on the use of 80 octane fuel. Some literature quoted a 450hp rating but this only referred to a take-off rating when 87 octane fuel was used. The two "Wasp Junior SB" nine-cylinder air-cooled radials were mounted on the leading edge of the wing centre section and drove 8ft 6in diameter two-blade, constant-speed,

baggage compartment/lavatory which sometimes included a small refreshment preparation area.

The tail compartment, like the bow, was permanently sealed providing no stowage.

The all-metal (24ST) wing of NACA 23000 series aerofoil section was constructed of a simple box-beam spar and consisted of three sections. The centre section was integral with the fuselage to a point just outboard of the engine nacelles. This section of the box-beam was sealed

off on each side and divided to provide two fuel tanks of 110 US gallons each, giving a total fuel load of 220 US gallons.

The outer wing sections were continued on the box-beam spar with all-metal (24ST) ribs. The forward part of the wings was covered in smooth (24ST) metal sheet while the rear was fabric covered. Control surfaces consisted of split trailing-edge two-position flaps which were connected to the wing by four hinges. The ailerons were fitted outboard of the flaps and were

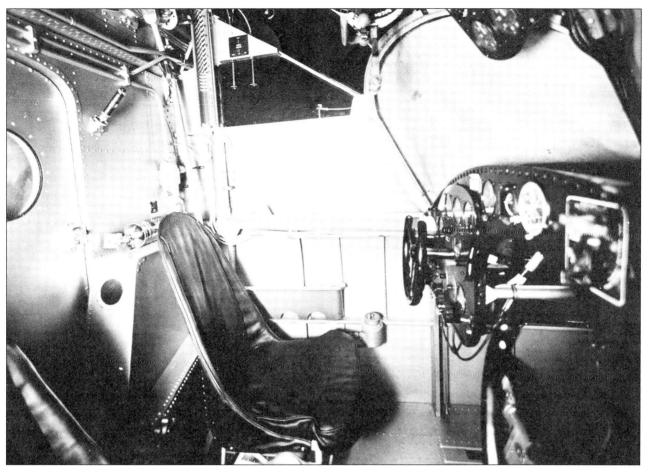

The left-hand side of the G-21 Goose cockpit showing the small porthole behind the seat through which a check could be made as to whether the landing gear was up or down. The portable fire extinguisher can be seen behind the seat. (Grumman photo 6093)

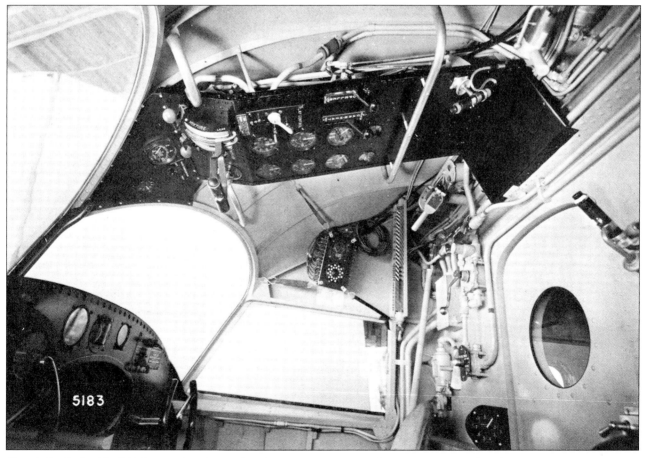

The right-hand side of the G-21 Goose cockpit showing the radio transmitter frequency selector and meter above the side window. Aft of that is the striped glass fuel sight gauge with shut-off. (Grumman photo 5183)

controllable-pitch Hamilton Standard propellers. To reduce noise levels in the cabin the engines were fitted with collector rings which led to exhaust exits above the wings.

The decision to start production of the G-21 was taken in late 1936 on the basis of the 10 orders received from the syndicate. The feel-good factor engendered by the prospect of building the company's biggest aircraft to date was tempered by the fact that cash flow was a problem, and so the Grumman board decided to limit initial production to three aircraft. Another factor which must have hindered the project was the move of production facilities from Farmingdale, Long Island, to the new factory at nearby Bethpage, which was only completed in April 1937. So the fact that the first G-21 off the production line (c/n 1001, registered NX16910 – the 'X' denoting prototype or experimental) made its first flight on 29th May 1937 is somewhat remarkable, when compared to present day development schedules.

The Grumman test pilots, Bud Gillies and Bob Hall, immediately demonstrated the amphibious capabilities of the new aircraft. After an hour-long first flight they put the G-21 down on the waters of Manhasset Bay, off Port Washington, Long Island, picked up Roy Grumman and gave him a 15-minute demonstration flight. Three more flights were made that day and were followed by two more flights on each of the next two days so that by the end of

G-21 Goose, VH-AAY, crated for shipment circa November 1937 displays the integral wing centre section with nacelles attached. *(Grumman photo)*

the month the G-21 had flown six hours and ten minutes.

Fully loaded, the Goose could take off from calm glassy water in 15 seconds, while a take-off from terra firma into a 3mph wind was achieved in only 10½ seconds. The pilots reported that they had

an aircraft with nice handling qualities and which was very good in the water, although minor modifications to the hull were necessary to facilitate better spray control during take-offs and landings. It was thought that this could be achieved by moving the step aft by some 4½ inches. To

G-21 Goose wing assembly line at Bethpage, NY circa 1937. *(Grumman photo)*

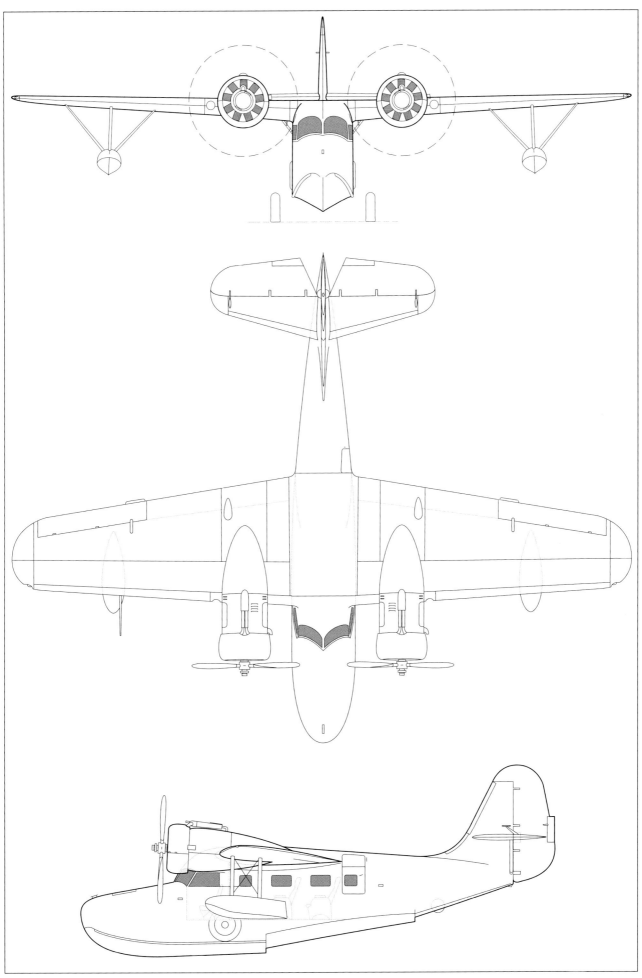

Three-view drawing of the G-21/G-21A Goose.

(Michael Zoeller)

Wall Streeters commute by plane

to and from this Manhattan dock

Private flying in America climbs to its highest financial ceiling at Manhattan's Downtown Skyport (*above*) on the East River at Wall Street. Four minutes walk past the towering shadows of 120 Wall Street (*above, right*) and Cities Service Building (*left*) is the Stock Exchange. Men who use the Skyport most make up the most select group of air commuters in the land—H. P. Davison and Henry S. Morgan, of J. P. Morgan & Co., Marshall Field,

E. R. Harriman. Mr. Harriman lives 38 miles away, flies into Manhattan in 25 minutes, saving an hour.

Shown at Skyport is Rudolph Loening's Fairchild (*left*) and the Marshall Field-Wilton Lloyd-Smith $50,000 Grumman amphibian. Up to 16 planes a day land at the Skyport, taxi to the float, discharge passengers, are turned about on turntable (*white circle*), scoot out. The city-owned Skyport charges $1 up **per** landing. Parking more than a half-hour costs $1.

The first G-21 Goose at the Downtown Skyport on New York's East River waterfront shortly after delivery to Wilton Lloyd Smith and Marshall Field in July 1937. Seen at the bottom of the page is the original printed caption which accompanied this photograph.   *(Grumman photo)*

This photograph of G-21 Goose, NC16914 (c/n 1005) on skis is thought to have been taken, circa 1938, purely for publicity purposes, and the G-21 was not operated as such. The "Tribune" logo on the nose denotes ownership by the Chicago Tribune newspaper group. (Grumman photo 10141)

simulate the reconfigured step, wooden blocks were fitted to the hull and the aircraft was test flown on 3rd June 1937. The crude modification worked and the hull of c/n 1001 was re-modelled accordingly. All subsequent G-21s had the remodelled step incorporated during production.

The first G-21 was delivered to syndicate leader, Wilton Lloyd Smith and co-owner, Marshall Field III on 16th July 1937, only 48 days after its first flight. All projected performance figures were met or bettered and the "Grey Goose", as Leroy Grumman called the aircraft, became an instant success. The second and third aircraft followed, and were delivered to syndicate members, the banker Henry S Morgan, and E Roland Harriman, respectively.

However, building a large (Grumman's largest to date) twin-engined aircraft from scratch with a long lead time between purchase of components and receipt of final payment from the customer was not conducive to good cash flow. Add to this the fact that, at $60,000, Grumman had probably priced the aircraft too low (by some 10%), which produced only a minimal profit, and the money men at the company were soon scratching around for a solution. Should they go public and sell all that was held dear by Roy Grumman? After all, he had only ever wanted to design and build aeroplanes in a small private company. But needs must when the devil drives, and the devil in this instance, as in many cases before and since, was money – or, more precisely, the lack of fluidity of funds. Therefore in the late spring of 1937

the Grumman Board of Directors decided to go public in order to raise the necessary finance to keep the company going. Three Wall Street brokerage firms agreed to underwrite the issue of 100,000 shares. Because the stock market in mid-1937 was not in the best of health, the brokers were twice able to invoke a clause in the agreement which allowed them to postpone the issue for 30 days on each occasion. That was not a lot of help to Grumman who wished to press on with the building of another seven Grey Gooses.

And press on they did, with the help of some careful management and prudence, and before long they received orders for two additional aircraft, for which they increased the price to $66,000 each.

Then chance took a hand. A character with a glass eye, a bad arm and a willingness to bet on anything, arrived in the front office at Bethpage. Bernard E Smith, known as "Sell-'em Ben", was a Wall Street broker who had made a fortune by selling stocks cheaply during the Depression. His reason for arriving in Bethpage at that time was to place an order for a Goose for his friend Lord Beaverbrook, the Canadian-born British press baron. Having placed the order, Smith was told that there would be a delay in delivery – and the reason for that delay. He suggested that the problem could be overcome by his underwriting the share issue with the help of his associates at Bergen & Company, on the condition that Grumman terminate all previous agreements with the other underwriters. Smith's offer was taken up and 95,000 shares with

a par value of $1 were offered for sale to the general public, 60,000 of which were issued at $7.50 each. Of the remaining 5,000 shares, offered to Grumman employees, only 3,800 were issued.

With the company now on a sounder financial footing, Grumman set about building and selling Gooses. A worldwide distributorship was awarded to Gillies Aviation Corporation, based on Roosevelt Field, Long Island. Gillies was owned by Jack Gillies, brother of Bud, the Grumman test pilot, and handled all sales except those to the United States government.

The day after delivery of the fourth Grey Goose, NC16913, to Charles W Deeds, the G-21 was awarded its Approved Type Certificate, ATC No.654, on 29th September 1937. This meant that c/n 1001 could be re-registered as NC16910, losing the experimental 'X', and begging the question as to whether the second, third and fourth Gooses should also have carried NX registrations prior to 29th September 1937; however no evidence has yet been found to show that they did.

By December 1937 the G-21 line was producing G-21As incorporating the hull modifications intended to reduce water spray on take-off and landing and a redesigned tail-wheel. With up-rated 450hp Wasp Junior SB-2 engines and a gross weight increased from 7,500 to 8,000 lbs, the twelfth and last Grey Goose came off the line as a G-21A Goose for delivery to the powerboat racer, Gar Wood. These improvements were approved on 5th February 1938, also under ATC 654, and during 1938, all 11 G-21s, with maybe the

G-21 Goose NC16914 (c/n 1005) awaiting delivery in October 1937 to Colonel Robert McCormick of The Chicago Tribune newspaper.
(Grumman photo 6146)

A rare shot of G-21 Goose NC16915 (c/n1006) before delivery in October 1937 to Captain Boris Sergievsky, chief pilot of Sikorsky Aircraft,.
(Grumman photo)

G-21 Goose NC16917 (c/n 1012) which was delivered to Gar Wood in December 1937, but destroyed in a hangar fire the following April.
(Grumman photo)

A contemporary (circa 1938) magazine advertisement announcing the delivery of the first OA-9 Goose to the US Army Air Corps.

exception of c/ns 1009, 1010 and 1011 which had been exported, were modified to G-21A standard.

The remaining syndicate members, and Lord Beaverbrook, got their Gooses, and beginning with c/n 1013, a total of thirty G-21A Gooses were built and delivered between December 1938 and September 1942.

Apart from being a luxury private aircraft for wealthy individuals, the Goose was also used as a tool in the oil exploration industry, seeing service in the Dutch East Indies and both North and South America. Early examples of the G-21A also served as airliners in Puerto Rico, Bolivia and the Dutch East Indies, and with Pan-American Airways.

By 1938 the military were becoming very interested in the portly amphibian, which they envisaged filling many utility roles. The first military customer for the G-21A Goose was, in fact, the Royal Canadian Air Force which took delivery of c/n 1016 on 26th July 1938. The RCAF eventually operated a total of 31 Gooses.

However, the Army Air Corps was the first US military arm to order the Goose. This was to fill a requirement to replace the ageing Douglas OA-3s and OA-4s in the air-sea rescue (ASR) and personnel transport roles. Under the Grumman Design number G-31, and with the AAC designation OA-9, 26 were built between 1938 and 1939, to contract AC-11304. These six-seat aircraft were powered by Pratt & Whitney's military equivalent engine, the R-985-17 radial of 450hp.

The 21st Goose (c/n 1021) was the only design G-26 airframe. It was designated XJ3F-1, given the BuAer serial 1384, and delivered to the US Navy at NAS Anacostia on 9th September 1938 for evaluation. Built as an eight-seat utility amphibian, it was powered by 450hp R-985-48 radials.

Following evaluation of the XJ3F-1, the US Navy took delivery of five of each of the JRF-1 for light transport duties and

JRF-1A for aerial photography and target towing, both versions being designated G-38. The Navy contract C-66303 had called initially for seven JRF-1s, similar to the XJ3F-1, with three more on option, but this was amended to five of each version. Both models were powered by the R-985-48 engine and were identical except for the photographic and target-towing equipment facilities of the JRF-1A. The ten aircraft, c/ns 1066-1075, received the BuAer serials 1671-1680 in sequence with 1069-1072 and 1075 built as the JRF-1 and 1066-1068, 1073 and 1074 as the JRF-1A. The first aircraft, JRF-1A 1671, was accepted at NAS Anacostia, MD on 15th September 1939 and the last of the batch was received in January 1940.

Commercial production of G-21A

models continued in parallel with the increasing numbers of US military aircraft and among the former were four for the Peruvian Air Corps with c/ns 1050-1053, handed over at Bethpage between December 1938 and February 1939. Until the USA entered World War II in December 1941, all non-US military Goose sales were equipped with the commercial Wasp Junior SB-2 and this included the Peruvian and subsequently Canadian and Portuguese aircraft.

The US Coast Guard took delivery of seven JRF-2 models in two batches in 1939 and 1940. The JRF-2, known as the model G-39, was powered by the 450hp commercial Wasp Junior SB-2 and was essentially a G-21A with a capability to replace seats with stretchers. Three aircraft with c/ns 1063-1065 and USCG serials V174-V176 were ordered by contract TCG-29648 and were delivered between July and October 1939. A further four with c/ns 1076-1079 and serials V184-V187 followed on contract TCG-30750 in February and March 1940. A further three aircraft were ordered on TCG-33389 in September 1939, but the addition of autopilot and anti-icing equipment to enable these aircraft to operate in northern latitudes resulted in a new designation, the JRF-3. These aircraft, still to the basic G-39 specification and powered by the Wasp Junior SB-2, were c/ns 1085-1087 and wore serials V190-V192. They were delivered in October and November 1940.

By the close of 1939 the Goose was in service with the Air Corps, the Navy and the Coast Guard and other foreign military customers were now showing considerable interest in Grumman's erstwhile executive transport. On 19th December 1939 the Portuguese Government, acting on behalf of its Aviação Naval, signed a contract for

The G-21 Goose production line at Bethpage, NY. The aircraft in the foreground is the second for the Cuerpo Aeronáutica del Peru (Peruvian Air Corps), with serial number 2TP-2H.

(Grumman photo 6568)

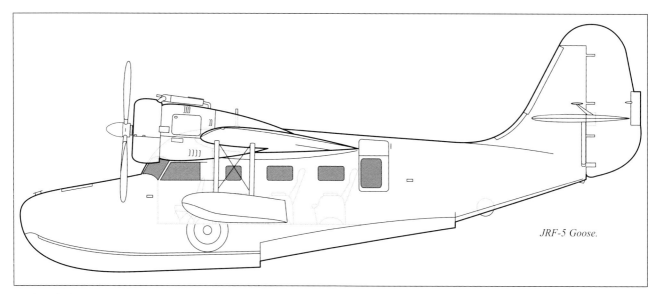

JRF-5 Goose.

12 aircraft that would be delivered without undercarriages. They would be known as the G-21B model and required special cradles for movement on land. Additionally these aircraft were equipped with hard points beneath each wing to allow the carriage of two 100lb bombs and fittings in the bow and dorsal hatches for two 0.30in machine guns. The Portuguese aircraft had c/ns 1088-1099 and were delivered by sea between April and July 1940. The G-21B model was to be the only true flying-boat built by Grumman, although in the post-war years small numbers of civilianised JRFs were modified by their owners to operate without wheels. Generally however the weight-saving and simpler construction benefits of the G-21B were heavily offset by the inflexibility of the design and no more G-21Bs were sold.

A further order for 25 JRF-1s was placed by the US Navy on contract C-75686 but ongoing development work resulted in changes to the aircraft leading to the appearance of the definitive JRF-5 model. The first 10 aircraft of this batch were thus produced with R-985-50 engines and were known as the JRF-4. Both the JRF-4 and the JRF-5 were known by Grumman as the G-38. Essentially the JRF-4 was a re-engined JRF-1 with the added provision of

The first G-21B Goose (c/n 1088) with flight-test registration NX97, at Floyd Bennett Field, NY prior to delivery to the Aviação Naval (Portuguese Navy), in whose service it would wear serial number 97. (Grumman photo 7297)

JRF-4 Goose 3854 (c/n 1108) spent most of the war assigned to US Naval Air Station Alameda. This photograph shows the aircraft in its original markings, although by now the prop-hazard warning line has been added to the forward fuselage. The undersides of the hull and floats were painted black.
(William Haines Collection)

hard points enabling the carriage of a 250lb depth charge outboard of each engine. These 10 aircraft with c/ns 1100-1109 and serials 3846-3855 were delivered between December 1940 and April 1941.

The JRF-5 (model G-38) became the final and main production variant of the Goose (the British JRF-6B version was essentially a JRF-5). Excluding the British aircraft, a total of 184 would be built between 1941 and 1945. The JRF-5 encompassed all the modifications of the earlier aircraft and was equipped with a camera hatch, target-towing gear, de-icing boots (on the leading edge of the wing and tail surfaces), auto-pilot and underwing hard points. The US Navy's JRF-5 standard engine was the 450hp R-985-AN-6, although four aircraft, sold new to Canada in 1944, were built with the dash 6B version (as installed on the JRF-6B). As explained above the first fifteen airframes were built under an option clause in C-75686 and were aircraft 1110-1124 with serials 6440-6454 delivered between April and December 1941. These particular aircraft were scheduled for production with the R-985-50 engine but were delivered with the new R-985-AN-6. A second batch of ten aircraft, 1176-1185 with serials 04349-04358, was added as a supplement to the contract on 5th November 1941 and they were delivered between July and October 1942. A further supplement to this Navy contract added two aircraft for Cuba, 1186 and 1187 with serials 39747 and 39748, which were delivered in October 1942.

Production of the early JRF-5 aircraft for the US Navy was complicated by the need to accommodate a large order for the United Kingdom. This appears to have caused the cancellation of a batch of 30 US Navy aircraft with serials 03713-03742, an allocation that would have been made (and cancelled) in 1941. Following the delivery of aircraft 6454 in November 1941, US Navy JRF-5 production continued with the delivery of 04349 in July 1942.

Subsequently, further contracts for an additional 168 JRF-5s (later reduced to 157), were placed by the US Navy and deliveries continued until December 1945 by which time aircraft were being sent directly into storage. These contracts, W&S 14088 (35 aircraft with c/ns 1189 - 1200 and B-1 – B-23), NAS463 (61 aircraft, c/ns B-24 – B-84) and NOa(S)3090 (72 reduced to 61 aircraft, c/ns B-85 – B-145) were all built to the basic US Navy specification with serials 34060-34094, 37771-37831, 84790-84818 and 87720-87751, but from early 1944 a number were diverted as new equipment to other users. In addition to six aircraft for the USCG and one for the USAAF, 16 were sold to Canada with another two going to Iceland. Four were temporarily supplied to the United Kingdom under Lend-Lease, another as aid to Colombia and one was sold to Humble Oil. Post-war, the JRF-5 remained in active US Navy service until 1956, although aircraft were released gradually to agencies

The pilot's station (left-hand seat) in the JRF-5 Goose. Note the round window on the bulkhead behind the seat, which afforded a view for the crew to check whether the undercarriage was up or down. The upper photograph on page 11 enables an evolutionary comparison with the G-21 Goose.
(Grumman photo 7524)

Cockpit of the JRF-5 Goose, showing the instrument panel and dual control wheels. The throttle controls are situated on the overhead panel. The hatch below and between the control wheels gave access to the bow compartment.
(Grumman photo 7520)

Left: JRF-6B Goose FP497 (c/n 1147) taken on 9th February 1942, while awaiting delivery to Great Britain. Note the large bubble window amidships which accommodated a compass to facilitate navigation training. (Grumman photo)

such as the USCG and friendly nations under MDAP. By 1969 the last surviving JRF-5 had been disposed of to the commercial market.

The JRF-5 was also produced for the United Kingdom as the JRF-6B. Powered by the R-985-AN-6B, the JRF-6B was visually distinguishable from the JRF-5 by virtue of a prominent Perspex 'bubble'

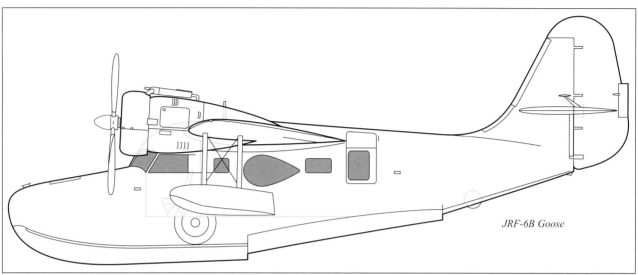

JRF-6B Goose

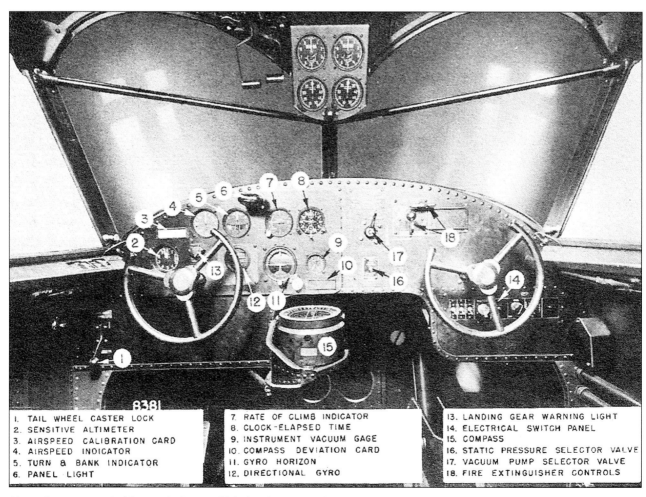

1. TAIL WHEEL CASTER LOCK	7. RATE OF CLIMB INDICATOR	13. LANDING GEAR WARNING LIGHT
2. SENSITIVE ALTIMETER	8. CLOCK-ELAPSED TIME	14. ELECTRICAL SWITCH PANEL
3. AIRSPEED CALIBRATION CARD	9. INSTRUMENT VACUUM GAGE	15. COMPASS
4. AIRSPEED INDICATOR	10. COMPASS DEVIATION CARD	16. STATIC PRESSURE SELECTOR VALVE
5. TURN & BANK INDICATOR	11. GYRO HORIZON	17. VACUUM PUMP SELECTOR VALVE
6. PANEL LIGHT	12. DIRECTIONAL GYRO	18. FIRE EXTINGUISHER CONTROLS

Above: *Instrument panel of the JRF-6B Goose, published in the JRF-6B Pilots Notes, A.P. 2090A.*　　　*(Grumman photo 8381)*

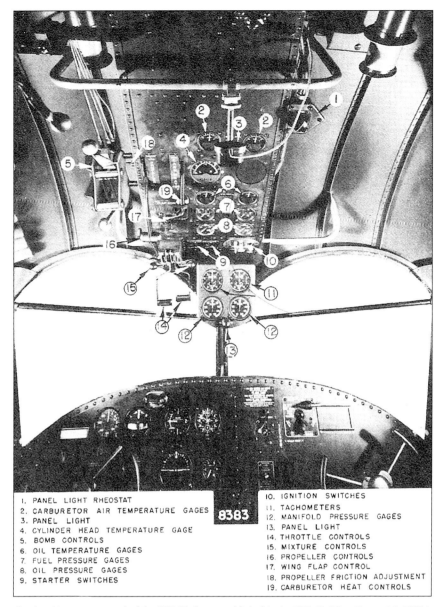

1. PANEL LIGHT RHEOSTAT
2. CARBURETOR AIR TEMPERATURE GAGES
3. PANEL LIGHT
4. CYLINDER HEAD TEMPERATURE GAGE
5. BOMB CONTROLS
6. OIL TEMPERATURE GAGES
7. FUEL PRESSURE GAGES
8. OIL PRESSURE GAGES
9. STARTER SWITCHES
10. IGNITION SWITCHES
11. TACHOMETERS
12. MANIFOLD PRESSURE GAGES
13. PANEL LIGHT
14. THROTTLE CONTROLS
15. MIXTURE CONTROLS
16. PROPELLER CONTROLS
17. WING FLAP CONTROL
18. PROPELLER FRICTION ADJUSTMENT
19. CARBURETOR HEAT CONTROLS

8383

Overhead instrument panel of the JRF-6B Goose, published in the JRF-6B Pilots Notes, A.P. 2090A.
(Grumman photo 8383)

window that replaced the normal second cabin window (port and starboard) and which facilitated navigation training (see side view drawing on facing page). The JRF-6B also lacked the camera hatch in the lower hull. British radio and navigation equipment (and, in a few aircraft, radar) was customer supplied. These 50 aircraft were supplied under Lend-Lease auspices on US Navy contract LL86447 and had c/ns 1125-1174. As will be explained later, six of these aircraft, 1150 and 1155-1159, were not delivered to the United Kingdom but were diverted instead as OA-9s to the USAAF (five) and Bolivia (one). The JRF-6Bs were delivered into British hands between January 1942 and March 1943.

The USA's entry into the war in December 1941 and the approval of the large British order had a disruptive effect on Grumman's production sequence. Commercial production of the G-21A ceased and any new US Navy JRF-5 orders could not be met until completion of the British aircraft. Existing US Navy orders (notably the batch with c/ns 1176-1187)

were therefore satisfied by administratively building 'out of sequence' although in reality this was just a paper exercise not affecting aircraft identities. Thus the production sequence of aircraft between July 1941 and March 1943 was approximately 1110-1124 July-November 1941, 1175 (a commercial G-21A) December 1941, 1125-1150 January-July 1942, 1176-1184 July-September 1942, 1188 (a civilian G-21A used for military research) September 1942, 1185-1187 September-October 1942 and 1151-1174 October 1942-March 1943. C/n 1189 (BuAer serial 34060) was delivered in April 1943 and all subsequent production was in c/n sequence. The last two civilian G-21As built (1175 and 1188) were delivered with Twin Wasp SB-3 engines.

In 1942 it was realised that orders for the JRF-5 would take Goose construction numbers beyond 1200 and that this would lead to confusion with G-44 Widgeon production which used a sequence commencing 1201. It was therefore decided that after 1200 was reached a new sequence

commencing with 'B-1' would be used for the Goose. Thus the complete range of Goose c/ns would eventually be 1001 to 1200 and B-1 to B-156, although B-146 to B-156 were cancelled in 1945.

Thus the Grumman Corporation built 345 Goose aircraft in various configurations to suit customer requirements. It is particularly curious to reflect that a project which set out to satisfy the needs of a group of exceptionally wealthy businessmen, socialites and sports personalities as an executive transport became a robust and widely used item of military hardware. After World War II many surplus aircraft entered commercial service as commuter and/or freight carriers in Alaska, the Caribbean and other parts of the world where runways were not available. In spite of the proliferation of airfields and the widespread use of helicopters and modern floatplanes the Goose still provides an essential service to remote Alaskan communities.

A summary of Goose production by basic type reference follows while fuller details of the aircraft's use by the world's air arms will be found in **Chapter 7**. **Chapter 8** provides similar details of all civilian and commercial users, while complete details of all individual aircraft in construction number sequence can be found in **Appendix 1**.

Goose Variants & Production Summary

A total of 345 aircraft of all models was produced between May 1937 and October 1945. A few of these aircraft were either re-defined with new designations while in production or shortly before delivery while others were delivered to customers who gave 'their' aircraft new designations or names. Transfers to the military after the outbreak of war, particularly those involving the USAAF, resulted in new and potentially confusing designations and this summary provides additional information for a few specific aircraft to assist understanding. The summary broadly categorises each aircraft as manufactured for either a civilian or military purchaser with additional detail in respect of primary military designations. Reference to the other sections of this book including individual aircraft histories will give greater insight into secondary modifications and projects and here only the 'administrative' USCG 'JRF-5G', the USN derivative JRF-6 and the grossly-modified 'K-16B' secondary designations are explained.

The Civilian Aircraft Models

G-21 The so-called 'Grey Goose'. 12 built in 1937 with c/ns 1001-1012. 1012 was modified to G-21A standard before delivery and all others are believed to have been converted subsequently to G-21A standard before delivery although there remains uncertainty about 1008, 1009 and

The prototype G-21 Goose, NX16910 (c/n 1001) during flight testing.   *(Grumman photo 5161)*

This unflattering photograph taken in 1937 shows the second G-21 Goose built, NC16911 (c/n 1002), awaiting delivery to the New York banker Henry Morgan.
(Grumman photo 6090)

The third G-21 Goose built, NC16912 (c/n 1003), taken in 1937 awaiting delivery to E Roland Harriman, a well-known New York businessman.
(Grumman photo 6131)

1010, which were delivered overseas. One aircraft, 1006, was acquired by the USAAF in March 1942 as 42-38215 with whom it was known as an OA-13A. Another, 1011, was gifted to the US Navy in 1941 with whom it was known as a JRF-1, with the BuAer serial 07004. Aircraft 1004, when with Pan American Airways in 1942 and used on behalf of the US Navy, was allocated the serial 48229 and administratively referred to as a JRF-5 (this designation had nothing to do with the technical standard of the airframe and appears to have been something of a clerical guess).

G-21A 30 built between 1937 and 1942 in addition to the modified G-21 aircraft. Although built to Grumman's commercial design number, several were for overseas military customers. C/ns were 1013-1020, 1048-1062, 1080-1084, 1175 and 1188. Some of these aircraft subsequently acquired US military designations when so acquired in later years. 1014 was sold to the US Navy in November 1942 where it became a JRF-1 with BuAer serial 99078 retrospectively allocated circa early 1945 (after its demise); 1017 was similarly acquired by the USN in June 1942 as a JRF-1, serial 09782; 1058 of Pan American was transferred to the USAAF as an OA-13A in March 1942 as 42-38214; 1060 was acquired by the USN in March 1942 as a JRF-4, serial 09767 and 1062, purchased by the USAAF in November 1942, became OA-13A 42-97055. C/n 1188, NX1604, was already undertaking naval research work with Columbia University when allocated BuAer serial 35921 in 1942 and was later taken on USN strength, probably in 1945. Initially it was referred to as a 'JRF-4' but then became a JRF-5.

G-21B 12 flying boat versions built without undercarriages for the Portuguese Navy in 1940. C/ns were 1088-1099.

Conversions **G-21C to G-21G** are described in **Chapter 5**.

The US Army Air Corps Variants

OA-9 Grumman design **G-31**. 26 aircraft delivered between November 1938 and October 1939 to contract AC-11304. C/ns 1022-1047 were given the serials 38-556 to 38-581. The USAAF re-used the designation when five JRF-6B (design **G-38**) were acquired in November and December 1942 for the use of US Air Attachés in the Caribbean and Central American region. These aircraft, 1155-1159 with serials 42-106979 to 106983, were diverted from the Naval Lend-Lease

Goose BuAer1384 (c/n 1021) was the prototype XJ3F-1, the first of the US Navy's aircraft. The photograph is probably an early Grumman publicity shot, taken circa September 1938, and shows the aircraft in its original silver colour scheme.

contract LL86447 and would otherwise have gone to the United Kingdom. In October 1947 and after virtually all previous OA-9s had been disposed of, a single US Navy JRF-5, c/n B-21 and serial 34092, was loaned to the USAF for research purposes as 48-128. In July 1948 it was re-designated ZA-9, reflecting its theoretical obsolescence as a type, and in April 1949 it was returned to the Navy.

OA-13A As explained above, all three OA-13A models, 1006 (42-38215), 1058 (42-38214) and 1062 (42-97055) were USAAF acquisitions of commercial **G-21A** models.

OA-13B The two OA-13B models, c/ns 1193 and B-120, were US Navy JRF-5s (**G-38**) diverted to the USAAF in March 1945 for use in North Africa. 1193, serial 34064, was already in USN service at the time of transfer becoming 45-49089 while B-120, serial 87726, became 45-49088 on the production line.

The US Navy/Coast Guard Variants

XJ3F-1 Grumman design **G-26**. One prototype built to US Navy contract C60242 in 1938. C/n 1021 was allocated the BuAer serial 1384.

JRF-1 Grumman design **G-38**. The first US Navy production contract, C66303, called for ten aircraft including three option aircraft. The option aircraft (numbers eight to ten) were all built but, when completed, the order had been reconstructed to call for five JRF-1 and five JRF-1A. The five JRF-1, c/ns 1069-1072 and 1075, were respectively numbered 1674-1677 and 1680 and were delivered between November 1939 and January 1940. As explained above, two subsequent civilian acquisitions (BuAer serials 07004 and 09782) were also known as JRF-1 in US Navy use.

JRF-1A Grumman design **G-38**. As explained above, the balance of five aircraft on C66303 were delivered as the JRF-1A. They were c/ns 1066-1068, 1073 and 1074 with serials 1674-1676, 1678 and 1679 and were also delivered between November 1939 and January 1940.

JRF-2 Grumman design **G-39**. A total of seven aircraft were built for the US Coast Guard against two purchase contracts. C/ns 1063-1065, serials V174-V176 were built for TCG-29648 and 1076-1079, serials V184-V187 were for TCG-30750. The two batches were delivered in October 1939 and March 1940 respectively. There was

Right: *Before the advent of the rescue helicopter, the US Coast Guard was almost totally reliant on its amphibians and sea-planes to undertake its primary role. Here, JRF-2 Goose V176 (c/n 1065) is seen on the water, probably near its final home station of CGAS Port Angeles.*
(US Coast Guard)

some fluidity of movement between USCG and USN aircraft during World War II and at least two of these aircraft eventually saw Fleet use with the Navy.

JRF-3   Grumman design **G-39**. A single batch of three aircraft was built for the US Coast Guard against contract TCG-33389. They were c/ns 1085-1087 with serials V190-V192, delivered in October and November 1940.

JRF-4   Grumman design **G-38.** In its original form Navy contract C75686 called for 25 aircraft with at least the first 10 to JRF-1 standard (and four of the early deliveries have movement record cards with 'JRF-1' corrected to JRF-4). However the first 10 were delivered to JRF-4 standard with the final 15, together with supplementary aircraft, built as the JRF-5. Thus there were 10 JRF-4 with c/ns 1100-1109 and BuAer serials 3846-3855 delivered between December 1940 and March 1941. As previously explained, two commercial G-21A aircraft were acquired as JRF-4 (becoming BuAer 09767 and 35921, the latter dubiously so and later re-designated JRF-5).

JRF-5   Grumman design **G-38**. The JRF-5 was the definitive Navy Goose and the production of 184 aircraft exceeded the combined total of all other models. It was procured against four contracts; C75686 for 15 with c/ns 1110-1124 and serials 6440-6454; C75686 (Supplementary) for 10 with c/ns 1176-1185 and serials 04349-04358 and two with c/ns 1186-1187 and serials 39747-39748 (for Cuba); W&S.14088 for 35 with c/ns 1189-1200 and B-1 – B-23 and serials 34060-34094; NAS463 for 61 with c/ns B-24 – B-84 and serials 37771-37831; NOa(S)3090 for 61 with c/ns B-85 – B-145 and serials 84790-84818 and 87720-87751. A further 11 aircraft on the final contract with serials 87752-87762 were cancelled.

Deliveries of the JRF-5 began in April 1941 and the final aircraft was accepted in December 1945. Orders and deliveries, together with those for the JRF-6B (below), sharply increased with the onset of war and reflected the concepts of Lend-Lease production and diversions from contract. Including some Coast Guard aircraft approximately 33 JRF-5 were delivered virtually from the production line into third-party hands and saw no service with the US Navy, although the UK's Lend-Lease aircraft were returned later. These recipients were the US Coast Guard (6), Canada (16), United Kingdom (four), Cuba (two), Iceland (two) with one aircraft diverted pre-delivery to the USAAF as an OA-13B and two released post-war to oil companies (Humble Oil and a subsidiary of Standard Oil).

JRF-5G   The JRF-5G designation was not initially an official BuAer identity although its eventual adoption by the USCG as a 'type' in the 1950s reflects the Bureau of Aeronautics' eclectic use of suffix letters as well as a USCG wish to standardise its designations. In this instance 'G' indicated 'Guard' for the US Coast Guard rather than any particular modification standard and it was a retrospective re-designation of the surviving JRF-5s in the early 'fifties. The aircraft was for all practical purposes a regular JRF-5 albeit with certain items of USCG kit. The complex World War II relationship between the Navy and the USCG is explained more fully elsewhere. As all JRF-5Gs were built as JRF-5 and a number had been lost or withdrawn before the adoption of the designation there is no production total. For a more complete understanding of the USCG operation the reader is referred to page 139 onwards.

JRF-6   Between July 1952 and June 1953 the USN at NAS Quonset Point, Rhode Island modified 15 JRF-5 aircraft to the JRF-6 standard (being known as 'JRF-6X' while under conversion). The modifications are believed to have included upgrades to radios, navigational instruments and flight controls. It is also believed that the Navy's intention was to modernise most and maybe all of its surviving fleet of JRF-5 but the programme probably fell foul of the post-Korean War budget cuts. The modified aircraft served with the handful of surviving Goose units in small numbers, most numerously at NAF Annapolis, Maryland, until the type was withdrawn. This modification had nothing to do with the British JRF-6B of an earlier era. The 15 modified aircraft were 34071, 37771, 37812, 37813, 37820, 37828, 84805, 84807, 84809, 84810, 87720, 87723, 87732, 87745 and 87750.

JRF-6B   Grumman design **G-38**. A single batch of 50 aircraft built for the United Kingdom and delivered between January 1942 and March 1943. Eventually ordered on US Navy contract LL86447, these aircraft had c/ns 1125-1174 and BAPC/Royal Navy serials FP475-FP524. Only 44 were delivered into British hands as six aircraft were diverted by the US Government to Bolivia (one, c/n 1150) and the USAAF (five as OA-9, c/ns 1155-1159 and see above). The aircraft were essentially JRF-5 models, the dash '6B' suffix indicating relatively minor customer requirements with a 'B' for Britain.

K-16B   The Kaman K-16B was a flight research vehicle that utilised the fuselage of JRF-5 04351 (c/n 1178). The research and development programme, funded by the Navy contract NOa(s) 56-549C was undertaken between February 1956 and September 1962. Although considered unsafe for flight without further development, the aircraft was, in September 1962, complete and 'airworthy' and the programme was only abandoned after funds were diverted to other more advanced projects (See page 77).

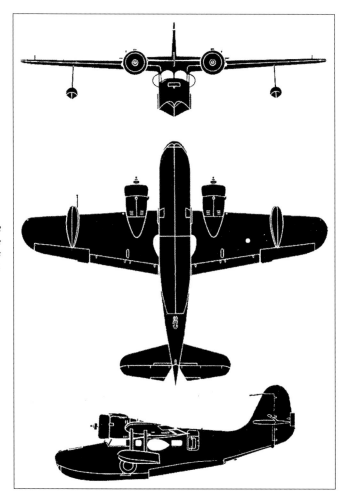

Right: JRF-6B silhouette. Note the blister windows amidships.

Not really a production line, but more a production corner, for the G-44 Widgeon at Bethpage in late-1940. Note the Goose fuselages on the right and the many F4F-3 Wildcats in the background.   *(Grumman photo 7635)*

CHAPTER 3:
G-44 WIDGEON DEVELOPMENT

THE SUCCESS OF THE GOOSE LED TO A demand for a similar aircraft at a more affordable purchase price and with lower operating costs. This demand came mainly from what we now know as "third level airlines" and also from wealthy individuals and sportsmen.

Roy Grumman recognised this interest and with his design team set about designing his "baby Goose" in August 1939. Like its successful forbear the Design G-44 sported a high wing carrying twin engines high above the waterline. Indeed, the engines chosen, being in-line Ranger 6-L-440-C5s with a high thrust line meant that the propellers were kept well away from any spray produced on landing.

Designed to be easy to fly and simple to maintain, the new amphibian was provided as standard equipment with a complete set of flight and engine instruments as well as two-way radio.

The semi-monocoque two-step hull displayed the graceful hallmark of Ralston Stalb and his design team. The all-metal structure, covered in "Alclad" aluminium alloy sheeting, was divided into three watertight compartments:

(i) The bow compartment for stowage of the mooring gear and anchor was accessed from outside by means of a hatch (well forward of the propeller line) and from there the main cabin was accessed through an opening under the starboard side of the instrument panel.

(ii) The main cabin which included the flight deck. The principal entrance to the main cabin was through a hatch in the upper left hull behind the wing. The cabin had seats for three passengers; one on a bench seat behind the pilot, and two fold-down seats at the rear, for use when needed. A bin, which could carry up to 150lbs baggage, was situated behind the rear seats.

The flight deck accommodated a pilot and co-pilot/extra passenger in side-by-side seats. The control yoke was of the "throw-over" wheel type mounted on a central column, allowing the aircraft to be flown from either seat without the need for dual controls. A Lear AMTR-12 two-way radio was also included as standard equipment and was operated from the aircraft's 12-volt battery. The cabin windows and windshield were of heavy gauge "Plexiglas".

(iii) The tail cone section which was permanently sealed.

The cantilever wing, of aerofoil section NACA-23015, consisted of three panels built around a single box-spar, set at one third of the chord back from the leading edge, and truss-type wing ribs. The outer panels joined the centre section just outboard of the engine nacelles. This all-metal framework was covered in "Alclad" sheeting to the rear of the box-spar with the remainder being fabric covered. The wings were less graceful than those on the G-21 with a taper on both leading and trailing edges, outboard of the engines, leading to squared-off wingtips. All-metal floats were attached to the outboard section of the wing to give stability while the aircraft was on the water. The centre section of the wing carried the twin Ranger 6-L-440-C5 engines with a 54-gallon fuel tank situated behind each. The oil tanks (total capacity seven gallons) were located within the engine nacelles. Hydraulically operated, slotted trailing-edge flaps were located between the ailerons and the hull. These were metal-covered and designed to facilitate take-off and climb at 15° setting and would deflect to up to 45° for landing.

The all-metal vertical tailfin was an integral part of the fuselage. The tail-plane was braced on each side by a strut attached to the hull and like the wingtips the top of the fin was rather squared-off. Movable parts of the tail-plane, including the ailerons, were fabric covered. The rudder and elevators boasted adjustable trim tabs while one aileron had a fixed tab that was only adjustable on the ground.

While on the ground, as opposed to on water, the G-44 was supported by a landing gear of two main wheels on oleo-spring shock struts and a 360° swivelling tail-wheel located at the second step. The 7.50ins x 10ins wheels were fitted with hydraulic brakes and the main gear was retracted to lie flush with the hull, as in the G-21. The tail wheel could be locked in the trailing position to reduce the possibility of ground-looping when landing on hard runways.

Both main and tail wheels were extended or retracted simultaneously by double-acting hydraulic cylinders, the operating pressure for which was supplied by an engine driven pump or in emergency by a hand pump. Landing gear movement was controlled by a lever on the left centre of the upper control panel on which the "DOWN" and "UP" positions were clearly marked.

If the engine driven pump (installed on

Gillies Aviation had handled all but the military sales of the Goose. This contemporary advertisement, dating from mid-1941, appeared in several magazines and bears witness to the fact that Gillies continued this function with the Widgeon.

The spartan G-44 Widgeon cabin, with the forward aspect dominated by a centrally-mounted "throw-over" control column yoke in the cockpit.
(Grumman photo 7820)

The G-44 Widgeon cabin looking aft, with the rear main door cut into both the side and the top of the fuselage. *(Grumman photo 7821)*

The G-44 cockpit, with the "throw-over" yoke moved across the front of the right-hand seat. Note the undercarriage position indicator at the top right of the panel. The door on the right of the instrument panel allows access to or from the bow compartment.

(Grumman photo G-11363, dated 19th February 1943)

This former US Coast Guard J4F-1 is seen here as G-44 N2770A operated by Kodiak Airways. The large hatch in the upper hull, which was a feature in the Coast Guard aircraft allowing the loading of stretchers is clearly visible.

(via Guy Denton)

The prototype XG-44 Widgeon, NX28633, is seen here at Bethpage in 1940.   *(Grumman photo P-1071)*

the left engine) failed, the emergency hand pump on the left side of the pilot's seat was used. Approximately 24 strokes were required to retract or extend the landing gear. Two red thumb latches were provided at the right of the lever slot to lock the landing gear control lever in the desired operating position, enabling the pilot to have one hand free in case hand pump operation was needed.

To check the position of the landing gear visually, small inspection windows were located at the top of each wheel pocket. Further safeguard was provided by a warning instrument designed to help prevent inadvertent landings with the gear in the incorrect position. Located on the top centre of the main instrument panel the signal was designed to light up when the right engine was throttled below 1,550rpm. "WHEELS UP" or "WHEELS DOWN" was signalled as appropriate, but in the event that the wheels were neither completely up or down – "DANGER WHEELS" was lit.

As noted above, the G-44 was powered by two six-cylinder Ranger 6-L-440-C5 inverted in-line air-cooled engines which produced 200hp each at 2450rpm, at sea level. The Rangers drove 82-inch two-bladed wooden Sensenich 82RS-72 propellers and gave the G-44 a maximum speed of 164mph at 3,000ft and a cruise speed on 75% power of 150mph at a similar height. Initial rate of climb was 700ft/min at sea level and the service ceiling was 14,600ft. A useful range of 800miles was available at a loaded weight of 4,525lbs.

Competitively priced at less than half that of the larger G-21A, the $30,000 Widgeon asking price bought items such as electric engine starters, carburettor heaters, a full set of engine and flight instruments,

navigation lights, fire extinguishers, mooring gear and anchor, two-way radio and a first aid kit, all included as standard.

The prototype Widgeon, designated XG-44, was given the c/n 1201 and was registered as NX28633. BA 'Bud' Gillies and Roy Grumman were at the controls for the first flight on 28th June 1940 which took place from Bethpage. No major problems were encountered and although the pre-production phase took several months, probably due to more pressing matters concerning the increasing volume of military aircraft then in development and production, the Widgeon was awarded its Approved Type Certificate (ATC No.734) on 5th April 1941.

By April 1941, Gillies Aviation, again acting as sales agent, had sold 10 G-44s, of which three had been delivered, and by August 1941 another 17 had been delivered. The US Coast Guard had also ordered a batch of eight aircraft to their contract TCG-33459 (c/ns 1222-1229 with serials V197-V204), the first of which was delivered on 7th July 1941. These aircraft were given the new BuAer type designation J4F-1.

The three-seat USCG J4F-1s were intended to replace earlier aircraft in the coastal patrol and Air-Sea Rescue (ASR) roles as well as undertaking routine communications duties. To facilitate the loading of stretchers, the J4F-1 had a hatch fitted in the upper hull just aft of the wing. This hatch also allowed a 0.30in machine gun to be fired from it, complementing a similar fitting in the bow.

The J4F-1 could also carry a single depth charge or bomb mounted on a rack beneath the starboard wing, inboard of the engine. However, carrying such a weapon,

even after reducing the crew to two, had a predictable effect on performance, affecting both rate of climb and range and rendering sustained single-engine flight impossible.

At the time of the Japanese attack on Pearl Harbor on 7th December 1941, approximately 40 aircraft had been delivered and all except the USCG aircraft had been commercial sales. A batch of 12 G-44 aircraft for the Portuguese Aviação Naval (c/ns 1241 to 1252) was in production with the first aircraft ready for delivery but other immediate future production was intended for commercial customers. After some consideration, the authorities released all the Portuguese aircraft for delivery and this took place between late December 1941 and February 1942. The final commercial G-44 to be released was c/n 1240 sold to the Canadian mining concern McIntyre Porcupine in December 1941, but in reality used to support the Canadian war effort. Ongoing production was diverted to military needs and the next 17 airframes (c/ns 1253 to 1269) were delivered to the USCG as V205-V221 on contract TCG-34026 between February and June 1942. While these deliveries were taking place, 15 of the earlier commercially sold G-44s were progressively acquired by the USAAF as OA-14s and the US Navy similarly acquired a small number of aircraft, eventually and notionally to be known as the J4F-2.

C/n 1270 was set aside to be the 'prototype' US Navy J4F-2 and was allocated the BuAer serial 30151. It was added initially to the Lend-Lease contract LL5229 (qv) that became NXs5229 (see below). This utility aircraft, the first true J4F-2, was accepted by the Navy on 10th

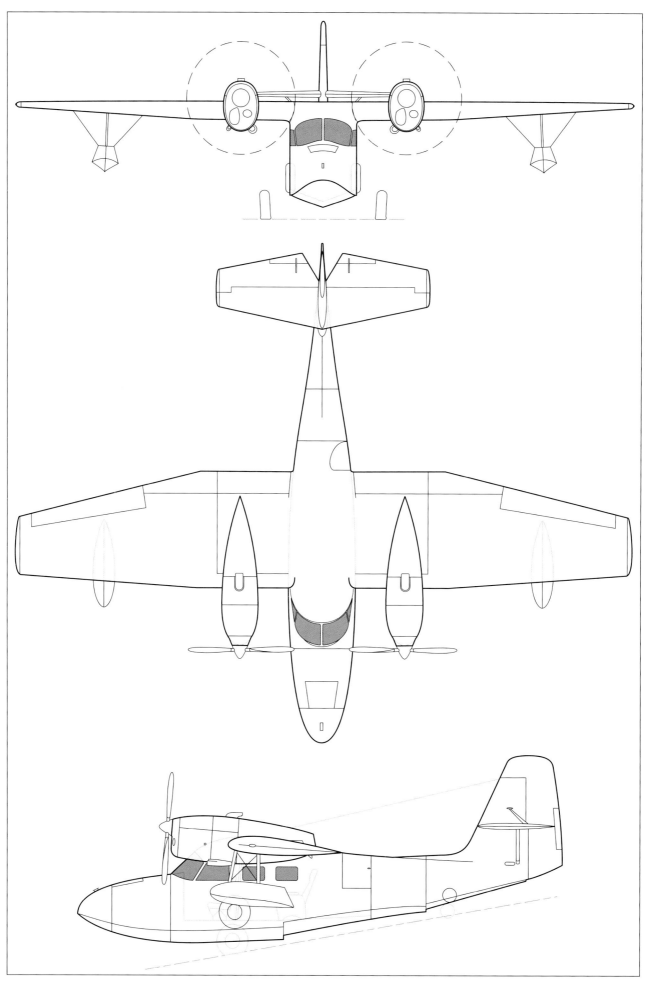

Three-view drawing of the G-44/J4F-1 Widgeon.

(Michael Zoeller)

July 1942. The J4F-2, still powered by the Ranger 6-L-440-C5 engine, lacked the stretcher-loading hatch of the J4F-1 but was otherwise identical to the Coast Guard aircraft.

The next batch of 20 aircraft (c/ns 1271-1290) was eventually approved for supply to Brazil (14) and Cuba (six) but after much complex negotiation the Cuban Aviación de Marina de Guerra declined to accept their aircraft and they were transferred to the US Navy becoming J4F-2s. The Brazilian aircraft were handed over at Bethpage between July and November 1942 and eventually the Cuban aircraft were accepted by the US Navy in September and October 1942. All 20 aircraft had been ordered originally on the US Navy Lend-Lease contract LL5229 that was later extended to become NXs5229 (the six diverted aircraft, c/ns 1273, 1274, 1277, 1278, 1281 and 1282, being given BuAer serials 33952-33957).

All subsequent war-time production aircraft (c/ns 1291-1400) were J4F-2s for the US Navy. The extension contract NXs5229 of August 1942 covered 50 aircraft (c/ns 1291-1340 with serials 32937-32986) and NOa(S)455 of November 1943 covered the final 60 aircraft (c/ns 1341-1400 with serials 37711-37770). Although early production plans were later scaled back there were no cancellations and production ran from December 1942 until February 1945. One aircraft was released for commercial sale in June 1944 and 18 were released under Lend-Lease to the United Kingdom (17 including one exchanged aircraft) and Uruguay (one).

G-44A Widgeon

Thus, by 1941, all Widgeon production was for military customers and it was not until 1944 that Grumman received US government approval to start work on another civil Widgeon project. In addition to the G-44 water-looping problem on smooth water landings (see Chapter 5), another problem was a tendency to "porpoise" during water take-offs. This problem was addressed by re-designing the forward hull. The hull was made deeper, from the bow to station 10 (see drawing below), and the keel line and step were modified to reduce spray. This modification was later offered as an update to existing G-44 aircraft.

Other minor improvements included a revised electrical panel and relocated pitot tube. The upgraded aircraft, allocated c/n 1401, was designated XG-44A, and registered as prototype NX41818 made its first flight on 8th August 1944. After the flight test programme, interspersed by some utility use, the XG-44A was certificated on 4th October 1945, under the G-44 Approved Type Certificate No.734.

Production models of the improved Widgeon were designated G-44A and deliveries started before World War II ended. Other improvements incorporated in the production models included oil coolers, exhaust mufflers, cabin heating and soundproofing. Some G-44As were fitted with an HF radio antenna which could be reeled out from a small mast on top of the vertical tailfin.

In November 1945, Grumman began a batch of 25 G-44A airframes, starting with c/n 1427, where changes were made to the hull to include two step vents aft of the step. Other improvements included adjustable pilot seats, two vacuum pumps, two landing lights and Sperry instruments. The new batch was powered by Ranger 6-440-C5s driving Sensenich 82RS-72 propellers. The engines for this batch of Widgeons were rebuilt at the Ranger factory and given "as-new" warranties.

In January 1946, starting with c/n 1434, changes were made to the hull to allow an increase in gross weight to 4,700lbs. These changes comprised removal of the false step and the internal keel connection and strengthening of the stringers at the cabin windows.

Between February and July 1945, 25 G-44As were delivered to civilian customers in the USA, and before production ended in May 1949 another 50 had been delivered of which only three went overseas.

SCAN-30 Widgeon

In 1948 as the G-44A production line slowed down, Grumman granted a licence to the small French company, Société de Constructions AéroNavales du Port Neuf (SCAN), to build Widgeons in France. The company, founded by Léon Douzille in 1938 with a head office in Paris, had been building SCAN-20 pusher flying boat trainers for the French Navy in a factory near La Rochelle on the west coast of France. The factory had been destroyed by the Germans in 1943 but with government help rebuilding was complete by 1948. With this limited experience of flying boat

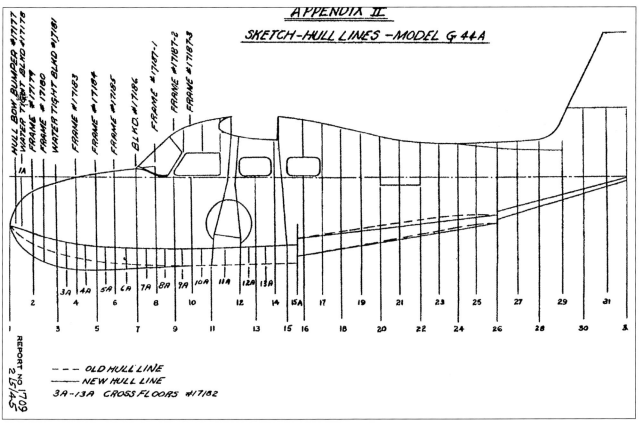

Hull lines sketch showing the difference in nose, forward keel and engine profile between G-44 and G-44A. (Grumman report dated 5th February 1945)

NOTICE
Weight and balance or operating limitation changes shall be entered in the appropriate aircraft record. An alteration must be compatible with all previous alterations to assure continued conformity with the applicable airworthiness requirements.

8. Description of Work Accomplished
(If more space is required, attach additional sheets. Identify with aircraft nationality and registration mark and date work completed.)

HULL MODIFICATION FROM G-44 TO G-44A

The hull bottom on the model G44A was redesigned from the bow to sta. 10 to eliminate a "porpoising " effect in water take-offs. The keel line from sta. 16 to sta. 26 was also altered slightly. The changes in the keel line from sta. 16 to sta. 26 have no effect on the structure as covered in the following report (page 97, paragraph 7). See attached Grumman Aircraft Engineering Corporation, Report No. 1709, Appendix II, pages 96, 97, 98 and 99 dated 2/5/45.

This modification is approved under the Aircraft Type Certificate Data Sheet No. A-734. See attached Data Sheet. Modification is only for the hull bottom.

This aircraft, a Grumman G-44 Widgeon, N144SL, S/N 1215 was inspected and verified the prior installation of revised hull bottom lines included in the Report 1709, Appendix II (List of Structural Changes and Their Effects on Structure), page 98 and 99.

See attached Report 1709 page 96 for Sketch of Hull Lines. Aircraft was previously reweighed with the hull bottom change.
---------- END ----------

Left: Details of the hull modification from G-44 to G-44A, as shown on FAA Form 337 for c/n 1215.

Above: An early G-44A Widgeon on a test flight from Grumman's facility at Bethpage, showing a distinct lack of colour, with an all-silver paint scheme except for the black hull bottom.
(Grumman photo)

Left: The XG-44A prototype NX41818 taken on 15th December 1944. The HF radio reel antenna with drogue cone attached to the small mast can just be discerned atop the rudder.
(Grumman photo G-13577)

construction it was a considerable gamble to embark upon building G-44As. Post-war optimism also produced an ambitious production target of some 40 aircraft, but with production financed by the government, Douzille was convinced that all 40 would be sold.

The aircraft, given the designation SCAN Type 30, differed from the

Left: SCAN Company logo. The outer circle, clouds and islands are silver, with the remainder of the design in various shades of blue. The darker parts of the winged boat are almost black.
(via Jean-Pierre Dubois)

Grumman originals in being built to metric measurements using non-anodised metal for the airframe and the hull. The engines chosen were also different. SCAN decided to install 190hp Mathis 8G40 eight-cylinder engines in the prototype. The production SCAN-30As had 240hp Salmson Mk8 AS-00 engines, with prospective customers being given the choice of the Salmsons, de Havilland six-cylinder inline Gipsy Queen IIs of 200hp, or 260hp Lycoming flat-six GO-435-C2s. Aircraft built with the Gipsys would be SCAN-30Gs while the Lycoming-powered examples would be SCAN-30Ls.

The prototype SCAN-30, F-WFDM (c/n 01), fitted with Salmson 8 AS-00 engines, seen here in early 1949. The aircraft was written-off in July 1949 after crashing into the river Seine at Les Mureaux near Paris during a demonstration flight.
(via PX Henry)

SCAN-30G F-BGTD (c/n 19), built in 1949, fitted with deHavilland Gipsy Queen engines. This aircraft was written-off after a crash landing off Calshot in Southampton Water, UK a day after delivery to a new owner in May 1961.
(via PX Henry)

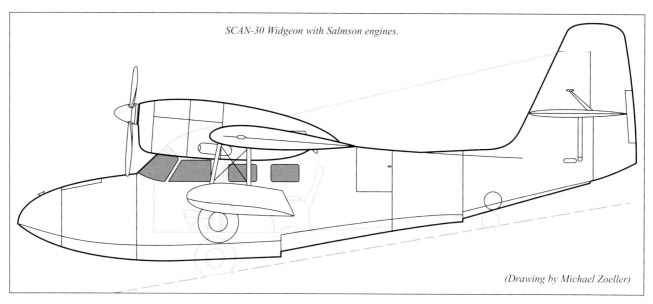

SCAN-30 Widgeon with Salmson engines.

(Drawing by Michael Zoeller)

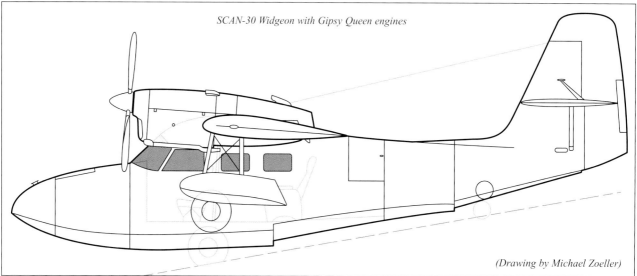

SCAN-30 Widgeon with Gipsy Queen engines

(Drawing by Michael Zoeller)

However, although offering a choice of engine is praiseworthy if the chosen engines are available, unfortunately for SCAN, obtaining the power-plants proved far from easy. Nevertheless, the company went ahead with airframe production and some reports claim that all 41 airframes had been completed before the prototype made its first flight!

In support of this a Bureau Veritas report dated 3rd April 1953, covering the inspection of construction numbers 2, 3, 4, 9, 10, 11, 12, 13, 14, 15, 16, 20, 21, 22, 23, 25, 31, 32, 33, 34, 37, and another report dated 23rd October 1956 covering c/ns 35 and 41, stated that their progress on the production line had been monitored (by the BV) from April 1948 until December 1949. The reports stated that as soon as the inspections were completed "the airframes have been prepared for long storage". The BV also noted that the construction was carried out in accordance with Grumman Widgeon drawings, except for the following main modifications:

- Modification of the firewall and engine controls for installation of Salmson AS-00 engines.
- Modification of the US instrument panel

and instruments systems for installation of French instruments.

- Modification of the oil circulation, and addition of an oil stop valve.
- Modification of the landing gear system for installation of French material (ERAM make).
- Modification of the Flettner control.
- Structural reinforcement in the area of the centre section - hull attachment to enable operation at the weight of 2,350kg. (To be operated at 2,350kg the additional following modifications should be embodied: a) Reinforcement of wing attachment fish plates; b) Modification of wingtips; c) Hull reinforcement in the projection of wheel housing)
- Installation of extinguishers.
- Additional locking of landing gear in high position.
- Replacement of standard parts with American dimensions by similar standard parts with French dimensions.

Before that, in 1947, the company had been in negotiation with the Aéronautique Navale for an order for SCAN-30s powered by the French Mathis engines of

190hp, producing a cruising speed of 149mph. In fact, the Aéronautique Navale did evaluate the Widgeon (albeit with Ranger engines) in the shape of the former US Navy J4F-2 c/n 1297 which was sold surplus and registered to Wallace Clair in 1946 as G-44 NC79801. It is believed that the aircraft was en route to the USA from Cairo (where it had been stricken by the US Navy) when it reached Croydon, UK in October 1946. It was then evaluated by the Centre d'Essais en Vol (CEV) at Istres in early 1947, flown from the Étang de Berre by a naval pilot between the 5th and 11th February 1947. When the aircraft crashed at Berre and was abandoned by the American owner, the Aéronautique Navale was not impressed, and SCAN did not receive their hoped for order.

The G-44 was sold by Clair to SCAN on 15th July 1947 who rebuilt it and sold it to Air Monaco in March 1948, described as "Widgeon G-44 SCAN nº 101", perhaps optimistically assuming production numbers would reach 100.

However, a tragedy befell the SCAN company on 24th April 1948 when Leon Douzille was killed returning from Lisbon to La Rochelle in G-44A NC86644. The aircraft crashed in mountains near the village of Pineda de la Sierra in the Burgos region of Spain.

Despite this set-back, the SCAN-30 prototype, c/n 01 registered F-WFDM, first flew in January 1949, from La Rochelle. Unfortunately about six months later the French-built Widgeon made headlines for all the wrong reasons, when on 11th July 1949 the pilot Paul Mingam misjudged his altitude and crashed into the River Seine at Les Mureaux during a low altitude demonstration flight. All four occupants survived but the incident was made all the more more newsworthy because Jacqueline Auriol, the daughter-in-law of the French President, had been on board in the co-pilot's seat and was seriously injured in the crash. Happily she recovered after several operations and went on to become a famous test pilot who set many records in French jet fighter aircraft. But, with orders for the amphibian already thin on the ground, the publicity was undoubtedly not good for SCAN.

It was thought that maybe the SCAN-30 would find a market in the numerous French colonies overseas, and this led to a West African sales tour late in 1950. Leaving Toussus-le-Noble on 18th November 1950, SCAN-30 c/n 4 F-BFHD, piloted by Paul Mingam, with Bernard Witt as co-pilot/radio operator and Camille Delaire as navigator/mechanic, called at La Rochelle/Laleu and ended the first day at Perpignan. Crossing to Tangier, Morocco on 20th November the SCAN-30 then followed the west coast of Africa reaching Pointe Noire in the Congo on 4th December. After flying inland to

Brazzaville, Mingam then flew north to Fort Lamy in Chad before heading westwards back to Dakar, Senegal, which was reached on 14th December. The SCAN-30 then headed northwards up the coast to Casablanca and from there, via Oran, reached Algiers on 19th December, ending the tour at Marseille-Marignane the next day.

This mammoth sales tour produced no orders and by February 1952 only eight aircraft had been delivered. Seven of these were to French colonial government agencies – four in French Guiana and three to the Health Ministry in Indochina. The eighth machine also went to Indochina, and was for the personal use of Emperor Bao-Dai of Vietnam. The remaining 33 airframes, not all complete and most without engines, were put up for sale by public auction at La Rochelle by the French government.

In late 1952, 20 largely engineless SCAN-30s were sold to Intercontinental Aviation, an American company managed by Alan H Sanstad, but about which no more is known. By 1954, all 20 were owned by Conair Corporation, Montreal, Canada, but none were entered on the Canadian Civil Aircraft Register. One of these 20, possibly c/n 4, was converted to SCAN-30L status with Lycoming GO-435 engines, at Sanstad's request. The eleventh test flight after conversion is known to have taken place on 18th March 1954. According to French registration records, ownership of c/n 4 had passed to Sanstad's wife, Marie Therese, on 10th April 1954 and was registered to her as F-BFHD on

17th May1954. It is thought that Sanstad then used the aircraft as a demonstrator in an effort to generate much-needed sales. Unfortunately, while demonstrating the aircraft to the Swiss company Farner SA, it crashed into the Bieler See in Switzerland on 28th May 1955. Sanstad was killed in the accident and the founder of Farner SA, Willi Farner, was injured. The aircraft overturned and sank, but whether it was recovered is not known.

At this point the story becomes confusing because the Conair Corporation of Montreal, Quebec, Canada is quoted as vendor on Bills of Sale in October 1954, seven months before the crash in Switzerland. The connection between Intercontinental Aviation and Conair has not been established but none of the aircraft were ever in Canada and therefore the transfers of ownership were only on paper. The fact that 19 of the airframes were on board the *"Cape Rodney"* destined for Los Angeles, California on 18th February 1953 would suggest that Sanstad had soon decided to sell them to Conair Corporation. Some of the airframes were then sold by Conair to Lee Mansdorf & Company in California as early as October 1954. According to FAA files c/n 4 was on a Bill of Sale from Conair to Mansdorf dated 26th October 1954 and on 8th November 1954 the aircraft was given an Experimental Certificate of Airworthiness after conversion to "PACE Gannet" status with Lycoming R-680 radial engines. The experimental certificate was requested by Mansdorf "to explore the flight characteristics of the aircraft fitted with the

SCAN-30 N57LM (c/n 4) was re-engined with Lycoming R-680 radials by Lee Mansdorf in 1954. The aircraft, now powered by 350hp Lycoming TIO-540 engines, is currently with an owner in Wisconsin.

(Art Krieger Collection)

300hp Lycomings". A Standard Certificate of Airworthiness was awarded on 7th October 1955, by which time the aircraft was registered as N57LM.

It is difficult therefore to reconcile the two sets of facts. The situation could be explained however, if it was c/n 24 (not c/n 4) that was the aircraft exported to the USA and converted to PACE Gannet status by November 1954. This is a possibility for two reasons: a) because the FAA only record the information given by the owner which in this case was incorrect, and b) because c/n 24 has no recorded history except that it was one of the 20 Sanstad aircraft. It could be assumed that Sanstad had c/n 4 converted to Lycoming power in order to use it as a sales demonstrator in Europe, and therefore did not allow it to go to the USA.

Most of this batch were re-engined with the 300hp Lycoming R-680 radials, and after other modifications, were sold as new "PACE Gannets". C/ns 25 and 35 were fitted with Fairchild Ranger 6-440 engines, as in the Grumman-built G-44. Details of these conversions are given in "Modifications & Projects" in Chapter 5.

The SCAN company obviously remained optimistic about their ability to sell all of the SCAN-30s and had projected two improvements to the original design.

These were the SCAN-31, which was to be a Widgeon with a large rear door fitted and the SCAN-32, a larger wingspan Widgeon. Neither design was progressed.

Widgeon Variants – A Production Summary

276 Widgeons of all models were produced by Grumman between 1940 and 1949, together with 42 SCAN-30 aircraft subsequently manufactured by the Société de Constructions AéroNavales du Port Neuf (SCAN). As with the Goose, some of these aircraft received new designations while in production or shortly before delivery, while others were delivered to customers who at various times gave 'their' aircraft new designations or names. World War II transfers to the US military forces from commercial and private sources as well as isolated inter-service exchanges and special re-designations resulted in potentially confusing new identities and this summary provides additional information for a few specific aircraft to assist understanding. The summary broadly categorises each aircraft as manufactured for either a civilian or military purchaser with additional detail in respect of the primary military designations. Reference to the other sections of this book including individual aircraft histories will give greater insights into any secondary modifications and projects. Post-war, virtually all the surplus military Widgeons passed into commercial and private hands and indeed a few post-war production aircraft eventually found their way into military use.

The Civilian Aircraft Models

XG-44 One built in 1940 with c/n 1201.

G-44 31 aircraft built for the civilian market in 1941 with c/ns 1202-1221 and 1230-1240 and 12 for the Portuguese Navy with c/ns 1241-1252 built in 1941 and early 1942. All except one of the civilian aircraft were sold initially to buyers in the United States and during the course of WWII many of them were acquired by the USAAF and the US Navy for military use. Those acquired by the USAAF in 1942 and 1944 as the OA-14 were 1202 (42-38218), 1203 (42-43460), 1204 (42-38355), 1205 (42-38340), 1206 (42-38223), 1207 (42-38216), 1208 (44-52997), 1209 (42-38356), 1211 (42-38285), 1218 (42-38217), 1219 (42-53003), 1230 (42-38219), 1232 (42-38221), 1233 (42-38339), 1234 (42-38220) and 1238 (42-38222). Five G-44s used by commercial airlines under contract to the US Navy were acquired by the Navy and allocated BuAer serial numbers and were given the USN designation J4F-2. These aircraft were 1214, 1215 and 1239 with serials 99074, 99075 and 99076 (linkage unknown), 1231 (09789) and 1235 (99077). The serials 99074-99077 were allocated circa early 1945 to Pan American Airways aircraft that had been in naval use since 1942 but which by definition had not been worn on the aircraft. The 12 Portuguese aircraft were considered briefly for acquisition by the US Navy in December 1941 and it is believed that the BuAer serials 09805 to 09816 were set aside for that purpose. Once the aircraft were released for Portugal the serial allocation should have been cancelled. This has led to the subsequent identification of this serial range in derivative naval records as being an allocation to 'J4F-2' aircraft although the designation J4F-2 did not exist in December 1941. Further details of the military contracts can be found on pages 125 and 144 onwards.

XG-44A One built in 1944 with c/n 1401.

G-44A 75 built for the civilian market between 1945 and 1949 with c/ns 1402 to 1476.

The US Army Air Force Variant

OA-14 The USAAF did not acquire any new production aircraft although the majority of the 15 OA-14s acquired from civilian owners in the spring of 1942 were standardised for Army use. An additional aircraft was acquired from the Corps of Engineers in 1944. Their details are included in the G-44 production listings in Appendix 2.

The US Coast Guard Variant

J4F-1 The BuAer designation J4F-1 was initially given to the version procured for the US Coast Guard in 1941 prior to the Widgeon's adoption by the US Navy in 1942. Thus the first eight aircraft were c/ns 1222-1229. These aircraft were produced against the contract TCG-33459 and were delivered in 1941 with the serials V197-V204. With the termination of civilian production in December 1941 and new Coast Guard commitments the USCG also took the next 17 available aircraft with c/ns 1253-1269 from the re-prioritised production line. These aircraft, also built as J4F-1, were acquired against contract TCG-34026 and were delivered in 1942 with serials V205-V221. Aircraft 1269 (V221) was renumbered administratively as a J4F-2 when it was transferred to the US Navy in October 1942.

The US Navy and Export Variants

J4F-2 The BuAer designation J4F-2 was assigned to the US Navy's version of the Widgeon in 1942. It was also used by the Navy to identify five G-44 models acquired in 1942 and 1943 and a batch of 20 aircraft approved for export to Cuba and Brazil in 1942 (the much-debated Munitions Assignments Committee's 'Case 88' aircraft), the first of which were laid down prior to the adoption of the J4F-2 designation and which were at that time referred to both as G-44 and J4F-1. It is important to understand that the 'dash 1' and 'dash 2' designations identified aircraft respectively procured for the USCG and the USN rather than to any precisely defined technical specification.

The first aircraft designated J4F-2 was c/n 1270, effectively assigned to the Navy as a prototype aircraft with the BuAer serial 30151 and which flew in June 1942. The batch of 20 aircraft with c/ns 1271-1290 was authorised for supply to Brazil and Cuba prior to the creation of the designation J4F-2 and they were known initially as J4F-1. However, at the point of delivery in July 1942, the six potential Cuban aircraft (c/ns 1273, 1274, 1277, 1278, 1281 and 1282) were rejected by the Cuban Navy and were taken on charge subsequently by the USN in September 1942. They were then re-designated J4F-2 and given BuAer serials 33952-33957. A further complication arises in respect of 33952 which is speculated to have been transferred further to the USCG as 221 (replacing c/n 1269) but which appears to have retained the designation J4F-2.

The 14 aircraft delivered to Brazil in 1942 were 1271, 1272, 1275, 1276, 1279, 1280 and 1283-1290. They received the local serials 01-14 and by the time of export were known as J4F-2. Although delivered under the auspices of a Defense Aid programme, these aircraft were at no time allocated BuAer serial numbers and the local type number 'UC4F-2' was created by the Brazilian Air Force some years later as part of a major administrative reorganisation.

There were therefore 110 true production

A rare photograph of an unidentified US Coast Guard J4F-1 in early-war US Navy two-tone grey colours, complete with red and white rudder and the 'red dot' roundel. These early 1942-vintage markings were soon abandoned, the roundel losing the 'dot', and the rudder stripes disappearing.

(Aeroplane Photo Supply Co via William Haines Collection)

This undated publicity photograph shows two production US Navy J4F-2s, perhaps up from Bethpage, prior to delivery. The bland markings and the style of the roundel suggest a 1943-44 timeframe for the photograph. By and large, the Navy saw the Widgeon as a somewhat fragile communications aircraft, and production ceased in 1945.

(US Navy photo)

J4F-2 aircraft with c/ns 1291-1400, delivered between December 1942 and February 1945. These aircraft were numbered 32937-32986 and 37711-37770. Their contractual details are explained on page 137 but in summary the early aircraft 30151 and 33952-33957 were added to LL-5229 of June 1942 and 32937-32986 to a contract extension NXs5229 dated August 1942. Although the serial allocation 37711-37770 dates from late 1942, this final contract, NOa(S)455, was not placed until November 1943. No aircraft were cancelled from contracts (J4F-2 production for the US Navy ceased well before the close of World War II) but further extensive production envisaged in 1943 did not materialise and a large number of serials earmarked for J4F-2s were not used.

One aircraft within the production run covered by serials 32937-32986 and

37711-37770, c/n 1370 (37740), was released for commercial sale to Union Oil in June 1944 and a total of 18 other aircraft was released under Lend-Lease to the United Kingdom (17 including one exchanged aircraft) and Uruguay (one). Virtually all the British aircraft were returned, some fairly quickly, and several subsequently saw some use with the US Navy. The local British name 'Gosling', abandoned in favour of 'Widgeon' after the receipt of about four aircraft, has no formal or separate status as a 'type'. Despite this, a three-view silhouette of the 'Gosling' was included in the 'Recognition Handbook of British Aircraft' AP 1480A Part 2, prepared for the UK Air Ministry under the direction of the Minister of Aircraft Production (see alongside).

Aside from cancelled serials and the previously explained G-44s 09789 and 99074-99077 there was one more 'J4F-2' that was assigned to the US Navy. This was the former US Coast Guard J4F-1, c/n 1269 numbered V221, that was transferred to the USN in October 1942. It was assigned the BuAer serial 34585 but this had not been applied at the time of its terminal accident late that month. US Navy records that were raised retrospectively to show its acquisition and strike (on 31st October 1942) refer to the aircraft as 'J4F-2' although its accident report describes it as 'J4F-1'.

XJ4F-2 NACA was loaned c/n 1326 (32972) in 1947 and it later acquired this designation which was retained by the Navy on its return in 1949 and was so used until 1954 when it was scrapped.

E-175 US Navy aircraft c/n 1330 (32976) received extensive modifications during research projects with EDO Aircraft (see page 77) and as a consequence the Navy recognised EDO's number 'E-175' as a type number in December 1952. 32976 remained on the Navy's books until February 1956 and all inventory records for this period refer only to the 'E-175'.

The SCAN-30

SCAN-30 There were 42 aircraft built under production licensed by Grumman to SCAN. Company records suggest that they were assigned the local c/ns 01 (for the prototype) and 1 to 41 for the production airframes. All those built went to the civil market.

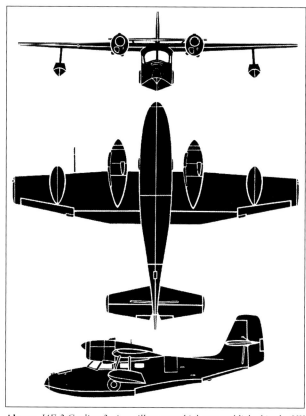

Above: *J4F-2 Gosling 3-view silhouette which was published in the UK Air Ministry's "Recognition Handbook of British Aircraft AP 1480A Part 2".*

Below: *Unfortunately, this photograph of the 'Petulant Porpoise', otherwise known as the E-175/J4F-2 32976 (c/n 1330), is undated, but is probably from the early 1950s, location unknown. The E-175 trialled a number of hull designs during its time with Edo, the National Advisory Committee for Aeronautics and the Naval Air Test Center, before spending nearly thirty years in storage, awaiting museum display. Since 1987, it has been on public view at Pima County Air Museum, Tucson, Arizona (now Pima Air & Space Museum).* (Warren Shipp via Art Krieger)

The prototype G-73 Mallard, NX41824, makes a low pass during flight testing, circa September 1946. (Grumman photo)

CHAPTER 4:
G-73 MALLARD DEVELOPMENT

AS IT BECAME APPARENT THAT WORLD War II was coming to an end, the Grumman management and design teams turned their thoughts to post-war aviation requirements, although the hell-for-leather pace of military production continued at Bethpage, indeed in March 1945, Grumman produced 664 military aircraft, which still stands today as an all-time production record for a single month.

Grumman optimistically expected that a post-WWII "feel-good factor" would produce a healthy order book for a feeder airliner. Based on their expertise in amphibian aircraft they imagined that a 10-15 seat twin-engined amphibian would fit the bill and thus in early 1945 development started on Design No.73, under the leadership of Gordon Israel.

An improved version of the Widgeon was also initiated, as Design No.74, but it was decided that the proposed improvements were not significant enough to warrant production.

Leroy Grumman had been influenced by studies suggesting a market for 250 or more G-73s and thus gave the go-ahead for production of the twin-engined amphibian. Gordon Israel's team included Hank Kurt

and of course Ralston Stalb, and between them they produced what is generally accepted as the finest looking amphibian ever built.

Design No.73 reached mock-up stage in September 1945. Ralston Stalb had been working on Design No.64 at the same time as the 73, and after much experimental work in the towing tanks of the Stevens Institute of Technology under the auspices of the US Navy Bureau of Aeronautics and the National Advisory Committee on Aeronautics, the two aircraft emerged with similar hull lines. Work with the Goose had suggested that a re-positioning of the step would be beneficial, whilst experiments with the Widgeon deemed a longer fore-body to be advantageous.

These two improvements coupled with the incorporation of a vented step, to eliminate drag on take-off, meant that the G-73 performed perfectly when the prototype, c/n J-1 NX41824, made its first flight on 30th April 1946 in the hands of Fred Rowley.

The G-73's large two-step hull, strong enough for rough water operations, was an all-metal (24ST) semi-monocoque structure covered in aluminium alloy sheet which was butt-jointed and flush-

riveted. To provide safe operation the 48ft 4in long hull was divided into six watertight compartments:

(i) Forward was a bow section measuring 30x36x60ins, incorporating stowage for an anchor and up to 350lbs of baggage. In the floor of this bow compartment was the nose-wheel housing. The hand-operated bilge pump was also located in the bow and all six watertight compartments could be drained from the pumping station in the bow or from another under the main cabin door step. A mooring hatch was cut into the top of the bow compartment and from there the cockpit could be reached through a watertight door under the instrument panel.

(ii) Aft of the bow section was the cockpit complete with controls for two pilots who sat on fully upholstered vertically adjustable seats. The control wheel stanchion was on the centreline of the airplane. The left-hand control wheel could be thrown over to the right-hand side or an auxiliary wheel stowed under the right seat could be attached quickly without the use of tools to allow dual control. The right-hand wheel had, however, to be removed to allow easy access to the bow

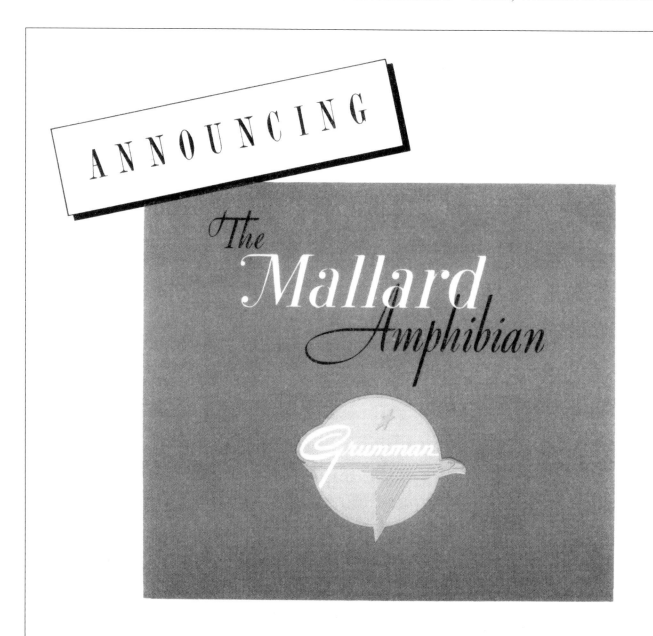

The cover of a Grumman sales brochure - "Announcing the Grumman Mallard", issued in 1946.

compartment. The rudder pedals were of the upright type and the pilot's pedals were adjustable fore and aft. The co-pilot's pedals hinged out of the way for access to the bow compartment. Brakes were provided for the pilot and an additional set of brakes could be provided for the co-pilot (at a slight additional cost) for scheduled air transport operation.

The elevator and rudder tab controls were located in the cockpit dome. Lateral trim, which was rarely required, was provided by an infinite position torque spring bungee located on the upper end of the control wheel stanchion.

Two views of the G-73 Mallard cockpit, showing the dual yoke (above) and the rudder pedals (below) folded back to allow access to the door into the bow compartment.
(Steve Hamilton)

A full instrument panel provided:
Kollsman Airspeed indicator
Kollsman Sensitive Altimeter
Sperry Artificial horizon
Sperry Directional gyro
Kollsman Rate of Climb indicator
Pioneer Turn and Bank indicator
Kollsman Magnetic Direction indicator
Kollsman Tachometer (fuel with built-in cyncroscope)
Kollsman Dual Manifold pressure indicator
2x Edison Engine gauge units
Weston Cylinder head temperature gauge
General Electric Dual Fuel quantity gauge
Lewis Engineering Dual Carburettor temperature gauge
Weston Outside temperature gauge
Hydraulic pressure gauge
Kollsman Suction gauge
General Electric Landing gear and Flap position indicator
Kollsman Electrically-heated Pitot tube
Clock

Like the main cabin, the cockpit was fully soundproofed and carpeted. Large ducts fed from the air-conditioning system were directed at each windshield panel to provide defrosting. According to Grumman literature, special efforts were made to provide "the best and most functional radio installation possible". This included the following Bendix equipment: an MN-31 automatic compass; an MN-26 receiver and anti-static loop; an RTA-1B transmitter-receiver (which incorporated a 50watt transmitter); and an MN-53A marker beacon receiver, together with accessories and antennae for all the above. All the controls for this Bendix radio package were custom built for the G-73 and the components were grouped for maximum operative convenience and mounted compactly on three panels. The volume controls and audio switches were located on the instrument board cowl and were readily accessible to either pilot. The tuning units and remainder of the controls were located in a control panel that was placed on a sloping shelf below the main instrument panel, also making them accessible to either pilot.

(iii) Moving aft, again through a watertight door, was the main cabin, access to which was also gained through a door on the port side at the rear of the cabin. An escape hatch was provided on the starboard side of the rear cabin. Passenger comfort was assured by the installation of heavy soundproofing to the cabin interior and provision of automatic air-conditioning, governed by a thermostat in the centre of the cabin. The two full-length divans in the forward main cabin and the four reclining chairs in the rear were upholstered in leather or heavyweight fabrics according to customer specifications. All seats and safety belt attachments were designed to withstand 20g load factors in all directions

in a crash landing. A portable card table was stowed in the rear baggage compartment when not in use. The floor was carpeted and dividers and panelling within the cabin were covered in real wood veneers. Adequate locker space for personal effects was provided and thirsty passengers were provided with a two-quart Thermos jug and drinking glasses in one of the wheel well lockers. In case of emergency, two one-quart Pyrene portable fire extinguishers were provided – one in the cockpit and one at the aft end of the main cabin.

(iv) A lavatory compartment was provided at the rear of the main cabin opposite the entrance door. This was equipped with a chemical toilet and a wash basin, complete with four gallon reservoir. A mirror and a shelf for toilet accessories were provided, and a First Aid kit was also located in the lavatory.

(v) A 36x48x60in compartment, again for up to 350lbs of additional baggage, was situated aft of the main cabin. This gave a total cargo/baggage capacity of 73cu.ft. The aluminium boarding ladder was stowed just inside the baggage compartment door.

(vi) The last compartment was the sealed aft compartment although this did contain two tubes containing parachute flares. These were incorporated to conform to CAA regulations that required their presence if the aircraft was to be operated for hire at night, and would have been used in the case of a forced landing in the dark. From c/n J-35 onwards they were not built-in and became an optional extra. From January 1948 owners of aircraft J-1 to J-34 were offered free cover plates for the holes in the fuselage skin, if they wished to remove the flares and gain an extra 46lbs useful load.

The tapered cantilever wing was an all-metal (24ST) semi-monocoque structure covered with flush-riveted aluminium alloy sheet, had a span of 66ft 8ins, and was set high on the fuselage. With NACA 23021 airfoil section at the root and NACA 23012 at the tip, the wings had an area of 444sq ft. The wing flaps, again of aluminium alloy construction but fabric-covered, were operated hydraulically and limited to 125mph. A blow-up device was incorporated to prevent damage to the flaps should the permissible speed limit be exceeded inadvertently. The ailerons, again fabric covered, were of the slotted-hinge type and to improve aileron control fixed wing-slots were positioned on the outer leading edges. Attached to the underside of the outer wings were all-metal wingtip floats suspended on tapering pylons. The beautifully aerodynamic floats were divided into three compartments of which the rear one could be used as an auxiliary fuel tank. The floats and pylons were also readily removable for extended land operations.

The cantilever tail assembly was of 24ST aluminium alloy semi-monocoque

construction with metal-covered fixed surfaces and fabric-covered moving surfaces. Elevator and rudder trim tabs were controllable from the cockpit and the rudder was provided with an internal seal for improved control during single engine flight. The horizontal tail had a span of 20 feet while the top of the vertical fin was 18ft 9ins above the ground.

The tricycle undercarriage employed on the G-73 was a major departure from the Goose design, and would also be used on the G-64 Albatross. The landing gear was fully retractable, using engine-driven hydraulic pumps, with a hand pump provided for emergency use. With a track width of almost fifteen feet, the under-carriage featured Bendix long-stroke shock struts and 9.50x16 wheels with hydraulic braking. With typical ingenuity, Grumman and Bendix managed to solve the problem of getting the wheels from eight feet below the wing into the wells in the fuselage side. The fully-castoring nose wheel had a centering device to assure correct wheel alignment on initial contact with the ground.

The G-73 design team sought an engine in the 700-800hp class to power the new larger amphibian, rather than the 450hp engines used on the Goose. Unfortunately there were no suitable engines available and so the tried and tested nine-cylinder Pratt & Whitney Wasp R1340-S3H1 air-cooled radial was chosen to power the G-73, rated at 600hp for take-off at 2250rpm at 3000ft, but more typically at 550hp at 2200rpm at 5000ft. The engines were fed from a 190-US gallon fuel tank in each wing inboard of the engine. The tanks were lined with a special Thiokol (polysulphide) compound bonded directly to the metal structure. Engine-driven fuel pumps were provided in an arrangement such that either engine could be fed from either tank. Electric motor-driven pumps were installed for use during take-off and landing or when the engine pump failed. The 380 US gallon fuel load could be increased to 480 US gallons when necessary by carrying 50 US gallons in each wing tip float. The float tanks were piped directly to each main tank with fuel transfer accomplished by means of electric pumps controllable by the pilot. The engines were started by means of 24-volt direct drive Eclipse starters and lubricated from ten US gallon oil tanks located in the top of the engine nacelle aft of the fire wall. The engines drove Hamilton Standard three-blade hydromatic propellers equipped with full feathering accessories and were exhausted through a collector ring with a venturi trough outlet on top of the cowl at the centreline. For use in an emergency a 15lb carbon dioxide engine compartment fire extinguisher was provided. Energised electrically, it could be directed to either engine or to the cabin heater compartment by means of solenoid operated valves.

Although not entirely satisfactory, the P&W Wasps provided the G-73 with a

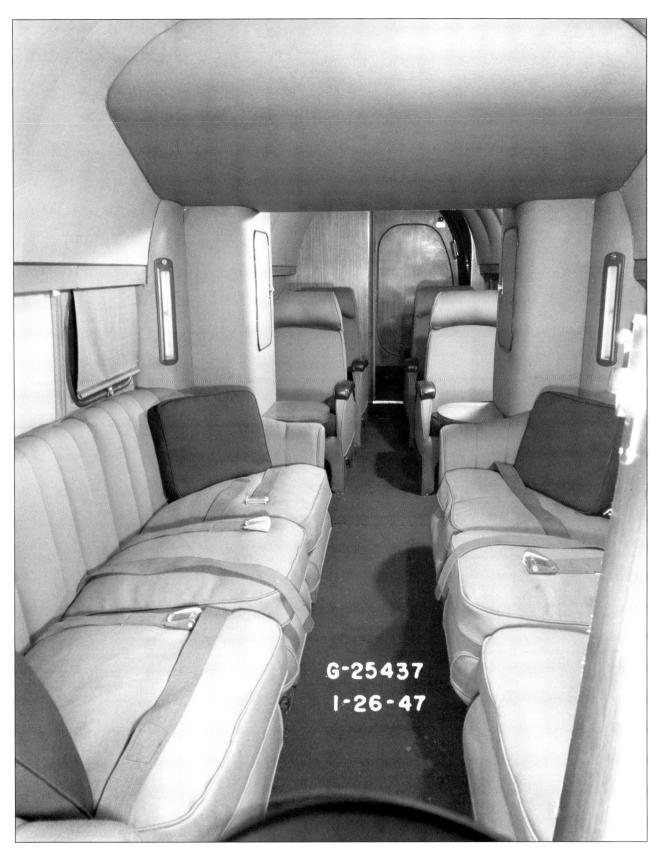

A G-73 Mallard interior looking aft, with the well-upholstered divans in the foreground.   *(Grumman photo G-25437 dated 26th January 1947)*

maximum speed of 203mph at sea level and a cruise speed of 160mph at 8,000ft on 55% power.

The maiden flight of the G-73 on 30th April 1946 went according to plan and all subsequent test flights showed that Grumman had an amphibian aircraft that met all the design parameters.

New post-war regulations were drawn up for the expected growth in air transport, including a new CAR 4B Transport Category, and the G-73 became only the second aircraft type, after the Martin 2-0-2, to be thus certificated. The G-73 was awarded Approved Type Certificate No.783 by the CAA on 8th September 1946 and deliveries began with c/n J-2 on 27th September 1946.

The successor to the Goose was named "Mallard" by Leroy Grumman and although the new amphibian was well received by owners and pilots alike, Grumman's ambitions for healthy sales were not realised. Despite the fact that Air Commuting Inc of New York ordered one Mallard with an option on a second, planning to provide services from the

Manhattan waterfront, there was little interest from other airlines. This was mainly due to the fact that the fledgling airlines could obtain war-surplus aircraft at a much lower price than that of a new Mallard, and thus the G-73 was destined to become a corporate aircraft, or a toy for the rich sportsman. A good example of this was the fact that Lofleidir, the Icelandic carrier, had acquired an option for an early delivery from Grumman of a G-73 Mallard. However, this option was sold in the summer of 1946 when the company acquired three military surplus JRF-6Bs instead. In combination with Air

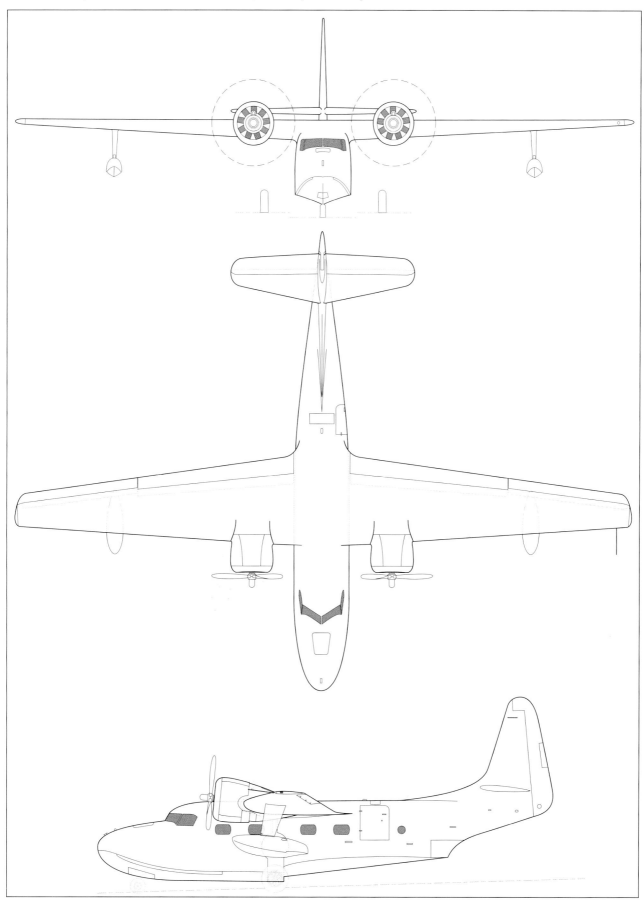

Three-view drawings of the G-73 Mallard.

(Drawings by Michael Zoeller)

The prototype G-73 Mallard NX41824 on the step, during a test flight circa September 1946.

(Grumman photo)

Commuting's failure to start their service Grumman halted production in 1951, with only 59 of the sleek amphibians built. Although partly due to poor sales figures, restrictions on the use of aluminium and other strategic materials implemented as a result of the Korean War played a role. It was not until much later in time that the Mallard was used as intended. Details of Mallard owners/operators can be found in Chapter 8 and Appendix 3.

G-73T Turbo Mallard

The main problem with a Mallard for airline use was the cost of operating and maintaining a 1940s-designed aircraft. The Mallard had been built from the outset with engines that did not provide the designed output, because there was none available at that time in the preferred 700hp range. It was plain, therefore, that fitting an engine with a higher take-off rating would be beneficial, and if that engine was a turboprop it would have other desirable effects such as a lower aircraft-empty weight and improved performance.

The idea of fitting the G-73 with turbine engines had occurred to J Fred Frakes and whilst flying his Safeways Mallard around Alaska he had considered the idea for a couple of years. However, the first person to do anything practical to solve the problem was Ray Peterson of Northern Consolidated Airlines. He had also wondered about turbine power for the amphibian and had then bought Mallard J-36 from Frakes in 1964.

Peterson decided to try out the idea, but in a rather unusual way. He took his G-73 to Victoria Air Maintenance on Vancouver Island and had them replace only one of the R-1340 radials with a Pratt & Whitney Canada PT-6 turbine engine. Peterson then returned to Alaska with his hybrid Mallard and, with his partner Bob Lampson, performed a programme of test flights to get some data on turbine performance. After 50 hours of tests with the hybrid by pilot John Waloka, assisted by Fred Cowley of Pratt & Whitney Canada, it was confirmed that water ingestion in the turbine would not be a problem, and that any corrosion within the turbine would

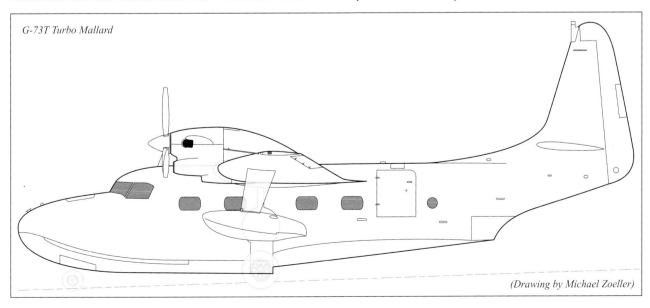

G-73T Turbo Mallard

(Drawing by Michael Zoeller)

Frakes Turbo-Mallard N2974, piloted by Fred Frakes, during a feasibility study in 1971, commissioned by the New York Department of Marine and Aviation, into the use of amphibian aircraft in the so-called "Northeast Corridor", linking Boston, New York, Philadelphia and Baltimore.
(Grumman via H Scanlan)

be manageable. The only problem was that at that time the PT-6 could only develop 550shp, which was less than the R-1340 which it was supposed to improve upon!

With the conclusion of the tests, J-36 was re-united with its starboard R-1340 and returned to service with Northern Consolidated. Frakes hailed Peterson's test programme as far-sighted but nevertheless had to wait for the right engine before he could embark on his project to produce an improved Mallard.

Meanwhile, Pratt & Whitney Canada continued development of the PT-6 and by 1967, by which time the engine-maker was known as United Aircraft of Canada Ltd (UACL) and Frakes had moved to California, the PT6A-27, producing 680shp, had been certificated.

Frakes re-purchased J-36, from Wien Consolidated Airlines and with his team at Angwin in the Napa Valley in California went about producing a turbine-powered Mallard.

On 5th September 1969, J-36 N2974 was rolled out as the G-73T prototype and took to the air powered by two PT6A-27 engines. Even with the -27 engines the G-73T, at a gross take-off weight of 14,000lbs, was still not able to meet the single-engine climb performance required by the FAA. Working with United Aircraft of Canada Ltd, Frakes designed a modified cowling which increased ram-air recovery, boosting engine power by some seven percent while not compromising the anti-icing provisions.

Under Supplemental Type Certificates SA2323WE and SA4410SW Frakes

modified G-73s for Chalk's, increasing the seating capacity from 10 to 17 seats. In all, 12 aircraft were converted by Frakes Aviation to G-73T standard, mostly at their new facility at Cleburne, Texas, and these were eventually re-engined with the PT6A-34 of 750shp.

"Hydroport"

With the advent of the Turbo-Mallard, Grumman saw a possible chance to realise its original aspirations for the aircraft. After all, with its improved performance figures, a single G-73T could do the work of two radial-engined Mallards. Would this be enough to persuade airlines to invest in the aircraft?

Another factor considered by Grumman was that the G-73T might be able to solve, at least in part, the increasing congestion in the "Northeast Corridor". Air traffic lanes to and from Boston, New York, Philadelphia and Baltimore were becoming very congested by the late-1960s and Grumman saw the use of amphibians as a means to ease the pressure on airports. After all, the G-21 had been commissioned so that business commuters in the 1930s could use the Downtown Skyport on New York's East River, so why not do something similar to solve the current problem?

The Department of Marine and Aviation in New York had investigated the use of amphibious aircraft for commuter transport in the Northeast Corridor, and in 1971 awarded a $50,000 contract to Grumman Aerospace to further the study. Using the G-73T N2974, with J Fred Frakes as pilot, the four-month programme was designed

as a technical feasibility exercise. Flights were made to and from the Downtown Skyport with the G-73T fitted with area navigation equipment and using a Talar microwave instrument landing system.

However, after some fifty hours flying, although the idea proved workable, the project highlighted some practical difficulties. Operations at night would require sophisticated flare-path lighting, a series of ramps would have to be built at locations other than New York and bad weather operations particularly at night in the winter would incur severe limits.

Whether or not Grumman had seriously considered restarting the Mallard production line following a positive outcome from the Hydroport study is open to question, but in the event Roy Grumman's dream of multiple Mallard sales to airlines was destined to remain a dream.

G-73AT

The Turbo-Mallard was further improved by the Paspaley Pearling Company in Australia, who produced the G-73AT ('AT' for Australian Turbine). The company "farmed" pearls in the warm waters to the west of Darwin, NT as far as Broome, WA on the Indian Ocean. The "farms" were in fact ships, and before the Mallards were put into service these were serviced by lighter.

Paspaley acquired their Mallards between 1990 and 1995 and had built up a regular service to the farms from a base in Darwin. Staff, mail and perishables were transported to and from the farms on a more or less scheduled basis, and medevac flights were operated on demand.

By 1995, the Mallards were showing their age prompting Paspaley to initiate an ambitious rebuilding programme. Under the auspices of the Australian Civil Air Regulations Bureau, the aircraft were rebuilt from scratch as if they were new aircraft. The project was carried out with the assistance of Sky West Engineering in Perth and overseen by the Australian airworthiness authorities. The rebuilds included a redesigned hydraulic system, complete re-wiring (which included relocation of junction boxes in the cockpit partition area), relocation of the battery from the engine nacelle to an under-floor rack near the junction boxes and a new cabin heating and ventilation system, all of which were covered by Engineering Orders as part of the rebuilding programme.

The main cabin door was modified to open upwards, while the bow hatch was made to open forward, both changes facilitating loading and unloading, again covered by Engineering Orders rather than Supplemental Type Certificates.

The modifications to the wings included the provision of droop tips on the ailerons, cuffs and seals on the leading edge of the flaps, aerodynamic balance horns on the elevators and the addition of vortex generators. Vortex generators were also fitted to the fin and rudder and small strakes were added to the engine cowlings.

The engine chosen for the "new" Mallard was the 680hp PT6A-34 but this too was modified with a re-designed intake cowling, improved ram-air recovery system and cowling extension beyond the

trailing edge of the wings. Engine installation was covered by Supplemental Type Certificate 226-1. Single engine performance and rate of climb were improved by fitting Hartzell HC-D4N-3T/D9511FK-2 four-blade propellers of 94 inch diameter. Passenger comfort was enhanced by a reduction in cabin noise levels. The conversion to turbine power required another Supplementary Type Certificate (STC 226-2) to cover the installation of aluminium auxiliary fuel tanks. These changes increased gross weight to 14,000lbs, which was covered by Supplemental Type Certificate ASA137ML.

A certification programme of 235 flights entailed 180 hours of flying and took eight months to complete. The G-73ATs were

G-73AT VH-PPT operated by Paspaley Pearling in northern Australia. The rear engine nacelle has been modified and the door opens upwards.
(Paspaley Pearling)

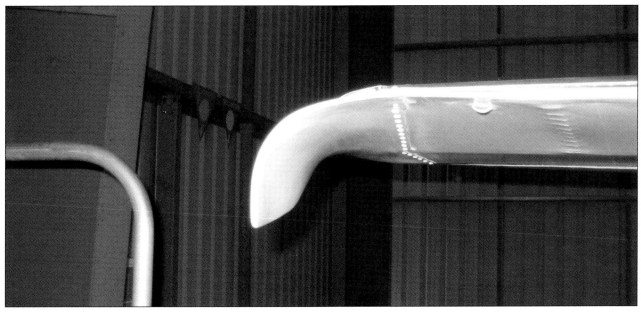

The modified wingtip on the G-73AT, seen from the rear.   *(Paspaley Pearling)*

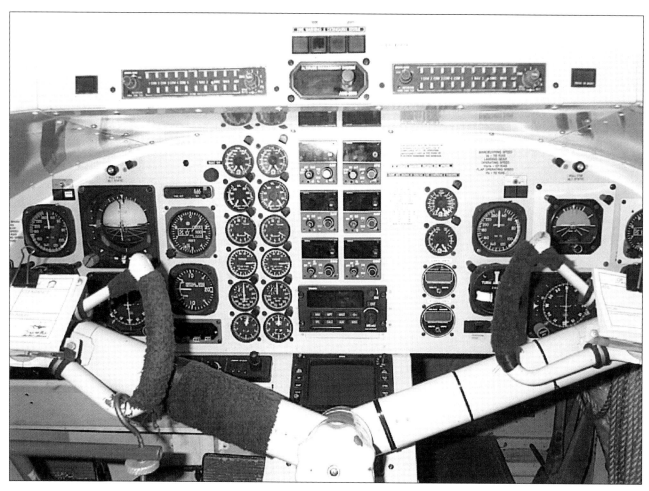

The array of modern avionics in the G-73AT is illustrated in this shot of VH-PPE's updated cockpit.   *(Paspaley Pearling)*

certificated in February 1998, starting with J-22, which was used as the "prototype" for the Paspaley Turbine Conversion programme. Certification of J-26 followed in July 2001, and finally J-23 in May 2005, ending a project which had taken over seven years to complete. The G-73ATs were continuing to support Paspaley's operations at the time of writing (late 2013).

Grounding

At about 1439hrs on 19th December 2005, tragedy visited the Mallard fleet. Chalk's Ocean Airways Flight 110 had flown from Fort Lauderdale/Hollywood International Airport at about 1305hrs, arriving at Miami Seaplane Base at Watson Island at about 1321hrs. The same aircraft then departed Watson Island at about 1438hrs as Chalk's Ocean Airways Flight 101, on a scheduled flight to Bimini in the Bahamas. About one minute after take-off from Watson Island, the Turbo Mallard N2969 crashed into the sea with eye-witnesses reporting the separation of the right wing and an in-flight fire prior to its impacting the water near a rock jetty. Eighteen passengers and the two pilots were all killed. The US Coast Guard, assisted by the Miami Beach Ocean Rescue and local fishermen, recovered all 20 bodies.

National Transportation Safety Board (NTSB) investigators found fatigue cracking of a wing spar, skin cracking and a broken z-stringer. The NTSB determined that the probable two causes of the accident were the in-flight failure and separation of the right wing during normal flight, which resulted from:

• the failure of the Chalk's Ocean Airways maintenance programme to identify and properly repair fatigue cracks in the right wing;

• the failure of the Federal Aviation Administration (FAA) to detect and correct deficiencies in the company's maintenance programme.

The FAA grounded all Mallards, except the Australian G-73ATs and Steve Hamilton's J-13, which had been completely rebuilt with a new wing centre section. The Emergency Airworthiness Directive (EAD) 2006-01-51, issued by the FAA on 30th December 2005, followed by the standard AD on 17th January 2006, were written in such a way that no aircraft could comply – essentially grounding the Mallards for ever.

A group of Mallard owners devised an "alternative means of compliance", known as an AMOC, but it was not until the autumn of 2008 that the FAA agreed to accept the AMOC. In the meantime some Mallards had been allowed to make flights under temporary permits that were valid for one year, or 200 hours. In reality most Mallards were grounded only for some six months, although no flights were made because of the length of time taken for the checks/repairs to the wing centre sections. This was followed by a period of temporary permits, until finally the FAA approved the AMOC. Thus, for example, in March 2009 John Fuller (J-5) reported that "we've always had our Certificate of Airworthiness, but were grounded by the Airworthiness Directive". (On a visit to Minden, Nevada in June 2007 the author saw the repairs to J-5 in progress). "Following compliance with the AD/AMOC we got a letter from the FAA, dated 27th March 2008, letting us go for another year or 200 hours, which we are about to renew. Our first flight after grounding was on 9th April 2008 and we've been flying regularly since then."

Mallard Variants & Production Summary

A total of 59 Mallards was built as follows:

G-73   59 Mallards built by Grumman and delivered to civil customers between September 1946 and May 1951.

G-73T   12 G-73s converted to UAC PT6A power by Frakes Aviation.

G-73AT   Two G-73s and one G-73T rebuilt with UAC PT6A-34 engines by Paspaley Pearling in Australia.

SCAN-30 CF-ODR (c/n 28) converted to Lycoming GO-480 power by McKinnon and operated by the Department of Lands & Forests, Toronto. The aircraft was noted for sale in October 2011 with only 4,405 total flying hours accrued. (MAP)

CHAPTER 5:
MODIFICATIONS & PROJECTS

OVER THE YEARS, THE GRUMMAN AMPHIBIANS HAVE BEEN MODIFIED in various ways by individuals and companies other than Grumman to meet specific requirements and tasks.

Widgeon Conversions

Pan American Airways

An early example of such a modification was the "Baby Clipper" flying classroom used by Pan American Airways. In July 1941 the first of four G-44 Widgeons was delivered to the airline's North Beach headquarters at La Guardia Field, Jackson Heights, New York.

The Ranger-powered aircraft featured modified interiors to accommodate a pilot station amidships, the conversion work for which was carried out by Aero Trades, Mineola, NY and Pan American, La Guardia, and completed in August 1941. Flown by the instructor from the left-hand seat, the modified Widgeon accommodated one pupil in the right-hand seat while the second pupil sat at the station amidships surrounded by black curtains which formed a hood.

At a height of about 1,500 feet the instructor turned over control of the aircraft

to the pupil amidships who then had to fly the aircraft to about 3,500 feet on instruments. Once there a series of QDM exercises were carried out for which the second student acted as radio operator. After about an hour the two students changed places.

Pan American technicians fitted intercom equipment and three radios to each of the Baby Clippers. Other additional

equipment fitted included a Kollsman direction indicator and visual light indicators for high-frequency markers.

The training programme, administered by Chief Instructor Donald Dionne, was designed to cater for students new to over-water flying as well as seasoned flying-boat captains and radio operators who needed a refresher.

DATE 19 *43*	FLIGHT FROM	FLIGHT TO	AIRCRAFT MAKE AND MODEL	AIRCRAFT CERTIFICATE MARK	CLASSIFICATION			DURATION	
					0-80 159:20	80-550 200:10	9600 142:23	CO-PILOT 715:28	32:33
3/18	BERMUDA	N.B., N.Y.	BOEING CLIPPER 314	NC18604			I:40	5':40	
5/15	NB	NB	GRUMMAN TWIN WIDGEON (400H) (C44)	NC28689		1:00		2:16	
5/16	NB	NB	''	''		.55		2:15	
5/24	NB	NB	''	''		.45		1:10	
5/25	NB	NB	''	NC28676		1:00		2:15	
5/29	NB	NB	''	''		.50		2:10	
5/30	NB	NB	''	NC1000		1:00		1:15	
5/31	NB	NB	''	NC28689		1:00		2:15	
6/3	NB	NB	''	NC28675		.55		1:15	
6/4	NB	NB	''	NC28676				1:00	
6/5	NB	NB.	''	NC28689		.50		1:50	
THE RECORD ON THIS PAGE IS CERTIFIED TRUE AND CORRECT:					159:20	208:20	145:13	738:48	32:3
PILOT *William Bowler Nash*					CARRY TOTALS FORWARD TO TOP OF NEXT PAGE				

William B Nash was a Boeing 314 Clipper pilot for Pan American Airways. He gained refresher training in the specially modified Widgeons, as witnessed in his logbook.

Photographed at the marine terminal—La Guardia Field, N. Y.

L*ittle sister ship* to the Clipper is the Grumman Widgeon . . . Three Widgeons, with full airline equipment installed, are used by PAA as instrument flight training ships in the Atlantic Division, and reported highly satisfactory . . . This small, smart handy bi-motored amphibian is also a favorite with the Coast Guard and private owners.

Designing, developing and building in quantity the Wildcat, Avenger, Widgeon and big JRF amphibian . . . have given Grumman so much unique experience . . . that Grumman has much to give to all aviation, today and tomorrow . . . Grumman learns more, builds better, with every passing day.

Grumman Aircraft Engineering Corporation • Bethpage, Long Island, N. Y.

Appearing in the August 1942 issue of "Aviation" magazine, this Grumman advertisement for the Widgeon features Pan American Airways "Little Sister Ship" NC28675 (c/n 1214), one of four used as flying classrooms.

Because of wartime restrictions these training flights were carried out within a fifteen mile radius of Port Chester, New York. Eight students were taken through the course each day, in each aircraft, adding up to ten hours to the flying log seven days a week. The Ranger engines were put through a check every 100 hours to conform to CAA regulations, and Pan American maintenance policy called for a change of engine every 400 hours. It is reported that the maintenance crew, led by Charles Hiller, could perform an engine change in 12 hours.

Widgeons converted for Pan American Airways were:

C/n	Registration
1214	NC28675
1215	NC28676
1235	NC1000
1239	NC37189

Water-Looping

After the initial test-flights with the G-21 Goose, the step was moved aft by some 4½ inches to facilitate better spray control during take-off and landing on water.

When the Widgeon was designed it was decided to emulate the Goose and go with a longer step design - to Station (Sta)15A, (see drawing on page 31). However, after the Widgeon had been in service for some time it was discovered that the long step had a tendency to drive the front of the hull deeper into the water and therefore increase the chance of a water-loop, especially when landing on calm water.

A water loop is a violent swerve to the side similar to a ground loop on land. In the case of a water loop to port, for example, the starboard wing float is slammed down by the centrifugal force. The high vertical loads thus produced cause the struts to fail and the wing and crippled float are plunged into the water, creating a large drag force which swerves the aircraft to starboard. The aircraft comes to rest pointing to starboard of the original course, with the damaged wing in the water.

The original Widgeon step vent was similar to the one on the Goose – a small hole on the side just forward of the step. The area between the afterbody and the forward hull between Sta 15 and 15A was open, and there were small holes in the step at Sta 15A to allow the air to escape.

Grumman suggested that the problem would be solved by cutting back the step from Sta 15A to Sta 15, and adding two tunnel vents in lieu of the original step vents, and the company produced drawings (No.1407 and No.17188) to demonstrate the change. This allowed the hull to ride on the water a little further forward, and thereby lessened the tendency for the forward hull to ride as deep. To replace the loss of structure caused by the removal of the outer hull at Sta 15, an internal keel stiffener was added. In combination with this, the stringer at the cabin window was re-inforced, making the air-craft structurally eligible for an increase in allowable gross weight.

A classic example of the problem was demonstrated by Widgeon c/n 1391, which had a history of serious water-looping incidents while in service in Tahiti. After the last of these incidents the remains of the G-44 were sold by Regie Aérienne Inter-insulaire to New Zealand Tourist Air Travel (NZTAT) in Auckland. The Widgeon was rebuilt and put into service by NZTAT, but the water-looping problems continued. With another of the NZTAT Widgeons (c/n 1432) suffering the same problem, the directors of the airline decided that a replacement aircraft type was needed and sent Captain Fred Ladd to the USA to find one. During his trip Ladd spoke with other Widgeon operators and was told that his problem aircraft needed to be modified with the shorter step. Ladd returned to New Zealand, had the two aircraft modified and experienced no more water-looping problems.

McKinnon-Hickman Company

Despite the success that Pan American Airways had with their flying classrooms a recurring theme had been the fact that Grumman amphibians were underpowered, leading to the need for regular replacement engines.

One company began providing that improvement in 1952. Originally known as the McKinnon-Hickman Company, based in Portland, Oregon, it later became McKinnon Enterprises Inc and moved to Sandy, Oregon. McKinnon began by converting its own G-44 Widgeon with 260hp Lycoming GSO-435-C2B engines, under Supplemental Type Certificate (STC) SA4-64. The improvement in performance thus achieved convinced McKinnon that there would be a commercial market for the conversion.

The Lycoming GSO series of engines was improved and soon McKinnon was installing 270hp GSO-480-B1Ds on the aircraft (under STC SA4-65), by then known as Super Widgeons. In all, some seventy aircraft were converted.

The McKinnon Super Widgeon, powered by two 270hp Lycoming GSO-480-B1D engines driving three-bladed Hartzell propellers, had a gross weight of 5,500lbs, a top speed of 185mph and a ceiling of 18,000ft. It could carry up to six passengers in a luxury custom interior over a range of 1,000 miles. This increase in range was

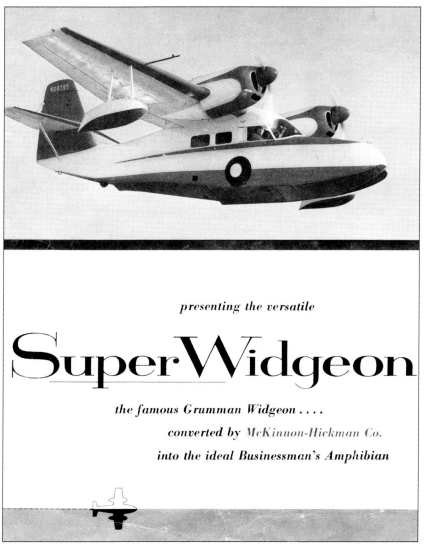

presenting the versatile

Super Widgeon

the famous Grumman Widgeon . . . .

converted by McKinnon-Hickman Co.

into the ideal Businessman's Amphibian

The cover of a contemporary brochure for the McKinnon Super Widgeon.

(McKinnon via Steve Hamilton)

McKinnon-Hickman's first Super Widgeon, N353CW (c/n 1298) which featured in company publicity brochures, is seen here at Oakland, California in 1961.   *(Douglas D Olson via Jennifer Gradidge)*

G-44 CF-IIQ (c/n 1265) converted to Lycoming-powered Super Widgeon, but with floats still fixed, at Vancouver, British Columbia in 1956.
(Douglas D Olson via Jennifer Gradidge)

Imperial Airways' Super Widgeon CF-IIQ (c/n 1265) with retractable floats fitted, seen at Vancouver, British Columbia, in June 1974.

(AJ Clarke)

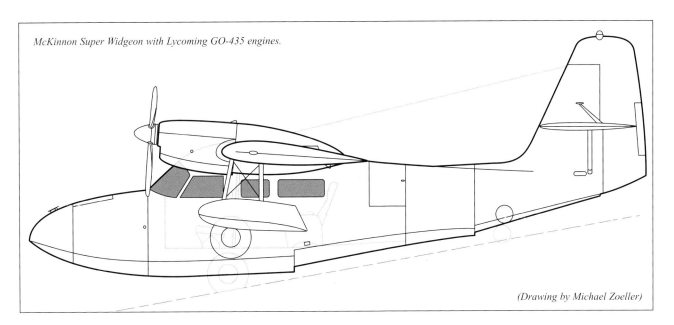

McKinnon Super Widgeon with Lycoming GO-435 engines.

(Drawing by Michael Zoeller)

achieved by the use of auxiliary fuel tanks in the outer wing and the reduction in drag facilitated by the retractable wing-tip floats. An optional extra was the provision of re-designed picture windows. Other improvements included a new instrument panel and a 24-volt electrical system. Installing the -480 engine also allowed an extra 200 hours between overhauls, thereby lowering operating costs. The cost of such a conversion was $55,000 but you had to have the aircraft first! McKinnon therefore also purchased five SCAN-30 airframes from Centravia SA in Paris in 1955 and converted them to Super Widgeons with Lycoming GO-480-B1D engines.

More recently, Lycomings have been installed, under SA4-64 or -65, by Viking Air Ltd and ACE Aviation Inc. The latter also amalgamated the two STCs, together with SA4-111 for the installation of Lycoming GO-480-G1D6 engines, to cover all three installations under one certificate – SA380WE, which was issued on 12th April 1963. As well as the engine installation, this composite STC allowed for associated modification of nacelles, electrical systems, propeller and engine controls, oil, fuel and vacuum systems; installation of new engine mounts and reinforced and modified wing structures; installation of spray rails, rudder boost systems and oil coolers, all in accordance with McKinnon technical data as required for each modification.

Widgeons, including SCAN-built models, when modified as above were eligible for the following gross weights:

(i) 4,700lbs gross weight for take-off and landing (land or water).

(ii) 5,500lbs gross weight, take-off and landing (land) and 4,700lbs gross weight take-off and landing (water) when approved landing gear was modified in accordance with McKinnon Enterprises drawings.

(iii) 4,700lbs gross weight, take-off and landing (land) and 5,500lbs gross weight take-off and landing (water) when hull was modified to meet buoyancy requirements of CAR 4a.490(a) per McKinnon Enterprises drawings.

(iv) 5,500lbs gross weight, take-off and landing (land and water) when landing gear and hull were modified as described in items ii) and iii) above.

Note: When more than five persons are carried, an FAA-approved emergency exit must be installed. The installation of such an emergency exit is covered by STC SA4-63 or SA4-967.

At least 45 Widgeons have been converted to McKinnon Super Widgeon standard. Known c/ns are: 1230, 1236, 1239, 1240, 1265, 1277, 1292, 1298, 1300, 1306, 1311, 1312, 1313, 1315, 1324, 1326, 1328, 1338, 1341, 1343, 1345, 1346, 1359, 1364, 1370, 1373, 1374, 1380, 1387, 1394, 1411, 1414, 1415, 1417, 1420, 1424, 1427, 1430, 1434, 1442, 1444, 1445, 1467, 1472 and 1475.

The SCAN Widgeons converted by McKinnon were c/ns 26, 27, 28, 29 and 30.

JC Udd's Lycoming-powered G-44 CF-HAC (c/n 1343). The prominent under wing exhausts suggest a Link conversion, but the aircraft was in fact converted to Super Widgeon by McKinnon.

(Art Krieger Collection)

Link-converted Super Widgeon N101PE (c/n 1386) of G Philip Ellsworth, visiting Ottawa, Ontario, circa 1965. Note the underwing exhaust allowing auxiliary fuel tanks to be installed in the rear section of the engine nacelles, increasing the aircraft's range. (KM Molson)

Link Aeronautical Corporation

Lockheed Aircraft Services also held a Supplemental Type Certificate (STC) for Widgeon conversions, but in 1954 this was purchased by Link Aeronautical Corporation of Endicott, New York. The purchase included the jigs, dies, patterns, tools, patents and CAA approvals to produce what Link also called a "Super Widgeon".

The conversion process was started by stripping down the aircraft to a bare shell. The hull was modified and strengthened and metal was replaced in the fuselage as necessary. The 200hp Ranger engines were replaced by two Lycoming GO 480-B1 "flat-sixes" of 270hp driving Hartzell HC-83X20-2B propellers, under STC SA4-65.

A feature of the conversion was the incorporation of Link engine exhausts underneath the wings. Link Corporation claimed that their exhaust system reduced noise and allowed installation of auxiliary fuel tanks in the rear section of the engine nacelles. These tanks each held 22 US gallons and fuel transfer to the main tank was controlled by an electrical solenoid switch actuated by means of a toggle switch on the instrument panel. A placard near the toggle warned the pilot: "*Use only in level flight when main tanks are below 25 gals.*"

The Widgeons were also re-wired throughout and equipped with new instruments and radios. Custom interiors were fitted, complete with soundproofing, and finally the completed aircraft was painted.

Thus the Link Super Widgeon was capable of a shorter take-off at higher gross weight and quieter operation over a longer range.

Like McKinnon, the Link Corporation later gained approvals for an even greater gross weight (to 5,500lbs), and for providing an escape hatch in the rear fuselage. This allowed an additional seat to be added in the rear compartment increasing the capacity to six. The company advertised the fact that the further improvements could be retro-fitted to any Super Widgeon.

It is uncertain how many Super Widgeons were produced by the Link Corporation, but thirteen aircraft, with c/ns 1206, 1213, 1315, 1364, 1368, 1386, 1404, 1419, 1441, 1444, 1454, 1457 and 1458, are known to have been converted.

Pacific Aircraft Engineering Corporation (PACE)

In 1953 nineteen of the French-built SCAN-30 Widgeons were crated and shipped to the USA where they were re-assembled, and re-engined with Lycoming radials.

The conversion programme was carried out by Pacific Aircraft Engineering Corporation (PACE) of Sun Valley, California, at their works at the Lockheed Air Terminal, Burbank, California. The converted aircraft, fitted with the 300hp Lycoming R-680-E3 nine-cylinder radial air-cooled engines, were known as PACE Gannets. The programme called for the conversion of 15 zero-timed SCAN-30 airframes. More than 30 major improvements were made during the conversion to Gannet standard under STCs which included SA4-2, 4-53, 4-60, 4-61, 4-62, 4-63, 4-773, 4-774 and SA603WE. These covered the major changes including the installation of the Lycoming radials with auxiliary fuel tanks and reinforcement of the airframe and landing gear to allow operation at 6,000lbs all-up weight. The five watertight compartments and the two longitudinal steps in the hull were re-engineered and the entire airframe, originally built in France with non-anodized metal, was given an anti-corrosion treatment. Both the main landing gear and tail-wheel were provided with a new up-lock system, and the hydraulic and

A PACE Gannet conversion of the Widgeon, N47CE (c/n 1371) with 300hp Lycoming R680E radials is seen here in the late-1950s. (MAP)

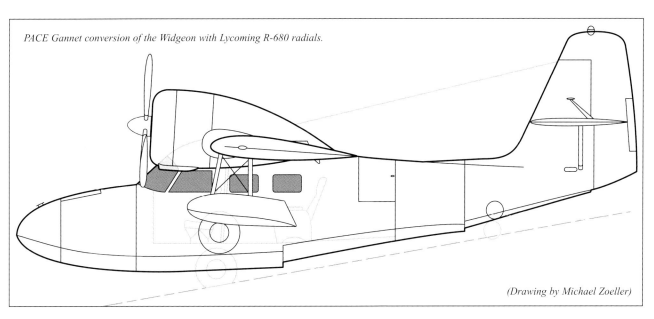

PACE Gannet conversion of the Widgeon with Lycoming R-680 radials.

(Drawing by Michael Zoeller)

G-44 Widgeon N9600H (c/n 1388) fitted with Lycoming R680E radials, with elongated rear nacelles. Seen here at Oakland, California in 1954, it was probably a one-off; to date no records of such a modification have been found. *(Chalmers Johnson via Jennifer Gradidge)*

SCAN-30 N57LM (c/n 4) after installation of Lycoming R-680 radials by Lee Mansdorf. The full story of this interesting aircraft is given on page 403. *(Art Krieger Collection)*

electrical systems were renewed. The engines were overhauled to zero-time standard, fitted with chrome cylinders, housed in full pressure cowlings and fitted with stainless steel over the wing exhaust augmentors to facilitate improved cooling, increased performance and lower cabin noise levels.

The wing trailing edge was re-engineered, producing an entirely metal-covered wing which included titanium engine fire-walls, two in-built 25 US gallon auxiliary fuel tanks, and the provision of landing lights.

The cockpit was provided with a one-piece windshield and the passenger cabin was fitted with bubble windows and an escape hatch. State of the art Lear avionics and full blind flying instrumentation were provided as standard.

The only SCAN airframe definitely identified as being converted by PACE is c/n 12.

However, Lee Mansdorf & Company, originally at Compton, CA, had moved to Sun Valley by 1955, and carried out "PACE Gannet" conversions under the same STCs. Whether or not this was done under contract to PACE is not known. Documents held by the FAA indicate that Mansdorf purchased up to 20 SCAN-30 airframes from the Conair Corporation in Montreal, Canada. The Canadian Department of Transport has confirmed that these aircraft were never registered in Canada. There is, however, some evidence that the airframes were shipped from La Rochelle direct to California and were never actually in Canada. It would seem therefore that the nineteen airframes that were shipped to California were actually owned by Mansdorf but his connection with Pacific Aircraft Engineering Corporation is not clear.

SCAN airframes known to have been re-engined with Lycoming radials by Mansdorf are c/ns 2, 3, 4, 9, 14, 15, 16, 21, 31, 32, 33, 34 and 41.

Franklin (Gander) Widgeon

Dean Franklin of Miami, Florida converted Widgeons, c/ns 1267, 1375 and 1381, to "Super Widgeon" standard with

Continental IO-470-M engines, under STC SA152SO. The company also converted a Widgeon (c/n 1340) with Continental IO-470-B engines in a flat nacelle. The wings of the original Widgeon were pitched at an angle of 3° from the fuselage with the engines a further 1½° above the wing. Franklin's conversion had the engines mounted in line with the wing chord giving a lower angle of attack which led to a tendency for the nose of the aircraft to go down when engine power was applied. Franklin reasoned that this change would make the aircraft fly faster. It did (by some 5knots), but this came at a price. The propellers suffered more erosion because they were closer to the water, and because the engine thrust was more downward than normal slightly more nose-up elevator was required at slow speeds. Franklin Widgeons were also limited to 5,400lbs maximum operating weight because they could not achieve the minimum stall speed above that weight.

J Ray McDermott Company

The J Ray McDermott Company, a major oil industry contractor based in Louisiana, also converted Ranger-powered Widgeons to Continental O-470 power, under STC SA2-13 issued on 31st January 1957. The O-470B and O-470M engines were of 240hp and some were fitted with pressure carburettors. The exhaust was channelled over the wing through augmentor pipes to provide cooling, as fitted to early Cessna 310 aircraft.

Following an Engineering Data Report (No.44) dated 7th July 1961, the STC was revised and issued as SA2-284, allowing the installation of the 260hp IO-470D engines (driving 84-inch Hartzell propellers) and for an increase in gross weight to 5,400lbs. This engine installation included the replacement of the (Grumman) wing fillets by Cessna wing fillets. Also included under SA2-284 were:
• landing gear modifications in accordance with Lee Mansdorf & Co data pertinent to SA4-60 (to accommodate the higher gross weight);

• hull compartment modifications to meet buoyancy requirements of CAR 4a.490(a), in accordance with Lee Mansdorf & Co data pertinent to SA4-61;
• outer wing panel modifications in accordance with Lee Mansdorf & Co drawing No.1201.

McDermott also held STC SA61SW, issued 1st January 1960, which allowed the Widgeon's horizontal stabiliser to be raised 5/8 inch "per STC SA2-13". The rudder trim tab was also enlarged to ease rudder pressure in engine-out situations.

19 McDermott conversions were carried out in-house. The first few were performed in their hangar at Alvin Callender Field in Belle Chasse, south of New Orleans. Subsequent conversions took place in the McDermott hangar at New Orleans Lakefront Airport. C/n 1453 was the first aircraft converted by McDermott, but the 240hp O-470B Continentals did not live up to expectations and subsequent conversions used the improved 240hp O-470M, or the 260hp IO-470D engines.

The following nine c/ns were converted in-house by McDermott: 1237, 1317, 1372, 1413, 1421, 1435, 1437, 1453 and 1464. All but 1437 and 1464 were owned by McDermott while c/n 1437 was converted for the Gulf Oil Company, and c/n 1464 for the Union Oil Company, which opted for 240hp O-470M engines with pressure carburettors. It is now operated by Chester Lawson in Florida.

The total of nineteen was made up with 10 further "McDermott" conversions. Work on c/ns 1221 and 1294 was performed in Alaska, while conversions to 1334, 1354 and 1463 were carried out by unknown companies. The remaining five conversions were hybrids, being a mixture of McDermott and Franklin modifications, carried out in New Zealand. New Zealand Tourist Air Travel (NZTAT) bought the McDermott conversion plans but modified their aircraft by removing the original "boat tail" nacelles and installing a new flat nacelle similar to Dean Franklin's Gander conversion (see above). The NZTAT

G-44 N67DF (c/n 1274) was converted to Continental IO-470 power by Dean Franklin. The aircraft is seen here at Opa Locka, Florida on 21st March 1979.
(Peter Vercruijsse)

Widgeons so converted were c/ns 1356, 1362, 1391, 1439 and 1466.

As well as these nineteen it is thought that a further three McDermott conversions were carried out (possibly including c/n 1381), but overall, the McKinnon conversion was considered a better product because the geared Lycoming engines had better pulling power and were quieter in flight due to the shorter radius propellers.

McDermott also held STC SA2-13 for the installation of Cessna Type landing lights in the leading edge of the left wing of G-44, G-44A and SCAN-built Widgeons, and c/n 1213 was modified in this way.

G-44 c/n 1317, converted to Continental power by McDermott in 1971, was used for two periods of oil support operations in Nigeria. Seen here in the UK circa 1991, where it was registered G-BTKJ, it was ferried back to the USA as N67867 in November 1997. (MAP)

Chester Lawson's G-44A N86638 (c/n 1464) powered by Continental O-470M engines, which with a pressure carburettor each produce 240hp. The aircraft is the 1955 McDermott conversion for Union Oil of California and was photographed at Oshkosh, Wisconsin on 26th July 1991.

(Jennifer Gradidge)

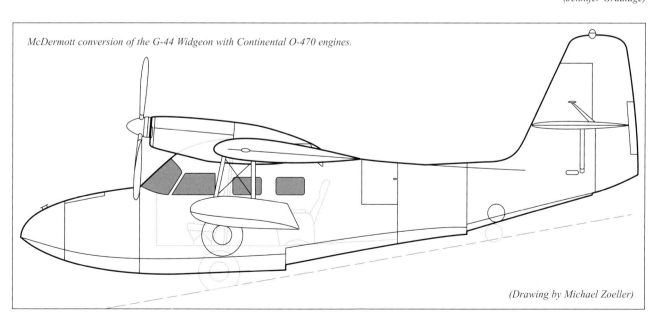

McDermott conversion of the G-44 Widgeon with Continental O-470 engines.

(Drawing by Michael Zoeller)

SCAN-30 N78X (c/n 32) marked "Experimental". Originally re-engined with Lycoming radials, it is seen here at Oshkosh, Wisconsin on 27th July 1994, with Continental IO-520 engines.   *(Jennifer Gradidge)*

Franklin-Morse Inc

Dean Franklin and Robert E 'Bob' Morse converted the SCAN-30, c/n 32, to 300hp Continental IO-520-E power in 1969, but the aircraft was only granted an Experimental Certificate of Airworthiness.

Other Widgeon Conversions

The installation of 300hp Continental IO-520-E engines was also tried by both

William Grenier and GJ Newell, but these were also both on an "Experimental" basis.

STC SA4774NM was developed by Ned Rice and Dennis Burke in 1990 and allowed installation of 300hp Lycoming TIO (& LTIO) -540-J2BDs, and is now owned by ACE Aviation Inc, Sausalito, California. Under the same STC, the largest engine fitted on a Widgeon was the 350hp Lycoming GTSIO-540, as used on the Piper Chieftain. The STC allows a manifold limitation equivalent to 300hp

maximum continuous power and the conversion uses slightly modified Chieftain nacelles. This conversion was known as the Magnum Widgeon, and five or six of these were carried out by Dennis Burke and others, between 1990 and 2005. Known airframes so converted are: G-44A c/n 1410 and SCAN-30s c/ns 3, 4 and 16.

EDO E-175 "Petulant Porpoise"

See comments on pages 38 and 77.

AERO-TOWING AND THE LOSS OF J4F-2 37736
During 1945 and 1946 the US Navy evaluated the techniques and value of aero-towing the Widgeon. The theoretical benefit was the ability to recover an unserviceable aircraft from a perhaps difficult location without repairing engines or certain other systems in situ. The trials were undertaken by the NAMU at Johnsville, PA and were initially successful. By June 1945 the Navy was able to publicly announce the successful recovery of an aircraft from NAAS Manteo, NC to Johnsville, a distance of 325 miles.

The aircraft in question was not identified but seems likely to have been NAMU's own aircraft 37736 (Manteo's only known assigned J4F, 37726, has nothing on its record to suggest any time under overhaul at Johnsville). The Widgeon had both propellers removed

with eye-bolts attached to the airscrew shafts enabling a 'Y' shaped bridle to be attached. The towing cable was attached to the bridle. The tug was a Curtiss SB2C Helldiver allegedly locally based at Manteo but which again seems more likely to have been a NAMU aircraft.

The contemporary press release together with an accompanying photograph suggested that the Widgeon had needed a double engine change and major overhaul, hence the need to tow it to Johnsville. Manteo's runway was 3,350 feet in length and although the Widgeon lifted off rapidly the Helldiver used most of the runway to get airborne. The flight lasted 2¼ hours and after casting off the cable the Widgeon made a safe dead-stick landing at Johnsville. Notwithstanding the Navy's determination to present this as a practical exercise to get an unserviceable aircraft to a depot it has all the hallmarks of an experiment.

J4F-2 37736 was then certainly used in further towing trials at NAMU Johnsville from prepared runways but it subsequently came to grief during the first attempt to tow it from water.

This happened on 23rd April 1946 off Betterton, MD, near Aberdeen, but unfortunately which aircraft was used as the tug on this occasion is unknown. The accident details are limited but it appears that on landing (presumably unsuccessfully) the pilot struck his head and was stunned. The aircraft became submerged and although two other occupants escaped, the pilot drowned.

The aircraft was a total loss and the accident report sententiously noted "Overconfidence in conduct of towing test. Insufficient planning", observing that the lack of a shoulder harness might have been a contributory factor in the pilot's death.

Aero-towing. This 1945 photograph shows a Curtiss SB2C Helldiver just leaving the runway while the J4F Widgeon on the end of the tow-rope is already some 20 feet off the ground.   *(US Navy photo)*

Goose Modifications and Conversions

The original Goose was based on Grumman Design No.21. The initial batch consisted of 12 aircraft, designated G-21, but before all were completed improvements were incorporated and the revised designation G-21A was applied to the aircraft. The G-21A featured an increased gross weight (up from 7,500 lbs to 8,000 lbs), improved R-985-SB2 engines and a redesigned tail-wheel. The 12th G-21 (c/n 1012) was modified to G-21A standard before being sold, and most of the original G-21s were upgraded by the end of 1938, except for c/ns 1008, 1009 and 1010, which were exported before the improvements could be made. A further 30 G-21As were built by Grumman between 1938 and 1942. At the request of the US Navy, commencing with c/n 1082, the Goose was built with a stronger axle on the main undercarriage to allow operation at a gross weight of 8,600lbs. This was confirmed in a letter, dated 29th October 1954, from the Grumman Aircraft Engineering Corporation Service Department to Bahamas Airways Limited (below).

GRUMMAN AIRCRAFT ENGINEERING CORPORATION

Bethpage, Long Island, New York.

October 29th, 1954.

Bahamas Airways Limited,
P. O. Box 65,
Oakes Field Airport,
Nassau, Bahamas.

Attention : Mr W. H. Llewellyn

Gentlemen:

We have received and noted with interest your letter of October 18th regarding your application to increase the gross weight of your Model G-21A "Goose" aircraft.

Starting with Grumman Serial #1082, all Model G-21A airplanes were equipped with axle member part #13638. The previous part # was 12601. This change was made to meet the structural requirements of the U.S. Navy for an airplane gross weight of 8600 lbs. The stronger axle member may be identified by the part number stamped thereon, however, most of them were made from forgings, whereas the original axle members were of welded construction, and this difference is the easiest way of telling them apart.

The CAA has granted partial approval for 8600 lbs. gross weight on serial numbers 1082 and up as follows:

a) The airplane is structurally satisfactory to the CAA for all flight conditions at 8600 lbs. gross weight. However, actual flight testing at this weight to determine the cooling, climb, controllability and other performance qualifications has not been made.

b) The airplane is structurally satisfactory to the CAA for water take-offs at 8600 lbs gross weight but no evaluation of stability, controllability and other characteristics of such take-offs has been made.

c) The airplane is structurally satisfactory to the CAA for land landings at 8600 lbs gross weight, however the present landing speed of 65 mph at 800 lbs is the maximum allowable. It is estimated that the landing speed at 8600 lbs would be 68 mph. 32 x 8 8-ply tires at 50 psi would be required to insure adequate load rating at 8600 lbs.

In order to meet the landing speed limitation, it would be necessary to install fuel dumping provisions to lower the gross weight to 8000 lbs. However, this has never been attempted since we believe that the G-21A would have difficulty in meeting the requirements for performance and cooling at gross weights above 8000 lbs.

Very truly yours,
GRUMMAN AIRCRAFT ENGINEERING CORPORATION

(sgd) E.H.L.Smith
Service Department.

A letter from Grumman Aircraft Engineering Corporation to Bahamas Airways Limited, dated 29th October 1954, with reference to an increase of the gross weight of the company's G-21A Goose aircraft.
(via WH Llewellyn)

The G-21B was a pure flying boat rather than an amphibian, being built without wheels by the Grumman factory. The contract placed by the Portuguese government on 19th December 1939 was for 12 "B" model flying boats fitted with two 0.30 calibre machine guns (one dorsal, the other mounted in the bow), and with the additional capability to carry two 100lb bombs as under-wing stores. Grumman built 12 examples with construction numbers 1088 – 1099. These aircraft supposedly carried temporary US civil registrations NX97 – NX108, later becoming NC97 – NC108, prior to being shipped to Portugal. The first (NX) registration would have been appropriate for any "experimental" test flights conducted before their eventual "commercial" certification – except that the Grumman G-21B was never recognized officially as an approved design under Approved Type Certificate 654. Aircraft were delivered to Portugal by sea between April and July 1940 and were assigned Portuguese Aviação Naval identification

numbers 97 – 108. In 1952 the nine G-21B aircraft which remained were transferred to the Força Aérea Portuguesa (FAP) (Portuguese Air Force).

McKinnon G-21C four-engined conversion

After the success with his Super Widgeon programme which began in 1952, Angus G "Mac" McKinnon of McKinnon Enterprises Inc, in Sandy, Oregon started on a series of Goose conversions in 1956, of which the G-21C was the first. The G-21C was a four-engine conversion because the Wasp Juniors could not be replaced on a one-for-one basis due to the lack of a suitable engine of comparable power. Accordingly, four 340hp Lycoming GSO-480-B2D6 six-cylinder, air-cooled, flat (horizontally-opposed), supercharged piston engines were installed, fitted with Hartzell three-bladed constant speed propellers. The conversion, as with the Widgeon, was carried out by McKinnon, with the help of AM "Abe" Kaplan, the owner and chief engineer of Strato Engineering Company Inc of Burbank, California.

The four-engined G-21C had an increased gross weight of 12,499lbs, which allowed up to nine people to be carried, and

it was approved under Type Certificate No. 4A24 on 7th November 1958. Fuel capacity was increased from 220 to 450 US gallons, allowing a normal range of 1,500 miles at a cruising speed of 225mph. Other improvements included retractable wing-tip floats, an extended radar nose, a dorsal fin and a one-piece wrap-around wind-screen with additional overhead cockpit "eyebrow" windows. Passenger comfort was enhanced by the installation of executive seating and the fitting of large "picture" windows measuring 54x18 inches. The landing gear, wing-tip floats, flaps and airscrew pitch were each operated using the 24-volt electrical system.

The two aircraft thus converted were:

- Grumman JRF-6B c/n 1147, which had been operated by the Fish & Wildlife Service in Alaska as NC709 until it was bought by McKinnon in January 1957 and converted into the first G-21C during the course of 1957 and 1958. It was given McKinnon c/n 1201 and registered as N150M.

- Grumman JRF-5 c/n B-78, registered as N3459C, was sold by McKinnon Enterprises Inc to Everbrite Electric Signs of Milwaukee, Wisconsin on 23rd March 1959. During the next four months,

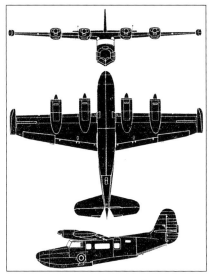

Above: *Three-view silhouette of the McKinnon G-21C Goose conversion. Note the "eyebrow" cockpit windows.*

McKinnon's second G-21C N3459C (c/n 1202) converted from Grumman c/n B-78. The aircraft was exported to East Pakistan in 1967, and from 1972 was in service with the Government of Bangladesh. The remains of the fuselage are currently at Dhaka. The photograph was probably taken in the early 1960s. *(Jennifer Gradidge)*

McKinnon's first G-21C conversion N150M (c/n 1147/1201) with four 340hp Lycoming GSO-480-B2D6 engines, fitted with Hartzell three-bladed constant speed propellers. The photograph dates from circa January 1958. *(Grumman photo G-79626)*

A rare shot of the G-21C (c/n B-78/1202) with Bangladeshi markings S2-AAD, showing the exhaust arrangement for the four Lycoming GSO-480-B2D6 engines. The photograph was taken at Seletar, Singapore on 12th March 1975. *(Ron Killick via Jennifer Gradidge)*

McKinnon converted it to the four-engine configuration under TC 4A24 and it was re-certified as a new (ie "zero-time") McKinnon G-21C c/n 1202 on 6th August 1959. Everbrite operated it until 9th January 1967, when they sold it back to McKinnon. During the course of 1967, it was refurbished by McKinnon and very soon after that work was completed it was exported to the government of East Pakistan as AP-AUY. After the 1970 civil war, East Pakistan became Bangladesh on 26th March 1971 and G-21C c/n 1202 was re-registered there as S2-AAD. It is reportedly still there, although derelict and partially disassembled.

The four-engined G-21C conversions did not attract a lot of customers. This was partly due to the high cost of the conversion and partly to the comparative unreliability of the GSO-480 engines. Part of McKinnon's investment in the programme was recouped however by offering various G-21C features such as the retractable wing-tip floats as STC kits to upgrade the standard G-21A Goose. The retractable floats permitted a gross weight increase to 9,200lbs per STC SA4-1467 on the basis that they provided effectively longer wings and therefore a greater total wing area. The floats had to be "up" for take-off at that higher gross weight. When operating on the water, the floats had to be retracted once the aircraft was "on the step" and prior to lifting off the water. The streamlining achieved by retraction of the floats also enhanced the single-engine performance of the G-21A Goose.

McKinnon G-21D four-engined conversion

Almost before the ink was dry on its brand new airworthiness certificate in December 1958, McKinnon started working again on N150M. His next big idea was to stretch the nose of the G-21C by 36 inches and make room for an additional four passenger seats in the area that until then had been the forward baggage area. The G-21D was just like a G-21C with four Lycoming GSO-480 engines but the longer nose was distinguished by two additional windows on either side. The aft window on the left side also doubled as an escape hatch. The total seating capacity increased from nine in the G-21C to 14 in the G-21D. After its second conversion in as many years, McKinnon G-21C c/n 1201 was re-certified as the McKinnon model G-21D in June 1960 and Type Certificate 4A24 was amended accordingly. It was re-registered as G-21D c/n 1251, all the while retaining the registration N150M (see page 245 for a photo).

McKinnon and Alaska Coastal interaction

With the advent of the United Aircraft of Canada (UAC) (later Pratt & Whitney Canada) PT6A series of turboprop engines, the problem of the one-for-one replacement of the Goose's engines was solved.

However, it was not a totally ideal solution, given the economic considerations and operational requirements of a turboprop engine. Because Strato Engineering already had experience with the four-engined conversions, McKinnon retained their services for his turboprop installation programme. Such a programme had been started already by Alaska Coastal-Ellis Airlines (ACE), who had expressed an interest in upgrading their entire Goose fleet. McKinnon collaborated with ACE on the design of the turbine engine installations but he never actually did either of the ACE conversions.

A one-time Supplemental Type Certificate, STC SA280AL, was granted to Alaska Coastal for the installation of two 550shp PT6A-6 engines on Grumman G-21A c/n 1164. The work was carried out in the company hangar at Juneau (with engines supplied by UAC and parts manufactured and supplied by Fairey Aviation Canada Ltd in Vancouver), under the supervision of Alaska Coastal president Shell Simmons and his chief engineer, Jack Bracelen. Registered as N95431, and

Alaska-Coastal's first PT6A-powered Goose N95431 (c/n 1164) converted "in-house" in 1964. The photograph was probably taken at the airline's maintenance base at Juneau, Alaska.

(Fred J Knight Collection)

Alaska Coastal Airlines' Turbo G-21A N95431 (c/n 1164) on a test flight in January 1966. The aircraft was rebuilt with P&W R-985 engines after an accident in 1968.   *(Alaska Coastal Airlines)*

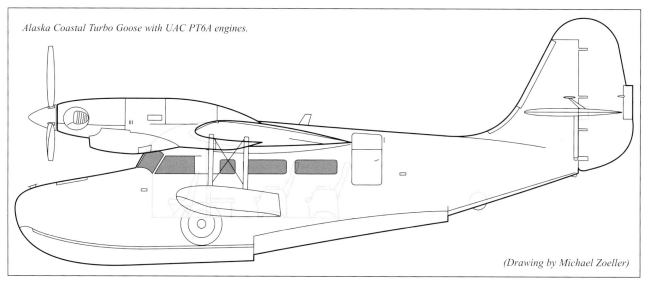

Alaska Coastal Turbo Goose with UAC PT6A engines.

(Drawing by Michael Zoeller)

painted in the revised colour scheme of Alaska Coastal Airlines, the Turbo Goose was granted an experimental certificate of airworthiness on 26th February 1966, and made its first flight two days later.

A report by Strato Engineering Corporation, dated 18th May 1966, stated that the Alaska Coastal-Ellis turbine conversion provided for a gross weight increase from 9,200 to 10,500 lbs, an increase in cruise speed from 211 to 220mph and an increase in size of rudder tab to 1.78sq ft. Two additional fuel tanks were incorporated into each outboard wing panel. Each inboard tank contained 715lbs with a further 325lbs of fuel in each outboard tank. The fuel feed system was arranged so that fuel was used from the inboard tanks while at the same time being replenished from the outboard tanks, so that when 325lbs of fuel had been used from each side the outboard tanks would be empty.

Alaska Coastal Airlines, as it had

become known by then, began regular scheduled operations with their Turbo Goose on 24th January 1967, and utilization averaged 2.3 hours per day. The data gathered from flying their first turbine G-21A allowed Alaska Coastal to obtain another one-time STC to cover the installation of newer PT6A-20 engines on Grumman G-21A c/n B-52, which was registered as N4773C. There was much speculation that Alaska Coastal would convert the rest of their Goose fleet (another 13 aircraft) to PT6A power, but with only the first two conversions completed, Alaska Coastal Airlines became part of Alaska Airlines in 1968 and the Goose routes were transferred to third-level carriers.

The difference between the Alaska Coastal installation and the conversions developed by McKinnon was that the former utilized the original Grumman engine nacelle positions on their wings, whereas McKinnon put into practice a

theory developed in Peru by Dr Alberto Alvarez Calderon of the Fabrica Nacional de Aeroplanos SA (FANASA) regarding a so-called "clean-wing." In order to minimize the turbulence generated by the normal transition between the wing and wing-mounted engine nacelles, the nacelles were relocated inboard against the fuselage. The engines were then canted upward and outward in order to improve the single-engine performance of the aircraft as well as reducing its single-engine minimum controllable airspeed (V_{mc}) by directing more of the propeller's slipstream over the vertical stabilizer and rudder.

As Alaska Coastal was completing its first turbine G-21A conversion of N95431 in early 1966, Angus McKinnon was close to completing his first turbine Goose conversion. Since it had served him so well already as a test bed to develop his previous ideas, McKinnon chose once again to modify N150M, his one and only model

G-21D. In addition to incorporating the Alvarez Calderon "clean-wing" with its relocated nacelles, McKinnon was interested in other innovations to further enhance the performance of his unique Goose. One such innovation was the installation of the rotating trailing-edge hinged wing flap system, also designed by Dr Alvarez Calderon. It gave the same aerodynamic benefits as Fowler flaps but used only a single hinge instead of the complicated double track mechanism that Fowler flaps required. STC SA1320WE was approved on 16th February 1967 but unlike the Alaska Coastal STCs that came before, it was not limited to one-time use. It covered the installation of the PT6A-20 engines on either a McKinnon G-21C or G-21D under Type Certificate 4A24 and also covered the installation of the Alvarez Calderon flaps on the G-21D. With the approval of this STC, N150M became a

G-21D "Hybrid" turbine Goose and was awarded a new certificate of airworthiness on the same day.

Even as it was in the process of being re-certified, N150M was sold to the Precision Valve Corporation of Yonkers, New York. In 1974, it was bought by Peyton Hawes of Portland, Oregon, co-owner of the PayLess Drug Store chain. In 1977, Hawes sold it to Hal Beale of On Mark Aviation. Visiting the Antilles Seaplanes shop in Gibsonville, North Carolina in around 2007, Hal Beale said that of all the airplanes that he ever owned, he loved – and missed – his turbine Goose the most. He said that it would fulfil any mission that he needed to fly and he never tired of flying it. For some reason unknown even to himself, he parted with N150M in March 1980 and sold it to the Whittington brothers, Bill and Don, who owned both aircraft and automotive racing teams, as well as the World Jet FBO at Fort

Lauderdale Executive Airport. N150M was re-registered eventually to Water Fowl Inc in Fort Lauderdale, Florida in July 1982.

Four years later, Bill Whittington pleaded guilty to income tax evasion and conspiracy to smuggle marijuana from Colombia and he was sentenced to 15 years in prison and ordered to surrender millions of dollars worth of property and other assets. In 1987, his brother Don pleaded guilty to money laundering charges associated with Bill's drug smuggling activities, receiving an 18-month prison sentence. The fate of N150M itself is unknown; rumours have circulated for years that it was seized in Haiti as a result of the Whittington brothers' drug smuggling activities and eventually scrapped – others say this happened in Cuba.

Meanwhile, after completing the turbine conversion of N150M in 1967, McKinnon

The original G-21C, after conversion to P&W PT6A power, as the McKinnon G-21D "Hybrid", N150M (c/n 1147/1251) takes-off with the Alvarez Calderon flaps fully extended. The photograph was probably taken in February 1967. (McKinnon photo)

On Mark Aviation's G-21D "Hybrid", N150M (c/n 1147/1251) fitted with PT6A-60 turboprops, seen here at EAA, Oshkosh on 2nd August 1979.
(Jennifer Gradidge)

had a very rosy perspective of his position in an exclusive niche market: *"The McKinnon development of the G-21D Turboprop Goose amphibian has proven to be the most outstanding, successful project in the known world of truly versatile multi-engined aircraft. It is now in full production and scheduling. Its performance plus TOTAL CAPABILITIES are far superior to any other aircraft in the global inventory of similar size, weight and capacity in anything less than pure Jet transport. In its maximum density seating version, it can accommodate a 17-place* configuration!"*

McKinnon's subsequent Goose conversions were accomplished using two 550shp UAC PT6A-20 turboprops rather than the four Lycoming piston engines and McKinnon described these aircraft as G-21C "Hybrids". Even so, McKinnon Enterprises Inc business records show that because so much of the early work on the turbine-powered Goose was done by Alaska Coastal-Ellis and he was able to copy it, McKinnon was required to pay a royalty of $10,000 to Alaska Coastal for each turbine engine kit that he produced for a Goose.

McKinnon G-21A conversions

Grumman G-21A c/n B-123, N640, was the next Goose converted by McKinnon and this was undertaken for the Bureau of Land Management in Alaska. The conversion of N640 was accomplished in conjunction with the many repairs that were required following a landing accident on 31st August 1966 in Alegnagik, Alaska after which the aircraft had sunk in 100ft of water. After recovery, it was shipped to McKinnon for both repair and conversion. Unlike the G-21C "Hybrids" that he eventually produced, at least nominally

---

* While drawings exist for this 17-place configuration, it was never approved under Type Certificate 4A24.

under both Type Certificate 4A24 and STC SA1320WE, the same PT6A-20 turbine engines were installed on N640 solely on the basis of STC SA1589WE. McKinnon applied to the FAA for this new STC on 4th April 1967 and an experimental certificate of airworthiness was issued for N640 on 27th July 1967. The aircraft completed its flight test programme that autumn and a new standard airworthiness certificate was issued on 12th January 1968, followed shortly thereafter by the approval of STC SA1589WE itself on 24th January 1968. N640 retained its identification as a "Grumman G-21A" under ATC 654 but the notation "Turboprop" was added to all of its official registration and airworthiness certificates until 2001, when it was eventually "scrapped".

Just like SA1320WE, but unlike the STCs used by Alaska Coastal, SA1589WE was a multiple use STC and could be licensed to install PT6A-20 turbines on any suitable Grumman G-21A airframe. Similarly, SA1320WE was the stated basis on which those turbine engines were installed later on two additional "McKinnon G-21C" aircraft. Aircraft modified by either of these McKinnon STCs were virtually indistinguishable, but nevertheless there was a significant difference. Without the requisite structural reinforcements used on a G-21C, the turbine G-21A was limited to its original certified gross weight of 8,000lbs. – unless it was also modified by McKinnon STC SA4-1467, the retractable wingtip float kit that permitted its gross weight to go up to 9,200lbs. G-21C "Hybrid" aircraft modified by STC SA1320WE were authorized to operate up to a gross weight of 10,500lbs (actually down from the 12,499lbs certified gross weight of the basic four-engine model G-21C), and with comparable empty weights, that 1,300lb difference was all payload.

Marshall of Cambridge

A second G-21A was converted in England by Marshall of Cambridge, and completed in 1968 using McKinnon STC kits as follows:

- PT6A-20 Turbine Engine Installation Kit No.2
- Auxiliary fuel tank Kit No.5
- Radar nose Kit No.3
- Windshield Kit No.6

Also incorporated under Marshall Modification No.222 were a revised instrument panel, crew harnesses and a new cabin seating layout, along with associated changes to air conditioning and interior furnishings. After being worked on for almost two years (having been started on 23rd August 1966), it made its first flight as a turbine Goose on 19th July 1968. Registered as G-ASXG for Grosvenor Estates, it was Grumman c/n 1083. Confusingly, it was subsequently (but improperly) re-registered as a "McKinnon G-21C" in the UK, but it still kept its Grumman serial number. In 1973, it was sold to a new owner in Canada and it was registered there as C-FAWH, once again properly identified as Grumman G-21A, c/n 1083. In 1986, while retaining its other McKinnon modifications such as the "radar" nose and the wrap-around windshield, it had its turbines removed and R-985 radial piston engines re-installed. Unfortunately, it crashed near Port Hardy at the north end of Vancouver Island in British Columbia on 12th May 1988. The wreckage was still in a dump near the end of the Port Hardy runway in July 2012.

McKinnon G-21C "Hybrid"

McKinnon completed two more examples in 1968 that he certified as models G-21C under TC 4A24 and in which he installed

Grosvenor Estates' G-21A Turbo Goose G-ASXG (c/n 1083) in flight over Booker, UK in the late 1960s. The conversion was carried out by Marshall of Cambridge Engineering Ltd in 1968, using McKinnon STC kits.   *(Brian Stainer via Air-Britain)*

Above: *G-21C "Hybrid" CF-BCI (c/n B-138/ 1203) of Air West, outside its hangar at Vancouver, British Columbia on 13th August 1973.*
(John P Stewart via PJ Marson)

Right: *G-21C Hybrid N642 (c/n B-137/1204) powered by PT6A-27 turbine engines, and registered to the US Department of the Interior. As a G-21A the aircraft was operated by the Bureau of Land Management in Alaska, but after conversion to turbine power was transferred to the Alaska Office of Aircraft Services. The photograph was taken at Merrill Field, Anchorage on 6th August 1972.*
(John P Stewart via PJ Marson)

turbine engines under STC SA1320WE – all at the same time. The first of these was Grumman c/n B-138, which had been operated since 1952 by the Fish & Wildlife Service in Alaska as N779. It was declared surplus to their requirements in April 1966 and was bought by Charles E Walters of Spokane, Washington, to whom it was registered N16484. A different registration, N501M, was reserved and was applied to the aircraft on 5th May 1966. McKinnon bought the Goose from Mr Walters a year and a half later on 24th August 1967 and on 19th December 1967 wrote a letter to the FAA informing them that the aircraft was to be sold to a Canadian owner, cancelling its US registration and transferring "N501M" to a G-44 Widgeon. McKinnon followed that letter with another on 22nd January 1968 including Form 1716 "Aircraft Accident Notice", using the section for Cancellation of Aircraft Registration Number, to de-register "Grumman G-21A, c/n B-138" on 2nd February 1968. When its conversion was complete on 26th June 1968, it was re-identified by McKinnon as "G-21C (ie Hybrid) c/n 1203" but he never certified it or registered it as such in the USA. It went directly to the British Columbia Division of Highways in Canada as CF-BCI and was operated later by Air West and Jim Pattison Industries.

In October 1984 C-FBCI went to Lindair Services Ltd in Richmond, British

Columbia for a major overhaul and was "upgraded" to a G-21G* with the installation of 680shp PT6A-27 engines and other modifications. After those "upgrades", it was operated by Crown Forest Products from 1985 until 1991, when it was transferred to a broker and eventually sold to Pen Air in Alaska. It went back on the US civil registry in 1991 as N660PA and was operated primarily in the Aleutian Islands until it disappeared on 11th August 1996, presumed to have crashed near Dutch Harbor, Alaska with the loss of the pilot and one passenger on board.

The second McKinnon turbine Goose for the Bureau of Land Management was built in 1968 using Grumman G-21A c/n B-137. Registered as N642, it became McKinnon

---

* Because Lindair Services Ltd was not the owner of TC 4A24, it was not valid for them to have re-identified C-FBCI subsequently as a "McKinnon G-21G" – only McKinnon Enterprises Inc ever had that authority. In October 1984 however, McKinnon no longer owned the TC either; it had been sold to Viking Air Ltd in June 1984. If Viking Air had performed the "upgrades" to C-FBCI (and if they had filed the appropriate paperwork), it would have become a "Viking G-21G" turbine Goose. Legally speaking, as a result of the Lindair "upgrades", the aircraft was then just a more highly modified McKinnon G-21 "Hybrid" that happened to resemble a model G-21G in many details.

G-21C (ie "Hybrid") c/n 1204. It was completed one month after c/n 1203 and was re-certified by McKinnon on 26th July 1968. McKinnon documented the conversion of N642, not with a Form 317 "Statement of Conformity" certifying production under 14 CFR Part 21 Subpart F, but rather using a standard FAA Form 337 "Major Alteration or Repair" (a 14 CFR Part 43 maintenance form) on which the aircraft was identified as "Grumman G-21 c/n B-137" and on which he listed each of the modifications by their various STC kit numbers as follows:

- Installed P & W PT6A-20 Turbine Engine Kit No.4 - STC SA1320WE, dated 22-4-68

- Wrap-around Windshield Installation Kit No.7 - STC SA4-680.

- Installed Picture Windows Kit No.2 - STC SA101WE.

- Installed Auxiliary Fuel Tank Kit No.3 - STC SA4-683

- Installed Radar Nose 15½in Extension Kit No.5 - STC SA4-678.

- Installed Left and right Leading Edge Landing Light Kit No.4 - STC SA4-1550.

According to this Form 337, McKinnon installed STC SA1320WE on a "Grumman G-21", but that STC was not (and still is not) eligible for installation on a G-21A. At least nominally speaking, the aircraft should have been certified as a McKinnon G-21C prior to the installation of STC SA1320WE. As N642 was a Grumman G-21A, the only approved means of installing the PT6A-20 turbine engines on it was by use of STC SA1589WE as McKinnon had done on N640, Grumman G-21A c/n B-123.

The N642 Form 337 goes on to detail all of the various repairs and minor detail changes that were accomplished at the same time. Nowhere in that list is there any mention of the installation of any of the structural reinforcements that were all necessary for the aircraft to be re-identified subsequently as a McKinnon model G-21C. The necessary modifications and reinforcements that were NOT installed were:

- McKinnon Engineering Order (EO) No. 1 to Grumman drawing no. 9603 – structural reinforcement of the main landing gear drag braces.
- McKinnon EO-2 to Grumman drawing No.12001 – structural reinforcement of the lower hull longerons between Hull Stations 10 – 13 and Stations 13 – 16.
- McKinnon EO-1, -2, and -4 to Grumman drawing No.12440 – the installation of doubler ribs on every original rib in the flaps.
- McKinnon drawing No.MPD-5011 – the reinforcement of the lower portion of the Station 13 bulkhead. (The Station 13 Bulkhead is the main bulkhead between the cockpit and the cabin; it carries the loads of both the wing and the landing gear, both of which bolt directly to it.)

The reinforcement of the flaps and the Station 13 bulkhead were particularly necessary because of the increased air loads that the basic or "pure" four-engine G-21C experienced operating at gross weights up to 12,499lbs. They were specifically required by McKinnon model G-21C Master Drawing List (MDL) No.7, dated 10th March 1958 as revised on 29th May 1959, as well as by MPD-90995, the MDL for the 12,500lb. model G-21G that was dated 24th April 1970. However, these reinforcements were not included in the separate MDL (MPD-9995) that McKinnon developed specifically for the interim G-21C "Hybrid" conversions. This was the basis for the "reduced" gross weight of only 10,500lbs for the so-called G-21C "Hybrids" and later for the model G-21E that was eventually certified under TC 4A24.*

A "true" model G-21C, whether modified in any subsequent manner or not (by any existing STC for example) is still required to have all of those reinforcements

installed; a model G-21E is not so required by its separate MDL. The aircraft that McKinnon nominally identified as G-21C "Hybrids" (serials 1203 and 1204) did not have any of these reinforcements – and therefore should never have been re-identified as "C" models. Although technically speaking, they may have eventually conformed to the G-21E type design, that model was not approved until July 1969 – a year or more after these aircraft were converted by McKinnon. By taking this "shortcut" McKinnon nominally approved them to operate at a gross weight of 10,500 lbs when in fact they should have remained limited to 9,200lbs. Furthermore, unlike all of the other aircraft that McKinnon converted under the authority of TC 4A24, these two aircraft were not "zero-timed" – whereas all of the other aircraft essentially "reborn" under TC 4A24 carried forward no "time in service" from their previous lives as Grumman G-21As, "McKinnon" c/ns 1203 and 1204 did in fact carry forward all of their existing times in service as "Grumman" aircraft.

In spite of these discrepancies, on the same day that McKinnon signed the Form 337 approving the installation of the "upgrades" to N642, he also filed an application for a new airworthiness certificate on which he re-identified it as "McKinnon G-21C c/n 1204." It was placed back into service by the Bureau of Land Management (BLM), who continued to operate it as a "public-use" aircraft for many more years. BLM also modified N642 with a static line to drop smoke jumpers – the Forest Service firemen who drop by parachute into the woods to fight forest fires (see also "Smoke-Jumper Door" on page 71). In August 1989, it was finally auctioned off by the General Services Administration as surplus property. It was purchased by Jack Mark, president of MA Inc, in Oshkosh, Wisconsin, who was among other things a noted collector of "warbird" aircraft. After flying it for many years, Jack Mark died in June 2007 and N642 was put up for sale, along with several other aircraft in his collection. A

new owner from the Seattle area finally bought it in April 2010 and started working to restore it to an airworthy condition after it had experienced several years of neglect and other accumulated issues.

McKinnon G-21E

The G-21C "Hybrid" configuration was finally approved as the model G-21E under Type Certificate 4A24 Section III on 17th July 1969. With the option to use either two 550shp Pratt & Whitney PT6A-20 or two 680shp -27 turboprops, the nine-place aircraft had a gross weight of 10,500lbs. McKinnon c/ns 1211 – 1225 were allocated for G-21E conversions, but only c/n 1211 was completed, in May 1970 with PT6A-27 engines. It was Grumman G-21A, c/n 1013, and it had been registered as N121H with the Halliburton Company in Oklahoma since 1954. In 1974, the G-21E conversion was still being offered at a cost of $486,305 (plus options) but there were no more takers.

McKinnon G-21F

The model "G-21F" proposed to McKinnon by the Fish & Wildlife Service (FWS) in Alaska was intended originally to be certified under TC 4A24. It was to feature the installation of two Garrett AiResearch TPE331-2UA-203D turboprops mounted in inverted Volpar-built Beech 18 nacelles (the "U" part of the engine designation indicated "upside down" and the "A" indicated aluminium instead of magnesium cases), a 40 inch fuselage extension in front of the wing leading edge and a long dorsal fin. The former was to accommodate two observers in the cockpit (forward of the Sta 13 bulkhead), and the latter to house the control cables that originally had been installed under the floor. The extension to the forward fuselage accommodated two observers, just behind the pilots, on those occasions when the FWS carried out marine mammal surveys over the Baring Sea. The extended dorsal fin allowed the control cables to be re-routed over the

The former G-21A (c/n 1013) became the only McKinnon G-21E in May 1970. Seen here as N121H (c/n 1211) attending the 1985 NBAA Show at New Orleans Lakefront.   *(EW Priebe)*

The former Alaska Fish & Wildlife Service's Volpar G-21G N780 (c/n B-72/1240) showing the long dorsal fairing which held the control cables to allow an extra fuel tank to be fitted under the cabin floor. The photograph was taken at Anchorage on 6th August 1972.   *(John P Stewart via P.J Marson)*

cabin, thus allowing an auxiliary fuel tank to be installed in the hull. All of the design and conversion work was done at the FWS aircraft maintenance facility in Anchorage, Alaska. Before FAA certification of the project was gained however, the conversion was re-designated as a McKinnon G-21G (STC) and, as a result, the model "G-21F" never officially existed.

McKinnon G-21G

Apparently, the Fish & Wildlife Service managers were not happy with the amount of engineering, drafting, and testing that the FAA would have required to fully certify a whole new model under TC 4A24. Therefore the project was reduced to modifying only a single aircraft by means of supplemental type certificates. The story that FWS subsequently told the FAA was that McKinnon would first convert the Goose into a standard model G-21G (under TC 4A24, Section IV), and then they (FWS) would use STCs to install the TPE331 engines, the 40-inch fuselage plug, a new dorsal fin and re-routed flight controls, a new fuel system with an additional 150-gallon header tank under the cabin floor, and a new hydraulic system for operating the flaps and the landing gear. In fact, FWS personnel in Anchorage installed all of those modifications and Volpar consulted on the engine installations, but there is no evidence that McKinnon ever worked on the aircraft in any way. So Grumman c/n B-72, registered as N780, was originally going to be a G-21F, but came to be registered as a G-21G in spite of the fact that there is a serious shortage of supporting documentation on file with the FAA.

The next aircraft in the McKinnon saga was US Navy JRF-5, BuAer serial 37809, which was originally built as Grumman c/n B-62. After being released as surplus, it was obtained by Flugfelag Islands (Icelandair) in September 1947 and registered as TF-ISR. It went back to the

USA in July 1967 as part of a deal that included a PBY-5A, having been purchased by Harold J Hansen of American Aviation, Inc in Seattle, Washington for only $5,000. A couple of months later in October 1967, then registered as N5558*, it was sold to McKinnon Enterprises. McKinnon in turn sold it to Charles E Walters of Spokane WA, and almost a year later, on 20th September 1968, Walters sold it back to McKinnon Enterprises and personally carried an inflated mortgage note on the aircraft, essentially handing the money necessary to convert it to McKinnon.

Over the course of several months

---

* *During all of the time since it came back from Iceland, N5558 was identified accidentally as c/n "B-1062" and its records in the FAA Registry archives in Oklahoma City, Oklahoma got mixed together with those for Grumman G-21A c/n 1062, which had been built in December 1939, and which had been owned and operated as NC3042 by the Gulf Oil Co of Pittsburgh, Pennsylvania. After the United States became more involved in WWII, Gulf Oil sold c/n 1062 to the War Department on 5th September 1942. It was impressed into military service as an OA-13A with serial 42-97055 but apparently did not survive its military service.*

between September 1968 and May 1969, McKinnon started the conversion of N5558. For the first time, the Form 337 that McKinnon used to record the individual modifications included the requisite reinforcements such as Drawing No. MPD-5011 for the Station 13 bulkhead and the various engineering orders detailed above for the landing gear, lower hull framing, and the flaps. Contrary to the claim of some previous histories of the McKinnon's turbine Gooses, N5558 was never identified as a G-21C, "Hybrid" or otherwise. There is one FAA Form 337 that McKinnon filed during the conversion process in order to document all of the specific modifications, including the turbine engines. While that one Form 337 identified N5558 as an "E" model, it may have been the result of a simple typographical error. While we may never know for sure, that was not nearly as important as the fact that, by the time McKinnon completed all of his modifications to N5558 and filed his final Form 317, the manufacturer's "Statement

Newly completed McKinnon G-21G N5558 (c/n B-62/1205) seen in August 1969 at Vancouver, British Columbia.   *(Ingvar Klett)*

Sea Bee Air's G-21E ZK-ERX (c/n B-62/1205) at Noumea-Magenta on 30th August 1981.   *(R Caratini)*

of Conformity" to an approved design per FAR 21 Subpart F on 5th September 1969, it was identified officially as a "McKinnon G-21G". It was identified similarly as a "G" model on the Forms 305 "Application for Airworthiness Certificate" for the experimental certificates it was issued on 13th June 1969 and again on 17th July 1969, and finally for its Standard Airworthiness certificate issued on 5th September 1969.

The model G-21G was a further development of the G-21E using the more powerful 680shp PT6A-27 turboprops. The fuel capacity was increased to 488 Imperial (586 US) gallons, and it incorporated all of the significant structural reinforcements that had been used in McKinnon's original four-engine "C" models, but that had been left out of each of his aircraft since. Accordingly, the model G-21G was certified once again to the maximum "small aircraft" gross weight limit of 12,500lbs. FAA approval was gained under TC 4A24 Section IV on 29th August 1969 and construction numbers 1226 – 1250 were reserved for future G-21G production.

Apparently, Angus McKinnon had over-stretched himself financially during the conversion of N5558. In addition to the original note from Mr Walters, the First National Bank of Portland, Oregon loaned him $200,000 on 25th September 1968 and McKinnon put up most of the remaining assets of McKinnon Enterprises Inc as additional collateral on the loan. Several months later, the bank realized that the engines had not yet been installed in the aircraft and were not part of their collateral. McKinnon did not get new engines for the aircraft until December 1968, when he was

extended "credit" to the amount of $74,930 from United Aircraft of Canada on the promise to pay for the engines out of the proceeds from the eventual sale of the aircraft. In February 1969, McKinnon borrowed an additional $150,000 from another individual, Mr James Eklem of Portland, Oregon. McKinnon stopped making payments on both of the loans in May 1970. By March 1971, James Eklem had sold the note that he held against N5558 to the US National Bank of Oregon. On 20th September 1971, the First National Bank of Portland filed suit against McKinnon Enterprises and for the first time, each of McKinnon's creditors learned of the others.

The court determined in favour of the plaintiff, the First National Bank of Portland and the aircraft, N5558, as well as the rest of McKinnon's property that had been put up as collateral, were all seized by the bank. First, the aircraft was re-registered to the bank, and then on 17th January 1972 an auction was held at McKinnon's airport in Sandy, Oregon to sell all of the assets paying off the other creditors from the proceeds. McKinnon G-21G c/n 1205, N5558, was sold to Peyton Hawes of Portland, co-owner of the PayLess Drugs Store chain. He operated it until December 1980, when it was sold to Sea Bee Air in New Zealand and registered as ZK-ERX. Between March 1980 and September 1983, Sea Bee Air operated services on behalf of the Tuvalu government, basing the G-21G at Funafuti, from which it flew non-scheduled services linking the nine atolls of the Tuvalu group and providing charters to the Tokelau, Samoa, Kiribati, Nauru and Cook groups of

islands. After the extreme wear it had experienced operating in the warm salt water environment around the South Pacific islands, the aircraft was then sent back to New Zealand for overhaul. Air New Zealand performed the restoration work on the promise that the Tuvalu government would fund the work in return for the aerial service that Sea Bee Air had provided them. Apparently, after over 15,000 man-hours of labour and a bill of close to $475,000, the government refused to pay and the conflict remained in litigation for several years; the eventual outcome is uncertain.

In December 1984, c/n 1205 was bought by Aero Quest Inc of Cleveland, Ohio, who shipped it back across the Pacific to Tacoma, Washington, off loaded it into the water and then flew it to Boeing Field in Seattle. From there, it was ferried to Cleveland, Ohio and finally delivered to Aero Quest. It spent most of 1985 being modified to have its unique large cargo door installed on the right side of the fuselage as well as new avionics and a new interior installed. It was operated by Aero Quest for only a few months before their insurance lapsed and they stopped flying it. It was transferred subsequently to Aero Quest's parent company, Kalt Manufac-turing Company in 1987, who sold it to its current owner in 1990. It was, in 2013, still maintained in pristine condition with the owner flying it frequently, often as far afield as the Bahamas and the Aleutian Islands in Alaska.

The second and final "true" G-21G built by McKinnon was converted from Grumman JRF-5 c/n B-125 (ex-USN BuAer serial 87731) and completed in

March 1970. After its US Navy service, the JRF-5 had been supplied to the Japanese Maritime Self-Defence Force (JMSDF) for use in a training role throughout the 1950s and into the early-1960s carrying the JMSDF serial 9013. It was purchased as surplus from the US Army Depot Command in Japan (probably in Sagamihara City) in September 1968 for the paltry sum of $5,555.56 by ex-Navy fighter pilot, crop duster and sometimes Hollywood stunt pilot, Tom Danaher of Wichita Falls, Texas who then sold it to McKinnon Enterprises in August 1969 for $15,000. (Apparently, McKinnon was using the multiple bank loans that he got for N5558 to simultaneously finance a second G-21G project as well.)

With the completion of McKinnon G-21G c/n 1226, as documented by his Form 317 "Statement of Conformity" on 16th March 1970, it was identified as "N70AL"* and was sold to US Plywood-Champion Papers Inc in Juneau, Alaska two days later. Champion Papers later

---

*In August of 1969, McKinnon tried to reserve "N-3060AL", which had too many characters in it for an official FAA registration and may have also simply been another typo on his part. That was on a typed letter to the FAA; he also requested, on a handwritten note, either "N3060A" or "N1970A". That was followed up with an official registration application form in September 1969 requesting "N60AL", but over-written "N70AL". That application was in turn followed by a chattel mortgage form on which the aircraft was identified as "McKinnon G-21G c/n 1226", but the registration was left blank. That was followed by another registration application form dated 23rd October 1969 on which the aircraft was identified as N70AL. McKinnon apparently also submitted an FAA Form AC 69-8070 "Reservation of Special Registration Mark" on which it was specified that while N60AL was its current registration, "N70AL" was reserved for future use. The chattel mortgage release showed the registration as N60AL on 10th March 1970.

became the Champion International Corporation and N70AL was later bought by Chevron Oil of California, who operated it from the New Orleans Lakefront Airport for many years in support of their Gulf of Mexico well-drilling operations. In 2013 it was still fully operational and flying with a private owner in Michigan.

In 1974 the G-21G conversion was offered at $550,000 including options, but with PT6A-powered commuter aircraft available brand-new, there was no longer much economic logic in converting a Goose (unless you needed a flying boat!)

Volpar Inc "Packaged Power"

The projected McKinnon "G-21F" was to have had two Garrett-AiResearch TPE331 turboprops fitted to replace the Wasps. Volpar Inc of Van Nuys, California had developed nacelles for their Turbo 18 conversion of the Beech Model 18. Following their success with the Turbo 18 nacelles, Volpar then marketed an installation dubbed "Packaged Power" which allowed installation of TPE331 engines with either over-engine or under-engine air intakes, as required. In the case of the Fish & Wildlife Service (FWS) Goose, the former was chosen and the nacelles were inverted to facilitate this requirement, a modification engineered under Volpar's STC SA551SW. (The TPE331 installation on the FWS Goose was facilitated by means of McKinnon STC SA2809WE). Grumman c/n B-72 was the only Goose so converted, using Garrett-AiResearch TPE331-2UA-203D engines of 715shp. It was never certified as a model "G-21F", and was later referred to as G-21G, c/n 1240. It was never designated officially as a G-21G by McKinnon, the FWS personnel involved or

by the FAA. There is no Form 337 on file documenting the installation of either STC SA514AL or SA2809WE, which served as the nominal basis of its unique configuration, and there is no manufacturer's Form 317 certifying its conformity to an approved type design for "production" under FAR 21 Subpart F. Apparently, FWS literally one day just started calling it a "McKinnon G-21G" with no official supporting documentation whatsoever!

Summary

G-21C 12,499lbs gross weight Goose conversion with four 340hp Lycoming GSO-480-B2D6 engines. Two built: c/ns 1201 and 1202.

G-21C "Hybrid" 10,500lbs gross weight Goose conversion with two 550shp UAC PT6A-20 turboprops per STC SA1320WE. Two built: c/ns 1203 and 1204.

G-21D same as G-21C, with four 340hp Lycoming GSO-480-B2D6 engines, but with a 36in nose extension that incorporated 4 additional seats. Only one was built, c/n 1251. It was later re-engined with two 550shp UAC PT6A-20 turboprop engines per STC SA1320WE, making it a G-21D "Hybrid". C/ns 1252 – 1255 were also allocated but none was built.

G-21E 10,500lbs gross weight Goose conversion with two 550shp UAC PT6A-20 or 680 shp PT6A-27 turboprop engines. One built: c/n 1211 (built with -27 engines). A second aircraft, c/n 1205, may have been started as a G-21E, but was eventually completed as a model G-21G.

McKinnon's second true G-21G Goose N70AL (c/n B-125/1226) operated by the Chevron Oil Company, and seen here at New Orleans, Louisiana in 1985.
(EW Priebe)

G-21F 12,500lbs gross weight projected Goose conversion with two 715shp Garrett AiResearch TPE331-2UA-203D turbo-props and a 40in fuselage extension for Fish & Wildlife Service (FWS) in Alaska. C/ns 1206 – 1210 were reserved, but the "G-21F" design was never certified under TC 4A24 by the FAA. The prototype was re-designated as "G-21G (STC)" on the unsubstantiated basis that it had been converted first to a G-21G by McKinnon Enterprises before being modified further to its own unique configuration by FWS per STC SA514AL and STC SA2809WE.

G-21G 12,500lbs gross weight Goose conversion with two 680shp UAC PT6A-27 turboprops. C/n 1205 was the first aircraft to be completed as a G-21G. Additional construction numbers 1226 – 1250 were allocated. C/n 1226 was the only additional G-21G built by McKinnon. The aircraft originally intended to be the FWS G-21F was registered eventually as a highly-modified G-21G, and assigned c/n 1240, in spite of its failure to ever demonstrate conformity to that design.

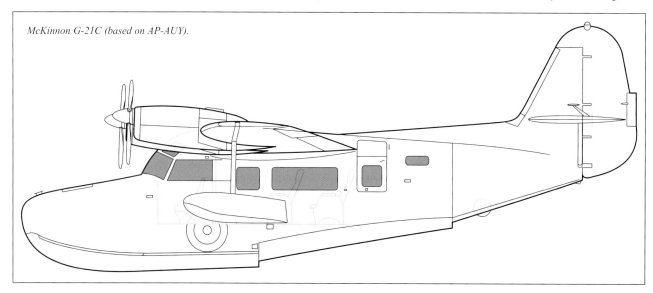

McKinnon G-21C (based on AP-AUY).

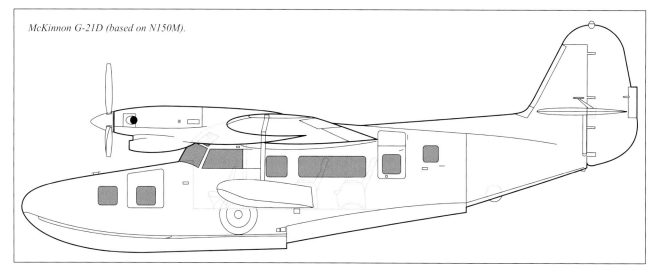

McKinnon G-21D (based on N150M).

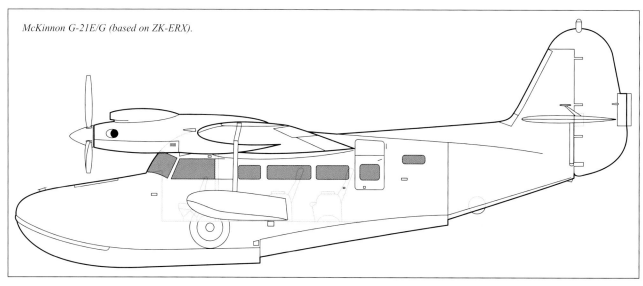

McKinnon G-21E/G (based on ZK-ERX).

(All drawings by Michael Zoeller)

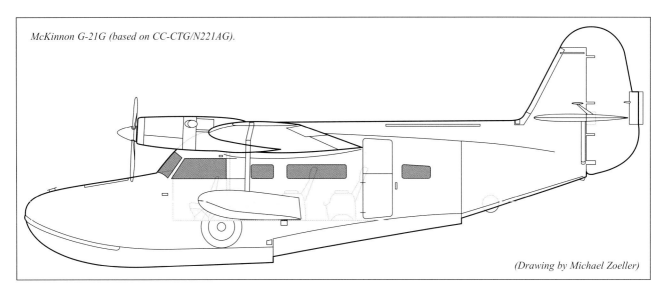

McKinnon G-21G (based on CC-CTG/N221AG).

(Drawing by Michael Zoeller)

"Smoke-Jumper Door"

The US Department of the Interior's Bureau of Land Management (BLM) was also responsible for a unique modification to the Goose.

To facilitate the rapid delivery of fire-fighters to the source of a bush fire, the BLM came up with the idea of parachuting "smoke-jumpers", or "Hot Shots" as they were also known, out of a Goose.

To enable this the BLM designed a door and fabrication was undertaken, in accordance with Supplemental Type Certificate SA1-439, at their workshops in Fairbanks, Alaska. The door, located on the right side of the rear fuselage in place of the escape hatch, was in two pieces (top and bottom) and opened inward so that it could be removed in flight. It was secured by a series of small dead-bolts. The bottom part of the door was cut below the waterline and designed so as to be watertight. The sequence of events was therefore that after locating the drop area, the doors would be removed, the smoke-jumper would jump from the aircraft, the doors would be re-fitted and the Goose would return to base (on the water or land). The BLM fitted several of their G-21As, in the N640 registration range, with the "smoke-jumper" door and its success led several Goose operators to decide that the "smoke-jumper" door would solve many of the logistical problems they had encountered with cargo handling into and out of the aircraft. Kodiak Western Airlines fabricated the doors in their own workshop and fitted them to c/ns B-100 and B-112. Each of these quickly became known as a "Big-Door" Goose.

The doors were never intended for heavy cargo, and with over exuberant ground crews, the loading of 55-gallon oil or fuel drums caused a few dents in the lower door sill. This prevented a water-tight seal being made when the doors were closed allowing water to leak in.

Water Rudder

According to Steve Harvey, of Harvey Flying Service, Louisiana, it is almost impossible to get a Grumman safely to a dock without a water rudder. In order to maintain any sort of directional control, speed must be kept up. Once the engines are shut down (to avoid killing anybody on the dock) all control is lost and the aircraft is headed towards the dock with no way to turn or stop. However, a water rudder gives the pilot excellent slow speed control in the water, and a competent pilot can put a fully loaded Grumman alongside a dock, with both engines shut down, at a very slow speed.

In the 1980s, G-21A N641 (c/n B-115) "Spirit of Alitak" was operated by Peninsula Airways. The Goose had been fitted with a "smoke-jumper" door by the Bureau of Land Management at Juneau, Alaska in May 1961.
(Steve Harvey)

A line-up of Widgeons in service with the Alaska Fish & Wildlife Service, seen here at Juneau, Alaska circa 1960. Water rudders can be seen fitted to the two aircraft in the centre and on the right of the picture.   *(Fred J Knight Collection)*

G-21A N2767A (c/n 1021) of Catalina Channel Airlines in October 1959 shows the water rudder which had been fitted by the Bureau of Land Management in Juneau, Alaska.   *(Harry Gann via Art Krieger)*

Most Grumman operators in Alaska lowered their wheels after landing on water and ran up a beach or a ramp, but in southeast Alaska pilots were instructed to only use docks, and not to lower their wheels for beach work. As Grumman did not provide a water rudder for the Goose or Widgeon the southeast Alaskan operators had to design one of their own. Situated behind the tailwheel, it was raised and lowered by the pilot. This led to another item on the landing checklist – "water rudder retracted". Failure to do this would result in (a) its being torn off in a runway landing, or (b) a water loop after

a water landing, causing much damage to the aircraft.

It is not known exactly how many aircraft were fitted with water rudders but the Alaska Fish & Wildlife Service fitted them to a number of their Juneau-based Goose and Widgeon aircraft, and operated them to and from docks.

Strange Bird Inc had a water rudder fitted to their G-44A c/n 1471 in 1994, in accordance with Thurston Aeromarine Corporation drawings.

Fred Frakes designed a water rudder for the Mallard. It looked very much like a boat's rudder and was attached at the rear

of the hull. Frakes gained FAA approval for his design and fitted it to his J-44 in 1963, for operations in Alaska.

"Water-bombing" Goose

Don McIvor, a pilot for B.N.P. Airways/West Coast Transport in British Columbia, developed a method of "water-bombing" forest fires by fitting external water tanks to Goose c/n B-107 CF-IOL. Attached to the fuselage just below the window line under each wing, the tanks were open-topped and could be swivelled downward in flight to release the water. Although not confirmed,

Above: *Don McIvor's water tank addition to Goose CF-IOL (c/n B-107) and* **below left** *CF-IOL in action, demonstrating its ability to help douse forest fires.* *(via Ingvar Klett)*

it appears from photographs that the tanks were able to be filled by skimming the surface of a body of water and collecting water through the pipe (in front of the tank) which projected just below the keel line.

McIvor left West Coast Transport in 1959 to form Forest Industries Flying Tankers, with the acquisition of four Martin Mars aircraft.

Hydrofoils and Floats – the EDO Aircraft

The Goose

Between 1947 and 1965 the US Air Force and then the US Navy worked with the EDO Corporation of College Point, New York on a series of research projects developing a hydrofoil-plus-float concept.

These projects involved several aircraft including at various times four JRF-5s and in a related project, a J4F-2 Widgeon.

The first Goose programme was Air Force funded and initially looked at the feasibility of operating a single aircraft from water, snow and ice. The 'Pantobase' system was intended to demonstrate that an amphibious aircraft could be enabled to operate from all these environments. Following experiments with models in water tanks the USAF's Air Materiel Command borrowed a JRF-5, BuAer 34092, from the Navy in late 1947 for EDO to modify as a full-scale test vehicle. When received it was in the standard glossy sea blue colour scheme and the USAF merely added basic markings in the form of the tail serial '8128' (48-128) and a large buzz number 'OA-128' reflecting its new identity as an 'OA-9'.

The initial 'hydro-ski' trials were conducted in a water-based configuration in which the aircraft was fitted with rigid, streamlined struts and floats in a four-point layout. There was a main ski, a tail ski and wing-tip float skis.

For trials on snow and ice the rigid struts were replaced by oleo shock absorbers.

These trials were successful and demonstrated that the aircraft's normal tip floats and aileron control negated any need for the float skis and that the tail ski was also unnecessary because the aircraft

The "Triphibian" ski system later used on the SA-16A Albatross was first tested by the EDO Corporation in 1948, using JRF-5 Goose 48-128 (c/n B-21) in 1948.   *(EDO Corporation)*

OA-9 Goose 48-128 (c/n B-21) testing the "Triphibian" gear during a snow landing in 1948.   *(EDO Corporation)*

remained stable on take-off until it had transitioned from the hull to the main ski. Finally 48-128 was configured with just the main ski and is illustrated on the next page. This 'Pantobase' concept would be incorporated into the 'Triphibian' modification that was adopted later by the SA-16A Albatross, primarily for use in Arctic operations.

48-128 (by now academically re-designated 'ZA-9' by the USAF) was returned to the Navy in April 1949 and after brief use by the Naval Air Test Center (NATC) at Patuxent River, Maryland, it was reduced to spares in March 1950. However the Navy was interested enough to award a further research contract to EDO to investigate the benefits of the single

'hydro-ski' to seaplane operations from rough water.

To that end another JRF-5, 37783, was bailed to EDO in August 1950 and modified with a single ski. Superficially the installation resembled the final USAF configuration but 37783's ski was supported from the hull by a shock strut which was taken from a conventional aircraft landing gear and was contained within a telescopic fairing. Initially the aircraft's hull was extended to prevent excessive pitch-up on take-off when the submerged ski broke the surface and transitioned from hull to ski support. These experiments confirmed that the ski created hydrodynamic lift while running under-

water and at low speed would lift the aircraft clear of the water eliminating the planing run.

When out of the water both 48-128 and 37783 required a specially created and spindly-looking beaching gear to provide safe clearance for the ski.

37783's successful EDO trials were concluded by September 1951 and the aircraft was transferred to the NATC where it was retired and eventually scrapped on 30th September 1953. Meanwhile, the Navy had funded another trials programme to test a twin hydro-ski fitting. A third aircraft, JRF-5 37805, was bailed to EDO in June 1951. The twin ski arrangement was intended to enable a seaplane to taxy up the ramp without the use of beaching gear. The skis were fitted with small wheels that were free to pivot when on a hard surface. Flight testing has been described as being only "moderately successful" with much spray generated and a tendency for one ski to rise while the other remained submerged. Moreover the 'shock absorber' concept, successful with the single ski, was less satisfactory with twin skis. Research data was also obtained in relation to twin-ski use in high-performance jet seaplanes.

37805 was returned to the NATC at Patuxent River in June 1953 and remained in use there until terminally damaged circa October 1955 after which it was scrapped. Hydro-ski research continued at EDO

using larger aircraft, most notably a PBM-5 Mariner, and it was not until 1958 that another Goose would feature in an EDO test programme.

By the late 1950s high-speed hydrofoil boat technology had advanced to the stage that the US Navy was prepared to experiment using supercavitating section hydrofoils on seaplane aircraft. Accordingly the Navy requested that a Gruenberg system be married to a Goose. The Gruenberg design comprised twin bow hydro-skis and a primary super-cavitating hydrofoil section configured to pierce the surface in a 'V'. However by January 1958 the Navy had more or less exhausted its stock of surplus JRF-5s and was obliged to borrow 37782

from Coast Guard storage, explaining its initial flight (in 1962) in a USCG colour-scheme.

When EDO modified the aircraft new, three-bladed propellers were fitted. The hydrofoil modification, although technically successful, caused the bow skis to create excessive spray that damaged the engines and propellers. According to an EDO source the aircraft was little flown by them. The aircraft, subsequently repainted in USN markings, remained at College Point, New York, until 1963 but was then transferred to the NATC for more Navy flying.

The US Navy's programme was terminated on 30th June 1965 and 37782,

Above: *Water ski-ing! OA-9 Goose 48-128 (c/n B-21) during a test flight by the EDO Corporation in November 1952.* *(EDO Corporation)*

Above: *The JRF-5 Goose 37783 (c/n B-36), perched on its spindly beaching gear, was used by the EDO Corporation to test a single Hydro-ski in 1950.* *(EDO Corporation)*

Above: *This series of photos from April 1953 shows JRF-5 Goose 37805 (c/n B-58) fitted with the double Hydro-ski configuration developed by the EDO Corporation under contract to the US Navy, to develop improved take-off and landing characteristics for high performance aircraft.*

(EDO Corporation)

JRF-5 Goose 37782 (c/n B-35) fitted with the complicated-looking "Gruenberg" hydrofoil system in 1964.   *(EDO Corporation)*

JRF-5 Goose 37782 (c/n B-35) seen here in November 1964 with the Hydro-skis and the "Gruenberg" hydrofoils retracted for beaching.   *(US Navy)*

minus its Gruenberg kit, was returned formally to the USCG for immediate retirement.

The Widgeon

In January 1947 EDO was contracted to modify a J4F-2, 32976, to incorporate a half-scale replica hull of the Martin XP5M-1 Marlin. Subsequently the aircraft was used to flight test other hull configurations of varying length-to-beam ratios, the greatest of which was 12.5:1. These modifications necessitated the replacement of the undercarriage with a new installation in which the 'retracted' undercarriage rotated upwards and remained in the air-stream while in flight. It was first flown with the XP5M-1 hull (with a ratio of 8.5:1) in May 1948 at the National Advisory Committee on Aeronautics' (NACA) facility at Langley Field, Virginia and the aircraft was later loaned by the Navy to NACA for further hull research work from early 1950 until June 1953. It was during these years that it acquired an all-over yellow colour scheme and the name '*Petulant Porpoise*'. During this loan period flight trials were undertaken at NATC Patuxent River and at the Torpedo Unit, NAS Quonset Point as well as at College Point. After December 1952 the USN ceased to refer to the aircraft as a J4F-2 and it became the 'E-175'. The E-175 remained on the strength of the Torpedo Unit until May 1953 when it was transferred to the NATC and remained there until retirement by October 1955. This curious aircraft was preserved subsequently for posterity by the NASM, Washington, District of Columbia and is currently on public display at the Pima County Air Museum, Tucson, Arizona.

McDonnell H-1B

The Platt-LePage Aircraft Company of Eddystone, Pennsylvania was an early player in the twin-rotor helicopter story having designed and built the XR-1 prototype for the US Army Air Force in 1941. Their connection with the Grumman amphibian story rests on the fact that having been acquired by the McDonnell Aircraft Company in 1944, the amalgamated company proposed a twin-engined twin-rotor helicopter for US Coast Guard air-sea rescue operations. This was designated the H-1B and would have used Grumman JRF-2 Goose hulls fitted with two Pratt & Whitney R-985-AN-1 radials driving twin Platt-LePage rotors. The proposed empty weight would have been 7,000lbs with a gross weight of 10,000lbs. With a 1,000ft per minute climb from sea level, the top speed was estimated at 148mph over a range of 540miles. The H-1B was not built, however, but McDonnell continued the theme by building the XHJD-1 *Whirlaway* prototype, which flew but did not reach the production stage.

Kaman K-16B

The Kaman K-16B was a grossly modified JRF-5 Goose that was the flight article element of a research programme undertaken by Kaman Aircraft of Bloomfield, Connecticut on behalf of the US Navy's Air Systems Command. This programme, to the US Naval contract NOa(S) 56-549C, was formalised in February 1956 and ended in September 1962 when funding ceased. It was one element of the US military's research into the development of troop-carrying vehicles that would combine helicopter features with the speed and capacity of conventional fixed-wing aircraft.

The programme specifically required analytical and experimental research to be conducted by Kaman to investigate the use of a variable camber, cyclic-controlled propeller, in combination with a partially-tilting wing with full-span flaps, enabling V/STOL aircraft operation. These features were incorporated in a full scale experimental aircraft (utilising a surplus JRF-5 airframe) designated the K-16B by Kaman. The K-16B was used to explore the feasibility of a unified propulsion-control system designed to reconcile the conflict between the requirements of static thrust in hover and high-speed propeller efficiency as well as providing helicopter-type control in hover without the need for auxiliary control devices. This was accomplished by installing trailing edge flaps in the blades of the propellers. Collective deflection of these flaps increased blade camber for high static thrust. The flaps would have been retracted in forward flight for a clean cruising-blade profile. Cyclic deflection of the flaps would furnish control moments in the hover. The system was investigated initially as a rig on ground bench stands and later, as the K-16B, first in full-scale powered tests at Bloomfield and then in the NASA Ames Research Center's 40ft x 80ft wind tunnel at Moffett Field, California. A full technical discussion of the K-16B, although fascinating, is unfortunately well beyond the scope of this book and the following is therefore but a brief summary of a complex and lengthy programme.

Kaman's tilt-wing concept accommodated symmetrically disposed power-plants (two 1,024shp General Electric T-58-GE-6

J4F-2 Widgeon 32976 (c/n 1330) named "Petulant Porpoise", was modified to incorporate a half-scale replica hull of the Martin XP5M-1 Marlin. Note the modified undercarriage, which was rotated upwards but remained in the airstream while in flight. (EDO Corporation)

Previously operated by Avalon Air Transport as G-21A N1523V (c/n 1178) JRF-5 04351 was modified by Kaman Aircraft under a US Navy contract for research into tilt-rotor development.
(Kaman Aircraft)

turbines in wing-mounted nacelles), each driving a propulsive-rotor of 15ft 2in diameter through a reduction gear-box. The rotors were interconnected to prevent asymmetric thrust in the event of a one-engine failure. Following four years of design and development between 1954 and 1958, during which time the Navy progressively increased funding, the

programme progressed from ground-rig devices to the stage when a flyable article became necessary. The Navy elected to use a surplus JRF-5 on the grounds of economy and overall weight and dimensions. The use of an amphibious fuselage with known hull characteristics had the perhaps optimistic additional benefit of enabling open-water trials. As recounted in the

individual aircraft history of BuAer 04351 (c/n 1178), the K-16B would be created from a previously commercially operated aircraft, Avalon Air Transport's N1523V, that was abruptly recalled by the Navy from its Californian lease.

The conversion of the K-16B involved Grumman in the initial preparation of the airframe. The new low aspect ratio wing of

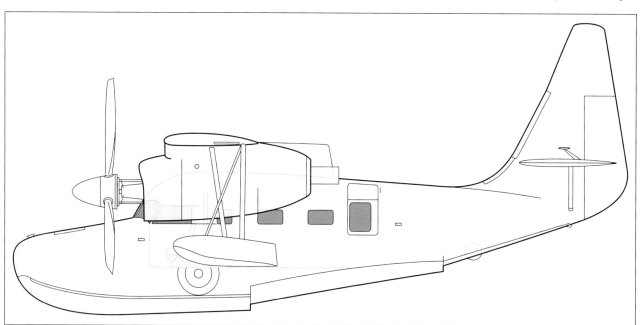

Kaman K-16B research vehicle.
(Drawing by Michael Zoeller)

34ft span was limited to a 50 degree tilt moment unlike those of contemporary experimental designs which could move through 90 degrees. However, this would not have detracted from the vertical lift component to any great extent because the wing contained large trailing-edge flaps that enhanced the downward force effect of the wing when in the partially tilted attitude. To compensate for the increased power of the T-58 turbines, the height of the vertical tail fin was increased. Transition from the use of the rotors' trailing-edge flaps would automatically take place above 80 knots after the conventional control surfaces had become effective. The longitudinal cyclic pitch was used to control yaw, while roll was controlled by use of the variable-pitch propellers. A maximum speed of 480kph was projected.

The K-16B was ground run at Bloomfield in 1960 where all systems underwent extensive evaluation. However, only functional testing in tie-down conditions was permitted by the Navy until such time that the aircraft could be demonstrated to be both aerodynamically and structurally sound. Tethered flight was therefore prohibited, although the airframe was lifted under power to full oleo extension. During these trials several mechanical problems became evident, principally with oscillating bearings in the blade-flap control system, although the system concept was proven sound. At that time Kaman believed the problems to be manageable with a redesign of the control-system geometry and with the ongoing development of high-capacity self-lubricating and elastomeric bearings.

Despite these problems it was decided to go ahead with full scale wind-tunnel testing at NASA's Ames Laboratory and the disassembled K-16B and its support equipment were flown to Moffett Field, California in September 1960. Further ground running and systems evaluations were followed by testing in the 40ft x 80ft

tunnel between 5th and 21st September 1962. These tests concluded that the K-16B in its existing configuration had insufficient thrust for vertical flight at its instrumented test gross weight; that lateral and directional control power was deficient; that severe wing and horizontal tail stall were encountered in portions of the transition region and that a number of detail design deficiencies had become evident. For these reasons, flight tests were not conducted. Data from the wind-tunnel tests, however, served to validate methods of analysis developed during the programme.

Kaman would have soldiered on with the project in the belief that both hardware and aerodynamic problems would be solved, but the project was terminated on completion of the wind tunnel testing when the Navy diverted funding to other more advanced projects such as the Vought-Ryan-Hiller (later Ling-Temco-Vought) XC-142 and the Bell X-22 research aircraft. With the project complete, the K-16B was returned to Bloomfield where it passed eventually into storage before being donated to the Connecticut Air Historical Association (Bradley Air Museum), Bradley, Connecticut in 1965. The museum, now known as the New England Air Museum, currently displays this fascinating aircraft as it looked in 1962.

A summary of Supplemental Type Certificates covering Grumman amphibian conversions can be found in Appendix 8.

Above: *The Kaman K-16B during ground runs at Bloomfield, CT in 1960.*

Above: *A much modified Goose (c/n 1178), the sole Kaman K-16B was used as part of a military-funded contract to produce a tilt-wing aircraft. The inadequacy of the bearings in the propulsive rotors caused the project to be abandoned and the K-16B never flew. It has, however, survived and is on display at the New England Air Museum, Bradley, Connecticut.* *(MAP)*

Three of Grumman's production test pilots who helped the war effort by flying the Goose (among other types): from left to right, Barbara Kibbee Jayne, Elizabeth Hooker and Cecile "Teddy" Kenyon seen here at Bethpage in 1943.   *(Grumman photo)*

This Grumman publicity shot from circa 1947 shows, from left to right, Widgeon (NC86635), an unidentified Goose and a Mallard (believed NC2948).
(Grumman photo by Harold G Martin)

Weldwood of Canada's G-21A C-GYVG (c/n B-117) in which Terry McEvoy made his first flight in the type, in 1980.   *(Gary Vincent)*

CHAPTER 6:
FLYING THE TYPES

AMONG THE MORE UNUSUAL PILOTS who have flown the Grumman amphibians must be the three ladies shown in the picture on the previous page.

- On the left is Barbara Kibbee Jayne. Mrs Jayne, the wife of a US Navy pilot, was a private pilot who had been helping the war effort by flying people and parts into Bethpage, on what was known as the "milk run".

- Elizabeth Hooker, a former Link trainer instructor, also helped with the "milk run".

- On the right is Cecile "Teddy" Kenyon, whose husband Ted had been involved with the development of the Sperry Corporation's auto-pilot, and joined Grumman in 1942 to investigate the incorporation of auto-pilots in Navy fighters. Cecile had been flying with the Civil Air Patrol and also helped Grumman by flying parts into Bethpage in the family Fairchild Argus.

Bud Gillies, who was responsible for flight testing at Bethpage, made a bold decision in the spring of 1942 and promoted the three women to the post of production test pilots. They were the pilots who first flew an aircraft when it left the production line, to ascertain whether it would fly, and how well it flew. After some familiarisation on the Widgeon, all three women were one day introduced to the Goose, and with no instruction, told to fly them! They got themselves and the aircraft back in one piece and from then on flew every type that came off the Bethpage production lines.

The ladies took their turn in rotation with their male counterparts, filling out a "crab list" of things that were not quite right with the aircraft. On average it was necessary to perform two or three test flights before an aircraft was handed over to the Navy pilot who would deliver it.

Goose

The following, written by Terry McEvoy, appeared in BC Aviator, Vol 3, No4, dated March/April 1994, and is reproduced by kind permission of Russ Niles/Canadian Aviator:

"My first experience at flying the Grumman Goose was to happen in 1980, and started with a check-out on Weldwood's Goose, C-GYVG – this, from legendary coastal pilot, Bill Cove.

Starting with the walk around, there were many differences from the other aircraft I have flown. In particular, draining the hull plugs and counting them to make sure none were missing (although the rule was you could never put one down until you put it back in the hull). We counted them every morning as you didn't want to be the pilot caught in the water with one missing.

Next, after unlocking the main hatch and opening it to facilitate climbing up on the wing, you would check the fuel, oil caps and quantities, as well as unlocking the bow hatch. While up there, we also paid particular attention to the lugs on the exhaust pipes, because if they cracked they would allow the pipes to rotate on the intensifier tubes for the heater. If this occurred, a hole would be burned through the top of the cowl causing all kinds of excitement in the cockpit. Another thing that required attention while up on the wing were the toggle bolts that held the cowls together around the engine. If over-tightened, they would break as the engine warmed up in flight and the cowls would leave the aircraft causing even more excitement!

Entering the Goose through the main hatch, you learned to duck your head just right, or you hit it!

Starting the Goose was similar to many other radial-powered airplanes. Our aircraft had a more simplified fuel system than most I have seen, and, similar to the Mallard, our Goose had electric boost pumps and electric primers for starting.

As I recall, to get the generators on line required 1,200rpm, but you could keep them on line at 1,000rpm after that. Another one of the differences typical to the Goose were the glass tubes, mounted to the rear corners of the cockpit, that measured fuel quantity – a pretty fool-proof system.

Adjusting the rudder pedals was important in order to taxi the Goose properly. Taxying was similar to other aircraft of the day having narrow gear and a tail wheel. C-GYVG had Mallard wheels and brakes which enhanced its ground handling ability.

Take off was normal as long as you paid attention and kept her straight on the runway from the start. Raising the gear after take off was a little different as you had to unlock it and move the ratchet pin in the hand crank to allow it to free wheel, or it would beat your hand and briefcase to death as you engaged the switch for the electric motor to raise the wheels. When the electric motor stopped two turns of the hand crank would finish the process. To lower the gear required moving the ratchet pin to the opposite side and turning the crank 41 turns clockwise until the gear locked down. During this time you could not let go of the crank handle or the gear would free-fall down and damage would occur.

The Goose was a good performer with both engines running and even manageable on one, as long as you didn't have to climb. This ability was demonstrated to us by Bill on several occasions with a full load of groceries going to camp – he liked to make training realistic.

Another of the different Grumman systems were the vacuum operated flaps. Vacuum was drawn from each engine and stored in a canister under the floor ready to operate the flaps. However, it wasn't strong enough to hold them down above 95kts and would automatically raise them if power was put on, as in a go-around.

We did a little IFR flying, although she didn't like to carry any ice. The Goose would reward the pilot who worked at her a little, with some of the smoothest water landings you could ever make. You knew you had got it just right when you heard the hiss of the water touching the hull.

A water take off in the Goose required about 15 seconds at 9,200lbs gross weight, and at this weight the aircraft splashed quite a bit of water around when you advanced the power for take off. An old time coastal pilot once told me, "if you saw green for more than seven seconds, you were probably under water."

Our aircraft had electrically retractable wing tip floats, and you only forgot to lower

them once for a water landing. A couple of Bill's rules for water landing were: if you porpoise the airplane on landing, go around; and in the event of porpoise on take off, abort the take off.

We routinely took our Goose into the strips at Clowhom Falls, Toba Inlet and Orford River and she would come off the strip with a good load in about the same 15 seconds. Because of our operation to water and land strips all day long, Bill had another good rule – you had to say out loud on final approach, "it's a water landing and the wheels are up", or, " it's a land landing and the wheels are down." This seemed to work well for us as no one ever landed in the wrong configuration.

The Goose was a pilot's airplane and I certainly enjoyed the time I spent on her."

The following first appeared as "Goose Stories (Kodiak Airways and the Grumman Goose)" on Timothy Smith's excellent website www.tanignak.com, and is reproduced with his kind permission:

"Travelling by Goose is no longer an everyday occurrence for most island passengers. The only way to re-create the ambiance of those adventurous days now is to let the memory play tricks with you and create a hybrid experience based on scores of memorable journeys.

Let's take a trip to Ouzinkie in the pre-airstrip days. Let's say it's a Saturday morning in early December of 1969. In a land famous for spruce trees, Kodiak Airways' little waiting room inexplicably boasts a silver aluminium Christmas tree, lighted by a spotlight with a rotating multicoloured plastic lens. The tree dramatically changes from yellow to blue as I approach the counter. I march my bag up to the counter, where Archie Zehe, legendary dispatcher for Kodiak Airways, is talking by short-wave marine radio to remote sites around the island in a near constant update of weather conditions. His radio conversation over, Archie looks up, addresses me by name and sends me and my bag out to the waiting Goose, painted in cheery Kodiak Airways red and white.

As the first one there, I happily clamber up the narrow aisle of recently upholstered brown and ochre seats, step over the aluminium housing for the landing gear with its little "double-check" window, and slide into the dark brown leather co-pilot seat. Any idiot knows to leave the controls alone, so I content myself with strapping in. Everything loaded, the pilot slides into his seat after unceremoniously slamming shut the sometimes-temperamental two-piece outer door. He is dressed as might be expected: olive coloured flight jacket, Air Force sunglasses, and (only because of the December weather) a cream coloured muffler. He knows his role in local lore, but any swagger or sneer is only in my imagination, for he greets me warmly and goes about his pre-flight check with appropriate dedication. He knows the drill; I know the drill. We start out without any of

the usual airline speeches, as is the universal custom. On the other hand, if he told me to go stand on my head in the tail cargo area I'd do it in a heartbeat; even more than on board a ship, his word is law and our lives are in his hands.

Various switches are switched and buttons are depressed and the starters are engaged. The big radial engines whine, cough and splutter to life, and the brakes and landing gear groan in protest as the seaplane is turned and forced down the beach into the water. Once safely away from the ramp, the pilot busies himself with making sure the wheels are up. This model has a little crank to guarantee the ancient motor got the job done. It is one of the most dangerous parts of the flight. As a true amphibian, landing a Goose on a runway wheels up is a very "iffy" proposition, but landing a Goose on water with wheels down will flip the plane and probably cost lives.

Satisfied that the landing gear is where it belongs, the pilot turns the Goose down the channel, pulls the yoke into his chest, gives it a half-turn, and holding it against him with one forearm, he reaches overhead to ram the twin throttles full forward. The roar of the radial engines is loud inside the cabin and near deafening outside, echoing off Pillar Mountain and Near Island as though a dozen Gooses are taking off. The thrust slams me back into the seat, and at first I feel as though the ocean is going to win, for the old seaplane is speeding faster than any speedboat and skimming the waves as smoothly as a hockey puck glides on ice. Abruptly the Goose leaps into the air, trailing a long stream of water from its bulbous underbelly. In one poetic moment of sheer power, a boat has magically converted to an airplane.

The plane pitches and yaws a bit as the pilot adjusts the trim and cuts back on the throttles. It may be only a ten-knot wind in Ouzinkie, but as we pass over the Loran station on Spruce Cape, the Goose finds a couple of drafts which give momentary roller coaster effects. The old plane seems to enjoy the little challenge, and roars defiantly towards its destination. I busy myself with trying to identify the boat traffic below, and look over the pilot's arms at the morning sun glinting off the snowy Three Sisters Mountains. Even though I am a local boy and supposedly used to such daily displays of beauty, I am completely transfixed. The pilot sees my satisfied expression. "Nice day!" the pilot states, matter-of-factly. He knows and I know that on days like this he has the finest job in the world."

Widgeon

The following is reproduced by kind permission of Steven T Hamilton, owner of c/n 1420, N111W:

"I have been flying my Widgeon since 1985 and in all the years have found it to be a wonderful magic carpet, that has carried my wife, myself and guests to far away and

Steve Hamilton's Lycoming-powered Super Widgeon, N111W, c/n 1420, at its Carson City, Nevada, base in June 2007.   (Fred J Knight)

wonderful places. It is a joy to fly because it possesses few bad flying characteristics in the air and on the land. It has to be respected on the water but mostly just to avoid rough sea situations.

My plane is a McKinnon conversion which gives the plane an adequate amount of power and reasonable fuel consumption. Most Widgeons have been converted away from the Ranger engines and this conversion is one of the most successful.

On the land and in the air the plane is easy to fly and does a wonderful job in all situations. I have never needed to use one tenth of my crosswind landing skills with the Widgeon as it has a lot of sail area and seems to want to go where it is pointed. It has heavy wing loading and this helps it resist gusts from the side, so it lands without too much drama. The wing on a Widgeon is the same wing that was used on the Grumman Wildcat of WWII fame and thus it is not an airfoil that likes to be flown in the slow, steep turn environment. I keep my airspeed between 90 and 100 kts unless I am in ground effect or over the fence. As such, the stall breaks clean so just before touchdown I increase the power just slightly and a smooth non-plopper landing is the result. I always three point the Widgeon as with any tail dragger most traumas occur on wheel landings gone wrong. The Widgeon, however, has a lot of weight on its tail wheel so a slightly tail up three pointer is the recommendation. Three points allow positive control to be achieved right after touchdown in a state where the plane is done flying, so that is my technique and I'm sticking to it.

On the water the Widgeon can bite if abused. This is true of any seaplane. There is a great book called "Water Flying" by Franklin T Kurt, that details the art of water landing and it is a must read and reference book for the seaplane pilot. In discussing the water handling characteristics of the Widgeon, I will try to avoid discussing general seaplane information as that is a book in itself.

When landing the Widgeon, I only use 25 degrees of flap as that achieves 80% effectiveness of the flaps without causing the nose to pitch down too much. Nose down can be offset by nose up trim, but the process puts too much stress on the stabilizer and can cause that assembly to stall, which is not good. The next thing on short approach is to not let the airframe touch down until you are around 60 kts. It

stalls at 55, but the faster you touch down the more it wants to suck the nose down and that is not good. At 60 it is always happy and makes the pilot look good. Slight nose up pressure needs to be immediately applied to offset the drag occurring on the keel at point of touchdown on a water landing.

On run out after pulling the throttles back to the stops, I always raise the flaps which has the effect of gluing the hull to the water so that in the event of a wave hitting the bow the plane does not want to go back into the air. As the plane slows and starts to come off the step, I apply full back pressure to keep the props out of the water since prop erosion can be expensive. In all it is a lovely airplane and I have never been scared in any of the situations that have occurred while flying it. I do fly it very carefully at all times and respect the water condition at all times. I avoid boaters, wakes, waves, etc as much as possible, remembering that a seaplane was designed to go from one relatively calm body of water to another and that a rough water landing is just as much an emergency as landing in a field full of rocks.

Take-off requires full left aileron to raise left wing and full back pressure. Power is applied slightly until a nose up attitude is established and then full on. The plane will rise up over the hump as it wants to come onto the step, where back pressure is relaxed to a slight nose up attitude. Just at this point is where a porpoise can occur and if it does, I immediately apply more back pressure accompanied by a slight reduction in power. If the oscillation seems to be worsening, I immediately come off the power and maintain a slight nose high attitude until it stabilizes, then returning with the power I continue the take off. A lot of people are afraid of this thing called the porpoise but it only happens on take off and it happens at under 20 kts so in any case a complete and immediate reduction in power will stop it. I then rotate at about 60 kts and let the machine build airspeed in ground effect to get above VMC (80 kts) before climbing beyond 15 or 20 feet. I only use flap in high altitude takeoffs and then only 10 degrees. I never use flap for take offs in general.

Widgeons seem to get bent on the water when pilots abuse the power or use poor judgment on where to land. I always err on the safe side in all situations. Like anything in life, it is being careful that keeps you and your passengers safe, so no hotshots are allowed in the Widgeon community, and practice even for a high time pilot is always important.

The Widgeon if flown within its envelope is a delightful plane and does a wonderful job. I have made numerous trips with pilots and non-pilots to Canada many times and our trips have always been magical. It is a machine that makes dreams come true and beautiful destinations a reality. I have loved having it in my life."

(The author had the pleasure of flying with Mr Hamilton in N111W, in 2007).

Mallard

The following is reproduced by kind permission of Steven T Hamilton, owner of c/n J-13, NC2950:

"The Grumman Mallard is the most beautiful Grumman ever designed and is a graceful lady in all situations. As with all planes, each was designed to do a specific task, and the Mallard being a rather large design for executive transport lives happily within that envelope.

I think of our Mallard as our yacht and it is not exactly a "turn the key and go" kind of an airplane. The pre-flight requires at least a half hour of looking at things and the props need to be pulled through being radials. However after all of that is accomplished she starts easily and makes me smile as I start my taxi to the runway. The take-off is a non event in terms of being tricky as it flies as easily as any Cessna on take-off. The main thing on take-off is to try and achieve VMC either on or near to the ground so that an engine out situation can be safely dealt with. The Mallard like the Widgeon is a checklist airplane and religiously following a checklist is a must in any seaplane.

In the air and on the land the Mallard is an easy plane to fly. All landings are easy and make the pilot look good. On the water the Mallard is also a joy to fly. I keep a couple of things in mind while flying the Mallard on the water. First, the Mallard is a large heavy plane and the larger waves can be hard on the hull, so even though it has a large hull I still try and put it down in relatively calm seas. Secondly, the Mallard is not particularly beach friendly or dock friendly without a ground crew so ramps, anchors, buoys, etc are the shutdown destinations. The Widgeon on the other hand loves beaches and being a tail dragger it is easily manoeuvred on the beach. Docks for seaplanes seem to be better suited to float type seaplanes.

The plane can make all but large swells seem like a graceful landing and rarely does it want to porpoise. When it does porpoise however, the recovery technique is different than the Widgeon. First, of course, coming off the throttles and aborting the take-off is always easy and is never a problem. Recovery on the step requires a nose up or down input opposite to the direction of travel. This sounds funny but once you get the hang of it you can immediately check the oscillation and continue your take-off run. I don't use this technique in the Widgeon because if induced at the wrong time it can have a bad accelerating effect whereas the Mallard seems to be happy most of the time no matter what.

There isn't much to say about the Mallard via the water and the land in that it is always a lady and a grand one at that. The only thing to avoid in a Mallard is a stall. When a full stall occurs in a Mallard it will be on its side in less than a second. The wing of the Mallard is a Davis wing, like the B-24, designed for speed and does

Steve Hamilton's Mallard NC2950 (c/n J-13) airborne over Nevada, circa 2001. J-13 was completely rebuilt to original Grumman drawings and was the only G-73 not grounded by the FAA after the Chalk's crash in 2005.   *(via Steve Hamilton)*

stop flying all at the same time in a stall. That is the bad news, the good news is that it stalls with lots of warning and a pilot has to be working hard to abuse it to enter a stall.

In all, the Mallard is a plane that is happy with a load of passengers and its rich teak interior wood is something that all passengers remember. I have taken it to a lot of destinations where a crowd soon appears and circles the plane after landing. Probably the nearest thing to the old China Clipper feel available today and also one of the easiest planes to fly, short of a Cessna." (The author had the pleasure of flying with Mr Hamilton in NC2950, in 2007).

The following, written by Capt James Cothron, appeared in Shell Aviation News No:422, dated 1974:

"The action here on Watson Island (Florida) on a Sunday afternoon is something to behold. The Goodyear Blimp is coming and going every fifteen minutes, helicopters are bouncing up and down every five, and sailboats, speedboats, tugboats, and even ocean liners, are manoeuvring around the harbour, and Chalk's flying boats are right in the middle of it all!

I am one of twelve pilots for Chalk's International Airline Inc, located in downtown Miami, Florida. We operate daylight VFR under part 135 of the Federal Air Regulations with Route 9 authority throughout the Bahamas. Last July, 1973, marked fifty-four years of continuous service.

At the present time we have seven Grumman Mallards with seating for fifteen passengers. The round trip fare to Bimini is $32.00, to Nassau $52.00, with five departures from Miami daily. Chalk's also will charter this aircraft for $250 per hour.

All of our flights penetrate the International Defense Zone so we file a DVFR flight plan with Miami Flight Service, although it is usually on a round-trip, no-arrival basis. The ADF is our best navigation aid because there are strong signals throughout the Bahamas; and here in Miami, we turn final around the WQAM tower (560 on your dial).

Flight 201 has just been announced over the PA system in the little terminal building where some of the passengers and I have been chatting. So, we all get up and amble out to the blue and white Mallard parked in the middle of the ramp. My trusty co-pilot, Kelly, will board last in order to get a head count, close the door, retract the squat strut – which keeps the tail from falling on the ground while everyone is in the rear – then make an announcement to the effect that everyone should fasten their seat belts, kindly refrain from smoking until after take off, and that the life jackets are underneath the seats.

By the time he reaches the cockpit, both engines are usually running. After a short taxi of one hundred feet or so we're in the water. Kelly trails the cowl flaps, and if the engines are warm enough, it's "gear up". The nose wheel retracts first: one can watch an indicator in the forward baggage compartment travel from down to up, plus see a small plexiglass window on the floor get dark as the wheel doors close. Then we can both watch the main gear from the cockpit windows. The panel gear indicators are unreliable. It amuses me sometimes to see one of them say 'up', another 'down', and the remaining one 'in transit'.

I sometimes start the take off run headed for Dodge Island, on the opposite side of Government Cut, so that when the automatic left turn takes place as the Mallard comes out of the water I can leave full power on both engines and we're headed

straight out the channel when we get some response out of the controls. We can also stop any bucking or porpoising that is going on but it will seem like ages before that left float comes out of the water.

By the time we reach 75mph the noise is so terrible I jam my telex in my ears another half inch to dampen it somewhat. Kelly will guard the throttles in case I decide to administer ten degrees of flaps to help facilitate lift off, which should come around ninety (mph). It does, and I nod to him that it should be alright to set up climb power.

A check of the surfers as we zoom past the South Beach pier and we're out over the blue. I've already spotted the extra large Cumulus that must be right over Bimini, almost 50 miles away!

We level off at 1,000 feet, close the cowl flaps and you-know-who sets up maximum cruise. He is still fiddling with the props when we begin our approach at Bimini twenty minutes later!

A visual check of the gear indicates that it is up and locked, so Kelly leans back and hollers for the passengers to "hook up and hang on".

People riding Chalk's for the first time are expecting anything, so the sound of the keel slicing through the smooth water is like music (you just can't make that kind of a landing on a runway). She slides gently to a halt amid a shower of water. We drop the gear immediately, in order to manouvre around the boats, and since we are now a boat ourselves we have no special right of way. Most of these boatmen know that we are unable to reverse or stop, so they give us a wide berth when possible.

The ramp at Bimini consists of steel plates, aluminium plates, rocks, pot holes, broken bottles and empty cans. So when we waddle ashore with salt water dripping from one end to the other, we're always glad to feel that the tires are not flat. Many a nose wheel and several main wheels have been changed at Bimini.

While we await the arrival of the Bahamian Customs and Immigration officials, Kelly huddles the passengers into the shade of the left wing of the Mallard, being careful not to stand directly under the engine, lest an occasional drop of oil or hydraulic fluid soil their vacation attire.

I have found it more expedient to allow the co-pilot to handle the paperwork, and since the ramp men know their job we're ready to depart in no time. Kelly takes us down to Cat Cay, where we deliver two passengers, the mail and newspapers, then off to Miami and Government Cut. The approach here is always a challenge and it is best to 'expect the unexpected', and never to land behind a tugboat underway! We splash down at about 70mph and have a few awkward moments as we skip to a halt among the boats. Once up the ramp, and through US customs, we're ready to go again.

I've made several thousand of these trips but still do not consider them routine.

Pilot's handling notes

The Mallard has a maximum gross weight of 12,750lbs, allowing 3,750lbs of useful load. Power is provided by two Pratt & Whitney 1340 radial engines. The design features a high speed slotted wing which allows a cruising speed of approximately 160mph while burning about 25 US gallons of fuel per engine per hour, yielding a range of at least 1,000 miles. The airplane has a complete hydraulic system which operates most services, leaving only fuel boost pumps as electric. Another unique feature of this Grumman is its free castering nose wheel which affords a greater degree of control on land.

The pre-flight walk around is similar to most other aircraft with one important addition – hull and wing floats plugs. These are removed to allow water to drain from the bilges after ramping. Failure to reinstall them before the aircraft is taxied into the water could result in sinking or at best could hamper or prevent take-off.

When starting the engines, the propellers are first rotated with the mixture controls in idle cut-off position and magnetos turned off to assure all oil is removed from the lower cylinders. Next, priming is accomplished by switching the boost pumps on with mixtures still at idle cut-off and pumping the throttles three or four times. Boost pumps are then shut off, mags turned on and the starter engaged. As the engine fires, mixture controls are moved to 'full rich', allowing engines to keep running.

Before taxying, the tail strut, a device for supporting the tail during loading, is raised. Directional control is achieved by the use of brakes and differential power as the nose wheel is non-steerable.

Once in the water, differential power is the controlling factor with some help from the rudder. Water taxi over a short distance is accomplished off the step allowing a forward speed of about 8 kts, which can be further reduced by lowering the gear. This also affords greater manoeuvrability.

Water taxi over long distance should be done with the aircraft planing on the step, to minimise spray damage to the propellers.

Land take-offs are similar to most other tricycle gear airplanes. Rudder control is quickly gained and lift-off comes around 80mph. The hydraulic gear is a pleasant change from the hand crank used in the Goose. Flaps are generally not used on land; however, during a water take-off 10° will shorten the run considerably.

After clearing the water and reaching V2 (100mph), power is reduced to a climb setting of about 30inches of manifold pressure and 2,000 rpm. Flaps are then retracted and cruise-climb of about 120mph set up to ensure adequate cooling.

Cruising altitude attained, the aircraft can be levelled off to build up a cruising

speed. Cowl flaps are then closed and power further reduced to 27 inches of manifold pressure and 1,700 rpm.

Approach is initiated at about 100mph, well below flap and gear extension speeds. The landing gear check is of prime importance as there is no landing gear warning device, and gear down during a water landing will prove more disastrous than a gear up on land.

Runway landings, again, are typical of most tricycle gear aircraft with good rudder control throughout.

Flaps are used on both land and sea. Although the flight manual approves the full 45 degree position, we have found a maximum of 30 degrees affords more positive elevator control in the event of a go-around.

For the smoothest water landing, a slight nose-high attitude is maintained to contact the water at the slowest possible speed, and as the keel starts knifing the water, some of the back-pressure is relaxed on the yoke. If swells are encountered, the nose can actually be pushed into the wave to prevent a porpoise from developing. If at all possible the Mallard should be held on the water while decelerating to prevent being thrown into a stall.

Once off the step, the landing gear can be lowered for ramping or the engines shut down for anchoring.

At this point, a word should be said about ramping, especially in high winds. Approaching a ramp upwind is no particular problem because the aircraft naturally tends to head into wind. Approaching downwind, however, requires special techniques and some fortitude. Getting turned downwind is the most challenging manoeuvre and should be planned so that, when completed, is as nearly upwind from the ramp as possible, for it is much easier to control with the wind directly over the tail than from the side. Once committed to the ramp, care should be taken not to backfire the engines by abrupt throttle usage. A good preventative measure is to use the boost pumps, and in extreme cases, carburettor heat."

Below: *Chalk's Mallard N2970 (c/n J-30) at Bimini, Bahamas in February 1976 while operating the Miami to Bimini schedules, as described by Capt James Cothron.*

(Jennifer Gradidge)

Seen here at Ushuaia, probably in 1955, JRF-6B 0294 '3-P-53' (c/n 1144) was by then serving with Argentina's Comando de Aviación Naval (COAN) Escuadra Aeronaval No3, nominally based at Punta Indio. This particular Goose was one of the final two aircraft to support an Antarctic campaign in 1955 but still had several years of military life to look forward to, later serving with Argentina's Prefectura Naval and the Misión Naval en Paraguay before being gifted to Paraguay in 1966. (via Jorge Nuñez Padin)

Following its service with the Prefectura Naval, JRF-6B 0294 (c/n 1144) was transferred to the Argentine Misión Naval (MNA) en Paraguay and was based in Asunción for two years before being donated to the Aviación Naval Paraguaya in 1966. As can be seen, the Goose essentially retained its markings from the Prefectura Naval days replacing the serial 'PM-8' with the new MNA code 'MNA-11'. The photograph can be dated to circa 1965 although the location is unknown. (via Jorge Nuñez Padin)

This early photograph, taken at Punta Indio circa 1948, shows the Aviación Naval's JRF-6B 0184 (c/n 1163) in its original Prefectura General Maritima (PGM) markings. Argentina's military politics ensured that these early naval markings reflected internal use rather than the intended open-sea operations. It would not be until 1950 that it would receive the more regular-style naval patrol markings of COAN's Escuadra Aeronaval No2. 0184 spent all its remaining life in Argentina, succumbing to the scrap-man in December 1960. (via Jorge Nuñez Padin)

CHAPTER 7:
MILITARY OPERATORS

ARGENTINA

COMANDO DE AVIACIÓN NAVAL - NAVAL AVIATION

Goose

ARGENTINA'S RELUCTANCE TO JOIN THE Allied cause against the Axis nations until very late in WWII ensured that no Lend-Lease aircraft were supplied by the United States and that modern aircraft such as the Goose could not be obtained until after the war. As post-war relations with the United States improved and Argentina indicated a willingness to become a signatory to the Inter-American Treaty of Reciprocal Assistance (the 'Rio Pact'), an Argentine Naval Commission was established in Washington, District of Columbia to procure much-needed new equipment. The

Goose, by now out of production, was a proven and ideal aircraft for coastal and riverine use and was an early target for the Comando de Aviación Naval (COAN) albeit after the evaluation of other options. In practice it was the Admiralty's Prefectura General Maritima (PGM) who would procure the aircraft, ostensibly for internal purposes policing the La Plata, Parana and Uruguay rivers.

In 1946, the only realistic source of aircraft was the pool of surplus JRF-6B aircraft formerly used by the Royal Navy in Trinidad and now returned to the USA under their Lend-Lease terms. These aircraft, some with low hours and in good condition, were being acquired rapidly by commercial dealers in the USA and the Commission sought competitive tenders for three aircraft from two such agents. The successful bid came from Efferson & Associates who had identified two aircraft

located at Lansdale, Pennsylvania and a third, still owned by the War Assets Administration (WAA), in California. Following inspection by Argentine naval officials, Efferson acquired the aircraft in January 1947 and sold them on to the Argentine Naval Commission on 30th January 1947. The Royal Navy had rarely used their aircraft on the water and neither of the two at Lansdale, NC74585 and NC74587, had recorded any such landings. Both these aircraft were subsequently overhauled by Dell Christensen of El Monte, Los Angeles, California and ferried to Argentina while the former BuAer 66344 (the WAA aircraft) was eventually prepared by Dade Brothers and shipped from Ontario, California by sea.

Details of crew training are sparse but the three aircraft were certainly operational in Argentina by mid-1947. The COAN allocated them the serials 0184 to 0186 and assigned them to the Escuadra Aeronaval N[o]2 at Punta Indio, Buenos Aires on 12th June 1947 although the aircraft were marked for internal PGM duties with the appropriate codes 'PGM-1' to 'PGM-3' (and were indeed delivered in these markings). Most noticeably they did not carry naval fuselage roundels. However two of these aircraft met with early accidents in February and March 1948 and although both were eventually repaired, it was clear that more aircraft were needed to sustain a viable fleet. Initially the COAN wanted a fleet of ten aircraft, later reduced to eight, but finally only another three were authorised in April 1948. In November 1947, Michael Efferson had identified three more JRF-6Bs which were available but in use at the time with Bay Valley Air Services of Stockton, California (NC95406, NC95429 and NC95431) but, by the time Argentina committed itself to the purchase, NC95431 was no longer available. The agent replaced this with a surplus JRF-5 recently released by the US Navy and registered NC68190. This aircraft had spent much of its short life in the Pacific theatre and a good deal of that time had been in maintenance facilities. Its early release by the US Navy in February 1947 may have been a reflection of its general condition. These three aircraft were sold to Argentina on 10th June 1948 and prior to delivery all were overhauled in California. NC95406 and NC95429 were refurbished by the Aircraft Service Company of El Monte and NC68190 by Aeromotive of Long Beach. These aircraft were eventually delivered to Escuadra N[o]2 on 19th November 1948. The JRF-6Bs were allocated serials 0293 and 0294 and the JRF-5 became 0295 and they were coded 'PGM-P-4' to 'PGM-P-6', the additional letter 'P' indicating 'Patrulla' (Patrol). In any event the 'PGM' codes would be short-lived.

Shortly before the delivery of the second batch, an aircraft was lost in a fatal accident when 0185/PGM-2 was wrecked at sea off Río Santo Cruz, Santa Cruz on 14th September 1948. All five crew perished and the pilot, Teniente de Fragata José Jubany, would later be honoured when the Argentine Antarctic base 'Jubany' was dedicated to his memory. The aircraft had been on a delivery flight from Punta Indio to Ushuaia, where it had been assigned for local rescue and general purpose duties.

In mid-1950, the five survivors were split between two units with, according to local historians, two aircraft (0184/2-P-20 and 0186/2-P-21) at Espora and three at Punta Indio with Escuadra Aeronaval N[o]3 (the latter three were coded '3-P-22', -23 and -24, but there is some confusion in secondary source data that lists four codes, '3-P-22' to '3-P-25' for three aircraft. Again, the 'P' indicated 'Patrulla' or patrol duty). From 1950 until 1956 these COAN aircraft also undertook the unique Goose summer duty supporting Antarctic operations while on detachment to the Campaña Antártica. Unfortunately this

would bring about the loss of a second aircraft on 3rd April 1951 when 0295/3-P-25 sank in heavy weather at the Melchior base, Antarctica. This particular aircraft, earlier transported to the region aboard *ARA Bahía Buen Suceso*, had been used intensively between December 1950 and March 1951, achieving 5,860 nautical miles of flight while undertaking aerial survey and sundry utility tasks. The aircraft was recovered by the *ARA Bahía Buen Suceso* and returned to Argentina for repair, but was eventually struck off charge in 1953. Reference to the individual aircraft histories will reveal that two aircraft were normally deployed each year until the summer of 1955/56. This was demanding work for both aircraft and crew and there were further accidents and incidents, including the rescue of 0186/3-P-51 by its support ship in February 1953.

By January 1953, the four airworthy JRF-6Bs had been re-grouped within the Escuadra Aeronaval N[o]3, Punta Indio, and re-coded, becoming 0184/3-P-50, 0186/3-P-51, 0293/3-P-52 and 0294/3-P-53. These codes were retained until another reorganisation in 1955 transferred them to a new, general purpose flight at Punta Indio. Within the Escuadrilla de Propósitos Generales they became 0184/3-G-6, 0186/3-G-7 and 0294/3-G-8. 0293/3-G-9 did not join the flight until, apparently, November 1958 and it is surmised that this may have been because of an extended and expensive repair (costing US$31,316) following its sinking in the Río de la Plata in July 1952.

By 1956, the fleet was ageing and the end was approaching for primary naval operations. 0184/3-G-6 was withdrawn in 1956 and eventually sold for scrap in 1960. 0293/3-G-9 was in fact the last to go in March 1960 and was also scrapped. The other two were however, to enjoy a new and slightly unusual lease of life. Circa 1958 0186 and 0294 were transferred to the Prefectura Naval where they received new serials-cum-codes 'PM-7' and 'PM-8'. They remained in Coast Guard service until January 1962, undertaking fisheries protection and SAR duties after which both were returned to COAN. Still airworthy, they were later transferred to the Argentine Misión Naval en Paraguay (MNA) at Asuncion, Paraguay. The first transfer appears to have been 0294, circa 1963, that then became 'MNA-11' in May 1964 and was followed by 0186/MNA-12 on an unknown date. 0294 was extensively overhauled and modernised between June

and July 1964 adding, among other equipment, new target-towing gear. The MNA worked in an advisory capacity with the Aviación Naval Paraguaya (ANP) who themselves were still using two JRF-5s in 1964. Eventually Argentina gifted both aircraft to the ANP, or at least that was their intention. Initially both aircraft were loaned to the ANP and in the case of 0186/MNA-12 there was a formal transfer on 28th March 1966, followed by a handover ceremony on 4th May 1966 by which date it was resplendent in ANP markings. The transfer of 0294/MNA-11 took place soon after the completion of its overhaul at Punta Indio in July 1966. However, it appears that, perhaps by accident, the legal ownership of 0294 was never transferred to Paraguay, and when the ANP finally disposed of the aircraft in 1968 to an American buyer, he had to purchase it from the MNA. He was, however, able to buy the former 0186 from the ANP! The date quoted by Argentine sources as being that of 0294's transfer to Paraguay, 13th September 1968, may therefore be the precursor to the sale of the aircraft by the MNA to the American purchaser on 3rd December 1968 (this very complicated transaction is more fully explored within the Paraguayan notes on page 108).

In Aviación Naval service, the small Goose fleet had performed faithfully for many years before succumbing to old age and, inevitably, newer and more efficient aircraft. Its achievements, however, particularly in the demanding Antarctic conditions, had earned it a permanent place in Argentine naval history. It is good to reflect that, at the time of writing, one of the old birds, 0186, is still airworthy as N3282.

Colours and Markings

Throughout their lives the fleet retained the same basic colour scheme of silver overall with national markings applied to the rudder and tail top. Black COAN anchor markings were carried beneath the wings, and codes were carried in full on the rear fuselage with the single-digit individual number frequently worn on either side of the nose. At various times smaller markings such as the titles 'Armada' or 'Armada Nacional' and the national flag would also be painted on the forward fuselage. The COAN four-digit serial, rarely visible on photographs, was carried on the tailfin in small characters. Aircraft used in the Antarctic received high-visibility markings.

Serial Numbers			
Serial	*Type*	*C/n*	*Circumstances*
0184	JRF-6B	1163	US civilian acquisition Jan47
0185	JRF-6B	1148	NC74587 acquired Jan47
0186	JRF-6B	1146	NC74585 acquired Jan47
0293	JRF-6B	1143	NC95406 acquired Jun48
0294	JRF-6B	1144	NC95429 acquired Jun48
0295	JRF-5	B-64	NC68190 acquired Jun48

AUSTRALIA

ROYAL AUSTRALIAN AIR FORCE

Goose

The Royal Australian Air Force briefly used one aircraft in North Africa when HK822 was transferred from the RAF Desert Air Force's Sea Rescue Flight to No.1 Air Ambulance Unit in late 1942. It was accepted by the unit at Heliopolis, Egypt on 1st December 1942 but following a ferry flight to Benina on 3rd December, the aircraft was lost during water landing practice on 9th December 1942, 15 miles North-North-West of Benghazi. The aircraft overturned and sank, although the seven occupants escaped and survived.

Serial Number			
Serial	Type	C/n	Circumstances
HK822	G-21A	1055	Transfer from RAF Dec42

BOLIVIA

CUERPO AÉREO BOLIVIANO - BOLIVIAN AIR CORPS

Goose

The Cuerpo Aéreo Boliviano received what is believed to have been its one and only Goose in July 1942 when a single JRF-6B (the intended FP500) was diverted from the UK Lend-Lease contract LL-86447. This aircraft became an early part of a US aid package to Bolivia but its initial purpose is not entirely clear, although it is said to have been for use in the Amazon region. The gift was unusual, inasmuch as Bolivia was the only nation in Latin America to receive a Goose as American aid, and it was delivered at a time when the type was in short supply and when requests from elsewhere on the continent were routinely refused. The short-notice diversion of an elsewhere urgently-needed British aircraft was perhaps indicative of a more complex purpose than simply providing a friendly state with a useful modern amphibian (five other identical aircraft were diverted simultaneously from the British line and assigned to the US Army Air Force Attachés in adjacent nations for purposes that included intelligence-gathering). The aircraft was delivered by air from NAS Anacostia, District of Columbia, presumably by a US crew, in the British grey colour-scheme with US roundels and without obvious Bolivian identity. Interestingly the aircraft was carrying the brand-new US Navy insignia in which the red central disc was now deleted from the white star. The suspicion remains that the aircraft was actually used in the early days by the US Air Mission to Bolivia.

Regardless of its early use, the Goose eventually passed into the hands of the new Fuerza Aérea Boliviano, and by 1952, the assumed original aircraft was being used by the Escuadrón de Entranamiento at the Base Aérea 3 at Santa Cruz, a unit equipped with T-6, PT-17 and BT-13 training aircraft, and it was still on unit strength in mid-1954. Its contemporary serial number is uncertain but subsequently it is reported to have been given the local serial TAM-15 suggesting an assignment to the the military airline Transporte Aéreo Militar (TAM) which had been created at La Paz in 1953 from the old Escuadrón de Transporte Aéreo (ETA). The Goose is reported to have been withdrawn in 1956 and was finally sold in the United States in early 1959.

The history of the Goose in Bolivian military service is not well understood and many sources vaguely suggest the receipt of a second aircraft. This is unlikely to have happened before the end of the war, and there is no known evidence to link any other aircraft to Bolivia.

Serial Number			
Serial	Type	C/n	Circumstances
(TAM-15)	JRF-6B	1150	US Aid Jul42

BRAZIL

FORÇA AÉREA BRASILEIRA - BRAZILIAN AIR FORCE

Widgeon

Brazil received extensive quantities of aircraft from the United States both before and after her formal involvement in WWII dating from 22nd August 1942. The Força Aérea Brasileira (FAB), formed in 1941 by the combination of army and naval aviation, was by 1942 a large and relatively sophisticated organisation capable of handling new and modern aircraft in large quantities. The decision to request the equivalent of a squadron of the G-44 'Grumman Amphibians' from the USA followed that of Portugal and pre-dated any US Navy orders for the Widgeon. The request was considered initially by the US Munitions Assignment Committee in March 1942 and was quickly approved, the aircraft being identified tentatively by the US authorities as the J4F-1 US Coast Guard model. By the time the first aircraft had been accepted by the FAB at Bethpage on 15th July 1942 the Brazilian aircraft had been identified as the J4F-2 in common with those that would shortly be coming off the production line for the US Navy. No US Navy/BuAer serials are known to have been allocated to the FAB aircraft.

The FAB aircraft were numbered '01' to '14' and were delivered into Brazilian hands at Bethpage, two in each of July, August and September 1942 with the final eight being handed over between 31st October and 30th November 1942. The aircraft were ferried to Brazil in groups of two and three between 20th August 1942 and early January 1943. In FAB service the Widgeons were all based at coastal sites and initially were reportedly used in support of larger aircraft in the maritime patrol and convoy protection roles where, although not the most suitable of aircraft, they were urgently needed in 1942-43. Initially the fleet was located at the Galeão, Belém and Florianópolis bases and in March 1943 two aircraft were assigned to the Seção de Aviões de Comando, Calabouço (the current Santos Dumont airport) where they were used by the FAB headquarters staff until 9th January 1945 when the unit was disbanded and its aircraft were transferred to the 1º Grupo de Transportes at Calabouço. In late 1943, aircraft were also based at Santa Cruz. Perhaps surprisingly, the entire fleet almost survived the war and all were considered available for re-numbering and reorganisation in July 1945 at which time the Widgeon was given a local type number that was incorporated into the new serial. The J4F-2 designation was modified to UC-4F2, appearing as 'UC4F2' on the aircraft, indicating its classification as a utility transport, and the aircraft were re-numbered 2667 to 2680. The application of the new serials was progressive and in view of the dates of some accidents (for example that of 2676 at Belém on 23rd May 1945) it is assumed that not all aircraft would have worn the new serials. Following this exercise, officially dated 30th July 1945, the fleet was organised as shown in the table at the top of the next page.

During the post-war years overhauls were undertaken at the Fábrica do Galeão but post-war the fleet suffered rapid attrition with several accidents occurring before 1950 and by 1952 only a few aircraft remained. Following yet another accident in April 1952 the fleet had dwindled to two aircraft by November 1952. Both surviving aircraft, officially listed as ZCA4F2 2668 and VZCAF2 2680, had by then received new designations although 2680's prefix may have been in error. The 'V' was indicative of VIP use, 'Z' that of ground-instructional status and 'A' that of an amphibian (and 2680 appears to have lost the digit '4'). ZCA4F2 2668 remained active until it was damaged, probably beyond repair, in August 1954 and was eventually struck-off charge in June 1956.

Base Aérea do Galeão, Rio de Janeiro

2667 (01)   2668 (02)   2671 (05)   2672 (06)

Base Aérea de Belém, Pará

2669 (03)   2670 (04)   2675 (09)   2676 (10)

Base Aérea de Florianópolis, Santa Catarina

2673 (07)   2674 (08)

1° Grupo de Transporte, Calabouço, Rio de Janeiro

2677 (11)   2679 (13)

Base Aérea de Santa Cruz, Rio de Janeiro

2678 (12)   2680 (14)

(The original two-digit serials are listed here only for information purposes)

VZCAF2 2680 was eventually saved from extinction when it was acquired by the Aerospace Museum at Campo dos Afonsos, Rio de Janeiro, where it is currently displayed as '14' in original markings. These early markings comprise light blue upper surfaces and fuselage with white undersides. The traditional green and yellow vertical colours are worn on the tailfin and rudder and the FAB roundel is worn beneath the wings and on the rear fuselage. The serial appears in white on the nose.

The FAB serials were revised on 30th July 1945 when the local type number and serial prefix 'UC-4F2' were adopted (all aircraft still survived officially on that date). There were subsequent alterations to the type number of some aircraft dependent on purpose and in some instances the aircraft's serial would be updated with new paintwork.

Serial Numbers

Serial	Type	C/n	Circumstances
01 (2667)	J4F-2	1271	US Aid Jul-Nov42
02 (2668)	J4F-2	1272	US Aid Jul-Nov42
03 (2669)	J4F-2	1275	US Aid Jul-Nov42
04 (2670)	J4F-2	1276	US Aid Jul-Nov42
05 (2671)	J4F-2	1279	US Aid Jul-Nov42
06 (2672)	J4F-2	1280	US Aid Jul-Nov42
07 (2673)	J4F-2	1283	US Aid Jul-Nov42
08 (2674)	J4F-2	1284	US Aid Jul-Nov42
09 (2675)	J4F-2	1285	US Aid Jul-Nov42
10 (2676)	J4F-2	1286	US Aid Jul-Nov42
11 (2677)	J4F-2	1287	US Aid Jul-Nov42
12 (2678)	J4F-2	1288	US Aid Jul-Nov42
13 (2679)	J4F-2	1289	US Aid Jul-Nov42
14 (2680)	J4F-2	1290	US Aid Jul-Nov42

The final Widgeon to enter service with the Brazilian Air Force in early 1943 was number '14' (c/n 1290). After lengthy service and many years of open storage, it was recovered by the Museu Aeroespacial in 1977 and, following restoration to its original colour scheme, was placed on public display at Campo dos Afonsos, Rio de Janeiro. Photographed in November 2011, the aircraft can be seen to be in excellent condition.   *(Colin R Smith)*

CANADA

ROYAL CANADIAN AIR FORCE

Goose

Variants and Acquisition

Canada initially procured a single, new G-21A from the Gillies Aviation Corporation, Long Island, New York, Grumman's primary agent, in 1938. Delivered on 26th July 1938 this was Grumman's first Goose sale to a military customer. Given the RCAF serial 917, the aircraft was acquired for utility and VIP duties and its acquisition reflected the RCAF's need for a robust, modern amphibian. However, initially it was not to be followed by further purchases and was intended to have been a 'one-off'.

On 12th September 1939, two days after Canada declared war on Germany, the prominent Canadian industrialist JP 'Jack' Bickell (later to become the president of Victory Aircraft, Malton, Ontario) gifted his Goose CF-BKE to the RCAF. Given the serial 924, it served initially alongside 917. Prior to the USA's direct involvement in the war Canada was subject to the vagaries of American law and consequently its subsequent Goose acquisitions were obtained by a number of complex and unorthodox transactions. That said, the next two G-21A aircraft (with serials 925 and 926) were obtained in straightforward fashion, being new production machines delivered from Grumman in July 1940 under the US government-approved Canadian contract CAN-2.

In September 1940, two early commercial aircraft, by now modified to G-21A standard, were acquired from their pre-war US owners and were re-registered CF-BTE and CF-BTF. These civilian registrations were retained for some time after their delivery to the RCAF as 939 and 940. Shortly after this, in November 1940, Jack Bickell passed a second aircraft, CF-BQE, to the RCAF as 941. Bickell had managed to acquire this new aircraft in December 1939 unofficially on behalf of the RCAF. Like all the 'commercially acquired' RCAF Goose aircraft, this was a civilian G-21A model.

By 1941 Grumman was fully extended, albeit within US 'peace-time' constraints, to meet new production orders from the US armed forces and US approved export customers. Any new orders for the RCAF effectively needed the tripartite approval of the US, Canadian and British governments. Against this background, the RCAF's agents continued to seek aircraft on the second-hand market and, with the assistance of Grumman and Gillies Aviation, three more were found in 1941. (It will be recalled that Gillies Aviation Corporation was owned by Jack Gillies, brother of 'Bud' Gillies, the Vice-President of Grumman Flight Operations). Delivered in March, August and September 1941, the former NC16912, NC16916 and NC2385 became 942, 943 and 944, respectively.

The Royal Canadian Air Force Goose 917 (c/n 1016) holds the distinction of being the first G-21A built for any military customer. Delivered in July 1938, it is here seen in an early posed photograph, probably at its home station of Ottawa (Rockcliffe) where it initially served with No.7 (General Purposes) Squadron. It would later crash in Alaska in July 1942, the survivors being recovered in an epic rescue mission.

(Aeroplane Photo Supply Co via DM Hannah)

CF-BKE (c/n 1013) was sold to the Royal Canadian Air Force on the outbreak of war by the industrialist 'Jack' Bickell and was allocated serial 924. While there were some early diplomatic benefits from retaining civil registrations, by the time this photograph was taken at Alliford Bay, Queen Charlotte Islands, BC, perhaps in 1940, they were probably irrelevant. Here the aircraft appears to have a broad nose stripe, probably to warn of the propeller hazard. 924 had many changes of unit during its time with the Western Air Command and then, later in the war, with units in eastern Canada and indeed survived, civilianised and much modified, until an accident in 1995 ended its flying career. *(British Columbia Museum via D Parker)*

All of the early Royal Canadian Air Force aircraft were built as G-21As and known simply as 'Goose' to the RCAF. Here 925 (c/n 1082) is seen at Bethpage prior to delivery in July 1940 wearing its temporary delivery registration NX925 and standard period RCAF markings. It was lost in a fatal accident in November 1942 when an unqualified pilot, ignoring standing orders, attempted a night landing in rough water off the Newfoundland coast. *(Royal Air Force Museum via MAP)*

926 (c/n 1083) was the second of the two new G-21A aircraft acquired by the Royal Canadian Air Force in July 1940. At the time of this 1941 photograph taken at Mount Hope, ON the Goose was on the strength of No.12 (Communications) Squadron, Rockcliffe. It was to survive a spectacular capsize in September of that year and following its wartime RCAF use it continued to fly for many more years, in many guises, before succumbing to an accident in 1989. *(via Ken Molson)*

For reasons that are not absolutely clear, Jack Bickell's former Goose CF-BQE (c/n 1061) did not wear its new Royal Canadian Air Force markings for some while after its delivery in November 1940 although its records show it as 941 from that date. This undated photograph, however, may well show the aircraft before its acquisition by the military. In RCAF service 941 had a typically busy existence with many changes of unit within western Canada before disposal in 1945. As with many former RCAF aircraft, this Goose enjoyed a long life as a civil aircraft and was still active at the time of writing.
(Peter M Bowers Collection)

The Goose II (JRF-5) fleet was delivered to the Royal Canadian Air Force with the 'Type C' roundels and fin flashes. Here 386 (c/n B-55) of 412 (Composite) Squadron, Rockcliffe is seen in its early post-war colours that included the red fuselage lightning flash and engine cowling leading-edges. A maple-leaf badge, similar to that of Trans-Canada Air Lines, is worn alongside the squadron markings.
(Fred J Knight Collection)

The RCAF's final acquisition of the commercial G-21A Goose came in early 1942 after the USA had entered the war. Although the circumstances are not absolutely clear the suggestion is that the RCAF accepted three aircraft that had been procured by the US Navy on behalf of the RAF for the latter's use as ASR aircraft. When the RAF eventually declined this offer the aircraft were sold to the RCAF as 796, 797 and 798 and the record cards of 796 and 798 note the US Navy as the vendor. NC20650 and NC20648 became 796 and 798 in April 1942 and NC2788 became 797 in June 1942.

The RCAF thus obtained 13 G-21A aircraft from all sources and in the process had become the owners of four of the original production batch. With the arguable exception of the custom-built 925 and 926, all aircraft had been built to

commercial specifications and were equipped with features unique to their original purchasers.

The aircraft performed well and certainly suited the Canadian environment but by 1943 the 11 survivors were showing their age. It was therefore agreed by the US Government that the RCAF should be allowed to purchase a fleet of new JRF-5 aircraft with deliveries to commence in the spring of 1944. These 16 aircraft, serials 382 to 397, were diverted from US Navy production and were received between March 1944 and January 1945. Their acquisition enabled the RCAF to withdraw the entire G-21A fleet and by November 1944, without exception, all the G-21As were awaiting disposal.

The RCAF also became the brief user of two Lend-Lease JRF-5s that were allocated to them by the British Air Commission

(BAC) for use under the BCATP scheme. Used by No.3 Training Command, FP471 and FP473 did not receive RCAF serials and were never owned by the RCAF. Both aircraft were returned to the British Air Commission in early 1945 and were transferred on to US Government agencies.

In summary, the RCAF purchased 13 commercial G-21A aircraft between 1938 and 1942, all of which had been disposed of by July 1945, and 16 military JRF-5 models in 1944, the last of which was sold in 1955. In Canadian use the G-21A model was simply known as the 'Goose' and the JRF-5 as the 'Goose II'. The two JRF-5 aircraft used by the BCATP were also known as 'Goose II'. The designation 'Goose I' was applied retrospectively to the G-21A fleet but this notation does not appear on any aircraft record card and appears to have been no more than an academic exercise.

Operations

The RCAF used the Goose initially, and then primarily, as a utility transport although it would later serve in multiple roles including flight-crew training, photographic, patrol and ASR functions. The first aircraft, 917 received in July 1938, was delivered to No.7 (General Purpose) Squadron at Rockcliffe, ON where it served with 'B' Flight, the unit's general purposes element. On the outbreak of war, 10th September 1939, it was joined by the newly acquired 924 and the unit was re-named No.12 (Communications) Flight. On 30th July 1940 the Flight became a 'Unit' and on 30th August 1940 it was elevated to full Squadron status. Serving the RCAF's Air Force Headquarters, the Goose would continue to serve in the communications role at Rockcliffe until its withdrawal in 1954.

In April 1940, 924 was transferred to the Western Air Command's (WAC) No.120 (Bomber Reconnaissance) Squadron at Sea Island, BC which then moved to nearby Patricia Bay in August 1940. Later in the year 924 is understood to have served with the co-located No.111 (Coastal Artillery Co-operation) Squadron and, after disbandment on 1st February 1941, the No.3 (Coastal Artillery Co-operation) Detachment, which replaced it.

The acquisition of five new aircraft after July 1940 enabled the RCAF to expand No.12 (Communications) Squadron's strength to three aircraft in September and to equip the recently formed No.13 (Operational Training) Squadron at Patricia Bay with three more. The arrival of 942 in April 1941 increased No.13 (OT) Squadron's strength to four and simultaneously one of the No.12 (Comms) Squadron's aircraft was released to join a new unit at Dartmouth, NS. This unit, Eastern Air Command's (EAC) Communications Flight briefly gained a second aircraft in August 1941 when the ninth RCAF aircraft, 943, entered service. The introduction of the Goose, particularly on the west coast, enabled the RCAF to replace larger aircraft such as the Stranraer on tasks more suited to the smaller, more economical Goose. The Goose was now also much used for lead-in training for the larger Catalinas and Cansos. In the autumn of 1941, the fleet entered a programme of major overhauls after which there was continual movement of aircraft between units. The west coast work was undertaken by Boeing Overhaul, Vancouver, BC, later to become part of Canadian Pacific Airlines. Noorduyn and Canadian Car & Foundry handled the Rockcliffe aircraft, and Clark Ruse those from Dartmouth and, later, Torbay.

The fleet continued to grow with a 10th aircraft received in September 1941 followed by the final three commercial acquisitions in April and June 1942. One of these aircraft, 796, was allocated to another new unit, No.145 (Bomber Reconnaissance) Squadron that formed at Torbay, Newfoundland on 30th May 1942. Although two aircraft were to be lost in accidents in late 1942, until then there had been no losses and following the delivery of the thirteenth and final G-21A Goose in June 1942 the fleet was dispersed as shown in the table at the top of this page.

Following the disbandment of No.13 (OT) Squadron on 9th November 1942 and the accidents that befell 917 and 925, the fleet was re-shuffled and streamlined into three core units. By February 1943 No.12 (Comms) and No.122 (Comp) Squadrons each had four aircraft with No.121 (Comp) Squadron using three. On 15th March 1943 the Communications Flight element of No.122 (Comp) Squadron moved to Sea Island, BC and on 15th July 1943 the unit

Air Force Headquarters		
No.12 (Communications) Sqn	Rockcliffe, ON	926, 939, 942, 943
Eastern Air Command		
No.121 (Composite) Sqn	Dartmouth, NS	797*
	Halifax, NS	925
No.145 (Bomber Reconnaissance) Sqn	Torbay, NL	796
Western Air Command		
No.122 (Composite) Sqn	Patricia Bay, BC	798, 917, 940, 941
No.4 Training Command (BCATP)		
No.13 (Operational Training) Sqn	Patricia Bay, BC	924, 942

* Allocation of 797 assumed. Aircraft was assigned to EAC in June 1942 and is known to have been with No.121 (Comp) Sqn in February 1943.

June 1942 dispersal of the Royal Canadian Air Force G-21A Goose fleet.

re-formed as No.166 (Communications) Squadron with four aircraft. A month later, on 15th August, the Communications Flight of No.121 (Comp) Squadron reformed at Dartmouth as No.167 (Communications) Squadron.

Aircraft continued to be shuffled within the units during the winter of 1943-44 and during this period two new Goose operators appeared. No.5 Communications Flight formed at Torbay at the turn of year (date is uncertain) and was allocated aircraft 797 and by February 1944 two aircraft were being used by No.7 (Bomber Reconnaissance) Squadron at Prince Rupert, BC. 797 was later to be used by No.161 (Bomber Reconnaissance) Squadron in April and May 1944 at Dartmouth.

Although there were to be no more G-21A terminal accidents, the Goose fleet was, by late 1943, very tired notwithstanding a major overhaul programme. Although robust, the commercial G-21As had not been constructed with wartime RCAF use in mind and indeed all were approaching the five-year mark that the US Navy (at that time) considered to be the end of useful life for the early aircraft. As explained above the solution was the

wholesale replacement of the G-21A fleet with the definitive military JRF-5. The US authorities approved the purchase of 16 aircraft and the first aircraft, 382, was delivered to No.167 (Comms) Squadron in early March 1944.

As the JRF-5 (Goose II) replaced the G-21A (Goose) on a one for one basis there were no major changes to the operating units or their roles during 1944. No.5 Communications Flight at Torbay was absorbed by the co-located No.1 Composite Detachment on 1st September 1944 and No.7 (BR) Squadron gave up their aircraft early in the year but towards the end of the year and with victory in sight, new aircraft were being delivered to storage. The two lend-lease JRF-5s, FP471 and FP473, saw brief use with No.3 Communications and Ferry Flight, St Hubert within No.3 Training Command but were also in storage by January 1945 (No.3 C&F Flight disbanded on 14th January 1945) pending return to the British Air Commission. In late January 1945 the fleet was dispersed as shown in the table below.

Two Goose IIs from No.166 (Comms) Squadron were written off early in 1945 following unrelated incidents, and with the cessation of hostilities, the run-down of

Air Force Headquarters		
No.12 (Communications) Sqn	Rockcliffe, ON	383, 386, 390
Eastern Air Command		
No.167 (Communications) Sqn	Dartmouth, NS	382, 387,
No.1 Composite Detachment	Torbay, NL	385
EAC storage (6 REMU)	Mont Joli, QC	391
EAC storage	Site uncertain	926 (awaiting disposal)
Western Air Command		
No.166 (Communications) Sqn	Sea Island, BC	384, 388, 389, 392, 395
No.22 Repair Depot	Sea Island, BC	942 (awaiting disposal)
No.1 Air Command		
No.1 AC storage	Site uncertain	393, 394, 396, 397
No.1 AC storage (BCATP)	Site uncertain	FP471*, FP473*

* Awaiting return to the USA via British Air Commission, Washington, DC.

January 1945 dispersal of the Royal Canadian Air Force JRF-5 Goose II fleet.

the fleet began almost immediately with several aircraft going to storage between August and October. By February 1946 only seven aircraft remained active. No.167 (Comms) Squadron disbanded at Dartmouth on 1st October 1945 and although it reformed briefly as the EAC Communications Flight it was to be without the Goose. Similarly No.166 (Comms) Squadron disbanded at Sea Island on 31st October 1945, reforming as the WAC Communications Flight and retaining three Goose aircraft. The first Goose II to be disposed of was aircraft 391 in February 1946, having spent its entire life in storage. When finally civilianised with the RCMP in April 1946 as CF-MPG, it had only 26 flight hours recorded. Perhaps ironically, but now with a further 24,000 hours on the clock, CF-MPG remains in storage at Rockcliffe with the Canadian Aviation Museum.

The WAC Communications Flight eventually became No.121 Composite Flight on 1st April 1947 although by then it had relinquished the Goose. In mid-1946 three more aircraft were released for sale and another was scrapped, probably following earlier damage. By January 1947, only four aircraft remained active with No.12 (Comms) Squadron, four more were in storage and another was in the process of disposal.

Perhaps surprisingly, the Goose was then to remain in active use until 1954 with the final disposal occurring in January 1955. In yet another re-organisation No.412 (Composite) Squadron reformed at Rockcliffe on 1st April 1947 and replaced No.12 (Comms) Squadron. No.412 (K) Squadron, re-titled No.412 (Transport) Squadron on 1st April 1949, appears to have had four Goose aircraft on strength

Serial Numbers

Serial	Type	C/n	Circumstances
917	Goose	1016	G-21A production 1938
924	Goose	1013	G-21A CF-BKE acquired Sep39
925	Goose	1082	G-21A production 1940
926	Goose	1083	G-21A production 1940
939	Goose	1005	G-21A NC16914 acquired as CF-BTE Sep40
940	Goose	1002	G-21A NC16911 acquired as CF-BTF Sep40
941	Goose	1061	G-21A CF-BQE acquired Nov40
942	Goose	1003	G-21A NC16912 acquired Mar41
943	Goose	1007	G-21A NC16916 acquired Aug41
944	Goose	1019	G-21A NC2385 acquired Sep41
796	Goose	1020	G-21A NC20650 acquired via US Navy Apr42
797	Goose	1059	G-21A NC2788 acquired Jun42
798	Goose	1018	G-21A NC20648 acquired via US Navy Apr42
382	Goose II	B-39	JRF-5 purchase from 1944/45 production
383	Goose II	B-40	JRF-5 purchase from 1944/45 production
384	Goose II	B-45	JRF-5 purchase from 1944/45 production
385	Goose II	B-50	JRF-5 purchase from 1944/45 production
386	Goose II	B-55	JRF-5 purchase from 1944/45 production
387	Goose II	B-54	JRF-5 purchase from 1944/45 production
388	Goose II	B-60	JRF-5 purchase from 1944/45 production
389	Goose II	B-61	JRF-5 purchase from 1944/45 production
390	Goose II	B-70	JRF-5 purchase from 1944/45 production
391	Goose II	B-77	JRF-5 purchase from 1944/45 production
392	Goose II	B-76	JRF-5 purchase from 1944/45 production
393	Goose II	B-83	JRF-5 purchase from 1944/45 production
394	Goose II	B-90	JRF-5 purchase from 1944/45 production
395	Goose II	B-98	JRF-5 purchase from 1944/45 production
396	Goose II	B-99	JRF-5 purchase from 1944/45 production
397	Goose II	B-107	JRF-5 purchase from 1944/45 production
FP471	Goose II	B-46	JRF-5 1944 production for BAC/BCATP
FP473	Goose II	B-59	JRF-5 1944 production for BAC/BCATP

FP471 and FP473 were Lend Lease deliveries to the British Air Commission in 1944 intended for RCAF/BCATP use. As they were not RCAF purchases and subject to return to the USA, they did not receive RCAF serials.

After 1946, the 'Type C' roundels were replaced by the Maple Leaf roundels. By the time of this photograph of 386 (c/n B-55) taken circa 1952, 412 (Composite) Squadron had adopted WWII style 'codes' on the Goose although in reality it was the radio call-sign – in this instance 'VC-AOQ'. Having the distinction of being the last Goose in the Royal Canadian Air Force inventory, 386 was sold to the civilian market in 1955 and continued to fly into the following century.

(via K Molson)

when formed in April 1947 but by January 1948 there were only two in use, 383 and 386. 386 went to storage in July 1949 leaving only 383 active. At that time the four stored machines were 386, 387, 393 and 394. Following the loss of 383 in a water-landing accident in August 1951, 386 was brought from storage at Trenton as a replacement and continued to serve with No.412 (T) Squadron until retirement in 1954. In the process it was perhaps unique among all Goose aircraft in that it served in a unit that also operated jet airliners (although it should be said that the RCAF's Comets were at Uplands, ON and the Goose was at Rockcliffe). 394 was lost in a disastrous hangar fire at Trenton, ON, on New Year's night 1951-52 leaving just 387 and 393 in long-term storage. After the withdrawal of 386, the last three aircraft were made available for disposal in August and September 1954. The last aircraft in the inventory appears to have been 386, sold in January 1955.

Thus was closed a long and meritorious career with the RCAF. The RCAF was the first air arm to purchase the commercial G-21A for military use and in its hands the Goose subsequently served in many unforeseen roles and conditions. The machinations of the commercial purchases made between 1939 and 1942 have been only lightly touched upon here but were part of a significant chapter in RCAF history. With the benefit of hindsight and official records it can also be seen that there were in effect two RCAF Goose eras; that of the wartime G-21A fleet and that of the post-war JRF-5 fleet.

Colours and Markings

The early aircraft were finished in a standard overall aluminium lacquer with black lower hull and floats. However, as the aircraft arrived from different sources at different times there were a number of minor variations, not all of which have been recorded for posterity. RAF type 'A' roundels with yellow outer rings were worn on the rear fuselage and above and below the wings. A very large fin flash was carried on the forward part of the tailfin extending almost to full height and the serial was carried beneath the wings as well as on the rear fuselage. As mentioned previously, several aircraft retained their civil registrations for much of their lives as well as their previous civilian paintwork. By and large this was a practical measure, delaying a costly and time consuming task until major overhaul.

Some aircraft were camouflaged using the same scheme as that of the Royal Navy's Goose IA fleet. Colours were therefore the so-called 'Temperate Sea' camouflage scheme that comprised the Extra Dark Sea Grey and Dark Slate Grey sides and upper surfaces and Sky undersides. The type 'A' roundels and large fin flashes were retained. Squadron and individual code letters were applied on either side of the roundel in the conventional RAF style and were frequently underlined. At least one aircraft was painted in an overall yellow scheme when active in a training role. High visibility red markings were added to some aircraft and on an aluminium-lacquered machine would appear typically on the rudder and fin-top and engine-cowlings.

In concert with the RAF, the RCAF adopted the type 'C' roundel and fin flash in 1942 and it is assumed that the Goose II fleet was delivered in these markings (they were certainly worn by the end of the war). Aircraft in the transport and communications roles retained their aluminium finishes and, post-war, several acquired a smart red 'lightning' fuselage stripe. From 1946 the type 'C' roundel was replaced by the new RCAF 'maple-leaf' roundel and individual unit titles and badges became regular features, typically on the aircraft's forward fuselage. The two Lend-Lease aircraft, FP471 and FP473, were delivered in the British 'Temperate Sea' camouflage with type 'C' roundels.

Widgeon

While it is true that the RCAF did not acquire the Widgeon (in spite of considerable pressure from Grumman and its agents) there are good reasons for mentioning three aircraft here. The first is NC26877 (c/n 1216) owned by Grumman's agent Gillies Aviation of Hicksville, New York. This was used by No.12 (Communications) Squadron, Rockcliffe under US registration for a brief period, date unknown, and this is assumed to have been under some kind of evaluation or loan agreement. Given the level of formal RCAF antipathy for the Widgeon, this may have been a very short and possibly unofficial loan.

CF-BVN (c/n 1240), owned by Jack Bickell, is noteworthy in this context because it was the first Widgeon to be registered outside the USA and was so registered in December 1941 at a time when export approval would have been complicated. Bickell had previously passed two Goose aircraft to the RCAF and, in his capacity as industrialist and occasional politician, his war-time Widgeon might be considered a quasi-military aircraft.

The third aircraft is the RAF Lend-Lease aircraft FP458 (c/n 1352) that was delivered to the British Air Commission in January 1944. Some US Government documents formally record the aircraft as "exported to Canada" but this appears to have been linked to a misunderstanding of British use. While no conclusive records have yet surfaced, it is assumed that FP458 was used by the RAF in Canada and not by the RCAF.

CUBA

AVIACIÓN DE MARINA DE GUERRA - NAVAL AVIATION

Goose

Cuba was a close ally of the United States in 1941 and was an early recipient of American aid. As a Caribbean state, Cuba's wartime involvement was immediate and closely linked to that of the USA which maintained a number of installations on the island during WWII. The 1942 decision to make two JRF-5s available to the Aviación de Marina de Guerra came about after lengthy consideration by the US Joint Aircraft Committee and was probably linked to an eventual agreement not to supply the J4F Widgeon to Cuba (see later). This decision resulted in the supply of two new aircraft under Lend-Lease conditions which were added as a supplement to a US Navy production contract, C75686. As Lend-Lease aircraft, new BuAer serials were allocated once production was authorised.

The two aircraft were delivered circa October 1942 and are assumed to have been based at the Mariel naval base situated to the west of Havana (the aircraft were also to be seen at the city's main aerodrome at Rancho Boyeros). They were numbered 56 and 57 in the contemporary naval serial system and appear to have remained so numbered after a new system was introduced in November 1946 (the number range '50' to '69' was now to be restricted to 'patrol, scout and observation [types] with less than 12 hours range'). Little is known of their precise use but it can be assumed to have been the usual mixture of operational tasks and official VIP duties. Aircraft serial 56 does not appear to have survived its military service while 57 remained in active use until about 1954 when it was withdrawn. It is said to have been used by President Fulgencio Batista, presumably only after his return to the island in 1952, and by 1955 it had been sold in the United States as N2720A.

Colours and Markings

The Cuban JRF-5s appear to have been delivered in the standard US Navy blue-grey non-specular shade camouflage. Cuban roundels were applied either side of the nose and above and beneath the wings

Serial Numbers			
Serial	Type	C/n	Circumstances
56	JRF-5	1186	Lend-Lease acquisition 1942
57	JRF-5	1187	Lend-Lease acquisition 1942

and the fin flash, a stylised version of the national flag, encompassed the complete rudder. The serial was worn in large digits aft of the cabin door.

Widgeon

Cuba formally requested the supply of six Widgeons for the Aviación de Marina de Guerra circa March 1942 as part of pre-Lend-Lease aid. The aircraft were built as part of a production batch of 20 J4F-1 models, the balance being for Brazil and were added to contract LL-5229 on 10th June 1942. Deliveries were scheduled for July, August and September 1942 with two aircraft due each month. The first four aircraft were available on schedule at Bethpage. Although absolute evidence is lacking, it would appear that Cuba was either prevailed upon by the United States to give up these aircraft or, for an unexplained reason, rejected them for their own reasons. The first of these aircraft, c/n 1273, (the others being 1274, 1277, 1278, 1281 and 1282) was actually flown by a Brazilian pilot on 1st August 1942, the inference being that such a decision had been made by then. The formal reason for rejection, as noted on US Navy documentation in early September, was that "the Vice Chief of Naval Operations has received advice that Cuba no longer desires

these airplanes". A memo from the Vice Chief dated 28th August 1942 noted that "the Cuban Government have indicated that they do not desire the six J4F-1…. assigned to them". The aircraft were then taken on strength by the US Navy as the J4F-2 model with new BuAer serials 33952 to 33957 and, on entering immediate service with Eastern Sea Frontier squadrons, they became the US Navy's first operational Widgeons.

A decade later and in more relaxed times, the Aviación de Marina de Guerra purchased three second-hand commercial G-44A Widgeons from the US broker Smith, Kirkpatrick & Co Inc of New York although the export licence (A8184 of 12th August 1952) was for four aircraft. However only three aircraft were delivered subsequently from Miami, FL on 28th December 1952 and the vendor's correspondence is explicit that only three were sold to Cuba. In Cuban service they

were reportedly allocated the serials 81, 82 and 83 and were probably based at Mariel but this is supposition and the operating unit is unknown. In April 1953 the Cuban Navy's Air Order of Battle was however reporting four aircraft on strength and the additional aircraft is unexplained. [The new naval serial system reserved the range '80 and up' for 'General Utility' types. The serial '80' has been quoted as seen on a Widgeon but the sighting date and the identity of the aircraft remain unknown.] Early operations appear to have been impeded by a shortage of spare engines, a not unfamiliar story, but all three remained intact until their disposal to a US buyer in August 1956 after which they were collected in an airworthy condition and ferried to the United States. Suggestions that at least one aircraft remained in use in 1957 might be explained by the ongoing existence of an un-related civilian aircraft, CU-N346, which was not sold until 1959.

Serial Numbers

Serial	Type	C/n	Circumstances
Uncertain	G-44A	1411	N41980 acquired Dec52
Uncertain	G-44A	1450	N86624 acquired Dec52
Uncertain	G-44A	1473	N86647 acquired Dec52

These three aircraft were numbered 81, 82 and 83, sequence uncertain. See above text for speculation in respect of a fourth aircraft.

EGYPT

ROYAL EGYPTIAN AIR FORCE

Mallard

Two new Mallards were acquired by the Egyptian Royal Flight in 1949, for the use of the monarch, King Farouk. Both aircraft

were delivered to Cairo via London with the first aircraft, serial F7 (c/n J-47) flown by Gp Capt Hassan Aqif, handed over to the Royal Flight on 30th March 1949. The second aircraft, F8 (c/n J-48), was ferried from Bethpage to London by Capt John Hackett and thence to Cairo by Hassan Aqif on 30th August 1949.

Not surprisingly both were regally

furnished in a manner befitting Farouk's extravagant life-style.

At its zenith Farouk's Royal Flight comprised some ten aircraft including helicopters, maintained within, but separate from the regular air force. Although these aircraft were essentially Farouk's personal possessions, the Royal Flight constituted No.3 Squadron, Royal Egyptian Air Force.

Given the extravagance of King Farouk of Egypt and his personal relationships with western nations it came as no surprise that he should acquire not one, but two Mallards for his own use. Here F7 (c/n J-47) of the Royal Flight is seen on delivery at London Airport in September 1949. Following Farouk's abdication in 1952 the aircraft remained in use as a VIP transport with the Air Force.   *(unknown via Air Pictorial)*

Mallard F8 (c/n J-48) of the Egyptian Royal Flight is here seen up from Bethpage for pre-delivery publicity photography in 1949. Following its delivery to Egypt in August of that year the aircraft was used by the King and other VIPs until Farouk's abdication in July 1952. At some later stage F8 was renumbered but was eventually withdrawn from use for unknown reasons with considerably fewer flight hours than those of sister ship c/n J-47.

(Grumman photo by Harold G Martin, via PJ Marson)

Following King Farouk's abdication, the Mallards continued to operate in a VIP role, reportedly being used by Presidents Naguib and Nasser, and both aircraft were eventually renumbered. Here 763 (c/n uncertain) is seen circa 1959, at Almaza, Cairo in a revised colour scheme, by which time the nation was known as the United Arab Republic. Both aircraft were eventually withdrawn from use at Almaza in the 1960s. *(Noam Hartoch via Colin R Smith)*

United Arab Republic flag prominent on the tail. It has also been suggested that attempts to sell the aircraft on the commercial market were thwarted by a lack of documentation in the wake of Farouk's abdication.

The Egyptian Air Force eventually stopped reporting flight hours to Grumman and it became uncertain how the aircraft were being maintained. However the final reported flight hours are instructive (J-48 with 1,960hrs and J-47 with 3,360hrs) because they support the reports that one aircraft was withdrawn from use after striking an obstruction in the Nile during a landing. The same reports suggest that this aircraft, presumably J-48, was then cannibalised to keep the other airworthy and the disparity in flight hours suggests that this enabled the surviving aircraft to fly on for a few more years. A photograph of 763 at Almaza, dated to circa 1959, suggests that 763 may therefore have been aircraft J-47.

The second aircraft appears to have been withdrawn by the early-mid 1960s and although there are conflicting reports in respect of whether one or both aircraft were derelict at Almaza, the more specific references suggest that just one aircraft was present in a compound there between at least 1968 and 1975. Later reports place it in a scrap yard at nearby Heliopolis and this was presumably the aircraft that was still to be seen with other derelict aircraft in a compound in a northern suburb of Cairo as late as 1984.

Following Farouk's abdication on 26th July 1952 and the abolition of the monarchy the following year, the Mallards were inducted into the new Egyptian Air Force where they remained in use as VIP and Presidential transports. Although the exact date of change is unknown the aircraft were re-numbered after Farouk's departure, gaining regular three-digit Air Force serials, one of which was 763. Reflecting their use as Presidential aircraft as well as inherent and obsessive Egyptian security, their subsequent careers are not well understood, although both continued

in service for several years. By 1956 they are reported to have been transferred to No.11 Communications Squadron at Almaza, Cairo and by the late fifties aircraft 763 had acquired a more toned-down colour scheme with the prominent green fuselage flash removed and the new

Serial Numbers			
Serial	*Type*	*C/n*	*Circumstances*
F7 (763?)	G-73	J-47	Commercial acquisition 1949
F8	G-73	J-48	Commercial acquisition 1949

The Escadrille 8.S JRF-5s were fighting machines and this unidentified example, equipped with rocket-rails, is seen working with naval patrol boats, probably in the Delta region of South Vietnam. *(ECP-Armées)*

FRANCE

AÉRONAUTIQUE NAVALE - NAVAL AVIATION

Goose

Acquisition

France received a total of 17 JRF-5s from the United States in the form of MDAP aid on a special account for the Far East, distinct from the European MDAP assistance. These aircraft were supplied to the Aéronautique Navale in Indo-China in two batches of 12 and five aircraft in early 1952 and early 1954, the second batch comprising attrition replacements. All the aircraft were taken from US Naval storage and overhaul at NAS Quonset Point, Rhode Island. They were part of larger US aid packages designed to support the French forces in their war with the Viet Minh nationalist movement. Following military defeat and the Geneva agreement and its withdrawal from the region in 1956, France was permitted to keep the surviving aircraft as MDAP equipment for ongoing use within Europe. With Algeria having been recognised previously by the United States as part of metropolitan France (and therefore within NATO), France was therefore able to use them in its ongoing battle against the Algerian independence movement. Although uncomfortable with France's use of MDAP-supplied equipment in Algeria, the United States did not seek to prevent their deployment to that theatre.

Operations

France was unique in using the Goose as a first-line combat aircraft. Whereas many other nations may have used it in extreme and demanding circumstances, sometimes in combat theatres, the French actually fought with it and fought hard. To that end the aircraft was modified locally to carry weapons and munitions never previously seriously envisaged, and although not all were totally successful, this late and radical use of the Goose is of particular interest.

The Goose was supplied to the French of necessity. By 1950, the struggle with the Viet Minh in Indo-China and its perceived wider implications had reached a stage when American intervention in the form of aid was inevitable and the replacement of ageing French equipment a matter of urgency. In this respect, the United States had changed direction sharply following the outbreak of war in Korea in June 1950. Prior to then the United States had to some extent sympathised with Ho-Chi-Minh and his efforts to remove the French colonialists from their pre-war empire, but the Communist invasion of southern Korea brought about a rapid reappraisal of American priorities. Thus the United States began to pour money and equipment into Indo-China in an effort to bolster French opposition to what was now seen as a Communist threat to the region rather than a legitimate independence movement.

Fighting was taking place at varying levels of intensity throughout what is now modern Vietnam and to a more limited extent in Cambodia and Laos. Within a diverse force of military aircraft, the Aéronautique Navale provided an amphibious element intended to combat the enemy in the marine and extensive riverine environment. Within Indo-China this included rivers, lakes, rice-paddies, swamps, mangroves and a very extensive length of coast-line. Historically this task had been undertaken by a number of aircraft of which the obsolete Supermarine Sea Otter was the principal type, but which also included the PBY-5A Catalina and sundry land-planes.

The decision to release 12 JRF-5 to France was taken in early 1951, when the French realised that the Sea Otter situation was becoming untenable. US Navy records suggest that the aircraft were taken from storage on 14th May 1951 and were formally stricken on 13th July 1951, for delivery to France. Delivery was by sea although the actual date of arrival in Saigon is unclear (the first dated reference for any aircraft in theatre is 28th January 1952). The situation on the ground on 1st January 1952 was that the Aéronautique Navale had two operational amphibious units stationed at Cat Lai, Saigon, both of which were only marginally equipped. The long-standing Sea Otter unit, Escadrille 8.S, had recently given up these aircraft to Escadrille 9.S and had been using the war-weary PBY-5A delivered back in 1944 as temporary equipment pending the arrival of the Goose. By January 1952 they were virtually grounded. Meanwhile Escadrille 9.S was nominally using four Sea Otters, only two of which were airworthy. The Goose was desperately needed. The earliest reference to any Goose from surviving records (28th January 1952) suggests that 04349 was assigned initially to Escadrille 9.S as '9.S-21', apparently earmarked for the personal use of the Amiral FMEO (the admiral commanding all French naval forces in the Far-East, the Forces Maritimes d'Extrême-Orient). However 9.S was only intended to provide operational cover with the Sea Otter while 8.S worked-up on the new aircraft and in the event this

JRF-5 358 '8.S1' (c/n 1185) and the propeller-less 826 '8.S-12' (c/n B-79) are here seen on the slip-way at Cat-Lai early in the early days of French operations, the latter aircraft meeting its end in an accident in Cambodia in March 1954. *(ECP-Armées)*

Above: *Virtually all the Escadrille 8.S JRF-5s are here seen on parade at Cat Lai on the bank of the Dong Nai River, Saigon. The occasion was the hand-over ceremony, which presumably dates the picture to 13th March 1952. At this early stage no unit markings had been applied. (ECP-Armées)*

assignment was short-lived and, like all others, 04349 joined Escadrille 8.S and Escadrille 9.S disbanded on 1st April 1952.

From limited evidence, it appears that the aircraft were prepared and modified at Cat Lai before acceptance by Escadrille 8.S in three batches of four on or about 29th February, 4th March and 17th March 1952 with the formal handover ceremony taking place on 13th March. The Escadrille 8.S codes '8.S-1' to '8.S-12' appear to have been applied in sequence as these batches were accepted by the unit ('9.S-21' became '8.S-3' and was one of the first batch). In Aéronautique Navale service the JRF-5 fleet retained their BuAer serial identities although, in then typical MDAP fashion, this was abbreviated on the aircraft to the 'last three'. These individual aircraft codes, while theoretically movable, remained permanently assigned and within 8.S became recognised as a fixed identity. The allocation of codes was as follows:

358/8.S-1	799/8.S-5	741/8.S-9
784/8.S-2	453/8.S-6	742/8.S-10
349/8.S-3	454/8.S-7	818/8.S-11
791/8.S-4	727/8.S-8	826/8.S-12

The aircraft received extensive modifications to equip them to French standards (and in the process modernise them) and to add a weapons capability. To use a modern term, updated avionics were added progressively to improve flight safety, while enhanced communications equipment made the aircraft more militarily useful. The fleet was fitted with twin 7.62mm machine guns at the side doors and one aircraft was fitted temporarily with forward-firing guns. The aircraft were also capable of carrying a variety of light bombs (including cluster-bombs), rockets and even jury-rigged napalm canisters and all were to be used extensively during the coming years. By 1952 the French were under no illusions as to what was expected from the Goose – even if had never been tried before!

The first operational missions were undertaken from 1st March 1952 although somewhat cautiously. Initial operations were restricted to the Mekong Delta area although one aircraft was based temporarily at Phnom-Penh, Cambodia for work in the Gulf of Thailand. Coastal surveillance, including the interdiction of shipping, was undertaken frequently in conjunction with the seaplane tenders *Commandant Robert Giraud* (A643) and *Paul Goffeny* (A644), both being able to carry a Goose for such work. Gradually the number of missions increased and by the summer of 1952 8.S aircraft were active throughout the Delta and the nearby coastal waters. Aircraft were detached to nearby Soc Trang and, eventually, to distant Haiphong where they joined the unit's two Morane-Saulnier MS.500 Criquet observation aircraft and their borrowed C-47 at Cat Bi. However while the return 'up north' took the Goose closer to the more serious fighting, much of the northern combat was taking place in the western part of Tonkin, an area beyond Hanoi and the normal range of the Cat Bi-based aircraft.

Late in the year, the unit experienced the inevitable spares shortages problems that appear to have followed US supplied MDAP aircraft the world over. The unit was also finding out that the Goose could be a tricky aircraft to handle. There had been a number of repairable accidents during 1952, including that of 741 '8.S-9' on 11th September which is thought to have put it out of action for much of 1953. Perhaps inevitably, on 8th November 1952 8.S lost its first aircraft, when 727 '8.S-8' overturned on landing at Nha Trang and was written-off.

1953 was a very busy year, with six aircraft required to be available at all times and aircraft routinely deployed away from Cat Lai. In addition to the Cat Bi aircraft, single ship detachments were regularly made to Soc Trang and Can Tho in the Delta. 1953 saw action in all theatres from the Gulf of Thailand to the Gulf of Tonkin with the Goose undertaking missions ranging from sampan interdiction through artillery direction to medical evacuation. In July 8.S used cluster bombs and napalm in the Delta area in support of ground troops. All this came at a price and three more aircraft were lost in 1953. 818 '8.S-11' sank in the Dong Nai River near Cat Lai following a landing accident on 25th April, 454 '8.S-7' was similarly lost in a landing accident on the Mekong at Can Tho on 6th July and 349 '8.S-3' was damaged in unknown circumstances on 24th September 1953. The airframe damage, maybe following a heavy landing or ground-loop, was considered to be non-repairable and the aircraft was eventually struck off charge.

With the war at a critical stage, the United States was obliged to make good these losses and on 19th May 1953 another five aircraft were taken from storage and readied for delivery to French Indo-China although, as with the previous batch, they would take six months to reach Saigon, by which time the outlook for the French forces was bleak. These new aircraft were:

| 078/8.S-7 | 738/8.S-11 | 063/8.S-15 |
| 831/8.S-8 | 827/8.S-14 | |

Their formal acceptance by 8.S appears to have taken place on 10-11th February 1954, although their arrival at Cat Lai may have been some weeks previously. The

allocation of codes was presumably made before 349 '8.S-3' was perceived to be a write-off.

Activity in early 1954 was frantic with aircraft deployed throughout the region where they were engaged in metaphorical and literal fire-fighting. In January, four aircraft were deployed to Nha Trang in support of an Army offensive, while other resources were concentrated in the Gulf of Thailand theatre. Actions took place west of Saigon at Dong Thap Muoi (the Plaine des Joncs or Plain of Reeds) and elsewhere in the Delta. By February, two Goose remained at Cat Lai, two were at Pleiku in the central highlands, two more were at Nha Trang and the rest of the airworthy aircraft were at Ream on the Cambodian coast. In early March, three were sent to

Cat Bi and another to Pakse in Laos. By now aircraft in all theatres were routinely collecting small-arms fire damage (usually Japanese 7.7mm) and on 6th March 1954 826 '8.S-12' was damaged beyond repair in a landing accident at Phnom-Penh while undertaking a medical evacuation task.

While the French (and Vietnamese allies') garrison at Dien-Bien-Phu fought for their lives, 8.S aircraft were flying sorties in the Mekong Delta, over the Red River, in Cambodia and in Laos, in the process undertaking just about every kind of mission imaginable in support of an increasingly desperate situation. Inevitably, Dien-Bien-Phu fell on 8th May 1954, but for a few weeks more the French continued to fight the Viet Minh forces and 8.S continued to be active, particularly in the

This classically posed photograph shows contented natives strolling through the operational area while smartly dressed, diligent Escadrille 8.S ratings discuss the JRF-5's tyres. In view of the later-styled 'danger' fuselage markings this typically naïve publicity photograph probably shows the second '8.S11', 738 (87738 c/n B-132), taken some time after its arrival at Cat Lai in February 1954. (ECP-Armées via J-P Dubois)

The wearing of red-cross decals was no guarantee of safety, but clearly the French were maximising their chances when they adopted these over-sized markings, shown here on 784 '8.S-2' (c/n B-37) at Cat Lai. The markings were applied circa May 1954 for casualty evacuation, particularly in the north of Vietnam, and were apparently retained for subsequent work with the armistice authorities. (ECP-Armées)

Probably photographed in the Mekong Delta in the vicinity of Saigon, this is an early photograph of 741 '8.S-9' (c/n B-135) as indicated by the absence of the later, high-visibility 'Danger' markings that would bracket the propeller warning line. Like all the French aircraft, this hard-worked Goose never saw subsequent civilian use, being withdrawn from use in 1959 with terminal corrosion. (ECP-Armées)

Delta. The number of combat missions decreased however, and in July the first peacetime Évacuation Sanitaire (EVASAN) missions were undertaken with at least two aircraft wearing highly visible 'red cross' markings. This was a very necessary step as the 8.S gunships were still very much a target for Viet-Minh ground-fire and as late as 16th June 738 '8.S-11' and 741 '8.S-9' both took hits from 7.7mm fire in the Delta. Two days later, 741 was damaged more seriously in an accident at Tan Son Nhut, Saigon when the undercarriage collapsed on landing. The repairs took four months. Much of the work in July 1954 centred on protecting and assisting the withdrawal of French forces in the north to safer ground and some combat missions were still being flown in the Haiphong and Delta regions. Finally, on 21st July, with the signing of the 'Geneva Accords', a general cease-fire was declared. Prior to that the final 8.S mission had been to escort the former aircraft

carrier, now fleet transport, *Dixmude* (the former HMS *Biter*) down the Mekong from Saigon to the sea.

Following the cease-fire, the dispersed fleet was returned to Cat Lai, initially leaving only one aircraft at Nha Trang. With French influence in Vietnam waning rapidly, the 8.S aircraft were used in communications and transportation work, frequently undertaking such duties at the behest of the Armistice Commission members and, as far as is known, there were no serious accidents that befell 8.S during this period. Between 1st April 1952 and July 1954 the 8.S Goose fleet had flown 6,500 hours, undertaking 3,800 operational sorties.

Eventually the unit moved to Tan Son Nhut, Saigon, from where it operated in a more low-key mode while preparations were made for the departure from South Vietnam in the summer of 1956. At the time of withdrawal, Escadrille 8.S

possessed 12 aircraft, all of which were potentially airworthy although at least one aircraft (741) had been earmarked earlier for withdrawal but had been reprieved. The intention appears to have been to transfer three or four aircraft to Escadrille 9.S at Nouméa-Tontouta in New Caledonia and to return the others to France where they would, where necessary, be overhauled before use in Algeria. In practice what seems to have happened is that eight aircraft, 358 '8.S-1', 784 '8.S-2', 799 '8.S-5', 453 '8.S-6', 078 '8.S-7', 831 '8.S-8', 741 '8.S-9' and 063 '8.S-15' were taken to France in the carrier *La Fayette* (R96) in May 1956, arriving in June, and that a ninth aircraft followed shortly afterwards, process unknown (this might be linked to an incident involving 827 '8.S-14' at Tan Son Nhut on 19th May 1956 which was still under repair at Saint-Mandrier naval base near Toulon in France in March 1957). Three aircraft, including 791 '8.S-4', were

Escadrille 8.S re-mustered at Maison Blanche near Algiers in the late summer of 1956. 453 '8.S-6' (c/n 1123) was an early arrival there following overhaul at Saint-Mandrier. By 1957, the Goose was beginning to show its age and its time in Algeria was limited. 453 was eventually withdrawn in 1959 for spares recovery and was probably scrapped soon after. (Baron via C Morin)

Seen here at Maison Blanche in 1959, Escadrille 8.S JRF-5 799 '8.S5' (c/n B-94) was withdrawn from use later that year and was held in reserve covering the two aircraft deployed to Dakar. It would be struck off charge and scrapped in December 1961. *(L Morareau Collection via Le Bloa)*

simultaneously carried as deck cargo from Saigon to Nouméa, New Caledonia, in the LST *Golo* (L9008) but attempts to use them in New Caledonia with 9.S were blocked by the United States. Correspondence dated August 1956 makes it clear that by then there were nine aircraft in the Mediterranean theatre and three remaining in the Pacific area, although it is uncertain exactly where they were located. It is certain, however, that the three aircraft were never used in Nouméa and that they subsequently returned to France. As a postscript to this episode, the correspondence confirms that the Aéronautique Navale had been considering the use of three SA-16 Albatross to undertake this work but was also considering the acquisition of two or three more second-hand Goose aircraft. In the event neither option was pursued.

The US Government had authorised the supply of the JRF-5 to France for the express purpose of limiting communist activity in Indo-China and presumably, to the relief of the French, the US extended this approval to use in Algeria where, since 1954, France had been fighting a bitter and complex war with another independence movement. Accordingly, Escadrille 8.S was relocated to Maison-Blanche, near Algiers, and tasked to support French forces, this time only in the more convenient role of maritime patrol, joining the SURMAR (Maritime Surveillance) organisation of land-based P2V Neptunes and PB4Y Privateers. The aircraft was now older and less well equipped for this kind of war.

Although it undertook coastal surveillance work in the early days (to interdict arms smugglers and enforce a more general blockade of traffic from eastern European countries and elsewhere), it was eventually relegated to a largely communications and transport role. Depot maintenance and some flying were undertaken at the Saint-Mandrier naval base near Toulon in France. One aircraft, serial unknown, is known to have spent time in 1956 wearing the code 'CS-20' (for Casablanca, French Morocco) and is presumed to have been based at Camp Cazes serving with the naval headquarters flight known as the Section

de Liaison de l'Aéronautique Navale au Maroc.

Escadrille 8.S became operational at Maison-Blanche, Algiers in the late summer of 1956 initially with three aircraft, believed to have been 358 '8.S-1', 784 '8.S-2' and 831 '8.S-8', which were soon followed, post overhaul, by 453 '8.S-6'. The other four initial arrivals, 799 '8.S-5', 078 '8.S-7', 741 '8.S-9' and 063 '8.S-15' were intended to remain at Saint-Mandrier

until the completion of 240-hour checks. Escadrille 8.S aircraft were also operated from Naval Air Station Lartigue, not far from Oran, Algeria and it was from Lartigue that 831 '8.S-8' was lost while on operations on 14th October 1956. The aircraft struck an off-shore rock at Cape Tenes, crashed and was destroyed by fire while on a low-level over-water flight between Cape Carbon and Cape Tenes. One crew-member was killed on impact, the other four survived.

1957 and 1958 was a period when several aircraft underwent major overhauls at Saint-Mandrier, on the French Riviera, and it was during such a check of 741 '8-S-9' in 1958 that terminal damage was discovered. 738 '8-S-11' was struck off charge in January 1959 with serious accident damage and is assumed to have been the aircraft involved in an aborted water take-off the previous year. By 1959, 8.S had almost reached the end of the road. Spares were in short supply, aircraft were being withdrawn and cannibalised and some were no longer capable of safe operations from water. In all six aircraft were struck off charge at Saint-Mandrier in 1959-60. Although it continued to fly operationally until disbandment on 1st October 1959 (784 '8.S-2' was still active in September), only three or four aircraft were active at any given time. However,

Above and below: *These two photographs of JRF-5 078 (c/n B-7) of 27 Flotille taken at Dakar, Senegal, appear to show that the aircraft was marked as '27.F-11' complete with unit badge before losing the 'dash 11' part of the code and much of the badge to weathering by the time of the second (lower) picture, reported to have been taken in 1960. This was the ill-fated aircraft that crashed in January 1961 leading to the rapid but inevitable final withdrawal of the Goose from French use.*

(both Roger Caratini via MAP)

JRF-5 827 (c/n B-80) of 27 Flotille was the last Goose to fly with the Aéronautique Navale following the accident to 078, eventually being withdrawn in December 1961. Here seen at Dakar in 1960, the aircraft is devoid of unit markings or the full code '27.F-12' which it reportedly wore during its early days in Sénégal. (R Caratini)

prior to disbandment at least two aircraft were assigned to Flotille 27.F, a P5M-2 Marlin unit based at Bel Air, Dakar in Sénégal although the Goose were actually based on land at nearby Ouakam.

At Ouakam two aircraft, 078 '27.F-11' and 827 '27.F-12', were maintained in airworthy condition for local communications and sundry general purposes duties with others acting as a spares source. The four reserve aircraft were 358, 063, 799 and 742. Unfortunately there was to be a very sad ending to the history of the Goose with the Aéronautique Navale when 078 '27.F-11' was lost in a fatal accident on 27th January 1961. The aircraft departed Tambacounda, Sénégal with Rear-Admiral Pierre Ponchardier, his wife and others but failed to maintain height and crashed, killing all on board. Ponchardier, a senior

serving officer, was a popular character with a distinguished war record. Although the Goose was not withdrawn immediately, its demise was close and on 5th December 1961 the five surviving aircraft were struck off charge, although it is unclear whether they were scrapped in situ (they were released for disposal on 19th December 1961). This brought to an end a decade of constant and often dramatic activity for the French Goose in a role that surely could never have been envisaged by its designers and which was unparalleled by any other user.

Colours and Markings

All aircraft were supplied to France in standard US Navy 'Glossy Sea Blue' colours to which were added standard French naval rudder markings with anchor

and roundels above and below both wings. There were no fuselage roundels. This dark blue scheme was retained on all aircraft throughout their service lives although in French use additional and more obvious warning notices were added fore and aft of the propeller line. The individual Escadrille or Flotille white aircraft codes were carried in full on the upper rear fuselage and, as a single-digit code, high on the tail-fin. The truncated three digit serial and aircraft designation 'JRF-5' were carried, US Navy style, beneath the tail-plane. As explained above, some aircraft carried EVASAN roundels in Indo-China. Early applications were modestly sized and located on the rear fuselage and under the wings while later applications were considerably larger, obliterating the aircraft code, and with a second smaller roundel added to the

827 '8.S-14' (c/n B-80) was one of the batch of attrition replacement JRF-5s that France received in 1954. The exact place and date of the photograph are unknown but would probably be at Cat Lai or Tan Son Nhut, Saigon circa 1955. 827 would survive Indo-China and another war in Algeria before retirement in Senegal, having become by then the last active French Goose. (MAP)

tail. It is of interest that, owing to the stubby fuselage and a lack of available space, squadron codes did not follow Aéronautique Navale regulations with dot and dash inserted in the code (eg 8.S-3) and were painted with a small 's' (eg 8s3).

Although not externally worn, the Escadrille 8.S aircraft in Algeria were assigned permanent radio call signs in the range F-YCHA/Z with the individual code aligned with final letter. Thus 784 '8.S-2' was F-YCHB.

Aircraft Disposal

All surviving aircraft were administratively returned to the United States, which in metropolitan France meant the MAAG in Paris, and this procedure probably applied to the aircraft in Sénégal.

Without exception, the aircraft were in poor condition and many had been cannibalised to the extent they were reduced to carcasses. As far as is known all were scrapped.

located at Tan Son Nhut, operated two aircraft under civil registration on behalf of the High Commission (as part of the Escadrille du Haut-Commissariat) and the local Medical Service (Service du Santé). They were respectively, F-BFHE (c/n 5) and F-BFHF (c/n 6), and both are believed to have been lost in or following accidents in 1951. F-BFHF was eventually written-off following an accident on 25th July off Cap Saint Jacques, near Saigon, and F-BFHE appears to have been lost following an incident at Cao Lanh, southwest of Saigon, on 29th December 1951.

It is unclear to what extent, if at all, Armée de l'Air resources were used to support SCAN-30 F-BFHG (c/n 7), used by the Emperor Bao-Dai between 1951 and 1954, when it was terminally damaged by fire at Tan Son Nhut.

Widgeon

The Widgeon was never used by the French armed forces but, prior to the manufacture of the SCAN-30, one former US Navy aircraft was evaluated by the Centre d'Essais en Vol (CEV) at Istres in February 1947. This was the G-44 c/n 1297, BuAer 32943, thought to have been registered NC79801 at the time of the trials, although it is uncertain what markings were worn (the pilot recorded its identity as '1297'). The aircraft was flown by at least one seconded naval pilot and the trials are assumed to have been undertaken on behalf of both the Armée de l'Air and the Aéronautique Navale. Following (or perhaps in the course of) these trials the aircraft was damaged and the American owner subsequently sold the aircraft to SCAN by whom it was rebuilt becoming F-BDAE (and see the individual history of c/n 1297).

Serial Numbers			
Serial	Type	C/n	Circumstances
6453	JRF-5	1123	MDAP Aid 1951
6454	JRF-5	1124	MDAP Aid 1951
04349	JRF-5	1176	MDAP Aid 1951
04358	JRF-5	1185	MDAP Aid 1951
37784	JRF-5	B-37	MDAP Aid 1951
37791	JRF-5	B-44	MDAP Aid 1951
37826	JRF-5	B-79	MDAP Aid 1951
84799	JRF-5	B-94	MDAP Aid 1951
84818	JRF-5	B-113	MDAP Aid 1951
87727	JRF-5	B-121	MDAP Aid 1951
87741	JRF-5	B-135	MDAP Aid 1951
87742	JRF-5	B-136	MDAP Aid 1951
34063	JRF-5	1192	MDAP Aid 1953
34078	JRF-5	B-7	MDAP Aid 1953
37827	JRF-5	B-80	MDAP Aid 1953
37831	JRF-5	B-84	MDAP Aid 1953
87738	JRF-5	B-132	MDAP Aid 1953

Aéronautique Navale documentation often presented the full BuAer serial in a 'split' format typical of the 'fifties, thus: '6.453', '4.358', '34.078', '37.784', '84.799' etc.

ARMÉE DE L'AIR – AIR FORCE

SCAN-30

Although the French-built SCAN-30 was not adopted for regular use by any of the armed forces, the Armée de l'Air did provide crews and support for at least two aircraft used by government agencies in Indo-China in the early 1950s. Escadrille de Liaison Aérienne 00.052 (ELA 00.052),

Serial numbers			
Serial	Type	C/n	Circumstances
No.5/F-BFHE	SCAN-30	5	New production 1950
No.6/F-BFHF	SCAN-30	6	New production 1950

GUATEMALA

CUERPO DE AERONÁUTICA MILITAR - MILITARY AIR CORPS

Goose

The Cuerpo de Aeronáutica Militar received a single, former British JRF-6B from US Navy surplus stocks, probably in late 1946. As no previous US civil registration has been identified it remains open to speculation as to whether or not it was obtained via a broker, its last US Navy reference being its strike as surplus from NAS Miami in June 1946. FAA documentation notes the purchaser as being the 'Government of the Republic of Guatemala'. However, in view of its subsequent VIP use there has to be an assumption that the aircraft was overhauled

and re-fitted to G-21A standard prior to its delivery.

The aircraft's use with the Cuerpo de Aeronáutica Militar (which became the Fuerza Aérea Guatemalteca in 1948) is poorly understood, but it is believed to have been used by the president, Juan José Arévalo, and was frequently to be seen moored at the presidential chalet at El Morlón on Lago Amatitlán, south of Guatemala City. Neither local serial nor operating unit is known although the aircraft was doubtless based at Los Cipresales, Guatemala City.

The Goose appeared on the AOB in 1947

and 1948 as a single 'OA-9' but there seems little reason to doubt its naval pedigree. The final known AOB reference was dated 5th May 1948 and a few days later on 8th May 1948 it was sold to an American buyer to whom it was registered briefly as NC66327 in July 1948. The use of the former US Navy identity as a registration is unusual and might indicate that there was no other identity prior to its delivery to Guatemala. Always assuming that the JRF-6B 66327 was indeed the FAG's 'OA-9' of 1947-1948, this is believed to have been the only Goose to have seen military use in Guatemala.

Serial Numbers			
Serial	Type	C/n	Circumstances
Unknown	JRF-6B	1153	Commercial acquisition 1946

HONDURAS

AVIACIÓN MILITAR - MILITARY AVIATION

Goose

The Aviación Militar (AM) acquired a single aircraft, a former British-used JRF-5, from US naval surplus stocks in 1946, presumably via an American broker and an unidentified civil registration. The Aviación Militar was a small organisation at that time and the aircraft was based nominally at the Toncontín airfield, Tegucigalpa. The AM allocated serial numbers according to purpose and the Goose was numbered 110 in a series used by communications aircraft. Its formal unit

allocation, if any, is uncertain. Little is known of its use and in June 1951 it was sold back to the US commercial market.

In 1954 the Fuerza Aérea Hondurena (FAH) was formed and the independent Air Force began a re-structuring and re-equipment process. Perhaps surprisingly in view of its previous use, another Goose was acquired in 1956. This was another surplus US Navy aircraft but this time a recently modernised JRF-6 that had been active at NAF Annapolis, MD until March 1956. This aircraft, also based nominally at

Toncontín, was numbered 811 in a sequence used by fixed-wing aircraft and (later) helicopters in a primarily search and rescue role. By 1956 it would probably have been organised within a formally titled flight or squadron, but such details remain unconfirmed. Like its predecessor, 811 would have but a short life with the FAH and it was sold to an American buyer in April 1959.

No official Honduran records have been seen by the authors but there is no evidence to suggest that other aircraft were used.

Serial Numbers			
Serial	Type	C/n	Circumstances
110	JRF-5	B-49	Commercial acquisition 1946
811	JRF-6	B-65	Acquisition from US Navy 1956

INDONESIA

ANGKATAN UDARA REPUBLIK INDONESIA - INDONESIAN AIR FORCE

Goose

Although several G-21 and G-21A had been operated commercially by oil exploration companies in the Netherlands East Indies, none survived the Japanese onslaught of 1941-42. Post-war, the Goose returned to Indonesia with the acquisition of two G-21As (a former JRF-4 and a JRF-5) by the Shell Oil subsidiary, NV De Bataafsche Petroleum Maatschappij (BPM). PK-AKA and PK-AKB were both registered in October 1946 and were used to support operations at Balikpapan, Kalimantan (Borneo). Their acquisition by the Angkatan Udara (AURI) came as an indirect result of the nationalisation of

Dutch assets announced in December 1958. Although not itself seized, BPM was to undergo significant change in the coming years and, as a small part of this process, both aircraft passed into Indonesian state ownership.

PK-AKA's registration was cancelled on 17th October 1958 and it is assumed that PK-AKB was cancelled at the same time, although it is unclear exactly when the aircraft took up the AURI identities PB-518 and PB-521. Their transfer to the AURI is understood to have taken place in 1957. Within the AURI they were operated by Skadron Udara 5 at Lanud Abdul Rahman Saleh, Malang alongside the recently

acquired SA-16A Albatross fleet (a squadron history shows two Gooses on strength in 1957).

Little is known of their use by the AURI (or Tentara Nasional Indonesia – Angkatan Udara (TNI-AU) as it became known on 5th October 1971) and they may well have continued to be used in support of the oil industry. Eventually PB-518 (c/n 1107) re-appeared on the civilian register as PK-RAM in 1977, its owner listed as Merpati Nusantara Airlines, while PB-521 remained in military markings, probably used for ground instructional purposes before storage at Kalijati near Bandung from at least 1986 until at least 2009.

Serial Numbers			
Serial	Type	C/n	Circumstances
PB-518	G-21A	1107	PK-AKA acquired circa 1957
PB-521	G-21A	1115	PK-AKB acquired circa 1957

Tentara Nasional Indonesia – Angkatan Udara (TNI-AU) Goose PB-521 (c/n 1115) was one of two examples probably used in support of the oil industry. It remained in military markings, and was probably used later for ground instructional purposes, before storage at Kalijati near Bandung, where this photograph was taken, from at least 1986 until at least 2009.
(Roland Adrie via Marc Koelich)

ISRAEL

HEYL HA'AVIR - AIR FORCE

Widgeon

Two G-44A Widgeons were obtained for Israel in the early summer of 1948 at the time of the creation of the nation state and they subsequently featured in the War of Independence. Their acquisition was typically complex, combining the usual elements of deception and misfortune. The two originally intended aircraft appear to have been a pair of unsold G-44As, NC86607 (c/n 1433) and NC86644 (c/n 1470) that were acquired by Bernard E Smith of New York ('Sell 'em Ben', see page 278) on 6th May and 27th June 1947 respectively. Smith was an associate of the Dutch pilot Wim Van Leer who reportedly later facilitated the delivery of two Widgeon aircraft to Israel via an organisation known as Mayfair Air Services, based at Croydon, England. Both aircraft arrived in Europe by unknown means but are known to have been used by Léon Douzille at La Pallice, France in the spring of 1948 (and perhaps earlier). Douzille's company, SCAN, was located at La Pallice and was in the early stages of manufacturing the Widgeon under licence as the SCAN-30 (the prototype SCAN-30 would not fly until January 1949) and their presence there was both visible and unsurprising in the circumstances. However NC86644 was soon destroyed, sadly killing Douzille and two others, in a high-ground crash in Spain on 24th April 1948 while en route Lisbon-La Rochelle.

Subsequent events are uncertain. It would appear that soon afterwards NC86607 was delivered to Israel and it is assumed to have been this aircraft that appeared on the order of battle summary of 14th May 1948 although Israeli documents clearly state that the delivery of NC86607 took place on 26th June 1948. The second aircraft, also reported to have been delivered in June 1948, was NC41995 (c/n 1426). This had earlier been a Grumman demonstration aircraft but the immediate vendor details are unknown. The cautious assumption is that NC41995 was a replacement for NC86644 although we have only the above circumstantial evidence to support this theory. If NC41995 was a replacement aircraft then the acquisition process was impressively rapid. If not, then it is possible that there were three aircraft originally intended for Israel.

More or less coincident with the arrival of the first Widgeon in Israel, the Air Service became known as the Heyl Ha'Avir or Israeli Air Force (IAF). The two aircraft that actually arrived were marked as B-72 (c/n 1433) and B-73 (c/n 1426) and initially at least one was used by A Squadron at Sde Dov. A Squadron became 1 Squadron in June 1948 and both aircraft were immediately plunged into the 'War of Independence'. In November 1948 the IAF renumbered its aircraft and B-72 and B-73 became 1201 and 1202 in a new type-specific sequence. Unfortunately B-73 would never wear the new serial as it was destroyed in a fatal accident on 7th December 1948. While undertaking practice water landings, the aircraft crashed into Lake Kineret (Sea of Galilee) killing all four occupants.

1201 survived a little longer, although its fate is less clear than that of 1202. It survived long enough to be acquired by the newly created 103 Squadron (head-quartered at Ramat David) but had dis-appeared from the IAF order of battle by late 1949. There are equally vague reports of it crashing and being sold to a US buyer in 1952 (and both versions could be correct) but c/n 1433 is not known to have re-appeared, anywhere, as an airworthy aircraft.

Colours and Markings

The aircraft are thought to have been flown in a three-tone camouflage scheme with roundels worn on the rear fuselage and above and below the wings. The serial was applied to the rear fuselage. It has been suggested that the rudder may have been painted red.

Serial Numbers

Serial	Type	C/n	Circumstances
B-72 (1201)	G-44A	1433	Commercial acquisition 1948
B-73 (1202)	G-44A	1426	Commercial acquisition 1948

JAPAN

JAPANESE MARITIME SELF DEFENCE FORCE

Goose

In March 1954, shortly before the official formation of the Japanese Maritime Self Defence Force (JMSDF) on 1st July 1954, it was agreed that Japan should receive four low-houred USN JRF-5 aircraft from US Navy stocks. Accordingly four aircraft at NAS Quonset Point were identified for future Japanese use although it would be nearly another eighteen months before their formal handover to an operational JMSDF unit. The aircraft were shipped to NAF Oppama near Tokyo where they were de-preserved and readied for JMSDF use by US Navy personnel. Initial training and work-up was undertaken with the US Navy's FASRON-11 at Oppama before the aircraft were transferred formally to the Second Kanoya Kokutai at Kanoya in southern Kyushu which formed on 16th December 1955. The Second Kokutai, which also used two PBY-6A Catalinas, subsequently moved to Omura in north-west Kyushu on 1st December 1956 becoming the Second Omura Kokutai in the process.

The relatively primitive JRF-5 was used by the JMSDF essentially for early training while the force grew in size and rapidly re-equipped with new and more capable aircraft. Although delivered in the standard USN dark blue colour-scheme, the JMSDF eventually re-painted them in an overall grey scheme. In addition to the JMSDF serial, prefixed by the Omura kana code, the aircraft continued to wear the 'last three' of the BuAer serial and a large 'last two' of the JMSDF serial on the nose. None of the JMSDF aircraft were lost although their operational lives were relatively brief and the fleet was withdrawn circa late 1960.

After lengthy periods of open storage two aircraft were sold eventually to US buyers and the others are presumed to have been scrapped in Japan.

Goose aircraft for spare parts and/or instructional purposes

In June and July 1955 six surplus USN JRF-5 aircraft, five of which were former USCG JRF-5Gs, were taken from the USN storage depot at Litchfield Park, AZ to NAS Alameda, CA where they were prepared for delivery by sea to a recipient under MDAP auspices. The aircraft were identified by the US Navy for MDAP use on 20th May 1955 and according to Navy records they were not re-worked prior to delivery. Two were moved to Alameda during June 1955 with the other four following in July. All aircraft departed Alameda in September 1955 and were struck off US Navy charge formally on 21st September 1955. Their strike code indicated a transfer to a 'non-USN' recipient with delivery by sea.

Serial Numbers

Serial	Type	C/n	Circumstances
9011 (84797)	JRF-5	B-92	MDAP aid 1955
9012 (35921)	JRF-5	1188	MDAP aid 1955
9013 (87731)	JRF-5	B-125	MDAP aid 1955
9014 (84800)	JRF-5	B-95	MDAP aid 1955

Seen here in the bone-yard at Shimofusa, Japan in October 1968 among Avengers and WS-51s, the JMSDF's JRF-5 9013 (c/n B-125) looks to have seen better days. However, following several years of storage this MAP-supplied Goose, still American government property, was being sold to a US-based buyer at the start of a new and lengthy lease of life. Later converted to turbine power, the aircraft is currently active as N70AL. The photograph shows the aircraft in its final overall grey JMSDF colour-scheme, still wearing the 'last three' of its former BuAer identity, 87731.

(JM Friell/FL Cooper)

The recipient of these six aircraft has not been found in any easily accessible official US documentation (although further research in USN records would almost certainly identify the end-user) and, with one exception, none of these aircraft has been identified subsequently from any other source. The exception is aircraft 34089 which was sold by the US Army Depot Command, Japan for $1,515 to Allied Aircraft Sales of Phoenix, AZ on 25th July 1967 (it subsequently became N12681). The Army Depot Command Japan provided a range of logistical activities, including the disposal of assets, on behalf of Pacific Command MAP nations. Given the relatively hard-use to which these six aircraft had been put previously, their generally high flight hours and the lack of any pre-delivery rework, the suspicion is that they were delivered to Japan for use as spare parts or instructional purposes. Japan received other former USN aircraft for spares recovery at this time and such aircraft did not receive JMSDF serials. The transfer of these surplus JRF-5s to Japan, an important MDAP nation, seems highly likely given that the USN would soon cease to be a Goose operator.

It is uncertain whether 34089 was the only aircraft from this group to be sold off as surplus. The modest 1967 sale value suggests that it was disposed of as non-airworthy and it is conceivable that other hulks were released similarly by the Army Depot Command as components or scrap. Although the fates of two of the four 'active' JMSDF JRF-5s are uncertain there is some evidence that 34089 and at least one of the other two former Japanese aircraft found their way to the USA by similar process. It is not unrealistic to envisage a scenario in which other hulks were purchased as components and returned to the USA during the period 1960-1968.

Serial Numbers			
Serial	*Type*	*C/n*	*Circumstances*
34089	JRF-5*	B-18	MDAP aid 1955
37772	JRF-5*	B-25	MDAP aid 1955
37773	JRF-5*	B-26	MDAP aid 1955
37789	JRF-5*	B-42	MDAP aid 1955
84792	JRF-5*	B-87	MDAP aid 1955
84813	JRF-5	B-108	MDAP aid 1955
Aircraft marked * were considered by the USCG to be JRF-5G when placed in storage in 1954. All were delivered from Alameda as JRF-5.			

PARAGUAY

AVIACIÓN NAVALE PARAGUAYA - NAVAL AVIATION

Goose

The Aviación Navale Paraguaya (ANP) purchased three surplus JRF-5 aircraft from the US Naval Reserve Surplus in 1958 under the auspices of the Military Assistance Sales programme. In practice these three aircraft were former US Coast Guard aircraft (known to the US Coast Guard as the JRF-5G) and were among the very last US military Goose aircraft remaining in storage. Prior to delivery, they were to be overhauled by TEMCO Aircraft in Texas, but for uncertain reasons this work was completed by the Aero Corporation of Atlanta, GA and it was from Atlanta that they were ferried to Asunción. The three aircraft were given the serials T-001 to T-003 and the delivery flight was eventually scheduled for the second fortnight of November 1959.

Delivery was undertaken by Paraguayan crews under the command of Rear Admiral Guillermo Haywood although one pilot, an American named Jones, was apparently contracted to fly one of the aircraft. They routed initially from Atlanta to Miami, then via Nassau and on to San Juan, Puerto Rico but unfortunately T-001, flown by Jones, was lost between Nassau and San Juan on 17th November 1959. In spite of an extensive search by the US Coast Guard, instigated by Haywood, no trace was found of the aircraft and its loss remains a mystery. The other two aircraft arrived safely in Asunción more than a week later.

T-001 was not replaced and the two surviving aircraft entered service with the ANP at the Sajonia naval base, Asunción where they replaced the Republic RC-3 Seabee. For several years they were engaged in all the sundry tasks, operational and informal, for which the Goose's unique qualities are renowned, and from about 1964 the ANP appears to have been supported in its endeavours by the Argentine Naval Mission to Paraguay (the MNA). The MNA brought with it two elderly JRF-6Bs that had seen use most recently with Argentina's coastguard, the Prefectura Naval.

In 1966 the ANP began to operate a quasi-airline service with the JRF-5, undertaking ad hoc passenger, mail and cargo services to various locations on the Paraguay River. This revenue-earning venture was intended to provide funds to reduce the running costs of the JRF-5 operation. The new operation, known as the Servicio Aeronaval (SAN), was helped considerably by the receipt of one of the MNA's JRF-6Bs. Shortly before this gift of the Argentine aircraft 0186 'MNA-12' (c/n 1146) the ANP aircraft had been re-numbered as 126 and 127 (although it is possible that T-003 was never repainted) and the new JRF-6B became 128. The formal handover ceremony took place on 4th May 1966. On 23rd July the existing SAN service, now known as the Línea del Correo Norte and linking Asunción with Bahia Negra, became a scheduled weekly service and on 15th October 1966 the Línea del Correo Sur, linking Asunción and Pilar, was established as a daily service.

The SAN operation continued until

1968, by which time only 128 was airworthy, the others having succumbed to time-expired components and a shortage of increasingly expensive spare parts. The second Argentine aircraft, 0294 'MNA-11', had by then also been given to the ANP, although according to local sources it was never airworthy and the application of the serial '129' is by no means certain. Moreover, as will be seen, it was not transferred formally to Paraguay until late in 1968 by which time the ANP was seeking to sell it.

The disposal of the ANP Goose fleet was particularly complicated and is explained separately below but, in summary, the ANP was approached by one of the owners of Catalina Airlines of Long Beach, CA, who expressed an interest in buying two of the aircraft. This approach probably took place in 1967 and it was not until 1969 that the deal was completed. By then the American had apparently acquired all four aircraft and two new Cessna U-206s had passed into ANP hands as part of the arrangement.

Colours and Markings

Little is known of the early markings of the original ANP aircraft although a poor quality monochrome photograph of T-003 shows it to be in a silver colour scheme with national roundels on the extreme forward section of the nose and beneath the wings. The serial was carried on the nose. An inscription on the nose appears to read 'Marina de Guerra' (Navy). 126's colour-scheme is unknown. The former Argentine aircraft were apparently left in the MNA silver scheme although stripped of all Argentine markings except the under-wing anchor devices. The new ANP serial 128 was inscribed on the nose in large numerals.

Serial Numbers			
Serial	Type	C/n	Circumstances
T-001 (6440)	JRF-5	1110	1959 MAS acquisition from USA
T-002 (37800) & 126	JRF-5	B-53	1959 MAS acquisition from USA
T-003 (37776) & 127	JRF-5	B-29	1959 MAS acquisition from USA
128	JRF-6B	1146	1966 gift from Argentina
129	JRF-6B	1144	1966 gift from Argentina

Aircraft T-001 to T-003 were previously active with the US Coast Guard where they were locally known as 'JRF-5G'. T-001 was lost on 17th November 1959 in the course of delivery. Aircraft 127 and 129 are not confirmed as having worn the new serials. The previous identity of T-001 is based on incidental evidence provided by the US Coast Guard (see below).

The Registration of N3282, N3283 & N3284 to Walter B von Kleinsmid

The disposal of the four ANP Goose aircraft in 1968-69, three of which were subsequently to fly in the USA, led to a most complicated dialogue between the buyers, Walter B von Kleinsmid and Wilton R Probert of Long Beach, CA and the FAA. The correspondence further involved Grumman, the US Coast Guard and the Paraguayan and Argentine Navies, all of whom offered assistance in identifying the original aircraft. The outcome of the FAA's attempts to understand the true provenance of the three offered aircraft and the switching of airframes by the buyers was that only one aircraft would be registered 'correctly'.

N3282 – This registration was initially applied for in connection with G-21A c/n

'1130' before it was amended to '1110'. However there is post-delivery photographic evidence from the USA that shows N3282 still wearing the former ANP serial 128 and there is no reason to think that it is anything other than the old Argentine JRF-6B 0186/MNA-12 (c/n 1146). However it was registered as a G-21A c/n 1110 – and this is why. The correspondence referred to is from the FAA files for all three aircraft.

The correspondence commenced on 18th April 1968 with von Kleinsmid discussing two aircraft, 128 and T-003, and on 25th April 1968 he was given the registrations N3282 and N3283. In an effort to find a c/n for 128 (N3282) Argentina correctly identified it as their former aircraft 0186. Grumman, involved in the conversation by the FAA, apparently misunderstood this and believed that they were talking about an aircraft known to them as 0186B (the obscure 1942 BuAer identity for c/n 1130, built as FP480 for the Royal Navy and still active in 1968 as N93G).

The Bill of Sale from the ANP to von Kleinsmid dated 27th May 1968 thus quoted 1130 as the c/n and 128 as the previous identity and that same day a Certificate of Registration was applied for using the c/n 1130. This was rejected by the FAA and von Kleinsmid turned to the US Coast Guard for help (Grumman having by then suggested that it might be c/n 1110, the JRF-5 6440 that Grumman

The Aviación Navale Paraguaya's JRF-6B 128 (c/n 1146) may well have the distinction of being the world's last operational military Goose. This picture, taken circa 1967 shortly before its retirement, sees the aircraft moored on one of Paraguay's major rivers. The aircraft was used largely on mail and general freight and passenger-carrying activities by the Servicio Aeronaval with regular calls made to otherwise remote communities. (via B Risseeuw)

Seen here, probably at Long Beach, CA, in late-1968, N3282 was registered to Walter B von Kleinsmid as a G-21A with the c/n '1110'. The photograph shows the aircraft still to be wearing the Aviación Navale Paraguaya (ANP) serial 128. As explained in the text, 128 was in reality the former Argentine Misión Naval Paraguaya JRF-6B 'MNA-12' and the true c/n was therefore 1146. The black painted hull line is typical of the Argentine naval aircraft and unlike those of the original ANP JRF-5s. (S Krauss)

Also seen soon after delivery, N3283 (c/n 1144) still wears its one-time Argentine naval serial 0294 albeit perhaps freshly applied. Before becoming N3283 in 1968, 0294 had served most recently with the Argentine mission in Paraguay as 'MNA-11' prior to its donation to the ANP as 129. There is however some doubt whether the serial number '129' was ever worn in ANP use and this might explain its absence at the time of this photograph. Close examination of the picture reveals a trace line of the former blister window unique to the JRF-6B and, as with N3282, the previous Argentine black hull paintwork is also diagnostic and can be seen to be identical to that of MNA-11 illustrated on page 86. Thus the c/n of N3283 should be 1144 and not 'B-29' as it was registered. (Fred J Knight Collection)

Although the history of N3283, explained elsewhere, is complex and not absolutely confirmed by known documentation, this photograph goes some way to explaining why N3283 was registered with the incorrect c/n 'B-29'. Here the former ANP JRF-5 T-003 (127) can be seen at Asunción in 1968 with the last digit of 'N3283' deliberately erased. T-003 was the former USCG aircraft 37776 (c/n B-29) and it is thought to have been the intended N3283. For reasons that are assumed to have been more about the state of the airframe rather than any legal problems, the registration N3283 was switched from JRF-5 T-003 to JRF-6B 129. This airframe was apparently abandoned and stripped of parts at Asunción. (Alex Reinhard via Tony Sapienza)

The only one of the three von Kleinsmid/Probert Gooses to be correctly registered with the FAA, N3284 (c/n B-53) was the former ANP JRF-5 126 (once T-002). Seen here post-delivery, paintwork on the engine cowlings and the fuselage/hull can be seen to be similar to that of the 'N3283' (c/n B-29) abandoned at Asunción and dissimilar to that of the JRF-6Bs N3282 (c/n 1146) and N3283 (c/n 1144). The title 'Miss Mañana' was applied during the sale and overhaul process at von Kleinsmid's request and reflected his frustration with certain bureaucratic processes. (S Krauss)

knew to have been prepared for the ANP in 1959 but which, of course, had been lost on delivery). Eventually, on 26th July 1968, a CofR using c/n 1110 was issued.

N3283 – This registration was always assigned to a G-21A, c/n B-29. However it is almost certain that N3283 is actually c/n 1144. This is why:

Walter von Kleinsmid's first correspondence was in connection with aircraft 128 and T-003 and it is assumed that as 128 became N3282 it was his intention that T-003 (c/n B-29) should become N3283 (the N3282 file has a letter dated 21st June 1968 noting that von Kleinsmid had also bought B-29). Correspondence in the N3283 file from 6th August 1968 until the application for a CofR on 2nd October 1968 (issued 7th November 1968) repeatedly refers to this aircraft as the former '0127' c/n B-29 and once 37776 (suggesting, amongst other things, that '0127' was a paper reference for T-003). It was registered as a G-21A, with c/n B-29. However post-delivery photographic evidence from the USA shows N3283 displaying the Argentine serial 0294 on the tail and with other paintwork identical to that of MNA-11. Moreover the photograph appears to show an aircraft with a rivet line trace indicating that a JRF-6B blister window had once been fitted. However, a previous photograph of an aircraft marked

'N3283', reportedly taken at Asunción in 1968, shows different hull paintwork. Moreover, the last digit of the registration has been scrubbed out (thus appearing to be 'N328') as were any traces of the ANP serial.

The logic of this is that N3283 was originally planned for T-003 (B-29/37776) which may never have worn the allocated new serial 127. However, for unknown reasons, von Kleinsmid and Probert replaced it with 0294 (ANP serial 129) without telling the FAA. Thus the original N3283 needed to have its registration adjusted to 'N328' once it had been replaced. It has to be assumed that the hulk of 'N328' (c/n B-29) was picked clean of useful parts and remained in Paraguay.

There is, in the N3284 file, a Bill of Sale dated 3rd December 1968, signed by the Chief of the Argentine Naval Mission in Paraguay, selling an aircraft to Probert. This can only refer to c/n 1144 (ANP 129) that was not officially struck off Argentine charge until 13th September 1968. This transaction would have enabled Probert to swap c/n 1144 for B-29. It is unclear why the FAA would not have been notified of this change.

N3284 – This registration is correctly assigned to G-21A, c/n B-53. However, while the registration is correct there is within the FAA file some bemusing correspondence concerning the provenance

of aircraft 126 (B-53, the former T-002 and US Coast Guard 7800). The file contains a letter from Probert to the FAA dated 9th June 1969 trying to expedite the registration, noting it to be B-53 ex 37800, previously with the Argentine Navy. Of course this was not true - 37800 was never an Argentine aircraft (unless the ANP had sold it to them!). The Bill of Sale dated 3rd December 1968 in this file selling an aircraft from the MNA to Probert must refer to ANP 129 (c/n 1144).

Summary

von Kleinsmid's original intention seems to have been to acquire only two aircraft, 128 and T-003 (127), but it was decided subsequently that he should take a third, 126. The fourth aircraft, 129 which was probably never active with the ANP, was added to the deal later and used to replace T-003 (127). It was probably not realised until late in the day that one of the former Argentine aircraft (almost certainly 129) had not been transferred legally to Paraguay and thus had to be purchased from Argentina.

The confusion about aircraft identities seems to stem from perhaps understandable Paraguayan ignorance of the aircraft histories, Grumman's innocent muddying of the waters and some very complicated footwork by von Kleinsmid and his partner Probert.

PERU

CUERPO AERONÁUTICA DEL PERU - THE PERUVIAN AIR CORPS

Goose

In 1938, as part of a modernisation programme, the Air Corps, or more precisely the Cuerpo Aeronáutica del Perú, was authorised to purchase four new G-21A Goose aircraft together with ten Douglas 8A-3P and seven North American NA-50s. The Air Corps intended to use the four G-21As as multi-purpose transport aircraft joining their existing diverse fleet of floatplanes. They would find considerable use in the jungle and rural areas and were referred generally to as 'Grummans' or, more officially, as 'G-21'. The first aircraft was handed over at Bethpage on 24th December 1938 and the last on 1st February 1939. Reportedly three of the aircraft were delivered to Peru on 24th March 1939 while the fourth, coded '2TP-2H', passed through Albrook Field, Panama on delivery on 21st August 1939. The reasons for this apparently late delivery are unknown.

The four aircraft were delivered to the Sección de Transporte of the Escuadrón de Aviación No.2 and wore the appropriate codes '2TP-1H' to '2TP-4H' (the 'H' suffix was indicative of a Hydroaviacion type). Escuadrón de Aviación No.2 was based at Santiago de Surco/Las Palmas, Lima. However, during the acquisition and delivery process there was a major reorganisation of the Cuerpo Aeronáutica's structure and by March 1940 the G-21s were with new users. Three were operational with the 101 Escuadrilla de Transporte at Iquitos and one with the 82 Escuadrilla de Información Maritima at Ancón. Within the new, more complex,

organisation the 101 Escuadrilla was a component of the 51 Escuadrón (written LI) and the 82 Escuadrilla that of the 32 Escuadrón (XXXII). At this stage of their lives all aircraft were involved in the delivery of mail to the remote areas of Peru. The G-21s are not known to have taken any direct rôle in the war with Ecuador in July 1941.

The appearance of two aircraft at Albrook, Panama in August 1941, reportedly coded 'XXII-84-9' and 'XXII-84-10', suggests that by then two aircraft had been transferred to the 84 Escuadrilla, a component of the 22 Escuadrón. As will be realised, the new coding system continued to show Escuadrón, Escuadrilla and 'plane-in-Escuadrilla' references. Both the 84 and 101 Escuadrilla were single-purpose, composite flights operating several types of aircraft, but by October 1941 there had been further changes with two aircraft now assigned to the 32 Escuadrón and two assigned to the 51 Escuadrón. The 84 Escuadrilla would appear to have been but a brief user of the Goose.

On 24th April 1942 the Servicio Aerofotográfico Nacional (SAN) was created and its initial equipment at Lima-Las Palmas comprised two G-21s and a light aircraft. From now on aerial survey and general photographic duties would be an important rôle for the aircraft and the first such task was the comprehensive photography of the capital city, Lima. One of the two aircraft on strength in September 1942, assumed to have been transferred from the 32 Escuadrón, was coded '29-3-2'. Escuadrón 29 de Comando was a headquarters unit, based at Lima-Collique and the relevance of the code is unclear and could indicate an allocation unrelated to the SAN. This aircraft retained the original

delivery colour scheme although the pre-delivery unit badge had by now been either removed or weathered off. The SAN was organised within the Cuerpo Aeronáutica's 2nd Air Region, Lima, and continued to operate the photo-modified G-21s for several years. In mid-1942 a single aircraft coded 'XXXI-82' was reportedly in use with 31 Escuadrón.

On 27th May 1943 Peru formally requested the supply of three more aircraft from the USA under Lend-Lease conditions as part of a larger aid package but the request was refused. As far as is known, neither the Cuerpo Aeronáutica nor the later FAP received any more Goose aircraft from any source.

By June 1943 the two Iquitos-based aircraft were being used by the 57 Escuadrón within the local 5th Air Region, one of which was coded '57-2-1'. As was often the case with the codes of this era the '57' was presented within a pennant, forward of the '2-1' marking. On 6th December 1943, the first loss occurred when an unidentified aircraft (but either c/n 1050 or 1052) was written off after an injury-free accident on a tributary of the Madre de Dios River in south-east Peru. Subsequent to the accident, the Cuerpo Aéreo continued to station two aircraft at Iquitos but it is unclear whether the aircraft lost in December 1943 was from the SAN or the 57 Escuadrón.

In January 1944 the SAN was using at least one camera-ship from Las Palmas with the code '20-1-1' (the inference being that the SAN flight unit was the 20 Escuadrón, although this remains unconfirmed. From photographic evidence '29-3-2' and '20-1-1' could be the same aircraft). In March 1944 there were two aircraft on strength at Las Palmas but in July only one and that was on loan from

The Cuerpo Aeronáutica del Perú was an early pre-war purchaser of the G-21A. '2TP-1H' (c/n 1050) is seen here, factory-fresh, at Bethpage in late 1938 probably at the point of delivery. The somewhat complicated code, explained in the text, would be short-lived reflecting a major reorganisation of Peruvian Army aviation. While two of the Peruvian aircraft would enjoy long lives '2TP-1H' would unfortunately not be one of them, it being one of the aircraft lost in accidents in December 1943 and April 1945. (Harold G Martin via A Krieger)

Iquitos. At Iquitos the 57 Escuadrón appears to have been inactivated by March 1944 by which time a new unit, the 54 Escuadrón de Transporte had one G-21 on strength. By July its strength had been increased to two, one of which was on loan to the SAN. Strength was further reduced to only two aircraft after an unidentified Goose was lost in an accident in Ancón Bay on 10th April 1945. Again there were no injuries. By October 1946 a new user-unit had emerged. This was the 61 Escuadrón Fotográfico at Las Palmas operating one Goose as part of a mixed fleet (the second aircraft was not on strength at that time). There was still one on strength in January 1949 operating alongside a Douglas 8A-3P, a Curtiss-Wright T-32, a Fairchild PT-26 and a Lockheed PV-2, but by June 1950 both surviving G-21s were now on strength.

On 18th July 1950 the Fuerza Aérea del Perú (FAP) was created. Among a number of organisational changes a new three-digit serial system had already appeared, grouping aircraft by operational purpose. The two G-21A became 323 and 324 although it is not clear exactly when this took place.

By mid-1954, the two surviving aircraft were both on the strength of the 31 Escuadrón de Información Estratégica based at Piura in northern Peru. The 31 Escuadrón was a mixed-type unit using the venerable Douglas 8A-5 (A-33) and Lockheed PV-2 as primary equipment. Given the squadron's primary role, it is assumed that at this stage of their lives the aircraft were used as general utility aircraft albeit with a photographic capability. They remained assigned to the 31 Escuadrón until at least June 1958 but were sold as surplus soon after on 15th July 1958. They were acquired on behalf of the Californian airline Avalon Air Transport both aircraft being overhauled on their behalf by the FAP prior to delivery in November 1958.

Colours and Markings

Pre-delivery monochrome photographs of the aircraft show what appears to have been a silver or white fuselage with a dark lower hull and anti-glare area forward of the windscreen. Engine and cowlings were dark (red?) and a harpoon-styled flash ran the length of the fuselage. The standard Cuerpo Aeronáutica roundels were worn above and below the wings and the traditional rudder stripes were full-height. An elaborate winged globe was painted on both sides of the nose and the original code was worn high on the tail-fin. As previously explained the aircraft changed units many times and the original markings became progressively more weathered as time passed. New codes were applied, usually to the fuselage area, and the globe device was lost.

The Cuerpo Aeronáutica and subsequently the Fuerza Aérea regarded manufacturer's numbers (or previous identities such as US military serials) to be the permanent aircraft identity and the complex unit codes, carried on virtually all aircraft, were changed regularly as aircraft moved between units. This was still the situation after the introduction of the first post-war three-digit serial system although the two surviving Goose aircraft retained their new numbers 323 and 324 until withdrawal in 1958.

Serial Numbers (with Initial and Final Codes)			
Serial	*Type*	*C/n*	*Circumstances*
2TP-1H	G-21A Goose	1050	G-21A production 1938/39
2TP-2H (323)	G-21A Goose	1051	G-21A production 1938/39
2TP-3H	G-21A Goose	1052	G-21A production 1938/39
2TP-4H (324)	G-21A Goose	1053	G-21A production 1938/39

PORTUGAL

AVIAÇÃO NAVAL - NAVAL AVIATION

Goose

The Goose was recognised by the Aviação Naval as potentially the most suitable of all available aircraft to meet their multiple needs and obligations at a time when Portugal was anxious to preserve its neutrality and to prevent the occupation of the Azores. In defining a suitable specification to meet these needs, the Portuguese government and the manufacturer would create a unique Goose model, the G-21B, which would become at the same time Grumman's only true seaplane. Driven by a need to maximise range in order to fly from mainland Portugal to the Azores, the Aviação Naval sacrificed the weight of an undercarriage (some 300lbs) for increased fuel uplift, the defining feature of the G-21B. The G-21B was fitted additionally with bow and dorsal .303in machine guns and two racks for 100lb bombs. The contract for 12 aircraft that were given the serial numbers 97 to 108, was signed on 19th December 1939.

The aircraft were manufactured rapidly

Portugal was the sole purchaser of the G-21B seaplane variant of the Goose. It was built to the Aviação Naval's unique specification and as such it served well both in Portugal and the Azores although its inherent limitations probably made it an unattractive second-hand purchase and none saw any subsequent civilian use. 97 (c/n 1088) was effectively the prototype aircraft and is here seen at Montijo, soon after the transfer of the fleet from Bom Sucesso in 1953, sitting on its beaching trolley, a necessary feature of the G-21B's operation. The colour-scheme is that of the Aviação Naval with the anchor marking displayed on the tail.
(FAP/BA.6 Montijo via Luís Tavares)

Serial Numbers

Serial	Type	C/n	Circumstances
97 to 108	G-21B	1088 to 1099	G-21B production 1940

and after local test flying were delivered by sea to the Centro de Aviação Naval (CAN) at Bom Sucesso, Lisbon. Deliveries took place in the spring and summer of 1940 with two received in April, four in each of May and June and the final pair in July. The aircraft entered operational service in June and were immediately involved in a wide variety of tasks including air-sea rescue, transport and sundry photographic and reconnaissance work. Although Portugal was a non-belligerent, the European war was very close. In December 1940 three aircraft, 100, 103 and 105, were flown to the Azores where they would remain at the Ponta Delgada base on São Miguel until the end of the war. 100 was lost in a storm in November 1941 and was replaced by 102. These aircraft saw considerable action in the search and rescue roles, eventually working alongside the allied forces and featuring in a number of high-profile rescue actions. In metropolitan Portugal the force was split between Bom Sucesso and Aveiro, with two aircraft maintained at the latter base. Another aircraft, 108, was lost when it crashed on take-off at Lisbon in August 1943 killing one of the crew who was drowned.

The Ponta Delgada base was closed in 1946 and the aircraft, now replaced in the Azores by more efficacious land-based types, returned to Portugal where the primary base continued to be Bom Sucesso with aircraft routinely detached to Aveiro. On 27th May 1952 Portugal created an independent air force, the Força Aérea Portuguesa (FAP), and all naval aircraft were reassigned to the FAP. The Goose fleet was transferred additionally in 1953 to a new station at Montijo in Lisbon and in June 1954 this base was re-titled, Base Aérea 6 (BA-6) Montijo. Nine aircraft were so transferred, the 'missing' aircraft, 98, having been lost to the inventory by then. By 1953, most of the Goose fleet had acquired the prefix letter 'G' to their serials but it appears that no attempt was made to renumber the Goose into the new FAP four-digit serial system (the range 9401 etc was allocated and it may be that no-one bothered because of the obsolescence of the Goose).

It would appear that the new FAP was not entirely thrilled to acquire a fleet of elderly seaplanes and the evidence is that they were little used, although one or two were to have several more years of service ahead of them. By mid-June 1953, G-99 was engineless at Montijo awaiting scrapping and what may have been the only five airworthy aircraft were soon re-located to BA-7, Aveiro. The fleet then faded away with aircraft progressively scrapped at Aveiro, presumably as they ran out of flight hours. One aircraft, G-105, was reportedly allocated a civil registration (CS-AHF) circa 1956 but this was apparently not used

and may be a reflection of the limited commercial appeal of a pure seaplane. The last three airworthy aircraft appear to have been G-97, G-103 and G-107, all active in the mid-late 1950s with G-103 still flying on 13th May 1959, the last reliably reported date. The final recorded sighting of any FAP Goose was that of the scrapped G-106 at OGMA, Alverca in April 1963. Sadly no Portuguese Goose was preserved by the FAP, a fact made the more significant by the unique nature of the G-21B.

Aircraft Colours and Markings

Throughout their lives the Goose remained in a natural metal finish with the keel painted black. In naval service the 'Cross of Christ' markings were applied only to the upper and lower wing surfaces. The rudder was green (forward) and red (rear) and the serial was applied in black numerals on the rear fuselage. A small anchor marking was displayed on the tail. Aircraft based at Aveiro wore the 'black swallow' base markings. After transfer to the FAP, the 'Cross of Christ' markings were also applied to the fuselage sides and one of each of the under and over wing markings was replaced by the serial, by now with the 'G' prefix. New tail markings comprised the rectangular Portuguese flag with the serial above. Where relevant, the Aveiro 'swallow' motif was retained.

Widgeon

Following the successful introduction of the Goose, the Aviação Naval saw the smaller, more flexible Widgeon as a complementary aircraft at a time when Portugal's ASR commitments, particularly in the Azores, were increasing rapidly. The Portuguese order for 12 model G-44s was placed shortly after the US Coast Guard had ordered their first aircraft and was therefore arguably the first true 'military' order for what had been seen previously as a corporate and leisure type.

The first aircraft were on the point of delivery to Portugal when Japan attacked US installations at Pearl Harbor on 7th December 1941 and brought the United States into WWII. One immediate effect was a US moratorium on the export of military supplies to foreign nations, pending clarification of individual circumstances and the investigation of any potential benefit to the United States of retaining appropriate goods for domestic use. Although no documentary evidence has been discovered it is certain that these 12 aircraft, several completed and the others in production, would have been so scrutinised and it is suspected that a batch of BuAer serials, 09805 to 09816, was set aside for their potential emergency acquisi-

tion. In the event the order was cleared for export and deliveries began immediately with the first aircraft handed over on 22nd December 1941. Two more followed in December with seven more in January and two in February 1942.

As was the case with the Goose, the fleet was split between the CAN's home headquarters at Bom Sucesso and the Azores base at Ponta Delgada, although a higher proportion of the Widgeon fleet, perhaps six aircraft, was assigned to the latter base. As with the Goose, the Ponta Delgada-based Widgeons had a busy war and they remained in-theatre until 1945 when they were brought back to metropolitan Portugal although three are reported to have been returned to Ponta Delgada in 1947. Unlike the G-21B Goose, the amphibious Widgeon could be used from conventional airfields and by 1947 at least three of the 11 surviving aircraft were operating from Portela airfield, Lisbon. Post-war, the Widgeon found further use on special missions in support of government agencies. Between 1946 and 1947 aircraft 130 supported the Hydrographic Mission to Cabo Verde (Cape Verde) and then between 1948 and 1952 to Guinea (Guinea-Bissau). Similarly, 129 supported the mission to Mozambique between 1947 and 1952 after which it was retained for the governor's use (it was eventually returned and is now displayed at the FAP Museum, Alverca). For such tasks, the Widgeon was an ideal aircraft.

An audit in January 1949 recorded six aircraft at Bom Sucesso, 119, 123 to 125, 127 and 128. 129 and 130 were overseas and 120, 122 and 126 are assumed to have been elsewhere in Portugal with 121 already lost to the inventory. There were no further losses or formal withdrawals by May 1952 when the FAP was created and all the aircraft in Portugal were reassigned to BA-6 Montijo. Like the Goose, the Widgeons, or at least some of them, had acquired the letter 'W' as a serial prefix but, unlike the Goose, a small number of them would eventually wear new four-digit FAP serials. While the fleet was based at Montijo in the mid-1950s, aircraft were regularly deployed away to AB-1 Portela where a naval detachment, the Portela Aeronaval Aircraft Section, was maintained, as well as to BA-7 Aveiro. Major overhauls were normally undertaken by OGMA at Alverca, north of Lisbon.

The run-down of the Widgeon fleet began in the mid-1950s. By November 1954 the fleet was no longer apparently being used on the water and it was suggested that the time between overhauls might therefore be extended from 500 to 600 flight hours. By 1956, the FAP appears to have had six airworthy aircraft W-123, W-125, W-127, W-130, 2401 (which was probably the former W-126) and 2405. W-119 and W-120 had by then been, or were in the process of becoming, civilianised as CS-AHE and CS-AHG.

The final years of the Widgeon are not well understood. Aircraft 2401 was based

Right: *When the Portuguese Air Force disposed of Widgeon W-120 (c/n 1242) in the mid-1960s it passed into civilian registration for several years. After final retirement as CS-AHG circa 1970 it remained unused at Lisbon for several years before being acquired by the Museu de Marinha, Lisbon. Beautifully restored in original Aviação Naval colours, the aircraft is currently displayed as '128'.* (Fred J Knight)

at Portela from 1956 until at least late 1958, by which time it was on the strength of the local Esquadra 31 while 2405 was based at Aveiro in 1956 and was seen at Portela in 1959. The last reliable report of a Widgeon flying is from Aveiro in 1963, although the serial has not been identified. 2401 and 2405 remain the only reported aircraft with the four-digit serials, but the assumption is that others were at least allocated. What is unclear is how many, if any, of the other aircraft actually wore the new serials post-1956. Happily two of the fleet survive on permanent display in Portuguese museums.

Aircraft Colours and Markings

Like the Goose, the Widgeon remained in a natural metal finish with the keel sometimes painted green. In naval service the 'Cross of Christ' markings were only applied to the upper and lower wing surfaces. The rudder was green (forward) and red (rear) and the serial was applied in black numerals on the rear fuselage. A

small anchor marking was sometimes displayed on the tail. Aircraft based at Aveiro wore the 'black swallow' base markings. After transfer to the FAP the 'Cross of Christ' markings were also applied to the fuselage sides and one of each of the under and over wing markings was replaced by the serial, by now with the 'W' prefix. New tail-fin markings comprised the rectangular Portuguese flag

with the serial above. Where relevant, the Aveiro 'swallow' motif was retained.

As explained above, a new serial range was allocated to the fleet when it was transferred to the FAP although it is not known how many or which aircraft received them. These serials, of which only 2401 and 2405 are confirmed, were then applied only to some (two?) aircraft, presumably reflecting the low priority of the task.

Serial Numbers			
Serial	Type	C/n	Circumstances
119 to 130	G-44	1241 to 1252	G-44 production 1941/42

SWEDEN

FLYGVAPNET - ROYAL SWEDISH AIR FORCE

Goose

The Flygvapnet acquired a single Goose from Norway in 1951 to provide air ambulance and search and rescue services in northern Sweden. Officially authorised to replace the Flygvapnet's sole Beech 18R, transferred to other duties, the Goose would remain in military service until its unfortunate demise in 1962.

LN-SAB, originally the Royal Navy JRF-6B, FP484, was acquired from Lars Solberg of Bergen in 1951, although the precise purchase date is uncertain. It entered service with the F21 (Norrbottens Flygbaskar) wing at Kallax, Luleå on 9th November 1951 assigned to the Ambulance Flight. In Swedish use the Goose was designated the Tp81 and was accordingly

numbered 81001, carrying the individual code '31' (this became '60' in 1955). It was painted in an overall high-visibility orange colour scheme and, in addition to normal Flygvapnet national markings, it also carried prominent red crosses. For winter operations the Goose was fitted with skis.

Although very successfully operated in its intended role, its tasks were transferred

progressively to more modern equipment in the private sector and its Flygvapnet duties became those of general transport and communications. Its career was brought to an abrupt end on 5th April 1962 when it crashed on take-off from the civilian airfield at Hemaven in central Sweden. The crew escaped with minor injuries.

Serial Number			
Serial	Type	C/n	Circumstances
81001	G-21A	1134	LN-SAB acquired Oct51

Right: *Sweden's Flygvapnet acquired its only Goose, 81001 (c/n 1134), from a civilian source in Norway in 1951. It spent its entire 11 year service life with the F21 (Norrbottens Flygbaskar) wing at Kallax, Luleå, initially operating as a medical evacuation aircraft. In this posed, post-1955 photograph it can be seen in full ambulance markings and in the winter, ski-equipped configuration.* (Fred J Knight Collection)

TAIWAN

REPUBLIC OF CHINA AIR FORCE

Goose

There is some evidence that a single aircraft, owned and used by the CIA in bogus RoCAF markings, was 'evaluated' by the RoCAF circa 1955 for potential use by the Air Force's VIP flight. The existence of this Goose with the serial 'OA9-0002' is considered justification for some explanatory comments here, although it is evident that the RoCAF did not actually own or operate the Goose, and that 'OA9-0002' was a bogus serial.

In July 1952 Western Enterprises Inc (WEI), a CIA cover company, acquired a former JRF-6B (G-21A), N1376V, for use in Taiwan. This aircraft had been owned previously by the Far Eastern Foundation of San Francisco, CA and the Air Carrier Service Corporation of Washington DC, and although its date of arrival in Taiwan is uncertain, it is likely to have been in late 1952, and it was certainly in place by November of that year. N1376V was maintained and flown by Civil Air Transport (CAT) personnel in the early

1950s, on behalf of Western Enterprises Inc, and was primarily used in a communications role supporting WEI activities on the disputed offshore Chinese Islands. In this role it frequently acted operationally in support of a PBY-5A, but was also used routinely as a VIP communications vehicle. In such circumstances it was an occasional visitor to Taoyuan AFB.

Monochrome photography shows the aircraft to be devoid of markings apart from the invented serial 'OA9-0002' beneath the port wing. Between 1952 and 1955, the American CAT crews used the aircraft in support of their activities in and around the islands off the coast of mainland China. Known to its pilots as '002', the Goose was apparently retired in 1955 and then became available for sale and at that time it was viewed as a potential personal aircraft for the President, General Chiang Kai-shek. According to local sources this plan failed after the aircraft was damaged in Chinese

hands. Again, according to the local sources, two RoCAF pilots crashed the aircraft when attempting a water landing at Tongkang, Pintung in southern Taiwan, and this accident could have occurred at any time between 1955 and May 1957 when the aircraft was sold to James Walker Lassiter of Falls Church, VA (its value in April 1959 was stated to have been $9,156.74). Lassiter, it should be noted, was a long-term WEI employee who had been involved in Chinese training programmes since at least 1952.

Ownership of the aircraft subsequently passed through the hands of several US agencies (see the individual aircraft history), until finally reaching the Air Carrier Service Corporation of Washington, DC on 5th July 1960, after which it was fitted with ferry tanks in August and was flown, presumably from Taiwan, to Japan. It was officially exported to Sekiya & Co Ltd of Tokyo on 13th September 1960, and became JA5063.

Serial Number			
Serial	Type	C/n	Circumstances
N1376V	G-21A	1153	CIA use 1951-1957
Marked as 'OA9-0002' in the style of the RoCAF.			

Right: *Many of the Grumman Goose had highly colourful careers and this was most certainly one of them. Following its wartime service with the Royal Navy, this JRF-6B (c/n 1153) spent time in Guatemala in quasi-military service where it was known as an 'OA-9'. Via several changes of ownership it became N1376V and by 1952 it was in the hands of the CIA in Taiwan being flown by Civil Air Transport pilots with the bogus ROCAF serial 'OA9-0002'. N1376V was eventually sold and continued to fly in Japan before returning to the USA in 1965. Before its untimely destruction in a Canadian hangar fire in 1999 it found time to feature in the appropriately-titled 1985 Arnold Schwarzenegger movie 'Commando'. '002' is seen here outside the maintenance shop at Tainan in the early 'fifties.*

(Leon Callaghan via Clarence Fu – Leon's father took the photo)

THAILAND

ROYAL THAI NAVY

Widgeon

Thailand's naval air arm was a brief and poorly-understood user of the Widgeon. Its mixed fleet of aircraft at Chantaburi included perhaps as many as six aircraft that were obtained commercially during the late 1940s and 1950. Only one of these acquisitions (c/n 1449 received circa 1950) has been identified positively. However, following its involvement in the failed coup of June 1951, the naval air arm was disestablished and its assets were passed to the Royal Thai Air Force.

Thus the Royal Thai Air Force became the accidental operators of the naval

The Royal Thai Air Force museum at Don Muang, Bangkok had acquired its G-44A Widgeon B.S6-2/94 (c/n 1449) by the mid-1960s and it remains on public display to this day. The Thai Widgeons were commercial purchases made by the Navy in the late 'forties but which fell into Air Force hands in 1951 after a failed coup attempt by the Navy. This photograph was taken on 8th March 2012 and shows the aircraft in remarkably good condition after the whole museum site was under three feet of water in the late-2011 floods. The rear fuselage band and 'Rescue' title are in yellow, with the national insignia on the rudder.

(Robert J Ruffle)

Widgeon fleet on 12th July 1951 when the naval air arm was disbanded. The naval aircraft, located at Chantaburi, were then re-formed into 7 Wing of the Royal Thai Air Force. Five Widgeons were so adopted in 1951 (the Thai year 2494) and although little is known of their serials or history they remained in service until 1956. Only two aircraft, however, one of which is c/n 1449 currently displayed at the Royal Thai Air Force museum, have been identified. Widgeon c/n 1403, previously NC41972, was delivered originally to the 'Civil

Aviation School, Bangkok' before transfer to the Air Force in June 1951. In Thai Air Force use the serial type prefix 'B.S6' was used by the Widgeon and the individual

aircraft number was appended with the year of acquisition. The previous naval serials are unknown and are therefore ignored here.

Serial Number			
Serial	Type	C/n	Circumstances
B.S6-2/94	G-44A	1449	N86623 gained by Navy circa 1950
'No.4'	G-44A	1403	Domestic acquisition Jun51
'No.4' would presumably have been BS.6-4/94 but this remains unconfirmed. Assumed aircraft B.S6-1/94 and B.S6-3/94 may have been either G-44As or former military J4F/G-44s.			

UNITED KINGDOM

ROYAL NAVY & ROYAL AIR FORCE

Goose

Variants and Acquisition

To understand the acquisition, numbering and use of the British Goose fleet is to understand considerably more than merely the brief history of 50 aircraft, none of which survived in the inventory beyond 1946. Here the various threads of the subject are considered chronologically, regardless of which particular element of the military (or indeed the Empire) was involved.

During the early stages of World War II British industry struggled to produce the vast quantities of military equipment urgently required by its forces and consequently increasingly large aircraft orders were placed in the United States. The US Lend-Lease Act of March 1941 permitted the purchase of war material by the US armed forces for loan or lease to countries whose defence was considered to be essential to the United States of America. In 1941 this most notably affected the United Kingdom, enabling it to receive urgently-needed equipment without the previous financial or production constraints. With the British Air Commission (BAC) in Washington acting as the UK's purchasing agent, there had already been considerable negotiation with the US government in respect of the Goose as Grumman struggled to balance the demands of three major customers – the US Navy, the RCAF and the British. A major problem, by no means unique to Grumman, had been a shortage of engines with Pratt & Whitney and their subcontractors unable to keep pace with the demand for the R-985 Wasp Junior radials. Lend-Lease would enable Grumman and its suppliers to increase output while remaining within the US neutrality constraints.

The acquisition of the Goose by the British had been a subject of discussion for some considerable time before the British Air Commission formally submitted a requisition (BSC.666 dated 21st April 1941) for 50 G-21A models together with

spares and support equipment to be supplied under Lend-Lease terms. The British had been attracted to the Goose initially for much the same reasons as other early customers, perceiving it as a robust utility aircraft that could fulfil a number of functions. These included Air Sea Rescue (ASR), the training of wireless operators, observers and navigators and, in an emergency, casualty evacuation.

There were, however, several reasons for the delay in finalising the 'order'. On the British side, funds were moved constantly between projects as priorities changed and it is believed that 50 serials (BW778 to BW827) were previously 'pencilled in' for the project before it was cancelled temporarily (the serials were subsequently reallocated to another project which was itself subsequently cancelled). On the American side, Grumman's capacity was limited by local peace-time politics, the conflicting needs of home customers, component shortages and supply bottlenecks. As mentioned previously there were, most significantly, shortages of the Pratt & Whitney Wasp Junior engines and Great Britain had accordingly purchased these and other engines independently as part of the greater procurement strategy.

The 50 G-21A as specified on the Requisition for Defense Articles (RFDA), reproduced on the next page, were to be fitted with the Wasp Junior SB-2 engine (17 ship-sets to come from British reserves) or the Wright R-975-E3 but, as delivered, the aircraft came with the Pratt & Whitney R-985-AN6 as per the normal JRF-5 fit. They were ordered for Britain by the US Navy on contract LL-86447 and were referenced as the JRF-6B (the 'B' suffix indicated Britain). Essentially this was a JRF-5 with large fuselage blister-type windows and customer-specific instrumentation and radios but lacking the camera hatch in the hull. In Royal Navy use, the aircraft was to be known as the Goose Mk IA to distinguish it from the originally planned version with the Wasp Junior SB-2 engine. The serial block FP475 to FP524 was allocated and deliveries ran from January 1942 until March 1943. Shortly before deliveries commenced, it was realised by the US Navy that these Lend-Lease aircraft possessed no formal

US identities and, being US property, they were therefore given the naval administrative identities '0181B' to '0230B'. These were not the manufacturer's numbers nor were they BuAer serial numbers; they were simply clerical references identifying US property. As delivered, FP496 to FP499 and FP521 to FP523 were fitted with radar.

This was a major production order for Grumman, coming as it did prior to the US entry into the war, and its inevitable effect was to temporarily slow production of the JRF-5 for the US Navy in the early months of 1942 at the point when the US Navy desperately needed the aircraft for coastal defence. It also meant that when the USAAF urgently needed a batch of aircraft in late 1942 there was nowhere else to go for them except to the British line. Thus FP500 and FP505 to FP509 were appropriated for American use prior to delivery with FP500 going to the state of Bolivia and the others to sundry US military attachés in Central America. This decision appears to have been made when construction was well advanced and circumstantial evidence suggests that three of these aircraft would have been radar-equipped for the Royal Navy and that this equipment eventually found its way into the late-production aircraft FP521 to FP523.

While the JRF-6B acquisition process rumbled on, the first British military Goose entered service in November 1941. G-21A NC3022 (c/n 1055) was purchased on 22nd September 1941 by the charity British American Ambulance Corps Inc, of Lexington Avenue, NY. This was then gifted to the British Government for use as an air ambulance (and had this not happened NC3022 would doubtless have found itself serving with the US military within a few months). It was allocated to RAF Air Headquarters, Middle East and was shipped to Egypt, where it was locally allotted the serial HK822, and simply referred to as a Goose. Its subsequent service life and ultimate demise in the hands of the RAAF is detailed below and in its individual history.

The convoluted history of Lord Beaverbrook's Goose, G-AFKJ (c/n 1049) is a story in itself but, in brief, this aircraft was brought to the United States prior to

ROUTING (Not to be filled in by requisitioner)	FORM 1	*666* No.
☐ War ☐ Maritime Comm. ☐ Navy ☐ State ☐ OPM ☐ Treasury ☐ Agriculture ☐	REQUISITION FOR DEFENSE ARTICLES (Under the Act of March 11, 1941)	April 21, 1941 Date United Kingdom Requisitioner

British Refs: BAC/ 2301	Air No. 2004	BAC/23- B	AL. 52

1. Will orders placed by the United States Government for the material requisitioned herein be covered by direct cash reimbursement to the United States Government?...No......

2. Articles (If possible, use continuation sheet(s) for detailed specifications; otherwise attach one complete set of drawings and specifications to each copy of form):

   A. Quantity and description (include mark, model, or other identifying designation).

   50 Grumman G.21A Aircraft, including engines (except as shown in Para. 5) and propellers, less guns but including all other military equipment. It is also desired that the aircraft be supplied with a full range of Spares, such as Airframe spares, Spare Engines, (except as shown in Para. 5) Engine Spares, Spare Propellers, Propeller Spares, Spare Instruments and Instrument Spares and spares for all other equipment. P.N.R. Nos. 447-R and 794-A. Certain modifications are required to adapt these aircraft for navigational training.

   B. Specifications...........U.S. Modified.......C. Use....................Air....................
                   U. S., British, other   Army, Navy, Air, other

3. If the articles requisitioned herein are to be installed in or used in the construction of some other article(s), name and identify the basic article(s), indicate number of requisition (Form 1 or 2) or PNR number, or both, covering request for basic article(s), and indicate contract number if contract has been negotiated for basic article(s).

   A. Name and identification of basic article(s):

   Not applicable

   B. Requisition No..............................C. PNR. No............................D. Contract No...........................

4. Delivery desired (by check [X] or, if possible, by quantitative breakdown)

   As soon as possible, schedule to be agreed.

1941			1942			
2nd Quarter	3rd Quarter	4th Quarter	1st Quarter	2nd Quarter	3rd Quarter	4th Quarter

5. Remarks (Justification of request, urgency, general information, etc.):

   The British Ministry of Aircraft Production requested the purchase of the above aircraft and it is understood that the above mentioned P.N.Rs were duly recommended.

   It is the intention that 17 of the above aircraft (PNR 447-R) should be fitted with 34 out of 40 P&W R985-SB2 Engines off a British Air Commission Contract, the six engines over to be used as Spare engines. The remaining 33 aircraft (PNR 794-A) should be fitted with P&W R985-SB2 Engines or Wright R-975-E3 Engines.

   Further particulars may be obtained from the Airframe Section of the British Air Commission, 1785 Massachusetts Ave., Washington, D.C., Telephone, Hobart 9000, Ext. 112.   (Signed)---------------------------------------
                                  F.W. Musson
                  (Title) ...BRITISH AIR COMMISSION...............

   GOVERNMENT OF THE UNITED STATES

mbg

The Requisition for Defense Articles No.666 submitted on 21st April 1941 by the British Ministry of Aircraft Production for 50 G-21A aircraft, plus spares.

Seen here in the United States in 1941 before delivery into the hands of the RAF, G-21A NC3022 (c/n 1055) wears the title of its then owner, the charity British American Ambulance Corps, and the inscription 'Gift Of Baltimore & Ohio-Alton Railroad Employees USA Through Railway Men Of Britain'. NC3022 was delivered eventually as HK822 to the RAF Desert Air Force's Sea Rescue Flight in North Africa in November 1941 and remained in RAF hands until December 1942 when it was given to the RAAF for ambulance duties. Unfortunately it was to be carelessly lost near Benghazi within a few days of its acceptance, making Australia probably the briefest of all military users of the Goose. (Peter M Bowers Collection)

WWII for his occasional use. During his time as Churchill's Minister of Aircraft Production (May 1940 to May 1941) it was in storage at Red Bank, NJ but was released to a US organisation in March 1941 to undertake an extensive intelligence-gathering tour of Latin America. At the conclusion of this tour the aircraft was parked up at the USAAC base at Bolling Field, DC. Both the Army and others attempted to persuade Beaverbrook to sell the aircraft to them but he was reluctant to do so. Beaverbrook's refusal to sell to anyone (he was now the UK's Minister of Supply) was particularly aggravating as the RCAF, the RAF and the USAAC were all urgently seeking second-hand Goose aircraft and the Americans were becoming increasingly sarcastic about strident British

requests for new aircraft! Had the aircraft been located in the UK it might have been impressed long before, but in the United States Beaverbrook could not be forced to sell. Of course the events at Pearl Harbor changed the situation rather suddenly and by January 1942 he had handed over the aircraft to the UK Air Ministry, although by then he had created enough confusion to cause the Ministry of Aircraft Production to initially allocate the aircraft to the RCAF rather than the RAF. It was then taken on RAF charge on 18th February 1942 and overhauled at the Naval Aircraft Factory at Lakehurst, NJ using Lend-Lease funds. Following further delays, it was eventually shipped (as a G-21A) to the UK, where it was allotted the RAF serial MV993 on 31st July 1942,

and was initially used by the Air Transport Auxilliary (ATA).

Three more aircraft that were intended, at least in American minds, for the RAF were the three civilian G-21As that eventually became RCAF 796 to 798 in April 1942. They were acquired by the US Navy reportedly to meet an RAF need for ASR aircraft, theatre unknown, but were rejected by the UK after which they were sold to the RCAF. It has been suggested that the RAF, who allegedly had a need for 15 such aircraft, regarded a batch of three 'civilians' as not worth the acquisition and the deal fell through. There must have been a good deal of confusion here as it will be obvious that there were nowhere near 15 G-21As available on the commercial market in early 1942, the US and Canadian forces already having acquired virtually everything that could be found for their own use.

The final British acquisition was only slightly less complicated. In 1943, the BAC identified a need for four new JRF-5s and accordingly requested them on the British Supply Commission (BSC) requisition N-1147. These aircraft, FP470 to FP473 (see below for c/ns) were delivered from new US Navy production between January and May 1944. It is believed that they were ordered against a Fleet Air Arm requirement and were actually delivered with 'Royal Navy' fuselage titles although none were in fact used by the Fleet Air Arm. Two, FP470 (c/n B-34) and FP472 (c/n B-49), were delivered to the RAF at Oakes Field, Nassau ostensibly for use as ASR aircraft, while FP471 (c/n B-46) and FP473 (c/n B-59), intended for similar duties with the British Commonwealth Air Training Plan (Canada) were delivered to the No.3 Training Command of the Royal

Lord Beaverbrook's much-travelled G-21A Goose G-AFKJ (c/n 1049) came late to national service after much prevarication by the owner. By the time MV993 finally arrived in ATA hands in the summer of 1942 it was wearing regulation camouflage with 'C' type fuselage roundels with yellow rings. This picture is thought to have been taken at its White Waltham base in August 1942. After a busy war, much of it spent in Scotland, it was lost in 1945 after a relatively minor accident on Southampton Water and is thought to have spent the next several years ignominiously dumped on the mud of the nearby River Hamble. (Negative RTP10950c via Fred J Knight Collection)

Canadian Air Force in April and May of 1944. These four aircraft were standard JRF-5 models powered by the R-985-AN-6 engine and were identical to a batch of aircraft being delivered to the RCAF. Thus FP471 and FP473 were delivered to the RCAF at the same time as it was receiving new JRF-5s from the same line (hence RCAF Lend-Lease FP473 c/n B-59 and RCAF Purchase 388 c/n B-60). After some consideration the Canadians, presumably in discussion with the British, called all their new aircraft Mk II (Goose II) and retrospectively identified all their earlier aircraft (powered by Wasp Junior SB engines) as Mk I (Goose I). It is unclear exactly which Mk number the RAF knew FP470 and FP472 as, but we here assume them to have all been the Mk II. The two Canadian aircraft were little used and were returned to the BAC early in 1945 (all other RCAF Goose aircraft were purchases and consequently were retained post-war) and all four Lend-Lease aircraft were returned subsequently to the US Government.

Royal Navy

During the first year of the European war, the Fleet Air Arm undertook its observer training at the increasingly vulnerable HMS *Peregrine* at Ford on the south coast of England. This activity needed urgent relocation and a site at Piarco Savannah, Trinidad was identified for that purpose. The airfield at Piarco was situated about 11 miles to the south-east of Port of Spain and was used already by Pan American Airways and other traffic. An improvement programme, including the laying down of paved runways, was underway, and HMS *Goshawk* as it became was commissioned on 6th November 1940 and became the home of No.1 Observer School. No.749 Squadron formed on 1st January 1941 as the primary training squadron within the school and was equipped initially with the efficacious, albeit primitive, Supermarine Walrus.

Although in practice the Walrus would remain in use with 749 Squadron throughout the war, the rapidly increasing workload demanded a more sophisticated aircraft. Enter the Goose.

The extended procurement process meant that the first Goose did not reach Piarco until January 1942, although further deliveries were rapid and 25 had been received by June of that year. Initial conversion was undertaken with the assistance of US Navy instructors, one of whom was unfortunately killed in the first Goose accident to befall 749 Squadron on 24th February 1942 (a collision involving FP478 and a 750 Squadron Shark). Of the 44 Goose IA delivered to the Royal Navy, only the final aircraft, FP524, did not serve with 749 Squadron and was instead allocated to the Senior British Naval Officer at Roosevelt Field (NAF Mineola), New York in May 1943. Lt (later Capt) Ed Walthall was at Roosevelt Field to oversee the acceptance of aircraft for the Fleet Air Arm and used the Goose IA in furtherance of these duties. With the exception of a handful of others that spent some of their time elsewhere, all the FAA aircraft served with 749 Squadron at Piarco. Of the 43 aircraft so used by 749 Squadron, five were lost in known flying accidents while two others (FP477 and FP485) were withdrawn from use while at Piarco, reasons uncertain. While two of the serious accidents were water-related, neither involved a take-off or landing. Most incidents occurred during the first year of operations and it was unfortunate that after almost three years without a fatal crash, three lives would be lost in an accident in August 1945 only weeks before the squadron would disband. Its task completed, 749 Squadron disbanded on 9th October 1945 and *Goshawk* was paid off in February 1946.

A dearth of official records makes it difficult to be certain exactly when or indeed to what extent any of the Goose IA fleet served elsewhere. As noted above, FP524 was retained on the US mainland, at NAF Roosevelt Field, NY (Mineola) where the Royal Navy had established a modifica-

tion centre, and it was there that it came to grief in February 1944. FP518 was certainly in use with 738 Squadron at Lewiston, ME (HMS *Sakar*) in September 1943 as a utility ship typically ferrying crews to US factories. It was later assigned to NAF Roosevelt Field for use of the Senior British Naval Officer who flew it between February and April 1944, after losing the use of FP524. FP522 was appropriated for a while in 1943 by the Chief British Naval Officer (CBNO) at NAS Norfolk, VA, but there is little evidence to confirm use at stations such as Palisadoes, Jamaica (HMS *Buzzard*) where they have been reported previously by some sources.

To the best of our knowledge, 36 of the FAA's Goose IA fleet were returned to the US Government in late 1945 under the terms of their Lend-Lease acquisition. Those that were not returned were FP477, FP478, FP481, FP485, FP492, FP504, FP519 and FP524 and of these eight only FP477 and FP485 have uncertain fates. The 36 survivors were ferried initially to Miami, FL and temporarily passed into US Navy hands pending their sale as war surplus stock. In January 1946 the aircraft were given the US BuAer numbers 66325 to 66359 (35 randomly allocated) and in December 1946 89492 was belatedly allocated to FP482, presumably correcting a clerical oversight. Subsequently many of these aircraft went on to enjoy lengthy lives in various guises and locations and several survive at the time of writing.

Operations – The British Air Commission (RAF & BCATP/RCAF)

As explained above, four JRF-5s were acquired by the BAC in 1944 under Lend-Lease conditions and were known to the British and Canadians as the Goose II. Two of them, FP471 and FP473, were acquired for ASR and related tasks with the British Commonwealth Air Training Plan (Canada) and were delivered to the No.3 Training Command of the Royal Canadian Air Force in the spring of 1944 and their brief RCAF use is explained on page 92.

The two RAF Goose II, FP470 and FP472, were also delivered in the spring of 1944 and were ferried to Oakes Field, Nassau, Bahamas where they were ostensibly used by 111 Operational Training Unit (OTU). 111 OTU undertook general reconnaissance training on US aircraft and primarily operated Mitchells and Liberators. The two aircraft officially replaced the Walrus in the local ASR role. In July 1945, 111 OTU began its drawdown at Oakes Field in preparation for the return to the UK and had departed officially by 12th September 1945. However, the two Goose aircraft remained at Oakes Field, passing into the hands of 1318 (Communications) Flight which was formed within No.45 Group on 15th January 1946 (the aircraft had previously been taken on charge by 45 Group on 29th November 1945). While with 1318 Flight, the aircraft were used officially for communications

Far and away the largest concentration of operational Goose aircraft during WWII were the aircraft of the Royal Navy's No.749 Squadron based at Piarco, Trinidad. FP480 'W2E' (c/n 1130) was a typical example. These aircraft, known to the US Navy as the JRF-6B and to the British as the Goose IA, were returned to the US authorities in 1945-46 under their Lend-Lease terms and were sold rapidly on the commercial market. By definition a valued type, the JRF-6B fleet was in good condition with generally low hours with some aircraft never used on the water. 65 years later several of them still survive.

(Fred J Knight Collection)

Photographed here at Oakes Field, Nassau in early 1946, Goose II FP470 'GA' (c/n B-34) was one of a pair of Special Duties aircraft delivered under Lease-Lend to No.111 OTU in the spring of 1944. (Special Duties aircraft referred to aircraft retained in the USA/Canada and not delivered to the UK). The aircraft's primary duties are thought to have been of the general and VIP communications nature rather than the support of any training activities and post-war both aircraft passed into the hands of No.1318 (Communications) Flight before being returned to US hands in April 1946. The camouflage scheme was identical to that of the Goose IA fleet albeit with 1944 era 'C' type roundels with yellow rings and including what appears to be the 'Royal Navy' stencilling of the earlier aircraft above the serial.

(W Wass)

activities including the carriage of the Governor and his wife (until mid-1945 they had been the Duke and Duchess of Windsor) on formal business. Of course all good things come to an end, and in February 1946, FP470 and FP472 were officially returned to the US Government and US BuAer numbers 66360 and 66361 were allocated. However, while the US Navy clerk dutifully recorded them as 'unreported' in the accounts for February and March 1946, both aircraft remained at Oakes. Eventually they were ferried to Miami on 3rd April (FP472) and 14th April 1946 (FP470) where they were subsequently reconditioned and sold as surplus to US requirements. FP470 went to Ecuador as HC-SBT with Shell Oil, while FP472 went to Honduras for military service.

Operations – the RAF's Miscellaneous Acquisitions (HK822 & MV993)

Following its transfer into RAF hands, NC3022 was shipped to 107 Maintenance Unit, RAF Kasfareet, Egypt where it was reassembled and made airworthy. It was then 'militarised' at RAF Habbaniyah, Iraq, where it was repainted in an overall matt black colour scheme, given the serial HK822 and the code letter 'N' applied. The actual dates of these events are uncertain but serial allocation is thought to have been in November 1941 with HK822 being allocated to the Desert Air Force's Sea Rescue Flight in North Africa on 25th November 1941, where it served alongside the similarly acquired Fairchild 91 NC16690/HK832 (the unit's headquarters was then at Burg El Arab near Alexandria, Egypt). HK822 was transferred eventually

to 1 Air Ambulance Unit, RAAF in late 1942 and was accepted by the unit at Heliopolis, Egypt on 1st December 1942. Following a ferry flight to Benina on 3rd December, the aircraft was lost during water landing practice on 9th December 1942, 15 miles NNW of Benghazi. The aircraft overturned and sank although the seven occupants escaped and survived.

MV993 was finally accepted by the RAF from Lockheed, Speke on 21st August 1942 and was allocated initially to the Air Transport Auxiliary (ATA) and based at White Waltham. Probably because of its plush interior and pedigree MV993 was transferred to No.24 Squadron, RAF Hendon by February 1943 and was used in the VIP communications role with the name 'Thurso Castle' until July 1944 when it migrated to the recently formed Metropolitan Communications Squadron (MCS) at Hendon (the MCS was created from elements of 24 Squadron and other units on 8th April 1944). Formal transfer appears to have taken place in January 1945. The aircraft was lost at Calshot in September 1945 after a collapsed strut punctured a float which then filled with water leading to its capsizing. MV993 had been the only British military Goose to see any service in the United Kingdom.

Colours and Markings

The Royal Navy's production Goose IA (JRF-6B) fleet was delivered in the so-called 'Temperate Sea' camouflage scheme that comprised the Extra Dark Sea Grey and Dark Slate Grey sides and upper surfaces and Sky undersides. Roundels were traditional 'A' type with yellow outer rings and aircraft were so delivered until at

least November 1942 (it is unclear when or whether the later 'C' roundels – as used on the Navy's Widgeons with yellow outer rings from late 1943 – were ever adopted by 749 Squadron). The over-wing roundels were type 'B' (no white) and without the yellow outer ring. There were no under-wing roundels or serials. Fin-flashes were initially of the 'three equal' design but they may have been replaced by the 'narrow white' design that was introduced in 1942 and was used on the Widgeon fleet. Small black 'Royal Navy' titles were worn on the rear fuselage above the serial number. The large individual aircraft codes applied by 749 Squadron to the forward fuselage were in yellow.

Of the other aircraft, HK822, as explained above, acquired an unusual matt black colour scheme for service with the RAF's Desert Air Force, probably with 'A' type roundels. MV993, however, received a more conventional 'Temperate Land' camouflage of Dark Green and Dark Earth for use within the United Kingdom. Its roundels were 'C' style on the fuselage and 'B' without yellow outer rings above and beneath the wings. The fin flash was of the 'narrow white' style. The serial was applied conventionally to the rear fuselage in black but was not carried beneath the wings. FP470 to FP473 are believed to have been delivered in camouflage identical to that of the Goose IA fleet albeit with 1944 era 'C' type roundels. When photographed in early 1946 use with 1318 Flight, FP470 was coded 'GA' in large white (?) letters on the nose and FP472 is understood to have been 'GB'. FP470 appears to have retained the 'Royal Navy' titles on the lower rear fuselage, notwithstanding its RAF use.

Serial Numbers

Serial	Type	C/n	Circumstances
FP470	JRF-5/Goose II	B-34	Production for BAC
FP471	JRF-5/Goose II	B-46	Production for BAC/BCATP
FP472	JRF-5/Goose II	B-49	Production for BAC
FP473	JRF-5/Goose II	B-59	Production for BAC/BCATP
FP470 to FP473 were Lend-Lease deliveries in 1944.			
FP471 and FP473 were used by the RCAF.			

Serial	Type	C/n	Circumstances
FP475 to FP499	JRF-6B/Goose IA	1125 to 1149	Production for Royal Navy
FP501 to FP504	JRF-6B/Goose IA	1151 to 1154	Production for Royal Navy
FP510 to FP524	JRF-6B/Goose IA	1160 to 1174	Production for Royal Navy
FP475 to FP524 were Lend-Lease deliveries in 1942 and 1943. FP500 and FP505 to FP509 were diverted on the production line and not delivered into British hands.			

HK822	G-21A Goose	1055	NC3022 acquired Nov41
MV993	G-21A Goose	1049	G-AFKJ acquired Feb42

Widgeon

The history of the Widgeon in British hands is almost as complex as that of the Goose and nearly seventy years later some aspects of its brief use remain uncertain. This is most certainly true of the first aircraft to be acquired, the G-44 NC28673. Its appearance at RAF Kasfareet, Egypt in May 1942 has never been fully explained, but it is widely assumed that the aircraft was acquired by or gifted to the British American Ambulance Corps for subsequent presentation to the RAF (it remained registered in the USA as a civilian until 1947). Its RAF career in Africa saw it at 107 MU, Kasfareet from May 1942 but its later movements, probably within West Africa, are unknown until it was reported with a detachment of 1314 Flight at Waterloo, Sierra Leone in 1945 still marked as NC28673 (1314 Flight was headquartered at Accra, Gold Coast). Its fate remains uncertain although it was probably scrapped in West Africa. The reason for the ongoing operation by the RAF wearing a civil registration is also unclear, but it may well have been that it did have a RAF serial, albeit unknown, locally allocated by 206 Group, RAF Middle East, Cairo.

All other British Widgeon acquisitions were Lend-Lease aircraft supplied in 1943 and 1944, the last of which was returned to the US Government in early 1946. To the best of knowledge all of these aircraft remained in North America throughout this period.

The first of these aircraft was JS996, acquired new from US Navy production by the BAC under requisition BSC N-262 in May 1943 on behalf of the RAF. It was used officially by 111 Operational Training Unit at Oakes Field, Nassau for ASR and general communications duties before passing eventually to No.45 Group and then to 1318 (Communications) Flight with whom it remained until its return to the US Government in February 1946. The unusual presence of the Widgeon and the two Gooses in the Bahamas may be safely

linked to the status of the Governor and his wife – the Duke and Duchess of Windsor who were present from 1940 until 1945.

All other British Widgeons were used by the Fleet Air Arm, although many of their duties were of a general purposes nature on behalf of the many British agencies active in the United States in the later stages of WWII. Initial interest in the Widgeon had been expressed in 1942 with a potential acquisition of twenty aircraft discussed. This request was withdrawn at an early stage and was replaced by requisition BSC N-1117 in September 1943 requesting 15 J4F-2 aircraft to be used for "special duties". These aircraft, FP455 to FP469, were diverted from US Navy production and were delivered between October 1943 and August 1944. Aircraft FP461, delivered 16th March 1944, was returned to the US Navy shortly after delivery and was replaced by FP474 (an older aircraft) which was stricken by the US Navy on 27th March 1944. Documentation dated September 1944 shows FP474 listed under N-1117 (FP461 is omitted). There is however an 'outstanding' BAC requisition, N-634, for one unidentified J4F-2 which cannot otherwise be accounted for and it may be that it superseded N-262 in respect of JS996.

The FAA Widgeons were used by naval

The Royal Navy's fleet of J4F-2 Widgeons saw brief use as FAA communications aircraft, mainly in the north-eastern United States and the Canadian Maritimes. FP456 (c/n 1340) spent most of its time at NAS Brunswick supporting FAA squadrons working up on US-built types such as Corsairs, Avengers and Helldivers. At the end of the war several Widgeons were returned to the US Navy for further use while others like FP456 were handed over to the War Assets Administration for disposal. FP456, here seen at Westchester County AP, NY in August 1945, went on to enjoy a lengthy life and survives at the time of writing as N9311R.
(William T Larkins)

FP458 (c/n 1352) was a Fleet Air Arm J4F-2 Widgeon about which little is known other than it saw wartime service in Canada. Like FP456, it was handed over to the War Assets Administration for disposal in 1945 and was with FP456 at Westchester County AP, NY in August 1945 awaiting a buyer. This photograph is undated and could have been taken before or after its time at Westchester. Unlike FP456 its future civilian life was brief and it was lost as NC94527 in a crash in December 1949.
(Harold G Martin)

squadrons and base flights in the United States and Canada and by the Commission itself to undertake routine visits to sundry industrial and military establishments. Contrary to previously received wisdom, all aircraft appear to have remained based within the United States although FP458 was probably assigned to the BCATP in Canada (but not to the RCAF). The naval aircraft saw considerable use ferrying crews and other personnel to and from factories and training fields, a task that in many respects mirrored the US Navy's use of the Widgeon. British assignment records are few but user units included Station Flights at Lewiston and Brunswick for 738 Squadron and 1835 Squadron, and Squantum for 857 Squadron, while the Senior British Naval Officer (SBNO) at NAF Roosevelt Field, Mineola, New York had the use of several different Widgeons from November 1943 until July 1944. The SBNO at NAS St Louis, Missouri had the use of FP468 from September 1944 until October 1945. Aircraft were also assigned to FAA and BAC activities at Pensacola, Miami, Norfolk and Bunker Hill in the United States, Argentia and Dartmouth in Canada and presumably elsewhere in both countries.

As far as can be ascertained from surviving records, only two aircraft appear to have been lost in accidents while in British hands. FP457, flown by an 1835 Squadron crew, was lost with four fatalities in Long Island Sound, NY on 17th February 1945 following an engine failure and FP466 was damaged beyond economic repair in a landing accident on 27th March 1945 (although it was later resurrected as a civilian). Nothing specific however, is known about FP455, the only other FAA aircraft that cannot be identified as having been returned to the US Navy in an airworthy condition (all other aircraft have

subsequent US Navy records and/or post-war civilian registrations). US records suggest that six aircraft, FP459, FP460, FP462 and FP467 to FP469 were returned into US Navy hands in October and December 1945 and were used briefly by the US Navy while the others went into storage awaiting disposal.

In passing it should be mentioned that, for a while, the Fleet Air Arm's J4F-2 Widgeons were known to their Lordships at the Admiralty as the 'Gosling'. The name 'Widgeon' however, was adopted in January 1944 before the majority of the fleet was delivered.

Colours and Markings

The Royal Navy aircraft were delivered in the same dark 'temperate sea' camouflage that was applied to the earlier Goose fleet. Fuselage roundels (with yellow outer rings) and fin flashes were of the 'C' type and the over-wing roundels were 'B' class, as with the Goose. The 'Royal Navy' title and serial number were applied to the lower rear fuselage as on the Goose. No Widgeons are known to have worn codes or other obvious titling, but evidence is limited. JS996's scheme, and indeed that of NC28673, are not known.

Serial Numbers			
Serial	Type	C/n	Circumstances
Unknown	G-44	1212	NC28673 acquired May42
FP455	J4F-2	1336	Production for BAC
FP456	J4F-2	1340	Production for BAC
FP457	J4F-2	1344	Production for BAC
FP458	J4F-2	1352	Production for BAC
FP459	J4F-2	1353	Production for BAC
FP460	J4F-2	1357	Production for BAC
FP461	J4F-2	1358	Production for BAC
FP462	J4F-2	1362	Production for BAC
FP463	J4F-2	1363	Production for BAC
FP464	J4F-2	1367	Production for BAC
FP465	J4F-2	1368	Production for BAC
FP466	J4F-2	1371	Production for BAC
FP467	J4F-2	1375	Production for BAC
FP468	J4F-2	1376	Production for BAC
FP469	J4F-2	1377	Production for BAC
FP474	J4F-2	1332	Production for BAC
JS996	J4F-2	1310	Production for BAC

FP455 to FP469, FP474 and JS996 were Lend-Lease deliveries in 1943 and 1944. The spurious serial 'MV989' has been linked to NC28673 but is clearly incorrect. The true serial of NC28673, assuming that one existed, is likely to have been one of the unidentified aircraft in the range HK820 to HK999, allocated to 206 Group for their use in September 1941.

Widgeon FP460 (c/n 1357) served with the Royal Navy from February 1944 until it was returned to the US Navy in 1945. Notwithstanding this undated photograph, nothing of its FAA use appears to be known. The FAA Widgeons were delivered in the same dark 'temperate sea' camouflage that was applied to the earlier Goose fleet with the 'C' type fuselage roundels and fin flashes. As with the Goose, the over-wing roundels were 'B' class. The accompanying pictures of FP456, FP458 and FP460 show that, by the war's end the fin flashes and roundels were by no means uniformly applied. FP460 (as BuAer 37727) remained in US Navy use until September 1946 when sold to a civilian buyer.   *(Real Photos via MAP)*

UNITED STATES OF AMERICA

UNITED STATES ARMY AIR CORPS

Goose

Variants and Acquisition

The Army Air Corps placed its one and only production order for the Goose in June 1938. The OA-9, known to Grumman as the model G-31, was powered by R-985-17 engines developing 450hp and was intended to serve as a general purpose, amphibious utility aircraft. 26 aircraft were ordered on contract AC-11304 and given the serials 38-556 to 38-581. The Army was the first of the US military services to order the Goose but this would be its only true purchase. All subsequent acquisitions were transfers, diversions or acquisitions from civilian sources. Unlike the Navy and Coast Guard, the Army's use of the Goose was restricted essentially to the WWII years.

In 1941, the US Army Air Corps merged with the Air Force Combat Command to form the US Army Air Forces (USAAF).

In December 1941 the Army and the Navy were authorised to acquire from civilian sources any aircraft deemed appropriate to the war effort. Very few commercial G-21A aircraft were available, but the USAAF was able to acquire two in March 1942 that were given the serials 42-38214 and 42-38215. They were given the new designation OA-13A. A third OA-13A, 42-97055, was subsequently obtained in November 1942. The first pair of acquisitions was part of Army contract DA 415 while the latter was on AC-22047, retrospectively approved in February 1943.

In January 1943, the authorities approved the urgent transfer to the USAAF of five JRF-6B aircraft originally intended for the United Kingdom under the Lend-Lease contract LL86447. Again, this was a retrospective approval as the first delivery into USAAF hands had been made in November 1942. These aircraft, although effectively manufactured to the standard US Navy JRF-5 design, were surprisingly identified as OA-9, perhaps in ignorance of the existence of the OA-13A designation. Aircraft serials were 42-106979 to 42-106983.

In March 1945 the USAAF negotiated the transfer of two US Navy JRF-5 aircraft as attrition replacements for the Pan American-operated aircraft 42-38214 and 42-38215. These aircraft had been working in West Africa and while one of the replacement aircraft was from new production, the other was an in-theatre transfer from the Navy. These standard JRF-5s were given the serials 45-49088 and 45-49089 and were designated OA-13B by the USAAF's Air Technical Service Command who uniquely understood the logic of their Goose

designations. Interestingly, these two aircraft were valued by the USAAF at $76,639 each. Again, this acquisition was to be approved retrospectively in May 1945 on contract AC-13341.

Under the National Security Act of 1947 the USAAF became the US Air Force (USAF) on 18th September 1947.

The final USAF Goose was a JRF-5 (BuAer 34092) loaned to the new Air Force by the Navy in November 1947 in connection with contract work to be undertaken by the EDO Corporation of College Point, NY. This project is discussed elsewhere in this book, but in contractual and specification terms this was an unusual acquisition. The aircraft was given the serial 48-128 for the period of the loan (it is believed that there was no contract raised) and was initially designated OA-9 (logically it should have been an OA-13B). The reason for it becoming an OA-9 was that one other Goose, 38-564, remained on the inventory in November 1947 and thus there were now two. This time, however, someone noticed that there were a few differences (very noticeably so after EDO got to work on the aircraft) and in the more general tidy-up of 1st July 1948 38-564 became a ZA-9A and 48-128 became a ZA-9. The 'Z' prefix indicated that the OA-9 was an obsolete type but it remains unclear why 38-564 justified the 'A' suffix! 48-128 was returned to the Navy in April 1949 and for a few months more 38-564 remained the only Goose in the inventory.

Aircraft used by, or contracted to, the Army Transport Command continued to fly with commercial registrations.

Operations

Notwithstanding gathering war clouds in Europe and Asia, USAAC aircraft procurement in the years 1937 to 1939 could best be described as 'limited' with about 650 new aircraft ordered in each of these years. Against this background, the acquisition of a fleet of 26 OA-9s in 1939 was a significant purchase, reflecting considerable confidence in the commercial model G-21A. Intended to replace the ageing OA-3s and OA-4s in the all-encompassing utility transport and air-sea rescue roles, the Goose fleet was ordered at a time when few in the Army could have foreseen the extent of its ultimate use.

The first aircraft was delivered to Wright Field for acceptance trials in November 1938, with production deliveries commencing in March 1939 and continuing until October of that year. Aircraft were allocated initially in ones and twos to all the major bases of the period, and unit allocation at station level appears to have been a matter of local decision at those stations where they were intended to be permanent fixtures. In some instances they were taken on the charge of the local Air Base Squadron or similar organisation, while elsewhere the allocation was to an Observation Squadron, or even a Pursuit or

Bomber Group. It would be a feature of the OA-9's service life that individual aircraft would serve with many units, reflecting organisational, location and role changes.

In August 1939, by which time 20 aircraft had been delivered (and two lost), 10 aircraft were shipped overseas to reinforce the US Army in areas of traditional interest. Here they would supplement and replace the OA-3s and OA-4s working in demanding amphibious environments. They were sent to the Philippine (two), Panama Canal (four) and Hawaiian (four) Departments and this followed an earlier delivery of one aircraft to the Puerto Rican Department. These organisations saw several changes of title during later years, and by 1945, the first three had respectively become the 5th, 6th and 7th Air Forces (the Puerto Rican Department was subsumed by the 6th Air Force). Allocation within the Canal Zone area of Panama was of considerable strategic importance, with two aircraft allocated to Albrook Field on the Pacific coast (15th ABS) and France Field (16th ABS) on the Atlantic/Caribbean coast.

The Army's Goose fleet suffered significant attrition throughout its short life and losses, by modern peace-time standards, were unusually high with 12 lost before Pearl Harbor – indeed only three of the original fleet of 26 would survive WWII. In mid-1940, by which time five had been delivered, the fleet was dispersed as shown in the table overleaf.

Notwithstanding the increasing relevance of the European war and the deteriorating situation in eastern Asia, the OA-9 fleet was little affected prior to Pearl Harbor other than that there was a very gradual shift of aircraft to arguably more operational roles. Most noticeably, two aircraft were transferred in July 1941 to the recently created 1st Air Force at Mitchel Field, NY.

Of course, the events of 7th December 1941 galvanised the Army into dramatic expansion and the USAAF very rapidly grew to gigantic proportions. Within this behemoth the Goose was but a very small element indeed. Pearl Harbor and its aftermath effectively cost two more aircraft with one, already heavily damaged in an accident, never to fly again and another soon to be lost in the Philippines. The USAAF thus entered 1942 with just 13 aircraft. For the rest of the war the Goose was used effectively in two major roles. One of these can be described broadly as a rescue/utility role and in this respect would serve most noticeably with the Air Transport Command in the Atlantic and African theatres supporting ferrying operations. The other role can be loosely described as that of diplomatic and military intelligence activities including mapping and reconnaissance work, typically within Central and South America. Within Panama the 6th Air Force continued to use the aircraft to support isolated jungle sites on both coasts.

As explained above, the OA-9 fleet was reinforced numerically in 1942 by the acquisition of three OA-13As and five new

The OA-9 Fleet Disposition – June 1940

Army Air Corps Allocations – Continental United States

Air Base Flight Section, GHQ Air Force	Langley Field, VA	1
HQ Sqn, Technical School	Chanute Field, IL	1
3rd Observation Sqn, Coast Artillery School	Langley Field, VA	1
97th Observation Sqn, IV Army Corps	Mitchel Field, NY	1
13th Air Base Sqn, Air Corps Tactical School	Maxwell Field, AL	2
91st Observation Sqn, IX Army Corps	Fort Lewis, WA	1
82nd Observation Sqn, IX Army Corps	Moffett Field, CA	1
1st Staff Sqn (for use by Chief of Staff)	Bolling Field, DC	1
5th Air Base Sqn	Hamilton, CA	1
Army Academy, Air Corps Detachment	West Point, NY	1
Flying Branch	Wright Field, OH	1

Army Air Corps Allocations – Overseas Commands

17th Air Base Sqn	Hickam Field, HI	1
19th Pursuit Sqn, 18th Pursuit Grp	Wheeler Field, HI	1
78th Pursuit Sqn, 18th Pursuit Grp	Wheeler Field, HI	2
15th Air Base Sqn	Albrook Field, Canal Zone	1
16th Air Base Sqn	France Field, Canal Zone	2
2nd Observation Sqn	Nichols Field, Philippines	1
Air Corps Detachment (in repair, Olmsted Field)	Borinquen Field, PR	1

OA-9s as well as a number of OA-14 Widgeons which could undertake similar tasks and were sometimes regarded as interchangeable assets by both the USAAF and the US Navy. In practice, two of the OA-13As were assigned permanently to Pan American Airways to support their African operations and the new OA-9s were assigned immediately to military attachés in the Central American and Caribbean states of Guatemala, Colombia, Venezuela, Cuba and Haiti. Bolivia, curiously, was given its own aircraft. The attachés in Peru and Honduras both received aircraft from the original batch while Brazil would see several aircraft undertake military intelligence activities between 1942 and 1944. Aircraft so used for mapping and related activities were assigned to the 16th Photographic Squadron, 1st Photographic Charting Group headquartered at Bolling Field, MD. One of the early tasks of the Goose in Central America was the location of suspected German activity, including airfield construction, a task undertaken in great secrecy. Reference to the individual aircraft histories will assist the reader to understand many of these changes but it has proved impossible to identify with certainty the specific aircraft based at St Johns, Newfoundland in 1941-1942, initially with the 21st Reconnaissance Sqn and then the 41st Reconnaissance Sqn. All other known user units appear within the individual histories.

Although two new naval JRF-5s were acquired as OA-13Bs in 1945 to replace the two African Pan American OA-13As, there were no more Goose acquisitions after 1942 and the fleet inevitably continued to dwindle in size. By January 1944 only eight of the original aircraft survived and a year later there were only four airworthy examples, together with three of the 1942 acquisitions.

The Goose has always had something of a reputation as a 'recreational' aircraft and one, sadly anonymous, came to grief in Newfoundland when so used by none other than 'Hap' Arnold, the Commanding General of the USAAF. Arnold's Goose was holed by a rock during a fishing trip to a remote lake in northern Newfoundland, remote to the extent that search parties took 36 hours to find the beached aircraft. Eventually, it was recovered, temporarily patched with hessian sacking and cement, and flown back to Harmon Field where it landed safely although not without incident. Overweight and unintentionally carrying 60 gallons of water ballast, the nose split on landing! Attempts to identify this aircraft via formal reports have, perhaps unsurprisingly, proved particularly difficult. One candidate, however, is c/n 1047 (see aircraft history).

When Japan surrendered in August 1945 the USAAF appears to have had about four airworthy aircraft in the Caribbean area as well as the two recently acquired OA-13Bs in Africa (both of which were disposed of almost immediately). Two of the Caribbean aircraft were sold as airworthy in 1945, while at least one, 38-566, continued to fly with the ATC in the Caribbean area until mid-1946. Others appear to have lingered in non-airworthy condition (and perhaps only so on paper) until progressively stricken from the inventory. The last airworthy aircraft, 38-564, ought perhaps to have been called a Phoenix rather than a Goose as it was returned to service by Caribbean Air Command at Atkinson Field, British Guiana in February 1947 and would remain active until November 1949. Re-designated ZA-9A on 1st July 1948, its final operating unit would be the 5920th Air Base Group, Waller AFB, Trinidad.

Although one US Navy JRF-5 (BuAer 34092, USAF 48-128) had been borrowed by the USAF for project work as a ZA-9 (see above), it had already been returned to the Navy when 38-564 was finally retired. Very few of the USAAF's aircraft survived to see post-war commercial use, a reflection perhaps of some pre-war carelessness, but more typically of a tough little aircraft pushed to the limit by the brutal environment of WWII. If aircraft thought like humans one might imagine a lonely 38-564 at Waller thinking of its salad days with the USAAC at Fort Lewis and Hunter Field, a far cry from the USAF of 1949.

Colours and Markings

The production aircraft, delivered in 1938 and 1939, were brightly and, of course, hopelessly inappropriately coloured for their future jungle-warfare role. The fuselage, floats and engine nacelles were light blue with a black lower hull below a yellow-striped waterline. The wings and horizontal and vertical tail surfaces were high-visibility yellow and, aft of a vertical blue tail band, the rudder was horizontally striped red and white. 'Red centre' roundels were carried on the wings but not on the fuselage. The letters 'U S' were written beneath the starboard wing and 'Army' beneath the port wing.

As was the fashion of the time, the serial number was carried only as part of a minutely scripted data block on the left-hand side of the fuselage forward of the cockpit. Once in the hands of the operating unit, the relevant owner was able to add an individual identity in the form of a code on the tail indicating the user and a 'ship in group' number. Thus an aircraft (thought to have been 38-566) in 1941 was wearing '10 9-AB' indicating the 10th aircraft of the 9th Air Base Group, Moffett Field, CA. The 'ship in group' number was sometimes worn on the nose and the unit badge might be applied to the rear fuselage.

After January 1942 the surviving OA-9s and the newly acquired OA-13s began to acquire camouflage, comprising Olive Drab upper and side surfaces and Grey lower surfaces. Subsequently some aircraft are thought to have acquired overall silver surfaces, but there is little reliable evidence of post-1942 USAAF OA-9 colour schemes and, given the dispersed nature of the fleet, there was probably considerable local variation. The post-war ZA-9, 48-128, retained its US Navy 'Midnite Blue' scheme but with a new USAF buzz-number 'OA-128' on both the fuselage and lower wing surfaces.

Serial Numbers
The following list includes all aircraft that received USAAC (USAAF) serial numbers regardless of purpose or the circumstances of the allocation.

Serial	Type	C/n	Circumstances
38-556 to 581	OA-9	1022 to 1047	Production for USAAC
42-38214	OA-13A	1058	G-21A NC3021 acquired Mar42
42-38215	OA-13A	1006	G-21A NC16915 acq Mar42
42-97055	OA-13A	1062	G-21A NC3042 acquired Nov42
42-106979 to 106983	OA-9	1155 to 1159	JRF-6B from UK production
45-49088	OA-13B	B-120	JRF-5 from US Navy production
45-49089	OA-13B	1193	JRF-5 tfd from US Navy
48-128	OA-9 (ZA-9)	B-21	JRF-5 loan from US Navy
NC16910	G-21A	1001	Army Transport Command use

USAAF never purchased new aircraft from Grumman but between 1948 and 1956 the Corps of Engineers operated a new G-44A, NC86635, in Greece. This aircraft was used by the District Engineer, Grecian District and was based in Athens in support of the US-aided reconstruction programmes in post-war Greece.

Operations

The OA-14 fleet enjoyed but a brief life with the USAAF but was a popular and useful aircraft albeit with all the problems attendant to a small fleet in a large Army. The Widgeon entered USAAF service in March 1942 with the acceptance of ten aircraft at Bolling, DC from whence they were distributed to various users in several commands. One aircraft, the almost new 42-38222, was immediately wrecked on the Potomac River by its Ferry Command pilot. The balance of five aircraft was accepted progressively between April and July 1942 as they became available. Early use paralleled that of the Goose, with many aircraft assigned to the 6th Air Force in the Caribbean and to Ferry Command in the Caribbean and north-eastern theatres. As a sign of things to come for the Widgeon, one aircraft was assigned to the 11th Air Force in Alaska where it was to be lost in October 1942. One or two saw brief use with Air Attachés in the Central American theatre.

The Alaskan aircraft was replaced and 1943 was a generally safe year for the fleet as it continued to operate in its specialised communications role. One aircraft was withdrawn from flight use at Hamilton, CA in unexplained circumstances but there were to be no more (known) major accidents until late 1944. Unfortunately the paper record of these aircraft, particularly as recorded on their movement cards after 1942, is abysmal and their very regular unit

The curious history of OA-13B 45-49089

In February 1945 the Navy found itself obliged to transfer two urgently needed JRF-5s to Pan American for their use in Africa. One aircraft, BuAer 87726, was to be delivered into USAAF hands from the production line and was to be numbered 45-49088. As will be read in the individual history, this transfer took place as planned and the aircraft was duly shipped to North Africa in March 1945. Presumably because the need for the other aircraft was particularly urgent, that aircraft, 45-49089, was to be a field transfer from the local US Navy unit at Port Lyautey, French Morocco. USAAF documentation seems to suggest that they were expecting to receive 37809 that had been operational with the Navy at Dakar, French West Africa and which was (at least on paper) with Fleet Air Wing 15 at Port Lyautey by January 1945. However, the aircraft stricken from Navy records on 28th February 1945 was 34064, another of FAW-15's aircraft.

This appears to have generated (unseen) correspondence by 8th March 1945 and caused the Chief, Aircraft Distribution Office (AAF, Wright Field) to write to the Director of the Air Technical Service Command on 17th March 1945. His letter definitively tells one Master Sergeant Smith that '44-34064' [sic] is in error and that its correct identity is in fact 37809. The letter is closed with the routine 'by command of General Arnold'. Unfortunately it appears that the Navy paid no heed to the General and, as reference to the individual histories will show, the USAAF received 34064 and not 37809 – as one assumes that Sgt Smith was trying to explain.

Widgeon

Variants and Acquisition

In the aftermath of the declaration of war, the US armed forces received new, non-combat aircraft in a number of ways, one of which was by purchase directly from the owner. In the case of the G-44 Widgeon, the great majority of those in private ownership that were not considered essential to the owner's part in the war effort, were thus acquired by the USAAF in early 1942. Some of those acquired were virtually new and none was more than one year old. In all 15 were obtained in 1942, the majority coming on the Army's large miscellaneous aircraft contract number DA 415 and they were given the designation OA-14. A sixteenth was acquired in November 1944 when the USAAF purchased NC28669 hitherto owned and operated by the Corps of Engineers. The

The OA-14 Fleet Disposition – September 1944
First Air Force

132nd Base Unit, Suffolk AAF, NY	42-38339

Second Air Force

215th Base Unit, Pueblo AAF, CO	42-38221
265th Base Unit, Pocatello AAF, ID	42-38218

Third Air Force

332nd Base Unit, Lake Charles AAF, LA	42-38223

Eleventh Air Force

Unit assignment uncertain, Elmendorf AAB, AK	42-38340

Air Force Air Training Command

2117th Base Unit, Buckingham AAF, FL	42-38355
2135th Base Unit, Tyndall AAF, FL	42-38219*
2539th Base Unit, Foster AAF, TX	42-38216** & 42-38217

Air Transport Command (Caribbean Division)

1103rd Base Unit, Morrison AAF, FL	42-38356

*Assignment assumed. **Accident date uncertain. Status of 42-53003 (Sixth AF/Curacao) uncertain. 42-38220, 42-38222, 42-38285 & 42-43460 previously lost.

The USAAF acquired several commercial Widgeons in early 1942 but by the time that NC28669 (c/n 1208) came on strength as OA-14 44-52997 in November 1944, several of them had been lost and the type was soon withdrawn. The Army acquired 'The Stud Duck' (as later named) from the Corps of Engineers at Borinquen Field, PR and used it in the local theatre until withdrawn in August 1945. Eventually sold, it found its way to Oakland MAP, CA where it was photographed in January 1948. Later registered N1250N and returned to civilian flying it went on to enjoy a lengthy life.

(William T Larkins via MAP)

changes are often unrecorded or unintelligible. At least one aircraft, struck off charge in 1945, could have succumbed at any time after late 1943.

Gradually the aircraft began to return to mainland use where they began to serve with various elements of the AAF Training Command and, in a similar role, at a few stations that supported bomber and fighter training programmes. Generally, and unsurprisingly, these were at coastal or lakeside sites. The Army Academy at West Point, New York saw several aircraft come and go

at Stewart AAF in 1943 and 1944. Until mid-1944, aircraft assignment at station level might be to any one of several flying organisations ranging from base flights to combat squadrons, but after the creation of the uniform 'Base Unit' structure in the spring of 1944, allocation also became more uniform. The approximate distribution of the fleet in September 1944 can be seen on the previous page.

In November 1944, the Army purchased NC28669 from the Corps of Engineers at Borinquen Field, PR and assigned it the

serial 44-52997. By January 1945 only seven OA-14s, including 44-52997, remained airworthy and withdrawal began before the end of the European war. Five aircraft, including two that would not fly again, were stricken from the inventory in April and May and the other four followed in August 1945, with all the airworthy aircraft later sold to commercial buyers. Although it was undoubtedly one of the USAAF's minor types, the OA-14 Widgeon served the Army well from the tropics to Alaska and in roles far removed from those intended for their 1941 owners.

Colours and Markings

There is little specific evidence of the initial colour scheme used by the fleet of OA-14s but, as acquisition took place in 1942 in a consistent fashion, the probability is that all the original aircraft received the then standard USAAF transport camouflage with olive drab upper surfaces and sides and grey lower surfaces. By the latter stages of the war it can be assumed that there would have been variations and those aircraft assigned to base rescue work would probably have acquired high visibility markings. 44-52997, acquired in 1944, appears to have ended the war in a silver colour scheme that included some splendid nose art.

Mallard

The US Army Corps of Engineers, based in Vicksburg, MS, purchased Mallard c/n J-24 new in April 1947. The aircraft was named "*Black Mallard*", perhaps giving a clue to its paint scheme. After 23 years' service, the aircraft was transferred to the Mississippi River Commission in 1970.

Serial Numbers (Widgeon)

Serial	Type	C/n	Circumstances
42-38216	OA-14	1207	G-44 NC28668 acquired Mar42
42-38217	OA-14	1218	G-44 NC28679 acquired May42
42-38218	OA-14	1202	G-44 NC28664 acquired Jly42
42-38219	OA-14	1230	G-44 NC1700 acquired Mar42
42-38220	OA-14	1234	G-44 NC37184 acquired Mar42
42-38221	OA-14	1232	G-44 NC37182 acquired Mar42
42-38222	OA-14	1238	G-44 NC37188 acquired Mar42
42-38223	OA-14	1206	G-44 NC28667 acquired Apr42
42-38285	OA-14	1211	G-44 NC28672 acquired Mar42
42-38339	OA-14	1233	G-44 NC37183 acquired Mar42
42-38340	OA-14	1205	G-44 NC777 acquired Mar42
42-38355	OA-14	1204	G-44 NC28666 acquired May42
42-38356	OA-14	1209	G-44 NC28670 acquired Mar42
42-43460	OA-14	1203	G-44 NC28665 acquired Mar42
42-53003	OA-14	1219	G-44 NC28680 acquired May42
44-52997	OA-14	1208	G-44 NC28669 acquired Nov44
NC86635	G-44A	1461	Corps of Engineers, acquired Apr48

Serial Number (Mallard)

Serial	Type	C/n	Circumstances
NC2965	G-73	J-24	New production Apr47

UNITED STATES NAVY

Goose

Variants and Acquisition

In common with the Air Corps and the Coast Guard, the Navy quickly recognised the potential of the Goose as a robust amphibian capable of fulfilling a number of utility and utility/transport tasks – the Navy's VJ and VJR functions. The purchase of a single aircraft in 1938 to contract C60242, the unique model G-26 known to the Navy as the XJ3F-1, enabled the Navy to evaluate the Goose, while much of the 1939 production was delivered to the Air Corps.

The XJ3F-1, BuAer serial 1384, was delivered to the Navy at NAS Anacostia, DC on 9th September 1938. Powered by 450hp R-985-48 engines, 1384 was configured as an eight-seat, passenger aircraft and, following early trials, spent

most of its time acting as a utility transport at Anacostia. After February 1941 it was used to support test and development work at NAS Lakehurst, NJ and NAF Philadelphia, PA before post-war disposal to the civilian market.

The Navy's first production order followed rapidly. In the pre-war Navy, non-combat types were still being ordered in small quantities for specific purposes and the 1938 order for 10 aircraft on contract C66303 was defined into two variants. The JRF-1 would be a conventional light transport powered by R-985-AN-6 engines giving 450hp while the JRF-1A, retaining the -48 engines of the XJ3F-1, down-rated to 400hp, was intended for photographic and target-towing activities. To that end the JRF-1A was manufactured with a camera hatch in the hull bottom and provisions for all the target-towing gear. When not employed in either of these roles, the JRF-1A could be returned to a standard

transport configuration. The JRF-1/1A was known to Grumman as the model G-38.

The five JRF-1 received serials 1674 to 1677 and 1680 and the five JRF-1A were 1671 to 1673, 1678 and 1679. They were delivered between September 1939 and January 1940, in serial order. Reference to the individual aircraft histories and the following section will provide more precise details of their use but in summary almost all aircraft spent their relatively short lives beyond the continental USA.

The order for JRF-1/1As was soon followed by a larger contract, C75686, for 35 aircraft which would eventually be delivered in three batches, between December 1940 and October 1942. By then, the USA had entered WWII and the Navy had placed significantly greater ongoing production orders. The first batch of 10 (serials 3846 to 3855) was delivered as the JRF-4, the JRF-2 and -3 designations having been allocated to US Coast Guard models. The JRF-4 differed from the JRF-1 in having -50 450hp engines, and provision for a 250lb bomb or 325lb depth charge beneath each wing. The JRF-4 was considered by Grumman to be a derivative of the basic model G-38.

Notwithstanding this weapons-carrying potential the ten JRF-4s were delivered into the hands of the larger naval establishments within the continental US where they served initially as utility aircraft, in some instances assigned to Flag Officers. One aircraft, 3846, was assigned to the US Marine Corps from early 1941 until mid-1944. Eventually most aircraft gravitated to less glamorous duties within the Navy's much enlarged world. Delivered between December 1940 and April 1941, only four aircraft survived the war and three of these would eventually find their way to post-war owners. The fourth, 3854, lingered in

The blue-grey colour scheme probably dates this photograph of JRF-4 3846 (c/n 1100) to 1942. Assigned by the Navy to the US Marine Corps for most of its short life, the code '2-W-1' indicated an allocation to the 2nd Marine Air Wing at San Diego. Like many JRF-4s, it failed to survive the war and was stricken in 1945. (Fred J Knight Collection)

In this later photograph, JRF-4 3854 (c/n 1108) is wearing the 1943-style national markings although a lack of visual clues prevents accurate dating. Probably photographed post-war, 3854 was the longest-serving JRF-4 and survived with the Navy until 1952 when it was broken up.

(Real Photos via MAP)

Built in early 1943, US Navy JRF-5 34062 (c/n 1191) probably acquired its glossy sea blue colour scheme in the post-war years. Here marked anonymously, the photograph is thought to date from the mid-1950s and may have been taken shortly before civilianisation as N323 with Avalon Air Transport.   *(Jennifer Gradidge Collection)*

naval storage until February 1952 when it was scrapped.

The second batch of 15 aircraft, within C75686, was delivered to the definitive JRF-5 standard, although still considered by Grumman to be the model G-38 design. The JRF-5 was powered by dash AN-6 engines giving 450hp, and retained all the features of the JRF-1A and JRF-4 as well as the de-icing boots and autopilot provision of the US Coast Guard's JRF-3 model. These aircraft, delivered between April and December 1941, had serials 6440 to 6454 and had early histories much as those of the JRF-4 fleet. Once the USA had entered WWII and dozens more JRF-5s were in use, these early aircraft were then spread far and wide. Some of those that survived the war, and most did so, went on to enjoy lengthy US Navy careers. Virtually all JRF-5s that survived their naval service were eventually disposed of to civilian owners.

The final batch of aircraft within C75686 was that of a further 10 JRF-5s, with serials 04349 to 04358. These were to be the final Goose aircraft ordered before Pearl Harbor and their delivery would be delayed by the consequences of the European war. After much wrangling, Grumman had been authorised to commence work on a batch of fifty JRF-5s for the United Kingdom and these aircraft, known as the JRF-6B, were to be delivered from January 1942, with the final delivery taking place in March 1943. Thus the batch of ten US Navy aircraft would be delivered between July and October 1942 from an integrated production line temporarily geared to the needs of a foreign customer. A 1941 BuAer allocation of thirty serials to US Navy JRF-5s, 03713-03742, was subsequently cancelled, presumably as a result of the greater priority afforded to the British aircraft.

America's entry into WWII generated new and much larger production contracts for the JRF-5 model, as the Navy expanded into a massive global force. They were W&S 14088 for 35 aircraft, 34060 to 34094, delivered April to November 1943, NAS 463 for 61 aircraft, 37771 to 37831, delivered November 1943 to September 1944 and NOa(S) 3090 for 61 more, 84790 to 84818 and 87720 to 87751, delivered September 1944 to October 1945. Ongoing production was terminated abruptly in August 1945 and the balance of NOa(S) 3090, 87752 to 87762, was cancelled.

Production JRF-5s were delivered exclusively to the US Navy until January 1944 when the first Lend-Lease aircraft was diverted into British hands. In February 1944 the first Canadian-purchased aircraft was diverted to the RCAF and, in all, 25 aircraft were diverted from the new-build contracts during 1944 and 1945 (two more aircraft, 39747 and 39748, delivered to Cuba as a supplementary call-off to C75686 were never intended for the US Navy). Thus it will be appreciated that the US Navy accepted 157 production JRF-5s for its own use, inclusive of six aircraft transferred internally to the US Coast Guard in August 1943 and another 24 that were used exclusively by Coast Guard Operations within the US Navy during WWII (and many of these aircraft were transferred formally to the US Coast Guard in July 1946). As will be seen, the JRF-5 enjoyed a relatively long life with the US Navy after 1945, with the last aircraft withdrawn from active use in July 1956. Others lingered in storage and in test work for another year or so.

The onset of war in December 1941 resulted in the acquisition and adoption of a small number of private, corporate and airline-owned G-21A aircraft which received BuAer serials and designations that were by no means always relevant. The individual histories in Appendix 1 provide more background but in summary they were as follows (all were described formally as 'miscellaneous acquisitions'). 07004, a JRF-1 taken on strength in January 1942; 09767, a JRF-4 in March 1942; 09782, a JRF-1 in June 1942; 35921, a JRF-5 in test work with a serial assigned in 1942; 48229, a JRF-5 in 1942 and 99078, a JRF-1 in 1942. For one reason or another all except 35921 had gone from the inventory by late 1944. 35921 became a regular fleet aircraft and survived in naval use until 1954, when transferred out as MDAP aid to Japan.

In 1953, the Navy modified 15 JRF-5 aircraft to JRF-6 standard in a little-publicised programme undertaken at NAS Quonset Point, Rhode Island. The specific nature of the modifications are uncertain but are assumed to have included upgrades to the radio and navigational aids and probably some of the flight controls. The re-use of the 'JRF-6' variant number is intriguing and could have been done in ignorance of the earlier JRF-6B, or perhaps because there were no US Navy JRF-6Bs extant in 1953. The 15 JRF-6 aircraft were 34071, 37771, 37812, 37813, 37820, 37828, 84805, 84807, 84809, 84810, 87720, 87723, 87732, 87745 and 87750.

Naval Operations 1939 to 1945

The Goose enjoyed a deceptively lengthy and varied career with the Navy and the varied nature of its operations further complicates its story. With the notable exception of the Annapolis fleet, no individual unit used more than two or three aircraft at any given time and there were many, many organisational changes during its 17-year operational career. Reference to the individual aircraft histories will provide greater unit detail than can be included realistically in this summary but with the assistance of 'snapshot' inventories the reader should be able to gain a clear understanding of the Goose's role within the US Navy.

The early versions of the Goose were essentially WWII-only aircraft and only one survived beyond December 1945. In contrast, the JRF-5 fleet which entered service in April 1941 did not reach full strength until late 1945, but then remained virtually intact for several years until a run-down began in the early-mid 1950s. If one ignores the administrative transfer of Coast Guard aircraft in 1946, there were only a handful of disposals of damaged aircraft before the early 1950s, and until 1956 virtually all disposals of airworthy aircraft were to US Government agencies and MDAP recipients. It should also be appreciated that the 25 JRF-5s diverted from US Navy contracts to other users in 1944 and 1945 saw no prior US Navy service. The picture is therefore that of an aircraft that was as much an asset post-war as it was during WWII.

The Goose was procured by the Navy as a utility amphibian and its allocation at unit level very much depended on the necessity of having such an aircraft within a mixed fleet of other utility types. Amphibious operations brought unique problems and the JRF was not used if a conventional aircraft was more appropriate, and by the later stages of WWII it was to some extent considered an interchangeable asset with the J4F Widgeon. Initially classified by the US Navy as a 'VJR' (Utility Transport), it became a 'VJ(M)' (Multi-engined Utility) during WWII alongside the JD, JRB and the J4F types, before further re-classification to 'VU' (Utility) in 1949. This 'VU' class added the TBM-3U and J2F to the mix, but further refinement arrived in 1951, when the JRF-5s (and later the JRF-6s) were classified uniquely as 'VU-GEN' (Utility-General). 'VU-S&R' was created simultaneously for the new UF-1 Albatross fleet and 'VU-TOW' for the JD-1 and TBM-3U. Thus it can be seen by 1951 that the Search and Rescue and Target Towing functions were officially a thing of the past for the Navy Goose.

As indicated above, the initial fleet of ten JRF-1 and JRF-1A entered service in late 1939. Three of the target-towing JRF-1As were assigned to fleet support units in the Hawaiian Islands, and ultimately the western Pacific, another to NAS Coco Solo, Panama while 1673 was permanently with VMS-3 at MCAS St Thomas, US Virgin Islands. Relatively few JRFs were assigned by the Navy to US Marine Corps units and those that were tended to be long-stayers. Three of the JRF-1 fleet were assigned rapidly to the Naval Attachés to Colombia, Cuba and Venezuela, reflecting the USA's determination to strengthen their influence in the region. Only two JRF-1/1As were lost in accidents, but the fleet appears to have fallen foul of a US

Navy policy to limit their lives to 60 months, with the result that all were withdrawn and struck off charge between August and December 1944. As none of these aircraft subsequently went to the civilian market, it is assumed that they were scrapped, probably in situ.

Between December 1940 and April 1941 the ten JRF-4s were delivered to the Navy against the background of a bitter European war and the ever-increasing pressure on the USA to protect not only its own coasts and sea-lanes, but those of its allies in the north and south Atlantic. JRF-4 production flowed into JRF-5 production and the first batch of 15 was in Navy hands by December 1941. The 1941 allocations were biased heavily towards the Atlantic seaboard stations, old and new, although several aircraft went to stations beyond US borders. Thus San Juan, Trinidad, Guantanamo Bay and Argentia joined Miami, Pensacola, Jacksonville, Quonset Point and the major base of Norfolk as recipients of the new tough little utility aircraft. Kodiak and Sitka were also 1941 allocations, reflecting growing concerns about the vulnerability of remote Alaska. In practice, the allocation of the Goose to US Navy and US Marine Corps field commanders would see the aircraft effectively follow the naval forces into South America, North Africa, Europe and, most obviously, across the Pacific. In the course of the next four years the Goose would operate in just about every imaginable environment and establish a reputation as a robust and versatile aircraft, albeit one that required careful handling.

Although not a declared belligerent in 1941, and therefore not on a war footing, the US armed forces were being reinforced and reorganised in recognition of the existing situation, and in anticipation of more serious future involvement. One consequence of this was the progressive absorption of US Coast Guard activities into US Navy operational hands. The final step was undertaken on 1st November 1941 when all remaining elements, including aviation, were transferred from the Treasury Department to the Navy Department for what transpired to be the duration of the war. From the narrow perspective of the Goose operations, this had a number of ramifications. The small fleet of widely-dispersed JRF-2s and JRF-3s essentially became US Navy assets for the duration of the future war, and although they were largely retained at their previous Coast Guard Air Stations undertaking historic duties, this was not always the case. For example, as early as August 1941, one JRF-2 was transferred to NAS Honolulu and subsequently would see naval use with two Carrier Aircraft Service Units (CASUs). From 1943, new production JRF-5s would be diverted to Coast Guard Operations within the US Navy and many of these aircraft were transferred formally to the post-war US Coast Guard, by then back in the Treasury's hands. For simplicity, wartime Coast Guard Opera-

tions are discussed within the US Coast Guard section of this book.

At the time of the Japanese attack on Pearl Harbor on 7th December 1941, the US Navy possessed a total of 34 Goose aircraft of all marks (one JRF-1 having been lost in 1940) as well as the prototype, and a single G-21A recently gifted to the Navy. This aircraft, 07004, would eventually be taken on strength in January 1942 as a JRF-1. Another production batch of ten JRF-5s (04349 to 04358) would not appear until July 1942, largely because they were to be preceded by the early part of the British order for 50 JRF-6Bs (the US Navy batch was delivered between July and October 1942 while British deliveries commenced in January 1942 and stretched until March 1943).

Although theoretically a number of civilian G-21As were available to the US Navy and the US Army Air Force for acquisition in the days after Pearl Harbor, in the event few were acquired, for a number of reasons. In the first instance a number had passed already into Canadian hands. Of those remaining, some were used by strategic industries and would not be called upon initially, while others would be only notionally 'drafted' later in the war. There is also evidence that three more US civilian aircraft, initially intended for the Royal Air Force but ultimately delivered to Canada in April and June 1942, were helped on their way by the US Navy, the inference being that the Navy (like the British) would rather wait for custom-built JRF-5s for their own use. The upshot of this was that only two civil G-21As, JRF-4 09767 and JRF-1 09782, were taken on strength, in March and June 1942 respectively. It remains unclear why they received different designations!

In the months following Pearl Harbor, the US Navy placed substantial orders for the JRF-5 and production continued until the end of the war. However, the Navy's need for the specialised amphibian proved to be less than anticipated, and by January 1944, aircraft were being diverted from the production line to other users. As mentioned above, deliveries to the fleet recommenced in July 1942, continued until October of that year, and then resumed in April 1943. Production, including diversions, was typically in the order of one aircraft weekly, with peak output achieved in the fall of 1944. By the spring of 1945, some aircraft were going directly to long-term storage, and all production ceased shortly after VJ Day.

The vast majority of new aircraft were delivered to NAS New York for collection and distribution within and beyond the USA. Aircraft destined for Central and South America would be ferried by air, while those bound for the Pacific and North African theatres were shipped, typically via Alameda, San Diego or Norfolk. Aircraft records suggest that few aircraft received major overhauls until 1945, after which all aircraft progressively passed through any one of several depots. A number of aircraft that received significant but repairable damage during the war were apparently set aside, and it was sometimes a matter of chance whether the intended repairs actually took place. Those most vulnerable were aircraft damaged in the western Pacific and South American theatres.

After mid-1943, the Goose began to be delivered to command centres in the Pacific with one of the first recipients, Commander Air Forces South Pacific, Guadalcanal, being allocated two aircraft in June of that year. While no US Navy Goose is known to have been lost to direct hostile action its general vulnerability became more obvious by 1943. Setting aside the more routine hazards of weather, pilot error and mechanical failure the Goose, like the Widgeon, had particular weaknesses and idiosyncrasies that contributed to a spate of accidents in 1943. The Goose was well suited to inland waterways and coastal lagoons but the open sea was more demanding, and operations in the Pacific and Atlantic routinely produced situations which occasionally broke the aircraft. This could mean an experienced pilot forced by circumstances to undertake a sortie in marginal sea conditions or a pilot, experienced or otherwise, simply making an error from which there was no recovery.

Landings on prepared surfaces could be equally problematic and in one respect the Goose was really very vulnerable. It was unfortunately an easy matter for the un-wary pilot to believe that his undercarriage was down and locked when, for more than one reason, it might not be. This design weakness was never properly resolved, and by the 1950s the US Navy introduced extreme training measures to demonstrate the problem to all pilots (the aircraft was lifted by crane or jacks and the pilot was shown the cycling process and this became a 'ticket' item). The undercarriage was also vulnerable to heavy lateral loading and many broke on landing, or even when taxying. Eventually greater awareness and improved training significantly improved the Goose's serious incident record, and after 1944 very few featured in fatal accidents.

Throughout 1944 and 1945, the Goose continued to join newly forming organisations working up for overseas deployment and was allocated increasingly to new and greatly enlarged homeland stations in support of massive training programmes.

At some of these establishments the aircraft saw significant use as crash-boats, as well as more prolonged Air-Sea-Rescue activities. Typical operational users were the Fleet and Marine Air Wings, Utility Squadrons (the 'VJ' units) and the Carrier Air Service Units, as well as a miscellany of depot organisations. By early 1945, the supply of new aircraft was such that some could be delivered new into what might be described as second-line activities. These activities included contractor-use and the Annapolis support squadron VN8D5. This unit traditionally provided indoctrination

training for the Naval Academy's midshipmen and flight proficiency opportunities for naval aviators in the Washington area. Post-war the unit would become far and away the largest single user of the Goose.

The formal surrender of Japan on 2nd September 1945 virtually coincided with the closure of the Goose production line (five aircraft would be delivered subsequently at a leisurely pace). At that time the US Navy

and US Marine Corps had approximately 140 aircraft on strength, including those allocated to Coast Guard operations, and a handful of damaged aircraft that would shortly be scrapped. The tables below and opposite show the approximate disposition of the fleet (exclusive of the Coast Guard aircraft) in early September 1945, but it should be remembered that the Pacific-based aircraft were not always where the planners intended them.

The JRF-5 Fleet Disposition – September 1945

Combat Elements – Pacific Fleet

Fleet Marine Force Pacific/First Marine Aircraft Wing:

Hedron MBG-61 MCAF Emirau, New Ireland		1

Utility Wing Pacific:

VJ-1	NAS Moffett Field, CA	1
VJ-2	NAAS Shelton, WA	1
VJ-3	NAS Puunene, HI	1
VJ-7	NAS Pearl Harbor, HI	1
VJ-8	NAB Samar, Philippines	1
VJ-9	San Marcelino, Philippines	1
VJ-12	NAS San Diego, CA	1
VJ-13	NAB Samar, Philippines	1
VJ-14	NAS Pearl Harbor, HI	1
VJ-17	NAB Agana, Guam	1
VJ-18	NAB Eniwetok, Marshall Islands	1
VJ-19	NAS Engebi, Marshall Islands	1

Service Units:

CASU-1	NAS Pearl Harbor, HI	1
CASU-31	NAS Hilo, HI	1
CASU-32	NAS Kahului, HI	1
CASU-36	NAAS Santa Rosa, CA	1
CASU-37	NAAS Hollister, CA	1
CASU-63	NAAS Vernalis, CA	1
CASU-64	NAAS Watsonville, CA	1

Flag Units:

ComAir 7th Fleet	NAB Samar, Philippines	1
	Sangley Point, Philippines	2
ComFltAir Seattle	NAS Seattle, WA	1
Commander Marianas	NAB Agana, Guam	1
ComPhilSeaFron	Tolosa, Leyte, Philippines	1

Combat Elements – Atlantic Fleet

Fleet Air Wing 5:

Hedron FAW5	NAS Norfolk, VA	1
NACTU Atlantic	NAAS Boca Chica, FL	1

Service Units:

CASU-21	NAS Norfolk, VA	1
CASU-24	NAS Wildwood, NJ	1

Flag Units:

ComAllForcesAC	NAS San Juan, Puerto Rico	1
ComNavEu London	RAF Hendon, United Kingdom	3
ComEastSeaFron	NAS New York, NY	1
ComGulfSeaFron	NAS Miami, FL	2 (forming)
ComFltAirships Atlantic	NAS Richmond, FL	1

Non-Combat Elements – United States:

NAS Alameda, CA 1*; NAS Anacostia, DC 1; VN8D5 NAF Annapolis, MD 1; NAS Astoria, OR 1; NAS Atlantic City, NJ 1; NAS Attu, AK 1; BAR Bethpage, NY 1 (in acceptance); NATB Corpus Christi, TX 1; NATTC Corpus Christi, TX 1; NAF Dutch Harbor, AK 1; MCAS Ewa, HI 1; VTB-OTU-1 Fort Lauderdale, FL 1; NAS Glenview, IL 1; NAS Jacksonville, FL (OTU VM) 1; NATTC Jacksonville, FL 1; NAS Lakehurst, NJ 1; NAS Miami, FL 2; NAS New York, NY 1 (delivery); NAS Norfolk, VA 1; NAS Oakland, CA 1; NAS Palmyra Island, HI 1; MCAS Parris Island, SC 2: NAS Patuxent River, MD 1; NAS Pearl Harbor, HI 1; NAF Philadelphia, PA 1 (overhaul); NAS Puunene, HI 1; Pool NAS Quonset Point 2; NAS Richmond, FL 1; NAS San Diego, CA 1; VJ-11 NAS Santa Ana, CA 1; MCAS Santa Barbara, CA 1; NAS Seattle, WA 7 (including overhauls); Pool NAS South Weymouth, MA 6 (storage); NAS Squantum, MA 1; NAS Whidbey Island, WA 1

Non-Combat Elements – Overseas:

NAF Argentia, Newfoundland 2; NAF Bermuda 1; US Naval Mission Brazil 1; NAS Coco Solo, Panama 2; US Naval Attaché to Cuba 1; US Naval Attaché to Dominican Republic 1; NAS Guantanamo Bay, Cuba 1; US Naval Attaché to Guatemala 2; CNAB Mactan Islands (Cebu), Philippines 1; CNAB Manus, Admiralty Islands 1; AROU-1 Manus, Admiralty Islands 1 (awaiting strike); NAB Samar, Philippines 1; NAS San Juan, Puerto Rico 1; NAS Trinidad 2*; US Naval Attaché to Venezuela 1

Loan and Project Aircraft:

BAR Goodyear, Akron, OH 1; Columbia University, NY 1; NACA Langley Field, VA 1

* The Alameda aircraft and one of the Trinidad aircraft were JRF-4

The final five JRF-5s for the US Navy were received subsequently between October and December 1945.

Post-War Naval Operations

As already indicated, the JRF-5 Goose was not simply a WWII aircraft, indeed far from it. It remained in use for a further decade and it was not until the acquisition of the UF-1 Albatross in quantity in the early-mid' fifties that it would be stood down from its niche role as an amphibious utility aircraft.

Eventually, in the aftermath of the war, many aircraft were shipped home to the USA and placed in temporary storage, pending overhaul or repair. A few, beyond economic repair, were scrapped locally, but in 1946, only a handful of aircraft were dropped from the inventory. 1946 also saw the transfer of all the US Navy Coast Guard operations aircraft into US Coast Guard hands, in line with the return of the US Coast Guard to the US Treasury Department on 1st January 1946. This involved not only the survivors of the pre-war JRF-2/3 fleet, but all the JRF-5s allocated to Coast Guard Operations duties during the war, and thus 17 JRF-5s were transferred formally to the US Coast Guard on 31st July 1946.

The Navy was also directed to manage the repatriation of surviving naval Lend-Lease aircraft. In practice, this really only affected the Royal Navy's fleet of JRF-6Bs in Trinidad and a few others in the region, including the two outstanding JRF-5s that had been used by the British Air Commission (two others similarly used by the RCAF had been returned before the end of the war). Thirty-six aircraft were recovered in this way from the Royal Navy (see box on page 136) and were stored initially at Miami and Jacksonville, prior to overhaul and disposal. Virtually all were refurbished subsequently at Seattle and Miami, and were sold progressively to civilian buyers.

Together with a few war-weary 'regular Navy' aircraft released in 1946-47, these JRF-6Bs were the only US Navy Goose disposals for some years, of which many were destined to survive in civilian use for several decades.

This Grumman publicity photo taken by the late Harold G Martin reportedly shows the brand-new JRF-5 37818 (c/n B-71) and would therefore have been taken circa July 1944. However, 37818 was not delivered to the US Navy but was diverted instead to Iceland to become TF-RVK of Loftleidir. This may have been the reason for the photograph.
(Harold G Martin via MAP)

By early 1947, strength was less than 100 and of these, fifteen equipped the growing VN8D5 and another ten were in long-term storage at South Weymouth, MA. The balance was roughly equally divided between those in storage or overhaul at major stations and depots such as Alameda, Pearl Harbor, San Diego, Norfolk and Bethpage, and those active and attached to US Navy stations. The latter group included allocations to the ALUSNA Naval attaché programme, and to the first of the newly created Fleet Air Service Squadrons. The FASRONs were a feature of the Navy organisation for the remainder of the fleet's service life, but their multi-function role can sometimes lead to confusion in respect of their use. While some FASRONs had JRF-5s attached permanently as part of their establishments, many aircraft were attached to them as part of a transit or delivery process, while others might be briefly held in a state of semi-storage pending overhaul.

Between 1947 and 1950 there was little movement within the Goose fleet, although aircraft were shuttled between depots as stations closed, and overhaul and storage functions were re-allocated. As demonstrated by the data for January 1949 (see alongside), an increasing proportion of the fleet was now in storage or extended maintenance, and the Annapolis operation was continuing to grow in numbers (and was also providing the statisticians with an ever-increasing number of accidents and incidents). The VN8D5 squadron identity gave way to a snappy new identity 'Naval Air Activities Severn River Command' (NavAirActSRC) in August 1947, but perhaps unsurprisingly this was soon dropped in favour of plain NAF Annapolis in March 1950. The unit continued to grow and ultimately peaked at an establishment figure of 22 in 1949, with typically 20 active. While in the years before the Korean War many of the Annapolis sorties would be of questionable military value, the unit nevertheless served an important function, and the last operational JRF-5 would be an Annapolis aircraft. The 1949 data also highlights the work of the manufacturer as a maintenance contractor.

In 1950, Quonset Point became the primary support station for the JRF-5, undertaking all major overhaul and modification programmes until withdrawal of the fleet in 1956. 1950 was also one of the safest years of US Navy Goose operations, with only one accident resulting in a write-off. Only one aircraft was actually stricken in 1950, the EDO-modified ex-USAF 48-128, which was found to be operationally useless after its return. 1951 marked the beginning of the fleet run-down as the US Navy began the process of releasing from storage and overhaul some of the more battered aircraft, together with others that were almost unused. The major event in this respect was the release of 12 aircraft at Quonset Point under MDAP auspices to France, for use in Indo-China. In October 1952, another batch of 12 aircraft was made available to other US Government agencies, with four passing to the US Wildlife Service, and eight to the US Coast Guard. In December 1952, a further three were promised to the US Civil Aeronautics Administration. With other attrition, the inventory had been reduced to approximately 55 aircraft by December 1952.

Aircraft allocation was little changed in 1952, although from January 1952 until October 1955, the seaplane tender *Currituck* carried one aircraft. A second aircraft was aboard the *Curtiss,* from December 1953 until May 1954, during which time the ship took part in the 'Operation Castle' Pacific nuclear test programme. Another aircraft was loaned to the US Department of the Interior, from November 1950 until June 1953, for use in Greece in support of US Government reconstruction programmes.

The JRF-5 Fleet Disposition - January 1949

Air Force Atlantic Fleet

VX-1	NAS Key West, FL	1
Pool FASRON-102	NAS Norfolk, VA	1
FASRON-104	NAS Bermuda	1
Naval Attaché Greece	Athens, Greece	(1 not on hand)
Naval Attaché Norway	Oslo, Norway	(1 not on hand)
Naval Attaché Sweden	Stockholm, Sweden	1
NAS Argentia	NAS Argentia, Newfoundland	1
NAS Bermuda	NAS Bermuda	1
NAF Narsarssuak	NAF Narsarssuak, Greenland	(1 not on hand)
NAS Port Lyautey	NAS Port Lyautey, Fr Morocco	1
10th Naval District	NAS Trinidad	1

Air Force Pacific Fleet

14th Naval District	NAS Pearl Harbor, HI	1
17th Naval District	NAS Kodiak, AK	1

Naval Air Bases Continental

1st Naval District	NAS Quonset Point, RI	1
5th Naval District	NAS Norfolk, VA	1
6th Naval District	NAS Key West, FL	(1 not on hand)
12th Naval District	NAS Alameda, CA	1
13th Naval District	NAS Seattle, WA	(1 not on hand)
13th Naval District	NAS Whidbey Island, WA	1
AES 46	MCAS Cherry Point, NC	1

Potomac and Severn River Naval Commands:

NAS Anacostia	NAS Anacostia, DC	2
NAVAIRACTSRC	NAF Annapolis, MD	20

Research and Development and Design and Engineering (RD&DE)

Administrative and Flight Proficiency Aircraft:

RD&DE Administration	NAS Patuxent River, MD	1
RD&DE Administration	NAAS Mustin Field, PA	1

Project Aircraft:

RD&DE Projects	Sundries	4
NAS Patuxent River	NAS Patuxent River, MD	1
NACA Langley	Langley Field, VA	1
NAF Philadelphia (Mustin)	NAF Philadelphia, PA	1
Pool BAR Bethpage	Bethpage, NY	1 (in modification)

BuAer Materiel & Services Group – Non-operational Aircraft

Pool MCAS Cherry Point	MCAS Cherry Point, NC	7 (storage)
Pool BAR Bethpage	Bethpage, NY	11 (overhaul)
Pool NAS Norfolk	NAS Norfolk, VA*	10 (repair & overhaul)
Storage Litchfield Park	NAF Litchfield Park, AZ	2 (storage)
Storage South Weymouth	NAF South Weymouth, MA	13 (storage)

* Norfolk total includes one JRF-4 (3854) awaiting overhaul

A number of JRF-5s were assigned to the American Legation US Naval Attaché (ALUSNA) programme in the late 1940s and early 1950s. The Naval Attaché to Norway possessed an aircraft from 1949 until 1953 when it was replaced by a UF-1 Albatross. 37813 (c/n B-66) was on strength in 1950-51 and here shows the large US flag, typical of the ALUSNA aircraft. The ALUSNA aircraft were particularly well looked after and perhaps unsurprisingly this was one of the machines later brought to JRF-6 standard. (via AJ Jackson)

The JRF-5 Fleet Disposition - January 1953

Air Force Atlantic Fleet

FASRON-104	NAF Port Lyautey, Fr Morocco	1
FASRON-795	NAS Bermuda	1
AV & CV Fleet Training	AV-7 USS *Currituck*	1
10th Naval District	NAS Guantanamo Bay, Cuba	1
Naval Attaché Greece	Athens, Greece	1
Naval Attaché Norway	Oslo, Norway	1

Air Force Pacific Fleet

FASRON-113	NAS Seattle, WA	1
FASRON-114	NAS Kodiak, AK	1

Naval Air Bases Continental

1st Naval District	NAS Quonset Point, RI	1
12th Naval District	NAS Alameda, CA	1
Potomac River Naval Cmnd	NAS Anacostia, DC	1
Severn River Naval Cmnd	NAF Annapolis, MD	10

Naval Reserve

NARTU Anacostia	NAS Anacostia, DC	1

Research and Development

Project Aircraft	Sundry	1
NACA Langley	Langley Field, VA	1
R&D Patuxent River	NATC Patuxent River, MD	1
BAR College Point (EDO)	College Point, NY	1

BuAer Overhaul & Repair Activities

BuAer Cherry Point	MCAS Cherry Point, NC	6 (storage)
BuAer Quonset Point	NAS Quonset Point, RI	15* (overhaul & upgrade)
BuAer San Diego	NAS San Diego, CA	1 (overhaul)
Miscellaneous Activities:		
Dept of Interior (loan)	USA	1 (loan)
Dept of Interior (loan)	Greece	1 (loan)
Storage Facilities:		
Storage Litchfield Park	NAF Litchfield Park, AZ	1 (for disposal)

* Quonset Point total includes seven aircraft in conversion and known as JRF-6X at time of census, and aircraft in preparation for disposal to the US Coast Guard and other agencies.

1953 saw 15 JRF-5s overhauled and modernised at Quonset Point, after which they were known officially as the JRF-6. The records suggest that the modified aircraft were not intended to fulfil any new or special functions and were allocated to the dwindling number of user units much as before. Annapolis received several of the enhanced aircraft and used them alongside un-modified JRF-5s. In December 1953, the JRF-6 fleet constituted almost half of the total Goose force. MDAP and other US Governmental agencies continued to receive surplus aircraft, and in July 1953 another batch of five aircraft was released from Quonset Point for supply to the French in Indo-China. The previous batch of French aircraft had been worked very hard and these were urgently needed attrition replacements. In September 1953, five of the late production JRF-5s were released to the US Department of the Interior (Land Management), and four more were disposed of in non-flyable condition.

By 1954, there was only one significant user of the Goose and that was the Annapolis academy, which retained a unit establishment of 12 aircraft (typically including up to 10 JRF-6s) until mid-1955, when a gradual run-down process commenced. 1954 witnessed the last withdrawal of an 'overseas' aircraft when it was withdrawn from Bermuda in August, and after Kodiak's machine was withdrawn in January 1955, only Annapolis, Norfolk and *Currituck* remained active users. The inventory was increased briefly when seven surplus US Coast Guard JRF-5s were taken on charge in May 1954, all aircraft going to the Storage Facility, Litchfield Park (the US Navy did not recognise 'JRF-5G' as a separate type reference and these aircraft were inventoried as the regular JRF-5). That same month four aircraft were released under MDAP for transfer to Japan. Including sundry loan and BuAer project aircraft, approximately

This undated photograph is said to be that of JRF-5 34083 (c/n B-12), presumably after its disposal by the US Navy at Quonset Point in 1953. Although obviously here seen in a substantive state, nothing more is known about the aircraft after leaving the service. (Collect-Air Photos)

34 JRF-5 and JRF-6s remained on strength at the end of 1954, with only 16 in active use with US Navy units.

The final run-down began in earnest in the summer of 1955, when a number of the stored aircraft at Litchfield Park were declared surplus. Six other aircraft, five of which had come earlier from the US Coast Guard, were ferried from Litchfield Park to Alameda in June and July 1955 for preparation for an undisclosed MDAP recipient (see page 106). These aircraft eventually departed Alameda by sea in September 1955. By February 1956 only Annapolis remained a US Navy user, with seven JRF-6s. Aircraft were now being sold to the civilian market, although Government agencies continued to receive odd examples, usually those with fewer flight hours.

The last Goose in regular US Navy use appears to have been JRF-6 37813, that was withdrawn to Litchfield Park, AZ from Annapolis, MD in July 1956, and which happily survives to the present day. However, the JRF-5 lingered in the inventory, and in January 1957, there were still four on the books; two on loan to Alaska Coastal Airlines, one with Kaman Aircraft in the process of becoming the K-16B and another with NACA at Langley Field. The two loan aircraft were the last to go, with a formal strike date of December 1958. This, however, was not quite the end of the story of the US Navy Goose.

For many years the US Navy and the EDO Corporation of College Point, NY had worked closely on various hull and float design concepts, and indeed several JRF-5s had been bailed to EDO for such projects. In 1957-58 work was continuing with evaluation of the Gruenberg hydrofoil system (see page 75), and EDO was loaned a former US Coast Guard JRF-5 (which by now the US Navy was prepared to call a JRF-5G!). This aircraft had not been on the Navy's books since 1946, but was re-adopted by the Navy for the duration of the work (the individual aircraft history of 37782 provides details of the 'owning' naval units). Initially the aircraft retained US Coast Guard markings, but by the time it was evaluated at NATC Patuxent River in 1963-64, it had acquired US Navy/NATC markings. 37782 was returned

eventually to the US Coast Guard, circa June 1965, and ultimately became a museum exhibit, thus finally ending its 25 year naval career.

Colours and Markings

The US Navy and US Marine Corps JRF fleet wore a wide variety of markings that reflected both formal instructions and local style. Over the course of time individual aircraft frequently changed markings and a good number changed the basic colour scheme at least once in their lives, usually during the course of depot maintenance. Given the complexity of the subject, only a limited summary of basic colours and markings is included here.

Although there were many unusual colour schemes applied for various diverse purposes, there were essentially four basic schemes applied to new production aircraft. The first of these was a bland silver scheme overall with black hull and lower floats. The aircraft type and serial number were applied in small characters on the tail-fin and rudder and the title 'U.S. Navy' or 'U.S. Marines' appeared on the lower rear fuselage. The early 'red centre' roundels were applied to the upper and lower wings, but not to the fuselage. Unit markings and

code letters appeared on some aircraft, and before late-1941 they might reflect the station by name, command by title, or the squadron by name and 'plane in squadron' number. Thus, JRF-1A 1671 of VJ-1 wore the code '1-J-11' in December 1939, as well as high-visibility (red?) tail markings reflecting its role as a target-tug. The JRF-4 3846, used by the commanding general of the Fleet Marine Force at San Diego in 1941, used the code '2-W-1' indicating that it was on the strength of the Headquarters Squadron of the 2nd Marine Air Wing. Such markings were typical of the pre-war Navy and Marine Corps.

Silver was abandoned as a basic scheme in October 1941 and was replaced by the 'blue-grey' scheme. The aircraft's upper surfaces and sides were painted in a non-specular blue-grey shade while the lower surfaces remained light grey. External titling disappeared, although some codes remained in use. Prior to May 1942, the 'red centre' roundel was applied to the rear fuselage, as well as to the wings. This camouflage was retrospectively applied to the earlier aircraft. After June 1942, the 'red centre' disappeared from all US military roundels.

A third scheme appeared in 1943 in which a dark non-specular blue on the upper surfaces and fuselage top graduated to a Light Grey-Blue on the lower sides which gave to way to White under-surfaces. In July 1943, the 'star and bar' roundel began appearing on the forward fuselage (nose), initially being outlined in red and then, post-September 1943, in blue. The final basic change that affected new-production JRF-5s was the introduction of the Glossy Sea Blue ('Midnite Blue') over-all scheme in early 1944. In this scheme the roundel was reduced to a white star flanked by solid White blocks (the Red 'bar' was not added to the white block until January 1947).

By 1946, the fleet, some of which were migrating to storage, reflected all four schemes, and variations thereof. A number

This anonymous JRF-5, assumed to be a Navy rather than a Coast Guard aircraft, is seen here in the post June 1942 'blue-grey' colour scheme. The Goose is carrying a 325lb Mk17 Depth Bomb beneath the starboard wing. (Grumman photo)

Taken after its disposal by the Navy in 1956 and prior to its becoming N789 with the US Wildlife Service, this photograph of JRF-6 84807 (c/n B-102) is noteworthy as an excellent example of 1953-era second-line US Navy training markings. Fresh from modification at Quonset Point in 1953, it would serve at NART Grosse Ile for only a few months before retirement. The passage of time has enabled earlier markings to reappear.

(Douglas O Olson via Jennifer Gradidge)

The US Naval Academy at Annapolis was, by a distance, the greatest single user of the naval Goose. In varying numbers, peaking at about 20 active in 1950, it was used from 1945 until 1956, mainly providing basic familiarisation and proficiency opportunities to both cadets and those desk-bound in Washington. JRF-6 84810 '5' (c/n B-105) came on strength in September 1953 and came to grief like several of its sister-ships in a local accident the following year.

(via AJ Jackson)

of aircraft, including some of the 'Midnite Blue' aircraft, reverted to silver schemes and a plethora of unit codes and local markings could be seen. A number of aircraft began to acquire the 'last three' of the serial on the fuselage, either on the nose or rear fuselage, and command titles began to appear. By the early 1950s, a typical 'midnite' aircraft might have 'United States Navy' block titles and a large 'last three' on the rear fuselage together with the station name or, for example, the FASRON identification across the tail-fin and rudder. From 1950, the abbreviated fuselage title 'NAVY' was re-adopted, and some aircraft were also marked by letter codes to indicate their home station. Thus, in 1953, the Midnite Blue JRF-6 84807, used by NART Grosse Ile, wore the station code 'I' on the tail as well as the station name on the

fuselage. This name was contained within a high visibility ('International Orange') fuselage band, markings typical of many US Navy aircraft of the period. The Annapolis academy aircraft of the early-mid 1950s, befitting their 'parade' status, were turned-out uniformly and smartly with individual aircraft code numbers and 'Annapolis' tail-fin titles. The word 'Annapolis' was painted in white beneath the starboard wing and 'Navy' beneath the port wing. Equally smart were the ALUSNA aircraft, which invariably had formal fuselage titles reflecting their diplomatic credentials. Aircraft elsewhere often wore the 'last three' beneath the port wing, and the Grosse Ile aircraft mentioned above wore '807 I NAVY'.

It will be appreciated that many aircraft will have worn unique colour schemes and

individual markings that will have passed sadly un-noticed and un-recorded. This short summary will hopefully have provided an overview of a very detailed subject.

Serial Numbers

The following list includes all aircraft that received BuAer serial numbers, regardless of purpose or the circumstances of the allocation. It also includes all aircraft allocated BuAer serials, but which were transferred as new equipment to non-US Navy users, including allotments to the US Coast Guard during WWII. Brief explanations of such use are included but fuller details will be found elsewhere in the text. The designations of the miscellaneous acquisitions are from US Navy records.

BuAer serial	Type	C/n	Circumstances
1384	XJ3F-1	1021	Prototype US Navy aircraft
1671 to 1673	JRF-1A	1066 to 1068	Production for US Navy
1674 to 1677	JRF-1	1069 to 1072	Production for US Navy
1678 to 1679	JRF-1A	1073 to 1074	Production for US Navy
1680	JRF-1	1075	Production for US Navy
3846 to 3855	JRF-4	1100 to 1109	Production for US Navy
6440 to 6454	JRF-5	1110 to 1124	Production for US Navy
03713 to 03742	JRF-5	None	Cancelled 1941 allocation
04349 to 04358	JRF-5	1176 to 1185	Production for US Navy
07004	JRF-1	1011	G-21A NC1294 acquired Jan42
09767	JRF-4	1060	G-21A NC2786 acquired Mar42
09782	JRF-1	1017	G-21A NC20643 acquired Jun42
34060 to 34071	JRF-5	1189 to 1200	Production for US Navy
34072 to 34094	JRF-5	B-1 to B-23	Production for US Navy & US Coast Guard
35921	JRF-5	1188	G-21A NX1604 acquired 1942
37771 to 37831	JRF-5	B-24 to B-84	Production for US Navy, US Coast Guard, Lend-Lease and other Foreign Sales
39747 to 39748	JRF-5	1186 to 1187	Production for Cuba
48229	JRF-5	1004	1942 allocation for G-21A NC16913. Probably not used
50660 to 50689	JRF-5	None	Cancelled allocation
66325 to 66359	JRF-6B	See box alongside	1946 allocations to Lend-Lease aircraft returned by the United Kingdom
66360 to 66361	JRF-5	See box alongside	1946 allocations to Lend-Lease aircraft returned by the United Kingdom
84790 to 84818	JRF-5	B-85 to B-113	Production for US Navy, US Coast Guard, Lend-Lease and other Foreign Sales
87720 to 87751	JRF-5	B-114 to B-145	Production for US Navy, US Coast Guard & sundry transfers
87752 to 87762	JRF-5	B-146 to B-156	Cancelled aircraft
89492	JRF-6B	See box alongside	1946 allocation to Lend-Lease aircraft returned by the United Kingdom
99078	JRF-1	1014	G-21A NC20620 acquired 1943

USN	c/n	UK	BuAer
JRF-6B			
66325	1138	FP488	0194B
66326	1146	FP496	0202B
66327	1153	FP503	0209B
66328	1167	FP517	0223B
66329	1171	FP521	0227B
66330	1133	FP483	0189B
66331	1161	FP511	0217B
66332	1165	FP515	0221B
66333	1172	FP522	0228B
66334	1126	FP476	0182B
66335	1173	FP523	0229B
66336	1164	FP514	0220B
66337	1162	FP512	0218B
66338	1170	FP520	0226B
66339	1130	FP480	0186B
66340	1134	FP484	0190B
66341	1168	FP518	0224B
66342	1139	FP489	0195B
66343	1160	FP510	0216B
66344	1163	FP513	0219B
66345	1144	FP494	0200B
66346	1148	FP498	0204B
66347	1149	FP499	0205B
66348	1137	FP487	0193B
66349	1166	FP516	0222B
66350	1151	FP501	0207B
66351	1145	FP495	0201B
66352	1143	FP493	0199B
66353	1140	FP490	0196B
66354	1141	FP491	0197B
66355	1125	FP475	0181B
66356	1136	FP486	0192B
66357	1147	FP497	0203B
66358	1152	FP502	0208B
66359	1129	FP479	0185B
89492	1132	FP482	0188B
JRF-5			
66360	B-34	FP470	37781
66361	B-49	FP472	37796

Lend-Lease Returnees

The circumstances of the United Kingdom return process are explained elsewhere. There appears to be no surviving single document neatly listing the returned aircraft, indeed all evidence points to a confused allocation process, probably resulting from uncertainty over just how many aircraft would be returned. The serial block 66325 to 66361 was part of a cancelled batch of PB4Y-2 Privateers and thus their re-use in early 1946 is of itself confusing. 89492 was an inconsistent allocation within a block of serials otherwise re-used for SNB-5 Lend-Lease returns from the United Kingdom. The movement record card incorrectly quotes the type as 'JRB-6B'.

The primary source of data linking British serials (and hence the c/ns) with the BuAer serials is the microfilmed record of the BuAer movement cards, but some are illegible. British records appear to be non-existent. Fortunately, many of the surviving British aircraft went on to have long lives in private and non-American ownership, and in many instances their subsequent records have provided supplementary intelligence. A lack of certainty in respect of British attrition has further clouded the picture. Ultimately, 36 of the 44 British JRF-6Bs were returned to the USA as 66325 to 66359 and 89492, while 66360 and 66361 were allocated unnecessarily to two JRF-5s that had previous BuAer allocations.

The table includes the BuAer reference numbers allocated to the British aircraft before their delivery in 1942-43 (see page 116 for an explanation of these numbers).

Widgeon

Acquisition

Unlike the JRF Goose, the G-44 Widgeon was not perceived to be appropriate equipment for the US Navy until after the United States was attacked on 7th December 1941, and the nation went to war. At that time, approximately 40 aircraft had been manufactured, mainly for the US corporate and private market, but including eight recently delivered to the US Coast Guard, as the J4F-1 model. Further US Coast Guard aircraft were in production, and a batch of 12 G-44s was almost ready for delivery to the Portuguese Navy. In the changed circumstances, the Widgeon was quickly recognised as having military potential, albeit mainly in the communications role in areas where the little amphibian's adaptability made it an ideal 'taxi'. Notwithstanding the US Coast Guard's anticipated use of their J4F-1s for important inshore coastal patrol and anti-submarine activities, the Widgeon was not seen by the Navy as a potential combat aircraft.

The great majority of the civilian-owned G-44s available to the military were acquired by the Army Air Corps, leaving just one aircraft, the future 09789, to be purchased by the Navy, and given the designation J4F-2, the '-2' suffix being indicative of US Navy use rather than signifying any specific modifications. It is also useful to note that this particular BuAer serial was one of a block allocated in December 1941 for miscellaneous acquisitions. In fact, this Widgeon, the former NC1055, was acquired in February 1942 by American Export Airlines (AEA) on behalf of the US Navy, but was not sold to the Navy until August 1942 (contract C97456), after which it was used by AEA, under contract to the Naval Air Transport Service (NATS).

Immediately following the declaration of war in December 1941, the US Government briefly suspended all exports of military equipment, pending decisions on their potential value to the US armed forces. Although no confirmatory documentary evidence has been located, it seems highly likely that the unused serial block 09805 to 09816, dating from December 1941, was set aside for the potential acquisition of the Portuguese G-44s that were about to be delivered. In the event this plan was short-lived and the Portuguese Widgeons were delivered to the customer with little delay, between December 1941 and February 1942.

The first truly naval J4F-2 was 30151 (c/n 1270), although its origins are unclear. It was acquired on contract LL5229, a Lend-Lease contract dated 10th June 1942, that also covered six aircraft intended for the Cuban Navy. However, as 30151 was accepted by the Navy on 10th July 1942, it is possible that this was also an 'acquisition', albeit of a new airframe, rather than a conventional prototype order. It remained at Bethpage throughout the war, assigned to the local Bureau of Aeronautics Representative (i.e. on Grumman's charge).

There were only two US Navy production contracts awarded to Grumman for the Widgeon, in 1942 and 1943. The first was NXs5229, dated 15th August 1942, for 50 aircraft, with serials 32937 to 32986, and this was followed by NOa(S)455, dated 6th November 1943, for 60 aircraft, numbered 37711 to 37770. The first batch was delivered between December 1942 and November 1943, and this was followed by the second batch, with deliveries continuing from November 1943 until the final acceptance, which took place on 26th February 1945. Further planned production for the US Navy did not take place, and although serial numbers were apparently allocated, no contracts were placed. Of the 110 production aircraft, a total of 17 spent some of their time with the British forces in North America under Lend-Lease terms, but all except two were returned later into US hands. Six of these, returned in October

and December 1945, subsequently served with active naval units prior to their retirement. Two other production aircraft were made available to third-parties and saw no US Navy service. These were 37712, delivered to Uruguay under Lend-Lease in November 1943, and 37740 released to Union Oil as NC1004 in June 1944.

The Navy additionally acquired several other Widgeons, all of which have complicated and poorly understood histories. The first of these was a batch of six aircraft built for the Cuban Navy between July and September 1942. These aircraft were produced for Cuba under what became Lend-Lease arrangements prior to the adoption of the J4F-2 model for the US Navy, and were thus laid down as the J4F-1 model as part of a larger group of 20 airframes, the balance of which went to Brazil. For reasons that are not at all clear, Cuba rejected these aircraft, probably prior to 1st August 1942, and by early September 1942 these six aircraft had been acquired by the US Navy as J4F-2s on contract NXs5229. The US Navy took delivery of at least five aircraft (33953 to 33957) in September and October 1942, but the early history of 33952 is obscure and it is possible that it was diverted to the US Coast Guard as a replacement for the aircraft that had earlier become 34585. This complicated situation is explored below in the US Coast Guard notes.

34585 (c/n 1269), acquired in October 1942, was the final production US Coast Guard J4F-1 V221, delivered to the US Coast Guard in June 1942. It was transferred to the US Navy for the use of the Naval Attaché to the Dominican Republic, but was lost in a fatal accident in Santo Domingo on 24th October 1942. While it is evident from the Navy's movement card that 34585 was the serial allocated to V221, the accident report speaks only of V221, and the assumption is that BuAer 34585 was never physically applied to the aircraft.

Serials 99074 to 99077 were allocated to four Pan American Airways Atlantic Division G-44s that were acquired by the Navy in 1943 as J4F-2s. The precise purchase date is uncertain as is the date of serial allocation, the BuAer numbers in question being part of a larger allocation of 'miscellaneous acquisitions', retrospectively allocated as part of an administrative tidying-up process. It does, however, seem certain that the serials were never applied to the aircraft during WWII. Pan American had used these aircraft as instrument and lead-in trainers for their larger equipment (also acquired by the Navy and the USAAF) and the aircraft remained based at La Guardia, New York, where they were used by Pan American in support of NATS operations (09789 was similarly used by AEA at New York). Eventually 99074 to 99076 were sold back to Pan American in August 1945, while 99077 remained with the US Navy until its disposal, with others, in February 1947.

Establishing the exact number of Widgeons that served with the US Navy is

a complex and perhaps unnecessary exercise as any total depends upon personal definitions of 'use'. However, it can be seen that five former G-44s (09789 and 99074 to 99077) were used together with 118 J4F-2s (30151, 32937 to 32986, 33952 to 33957, 34585 and 37711 to 37770). However this total of 118 includes two aircraft that saw no US Navy service (the Uruguayan and Union Oil aircraft) and, in all, 17 aircraft that were used by the British services and which saw varying levels of use by the US Navy. A point of additional confusion would also be the designation of 34585. This was a J4F-1 that was recorded administratively as a J4F-2 during its brief naval life.

While the Widgeon's relatively quiet operational US Navy history is dealt with more fully below, two aircraft had particularly unusual histories and served the Navy considerably longer than did the rest of the fleet, all of which were withdrawn by March 1947. J4F-2 32972, having been transferred to the US Coast Guard in July 1946, and from there to NACA Langley, was formally taken back by the Navy on 31st October 1949 as the XJ4F-2, remaining on the books until stricken at the NATC Patuxent River in October 1954. 32976 was transferred to EDO Aircraft of College Point, New York in January 1947, where it was grossly modified and became known as the E-175, a designation formally recognised and subsequently reported on by the Navy. The E-175 was to be the longest serving US Navy Widgeon and was not withdrawn until February 1956.

Operational History

Unlike the Goose, the Widgeon was most definitely only a war-time aircraft with the US Navy. As explained above, it did not enter the inventory until late in 1942, production ceased in February 1945, and virtually the entire fleet was withdrawn in 1946. For all practical purposes there was only one production model, the J4F-2, and this was essentially a uniformed, civilian G-44. However, it was a versatile and popular aircraft, and was used in most naval theatres, suffering agreeably low attrition in naval hands.

Service introduction was complicated by the unexpected and premature arrival of the six intended Cuban aircraft in late 1942 which, in practice, became the first aircraft to enter operational service. At least five of these aircraft were assigned to Inshore Patrol Squadrons operating on the north-east seaboard within the Eastern Sea Frontier, where they remained through a number of organisational changes until late 1944. The sixth aircraft, 33952 and the first of the batch, has a poorly recorded history and may have served with the US Coast Guard.

The definitive production J4F-2 aircraft began to reach the fleet in January 1943. Like the JRF-5 Goose, it was classified as a 'VJ(M)' or Multi-engined Utility type, and

This particular Widgeon's record reveals a most complicated movement history during the immediate post-war years that is unfortunately still not fully understood. J4F-2 32943 (c/n 1297) is seen here at Croydon, UK on 20th October 1946, by which time it had been registered NC79801 to a New York-based dealer. Still in US Navy markings, it had been declared surplus in March 1946 when on the strength of the US Naval Attaché to Egypt and the aircraft is presumed to have been ferried from Cairo to the UK later in the year. A typical US Navy 'Plain Jane' J4F-2, 32943 wears no obvious unit (or trace of) markings and the significance of the tail-fin character is unknown. Subsequently it went to France for military evaluation and other adventures and was last heard of in 1960 registered in the Cape Verde Islands.   *(Peter Barrington via DM Hannah)*

was assigned in general to units and stations in ones or twos, operating within a pool of mixed types. In US Navy use it was typically flown by one or two crew and would carry up to three passengers. Aircraft were usually accepted by the Navy at Bethpage and delivered through NAS New York, with aircraft destined for overseas use normally ferried to Alameda or San Diego on the west coast and Norfolk on the east. Production in 1943 and 1944 was about one aircraft every week, inclusive of those delivered into British hands.

Normally the Widgeon was assigned at Air Station or Air Facility level within the United States and Alaska, but as the war progressed and naval aviation grew in size, aircraft began to be assigned to an increasing number of Auxiliary Air Stations and training units, some of which had very short lives. By 1944, aircraft were assigned to units of all kinds, including Fleet and Marine Air Wings, Fleet Airship Wings and Carrier Air Service Units. The aircraft were used extensively for local communications and ferrying activity, most obviously where a marine environment necessitated the use of an amphibian. By 1945, several aircraft were on permanent assignment to Bureau of Aeronautics Representatives (BAR) at supplier factories, and it is appropriate to note that some of the British Lend-Lease Widgeons were used by the BAC in identical fashion. A small number of J4F-2s were used by the US Marine Corps, but none were supplied to the US Coast Guard from naval stocks until after the war.

Beyond the United States, the Widgeon was used extensively from bases in the Hawaiian Islands, the Caribbean and in Brazil, with FAW-16. Elsewhere in the

The J4F-2 Widgeon had only a brief service life with the US Navy and post-war the great majority of them were sold off rapidly to the commercial market. 32980 (c/n 1334) is a typical aircraft, stricken from naval charge in July 1946 as 'obsolete and surplus'. The markings are typically austere, Carrier Aircraft Service Unit 27, NAS Chincoteague being its final operational unit in early 1946. The photograph is assumed to have been taken on a civilian field after its naval service was concluded. Happily the aircraft continues to fly in Alaska as N90727.   *(via Collect-Air Photos)*

Pacific, a few were used in the Philippines and Guam theatres late in the war but such use was markedly less than that of the more robust Goose. FAW-15 at Port Lyautey, Morocco also used one, and two were used later by the Air Attaché, Cairo, but these were the only J4F-2s to operate in Africa or Europe.

Including the five NATS aircraft used by Pan American and American Export Airlines, peak strength was achieved in February 1945 when, excluding the British aircraft, slightly fewer than 100 were on the inventory. In all 12 aircraft were lost, never to fly again, by the Navy during the life of the Widgeon with almost all accidents

blamed at least in part on pilot error. In the hands of an experienced pilot the Widgeon was a very safe aircraft. Prior to 1945, very few non-damaged aircraft received major overhauls and it was not until mid-1945 that NAS Seattle began to receive the aircraft in quantity. While other depots also undertook J4F overhauls, the great majority of work and storage was undertaken at Seattle.

Run-down of the fleet began a few days before the defeat of Japan, when three damaged aircraft were stricken at Pearl Harbor, but the great majority of the Widgeons were released in 1946, leaving only ten on strength at the year end. In June 1946, twelve Widgeons were transferred to

Coast Guard operations, and on 31st July 1946, all of them were transferred formally to the US Coast Guard. Of the ten US Navy aircraft that survived into 1947, one was released in January, six in February, one in June and one in July 1947, leaving only 32976 with the EDO Corporation. As previously explained, 32972 would return eventually into naval hands from NACA, and 32972 and 32976 would survive for many more years, undertaking test work that could never have been envisaged in 1940.

(32972 was not on the Navy's books in 1947 (it went from the US Coast Guard to NACA) so was not one of the ten on strength. 32976, although with EDO, was on Naval strength throughout.).

The British Lend-Lease aircraft were returned into US Navy hands in October and December 1945, with others seeing no subsequent naval use and passing directly to a disposal process. As all aircraft had recognisable BuAer identities there was no need to raise new serials (as had been necessary in respect of the British JRF-6B fleet). Although many Widgeons were stricken and disposed of at remote locations (such as Cairo, Egypt) it was testimony to the strength and popularity of the aircraft that, almost without exception, every aircraft was registered subsequently for civil use, and eventually made flyable. Moreover, many have survived to the present day.

Serial Numbers			
Serial (BuAer no.)	*Type*	*C/n*	*Circumstances*
09789	J4F-2	1231	G-44 NC1055 acquired Aug42
09805 to 09816	'J4F-2'	None	Cancelled allocation
30151	J4F-2	1270	Production for US Navy
32937 to 32986	J4F-2	1291 to 1340	Production for US Navy
33952 to 33953	J4F-2	1273 to 1274	Gain for US Navy from Cuba Sep42
33954 to 33955	J4F-2	1277 to 1278	Gain for US Navy from Cuba Sep42
33956 to 33957	J4F-2	1281 to 1282	Gain for US Navy from Cuba Sep42
34585	J4F-1	1269	V221 from US Coast Guard Oct42
37711 to 37770	J4F-2	1341 to 1400	Production for US Navy
50889 to 51022	J4F-2	None	Cancelled allocation
67807 to 67831	J4F-2	None	Cancelled allocation
99074	J4F-2	Uncertain	G-44 acquired from PAA 1943
99075	J4F-2	Uncertain	G-44 acquired from PAA 1943
99076	J4F-2	Uncertain	G-44 acquired from PAA 1943
99077	J4F-2	1235	G-44 NC1000 from PAA 1943

The uncertain c/ns of the three former Pan American G-44s were 1214 (NC28675), 1215 (NC28676) and 1239 (NC37189), sequence unknown. The serial block 09805 to 09816, allocated to 'J4F-2' and dating from December 1941, was not used and probably relates to the potential acquisition of the G-44 production batch that was delivered to Portugal.

Colours and Markings

In general, the US Navy J4F-2s followed the same naval rules in respect of basic colours as did the JRF fleet, although the 'Midnite Blue' scheme of 1944 does not appear to have been used by the Widgeon. The type's early withdrawal in 1946 generally limited individual markings to the 'minimalist' functional stencilling of the later war years, and many aircraft accordingly had an anonymous appearance.

UNITED STATES COAST GUARD

Goose

Variants and Acquisition

The US Coast Guard, in common with the Army and Navy, was quick to recognise the eminent suitability of the commercial G-21A Goose to meet its need for a multi-purpose amphibian to replace other increasingly obsolescent types within its inventory. The pre-war Coast Guard's aviation assets were nothing if not varied and there was a real need for modern, purpose-built equipment. That said, budgets were tight and the Goose was procured initially in small batches, with some aircraft equipped for station-specific use.

The Coast Guard placed its first order (contract TCG-29648) for three aircraft in 1938. It specified an aircraft with the standard commercial 450hp Wasp Jr SB-2 engines and an interior equipped for general purpose work, with easily removable seats and stretcher fittings. The aircraft was identified by Grumman as the model G-39 and was given the BuAer identity JRF-2. The serials would be V174 to V176 and the aircraft were delivered in September and October 1939. By then further orders had been placed for additional JRF-2s, and for an enhanced version, to be known as the JRF-3.

The follow-on order for the JRF-2s (contract TCG-30750) called for four aircraft, serials V184 to V187, that would be delivered in February and March 1940. The three modified aircraft (contract TCG-33389), serials V190 to V192, were intended for use in cold weather environments and were equipped with de-icing boots on the leading edges of the wings and tail. They were also fitted with an autopilot, and these three aircraft were considered significantly different enough from the JRF-2 to warrant the designation JRF-3. The JRF-3s were delivered in October and November 1940.

Although the custom-built JRF-2 and JRF-3 performed outstandingly well throughout the future war (and most survived), it would be the Navy's JRF-5 that proved to be the definitive US Coast Guard model and ultimately would remain in service with the USCG until 1956. The acquisition of the JRF-5 would not happen until 1943, by which time the US Coast Guard would be operating within the Navy Department and undertaking a role defined by the US Navy. Eventually the order of 36 JRF-5s would see use with the US Coast Guard in various ways at various times, and their somewhat complicated

The first of the US Coast Guard's JRF-2 aircraft is seen at the end of the line at Buchanan Field, Concord, CA on 21st January 1947. V174 (c/n 1063) wears its war-time Navy blue colours with the post-war high-visibility yellow bands and floats. The pre-war practice of wearing the serial on the hull had returned. Although sold on the civilian market as NC68902, probably before the date of the photo, nothing is known of any further use. (William T Larkins)

US Coast Guard JRF-3 V191 (c/n 1086) is probably seen here pre-delivery at Bethpage. The decision to adopt the 'dash 3' suffix reflected relatively minor modifications to the 'dash 2' model and might explain the apparent mistake in temporarily stencilling 'JRF-2' on the fin. This aircraft survived the war and many years later it was placed on display at the National Museum of Naval Aviation at Pensacola, Florida, albeit incorrectly marked as 'V190'.

(Real Photos via MAP)

As far as is known, this familiar but glorious publicity shot of three Coast Guard JRF-2s dates from circa 1940 and shows V175, V185 and V186 (c/ns 1064, 1077 & 1078 respectively) probably up from CGAS Elizabeth City in their colourful pre-war uniforms. Courtesy of a dearth of surviving official records, we do not know the final fates of any of these aircraft, although the assumption is that all were eventually withdrawn from use as 'war-weary'.

(US Coast Guard photo)

changing as the implications of this not-so-distant conflict became ever more serious. The Goose took its place with the rest of the pre-war fleet undertaking neutrality patrols and increasing numbers of search and rescue missions, alongside other more traditional tasks. The winterised V192 reportedly undertook 18 reconnaissance sorties over the Great Lakes in support of ice-breaking operations during the first two weeks of April 1941. As the Atlantic war increased in ferocity, and the United States became actively involved protecting its interests, Coast Guard aircraft augmented the Navy's anti-submarine and convoy defence activities. The Goose fleet reached full strength in November 1940 and, almost incredibly in the circumstances, all ten aircraft would survive until after the United States entered the war a year later. As will be seen below the fleet was widely dispersed.

During 1941, a number of Coast Guard functions were transferred to US Navy

story is recounted below. As will be explained, the 'JRF-5G' designation used by the US Coast Guard in the 'fifties does not describe a technical specification, and will not be used here.

Coast Guard Operations 1939 to 1945

Following trials, training and acceptance activities at Bethpage, the first three JRF-2 aircraft were delivered into Coast Guard hands at CGAS Brooklyn in October 1939. By now there was a war in Europe, and the role of the US Coast Guard was rapidly

The JRF-2/3 Fleet Disposition – December 1941			
CGAS Salem	Salem, MA	JRF-2	V185
CGAS Brooklyn	New York, NY	JRF-3	V190, V191
CGAS Biloxi	Biloxi, MS	JRF-2	V184
CGAS Port Angeles	Port Angeles, WA	JRF-2	V176
CGAS Elizabeth City	Elizabeth City, NC	JRF-2	V175, V186
Air Patrol Det Traverse City	Traverse City, MI	JRF-3	V192
Senior CG Officer, 14th Naval District	NAS Pearl Harbor, HI	JRF-2	V187
Senior CG Officer, 7th Naval District	NAS Charleston, SC	JRF-2	V174

control and finally, on 1st November 1941, the remaining assets and activities of the US Coast Guard were transferred from the Treasury Department to the Department of the Navy, until further notice. This move, pre-dating Pearl Harbor, placed all US Coast Guard aviation activity under US Navy control. In practice, this typically allowed the senior Coast Guard officer to continue to manage his station logistically, while operations were controlled entirely by the Navy. Thus, for example, CGAS Brooklyn was subordinated to NAS New York on 16th December 1941. US Coast Guard aircraft were now needed urgently by the Navy to augment the limited naval air strength defending coastal shipping and harbours against the submarine threat. In early 1942, the Eastern seaboard was particularly vulnerable, and therefore in February 1942, aircraft at New York, Salem and Elizabeth City were assigned to the Commander Eastern Sea Frontier, and became combat aircraft. Elsewhere, the change of command would mean the re-assignment of aircraft to US Navy units. Thus the JRF-2, recently re-assigned to the Senior CG Officer 14th Naval District on Ford Island, Pearl Harbor, would soon be transferred to a Carrier Air Support Unit at Pearl.

As the war progressed, the Goose featured in countless searches, rescues and even direct, albeit unsuccessful, attacks on enemy submarines. Inevitably, aircraft were damaged and lost, and by mid-1943, the fleet needed to be augmented with new equipment. However by mid-1943, other events were unfolding that would signi-ficantly increase the size of the Coast Guard's Goose fleet. A Coast Guard proposal that it be designated the single Air-Sea Rescue (ASR) organisation within the United States was rejected as unrealistic, but the US Coast Guard was directed to create an Office of Air Sea Rescue to co-ordinate and develop equipment and operational procedures. While the Army and the Navy would continue to provide their own rescue

facilities, the Navy delegated ASR responsibility for the Continental Sea Frontiers to the US Coast Guard. This decision would more than double the size of US Coast Guard aviation.

Initially, six new JRF-5s were diverted to the US Coast Guard from the production line in August 1943, in part to replace earlier attrition. These aircraft, the last to be allocated serials in the old, pre-war three-digit range (224 to 229, now without the 'V' prefix), were received between August and October 1943, and went into imme-diate use at existing sites. It should be remembered that there had been a lengthy pause in US Navy deliveries (effectively between August 1942 and April 1943) while the manufacturer had been producing JRF-6Bs for the United Kingdom, and thus by mid-1943, new aircraft were needed urgently by both the Navy and the US Coast Guard. The decision, however, to delegate coastal ASR work to the US Coast Guard required still more resources, and between October 1943 and May 1945, 24 aircraft were delivered to Coast Guard operations for ASR work (21 ex-factory and four from the Navy, one of which was returned to the Navy in 1945). These aircraft were considered US Navy assets and retained BuAer serial numbers for the duration of the war. Until stricken in 1946, these aircraft were, in most respects, maintained and managed by the US Navy.

By September 1944, Goose operations had been concentrated at eight continental Air Sea Rescue sites. They comprised five Atlantic fleet stations at Biloxi, St Petersburg, Miami, Elizabeth City and Salem, and three Pacific fleet stations at Port Angeles, San Francisco and San Diego. Serious accidents in 1944 and 1945 were happily rather few and the most numerically significant losses of these years would be three to a Miami hurricane in September 1945.

From late 1944, the Goose fleet had been engaged almost exclusively in ASR work, reflecting the greater ability of other aircraft to undertake patrol functions and a

considerable increase in the number of accidents to airmen and sailors in coastal waters. Following the creation of the National Air Sea Rescue Agency in April 1944, the Navy and Coast Guard worked towards a post-war strategy that would see the US Coast Guard maintain account-ability for coastal ASR. In practice, negotiations with the Army on global and internal accountabilities was protracted and continued for some years. Following Japan's surrender in August 1945, the Navy therefore began the process of divesting itself of ASR units, and in December 1945 the US Coast Guard acknowledged that it would subsequently undertake the function, eventually to be universally known as Search and Rescue (SAR).

The combined strength of the US Coast Guard and US Navy/Coast Guard Operations Goose fleets was in the order of 30 aircraft in December 1945. This total included up to six survivors of the pre-war JRF-2/3 fleet, some of which were in poor condition. This was the numerical high-point of the Goose years.

Post-War Coast Guard Operations

The US Navy returned the US Coast Guard to the Treasury Department on 1st January 1946 and the great majority of the Coast Guard Operations JRF-5 fleet was stricken formally from naval records on 31st July 1946 and transferred to the Coast Guard as part of a wider transfer of assets. Following a conference in February 1946, 26 'JRF' aircraft (presumably all JRF-5 models) were authorised for transfer to the US Coast Guard for ASR work, but in the event, the Coast Guard received only 16 aircraft that were assigned to the stations already, and one additional aircraft recently transferred to Coast Guard Operations in April 1946, and apparently overlooked by the original transfer request. These 17 aircraft comprised the survivors of the 24 aircraft received from the US Navy. It is surmised that the additional 10 aircraft initially agreed upon might have been intended replacements for the 10 US Coast Guard-purchased aircraft that are thought to have survived until February 1946 (JRF-2 174, 185 and 186; JRF-3 191 and 192 and JRF-5 224 and 226 to 229). Of course, it is also feasible that these aircraft were somehow double-counted in February 1946!

The 17 JRF-5s transferred by the US Navy were as follows:

04356	37788	37814	84792
37775	37789	37821	84816
37776	37800	84790	87730
37782	37804	84791	87733

The additional aircraft is thought to have been 87725, located at the Coast Guard detachment, NAS Kaneohe Bay, HI.

37821 (c/n B-74) was a JRF-5 delivered new from the factory to the wartime US Coast Guard in August 1944. Later becoming a 'JRF-5G' it remained in use until October 1953 when it passed into storage at the AR&SC Elizabeth City. It is seen here prior to its sale to Mackey Airlines of Miami, FL in 1956 as N2579B. After an eventful few years in the Bahamas it ended its days in Florida, and the Certificate of Registration expired on 31st March 2011. (US Coast Guard photo)

To some extent 1947 was spent re-organising and re-establishing bases and creating new operations overseas, most

The JRF Fleet Disposition – January 1947		
CGAS Salem	Salem, MA	2
CGAS Elizabeth City	Elizabeth City, NC	2
CGAS San Francisco	San Francisco, CA	3
CGAS Biloxi	Biloxi, MS	2
CGAS Port Angeles	Port Angeles, WA	2
CGAS St Petersburg	St Petersburg, FL	2
CGAS Miami	Dinner Key, Miami, FL	2
CGAS San Diego	San Diego, CA	3
CGAS Traverse City	Traverse City, MI	1
10th CG District, San Juan	NAS San Juan, Puerto Rico	1
14th CG District, Honolulu	CGAS Barbers Point, HI	1
17th CG District, Ketchikan	Air Det Annette Island, AK	2

US Navy records do not show the type variant, but the inventory at this time was almost entirely comprised of the JRF-5. This list probably reflects an active force of 21 JRF-5, and probably two of the JRF-3 models, both of which were withdrawn by 1948. The total of 23 aircraft, sustained from January to March 1947, was to be the post-war peak strength of the Goose fleet.

notably in the Pacific. In small numbers, the Goose would be deployed to some of these stations. During 1946, US Coast Guard JRF-5s appeared at Annette Island, AK, Kaneohe Bay, HI, San Juan, PR and as a detachment at Traverse City, MI. At the year-end, the nominal establishment strength at the stations was 17 aircraft, to be brought to 23 in early 1947, as shown in the table above.

The Coast Guard Air Stations continued to operate a miscellany of fixed wing aircraft and, in later years, helicopters. Individual stations used the Goose according to local circumstances in ones, twos or occasionally threes. Servicing was undertaken initially at US Navy stations such as Seattle, but the establishment of the

US Coast Guard's Aircraft Repair and Supply Center (AR&SC) at Elizabeth City in 1946, enabled much of the future work to be undertaken in-house. Between 1946 and 1950, there were no more transfers of aircraft from the Navy and, with the withdrawal of the remaining JRF-2/3s, the fleet had dwindled to 19 JRF-5s by January 1950. In 1951, the first of the new UF-1G Albatrosses entered service and the slow process of rundown would soon begin for the JRF-5 (which had now acquired the new designation 'JRF-5G'. 'G' indicated Coast Guard ownership but little else). The JRF-5G, however, still had several years of use left, and the fleet was strengthened by the acquisition of eight surplus aircraft transferred from US Navy storage

at Quonset Point in October 1952. This enabled the early retirement of a few weary aircraft, bringing the inventory once more back to approximately 22 aircraft.

There was little change in role for the JRF-5G during the Korean War years, and the trickle of UF-1G deliveries eventually enabled the US Coast Guard to return seven of the original aircraft to the US Navy in 1954. As far as is known, these aircraft were needed by the Navy to meet MDAP commitments, and future Coast Guard retirees would not return to the US Navy inventory. Other JRF-5Gs passed into storage or were sold 'as is, where is' from 1954. The US Coast Guard continued to use the JRF-5G as a training aid at the AR&SC Elizabeth City and, in the mid-'fifties stationed one aircraft at the Coast Guard Academy, located at New London, CT. In 1955, aircraft were being stored at Elizabeth City, while others were sold in situ at their stations. The last aircraft were released from storage circa 1958 with one, 37782, ironically being loaned to the US Navy, for ongoing use by the EDO Corporation at College Point, NY. Although never physically returned to the US Coast Guard, this would remain a Coast Guard asset until 1965.

Colours and Markings

The pre-war JRF-2 and JRF-3 aircraft were delivered in very colourful markings. The aircraft were basically in a natural metal finish with the rear large fuselage title 'U.S. Coast Guard', and serial below. The upper one-third of the rudder and tail-fin was Dark Blue and carried the aircraft type number, with the lower two-thirds

Seen here with the back-drop of Long Island, NY, JRF-2 V185 (c/n 1077) was delivered initially to CGAS Brooklyn in February 1940. This early official photograph shows the pre-war US Coast Guard markings to excellent effect. As with a number of the US Coast Guard Goose fleet, its precise fate remains a mystery to the authors and to the Coast Guard.
                                                                                        (US Coast Guard photo)

vertically striped Red and White. There was a Black fuselage cheat line above the hull and through the wheel-well. The upper wing surface was Yellow, 'USCG' letters were worn beneath each wing, a huge serial was carried on the lower hull surface and the US Coast Guard badge was worn beneath the cockpit window on both sides. In the first weeks of the war, the period US Navy roundel replaced the large 'U.S. Coast Guard' and serial number on the rear fuselage, these markings being displaced to appear in tiny characters on the tail.

Wartime colours reflected US Navy policy, and indeed most of the JRF-5s were delivered from the production line in standard colours, with the early aircraft being repainted progressively, to match the current Navy standards. Prior to mid-1943, a Dark Blue-Grey was applied to the fuselage and upper surfaces, with the lower surfaces Grey, and the US Navy-style roundel, in use on the rear fuselage and beneath the wings, had lost its earlier Red centre. After mid-1943, new JRF-5s appeared in the so-called 'tri-color' scheme in which the upper surfaces were Dark Blue and the sides and lower surfaces were a Light Grey-Blue. The roundel had now moved to the nose and had acquired the now familiar side bars.

By the end of the war, there were several schemes visible in the fleet, and post-war features were added as fashion changed. Thus JRF-2, V174, that survived in use until 1946, retained its 1942-era Dark Blue-Grey scheme, but had lost its roundels for Yellow rear fuselage bands with Black trim and a Yellow, forward-fuselage block, edged in Black, inscribed 'ASR174'. Gradually the JRF-5 fleet, augmented by new arrivals from the Navy, returned to natural metal/Silver paint with Yellow rear-fuselage bands, floats and wing-tips. The 'U.S. Coast Guard' title reappeared on the lower rear fuselage, and by the nineteen fifties, the familiar 'star and bar' national markings were applied to the centre fuselage and wings, where they replaced the 'USCG' title. The microscopic tail-fin serial also gave way to larger side numbers, ultimately on both the nose and rear fuselage. The serials of the 'fifties were presented as three or four-digit numbers, with five-digit serials truncated to four by dropping the first digit.

Serial Numbers

The list shown on the right includes all aircraft that are known to have served with the US Coast Guard at any time. The complex wartime relationship between the US Navy and the US Coast Guard, and the allocation of aircraft to Coast Guard Operations within the US Navy, creates complications when trying to produce a neat list of such aircraft. Anomalies include one US Navy aircraft only temporarily used between 1943 and 1945, and those lost during these years and thus never 'officially' on US Coast Guard books.

Serial (BuAer no.)	Type	C/n	Circumstances
V174 to V176	JRF-2	1063 to 1065	1939 production for US Coast Guard
V184 to V187	JRF-2	1076 to 1079	1940 production for US Coast Guard
V190 to V192	JRF-3	1085 to 1087	1940 production for US Coast Guard
224 (34079)	JRF-5	B-8	1943 production for US Navy
225 (34082)	JRF-5	B-11	1943 production for US Navy
226 (34087)	JRF-5	B-16	1943 production for US Navy
227 (34090)	JRF-5	B-19	1943 production for US Navy
228 (37772)	JRF-5	B-25	1943 production for US Navy
229 (37773)	JRF-5	B-26	1943 production for US Navy

Aircraft 224 to 229 were permanent transfers from new production for the US Navy. They were stricken from US Navy charge on 21st August 1943, on which date the first aircraft was delivered to the US Coast Guard. They were permanent US Coast Guard assets.

Serial (BuAer no.)	Type	C/n	Circumstances
34073	JRF-5	B-2	1943 production for US Navy
34075	JRF-5	B-4	1943 production for US Navy
34076	JRF-5	B-5	1943 production for US Navy
37775*	JRF-5	B-28	1943 production for US Navy
37776*	JRF-5	B-29	1943 production for US Navy
37780	JRF-5	B-33	1943 production for US Navy
37782*	JRF-5	B-35	1944 production for US Navy
37788*	JRF-5	B-41	1944 production for US Navy
37795	JRF-5	B-48	1944 production for US Navy
37798	JRF-5	B-51	1944 production for US Navy
37800*	JRF-5	B-53	1944 production for US Navy
37804*	JRF-5	B-57	1944 production for US Navy
37814*	JRF-5	B-67	1944 production for US Navy
37821*	JRF-5	B-74	1944 production for US Navy
84790*	JRF-5	B-85	1944 production for US Navy
84791*	JRF-5	B-86	1944 production for US Navy
84792*	JRF-5	B-87	1944 production for US Navy
84816*	JRF-5	B-111	1945 production for US Navy
87722	JRF-5	B-116	1945 production for US Navy
87730*	JRF-5	B-124	1945 production for US Navy
87733*	JRF-5	B-127	1945 production for US Navy

The above aircraft were accepted by the US Navy and were allocated immediately to Coast Guard Operations, where they remained permanently assigned. Those marked * survived the war, and were transferred formally to the US Coast Guard on 31st July 1946.

Serial (BuAer no.)	Type	C/n	Circumstances
04356*	JRF-5	1183	WWII transfers within US Navy
37789*	JRF-5	B-42	WWII transfers within US Navy
84808	JRF-5	B-103	WWII transfers within US Navy
87725*	JRF-5	B-119	WWII transfers within US Navy

The above aircraft were transferred to Coast Guard Operations from other activities during the war, and those marked * were permanently transferred to the US Coast Guard on 31st July 1946. 84808 was briefly assigned to Coast Guard Operations in 1945. However, it would subsequently be transferred to the US Coast Guard in 1952 (see below).

Serial (BuAer no.)	Type	C/n	Circumstances
6440	JRF-5	1110	1952-53 transfers from US Navy
6452	JRF-5	1122	1952-53 transfers from US Navy
34085	JRF-5	B-14	1952-53 transfers from US Navy
34089	JRF-5	B-18	1952-53 transfers from US Navy
37779	JRF-5	B-32	1952-53 transfers from US Navy
37794	JRF-5	B-47	1952-53 transfers from US Navy
37825	JRF-5	B-78	1952-53 transfers from US Navy
84808	JRF-5	B-103	1952-53 transfers from US Navy

The above aircraft were stricken by the US Navy in two tranches of four in October 1952 and January 1953, but the US Coast Guard acceptance dates are uncertain (see individual histories).

JRF-5 37794 (c/n B-47) was acquired by the US Coast Guard from the US Navy in January 1953 and remained in use as a 'JRF-5G' until the fleet was retired a few years later. 37794 was then sold to the US Fish and Wildlife Service in 1958 as N782 but, as can be seen from this photograph taken at Anchorage, Alaska on 6th August 1972, the aircraft remained unconverted for many years. 37794 can here be seen in the final mid-1950s US Coast Guard scheme without station titles. *(John P Stewart via PJ Marson)*

Explaining this in tabular form is cumbersome, and hampered by a dearth of accessible official US Coast Guard records. Much of the JRF-5 data is derived from official US Navy records. As explained above, the 'JRF-5G' designation can be something of a source of confusion, and is therefore not used here. JRF-5 aircraft acquired post-1943 are shown here with the complete BuAer serial, although those formally transferred to the US Coast Guard post-war and those subsequently obtained from the US Navy had their serials modified from five to four digits by dropping the first digit. JRF-5s with four-digit BuAer serials were unchanged.

Widgeon

Variants and Acquisitions

The US Coast Guard was the first military customer for the diminutive Widgeon. The initial pre-war order was for eight aircraft (contract TCG-33459) that were delivered in July and August 1941. They were given the US Navy type number J4F-1, and the serials V197 to V204. The second production order (contract TCG-34062) was placed immediately following the Japanese attack on Pearl Harbor in December 1941, and reflected the decision to terminate commercial production of the

G-44 in favour of military aircraft. Thus this order for 17 J4F-1 aircraft, serials V205 to V221, followed the delivery of 12 aircraft already committed to Portugal and accounted for all production between February and June of 1942.

There would be no more Widgeons acquired by the US Coast Guard until 1946, although the history of aircraft V221 requires explanation. The original V221, the last J4F-1 of the order delivered in June 1942, was transferred to the US Navy as BuAer 34585, for diplomatic support duties in October 1942, and was lost immediately in a fatal accident. It was replaced in the US Coast Guard inventory by a second 221 (on

Notwithstanding the gathering war clouds, the US Coast Guard's early J4F-1 Widgeons were delivered in the colourful pre-war markings. V199 (c/n 1224) is here seen at Bethpage shortly before delivery to the Coast Guard in July 1941. Unfortunately, although most official US Coast Guard aircraft records of this era have been lost, V199 is known to have been delivered to CGAS Elizabeth City in 1941 and to have met an early end in an obscure accident in December of that year. *(via Collect-Air Photos)*

an unknown date, but which was prior to March 1943) that is believed to have been the former US Navy J4F-2 33952. This episode is explained more fully below. In June 1946, the US Navy transferred 12 surplus J4F-2 aircraft to the Coast Guard, allowing the retirement of many of the original J4F-1 aircraft.

The J4F-1 was essentially the commercial G-44 model, with the Ranger 6-440-C5 engine but with the addition of a large upper-fuselage hatch situated behind the wing. This hatch enabled the safe loading of bulky cargo and stretchers. A hard point, facilitating the carriage of various munitions and stores, was located inboard of the starboard engine and this was normally used to carry a depth charge, or raft and rescue equipment. This feature is thought to have been fitted to the second batch when in production, and retrospectively to the first batch.

The J4F-1 Fleet Disposition – December 1941		
CGAS Salem	Salem, MA	V197
CGAS Brooklyn	New York, NY	V198
CGAS St Petersburg	St Petersburg, FL	V200
CGAS San Francisco	San Francisco, CA	V201
CGAS Biloxi	Biloxi, MS	V202
CGAS Port Angeles	Port Angeles, WA	V203
CGAS Elizabeth City	Elizabeth City, NC	V199
Air Patrol Det Traverse City	Traverse City, MI	V204

The Widgeon's immediate contribution to the war was limited. There were few of them, and it would not be until well into 1942 that they would receive limited armament. The Air Stations were placed under the command of the Naval Area commanders, who in turn reported to their respective Sea Frontiers. Thus, for example, aircraft at Salem, Brooklyn and

Guard aircraft. The Widgeon, however, came very close to achieving a kill, and for many years one crew was so credited.

In the summer of 1942 CGAS Biloxi, MS was operating five Widgeons, detached to nearby NAS Houma in support of their Gulf Sea Frontier commitments. On 1st August 1942, V212, flown by CAP Henry White and crewed by RFC George Boggs

US Coast Guard J4F-1 V203 (c/n 1228) was delivered in August 1941 and served initially at CGAS Port Angeles. This delightful air to air photograph was taken in 1941, soon after delivery to Port Angeles, and shows the hull serial to good effect. V203 not only survived the war, serving at Port Angeles throughout, but still flies as N1340V in faithfully restored 1941 US Coast Guard colours.   (Gordon S Williams)

Operations

The early US Coast Guard Widgeons were delivered in the summer of 1941, at a time when the United States was already embroiled in a deteriorating situation in the North Atlantic. American shipping was being lost to German U-boats, and the Navy simply did not possess adequate aviation assets to protect its coastal waters. The fleet of eight aircraft was distributed to the principle Air Stations, where they served alongside the new JRF Goose and several older types. Each station thus possessed a miscellany of aircraft intended to meet specific emergencies or routine obligations. Initially, none of the J4F-1s were armed and sea patrols were largely observational, although occasional rescue missions were possible subject to the sea state, and other weather conditions. At the time of Pearl Harbor, the fleet was distributed as shown at the top of the page.

Elizabeth City were assigned respectively to the Salem, Rockaway and Currituck Air Patrol Groups, all of which were assigned to the Eastern Sea Frontier, a mixed force of US Navy and US Coast Guard patrol aircraft. Elsewhere, stations were assigned to the Gulf and Western Sea Frontiers. The arrival of the second batch of aircraft allowed the same stations to maintain standing patrols with armed aircraft, a small but significant step forward in the U-boat war.

Of course, equipping the little J4F-1 with a single 325lb depth charge did not turn the aircraft into a serious warplane, and indeed, its flying characteristics now became marginal. The armed aircraft, with a crew of two, could not maintain level flight on one engine, and the loss of an engine on take-off could lead to disaster. Weapon delivery was primitive and it is perhaps not surprising that no U-boats were lost to Widgeons, or indeed to any other US Coast

Jr, was on routine patrol south of Isles Dernieres, LA when it found U-171 on the surface. The submarine chose to dive rather than fight – which was perhaps fortunate for White and Boggs - and was submerged by the time the steep-diving Widgeon had released the depth-charge. The weapon missed by about 20 feet, but an oil-slick was sighted although the submarine was in fact undamaged. Post-war, the US authorities came to the perhaps understandable, but wrong, conclusion that V212 had actually sunk the U-166 that was active in the area at that time, and which had torpedoed the *Robert E Lee* on the 30th July off the Mississippi delta. In fact, U-166 had gone down that same day close to the *Robert E Lee*, having been depth-charged successfully by the US Navy escort PC-566. U-171 returned to Europe undamaged but was then lost to a mine off Lorient, France on 9th October 1942, taking with her all logs and records. Her

US Coast Guard J4F-1 203 (c/n 1228) is seen here in its final war-time colours. Having passed through an interim stage in 1942 in which at least some of the fleet was re-painted in the dark blue-grey colours while adopting red and white tail-fin stripes and the 'red dot' roundel, the Widgeons lost the stripes and the 'dot'. Of probably greater interest here however is the 325lb Mk17 Depth Bomb beneath the starboard wing. According to those who flew the aircraft, level flight with two crew (as seen here) and the Mk17 was unsustainable with one engine out.   *(Grumman photo)*

captain survived, and subsequently recorded an incident, date un-remembered, in which U-171 had been attacked by a 'flying-boat'. It would not be until 2001, and the accidental discovery of U-166, that the historians would finally concur that White and Boggs could not have destroyed the U-166, and must have attacked the U-171. However, the long-held belief in the story led to the eventual if some-what fortunate preservation of V212, now displayed resplendently at the National Museum of Naval Aviation at Pensacola, FL.

The Widgeons continued to fly armed patrols throughout 1942 and 1943, and by early 1943, only one aircraft had been lost – no mean achievement in the circum-stances. A routine inventory of the fleet, shown below, gives the following disposition at the end of February 1943.

After early 1944, the US Coast Guard mission became more focussed on air-sea rescue (ASR) work, with the Navy becoming fully responsible for all aspects of ocean and coastal patrol and offensive operations against the dwindling U-boat fleet. In practice, the ASR work was considerable, and from October 1944 became the formal tasking. War-time J4F-1

losses were few, but it was a very tired US Coast Guard fleet that was returned to the Treasury on 1 January 1946. In late February 1946, the US Navy agreed to transfer 12 J4F-2s to the US Coast Guard for future ASR activities, as part of a wider transfer of assets, and this acquisition enabled many more J4F-1s to be with-drawn.

Although formal aircraft movement records for the older aircraft are now non-existent, it would appear that by mid-1946, a number of the J4F-1s were in storage, and in June 1946, the US Navy, now in the

process of divesting itself of all Widgeons, transferred the promised 12 J4F-2s to the Coast Guard. As a result of this acquisition, many US Coast Guard J4F-1s were declared surplus from November 1946 and were disposed of to the civilian market. With official disposal records no longer surviving, it is now unclear what happened to all surplus aircraft, but circumstantial evidence suggests that maybe as many as six aircraft were perhaps stripped for spares and scrapped, although dates and locations are not known. The fleet situation at the end of January 1947 was as follows:

The J4F Fleet Disposition – January 1947

CGAS Salem	Salem, MA	2
CGAS Brooklyn	New York, NY	2
CGAS St Petersburg	St Petersburg, FL	3
CGAS San Francisco	San Francisco, CA	1
CGAS Biloxi	Biloxi, MS	1
CGAS Port Angeles	Port Angeles, WA	3
CGAS San Diego	San Diego, CA	3
CGAS Elizabeth City	Elizabeth City, NC	3

This list reflects an active force of six J4F-1 and 12 J4F-2 aircraft. The total of 18 aircraft, sustained from December 1946 to March 1947, was to be the post-war peak strength of the Widgeon fleet.

The J4F Fleet Disposition – February 1943

CGAS Salem	Salem, MA	V197, V218
CGAS Brooklyn	New York, NY	V198, V205, V210, V215
CGAS St Petersburg	St Petersburg, FL	V200, V209, V213, V216
CGAS San Francisco	San Francisco, CA	V201
CGAS Biloxi	Biloxi, MS	V202, V211, V212, V214, V217
CGAS Port Angeles	Port Angeles, WA	V203, V206, V207, 221
CGAS San Diego	San Diego, CA	V204, V219, V220
CGAS Elizabeth City	Elizabeth City, NC	V208

Aircraft V199 (CGAS Elizabeth City) had been lost in December 1941.

After March 1947, the fleet began to run down. Aircraft remained at traditional stations, albeit in dwindling numbers, with only Traverse City appearing briefly in March-April 1947 as a 'new' user. As aircraft continued to be sold off, the fleet drifted down to just seven active aircraft in July 1947 (there were two at Port Angeles and one each at Elizabeth City, San Francisco, Brooklyn, St Petersburg and San Diego). Between February and October 1948, it was increased to ten with extra aircraft at Salem, Port Angeles and now at the AR&SC Elizabeth City, where the first J4F overhauls took place in 1948. In

November 1948, there was a sharp reduction to six aircraft (at Elizabeth City, San Francisco, Port Angeles, Brooklyn, St Petersburg and San Diego).

US Coast Guard records are extremely vague as to when the Widgeon was withdrawn formally from use, but it may well have been in December 1948. Aircraft continued to be sold as surplus, but four apparently remained on the inventory in January 1950, presumably in storage and perhaps non-airworthy. All things considered, the Widgeon had performed remarkably well in Coast Guard colours.

Colours and Markings

The first batch of pre-war J4F-1 aircraft, serials V197 to V204, was delivered in the same colourful finish as the JRF-2 and JRF-3 aircraft, and they were in every way identical. The second batch was finished in the 1942 wartime markings with Dark Blue-Grey applied to the fuselage and upper surfaces, with the lower surfaces Grey. After mid-1943, the rear-fuselage roundel was replaced by the early 'star and bar' markings. The early aircraft were re-painted progressively in the same colours, and the serial, less the 'V' prefix, was carried in small white digits on the nose as

Serial Numbers			
Serial (BuAer no.)	Type	C/n	Circumstances
V197 to V204	J4F-1	1222 to 1229	1941 production for US Coast Guard
V205 to V221	J4F-1	1253 to 1269	1942 production for US Coast Guard
221 (33952)*	J4F-2	1273	1942 acquisition from US Navy
32940	J4F-2	1294	1946 transfers from the US Navy
32949	J4F-2	1303	1946 transfers from the US Navy
32959	J4F-2	1313	1946 transfers from the US Navy
32965	J4F-2	1319	1946 transfers from the US Navy
32966	J4F-2	1320	1946 transfers from the US Navy
32972	J4F-2	1326	1946 transfers from the US Navy
32973	J4F-2	1327	1946 transfers from the US Navy
32977	J4F-2	1331	1946 transfers from the US Navy
33956	J4F-2	1281	1946 transfers from the US Navy
37711	J4F-2	1341	1946 transfers from the US Navy
37730	J4F-2	1360	1946 transfers from the US Navy
37765	J4F-2	1395	1946 transfers from the US Navy
* The second use of serial 221 is certain, the linkage with BuAer 33952 is speculative – see panel below.			

well as the tail-fin (the US Coast Guard appears to have dropped the 'V' from routine documentation in 1944). The aircraft received from the US Navy in 1946 initially retained the US Navy 'tri-color' scheme, with Dark Blue upper surfaces and Light Grey-Blue sides and

lower surfaces. Prior to their withdrawal in 1948, several aircraft had returned to a natural metal finish and acquired high-visibility Yellow bands on the rear fuselage, wing-tips and floats, effectively mirroring the JRF-5 markings of that period.

The Identity of Widgeon V221

The original V221 was a J4F-1 (c/n 1269) delivered to the US Coast Guard in June 1942, by which time the US Coast Guard was under the operational control of the US Navy. In October 1942, V221, the newest and last of the J4F-1 fleet, was transferred to the US Navy for the use of the Naval Air Attaché to the Dominican Republic at Trujillo City, Santo Domingo and was allocated the new BuAer serial 34585. It is not clear why this particular aircraft was selected, but it should be remembered that in September 1942 the US Navy would have had no other J4F available for the task. However, carrying a mixed US Navy and US Coast Guard crew of five, V221 was destroyed in a fatal crash at Santo Domingo on 24th October 1942 (the report uses the word "demolished"), and the aircraft was stricken by the US Navy on 31st October 1942. The accident report describes the aircraft as a J4F-1, and quotes the serial as 'V-221'.

US Coast Guard WWII aircraft records are at best fragmentary, but a J4F with the serial V221 was on active strength at CGAS Port Angeles in February 1943, and an

entry in the surviving Port Angeles War Diary, dated 27th March 1945, shows it still to be on strength. A formal US Navy accident report describes a category 'C' landing accident befalling J4F-2 221 at Port Angeles on 5th September 1945. This evidence thus suggests that a second 221, a J4F-2, was active at CGAS Port Angeles, from at least February 1943 until September 1945, and that this aircraft cannot be the aircraft destroyed in 1942. As all construction numbers are accounted for, the assumption is that the second 221 would have come from the Navy, as a replacement for the original aircraft.

The later service history and fate of virtually every US Navy J4F-2 is known, although some aircraft lack pre-August 1944 details. There are almost no credible candidates for a second '221', but one such is aircraft 33952 (c/n 1273), about which little is known from the US Navy movement record card (there are no pre-August 1944 details, and from then on it was at an unknown location until 31st March 1945 when stricken). BuAer 33952 was, however, reinstated without explanation on 31st October 1945 at

South Weymouth, after which the record is unhelpful, until it was stricken without a disposal code on 30th April 1946. Uniquely, for a theoretically airworthy Widgeon, no subsequent details are known. A convenient explanation for this vague history might be that 33952, the first J4F-2 acquired by the US Navy from the cancelled Cuban order, was passed to the US Coast Guard, by February 1943, to replace the original aircraft. In March 1945, the clerical record was perhaps belatedly updated, and the aircraft stricken from Navy records (as would have been standard practice for such a permanent transfer), only for it to be reinstated in October 1945, following its accident at Port Angeles. The damage was substantial ('C'), although repairable and would perhaps have required depot work.

It is conceivable that, in the post-war environment, the aircraft was returned to the US Navy for repair only for the Navy to lose interest and scrap it. While this remains a hypothesis, 33952's strike is unexplained, and there are no other obvious candidates for the second 221.

ASSIGNMENTS OF AIRCRAFT TO US MILITARY UNITS AND ESTABLISHMENTS BETWEEN 1938 AND 1958

This listing is intended to assist the reader with the identification of all aircraft used by any given unit or establishment. The complete details of such assignments will be found in the individual aircraft histories and lists of serials with their manufacturer's numbers are included at the foot of each section to assist the cross-referencing process. These lists are not intended to provide complete histories of the units or establishments but do include all aircraft assigned at any time and for any purpose, including those of maintenance, storage and transit. The lists are in alphabetic sequence where the station or agency is the primary identifying feature and then by alpha-numeric sequence where typically a numbered unit is the primary identifying element. The numbered units

and titled commands are grouped to ease identification, but these groupings have no organisational significance.

United States military aviation during WWII was both complex and fluid and involved vast numbers of organisations. Although relatively few of them used these Grumman aircraft it is no easy matter to neatly compartmentalise those users and, bearing in mind the purpose of this listing, a number of organisations evident within the individual histories have been ignored here and the aircraft listed typically under the holding station. Thus a Navy aircraft assigned to 'NAMC Philadelphia' appears under 'NAF Philadelphia' and a typical USAAF aircraft under the holding station, in part reflecting the nature of the recording of aircraft

allotments during WWII and in part allowing for changes in recording that took place over time. It will be apparent that some anomalies exist, generally the result of inconsistent recording and unit and base title changes.

The list excludes establishments to which aircraft were delivered from the factory except in those instances where the aircraft remained there for an extended period of time (typically in excess of one month) or where no other details are known. Also excluded are occasional card references to naval aircraft simply allocated to the 'Atlantic Fleet', 'Pacific Fleet' and a few other similarly vague references. To repeat, this analysis is only a list of the units and establishments mentioned in the individual histories and it has no organisational relevance.

THE JRF GOOSE

Naval, Marine Corps and Coast Guard Establishments

NAF Adak, AK

6442, 34071

NAS Agana, Guam
- see CASU-F12

NAS Alameda, CA

1679, 3846, 3854, 6440, 6441, 6442, 6448, 6449, 09782, 34061, 34068, V225/34082, 34083, 34089, 34091, 34094, 37771, V228/37772, V229/37773, 37778, 37783, 37789, 37790, 37791, 37794, 37810, 37812, 37813, 37819, 37822, 37825, 37826, 37828, 37829, 37831, 84792, 84793, 84794, 84796, 84799, 84806, 84807, 84808, 84809, 84810, 84811, 84813, 84814, 84815, 87721, 87723, 87725, 87727, 87728, 87731

NAS Anacostia, DC

1384, 1675, 3852, 3854, 3855, 6452, 6453, 04349, 04352, 34071, 34077, 34085, 37784, 37799, 37816, 84808, 87723, 87724, 87729, 87731, 87732, 87744

NAF Annapolis, MD (including VN8D5 and Naval Air Activity Severn River Command)

3852, 6440, 6441, 6448, 6452, 6453, 04349, 04351, 04354, 04355, 04357, 04358, 09767, 34061, 34062, 34063, 34069, 34071, 34083, 34088, 34089, 34092, 34094, 35921, 37771, 37779, 37783, 37790, 37791, 37794, 37799, 37803, 37805, 37812, 37813, 37816, 37819, 37822, 37825, 37826, 37827,

37828, 37831, 84797, 84798, 84800, 84805, 84808, 84809, 84810, 84813, 84814, 84815, 84817, 84818, 87720, 87721, 87723, 87727, 87728, 87731, 87732, 87734, 87736, 87737, 87738, 87741, 87742, 87743, 87744, 87748, 87750, 87751

CGAD Annette Island, AK

37821, 84791

NAF Aratu, Brazil

34080

NAAS Arcata, CA
- see CASU-36

NAS Argentia, Nfld (including Commander Task Force 24)

6441, 6451, 04351, 34078, 37790, 87748

NAS Astoria, OR

37826

NAS Atlantic City, NJ

37784

NAS Attu, AK

34068

NAS Banana River, FL

84802

CGAF Barbers Point, HI

34085, 37825

NAS Barbers Point, HI

34083

NAAS Barin Field, FL - see VN4D8-N

NAS/NAF Bermuda

34071, 34078, 37803, 37820, 84800

CGAS Biloxi, MS

V174, V184, 04356, 37782, 84791

NAS Boca Chica, FL

34086

NAAS Bronson Field, FL
-see VN8D8-B

CGAS Brooklyn, NY

V174, V175, V185, V187, V190, V191, V192, 37776, 37804, 84816, 87722, 87730, 87733

Carlsen Field, Trinidad
- see BlmpHedron 5

NAB Cebu, Philippines

84813

NAS Charleston, SC

V174, 04355

MCAS Cherry Point, NC

04351, 04357, 07004, 37771, 37816, 37820, 84796, 84805, 84807, 84817, 87720, 87732, 87735, 87737, 87738, 87739, 87750

NAAS Chincoteague, VA

6454, 34061, 34071

NAS Clinton, OK

34088

NAS Coco Solo, Panama CZ

1675, 1678, 04349, 34072, 84799

NAS Corpus Christi, TX (including NATTC Ward Island)

3850, 6454, 04358, 09767, 34085, 84800, 84802

NAIT Corry Field, FL

04357, 34085, 34093

Station Operations Dakar, French West Africa

37809

NAS Dallas, TX

84807, 84809, 84810

NAS Dutch Harbor, AK

6440, 34071

Efate Naval Base, New Hebrides - see VJ-8 and VJ-11

CGAS Elizabeth City, NC (including AR&SC)

V175, V184, V185, V186, V227/34090, 37814, 37821, 84790, 84816, 87725

NAS Engebi, Eniwetok Atoll (Wrigley Field)

34063

Espiritu Santo Naval Base, New Hebrides

1672

MCAS Ewa, HI

87725

NAAS Fallon, NV
- see CASU-54

NAS Fort Lauderdale, FL
- see VTB OTU-1

NAAS Franklin, VA

37816, 87732

NAS Glenview, IL

3853, 04354, 84796, 84800

NAS Grosse Ile, MI

84807

**Guadalcanal Naval Base,
Solomon Islands** - see ARUSOLS

NAS Guantanamo Bay, Cuba

1673, 6445, 04352

NAC Hampton Roads, VA
- NAS Norfolk, VA

RAF Hendon, London, UK
- see FASRON-76

NAAS Hollister, CA
- see CASU-37

NAS Honolulu, HI

V187, 37812

NAS Houma, LA

34088

NAF Ipitanga, Brazil
- see Fleet Airship Wing-4

NAS Jacksonville, FL

3847, 6442, 6445, 04354,
04357, 34089, 66335, 66337,
66338, 66342, 66344, 66345,
66347, 66350, 66353, 66355,
66356, 66357, 66358, 66360,
66361, 84802, 87722

NAMU Johnsville, PA

04351, 04354, 04358, 34077

CGAD NAS Kaneohe Bay, HI

87725

NAS Kaneohe Bay, HI

6446, 37778

NAS Key West, FL

37822, 87729, 87748

NAS Kodiak, AK

6440, 6448, 6449, 04354, 34068,
34071, 37826, 99078

NAS Lakehurst, NJ

1384, 35921, 37799, 37812,
37827

NAAF Lewiston, ME
- see Royal Navy in Military
Operators section

NAS Litchfield Park, AZ

34083, 84817, 87732, 87750

SF Litchfield Park, AZ

04351, 04357, 34062, 34063,
34071, 224/34079, 34089,
228/37772, 229/37773, 37789,
37799, 37812, 37813, 37816,
84792, 84798, 84805, 84807,
84809, 84813, 84817, 87720,
87721, 87723, 87730, 87732,
87748

NAS Livermore, CA

6440

**Los Negros Naval Base,
Admiralty Islands**
- see AROU-1

**NAB Mactan,
Philippines**

84813

**NAF Manus Island,
Admiralty Islands**

37815, 84793

NAS Maui, HI

09782

NAS Mayport, FL

V226/34087

CGAS Miami, FL

V185, 34073, 34076,
V227/34090, 37780,
37798, 37804, 87722

NAS Miami, FL

3847, 3848, 3853, 04354, 04356,
34089, 34093, 66325, 66326,
66327, 66328, 66329, 66330,
66331, 66332, 66334, 66336,
66337, 66339, 66340, 66341,
66342, 66343, 66344, 66345,
66346, 66347, 66348, 66349,
66350, 66351, 66352, 66354,
66355, 66360, 66361, 84800

NAS Minneapolis, MN

37803

NAS Moffett Field, CA

6440, 6448, 6449, 6453

MCAS Mojave, CA

37827

NAAS Mustin Field
- see NAF Philadelphia, PA

**NAS Natal,
Brazil**
- see FAW-16

**CG Academy (New London),
CT**

6440

NAS New Orleans, LA

37803, 84800

NAS New York, NY

6449, 04356, 09782, V224/34079,
34093, 87742, 87750, 87751

**NAS Norfolk, VA
(including Atlantic Fleet
& NOP/NAC Hampton
Roads)**

1384, 1671, 1675, 3847, 3851,
3852, 3853, 3854, 3855, 6441,
6443, 6444, 6451, 6452, 6453,
6454, 04349, 04351, 04352,
04353, 04354, 04355, 04357,
04358, 07004, 09767, 34062,
34066, 34070, 34071, 34074,
34077, 34078, 34080, 34083,
34085, 34088, 34089, 34094,
35921, 37779, 37782, 37784,
37790, 37791, 37794, 37803,
37805, 37809, 37813, 37816,
37820, 37827, 37828, 37831,
89492, 84796, 84797, 84799,
84800, 84810, 84814, 84815,
84817, 87721, 87723, 87727,
87729, 87731, 87732, 87742,
87744, 87748

NAAS North Bend, OR

V174

**Noumea Naval Base,
New Caledonia**
- see FABU-1

NAS Oakland, CA

6452

NAS Orote, Guam
- see CASU-F12 and
FASRON-13

NAB Palawan, Philippines

84809

**NAS Palmyra Island,
Line Islands**

1679, 09782, 37778

MCAS Parris Island, SC

37813, 84796

NAS Pasco, WA

37826

**NAS Patuxent River, MD
(includes NATC)**

3855, 6444, 34062, 34068,
34092, 37782, 37783, 37805,
84814, 87721, 87744

NAS Pearl Harbor, HI

1672, 1679, 6451, 09782, 34061,
34083, 34091, 37771, 37778,
37783, 37790, 37791, 37810,
37811, 37812, 37829, 84793,
84794, 87723, 87725

NAS Pensacola, FL

3849, 04357, 34085, 34093

**NAF Philadelphia, PA
(including NAAS Mustin Field)**

1384, 34069, 34071, 37812,
37816, 84810, 84813, 87729,
87734, 87736, 87743, 87751

CGAS Port Angeles, WA

V174, V175, V176, 34075,
37779, 37814

NAS Port Lyautey, Morocco

37785, 37809, 37813, 84800,
87721, 87731

MCAS Quantico, VA

37782

NAS Quonset Point, RI

3854, 6440, 6441, 6450, 6451,
6452, 6453, 6454, 04349, 04351,
04355, 04357, 04358, 34062,
34063, 34071, 34078, 34083,
34085, 34089, 34094, 35921,
37771, 37779, 37783, 37784,
37791, 37794, 37799, 37803,
37812, 37813, 37816, 37819,
37820, 37822, 37825, 37826,
37827, 37828, 37831, 84796,
84797, 84798, 84799, 84800,
84805, 84807, 84808, 84809,
84810, 84813, 84815, 84817,
84818, 87720, 87721, 87723,
87727, 87728, 87729, 87731,
87732, 87734, 87735, 87736,
87737, 87738, 87739, 87741,
87742, 87743, 87744, 87745,
87748, 87750, 87751

NAF Recife, Brazil - see FAW-16

NAS Richmond, FL

84801, 87748

Roosevelt Base
- see NAS Terminal Island, CA

**NAF Russell Island,
Solomon Islands**

37831

St Louis, MS

V174

CGAS Salem, MA

V185, V192, V226/34087, 84790,
84816, 87725, 87733

NAB Samar, Philippines

34061, 37783, 37825, 37831, 84809, 84810, 84813, 84814

NAAS San Clemente, CA

84807

CGAS San Diego, CA

37789, 37795, 84808, 87743, 87745

NAS San Diego, CA

V175, 1680, 3854, 6446, 6451, 04354, 34060, 34061, 34063, 34075, 34083, 37771, 37811, 37825, 37826, 37831, 84798, 84806, 84807, 84809, 84810, 84813, 84814, 84817, 87723, 87732

CGAS San Francisco, CA

V176, V225/34082, 37775, 37782, 37800, 84792, 84816, 87733

CGAS San Juan, PR

87730

NAS San Juan, PR

1676, 3852, 3853, 04357, 34081, 34085, 84805

NAS San Julian, Cuba

37799

San Marcelino Naval Base, Philippines
- see VJ-9

NAB/NAS Sangley Point, Philippines

34083, 37825, 84809

MCAS Santa Barbara, CA

37828

NAS Seattle, WA

1674, 3854, 6440, 6441, 6442, 6447, 6448, 6449, 6451, 04349, 04352, 04354, 04355, 04357, 34062, 34063, 34071, 34075, 34078, 34085, 34088, 34089, 34092, 34093, 34094, 37775, 37776, 37777, 37779, 37782, 37784, 37788, 37789, 37800, 37804, 66325, 66328, 66330, 66331, 66333, 66334, 66335, 66336, 66338, 66339, 66340, 66342, 66344, 66345, 66348, 66349, 66350, 66351, 66352, 66353, 66354, 66355, 66356, 66357, 66358

NAS Sitka, AK

6447, 6448

NAS South Weymouth, MA

04351, 34061, 37771, 37816, 84796, 84805, 84807, 87720, 87734, 87735, 87736, 87737, 87738, 87739, 87743, 87744, 87745, 87750, 87751

NAS Squantum, MA

04355

CGAS St Petersburg, FL

04356, 37788, 84792, 84816

NAS Tanapag, Mariana Islands

84814

NAS Terminal Island, CA (Roosevelt Base)

6453

NAF Tinian Island, Mariana Islands - see VJ-3

CGAS Traverse City, MI

V192, 37776, 87733

NAS Traverse City, MI

34084, 37784

NAS Trinidad

1675, 3852, 6443, 04349, 34077, 37779, 37816, 87748

NAF Tutuila, American Samoa

3846, 37811

NAAS Vernalis, CA
- see CASU-63

NATTC Ward Island
- NAS Corpus Christi, TX

NAAS Watsonville, CA
- see CASU-64

NAF Weeksville, NC
- see ZP-1

Wheeler Field
- see NAS Pearl Harbor, HI

NAS Whidbey Island, WA

6441, 34094, 37819

NAS Willow Grove, PA

84807, 84810

Warships

USS Antietam (CV36)

84814

USS Currituck (AV-7)

34078, 37820, 37831

USS Curtis (AV-4)

84813

Naval and Marine Corps Commands

Commander Air Center Manus Island, Admiralty Islands (including Commander Naval Air Base Manus)

37815, 37825, 84793

Commander Air Forces 7th Fleet (Brisbane, Australia and NAB Samar, Philippines)

37811, 84809, 84810

Commander Air Forces Atlantic Fleet (NAS Norfolk, VA)

87748

Commander Air Forces Philippines (NAB Samar)

84810

Commander Aircraft South Pacific Force (Guadalcanal Naval Base, Solomon Islands)

3846, 34060, 34061

Commander Airships Atlantic (NAS Norfolk, VA)

34066

Commander All Forces Aruba-Curaçao (Curaçao)

37799

Commander Atlantic Fleet (NAS Norfolk, VA)

6440, 6444, 04352

Commander Eastern Sea Frontier (NAS New York, NY)

04350

Commander Fleet Air West Coast (NAS San Diego, CA)

04349

Commander Fleet Airships Atlantic (NAS Lakehurst, NJ)

34080

Commander Fleet Airships Wing (unidentified station)

34066

Commander In Chief Atlantic (NAS Quonset Point, RI)

3847

Commander Marianas (NAS Agana, Guam)

34091

Commander Naval Air Bases Mactan Islands, Philippines

84813

Commander Naval Air Bases Philippines

84814

Commander Naval Command Reserve Forces (NAS Norfolk, VA)

37820

Commander Naval Forces Eastern Atlantic and Mediterranean (RAF Hendon, London, UK)

37805

Commander Naval Forces Europe (RAF Hendon, London, UK)

37805, 84797, 84798

Commander Naval Forces North African Waters (NAS Port Lyautey?)

3847

Commander Philippine Sea Frontier (Tolosa Naval Base)

37811

Commander Support Force (NAS Norfolk, VA)

6440

Commander Task Force 24 (NAS Argentia, Nfld)

Aircraft listed under NAS Argentia

Commander United States Ports and Bases (France)

37805, 84798

Fleet Marine Force (NAS San Diego, CA)

3846

Naval Organisations and Units

ACORN-47 (NAB Palawan, Philippines)

84811

ACORNTRADET (Port Hueneme, CA)

37828

**AR&OH-1
(NAB Manus Island,
Admiralty Islands)**

37811, 37815, 84794

**AROU-1 (Los Negros Naval
Base, Admiralty Islands)**

37783, 84794

**AROU-2 (NAB Samar,
Philippines)**

37783, 37811, 84809, 84811

**ARUSOLS
(Guadalcanal Naval Base,
Solomon Islands)**

37831

**BlmpHedron 5 (Carlsen Field,
Trinidad)**

34074

**CASU-1
(NAS Pearl Harbor, HI)**

V187, 37791

CASU-4 (NAS Puunene, HI)

V187

CASU-6 (NAS Alameda, CA)

84808, 87721, 87727, 87728

CASU-7 (NAS Seattle, WA)

04349, 87731

CASU-F12 (NAS Orote, Guam)

34061, 37810, 37829

CASU-F12 (NAS Agana, Guam)

34091, 37783

CASU-F13 (Admiralty Islands)

84809, 84810, 84811, 84813,
84814

CASU-21 (NAS Norfolk, VA)

6451, 34094, 87729

**CASU-22
(NAS Quonset Point, RI)**

04352

CASU-24 (NAS Wildwood, NJ)

87732

CASU-31 (NAS Hilo, HI)

37771, 37812

CASU-32 (NAS Kahului, HI)

37783

**CASU-35 (NAF Eniwetok,
Marshall Islands)**

37829

CASU-36 (NAAS Arcata, CA)

84808

**CASU-36
(NAAS Santa Rosa, CA)**

87727

CASU-37 (NAAS Hollister, CA)

87728

CASU-F43 (Guam)

34091

CASU-54 (NAAS Fallon, NV)

87721, 87728

CASU-63 (NAAS Vernalis, CA)

87727

**CASU-64
(NAAS Watsonville, CA)**

87721, 87728

CASU-67 (NAS Memphis, TN)

34078

**FABU-1 (Noumea Naval Base,
New Caledonia)**

34060

**FASRON-7
(NAS San Diego, CA)**

6451, 34063

FASRON-8 (NAS Alameda, CA)

34083

FASRON-9 (NAS Seattle, WA)

04349

**FASRON-11
(NAS Pearl Harbor, HI)**

6451, 87723

**FASRON-13
(NAS Orote, Guam)**

84793, 84814

**FASRON-76
(RAF Hendon, London, UK)**

34062

**FASRON-101
(NAS Quonset Point, RI)**

04351, 04355, 34077, 34078,
35921, 37820, 84805

**FASRON-102
(NAS Norfolk, VA)**

6451, 6454, 04357, 34062,
34069, 34071, 34085, 37783,
37784, 37790, 37799, 37803,
37813, 37820, 37831, 84800,
84809, 84818, 87721, 87745,
87748

FASRON-104 (NAS Bermuda)

6453, 34078

**FASRON-104 (NAF Port
Lyautey, Morocco)**

34062, 37813, 87721, 87723,
87745, 87748

**FASRON-109
(NAS Jacksonville, FL)**

04351

**FASRON-110
(NAS San Diego, CA)**

37771

FASRON-111 (NAS Bermuda)

84800

**FASRON-112
(NAS Whidbey Island, WA)**

04354, 34063, 37771, 37826

**FASRON-113
(NAS Seattle, WA)**

84813

**FASRON-113
(NAS Whidbey Island, WA)**

84813

**FASRON-114
(NAS Kodiak, AK)**

34063, 37771, 84798

FASRON-115 (NAS Trinidad)

37813

**FASRON-119 (NAS Sangley
Point, Philippines)**

34083

**FASRON-201
(NAS Norfolk, VA)**

37803, 37820

**FASRON-795
(NAS Jacksonville, FL)**

84800

**FASRON-895
(NAS Seattle, WA)**

84813

FASRON-915 (NAS Trinidad)

34078

**FAW-3
(NAS Coco Solo, Panama CZ)**

6451, 34072

FAW-5 (NAS Norfolk, VA)

6444, 04352, 34078, 37794,
37805, 37809, 37820

**FAW-7 (Plymouth/NAF
Dunkeswell, UK)**

37805, 84797, 84798

FAW-11 (NAS San Juan, PR)

34070, 34094, 66333, 66335,
66338, 66352, 66353, 66354,
66355, 66356, 66357, 66358

FAW-12 (NAS San Julian, Cuba)

04352, 34086

FAW-12 (NAS Miami, FL)

34065

**FAW-15 (NAS Port Lyautey,
Morocco)**

3847, 34064, 37785, 37809

FAW-16 (NAF Recife, Brazil)

6444, 34080, 37774

FAW-16 (NAS Natal, Brazil)

04352

**Fleet Airship Wing-4
(NAF Ipitanga, Brazil)**

34066

**Fleet Airship Wing-5
(NAS Trinidad)**

34074

**Naval Air Activities Severn
River Command
(NAF Annapolis, MD)**

Aircraft listed under
NAF Annapolis

**1st Naval District
(NAS Quonset Point, RI)**

35921, 84797

**4th Naval District
(NAS Atlantic City, NJ)**

37784

**5th Naval District
(NAS Norfolk, VA)**

37828, 84813

**6th Naval District
(NAS Key West, FL)**

37822

**6th Naval District
(NAS Sanford, FL)**

84814

**6th Naval District
(NAS Jacksonville, FL)**

87743

**10th Naval District
(NAS Trinidad)**

37784

**10th Naval District
(NAS Guantanamo, Cuba)**

84796

**12th Naval District
(NAS Alameda, CA)**

37827, 84808, 87736

**13th Naval District
(NAS Whidbey Island, WA)**

34094, 37819

**17th Naval District
(NAS Kodiak, AK)**

87745

SOSU-2 (NAS Norfolk, VA)

37820

VJ-1 (NAS Pearl Harbor, HI)

6453, 87723

VJ-1 (USS Rigel)

1671, 6453

VJ-2 (NAS Moffett Field, CA)

6453

VJ-2 (NAAS Shelton, WA)

87731

VJ-3 (NAS Pearl Harbor, HI)

1671, 1672

VJ-3 (NAS Puunene, HI)

1671, 37790

VJ-3 (USS Rigel)

1671, 1672

**VJ-3
(NAF Tinian Island,
Mariana Islands)**

37810

VJ-7 (NAS San Diego, CA)

84806

VJ-7 (NAS Pearl Harbor, HI)

6453, 34083, 87723

**VJ-8 (Efate Naval Base,
New Hebrides)**

1672, 37831

VJ-8 (NAS Santa Ana, CA)

34063

VJ-9 (NAS San Diego, CA)

84806

**VJ-9 (San Marcelino Naval
Base, Philippines)**

37783

VJ-10 (NAAS Shelton, WA)

37810, 87731

VJ-11 (NAS Puunene, HI)

1672, 37790, 87723

**VJ-11 (Efate Naval Base,
New Hebrides)**

1672

VJ-11 (NAS Santa Ana, CA)

34063, 37810

VJ-12 (NAS San Diego, CA)

84806

VJ-13 (NAAS Shelton, WA)

37771

**VJ-13 (Guadalcanal Naval
Base, Solomon Islands)**

34061

VJ-14 (NAS Pearl Harbor, HI)

87723

VJ-18 (NAS Moffett Field, CA)

37829

**VJ-18 (Ulithi Naval Base,
Ulithi Atoll, Caroline Islands)**

37829

**VJ-18 (NAF Eniwetok,
Marshall Islands)**

37829

VJ-19 (NAS Moffett Field, CA)

37771

VJ-19 (NAS Puunene, HI)

37771

VJ-19 (NAS Santa Ana, CA)

34063

**VMJ-353 (NAF Tutuila,
American Samoa/Funafuti
Marine Base, Ellice Islands)**

3846

**VMS-3 (MCAS St Thomas,
US Virgin Islands/
NAS San Juan, PR)**

1673

**VN4D8-N
(NAAS Barin Field, FL)**

04357

VN8D5 (NAF Annapolis, MD)

Aircraft listed under NAF
Annapolis

**VN8D8-B
(NAAS Bronson Field, FL)**

04357

VPB-153 (NAS Clinton, OK)

34088

**VS-51 (NAF Tutuila,
American Samoa)**

3846

VS-63 (NAS San Juan, PR)

34070

**VTB OTU-1
(NAS Fort Lauderdale, FL)**

34089

VU-6 (NAS Puunene, HI)

87723

VU-7 (NAS San Diego, CA)

84806

VU-8 (NAS Santa Ana, CA)

34063

ZP-1 (NAF Weeksville, NC)

04355

*Marine Corps
Organisations and Units*

**AES-46
(MCAS Cherry Point, NC)**

84799

MAG-24 (Hawaii)

3846

**1st MAW (Emirau Marine
Base, St Matthias Islands,
Bismarck Archipelago)**

34067

**2nd MAW
(NAS San Diego, CA)**

3846

**3rd MAW (MCAS St Thomas,
US Virgin Islands)**

1673

**4th MAW (NAF Tutuila,
American Samoa)**

3846

**9th MAW (MCAS St Thomas,
US Virgin Islands)**

1673

*Naval Missions and
Attachés*

**Naval Attaché to Colombia
(Bogota, Colombia)**

1675, 1677

**Naval Attaché to Cuba
(Havana, Cuba)**

1676, 37822

**Naval Attaché to Dominican
Republic (Ciudad Trujillo,
Dominica)**

34077

**Naval Attaché to Greece
(Athens, Greece)**

87721, 87723

**Naval Attaché to Guatemala
(Guatemala City, Guatemala)**

04349, 04357, 84818

**Naval Attaché to Norway (Oslo,
Norway)**

34062, 37813, 84800, 87745

**Naval Attaché to Sweden
(Stockholm, Sweden)**

34077, 87749

**Naval Attaché to Venezuela
(Caracas, Venezuela)**

1675, 37820

**Naval Mission to Brazil (Rio de
Janeiro, Brazil)**

34069

**Naval Mission to Havana
(Havana, Cuba)**

04351

**Joint US-Brazilian Mission
(Rio de Janeiro, Brazil)**

87748

Other Users and Agencies

**Ames Laboratory (NASA),
Moffett Field, CA**

04351

**Bell Aircraft Corporation,
Buffalo, NY**

87750

Columbia University, NY

35921

**Curtiss-Wright Corporation
(probably Buffalo, NY)**

34091

**Department of the Interior,
Washington, DC**

34077, 87731

**EDO Corporation, College
Point, NY**

37782, 37783, 37805

**BAR Goodyear, (Goodyear
Aircraft Co, Akron, OH)**

84815

**INA/BAR Bethpage (Grumman
Aircraft), Long Island, NY**

1384, 1675, 3846, 6451, 6452,
6454, 04349, 04351, 04354,
04357, 04358, 34061, 34063,
34068, 34069, 34071, 34077,
34078, 34083, 34088, 34092,
34094, 37771, 37778, 37782,
37783, 37790, 37791, 37794,
37799, 37803, 37805, 37812,
37813, 37816, 37819, 37820,
37822, 37825, 37826, 37827,
37828, 37831, 84796, 84797,
84798, 84799, 84800, 84805,
84807, 84808, 84809, 84810,
84813, 84814, 84815, 84817,
84818, 87720, 87721, 87723,
87728, 87729, 87732, 87741,
87742, 87744, 87745

**Kaman Helicopter Corporation,
Bloomfield, CT**

04351

NACA Langley Field, VA

34088/NACA103,
34094/NACA103,
37778/NACA103,

37816/NACA103,
87748/NACA103,
87748/NACA202

NASA - see Ames Laboratory,
Moffett Field, CA

**Pan American Airways Inc,
New York, NY**

48229

*Serials and corresponding
manufacturer's numbers:*

1384 (1021), 1671 to 1680
(1066 to 1075), 3846 to 3855
(1100 to 1109), 6440 to 6454
(1110 to 1124), 04349 to 04358
(1176 to 1185), 07004 (1011),
09767 (1060), 09782 (1017),
34060 to 34071 (1189 to 1200),
34072 to 34094 (B-1 to B-23),
35921 (1188), 37771 to 37831
(B-24 to B-84), 39747 to 39748
(1186 to 1187), 48229 (1004),
66325 (1138), 66326 (1146),
66327 (1153), 66328 (1167),
66329 (1171), 66330 (1133),
66331 (1161), 66332 (1165),
66333 (1172), 66334 (1126),
66335 (1173), 66336 (1164),
66337 (1162), 66338 (1170),
66339 (1130), 66340 (1134),
66341 (1168), 66342 (1139),
66343 (1160), 66344 (1163),
66345 (1144), 66346 (1148),
66347 (1149), 66348 (1137),
66349 (1166), 66350 (1151),
66351 (1145) 66352 (1143),
66353 (1140), 66354 (1141),
66355 (1125), 66356 (1136),
66357 (1147), 66358 (1152),
66359 (1129), 66360 (B-34),
66361 (B-49), 84790 to 84818
(B-85 to B-113), 87720 to 87751
(B-114 to B-145), 89492 (1132),
99078 (1014)

V174 to V176 (1063 to 1065),
V184 to V187 (1076 to 1079),
V190 to V192 (1085 to 1087)

OA-9 & OA-13 GOOSE

*Army Air Corps and
Army Air Force Establishments*

**Albrook Field, Panama, CZ
(including assignment to
6th Air Force)**

38-559, 38-562, 38-564, 38-566,
38-571, 38-572, 38-573, 38-574,
38-579, 38-580

**Atkinson Field, Georgetown,
British Guiana**

38-564, 38-570, 38-576

Barksdale Field, LA

38-573, 38-574

Bolling Field, DC

38-559, 38-562, 38-563, 38-565,
38-566, 38-570, 38-576, 38-578,
38-579, 42-97055

Borinquen Field, PR

38-570

Bush Field, GA

42-106981

Clark Field, Philippines

38-567

Chanute Field, IL

38-557

Drew Field, FL

38-559

Eglin Field, FL

38-562, 38-578, 38-579

Fairfield Air Depot
- see Patterson Field, OH

Fort Lewis (Gray Field), WA

38-564

**Fort Pepperrell
(St Johns), NL**

38-557, 38-581

**France Field
(Panama Air Depot), CZ**

38-566, 38-571, 38-572, 38-573,
38-574, 38-579, 42-106979,
42-106983

Gray Field
- see Fort Lewis, WA

Hamilton Field, CA

38-561, 38-566, 38-570, 38-577

Hawaiian Air Depot
- see Luke Field, Ford Island, HI

Hickam Field, HI

38-558, 38-568, 38-569, 38-575

**Hunter Field,
Savannah, GA**

38-564

**Kelly Field
(San Antonio Air Depot), TX**

42-97055

Langley Field, VA

38-558, 38-559, 38-570, 38-571,
38-572, 38-578

**Luke Field (Hawaiian Air
Depot), Ford Island, HI**

38-558, 38-569

McChord Field, WA

38-570

MacDill Field, FL

38-559

March Field, CA

38-567, 38-568, 38-569

Maxwell Field, AL

38-562, 38-579

Miami Air Depot
- see 1105th and 4006th Base
Units below

Middletown Air Depot
- see Olmsted Field, PA

**Mitchel Field, NY
(including 1st Air Force)**

38-557, 38-560, 38-575, 38-581

Moffett Field, CA

38-566

Morrison Field, FL
- see 1103rd Base Unit

**Nichols Field
(Philippines Air Depot)**

38-561, 38-567

**Olmsted Field
(Middletown Air Depot), PA**

38-559, 38-564, 38-570, 38-576,
38-578, 38-579, 38-581

Panama Air Depot
- see France Field, CZ

**Patterson Field
(Fairfield Air Depot), OH**

38-556, 38-562, 38-566

Philippines Air Depot
- see Nichols Field

Pope Field, NC

38-565

St Johns, NL
- see Fort Pepperrell

San Antonio Air Depot
- see Kelly Field, TX

Savannah - see Hunter Field, GA

Stewart Field, NY

38-559, 38-579

Waller AFB, Trinidad - see 5920th Air Base Group

West Point Academy, NY

38-559, 38-560, 38-564, 38-579, 38-580

Wheeler Field, HI

38-558, 38-568, 38-569, 38-575

Wright Field, OH

38-556, 38-579, 38-581, 42-38214

Zandery Field, Surinam

38-576

Army Air Base Units, ATC and post-war Organisations

1103rd Base Unit, Morrison Field, FL (West Palm Beach Field)

38-562, 38-566, 38-578

1105th Base Unit, Pan American Field, Miami, FL (36th Street Airport)

38-564

1455th Base Unit, Gore Field, MT

38-578

4000th Base Unit, Wright Field, OH

48-128

4003rd Base Unit, Newark, NJ

45-49088

4006th Base Unit, Miami (Miami Air Depot), FL (36th Street Airport)

38-562, 42-106981

4121st Base Unit, Kelly Field, TX

42-106981

5918th Air Base Squadron, Atkinson Field, Georgetown, British Guiana

38-564

5920th Air Base Group, Waller AFB, Trinidad

38-564

Air Transport Command, North Atlantic Wing

38-562

Air Transport Command, South Atlantic Wing

38-562, 38-578

Air Transport Command, North Africa

45-49088, 45-49089

Caribbean Transport Wing, ATC, Morrison Field, Miami, FL

38-562, 38-566

Army Air supported Missions, Attachés and Foreign Intelligence Activities

Military Attaché to British Guiana

42-106979

Military Attaché to Colombia

42-106980, 42-106983

Military Attaché to Cuba

42-106982, 42-106983

Military Attaché to Guatemala

42-106979, 42-106981

Military Attaché to Haiti

42-106983

Military Attaché to Honduras

38-579

Military Attaché to Venezuela

38-564, 42-106979, 42-106981

Military Intelligence, Brazil

38-562, 38-566, 38-570, 42-97055

Military Intelligence, Peru

38-578, 42-97055, 42-106983

Other Users and Agencies

EDO Corporation, College Point, NY

48-128

Pan American Airways Inc, New York, NY

42-38214, 42-38215

Serials and corresponding manufacturer's numbers:

38-556 to 36-581 (1022-1047), 42-38214 (1058), 42-38215 (1006), 42-97055 (1062), 42-106979 to 42-106983 (1155-1159), 45-49088 (B-120), 45-49089 (1193), 48-128 (B-21)

J4F WIDGEON

Naval, Marine Corps and Coast Guard Establishments

NAS Adak, AK

32951

NAS Alameda, CA
- see also CASU-6

32937, 32938, 32942, 32961, 37758, 37766, 37767, 37769

NAS Anacostia, Washington, DC

32944

NAF Annapolis, MD (including VN8D5)

32967, 37743

NAF Aratu - see FAW-16

NAS Argentia, NL

32978

NAAS Arlington, VA

37713, 37717

NAS Astoria, OR

32941, 37713, 37717, 37721

NAS Atlantic City, NJ

32965, 32980

NAS Banana River, FL
- see also VPB 2 ATU 3

32945, 32969, 32972, 37749, 37750, 37756

NAS Barbers Point, HI

32941, 32963

NAS Beaufort, SC
- see also OTU VB2-1

32972

NAF Belem
- see FAW-16

CGAS Biloxi, MS

V198, V202, V210, V211, V212, V214, V217, 33956, 37765

NAS Boca Chica, FL

32960

CGAS Brooklyn, NY (Floyd Bennett Field)

V198, V205, V210, V215, 32965, 37730

NAS Brunswick, ME
- see also VJ-15

32955, 32966, 37720

NAS Bunker Hill, IN

37746

NAS Cape May, NJ
- see VS1D4 and VS-36

NAS Charleston, SC
- see CASU-28

NAAS Charlestown, RI

32967

MCAS Cherry Point, NC

33956, 37754

NAAS Chincoteague, VA
- see also CASU-27

37725, 37726, 37735

Chorrera Field, Panama, CZ
- see Fleet Airship Wing-2 and ZP-23

NAS Coco Solo, Panama, CZ
- see FAW-3

NAS Daytona Beach, FL

32945, 37756

NAS Dutch Harbor, AK

32950

MCAS Eagle Mountain Lake, TX

37754

NAS Edenton, NC
- see also CASU-67

32970, 37715, 37739

CGAS Elizabeth City, NC (including AR&SC)

V199, V208, 32959, 33956

NAS Elizabeth City, NC
- see FAW-9

MCAS Ewa, HI

32944

NAS Ford Island, HI

32963

NAAS Franklin, VA

32949, 32965, 33954, 33955, 33956, 33957, 37751, 37759

NAS Glenview, IL

32969, 37734

NAS Glynco, GA

09789, 37728

NAS Great Exuma Island, Bahamas

32962

NAS Grosse Ile, MI

37735

NAS Groton, CT
- see CASU-28

NAS Guantanamo Bay, Cuba

32939, 32958

NAAS Harvey Point, NC

32940, 32974, 37735

NAS Hilo, HI
- see also CASU-31

32963

NAS Honolulu, HI

32984

NAS Houma, LA

37754

NAS Jacksonville, FL
- see also VPB2 OTU-4

32945, 32969, 37728, 37749, 37750, 37756

NAS Johnston Island, Johnston Atoll

32941

NAMU Johnsville, PA

32952, 37736

NAS Kahului, HI

32979

NAS Kaneohe Bay, HI
- see CASU-38 and FAW-2

NAS Key West, FL
- see also FAW-12

32949, 32960, 33953

NAS Kodiak, AK

32947, 32951

NAS Lakehurst, NJ

32981, 33956, 37770

NAS Los Alamitos, CA

37761

NAAS Manteo, NC

37726

NAAS Martha's Vineyard, MA
- see also NACTULANT

37744

NAAS Mayport, FL

32969, 32972

NAS Memphis, TN
- see CASU-67 and FASRON-4

NAS Miami, FL

32945, 37756

NAF Middle River, MD

37735

NAS Moffett Field, CA

32942

Mustin Field, PA
- see NAF Philadelphia

NAS New Orleans, LA

32983

NAS New York, NY (Floyd Bennett Field)
- see also VS1D3 and VS-34

32937, 32938, 32939, 33954, 33955, 33956, 33957, 37712, 37752, 37757

NAF Newport News, VA

37742

NAS Norfolk, VA
- see also CASU-21, FAETULANT, FAW-5 VS2D5 and VS-38

32939, 32940, 32944, 32945, 32948, 32952, 32962, 32964, 32968, 32970, 32972, 32974, 32976, 33955, 37715, 37718, 37723, 37725, 37726, 37727, 37732, 37735, 37739, 37745, 37746, 37747, 37759, 37762, 99077

NAAS North Bend, OR

32940

NAS Orote, Guam
- see CASU-F12

NAAF Otis Field, MA
- see CASU-26

NATC Patuxent River, MD

32972, 32976, 37723

NAS Pearl Harbor, HI
- see also CASU-1

32937, 32938, 32941, 32944, 32946, 32961, 32963, 32979, 32984, 37719, 37763, 37769

NAF Philadelphia (including the Naval Air Factory, Mustin Field which became the Naval Air Materiel Center in 1943)

32940, 32952, 32972, 33953, 33954, 33957, 37736, 37748

CGAS Port Angeles, WA

V203, V206, V207, 32959, 32973, 221/33952, 37711

NAS Port Lyautey, Morocco
- see FAW-15

NAS Puunene, HI

32984

MCAS Quantico, VA

37718, 37755

NAAS Quillayute, WA

37717

NAS Quonset Point, RI
- see also CASU-22

32952, 32967, 32976, 221/33952, 33953, 33954, 37724, 37744, 37759

NAAS Ream Field, CA

37753

NAF Recife, Brazil
- see FAW-16

NAS Richmond, FL

32949, 32981

NAF Rio de Janeiro
- see FAW-16

CGAS St Petersburg, FL

V200, V209, V213, V216, 32949, 32972

NAS St Simons, GA

37749

CGAS Salem, MA

V197, V218, 32940, 32966

NAAS Salton Sea, CA

37760

NAB Samar, Philippines
- see also AROU-2

37763, 37769

NAS Sanford, FL
- see also VF-OTU-6

32969

NAAS San Clemente, CA

32971, 37753, 37760

CGAS San Diego, CA

V204, V219, V220, 32977

NAS San Diego, CA

32937, 32938, 32941, 32942, 32946, 32950, 32951, 37757, 37760, 37761, 37763, 37764

CGAS San Francisco, CA

V201, V206, V215

NAS Sangley Point, Philippines
- see CASU-F58

NAS San Juan, PR
- see FAW-11

NAAS San Nicolas, CA

37753

NAS Santa Ana, CA
- see ZP-31

NAAS Santa Rosa, CA
- see CASU-36

NAS Seattle, WA

09789, 30151, 32942, 32947, 32949, 32953, 32957, 32959, 32960, 32965, 32966, 32967, 32969, 32970, 32971, 32972, 32973, 32974, 32975, 32976, 32977, 32980, 32983, 32985, 33955, 33956, 37711, 37713, 37716, 37717, 37720, 37721, 99077

NAS South Weymouth, MA

221/33952, 33953, 33954

NAS Squantum, MA
- see FAW-9 and VS1D1

NAS Terminal Island, CA (Roosevelt Base)

32977, 37757

NAF Thermal, CA

37761

NAS Tillamook, OR

32954, 37713, 37717

CGAS Traverse City, MI

V204

**NAF Trenton, NJ
(Mercer Field)**

32977

NAS Trinidad

32964, 32975

NAAS Ventura County, CA

37757

NAS Vero Beach, FL
- see OTU VFN-1

NAS Whidbey Island, WA

32959

NAS Wildwood, NJ
- see also CASU-24

37729

*Naval and Marine Corps
Commands*

**Commander Air Forces Atlantic
Fleet (NAS Norfolk, VA)**

37751

**Commander Alaskan Sector
(NAS Kodiak, AK)**

32942

**Commander All Forces Aruba-
Curacao (Curacao)**

32960

**Commander Destroyers
Atlantic Fleet (NAS Brunswick,
ME)**

32955

**Commander Fleet Air Quonset
(NAS Quonset Point, RI)**

37716

**Commander Fleet Airships
(NAS Moffett Field, CA)**

37766

**Commander Naval Air Bases
8th Naval District (NAS New
Orleans, LA)**

37754

Eastern Sea Frontier

33953, 33955, 33956 & 33957

*Naval Organisations
and Units*

**AROU-2 (NAB Samar,
Philippines)**

37763, 37769

**CASU-1
(NAS Pearl Harbor, HI)**

32938

CASU-6 (NAS Alameda, CA)

37767

**CASU-F12 (NAS Orote,
Guam)**

37763, 37764, 37769

CASU-21 (NAS Norfolk, VA)

32953, 37716, 37730, 37762

**CASU-22
(NAS Quonset Point, RI)**

32985, 37716

**CASU-24
(NAS Wildwood, NJ)**

32980

**CASU-26
(NAAF Otis Field, MA)**

33954, 37731

**CASU-27
(NAS Chincoteague, VA)**

32980, 37730, 37759

CASU-28 (NAS Groton, CT)

33955, 37768

CASU-28 (NAS Charleston, SC)

37768

CASU-31 (NAS Hilo, HI)

32946

**CASU-36 (NAAS Santa Rosa,
CA)**

37768

**CASU-38
(NAS Kaneohe Bay, HI)**

32938

**CASU-F58
(NAS Sangley Point,
Philippines)**

37764

CASU-67 (NAS Edenton, NC)

33956, 33957

CASU-67 (NAS Memphis, TN)

32953, 32957, 32974, 32976,
37723, 37727, 37732, 37745,
37746, 37751, 37762, 37765

**FAETULANT
(NAS Norfolk, VA)**

37762

**FASRON-4
(NAS Memphis, TN)**

32953, 32957, 32974, 32976,
33957, 37723, 37727, 37732,
37745, 37746, 37751, 37762

FAW-2 (NAS Kaneohe Bay, HI)

32937

**FAW-3 (NAS Coco Solo,
Panama CZ)**

32949

FAW-5 (NAS Norfolk, VA)

32940, 33957, 32976, 37751,
37762

**FAW-5
(NAS Boca Chica, FL)**

32976

**FAW-9
(NAS Elizabeth City, NC)**

33953

FAW-9 (NAS Squantum, MA)

33955

FAW-11 (NAS San Juan, PR)

32953, 32957

FAW-12 (NAS Key West, FL)

32948, 37715

**FAW-15 (NAS Port Lyautey,
Morocco)**

32943

**FAW-16 (NAF Recife, Brazil,
also with aircraft at
NAF Aratu, Belem and Rio de
Janeiro)**

37716, 37730, 37759, 37762

**Fleet AirshipWing-2
(Chorrera Field,
Panama, CZ)
(La Chorrera AAF)**

32952, 32981

**NACTULANT (NAAS
Martha's Vineyard, MA)**

32976, 37765

**SOSU-2
(NAS New York, NY)**

32940

**OTU VB2-1
(NAS Beaufort, SC)**

32972

**OTU VFN-1
(NAS Vero Beach, FL)**

37750

**VF-OTU-6
(NAS Sanford, FL)**

37750

VJ-15 (NAS Brunswick, ME)

32955

VN8D5 - see NAF Annapolis

**VPB2 OTU-4
(NAS Jacksonville, FL)**

37750

**VPB2 ATU-3
(NAS Banana River, FL)**

37750

VS1D1 (NAS Squantum, MA)

33955

VS1D3 (NAS New York, NY)

33955, 33957

VS1D4 (NAS Cape May, NJ)

33953, 33954, 33956

VS2D5 (NAS Norfolk, VA)

33956

VS-34 (NAS New York, NY)

33957

VS-36 (NAS Cape May, NJ)

33954

VS-38 (NAS Norfolk, VA)

33956

**ZP-23 (Chorrera Field,
Panama, CZ)**

32952

**ZP-31
(NAS Santa Ana, CA)**

37766

ZP-51 (base unspecified)

32945

Naval Missions and Attachés

Naval Attaché to Dominican Republic (Trujillo City, Dominican Republic)

V221/34585, 32940

Naval Attaché to Egypt (Cairo, Egypt)

32943, 33955

Naval Attaché to Haiti (Port-au-Prince, Haiti)

32939

Other Users and Agencies

American Export Airlines Inc, New York, NY

09789

BAR Beech Aircraft Corporation, Wichita, KS

37729

BAR Convair, Allentown, PA

37728

EDO Corporation, College Point, NY

32976

BAR General Motors Eastern Aircraft Division, Linden Field, Trenton, NJ

32973, 37739

BAR Bethpage (Grumman Aircraft), Long Island, NY

30151

NACA Langley Field, VA

32972, 32976

BAR Nash-Kelvinator Co, Kenosha, WI

37751

Pan American Airways Inc, New York, NY

99074, 99075, 99076, 99077

BAR Wright-Patterson Field, OH

37731

Serials and corresponding manufacturer's numbers:

09789 (1231), 30151 (1270), 32937 to 32986 (1291 to 1340), 33952 to 33953 (1273 to 1274), 33954 to 33955 (1277 to 1278), 33956 to 33957 (1281 to 1282), 34585 (1269), 37711 to 37770 (1341 to 1400), 99074 to 99076 (1214, 1215 and 1239, sequence uncertain), 99077 (1235)

V197 to V204 (1222 to 1229), V205 to V221 (1253 to 1269)

OA-14 WIDGEON

Army Air Force Establishments

Albrook Field, Panama, CZ

42-38219

Atlanta Field, GA

42-38221

Aruba

42-53003

Bahamas

42-38217

Bolling Field, DC

42-38216, 42-38219, 42-38220, 42-38221, 42-38222, 42-38285, 42-38339, 42-38340 42-38356, 42-43460, 42-53003

Borinquen Field, PR

44-52997

Buckingham Field, FL
- see 2117th Base Unit

Columbia Field, SC

42-38223

Curacao

42-53003

Drew Field, FL

42-38221, 42-38223

Eglin Field, FL

42-38216

Elmendorf Field, AK

42-38340, 42-43460

Fairfield Air Depot
- see Patterson Field, OH

Foster Field, TX
- see 2539th Base Unit

France Field (Panama Air Depot), CZ

42-38219, 42-38221

Gravelly Point Field, VA
- see 503rd Base Unit

Great Falls Field, MT

42-38340

Greensboro Field, NC
- see 571st Base Unit

Hamilton Field, CA

42-38285

Harlingen Field, TX
- see 2123rd Base Unit

Hensley Field, TX

42-38223

La Guardia Field, NY

42-38339

Ladd Field, AK

42-38340

Laguna Madre Field, TX
- see 2124th Base Unit

Lake Charles Field, LA
- see 332nd Base Unit

Laredo Field, TX

42-38221

MacDill Field, FL

42-38220

Matagorda Island Field, TX
- see 2541st Base Unit

Miami Air Depot (36th Street Airport), FL

42-38218

Mitchel Field, NY
- see 110th Base Unit

42-38339

Morrison Field, FL
- see 1103rd Base Unit

42-38217, 42-38218, 42-38221, 42-38355, 42-38356

Panama Air Depot
- see France Field, CZ

Patterson Field (Fairfield Air Depot), OH

42-38340, 42-43460

Pocatello Field, ID
- see 265th Base Unit

Ponce Field, PR

42-38221

Presque Isle Field, ME

42-38356

Pueblo Field, TX
- see 215th Base Unit

Robins Field (Warner Robins Air Depot), GA

42-38223

San Juan, PR

42-38221

Stewart Field, NY (West Point Academy)
-see also 2002nd Base Unit

42-38216, 42-38217, 42-38218, 42-38219, 42-38355

Suffolk County Field, NY
- see 132nd Base Unit

Tyndall Field, FL
- see 2135th Base Unit

Waller Field, Trinidad

42-53003

Warner Robins Air Depot
- see Robins Field, GA

West Point Academy, Stewart Field, NY
- see also 2002nd Base Unit

42-38216, 42-38217, 42-38218, 42-38219, 42-38355

Wright Field, OH

42-38339

Wright-Patterson Field(s), OH
- see 4020th Base Unit

Army Air Base Units and ATC Organisations

110th Base Unit, Mitchel Field, NY

42-38339

132nd Base Unit, Suffolk County Field, NY

42-38339

215th Base Unit, Pueblo Field, TX

42-38221, 42-38223

265th Base Unit, Pocatello Field, ID

42-38218

332nd Base Unit, Lake Charles Field, LA	2117th Base Unit, Buckingham Field, FL	2541st Base Unit, Matagorda Island Field, TX	Military Attaché to Peru
42-38223	42-38355	42-38217	42-38219
503rd Base Unit, Gravelly Point Field, VA	2123rd Base Unit, Harlingen Field, TX	4020th Base Unit, Wright-Patterson Field, OH	*Serials and corresponding manufacturer's numbers:*
42-38217	42-38355	42-38217	
571st Base Unit, Greensboro Field, NC	2124th Base Unit, Laguna Madre Field, TX	Caribbean Transport Wing, ATC, Morrison Field, FL	42-38216 (1207), 42-38217 (1218), 42-38218 (1202), 42-38219 (1230),
42-38217	42-38355	42-38217, 42-38356	42-38220 (1234), 42-38221 (1232), 42-38222 (1238),
1103rd Base Unit, Morrison Field, FL	2135th Base Unit, Tyndall Field, FL		42-38223 (1206), 42-38285 (1211), 42-38339 (1233),
42-38356	42-38219	*Army Air supported Missions, Attachés and Foreign Intelligence Activities*	42-38340 (1205), 42-38355 (1204), 42-38356 (1209),
2002nd Base Unit, Stewart Field, NY	2539th Base Unit, Foster Field, TX	Military Attaché to Guatemala	42-43460 (1203), 42-53003 (1219),
42-38218	42-38216, 42-38217	42-38340	44-52997 (1208)

URUGUAY

SERVICIO DE AERONÁUTICA DE LA MARINA - NAVAL AIR SERVICE

Widgeon

As part of a larger aid package to Uruguay, the Servicio de Aeronáutica de la Marina Uruguaya received a single J4F-2 in late 1943. This was a new aircraft taken from US Navy production, and although the records show it as delivered to the US Navy on 25th November 1943, it was soon in Uruguayan hands. It was delivered to the

Base Aeronaval No.1, located on the Isla del la Libertad, Montevideo, probably in early 1944, and was serialled SG-1. The aircraft was very active in patrol, photographic and ASR roles, and was used occasionally as a target-marking aircraft for the naval OS2U Kingfishers. It also featured in the dramatic rescue of passengers from the Air France Latécoère 631, F-BDRC, that had made an emergency landing on Laguna de Rocha on 31st October 1945. The aircraft is assumed to have moved to the new Base Aeronaval No.2, at Laguna del Sauce, after 1947 (BA

No.1 was closed in 1950), and in 1948 it was re-numbered A-751, the 'A' indicating 'Armada'. A-751 enjoyed a long and safe life with the Armada before eventual withdrawal on an unknown date in the 1960s, and survives to the present day with an owner in California.

Colours and Markings

SG-1 wore dark blue upper surfaces and grey sides and lower surfaces. The national flag was worn on the upper rudder, and roundels and the naval anchor device were worn above and below the wings. Roundels were not worn on the fuselage. The serial was presented in large characters on the rear fuselage. The colour scheme remained unchanged until at least the late 'fifties, by which time the serial had become A-751.

Serial Number			
Serial	*Type*	*C/n*	*Circumstances*
SG-1, A-751 (37712)	J4F-2	1342	Lend-Lease Acquisition 1943

The Servicio de Aeronáutica de la Marina J4F-2 Widgeon SG-1 (c/n 1342) served Uruguay's Navy with some distinction for twenty years. It was used in patrol, photographic and ASR roles and as a target-marking aircraft for the naval OS2U Kingfishers. In this undated but early picture, the J4F-2 is seen apparently under maintenance and without an obvious serial. Presently registered to a Californian owner as N1944W, its current status is uncertain.

(Rolando Grasso Alfaro)

Air Catalina G-21A N14CS (c/n 1048) taxies out at Long Beach, California, for a flight to Santa Catalina Island in 1974. The registration N14CS reflects previous ownership by Catalina Seaplanes. (MAP)

CHAPTER 8:
CIVILIAN OPERATORS

THE G-21 WAS DESIGNED AND BUILT FOR A SYNDICATE of wealthy businessmen, to enable them to commute from their homes on Long Island across to the East River waterfront in downtown Manhattan where their offices were located. The first 20 aircraft were delivered as G-21 or G-21A but the United States military soon became interested in the Goose, so that by the end of 1939 it was in service with the Army Air Corps, the Navy and the Coast Guard. With military versions going to the Royal Canadian Air Force, the Peruvian Air Corps and a flying boat version (G-21B) going to Portugal, the remainder of Goose production, until 1945, was with few exceptions for military customers. The G-44 Widgeon followed a similar pattern until 1944, when Grumman received permission to proceed with development of an improved Widgeon for the civilian market. The G-44A first flew in August 1944 and deliveries to civilian customers began in February 1945.

From 1946, enabled by the Surplus Property Act of 1944, the US government was able to sell a large number of the war-surplus Goose and Widgeon aircraft to the civilian market through the War Assets Administration. Similar sales were made through the War Assets Corporation in Canada. Many were acquired by entre-preneurs who in some instances sold the aircraft within a day or two at a substantial profit. In these cases the aircraft were not converted to civilian (G-21A or G-44) status and were not registered with the Civil Aeronautics Administration (CAA). It was sometimes the third owner that had the aircraft civilianised and then registered. This has caused a problem with the compilation of accurate ownership records because although the CAA published a "first registrant" list, this clearly was not a list of first *owners*. This ownership information can only be gleaned from the aircraft file held by the Federal Aviation Administration (FAA) in Oklahoma City. Obtaining files on non-current aircraft is notoriously difficult, and in some cases impossible (because the file has been lost or destroyed), but the following list of owners is without doubt more complete than any-thing published hitherto.

The versatility of the Grumman amphibians is demonstrated by the fact that they have been purchased for many and various reasons over the past seventy-five years. The initial syndicate of businessmen wanted a private air-yacht in which to commute to the office, oil companies wanted a tool to facilitate support of drilling operations, and small airlines wanted a versatile aircraft that could operate anywhere, without the need of paved runways or indeed to operate only from water. The US Department of the Interior's Fish & Wildlife Service used Grummans since World War II ended, particularly in Alaska, managing forestry, water resources and wildlife conservation projects.

The world's oil companies have used Grumman amphibians as personnel transport and freight carriers to support exploration and drilling in all continents except Europe. Notable among these was the Shell Oil Company which maintained large aviation departments in both South America and the Dutch East Indies, which both used the Goose and, in the latter location, the Mallard amphibians as well.

The islands of the East Indies, the West Indies, the South Pacific and New Zealand, and the wilds of Alaska and Canada have all benefitted from the services provided by Grumman amphibians. The warm salt-water environment of the former locations and the harsh weather encountered in the latter have not made for easy operation, but in Alaska and Canada the durable Grummans are still providing vital local passenger and freight services, interspersed by medevac flights, which have been a part of daily life for many communities in these remote areas.

The first airline to order a Grumman amphibian was Lloyd Aero Boliviano, based in La Paz, Bolivia, who took delivery of Goose c/n 1015 in June 1938. The first oil industry utilization of the Goose came in the developing East Indies sector, where KNILM, the subsidiary of Dutch airline KLM, sought to set up a network of scheduled services among the many islands in the archipelago. Lockheed L-14s were in use for a service from Batavia via Soerabaya to Makassar and on 21st August 1940 a Goose inaugurated the service from Makassar via Ambon to Manokwari, in Dutch New Guinea (*see the first flight postal cover in the Colour Gallery*).

Since 1946, many airlines, large and small, have operated Grumman amphibians all over the world. In New Zealand, Tourist Air Travel, Mount Cook Airlines, Sea Bee Air, and others operated Widgeon and Goose services from 1955 until the 1990s. In the USA, pioneers like Ellis, Reeve and Simmons all used Grummans, to provide local air services to isolated communities in Alaska, including the Aleutian Islands. As well as the many airlines serving Alaska, Chalk's International Airline has provided air services from Miami to the Bahamas islands, while from Long Beach, California services across the 26 miles of ocean to the island of Santa Catalina have been provided by a variety of airlines, including Air Catalina, Catalina Airlines, Catalina Channel and Golden West Airlines.

Airlines serving Santa Catalina Island with Grumman amphibians:	
Air Catalina	1973-1978
Amphibian Air Transport	1947-1949
Avalon Air Transport	1953-1968
California Amphibious Transport	1981-1982
Catalina Air Lines	1963-1968
Catalina Airlines	1973-1981
Catalina Amphibian Air Lines	1963
Catalina Amphibious Transport	1979-1982
Catalina Channel Airlines	1959-1966
Catalina Flying Boats	1984-1989
Catalina Seaplanes	1967-1973
Catalina-Vegas Airlines	1962-1967
Golden West Airlines	1968-1972
Trans Catalina Airlines	1978-1979

Antilles Air Boats, founded by the former USAF Brigadier General Charles F Blair, served the US Virgin Islands from 1964 until 1981, using up to eighteen of the Goose aircraft, and latterly Mallards, to provide inter-island air services.

Canada has also been served by many operators providing passenger, freight and medevac flights, and oil exploration, civil engineering projects and forestry have all benefitted from the support provided by Grumman amphibians.

With the exception of the two VIP aircraft for the Royal Egyptian Air Force, none of the 59 Mallards were built for military customers, although c/n J-24 did serve with the US Army Corps of Engineers before going to the Department of the Interior in Alaska. Although many have been used as private air-yachts, the Mallard has seen extensive airline use in many parts of the world, albeit not in the numbers originally envisaged by Leroy Grumman.

It was not until 1954 that the Mallard was put into airline use in Canada. Central British Columbia Airways had been formed in 1945 by bush pilot Russ Baker and mining executive Karl Springer. When the Aluminium Company of Canada (Alcan) decided in 1949 to build a huge hydro-electric powered bauxite smelter in Kitimat, BC local air operators fought over the lucrative contracts on offer, with Central BC Airways getting the lion's share, and leaving the rest to Jim Spilsbury's Queen Charlotte Airlines (QCA). By 1953, Central BC Airways had acquired Kamloops Air Service, Skeena Air Transport and Associated Air Taxi, to become Pacific Western Airlines (PWA). To better serve the scheduled route from Vancouver to Kitimat, acquired from Associated Air Taxi, PWA bought three Mallards, the first two of which entered service on 4th June 1954.

Other operators who used Mallards for airline schedules in Canada were:
Air BC (1980-83)
BC Air Lines (1959-67)
North Coast Air Service (1973-80)
West Coast Air Services (1967-84)
In the USA:
Antilles Air Boats (1974-81)
Catalina Amphibious Transport (1979-82)
Chalk's International Airline (and affiliates) (1967-2005)
Northern Consolidated Airlines (1964-68)
Safeway Airways (1962-64)
Swift Air Service/ Catalina Vegas Airlines (1962-67)
Trans Catalina Airlines (1978-79)
Tyee Airlines (1978-79)
Virgin Islands Seaplane Shuttle (1982-89)
Elsewhere:
Air Pacific, Fiji (1969-71)
Air Whitsunday, Australia (1983-88)
East Coast Airlines, Australia (1962)
Nitto Aviation, Japan (1960-64)
Seair Pacific/Reef World Airlines, Australia (1988-95)
Tahiti-Hawaii Airlines, Papeete (1951-56)
Trans Australia Airlines (TAA) (1953)
Tropical Sea Air, Thailand (1992-93)

Details of all owner/operators are listed alphabetically in the following pages, and aircraft owned or operated are denoted by construction number as follows:

Goose	c/n 1001 to 1200 and B-1 to B-145
Widgeon	c/n 1201 to 1476
SCAN-30	c/n 01 & 1 to 41
Mallard	c/n J-1 to J-59
NB: McKinnon Goose conversions are identified by their original Grumman c/ns.	

Individuals and companies listed in more than one entry in this section are denoted in italics. For example Joseph Maugeri, owner of A B C Services, is also listed under Maugeri, Joseph, and Seaplane Service Inc.

A & W INC, Eunice, LA 1380
Mitchell Ashy, President and *Monroe J Wolfe* as partner.

A/S LUFTTRANSPORT,
Åalesund, Norway
1278
Used the G-44 on regular and charter services along the west coast and to Oslo from 1947 to 1951.

AB AERO SERVICE, Stockholm, Sweden
1367

ABANDONATO, Joe,
Huntington Beach, CA (co-owner)
1132

ABBOTT, Danny, Salem, WI
1351

A B C SERVICES, Miami, FL 1210
1214
Previously known as *Amphibian Bahamas Charters Inc*, and owned in 1961 by *Joseph W Maugeri*, who was also President of *Seaplane Service Inc*. By 1964 *Frank W Cuttrelle* was President of A B C Services.

ABELARDO, Hernandez B,
Caracas, Venezuela
1293

ABITIBI AVIATION Ltd, Hamilton, ON
1187
The Goose was leased from *MJ Boylen* from June 1969 until Boylen died in 1970.

ABITIBI PAPER Co Ltd, Toronto, ON
J-7
TJ Bell, President. The paper company bought the Mallard from *BC Airlines* in 1970 and after some re-skinning of the rear fuselage carried out by Field Aviation used it to supply a fishing camp on the east coast of Hudson's Bay. In 1973 the G-73 was sold to *North Coast Air Services* via Dean Franklin.

ABPLANALP, Josephine,
Revocable Living Trust
- see *Precision Valve Corp*

An anonymous JRF-5 Goose in wartime camouflage, probably painted up ready for the US Navy. (Grumman photo)

The long-serving G-21A Goose, CF-MPG, c/n B-77, in the early livery of the Royal Canadian Mounted Police Air Division. The aircraft served them for forty nine years.

(RCMP photo)

On delivery through Miami, Florida, in September 1968, N3282 was destined for Walter von Kleinsmid, in California. The Goose is still wearing the Aviación Navale Paraguaya (ANP) serial 128. As explained in the text, 128 was in reality, the former Argentine Misión Naval Paraguaya JRF-6B, 'MNA-12', and the true c/n was therefore 1146. The black-painted hull line is typical of the Argentine naval aircraft, and unlike those of the original ANP JRF-5s.
(TR Waddington)

John W Pletcher's beautifully restored JRF-6, N703, c/n B-81, resting in a sylvan Alaskan setting. The former US Navy aircraft was totally restored at The Goose Hangar, Lake Hood, Alaska between June 1994 and February 1996. After crashing on landing at Anchorage, Alaska on 6th May 1996 it was rebuilt and painted in blue US Navy scheme as "37828".
(via JW Pletcher III)

In Swedish use the Goose was designated the Tp81, and was accordingly numbered 81001, carrying the individual code '31' (this became '60' in 1955). It was painted in an overall high-visibility orange colour-scheme and carried the normal Flygvapnet national markings. The Goose is seen here fitted with skis for winter operations.
(via Leif Hellström)

Former JRF-6B, c/n 1125, which had seen service with Loftleidir and Avalon Air Transport, is seen here as N1583V, of Kodiak Airways Inc, taxying for take-off. The Goose was sadly lost en route from Old Harbor to Kodiak, Alaska with five on board, on 11th December 1974. *(Guy Denton)*

Goose, C-FVFU, c/n B-101, of Forest Industries Flying Tankers Ltd, waddles up the ramp at Sproat Lake, Vancouver Island, in September 1989. The Goose was used as a personnel transport and as a "bird-dog" for the Martin Mars water bombers, one of which is seen at anchor on the lake. *(Fred J Knight)*

The former Royal Canadian Air Force Goose II, c/n B-46, having then seen more than 25 years service in British Guiana (and later Guyana), was sold to Antilles Air Boats for service in the US Virgin Islands. It is seen here as N1048V, taxying in to Christiansted, US Virgin Islands, in October 1979. *(Stephen Piercey)*

The following information should help to make your Sun Tours Air Flight even more enjoyable.

Check in time: 15 minutes prior to departure. Late check-ins could lose their seat, if not holding tickets.

Free Baggage Allowance: 20 kilograms per passenger adult or child, plus one cabin bag per passenger. (Excess baggage will be carried at a charge of 20 cents per kilogram subject to space availability).

Re-confirmation of Flights: Please reconfirm your flights 24 hours before departure.

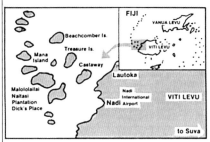

For reservations and flight information please contact SUN TOURS AIR.
PO Box 9403, Nadi Airport.
Telephone: 72723 or 72268.
Telex: FJ5213 or see your travel agent.

sun tours air

the vacation
airline that's pure
pleasure to fly

Above and right: *Sun Tours Air timetable for local services in Fiji, valid from October 1982 until December 1983. (Fred J Knight Collection)*

From Nadi International airport to the vacation playgrounds of Fiji fly Sun Tours Air — the airline that cares for your comfort.

For Sun Tours is the amphibious airline, at home on land as well as water, so our service to your favourite island resort is a doorstep service — we deliver you right to the resort not to an airstrip.

And we do it in Sun Tours comfort onboard our Grumman Goose very comfortable 10 seater amphibious aircraft.

From take off to landing turn to the vacation airline that's pure pleasure to fly — Sun Tours Air "we care for your comfort".

FLIGHT TIMETABLE (Non-scheduled)

DAILY SERVICE (Except Friday and Saturday)

	FLT.	DEPT.	ARR.
Nadi to Mana	ST1	7.45am	8.00am
	ST7	5.00pm	5.15pm
Mana to Nadi	ST2	8.15am	8.30am
	ST8	5.25pm	5.40pm
Nadi to Mana (via Plantation, Naitasi, Castaway, Treasure, Beachcomber)	ST3	8.45am	9.15am
	ST5	2.00pm	2.30pm
Mana to Nadi (via Castaway, Naitasi, Plantation, Treasure, Beachcomber)	ST4	9.30am	10.00am
	ST6	2.45pm	3.15pm

FRIDAY SERVICES:

	FLT.	DEPT.	ARR.
Nadi to Mana	ST1	8.00am	8.15am
Nadi to Mana (via Plantation, Naitasi, Castaway Treasure)	ST3	9.15am	9.45am
Mana to Nadi (via Castaway, Naitasi, Treasure, Plantation)	ST2	8.30am	9.00am
Mana to Nadi	ST4	10.00am	10.15am

SATURDAY SERVICES

	FLT.	DEPT.	ARR.
Nadi to Mana	ST1	11.10am	11.15am
Nadi to Mana (via Plantation, Castaway, Naitasi, Treasure)	ST3	12.15pm	12.45pm
Mana to Nadi via Castaway, Castaway, Naitasi, Treasure)	ST2	12.15pm	12.45pm
Mana to Nadi via Castaway, Naitasi, Treasure, Plantation).	ST2	11.30am	12.00pm
Mana to Nadi	ST4	1.00pm	1.15pm

Services to or from Mana via other islands operates if firm bookings are held.

FARE STRUCTURE 1983

The following fares are applicable from October 1st 1982 till December 31st, 1983.

A. Nadi Airport to:	ONE WAY	RETURN
— Mana Island Resort	$35.00	$70.00
— Castaway Resort	$35.00	$70.00
— Plantation/Dick's Place	$35.00	$70.00
— Club Naitasi	$35.00	$70.00
— Child's Fare	$17.00	$35.00
— Infant (On parent's lap)	FREE	FREE
B. Nadi Airport to:		
— Treasure Island/Beachcomber	$38.00	$76.00
— Child's Fare	$20.00	$38.00
— Infant (On parent's lap)	FREE	FREE

NOTE: The tariff per flight between resorts is $35.00 one way.

CHARTER RATES

A. Nadi to/from:	RATE
Mana Island	$250.00
Castaway Is./Naitasi	$250.00
Plantation/Dick's Place	$250.00
Treasure/Beachcomber	$250.00
B. Lautoka to/from:	
Nadi Airport	$250.00
Mana Island	$350.00
Castaway Is./Naitasi	$350.00
Plantation/Dick's Place	$350.00
Treasure/Beachcomber	$350.00
C. Nadi Airport to/from:	
Pacific Harbour	$550.00
Tradewinds Hotel	$700.00
Nausori Airport	$850.00
Outer Island Resorts to/from	
(as listed in A.)	
Pacific Harbour	$550.00
Tradewinds	$850.00
Nausori	$900.00

Right and below: *Tuvaluan Government brochure. Between March 1980 and September 1983, Sea Bee Air operated services on behalf of the Tuvaluan government. Based at Funafuti, the non-scheduled services linked the nine atolls of the Tuvalu group and provided charters to the Tokelau, Samoa, Kiribati, Nauru and Cook groups. Widgeon, ZK-CFA (c/n 1439), was used until August 1981 when G-21G, ZK-ERX (c/n B-62/1205) took over. In December 1982, 'ERX became the first aircraft to land at the newly-opened airport at Rakahanga in the Cook Islands. The British Overseas Development Agency withdrew funding for the Tuvalu service, and Sea Bee Air discontinued it in September 1983.*

(Fred J Knight Collection)

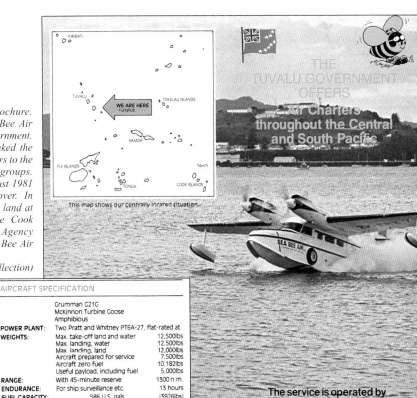

A NEW ERA IN LOCAL AIR TRAVEL

The Grumman G21G McKinnon TURBINE GOOSE amphibian ushers in a new era in the internal air services linking the nine atolls of Tuvalu.

But more than that, TURBO GOOSE is able to provide a vital air capability over 1300 nautical miles (1500 statute miles; 2400 kilometres) of the Pacific Ocean — and that takes in Fiji, Samoa, Kiribati, Vanuatu, Solomon's, New Caledonia, Tokelaus and even Tahiti and the Northern Cooks!

The two pilot, 12-passenger TURBO GOOSE — operated under exclusive contract to the Government of Tuvalu by Sea Bee Air, of Auckland, New Zealand — takes over the Tuvalu Government Air Service from its much smaller and older piston-engined brother, the Grumman Widgeon, which has been operated by Sea Bee Air for the islands for the past 18 months.

In acquiring the TURBO GOOSE, with its power, range, endurance, load capacity and sophisticated navigation and safety equipment, plus its ability to operate on land and water, *the Tuvalu Government is now in a position to provide air transport capability beyond its own shores and in an area that is not immediately accessible by conventional aircraft.

This amphibious aeroplane, specially modified for its role by the installation of twin, 715hp turbine engines and highly-sophisticated avionics, *is particularly suited for:
* Short or long-range charter flights for freight, passengers — or both.
* Search and rescue operations.
* Surveillance of shipping over a wide area and for 13 hours at a stretch.
* Provision of fast, ample freight and passenger capacity for aid and development agencies operating in the Pacific area bounded by Fiji, Samoa, the Tokelaus, Tahiti and the Northern Cooks. (Already, the Government of Tuvalu and Sea Bee Air have accepted a charter from the New Zealand Government to service the Tokelau Islands).

THE OPERATORS:

SEA BEE AIR has been operating and servicing Grumman amphibian aircraft in New Zealand and the Pacific since 1955. Thus, the flying and maintenance of the TURBO GOOSE is backed by 26 years of experience. The TURBO GOOSE will be serviced and maintained by New Zealand-licensed aircraft maintenance engineers in the Tuvalu Government Hangar at Funafuti.

Safety is, and always has been, the prime concern of Sea Bee Air. Hence, it is not insignificant that the TURBO GOOSE is equipped with the world-wide OMEGA long-range navigation system as well as several other sophisticated navigation and communication systems, weather radar and mapping, and oxygen.
* See aircraft specification box

AIRCRAFT SPECIFICATION

	Grumman G21G		
	McKinnon Turbine Goose		
	Amphibious		
POWER PLANT:	Two Pratt and Whitney PT6A-27, flat-rated at		
WEIGHTS:	Max. take-off land and water	12,500lbs	
	Max. landing, water	12,500lbs	
	Max. landing, land	12,000lbs	
	Aircraft prepared for service	7,500lbs	
	Aircraft zero fuel	10,182lbs	
	Useful payload, including fuel	5,000lbs	
RANGE:	With 45-minute reserve	1300 n.m.	
ENDURANCE:	For ship surveillance etc.	13 hours	
FUEL CAPACITY:	586 U.S. gals	(3926lbs)	
SPEED:	Maximum 200kts; 230mph;	368k/mh	
	Cruise 170kts; 195mph;	313k/mh	
PASSENGERS:	Seating for up to 12		
AVINOICS:	Dual VHF Comm; dual HF SSB Comm;dual VOR; dual ILS; dual marker beacons; dual ADF; RMI; HSI; dual DME; COL WX Radar with mapping; CMA 734 OMEGA/VLF long-range navigation system.		

FURTHER INFORMATION

Further information on charter costs and availability of the TURBO GOOSE, can be obtained from:

The Secretary
Communications and Transport
Funafuti, TUVALU
CABLES: Comtra, Funafuti

Captain Murray Pope
General Manager
Sea Bee Air
P.O. Box 1971
Auckland, NEW ZEALAND
TELEX: Sea Bee 21253
PHONE 774-406

Raymond G. Brooks,
P.O. Box 10217 Honolulu,
Hawaii 96816.
Telephone 808/8330026
Telex 723 8217

The High Commissioner
for Tuvalu
National Bank of Fiji Building,
Victoria Parade,
Suva, Fiji.
Telephone 22697

Casual charter rates for the TURBO GOOSE and estimates of journey costs will be provided on request. A deposit of 25% of the estimated cost is required on reservation and payment in full before the charter commences.

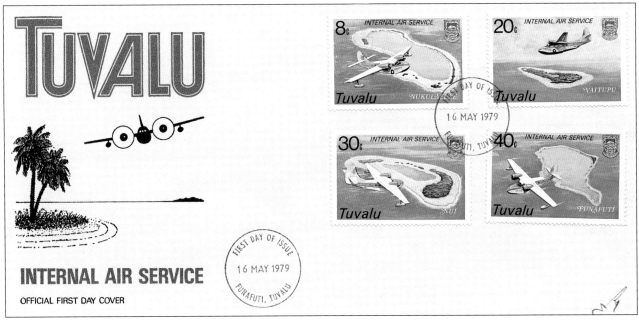

Above: *First Day Cover for the Tuvalu Air Service, dated 16th May 1979, showing a cross between a Goose and a Mallard!* (Fred J Knight Collection)

Sea Bee Air Goose, ZK-DFC, c/n B-104, and ZK–ENY, c/n 1145, over their home base at Mechanics Bay, Auckland. C/n 1145 was last reported under rebuild in Germany, whilst c/n B-104 crashed during a water landing off the coast of Caicos Island in December 1992, and the wreck has not been recovered.
(CJ Mak)

Goose, N2751A, c/n 1184, in the white, gold and red colours of Alaska Airlines and wearing the "Golden Nugget Service" logo on the tailfin. Note the rudimentary runway levelling device!
(Alaska Airlines)

The former Air Transport Services Inc Goose, N22932, c/n B-139, on the beach at Cape Douglas, across the peninsula from Homer, Alaska. The aircraft was rebuilt after an accident on 4th April 2004 and was in service in 2012 with Peninsular Airways Inc, based at Anchorage.
(Fred J Knight Collection)

Goose, N2021A, c/n B-114, of Hal's Air Service, about to leave an Alaskan beach in the 1970s. The Goose crashed and sank near Ouzinkie, off Spruce Island, 5 miles north of Kodiak, en route to Larsen Bay, while flying in dense fog on 21st July 1984. Harold W Dierich (owner/pilot) and three passengers were killed in the tragedy.
(Guy Denton)

A rare photo of the first McKinnon G-21C, c/n 1201, N150M, passing Mount Hood in Washington State, circa 1960. The aircraft, originally Grumman c/n 1147, was later re-engined with two PT6A-20 turboprops, thereby becoming a G-21D "Hybrid", c/n 1251, later in 1960. (via Ingvar Klett)

The second McKinnon G-21C, c/n 1202, AP-AUY, on delivery to Pakistan through London-Gatwick in September 1967. The aircraft, originally Grumman c/n B-78, became S2-AAD for the Government of Bangladesh in the 1970s. The fuselage was reported, in a poor state, at Dhaka in February 2011. (AJ Clarke)

The former Royal Canadian Air Force G-21A, c/n 1013, was converted to McKinnon G-21E, c/n 1211, in 1970. Seen here as N121H, at New Orleans (Lakefront) in October 1978. (John P Stewart via PJ Marson)

Larry Teufel's immaculate G-21G conversion, N640, c/n B-123, is seen here taking off from Victoria on Vancouver Island, British Columbia on 24th July 2010. (Tim Martin)

G-21A, c/n B-117, was registered N525 to the Ada Oil Company of Houston, Texas, in January 1957. It was then sold to Aviation Sales & Engineering, also based in Houston, in May 1957. It is therefore likely that this 1957 picture was taken in Houston, but the ownership of the aircraft is not clear.
(DM Hannah)

Chalk's Goose Number 1, N2721A, c/n B-54, named "Bimini Bonefish". Seen here at Miami, Florida in April 1970, the aircraft departed for Australia in 1974 and then, in 1978, to Indonesia where it was eventually withdrawn from service in 1990.   *(DM Hannah)*

The former Bolivian Air Force Goose, c/n 1150, seen here in Tropic Bird Airways' colours, as N5548A, at Fort Lauderdale, Florida, in March 1999. The aircraft was named "Pappy's Choice" in honour of "Pappy" Chalk.   *(Lothar Grim photo, published as a postcard)*

G-21A Goose, CF-SBS, c/n 1153, in the colours of Rainy Lake Airways of Fort Francis, Ontario. The aircraft is seen here at Miami in February 1978, after sale to Dean Franklin. (Nigel P Chalcraft)

The first of two pictures of the much travelled former JRF-6B, c/n 1145. As ZK-ENY, of Canterbury Planes, resting at Hamilton, New Zealand in late 1988, before going to Thailand via Australia. (Tony Arbon)

The second picture of c/n 1145, seen here as Tropical Sea Air's Goose, HS-TOM, in 1991, with company logo on the tail-fin and legend "Yellowbirds" reflecting the colour scheme. The company's Mallard was also painted in the same scheme. (MAP)

The former RCAF Goose, C-FBXR, c/n 1059, seen here in British Columbia in the summer of 1981. The G-21A had spent some six months in California before returning to service with Trans Provincial Airlines in December 1978. The aircraft is still flying in 2013, with an owner in Oregon. (Gary Vincent)

Goose, HK-2058, c/n 1084, of Aerolineas La Gaviota, in Florida in April 1978. The aircraft was displayed in the Museum of Transport in Cali, Colombia for some years, from perhaps 2002 until 2007, when it returned to the USA and was registered to its current owner in Delaware.

(Fred J Knight Collection)

Bob Keys' much-travelled G-21A, c/n 1164, painted in the colours of the Yaukuve Island Resort, in 2005, for planned operation in Fiji as DQ-AYL. The project was cancelled and, in 2011, the Goose was being prepared for operations in the Solomon Islands.   (via Steve Harvey)

Goose, N69263, c/n 1132, boldly titled as "Catalina Seaplanes", at Long Beach, California, in March 1984. In fact, Catalina Seaplanes Inc had ceased operations in 1973, and the aircraft was actually operated by Catalina Flying Boats.   (John Wegg)

Gulf Air's Goose, CF-EFN, c/n 1157, leaving an unknown location in August 1979. When seen here, the aircraft was on lease from Alert Bay Air Services Ltd, but can now be seen on display at the Tongass Historical Society Collection in Ketchikan, Alaska.

(John Kimberley via PJ Marson)

The Royal Canadian Mounted Police – Air Division's Goose, CF-MPG, c/n B-77, in a later colour scheme, patrols over British Columbia. After more than 24,000 flying hours, the aircraft was retired from RCMP service in January 1994 and is currently in storage at the National Aviation Museum in Ottawa. (RCMP photo)

McKinnon G-21C Hybrid Goose, N660PA, c/n B-138/1203, of Peninsula Airways Inc, seen here in 1993. The aircraft was lost in a fatal accident near Dutch Harbor, Alaska in August 1996, some of the wreckage not being found until the Spring of 1998. (MAP)

"McKinnon" G-21G, c/n B-72/1240, "The Aleutian Goose", seen here as N780, at Anchorage, Alaska, in June 1979. The aircraft was destroyed in a fatal accident in the United Arab Emirates on 27th February 2011, killing Landon Studer, owner of Triple S Aviation, and three others on board. (EMCS)

Willing locals trying to move Shell Ecuador's Goose, HC-SBA, c/n 1048, off a sand-bank in the River Napo on 27th November 1947. The Goose flew 4,110 hours in service with Shell Oil and affiliated companies and is now displayed as NC702A in the Steven F Udvar-Hazy Center, at Washington-Dulles, DC.
(HC Kavelaars Collection)

Goose, c/n B-73, N322, in the colours of Catalina Airlines Inc, taxying out of San Pedro, California, in August 1978. The aircraft force landed in a field and nosed over at Big Spring, Texas due to a blocked fuel system vent on 6th July 1987. It has since been repaired and is still registered as airworthy in 2013.
(Nigel P Chalcraft)

Goose, N703A, c/n 1141, in the colours of Southeast Airlines Inc, in the mid-1960s. The aircraft had briefly served with Shell-Ecuador, as a replacement for c/n 1005, in late 1949 and early 1950.
(via James Cothron)

Goose, c/n B-126, N87U, in the colours of Kodiak Airways Inc, visiting Boeing Field, Seattle, Washington, on 7th February 1970. The aircraft was transferred to Kodiak Western Alaska Airlines in 1975 and in 2012 was operated by Blue Goose Enterprises Inc, Las Vegas, Nevada. (Peter Kirkup)

Goose, c/n B-115, N641, in the colours of Webber Airlines Inc, visiting Boeing Field, Seattle, Washington, on 6th January 1979. The aircraft was completely dismantled by Antilles Seaplanes Inc during a "reverse engineering" project. (Peter Kirkup)

The former Alaska Airlines Goose, c/n 1184, N2751A, awaiting attention at Renton, Washington, on 15th May 1974 before going into service with Coast Air. Note the water rudder behind the tail-wheel. (Howard Valiant)

Above: *A rare First Day Cover, for the extended KNILM service from Batavia to Manokwari, via Soerabaja and Ambon. The cover is date-stamped 19th August 1940 at Batavia, with a back-stamp, dated 23rd August 1940, for arrival at Manokwari, Dutch New Guinea.*   *(Fred J Knight Collection)*

Right: *Another First Day Cover, dated 25th February 1939, flown from Port Moresby to Darwin via Thursday Island, with added comment "per Grumman Amphibian VH-AAY". This is, of course, Goose, c/n 1008. The cover is signed by the pilot, WF Eddy.*
(Fred J Knight Collection)

Left: *First Day Cover, dated 25th February 1939, announcing the first airmail service from Port Moresby to Darwin, via Thursday Island.*

(Fred J Knight Collection)

Right:
Isle Royale Airways timetable cover, dated August 1963.

General Information
—

Reservation:

Reservations should be made with Isle Royale Airways or authorized agents. Passengers are requested to present themselves at departure points at last 20 minutes before scheduled departure times.

Baggage:

40 pounds baggage is carried free with each adult passenger. Children paying half fare are allowed 20 pounds. Excess baggage can be transported air freight.

Schedules:

Schedules show expected departure and arrival times. Isle Royale Airways will not be responsible for consequences arising from delays or cancellations.

Fares:

Fares shown are one way per adult passenger. One child under 2 years not occupying a seat will be carried free with each adult. Children under 12 will be charged one-half the adult fare.
Between:

Houghton and Copper Harbor ...	$ 7.50°
Houghton and Rock Harbor	$12.00
Copper Harbor and Rock Harbor	$11.00
Copper Harbor - Rock Harbor round trip	$19.00
Rock Harbor and Windigo	$ 7.50
Grand Portage and Windigo	$ 7.50
Special scenic round trip between Rock Harbor and Windigo and return	$13.00

Air Freight:

Air freight from any departure point in Michigan or Minnesota to nearest point on Isle Royale $4.50 per 100 pounds, min. $5.00; between Rock Harbor and Windigo, $4.00 per 100 pounds, min. $5.00.

Special charter rates to any point in U.S. on request.

Schedules and fares are subject to change without notice.

* Not applicable to Rock Harbor passengers traveling via Copper Harbor.

FLY...
Isle Royale AIRWAYS

HOUGHTON MEMORIAL AIRPORT
Post Office Box 50
Houghton, Michigan 49931

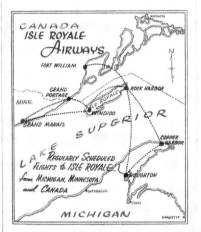

make your LAKE SUPERIOR VACATION *complete!*

FLY TO BEAUTIFUL
Isle Royale National Park
from
Michigan and Minnesota

The Wilderness Paradise of Isle Royale
Is Only 30 Minutes Away

with

Isle Royale Airways
GRUMMAN "SUPER GOOSE" SERVICE

—

ISLE ROYALE AIRWAYS
HOUGHTON MEMORIAL AIRPORT
POST OFFICE BOX 50
Houghton, Michigan 49931

TELEPHONE 482-4343

JUNEAU
Alaska's Capitol is nestled at the foot of Mt. Juneau in Gastineau Channel. A.C.A.'s offices and hangars are situated in the heart of town three blocks from the farthest hotel.

SITKA

Only forty minutes from Juneau by air, is served on daily schedules by A.C.A. Now principally a fishing center, historic Sitka was the Capitol of Alaska when Alaska belonged to Russia.

WINGING OVER THE ICE CAP
In back of Juneau, only mountain peaks extend above the gigantic sea of ice from which eminate Twin, Taku, Mendenhall, and Norris Glaciers. With no wing obstructing his vision the Alaska traveler can watch in comfort as rugged enchanting Alaska unfolds before his eyes.

Courteous, efficient, uniformed personnel are at your service to make every trip a pleasure.

Really see ALASKA
by ALASKA COASTAL AIRLINES

ALASKA COASTAL AIRLINES

TWIN GLACIER LAKE

Serving Southeastern Alaska

DAILY SCHEDULED
SERVICE OVER
ALASKA'S SCENIC
SKYLANES

By ALASKA COASTAL AIRLINES
MAIN OFFICE: BOX 2808, JUNEAU, ALASKA
EFFECTIVE DATES INSIDE

Above: *Alaska Coastal Airlines timetable cover, dated March 1953.*

An undated picture of Chalk's Goose, c/n B-104, N1621A, (Fleet number 3), leaving an unidentified beach. The aircraft was exported to New Zealand in 1972.
(DM Hannah)

Catalina Golden West Goose, c/n 1130, N93G, taxying in at Avalon (Pebble Beach), on Santa Catalina Island on 29th August 1973. Another of the company's Goose aircraft is following in.
(PJ Marson)

Sea Bee Air's Goose, c/n 1145, ZK-ENY, prior to conversion to turbine engines, taxying in at Mechanics Bay, Auckland on 11th October 1980.
(Richard Currie via PJ Marson)

A/S Lufttransport (Norway) operated G-44 Widgeon LN-HAW (c/n 1278) in the late 1940s.
(Photo courtesy Norwegian Aviation Historical Society)

The Admiral Corporation's Mallard N2982 (c/n J-52) at Oakland, California in 1950, with the legend "Admiral Flagship" under the cockpit window. *(Douglas D Olson via Jennifer Gradidge)*

ABRAHAMSEN, Olaf,
Jamaica Estates, NY
- see *Anthony Stinis*
35, 36, 41

ACCEPTANCE MORTGAGE Corp,
Vancouver, BC Kenneth Seed, President.
1312

ACE AVIATION Inc, San Rafael, CA
1438, 31
Ronald C Broyles, President. Ace Aviation Inc was based at Marin Ranch Airport, San Rafael, CA. In November 2000 the Marin County Court awarded ownership of the SCAN to *Leon C Felton*. In March 2003 the company moved to Sausalito, CA and by 2004 Ace had acquired many of the STCs pertaining to Goose and Widgeon modifications. The current status of the company is in doubt.

ACES HIGH Ltd, London, UK
(based at North Weald Airfield)
B-63

AD PROPERTIES Inc, New York, NY
J-49
Owned by *Adolph J Toigo*. John D Spiers, Pres. Ownership of the Mallard was transferred into Toigo's name, before being sold in 1956.

ADAMS, Charlene,
North Miami Beach, FL
1233

ADAMS, Jack
- see *Jack Adams Aircraft Sales Inc*

ADAMS, Jackson, Phoenix, AZ
1267

ADAMS, Joseph Q, Miami, FL (co-owner)
dba *Gander Aircraft Corp.*
1132, B-65

ADA OIL Co, Houston, TX
B-117
KS Adams Jr, President.

ADIRONDACK AERO SERVICE
- see *VL Johnson*
1357

ADIRONDACK SEAPLANE SERVICE
- see *MT Windhausen*

ADMIRAL Corp, Chicago, IL
J-52

ADVOCATE MINES Ltd, Toronto, ON
1187
Mathew James Boylen, President. The G-21A was operated in the name of Advocate Mines between 1956 and 1958. Another of Boylen's companies, *Lanson Holdings Ltd*, was the registered owner of 1187 from June 1955 until July 1956. Boylen himself was the registered owner from October 1958 until June 1969 when he leased the aircraft to *Abitibi Aviation Ltd*. The aircraft was sold in the USA after Boylen died in 1970.

AEREX Inc, Wilmington, DE
1419

AERO ACCESSORIES Inc,
Gibsonville, NC
B-46, 1274
T Henderson, President.

AERO AIR Inc, Hillsboro, OR
- see *Dan Vollum*
1059, B-62

AERO CLUB de FRANCE, Paris
19
Aircraft based at Buc.

AERO COMMUTER Inc,
Long Beach, CA
1130, B-59, B-66, B-73, B-119
Fred L Austin, President; Chief Execs: *WR Probert & WB von Kleinsmid*. Aero Commuter Inc was formed at Long Beach, CA in December 1967. After merging with *Catalina Air Lines Inc,* it was operating five G-21As between Long Beach and Santa Catalina Island during 1968/69, before becoming part of the re-formed *Golden West Airlines Inc.*

AERODEX Inc, Miami, FL
1388
A CAA-approved repair station that had converted many military Lockheed L-18s to civil use in the late 1940s.

The Aero Club of France's SCAN-30G Widgeon F-BGTD (c/n 19) at the de Havilland factory at Hatfield circa 1954. *(DAS McKay via Jennifer Gradidge)*

Aerolineas la Gaviota had their G-21A Goose HK-2059 (c/n 1019) being maintained at an unknown Florida location in 1977.   (MAP)

AERODYNE ENTERPRISES Inc,
Goleta, CA
1388

AEROFLOAT G21a Inc (Trustee),
Wilmington, DE
B-120
Owned by Ossie Kilkenny, a Dublin-based accountant who had many show business people among his client list. The G-21A was based at Weston, near Dublin, from 1997, and was used to fly clients to the lakes in the west of Ireland. From January 2006 until January 2007 the aircraft was based at Duxford, UK and from May 2007 continued operations from Weston.

AERO HOLDINGS, Salt Lake City, UT
1230

AEROLINEAS del LLANO Ltda,
Villavicencio, Colombia
1084

AEROLINEAS LA GAVIOTA,
San Andrés, Colombia
1019, 1084
The G-21As were delivered in November 1977 to provide services between Isla de Providencia and the Isla de San Andrés off the east coast of Nicaragua. 1019 was written-off after going missing on a flight between the two islands on 30th November 1979. The other G-21A was transferred to *Aerolineas del Llano Ltda* in 1984 but operations ceased by 1985. 1084 was then preserved as HK-2058-P in the Transport Museum at Cali, Colombia, but was sold to an American owner in December 2007.

AEROMAR Inc, Miami Beach, FL
1230
Arthur C Stifel III, President.

AEROMAR 8 Inc
1230

Aeromar Inc's McKinnon Super Widgeon N1AS (c/n 1230) without its rudder, at Opa Locka, Florida on 4th October 1977. The registration reflects the initials of Aeromar's President, Arthur C Stifel III.
(Ian MacFarlane via Jennifer Gradidge)

AEROMAR SA, Panamá
1277
The G-44 was abandoned while in for repairs, and repossessed by *Banco Nacional de Panama* in 1974.

AEROMARINE SKYWAYS,
Bayfield, WI
1324

AEROMOBILE EQUIPMENT Co,
Hempstead, NY
1371
Owned by *Paul & Mildred Nyholm*.

AERO PLAN LEASING Inc, Dayton, OH
1463
Daniel G Stanley, President.

AEROPLAN EXECUTIVE FLEET Inc,
Dayton, OH
1463
Known as *Aero Plan Leasing Inc* (see above), until March 1970. The company

had an address in Delray Beach, FL by April 1975, when the G-44A was sold.

AEROPLANES LLC, Hillsboro, OR
- see *Dan Vollum*
B-125

AERO PUNTA, Montevideo, Uruguay
1342

AERO QUALITY SALES Co, Detroit, MI
J-34, J-45
Owned by *George W Sherwood*, who was also company President. J-45, based at Detroit City Airport, was operated under the name *Land-Sea-Airways* from April 1969. J-34 was owned from March 1966 until being sold to Canadair in July 1966.

AERO QUEST Inc, Cleveland, OH
B-62
Had a large cargo door installed in the right side of the fuselage in 1985. The company's insurance lapsed after a few

months and the Goose was transferred to Aero Quest's parent company *Kalt Manufacturing Co* in 1987. They in turn sold the aircraft in 1990.

AERO SALES & LEASING Ltd,
Campbell River, BC
1299
The G-44 was bought as a restoration project in 1996 but was never completed and the aircraft was returned to the USA in 2005.

AERO SERVICES, Manila, Philippines
1436
Owned by a US citizen, Blaine Gardner, who also operated a C-47.

AERO TECHNOLOGIES,
Long Beach, CA
1160, B-140
Richard L Probert, President. Richard, the son of *Wilton R (Dick) Probert,* had registered the G-21A (B-140) as N931RP, but transferred the registration to his Beech Duke (ex JA5260). B-140 was then registered as N329 in November 1999 in homage to one of his father's aircraft, and

was under rebuild/restoration in 2000. Richard Probert was killed in a road accident in 2007, but restoration of the aircraft was continued by Auggie Swanson at Warbird Connection in Chino, CA. It was then sold to *Charles Nichols* for proposed display at the Yanks Air Museum in Chino.

AERO TRADES Inc,
Mineola, Long Island, NY
1352
Aircraft repairers based at Roosevelt Field and later at MacArthur Airport, Ronkonkoma, NY.

AEROVIAS NACIONALES de COLOMBIA, Barranquilla, Colombia
1045
Owned the Goose from September 1944 until May 1945.

AEROVIAS NACIONALES PUERTO RICO Inc, San Juan, PR
1001
N Basso Jr, President. The G-21A was purchased from the estate of Wilton Lloyd-Smith for $40,000 in September 1940, and

converted from 8 to 10-place in November 1940. Aerovias Nacionales was authorised to fly the aircraft from San Juan, PR to Miami, FL, via the Dominican Republic, Haiti and Cuba in late 1942 for an engine change.

AFRICAIR Inc, Miami, FL
1381
Connected with Nigerian operator *Pan African Airlines*.

AG NORTHWEST Inc, Hermiston, OR
1291

AHLERS, Tom, St Charles, MO
B-35
Co-owned the G-21A with *William Sims & Fred Niedner*.

AHRENS, Peter, Coolangatta, QLD
J-13
Ahrens, a Swede, was founder of *East Coast Airlines* and purchased the G-73 from the *Dutch New Guinea Petroleum Company* in 1962.

AIR ALASKA COMMUTER HOLDINGS Inc, Hurst, TX
J-28, J-30, J-38
Thor K Tjonveit, CEO. Another of Tjonveit's companies that failed. The G-73s were passed to his *World Pacific Air Lease Inc*, which in 2000 also ended up in the bankruptcy court.

AIR AQUATIC Inc, Weatherford, OK
1132
Had the G-21A briefly registered in 1983, but it was re-registered in the joint names of *Jerry P McLean*, the Air Aquatic company secretary, and a *Shaun V Baldachino*. The aircraft had been mortgaged for $75,000 by JP McLean with the American Federal Savings & Loan Association (AFSLA) in March 1983. In November 1983 the AFSLA repossessed the aircraft and in February 1984 applied for a certificate of registration, but at the same time issued a disclaimer of re-possession, dated 12th January 1984! McLean and Baldachino sold the G-21A to *Bill Carroll* and partners, on a Bill of Sale also dated 12th January 1984.

AIR BC Ltd, Richmond, BC
(*Jim Pattison Industries Ltd*)
1059, 1077, 1083, 1157, B-129, B-138, B-145, J-22, J-26, J-53
By October 1980, Pattison had acquired most of the British Columbia-based commuter airlines and amalgamated them into Air BC, which was divided into two operating companies: *Trans Provincial Airlines (TPA)* and Air BC. The former adopted the red and blue colour scheme of Air BC but carried TPA titles and the TPA logo on the tailfin. Services out of Prince Rupert, BC were operated by TPA, using the G-21As, serving the Queen Charlotte Islands, north-western BC and south to Ocean Falls. The Air BC division under Iain J Harris operated the G-73s on

PHONE: GARDEN CITY 4989

AERO TRADES COMPANY
ROOSEVELT FIELD
MINEOLA, L. I., N. Y.

GOVERNMENT APPROVED
STATION NO. 115

Supl. # 1 to Form 337

REPAIR AND ALTERATION FORM

The Texas Co.
135 East 42nd Street
New York City

Aircraft Manufacturer and Model - Grumman G-44   Serial #1236

NC 37186

Installed two new propellers,

    Left Des. 82RS72 Serial No. 49847
    Right Des. 82RS72 Serail No. 49849

Installed two Factory built wing floats, including struts and brace wires

Installed left and right Factory built ailerons

Recovered wings, rudder, flaps and ailerons

Assembled airplane for flight

Date: October 16, 1942

    Paul Nyholm
    Mechanics Signature

    A & E 16576
    Rating

Aero Trades Company letterhead showing a supplement to a FAA Form 337 dated 16th October 1942 and signed by Paul Nyholm.

Mallard C-GIRL (c/n J-53) in the colours of Air BC at Vancouver, British Columbia on 5th February 1983.   *(Jennifer Gradidge Collection)*

scheduled services out of Vancouver International Airport to points in southern coastal BC and north to Campbell River, Port Hardy, Bella Coola and Ocean Falls. The G-73s were sold in 1983. On 28th November 1986 Air BC was purchased by Air Canada, and by 1989 all the G-21As had been sold.

AIRBORNE ATTITUDE LLC, Brier, WA
12

AIR CARRIER SERVICE Corp,
Washington, DC
1153
Francis L Duncan, President.

AIR CATALINA, Long Beach, CA
1007, 1048, 1086, 1166, B-59
Owned by Jackson Hughes, Air Catalina began operations in 1973 after acquiring most of *Catalina Seaplanes'* G-21As. Scheduled services were flown all year round from San Pedro and Long Beach to Santa Catalina Island, until the G-21As were grounded for three months in October 1977. During this time the services were provided by Air Catalina's own amphibious Sikorsky S-62A and two leased Bell Jet Rangers, while the G-21A fleet was refurbished. In the summer season of 1978 the company provided up to eight flights a day from San Pedro to Avalon Bay and two flights daily to Two Bays, Santa Catalina.

**AIR CLASSICS MUSEUM
OF AVIATION**,
Aurora, IL
1013

AIR COMMUTING Inc, New York, NY
J-11, J-12
The company was certificated by the CAB for CAR 4B operation and awarded routes from Manhattan to points in the New York City area and Long Island. Flights were for passengers and cargo only (not mail) and were to be conducted under Visual Flight Rules (VFR). Grumman produced a manual detailing the procedures necessary for non-scheduled air-carrier operations using a G-73, with detailed instructions to the named crew and details of the maintenance schedule to be carried out at

Bethpage. On 17th September 1947 the public and press were invited to take part in demonstration flights and Air Commuting Inc announced that services would begin within a week. It is however doubtful whether services were ever operated and on 30th June 1948, J-11 was sold to Texaco. J-12 was on option for Air Commuting and a Grumman Certificate of Airworthiness application dated 4th March 1947 shows the airline as owner, but the aircraft went to *Joseph Ryan*.

AIRCORP III Inc, Dallas, TX
(base Anchorage, AK)
B-72
Terry Smith dba *Aleutian Goose Adventures.*

**AIRCRAFT FACILITIES
INTERNATIONAL Inc**, Wichita, KS
1182
This company prepared the G-21A for the ferry flight to New Zealand, but it crashed after take-off from Wichita on the 9th October 1974.

AIRCRAFT HOLDINGS Inc,
Washington, DC and at Miami, FL
J-6, J-26
Affiliate company of *Lloyd Helicopters Ltd*, Miami, FL owned J-26 from 4th May 1990 until its transfer to *Lloyd Helicopters (Singapore) Pte* in 1992.

**AIRCRAFT INDUSTRIES OF
CANADA Ltd**
B-39
AL Brown, President. Although the G-21A was owned by *WRG Holt*, the registration CF-ESZ was allocated to Aircraft Industries of Canada, but then the Certificate of Registration was issued to Holt!

**AIRCRAFT INNSBRUCK
LUFTFAHRT GmbH**
30
The aircraft was painted in Red Bull colours and operated from 1998 until 2005.

AIRCRAFT LEASE CHARTER Inc,
Oklahoma City, OK
B-127

AIRCRAFT LEASING Corp, Chicago, IL
Joseph F MacCaughtry, President
3

Catalina Seaplanes' Goose N11CS (c/n 1166) at Long Beach, California on 20th May 1972 with the starboard engine running. Note the rear emergency exit which was mandatory on passenger carrying aircraft.   *(John P Stewart via PJ Marson)*

Air Catalina Goose N12CS (c/n 1086) awaiting passengers on the company ramp at Long Beach, California in May 1975.   *(John P Stewart via PJ Marson)*

AIRCRAFT Ltd, Davidson, NC
1364, 32
The trading name of *Donald J Anklin*. See also *Aircraft Sales Inc*, below. Also at Mooresville, NC.

AIRCRAFT SALES Co, Anchorage, AK
1377

AIRCRAFT SALES Inc, Charlotte, NC
1233, 1315, 1364, 1370, 1438, 31
By 1980, the company was based at Mooresville, NC. *Donald J Anklin,* President.

AIRCRAFT SALES & BROKERAGE Co, Long Beach, CA
1300

AIRCRAFT SALVAGE & REBUILD, Omak, WA
1431

AIRCRAFT SPECIALTIES Inc, Fort Pierce, FL
1374, 36
Associate company of *Mirabella Aviation Inc*, Palm Beach, FL. It is not known whether this company is connected with the one of the same name, below.

AIRCRAFT SPECIALTIES Inc, Belle Chasse, LA
1277, 1372, 1408
George E Potter, owner/President.

AIRCRAFTSMAN Inc, Oklahoma City, OK
J-4
The company began operations in 1949, providing an air-taxi service as well as a repair/overhaul facility.

AIR CRANE Inc, Opa Locka, FL
32
James T Robinson, President, and owner, also owned *Island Flying Boats Inc*.

AIREX Inc, Wilmington, DE
1419
JR Collins, President.

AIREXEC SERVICES Ltd, Fort St John, BC
15
JW Burroughs, President.

AIR FAST FREIGHT, Long Beach, CA
B-73

AIR FRONTIER Pty Ltd, Darwin, NT
B-49
- see also *Hunt Aerospace Pty Ltd*. The Goose is operated on charter flights from Darwin.

AIR JOURNEYS Inc, Little Rock, AR
4

AIRLEASE Corp, San Francisco, CA
1267

AIRMARINE LEASING Corp, Gainesville, FL
1328

Air Pac Inc's G-21A Goose N95467 (c/n 1161) at Anchorage on 27th September 1978 sporting a Shamrock emblem on the forward fuselage. *(EC Power)*

AIR MART INTERNATIONAL, Panama
1084

AIR METAL FABRICATORS Inc, Arlington, WA
1161

AIR MONACO
1297
The former US Navy J4F-2 was evaluated by the Centre d'Essais en Vol (CEV) at Istres, France in early 1947. It was flown from the Étang de Berre by a naval pilot between the 5th and the 11th February 1947 but crashed at Berre. Abandoned by its American owner, it was sold to SCAN on 15th July 1947 and rebuilt. When sold by SCAN to Air Monaco in March 1948 it was described as "Widgeon G-44 SCAN No 101".

AIR NORTH Inc, Burlington, VT
1410
Edward A Deeds, President. The company was founded in 1956 as *Northern Airways Inc.*

AIR PAC, Seattle, WA
and later out of Dutch Harbor, AK
1161, B-70, B-128

AIR PACIFIC AIRLINES Inc, Seattle, WA
Richard Maloney, President. Later out of Dutch Harbor & Anchorage, AK dba *AirPac (see above).*

AIR PACIFIC Ltd, Suva, Fiji
J-13
Air Pacific's involvement with this G-73 was something of a political fix. By December of 1967, the New Zealand government had decided to withdraw the RNZAF Sunderland flying boats from their base at Lauthala Bay in Fiji. The Sunderlands had been used for search and rescue operations and mercy flights and to compensate for the withdrawal of the service the government suggested that Air Pacific could operate a Mallard. The NZ government had their eye on J-13 which was supporting the Manapouri Power project in the South Island of New Zealand, but their proposal that the Mallard's role

could be filled by Mount Cook Airlines' Widgeons was firmly rejected by Utah Construction, the project's lead contractor.

However in December 1968 with the Manapouri project completed, the NZ government had their way and Don Nairn flew the Mallard to Christchurch for overhaul by NZ National Airways Corporation. In February 1969 Nairn carried out the post-overhaul test flights and then checked-out the pilot who would fly J-13 in Fiji. The G-73 was registered as VQ-FBC to Air Pacific Ltd on 25th February 1969 and was delivered to Fiji in March 1969, but nothing is known of the services it provided. Back in Auckland for maintenance by Air New Zealand, J-13 suffered minor damage during a water landing in Auckland Harbour on 5th December 1969.

Greater ignominy was to follow, however, when in 1970 an unqualified crew was flying the aircraft and operated the emergency shut-off valve for fuel to the starboard engine. Somehow they managed to land the aircraft on one engine but overshot the runway by 500 feet and ended up in the jungle at Suva in Fiji.

Air Pacific was finding it difficult to justify the expense of operating a G-73 and this was seen as the perfect opportunity to sell the aircraft. It was advertised in the US "*Trade-a-Plane*" for sale "as-is" for US$50,000 and was purchased along with a spares inventory by *Crow Inc* for US$35,000. The G-73 was removed from the Fijian register on 31st March 1971.

AIR PARK AVIATION Ltd, Lac du Bonnet, MB
B-49
Charles *Weyerhaeuser*, owner. The aircraft was based at Hangar T.68, Winnipeg.

AIR POLYNESIE, Papeete, Tahiti
1152
Founded in 1958 and acquired the G-21A in 1964, operating it from the Quai Bir Hakeim in Papeete. The company was bought by *Régie Aérien Interinsulaire* in the summer of 1965 and the aircraft was sold to *Antilles Air Boats* in December 1967.

The infamous water-looper! G-44 Widgeon F-OAGX (c/n 1391) was operated in Tahiti in the early 1950s. After a water-looping crash in 1953, the remains were bought by New Zealand Tourist Air Transport. *(RF Killick)*

Air Tahiti Mallard F-OAII (c/n J-29) seen here in California in 1956. The legend on forward hull reads "Ciel de Polynesie". *(William T Larkins via Jennifer Gradidge)*

AIRPORT FACILITIES Inc,
Miami Springs, FL
J-13

AIR POWER Ltd, Hillsboro, OR,
and later at Medford, OR
1013

AIR QUASAR Ltée, (Aerotaxi),
St Hubert, PQ
1414
Sylvain Michaud, President.

AIRQUEST see *Kalt Manufacturing*
B-62

AIR RANGER Ltd, The, Winnipeg, MB
B-120
Sam K Haladay, President.

AiRESEARCH AVIATION Co,
Los Angeles, CA
1450, J-54

AIR-SEA CHARTERS Inc,
Miami Beach, FL
1130

AIR TAHITI, Papeete
1391, J-29
aka Tahiti-Hawaii Airlines & later *RAI*
The G-44 was registered on 24th October 1951, and piloted by Capt J Pommier,

provided services between Papeete and the Society Islands and also to Bora Bora and Aitutaki, to connect with the New Zealand National Airways DC-3 service to Fiji and New Zealand. It flew some 30,000 kilometres, carrying 650 passengers and 7,200 kilos of cargo, in service with Air Tahiti. Unfortunately, the G-44's tendency to water-loop when landing on glassy water culminated in an accident in 1953, after which the remains were sold to *Tourist Air Travel* in New Zealand.

The G-73 was registered to the French government and operated by Air Tahiti. An attempt was made to start mail services from Papeete to Bora Bora, and to Aitutaki in the Cook Islands, with the G-73 on 3rd May 1951. The Cook Islands were administered by New Zealand, and in New Zealand eyes, Tahiti was a breeding ground for polio so that anything Tahitian had to be treated with caution. The G-73 landed at Aitutaki with its mail but was not allowed to unload and was duly dispatched back to Papeete. The aircraft flew services to the islands of Raiatea, Huahine and Bora Bora, and also transported officials of the Government of French Polynesia to the more outlying islands. In June 1953 Captain Frame piloted the G-73 on a six-day tour through the Tuamotu Islands with ten government officials, but by then Air Tahiti was in financial trouble. To avoid

losing the mail service to Aitutaki, the colonial government bought Air Tahiti and it was renamed *Régie Aérienne Inter-insulaire (RAI)* in August 1953. On 2nd October 1953 the G-73 made the inaugural flight to Nuku Hiva in the Marquesas Islands. On arrival the Chief of Nuku Hiva re-named the aircraft *"Te Manu Nui o Nukuhiva"* (the Big Bird of Nuku Hiva), which legend was painted later on the aircraft's bow. In 1954 TAI of France took a controlling interest in RAI. On 23rd June 1954 the G-73 suffered an engine fire on the water at Bora Bora and because of difficulties in getting it repaired the aircraft was replaced with Catalina F-OAVV. After repairs the G-73 was sold in the USA.

AIR TRANSPORT Ltd, St John's, NL
1447
The G-44A was leased for 5 years from *Carl Millard Ltd* but within a year the aircraft was lost at sea.

AIR TRANSPORT SERVICES (ATS) Inc,
Kodiak, AK
B-139
Dave Klosterman, President. ATS acquired the G-21A in 1981 and flew it from Kodiak until the company was bought by *Peninsula Airways* in the 1990s.

AIRTRONICS DEVELOPMENT Corp,
Dayton, OH
1218

AIR WEST AIRLINES Ltd,
Vancouver, BC
1083, 1145, B-138
NA Gold, President. The company was formed in 1959 by Norman Gold under the name Powell River Airways and operated charters out of Powell River, BC. It took over C & C Air Taxi of Vancouver in 1964, thereby acquiring authority to operate a scheduled service between Vancouver, Texada Island and Powell River. In 1965 Powell River Airways merged with Nanaimo Airlines to form Air West Airlines Ltd. Scheduled services between Vancouver Harbour, Nanaimo Harbour and Victoria Harbour, and between Vancouver, Duncan and Qualicum were commenced in 1968. Further expansion in 1977 provided a service from Victoria Harbour, BC to Lake Union, Seattle, WA. Re-named *Airwest Operations Ltd* in 1979.

AIR WHITSUNDAY, Airlie Beach, QLD
J-22, J-26
The company was founded in 1973 by Kevin W Bowe with a Lake Buccaneer to provide sight-seeing flights to the Outer Barrier Reef, 80 kilometres off the coast. The G-73s were acquired from *Air BC* in 1983 and given US registrations in the name of Bowe with a Santa Paula, CA address. Long range fuel tanks were fitted in the passenger cabins at Santa Paula to facilitate the ferry flight to Brisbane, Australia where they arrived in April 1983. Entering service with Air Whitsunday in June that year, they operated tourist and

Air West's G-21A Turbo Goose CF-AWH (c/n 1083) which was the former G-ASXG, converted by Marshall of Cambridge in the UK to McKinnon specifications. (AJ Clarke)

Air West's G-21A Goose CF-RQI (c/n 1145) on the company ramp at Vancouver Harbour, British Columbia, in July 1972. (Harrie Vercruijsse Sr via Peter Vercruijsse)

Air Whitsunday's Turbo Mallard VH-JAW (c/n J-26) anchored in Sydney Harbour, New South Wales, on 21st August 1983. The sub logo reads "The Great Barrier Reef Airline" and the aircraft also carries a small "Qantas" logo on the rear fuselage. (NM Parnell via ED Daw)

sightseeing flights to the Whitsunday Islands and the Great Barrier Reef, as well as a scheduled service from Airlie Beach to Townsville (to connect with Ansett and Qantas services) and Orpheus Island, where they landed on water.

AIRWING INTERNATIONAL Inc,
Fort Lauderdale, FL
21
Robert G Eby, President. The financing agreement between Airwing/Eby and

Vacation Inc was breached on 5th May 1982 and the aircraft was re-possessed by Vacation Inc on 22nd June 1982. The re-possession was covered by a Bill of Sale dated 16th August 1982 and the aircraft was registered to Vacation Inc on 21st August 1982. However, a Bill of Sale dated 24th August 1982 transferred ownership from Airwing International Inc to *Transportation Locators Ltd* in Tulsa, OK. A later Bill of Sale, dated 2nd May 1983, transferred the aircraft to 'Red' Stevenson

but this sale was not recorded by the FAA until 13th August 1983, after the aircraft was involved in an accident on 5th August. The aircraft was listed as "destroyed" but a Certificate of Registration was issued to Stevenson on 13th August 1983.

AITKENS, Dan
dba *California Amphibious Transport*
J-18

AKWISSASNE FLYING SERVICE,
Northville, NY
1452
Anthony B Farrell, owner.

ALASKA AEROMARINE,
King Salmon, AK
1373
Richard H Jensen, owner.

ALASKA AERONAUTICAL INDUSTRIES
1351
The company was originally at Spenard, AK with Jack Peck as a partner and later at Anchorage, AK. By 1964 Peck was the owner of the company and on a mortgage dated 10th June 1966 he was described as Jack Peck, dba Alaska Aeronautical Industries.

ALASKA AIRCO Inc, Fairbanks, AK
1463
John Hajdukovich, President. - see also *Frontier Flying Service.*

ALASKA AIR GUIDES Inc,
Anchorage, AK
1260, 1377
William D Cunningham, President.

ALASKA AIRCRAFT SALES Inc,
Anchorage, AK
1206
K Gene Zerkel, President.

ALASKA AIRLINES Inc, Seattle, WA
1061, 1138, 1149, 1157, 1164, 1165, 1172, 1184, B-8, B-30, B-52, B-60, B-63, B-86, B-88, B-131, 1215, 1265, 1270, 1338, 1355, 1411
The company was started in 1937 as Star Air Lines Inc and became Alaska Airlines Inc on 6th June 1944. The Widgeons were acquired in the 1950s and by 1968, after acquiring *Cordova Airlines* and *Alaska Coastal-Ellis Airlines,* the airline boasted no less than 14 Goose aircraft, one of which was turbine powered, and operated services from Seattle-Tacoma to Alaska, and within Alaska. By May 1971 the Seattle service was being flown by Boeing 727 and with other local routes being flown by de Havilland Canada DHC-6 Twin Otter, the G-21As were used only on routes from Ketchikan to Annette Island and Wrangell. Flight number 401 left Ketchikan at 0715 to arrive in Wrangell at 0800, while flight 403 departed Ketchikan 0955 for arrival in Wrangell at 1035. A return flight to Ketchikan left Wrangell at 0840 daily as flight 300 and arrived at 0925. The flight

continued with a departure from Ketchikan at 0935 that arrived at Annette Island at 0950. The return, as flight 311, departed Annette Island at 1015. Flight 406 left Wrangell at 1115 to arrive in Ketchikan at noon. In this case the continuation flight to Annette Island was by Twin Otter. The six G-21As still in service in 1973, operating the ferry service between Ketchikan and Annette Island, were deemed surplus to requirements with the opening of the new airport on Gravina Island, across the Tongass Narrows from Ketchikan. In fact four of them had already been sold by the time jet services began at the airport in June 1973.

ALASKA COASTAL AIRLINES (ACA),
Juneau, AK
1061, 1114, 1121, 1138, 1149, 1164, 1165, B-52, B-60, B-93, B-131, 1321, 1325
ACA was formed on 27th May 1939 when Sheldon "Shell" Simmons merged his Alaska Air Transport with Alex Holder's Marine Airways. In February 1945 Alaska Coastal became the first airline in Alaska to fly the G-21A. ACA received CAB approval in May 1947 for a joint operation on the Juneau – Ketchikan route (with *Ellis Airlines*) and by 1954 was serving 21 points in southeast Alaska with a fleet of seven G-21As. Alex Holder died in 1953 and was succeeded by OF Benecke. G-21A B-52 was leased from the US Navy on contract NOaS55-21m on 4th March 1955 (until bought outright in May 1958). The lessee was described as "Marine Airways and Alaskan Air Transport dba Alaska Coastal Airlines". By 1955 ACA had a fleet of nine G-21As providing services in south-eastern Alaska, including a 3-times weekly service from Juneau to Ketchikan, which by 1957 had been increased to a daily service and included intermediate stops at Petersburg and Wrangell. In April 1962 ACA merged with Ellis Airlines to form *Alaska Coastal-Ellis Airlines*, which then boasted a fleet of nineteen G-21As.

ALASKA COASTAL AIRLINES Inc,
Juneau, AK
Alaska Coastal-Ellis Airlines was renamed as Alaska Coastal Airlines Inc in June 1966. The company was then merged into *Alaska Airlines Inc*, Seattle, WA on 27th March 1968.

ALASKA COASTAL-ELLIS AIRLINES,
Juneau, AK
1028, 1061, 1114, 1138, 1149, 1157, 1164, 1165, 1172, 1184, B-8, B-30, B-52, B-60, B-63, B-86, B-88, B-93, B-131
Alaska Coastal Airlines and *Ellis Airlines* were duplicating services to such an extent that in July 1961 they applied to the CAB for consolidation. The merger was approved on 1st April 1962. Simmons became President with Ellis and Benecke as Vice-Presidents. The combined fleet of nineteen G-21As continued to provide local services within south-eastern Alaska connecting with jet schedules out of Annette and Juneau. Many charters were

Alaska Airlines Goose N1019N (c/n B-30) in the company's white, gold and red Golden Nugget Service colour scheme. (via Will Blunt)

The former Alaska Airlines G-21A Goose N74676 (c/n 1172) with its "Golden Nugget Service" logo on the tail is seen here in the 1970s after operating in Alaska since 1947. (Steve Krauss)

The former Alaskan Airlines G-21A Goose N2751A (c/n 1184) awaiting refurbishment in 1973, before joining Coast Air of Ketchikan, Alaska. (AJ Clarke)

Alaska Coastal Airlines' G-21A Turbo Goose N95431 (c/n 1164) at Juneau, Alaska, circa February 1966. (James Davis photo, published as a postcard by International Airline World Publishing Co in April 1990)

Alaska Coastal Ellis Airlines' G-21A Goose N4773C (c/n B-52) under lowering skies at Ketchikan, Alaska on 26th May 1964. The water rudder can be seen behind the tail-wheel and the "last three" of the registration under the cockpit window. *(KM Molson)*

also flown to provide service to logging camps, salmon canneries and hunters and trappers. The Goose aircraft also provided the area's main ambulance service. It was once said that every inhabitant of south-eastern Alaska has probably flown with the airline at some time! In June 1966 the airline's name was shortened to *Alaska Coastal Airlines Inc.,* and by February 1968 the Goose fleet had been reduced to twelve. Two of these, 1164 and B-52, were G-21A Turbo conversions (see Chapter 5), the former entering service on 24th January 1967. As part of the turbine conversion programme Goose N2751A was used to test-fly the nacelle. A mock-up nacelle was fitted in place of the starboard engine. The whole conversion programme was undertaken by Alaska Coastal personnel under the supervision of 'Shell' Simmons and Jack Bracelen and took eighteen months to complete at a cost of $250,000. Alaska Coastal Airlines Inc was merged into *Alaska Airlines Inc* on 27th March 1968.

ALASKA FISH & WILDLIFE SERVICES,
Juneau, AK
aka Alaska Fish & Game Department
1129, B-22, B-24, B-28, B-47, B-56, B-72, B-81, B-97, B-102, B-115, B-122, B-123, B-130, B-142, B-144, 1294, 1319, 1341, J-24
A department of the US Department of the Interior – see *US Government* (pages 293-295).

ALASKA GRUMMANS LLC,
Anchorage, AK
1378

ALASKA ISLAND AIR Inc,
Petersburg, AK
1138
Alaska Island Air commenced operations in 1961 as Lons Flying Service and was certificated on 8th September 1964. The

Alaska Island Air Inc letterhead (October 1985).

company name was changed in 1968 when it was acquired by Lloyd Roundtree. Regular flights were operated from Petersburg to Port Alexander, Port Walter, Saginaw Bay, Baranof and Kake whilst charters were flown throughout south-eastern Alaska and to British Columbia. The G-21A was acquired in 1971, rebuilt at Victoria, BC, and returned to service in 1972, alongside a Beaver and three Cessna 180s, and eventually sold in 1989.

ALASKA ISLAND AIRLINES Inc,
Petersburg, AK
1325
Operated the G-44 from bases at Petersburg and Wrangell from 1947 until 1954 when it was sold to *Alaska Coastal Airlines,* who had been performing maintenance for Alaska Island Airlines. Some maintenance documents also suggest that Alaska Coastal Airlines had leased the aircraft in 1951.

ALASKA JUNEAU AERONAUTICS Inc,
Juneau, AK
1327

ALASKAN AVIATION HERITAGE MUSEUM, Anchorage, AK
B-102, 1312
Both the G-21A and G-44 have been beautifully restored and are displayed at the museum overlooking Lake Hood.

ALASKA TURBINES STOL LLC,
Battle Ground, WA
1437
Robert G Tebo, Manager. Robert G Tebo was a partner in Tebo Brothers Rock Products which owned the G-44A from July 1991.

After his brother and partner Gerald L Tebo died in 2003, Robert G Tebo transferred ownership of the aircraft to Alaska Turbines STOL, of which he was manager.

ALASKA USA FEDERAL CREDIT UNION, Anchorage, AK
1213

ALBERT, Frank W, Philipsburg, PA
1153

ALCAN AIRWAYS - see *Gentry W Shuster*

ALERT BAY AIR SERVICES,
Campbell River, BC
1157

Algoma Steel's Mallard CF-FOD (c/n J-16) gracing the ramp at Montreal-Dorval in May 1948. Note the extended tail strut to prevent the aircraft from tipping tail down when loading. *(Jack McNulty)*

ALEXANDER, Elwood R,
Lima, Peru
1051, 1053
Alexander facilitated the purchase of the two Peruvian Air Force G-21As for Avalon Air Transport.

ALGOMA STEEL,
Sault Ste Marie, ON
1441, J-16
Sir James H Dunn, President. Formed a subsidiary company, Algoma Airways Ltd, to operate the G-44A and used the G-73 as transport for Sir James Dunn, Company Chairman, between Sault Ste Marie, ON and his home in New Brunswick.

ALLEN, Antony F,
St Albans, UK
1317
The G-44 was rebuilt by Mark Hales and sold to *Warren F Chmura* in 1994.

ALLEN, Charles P, Anchorage, AK
1380
dba Charlie Allen Flying Service (in 1984), and had the G-44 registered in the names of CP Allen and Marlyn A Allen before selling it in 1986.

ALLEN, Sam, Jr, Alexandria, MN
14
dba *Frontier Enterprises Inc.* Allen also had an address in Fort Frances, ON when he bought the SCAN-30 from *Atlas Acceptance Corp* in April 1973.

ALLEN, Telford M, Rockwood, ME
29

ALLEN TOOL & MANUFACTURING DIVISION, WOLAB Corp,
Columbus, OH
1216

ALLEY BROTHERS, Medford, OR
B-117

ALLEY LUMBER Co Inc, Medford, OR
B-117
BH Alley, President.

ALLIED AIRCRAFT SALES,
Phoenix, AZ
B-18
Robert A Gallaher, President. Allied bought the JRF-5 from the US Army Depot Command at Sagamihara City, Japan in July 1967. This was one of the six JRF-5 aircraft supplied as MDAP aid by the United States in 1955 and believed to have been used for spares by the JMSDF. It is conceivable that Gallaher also acquired other components from the same source (see page 107).

ALL SEASONS AIR PACIFIC
dba *Trans Catalina Airlines.*
J-18, J-19, J-42, J-58

ALLUVIAL GOLDS Inc, Fairbanks, AK
1440
Ernest N Patty Jr, President. Alluvial Golds Inc bought the G-44A from *Grumman Aircraft Engineering Corporation*, but had it registered in the name of Ernest N Patty Jr because less than 75% of the company stock was owned by US citizens.

ALMON LANDAIR Ltd, Whitehorse, YK
1153
Alexander Landolt, President. The G-21A was imported from the USA in 1994, fully restored and updated with modern avionics. Used for charter and sightseeing flights, it was lost in a hangar fire in 1999.

ALPINE AIRWAYS Inc, Fitchburg, MA
1452
The company was incorporated in Maryland on 6th September 1931. When the G-44A was bought new from Grumman in June 1946, George R Wallace III was President. In January 1957, the registration N808W was transferred to the Widgeon from the company Sikorsky S-39, which had been operated from 1931 to 1941.

ALPINE AVIATION LLC, Alpine, WY
12
William J Wiemann, Owner/President.

ALSWORTH, Wayne, Port Alsworth, AK
14

ALTSCHULER, Elmer E, Soldotna, AK
1267
Co-owner with *Alvan G Schadle.*

AMERICAN AIRCRAFT MANAGEMENT, Scottsdale, AZ
J-57

AMERICAN AIRCRAFT SALES Inc,
Renton, WA
1371

AMERICAN AVIATION Inc,
Brooksville, FL
1013, 1364
John Petrick, President.

AMERICAN AVIATION Inc, Seattle, WA
B-62
Also at Renton, WA. - see *Harold J Hansen.*
1346

AMERICAN-BAHAMIAN AIR SERVICE Inc,
Lantana, FL
B-100
AC Clewis, President. Aircraft based at *Florida Airmotive Inc*, Lantana.

AMERICAN CITY CONSTRUCTION Co,
New York, NY
B-120
One of *Peter de Savary*'s companies.

AMERICAN COSMOPOLITAN DEVELOPMENT Co,
New York, NY
J-26
Ben E Smith took delivery of the G-73 in August 1947. When it was registered jointly to Smith and American Cosmopolitan Development in May 1948 it was named *"The Golden Jennababe"* and visited Haifa, Israel as such. The G-73 was transferred to another of Smith's companies, *Van Leer's Metal Products Inc* of New York City in April 1950.

AMERICAN CYANAMID Corp,
New York, NY
J-57
A multinational that has used aircraft for corporate purposes since 1951.

AMERICAN EXPORT AIRLINES Inc,
New York, NY
1231
Formed by the shipping company American Export Lines in 1938, AEA flew transatlantic services with VS-44 Excalibur aircraft from June 1942 until 31st December 1944. Whether the G-44 was used for training (as with Pan American Airways) or as a company hack is not known. It was donated to the US Navy in August 1942, allotted BuAer 09789, and albeit maybe with a civil registration was certainly used by the Naval Air Transport Service (NATS) during WWII. (FAA 337s during WWII show American Export as owner.)

AMERICAN LEASE PLANS Inc,
Anderson, SC
1233
The G-44 was purchased from *Aircraft Sales Inc* in July 1973, then leased back to them in October 1973, and finally sold back to them in October 1975.

AMERICAN NATIONAL BANK & TRUST of NEW JERSEY, Morristown, NJ
1438

AMERICAN SKYPORTS Inc,
New York, NY
1237, 1438
The company was incorporated in Delaware on 29th November 1945 and had *William F Zelcer* as President.

AMPHIB Inc, Lake Zurich, IL
1129, B-52, B-129
Charles Greenhill, President.

AMPHIBIAN AIR TRANSPORT,
Long Beach, CA
1138, 1140, 1161
Owned by *Kenneth F Brown* and was the first airline to operate services to Catalina Island with G-21As, three of which, along with three Sikorsky S-43s, flew 12 daily round trips from Long Beach to Avalon on Catalina Island and six round trips from Burbank, California. Passengers were boarded from a floating barge moored near the Casino in Avalon Bay. Services operated from 1947 to 1949.

AMPHIBIAN AIRWAYS,
Invercargill, NZ
1362, 1466
Founded by Harry English and Jim Monk, Amphibian Airways was registered as a company on 27th February 1951 to operate non-scheduled passenger & freight charters across southern New Zealand. The G-44A (1466) had arrived in December 1950, after being shipped as deck cargo on the *"Aorangi"* from Australia to Auckland. After transfer to Mangere Airport on 12th December 1950 it was re-assembled and then flown south to Invercargill by chief pilot Jim Monk. Service to Stewart Island was started on 1st October 1951 when the G-44A left Invercargill at 1418hrs and landed twenty minutes later at Half Moon Bay. The aircraft left Invercargill again at 1800hrs for a second service that day, this time landing at Paterson's Inlet and returning to Invercargill at 1850hrs.

The second G-44 (1362) arrived in November 1952 and together they were also used to fly crayfish being shipped from Australia to Auckland direct from the fishing boats to the shore. The first such flight was made in November 1951. In one year it is recorded that no less than 121,000lbs of crayfish were airlifted by Widgeon. In 1953 a regular three-weekly service to the Puysegur Lighthouse was started, taking supplies and personnel to one of the most isolated places in New Zealand. Even by Widgeon the journey from Invercargill took an hour. Tourist/sightseeing flights were also operated from Invercargill to Queenstown, Wanaka and Te Anau and over Fjordland and the southern lakes.

By 1961, when the company was taken over by *New Zealand Tourist Air Travel,* flights from Invercargill to Stewart Island were being flown on Mondays/

Amphibian Airways' G-44 Widgeon ZK-BAY (c/n 1362) at Lake Te Anau, near Queenstown on New Zealand's South Island in January 1955. (HC Kavelaars)

Amphibian Bahamas Charters' G-21A Goose NC1080M (c/n 1136) in 1949. The company was later known as A B C Service. (MAP)

Wednesdays/Fridays twice daily, departing Invercargill at 0800 & 1700 in summer, and 0900 & 1600 in winter. After a 20 minute flight the return journeys were made at 0840/1740 & 0940/1640 respectively.

AMPHIBIAN BAHAMAS CHARTERS Inc,
Miami, FL
1136, 1210
The company was later known as *A B C Services*, Miami, FL under the presidency of *Frank W Cuttrelle.*

AMPHIBIAN MODIFICATIONS Inc,
Mooresville, NC
32
Paul S Array, President, *Donald J Anklin,* Secretary/Treasurer

AMPHIBIAN PARTS Inc, Miami, FL
1153, B-141, 1210, 1306, 1340, 1370, J-3, J-13
One of the *Dean H Franklin* group of companies.

AMPHIBIAN SALES Inc, Miami, FL
aka AMPHIBIANS Inc.
1061, 1132, 1150, 1153, 1166, B-29, B-46, B-76, B-128, 1215, 1299, 1359, J-10, J-25
One of the *Dean H Franklin* group of companies. Louise Franklin was President while Dean Franklin was Vice-President. By 1999 Joanne Franklin was President.

AMPHIBIOUS AIRWAYS Inc, Miami, FL
1048, J-56
Reportedly affiliated with *Chalk's Flying Service.*

AMPHIBIOUS CHARTERS Inc,
Beaver Falls, NY
1306

AMPHIBIOUS SALES Co,
Cincinnati, OH
16
Owned by *Thomas H Noonan.*

AMTOR Corp Ltd, Toronto, ON
1423
Louis Cadesky, President. Amtor bought the G-44A from *Carl Millard* in May 1952

but in September 1952 the aircraft was sold to *Field Aviation Co Ltd* "in a damaged condition, for rebuild". In November 1954 it was again registered to *Carl Millard.*

ANACONDA COPPER MINING Co,
New York, NY & Rio de Janeiro, Brazil
1170
Company pilot was Capt Harold Curtis. When authorisation was requested for Curtis to fly the G-21A from Brazil to Bethpage for overhaul in January 1948, the request was in the name of Alberto B Lee. The aircraft was re-registered in the USA in April 1948 and sold in November 1950.

ANCHOR AIR Inc, Miami, FL
1160
WW Watson, President

ANDERSON MANUFACTURING Co,
Englewood, CO
1364
The President, Russell T Anderson, was also President of *Englewood Airport,* also with an address in Englewood. The company was registered at an address in Denver, CO in June 1962. A title disclaimer, dated 15th May 1973, was signed by Russell T Anderson, President of Anderson Manufacturing Company dba Englewood Airport.

ANDERSON, RJ, Co, Anchorage, AK
1260

ANDERSON, Robert J, Orlando, FL
J-43

ANDERSON, Ted T, North Miami, FL
1359, 1448

ANDIAN NATIONAL Corporation Ltd,
Cartagena, Colombia
B-140, B-141
A subsidiary of International Petroleum Corporation, Montreal, Canada which itself was a subsidiary of Standard Oil Co (New Jersey). Andian was based at Corta, Colombia and operated the G-21As on behalf of Esso in the early 1950s.

ANDRUS, Herbert E Jr, Granby, CT
1451, 1458

The Anderson Manufacturing Company's Link Super Widgeon N4617N (c/n 1364) at Ottumwa, Iowa, on 5th September 1970. (W Haines Collection)

ANGELS Inc, Tampa, FL
1340
Bernard Little, President.

ANGELS AVIATION Inc, Tampa, FL
1340
ER Cantrell, President. Aircraft based at Peter O'Knight Airport, Tampa. In November 1963 ownership of the G-44 was passed to *Pasco Aviation* of which Cantrell was also President. Ownership passed back to Angels Aviation in January 1964 but the aircraft was re-possessed by *Appliance Buyers Credit Corporation* on 24th August 1964 after the obligations of the finance agreement were breached.

ANGLO-CANADIAN AVIATION Ltd,
Pitt Meadows, BC
B-24

ANKLIN, Donald J,
Davidson, NC
1315, 1364, 1370, 32
Aircraft dealer dba *Aircraft Sales Inc* at Mooresville and Charlotte, NC. See also *Amphibian Modifications Inc*.

ANTHONY, E & Sons Inc,
New Bedford, MA
1422

ANTILLES AIR BOATS,
Christiansted, St Croix,
US Virgin Islands
1053, 1061, 1141, 1149, 1150, 1152, 1161, 1162, 1165, 1172, 1187, 1191, B-19, B-29, B-46, B-46, B-53, B-60, B-63, B-81, B-88, B-111, B-131, B-141, J-4, J-10, J-13, J-38, J-42, J-44, J-56
Antilles Air Boats (AAB) was founded in February 1964 by former USAF Brigadier General and Pan American Airways captain Charles F Blair, and started with one G-21A providing services between the harbours of St Croix and St Thomas. By 1974 AAB was operating over 100 daily scheduled inter-island seaplane services with eighteen G-21As. The services from Christiansted served Charlotte-Amalie (St Thomas), West End (Tortola), Cruz Bay (St John), Marigot (St Maarten), Isla Grande (San Juan, Puerto Rico) and Puerto Real (Fajardo, Puerto Rico). AAB began G-73 operations in March 1974 and also operated PBYs, Short Sandringhams and a Vought-Sikorsky VS-44A. When Blair was killed in a G-21A crash in 1978, his wife, the actress Maureen O'Hara Blair, took over the operation. However, in April 1979, she sold the company to Resorts International of Miami, FL. In September 1981, Resorts pulled out and the AAB operation was shut down at short notice. During the seventeen years of service AAB had operated more than 400,000 flights and carried almost three million passengers. Services were continued some six months later by *Virgin Islands Seaplane Shuttle*.

Antilles Air Boats' G-21A N1048V (c/n B-46) ready to go at Tortola-West End, British Virgin Islands on 7th February 1980. In February 2004, the Goose was sold to Aero Accessories Inc who in turn sold the fuselage to Sam Damico for the use in the rebuild of c/n 1051. (Peter Vercruijsse)

Antilles Air Boats' G-21A N79901 (c/n B-63) receiving attention to its Wasp Junior R-985s at Carrier Aircraft in Long Beach, California. Note the water rudder installed behind the tail wheel. The aircraft was reported in storage in Sweden in 2011. (Steve Krauss)

Antilles Air Boats' Mallard N7338 (c/n J-38) taxiing at Charlotte Amalie, St Thomas, US Virgin Islands on 6th February 1980. The company logo appears under the cockpit window and the US Virgin Islands flag on the tail-fin. (Peter Vercruijsse)

ANTILLES SEAPLANES LLC,
Gibsonville, NC
1054, B-115, B-129, B-145
The company was set up by VL Manuel and his anonymous partner with the goal of rebuilding G-21As, with both piston and turbine engines, and ultimately to build new Gooses. In the autumn of 2000 the company purchased the G-21 technical design data and a warehouse full of spares from *Dean Franklin Aviation Enterprises*, which had been supporting the Grumman amphibian fleet for many years. Antilles also acquired the remains of *McKinnon Enterprises* from *Dan Vollum*, which gave them the FAA type certificates for all the Turbo Goose conversions.

In August 2007 a business syndicate based in North Carolina invested "several million dollars" in Antilles with a promise that more investment would follow if targets were met. One of the key targets was the roll-out of the first Antilles-built Goose by the first quarter of 2009.

In January 2008 the company received a set-back when G-21A c/n B-129 crashed into the sea five miles off Marathon, Florida, while on a test-flight.

Details of progress towards that roll-out are not known at the time of writing (March 2013) and the current status of the programme is uncertain (see Chapter 9).

ANTIQUE AIRCRAFT Inc, Chelsea, MA
16
Dennis K Burke, President.
Dennis Burke has converted several Widgeons to Lycoming GTSIO-540 power and named them "Magnum Widgeons" (see Chapter 5).

ANTIQUE AVIATION SALES Corp,
Colonia, NJ
1457

ANTL Inc - see *Resorts International*

APPLEBAUM, Garry, Hopkins, MN
and later at Kenosha, WI
1228

APPLIANCE BUYERS CREDIT CORP,
St Joseph, MI
1340, 29
The company re-possessed both aircraft in 1964 after the credit agreements were breached.

AQUA AIR LLC, Wilmington, DE
1377
The G-44 was operated by *Patrick J Coyle*, Orange Park, FL.

AQUATIC Inc, Weatherford, OK
1132
see *Baldachino & McClean.*

AQUATIC & VINTAGE AIRWAYS Ltd,
Paihia, Auckland, NZ
1356, 1432, 1439, 1466
The original operating name of the company owned by Owen Harnish and his son Grant that purchased the Widgeons

Operated in Nigeria by Arax Airlines, G-44 N3103Q (c/n 1218) is seen here visiting Luqa, Malta in 1971. The Widgeon was owned by ATC Inc of Reno, Nevada and has been preserved at Biscarosse in France. (via MAP)

Kenny Ashby's Continental-powered G-44 Widgeon N23456 (c/n 1270) "Sea Straight", in 1992. (MAP)

formerly operated by Sea Bee Air. Charter flights were operated from Auckland to the Bay of Islands from 1992. According to Owen Harnish, because the company name was "a bit of a mouthful for the tourists" it was changed to *Salt Air* in 1996.

AQUILA HOLDINGS Ltd, Parksville, BC
1265
RA Fouty, President. Leased the G-44 along with two Cessna 172s to *Trans Mountain Air Services Ltd* for 30 days in May 1975. The aircraft was based at Qualicum, BC until sold in January 1977.

ARAX AIRLINES, Nigeria
1218, 1341
Operated the G-44 owned by *ATC Inc* in support of oil operations.

ARCHBOLD EXPEDITIONS,
New York, NY
1205
Richard Archbold, the zoologist and philanthropist, had sponsored a series of biological expeditions to New Guinea in the 1930s for the American Museum of Natural History. In 1941 he established the Archbold Biological Station at Lake Placid in Florida, where the G-44 was based.

ARKANSAS AVIATION SALES Inc,
Little Rock, AR
1213, 1438, 4
Fred Smith, President. Aircraft based at Adams Field, Little Rock.

ARMETTE Ltd, Sun Valley, CA
16

ARNOLD, Patrick R,
Anchorage, AK
1305

ARRAY, Paul S, Delray, FL
1370

ARROWHEAD SKYHAVEN Inc,
Isabella, MN
1317
RV Hedin, President.

ARSDALE, Rickford van, Salem, OR
1380

ARTCO INTERNATIONAL Corp,
Coral Gables, FL
1019, 1084
Sold the two G-21As to *Aerolineas La Gaviota Ltda* in 1977.

ARTHUR, Melvin L, Phoenix, AZ
dba Arthur Corp
J-57

ASHBY, Kenny,
Anchorage, AK
1270

ASHY, Mitchell, New Orleans, LA
1377
Briefly co-owned the G-44 with *Monroe J Wolfe* in late 1956, and see also *A & W Inc.*

Ordered by Asiatic Petroleum Corp, G-21A Goose PK-AKA (c/n 1056) at a New York airfield in June 1937, awaiting delivery to NNGPM in Babo, Dutch New Guinea.

(Karl F Lunghard photo via HC Kavelaars Collection)

Bataafsche Petroleum Mij (Batavia Petroleum Company) Mallard PK-AKD (c/n J-35) at the Grumman factory in Bethpage, New York in 1948, awaiting delivery to Batavia, Dutch East Indies.

(Grumman photo via HC Kavelaars)

ASIATIC PETROLEUM Corp,
New York, NY
1008, 1010, 1018, 1048, 1056, 1057, 1106, 1107, 1115, B-34, J-13, J-17, J-35, J-37, J-41

The Asiatic Petroleum Corp (APC) acted as the purchasing agency for Shell Oil Company affiliates around the world. The G-21As were purchased for use by *NV de Bataafsche Petroleum Mij (BPM)* who joined with Ned Koloniale Petroleum Mij and Ned Pacific Petroleum Mij to form the Netherlands New Guinea Petroleum Mij (NNGPM). NNGPM used the aircraft to survey ten million hectares in western Dutch New Guinea (Irian Jaya) exploring for new oilfields. 1056 and 1057 were shipped to the Dutch Navy yard at Soerabaya where they were re-assembled and flown to the NNGPM base at Babo without their wheels (as in the G-21B). This allowed an extra 300lb of cargo to be carried but also called for a special docking cradle to be built at Babo to facilitate the removal of the aircraft from the landing area in the river.

APC also procured a G-21A (c/n 1048) for the Venezuelan Oil Development Company in 1938. In April 1942 this aircraft was transferred to Shell Ecuador for whom APC procured more G-21As for exploration and supply work from their base at Mera on the Pastaza River.

After WWII, APC procured the G-73s

for NNGPM for use in support of seismic and drilling teams based at Sorong, Dutch New Guinea.

ASPOSTOLICO, Vicaritario, Iquitos, Peru
B-111

ASSETS PROTECTED – TRUSTEE,
Salt Lake City, UT
1230

ASSOCIATED AERO SERVICES Ltd,
Vancouver, BC
1309
Registration CF-GYZ was allotted to the company on 28th March 1951 for the

purposes of preparing the aircraft for its Certificate of Airworthiness, but the Certificate of Registration (10075) was issued to the aircraft's owner *Realite Ltd*, Vancouver, BC on 3rd April 1951. The G-44 was then leased by *Associated Air Taxi Ltd* for one year from 12th April 1951.

ASSOCIATED AIR TAXI Ltd,
Vancouver, BC
1230, 1309
Robert B Gayer, President. Operated 1230 within British Columbia from 1949 until 1955, piloted by JD Hannay and George S Phillips. 1309 was leased from *Realite Ltd* for one year from 12th April 1951.

ASSOCIATED AIRWORKS,
Dum Dum Airport, Calcutta, India
1171
Owner, D Ghosh? The aircraft was listed in McKinnon Enterprises records as "Calcutta Goose" and was fitted with McKinnon Radar Nose Kit No.7 in 1968. No specific conversion or modification information has been found and it is not known whether the aircraft was ever exported to India.

ASSOCIATED CONSULTANTS INTERNATIONAL,
St. Croix, US Virgin Islands
J-10, J-30, J-38, J-51
Michael Braunstein, the president of *Virgin Islands Seaplane Shuttle*, was a co-partner in this company, with Vincent Condello. The G-73s were actually owned by the Manufacturers Hanover Trust Co / CIT Group, and were re-possessed by them in September 1991, and sold to *Frakes*, except J-51 which went to *Caribbean Airline Services*.

ASSOCIATED SERVICES Inc,
Anchorage, AK
1371
Previously known as *City Electric of Anchorage Inc*, with the same address and the same President: RC Sweezey.

ASTOR, Vincent, New York, NY
J-27
Astor (1891-1959) took over his father's real estate business empire in 1912. He used the G-73, named "*Flying Neurmahal*", between 1947 and 1959.

Vincent Astor's Mallard N2969 (c/n J-27) seen here at Teterboro, New Jersey on 3rd April 1958, carried the legend "Flying Neurmahal" under the cockpit window.

(Charles N Trask via Jennifer Gradidge)

ASTRON Corp, Houston, TX
1310

ATC Inc, Reno, NV & Santa Rosa, CA
1218, 1341
ATC was connected with the *International Aviation Development Corp*, with an aircraft maintenance base in Malta for many years. The G-44s were operated in Nigeria by *Arax Airlines*.

ATLANTIC AIR CHARTER SERVICE, Portland, ME
1411
Milton V Smith, President.

ATLANTIC AMPHIBIAN Inc, Highlands, NJ
1160

ATLANTIC AVIATION Co, Teterboro, NJ
1353, 1378, J-51
Aircraft dealer.

ATLANTIC CREOSOTING Co Inc, New York, NY
1233

ATLAS ACCEPTANCE Corp, Montreal?, QC
- see *Riverton Airways Ltd*
14
The aircraft file does not make clear how *Atlas Acceptance Corp* came into ownership of the SCAN-30, but in April 1973 it was sold by them to *Sam Allen Jr*.

ATLAS AIRCRAFT ENTERPRISES Inc, Fairfield, NJ
1438

ATLAS LEASING Co, Portland, OR
1380
WG McCall, President.

ATWOOD VACUUM MACHINE Co, Rockford, IL
1086, 1309
Owned by the Atwood family. Seth Atwood later formed *United Capital Corp*, which later bought *Chalk's International Airlines*.

AUSTRALIAN PETROLEUM Co (Pty) Ltd (APC), Melbourne, Australia
1466
The G-44A was used in support of oil operations in Papua from 1947 in a joint venture between British, Australian and US interests. Having been shipped to Australia, the aircraft was assembled at Rose Bay and issued with a Certificate of Airworthiness on 29th April 1947. Based at Port Moresby, Papua New Guinea, it was flown by Qantas Empire Airways crews. Between 1948 and 1950 it was flown by Qantas Captain Phil Oakley. When the G-44A was sold to *Amphibian Airways*, Invercargill, NZ in October 1950 it was nominally owned by the Vacuum Oil Company of Australia. (Vacuum Oil had a forty per cent stake in the APC).

The G-44A crashed at Rose Bay while pilot Hugh Birch was giving conversion

The Australian Petroleum Company's G-44A Widgeon VH-AZO (c/n 1466) seen here, probably in April 1947 at Brisbane. The aircraft was flown by Qantas Empire Airways crews and was based at Port Moresby for operations in New Guinea. (Grulke Collection via ED Daw)

training to Capt Fred Adams of Amphibian Airways. The damage sustained to the forward plates under the bow meant that plans for Fred Adams to fly the aircraft to New Zealand were cancelled, even though work to fit extra fuel tanks and radio equipment had started already. Instead the aircraft was shipped to Auckland as deck cargo aboard the "*Aorangi*", arriving on 11th December 1950.

AVALON AIR TRANSPORT, Long Beach, CA
1020, 1051, 1053, 1125, 1178, 1191, B-41, B-66, B-73, B-103, B-117, B-119, B-127
Founded by *Wilton R ("Dick") Probert* and Jean Chisolm in the summer of 1953, AAT began operations on 27th August 1953 with a single G-21A, N1503V, purchased from

Loftleidir. Chisholm's half-share was bought by *Walter von Kleinsmid* in 1954 and the airline quickly grew into a successful operation with seven G-21As, a Sikorsky S-43 and the legendary Vought-Sikorsky VS-44A. From 1st July 1955, all mail to and from Santa Catalina Island was carried by air by Avalon Air Transport. In 1956 the timetable showed 14 flights daily plus additional flights as required, flying every 30 minutes from Long Beach Municipal Airport to and from Avalon Harbour in summer, reducing to twice daily services in winter. A longshoreman strike in November 1958 left the island with no sea transport links, but the AAT Gooses saved the day by hauling some 6,000lbs of freight a day, at a 40% discount on the normal rate of 5 cents per pound. In late-1958,

Avalon Air Transport's first Goose N1503V (c/n 1020) Fleet Number 1, is seen here in California, circa 1954. The word "AVALON" is carried under the starboard wing with the registration N1503V under the port wing. (Douglas D Olson via Jennifer Gradidge)

Avalon Air Transport's G-21A N327 (c/n 1051) in the later company colour scheme at Oakland, California circa 1963. The Goose later starred in the 1980s television series "Tales of the Gold Monkey", and was being re-built in 2011 by an owner in New York State. (Douglas D Olson via Jennifer Gradidge)

Avalon Air Transport's G-21A N325 (c/n B-127) Fleet Number 9 is seen here at Long Beach, California in the late 1950s, showing its two-part passenger door.

(Gregory Kuhn via Jennifer Gradidge)

1051 and 1053 were purchased from the Peruvian Air Force. In 1963, when annual passenger numbers totalled 80,000, the company name was changed temporarily to *Catalina Amphibian Air Lines*. Only one G-21A (B-73) carried the new titles and Dick Probert soon decided on *Catalina Air Lines* as the new title.

The eleven G-21As in the Avalon fleet carried their fleet number on their nose, as follows:

No:1	N1503V	(1020)
No:1 (2)	N327	(1051)
No:2	N1583V	(1125)
No:2 (2)	N328	(1053)
No:3	N1513V	(B-103)
No:4	N1523V	(1178)
No:4 (2)	N329	(B-119)
No:5	N1543V	(B-41)
No:6	N322	(B-73)
No:7	N323	(1191)
No:8	N324	(B-66)
No:9	N325	(B-127)

AVALON INDUSTRIES Ltd,
St John's, NL
J-1
Charles E Hunt, President.
See also *Irving, KC*
Irving bought the ex-demonstrator G-73 in January 1949 and registered it in Newfoundland as VO-ACC. It crashed on 4th December 1951 after an engine fire on take-off from Millidgeville Airport, St John, NB (pilot James Wade).

AVAMERICA Inc, Anchorage, AK
1375
Acted as agents for the sale of the G-44 in 1992.

AVEMCO FINANCE Corp,
Silver Spring, MD
1424

AVERBUCK, Harold, Newton, MA
1213

AVEY, RL, Montreal, QC
B-14, B-70
Avey bought B-70 from *Massey-Harris Co Ltd* for $47,500 on 16th May 1952 and sold

it the same day to *Canadian Forest Products Ltd* (for an undisclosed sum). In 1956 Avey imported B-14 from the USA into Canada for the *Murdock Lumber Company*.

AVIACORP of FLORIDA Inc, Miami, FL
1359
The G-44 was based in Cyprus in 1989 and in France in 1990/91.

AVIATION ASSOCIATES Ltd,
Ketchikan, AK
1164
Owned the G-21A between 1982 and 1987, but it was operated by *Chuck Slagle's Westflight Aviation Inc*. Slagle was also a partner in Aviation Associates Ltd.

AVIATION ENTERPRISES Inc,
Miami, FL aka *Dean H Franklin Aviation Enterprises*.
B-104

AVIATION FACILITIES Inc, Miami, FL
1381

AVIATION MANAGEMENT INTERNATIONAL Inc,
Fort Lauderdale, FL
J-49

AVIATION REHAB Inc, Euless, TX
1474
JH Hornisher.

AVIATION SALES & ENGINEERING,
Houston, TX
B-117

AVIATION SERVICE CENTER Inc,
Fort Lauderdale, FL
1214

AVIATION 3C Inc, St. Hubert, QC
1414
The company leased the G-44A to *132802 Canada Ltée (Aerotaxi)*, St Hubert, QC in the early 1990s.

AYER, Frederick B & Associates,
New York, NY
1007, B-104, B-114, 1411, 1430, J-6, J-38, J-52, J-56
Aircraft dealers dba *TradeAyer Co*, Linden, NJ. See also *Ming-Ayer Inc*, *Welsch-Ayer Inc* and *Universal Trading Corp*.

AZTEC AIRCRAFT Inc, Long Beach, CA
31
CD Smith Jr, President. Aztec prepared the SCAN Widgeon for *James Langley* and requested reservation of N1JL, then N20JL and finally N69BJ for him, but the aircraft remained registered as N4453.

B A LEASING Corp, San Francisco, CA
1340
The G-44 was leased to *International American Advertising Corp*, dba American Graphics & Chromeprint in July 1985, registered to them in September 1985, but re-possessed by B A Leasing on 31st October 1985, after a breach in the finance agreement.

BABB, Charles H & Co,
New York, NY & at Glendale, CA & St John's, QC
1001, 1005, 1013, 1018, 1045, 1061, 1106, 1168, B-34, J-7
A well-known aircraft dealer for many years. This aircraft sales and service company was purchased by *Transocean Airlines* in 1957 & became a subsidiary of International Aircraft Services in 1959.

BACH, Richard D, Long Beach, CA
31
Bach, the famous author/pilot who wrote '*Jonathan Livingston Seagull*', was President of *Creature Enterprises Inc* which provided the SCAN Widgeon for use in the TV series '*Fantasy Island*'.

BAHAMAS AIR TRADERS Ltd,
Nassau, Bahamas
1077, 1084, 1168, 1424, 1445, 1455, 1462
Founded, in the early 1960s by *Gilbert A*

Bahamas Air Traders Ltd G-21A Goose N95400 (c/n 1077) at Nassau in the 1960s. The company name can be seen above the wheel well.

(MAP)

Hensler to provide charter services within the Bahamas and to Florida. Later became known as *Out Island Airways* which in 1973 became *Bahamasair*.

BAHAMAS AIRWAYS Ltd, (BAL)

Nassau, Bahamas
1002, 1007, 1084, 1109, 1126, 1162, B-74, 1208, 1340, 1448, 1462, 1468
Founded in 1936 by Sir Harry Oaks and Harold Christie to operate scheduled mail flights within the Bahamas and charter flights to the American mainland. The first G-44, registered in the name of Charles S Collar, arrived in April 1941 but was soon impressed by the US Army Corps of Engineers. From 1946 BAL operated limited scheduled flights to islands within the Bahamas and was certified by the US Civil Aeronautics Board (CAB) to operate scheduled flights between Nassau, Cat Cay and Miami from February 1948. In August 1948 the entire shareholding of BAL was bought by British South American Airways Corporation, which in turn was taken over by British Overseas Airways Corporation (BOAC) on 30th July 1949. Financial restraints meant that by 1955 BAL had been reduced to a fleet of five G-21As to provide local services and external charters.

On 30th November 1957 control was passed to BOAC Associated Companies Ltd. By 1959 some of these flights were being operated by DC-3/Dakota leaving the Goose flight schedule as seen in the lower table on the right (all from Nassau):

On 1st April 1959 a controlling 80%

Bahamas Airways Ltd Goose-operated services 1st July 1950:		
Flight #	Route	Frequency
25/26	Nassau-Bimini-Cat Cay (request)	one per fortnight
33/34	Nassau-Georgetown (Exuma)	one per four weeks
23/24	Nassau-Marsh Harbour-Hopetown-Man o'War Cay-Green Turtle Cay	one per fortnight
31/32	Nassau-Governor's Harbour-Rock Sound-Nassau	two per week
21/22	Nassau-Harbour Island-Spanish Wells-Nassau	three per week
21A/22A	Nassau-Spanish Wells-Harbour Island-Nassau	three per week

1959:		Frequency	
Flight #	Route	16th April-14th January	15th January-15th April
BH.21/22 37/38	Harbour Island-Spanish Wells	one service	four services
BH.15/16	Harbour Island-Spanish Wells	daily	daily
BH.35/36	Port Cay-Mangrove Cay	- Tuesday, Thursday, Sunday -	
BH.43/44	Sandy Point-Cherokee Sound	Mon/Fri	Mon/Wed/Sat
BH.51/52	Cat Island	Alternate Fridays	
BH.55/56	Long Island	Alternate Fridays	
BH.17/18	Governor's Harbour-Rock Sound	Tue/Sat/Sun	None
Note: BH.17/18 was an evening service.			

interest was sold to *Skyways (Bahamas) Holding Company Ltd*, in the names of J Eric Rylands and David Brown. By February 1961, BAL was facing bankruptcy and in order to secure its interests, including the lucrative Nassau to New York route, BOAC again took control of BAL and on 20th June 1962 BAL

The Bahamas Airways fleet of four Goose, a Widgeon and a Catalina posing on the ramp at Nassau circa 1953. The four Goose aircraft visible are VP-BAM, BAL, BAH and one other, plus Widgeon VP-BAC and PBY-5A Catalina VP-BAB. *(Colyn L Rees photo via WH Llewellyn)*

G-44A Widgeon VP-BAC (c/n 1448) was operated in the Bahamas from December 1946 until December 1954. It was operated by Bahamas Airways Ltd and named "Exuma" from May 1951 until returned to Skyways Ltd in October 1953. *(via Brian Stainer)*

Bahamas Airways' G-21A Goose VP-BBK (c/n B-74). Originally registered as VP-BAB, the aircraft returned to Bahamas Airways as N5542A after crashing and being rebuilt in 1959, and was re-registered as VP-BBK in 1960. *(Harold G Martin)*

became a wholly-owned subsidiary of BOAC-Cunard Ltd. Vickers Viscounts had been introduced by then and a decision was made to replace the remaining G-21As with Aero Commander 500As. BAL was declared bankrupt in 1970.

BAHAMAS ISLAND AIR SERVICE,
Nassau, Bahamas
1445

BAHAMASAIR, Nassau, Bahamas
1084, 1168, 1445
Formed in 1973 as the flag-carrier for the newly-independent island nation by the amalgamation of Flamingo Airlines and *Out Island Airways*. By 1977 the Grummans had been sold or withdrawn from service.

BAILEY LEASING Corp, Fort Wayne, IN
aka George H Bailey Co Inc.
1420
George H Bailey, President,

BAIRD, James Randall, Naples, FL
1210

BAKER, George F, Jr, New York, NY
1204, 1447

BAKER, Kane K, New York, NY
B-29

BAKER, George T, Aviation School,
Miami, FL
1182
This FAA approved school (#3460) was operated under the auspices of the *Dade County Board of Public Instruction*, Miami, Florida.

BAKER & FORD Company,
Bellingham, WA
1327

BALDACHINO, Shaun V,
Weatherford, OK dba *Air Aquatic Inc.*
1132

BALL, Fred - see *Island Hoppers Inc.*
Fred Ball is a legendary Alaskan Goose pilot, having been associated with the type since 1958, and while flying seventeen different G-21As had amassed more than 11,300 hours (as of 1996). He can also claim to have trained many pilots to fly the G-21A. Ball flew N327, "Cutter's Goose", before it was used in the TV series, and claims that it probably flew the best of all the G-21As he had flown.

BALTIMORE & OHIO RAILROAD
1055

BANCO NACIONAL de PANAMA,
Panama City, Panama
1277
The G-44 was abandoned by Aeromar SA while being repaired, and re-possessed by the bank in 1974. The aircraft was noted on the sales contract (to *John Morris Wells*) as being located at Punta Paitilla Airport, Panama City.

Operated jointly by Bahamasair and Out Island Airways (OIA), G-44A Widgeon N86619 (c/n 1445) is seen here at Nassau in October 1973 with its OIA logo on the tail. *(William Blunt via Jennifer Gradidge)*

G-21A Goose N75333 (c/n 1182) at the George T Baker Aviation School, Miami, Florida in 1974. The Goose was destined for Mount Cook Airlines in New Zealand as ZK-MCC, but crashed at Wichita, Kansas, after take-off for the delivery flight. *(RH Milne)*

BANGLADESH FLYING CLUB Ltd,
Dhaka, Bangladesh
1451, 1471, 1474
Anisul Islam Mahmud, President. Founded in 1948, and based at Tejgaon Airport, Dhaka. The three G-44As were stored there from 1981 until August 1989, when they were exchanged for two Piper Senecas by *Northern Aircraft Traders*, Anchorage, AK. The Bill of Sale was signed by Captain ANM Rafiqur Rahman (Secretary/Treasurer) and Mr AR Shaikh (Chief Engineer).

BANGLADESH GOVERNMENT AIRCRAFT WORKSHOP,
Dhaka, Bangladesh
1451, 1471, 1474

BANGLADESH GOVERNMENT,
Dhaka, Bangladesh
B-78, 1474
A document from the Bangladeshi CAB states that c/n 1474 was never registered in Bangladesh.

BANK OF AMERICA NATIONAL TRUST & SAVINGS ASSOCIATION,
Los Angeles, CA
1300, 16, 25
The bank re-possessed the G-44 from *Early J Moore* on 3rd May 1949. The SCAN-30s were re-possessed from *Pacific Aircraft Engineering Corp* on 3rd June 1963. C/n 16 was sold to *Armette Ltd* on 8th August that year, while c/n 25 went to *SF DeYoreo* on 29th January 1964.

BANNOCK AEROSPACE Ltd,
Toronto, ON
J-34
Bannock acted as broker for the sale of the Turbo-Mallard by *Canadair* to *Sandy Mactaggart* in mid-1984.

BARNES, Gay George, Miami, FL
41
The ownership of this aircraft is complicated. Barnes married *Isabella Johnstone* in the British Embassy in Kinshasa, Zaire on 28th January 1969. Isabella Johnstone was given as the name of the purchaser when the SCAN-30 was sold by the *Modern Furniture Co of Greeneville Inc* on 23rd October 1969. Mrs Barnes died in hospital in Glasgow, Scotland, of acute renal failure associated with malignant malaria, on 15th May 1970. The ownership of the aircraft therefore passed to her husband, but Bills of Sale dated September 1976 show the SCAN-30 being transferred between the Modern Furniture Co arms in Greeneville, TN and Elizabethton, TN; and then from the latter to *Flying Sportsmen Inc*, Sussex, NJ.

According to a magazine article, Tom Neumeister, President of Flying Sportsmen, found the SCAN-30 in Kinshasa in the Spring of 1976, and stated that it had been there for six years and had not flown in that time. So perhaps the Bills of Sale dated September 1976 were merely a case of the paperwork catching up with the facts! This does not, however, explain how the aircraft left the ownership of Gay George Barnes after his wife's death. This confusion is compounded further by a Bill of Sale dated 29th March 1977 transferring ownership *from* Flying Sportsmen Inc *to* Gay G Barnes, who got a Certificate of Registration on 1st June 1977. However, on 8th May 1978 Barnes transferred ownership back to Flying Sportsmen Inc, with a Certificate of Registration dated 20th June 1978.

BARNETT LEASING Co Inc,
Fort Lauderdale, FL
J-13
Barnett leased the Mallard to *Peter M Davis* dba *Seagull Air Service*.

BARNUM, Leon E, Alpena, MI
and at Whitehouse, OH
1436, J-42
"Tony" Barnum started charter flying with the G-44, dba Thunder Bay Flying Service, and built up a large customer base. The hunting & fishing charters continued after he teamed up with Walter R Crow and became joint-owner of *Crow Inc* using the G-73 for the charter work. The G-73 starred in the 1968 film, "*Target: Harry*" with Vic Morrow, Suzanne Pleshette & Charlotte Rampling.

BARON AVIATION SERVICES Inc,
Vichy, MO
1132, 1421
CE Schmidt, President. The company operated out of Rolla National Airport, Vichy. The G-44A was transferred to company president CE Schmidt in 2004, before being sold to *Dixie Air Leasing LLC*, of which Schmidt was a member.

BARON Corp, New York, NY
1410
The G-44A was transferred by Bill of Sale from *Edward A Deeds* to the Baron Corporation in August 1964, but the ownership chain is clouded because by March 1965 *Federal Airlines Inc* was given as owner on a Form 337. A mortgage document dated 7th December 1965 signed by William B Wilson as President of Federal Airlines, included G-44A (c/n 1410) in the list of aircraft covered under the mortgage. By January 1966 Federal Airlines was recorded at an address at Burlington Municipal Airport, whilst a Certificate of Registration for the G-44A was issued to *Northern Airways Inc*, Burlington, VT on 30th August 1967. Edward A Deeds was President of Northern Airways Inc.

BARRATT, William B, Spokane, WA
1427

BARRATT, William Scott & Jeneen Dee,
Spokane, WA
1427
William B Barratt transferred ownership of the G-44A to William Scott & Jeneen Dee Barratt prior to its sale in February 2001.

BARRETT, OH, Toronto, ON (co-owner)
1240

BART, Jack, c/o Lac Management Inc,
Spotswood, NJ
J-18
Jack Bart was owner of *Lac Management Inc*.

BASCARO, Antonio, Ciudad Guatemala, Guatemala
1311

BASIC BIBLE CHURCH OF AMERICA,
Deatsville, AL
1394
Jerome Daly, DD, President.

BASLER FLIGHT SERVICE Inc,
Oshkosh, WI
J-5
Operated passenger and cargo charter services.

BASLER TURBO CONVERSIONS LLC,
Oshkosh, WI
J-31

BATAAFSCHE PETROLEUM MAATSCHAPPIJ (BPM)
- see *Batavia Petroleum Co.*

BATA SHOE Co, Bekcamp, MD,
and in Czechoslovakia
J-26

BATAVIA PETROLEUM Co, (BPM),
Jakarta, Dutch East Indies
1008, 1010, 1107, 1115, J-41
The exploration and production arm of Royal Dutch / Shell Oil Co in the Dutch

Bataafsche Petroleum Maatschappij (Batavia Petroleum Company) G-21A Goose PK-AKR (c/n 1010) on the KNILM ramp at Soerabaja, Java.
(HC Kavelaars Collection)

East Indies. The use of c/n 1008 is debatable but c/n 1010 (PK-AKR) was reassembled by KNILM and shipped to Soerabaya for use by BPM on survey and mapping operations in Dutch New Guinea. From late August 1940 pilot John Claringbould flew PK-AKR in support of oil exploration and production in Borneo and Sumatra, while based at Manggar Airport, Balikpapan. BPM also used a two-storey houseboat as an advance base for the survey work. This was moored in the Mahakan River at Tandjungselor, with the G-21A moored alongside ready to take advantage of any break in the weather and make a quick take-off from the river, to continue the photo-survey work. Most of 1941 saw intensive survey operations from the houseboat. With the Japanese advance in the area, PK-AKR was evacuated from Borneo to Java in February 1942, but despite this, was probably captured by the Japanese.

The later machines were used by BPM, based at Balikpapan on the east coast of Borneo, from 1947 until 1958 in support of oil exploration and production. When Indonesia became independent in 1949, the company was renamed P.T. Shell Indonesia.

BAUMGARDNER, Marvin Dodge,
Bennington, VT
41
The SCAN-30 was converted to a PACE Gannet by *Lee Mansdorf* in 1963.

BAWDEN DRILLING (1964) Ltd,
South Edmonton, AB
1415

BAWDEN DRILLING Ltd, Peter,
Calgary, AB
1415

BAY VALLEY AIR SERVICES,
Stockton, CA
1143, 1144, 1164
BVAS bought the war-surplus JRF-6Bs and operated passenger services between San Francisco and Sacramento.

BC AIR LINES Ltd, Vancouver, BC
1077, 1145, 1195, B-45, B-142, J-7, J-9, J-21
Founded by Bill Sylvester, BC Air Lines set up a fixed base at Sea Island, Vancouver in December 1943 and received its first charter licences on 17th November 1945. Some services were operated on behalf of Queen Charlotte Airways and from 1953 the airline was licensed to operate feeder services. In 1959, under the leadership of Francis G Winspear, BC Air Lines took over several of *Pacific Western*'s routes, including Vancouver to Tofino and Tahsis on Vancouver Island and to Ocean Falls, BC. Queen Elizabeth II and Prince Philip used J-9 during the Royal Tour of Canada in 1959. In 1960 J-21 joined the fleet. Goose c/n 1195 was lost in an accident in December 1964 and replaced by c/n 1145. By April 1965, BC Air Lines was a fully-owned subsidiary of Canadian Aviation

G-21A NC95431 (c/n 1164) of Bay Valley Air Service crossing San Francisco Bay in 1947.
(William T Larkins)

BC Air Lines' Goose CF-UAZ (c/n 1077) in the company's red, white and grey colour scheme. No further details are known. *(Jack McNulty via Jennifer Gradidge)*

BC Air Lines' Mallard CF-HPU (c/n J-9) which was used to transport Queen Elizabeth II and Prince Philip during the Royal Tour of Canada in 1959. It is reported that Prince Philip took the controls of the Mallard on one occasion. *(Jennifer Gradidge Collection)*

BC Air Lines' Mallard CF-HPU (c/n J-9) in a new colour scheme and wearing company Fleet Number 101 on the tail in June 1973. By this time Pacific Western Airlines had taken over the BC Air Lines' route network. *(Steve Krauss)*

Electronics of Montreal under President WM Anderson, and was operating scheduled and charter services from ten major bases between Vancouver and Prince Rupert, and on Vancouver Island and the Queen Charlotte Islands. Another Goose, c/n 1077, was added to the fleet in 1966, but all Grummans had been sold by 1970 when *Pacific Western Airlines* took over the BC Air Lines' route network at the government's request, until a new operator could be found. In the meantime, the routes were flown by *West Coast Air Services*.

BC GOVERNMENT, Vancouver, BC
B-98, B-138, 1230
Department of Public Works, Highways Department & Hydro-Power Authority.
The G-44, operated by the Public Works Department, was based at Patricia Bay, BC from July 1955. After being re-engined with Lycoming GO-480-C1D6s it was transferred to the Highways Department in July 1957 where it served until September 1967.

BEACON WEST LLC, Billings, MT
1427
also c/o *Robert G Williams*, Coeur D'Alene, ID 1230

BEARDSLEY, Elmer O, Lilliwaup, WA
1215
Bought the G-44 from Pan American Airways for pleasure purposes, and employed Alton C Mosley as his pilot.

BEAVER AVIATION SERVICE Inc,
Grove City, PA
J-42

BEAVERBROOK, Lord, London, UK
1009, 1049, J-13
See also *Canprint Securities Ltd.*
The Canadian industrialist, born William Maxwell Aitken, moved to England where he entered Parliament. He was elevated to the peerage in 1911, becoming Lord Beaverbrook, and later bought London's *Daily Express* newspaper. G-21A c/n 1009 was owned briefly in 1937 and was replaced in 1938 by c/n 1049. Beaverbrook used the aircraft for a hunting trip to Africa in 1939 after which it was shipped to the USA for storage. Lord Beaverbrook was appointed Minister for Aircraft Production on 14th May 1940 in which role he served in the UK wartime government. When WWII started the G-21A remained in storage except when used by the Inter-American Escadrille Inc (IAE) for a Civil Air Mission to South America. Franklin Field, President and Laurance S Rockefeller, a director of IAE, left Washington, DC on 5th March 1941 to tour Latin America with the hope of forming branches or "wings" of IAE. The mission had already visited Cuba, Puerto Rico, Santo Domingo, Haiti, Venezuela, Brazil and the Argentine when Field wrote to CR Fairey of the British Purchasing Commission, Washington, DC on 30th April 1941, stating that the mission was in Buenos Aires, "leaving for Uruguay on Sunday and

Lord Beaverbrook's Goose G-AFCH (c/n 1009) at Andir Airport, Bandung, West Java, on delivery to KNILM in 1938 for survey work. *(AeroHobby via Fred J Knight)*

proceed to Chile Tuesday next." The tour was completed with visits to Ecuador, Bolivia, Peru, Colombia, Panama, Honduras, Nicaragua, Guatemala and Mexico. Rockefeller was obviously impressed by the G-21A and in May 1941 wanted to buy the aircraft to help equip a south American airline.

In June 1941 the US Army Air Corps wanted c/n 1049 to replace their losses in the Panama Canal Zone. On 30th July 1941 the aircraft was reported "lying at Bolling Field", with a request to "return it from whence it came, which I gather is some airport near New York". This request was agreed but repeated requests to buy the aircraft were all refused. However, Beaverbrook's refusal to sell was having an adverse affect on the British requests for the USA to supply second-hand G-21As and Sikorsky S.43s to the RAF for rescue duties. The Americans rightly pointed out that if Beaverbrook would not make his own aircraft available, then the British need could not be as urgent as was being portrayed, so why should the USA put themselves out to fill that need? Eventually, by January 1942, Lord Beaverbrook had decided to hand over the G-21A to the UK Air Ministry. Surprisingly, the UK Ministry of Aircraft Production was in ignorance of Beaverbrook's decision and re-allocated the aircraft to the Royal Canadian Air Force in February 1942! The confusion was overcome, however, and on 18th February 1942 the G-21A was impressed into RAF service with serial MV993, and the UK civil registration cancelled. On 31st March 1942 a cable stated that the Goose had been delayed because of trouble with the fuel tanks, but "should be ready for shipment to England by April 9th".

Beaverbrook took delivery of the G-73 in 1947 and used it during his frequent trips to Canada and the Bahamas. It was registered in the name of *Canprint Securities Ltd,* and was sold in 1948.

BEBCO Inc, New Orleans, LA
B-140
Frank B Williams, President.

BECKER, Roberta E & John A,
Long Beach, CA dba *Catalina Seaplanes.*
1153

BEEK, Dudley, Miami, FL
1215

BELDEX Corp, St Louis, MO
1145, B-100, B-128, J-32, J-44
William F Remmert, President. Beldex Corporation was an affiliate of *Remmert-Werner Inc*. B-100 was purchased from the US Navy in October 1956 and converted to G-21A standard at Remmert-Werner's Pompano Beach, FL facility. B-128 was similarly converted and ferried from there to Montreal, PQ on delivery to the *Hudson's Bay Company* in March 1961.

BELIZE GOVERNMENT,
Belize City, Belize
1054
The G-21A was confiscated by the government of Belize for alleged drug running in November 1982, and it was sold for Bel$20,000 in July 1983.

BELL, Douglas T, Detroit, MI
dba *Mercury Aviation Service*.
1368

BELLE CONSTRUCTION Ltd,
Ville d'Alma, PQ
1334
JP Tessier, President.

BELLINGHAM CANNING Co,
Bellingham, WA
1323
Jeanice M Welch, President, who also presided over the Icy Straits Salmon Company, to whom the G-44 was mortgaged.

BEN BRANSOM CHARTER SERVICE
J-18

BENDER, Thomas B, Mobile, AL
1409

BENDIX AVIATION Corp,
Detroit, MI
J-13, J-17

BENEDICT, Thomas M, Portland, O
1452
Benedict was President of *Portland Amphibians Inc,* to whom the G-44A was registered in January 1970.

BEN GINTER CONSTRUCTION Co Ltd,
Prince George, BC
1265
The G-44 was officially leased by Ginter's *Imperial Airways* to his construction company for six months, beginning on 1st December 1959, but was used on construction support flights during the 1960s and early 1970s without being officially leased. In December 1960 the aircraft was ferried from Portland, OR to Vancouver, BC after conversion to Lycoming GO-480-B1D power by McKinnon.

BENSON, John T, Naples, FL
1467, 1475

BENSON, Richard K, Beaver Falls, NY
1452

BENTLEY, Michael D, Nassau, Bahamas
1359

BERARD, Norman, Mission, BC
B-24

BERGT Corp, Anchorage, AK
1324

BERKINSHAW, RC, Toronto, ON
(co-owner)
1240

BERMINGHAM, Henry T, Jr,
New Orleans, LA
and later at Slidell, LA
31

BESTONE AVIATION Inc, Chardon, OH
4
Walter C Best, President. Started operations in 1955 with a charter and instruction service. The SCAN-30 was in use from 1957 until 1969.

BETTENCOURT, David, Honolulu, HI
1165

BETZOLDT, Raymond, Clinton, MI
dba Tecumseh Aviation, a Division of *Meyers Industries Inc*.
1240

BEVAN INVESTMENT Co,
Anchorage, AK
1239
Owned the G-44 after it was sold to the company by Robert Denny, one of the partners in the company that co-owned the aircraft with *Yukon Office Supply Inc*.

BFD Co, New York, NY
1423

BICKELL, JP, Toronto, ON
dba *McIntyre Porcupine Mines Ltd*
1013, 1061, 1240, J-2
John Paris "Jack" Bickell was a millionaire by the age of 30. He took over the gold mining company of *McIntyre Porcupine Mines Ltd* and used the Grummans to commute from Toronto to his various

The first Widgeon registered in Canada was JP Bickell's CF-BVN (c/n 1240) seen here at Uplands, Ottawa in December 1946. Note the "Goodyear" logo on the bow. Jack Bickell, a friend of Lord Beaverbrook, had transferred both of his Goose aircraft to the Royal Canadian Air Force by November 1940, and it is thought that he also used his G-44 to help the war effort. (Jack McNulty)

business interests. Bickell donated his first G-21A, c/n 1013, to the Royal Canadian Air Force (RCAF) in 1939 replacing it with c/n 1061, which he sold later to the RCAF in 1940. His commitment to helping the war effort was also demonstrated when he went to England to work with *Lord Beaverbrook* in London on matters of aircraft production and subsequently became President of Victory Aircraft. The second G-21A was replaced in turn by the G-44 which is believed to have been based at Malton, ON (the primary Victory Aircraft factory) from 1942 until 1945. Bickell's role in allied munitions production probably facilitated the export of the G-44 in 1941.
The registration CF-BKE was used on the original G-21A and used later on the G-73, which was delivered in September 1946.

BIG RED'S FLYING SERVICE Inc,
Anchorage, AK
1424
Operated from a hangar on the west shore of Lake Hood.

BIGGS, Leo M, Inc, Detroit, MI
1467
The G-44A was cancelled from the US Register on 4th September 1953, after an accident on 19th May 1953. The FAA file next (spuriously) reports a sale from a "J

Perry" to Virginia and Urbano DaSilva, for $27,500, on 17th April 1985. However, what appears to be the correct chain of events is shown by a Bill of Sale, dated 29th April 1987, from Biggs to *Urbano M & Virginia G DaSilva*, to whom the aircraft was registered on 30th July 1987.

BILZI, Vincent, Centerport, NY
1382
Co-owner with *Henry O Moffett*.

BINGHAMPTON CONTAINER Co,
Binghampton, NY
1220

BINGMAN, Lester LR, Dillingham, AK
dba *Fresh Water Adventures Inc*
also at Fairbanks, AK.
B-55, 1375, J-54

BINGMAN, Philip L, Anchorage, AK
B-55, B-86, B-140, 1375, J-54
Philip Bingman founded *Yute Air Alaska* in 1963, and was later dba *Fresh Water Adventures Inc*, operating fishing charters and on-demand air-taxi flights under a Part 135 Air Taxi Commuter licence.

BLADE, Walter William Jr
1187
Co-owner of the G-21A with the *Holmstedts* in 1996 before selling it to *Pacific Coastal Airlines*.

The former Tropical Sea Air Mallard (c/n J-54) seen here in 2000 possibly in Alaska, registered to Philip Bingman as N7777Q. *(MAP)*

BLAIR, Charles F see *Antilles Air Boats.*

BLAIR, Maureen O'Hara see *Antilles Air Boats* and *Caribbean Flying Boats Inc.*

BLAIR, Gordon W, Huntingdon Valley, PA
J-23
Blair was President of *St Lawrence Aviation Company*. The G-73 was named "Patricia".

BLAKE, Norman, Oklahoma City, OK
1364
The G-44 was based at Will Rogers Airport, Oklahoma City, OK.

BLUE ARROW CHALLENGE Inc,
New York, NY
B-120
The company was set up to operate the G-21A in support of *Peter de Savary*'s Americas Cup challenge in 1988, after the aircraft had been used successfully in support of the 1983 challenge. In October 1988 a survey showed that the G-21A was badly corroded and would need a complete overhaul. It was shipped to the UK in April 1989 and was rebuilt by Doug Wyatt's team at Leavesden. The de Savary yacht "Blue Arrow Challenge" was ruled ineligible for the 1988 Americas Cup race, and although he had intended to challenge again in 1992, his business empire was collapsing and the G-21A was sold in 1994.

BLUE GOOSE ENTERPRISES Inc,
Las Vegas, NV
B-126
The G-21A took part in the 50th Anniversary of VJ Day celebrations in Hawaii in 1995. It was also used during summers to fly the owner to a private island in Moosehead Lake, ME.

B.N.P. AIRWAYS, Vancouver, BC
1003, B-45, B-55, B-76, B-83, B-98
Formed, in 1950, out of *Malibu Seaero* and carrying out corporate flying operations for three local operators: BC Electric (later BC Hydro), Northern Construction &

Gordon Blair's Mallard N2964 (c/n J-23) "Patricia", parked at the General Aviation Terminal at London-Gatwick, probably on 5th May 1969. *(MAP)*

JW Stewart Ltd., and the Powell River Company (later merged into *MacMillan Bloedel*) – hence the initials B.N.P. In 1952, T Ingledow was company president. Northern Construction was a subsidiary of the Morrison Knudsen Construction Company which was engaged in the building of the dam, tunnel and power house at Shalath on the Bridge River for BC Electric. In support of this huge project, maintenance and hangar facilities were provided by B.N.P. under contract to *Canadian Forest Products* and *West Coast Transport*. In 1955, *Crown Zellerbach* joined B.N.P. and thus B-76 joined the fleet, to replace 1003 which had been sold to *Central BC Airways*. Former RCAF aircraft, B-55 and B-83, were acquired in 1955 and put into storage. In May 1959 B-55 was sold and B-83 was put into service.

BC Electric was taken over by the BC Government and renamed BC Hydro, and their interest in B.N.P., but not their G-21A, was acquired by *Crown Zellerbach*. Northern Construction sold their interest in B.N.P. to *MacMillan Bloedel*. B.N.P. was disbanded in 1965 when *MacMillan*

Bloedel bought out the *Crown Zellerbach* (CZ) interest in the partnership, but CZ kept their G-21A.

BOARD, Mark R, & Gregory R,
Miami, FL
J-4
The G-73 was registered to Gregory R Board, Miami, FL on 16th January 1976. He then flew it to Australia where it was registered as VH-SPL to his *South Pacific Airlines* on 30th August 1976 and parked at Sydney-Bankstown. Ownership was transferred to Mark R Board (Greg's son), Miami, FL on 29th June 1977, registered as N83781, and the aircraft was based in Singapore and maintained by Heli Orient Pte Ltd at Seletar. The G-73 was chartered by John McCallum Productions Pty Ltd for film work in Penang. At 0800hrs on 14th October 1977 the aircraft flew from Penang Airport to Telok Bahang Bay (on the north side of Penang Island) and moored to a wharf as a backdrop for filming. At about 1600hrs pilot Greg Broad was asked to taxi from the wharf and then taxi back to the wharf through a fishing vessel anchorage, whilst being filmed. During taxying the

The B.N.P. Airways Ltd fleet of Goose aircraft, on the ramp at Vancouver International Airport, British Columbia, circa 1956. Visible are CF-BAE, GEB, GEC, IOL and the RCMP aircraft CF-MPG on the right. *(via Ingvar Klett)*

G-73 turned sharply to avoid a collision with fishing vessel ST2956 but collided with a moored boat, sustaining slight damage. After inspection it was flown to Seletar for repair by Heli Orient, leaving Singapore on or about 20th November 1977 and returning to Florida via France and the UK (Jersey, Bournemouth, Hatfield 29th January 1978, Kidlington 23rd February (for radio checks) and Prestwick 2nd March 1978), and via Iceland on 4th March 1978.

BOB HALL'S AIR SERVICE, Kodiak, AK
1231
Owned by Robert L Hall, who later became President of *Kodiak Airways Inc.*

BOB'S AUTO SALES, Iron Mountain, MI
1267
Bob Forgette, owner

BOEING, William E, Seattle, WA
J-21
William ("Bill") Edward Boeing learned to fly in 1915, and in July 1916 formed Pacific Aero Products which grew into Boeing Air Transport. In 1928 he formed United Aircraft but was forced to dismantle the consortium in 1934 under the terms of the Black-McKellar Act. Boeing used the G-73, named "*Rover*", as a personal transport from 1947 until his death in 1956.

BOGART, John B, Caracas, Venezuela
1030
Bogart bought the OA-9 from the USAAF for $4,000 in November 1949 and sold it to an owner in Canada in May 1953.

BONANZA AIRLINES INTERNATIONAL Inc,
Woodland Hills, CA
B-35
Donald E DeTemple, President. The G-21A was based at Burbank-Glendale-Pasadena A/P for some three years before being re-possessed by the Liquidator in November 1983. The last Form 337 in the FAA Airworthiness file is dated October 1981 which would suggest that the aircraft was little used.

BONEBRAKE, Bill W Inc, El Reno, OK
1358

BOOTHE LEASING of CANADA Ltd,
Toronto, ON
1311, 1312
RL Borden, President. Owned c/n 1311 between April 1965 and February 1967, during which time it was based in Prince George, BC. In October 1966 the company changed its name to *Greyhound Leasing & Financial of Canada Ltd.*

BOSWELL, Perry Jr, Delray Beach, FL
1334, 1377, 1417

BOUSSAC, Marcel, Paris, France
J-26
Although the G-73 was registered to his fashion house '*Christian Dior*', Boussac regularly used the aircraft from its base at Toussus-le-Noble, near Paris. Boussac had previously and notoriously contributed to famous RAF pilot Sidney Cotton's downfall when bribing him to aid his escape from Paris in 1940.

BOWATER NEWFOUNDLAND PULP & PAPER MILLS Ltd, Corner Brook, NL
1167
The G-21A was transferred from the US parent company in 1950 and used by company president, Sir Eric V Bowater, until sold in 1956.

BOWATER PAPER Co Inc, New York, NY
- see above
1167

BOWER ROLLER BEARING Co,
Detroit, MI
J-10
Became *Federal Mogul Bower Bearings.*

BOYEAUX, Mr,
7
Boyeaux operated the SCAN-30 for Emperor Bao Dai from its base in Saigon.

BOYLE, Edward M, Pittsburgh, PA
(co-owner)
1458

BOYLEN, MJ, Toronto, ON
1187
Mathew James Boylen controlled *Lanson Holdings* and *Advocate Mines Ltd* and operated the G-21A from June 1955 until it was leased to *Abitibi Aviation* in June 1969. Mr Boylen died in 1970 and the aircraft was sold in the USA.

BOYNE MOUNTAIN LODGE Inc,
Boyne Falls, MI
J-26
Everett Kircher, a self-made entrepreneur from Detroit, bought a parcel of land in Michigan for $1.00 in 1947 and developed it into a ski and golf resort, which he named Boyne Mountain Lodge. Kircher bought the G-73 in 1966 to further his interest in fishing, and in 1972 had it converted to turbine power.

BRACE, Maxwell, Sr.
- see *See, Clarence, Jr.*

BRADLEY AIR MUSEUM, Bradley, CT
1178
see *New England Air Museum.*

BRADLEY AIR SERVICES Ltd, Carp, ON
1315
RL Bradley, President. Based at Carp Airport, the G-44 was operated from 1970 until 1974 when it was sold in the USA.

BRAMAN, DH, Victoria, TX
1328, J-53
After owning the amphibians, Braman, an oil tycoon, traded up to a Howard 350 and then a G-159 Gulfstream I.

William Boeing's Mallard N2961 (c/n J-21) "Rover" at Oakland, California in 1959.
(Douglas D Olson via Jennifer Gradidge)

Bradley Air Services' McKinnon Super Widgeon CF-HPD (c/n 1315) out to grass at Carp, Ontario on 23rd September 1973. The aircraft was sold in the USA in 1974.   *(KM Molson)*

CARL BRANDENFELS ENTERPRISES,
St Helens, OR
1393

BRANDT JORDAN CORP,
New Bedford, MA
1353

BRANHA, EG,
Anchorage, AK
1301

BRANHAM, Bud, & SAVAGE, Joe Jr,
Anchorage, AK
dba *Rainy Pass Lodge*
1375

BRANHAM, James R, Anchorage, AK
1329

BRAUNSTEIN, Michael B,
Weirs Beach, NH
and later at New York City and
Craryville, NY
1315
"Mickey" Braunstein started *Virgin Islands Seaplane Shuttle* with his co-founders Donald Lewis and Vincent J Condello in late 1981. Previously, Braunstein had been an insurance and pension fund consultant and bought his G-44 in 1978 to commute from Manhattan to his country estate in upstate New York. Sadly, he was killed when the Widgeon crashed into the Hudson River near Germantown, New York, on the afternoon of 2nd May 2013. Braunstein's body was recovered by divers the following day. Initial reports indicated that the aircraft was destroyed in the crash and subsequent fire.

BRESEE CHEVROLET Co Inc,
Liverpool, NY and Syracuse, NY
1334, 1431
Herbert A Dunn, President in 1960, followed by William Dunn in 1961.

BILL BRENNAND AIRCRAFT SALES,
Neenah, WA
1233
William Brennand and Byron Fredericksen, partners

BRIGGS MANUFACTURING Co,
Detroit, MI
J-45
Walter "Spike" Briggs, President. Briggs also owned the "Detroit Tigers" baseball team. The Mallard was based at the Briggs hangar at Detroit City Airport. In 1949, *George Sherwood* became the company pilot. In 1960, the company sold their auto-body division to Chrysler Corporation and also decided to sell the Mallard.

BRIGNAC, Donald D, Houma, LA
1377
dba Donald's Air Service, also operated a Cessna 180 in the late 1950s.

BRINSON AIR Inc, Miami, FL
J-13

G-21A Goose NC3022 (c/n 1055) was gifted by the railway workers of the USA to their counterparts in Britain, to be used by the British American Ambulance Corps. The Goose was later operated by the RAF and No.1 Air Ambulance Unit, Royal Australian Air Force, as HK822.
(Peter Bowers via grummangoose.com)

BRISTOL AERO INDUSTRIES,
Winnipeg, MB
J-19
Sir Reginald Verdon Smith, Chairman. Owned the G-73 briefly during 1961.

BRITISH ACCEPTANCE Corp, Canada
26
Sold the SCAN-30 in the USA as salvage, after the crash in July 1971.

**BRITISH AMERICAN
AIR TRANSPORT Ltd**
- see *British American Oil Co Ltd*

BRITISH AMERICAN AMBULANCE CORPS, Inc, New York, NY
1055, 1212
On a Certificate of Airworthiness application, the Corps stated that the G-21A was used "to tour the US to publicise the Ambulance Corps". An internal CAA letter dated 26th July 1943 confirmed that the aircraft "had been sold to the British government and removed to Africa". It was then cancelled from the register on 21st August 1943.

BRITISH AMERICAN OIL Co Ltd,
Toronto, ON
B-50, B-76
WK Whiteford (1947) & AL Ellsworth (1948), Presidents. The aircraft were operated by subsidiary, British American

Air Transport Ltd, based at Toronto-Malton, for transportation of executives. B-76 was allowed to carry the marks CF-BAE only because Mr SR Bernado agreed to the re-allocation of the registration which he had originally received for a Stinson, but which he never registered. Similarly, B-50, had both the Certificate of Registration and Certificate of Airworthiness backdated to the date on which the application had been made by the previous owner, *John G Sharp*. These allocations were not taken up by Sharp, who had quickly sold the aircraft to British American Oil (BAO), but the Canadian authorities issued the certificates (to BAO) with effect from the date on which Sharp had applied for them!

BRITISH GUIANA AIRWAYS Ltd,
Georgetown, British Guiana
1007, 1015, B-46
Founded as British Guiana Air Services in 1934 by US citizen, *Mr Arthur James Williams*, who later flew for the USAAC, attaining the rank of Major. Authorised by the British Guiana government to operate an internal air service, the company was reformed as British Guiana Airways Ltd in 1939, with Williams and *John Henry Hunter*, a British citizen resident in New York as partners, and *Captain Harmon Edgar Wendt* as pilot. The company was capitalised by the issue of 50,000 $1 shares, of which Williams held 39,800, Mrs

British Guiana Airways' Goose VP-GAC (c/n B-46) at Piarco, Trinidad on 20th November 1953. Note the BGA "wings" logo on the forward fuselage. The Goose also carries an unreadable legend under the tailplane.
(DAS McKay via Jennifer Gradidge)

Williams 200, and Hunter 10,000. Only charter services had been allowed under the original contract but regular passenger/mail/freight services were started in June 1944 with fortnightly services to the Mazaruni district and monthly flights to the Rupununi savannahs. Pan American Airways had provided a flying boat service from Trinidad to the Marine Airport at Georgetown but this had stopped by 1945. From 1st September 1945, *British West Indian Airways(BWIA)* flew a landplane service from Port of Spain, Trinidad to the bauxite town of Mackenzie, from where a BGA Goose provided a shuttle service to Georgetown, 60 miles away. The service started with two flights a week (Sunday & Thursday), but from 1st November 1945, the frequency was doubled with two flights on both Sundays & Thursdays. Two more G-21As were added in 1946, with two Douglas C-47s following in 1947. On 28th March 1947 Major Williams and Captain Wendt were awarded medals by the British Government for their extensive work in the development of air transport within the colony during the years 1934-47. When the road network improved, the service to Mackenzie was no longer required and the G-21As were sub-contracted to *BWIA* and based on St Vincent in the Windward Islands to provide third level services into strips where C-47s could not land. In 1953 this included Flight No:121/122 from St Vincent to Piarco, Trinidad and return. In July 1955 Williams sold his interest in the company to the colonial government for £170,000, and the company was renamed British Guiana Airways (Government). Williams returned to America but Wendt stayed on as a pilot. BWIA were contracted to manage the BGA feeder operations into BWIA's network and the internal routes were suspended. On 5th December 1957 Captain Wendt was awarded the Order of the British Empire (OBE) for his "exceptional flying and engineering skill." As the colony moved towards independence, however, the airline's name changed to *Guyana Airways Corporation* on 1st September 1963, and the domestic network was expanded. Re-equipment took place and by the 1970s the Grummans were no longer in service.

BRITISH WEST INDIAN AIRWAYS (BWIA),
St Vincent
1007, 1015, B-46
BWIA provided services for the St Vincent Government Air Service using the G-21As of *British Guiana Airways*. In April 1953 these consisted of services from St Vincent, weekly to St George's, Grenada and twice weekly to both Port of Spain (Piarco), Trinidad and Bridgetown, Barbados. This latter service continued to Dominica and later routed through Fort de France on Martinique. The St Vincent-Piarco and return flights were numbered 121/122.

BROOME, John Spoor, Oxnard, CA
1347

BROWN & ROOT Inc, Houston, TX
1370, 1441
The oil company has used many corporate aircraft, including a Grumman Gulfstream, which was operated alongside the Widgeons in support of the company's oil exploration operations.

BROWN, David B, Anchorage, AK
1334
Co-owner with *Shirley J Rohl*.

BROWN, Kenneth F, Long Beach, CA
1138
- see also *Amphibian Air Transport*.

BRUNDAGE, HL, Miami, FL
1293, 1312

BRUNQUIST, Norman E, Anchorage, AK
B-81

BRUNTON, FK, Bellevue, WA
1208, 1265

BRUNTON, William R,
Freeport, Bahamas
1270

BUEHN, Dennis G, Compton, CA
and later at Carson City, NV
B-66, B-86, 1388
After leaving the US Navy in 1972, Dennis Buehn formed his first company, *Warbirds West*, in Compton, CA to restore warbirds, his first being Grumman HU-16C, 137927. Moving to Carson City, NV in 1989 he formed a new company named *American Warbirds, Inc* and although known as "*Mr Albatross*", he worked on G-21As and G-44s and can also boast the restoration of many AT-6 Texans, S-2 Trackers and C-117 Skytrains et al, as well as nearly twenty HU-16s.

BUFFET, Jimmy - see *Strange Bird Inc*.

BUEKER, Walter, Warri, Nigeria,
and at Neustadt, Germany.
1317
Bueker bought the G-44 and spares from *McDermott* in Nigeria, shipped them back to Germany, and sold them to *Tony Allen*.

BUNCH, Kenneth H, Glenallen, AK
1375
dba *Gulkana Air Service*. Ken Bunch of Gulkana Air Service was credited with providing logistic assistance for the US Geological Survey Trans-Alaska Crustal Transect field-mapping programme in 1984 and 1985. The G-44 was sold by Evelyn M Bunch on behalf of the Estate of KH Bunch in March 1992.

BURCHFIELD, Albert H, III,
Pittsburgh, PA
35

BURCHFIELD, Albert H, III, & Janice K,
Pittsburgh, PA
1458
Co-owners with *EM Boyle*.

BURDIS, William J, Coraopolis, PA
dba *Classic Wings Inc*.
B-76

BUREAU OF LAND MANAGEMENT,
US Dept of Interior
- see *US Government*

BURKE, Dennis K,
Pembroke, MA & Chelsea, MA
and later at Vero Beach, FL
1349, 1438, 1471
President of *Antique Aircraft Inc*, Burke also presides over the fuel distribution company, Dennis K Burke, Inc. In November 1994 he bought the remains of 1438. Similarly in 2003, he bought the remains of 1349 and had them reassembled by North River Aviation Inc, Halifax, MA. Over the years Burke has fitted his G-44s with a variety of Lycoming engines (see below and Chapter 5).

BURKE, Dennis K, Vero Beach, FL
1471, 16
In 1990 Burke developed the STC (SA4774M), with *Ned Rice*, to re-engine Widgeons with 350hp Lycoming TIO-540-J2BD. Both aircraft were so converted.

BURKE, Maureen C, Pembroke, MA
16

BURLINGTON MILLS Corp,
Greensboro, NC
J-32

BURNS BROS PLUMBERS Inc,
Syracuse, NY
1343

BURNS, Janet Y, Hampshire, IL
1265

BURNS, Richard O, Jr, Chicago, IL
1441

BURNS, Richard O, III, Lake Bluff, IL
1441

BURNS, Richard Owen, Hinsdale, IL
1441

BURNSTEIN, Stan, Tulsa, OK
dba *Continental Aviation Co*.
16

BURR, James B, Provo, UT
1340
Burr was President of Rocky Mountain Helicopters Inc.

BURRUS MILLS Inc, Dallas, TX
J-18
formerly *Tex-o-Can Flour Mills Inc*.

BUSINESS AIR SERVICES Ltd,
Goderich, ON
J-34
BA Sully, President. The G-73T was based at Cartierville, PQ, and was leased to *Canadair Ltd* in 1981 before being bought by them the following year.

BUSINESS AIRCRAFT Inc,
Green Bay, WI
J-5

BUSINESS AVIATION SERVICES Corp,
Spring Park, MN
31

BUTCHER-ARTHUR Inc, Houston, TX
1370
The G-44 was operated for almost five years from 1948 including a nominal change to *Commercial Petroleum & Transport Co* in December 1950.

BUTTERWORTH SYSTEMS Inc,
Bayonne, NJ
J-38
Division of *Standard Oil of New Jersey*.

CABLE AIRPORT Inc
1130
The airport sold the G-21A for $6,000, in March 1967, in lieu of storage charges unpaid by *Inlet Airlines Inc*.

CALIFORNIA AMPHIBIOUS TRANSPORT – CAT
J-18
CAT's owner, Dan Aikens, bought the G-73 when *Trans Catalina Airlines* ceased operations in 1979, and used it to continue the services on *"The Route of the Seagulls"* from Long Beach, California to Santa Catalina Island until 1982.

An undated picture of the California Oil Company's Goose N60X (c/n 1045) at New Orleans. The California Company was a Division of Chevron Oil.
(Art Krieger Collection)

CALIFORNIA OIL Co, New Orleans, LA
1045, J-57
A Division of *Standard Oil of California*.

CALIFORNIA WESTGATE Corp
-see *Golden West Airlines*

CALKINS, Dwight L, Spokane, WA
1292
The G-44 was bought in 1950 and transferred to the *Calkins Manufacturing Co* in 1956.

CALKINS MANUFACTURING Co,
Spokane, WA
1292, 1427

CALLANAN, John H, Clifton Park, NY
1300

CALM AIR INTERNATIONAL Ltd,
Lynn Lake, MB
B-117
Carl Arnold L Morberg, President. Calm Air provided services to the scattered communities of northern Manitoba and the Keewatin District of North West Territories,

and operated the G-21A in 1978/79, on lease from *Keewatin Arctic Camp Company*.

CAMPBELL, Bruce, Ltd,
Hamble, UK
19
Bruce Campbell was a former de Havilland test pilot who became a boat-builder. With his company based on the River Hamble, in Hampshire, he had planned to use the SCAN-30 for sales tours to Europe and the Middle East. Unfortunately the plane crashed into Southampton Water near Calshot only 24 hours after delivery in May 1961.

CAMPBELL, Carroll J, Toomsuba, MS
1208

CAMPBELL, James J,
Morton, and Woodinville, WA
1208, 1311

CANADA COACH LINES Ltd,
Hamilton, ON
B-39
Bought from the Holt family for $20,000, the G-21A was operated for private use

Bruce Campbell's SCAN-30G Widgeon G-ARIX (c/n 19) was the first of the type to appear on the UK register and is seen here at Biggin Hill, where it was awarded a Certificate of Airworthiness on 11th May 1961. The aircraft was delivered to Eastleigh after which it unfortunately crashed on 19th May 1961, only 24 hours after delivery.
(MW Prime)

Canada Coach Lines' Goose CF-ESZ (c/n B-39) in the sunshine at Malton, Ontario on 14th May 1949. The aircraft was sold in the USA in 1951 and cancelled from the US register in September 1957 as "exported to Guatemala".
(Jack McNulty)

California Amphibious Transport timetable dated 1981.

Above: Canadian Breweries operated Mallard CF-GEV (c/n J-34). Seen here in 1954, the aircraft displays the company monogram on the forward hull. (Brian Baker via Jennifer Gradidge)

between January 1949 and May 1951 from Malton Airport, Toronto. At least two attempts to sell the aircraft in 1951 were unsuccessful, but it went to an American buyer in June 1951.

CANADA KELP Co Ltd,
Sproat Lake, BC
1334
Harold R Hine, President. Having acquired the G-44 in 1969, the company went into receivership in 1970, and the aircraft was sold to *Flying Fireman Ltd.*

CANADAIR Ltd, Montreal, QC
J-34
The G-73 was used during the construction of the company's fishing lodge at Lac Piraube, QC and was then sold to *Nordair,* during whose ownership it was converted to turbine power. In September 1981 Canadair leased the aircraft from *Business Air Services Ltd* of Goderich, ON and bought it from them in August 1982.

CANADIAN AIRCRAFT RENTERS Ltd,
Toronto, ON
1030
Formed in 1946 as Savage Aircraft Services Ltd, renamed as Lorne Airways Ltd in September 1947, and as Canadian Aircraft Renters in late 1953. Although the G-21A was reportedly based in Montreal, PQ, the company operated charters in southern Ontario. The aircraft was sold in October 1957.

CANADIAN BREWERIES Ltd,
Toronto, ON
J-34
Edward Plunket Taylor formed the Canadian Breweries conglomerate by buying up independent breweries in the 1930s. He then combined Canadian Breweries, Dominion Stores and Standard Broadcasting to form the Argus Corporation. J-34 was their first aircraft and was operated for Canadian Breweries during the years 1948-1961.

CANADIAN FLYING MACHINES,
Langley, BC
1265
Acted as sales agent for the G-44 in June 1975.

CANADIAN FOREST PRODUCTS Ltd,
Vancouver, BC
B-70
JG Prentice, President. Used the G-21A for corporate transportation, amassing only 4,000 flying hours from 1952 until selling it to *Air Pacific Inc* in 1982. Maintenance and hangar facilities were provided by *B.N.P. Airways* at Vancouver.

CANADIAN INSPECTION & TESTING Co Ltd, Montreal, PQ
1334
W Howard Wert, President. Associate company of the Warnock Hersey group.

CANADA VENEERS Ltd, St John, NB
1083, J-5
One of *KC Irving*'s companies.

CANADIAN WARPLANE HERITAGE MUSEUM, Mount Hope, ON
28
The long-serving, but low-time (4,405hrs) SCAN-30 was displayed here from 2001 until offered for sale in October 2011.

CANADY, Sam W, Lexington, NC
1228
Canady purchased the ex-Coast Guard J4F-1 from the War Assets Administration in February 1947 for $5,000. The FAA file does not contain a Certificate of Registration in his name, despite the fact that he owned the aircraft until May 1950.

CAN-AM AIRCRAFT Ltd, Kenora, ON
B-120
One of *Barney Lamm*'s companies, to which the G-21A was registered in 1966.

CANDY, Lt Cdr William,
USNAS Glenview, IL
1430
dba *Western Continental Airlines Inc* out of Grand Central A/P, Glendale, CA. Candy was President of the airline, which was described as a charter operator on the

mortgage documents raised by Pacific Finance Corporation. When the G-44A was wrecked on 15th June 1946, it was declared a total loss and Pacific Finance Corporation became entitled to the salvage rights, and Western Continental went out of business.

CANNING, Henry A, Cleveland, OH
1210

CANPRINT SECURITIES Ltd,
Montreal, QC
J-13
GE Hoult, President. *Lord Beaverbrook*'s company in which name the G-73 was registered until sold to *New Brunswick Holding Co Ltd.*

CANTERBURY PLANES,
Christchurch,
New Zealand
1145
Operated a tourist service from Christchurch to the southern lakes.

CANYON de CHELLY MOTEL Inc,
Albuquerque, NM
J-14
Canyon de Chelly is the second largest canyon in the USA and is a magnet for campers, hikers and fishermen. The motel is situated at the mouth of the canyon.

CAPPER, Cynthia A, Anchorage, AK
1464

CARIBBEAN AIRLINE SERVICES Inc,
Carolina, PR
J-9, J-11, J-28, J-32, J-51, J-53, J-55
Anthony C Tirri, President. Leased the Mallards to *Sea Air Shuttle Corp*, headed by Arnaldo Delio and dba *Virgin Islands Seaplane Shuttle*. At the end of 1990 Caribbean Airline Services (CAS) joined with Sal Labate's *Labate Aviation Inc* in co-ownership of the seven Mallards abandoned by Virgin Islands Seaplane Shuttle to the *Manufacturers Hanover Trust Company*. The aircraft were in varied condition, from airworthy to un-repairable. CAS then put forward a proposal to the Virgin Islands Port Authority (VIPA) in competition with two other bidders, to lease the seaplane ramps at St Thomas and St Croix, and thereby continue the inter-island air service. After much backroom political manoeuvring, VIPA awarded the right to negotiate for the lease to Caribbean Air Boats who had no aircraft and no experience of seaplane operation. Not surprisingly, Caribbean Air Boats were not able to provide a service and after several years the lease was put out to tender again. This time the lease on the seaplane ramps was awarded to Caribbean Airline Services Inc, but again, after two years the lease was nullified for lack of performance. A few more years passed and finally the lease was awarded to Seaborne Seaplanes who had been operating between St Thomas and St Croix with DHC-6 Twin Otters on straight floats. After some ten years (circa 2001),

the seaplane ramps were rebuilt and put into use together with floating docks to support the DHC-6 operation.

CARIBBEAN CLIPPER Inc,
Isle of Islay, Scotland
B-76
Owned by former Grumman test pilot Capt Thomas Friedrich. The G-21A was flown across the Atlantic in 1994 and appeared at the Farnborough (UK) Airshow. Friedrich planned to operate safari charters in Uganda, Tanzania and southern Africa in 1995 under the auspices of Bush-buck Safaris, Hungerford, UK, but the aircraft was stored at Westcott Airfield, near Aylesbury, UK until October 1996. The starboard undercarriage collapsed landing at Elstree, UK in October 1996 and was repaired by Light Aircraft Engineering Ltd. The aircraft was exported to Canada in March 2007.

CARIBBEAN FLYING BOATS Inc,
San Juan, PR
1141, B-29, B-53
Charles F Blair was succeeded as President, after his death, by his wife *Maureen O'Hara Blair*. On the Bill of Sale for c/n B-29 the company address is given as Isla Grande Airport, San Juan but on the application for aircraft registration this has been amended to c/o Antilles Air Boats Inc, Christiansted, St Croix. The company was later divided into two: *CFB PR Inc & CFB VI Inc* (see below). FAA 337s for these aircraft show the address as c/o Antilles Air Boats.

CARIBBEAN FLYING BOATS - PR Inc,
San Juan
1162, B-29

CARIBBEAN FLYING BOATS - VI Inc,
Christiansted, St Croix.
1150, 1162, 1187, B-29, B-53

CARIBBEAN PETROLEUM CO.
B-34
A subsidiary of *Shell Oil*.

CARL BRANDENFELS ENTERPRISES
St Helens, OR
1393

CARLSON, Professor Fred,
Sun Valley, CA
1337
The FAA file contains a Bill of Sale showing that Carlson bought the remains of the G-44 from Robert L Hall, President of *Kodiak Airways*, in March 1993 and immediately sold them to *Edwin E Forsberg*. However, in a letter to the author, Forsberg states that he bought the aircraft from Professor Carlson, (who was living in a Spartan trailer-house parked in his hangar at the Whiteman Airport in Pacoima, near Burbank, CA) "in about 1984".

CARNER, James E, Fairbanks, AK
1328

G-21A N93GS (c/n B-76) of Caribbean Clipper Inc, at Shannon, Ireland in 1994. The former Royal Canadian Air Force Goose II served civilian owners in Canada for almost forty years. After returning to Canada in 2007, the Goose was lost in a fatal crash in August 2008. (M Nason)

The former Fuerza Aérea Boliviana JRF-6B Goose (c/n 1150) in the colours of Cat Cay Airways as N5548A in Florida, circa 1961. (MAP)

Catalina Air Lines' G-21A N329 (c/n B-119) seen here at Long Beach, California in August 1966, was sold in Indonesia in 1976. (John P Stewart via Jennifer Gradidge)

CAROLINA AIRCRAFT Corp,
Fort Lauderdale, FL
16

CAROLINA FLYING SERVICE
- see *Ruebush, Lee Jr.*

CAROLINA PAPER BOX Co Inc,
Burlington, NC
1375
Bill Price, President. The remains of the G-44 were bought by *Fred Fenn* after it crashed in Cuba in 1958. Fenn rebuilt it at his hangar on North Perry Airport in Hollywood, Florida and sold the aircraft in April 1961.

CARRIER AIRCRAFT, Long Beach, CA
1051

CARROLL, Bill, Huntington Beach, CA
(co-owner)
1132

CARSTAIRS ENTERPRISES Inc
1462

CARTER, Garrett,
Anchorage, AK
1415
dba *Tri-Negro of Alaska*, co-owner with *Chaos Consulting*.

CASSULO, John,
Cove Neck,
Long Island, NY
1141

CAT CAY AIRWAYS Inc,
Miami, FL
and at Lubbock, TX
1141, 1150
Irving L Jones, President.

CATALINA AIR LINES Inc,
Long Beach, CA
1059, 1130, 1191, B-59, B-66, B-73, B-119
The former *Avalon Air Transport* became *Catalina Amphibian Air Lines* briefly in 1963 before becoming Catalina Air Lines Inc on 30th October 1963. The company operated G-21As between Long Beach Municipal Airport, CA and Santa Catalina

The former Peruvian Air Corps Goose, seen here with Catalina Airlines Inc as N328 (c/n 1053) at Long Beach, California in April 1967, having been repaired after an accident in February that year.
(Steve Krauss)

Island (Avalon Bay) with the November 1965 timetable showing five flights per day. In 1968, Aero Commuter Inc merged with Catalina Air Lines and the merged entity then swallowed up Cable Commuter, Skymark Airlines and the original Golden West Airlines to form *Golden West Airlines Inc*. The aircraft, although registered to Golden West, were operated with '*Catalina Golden West*' titles.

CATALINA AIRLINES Inc, Gardena, CA
1048, 1053, 1086, 1130, 1153, 1166, 1188, 1191, B-59, B-66, B-73, B-119, B-139
Began operations in 1973 after taking over the *Golden West Airlines* Goose routes to Santa Catalina Island. There was no connection between this airline company and the former *Catalina Air Lines*, owned by *Wilton R "Dick" Probert*. *Walter von Kleinsmid*, a one-time partner of Probert, was however Vice-President of Catalina Airlines Inc which flew nine daily returns to Avalon Bay and two returns to Two Harbors, both from Long Beach. In 1977, Briles Aviation took over the operation but the G-21As were grounded the same year by the FAA due to salt water corrosion. They were flying again by 1979 but suffered two fatal crashes and Catalina Airlines Inc ceased operations in 1981.

CATALINA AMPHIBIAN AIR LINES,
Long Beach, CA
B-73
A temporary name, adopted for a short time in 1963, for *Avalon Air Transport*. Only the one G-21A was painted with the new titles.

CATALINA CHANNEL AIRLINES Inc,
Long Beach, CA
1007, 1021, 1030, 1166, B-14, B-127
Founded by former *Amphibian Air Transport* pilot, Robert "Bob" J Hanley, in

1959, Catalina Channel Airlines developed the amphibian ramp at Pebbly Beach on Santa Catalina Island and flew services from there and from Avalon Harbor to Long Beach, CA. Ray McClure was chief pilot.

Five G-21As were used between 1959 and 1966, when the operation was taken over by *Catalina Seaplanes*. B-14, bought on 20th June 1960, was sold on 9th September 1960 and was therefore probably not put into service.

CATALINA FLYING BOATS,
Long Beach, CA
1132, 1153, 1184
Founded by Frank and Irene Strobel in 1984, the company operated a passenger and cargo service between Long Beach, CA and Pebbly Beach on Catalina Island. Using two of the G-21As (1132 and 1184), the operation was not profitable and was sold in 1989.

Avalon Air Transport was re-named as Catalina Amphibian Air Lines in October 1963. This rare photograph shows Goose N322 (c/n B-73) wearing the new titles and Fleet Number 6. Owner Dick Probert very quickly changed his mind, however, and by the end of 1963 the company was re-named Catalina Air Lines Inc.   *(Ed Coates Collection)*

The original XJ3F-1 Goose (c/n 1021) seen here at Long Beach, California on 17th January 1959. By then it had been converted to G-21A standard and registered N2767A to Catalina Channel Airlines.   *(Ed Coates via Jennifer Gradidge)*

This former US Navy JRF-6 Goose provided services to Santa Catalina Island with various operators since 1956. It is seen here with Catalina Airlines Inc as G-21A N324 (c/n B-66) named "Michelle". The Goose is now owned by Flight Data Inc and is based at Carson City, Nevada.
(R Caratini)

Catalina Flying Boats' G-21A Goose N1257A (c/n 1184) looking the worse for wear at Long Beach, California circa 1985.   *(EW Priebe)*

Catalina Seaplanes' G-21A Goose N12CS (c/n 1086) seen here at Long Beach, California in November 1969. This Goose was used at Universal Studios' back-lot as a prop in the TV series "Tales of the Gold Monkey" in the 1980s. It is now displayed at the National Museum of Naval Aviation in Pensacola, Florida, with the (incorrect) serial "V190". *(Steve Krauss)*

Mallard N2968 (c/n J-25) in the colours of Catalina-Vegas Airlines on 10th April 1966. The airline titles are on the rear cheat-line. *(K Measures Collection)*

Chalk's G-44 Widgeon N1059M (c/n 1274) parked at McArthur Causeway, Miami, Florida on 12th October 1961. The Widgeon has spent most of its life in the same area and currently resides with an owner in Hollywood, Florida. *(Fred J Knight Collection)*

CATALINA GOLDEN WEST AIRLINES
- see *Golden West Airlines*
Although the G-21As displayed "Catalina Golden West" titles the operator's title was always only Golden West Airlines.

CATALINA SEAPLANES Inc,
San Pedro, CA
1007, 1086, 1153, 1166, B-29, B-59
Robert B Sprague, President; *Wilton R Probert,* Chief Executive. Founded by the owners of the SS Catalina steamship (Manley & the Beckers), the company took over the *Catalina Channel Airlines* operation at Pebbly Beach in 1966. A fleet of six G-21As operated until 1973, flying from Berth 96, San Pedro, CA to Avalon Bay on Santa Catalina Island. By 1974 the aircraft were in service with *Air Catalina*.

CATALINA-VEGAS AIRLINES,
San Diego, CA
J-25
JW Dowdle, President; Lloyd Smith, Chief Executive. One of the trading names used by *JW Dowdle,* who also used the name

Swift Air Service. Scheduled services were flown from Lindbergh Field, San Diego to Las Vegas and Santa Catalina Island. The G-73 crashed during a training flight and sank off Santa Catalina Island on 22nd May 1967, killing one and injuring three others.

CATER, Richard Eugene Stader,
Guatemala City, Guatemala
1311
Registration documents held in Guatemala state his name as Richard Eugene Stader Cater, but when he sold the G-44 in June 2002, he signed the Bill of Sale as *Richard E Stader* (omitting the Cater).

CAV Air Inc, Fort Lauderdale, FL
J-35

CELCER, Alvin, Casa Grande, AZ
1340
Co-owner with *William E Hamilton*. Celcer and Hamilton breached the financing agreement and the G-44 was re-possessed by *Martin Aviation Co* and assigned to *William A Thompson* on 10th November 1978.

CENTERLINE HOLDINGS Inc,
Camden, DE
J-49

CENTRAL BRITISH COLUMBIA AIRWAYS Ltd, Vancouver, BC
1003
Central BC Airways had been formed on 1st July 1945 by bush pilot Russ Baker and mining executive *Karl Springer*. When the Aluminium Company of Canada (Alcan) decided in 1949 to build a huge hydro-electric-powered bauxite smelter in Kitimat, BC local air operators fought over the lucrative contracts on offer. The project was so large that it required the building of a new town (Kitimat) and a new port (Kemano). Central BC Airways were awarded the lion's share of the airlift contracts to support this major undertaking, leaving the rest of the work to Jim Spilsbury's Queen Charlotte Airlines (QCA). By 1953 Central BC Airways had acquired Kamloops Air Service, Skeena Air Transport and Associated Air Taxi and become *Pacific Western Airlines Ltd* (PWA).
The G-21A was operated from May 1952 until it crashed en route to Kemano on 27th January 1953.

CENTRAL JAPAN AIRLINES
- see *Naka Nihon Koku*

CENTRAVIA SA, Paris, France
26, 27, 28, 29, 30
Centravia sold the SCAN-30s to *McKinnon-Hickman Company* in September 1955. (For further details see *McKinnon Enterprises*)

CENTURY MOTOR SALES Ltd,
Toronto, ON
1240

CESSNA AIRCRAFT Co, Wichita, KS
1059
Took the Goose in part exchange for a Cessna 208 Caravan.

CF-BGS Aircraft Inc, Oakville, ON
1327
Barry G Smith, President. Bought the G-44 in April 2003 and based it at Brantford, ON.

CHALK, Arthur Burns, Miami, FL
1274
"Pappy" Chalk bought the G-44 in 1949 (see following entry).

CHALK'S FLYING SERVICE,
Watson Island, Miami, FL
1019, 1048, 1162, B-54, B-100, B-104, 1274, J-4, J-6, J-9, J-13, J-19, J-27, J-28, J-36, J-38, J-42 - J-44
Chalk's has operated services from Florida to the Bahamas since the end of WW I. The airline was founded in 1917 by Arthur Burns "Pappy" Chalk as Red Arrow Flying Service, flying a Curtiss JN-4 Jenny from Miami to Bimini and Nassau, and became Chalk's Flying Service in 1919. The CAA

granted Chalk's an air carrier certificate on 18th July 1950 by which time the G-44 and G-21As were in service. "Pappy" Chalk retired in 1966 and chief pilot *Dean Franklin*, who had been with Chalk since 1936, took over the operation of the company. The fleet was augmented progressively by the 15-seat G-73s from 1967. Franklin implemented a STC which limited the aircraft's gross weight to 12,499lbs to allow legal operation with a single pilot. In 1970 the operation became known as Chalk's International Airline.

Chalk's Goose Fleet Numbers:

F/N 1	c/n B-54	N2721A
F/N 3*	c/n B-104	N1621A
F/N 5	c/n 1162	N5521A
F/N 7	c/n B-100	N88U
F/N 9	c/n 1048	N702A

Note the use of odd numbers only. *It is not known whether c/n 1019, which assumed the registration N1621A in 1975, also took the Fleet number 3.

Mallard, J-43, was hijacked to Havana, Cuba on 7th March 1972. Two armed men entered the aircraft which was about to depart for Bimini, Bahamas with five passengers, and demanded to be flown to Cuba. Pilot James Cothron shut down the engines, stating that he was not going to Cuba, but he was shot three times and thrown off the aircraft. Co-pilot Robert Wallis decided that it might be prudent to accede to the gunmen's wishes, and flew the Mallard to Cuba. The aircraft returned to Miami next morning with five relieved passengers, and a few bullet holes in the cabin.

Franklin sold a controlling interest in Chalk's to *Edward F Dixon*, a Pennsylvania businessman, in 1973. Dixon fell foul of the IRS and having paid his dues to the revenue service by handing over Mallard J-19, sold Chalk's to James Crosby, owner of *Resorts International*, the casino operator, in 1978. The Frakes G-73T demonstrator was evaluated in 1979 (with 17 seats and two pilots) and purchased in 1981. The G-21As were sold and the other G-73s converted to turboprops. Albatrosses were purchased with a view to converting them to G-111 standard, to carry 28 passengers. The first G-111, N112FB, entered service with Chalk's on 15th December 1981, flying from Miami to Paradise Island in the Bahamas, and by 1984 Paradise Island was being served from Fort Lauderdale and West Palm Beach as well. Meanwhile the G-73Ts were flying services from Miami and Fort Lauderdale to Bimini and Paradise Island, and from Miami to Cat Cay, as well as supplementing the G-111s on their routes to the Bahamas *(see timetable)*.

Crosby died suddenly in 1986 and control of the airline passed to his sisters, who in 1988 sold Resorts International to *Donald Trump*, the New York real estate magnate. He wanted to maximise the use of Chalk's Part 121 licence for services to Paradise Island and set up a subsidiary

Chalk's G-21A Goose, Fleet number '1', N2721A (c/n B-54) poses with pilot James Cothron in the ocean off the Florida coast in October 1969. The former Royal Canadian Air Force Goose II ended its career in Indonesia as PK-LEH. (James Cothron)

Chalk's G-21A Goose, Fleet number '7', N88U (c/n B-100) parked at McArthur Causeway, Miami, FL in 1967. After service in Alaska during the 1970s and various owners since, the Goose is currently airworthy with an owner in Maryland. (MAP)

Chalk's Mallard N123DF (c/n J-9) "City of Nassau", taxying in to the Bimini Seaplane Base, Bahamas on 15th March 1979. Converted to G-73T Turbo Mallard by Frakes in 1984, it was damaged by Hurricane 'Hugo' on 17th September 1989 while in service with Virgin Island Seaplane Shuttle. (Peter Vercruijsse)

Chalk's G-73T Turbo Mallard N1208 (c/n J-44) coming up the ramp at Watson Island, Miami, Florida in March 1983. Before service with Chalk's, J-44 had seen service in Alaska during the 1950s and '60s. (Stephen Piercey)

While on Paradise Island, Nassau, enjoy a Chalk's seaplane sightseeing tour for 30 minutes over Nassau, New Providence, Paradise Island, and surrounding Cays.

For information contact your travel agent, hotel superintendent of service, or Chalk's International Airline in Nassau for frequency, cost, and minimum seat requirements.

CHALK'S INTERNATIONAL
The World's Oldest Airline.
(305) 377-8801

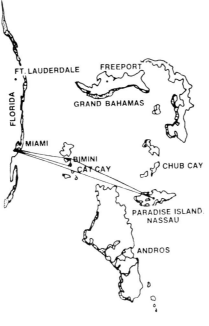

ROUND TRIP FARES BETWEEN:

Miami	Bimini	*96.00*	$75.00
Miami	Cat Cay	*102.00*	$94.00
Miami	Nassau	*105.00*	$86.00
Nassau	Bimini	*84.00*	$76.00

All fares are round trip plus departure tax.

Schedules and rates subject to change without notice.

CHALK'S AIRLINES

Watson Island - Miami, Florida	(305) 377 8801
Nassau - Paradise Island	325-2845/2846
Bimini	(809) 347-2024
Cat Cay	(809) 2322

On 1st January 1991 *United Capital Corporation* of Rockford, IL, owned by the *Atwood* family, became the owners of Chalk's International Airline, leaving Merv Griffin with PIA to operate his DHC-7. The FAA issued a Part 135 certificate to Chalk's in the name of their subsidiary *Flying Boat Inc* and with the injection of fresh capital the airline began to flourish again. Also in 1991 four Albatrosses were removed from storage at Evergreen Air Center Inc, Marana, AZ. One was leased for services from Okinawa, while the others (N117FB, N120FB and N121FB) were returned to Grumman-St Augustine for overhaul and internal refurbishment, while Chalk's looked at the possibility of services to Cuba. The Albatrosses did not go into scheduled service but were used for charters as necessary, N121FB being used in Singapore. In August 1992 Hurricane Andrew caused major damage at Watson Island and Bimini, and the terminal at Cat Cay was destroyed. Chalk's was back on track very quickly using three Albatrosses for the winter 1993 season, but their operation was not as economic as the G-73Ts and they went back to desert storage in 1994. The 18th March 1994 was a sad day for Chalk's in that it recorded the airline's first fatal accident in 75 years of operations when Mallard J-51, N150FB, crashed off Key West, FL during a positioning flight, killing the two pilots. Also in 1994, Chalk's reached agreement with Robert Abplanalp to take over the

Above and right: Chalk's timetable of services from Florida to the Caribbean, dated 27th April 1980.

named Paradise Island Airways (PIA) to operate DHC-7 services to the island day and night rather than the daylight-VFR Mallard services. As a consequence the Mallard operation declined, much to the chagrin of the locals who relied on the Grummans for local travel, and the situation did not improve when Trump sold Chalk's (and PIA) to *Merv Griffin* in November 1988. Following losses of $2.3million in the first half of 1989 Griffin put Resorts International up for sale. With four G-73Ts (J-27, J-36, J-42 and J-44) in service, only 3,900 flight hours were recorded in 1989, and by January 1990 only three return flights a day were being flown from Watson Island to Bimini. The first left the airline's engineering base at Fort Lauderdale at 0715hrs positioning for a 0745hrs departure from Watson Island to Bimini. The second flight left Watson Island (MPB) at 1000hrs for Bimini and continued to Nassau, while the third, to Bimini only, left MPB at 1515hrs. The return flight from Bimini to MPB at 1615hrs continued to Fort Lauderdale. The MPB-Fort Lauderdale sector was only available to international passengers, i.e. those travelling to or from the Bahamas. With only one of the aircraft being used each day, with a second on standby at Fort Lauderdale, the G-73T fleet was only achieving 150 hours a month by early 1990.

CHALK'S
SALES TIPS AND INFORMATION

LEAVING FROM NASSAU

1. Free 24 hour parking within 50 feet of Chalk's terminal on Paradise Island, Nassau.

2. Five flights daily to Miami:
   a) Two direct non-stop flights
   b) Three flights to Miami stopping in Bimini.

3. Three non-stop direct flights to Bimini.

4. While in Nassau, take advantage of Chalk's 8:30 a.m. flight to Bimini and enjoy the world-famous, big game fishing resort island for the day. Return to Nassau 2:00 P.M. same day.

LEAVING FOR MIAMI

1. Free 24 hour parking within 50 feet of Chalk's terminal on Watson Island just off the MacArthur causeway in downtown Miami.

2.* Five flights daily to Paradise Island:
   a) Two non-stop flights
   b) Three flights to Paradise Island stopping over in Bimini.

3. Nine non-stop direct flights to Bimini.

4. Two convenient non-stop flights to Cat Cay.

ADDITIONAL CONVENIENCES

- All Chalk's terminals have their own customs and immigration.

- All flights are during daylight hours.

- All flights are non-stop unless otherwise indicated.

- Chalk's Charter flights are available at $600.00 an hour. In Miami call 377-8801. On Paradise Island, Bimini and Cat Cay, see terminal agent.

* Before returning to Miami or before landing on Paradise Island, whether east or west bound, for only $22.50 stop over in Bimini, world famous big game fishing resort. Stay for a few hours or for a few days -the fare remains the same.

FLIGHT SCHEDULE
Effective April 27, 1980

EASTBOUND

FROM	TO	FLIGHT		Departure	Arrival
Miami	Bimini	111	T	07:00 am	07:20 am
Miami	Bimini	501		08:30 am	09:00 am
Miami	Bimini	101		10:30 am	11:00 am
Miami	Bimini	505		11:00 am	11:30 am
Miami	Bimini	503		02:15 pm	02:45 pm
Miami	Bimini	115	T	01:30 pm	01:50 pm
Miami	Bimini	103	T	04:30 pm	04:50 pm
Miami	Bimini	117		05:30 pm	06:00 pm
Miami	Bimini	105		03:00 pm	03:30 pm
Miami	Cat Cay	403	FSS	09:00 am	09:30 am
Miami	Cat Cay	401	T	03:00 pm	03:20 pm
Miami	Nassau	501/301·		08:30 am	10:30 am
Miami	Nassau	211	T	09:00 am	10:00 am
Miami	Nassau	505/305·		11:00 am	01:00 pm
Miami	Nassau	503/303·		02:15 pm	04:15 pm
Miami	Nassau	203		05:15 pm	06:30 pm
Bimini	Nassau	301		09:30 am	10:30 am
Bimini	Nassau	305		12:00 pm	01:00 pm
Bimini	Nassau	303		03:15 pm	03:45 pm

WESTBOUND

Bimini	Miami	112	T	08:00 am	08:20 am
Bimini	Miami	102		11:30 am	12:00 pm
Bimini	Miami	504	T	12:00 pm	12:20 pm
Bimini	Miami	502		02:00 pm	02:30 pm
Bimini	Miami	116	T	02:15 pm	02:35 pm
Bimini	Miami	500		03:15 pm	03:45 pm
Bimini	Miami	106		04:00 p.m.	04:30 pm
Bimini	Miami	104	T	05:15 pm	05:35 pm
Bimini	Miami	118		06:30 pm	07:00 pm
Cat Cay	Miami	404	FSS	10:00 am	10:30 am
Cat Cay	Miami	402	T	03:45 pm	04:05 pm
Nassau	Miami	202		08:30 am	09:15 am
Nassau	Miami	304/504·	T	10:45 am	12:20 pm
Nassau	Miami	302/502·		12:30 pm	02:30 pm
Nassau	Miami	300/500		01:45 pm	03:45 pm
Nassau	Miami	204		05:15 pm	06:30 pm
Nassau	Bimini	304	T	10:45 am	11:30 pm
Nassau	Bimini	302		12:30 pm	01:30 pm
Nassau	Bimini	300		01:45 pm	02:45 pm

FSS| Flight 403 from Miami to Cat Cay, and flight 404 from Cat Cay to Miami operates on Fri, Sat, and Sunday only.

NOTE: Miami Eastern Savings Time

* Stop over in Bimini   T Turbo-Prop

route from Fort Lauderdale to Walker's Cay, in the Bahamian Abaco chain, previously operated by *Walker's International*. However, by 1995 only three G-73Ts were in service and the only scheduled route was from Watson Island to Bimini and Paradise Island with an extension to/from Fort Lauderdale-Hollywood International only for passengers travelling from or to the Bahamas.

The consortium, led by Miami businessman Charles Cobb, that was in the process of resurrecting *Pan American World Airways* decided in 1996 to buy Chalk's with the idea that it would eventually act as a feeder line to the projected Pan Am services from Miami. Two G-73Ts were repainted with the new name of "*Pan Am Air Bridge*".

Flying Boat Inc, which had been retained by Atwood, was bought by *Thor Tjonveit*, a Norwegian living in Irving, TX, and five G-73Ts were registered to his *World Pacific Air Lease* operation in January 1998.

In February 1998 the new Pan-Am filed for Chapter 11 bankruptcy protection followed in January 1999 by Flying Boat Inc, who filed similarly. In August 1999 *James Confalone* bought the assets of Flying Boat Inc from the court and on 17th December 1999 he changed the name of the operation to *Chalk's Ocean Airways*. Of the six G-73Ts on strength only two were operational. To bring the others to service Confalone bought *Dean H Franklin Enterprises Inc* of Miami, which had the largest inventory of Grumman amphibian spares in the world. Confalone retained the Mallard spares and sold the rest to *Antilles Seaplanes Inc*. With two G-73Ts in service and the others being repaired, Confalone even thought of converting the stored Albatrosses to turbine power but the terrorist attacks of 11th September 2001 created a severe downturn in traffic and thoughts of expansion were shelved. The crash of G-73T J-27 with the loss of all on board on 19th December 2005, sadly recorded the first passenger fatalities in

Chalk's long history, and the Mallard fleet was grounded by the FAA pending NTSB investigations.

The workforce was cut from 87 to 18, and a Beech 1900D was leased from Big Sky Airlines in Montana. Services were flown from Fort Lauderdale-Hollywood International Airport to Bimini and Nassau on Mondays, Thursdays, Fridays and Sundays from 8th August 2006. The Beech 1900D was replaced by Saab 340As during 2006 and other types were wet leased as necessary.

However, when Chalk's had not flown out of Fort Lauderdale since 3rd September 2007, the US Department of Transportation revoked its operating licence on 30th September 2007, on the grounds that it had neither re-certificated the Mallards nor bought replacement aircraft.

In late February 2009, a spokesman for Chalk's stated that "their Part 135 Certificate was still technically in effect, and the corporation had not gone into bankruptcy". Attempts were being made to get funding to re-start operations.

Two G-73Ts, c/ns J-30 and J-36, were in the hangar at Fort Lauderdale with wings removed, to facilitate work on the centre sections, while N142PA, c/n J-42, was stored outside on the ramp, essentially complete.

J-36 and J-42 were not made airworthy

and cancelled from the US register in 2010, but J-30 was sold and is currently flying with an owner in Delaware.

**CHALK'S INTERNATIONAL AIRLINES
CHALK'S OCEAN AIRWAYS**
- see *Chalk's Flying Service* above

CHAMCOOK AIRWAYS Ltd,
Montreal, QC
1235
G Blair Gordon, President. Aircraft based at Dorval.

CHAMPION PAPERS - see *US Plywood*

CHAMPLAIN ENTERPRISES Inc,
Miami, FL
J-13

CHANDLER, Dr Robert H,
Downers Grove, IL
1323

CHANDLER-EVANS Corp,
South Meriden, CT
1231
Charles W Deeds, President.

CHANNEL FLYING Inc, Juneau, AK
B-8, B-52
Ken Loken, President. Founded in 1954, Channel Flying bought the former *Alaska*

Chalk's Ocean Airways operated G-73T Turbo Mallard N130FB (c/n J-30) from 2000 until 2005, when the Mallard fleet was grounded. *(Fred J Knight Collection)*

Channel Flying's G-21A Goose N37487 (c/n B-52) seen at Juneau, Alaska in October 1982. The aircraft was previously Alaska Coastal Airlines' second Turbo Goose conversion, but was returned to piston power in 1980. *(Ueli Klee)*

Grumman Mallard (N2990) taking off at Leeville, La.

HOT, REDLINE TAKEOFFS! BUT ENGINES STAY SLUDGE-FREE WITH RPM AVIATION OIL

Hot engines form sludge, varnish; coke piston bottoms . . . but not with compounded "RPM!" These engines get hot! Manifold pressure and rpm are at top limits for the full allowable time because water traffic and dead-ends force short-run takeoffs at close to maximum allowable gross load.

Making it worse, there may be no head wind . . . or a 35 mph cross wind. Outside temperature may be 100° and river current 10 mph against the take-off.

Yet due to compounded "RPM", Carl Trippi (Chief Pilot of The California Company division of Chevron Oil Company) is 100% confident. "The other day, taking off on the Mississippi River, a submerged log suddenly appeared. It was close, but I was able to suck her out just in time!"

Further proof! Aviation Power Supply, Inc., Burbank, California, which has overhauled their radial engines for 10 years, gives this disassembly summary: All parts normal—operating satisfactorily.

The Chevron ABOVE ALL ...means service

Overhaul Report (T.S.O.: 912 Hours. T.T.: 3474 Hours)

Pratt & Whitney R1340-S1H1 (P328082) from Grumman G-73 (N2990). Nose Section: Normal—no sludge build up noted. Power Section: no sludge build up noted. Blower Section: Normal—no sludge build up noted. Cylinders: Normal—no sludge build up noted.

We take better care of your PLANE

The Chatham Manufacturing Company operated Mallard N2968 (c/n J-25) in the 1950s, and it is seen here at San Francisco, California, circa 1951.   (Lee Stoller via Jennifer Gradidge)

Airlines Turbo Goose (B-52) from *Viking Air,* after they had converted it back to P&W R-985 power in 1980. The G-21As were sold in 1987/88.

CHAOS CONSULTING UNLIMITED, Anchorage, AK
1415
Co-owner with *Garrett Carter* dba *Tri-Negro of Alaska.*

CHARLIE ALLEN FLYING SERVICE, Anchorage, AK
1380

CHATHAM MANUFACTURING Co, Elkin, NC
J-25

CHEER, Omar H Jr, New Orleans, LA
dba Air Transport Corp.
1398

CHELSEA HOLDINGS Ltd, Montreal, QC
1447

CHEMICAL EXPRESS Inc, Dallas, TX
J-5
Chemical Express Inc was the owner of the *Club de Pesca de Panamá,* a well-known marlin fishing organization.

CHEROKEE AIRWAYS Inc, St Paul, MN
1448

CHEVRON OIL Co, California Division
B-125, J-57

Left: A 1965 advert for Chevron Oil featuring the company's own Mallard, N2990, taking off at Leeville, LA. The advert is also remarkable in that it reports the Total Flying Hours (TFH) for the aircraft.

Chibougama Express Ltée operated G-44 Widgeon CF-PNT (c/n 1334) seen here at Toronto, Ontario, on 20th January 1969. The legend "Hamel" on the tail-fin refers to Alfred Hamel, the company president.   *(W Haines Collection)*

CHEVRON USA Inc, New Orleans, LA
1437, J-57

CHIBOUGAMA EXPRESS Ltée,
St Félicien, QC
1334
Alfred Hamel, President. Operated the G-44 from 1961 until 1968.

CHICAGO STEEL SERVICE Co,
Chicago, IL
J-53
Later known as *House of Stainless Inc.*

CHICAGO TRIBUNE, The, Chicago, IL
1005, 1060
Colonel Robert McCormick ran the Chicago Tribune newspaper, which had been started by his grandfather Joseph Medill for 45 years. To counteract the shortage of newsprint, McCormick built a paper mill at Thorold, Ontario, Canada and formed the *Ontario Paper Company* to operate it. Meanwhile McCormick's cousin Joseph Patterson started the *New York Daily News* and in the 1920s McCormick bought more land on the north shore of the St Lawrence river to satisfy the ever-growing demand for newsprint. The Grummans were used to commute between Chicago and the mills at Thorold and Baie Comeau. Goose 1060 replaced 1005 which was damaged in an accident in August 1939.

CHMURA, Warren F, (Trustee),
Norwich, UK
1317
By 1996 Chmura was dba Southern Trust, St Just, UK.

CHOQUETTE, Paul D, Homer, AK
1130
dba *Inlet Airways* which became *Inlet Airlines Inc* in September 1959.

CHRISTENSEN AIR SERVICE,
Anchorage, AK
1305
Hakon Christensen, President. When Christensen died in 1956, the G-44 was sold as part of his estate, and the registration N79906 was transferred to c/n 1327, with *Sea Airmotive Inc*. The company was acquired by *Cordova Airlines Inc*.

CHRISTENSEN, Dall L, Long Beach, CA
1141
Although only c/n 1141 was registered to him, and later went to Shell Ecuador, Christensen also prepared G-21As c/ns 1146 and 1148 which went to Argentina in 1947.

CHRISTIAN DIOR (New York) Inc,
New York, NY
J-26
Christian Dior's high-fashion business was developed with the help of *Marcel Boussac*, the textile manufacturer. The company bought the G-73 in 1950, and although registered to Christian Dior (NY) Inc, it was based at Toussus-le-Noble, near Paris, France, and operated by Marcel Boussac. Dior often flew the Aga Khan and other horse-racing luminaries into Croydon Airport for the Epsom Derby or Ascot Week. When Dior died suddenly in 1957 Boussac continued to use J-26 until 1966, often visiting Goodwood races (via Gatwick or Eastleigh). The G-73 had spent a lot of time on the ground, however, accruing only 1,659hrs flying time by 1964. Curiously, the aircraft used the early post-war US radio call-sign "*WMHEZ*".

CHRISTIASON, MG, Minneapolis, MN
16

CHRYSLER, James W, Seattle, WA
dba Chrysler Air / Seattle Seaplanes.
1051

CHURUTON, Benjamin L,
c/o Frost Box, Pawtucket, RI
1307

CINCINNATI AIR TAXI Inc,
Cincinnati, OH
16
Based at Hangar #6, Lunken A/P. *Thomas H Noonan*, President, for whom the aircraft was registered before it was sold to another of his companies – *Amphibious Sales Co.*

G-21A NC16914 (c/n 1005) was delivered to Colonel Robert McCormick of the Chicago Tribune newspaper in October 1937. The aircraft is seen here, possibly at Glendale, California. It later served with the Royal Canadian Air Force, before going to Shell Oil in Ecuador.

(Art Krieger Collection)

Christian Dior's Mallard N2966 (c/n J-26) was a frequent visitor to the United Kingdom in the 1950s, and is seen here at Blackbushe in October 1956.   *(Jennifer Gradidge)*

CINEMA AIR, Carlsbad, CA
B-126
A superb collection of warbirds which is housed at the Carlsbad Airport, four miles east of the town includes this G-21A.

CIRCLE Inc, Harvey, LA
1361

CIRCLE BAR DRILLING Co,
New Orleans, LA
1281

CITIES SERVICES Corp, New York, NY
1235
The aircraft operating arm of *Swiflite Corp* which has used many corporate aircraft, including Grumman Gulfstreams.

CITY ELECTRIC of ANCHORAGE Inc,
Anchorage, AK
1371
Later became *Associated Services Inc* at the same address and with the same President: RC Sweezey.

CIVIL AERONAUTICS ADMINISTRATION, Washington, DC
B-110, B-129, B-133, 1303
Originally known as the Civil Aeronautics Authority and later the Civil Aviation Administration before becoming the Federal Aviation Agency (FAA) on 1st January 1959. The G-21As were used in Alaska. The G-44 was based in Juneau, Alaska from 1949 until 1952, when it was assigned to the Aeronautical Center in Oklahoma City, to be used for seaplane training.

CLACKAMAS LOGGING Co,
Portland, OR
1337

CLAIR, Wallace, New York, NY
1297
The former US Navy J4F-2, c/n 1297, was sold surplus and registered to Wallace as G-44 NC79801 in 1946. It is believed that it was en route from Cairo, where it had been stricken by the US Navy, to the USA when it was evaluated by the French Navy at Centre d'Essais en Vol (CEV), at Istres in early 1947. It was flown from the Étang de

Mullard IIP 383 (c/n J-5) operated by the Club de Pesca de Panama, who provided the "world's finest Marlin fishing", according to the legend on the aircraft. The aircraft is seen here, possibly in Miami, Florida, in 1963. *(Art Krieger Collection)*

Operated by Coast Air, G-21A Goose N2751A (c/n 1184) is seen here at Victoria, British Columbia, on 16th September 1975. Coast Air's operational base is shown by the "Ketchikan, AK" logo under the cockpit window. *(John P Stewart via PJ Marson)*

Berre by a naval pilot between the 5th and the 11th February 1947. The aircraft crashed at Berre and was abandoned by the American owner, sold to *SCAN* 15th July 1947 and rebuilt.

CLAIRE AVIATION, Wilmington, DE
1228
Thomas J Duffy, President. The aircraft disappeared from FAA records between July and October 2010, reason unknown.

CLARK AUTO
1458

CLARK, Walter G, Co, Charleston, WV
1228
Walter Gerald Clark bought the aircraft on 23rd May 1950 and sold it the next day.

CLASSIC RESTORATIONS Inc,
Wilmington, DE
1051

CLASSIC WINGS Inc, Coraopolis, PA
B-76, 1270

CLEWIS, AC, Jr, Tampa, FL
B-100
Clewis was president of *American-Bahamian Air Service Inc*.

CLOT, Oscar A, Miami, FL
1381

CLUB de PESCA de PANAMA,
Bay of Penas, Panama
J-5
A Division of *Chemical Express Inc* of Dallas, TX which operated the G-73 from 1963 to 1966, and although nominally based at Tucumen International Airport, it was docked at the club's remote fishing enclave in Penas Bay on the Pacific coast of Darien province. According to the legend painted on the aircraft the club provided the "World's Finest Marlin Fishing".

COAST AIR Inc,
Ketchikan, AK
1184 and one other
Coast Air was formed as Simpson Air Service in 1947. Two G-21As were obtained from *Alaska Airlines* to provide seasonal passenger, freight and mail services to Klawock, Craig and Hydaburg, but only one has been identified.

The Civil Aeronautics Administration's only G-44 Widgeon (c/n 1303) registered as N99, and seen here in 1959 in California, shortly before the Administration was re-named the Federal Aviation Agency. *(Douglas D Olson via Jennifer Gradidge)*

COASTAL AERO, Houston, TX
1200

COASTAL AIR Inc, Miami, FL
B-84, 1274, 1340, 1468, J-3
Dean H Franklin, Vice-President.

COASTAL AVIATION, Orlando, FL
Certificated by the FAA on 10th October 1964 & operated Grummans (identities unknown) on a route network from Orlando-Tallahassee-Tampa-Nassau. It is not known whether this company was affiliated to *Coastal Aviation Company Inc* of West Trenton, New Jersey (see below).

COASTAL AVIATION Co Inc,
West Trenton, NJ
J-28, J-43
Originally known as Coastal Cargo, Coastal Aviation Co was a non-scheduled carrier based at Mercer County Airport and licensed by the CAB to operate G-73s on regular or irregular services between 1963 and 1969. In 1967 the company changed its name to Coastal Air Lines Inc, and in 1968 it was operating scheduled services from Herndon Airport, Orlando, Florida to the Bahamas. Robert J Anderson was president of Coastal Aviation Co, while Charles R Baird was president of Coastal Air Lines. The aircraft were re-possessed by the National Community Bank, Rutherford, NJ in September 1969 and sold.

COBAS, Washington Martinez,
Montevideo,Uruguay, dba *Aero Punta.*
1342

COCKRELL, Ernest C, Jr, Houston, TX
9

COFFEY, Harry K, Portland, OR
1173

COFFEY, Thomas A,
c/o American Express Co, New York, NY
1317
Coffey was President of *Onal Air Transport Corp.*

COFFIN, Dexter D, Jr, Palm Beach, FL
dba *Palm Beach Yacht Sales.*
16

COFFIN, WH, Los Angeles, CA
1346
dba WH Coffin Air Service at Vail Field Airport, in Los Angeles.

COGUENHEM, Paul E, New Orleans, LA
1133
Coguenhem was the President of *Comor Inc.*

COKER AIR TRANSPORT Ltd,
Anchorage, AK
1267
Donald A Coker, President. The G-44 was registered initially to DA & Taeko W Coker in July 1982 but transferred to company ownership in November 1985.

COLLAR, Charles S, Nassau, Bahamas
dba *Bahamas Airways.*
1162, 1208

COLLINS AIR SERVICE,
Anchorage, AK
1338
Grenold Collins, partner.

COLLINS BROTHERS Corp,
Las Vegas, NV
B-100
The G-21A was operated by *Sport Aero Co* of Las Vegas in the early 1980s.

COLLINS BROTHERS Inc,
Mechanicville, NY
1210

COLUMBIA UNIVERSITY,
New York, NY
1188
Division of War Research, based at LaGuardia Field. Used by the University's Airborne Instrument Laboratory in magnetic anomaly detection projects (anti-submarine operations) conducted on behalf of the National Defense Research Committee. The G-21A also ferried scientific personnel and apparatus between commercial, Army and Navy airfields.

COMBS AIRCRAFT Inc, Denver, CO
J-5
Based at Stapleton Intl Airport, Denver.

COMMANDAIR Inc, White Plains, NY
1236
Based at Hangar D, Westchester County Airport, NY.

COMMANDER AVIATION Ltd,
Montreal, QC and Toronto, ON
1235, 1312, 1431, 1473
DG Seagrove, President. Aircraft sales agent.

COMMERCIAL BARGE LINES Inc,
Houston, TX
1370

COMMERCIAL CENTERS Inc,
Los Angeles, CA
J-52

COMMERCIAL PETROLEUM & TRANSPORT Co, Houston, TX
(previously *Butcher-Arthur Inc*)
1370

COMMERCIAL TRANSPORT Corp,
Houston, TX
1370

COMMONWEALTH AVIATION Corp,
Port Orange, FL
1324

COMMONWEALTH PETROLEUM Co,
Chicago, IL
1329
RB Danley, President.

COMMUTE AIR Inc, Kalispell, MT
1371
The G-44 was based at Flathead County Airport, Kalispell, but was re-possessed in July 1969 due to the breach of a financing agreement.

COMOR Inc, New Orleans, LA
1130, 1133, B-139, B-140, 1214
Paul E Coguenhem, President. Comor operated a charter / leasing service out of New Orleans. An Experimental Certificate of Airworthiness (CofA) was granted for B-140, to test a modified extended wing tip, wing float and aileron configuration in March 1962. Another Experimental CofA in July 1962 allowed tests on retractable wing floats. All G-21As were also registered at various times to affiliated company *Pan-Air Corporation.*

COMPTON, Charles E, Chicago, IL
1398

COMPTON, Steven J & Karen M,
Anchorage, AK
1378

CONAIR Corp, Montreal, QC
2-4, 9-13, 15,16, 20-23, 25, 31-34, 37
It appears that all the above SCAN-built Widgeons were owned by Conair circa 1954, but a letter from the Canadian DoT to the FAA in Washington, dated 12th March 1959, confirms that none of the aircraft were ever registered in Canada. Indeed, because a number of them were exported by sea from France bound for California, it is doubtful whether the airframes were ever physically in Canada.

CONANT, Raymond A, Whitehorse, YK
26
Conant owned the SCAN-30 for two months before crashing it into Tincup Lake,YK, where it sank in several hundred feet of water. Salvaged to the USA.

CONDOR AVIATION
- see *William E Harrison*

CONFALONE, James Jr, Rye Beach, NH
J-32
James Confalone was a pilot for Eastern Airlines for 26 years, had many business interests and owned his own aircraft. He bought *Chalk's* for $925,000 and in August 1999 he bailed *Flying Boat Inc* out of the bankruptcy court. On 17th December 1999 he changed the name to *Chalk's Ocean Airways* and then bought out *Dean Franklin Aviation Enterprises Inc,* to ensure a good inventory of spares for the Mallards. By 2005 he was doing good business with the Turbo Mallards, but unfortunately, on 19th December 2005 the crash of J-27 with the loss of all on board caused the grounding of the Mallard fleet.

CONKLIN, EJ, AVIATION Corp,
Richmond, VA
1345
Based at Byrd Airport, Richmond.

CONN-AIR Inc, Danbury, CT
1378

CONROY, James F, Long Beach, CA
1388, 1430
dba Long Beach Airmotive. Conroy bought the salvage rights to the G-44A in 1946, and co-owned the G-44 with *Lee Mansdorf* in the mid-1950s.

CONROY, John F, Van Nuys, CA
(co-owner)
B-101, 1388
Founder of Conroy Aircraft Corp and Aero Spacelines, owned and later co-owned the G-44 in the 1960s. The registration N404Q was on a Boeing 377 but was transferred to the G-44 on 1st March 1967. Conroy Aircraft Corp was later instrumental in the development of the Turbo Albatross.

CONROY, John M, Goleta, CA
1388

CONRY, Edward R, Minneapolis, MN
1390

CONSOLIDATED COSMETICS Inc, Chicago, IL
1160

CONTINENTAL AVIATION Co, Tulsa, OK
16
Stan Burnstein, owner.

CONTINENTAL CAN Co of CANADA Ltd, Thorold, ON
J-2
Owned a 10% share in the G-73 from May 1973 until April 1997 by which time the company had become Continental Group of Canada Ltd, then Continental Can Canada Inc, and finally *Crown Cork & Seal Canada Inc.*

CONTINENTAL OIL Co, Houston, TX
1328
Conoco is a multi-national oil company that has operated many aircraft types for personnel transportation and oil support operations.

CONTRACT CARTAGE Co
- see *Motorcar Transport Co*

COOK, William H, Jr, Mercer Island, WA
1365
Shared the ownership of the G-44 with *Richard L Rouzie* from 1951 until 1971, then becoming sole owner with an address in Bellevue, WA.

COOK, Wyatt F, Wilson, WY
1445

COOKE, J (Concrete Blocks) Ltd, Aldershot, ON
1423
The aircraft was based at Hamilton, ON from 1955 until 1963.

COOL, Leon D, Rockville, MD
1329

COOPER, Douglas O & Kathleen E, Anchorage, AK
1267

COOPERS & LYBRAND Ltd, Vancouver, BC
Acted as Receivers for *Trans Provincial Airlines.*

COPANO OIL Co, Victoria, TX
J-53

CORAL SEA AIRWAYS Pty Ltd, Mena, AR
32

CORAL WINGS, Cairns, QLD
1466
Owner/pilot John Jones operated charters, mainly ferrying crews and supplies to prawn fishing boats in remote areas off the Queensland coast.

CORDOVA AIRLINES Inc, Anchorage, AK
1325, 1327, 1346, 1355, 1369
Merle K Smith, President. Acquired Christensen Air Service in March 1956 and operated mail, passenger and freight services out of Anchorage to the Cordova and Seward area, and up to Fairbanks. By April 1965 services were being flown from Anchorage to Cordova, Seward, Homer, Dawson City and Yakutat.

CORDOVA AIR SERVICES, Anchorage, AK
1020
The company began operations in 1934 and was renamed *Cordova Airlines Inc* in February 1956 (see above).

Above: *G-44A Widgeon CF-FCH (c/n 1423) at Mount Hope, Ontario in May 1962, with the J Cooke Concrete Blocks Ltd company logo on the forward fuselage.* (Jack McNulty via Jennifer Gradidge)

Below: *Cordova Airlines Inc operated G-44 Widgeon N67586 (c/n 1346). The aircraft is seen here at Oakland, California in 1955, after McKinnon conversion to Lycoming power.*
(Douglas D Olson via Jennifer Gradidge)

Lorne Corley's much-travelled but low-time McKinnon Super SCAN Widgeon CF-ODR (c/n 28) is seen here at Toronto Island Airport on 3rd September 1977. Countries visited are denoted by flags on the tail-fin. The aircraft is now displayed at Mount Hope, Ontario. *(KM Molson)*

history of aviation on Long Island. Dade, a lifelong aviation enthusiast, developed a method of securely transporting wrecked aircraft, and with his brother Bob, perfected a bi-axial support system which prevented airframes from twisting during transport.

During WWII the Dade brothers grossed more than $50 million, packing and shipping some 33,000 aircraft, including some Grummans, overseas. Dade died in 1996 aged 85, but left the museum as a legacy for future generations. The Goose, 1051, was reported stored here in 1992 but was sold and subsequently crashed. Another Goose was acquired in 1993 and is currently displayed in Pan American Airways colours.

CORLEY, Lorne Francis, Islington, ON
28
Owned the SCAN-30, based at Toronto Island Airport, from 1969 until selling it to the Canadian Warplane Heritage in 2001, at a low total flying time of only 4,402.6hrs.

CORMACK AIRCRAFT SERVICE Ltd, Glasgow, Scotland
B-86
George Cormack planned to operate tourist flights over the Scottish moors in 1992. Acquisition of the aircraft was allegedly unsuccessful because of Scottish bureaucracy, and the G-21A did not leave Alaska.

CORPORATION ARCHIEPISCOPALE CATHOLIQUE ROMANE de ST BONIFACE,
St Boniface, MB
B-111
Monseigneur Baudaux Maurice, President. The G-21A was operated in Peru by Father AL Bedard on behalf of a group of Canadian Franciscans who ran schools and missions in the jungle.

COSMOPOLITAN BROADCASTING Corp,
New York, NY
aka *Seaplane Shuttle Transport Inc.*
1153

COTARIU, Alan R, Los Angeles, CA
1394
According to the Bill of Sale from the *Foreign Liquidation Commission*, Cotariu was an Ensign based at MAB Guam, in the Marianas Islands when he purchased the J4F-2 for $5,250 in April 1947.

COTE, Elmer L, Newport Beach, CA
(co-owner)
1165

COULON, Charlotte, Pantin, France
19

COULSON HELICOPTERS Ltd,
Port Alberni, BC
1045

The Dade brothers, George and Bob, developed a method of securely transporting wrecked aircraft and perfected a bi-axial support system which prevented airframes from twisting during transport. Here a J4F-1 is being crated for delivery to the US Navy. George Dade leaves as his legacy, the Cradle of Aviation Museum in Garden City, NY which he set up in the early 1980s. *(Fred J Knight Collection)*

COUNTRY CLUB FLYING SERVICES Inc,
Hicksville, Long Island, NY
1216

COURIER TRADING & ENTERPRISES Ltd, Winnipeg, MB
B-98, J-19
Peter M Lazarenko, President. Reportedly used the G-21A to carry cargoes of fish in 1969. The G-73 was transferred to *Northland Fisheries Ltd*, another of Lazarenko's companies.

COYLE, Patrick J, Orange Park, FL,
and at Clymont, DE
dba *Aqua Air LLC*, Wilmington, DE
1337, 1445

COZAD, Michael L, Las Vegas, NV
1311

CRADLE OF AVIATION MUSEUM,
Garden City, NY
1051
The museum was set up in the early 1980s by George C Dade and others to display the

CRANE ENGINEERING Corp,
Greendale, WI
1383
- see *Milwaukee Crane & Service Co.*

CREATURE ENTERPRISES Inc,
Bridgehampton, NY
31
Richard D Bach, President. The G-44 was used in the TV series 'Fantasy Island'.

CREEFT, William J de,
Montclair, CA,
and later at Carpinteria, CA
B-14

CRESCENT HOLDINGS Inc,
Harvey, LA
1455

CRILE, Vaughn W, Washington, PA
31
Crile was President of aircraft dealer *Red Carpet Helicopters Inc.*

CROSBY, James
- see *Resorts International Inc*

CROSLEY, Powel, Jr, Sharonville, OH
1002, 1007, J-7
The President of Crosley Radio Corp, Cincinnati, OH was an aviation entre-preneur who had sponsored many of the flights made by the American aviatrix, Ruth Nichols during 1930/31. Crosley took delivery of 1007 on 2nd November 1937 and named it "*Lesago*". The G-21A was sold to the RCAF in 1941 but after the war he bought the former RCAF Goose (1002) before taking delivery of the G-73 in December 1946 to commute between his business interests and his beach home in Sarasota, FL. The Mallard was sold in Canada in 1954.

CROSSLANDS Inc, Wilmington, DE
1457

CROTHERS Ltd, Geo W,
Leaside & Toronto, ON
B-76, J-19
James F Crothers, President. The aircraft were based at Toronto-Malton and carried the "personalised" registration, CF-*JFC*.

CROW Inc, Toledo, OH
J-13, J-32, J-42, J-44, J-45, J-58
Crow Inc was owned by Walter R Crow & *Tony Barnum*. They operated a distributorship for Piper aircraft, Piaggio Royal Gull and Aero Commander, and flew charters for fishermen and huntsmen. Their first Mallard (J-42) was purchased in 1965 and the fishing charters to Canada increased. J-13 was purchased from *Air Pacific Ltd* in Fiji. The aircraft had ended up in the jungle 500 feet off the end of a runway and had been left there to rot. Offered for sale "as-is" together with 45 boxes of spares for US$50,000, Tony Barnum managed to buy the lot for US$35,000. There was no major damage to the aircraft and it only needed a new starboard engine.

This was duly fitted at Suva Airport by Barnum and Crow's service manager, Bill Tanner. The job of getting the Mallard airworthy took six weeks and in November 1971 the delivery flight across the Pacific to the USA began. The route was via Funafuti in the Ellice Islands, Tarawa, Johnston Island, Honolulu, Hilo and then, after a take-off at 17,000lbs all-up weight, a 16-hour flight to Hayward Field, east of San Francisco. Once in Toledo, J-13 was given a thorough overhaul and a new paint scheme to match J-42. The spares arrived by ship some eighteen months later! J-13 was sold to *Pelican Seaplanes Inc* in Fort Lauderdale, FL in December 1973. The post-crash remains of J-45 and J-58 were purchased for spares.

CROWLEY LAUNCH & BARGE Corp,
San Francisco, CA
dba *Puget United Transportation Companies.*
J-21

CROWN CONTROLS,
New Bremen, OH
J-56
A forklift truck manufacturer which used a variety of aircraft for corporate transportation.

CROWN CORK & SEAL CANADA Inc,
Toronto, ON
J-2
Formerly known as *Continental Can Co of Canada,* and owned a 10% share in the G-73 until April 1997.

CROWN FOREST INDUSTRIES
B-76
Became **CROWN ZELLERBACH CANADA Ltd**,
Vancouver, BC
FN Youngman, President.

CRUISES & TRAFFIC SALES Ltd,
Mount Hope, ON
B-39
Canada Coach Lines drew up a Bill of Sale for the G-21A but the sale did not go through. Although Mary Doyle, the Treasurer of Cruises & Traffic Sales Ltd, gave her address as Hamilton, ON, the company was not registered in Hamilton. However, when the aircraft was eventually sold to *The Diamond Match Co* in May 1951 the seller was Cruises & Traffic Sales Ltd!

CRYSTAL TRANSIT Co, Buffalo, NY
- see *George C Hall*

C-TEC Ltd, St John, NB
B-101
A company set up to oversee the transfer of the G-21A from Canada to Croatia.

CUMMINGS, Veigh,
Boulder City, NV
1429

CUNNINGHAM, William,
Anchorage, AK
1260

CURREY FLYING SERVICE,
Galesburg, IL
1328

CURTIS, Robert E & SMITH, Hugh Z,
Anchorage, AK, dba *Goose Leasing.*
B-115

CUSACK, Mike, Anchorage, AK
B-86
Cusack used the G-21A for charters to his fishing lodge on the Alaska Peninsula but wintered the aircraft at Merrill Field, Anchorage.

CUSHNIR, David, New York, NY,
and later at Opa Locka, FL
B-29

CUTTRELLE, Frank W, Miami, FL
1130, 1214
Cuttrelle was president of *Air-Sea Charters Inc.*

Crow Incorporated operated Mallard N51151 (c/n J-42) seen here visiting Toronto Skyport on 21st July 1968. J-42 ended its days being grounded after the Chalk's accident in 2005 and was cancelled from the US register in 2010. (William Haines Collection)

DADE, George C
- see *Cradle of Aviation Museum*

DADE COUNTY BOARD OF PUBLIC INSTRUCTION AVIATION SCHOOL,
Miami, FL
1182
Otherwise known as FAA approved school #3460, which was the *George T Baker Aviation School.*

DAGENS NYHETER AB,
Stockholm, Sweden
1367
The Swedish newspaper publisher owned the G-44 between 1949 and 1958.

DALY, Vince, Kodiak, AK
1195
Daly operated a charter business in Kodiak using a Republic Seabee and the G-21A, the latter acquired from *Hardy Aviation Inc* and operated until 1962.

DAMICO, Samuel P, Pittsford, NY
1051, B-46, B-97, B-145
Damico bought the remains of 1051, which crashed in February 2005 and embarked on a re-build programme using parts from the other three G-21As.

DANAHER, Tom, Wichita Falls, TX
B-125, 1188
dba *Tom Danaher Autos.* Tom Danaher is an ex-US Navy fighter pilot credited with the last aerial kill in WWII in Okinawa. He was also a crop duster and sometime Hollywood stunt pilot. Unfortunately,

while on a visit to the Farnborough Air Show in 2010, Danaher was taken ill, and after hospitalisation in London, UK returned to Texas to recover.

DANKO, Bill, Opa Locka, FL
1439
Real estate investment broker, Bill Danko, purchased the G-44A from *Okeechobee Farms* in April 1962 and sold it to New Zealand in 1963.

DASATOUR TRAVEL AGENCY,
Lima, Peru
1051, 1053
According to Bills of Sale, a Mr Alexander of Dasatour Travel Agency acted as agent for the purchase of the G-21As from the Peruvian Air Force in July 1958.

DASILVA, Urbano M & Virginia G DaSilva,
Dexter, MI
B-52, 1467
Urbano ("Bill") DaSilva was an airline pilot who rebuilt Goose, Widgeon and Albatross aircraft.

DAVIDSON, Walter J, Sun Valley, CA
12, 16, 25
Ownership of c/n 12 was transferred in January 1959 from *Lee Mansdorf & Co* to Davidson, with *JG Spielman, Charles H Harris* and *Tom Katsuda* at the same address as the *Pacific Aircraft Engineering Corp (PACE).* C/ns 16 and 25 were transferred in the same way in March 1959. Ownership of c/n 12 then passed from the

four partners to PACE in February 1959 with c/n 16 following in March 1959, and c/n 25 in April 1959. Davidson was Secretary/Treasurer of PACE.

DAVIS, Connie M, Knightsen, CA
1371
Davis inherited the G-44 in 1999, after the death of *Robert L Nelson.*

The HB DAVIS Co, Baltimore, MD
1317

DAVIS, Peter Michael, Miami, FL
dba *Seagull Air Service.*
J-13

DAVISON, Endicott P, New Canaan, CT
1306

DB AERO Inc, Wilmington, DE
B-129

DEALERS TRANSPORT Co,
Chicago, IL
1385

DEAN CHANNEL FOREST PRODUCTS, Nanaimo, BC
B-45
RS Mayo, President. Owned the G-21A between May 1964 and April 1965, when it was sold to *BC Airlines.*

DEARBORN MOTORS Co, Detroit, MI
J-3

DEBIAN AVIATION Inc, Miami, FL
1359

DECATUR AVIATION Co, Decatur, IL
1214, 1239
Owned by *Hunter C Moody,* an aircraft dealer who bought war-surplus aircraft and converted them for civilian/executive use. He handled the G-44s during 1947.

DEEDS, Charles, W,
West Hartford,
and South Meriden, CT
1004, 1231, 1410
Charles Walton Deeds was a co-founder in 1926 of the Pratt & Whitney Aircraft Company which in 1928 became the engine division of the United Aircraft Corporation. Deeds used the Grummans as personal transports.

DEEDS, Edward A, Chester Springs, PA
1410
Edward Deeds had founded the Wright Aeroplane Company with Orville Wright and *Charles Kettering.* He used the G-44A as a personal transport in the early 1960s, but in 1964 it was sold to the *Baron Corporation* of New York City. Documents dated 1965 and 1966 give the owner as *Federal Airlines Inc* of New York City, but a Certificate of Registration was issued to *Northern Airways Inc*, with Edward A Deeds as President. The aircraft was used by his son, *Edward A Deeds II,* in the 1970s and it finally left the family in November 2006.

Dagens Nyheter operated G-44 Widgeon SE-APO (c/n 1367) out of Stockholm, Sweden in the early 1950s. Unfortunately, the aircraft suffered a fatal crash at Malmi, Finland on 18th November 1968.
(Fred J Knight Collection)

Vince Daly's G-21A Goose N69264 (c/n 1195) with the name "Anna M" on the bow at Kodiak, Alaska in the late 1940s. The owner's logo, "Vince Daly, Kodiak", appears on the upper rear fuselage.
(Fred J Knight Collection)

The John Deere Company operated G-44A Widgeon N41990 (c/n 1421) in the late 1940s with the company logo on the bow. Converted to Continental IO-470-D power by McDermott in 1963, it is currently flying with an owner in Missouri. (Art Krieger Collection)

DEEDS, Edward A, II, Charlotte, VT
1410
Son of the above.

DEEDS, Brigit W, Charlotte, VT
1410

DEERE & Co, John, Moline, IL
1421
The well-known agricultural machinery manufacturer, who has used many aircraft as corporate transports over the years, bought the G-44A in June 1945 and based it at Quad City Airport, Moline.

DEFENSE PLANT Corp, Seattle, WA
1141, 1233
The surplus JRF-6B was sold by the War Assets Administration to the Defense Plant Corp in October 1946.

DEFENSE SUPPLIES Corp,
Washington, DC
1015, 1206, 1232, 1233
Purchasing agent for the US War Department.

De HAVILLAND AIRCRAFT of CANADA Ltd, Downsview, Toronto, ON
B-76
Acted as agent for the sale of the G-21A from *Geo W Crothers Ltd* to *The British American Oil Co Ltd* in November 1948, with Stewart, Smith (Canada) Ltd acting as adjusters.

DE KROONDUIF,
Biak, Dutch New Guinea
J-13
Leased the G-73 from *Dutch New Guinea Petroleum Co (NNGPM)* from 25th October 1959 until 31st August 1960.

Flew the aircraft for NV Ost-Borneo Maatschappij during March 1960, but it was withdrawn from use and abandoned at Biak on 31st August 1960 where it remained until purchased by *Peter Ahrens* in 1962.

DEMOLA, Louis, Red Bank, NJ
1214
The proposed purchase of the G-44 from *A B C Services* in June 1966 was not completed.

DENHOLM, Warren,
Auckland, New Zealand
1466
Warren Denholm and his wife Shona formed Avspecs Ltd in 1997. The Widgeon was acquired from *Owen Harnish* in May 2012, the same year that the company provided parts for the restoration of a DH Mosquito being carried out by Mosquito Aircraft Restoration.

DENNIS, Reid W, Woodside, CA
J-8
Reid Dennis has the distinction of being the first person to circumnavigate the globe in a Grumman Albatross. Leaving Oakland, CA on 17th March 1997, N44RD accompanied a Lockheed 10 following Amelia Earhart's route, returning to Oakland on 29th May after a 26,347 nautical-mile adventure. Dennis also used the G-73 for less adventurous trips along the west coast of North America, from Lower California to Alaska.

DENNY, Leiann, Anchorage, AK
1464

DENNY, Robert O, Anchorage, AK
1239

DENT, RK, Seattle, WA
1383

DEPARTMENT OF INTERIOR
- see *US Government*

DEPARTMENT OF NATIONAL DEFENSE,
Ottawa, ON
The government agency for the purchase of aircraft for the Royal Canadian Air Force at the beginning of WWII (see Military Operators, Chapter 7).

DEPARTMENT OF PUBLIC INSTRUCTION,
Honolulu, HI
B-78

De SAVARY, Peter John, London, UK
dba *Blue Arrow Challenge*
B-120

De TEMPLE, Donald E,
Woodland Hills, CA
dba *Bonanza Airlines International*.
B-35

DETROIT SCHOOL OF AVIATION Inc,
Royal Oak, MI
1307

DEVCON CONSTRUCTION Inc,
Tualatin, OR
1059

DEVINE, George W, Corpus Christi, TX
1374

DEXTER AIRCRAFT SALES Inc,
Pebble Beach, CA
1364

DEYOREO, Silvio F,
Rochelle Park, NJ, and later at
Fort Worth & Bedford, TX
1293, 25
DeYoreo failed to return a Triennial Aircraft Registration Report for c/n 25 in July 1981 with the result that the FAA revoked the registration on 12th February 1982. Continued attempts at contact by the FAA were to no avail and letters were returned as "not at this address".

**DGAC –
Direção-Geral da Aeronautica Civil**,
Lisbon, Portugal
1241, 1242

G-44 Widgeon CS-AHE (c/n 1241) without floats at Dakar, Senegal in 1958, probably en route to Angola. The former Portuguese Air Force aircraft ended its days with Transportes Aereos de Cabo Verde as CR-CAF. (Roger Caratini via Jennifer Gradidge)

G-44 Widgeon CS-AHG (c/n 1242) is seen here withdrawn from use at Lisbon in July 1974. It is now displayed in the Museu de Marinha in Lisbon as '128'. (John Wegg)

G-44A Widgeon N444M (c/n 1411) at Biggin Hill, England after a rebuild which included the fitting of 260hp Lycoming engines acquired from Aero Commander G-ASJU.   *(Don Conway)*

After 1,030 hours of flying in Canada, G-21A (c/n B-39) was registered N60093 to the Diamond Match Company in December 1951. It is seen here at an unknown location sometime before September 1955 when it was sold to William J During of Fayetteville, NY.   *(R Stuckey)*

DHF REALTY Inc, Miami, FL
& Chicago, IL
1411
Michael Dunkerly, President, operated the G-44A from Biggin Hill, UK doing business as Shipping & Airlines Ltd.

DIAMOND CONSTRUCTION (1955) Ltd,
Fredericton, NB
1431
Burton D Colter, President.

DIAMOND DRILLING Co,
New Orleans, LA
1361, 1380, 1420
The oilfield exploration company crashed c/n 1361 circa 1970, and leased c/n 1380 from *McKinnon-Hickman Co* for about a year as a replacement, until c/n 1420 was put into service after it had been converted to Super Widgeon standard.

DIAMOND MATCH Co, The,
New York, NY
B-39
Howard M Leonard, Chief Pilot.

DIAMOND SERVICES W H T Corp,
Morgan City, LA
1420

DICKEY, Tod V, Phoenix, AZ
1270, 16

DICKRELL & SCHRAUFNAGEL,
Mason, WI
1324

DICKSON, Charles B, Cincinnati, OH
1375

DIEMERT, Robert E, Carman, MB
B-35
Obtained the G-21A from the USMC Museum, Quantico, VA in exchange for an A6M2 "Zero". Diemert had marks C-GOOS reserved but sold the aircraft to *James C McKinney* and the Canadian marks were not used.

DIESEL ACQUISITIONS LLC,
West Linn, OR
1059

DINCA Inc, Bear, DE
1084

DIONNE AUTOMOBILE Enrg,
Rimouski, QC
B-76
Elbert Dionne was also President of *Rimouski Airline* and his automobile company had acted as sales agent for the G-21A when it was purchased from *Kashower Air Service* in mid-1947 (the "Enrg" is an abbreviation of the French verb "Enregistrer", meaning "Registered" and indicates that the company was

more than a partnership but less than an incorporation.

DIOR, Christian
- see *Christian Dior*

DIXIE AIR LEASING LLC, Vichy, MO
1421

DIXON, David G & HILL, H Dan,
Santa Ana, CA
J-19, J-42
dba *Dixon/Hill Aircraft Leasing Co* which bought the remains of J-19 after the crash in 1979 before selling them to Chalk's for parts. J-42 was leased to *Trans Catalina Airlines*.

DIXON, Edward F, Frackville, PA
and Mt Carmel, PA
J-5, J-19
Dixon was the Pennsylvania businessman who bought *Chalk's International Airlines* from *Dean Franklin* in 1973. J-19 was based in Nassau, Bahamas. The US IRS however charged Dixon with tax evasion, which he admitted, and paid the bill by handing over J-19 as payment! He sold Chalk's soon afterwards to James Crosby of *Resorts International*, and the second G-73 went to *Visair* in the Bahamas in 1978.

DOCKERY, Joe R, Cleveland, MS
1455

DODERO, Alberto A,
Corrientes, Argentina
1432

DODGE, Earl 'Red', Anchorage, AK
B-112, 1378, 1423, J-36
A long-time Grumman operator, active in charter flying in Alaska for many years, Earl 'Red' Dodge died on 11th January 2004, aged 77.

DODSON, James L, Fairbanks, AK
1328
Dodson breached the financing agreement on the G-44. It was re-possessed by the *Key Bank of Alaska* on 14th December 1995, and was sold to *James E Carner* in July 1997.

DON L AIRCRAFT Inc, Delray Beach, FL
1457

DONAHUE, James Paul, New York, NY
1058

DONOGH, Stanley W, Bellevue, WA
1045

DONOHUE ACQUISITIONS Inc,
Montreal, QC
J-2
Gained the G-73 by merging with *QUNO Corp* to form Donohue QUNO Inc which later became Donohue Forest Products Inc.

DONOHUE FOREST PRODUCTS Inc
– see above

Tim Donut Ltd's G-44A CF-LGZ (c/n 1473) shortly after delivery at Mount Hope, Ontario on 11th April 1977. The Widgeon was sold to an American owner in 1986 and is currently flying with an owner in New Hampshire. (Jack McNulty)

DONUT, Tim, Ltd, Oakville, ON
1473
RV Joyce, President. The aircraft was based at Malton, ON until 1978, after which it was operated from Hamilton, ON.

DOUBLEDAY & Co Inc, Garden City, Long Island, NY
1404

DOWDLE, JW, Chula Vista, CA
1371, J-25
dba *Swift Air Service* and *Catalina-Vegas A/L*. Operated services between San Diego and Catalina Island from 1962 to 1966. The G-44 was based at Lindberg Field, San Diego, CA whilst the G-73 was registered with an address at San Diego, CA.

DOWLING, RE, Realty Corp,
New York, NY
1340
Robert W Dowling, President.

DRAPER MOTORS Corp, Detroit, MI
1431
The company was incorporated on 29th March 1943, with Dean A Draper as President. The G-44A was bought in January 1946.

DREEWES, James W & Linda M,
Snohomish, WA
1388

DRISCOLL, James Barnett, Wasilla, AK
1293

DUCHINI, Adolph, New York, NY
1352

DUKE, Roland N, Newport Beach, CA
(co-owner)
1165

DUKES, Robert L, Seattle, WA
1323
Acquired the G-44 with co-owner *John H Flynn* in September 1961. An un-dated, handwritten reply, presumably to a FAA request, stated "Mr Dukes no longer resident this address and I do not know where he can be reached. I do not know if he has the airplane in question at this time or not. (signed) Mrs Erma Jean Dukes". The FAA cancelled the registration on 25th May 1965.

DUNKERLY, Michael, Biggin Hill, UK
1411
dba *Shipping & Airlines Ltd* operated the aircraft for *DHF Realty Inc.*

DUPONT, F, dba T.......avon
Flying Service Inc, Easton, MD
1209
The full name of the Flying Service is unreadable in the FAA file.

DURING, William J, Fayetteville, NY
B-39

DUTCH NEW GUINEA MINING Co,
(MMNNG)
1008, 1009
Both aircraft were used in support of gold mining operations from 1937 until 1942. PK-AES (c/n 1008) is believed to have also operated for Shell affiliate *NNGPM* (below).

**DUTCH NEW GUINEA
PETROLEUM Co**, (NNGPM),
Babo, New Guinea
1056, 1057, J-13, J-17, J-35, J-37, J-41
The *Batavia Petroleum Co* (BPM) was the managing partner in a joint venture with the Dutch Colonial Petroleum Co and the Dutch Pacific Petroleum Co, formed in 1935 to explore for oil in Dutch New Guinea.
The G-21As were shipped to Soerabaya where they were re-assembled at the Dutch Navy Yard. They were then flown to Babo in New Guinea and were used to support oil

The Asiatic Petroleum Corp purchased G-21A Goose PK-AKB (c/n 1057) for NNGPM at Babo, Dutch New Guinea, seen here at one of the airports in the New York area on 15th August 1939.
(Carl F Lunghard via HC Kavelaars Collection)

NNGPM Mallard PK-AKU (c/n J-37) in the Steenkol River, Dutch New Guinea in February 1950. The aircraft's bow has turned downstream, while a company motor launch has arrived, with a rowing boat to transfer crew, passenger(s) and material from aircraft to launch. (HC Kavelaars)

exploration from 1937 until the Japanese advance in 1942. PK-AKA and AKB (c/ns 1056 and 1057) were both operated without wheels to improve cargo capacity. PK-AKA (c/n 1056) was reportedly leased to *KNILM* in November 1941. NNGPM moved their headquarters to Sorong, on Jef Man Island in 1946. The G-73s were delivered via Amsterdam in 1948 and were operated until 1960 in support of oil exploration for Shell Oil affiliates in the East Indies and New Guinea. J-41 was the most expensive Mallard to leave the factory, after modifications requested by Shell to the bow hatch, engine cowlings and radio equipment, elevated the price to $210,000. J-41 also encountered political problems with the delivery flight. India, Pakistan and Burma were restricting over-flights by Dutch-registered aircraft. This was circumvented by registering the Mallard as G-ALLJ to *Shell, London* (on the UK aircraft register) for the flight from Amsterdam to Batavia, and then reverting to the Dutch East Indies registration, PK-AKE on 25th April 1949. J-41 also suffered an unusual demise when, having been washed down with gasoline, it caught fire and was burned beyond repair on 27th January 1951. This happened in the hangar at Jakarta and thankfully airport personnel were able to pull PK-AKD from the hangar before it too was damaged. A former police pilot, Captain Sudaryono, began flying for Shell in December 1959 and his logbooks show regular flights, in both J-17 and J-35, from Balikpapan from August 1960 until 1963. The routine flights were to Sangga-Sangga, Kuaro, Samarinda, Tandjund and Tarakan. Capt Sudaryono also performed test-flights on the Mallards after they were transferred to the Indonesian Air & Water Police in 1963.

DUVAL, EJ, New Auburn, WI
1324

DWORAK, Frank, Stow, MA
B-86

DYER, Rex, Compton, CA
1231

DYNAIR Corp,
New Orleans, LA
1438
John L Freiberg, President. Freiberg was also president of *Trans Air Corp* and after transferring ownership of the G-44A from Trans Air to Dynair on 13th December 1965 transferred ownership to his own name on the same day. The aircraft was based at New Orleans-Lakefront Airport.

DYNAMIC AVIATION GROUP Inc,
Bridgewater, VA
27

EAST COAST AIRLINES,
Brisbane, QLD
J-13
East Coast Airlines was set up by *Peter Ahrens*, a Swede who emigrated to Australia

by flying his family there in a DH.89. Scheduled passenger services were planned from New South Wales coastal towns into Brisbane but Ahrens was never granted an airline licence from the Department of Civil Aviation. Ahrens bought the G-73 in 1962 and applied for registration VH-KWB, but this was never used and the aircraft flew in Australia with East Coast for more than six months as JZ-POB. After an emergency water-landing at Redland Bay, QLD on 16th July 1962 with the port undercarriage leg extended, the Australian certification was abandoned and the aircraft was offered for sale. The G-73 was purchased by *Trans Australia Airlines* in 1963.

EAST PAKISTAN FLYING CLUB
- see below

EAST PAKISTAN GOVERNMENT,
Dacca
B-78, 1354, 1471, 1474, 1476
The G-21C has been out of use for some years and not in good condition, but was reported to be in Dhaka in November 2010. The G-44 (c/n 1354) was operated by the East Pakistan Flying Club, set up by the government to promote interest in aviation among the country's young people. The G-44 crashed 24th January 1967, whilst the G-44A (c/n 1476) had been written-off in a crash in 1949 and the remaining two aircraft were part-exchanged (with c/n 1451) by the *Bangladesh Flying Club* for two Piper Senecas.

EASTMAN, Thomas C, Hicksville, NY
1210, 1434
A member of the Eastman family who founded the Kodak film empire, latterly known as Eastman Kodak Corporation. Eastman gave his address as the Aviation Country Club of Long Island when he registered the G-44 in May 1941 and as Monkton, MD when he bought the G-44A in 1946.

THE T EATON Co Ltd, Toronto, ON
B-70
JD Eaton, President. Bought the Goose as war surplus in 1947 and operated it for company transportation until sold to *Massey-Harris Co Ltd* in April 1950.

EDO Corp, College Point, NY
B-21, B-35, B-36, B-58, 1330
Known today for its range of seaplane floats, the EDO Corporation carried out much research on hydro-ski and hydrofoil operation, under contract to the US military in the 1950s and 1960s, using the JRF-5s. The J4F-2 was modified for research into the hull design of high-speed flying boats (see Chapter 5). The modified J4F-2, re-designated E-175, is now displayed at *Pima County Air Museum*, AZ.

EDSON & ASSOCIATES, Sitka, AK
1291
The G-44 was operated by *Sitka Sounds Seafood*.

EDWARDS ENGINEERING Co,
South San Francisco, CA
1385
Sterling Edwards, President.

EDWARDS, Jack H,
Kenora, ON
B-120
Edwards leased the Goose to *Parsons Airways Ltd* in June 1972.

EDWARDS TRANSPORTATION Co,
Houston, TX
1206, 1403, 1475
A partnership between CW Edwards of Houston, TX and *William Helis* of New Orleans, LA. The application for a Certificate of Airworthiness for 1206, dated 27th December 1940 stated: "This amphibian will be used to get to and from our many boats in the swamps of Louisiana". However in 1942, the G-44

The former US Marine Corps J4F-2 Widgeon (c/n 1385) seen here at Santa Barbara, California in the late 1960s as G-44 N65914 of Edwards Engineering Company.　　　*(Steve Krauss)*

was acquired by the USAAF and designated as an OA-14. It survived the war, becoming civilian registered again and is currently with an owner in Texas.

EDWARDS, Wilson C, Big Spring, TX
1110, 1138, B-8, B-24, B-73, J-21
"Connie" Edwards was born in 1934 and gained his private pilot's licence in 1951. He later gained a commercial licence and added instrument, multi-engine land and seaplane ratings. In 1968 he became chief stunt pilot for United Artists and appeared in several films, including "*The Battle of Britain*". Edwards has owned numerous warbird aircraft over the years and was inducted into the EAA Warbirds of America Hall of Fame in 2007.

EFFERSON, Michael P, Washington, DC
1141, 1143, 1144, 1146, 1148, 1163, B-64
dba MP Efferson & Associates who sold three of the G-21As to the Argentine Naval Commission (see Military Operators, Chapter 7) in January 1947, while 1141 was sold to the Shell Company of Ecuador in 1949.

EGELSTON, Dennis Michael, Mena, AR
32

EGGE, Lori, Wasilla, AK
1327
dba Sky Trekking Alaska, Fiskehauk Airways & Tikchik. Egge was in fact Lori Louise Egge-Gossett, a fact which she did not declare to the FAA. When she married in 1999 and became Lori L Michels, the FAA was in administrative confusion and much paperwork ensued!

E GENEVA Inc, Incline Village, NV
1328
Edward E Kirkpatrick, President.

EICHERT FRANKLIN Inc, Miami, FL
1019
One of the *Dean H Franklin* group of companies.

EISELE, Arthur, Carson City, NV
32
Eisele was a builder and trucker.

ELDRIDGE, WR, Austin, TX
1374

ELECTROANALYSIS Co, Victoria, TX
1328

ELLIS AIRLINES Inc, Juneau, AK
1028, 1157, 1165, 1172, 1184, B-8, B-30, B-63, B-86, B-88
Robert Ellis had started his airline in 1936 with a single Waco floatplane. In 1946, based at Ketchikan, Ellis started operations with three G-21As to provide a link to the airfield on Annette Island from which the landplane services to Seattle operated. By 1956 the Goose fleet had increased to ten and routes from Ketchikan were flown to Annette Island three times daily, to Sitka via Craig on weekdays, to Juneau via

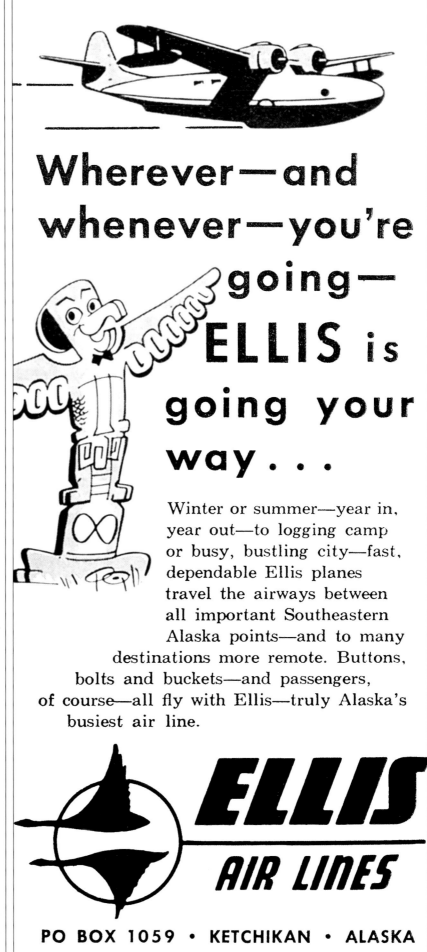

An advert for Ellis Airlines, dated July 1956.

Wrangell & Petersburg daily, and to Prince Rupert, BC three times weekly. In April 1962 Ellis merged with *Alaska Coastal Airlines* to form *Alaska Coastal-Ellis Airlines*.

ELLSWORTH, G Philip,
Wappinger Falls, NY
1386
dba Poughkeepsie Aviation Services at Dutchess County Airport. When Ellsworth died the Bill of Sale for the G-44 was signed by Hazel W Ellsworth, for the estate of GP Ellsworth.

ELLSWORTH, J William, Greenport,
Long Island, NY
1404

ENDICOTT-JOHNSON Corp,
Endicott, NY
1427
The G-44A was purchased new from Grumman in December 1945. Endicott-Johnson signed a conditional sales contract on 22nd September 1954 with *J Fred Frakes* for $33,000, to be paid in instalments including $30 per hour flown by the buyer in pursuit of his business. In 1962 Endicott-Johnson bought the G-44A from Frakes and sold it to *McKinnon Enterprises Inc*.

ENGELMAN, MW, Long Beach, CA
1138
Engelman was the assignee for *Amphibian Air Transport* on a *Bank of America NT&SA* mortgage document dated 18th November 1948.

ENGLEWOOD AIRPORT,
Englewood, CO
1364
The President, Russell T Anderson, was also President of *Anderson Manufacturing Co*, also with an address in Englewood. The company was registered at an address in Denver, CO in June 1962. A title disclaimer dated 15th May 1973 is signed by Russell T Anderson, President of Anderson Manufacturing Company dba Englewood Airport.

ENNOR, Paul, Burlingame, CA
1430
Ennor co-owned the G-44A with *Gerry Stroh* and *Andrew Robertson*.

ERHART, Lewis M, Anchorage, AK
1371

ERICKSON GROUP Ltd, Vancouver, WA
1420, J-13
Steven J Thomas, President. Steven Hamilton sold both his aircraft to the Erickson Group in late 1992, but bought back the G-44A in January 1993 and the G-73 in June 1993.

ESSO SHIPPING Co, New York, NY
B-141, J-38
A division of *Standard Oil of New Jersey*, renamed *Esso Tankers Inc* in January 1960.

G-21A Goose C-FVFU (c/n B-101) in the colours of European Coastal Airlines, Croatia circa 2008. Of the five purchased by the company this was the only one to be made airworthy and it was last reported stored in Croatia in 2008.   *(Fred J Knight Collection)*

Everbrite Electric Signs' McKinnon Super Widgeon N86646 (c/n 1472) is seen here at Mitchell Field, Milwaukee, Wisconsin.   *(Leo J Kohn via Jennifer Gradidge)*

The G-21A was operated in Colombia by the *Andian National Corporation Ltd*, who based it at Corta, while the G-73 was operated in Peru by *International Petroleum Co*.

EURIC, Carl, Seattle, WA
B-52

EUROPEAN COASTAL AIRLINES
(Klaus Dieter Martin)
- see *European Seaplane Services* below.

EUROPEAN SEAPLANE SERVICES,
Oberpfaffenhofen, Germany
(Klaus Dieter Martin) 1145, 1149, B-88, B-101, B-141
aka *European Coastal Airlines*. ECA used at least one Goose (B-101) painted in ECA colours but carrying registration C-FVFU, for services from Venice, Italy to Pula, Croatia and from Split to Hvar in Croatia. The Venice service took off from the Lido and delivered passengers to Pula harbour, whereas the other route was from Split International Airport to the beaches of Hvar, depending on which hotel the guests were booked into. It is thought that the service only operated for the summer of 2008, since when nothing has been heard of ECA, and the remaining G-21As were still in storage in Landsberied, Germany in 2012.

EVANS PRODUCTS Co, Plymouth, MI
J-45
When *Briggs Manufacturing Company* downsized in 1960, the aircraft was sold to Evans Products.

EVERBRITE ELECTRIC SIGNS,
Milwaukee, WI
B-78, 1460, 1472

EVEREADY SUPPLY Co, Bridgeport, CT
1167

EXCALIBUR AIR SERVICE,
Windham, NH
1473

EXECUTIVE AERO Inc,
Eden Prairie, MN
21, 31, 33, 34
Eugene P Bright, President. The company operated out of Flying Cloud Airport, Eden Prairie.

EXECUTIVE AIRCRAFT Co,
Broomfield, CO
16
See below.

EXECUTIVE AVIATION Co,
Broomfield, CO
16
These two companies had the same address. The Certificate of Registration

was issued to *NC Swanson*, Lander, WY who executed the financing agreement to Executive Aviation Co on 15th August 1963. On 24th November 1964 the aircraft was re-possessed by the National City Bank of Denver.

EXECUTIVE AIRCRAFT Co,
Kansas City, MO
1385

EXECUTIVE AIR SERVICE Inc,
Bellingham, WA
1325
The Certificate of Registration was revoked by the FAA on 24th September 1982 due to an undelivered Triennial Report and not re-instated until February 1987 after sale of the G-44 to *Robert E McCormick*.

EXECUTIVE BUSINESS TRANSPORTATION Inc,
Anchorage, AK
1377
Richard Rude, President.

EXECUTIVE DOGS Inc,
Wilmington, DE
1210, 1214, 1445, 1462, 1472
Marvin Good, President.

EXECUTIVE SEMINARS Inc,
Lincoln, NB
B-117
Jack R Cole, President.

EXETER Inc, Miami, FL
1141, 1150

FAA
– see *Civil Aeronautics Administration*

FAIKS, James L & Janice O,
Anchorage, AK
1213

FANDA Corp, Homer, AK
1213
Tony Neal, President. See also *Neal & Company Inc* and *Popsie Fish Co*, all owned by the Neal family and operating from the same address.

FANTASY OF FLIGHT, Polk City, FL
1388
aka Weeks Air Museum, Fantasy of Flight is the well-known museum housing the aircraft collection of *Kermit Weeks*. See also *World's Greatest Aircraft Collection Inc.*

FAR EASTERN FOUNDATION,
San Francisco, CA
1153

FARLEY, LE, Inc, Houston, TX
1214
LE Farley, President.

FARRELL, Anthony B, Northville, NY
dba *Akwissasne Flying Service*.
1452

FEADSHIP Inc, Fort Lauderdale, FL
1334
Chas M Donnelly, President. Sold the G-44 to The Warnock Hersey Co Ltd in February 1957.

FEDERAL AIRLINES Inc, New York, NY
1410
Although no Certificate of Registration has been found, ownership of the G-44A was recorded on both a form 337 dated March 1965 and a mortgage document dated 7th December 1965, signed by William B Wilson as President.

FEDERAL DEPOSIT INSURANCE Corp,
Costa Mesa, CA
B-35
Re-possessed the G-21A from *Bonanza Airlines International* while acting as Liquidator.

FEDERAL MOGUL BOWER BEARINGS,
Detroit, MI
J-10
Originally known as *Bower Roller Bearing Co*, operated the G-73 without floats to provide extra payload capacity.

FELTON, Leon C, Sausalito, CA
31
Felton took possession of the SCAN-30 after a court case against *Ace Aviation Inc* in November 2000.

FENN, Fred W, Ojus, FL
1375
dba Fred Fenn Aircraft Service, North Perry Airport, Hollywood, FL. Fenn bought the remains of the G-44 after it crashed in Cuba in 1958. He rebuilt it at his hangar on the North Perry Airport and sold it in April 1961.

FENWICK, Loel, Coolin, ID
dba *Tanglefoot Wing & Wheel Co.*
B-32, J-2, J-57

FERGUSON, Robert J, Lincoln, NE
1328

DENNIS FERRANTI METERS Ltd,
Bangor, North Wales, UK
J-55

DENNIS FERRANTI Co Ltd,
Oldham, Lancashire, UK
J-55
The G-73 was registered (Certificate of Registration R.7633/1) to Ferranti Meters on 7th August 1962. This was amended to Ferranti Co Ltd (R.7633/2) on 13th September 1962, but in both cases listing the companies as "charterer" not owner. The aircraft was based in Manchester and used to fly Mr Ferranti and friends to his estate near Mallaig, western Scotland for hunting and fishing, using Loch Morar as the "landing strip". Ownership of the aircraft was transferred to *FM Lawreys* on 1st November 1967.

FERRAZ, Manoel M de Figueiredo,
Sao Paulo, Brazil
1168
Senor Ferraz was a lawyer.

FIELD AVIATION Co Ltd, Oshawa, ON
1334, 1423
AF Soutar, President. Rebuilt the former *Amtor Corporation* G-44A between 1952 and 1954 and acted as sales agent for the G-44 in 1968.

FIELD LUMBER Co (1956) Ltd,
Sturgeon Falls, ON
1389
John H Hope, President. Originally based at North Bay, Ontario the Widgeon was operated from 1961 until 1983 and moved base during this time to Field, Guelph, and Stoney Creek, all of which were in Ontario.

FIELD, Marshall, III, New York, NY
1001
Field was a department store magnate, co-founder of the original syndicate that ordered the G-21 into production and co-owner of the first G-21.

FIJI AIR - see *Sea Bee Air*

Dennis Ferranti's Mallard G-ASCS (c/n J-55) showing a fine array of aerials at Cambridge, UK in the 1960s. After service in Canada in 1969/70, it served with Chalk's and Virgin Islands Seaplane Shuttle before being destroyed by Hurricane 'Hugo' on 17th September 1989.
(Fred J Knight Collection)

FIRST NATIONAL BANK OF ANCHORAGE, AK
1239
GW Shuster mortgaged the G-44 with the bank for $35,000. The bank re-possessed the aircraft when Shuster died, and applied for a Certificate of Registration on 24th March 1969. The G-44 was sold by the bank to *Robert O Denny* on 4th September 1969.

FISH & WILDLIFE SERVICE
- see *US Government*

FITZGERALD, Ronald L & Jennifer J, Hemet, CA
1424

FLAHART, LE, Anchorage, AK
1313, 1325

FLAHIFF, Terence F, Thorold, ON
J-2
Flahiff was attorney for the *Ontario Paper Co*, which registered the G-73 in his name between 1950 and 1958. The aircraft was based at Toronto-Malton.

FLANDES, RC, Madrid, Spain
1402

FLC - see *Foreign Liquidation Commission*

FLEET AIR TRANSPORT Inc,
Anchorage, AK
B-145

FLEET RENTAL Co, Clarksburg, WV
B-100

FLETCHER, Jordan, Norfolk, MA
1334
dba Fletcher Aviation at Franklin-Norfolk Airport, MA. Converted the J4F-2 to G-44 standard in January 1947.

FLIGHTCRAFT Inc, Portland, OR
32
Aircraft dealer.

FLIGHT DATA Inc,
Roanoke, TX and at Carson City, NV
1165, B-66

FLIGHT DEPARTMENT Inc, The,
San Francisco, CA
1059
David C Ketchum, President.

FLIGHT LEASE Inc, Columbus, OH
J-32

FLITEWAYS Inc, Milwaukee, WI
1356, 1374

FLOAIR Inc, Wichita, KS
B-104
KW Patterson, President. This ferrying and modification company, based in Hangar 17 at Wichita Municipal Airport, prepared the G-21A for delivery to New Zealand in September 1972. The flight was made during October 1972 under the captaincy of FLOAIR pilot, F Schlienz.

FLORIDA AIRMOTIVE SALES Inc,
Lantana, FL
1429
and at Fort Lauderdale, FL.
Wm R Eckhardt, President.
1371

FLORIDA INSTITUTE OF TECHNOLOGY, Melbourne, FL
1419

FLORIDA SEAPLANES Inc,
Opa Locka, FL
1462
Aviation training centre and FAR135 taxi service which used the G-44A for amphibian training during the 1980s and 1990s. The company is now using Maule M-7-235s.

FLORIDAYS Inc, Wilmington, DE
1215
Henry Ruzakowski, President.

FLUGFELAG ISLANDS hf,
Reykjavik, Iceland
B-62, B-134
aka Iceland Airways Ltd. Founded as Flugfélag Akureyrar hf (Akureyri Airways Ltd.) in 1937, and began operations with a Waco YKS-7 in April 1938. The company moved to Reykjavik in 1940 and changed name to Flugfélag Islands hf, under the ownership of the Icelandic Steamship Co. The first Goose, JRF-5 c/n B-134, was purchased directly from Grumman in July 1945 and after delivery to Iceland by sea, it entered service in early September 1945. This aircraft was damaged beyond repair in a landing accident at Nordfjördur on 20th March 1947, just one week after the fatal accident to *Loftleidir*'s TF-RVI (c/n 1139). In the accident at Nordfjördur there were no injuries, but the aircraft was a write-off. The second Goose (c/n B-62) also TF-ISR, was purchased in September 1947.

The Icelandic government's decision to choose Flugfélag rather than *Loftleidir* as the domestic carrier meant that c/n B-62 was the only Grumman in domestic service in Iceland after May 1952. The G-21A operated a weekly service between Reykjavik and Akureyri (Iceland's second city), and as well as herring spotting,

The first G-44A Widgeon to be exported (c/n 1402) was registered EC-AJU to RC Flandes, Madrid, Spain. The aircraft was named "Gavina I" and is seen in California prior to delivery in 1954.
(via Steve Krauss)

Flugfélag Islands' first Goose to be registered TF-ISR (c/n B-134). The aircraft served the airline from September 1945 until March 1947 and was replaced after an accident by c/n B-62, which carried the same registration.   *(Flugfelag Islands hf via PJ Marson)*

Lycoming-powered G-44 Super Widgeon N137B (c/n 1343) operated by Fly-by-Lease, Oswego, New York, visiting Toronto Island Airport circa 1961. The aircraft is now flying with an owner in Michigan.
(KM Molson)

The Ford Motor Company's Mallard N2971 (c/n J-29) at an unknown location circa 1950. The G-73 was operated by Air Tahiti in the early 1950s and although it is known to have returned to the USA in the mid-1950s, its ultimate fate is unknown. *(Art Krieger Collection)*

ambulance and charter flights to outlying communities until withdrawn from service in 1956.

The Goose had played more of a secondary role in Iceland Airways' operation, as the company's main domestic aircraft at the time were three Catalinas and a Douglas C-47. The G-21A was then used as a maintenance trainer until sold in the USA in July 1967.

FLY-by-LEASE, Oswego, NY
1343
Later known as Fly-by-Lease Corp, Syracuse, NY

FLYGVAPENMUSEUM
- see *Swedish Air Force Museum*

FLYHISTORIK MUSEUM, Sola, Norway
1332
The G-44 was originally donated to the Norwegian Technical Museum in Oslo in 1975, and was still there in 1995. It was last noted at Sola in November 2002.

FLYING BARNYARD Inc, The,
Greenwich, CT
1233, 1266

FLYING BOAT Co, Wilmington, DE
B-86

FLYING BOAT Inc, Miami,
and later at Fort Lauderdale, FL
J-27, J-28, J-30, J-32, J-36, J-42, J-44, J-51, J-55
Flying Boat Inc was a subsidiary of *Resorts International*, the leisure and gambling

group that bought *Chalk's International Airline* in 1974. Chalk's operated the G-73s, later converting them to turbine power. Meanwhile, Flying Boat Inc and Grumman initiated a programme to uprate their Albatrosses to G-111 standard, with 28 passenger seats. The first of these entered passenger service with Chalk's in January 1981 and was joined by a second in October that year. When James Crosby died in 1986 the enthusiasm for Chalk's died with him and his estate put Chalk's up for sale. Charles ("Chuck") F Slagle was president of Flying Boat Inc in 1996 and was replaced by William J Jones by 1998. After a convoluted series of ownership changes during which the airline lost much money, and indeed filed for Chapter 11 bankruptcy protection on 11th January 1999, *James Confalone* came to the rescue in August 1999. The G-73Ts were grounded, following the fatal crash of J-27 in December 2005.

FLYING FIREMAN Ltd, Victoria, BC
1334
RL Rude, President. The company operated from Victoria Airport on Vancouver Island employing a fleet of PBY Canso water bombers for forest fire control. The G-44 was owned in the early 1970s until the company went into receivership in June 1973 and the G-44 was sold in the USA.

FLYING SPORTSMEN Inc, Sussex, NJ
41
John T Neumeister, President. The ownership of this aircraft is complicated. Bills

of Sale dated September 1976 show the SCAN-30 being transferred between the *Modern Furniture Co* arms in Greeneville, TN and Elizabethon, TN; and then from the latter to Flying Sportsmen Inc.

According to a magazine article, John Neumeister found the SCAN-30 in Kinshasha in the Spring of 1976, and stated that it had been there for six years and had not flown in that time. So perhaps the Bills of Sale, dated September 1976, were merely a case of the paperwork catching up with the facts! This does not, however, explain how the aircraft left the ownership of *Gay George Barnes* after his wife's death. This confusion is further compounded by a Bill of Sale dated 29th March 1977 transferring ownership *from* Flying Sportsmen Inc *to* Gay G Barnes, who was issued a Certificate of Registration on 1st June 1977. However, on 8th May 1978 Barnes transferred ownership back to Flying Sportsmen Inc with a Certificate of Registration dated 20th June 1978.

Neumeister overhauled the aircraft before selling it to *Carl H Ludwig* in 1996.

FLYING "W" Inc, Medford, NJ
1371, 1445
William C Whitesell, President. Operated air-taxi and ambulance flights in the early 1960s, but the Widgeons were only owned for a few weeks, so the company may also have acted as brokers. Thunderbird Airways Inc was a subsidiary of Flying "W" Inc.

FLYNN, John H, Seattle, WA
1323
Co-owned the G-44 with *Robert L Dukes*.

FONTAINE, Oscar A, Westport, MA
29

**FONTANA SCHOOL of
AERONAUTICS,**
Iron Mountain, MI
1232
Operated by Mario & Joseph Fontana out of Ford Airport, Iron Mountain, MI. Mario held a commercial pilot's licence while Joseph held a private licence. Ownership of the G-44 was registered to M&A Fontana in January 1949 by which time the partners were named as Mario and Audrey Fontana.

FORD MOTOR Co, Dearborn, MI
1175, J-29
The multinational automobile manufacturer has operated many types of aircraft for personnel transportation over many years. The G-21A was bought direct from Grumman in December 1941 when Ford gave their address as "Willow Run Bomber Plant".

**FOREIGN & DOMESTIC
ENTERPRISES Inc**, Seattle, WA
1164, B-8, B-32, B-45, B-86, B-100, B-115, B-126, B-145
Aircraft maintenance & rebuild facility on Boeing Field owned by *Lloyd A Rekow*, who became noted for rebuilding G-21As.

Forstmann Woolens' Mallard NC2941 (c/n J-3)at Grumman's Bethpage facility awaiting delivery in October 1946. While owned by Dearborn Motors Company, the aircraft was damaged beyond repair when it crashed on landing at Charlotte, North Carolina on 24th May 1950.

(Fred J Knight Collection)

FOREIGN ECONOMIC ADMINISTRATION, (FEA), Washington, DC
B-59
The FEA was headed by Nelson Rockefeller and carried out economic warfare, propaganda and intelligence operations particularly in Central and South America. Research staff were based in Washington, DC with agents at various US Embassies around the world. The G-21A was registered to the FEA as NR1800 in 1945, but to what use it was put is not clear. The Administration was succeeded by the *Reconstruction Finance Corporation.*

FOREIGN LIQUIDATION COMMISSION, (FLC), Washington, DC
1394
The FLC was responsible for sales of government surplus located outside the USA.

FORESTER, Kenneth, Oradell, NJ
1389

FOREST INDUSTRIES FLYING TANKERS, (FIFT), Port Alberni, BC
B-101
JO Hemmingson, President. Formed in 1959 by a consortium of six companies in the BC logging industry to protect against forest fires. It operated from Sproat Lake with two Martin Mars water bombers and from April 1967 used the G-21A as a personnel transport and sometime bird-dog aircraft. In July 2001 the Mars aircraft were registered to *TFL Forest Ltd*, Vancouver, BC who leased them to Flying Tankers Inc in Port Alberni, BC until 31st December 2003. The G-21A was sold to *C-Tec Ltd* in October 2001, to be operated by *European Seaplane Services* in Croatia.

FORSBERG, Edwin E, Salem, OR
and later at Elk Grove, CA
1337, 30
A Boeing 747 pilot who started restoration of the G-44 in 1985. The SCAN-30 was trucked from Alaska to California circa 1st June 2012 and restoration was started. The restoration projects are being carried out by the owner with the help of Goran King, a former engineering supervisor at *Catalina Airlines.*

FORSTMANN WOOLENS Co,
Passiac, NJ
J-3
The company started as Forstmann & Huffmann Company in 1904. The founder Julius Forstmann died in 1939 and the company presidency was taken over by his son Curt E Forstmann. The G-73 was purchased new in October 1946 and sold in June 1949. In 1957 the company became part of JP Stevens & Company.

FORT DODGE AIRWAYS, Moorland, IA
1462

FORT SUMTER CHEVROLET Co,
Charleston, SC
J-51
The G-73 was fitted with R-1340-S1H1 (rather than the normal S3H1) engines and had an Experimental Certificate of Airworthiness issued for acceptance tests, before being granted standard airworthiness status in April 1950. It then acted as Grumman demonstrator before being sold to Fort Sumter Chevrolet on 30th August 1950.

FOUR WINDS AIR ASSOCIATION Inc
1462

FOWLER, Ronald B, Anchorage, AK
1464
Fowler co-owned the Widgeon with *Lynn W Wyatt Jr* before transferring it to Wyatt as sole owner in February 1983.

FRAKES AVIATION, Cleburne, TX
& Angwin, CA
J-9, J-10, J-19, J-27, J-30, J-32, J-36, J-38, J-45, J-50, J-51, J-53, J-58
J Fred Frakes bought J-36 in 1962 and flew charter services within Alaska from Anchorage. The aircraft was chartered to *Red Dodge Aviation* of Anchorage during 1962. Following sale to *Northern Consolidated Airlines,* J-36 was fitted with a PT6A-6 turbine on the starboard side (with the piston engine on the port side) and carried out a fifty-hour flight test programme. It was then returned to piston power, and after Frakes had moved to Angwin, CA in 1968, J-36 became the prototype G-73T conversion.
Frakes also operated J-44 during 1963 in the colours of his *Safeway Airways.*
J-30 & J-51 were "bought" by Frakes in exchange for a Beech B-200 in January 1986. The remainder of the above were converted to G-73T by Frakes at Angwin, and later at Cleburne, TX (see Chapter 4).

FRAKES, J Fred, Anchorage, AK
1427
Frakes operated the G-44A from 1954 until 1962, when he bought his first G-73 (see above).

FRANK, Randall D & Kathleen M,
Palmer, AK
1377

**FRANKLIN, Dean H,
AVIATION ENTERPRISES Inc**,
Miami, FL
(inc *Franklin Flying Service Inc*).
1053, 1061, 1086, 1109, 1126?, 1132, 1133, 1149, 1162, 1166, 1168, 1182, B-18, B-46, B-49, B-54, B-65, B-74, B-88, B-100, B-104, B-128, B-139, B-141, 1274, 1281, 1311, 1340, 1370, 1371, 1375, 1381, 1450, 1384, 1442, 1450, 1462, 1464, 1468, SCAN 13, J-4, J-6, J-7, J-11, J-18, J-19, J-22, J-23, J-35, J-38, J-43, J-52, J-54
Dean H Franklin became known as "*Mr Grumman Amphibian*", building up a repair/conversion business and setting up many operating /leasing companies, such as *Franklin Flying Service*. In the early post-WWII years he flew his personal

Dean Franklin overhauled the former JRF-6B Goose N333F (c/n 1166) in December 1957, fitting squared-off wing tips and oversized spinners. He dubbed the aircraft "The Golden Super Goose" which is seen here at Miami in 1959. Later used by various operators on the Santa Catalina Island routes, the aircraft suffered a fatal crash on 14th April 1979.   *(Dean Franklin photo)*

Above: *Dean H Franklin Aviation Enterprises letterhead from May 1995.*

Above: *Mallard N22DF (c/n J-35) at Shannon, Ireland on 11th July 1976 during the ferry flight from Indonesia to the USA for Dean Franklin. The legend on the nose reads "Lady Luck, Miami, Florida". The aircraft is currently active in Australia.* (Malcolm Nason)

G-21A south in the winter to fly services for *Chalk's*.

Franklin was also in partnership with Edward Moore and Joseph Adams, the latter doing business as *Gander Aircraft Corporation*.

In 1966 Franklin took over the running of Chalk's International Airline from "Pappy" Chalk, and in the following year introduced the G-73s to the fleet.

Although Franklin sold the airline to the Pennsylvania businessman, *Edward F Dixon* in 1973, he retained the spares inventory for himself. Over the years Franklin built up repair facilities for Grumman amphibians and a vast inventory of spares.

By 1998, Dean H Franklin Aviation Enterprises Inc was located at North Miami Beach, FL with Jeanne Franklin as President. The company was purchased by *James Confalone* to ensure a guaranteed supply of spares for his *Chalk's Ocean Airways* G-73Ts. The G-21A and G-44 spares, also acquired in the deal, were sold. See also *Amphibian Parts Inc* and *Amphibian Sales Inc*.

FRANKLIN-MORSE AIRCRAFT Corp, Miami, FL
10, 13, 32
Robert E Morse, President. The corporation's stationery proclaimed that they were "builders of the Franklin-Morse Super Widgeon". The southern office and manufacturing plant was at Miami, FL with a northeastern sales office in Utica, NY. By

1971 the company was known as *Morse Aero Inc* and specialised in aircraft salvage, repair and sales. In reply to an FAA request in October 1971, Morse stated that c/ns 10 and 13 were "uncompleted Grumman Widgeon hulls". In May 1998, a Bill of Sale dated 3rd December 1967 was recorded on the FAA file. This transferred c/n 10 from Franklin-Morse (DH Franklin, Secretary) to *DH Franklin Aviation Enterprises Inc* with a Certificate of Registration dated 11th July 1998.

FRAWLEY, RD, Dravosburg, PA
1384
Frawley based the G-44 at the Dravosburg Seaplane Base.

FREEPORT McMORAN Inc,
New Orleans, LA
J-49
See below.

FREEPORT-McMORAN RESOURCE PARTNERS, Ltd PARTNERSHIP
J-49
See below

FREEPORT MINERALS Co - see below

FREEPORT SULFUR Co,
New Orleans, LA
B-141, J-27, J-49
Operated the G-21A as N41996 before Chief Pilot, Richard D McNally, arranged for special registration N200S in January 1956. This was transferred to J-27 in October 1959 when the G-21A became N2003. The G-73s were used from the late 1950s in support of Freeport's mining activities. The company was known as *Freeport Minerals Co* from 1971. An attempt to register Mallard J-49 in the name of Freeport-McMoran Resource Partners, Ltd Partnership in June 1986 was deemed a prohibited conveyance under existing legal codes of practice and the Bill of Sale was rescinded. In 1990 the conglomerate became known as *Freeport McMoran Copper and Gold Inc*.

In the 1950s the aircraft were based at the Mitchell Hangar at New Orleans Airport. By 1989 J-49 was noted as based at Lafon Airpark, Kenner, LA. J-49 was later used in support of affiliate *PT Freeport Indonesia*.

The Freeport Sulfur Company's G-73T Turbo Mallard N300S (c/n J-49) seen here at New Orleans, Louisiana, during the NBAA show in 1985. (EW Priebe)

FREIBERG, John L, New Orleans, LA
1438
Freiberg was president of both *Trans Air Corp* and *Dynair Corp* and, after transferring ownership of the G-44A from Trans Air to Dynair on 13th December 1965, transferred ownership to his own name on the same day. The aircraft was based at New Orleans-Lakefront Airport.

FRENCH GOVERNMENT
In a bid to re-coup some of its investment in the SCAN-30 Widgeon project, the French government dispatched five of the aircraft to French overseas territories, more in the hope that this would generate some sales, rather than the fact that there was any need for the aircraft in those territories.

Ministère de la Finance
35, 36, 41
The French Ministry of Finance sold the SCAN-30s to *Anthony Stinis & Olaf Abrahamsen* on 14th August 1956. According to a Bureau Veritas report dated 23rd October 1956 airframe c/ns 35 & 41, "without power unit nor cabin fitting up and equipment", were inspected in December 1949 and then "prepared for long storage". An Affidavit dated 15th September 1956 and signed by Abrahamsen confirms that "the airplanes were never completely assembled by the factory therefore were never registered in France or any other country".
   C/n 36 was registered to the State Commissariat General for Productivity, Paris. Its registration F-OARB was cancelled on 23rd August 1956 on sale to Stinis & Abrahamsen.

Ministère de la France Outre Mer
Etablissements Française de l'Oceanie, Tahiti
J- 29
The government-owned Tahiti-Hawaii Airlines (aka *Air Tahiti*) purchased the G-73 in March 1951 for services from Papeete to Bora Bora and was the first Mallard to enter airline service. The aircraft was sold in 1956 when *RAI* took over the route using a Short Sandringham.

Département de la Guyane,
Cayenne-Rochambeau
36, 38, 39, 40
Little is known of the use to which the four SCAN-30s were put.

FRENCH INDO CHINA, Service du Santé
6
Similarly, little is known, but the SCAN-30 may have been used to provide medical services to outlying regions.

FRENCH, James B, Bakersfield, CA
1160

FRESH WATER ADVENTURES Inc,
Dillingham, AK
B-55 B-86, B-139, B-140, 1375
The company operated mainly fishing charters and an on-demand air taxi service

FRENCH-BUILT GRUMMAN
WIDGEON
SCAN-30

GIPSY QUEEN 30 MK. 2 ENGINES
D.H. CONSTANT SPEED PROPELLERS
CURRENT FRENCH C. of A.

TOTAL HOURS SINCE NEW 20 ONLY

FULL BLIND AND
NIGHT FLYING DUAL CONTROL
AIRLINE RADIO—24 VOLT
SEATING PILOT, CO-PILOT, 4 PASSENGERS

———————

AERONAUTIQUE LEGASTELOIS
17-19 CITE CANROBERT
PARIS 15e, FRANCE

CABLES: LEGASTAERO — PARIS
TELEPHONE: SUFFREN 80.00

A July 1956 advertisement, which appeared in "The Aeroplane", offering SCAN-30 F-OARB for sale.

under a Part 135 Air Taxi & Commuter licence and was owned by the *Bingman* family.
- see also *Kerriston Ltd Partnership* and *Widgeon Enterprises LLC*

FREUHAUF TRAILER Corp,
Detroit, MI
J-44
A manufacturer of truck trailers operated the G-73 during the late-1950s.

FRIEDKIN INVESTMENTS Inc,
Houston, TX
B-126

FRIEDKIN, Thomas H, Carlsbad, CA
dba Cinema Air Inc.
B-126

FRIEDRICH, Thomas,
San Antonio, TX
dba *Caribbean Clipper Inc.*
B-76

FROIS, E,
Montevideo, Uruguay
dba *Aero Punta.*
1342

FRONTIER ENTERPRISES Inc,
Alexandria, MN
14

FRONTIER FLYING SERVICE Inc,
Fairbanks, AK
1463
John Hajdukovich, President. By 2003 Robert Hajdukovich was presiding.

FROST, Robert A,
Newport Beach, CA (co-owner)
1165

FROST BOX Co, Pawtucket, RI
1307

FROTHINGHAM, Warren S &
Viola M, Mayburyport, MA
1365
dba *Plum Island Flying Service Inc* which did not actually operate the G-44, and it remained stored until sold in September 1949.

FUEHRER K, Federico,
Buenos Aires, Argentina
1004
It has been reported that this is only a phonetic version of his name and Fuehrer's true identity has not been established. He bought the Goose when *TARyTA* ceased operations in 1951 and was in partnership with Walter Roth, of *Roth y Compania Ltda* who operated the G-21A in Chile.

FUGU Ltd, Bellevue, WA
1380
Formerly known as *Octal Inc* with an address in Mountain View, CA.

FULLER BRUSH Co, Hartford, CT
1417, J-6

SCAN-30G Widgeon F-OARB (c/n 36) at Toussus-le-Noble in September 1955 before export to French Guiana. The aircraft was advertised for sale in July 1956 and sold in the USA the following month. It is currently owned by Rochester Amphibian Inc in Rochester, New York.
(DAS McKay via Jennifer Gradidge)

FULLER, Frank W, Hillsborough, CA
1020, J-8
dba WP Fuller Paint Company. Frank W
Fuller was a well-known air racer and won
the Bendix Trophy races of 1937 and 1939.
Fuller sold his G-21A to the US
government in 1942 and took delivery of
the G-73 in July 1946, following his stint as
a test pilot for Douglas in Santa Monica,
CA during WWII. As a proving flight
Fuller flew J-8 from Bethpage to San
Francisco and then to Alaska and British
Columbia for some fishing. Always used as
a personal transport, the aircraft was even
flown back to Bethpage each year for
inspection and re-certification. Because of
his advancing years Fuller reluctantly sold
J-8 in 1974.

FULLER, John M, Jr, Nashua, NH
1421
Fuller changed his address to Allied Bendix
Aerospace, Arlington, VA in 1986.

FULLER, Walter,
dba *Walter Fuller Aircraft Sales Inc*.
1213

FULWEILER, G Oscar, Piedmont, CA
1267

GALBREATH, John W & Co,
Columbus, OH
1213, J-46, J-55
Galbreath made his money from real estate.
The G-44 was owned from 1946 until
1950. The first Mallard, J-46, crashed
during a night training flight at the
Galbreath's Darby Dan Farm. He operated
the replacement (J-55) until 1952.
Galbreath was also a successful horse
breeder and won the Kentucky Derby in
1967. He later operated a Gulfstream II out
of Darby Dan Farm.

GALLISON, Frank A, Merced, CA
1383

**GANDER AIRCRAFT &
ENGINEERING Corp**, Miami, FL
1086, 1417, 1442, 1445
One of *Dean H Franklin's* group of
companies, set up by Franklin and a partner
in the late 1950s to re-engine G-21As with
Continental IO-720s. Unfortunately, the
partner was killed in an aircraft accident
and the plans for the Continental Goose
program were dropped. C/n 1086 was
modified with "canted engine mounts and
re-designed wingtips" and an Experimental
Certificate of Airworthiness was issued in
November 1961 to facilitate test flights to
evaluate the modification.

GANDER AIRCRAFT Corp
- see *Joseph Q Adams*

GANNET Corp - see *Tom Katsuda*

GANNETT, Guy, Portland, ME
1211, 1236
dba *Gannett Publishing Co Inc*. From 1950
known as Guy Gannett Publishing Co, and

Garland Aviation Company's G-21A Goose N95400 (c/n 1077) at an unknown location circa 1950, with the company logo displayed on the forward fuselage. After a long career providing airline service in the Bahamas and Canada, the Goose was withdrawn from service by Pacific Coastal Airlines in September 2012. (R Stuckey)

latterly as *Gannett Newspapers Inc*, the
different companies used a variety of
aircraft as executive transports over the
years. G-44 NC28672 (c/n 1211) was
impressed by the USAAC in 1942 and was
replaced by NC37186 (c/n 1236) in August
1944.

GARANT AVIATION Enrg,
St Francois, QC
14
A family company which registered the
SCAN-30 in the names of the family
members: Daniel, Irene, Jean Marie,
Marcel and Oscar Garant. In 1966 the
company became *Garant Inc* with Oscar
Garant as president.
    The aircraft, which Garant leased to the
Quebec City Flying Club in the second half
of 1966, was sold in 1967. (The "Enrg" is
an abbreviation of the French verb
"Enregistrer", meaning "Registered", and
indicates that the company was more
than a partnership but less than an
incorporation.)

GARBER, David S,
Menlo Park, CA & Leesburg, FL
1375, 1415
Garber kept the G-44A at his lakeshore
house on Lake Griffin, Leesburg, FL using
a purpose-built seaplane ramp.

GARDENER, Blaine,
Rizal, Manila, Philippines
1436

GARGIULO, Silvio,
New York, NY
1380

GARLAND, Harry, Detroit, MI
dba *Garland Aviation Co*.
1077, 1388, 1407

GARRISON, Fred R, Needville, TX
31
Garrison sold the SCAN-30 to *Rod Aero
Aircraft Brokerage Inc* in October 1991
and bought it back again the following
month!

GAR WOOD INDUSTRIES
- see *Wood, GA*

GAY, Alfred E,
Anchorage, AK,
and at Gringo Pass, AZ
1239, 1325, 1346
Gay had the *Sea Airmotive Inc* G-44 (c/n
1325) registered in his name in December
1955. There was almost certainly a family
connection with Sea Airmotive, which was
presided over by *Ward I Gay* at the same
address given by Alfred E. After selling the
G-44 to *Cordova Airlines Inc* in September
1956, he bought it back again in October
1959 and had it registered in April 1960 to
Gay Airways Inc, of which he was
president, before selling it to *LE Flahart*
the following month.
    In December 1972, six months after
registering it, Gay transferred ownership of
c/n 1239 to his company, *Gringo Pass Inc*,
of Lukeville, AZ.

GAY, Ward I, Anchorage, AK
1387
Ward I Gay was President of *Sea Airmotive
Inc*.

GAY AIRWAYS Inc, Anchorage, AK
1205, 1325, 1346
Alfred E Gay, President. Operated c/n 1205
from at least March 1956 until the crash in
1963, and owned c/n 1325 only briefly in
1959/60.

GAYLE AVIATION Inc,
Locust Valley, NY
41

GAYLER, Noel, Dept of Navy,
Washington, DC
1237
Admiral Gayler subsequently became
Director of the National Security Agency
and retired from the US Navy as
Commander, Pacific Command.

**GE CAPITAL CANADA LEASING
SERVICES Inc**
1077, B-129

GEE BEE Inc, Anchorage, AK
1206
K Gene Zerkel, President.

GEIER, James AD, Cincinnati, OH
1409, 1462

GEMO Inc
J-26

GENERAL CONSTRUCTION Co,
Seattle, WA
1351

GENERAL FOODS Corp, New York, NY
J-49, J-58
The company was founded in 1929. Since 1985 it has been part of the Philip Morris conglomerate, which later also acquired Kraft Foods, and combined it into Kraft General Foods. Since 1995 it has been known as Kraft Foods. The G-73s, used in the 1950s, were just two of the many executive aircraft used by the corporation.

GENERAL INDUSTRIES Inc,
Melbourne, FL
and later at New York, NY
1352

GENERAL MOTORS Corp, Detroit, MI
J-40, J-56
The multi-national car maker has used a large variety of aircraft types for executive transportation. The G-73s were used in the 1950s.

GENERAL TIRE & RUBBER Co,
Akron, OH
J-12
The tyre manufacturer has used a variety of corporate aircraft over the years.

GENESEE AIRPORT Inc, Rochester, NY
1045, 1368
Robert V Wilson, President.

GEORGE, Herbert W, Reno, NV
(co-owner)
1397

G G LEASING Co,
Anchorage, AK
1206, 1324
A partnership between *K Gene Zerkel* and *George S Patterson*.

GHOSH, D, - see *Associated Airworks*

GIBBS, J Gordon, Marion, MA
1232

GIBBS, John R, Rochester, MI
21

GIBBS, Thomas B, Delavan, WI
1368

GIBSON, Harvey G,
San Jose, Costa Rica
1184
The former TWA airline captain had retired to a farm in Costa Rica after a Boeing 727 he was piloting "fell from the sky" in 1979, an incident which engendered controversy and legal argument. Gibson owned the G-21A from 1990 until 1996 when it was sold after flying into a river bank on take-off the previous year. The aircraft featured in the 1994 film "*Endless Summer II*".

GIFFORD, John, Anchorage, AK
dba *Gifford Rentals*.
1328

GILBERT, William E,
Christiansted, US Virgin Islands
1438
The aircraft was based at Alexander Hamilton Airport, St Croix while in the Virgin Islands, but in 1972 Gilbert moved to Gibson Island, Maryland and based the G-44A at Friendship International Airport, Baltimore.

GILLES TREMBLAY AVIATION Inc,
Montreal, QC
1370
Sales agent.

GILLEY, CG, Lafayette, LA
1372

GILLIES AVIATION Corp,
Hicksville, Long Island, NY
1004, 1016, 1019, 1054, 1058, 1216, 1404
An aircraft distributor operating out of Roosevelt Field, Long Island, owned by Jack Gillies, brother of the Grumman test-pilot, Bud. It was awarded the worldwide distributorship for the G-21A, covering all sales except those to the US military, and subsequently also handled G-44 sales.

GILMORE, Ronald J,
Sellersville, PA
1233

GINTER CONSTRUCTION Co Ltd,
- see *Ben Ginter Construction Co Ltd*

GLASER CONSTRUCTION Co Inc,
Lafayette, LA
1329, 1438
Donald Morris Glaser, President.

GLOBE PRINTING Co
- see *Toronto Globe & Mail*

GODSALL, GH, Equipment Ltd,
Toronto, ON
1240

GOETZ, William,
c/o Universal International Pictures,
Universal City, CA
J-38

GOLD BAR DEVELOPMENTS Ltd,
Edmonton, AB
J-34
Sandy Mactaggart, President.

GOLD BOND STAMP Co
- see *Premium Service Corp*

GOLDEN WEST AIRLINES Inc,
Long Beach, CA
1051, 1130, B-59, B-66, B-73, B-119
Golden West Airlines Inc, owned by Bill Perara, already operated commuter services throughout southern California with DHC-6 Twin Otters when they acquired the *Catalina Air Lines* G-21A fleet in 1968.

Sandy MacTaggart's much-travelled G-73T C-FUOT (c/n J-34) on a visit to the United Kingdom in July 1991. The aircraft is seen here at London-Heathrow Airport and is currently registered as VP-CLK, stored in the USA. *(Dave Winyard)*

Catalina Golden West's G-21A Goose N93G (c/n 1130) taxies up the ramp at Pebbly Beach on Santa Catalina Island on 29th August 1973. After providing service to Santa Catalina Island for many years the aircraft was sold for scrap in 1981. *(PJ Marson)*

With dual Catalina Air Lines and Golden West Airlines titles, G-21A Goose N1133 (c/n B-59) is seen here at Long Beach, California in 1969. *(John P Stewart via PJ Marson)*

Repainted in Catalina Golden West colours, G-21A Goose N1133 (c/n B-59) is seen here in 1974, probably at Long Beach, California. After going to Catalina Seaplanes as N18CS, the Goose crashed and sank off Avalon on 10th April 1976. *(MAP)*

Earlier in 1968, *Aero Commuter Inc* had merged with Catalina Air Lines. Cable Commuter and Skymark Airlines were then added to the group and the merged entity became Golden West Airlines Inc. The five aircraft, painted with Catalina Golden West logos, were operated to Santa Catalina Island until 1973 by which time the airline was owned by the *California Westgate Corp*. The Golden West operation to Santa Catalina Island was taken over by *Catalina Airlines Inc*.

GOLDEN WEST AVIATION Ltd,
Vancouver, BC
B-66
Acted as agent for the sale of the G-21A in July 1980.

GOLDSCHMIDT, JA, Ltd, London, UK
J-55

GOLDSWORTHY, Robert F, Rosalia, WA
1371
Was granted ownership of the G-44 in 1969 after the owners breached a financing agreement.

GOLLANCE, Harold M, Waban, MA
1166
Based at Logan Airport, Boston, MA.

GONSOULIN, Jerry T, Houma, LA, and later at Pensacola, FL
1372

GONZALEZ, Hugo
1004

GONZALEZ, Gen Leopoldo Vivas
1293

GOOD AVIATION LLC, Oshkosh, WI
J-31
Address given as:
c/o *Basler Turbo Conversions LLC.*

GOOD, William S, Jr, New Orleans, LA
1421, 1454

GOOSE AVIATION Co,
New Brunswick, NJ
1168
later at Dayton, NJ, Fort Pierce, FL and then Princeton, NJ
The G-21A was owned by Seward Johnson of the *Johnson & Johnson Company*, and was operated out of Fort Pierce, FL by Capt James Cothron, who later flew G-73s for *Chalk's International Airline*, and famously got shot during a hi-jacking to Cuba in March 1972 (see J-43 in the Mallard production list.) See also *Chalk's Flying Service, Raritan Aviation,* and Chapter 6.

GOOSE LAKE AIRWAYS
- see *Tuthill Corp*

GOOSE LEASING, Anchorage, AK
B-115
- see *Smith, Hugh Z*

GOOSE TRANSPORT Inc,
Gainesville, FL
1054

GOPHER AVIATION Inc, Rochester, MN
1390
Based at Rochester Municipal Airport.

GORDON, G Blair,
Montreal, QC
1235
Gordon was President of *Chamcook Airways.*

GORMAN, John O & Ruth,
Carmichael, CA
1375

GOVERNMENT OF FRANCE
- see *French Government*

GOVERNMENT OF GABON,
Libreville, West Africa
J-52
The G-73, used by the President of Gabon, was unfortunately lost when it sank in the Atlantic Ocean in June 1975 after attempting the rescue of passengers from a ship.

GOWELL, Kathleen MacLean,
1317
After *Charles Stuart MacLean* died in 1961, his daughter Kathleen MacLean Gowell was appointed as Trustee (in 1967). A Bill of Sale dated 31st May 1967 transferred ownership of the G-44 from Citizens Fidelity Bank (Executors of the estate) to Mrs Gowell as Trustee.

GRANBY CONSOLIDATED MINING, SMELTING & POWER Co Ltd,
Vancouver, BC
1265
LT Postil, President.

Grand Touring Cars Inc of Scottsdale, Arizona operated this Franklin Widgeon conversion N9311R (c/n 1340) during 1984/5. It is seen here at its home base on 23rd March 1985.
(Peter Kirkup via Jennifer Gradidge)

GRAND TOURING CARS Inc,
Scottsdale, AZ
1340
Harley E Cluxton, President.

GRAUBART AVIATION Inc,
Valparaiso, IN
1340, 1389, 1463, 16, 29
Eli Graubart, President. Graubart Aviation Inc operated from an address in Chicago, IL in 1956. By the time that the company acted as sales agent for the G-44 in 1961 and 1962, and for the G-44A in 1963, it was situated in Valparaiso, IN. Graubart breached the financing agreement on c/n 29 in July 1964 and it was re-possessed by *Appliance Buyers Credit Corporation* on 11th July 1964, and registered to them on 28th July, before being sold to *North Country Airways* on 7th December 1964. C/n 16 was bought from the *National City Bank of Denver* in 1966.

GRAY AUDOGRAPH Corp,
New York, NY
- see below

GRAY DICTATING MACHINE Corp,
New York, NY
1438
This company was affiliated to the Gray Audograph Corp and shared the same address. Helen M Olson, who signed the Certificate of Registration applications, was Treasurer for both companies.

GREAT BARRIER AIRLINES Ltd,
Auckland, NZ
B-104
Founded in 1983, and operated the G-21A for *Sea Bee Air* from 1989 until 1991. The airline is still flying commuter services in New Zealand, currently with B-N Islanders, Trislanders and various Piper aircraft.

GREAT BEAR LAKE LODGE Ltd,
Winnipeg, MB
B-34, B-139
- see *Plummer Holdings* and *Sioux Narrows Airways*.

GREAT CIRCLE Corp, Bellevue, WA
33

GREATEST GENERATION NAVAL MUSEUM, San Diego, CA
1429

GREAT LAKES CHARTERS,
Camden, NY
1314

GREAT LAKES PAPER Co,
Fort William, ON
J-19
PM Fox, Chairman. Had the G-73 converted from photo-survey back to passenger configuration in 1961 and continued to operate it until 1969.

Great Bear Lake Lodge Ltd owned Goose CF-WCP (c/n B-139) from June 1964 until June 1966, and from June 1967 until May 1971, during most of which time it was leased to Sioux Narrows Airways Ltd. The aircraft is seen here at Winnipeg on 19th June 1970. *(Tim Martin)*

GREEN BAY PAPER & BOX Co,
Green Bay, WI
1359

GREEN VALLEY AVIATION Inc,
Granite Falls, and at Everett, WA
1215, 1235, 1239, 1266, 1442

GREENHILL, Charles,
Northbrook, and Mettawa, IL
B-49, B-52, B-142, 1394
G-21A B-52 was later registered to Greenhill's *Amphib Inc* with which it is current.

GRENOLD COLLINS FLYING SERVICES, AK
1151, 1270
Collins bought the war-surplus JRF-6B in 1946 but it crashed in 1948. It was replaced by the G-44, which Collins operated in Alaska until 1952 when it was sold to *Alaska Airlines*.

GREYHOUND LEASING & FINANCIAL of CANADA, Toronto, ON
1311
Previously known as *Boothe Leasing of Canada Ltd*.

GREYVEST FINANCIAL SERVICES Ltd
1077, B-129
Greyvest bought the G-21As from *Pacific Coastal Airlines* in 1989 and leased them

G-44 Super Widgeon N68395 (c/n 1359) of the Green Bay Paper & Box Company, seen here in June 1956. *(Art Krieger)*

Based in Seattle, Washington, Griffco Aviation's G-21A N2844D (c/n B-32) was leased to various operators in Canada between 1955 and 1961. The photo was taken on 4th July 1959 at Boeing Field, Seattle. *(Ed Coates via Jennifer Gradidge)*

Grosvenor Estates' G-21A Goose G-ASXG (c/n 1083) prior to turbine conversion waits with floats lowered at London-Heathrow, for another assignment in the mid-1960s. Converted to a G-21A Turbo Goose by Marshall of Cambridge in 1968, the aircraft returned to Canada but was unfortunately lost in an accident at Rivers Inlet, British Columbia on 12th May 1988. *(AJ Kemsley)*

back to them for 83 months. In 1994 the aircraft were sold back to Pacific Coastal via GE Capital Canada Leasing.

GRIFFCO AVIATION Co, Seattle, WA
- see below

GRIFFITH, Glynn K, Seattle, WA
1157, B-6, B-32, B-45, B-112, B-129, B-145
dba Griffco Aviation Co at Boeing Field, Seattle. B-32 was sold to *Ontario Central Airlines Ltd* on 5th June 1955 but the two parties quickly agreed that a lease arrangement would better suit their needs and the G-21A was sold back to Griffco on 15th June 1955. Ontario Central then leased the aircraft until it was returned to Griffco in August 1958. Griffco acted as agent for the sale of B-32 & B-129 to *Pacific Western Airlines* in 1960 & 1961 respectively; B-45 to the USA, and both B-6 and B-145 to *Pacific Western*, all in 1966. C/n 1157 was sold by Griffco to *Pacific Western Airlines* who apparently operated it with US marks in 1970/72.

GRIFFIN, Merv
G-73T
Griffin was the US television personality who briefly owned *Resorts International* (and therefore *Chalk's International Airline*) when it had filed for Chapter 11 bankruptcy protection in 1988. During 1988 to 1990 Chalk's reached its lowest ebb with only three daily G-73T services from Watson Island to Bimini.

GRIFFIN, S Stanley,
West Palm Beach, FL
1210

GRIFFIS, Jack L, Orange, CA
1377

GRIMES MANUFACTURING Co,
Urbana, OH
1424
Grimes made, among other things, navigation beacons, motors and micro switches for reversible propeller control. The G-44A was used as a flying test-bed for new products.

GRINGO PASS Inc, Lukeville, AZ
1239
Owned by *Alfred E Gay*.

GRIPPEN, Earl J, Endicott, NY
1386

GROSVENOR ESTATES, London, UK
1083, J-55
A management company set up to run the many properties and interests of the Duke of Westminster. The G-21A was used to commute to his various estates in Scotland and Ireland. The G-73 was not owned, but used briefly during 1968, while the Goose was being converted to turbine power by Marshall of Cambridge, UK.

GROVETON PAPERS Co, Groveton, NH
1299

GRUMMAN AIRCRAFT ENGINEERING Corp,
Bethpage, Long Island, NY
and later as
GRUMMAN AEROSPACE Corp
1001, 1141, 1054, B-34, 1201, 1216, 1401, 1406, 1408, 1410, 1411, 1420, 1424, 1425, 1426, 1427, 1429, 1434, 1442, 1445, 1452, 1465, 1467, J-1, J-9, J-10, J-11, J-17, J-40, J-42, J-50, J-54, J-59
Some of the above were registered to Grumman before sale to both civil and

Mallard NC2947 (c/n J-10) was used as a demonstrator by Grumman during 1947, before serving with many companies in the USA and Canada until 1984, when it was grounded because of corrosion. The remains of the Mallard are owned by Frakes Aviation of Cleburne, Texas.
(Grumman photo by Harold G Martin)

Grumman G-44A demonstrator N41975 (n 1406) at Timmerman in November 1955. It was later converted to Continental IO-470-D power and served in Canada, where it was written-off in January 1970. *(Jennifer Gradidge Collection)*

Gulf Air's G-21A Goose CF-EFN (c/n 1157) at Vancouver International Airport, British Columbia, on 19th January 1980. It later served with Air BC but crashed in February 1991. The remains were sold to the Tongass Historical Society in Ketchikan, Alaska, where it has been restored to airworthiness. *(Peter Kirkup)*

A Henry Clark drawing of Gulf Oil Goose NC3042 (c/n 1062).

military customers. Others were used as company hacks or demonstrators while further examples were registered to Grumman pending development work or conversion from military to civil use.

GUEST ENTERPRISES Inc,
New York, NY
1230

GUIBERSON, Gordon G,
Los Angeles, CA
1200

GULF AIR AVIATION Ltd,
Campbell River, BC
1157
Leased the Goose from *Alert Bay Air Services.*

GULF OIL Corp,
Pittsburgh, PA
1019, 1062, 1437
The oil company used Grumman aircraft over many years for executive transportation and oil operations support. G-21A NC3042 (c/n 1062) entered service in December 1939, while the G-44A served for almost 30 years from 1957.

GULF REFINING Co, Houston, TX
1437

GULF RESEARCH & DEVELOPMENT Corp,
Pittsburgh, PA
1045
Incorporated on 16th February 1933, it was a subsidiary of the *Gulf Oil Corp.*

GULF SOUTH AVIATION Inc,
Shreveport, LA
1377
Henry A Sibley Jr, President.

GULKANA AIR SERVICE,
Glenallen, AK
1375
Founded in 1963. *Kenneth H Bunch,* President.

GULLY, Guy W, Farrell, PA
1232

GUNDLACH, Charles R, Toledo, OH
1325
The Certificate of Registration was revoked on 22nd October 1976 due to Gundlach's failure to submit an Aircraft Activity Report to the FAA. The certificate was re-instated in May 1978 after the G-44 was sold to *Executive Air Service Inc.*

GUYANA AIRWAYS Corp,
Georgetown, Guyana
1015, 1170, B-46
Previously known as *British Guiana Airways* but renamed in 1963. The country became independent in 1966 and the G-21As were withdrawn from service by the 1970s. B-46 was sold by Guyana Airways Corporation to *Antilles Air Boats* in March 1973 for US$92,500, which included a spare engine, propeller and various spares. The aircraft was delivered at Timehri Airport on 28th March 1973 and ferried to the US Virgin Islands in April 1973, using registration N328.

HACKLEY, Sherlock D, Oxford, MD
and at Nassau, Bahamas
1084, 1168, 1424, 1445, 1455
Hackley was Chairman of *Island Flying Services of America Inc* and its affiliate *Out Island Airways Ltd,* both operating from Nassau.

HAGEN, Charles D, Edina, MN
1442

HAGGLAND, James P, College, AK
and at Fairbanks, AK
1338

HAJDUKOVICH, John, Fairbanks, AK
1463
dba *Frontier Flying Service Inc* and was also sometime President of *Alaska Airco Inc.*

HAL'S AIR SERVICE Inc, Kodiak, AK
B-114
Harold Dierich, President, bought the Goose from *Kodiak Western Alaska Airlines* for whom he used to fly it. The aircraft was operated on a daily basis until it crashed near Ouzinkie, AK on 21st July 1984, killing Dierich and his three passengers.

HALL, George C, Fort Lauderdale, FL
1375
Later dba *Crystal Transit Co,* Buffalo, NY

Sherlock Hackley's G-44A Super Widgeon N86619 (c/n 1445) at Nassau, Bahamas on 14th March 1970. After spending much of its life with various owners in the Bahamas and Florida, its status is currently uncertain. (William Haines Collection)

fishing expeditions to Canada. The G-73 was restored to its original state, by means of a nine-year rebuild at *Victoria Air Maintenance* on Vancouver Island, BC, and won the Classic Category Grand Champion award at Oshkosh, WI, in 2001. Because of the re-build it was not grounded after the 2005 Chalk's crash and is now based in Minden, NV.

HAMILTON, William E, Casa Grande, AZ
1340
Co-owner with *Alvin Celcer*. When Celcer and Hamilton breached a financing agreement, the G-44 was re-possessed by *Martin Aviation Co* and assigned to *William A Thompson* on 10th November 1978.

HALL, Robert L, Kodiak, AK
1051, 1110, B-100
See below

HALL, Helen C, Kodiak, AK
Hall was president of *Kodiak Airways Inc*. B-100 was his personal aircraft, co-owned with his wife Helen, but was leased to Kodiak Airways and later *Kodiak Western Alaska Airlines* until it was damaged while hauling live salmon from Akalura Lake, AK. The aircraft was left in the lake until the winter ice set in when it was hauled onto the ice so that it could be repaired enough to fly it back to Kodiak. It was sold, as is, to *Foreign & Domestic Enterprises* in Seattle and completely overhauled in January 1980.

HALLIBURTON OIL WELL CEMENTING Co, Duncan, OK
1013
Halliburton, founded in 1919 in Duncan, OK, has grown into one of the world's largest providers of products and services to the oil and gas industries, employing more than 50,000 people in nearly 70 countries. The company name was changed to Halliburton Company in August 1960. The G-21A was acquired in 1954 and was converted to McKinnon G-21E with P&W PT6A-27 turbine engines in April 1970.

HALLMARK LEASING Corp, Vancouver, BC
B-129, B-145
C/n B-145 was bought from Coopers & Lybrand (Receivers for *Trans Provincial Airlines*) in May 1993 and leased to *Waglisla Air*. Hallmark also bought the remains of c/n B-129 after its crash in June 1994, rebuilt it and sold it in the USA in 1998.

HALTER YACHTS Inc, New Orleans, LA
1372, 1421, 1453

HAMILTAIR Ltd, Vancouver, BC
1003

HAMILTON AERO Ltd, Beverly Hills, CA
1346

HAMILTON, Gladen R, Jr, Vashon, WA
and at Edgewater, MD
1230, 1319

HAMILTON, Steven T, Reno, NV
and at Carson City, NV
1260, 1420, J-13
dba Hamilton Restoration Ltd, Reno, NV. Widgeon c/n 1260 was transferred to the *National Museum of Naval Aviation* at Pensacola, FL and Hamilton bought the wreck of c/n 1420 for re-build, to replace it. It is now based in Carson City and used for

H & H AERO Inc, Wilmington, DE
1300

HANGAR ONE Inc, Wilmington, DE
1270

HANIFL, Howard, Robbinsdale, MN
1319

Halliburton Co letterhead dated 4th June 1954.

Gladen Hamilton's Ranger-powered G-44 N1595V (c/n 1319) visiting Oshkosh, Wisconsin in July 1983. The Widgeon is currently flying with an owner in Idaho. (Jennifer Gradidge)

Steve Hamilton's G-44 N212ST (c/n 1260) re-engined with Continentals is seen here at Oshkosh, Wisconsin. The Widgeon is now preserved in the National Museum of Naval Aviation, Pensacola, Florida. (Jennifer Gradidge)

HANSEN, Harold J, Seattle, WA
dba American Aviation Inc.
B-62
Hansen handled the transfer of the G-21A from Iceland to McKinnon Enterprises in 1967.

HANSEN, Paul B, Pacific Palisades, CA and later at Chugiak, AK
1338
Paul Hansen also made over 130 flights around Kodiak in c/n 1265 for *Alaska Airlines* between 4th March 1950 and 7th October 1950, before owning c/n 1338, which he flew on contract to Kadiak (sic) Fisheries, out of Port Bailey, until selling it to *James W Harvey* in April 1963.

HANSON, James B, Daytona Beach, FL
dba Hanson Aero.
1451, 1458

HANSON, Martin R, Ketchikan, AK
1337
dba *Ketchikan Air Service*, in partnership with *Stanley Oaksmith Jr.*

HARDER, Michael U, Dillingham, AK
1213, 1340
dba *Starflite Inc.* On 11th November 1993 Harder broke the financing agreement on c/n 1340 and it was re-possessed by the *US Small Business Administration*, Anchorage, AK on 25th July 1994. However, the re-possession was rescinded on 19th October 1994 and the G-44 was re-registered to Starflite Inc. In 2007, c/n 1340 was registered to Harder as an individual and was joined by c/n 1213 in October 2010.

HARDY, Malcolm L, Waynesboro, PA
dba Hardy Aviation, Inc.
1045, 1054, 1132, 1153, 1161, 1195, 1368

HAREIDE, D, Åalesund, Norway
1332

HARLEY, David W, Kodiak, AK
1324

HARNISH, Owen & Grant, Auckland, NZ
1356, 1432, 1439, 1466
dba *Aquatic & Vintage Airways Ltd* and later *Salt Air.* Owen Harnish and his son Grant were owners and operators of several small companies in New Zealand. Aquatic & Vintage Airways Ltd was started in 1992. The name was changed to Salt Air in 1996 and in 1999, Owen Harnish handed over the company to his son. Although no longer operational two of the Widgeons have been restored recently and put up for sale, while a third is used as a spares source. Between them the Harnish's have had 25 years accident-free flying with the Widgeons. C/n 1466 was sold in May 2012.

HARRIMAN, E Roland, New York, NY
1003, 1442
The G-21A was based at Roosevelt Field, Long Island, when sold to the Royal Canadian Air Force in 1941. On a Annual Inspection report dated 1st October 1949 it was noted that the G-44A was based at the Grumman airport, Bethpage, on Long Island. The Harriman family owned the G-44A from new until it was sold in 1972.

HARRIS AIRCRAFT SALES, Grafton, WI
1462

HARRIS, Albert C,
North Miami Beach, FL
1215

HARRIS, Charles H,
Sun Valley, CA
12, 16, 25
Ownership of the SCAN-30s was transferred from *Lee Mansdorf & Co* to Harris, with *JG Spielman*, *Walter J Davidson* and *Tom Katsuda*, at the same address as the *Pacific Aircraft Engineering Corp (PACE)* in January 1959 (c/ns 16 & 25 in March 1959).
Ownership then passed from the four partners to PACE in February 1959 (c/n 16 in March 1959 and c/n 25 in April 1959).

HARRISON AIRWAYS Ltd,
Richmond, BC
1235, 1431
JN Haldeman, President. Operated charters from Vancouver, BC.

The legend under the cockpit window reads "Paul Hansen", denoting the owner, who flew the aircraft on charter to Kadiak (sic) Fisheries, Port Bailey, Alaska in the 1950s. G-44 Widgeon N69067 (c/n 1338) is seen here at Renton, Washington on 6th July 1960.   *(Jennifer Gradidge Collection)*

Right: *Roland E Harriman's McKinnon Super Widgeon N86616 (c/n 1442) visiting Nassau, Bahamas on 14th March 1970. The aircraft is currently flying with an owner in Alaska.*
(William Haines Collection)

Albert Harris' Continental-powered Super Widgeon N37DF (c/n 1215) visiting Oshkosh, Wisconsin on 5th August 1986. This former Pan American Airways aircraft survives but its status is uncertain.
(Jennifer Gradidge)

McKinnon Super Widgeon CF-JXX (c/n 1235) of Harrison Airways at Vancouver, British Columbia in early 1969. The aircraft had been repaired after colliding with RCAF Canadair T-33AN Silver Star 21098 on 21st August 1968.   *(William Haines Collection)*

HARRISON, William E, Tulsa, OK
dba *Condor Aviation,*
21

HARRISVILLE COMBING MILLS Inc,
Harrisville, RI
1109
The company was later renamed *The Harrisville Co.*

HART & BLEDSOE INVESTMENT Co,
Jasper, TX
1340
Bought the G-44 from *Graubart Aviation* in October 1961 and sold it back to them in April 1962.

HARTER, David S, Camden, SC
1380
Harter made a quick profit on the war-surplus J4F-2, buying it for $7,500, and selling it next day for $10,000.

HART STUD MILL, Jasper, TX
J-4

HARVEY, James W, Kodiak, AK
1324, 1338, 1377, 1378
dba *Harvey Flying Service.* A family business, started by James W "Bill" Harvey in 1956 with a Republic Seabee. The first G-44, c/n 1378, was acquired in 1958 and sold a year later. It then crashed and was rebuilt by George Pappas. Harvey bought it back as N141R, selling it to *PenAir* in 1963 and replacing it with c/n 1338. Two months later c/n 1324 was added to the fleet. C/n 1377 was not owned initially by Harvey but leased to help out during the busy summer of 1961, although he did own it by 1963. The G-44s operated on-demand charters for the large fish canneries, fishermen and hunters, and were kept busy serving the outlying native villages. Bill Harvey was killed in 1967 when the wing came off his Twin Beech, and Harvey Flying Service closed for business soon afterwards.

It was resurrected in 2000 and is now run by Steve (see below) and Mary Ann Harvey and uses c/n 1360 for carrying freight, mail, hunters, fishermen and tourists around the Kodiak area of Alaska.

HARVEY, Charles Steve, Kodiak, AK
1360
dba Harvey Flying Service. Charles Steve Harvey was the son of *James Harvey*, founder of Harvey Flying Service. After his father's death Steve Harvey flew for other operators but in 1977 bought c/n 1360 and put it to work flying for the Afognak Logging Company on Kodiak Island for four years. From 1981 he flew the G-44 for Bob Stanford under Stanford's *Island Air Service* certificate until, in 1983, Stanford bought a DHC Beaver to do the work of the G-44. In 1985 Harvey leased the G-44 to *PenAir* and flew it for them until 1998 when PenAir closed its Kodiak base. In 2000 Harvey Flying Service was reborn and continues, in 2013, to serve the communities around Kodiak.

After earlier service in Alaska, New York and Brazil, Steve Harvey's Lycoming-powered G-44 Widgeon N17481 (c/n 1360) is still flying charters out of Kodiak, Alaska.   (Harvey Flying Service)

Helicopter Resources' G-73T Turbo Mallard VH-JAW (c/n J-26) was later re-built as a G-73AT and is currently operated from Darwin, Northern Territories for the Paspaley Pearling Company.

(Tony Arbon)

HARVEY, Jerry, Minneapolis, MN
J-4

HATELY, William & Joan C,
Anchorage, AK
1424

HAWES, Peyton, Portland, OR
dba Payless Drug Stores
1147, B-117, B-128, 1380

HAWKINS, Troy G, Wichita Falls, TX
B-18

HAYES AIRCRAFT ACCESSORIES Corp,
New York, NY
1213
Having bought the G-44 new in 1941, the company for some reason reversed its name to become the *Seyah Corp* in 1942. Both had *F William Zelcer* as president, and he allowed the aircraft to be used by the Civil Air Patrol (CAP) in 1942 where it was flown by his step-son John Haggin. 'Johnny' Haggin and Wynant Farr achieved fame within the CAP community for their subsequently unsubstantiated claim to have destroyed a U-boat while flying 1213.

HEALEY, George J, Detroit, MI
1388

HEALY, Kenneth W, Van Nuys, CA
(co-owner with *J Conroy*)
1388

HEDIN, RV, South Minneapolis, MN
1317

HELICOPTER RESOURCES Pty Ltd,
Tyabb, VIC
J-26
Formerly known as *Vowell Air Services* of Tyabb, VIC. The Mallard was based at Karratha, WA and used from 1985 to ferry oil and gas rig crews to and from Barrow Island. On 25th August 1988 an engine failed due to corrosion in the turbine section and the aircraft was damaged in the subsequent forced landing in the Indian Ocean, near Varanus Island, Western Australia. More serious damage was suffered in January 1989 when a wing float dug in and almost tore off the port wing. J-26 was repaired, however, and soon back in service at Karratha. In November 1989 the G-73T was returned to Tyabb, VIC for storage and then transferred to *Aircraft Holdings Inc/Lloyd Helicopters Ltd*, Miami, FL in May 1990.

HELIS, William G, New Orleans, LA
1407, 1469
The aircraft were registered to the Estate of WG Helis. William Helis was a partner in *Edwards Transportation Company* which had owned c/n 1206. C/n 1407 was cancelled from the US Civil Aircraft Register on 13th June 2012, but the registration (N41976) was reserved the same day for use by the Estate of WG Helis.

Charlie Hillard's restored G-44A Super Widgeon N44CH (c/n 1454) in Royal Navy colours as "FP469". The aircraft is currently owned by Royal Baby Duck LLC in Texas.
(Fred J Knight Collection)

HELITECO, San Jose,
Costa Rica (*John M Wells*)
1277

HENLEY, David W, Kodiak, AK
1324
dba *Henley's Air Service*. David Henley
was a pilot for the Department of the
Interior and flew G-21As for Kodiak
Western for eight years, including nearly
4,000 hours in N2845D. Before that he had
operated charters with the G-44 in the late
1960s/early 1970s, based at Kodiak.

HENSLER, Gilbert Anderson Jr,
Nassau, Bahamas
1077, 1084, 1168, 1424, 1445, 1455, 1462
dba *Bahamas Air Traders Ltd*, which he
founded in the early 1960s to provide
services within the Bahamas and to Florida.
He was also involved with *Island Flying
Services of America*.

HESSLER Inc, Wilmington, DE
1334

HEWITT, John Thomas,
Huntington Beach, CA
1342
Hewitt bought the J4F-2 in Uruguay and
had it registered there. Later it was
registered to him at El Segundo, CA and
then Rancho Palos Verdes, CA.

HEWITT, Stanley C, Ketchikan, AK,
and later at Wrangell, AK
4
The SCAN-30 was re-possessed by the
National Bank of Alaska in September
1982 and sold to *James D Perry*.

HICKOK MANUFACTURING Co Inc,
Rochester, NY
1217, 1233, 1425
On a Certificate of Airworthiness application, dated 9th October 1941, Hickok
declared that the aircraft would be used to
transport officials of the company.

HICKORY SPINNERS Inc,
Hickory, NC
1132, 1206
Originally known as Hickory Spinners,
which was a partnership between A Alex
Shuford Jr, PD Hutchison and JE Webber.
By mid-1946 the company had been
incorporated and was under the presidency
of JW Abernethy.

HILL AIR Co Inc, Fort Lauderdale, FL
1110, 1150, 1359
Founded by Frank A Hill and later joined
by *Anthony Stinis*, the company was a
fixed-base operator specialising in twin-
engined aircraft.

HILL, Gene N,
Huntington Beach, CA
(co-owner)
1132

HILL, H Dan, & DIXON, David G,
Santa Ana, CA
J-42
dba *Dixon/Hill Aircraft Leasing Co*. See
also *Trans Catalina Airlines*.

HILLARD, Charlie R, Fort Worth, TX
1451, 1454, 1458

HILTON BOX CO, Klamath Falls, OR
1296

HILTON, Lewis O, Greenville, ME
1136

HOFFMAN, C Chase, Tulare, CA
1153

HOFFMAN, James, Lawton, OK
1420
Hoffman was President of *Windjammer
Capitol & Leasing* and later had an address
in Oceanside, CA.

HOLEMAN, DeWiley, King Cove, AK
1265

HOLLADAY AERO Inc, Arlington, VA
1434
H Warren Holladay, President.

HOLLADAY AVIATION Inc,
Charlottesville, VA
1030
Possibly connected with Holladay Aero,
above.

HOLLIDAY, Frederick T, Indianapolis, IN
1239
dba *T O C Oil*. Holliday described himself
as a partner in T O C Oil Company under
which name he engaged in certain business
enterprises starting in July 1950. He had
intended to find a partner for these business
dealings but, in fact, no partnership was
formed and therefore T O C Oil Company
was solely FT Holliday doing business
under that name. The G-44 was sold by the
executor, Indiana Trust Company,
following Holliday's death in December
1951.

HOLLIDAY, WJ, Indianapolis, IN
1300

HOLLINGSHEAD Corp, RM,
Camden, NJ
1018, 1412, J-44

HOLLINGSWORTH, James P,
South Miami, FL
1364

HOLMES, Gerald, Chattanooga, TN
dba *Inland Marine South Corp.*
B-49

HOLMES, Gerald & ASSOCIATES,
Chattanooga, TN
B-49

HOLMSTEDT, Robert J, North Bend, OR
1187
The G-21A was also registered to *Peggy A
& James Holmstedt*, with *WW Blade*.

HOLT, Major Andrew P, Montreal, QC
J-2
Major Andrew Holt was one of the sons of Sir Herbert Holt, the Canadian millionaire. Holt Jr had business interests in South America as well as Canada and spent his summers in England and the winters in the Bahamas, using the G-73 to commute to the Caribbean. The aircraft was managed by the Montreal Trust Company which oversaw much of the Holt business empire.

HOLT, Herbert P Jr, Montreal, QC
B-39, J-13
Another of the three Holt brothers (see above) who based the G-73 in the Bahamas during the winter and returned it to Toronto during the summer. The aircraft were managed by the Montreal Trust Company which oversaw much of the Holt business empire.

HOLT, William Robert Grattan,
Montreal, QC
B-39
Holt bought the G-21A from the *War Assets Corporation* for use by *Aircraft Industries of Canada*. When WRG Holt died the aircraft was transferred to *Herbert P Holt* (see above).

HOMER AIR SERVICES, Homer, AK
1260

HONORBUILT TRAILER MANUFACTURING Co,
Lakeview, CA
32

HOOVER, Raymond Paul,
Chambersburg, PA
1107

HORVATH, Paul G, Miami, FL
1130, 1136, 1141
Horvath was vice-president of *Air-Sea Charters*.

HORVATH, William, Ida, MI
J-45

HOUGH, Richard,
Morristown, NJ
1306
The G-44 was registered to Richard Hough in January 1978. In November 1990 ownership passed to Richard R Hough, dba Fisher Forestry & Realty Co, and finally to Robert M Hough on 25th August 1992.

HOUGH, Robert M, Derry, NH
- see above

HOUGH, Richard R,
dba *Fisher Forestry & Realty Co*, Concord, NH
- see above

HOUSE OF STAINLESS Inc, Chicago, IL
J-53
Formerly known as *Chicago Steel Service Co*.

HOUSTON-BEECHCRAFT Inc,
Houston, TX
1300
Acted as sales agent for the G-44 in August 1966.

HOWARD AERO SERVICE Inc,
San Antonio, TX
1328
A company specialising in the conversion of Lockheed 18s and PV-1s into updated executive twins, including the Howard 250, 350 and 500. *DH Braman* sold the G-44 to Howard Aero Service in 1955 and took delivery of a Howard 350 in 1963.

HOWES BROTHERS LEATHER Co,
Boston, MA
J-19

HOWSER, Arthur J, West Linn, OR
B-128
Howser bought the G-21A from *Hudson's Bay Company* for Can$112,000 in April 1974, and paid an extra Can$800 for the delivery.

HUDSON FLIGHT Ltd, Pampa, TX
31
LR Hudson, President.

HUDSON, Oren B, Anchorage, AK
dba Hudson Air Service.
1294
Oren Hudson owned and flew his G-44 for 30 years. Work included charters for the US Geological Survey, Water Resource Division, operating to rivers, lakes and gravel bars all over Alaska. Hudson also served outlying villages, providing transportation of people and foodstuffs, and flew charters for oil companies and the Health Department, logging over 12,000hrs flying in the process. At the age of 92, he attended the Alaska Grumman Fly-in at Marion Lake near Anchorage in July 2012, by riding his motorcycle out from Anchorage!

HUDSON'S BAY AIR TRANSPORT Ltd
– see below

HUDSON'S BAY Co, Calgary, AB,
and at Winnipeg, MB
B-128, J-20
The G-21A, acquired in 1961 and based at Winnipeg, was fitted with long-range fuel tanks in the wings, and with retractable floats, for operation in the far north of Canada. The G-73 was operated by *Hudson's Bay Air Transport Ltd* (Thomas Creighton, President) and based at Channing, MB. The company also had hangar facilities at Flin Flon, MB, and it was here that the G-73 was destroyed by fire on 4th April 1963. The company also lost Otters CF-JOR and CF-KTI in the fire.

The Hudson's Bay Company's G-21A Goose CF-HBC (c/n B-128) seen here at Winnipeg in March 1962. The company title is displayed under the cockpit window, while the Dominion flag is on the tailfin. *(Jack McNulty)*

The Hudson's Bay Company also operated Mallard CF-FLC (c/n J-20) seen here at Winnipeg, Manitoba on 16th December 1959. Unfortunately, it was destroyed in a fire in the company hangar at Flin Flon, Manitoba in April 1963. *(Jack McNulty)*

**HUDSON'S BAY MINING &
SMELTING Co**
- see *CV Whitney*

HUFT, John M, Pagosa Springs, CO
1372

HUGHES, Howard, New York, NY
J-14
The legendary pilot and aircraft designer leased the G-73 from *Garfield Wood* in March 1955. In May 1955 the aircraft was reported "stolen" from Miami International Airport. It was found in the Everglades, ten miles north of Andytown, recovered from the swamp on a salvage barge, and then trucked to Miami for repairs. It is still not known how J-14 ended up in the swamp and the only clue to what might have happened is that Howard Hughes paid for the salvage.

HULEN, A Douglas, Anchorage, AK
1329
Hulen owned the G-44 from 1992 until 1994 when it was part owned by *James R Branham*. From March 1997 ownership was in the names of AD Hulen and Helen M Hulen until the latter died in 2001, and AD Hulen became sole owner once again.

HULEN, Helen M, Anchorage, AK
- see above

HUMBLE OIL & REFINING Co,
Houston, TX
B-141, J-53
HC Weiss, President. A large oil company, 80% owned by *Standard Oil Co (New Jersey)*, that has used many corporate aircraft over the years. The JRF-5 was declared surplus by the US Navy before service, returned to Grumman for conversion to G-21A standard, and delivered to Humble Oil in October 1945 at a cost of $79,243. The G-73 was operated in the early 1960s.

HUNSINGER, Charles E,
Long Beach, CA
1137, 1138

HUNT AEROSPACE Pty Ltd,
Howard Springs, NT
B-49
The Goose is operated on charter flights out of Darwin, NT, by *Air Frontier Pty Ltd*, of which Geoffrey W Hunt is a Director. Note that the Goose has been registered using Mr Hunt's initials.

HYDE, Charles G, Roanoke, TX
aka Glen Hyde, dba *Flight Data Inc*,
Carson City, NV.
1086, 1165, B-66
See also *TUCO Inc* and *IR3T Inc*. G-21A c/n 1086 was sold to the National Museum of Naval Aviation in Pensacola, Florida, in 1989.

HYDROXYL SYSTEMS Inc, Victoria, BC
B-117
Juergen Puetter, owner.

G-21A Goose CF-IOL (c/n B-107)of Imperial Oil Limited, at Malton, Ontario in April 1949, shortly after being purchased from the War Assets Corporation. The outline of the RCAF roundel can be seen behind the fuselage door.   *(Jack McNulty)*

Flagship of the Imperial Oil Ltd fleet, Mallard CF-IOA (c/n J-39) is seen here at Toronto-Malton, Ontario on 16th September 1950. The aircraft was sold to Pacific Western Airlines in April 1955 but crashed into a mountain while en route from Kemano to Kitimat, British Columbia on 3rd August the same year.   *(Jack McNulty)*

HYLAN FLYING SERVICE,
Rochester, NY
1368, 1444
Ray P Hylan, President. A Piper dealer, flying school and charter operator based at Rochester Municipal Airport. Hylan had c/n 1368 converted to Lycoming GO 435-C2B power, with auxiliary fuel tanks, by Link Aeronautical in 1955. In 1969 c/n 1368 was flown 50hrs on air taxi work and 50hrs on instruction, but in May 1971 the aircraft was de-registered as dismantled.

ICECAP LLC Trustee, Anchorage, AK
1463

**IDAHO STATE EDUCATIONAL
AGENCY for SURPLUS PROPERTY**,
Boise, ID
1121
The agency applied for Certificates of Registration for a Stinson OY-1 (N58989) and the JRF-5 (N58981) in 1950, but the Chief, Surplus Property Utilisation Program, Washington, DC requested CAA to return the applications and stated that the Idaho Agency would be advised to "transfer the aircraft to a more eligible institution where there is an existing educational requirement for such property". Rather bizarrely after such a request, the G-21A was purchased by Alaska Coastal Airlines for parts!

ILARDI, Agnes, Rochester, NY
36
Transferred ownership of the SCAN-30 in July 1970 to *Joseph P Ilardi*.

ILARDI, Joseph P, Rochester, NY
36

ILARDI, Ruth, Victor, NY
1386

ILFORD-RIVERTON AIRWAYS,
Winnipeg, MB
B-139, 14
HT Kleysen, President. Founded in 1953 and operated passenger and cargo charter flights in northern Manitoba and the Arctic. The G-21A was operated from 1970 until 1972.

ILLINOIS FISH & WILDLIFE,
Chicago, IL
1320, 1350

**ILLINOIS UNIVERSITY BOARD
of TRUSTEES**, Urbana, IL
1385

IMPERIAL AIRWAYS Ltd,
Prince George, BC
1265
Imperial Airways' president was Ben Ginter who also owned *Ben Ginter Construction Co Ltd*, and the G-44 was often used in support of construction contracts in British Columbia.

IMPERIAL OIL Ltd, Toronto, ON
B-107, J-39
Henry H Hewetson, President. The aircraft were operated by Imperial Oil Transport Ltd (JR White, President), based at Toronto-Malton, from 1949-55 in support of oil operations for the parent company.

INCON Corp, Roseburg, OR
1328, 4
JM Shanks, President.

INDAMER Corp, New York, NY
1210

INDIANAPOLIS MORRIS PLAN Corp,
Indianapolis, IN
1233
The finance company re-possessed the
G-44 from *Harold L Pitcher* in August
1962 and sold it to *Charlene Adams.*

**INDONESIAN AIR & WATER
POLICE FORCE**
J-17, J-35
The G-73s were purchased from *Shell Oil*
in November 1963. Test-flights were
performed by Capt Sudaryono, a former
police pilot, who had been flying for Shell
Oil from 1959 until 1963. Initially serials
PK-211 and PK-212 were used, later
changing to P-2011 and P-2012. The latter,
J-17, was destroyed in unknown circum-
stances, while P-2011, J-35, was "sold" to
Dean H Franklin in exchange for a new
Cessna 206 in June 1976.

INDUSTRIAL ACCEPTANCE CORP Ltd,
Vancouver, BC
1235
LE Nicol, President.

**INDUSTRIAL ENGINEERING &
MANUFACTURING Co Inc**,
Brimfield, IN
1329

INDUSTRIAL WINGS Ltd,
Vancouver, BC
1235

INGLE, John W, Naples, NY
1300

INGRAM CONTRACTORS Inc,
Harvey, LA
1266, 1361, 1420
The contracting arm of Ingram Oil
Company. Ingram was bought out by
Tidemark who took over c/n 1420 in the
process.

INLAND MARINE SOUTH Corp,
Chattanooga, TN
B-49
Gerald E Holmes, President. Flown in by
Jerry and Betsey Holmes, the G-21A was
voted Grand Champion Seaplane at Sun'n
Fun 1995.

INLET AIRWAYS, Homer, AK
1130
Paul D Choquette, President. Became *Inlet
Airlines Inc* in September 1959. (see
below).

INLET AIRLINES Inc, Anchorage, AK
1130, 1307
Paul D Choquette, President. In 1960 Inlet
Airlines was licenced to operate between
Anchorage and Seldovia, AK.

INSTITUTE of TECHNOLOGY,
Melbourne, FL
1419

INSTITUTE LINGUISTICO de VERAO,
Brasilia, Brazil
1360
The aircraft was donated to the institute by
Jari Indústria & Comércio SA, and was
operated by *JAARS Aviation* for missionary
work in remote areas of Brazil.

INTER-AMERICAN ESCADRILLE Inc
- see *Beaverbrook, Lord*

INTERCON DEVELOPMENTS Ltd,
Boca Raton, FL
B-104, 1457
Mark Woodring, President. The G-21A was
based at Providenciales, Turks & Caicos
Islands in the British West Indies.

INTERCONTINENTAL AVIATION
2, 3, 4, 9, 10, 11 12, 13, 15, 16, 20, 21, 22,
23, 25, 31, 32, 33, 34, 37
An American company, managed by Alan
H Sanstad, bought the twenty SCAN-30s at
auction in France on 4th October 1952. See
the SCAN-30 section in Chapter 3.

INTERIOR AIRWAYS Inc, Fairbanks, AK
1313, 1338, 1341, 1346, 27
James S Magoffin, President & Chief
Executive.

INTERIOR ENTERPRISES Inc,
Fairbanks, AK
1341, 1399
An operating division of *Interior Airways
Inc.*

**INTERNATIONAL
AIRCRAFT FUEL Ltd**,
Nassau, Bahamas
J-5

INTERNATIONAL AIR SERVICE Inc,
West Palm Beach, FL
J-31
The G-73 was operated by *Charles B
Wrightsman.*

**INTERNATIONAL AMERICAN
ADVERTISING Corp** (IAAC),
North Rafael, CA dba American Graphics
& Chromeprint.
1340
The G-44 was leased from *B A Leasing* in
July 1985, registered to IAAC in
September 1985, but re-possessed by B A
Leasing on 31st October 1985 after a
breach in the finance agreement.

**INTERNATIONAL AVIATION
DEVELOPMENT Corp**, Reno, NV,
and at Danville, CA
1218, 1341
A company specialising in management
and consulting services, in particular
providing aircraft for the oil industry. An
outpost was operated in Malta for many
years, from where the G-44s were operated
by *Libyan Aviation Co.*

INTERNATIONAL HOLDINGS,
New York, NY
B-59
International Holdings was a land holding
company with interests in Canada, the
United States and the Bahamas. The G-21A
was flown by Charles H Spurgeon and
based in Ontario, Canada.

INTERNATIONAL PAPER Co,
New York, NY
B-49
A multi-national company that has used
many aircraft in the personnel transporta-
tion role since 1939.

**INTERNATIONAL PAPER BOX
MACHINE Co**, The, Nashua, NH
1353

INTERNATIONAL PETROLEUM Co,
New York, NY
J-38
Subsidiary of the *Standard Oil Co (New
Jersey)* (now Exxon) who operated the
G 73 in support of oil operations from
Talara, Peru in the 1950s.

**INTERNATIONAL TELEPHONE &
TELEGRAPH Corp**, New York, NY
B-49
ITT has operated many corporate aircraft
since World War II, including Grumman
Gulfstreams, and owned the G-21A during
the 1970s.

INTRACOASTAL TERMINAL Inc,
Harvey, LA
1445

IOZIA, Robert J, Ruidoso, NM
1214
Iozia was a one-time Vice-President of
Seaplane Service Inc.

IR3T Inc, Pahrump, NV
1085
Another company set up by *Charles (Glen)
Hyde.*

IRISH HELICOPTERS LTD,
Shannon, Ireland
19 *(photo page 228)*
The SCAN-30 was actually based at Biggin
Hill, UK.

IRVING OIL TRANSPORT, St John, NB
1324, J-5 *(photo page 228)*
- see below.

IRVING, KC,
dba Avalon Industries, St.John's, NL
J-1
and dba Canadian Veneers Ltd,
St.John, NB
J-1, J-5
Kenneth Colin Irving served in the RFC in
WWI and went into the garage business in
the 1920s. He later formed the Irving Oil
Company and expanded into the forest and
paper business, as well as owning bus
companies. One of the richest men in
Canada, at the time, he saved some money

Irish Helicopters Ltd owned SCAN-30G EI-ALE (c/n 19) powered by DeHavilland Gipsy Queen engines. The aircraft is seen here at Biggin Hill on 31st January 1960.   *(Air-Britain photo)*

Irving Oil Transport operated Mallard CF-EIZ (c/n J-5) seen here visiting Miami, Florida in 1961, with the Irving Gas & Oil logo on the forward fuselage. The G-73 was sold in 1963 when the company upgraded to turbine-powered aircraft.   *(DM Hannah)*

by buying J-1, the ex-demonstrator Mallard, and some more money by importing the aircraft through Newfoundland (see *Avalon Industries*). J-1 was lost after crashing in March 1949 but Irving replaced it with J-5 in 1954. The G-73 was sold in 1963 when the company upgraded to turbine aircraft. Irving died in 1992.

ISLAND AIR SERVICE Inc, Kodiak, AK
1360
Island Air Service Inc was owned by Robert Stanford and flew services out of Kodiak-Municipal Airport. Stanford was short of suitable aircraft so contracted with *Charles Steve Harvey* to fly the G-44 under Stanford's Island Air certificate from 1981 until he (Stanford) bought a DHC Beaver to do the work in 1983.

ISLAND AIRLINES Ltd,
Campbell River, BC
B-139
RC Langdon, President. Operated scheduled and charter services out of Campbell River mainly in support of the logging industry, and used the G-21A between 1973 and 1978. Island Airlines Ltd became part of *Air BC* by June 1980, by which time the G-21A had been sold in the USA.

ISLAND AIRWAYS, New York, NY
1238

ISLAND AIRWAYS Inc, Miami, FL
1323
John C Monte Jr, President.

ISLAND AIRWAYS OF FORT LAUDERDALE Inc,
Fort Lauderdale, FL
1398, 1417

ISLAND CHARTERS Inc, Miami, FL
1445
James C Saunders, President.

ISLAND CHEVRON SERVICE,
Kodiak, AK
1235

ISLAND FLYING BOATS Inc,
Hollywood, FL
also listed at Miami and Opa Locka, FL
1215
Island Flying Boats, a subsidiary of Duncan Aircraft Sales, was founded by James T ('Jim') Robinson who also owned *Air Crane Inc*.

ISLAND FLYING SERVICES of AMERICA Inc, Miami, FL
and later at Nassau, Bahamas
1077, 1084, 1168, 1424, 1445
Presidents: *Sherlock D Hackley and Capt GA Hensler Jr*. Island Flying Services of America was listed in Janes AWA 1969/70 as operating four Super Widgeon and two Gooses, although c/n 1077 had been sold in 1965. By 1975 when c/n 1084 was sold, Dann H Lewis was President. Aka *Island Flying Service*.

ISLAND HOPPERS Inc, Kodiak, AK
1164
Fred Ball, President. The ownership of this G-21A is very complicated. The FAA file contains a Bill of Sale from Robert Sholton to *Island Hoppers Inc* and this is followed by another Bill of Sale jointly from Sholton/Island Hoppers/Kodiak Western/ Alaska Coastal and the BM Behrends Bank of Juneau to Wilton R Probert of Oakland, OR on 30th June 1979. Finally, on 2nd October 1979, the file records an undated Bill of Sale from Island Hoppers Inc to Probert, and he was issued a Certificate of Registration for the aircraft on 2nd October 1979.

ISLE ROYALE AIRWAYS, Houghton, MI
1166
There are references to Isle Royale Airways being based at Grand Marais, MN between 1954 and 1958, but by 1963 the G-21A was flying schedules across Lake Superior from Houghton, MI via Isle Royale to points in Canada and Minnesota (see map in Colour Gallery I). The flights were seasonal, being flown from 20th June until 30th October. Charter flights were also made by Cessna 180 from 1st May until 30th October. In 1964 the G-21A was only used from 20th June until 10th September. The company is

Island Flying Service's G-44A N41993 (c/n 1424) seen here on the company ramp in Nassau, Bahamas in 1971. Note the company's G-44A N86619 (c/n 1445) in the background.   *(MAP)*

Edwin Jameson's smart G-44 Widgeon N62095 (c/n 1349) at Teterboro, New Jersey on New Year's Day 1955. The Certificate of Registration was revoked on 10th July 1981 noting that the aircraft had last flown in 1967. (CN Trask via Jennifer Gradidge)

listed in Janes AWA 1969/70 as operating a G-73, possibly c/n J-45 on lease from *Land-Sea Airways*, on scheduled services within Michigan.

ISPAHANI Ltd, MM, Dacca, East Pakistan
1451

ISRMS Inc, Land-o-Lakes, FL
1364
Robert Del Valle, President.

JAARS AVIATION, Waxhaw, NC
1360
Jungle Aviation & Radio Service (JAARS) was a non-profit missionary group that flew charters to wilderness areas, and used this G-44 in Brazil, after it was donated by the previous owner to the *Institute Linguistico de Verão* in Brasilia.

JACK ADAMS AIRCRAFT SALES Inc, Walls, MS
1267, 1377, 1408, 29, J-4
Jack Adams, President. Based at Twinkletown Airport, Walls, MS.

Jack Adams Aircraft Sales, Inc.
TWINKLETOWN AIRPORT P.O. BOX 121 / WALLS, MISSISSIPPI 38680
PHONE 601 391-4435

Above: *Jack Adams Aircraft Sales' letterhead showing the quaintly-named airport address.*
(Fred J Knight Collection)

JACK & HEINTZ Inc, Bedford, OH
1210
Manufacturers of aircraft parts. William R Jack held an Airline Transport Pilot's licence. The G-44 was registered as NX28671 in June 1945, to allow flight testing of an experimental automatic pilot. By the time that the G-44 was sold in January 1947 the company was known as Jack & Heintz Precision Industries Inc.

JACKS, JE, Hollywood, FL
(co-owner with *Charles L Yuille*)
1274

JACKSON, John G,
Christiansted, St Croix, USVI
1445
Jackson, a certified aircraft mechanic, moved to La Luz, NM in March 1976 and

by June 1977 had a workshop in Lafayette, LA. By April 1979, after he had sold the Widgeon, he had a workshop in Miami Springs, FL.

JACKSON, Richard C,
Somersworth, NH,
and later at Rochester, NH
1394

JAMES, TL & Co Inc, Ruston, LA
1374

JAMESON, Edwin C Jr, New York, NY
1349, 1393
The G-44s were based at Roosevelt Field, Mineola, NY

JAMISON, Gussie R, Chickasha, OK
1364

JANSON, P, Panama?
J-54

JAPAN DOMESTIC AIRLINES/ NITTO AIRLINES, Osaka, Japan
- see *Nitto Air Lines*
1430, J-38, J-40, J-52, J-56

JARI INDÚSTRIA E COMÉRCIO SA,
Brazil
1360
An operator of container ships, Jari donated the G-44 to the *Institute Linguistico de Verão*, in Brasilia. It was operated by *JAARS Aviation* for missionary work in Brazil.

JENSEN, Richard H, Girdwood, AK
1373
The G-44 was originally registered to Jensen's company, *Alaska Aeromarine*, in 1959. Registration of the aircraft passed between members of the Jensen family, finally being sold by the estate of Richard H Jensen in 2003.

JENSEN, Richard LE, Fairbanks, AK
- see above

JETCRAFT Corp, Raleigh, NC
1051
Charles Oliver II, President. Aircraft based at Raleigh-Durham Airport.

JMH LEASING LLC, Fairbanks, AK
1463

JMQ Inc, Gulf Breeze, FL
1317
Julian B MacQueen, President. Aircraft based at Pensacola Regional Airport, FL.

JOHANSEN, K Gunner, Ferndale, MI
1329

JOHNSON & JOHNSON Co,
New Brunswick, NJ
1230
A multinational corporation that has used many different types of aircraft for corporate transportation based at Mercer County Airport, West Trenton, NJ.

JOHNSON, Don, Kenai, AK
1327

JOHNSON, Edmund Glen, Fort Worth, TX
B-126

JOHNSON, F Kirk, Fort Worth, TX
1300

JOHNSON, Jeffrey E & Robert A,
Fort White, FL
1054

JOHNSON, Samuel C, Racine, WI
B-49, 1214
President of SC Johnson & Son Inc and also of Johnson Air Interests Inc which operated the company aircraft.

JOHNSON VL, Warrensburg, NY
1357

JOHNSTON, John DH, Lake Stevens, WA
33
Johnston died when the SCAN-30 crashed on 27th May 1979.

JOHNSTON, Tom, dba Florida Charters
B-86
Johnston bought the G-21A from *Philip L Bingman* for $350,000 in 1999 and had it rebuilt by *Dennis Buehn*, who later bought the aircraft from Johnston.

JOHNSTONE, Isabella Anderson,
Kinshasa, Congo
41
The ownership of this aircraft is complicated. Isabella Johnstone married *Gay George Barnes*, in the British Embassy in Kinshasa, on 28th January 1969. Isabella Johnstone was given as the name of the purchaser when the SCAN-30 was sold by the Modern Furniture Co of Greeneville Inc on 23rd October 1969. Mrs Barnes died of acute renal failure associated with malignant malaria in hospital in Glasgow, Scotland on 15th May 1970. The ownership of the aircraft therefore passed to her husband, but Bills of Sale dated September 1976 show the SCAN-30 being transferred between the *Modern Furniture Co* arms in Greeneville, TN and Elizabethon, TN; and then from the latter to *Flying Sportsmen Inc*, Sussex, NJ.

According to a magazine article, *John Neumeister*, President of *Flying Sportsmen Inc*, found the aircraft in Kinshasa in the Spring of 1976, and stated that it had been there for six years and had not flown in that time. So perhaps the Bills of Sale, dated September 1976, were merely a case of the paperwork catching up with the facts. This does not, however, explain how the SCAN-30 left the ownership of Gay George Barnes after his wife's death. This confusion is further compounded by a Bill of Sale dated 29th March 1977 transferring ownership *from* Flying Sportsmen Inc *to* Gay G Barnes.

JONES, E,
Cairns, QLD
1466

JONES, Irving L, Miami, FL
1141, 1161
President of *Cat Cay Airways* and *Southeast Airlines Inc.*

JONES, Raymond J, Jr, Pontiac, MI
1398
Aircraft based at Oakland-Pontiac Airport.

JONES, Steve W & Mickie B,
Emmonak, AK
33

JOPLIN, William G, Monroe, WA
dba William G Joplin Leasing Co.
1328

JORD Corp, Wilmington, DE
1300

JOYCE LUMBER Co, Chicago, IL
J-32
Beatrice Joyce Kean inherited the fortune amassed by the lumber baron, David Joyce. In 1948 she set up the Joyce Foundation for philanthropic programmes to benefit the Great Lakes region. The G-73 was owned between 1953 and 1965.

JP AIR Inc, Cleveland, OH
1452
W James Priest, President

JRW AVIATION, Dallas, TX
B-72

KACHEMAK AIR SERVICE Inc,
Homer, AK
1265
William DeCreeft, President. Founded in 1967 and flew services out of Beluga Lake, Homer, AK.

KAHN, Roger Wolf,
New York, NY
1230
Kahn, head of Grumman's service department, owned the G-44 briefly before it was impressed in March 1942. From March 1949 he flew a G-58A (civilianised Bearcat) on company missions. Kahn retired from Grumman in 1960 and went to Cornell Laboratories.

KAIL AERONAUTICAL Corp,
Endicott, NY
1329, 1419
Karl A Kail, President. Associate company of *Link Aeronautical* with the same address. Kail was also Vice-President of Link Aeronautical.

K & J AIRCRAFT PARTS Inc, Miami, FL
J-30
James Confalone, President. Took the G-73 in lieu of unpaid bills in December 2005.

KALAMAZOO AIR ZOO MUSEUM,
Portage, MI
J-14
The G-73 was donated by Roland Lafont in 2007 and is displayed on the museum's main campus.

KALT MANUFACTURING Co,
Cleveland, OH
B-62
The parent company of *Aero Quest Inc.*

KALT, Nathaniel A,
Dallas, TX
dba NA Kalt & Co, North American Aviation Plant, Dallas
1230, 1355, 1375

KAMAN AIRCRAFT Corp,
Windsor Locks, CT
1178
The helicopter manufacturer, founded in 1945, became involved in the effort to produce a tilt-wing aircraft for the US military. Using the Goose airframe, Kaman mounted a tilt-wing complete with two propulsive rotors (see Chapter 5). The K-16B, as it was designated, only reached the ground test experimental stage and never flew. The project was abandoned due to the inadequacy of the bearings in the rotors (see Chapter 5). Kaman and Grumman joined forces in a later US Air Force competition for a similar concept but were unsuccessful. The K-16B is preserved at the *New England Air Museum.*

KASHOWER AIR SERVICE Ltd,
Oshawa, ON
B-76

KATHARINE GIBBS SCHOOLS Inc,
New York, NY
1220
Popular rumour has it that the chain of vocational schools was founded by Katharine Gibbs, a pioneering businesswoman. Be that as it may, Katharine senior was the mother of Katharine Edwina Gibbs (born 1905) who later became known as the actress Kay Francis. The G-44 was registered to the KG Schools in 1946 and used throughout the 1950s.

KATSUDA, Tom, Oxnard, CA
11, 12, 16, 25, 32
dba *Gannet Corp*, but described as a "farmer" in the mortgage deed for c/n 32! Ownership of c/n 12 was transferred from *Lee Mansdorf & Co* to Katsuda, with *JG Spielman*, *Charles H Harris* and *Walter J Davidson* at the same address as the *Pacific Aircraft Engineering Corp (PACE)* in January 1959 (c/ns 16 & 25 in March 1959). Ownership then passed from the four partners to PACE in February 1959 (c/n 16 in March 1959 and c/n 25 in April 1959). Katsuda was President of PACE.

KAWNEER Co, Niles, MI
1436

KAY EVELYN Co, The, Houston, TX
1406

KAYFES, James F, Prescott, WI
J-19
Kayfes financed *Northwestern Flying Services*, Nestor Falls, ON.

K C AIRCRAFT SHEET METAL Inc,
Long Beach, CA
1130, 1150, 1051, 1161, B-45, B-73, B-117, B-139
KC van der Riet, President.

KC MACHINE & TOOL Co, Detroit, MI
J-53

KEAN, Beatrice Joyce,
Grand Rapids, MI
dba *Joyce Lumber Co*, Chicago, IL (qv)
J-32

Kachemak Air Service's McKinnon Super Widgeon N99431 (c/n 1265) at Renton, Washington in May 1979(?). The photograph is dated May 1978, but this is 9 months before the Certificate of Registration was issued. The aircraft is currently with an owner in North Carolina.

(Peter Kirkup via Jennifer Gradidge)

KEARNEY & TRECKER Corp,
Milwaukee, WI
1454, J-31
The company used many corporate aircraft, including a Vickers Viscount. See also *Trecker, Francis J.*

KEELER, HF, Seattle, WA
B-101

KEEWATIN ARCTIC CAMP Co,
Winnipeg, MB
B-117
Leased the G-21A to *Calm Air International* between 1978 and 1980, when it was sold to *Weldwood Canada Ltd.*

KEILT, Walter H, Seattle, WA,
and later at Alderwood, WA 1393

KENAI AIR ALASKA Inc, Kenai, AK
1377
Founded in 1955 as Kenai Air Service Inc, the company bought the G-44 in December 1978. Vice-President, *Vernon L Lofstedt*, had the aircraft registered in his name from 1986 until it was sold to *Aqua Air* in 2002.

KENAI FLOATPLANE SERVICE Inc,
Kenai, AK
1327
Founded in 1957 and flew services out of Port Moller - Bear Lake.

KENMORE AIR HARBOR,
Kenmore, WA
1184
Kenmore Air Harbor was founded in 1943, and is the main seaplane base in the Seattle area. The company provides seaplane training courses, and is also a Cessna sales agent.

KENN-AIR LEASING Corp,
Gainesville, FL
1454

KERKORIAN, Kirk, Los Angeles, CA
1138
The former WWII ferry pilot and Las Vegas hotel and movie studio magnate was co-owner with *Rose Pechuls* and dba *Los Angeles Air Service Inc*, later re-named Trans-International Airlines.

KERRISTON Ltd Partnership, Kent, WA
1375
A Newton Ball & Carolyn P Ball, partners. The company was re-named *Widgeon Enterprises LLC* at the same address in 2009.

KERR-McGEE OIL INDUSTRIES Inc,
Oklahoma City, OK
1374

KETCHIKAN AIR SERVICE,
Ketchikan, AK
1337
Owned by *Stanley Oaksmith Jr & Martin R Hanson*, the company operated the G-44 in the early 1950s.

Kenmore Air Harbor's Goose N1257A (c/n 1184) tied down at its home base on 2nd November 1980. The G-21A was sold in Canada in 1998 and was reported being re-built by Pacific Coastal Airlines Ltd in Vancouver. In 2012, however, Pacific Coastal withdrew all their Goose aircraft from service.
(Fred Barnes)

G-21A Goose C-GRCZ (c/n B-49) of Keyamawun Lodge Ltd, undergoing repairs at St Andrews Airport, Winnipeg, Manitoba in July 1985. Note the wingtip float retraction mechanism.
(KM Molson)

KETCHUM, David, Reno, NV
1165

KETTERING, CF, Inc, Dayton, OH
J-42
Charles Kettering graduated from Ohio State University in 1904 and went to work for National Cash Register in Dayton, OH, where he invented the electric cash register. In WWI Kettering joined Orville Wright and *Edward A Deeds* (also of NCR) in forming the Wright Aeroplane Company. In 1919 Kettering became head of research for *General Motors* and after retiring in 1949, he bought the G-73 and named it *"The Blue Tail Fly"*. Although for his personal use, the aircraft was operated from Dayton by General Motors after his retirement, until his death in 1958.

KEY BANK OF ALASKA, Fairbanks, AK
1328
Repossessed the G-44 from *James L Dodson* in 1995 and had it registered to the Bank in February 1996, before selling it to *James Carner* in July 1997.

KEYAMAWUN LODGE Ltd,
Red Lake, ON
B-49

KEYS, Robert Harvey,
Noosa Heads, Qld
1164
Bob Keys, owner of *Paradise Air Services*, transferred his G-21A to his company, *Up Over Down Under* in 1992, and to the Australian register in 1999. In 2000 the aircraft was painted as US Navy "931-79" for the TV series *"South Pacific 2001"*, starring Glenn Close. In 2005 it was reported to have been sold to the Yaukuve resort in Fiji and was painted as DQ-AYL in preparation for delivery. The deal fell through, but another proposal was for the G-21A to operate services in the Solomon Islands. As of December 2010 it was still in Australia, painted as DQ-AYL, being prepared for delivery to *Solomon Islands Seaplanes Ltd*. The project was postponed due to financial restraints in 2011, and then cancelled due to bureaucratic delays with licensing. In March 2013 the Goose was at Wangaratta completing its rebuild to executive configuration by Precision Aerospace. It was then planned to base it in Noumea for charter work.

KEYSTONE HELICOPTER Corp,
Philadelphia, PA
B-100

KIDS INVESTMENT,
San Luis Obispo, CA
A California Ltd Partnership.
1424

KIEKHAEFER Corp, Chicago, IL
and at Fond du Lac, WI
B-54, J-42

KIECKHEFER CONTAINER Corp,
Camden, NJ
1160
HM Kieckhefer, President. See also *North Carolina Pump Co.*

KILKENNY, Osmond J,
Dublin, Ireland
B-120
'Ossie' Kilkenny is an accountant with substantial film, television and music interests. The G-21A was used mainly within Ireland to carry show-biz and other clients in connection with his business interests.

KILLA KATCHKA, West Bloomfield, MI
1051, B-125
Robert R Redner, President, flies the aircraft himself, enjoying fishing trips to northern Canada.

KIMBALL, Warner H, Fort Lauderdale, FL
B-100
Kimball was V-P of *American-Bahamian Air Service Inc*.

KIPNIS, JL, Jacksonville, FL
1374

KIRK, Charles M, El Rio, CA
11, 16, 32
The SCAN-30s were imported by *Lee Mansdorf*. C/n 11 was never in fact registered to Kirk because he did not support his application with the correct documentation.

KLEINBERGER, Moises Press,
Cali, Colombia
1084
Kleinberger sold the G-21A to *Air Mart International*, Panama in 2007.

KLEINSMID, Walter B von,
Long Beach, CA
1110, B-29
In 1954 Kleinsmid bought Jean Chisholm's 50% share in *Avalon Air Transport* and thus became *Dick Probert's* partner. Kleinsmid's business acumen was a perfect foil to Probert's "let's do it now" approach. Under their leadership Avalon Air Transport served Santa Catalina Island for some 15 years, an achievement that was recognised by the people of Avalon with the award of a plaque of appreciation. The complicated story of the purchase of the Paraguayan JRF-5s can be found under Paraguay in the Military Operators section in Chapter 7.

KNIGHT, Karl, Miami, FL
1334

McKinnon Super Widgeon N213K (c/n 1414) of Knox Gelatine Company, visiting Toronto Island Airport in July 1970. The G-44A was owned by the Knox family from new in 1945 until 1989. The aircraft is currently for sale in Calgary, Alberta.   (William Haines Collection)

KNILM
- see *Koninklijke Nederlandsch-Indische Luchtvaart Maatschappij*

KNOX GELATINE Co, Johnstown, NY
1414
Founded by Charles B Knox. The company took delivery of the G-44 in 1945 and used it as a personal and company transport. (see below)

KNOX, John, Lake Pleasant, NY
1414
Knox flew the company G-44A with a crew of three from Key West, FL to Cuba on 28th March 1950. The aircraft was converted to Lycoming power in 1954 by McKinnon and continued in service with the Knox family/company until sold in Canada in 1989.

KODIAK AIRWAYS Inc, Kodiak, AK
1020, 1125, 1132, 1147, 1173, 1195, B-100,
B-126, 1215, 1231, 1260, 1267, 1270, 1323,
1337, 1339, 1340, 1397, 1442
Robert L Hall, owner and President. Kodiak Airways Inc served outlying points on the island of Kodiak from 1950. The first G-44, c/n 1339, acquired in the early 1950s was named "Helen", after Hall's wife. Irregular charters were operated until

1954, when the company was awarded a contract to provide mail service to various points on the island. The first G-21A, c/n 1125, arrived in 1956, scheduled services started on 5th December 1960 and by April 1963 three routes were operated from Kodiak to Olga Bay, Parks and Port Williams. The former Pan Am G-44, c/n 1215, was purchased on 1st June 1961 for $24,000, bringing the ever-changing Widgeon fleet to three. On 27th March 1964 an earthquake in the Anchorage area caused a tidal wave which destroyed the Kodiak Airways hangar at Kodiak seaplane base. Unfortunately c/n 1173 was in the hangar at the time and was also destroyed.

By April 1965 the routes were from Kodiak to Lazy Bay, Karluk and Port Williams. By November 1965, Kodiak to Port Wakefield was flown six times weekly and on to Port Williams once weekly. Kodiak to Alitak was flown via Old Harbor six times weekly, and Kodiak to Larsen Bay via "San Juan" three times weekly. Kodiak Airways was merged with *Western Alaska Airlines* to form *Kodiak Western Alaska Airlines* on 1st April 1973.

Robert Hall's son Robbie was killed when c/n 1125, which he was piloting, crashed returning from Old Harbor to Kodiak on 11th December 1974.

A wing-walker features on a nice, but undated, shot of G-21A Goose N69263 (c/n 1132) of Kodiak Airways Inc, probably on Lilly Lake, Kodiak.   (Guy Denton)

The first Widgeon for Kodiak Airways, N58847 (c/n 1339), was named "Helen" after Bob Hall's wife. The blue and yellow Alaskan flag is painted on the forward fuselage. The undated photo was taken on the company's wooden ramp at Kodiak, Alaska. *(Guy Denton)*

A close-up of Kodiak Airways' founder Bob Hall fuelling Widgeon N58847 (c/n 1339) "Helen", on the company's wooden ramp at Kodiak, Alaska in the early 1950s. Note the company title and logo aft of the door. *(via Steve Harvey)*

KODIAK WESTERN ALASKA

AIRLINES, (KWAA), Anchorage, AK
1051, 1110, 1132, 1164, B-100, B-112, B-114, B-126, 1215, 1267, 1340, 1442, 1468
Kodiak Western Alaska Airlines was formed on 1st April 1973 when *Kodiak Airways* merged with *Western Alaska Airlines*, with *Robert L Hall* remaining as President. Head office was at Merrill Field in Anchorage and services were flown to outlying communities in the Kodiak and

Bristol Bay areas. KWAA also maintained a base at the Kodiak seaplane base. G-21A c/n 1164 was leased reportedly from *Northern Air Cargo*. However the FAA file contains a Bill of Sale from *Robert Sholton*, owner of Northern Air Cargo, to Kodiak Western dated 9th June 1977 (but no Certificate of Registration [CofR]), followed by another Bill of Sale that transfers the aircraft back to Sholton on 6th March 1978 with a CofR dated 16th May 1978. An undated Bill of Sale transfers the

G-21A from Sholton to *Island Hoppers Inc* and this is followed by another Bill of Sale (remarkably) from Sholton/Island Hoppers/ Kodiak Western/Alaska Coastal and the BM Behrends Bank of Juneau, to *Wilton R Probert* of Oakland, OR on 30th June 1979. Finally the file records, on 2nd October 1979, an undated Bill of Sale from Island Hoppers Inc to Probert, and he is issued a Certificate of Registration on 2nd October 1979.

G-21As B-100 and B-112 were modified with "smoke-jumper" doors to facilitate cargo handling (see Chapter 5). By 1980 the Grumman fleet was reduced to three G-21As and one G-44, and by 1985 all operations had ceased.

KOERTS, Albert J
1356

KOHLER, Terry J, Sheboygan, WI
B-72
also dba Terryair, Puerto Montt, Chile in support of the Rio Puelo Lodge. After returning to the USA in 1996 the G-21A was operated by Windway Aviation, Sheboygan, WI.

KONINKLIJKE NEDERLANDSCH - INDISCHE LUCHTVAART MAATSCHAPPIJ (KNILM) – ROYAL DUTCH INDIES AIRLINES,
Batavia
1009, 1056, 1080, 1081
KNILM was incorporated in Amsterdam on 16th July 1928 to provide commercial air services throughout the Netherlands East Indies as well as the connecting segment (Batavia – Sydney) of the KLM service from the Netherlands to Australia. C/n 1009 was used in survey work for *Shell Oil Co*. C/ns 1080 and 1081 were delivered to Batavia in March 1940. Lockheed L-14s were used for a service from Batavia via Soerabaya to Makassar. Departing Batavia on 18th August 1940, a G-21A left Makassar on 21st August 1940 to extend the service via Ambon to Manokwari in Dutch New Guinea (see first-flight cover in Colour Gallery I). On 1st October 1940 a G-21A inaugurated a route from Makassar to Ambon via Palapo, Kolonedale, Gorontalo, Menado and Ternate. C/n 1056 was leased from Shell in November 1941. During February 1942 evacuation flights were operated in advance of the Japanese

Kodiak Western Alaska Airlines' Super Widgeon N91040 (c/n 1267) under a misty Alaskan sky in July 1976. The engines are Continental IO-470-Ms fitted in August 1967. *(JB Hayes)*

G-21A N72PR (c/n 1164) known locally as "Peter Rabbit" in a non-standard Kodiak Western colour scheme in the late 1970s. The much-travelled Goose is currently being re-built in Australia. (via Guy Denton)

Goose (c/n 1081) for KNILM as PK-AFS, with remains of its NX- test registration still visible. The photo was apparently taken in the USA in 1940, before or during delivery. The G-21A was shot down over Timor during the Japanese advance in January 1942. (AeroHobby)

LABOMBARDE, Raymond A,
Nashua, NH
1353

LABRADOR AIRWAYS,
Goose Bay, Labrador
1415
Formed in 1969 when Eastern Provincial Airways sold its bush operations to a group of employees. Leased the G-44 from *Newfoundland & Labrador Air Transport Ltd* for scheduled and charter flights from Goose Bay, Deer Lake and St Anthony.

LAC MANAGEMENT, Lakehurst, NJ
J-18
Jack Bart, owner.

LAFLIN, Lloyd Alan,
Castle Hot Springs, AZ
1472

occupation. Three of the G-21As were destroyed by enemy action whilst the fourth was broken up to avoid capture by the Japanese.

KOZENY, Victor, Cayman Islands
J-34

KRAJCIRIK, Lisa & Dorothy, Glenn, CA
1214

KRAMER, Joseph,
Majuro, Marshall Islands, Micronesia
34
Leased the SCAN-30 from *Lagoon Aviation.*

KRANDALL, Jerry, Detroit, MI
1368

KRAUSE, George, Dillingham, AK
1232

KRECK, Steven C, Carson City, NV
31

KRUSE, William P, San Francisco, CA
1346

K-T FLYING SERVICE Ltd, Honolulu, HI
1292, 1298, 1300
Theodore R James, President. The company was formed on 24th August 1945 and incorporated on 29th August 1945. Charters were flown within the Hawaiian Islands from the company base at John Rodgers Airport, Honolulu.

KURTZER, Lana R, Seattle, WA
dba Kurtzer Air Service out of Seattle Harbor.
1291

LAB - see *LLOYD AEREO BOLIVIANO*

LABATE AVIATION Inc, Carolina, PR
J-28
The company co-owned the Mallard with *Caribbean Airline Services* until it was sold to *Flying Boat Inc* in 1992.

LABATE, Salvatore J, (Trustee)
Malvern, PA
J-11

Steven Kreck's SCAN-30 Widgeon N4453 (c/n 31) was re-engined with 300hp Lycoming R-680E radials and re-designated a PACE Gannet in 1967. The aircraft was used in the 1970s TV series "Fantasy Island" and is seen here in 1979. (MAP)

Jack Bart's Mallard N98BS (c/n J-18) with the legend "Ti-Loup du Lac" on the forward hull, seen here at New London, Connecticut on 15th July 1994. Jack Bart was the owner of LAC Management. (Robert Parmerter)

Lloyd Laflin's newly delivered G-44A Widgeon N86646 (c/n 1472) in 1947. After various owners before 2005, ownership was granted to Mirabella Aviation Inc of Fort Pierce, Florida in January 2007, after a court case. The aircraft was reportedly being rebuilt in 2008 but its current status remains uncertain. (R Stuckey)

Lagoon Aviation's PACE Gannet N4452 (c/n 34) under the palm trees at Majuro on the Marshall Islands. Unfortunately the aircraft was written-off on 31st July 1972. (via MW Prime)

SCAN-30G Widgeon VP-KNV (c/n 19) of Lake Air Charters Ltd, Mwanza, Tanganika seen here at Croydon, UK circa 1957. It was later registered as EI-ALE, and as G-ARIX the aircraft unfortunately crashed in Southampton Water, UK in May 1961. (DAS McKay via Jennifer Gradidge)

LAFONT, Roland, Albuquerque, NM
J-14
Lafont acquired the G-73 in 1993, had it refurbished and operated it until 2007 when he donated it to the *Kalamazoo Air Zoo Museum*.

LAGOON AVIATION,
Majuro, Marshall Islands
34
Leased the SCAN-30 to *Joseph Kramer* from 12th January 1971.

LAHMANN, Román Macaya,
San José, Costa Rica
1141
Bought the remains of the G-21A for $250. After major repairs by TACA Airways the aircraft was sold in the USA.

LAIGNELOT, Serge J, Denver, CO
1152

LAKE AIR CHARTERS Ltd,
Mwanza, Tanganika
19

LAKE AIR Inc, Fort Lauderdale, FL
1214, J-11
Ron Buccarelli, President.

LAKE NEW ENGLAND Inc,
Laconia, NH
1315
Armand Rivard, President.

LAMB, Stuart M, Jr, Marblehead, MA
1438
The G-44A was severely damaged in an accident on 9th November 1975 and although salvaged was cancelled from the US Civil Aircraft Register in January 1976.

LAMB RENTAL TOOLS Inc,
Lafayette, LA
1420
WC Lamb, President.

LAMBROS, George, Jr, Jupiter Beach, FL, and later at Ridgefield Park, NJ - see below
1319, 1469

LAMBROS SEAPLANE BASE,
Ridgefield Park, NJ
George Lambros Jr, President.
1228, 1319, 1378, 1398, 1444, 1450, 41
Lambros bought c/n 1228 on 24th May 1950. The FAA cancelled the Certificate of Registration on 31st May 1950 for failure to comply with Civil Air Regulations. The FAA recorded the aircraft as re-instated on 11th December 1953 and the Certificate of Registration was re-issued to Lambros on 15th January 1954.

LAMM, Barney E,
Kenora, ON and Gimli, MB
B-55, B-120
Lamm was owner of *Can-Am Aircraft Ltd*, and owner and President of *Ontario Central Airlines*.

Ontario Central's business was based on fishing charters to Ball Lake Lodge. In 1969, it was discovered that the local paper companies had, over many years, been polluting the river systems with mercury. In the light of this discovery the government banned all fishing activities in the Ball Lake and Wabigoon river system causing Lamm to close his fishing lodge. His response was to file a multi-million lawsuit against the pulp and paper companies in January 1971. He also started a publicity campaign against them which antagonised the local population, many of whom worked in the paper industry. The situation became so fraught that, in 1972, Lamm decided to move his family and airline out of Kenora. He sold the floatplane operation to *Parsons Airways* and moved the rest of his aircraft to the former RCAF base at Gimli, MB.

LAND MANAGEMENT Corp,
Lincoln, NB
B-117
President: Jack R Cole, who also presided over *Executive Seminars Inc.*

LANDRY, James E, Seattle, WA
1388

LAND 'N SEA AIRWAYS
- see *See, Clarence, Jr*

LAND-SEA-AIRWAYS Inc, Detroit, MI
J-34, J-45
William Horvath, President
Land-Sea-Airways operated hunting and fishing trips and was an affiliate of *Aero Quality Sales Co Inc*, owned by *George W Sherwood*. As the business expanded Sherwood included antelope hunting trips to Wyoming and deep-sea fishing trips to the Bahamas in the winter. The high volume of business occasionally necessitated the charter of a third Mallard. J-45 may have been leased to *Isle Royale Airways* in the late 1960s.

LANGLEY, James N, Ashland, OR
31
Langley's mailing address was Redondo Beach, CA.

LANOLIN-PLUS Inc, Chicago, IL
1160
Affiliate of *Consolidated Cosmetics* at the same address.

LANSON HOLDINGS Ltd, Toronto, ON
1187
President: *Matthew James Boylen*, who was also president of *Advocate Mines Ltd.*

LARRANCE, Clifford E,
Port Townsend, WA
dba *North Coast Aero*.
1051, 26

LARRANCE, Danae A, Port Ludlow, WA
26

LARSON, Kenneth, Anchorage, AK
1300

LARY, Albert G, & Co, Los Angeles, CA
1317

LASSITER, James Walker,
Falls Church, VA
1153
Assumed to have been the same James
Lassiter employed by *Western Enterprises
Incorporated* in Taiwan circa 1952.

**LAS VEGAS AIRCRAFT SALES
& LEASING**, Henderson, NV
1184

LATHAM, William C, Manassas, VA
1277
Latham operated his G-44 from a grass
strip on his farm at Haymarket, VA.

**LATSHAW DRILLING &
EXPLORATION Co,**
Broken Arrow, OK
1474
Trent B Latshaw, President. By 2011 the
aircraft was registered at an address in
Tulsa, OK.

LAURENTIAN AIR SERVICES Ltd,
Ottawa, ON
1059
Founded in 1936, Laurentian Air Services
(LAS) held a licence to operate non-
scheduled services, and in 1960 a regular
service was flown from Ottawa to St Jovite.
The G-21A was used between 1945 and
1975, and LAS became Air Schefferville in
1981.

LAVCO - see *Libyan Aviation Co*

LAWRENCE AIRCRAFT SALES Inc,
Homer, AK dba *Homer Air Services.*
1260

LAWREYS, Francois Maurice,
London, UK
J-55

LAWSON, Chester M, Ponce Inlet, FL
and later at Daytona Beach &
Port Orange, FL
1464
Lawson bought the G-44A in August 1990
and has used it to provide seaplane training
from the Spruce Creek Airport, FL.

**LAYMAN, BD, LAYMAN ER,
& OLDHAM, KD**, Anchorage, AK
1377
Oldham & B Layman were partners in
Northwest Airmotive.

LEASE, Nathan, Dublin, GA
1374
Lease bought the J4F-2 from the WAA for
$7,500 on 28th October 1946 and sold it
the same day to *Whitehead's Inc.*

LEBCA International - see *Perez, HR*

LEE COUNTY LAND & TITLE Co,
Miami Beach, FL
3

William Latham's Super Widgeon N54VT (c/n 1277) which he operated from a grass strip on his farm at Haymarket, Virginia. The photo was taken at Oshkosh, Wisconsin in 1989/1990. In October 1994, Latham landed on his home strip with the undercarriage up, substantially damaging the aircraft, although he was uninjured. (Jennifer Gradidge)

Latshaw Drilling & Exploration's Super Widgeon N474JH (c/n 1474) was one of the G-44As that went to Pakistan/Bangladesh. Now restored and re-engined with Lycomings, the aircraft is seen here at Boeing Field, Washington in October 1999. (Fred J Knight Collection)

Laurentian Air Services' Goose CF-BXR (c/n 1059) at Uplands, Ottawa in May 1965. Note the rear emergency door, mandatory on passenger carrying aircraft. (Jack McNulty)

Chester Lawson's G-44A Widgeon N86638 (c/n 1464) powered by Continental O-470-M engines, which with a pressure carburettor produce 240hp. Lawson used the Widgeon to provide seaplane training from Spruce Creek Airport in Florida. (Mike Moore)

LEE MANSDORF
- see *Mansdorf & Company*

LEE, Thomas S, ENTERPRISES
J-38

**LEEWARD AERONAUTICAL
SALES Inc,**
Miami, FL
1132
This company was owned by Albert J
Leeward, with a head office in Fort Wayne,
IN, and specialised in the leasing and sale
of executive aircraft and parts.

LEHIGH ACRES DEVELOPMENT Corp,
Miami Beach, FL
3
On a FAA Form 337, dated 30th March
1964, the aircraft's owner was noted as
Tursair Executive Aircraft Services Inc in
Opa Locka, FL. It is therefore likely that
Tursair operated the aircraft on behalf of
Lehigh Acres Development Corp.

LEHIGH VALLEY OIL Co, Allentown, PA
1411
DE Leber Jr, President. Operated the G-44A
during the 1960s.

LEHMAN, Robert, Long Island, NY
1059

LEISURE LIVING COMMUNITIES Inc,
South Casco, ME
4

LENTSCH, William J, Fairbanks, AK
dba *Tamarack Air Ltd.*
1338

LENOX, RE, Forest Grove, OR
1391

LEVY, Lionel K, New York, NY
1282

LEWIS, Clayton,
George Town, Grand Cayman,
Cayman Islands
dba *Mallard Aviation Corp.*
J-34
Lewis, with his wife Dragana, were flown
around the world in the G-73T in 2000/
2003, piloted by Glen Wales and Peter
McLeod. Glen Wales had flown J-34 for the
MacTaggart family and remained as captain
when Lewis bought the aircraft. Having
flown half way around the world to
Australia, Wales handed over the captaincy
to Peter McLeod, who had gained experience
with the Mallards of Paspaley Pearling Co.
McLeod flew the Lewises back home via
Asia, Europe and the North Atlantic.

LEWIS, Donald J, New York, NY
dba *Seaplane Shuttle Transport Inc,* aka
Cosmopolitan Broadcasting Corp, New
York, NY
1153

LEWIS, George, Miami, FL (co-owner)
J-388

G-44A N41988 (c/n 1419) in September 1966 after conversion to Link Super Widgeon with 280hp Lycoming GO-480-B engines and Hartzell HC-83-20-2B propellers. The aircraft is currently flying with an owner in Virginia. (Steve Krauss)

LEWIS PAPER Co, JP, Beaver Falls, NY
1306
Dick Benson was the Chief Pilot and used
to fly the G-44 with *"Bud" Windhausen.*

LIBERTY AIR, Hudson, NY
B-100
According to a Form 337 lodged with the
FAA, Liberty Air operated the G-21A
owned by *Richmor Aviation* during 1986.

LIBYAN AVIATION Co (LAVCO), Malta
1218
A company specialising in oilfield-related
work. The G-44 was operated in Nigeria
for *International Aviation Development
Corp.*

LILLEBERG, Martin K,
Mercer Island, WA
- co-owner with *John R Logan*
1325

**LINCOLN 1st FEDERAL SAVINGS &
LOAN ASSOCIATION,** Spokane, WA
President: Donald P Lindsay.
J-23

LINCOLN THOMAS AVIATION,
Milwaukee, WI
1171

LINDBURG, A Clinton, St. Louis, MO
1375

LINDEN FLIGHT SERVICE, Inc,
Linden, NJ
B-71
This Beechcraft sales & service agency and
charter operator bought the G-21A, of
which it was said: "suffered major damage,
and there is a good possibility that it will
never be rebuilt". Linden requested the
FAA to reserve the registration N30Y for
their future use and to assign N152M to the
G-21A.

LINDOW, David H,
Steamboat Springs, CO
1471

LINDSLEY, Fred O, Jr, Montclair, NJ
dba Lindsley Chevrolet.
1214

LINK AERONAUTICAL Corp,
Endicott, NY
1206, 1213, 1237, 1315, 1329, 1364, 1404,
1419, 1435, 1438, 1441, 1457
Link Aeronautical Corp started operations
in Cortland, NY in 1928, offering
maintenance and flight instruction. The
firm moved to Tri-Cities Airport, Endicott,
NY in 1936 and Link Aviation Inc was
formed to produce the flight simulators for
which *Edwin Link* is best known. During
the 1950s Link Aeronautical Corp carried
out modifications and conversions on
Widgeon aircraft. (see Chapter 5).

LINK, Edwin A, Binghampton, NY
1419, 1441
-see above

**LION ENTERPRISES
ETABLISSEMENT** 1381
This company is noted as the "seller" on a
Bill of Sale for the G-44 to Aviation
Facilities Inc, Miami, FL after the aircraft
had been removed from the Nigerian Civil
Aircraft Register in November 1968. This
company's connection, if any, with Pan
African Airlines (Nigeria) Ltd is not known.

LITTLE ROCK AIRMOTIVE,
Little Rock, AR
1213
Lucien M Taillac, President. The company
carried out a major overhaul of the G-44 in
1970/1 and flight tested the alterations
under an Experimental Certificate of
Airworthiness dated 3rd February 1971.
Only 105 minutes flying time was required
for this and a Standard Certificate of
Airworthiness (under CAR 4a) was issued
on 10th February 1971, and the aircraft was
sold on 20th February 1971.

LLOYD AEREO BOLIVIANO, (LAB)
Cochabamba, Bolivia
1015
LAB was formed in 1925 and used mainly
German aircraft. In June 1938 the G-21A
was delivered and named *"Moxos"*. The
use of registration numbers began in 1940
and these were issued retrospectively, the
G-21A being allocated CB-24 in May41,
although there is no evidence that these
markings were carried on the aircraft.

LLOYD HELICOPTERS Ltd
- see *Helicopter Resources Pty Ltd*

**LLOYD HELICOPTERS
(SINGAPORE) Pte**
- see *Helicopter Resources Pty Ltd*

LLOYD, Peter J, Nassau, Bahamas
1381

LOCKHART, Dr John A, Bath, NB
1441

LODATO, Joseph S & Carol, San Jose, CA
1385, 1475
dba *Westholm Aviation*, with a mailing address at Crystal Bay, NV. Joseph S Lodato, with an address at Gardnerville, NV, later became sole owner of c/n 1475.

LOFFLAND BROS Co, Tulsa, OK
1372
Based at New Iberia, LA in August 1957, but back to Tulsa by September 1958.

LOFSTEDT, Vernon L, Kenai, AK
1377
Lofstedt was Vice-President of *Kenai Air Alaska Inc*.

LOFTLEIDIR hf, Reykjavik, Iceland
1020, 1125, 1139, 1168, B-71
Loftleidir hf was formed on 10th March 1944 in Reykjavik by Alfred Eliasson, Kristin Olsen and Sigidur Olafsson, with one Stinson SR-8CM, purchased in Canada. Operations started in April that same year from an old seaplane base leased from the Reykjavík Harbour Authority. This facility included a hangar used earlier by a company that had operated Junkers F.13s between 1928 and 1931. The airline acquired its first Goose, JRF-5 c/n B-71, directly from Grumman in August 1944. After crew training was completed the aircraft, registered TF-RVK, departed Bethpage, Long Island for Reykjavik on 29th September 1944. The delivery flight is

said to be the first North Atlantic crossing by a Grumman Goose. According to the biography of Alfred Elíasson, one of the founding trio of Loftleidir and Chief Executive Officer for many years, this aircraft was prepared specially by Grumman for the delivery flight. This included the installation of de-icing boots and other equipment at no extra charge. It is said that Grumman made a point of using this North Atlantic delivery flight in advertising material. Bad weather was encountered en-route forcing extended stays in Goose Bay, Labrador and Iqateq, Greenland (Bluie East Two). Reykjavík was finally reached on 16th October 1944. On 23rd October TF-RVK flew its first passenger service for Loftleidir from Reykjavík to Isafjördur.

Loftleidir operated a total of five G-21As in the years between 1944 and 1953. They were operated on Loftleidir's scheduled services from Reykjavík to villages in the west and north of Iceland. In March 1946, the schedule included flights as follows: To and from: Ísafjördur week days (Monday through Friday); Patreksfjördur, Tuesdays, Thursdays and Saturdays; Bíldudalur Wednesdays; Thingeyri Wednesdays and Fridays; Flateyri Thursdays; Súgandafjördur Thursdays; Stykkishólmur Mondays; Búdardalur Mondays; Hólmavik Mondays; Siglufjördur Mondays, Thursdays and Saturdays.

The first six (Ísafjördur, Patreksfjördur, Bíldudalur, Thingeyri, Flateyri, and Súgandafjördur) are all in the Westfjords region, with Ísafjördur being the commercial centre for the region. When Loftleidir started operations in 1944 the company immediately focused its sights on the Westfjords as this area of the country had seen very little air service. Iceland Airways (*Flugfélag Íslands*), founded in Akureyri in 1937, had concentrated its operations from Reykjavík more on serving the north, east and southeastern parts of the country. Stykkishólmur is the commercial

centre for the Snæfellsnes peninsula and Búdardalur is a small village and commercial centre in the western part of the country. Hólmavík is another small village in the northwest.

Loftleidir's first Goose, TF-RVK, was heavily damaged in a landing accident at the seaplane base in Reykjavík while taking part in a Royal Air Force air-show on 15th September 1945. The cause of the accident was that the landing gear was still extended when the aircraft attempted a water landing. The pilot suffered minor injuries but there were no injuries to the six passengers in this accident, but the aircraft had to be shipped back to Grumman for rebuilding. After repair it was returned to Iceland by sea. The wooden container in which the Goose was shipped was of such fine material that it was used as the first part of a passenger terminal for Loftleidir at Reykjavik Airport. The container is still in use today, but now as a weekend cottage not too far from Reykjavik.

The second Loftleidir G-21A, c/n 1020, was acquired immediately to replace the crashed aircraft. This aircraft left Montreal on 5th October 1945 but again delays were encountered due to weather en route, and it eventually arrived in Reykjavík on 28th October.

According to Alfred Elíasson´s biography, Loftleidir had acquired an option for an early delivery from Grumman of a G-73. This option was sold in the summer of 1946 when the company acquired three military surplus JRF-6B's instead. According to Elíasson these aircraft were stored in a field in Georgia and were purchased at a very good price, with a US Military veteran serving as middleman. These three aircraft were flown to Iceland together in a group via Mont Joli, Quebec (overnight 2nd/3rd November), and Goose Bay, Labrador, where they remained until 16th November due to adverse weather in Greenland. All three departed Goose Bay en route for

Loftleidir's first G-21A Goose TF-RVK (c/n B-71). A former US Navy JRF-5, it is seen here in the New York area in the late 1940s. It was later owned by the New York Yankees and ended its life with McKinnon Enterprises as N152M. The registration was cancelled on 18th June 1965 after an accident.
(W Steeneck via Jennifer Gradidge)

Bluie West and arrived at Reykjavík on 18th November 1946.

An important part of Loftleidir's Goose operations were the seasonal herring spotting flights off the North Coast of Iceland. Loftleidir operated their herring spotting flights from a base at lake Miklavatn in Skagafjördur near the main herring centre in Siglufjördur, while *Flugfélag Íslands* (Iceland Airways) operated their herring spotting flights from the seaplane base at Akureyri. Aircraft were first used in Iceland for herring spotting in 1929 and continuously between 1938 and the early 1960s.

Landhelgisgæzlan (the Icelandic Coast Guard) would sometimes lease aircraft from Loftleidir and Iceland Airways for fisheries patrol work and offshore reconnaissance. For these flights Coast Guard personnel would form part of the crew. On at least one occasion, in late March 1948, six boats were caught fishing illegally when spotted from a G-21A leased from Loftleidir.

Loftleidir lost one aircraft, TF-RVI, in a fatal crash on 13th March 1947 at Búdardalur in Hvammsfjördur. Four lives were lost in this accident but there were four survivors, including the pilot.

One G-21A, TF-RVG, was sold in 1949 at the same time that Loftleidir acquired its first Catalina, which received the marks carried by the Goose it was replacing. Another G-21A, TF-RVA, was sold in 1951 when Loftleidir purchased its second Catalina, TF-RVR. By the time that the Icelandic government chose *Flugfélag Íslands* to be the only domestic carrier in Iceland and all services ceased on 3rd January 1952, Loftleidir had only one G-21A (B-71) in the fleet. This was sold in the USA in September 1952 but paperwork related to the sale was delayed due to a general strike in Iceland one result of which was that mail for the USA was diverted via Great Britain.

LOGAN, John R, Mercer Island, WA
1325
Logan was registered as co-owner of the G-44 with *Martin K Lilleberg* in November 1965, and then as sole owner in March 1967.

LONGINI, Georgia, Barrington, IL
1210

LONGINI, Georgia Y, Chicago, IL
4
dba Boats Inc. Bought the PACE Gannet direct from *Lee Mansdorf* "as new" in October 1955 after it had been fitted with Lycoming R-680 engines.

LONG ISLAND AIRLINES Inc,
Southampton, NY
1444, 1449, 1450
Formed by Royce Grimm on 20th March 1946 with a head office in Southampton, NY, with Grimm as President. In the company prospectus issued on 27th June 1946 the airline proposed to offer com-

muter services from a base at 23rd Street and East River Drive in New York City, to Montauk Point, Southampton, Easthampton and Westhampton. The services would be operated from 15th May to 15th October using "the most modern amphibious equipment available". The proposed schedule called for five non-stop flights daily each way to Montauk Point, and six non-stop flights daily each way to Easthampton, to Southampton and to Westhampton, using the G-44As.

The prospectus accompanied a stock issue, the proceeds of which were intended to be used for the purchase of G-73s, and rather optimistically, it was stated that "delivery of the first Mallard is expected some time in July" (1946). Whether the stock issue was successful is not known but Long Island Airlines, like many other aspiring operators, did not purchase a G-73.

The airline had negotiated free landing rights on Lake Montauk for three years from 15th April 1946, and thereafter a charge of 10 cents per passenger from New York would be levied until the end of the twenty-year contract. The Montauk Beach Company signed an agreement to provide a site for a seaplane ramp adjoining the Montauk Yacht Club for a period of ten years at a rent of $1 per annum. The Montauk Beach Company also agreed to pay $2,000 towards the estimated cost of $5,000 for the construction of the ramp.

Long Island Airlines was also granted the right to use the Easthampton Airport until 16th October 1948 for a payment of $1,000 per annum, providing the airline maintained a regular passenger service with at least one scheduled flight each day.

The village of Southampton, pending construction of a municipal airport, had designated a temporary landing area in the waters of "the township of Shinnecock Bay", which the airline was permitted to use. The village of Southampton also contracted to lease the Old Fort Pond (Southampton) for use as a seaplane base for three years at a rent of $1,000 per annum. It was agreed that the village would construct a seaplane ramp and dredge a suitable channel to the ramp. The airline agreed to operate the base at Old Fort Pond and provide scheduled airline services from there to New York City.

Services to Westhampton-Riverhead were reported to land at Suffolk Airport, (which charged 20 cents per passenger), while negotiations were taking place to allow the use of the nearby Suffolk County Airport which could provide hangar facilities.

C/n 1450 was delivered in June 1946, with the other two aircraft following in July 1946. C/n 1449 was fitted with "special cabin seating" and a third window on the starboard side before delivery. It is not known for how long the proposed services were actually operated, and the G-44As were sold in September 1949.

LONGLEY, Fuller, Chattanooga, TN
1392

LORRILARD, P, Co, New York, NY
J-49

LOS ANGELES AIR SERVICE,
Los Angeles, CA
1138
Founded by *Kirk Kerkorian* in 1948 to operate charter services from Los Angeles Municipal Airport. Non-scheduled passenger services began in November 1948. The G-21A (registered to Kerkorian and his sister *Rose Pechuls*) was added in July 1949 but was sold to *Alaska Coastal Airlines* in December 1949.

LOST IN TIME LLC, Rochester, NY
1444

LOUGHREA MARITIME II LLC,
Charlotte, NC
1324, 1472

LOUISIANA AIRCRAFT,
Baton Rouge, LA
1377

LOUISIANA STATE CIVIL DEFENSE AGENCY, Baton Rouge, LA
1303
The Bill of Sale from the US Department of Commerce stipulated that the aircraft was "to be used for aerial reconnaissance for Civil Defense use in disaster".

LOUISIANA STATE, WILDLIFE & FISHERIES COMMISSION,
New Orleans, LA
1361, 1445, 1454, 30

LOUISIANA SURPLUS PROPERTY AGENCY, Baton Rouge, LA
1303

LUCAYA AIR, Opa Locka, FL
1429
Operated services to the Bahamas in the late 1980s and was later based at Freeport on Grand Bahama.

LUDINGTON, Nicholas, Philadelphia, PA
1167

LUDLOW JUTE Co Ltd, Boston, MA
and later at Calcutta, India
1171
The log book of Ronald Keith Cannon shows that he flew Goose N79565 at Dacca, East Pakistan, in January 1958, doing circuits, including 5 water landings, with Capt H Law. The G-21A was cancelled from the US Civil Aircraft Register on 21st August 1962. McKinnon records show this as "*Calcutta Goose*" which was modified with a radar nose kit in 1968. The owner was listed as D Ghosh, and there is also mention of a company called Associated Airworks at Dum Dum Airport, Calcutta. Details of registration in India are unknown.

LUDWIG, Carl H, Peekskill, NY
and later at Irvington, NY
41

LUMANAIR Inc, Aurora, IL
1370

LUND AVIATION (CANADA) Ltd,
Montreal, QC
B-111, 1213
Aircraft sales agent.

LUNDE, Trygve,
Bergen, Norway
1134

LURA CORPORATION Ltd,
Montreal, QC
1447
co-owner with *Chelsea Holdings Ltd* & *RP Mills & Co Ltd*.
RP Mills was President of *Lura Corp* & *RP Mills & Co Ltd*.

LYON Inc, Detroit, MI
J-31

LYONS, Alan W, Sedro Woolley, WA
4

M A Inc, Oshkosh, WI
B-137, 1472, J-31
John (Jack) Mark, President, a noted collector of warbird aircraft. He died in 2007 and the aircraft were put up for sale.

MAAHS, Alice & Eugene F,
Hermiston, OR
1291

MABEE, Roy W, Anchorage, AK
& Anaheim,CA
B-47, B-128, 1398

MACDONALD CONSTRUCTION,
Miami, FL
1126

MACDONALD, Hugh A, Honolulu, HI
1349

MACKEY AIRLINES Inc,
Fort Lauderdale, FL
B-19, B-74
Founded by Colonel Joseph C Mackey in 1946 as Mackey Air Transport. The G-21As, obtained in 1956, were intended for use on the lucrative run to Nassau in the Bahamas, which Mackey had been flying with DC-3s, but it is doubtful that they were so used. Opposition to Mackey's plans were voiced by the people of Bimini at a CAB hearing into the case in 1956. Their petition stated that *"Bahamas Airways, Chalk's Air Service and Island Airways* had given excellent and more than adequate service". In a letter to Captain Fair of Bahamas Airways, dated 19th October 1956, Dean H Franklin said that he had *"reliable information that Mackey Airlines intends to start a schedule operation beginning November 1st (1956) between Miami and Bimini and possibly other points in the Bahamas, with Goose aircraft. They intend to cut the present fare practically in half hoping to eliminate all competition."* Ironically, B-74 was sold to Bahamas

Airways in February 1958, after B-19 had been sold to Suncoast Airways Inc of Palm Beach, FL in March 1957.

MACLEAN, Charles Stuart,
Louisville, KY
and later at Prospect, KY
1317
dba *Wood-Mosaic Co*. After MacLean died in 1961, his daughter *Kathleen MacLean Gowell* was appointed as Trustee (in 1967). A Bill of Sale dated 31st May 1967 transferred ownership of the G-44 from Citizens Fidelity Bank (Executors of the estate) to Mrs Gowell as Trustee.

MACLEAN, CS, as above?
1423
Sold the G-44A to *Millard Auto Aero Marine Ltd* in April 1952.

MACMILLAN BLOEDEL Ltd,
Richmond, BC
B-83, B-107
The two G-21As had been operated by *West Coast Transport* which was the corporate aviation department of the company based at Vancouver International Airport. A nominal change was made on 1st January 1980 when West Coast Transport became a division of the company, and was renamed MacMillan Bloedel Ltd Flight

Operations. The aircraft were sold to *Pacific Coastal Airlines* in October 1994. See also *Powell River Co Ltd*.

MACPHEE, Donna, Palm Springs, CA
1437

MACAYA, Robert, Oakland, CA
1141

MACTAGGART, Sandy Auld,
Edmonton, AB
J-34
Sandy Mactaggart was the property developer who headed *Gold Bar Developments*. He was an experienced sailor and also had a pilot's licence but he hired pilot/engineer Glen Wales to manage the G-73T which was used to visit the family estates in the Bahamas and the Isle of Islay in the Hebrides. The PT-6A-28s were replaced by PT-6A-34s in 1990, the aircraft given a complete overhaul by Viking Air in British Columbia, and, equipped with an inflatable boat, was ready to see the world. After touring South America in 1994, J-34 was ferried from Santa Barbara, CA to Honolulu using a ferry fuel tank in the fuselage. The Mactaggarts then crossed the south Pacific in J-34, calling at Samoa, Tonga, Fiji, New Caledonia, Papua New Guinea, Norfolk

Mallard N1888T (c/n J-31) owned by MA Inc of Oshkosh, Wisconsin who operated the G-73 under a Transport category Certificate of Airworthiness from 27th April 1988 until the Mallard fleet was grounded in 2006. The photograph was taken at Milwaukee, Wisconsin on 20th August 1980.
(Peter Kirkup via Jennifer Gradidge)

Mackey Airlines had purchased G-21A Goose N2579B (c/n B-74) for intended services between Miami and the Bahamas, in competition with Bahamas Airways Ltd, Chalk's and Island Airways. Local opposition to the airline's plans were voiced at a CAB hearing in 1956, and the aircraft was sold to Bahamas Airways in 1958.
(Art Krieger Collection)

The former Imperial Oil Company's G-21A Goose C-FIOL (c/n B-107) is seen here over the British Columbia forests while owned by MacMillan-Blodel, and named "Dryad" on the forward fuselage. *(John Kimberley)*

and Christmas Islands in the process. The journey back to Edmonton was via India and Scotland thus completing a circumnavigation of the globe. Mactaggart sold the aircraft when he was no longer medically fit to fly. The much-travelled G-73T circled the globe again in 2001/2003.

MADDEN & SMITH AIRCRAFT SALES,
Miami, FL
1324, J-5

MAGNOLIA Corp, Cypress, TX
1398
John B Kane, President.

MAGOFFIN, James S, Snr, Fairbanks, AK
1312, 1313,1359
Magoffin was President of *Interior Airways Inc*. N68395 (c/n 1359) was leased to *Transocean Air Lines* circa 1950.

MAGOFFIN, James S, Fairbanks, AK
1338

MAHIEU, Lew, Long Beach, CA
1130, B-66, B-73, B-119, 1327, 1388
Mahieu owned c/ns 1130, B-66 and B-73 in the mid-1970s before they went to *Catalina Airlines Inc*. He later moved to Willow, AK and owned the Super Widgeon c/n 1327 for 3 years.

MAKI, Arne A, Long Island City, NY
1352

MALIBU SEAERO SERVICE Ltd,
Vancouver, BC
1003
The company was owned by Tom Hamilton of the Hamilton Aircraft Propellor Company. Hamilton built and operated Malibu Lodge on Princess Louise Inlet, BC and used the G-21A to fly customers and supplies to the fishing lodge. Operated under a Commercial Class 4 Licence and based at Sea Island Airport, the aircraft was used from 1945 until it crashed and sank in January 1953. See also *Hamiltair Ltd.*

MALLARD AIRCRAFT Corp,
Wilmington, DE & Barrington, IL
J-35
William R Rose, President.

MALLARD AVIATION Corp,
George Town, Cayman Islands
J-34
Owned by *Clayton & Dragana Lewis*, J-34 flew to many places around the world between June 2000 and the end of 2003. The first part of the epic journey was under the captaincy of Glen Wales, who had come

Malibu Seaero's G-21A Goose CF-BHL (c/n 1003) seen circa 1948. The Malibu Lodge logo is shown on the tail above the legend "Sky Chief". The Goose was lost in an accident on 27th January 1953 while operating with Central British Columbia Airways . *(via Ingvar Klett)*

The Mallard Aircraft Corporation of Barrington, Illinois owned Mallard N100BR (c/n J-35) in the 1990s. The G-73 is seen here at Oshkosh, Wisconsin on 28th July 1993, and is currently registered in the USA but operating in Australia. *(Jennifer Gradidge)*

Management Associates' G-44A Widgeon NC41989 (c/n 1420) seen here at Boston-Logan Airport in 1953 prior to its sale to John Zimicki of Loudonville, New York. After conversion to Super Widgeon standard, the aircraft was used in support of oil exploration in Louisiana for many years and is currently flying with an owner in Nevada. *(David Rankin via Jennifer Gradidge)*

MANLEY BROTHERS, Chesterton, IN
1210

MANLEY, Phyllis (co-owner),
Long Beach, CA dba *Catalina Seaplanes.*
1153

MANNING, Norman, Ltd,
Vancouver, BC
1406
President, Norman B Manning, who leased the G-44A to *North Coast Air Services* for services out of Prince Rupert, BC.

MANOKOTAK AIR - see *Starflite Inc.*

MANSDORF, Harry, Los Angeles, CA
1351
Harry Mansdorf was a partner in the *Lee Mansdorf & Co* conversion & repair business (see below).

MANSDORF & COMPANY, Lee,
Compton, CA
1231, 1351, 1388, 2, 3, 4, 9 - 16, 20 - 23, 25, 31 - 34, 37
The company moved to San Valley, CA, and by 1967 used an address in Sherman Oaks, CA. The Mansdorf family (Lee, Harry and Norman) ran a conversion and repair business and re-engined SCAN-30 Widgeons with 300hp Lycoming R-680 radials. Most of the SCANs were purchased from *Conair Corporation*, Montreal, QC in October 1954. Ownership of some of the SCANs (eg c/n 25) was passed through officers of the *PACE Corporation* to the Corporation itself.

with the G-73 when it was bought from *Sandy Mactaggart*. From November 2002 the flights were made with Peter McLeod in the left-hand seat. The corporation later had an office in Seattle, WA and the aircraft was offered for sale/long lease in January 2012, stating that it was "in storage in the USA".

MANAGEMENT ASSOCIATES,
Boston, MA
1420

MANATEE Inc, Fort Lauderdale, FL
1445
Steve St Clair, President, who also presided over *Odyssey Aircraft Leasing Inc*, to whom the aircraft was transferred in May 1982.

M & F FISH FARMS,
Del Ray Beach, FL
1364
The Bill of Sale recording the "purchase" of this G-44 was signed by LS Frisk as Vice-President of M & F Fish Farms. However before the aircraft could be registered it was sold back to *Aircraft Ltd* and was then sold to *Seacoast Aircraft* of Riviera Beach, FL whose President was LS Frisk.

M & K AVIATION Inc, Jeffersonville, IN
21

SCAN-30 Widgeon N58LM (c/n 14) was converted to PACE Gannet with Lycoming R-680E-13 radial engines in 1958, before sale to Richmond Pulp & Paper Company of Canada on 15th December 1958. After returning to the USA in 1975, the aircraft suffered substantial damage in an accident at Point MacKenzie near Anchorage, Alaska on 9th October 2004. The plan was to remove the wreckage by sled when the ground was frozen sufficiently. The aircraft was recovered and rebuilt and is now flying with another owner in Alaska. *(Fred J Knight Collection)*

This 1960 photo shows SCAN-30 N63L (c/n 2) after conversion to Lycoming R-680E radial power by Lee Mansdorf. The PACE Gannet was exported to Pakistan in 1962 where it was used by the United Nations. *(Howard Levy via Jennifer Gradidge)*

MANSUR, Harold W, Fairbanks, AK
1206

MANTZ, A Paul, Burbank, CA
1346
dba Paul Mantz Air Services, based at Hangar #1 at the Lockheed Air Terminal in Burbank.

MANUFACTURERS HANOVER TRUST Co / C.I.T. Corp
J-9, J-11, J-28, J-32, J-51, J-53, J-55
This group was a 100% stockholder and secured creditor of the *Virgin Islands Seaplane Shuttle Inc* (VISS). On 14th December 1989 the assets of VISS were abandoned to them. The assets included: G-73s J-11 and J-28 irrepairable; J-53 damaged but repairable and J-55 irrepairable; G-73Ts J-9, J-32 irrepairable and J-51 badly damaged. This was after the ravages of Hurricane Hugo had put paid to VISS's already slim chances of economic survival.

MARCHANT, James C,
Roslyn, Long Island, NY
1013
Operated unscheduled charters with the G-21A in the late 1940s.

MARCO FLITE SERVICES Inc,
Margate, FL
1150
Received the wreckage of the G-21A after the crash on 25th March 1999.

MARDICK, JK, Honolulu, HI
1317, 1338
Mardick bought both the J4F-2s from the WAA for $2,500 each in 1947, and immediately sold them to *Fred C Richards* for $3,400 and $3,600, respectively.

MARINE AIRCRAFT Corp,
New York, NY
1334

MARINE AIRWAYS
- see *Alaska Coastal Airlines*

MARINE INDUSTRIES Ltd, Sorrel, QC
14, 15
Gerard Filion, President. SCAN-30 c/n14 was based at St Hubert, QC in 1969.

MARINE INVESTMENTS Inc,
Mobile, AL
1409

MARJIM CORPORATION Ltd,
Winnipeg, MB
1458
James R Shore, President.

MARJON REALTY Inc, San Carlos, CA
1453

MARK IV AVIATION,
Fort Lauderdale, FL
J-35
Mark Shubin, President. Bought the G-73 from the *US Customs Service* after it had been seized (reason unknown).

The Marjim Corporation's G-44A Super Widgeon CF-IJO (c/n 1458) at Winnipeg, Manitoba in August 1964. After many years' service with various owners in Canada, the aircraft is currently registered as N9GW with an owner in Connecticut. (Art Krieger)

William F Marshall's McKinnon Super Widgeon (c/n 1441) with personalised registration CF-WFM, seen at Mount Hope, Ontario in September 1966. Note the name "Kiska VII" on the bow. (Jack McNulty)

MARK, John J, Dunedin, FL
1472

MARK, John J,
Hales Corner, WI
dba *M A Inc,* Oshkosh, WI.
J-31

MARRS, Joe G, Opa Locka, FL
1167, B-49, 1334, 1384
Owner of *Marrs Aircraft*, Hollywood, FL which purchased salvaged aircraft and also sold aircraft and parts.

MARSHALL, William F, Oshawa, ON
1441

MARTIN AVIATION Co, Walla Walla, WA
1340

MARTIN, Douglas F, Boca Raton, FL
1150

MARTIN, Ernest, Kalispell, MT
c/o Rocky Mountain Aircraft Service.
J-56

MARTIN, Herman L, Walla Walla, WA
1215, 1396

MARTIN, James MW, Greenwich, CT
12
Martin was Secretary/Treasurer of the *Peekskill Seaplane Base Inc*. After his death in 2006 the SCAN-30 was sold to *Airborne Attitude LLC.*

MARTIN, Klaus Dieter, Munich, Germany
1145, 1149, B-88, B-101, B-104, B-141
Martin bought the ex-Forest Industries Flying Tankers' G-21A c/n B-101 the ex-Tropical Sea Air Goose c/n 1145, and the derelict ex-Antilles Air Boats aircraft, planning to operate services in Croatia. The aircraft were taken to Landsberied, near Munich to be prepared for service. C/n B-101 was operated briefly in *European Coastal Airlines* colours in 2002, but was last noted stored at Borovo Naselje, Vukovar, Croatia in October 2008. The remainder were still in various states of repair at Landsberied in 2011.

MARTIN, Timothy R, Anchorage, AK
1231, 1346, 1442, 30
Martin built his house in such a way that he could rebuild the Widgeon, c/n 1346, inside the house! He bought the salvaged remains of the SCAN-30, used parts in the rebuild of his G-44, and sold the remains to *Edwin Forsberg* in 2008. Widgeons c/n 1231 and 1442 were being rebuilt (as of April 2013), in partnership with *Grant A Stephens*.

MARYK, George,
Lac du Bonnet, MB
dba *Tall Timber Lodge.*
1381

MARZICH, Frank M, Rockford, IL
1394

MASSEY-HARRIS Co Ltd, Toronto, ON
B-70
JS Duncan, President. A manufacturer of agricultural machinery that used many other corporate aircraft as well as the G-21A, which was based at Toronto-Malton between 1950 and 1952.

MASSIM EXPEDITIONS & TOURS,
Rabaul, Papua New Guinea
- see also *Pacific New Guinea Lines.*
1466

MATTHEWS, Charles E,
Tegucigalpa, Honduras
1175
Matthews was associated with TACA, which had operated the G-21A before it was sold to *Texaco* in May 1944.

MATTHEWS, Rodney N,
- see *Rod Aero Aircraft Brokerage Inc*

MAUGERI, Joseph W, Miami, FL
1448
Maugeri, who operated an aircraft service facility in Miami Beach, FL, was also President of *Seaplane Service Inc.*

MAUGERI, Salvatore,
Miami, FL & Safford, AZ
1382

MAXWELL, Michael A & Adrienne J,
Anchorage, AK
dba DeBarr Dental Center.
1424, 1464
C/n 1464 was based at Merrill Field, Anchorage.

MAY, Malvern O, Pearl Harbor, HI
1393
On a Certificate of Airworthiness application dated 7th February 1948 May's address was stated as NAS Alameda.

MAYES, Brett R, Williams, CA
1165

MAYES, John, Austin, TX
J-56

McAVOY AIR SERVICES Ltd,
Yellowknife, NT
1240
In 1962 McAvoy Air Services was operating a Fairchild model 82D from the Seaplane Base in the Old Town in Yellow-knife. The G-44 was owned from mid-1963 until December 1964.

McCHESNEY, Lindsley, Troy, NY
1232

McCORMICK, Col Robert R, Chicago, IL
1005
- see *Chicago Tribune*

McCORMICK, Robert E, Renton, WA
1325
McCormick bought the G-44 in May 1982, but from May 1991 it seems to have been under overhaul or repair at Speciality

The Massey-Harris Company's G-21A Goose CF-ETJ (c/n B-70) a former Royal Canadian Air Force Goose II, is seen here at Malton, Ontario in June 1949. Note the re-inforced bow, possibly installed after the ground-loop accident in 1948.   *(Jack McNulty)*

McDermott's Continental-powered Widgeon 5N-AMD (c/n 1317) is seen here at Shoreham, UK in September 1974 en route from Nigeria to the USA. After an overhaul by McDermott, the aircraft returned to Nigeria as 5N-AMG in 1976. It was imported to the UK in 1991 in poor condition, where it was restored to flying condition by 1995 and exported to Florida in 1997, where it currently remains airworthy.   *(Peter J Bish)*

Aircraft Maintenance in Seattle, WA until at least 2004, with the total airframe flight time over that period remaining static at 6,371hrs.

McCRAY, George J, Jamestown, NY
1384

McCRAY, Neil R, Jamestown, NY
1384

McDERMOTT (NIGERIA) Ltd,
Ikeja, Nigeria
1221, 1237, 1317, 1372
The G-44s were transferred from the parent company in the USA (see below) to support oil exploration in Nigeria.

McDERMOTT, J Ray & Co Inc,
Harvey, LA
and at New Orleans, LA
1221, 1237, 1317, 1372, 1413, 1421, 1435, 1453, B-54
McDermott was an oilfield contractor and construction company. Having their own aviation department allowed them to initiate a Widgeon conversion programme, converting all their Widgeons to Continental power, and carrying out conversions for other owners (see Chapter 5). The company changed address to New Orleans, LA in 1969 and was known as McDermott Inc from December 1982.

G-21A, c/n B-54 was leased from *SAATAS* in support of operations in Indonesia in the early 1980s. In 1985 the company decided to sell all its prop-driven aircraft and all the remaining G-44s were disposed of.

McDONALD, HD, Seattle, WA
1393

McDONALD, J Gordon, Ann Arbor, MI
1356

McDONALD, Thomas,
Whitehouse Station, NJ
and at Clermont, FL
1051

McDONNELL, Edward O,
New York, NY
1212
A financier who had joined the consortium that backed Juan Trippe, John Hambleton and *Cornelius Vanderbilt Whitney* in financing the newly-formed *Pan American World Airways* in 1927.

McFARLAND, HJ, Construction Co Ltd,
Picton, ON
1441
HJ McFarland, President.

McGUIRE, Thomas E, Anchorage, AK
1206

McINTYRE-PORCUPINE MINES Ltd,
Toronto, ON
1240, J-2, J-16
JP Bickell, President. In December 1941 c/n 1240 was the first G-44 exported to Canada, with plans to put it to use in the war effort (see Chapter 7). The G-73, J-2, was owned during 1946/47, and J-16 briefly during 1961 before it was sold in the USA for US$142,500.

McKAY PRODUCTS Corp,
New York, NY
1445
The company, owned by S Earle Kay and S Zachary Kay, who was President, bought the G-44A new from Grumman in June 1946. The company was incorporated in Baltimore, MD on 31st Dec 1946.

McKEE, CD, Los Angeles, CA
1325
The Bill of Sale from the War Assets Administration gave McKee's address as c/o Nelson-Kelley Co in San Diego, CA. The G-44 was prepared for civilian service by Nelson-Kelley and was probably not used by McKee, who sold it two months later.

McKINNEY, J Curtiss, Titusville, PA

McKINNEY, James C, Titusville, PA
B-35, 1303, 1306, 1314, 1329, 1380, J-31
McKinney owned G-44 c/n 1306, apparently for the second time, a short time before his death, when it was sold to *Amphibian Parts,* Miami. In March 1964 c/n 1306 had been registered to J Curtiss McKinney, whereas in May 1976 he was recorded on the Bill of Sale as James C McKinney. It is assumed that the two names relate to the same person.

McKINNON, AG
- see *McKinnon Coach & McKinnon Enterprises* (below)

McKINNON COACH Inc, Sandy, OR
1045, B-128, 1313
AG McKinnon, President. Acted as sales agent for transfer of the G-21A, c/n 1045, from *Chevron Oil* to Canada in 1974, and c/n B-128 from *Hawes* to *Overtrade Inc* in 1978.

McKINNON ENTERPRISES Inc,
Sandy, OR
1054, 1147, 1153, B-62, B-71, B-78, B-117, B-123, B-125, B-137, B-138, 1230, 1266, 1299, 1312, 1343, 1346, 1380, 1414, 1427, 1430, 26 - 30
The company was founded in 1952 by Angus Gerald McKinnon as *McKinnon-Hickman Company* in Portland, OR. Since that time it has specialised in the overhaul, modernisation and conversion of Grumman amphibians. Some seventy Widgeons, including SCAN-30s, had been converted to Lycoming power by 1968. The G-21A conversions started in 1959 when c/n 1147 was re-engined with four Lycoming GSO-480s.

When G-21A c/n 1153 was sold by McKinnon to Warren Plummer in May 1965 the FAA were prompted to issue a memo, dated 18th May 1965, stating:
"Please note the bill of sale from McKinnon Enterprises Inc to Mr Plummer in Winnipeg is dated May 10th, 1965. This was due to a complicated financial arrangement between Nagasaki Airlines, Toyomenka Inc, McKinnon Enterprises Inc, Mr Plummer and the gentlemen who are purchasing the aircraft from Mr Plummer. Actually, all documents were completed when we issued the certificate of airworthiness for export to Canada, and all of the aforementioned parties were satisfied."
B-71 was bought after suffering major damage. No Form 337s are on file and it is therefore possible that it was not rebuilt, and only used for spares.
A second facility was opened at Victoria, BC, and was operated as McKinnon Enterprises Ltd. The business was later bought by *Dan Vollum* of Portland, OR and subsequently by *Antilles Seaplanes LLC* of Gibsonville, NC.

Full details of McKinnon conversions can be found in Chapter 5, while Chapter 9 gives the Antilles Seaplanes Super Goose story.

McKINNON-HICKMAN Co,
Portland, OR
- see above

McLEAN, Jerry P, Weatherford OK
(co-owner)
1132
McLean was company secretary of *Air Aquatic Inc* and had the G-21A registered in his name (with co-owner *Shaun V Baldacchino*) in August 1985.

McLOUTH STEEL Corp,
Detroit, MI
1170, J-18
Donald B McLouth, President. Company pilot: Don McLott.
The registration N10M was transferred from the G-21A to the G-73 in 1956.

McNALLY, Richard D, Miami, FL
1323

Above: *McKinnon G-21D N150M (c/n 1147/1251) on the company ramp on 10th May 1965. The property in the background is Angus McKinnon's family home.* **Below:** *The same aircraft after being re-engined with PT6A-20 engines and becoming the McKinnon G-21D Hybrid N150M (c/n 1147/1251). It is seen here doing engine runs on the McKinnon ramp at Sandy, Oregon on 31st August 1966.* *(both McKinnon photos via D Marion)*

McNEW, GH, South Miami, FL
1130, 1214

MEAD, Dudley H, San Francisco, CA
1453

MECOM, John W, Houston, TX
1281, 9
The oil magnate who owned *US Oil of Louisiana* which operated the G-44 in the 1960s and early 1970s. Ownership was registered to Mecom in 1977. An affiliate company, The John Mecom Oil Company, based in Salif, Yemen, operated the SCAN-30 in the early 1960s.

MELVIN, Dr Perry D, Warner Robins, GA
1435
The G-44A crashed into Lake Borgne, near New Orleans, LA in June 1975. It was salvaged and sold through *George Potter Aircraft* to Dr Melvin who restored it over a nine-year period between 1985 and 1994. The G-44A won the "Best All-Metal Amphibian" award at Sun 'n Fun 2008.

MEMPHIS FLYING SERVICE Inc,
Germantown, TN
1372
George Tamble, President.

MERCANTILE NATIONAL BANK,
Dallas, TX
B-100

MERCURY AVIATION SERVICE,
Detroit, MI
1368
The surplus J4F-2 was purchased in May 1946. The Bill of Sale notes that the aircraft identification number was "1801". Mercury Aviation Service was owned by *Douglas T Bell* and he was granted a permit to ferry the "Gruman", serial No. 1368, with US Army identification No. "U.S.1801" from Woodward Field, Camden, SC to City Airport, Detroit on 16th May 1946. Bell then sold the J4F-2 to *Jerry Krandall* on 23rd May 1946 and it was converted to G-44 status in June 1946.

MERILLAT, James N, Tecumseh, MI
1240

MERPATI NUSANTARA AIRLINES,
Jakarta, Indonesia
1107
The airline was formed on 6th September 1962 as Merpati Nusantara. It became

Midwest Airlines' Goose CF-PVE (c/n 1200)at Winnipeg, Manitoba on 31st July 1970. Midwest used the G-21A from June 1969 until selling it to West Coast Air Service in November 1972. Sadly, all on board were killed and the aircraft was destroyed when it crashed into Nitinat Canyon at the foot of Mount Hooper, British Columbia on 9th September 1974.
(Tim Martin)

Merpati Nusantara Airlines in 1969 and acquired the G-21A in late 1977.

MERRIMAC AIRCRAFT Inc, Dracut, MA
1213
Charles A Balch Jr, President. A FAA Repair & Alteration Form dated 4th May 1951 gives the owner as *Reebal Flying Service Inc*, Dracut, MA but this may have been a lease or loan.

J MESINGER CORPORATE JET SALES Inc,
Santa Fe, NM
1471
Handled the sale of the G-44A from *David Lindow* to *Strange Bird Inc* in October 1992.

**METZGER, Thomas R,
& BOSS, Hugh A**, Greenville, MI
1345

MEURER Co Inc, New York, NY
J-10

MEYERS INDUSTRIES Inc,
Tecumseh, MI
1240
AH Meyers, President. *Tecumseh Aviation* was a Division of *Meyers Industries Inc*.

MIAMI AVIONICS Corp, Opa Locka, FL
1215

MICHELS, Lori L, AK
- see also *Lori Egge*
1327

MIDET AVIATION, West Palm Beach, FL
1130
Nelson A Miles, President.

MID-HUDSON FLYING SERVICE Inc,
Kingston, NY
1214
Based at Kingston-Ulster Airport, NY.

MIDWEST AIRLINES Ltd,
Winnipeg, MB
1145, 1200, B-98, J-19, J-55
JS McBride, President. Formed in 1957, as Midwest Aviation which took over *Northland Airlines* to become Midwest Airlines Ltd in April 1969, acquiring the G-73s in the process. The company was then absorbed into *Transair* in November 1969.

MIHANOVICH, Carlos & Fernando,
Buenos Aires, Argentina
1004

MIJNBOUW MAATSCHAPPIJ NEDERLANDS NIEUW GUINEE –
(MMNNG)
- see Dutch New Guinea Mining Co

MILES, Nelson A,
West Palm Beach, FL
1130, 1363, 1380
dba *Midet Aviation*, based at the West Palm Beach Sea Plane Base, with aircraft also based at Mineola, NY (1363), and at Lake Success, NY (1380).

MILLARD, Carl, Ltd, Toronto, ON
B-34, 1235, 1311, 1324, 1389, 1423, 1441, 1447, 1458, 28, J-19
Carl W Millard, President. Founded in 1954 as an aircraft dealership, superceding the earlier Millard Auto Aero Marine Ltd, it later operated as *Millardair*, providing air services and FBO facilities from Malton Airport, Toronto.

Carl Millard's G-44A CF-IJO (c/n 1458) at Toronto on 22nd November 1958 prior to conversion to Super Widgeon. The aircraft is currently flying with an owner in Connecticut.
(KM Molson)

Having served with Shell Oil in South America, G-21A Goose (c/n B-34) was overhauled by Grumman and sold to Millardair in 1962. CF-OIA was photographed at its Malton, Ontario base on 2nd May 1964, shortly before it was destroyed by fire in an accident at Sioux Narrows Airport, Ontario on 28th May 1964.
(Jack McNulty)

Miller Brewing's G-44A Widgeon N86629 (c/n 1455) seen here at an unknown location in September 1954.The aircraft was reportedly destroyed by fire in Jamaica on 31st March 1974. (Art Krieger)

MILLER BREWING, Milwaukee, WI
1455

MILLER, The Carl, Co,
Milwaukee, WI
1374

MILLER, Malcolm A, Akron, OH
J-12

MILLER, Robert H, Jr, Eunice, LA
1372

MILLS, Michael D, Gustavus, AK
1327

MILLS, RP & Co Ltd, Montreal, PQ
(co-owner)
1447
RP Mills, President. See also Lura Corporation.

MILNE BAY AIR,
Port Moresby,
Papua New Guinea (*JR Wild*)
1164
John Wild bought the G-21A from *Chuck Slagle's Aviation Associates* in 1987 for $150,000. A telex from the Civil Aviation Department in Port Moresby in August 1987 requesting urgent confirmation that the aircraft had been cancelled from the USCAR, stated that "*the aircraft required for SAR/Medivac standby*".

MILWAUKEE CRANE & SERVICE Co,
Cudahy, WI
1345, 1383
Clarence G Nissen, President, who had the G-44 registered in his name from April 1956 and transferred the registration N1173V to c/n 1383, after c/n 1345 crashed in 1966, by which time the company was known as *Crane Engineering Corp*.

MIMS, Jeffrey H, Dallas, TX
J-28, J-30
Mims acted as Chapter 11 Bankruptcy Trustee for *World Pacific Air Lease Inc* and oversaw the sale of the Mallards to *United Capital Corporation of Illinois* in 2000.

MING-AYER Inc, Linden, NJ
B-104
Anthony J Ming, President. This was one of the many companies in the Ayer group. See also *Frederick B Ayer*.

MINISTERIO de DEFENSA NACIONAL-MARINA de GUERRA,
Havana, Cuba
1411, 1450, 1473
The Cuban government purchased the three G-44As through *Smith, Kirkpatrick & Co Inc* in December 1952.

MIRABELLA AVIATION Inc,
Fort Pierce, FL
1210, 1374, 36, 37
The G-44s and SCAN-30s were all acquired in March 2007 after legal action against *Executive Dogs Inc*, *Good Marketing Inc*, and Marvin Good individually. C/ns 1374 & 36 were then sold to associated company, *Aircraft Specialties Inc* in June 2007.

MIRON & FRERES Ltée, Montreal, QC
J-55
The G-73 was used as transport for company president, Gerard Miron, between April 1953 and June 1955.

MISCHIANZA Corp, The, St Charles, IL
1168

MISSISSIPPI RIVER COMMISSION
J-24

MISTY ACRES Inc
- see *Richard L Rude*

MITCHELL, Baxter E, Anchorage, AK
1324

MITCHELL, Harold F,
Majuro, Marshall Islands
1160, 1270

MMNNG – Mijnbouw Maatschappij Nederlandsch Nieuw Guinea
-see *Dutch New Guinea Mining Co*

MODERN DIE & TOOL Co, Detroit, MI
1329
Arthur R Evans, President.

MODERN FURNITURE CO OF ELIZABETHTON Inc, Elizabethton, TN
41

MODERN FURNITURE CO OF GREENEVILLE Inc, Greeneville, TN
41
The two above companies had Presidents with the same surname. The Certificate of Registration issued to the Greeneville arm of the company was revoked by the FAA in March 1972 because of "failure to sign and submit Aircraft Activity Reports, commencing 1 July 1970". However a Bill of Sale, dated 14th September 1976, transfers ownership from Greeneville to Elizabethton, and another Bill of Sale, same date, transfers the SCAN-30 to *Flying Sportsmen Inc*, Sussex, NJ and the Certificate of Registration is re-instated on 20th December 1976.

This in no way clarifies the ownership of this aircraft however, because a Bill of Sale dated 23rd October 1969 had transferred ownership from the *Modern Furniture Co* of Greeneville to *Isabella Johnstone*, with an address in Kinshasa, Republic of Congo.

MOEREFLY A/S, Ålesund, Norway
1332
Operated charters and ambulance flights from Ålesund along the west coast, and to Oslo, in the 1960s.

Moerefly's G-44 Widgeon LN-HAL (c/n 1332) without props (date & place unknown). The aircraft's Certificate of Airworthiness expired on 31st December 1970, and it was donated to the Norwegian Technical Museum, Oslo in 1975. It was last reported stored in the Stavanger area. (Kay Hagby)

MOFFETT, Henry Ober,
Kent, Barbados,
West Indies
1375

MOFFETT, Henry Ober, Centerport, NY
1382
When Moffett registered c/n 1375 in 1964, he certified that he was an American citizen, born in New York City. He sold 1375 in 1965 and co-owned c/n 1382 with *Vincent Bilzi* from 1967.

MOHAWK Ltd, Chadwicks, NY
35
Gordon J Newell, owner & President. Newell acquired the SCAN-30 in 1991 and registered it with his initials (N2GN).

Newell made many alterations/ improvements to the aircraft, resulting in it operating under a series of Experimental Certificates of Airworthiness, with the result that by December 1994 it had only flown a total of 103 hours. (see SCAN-30 Production List).

MOLLER, Bill A, Rancho Palos Verde, CA
1132, 1184

MONTAG, Clyde C, Portland, OR
1354, 1430
Clyde Montag was President of CJ Montag & Sons, who were general contractors of Portland, OR.

MONTGOMERY, Robert L,
Hollidaysburg, PA
1364

MOODY, Hunter C, Decatur, IL
1214, 1239
Moody owned the aircraft dealership *Decatur Aviation Co* and owned the ex-Pan Am G-44s during 1947.

MOORE, A Brown, New Orleans, LA
(co-owner)
1133, B-65

MOORE, Early J, San Carlos, CA
1291
and at Belmont, CA
1226, 1295, 1300, 1338

MOORE, Edward N, Miami, FL
(co-owner)
1132

MORAN, Robert C, Key West, FL
1364

MORGAN, Henry Sturgis,
New York, NY
1002
The New York banker was one of the original syndicate that ordered the G-21 into production. Henry Sturgis was the grandson of JP Morgan and the son of JP Morgan Jr, and was himself the co-founder of Morgan Stanley.

MORGAN, Iris K, Binghampton, NY
1329, 1457

MORGAN-ROURKE AIRCRAFT SALES, Bartlesville, OK
1364

MORRISON KNUDSEN Co Inc,
Anchorage, AK
1014
Bought the G-21A from *JJ Ryan* in June 1942, but the aircraft was requisitioned by the US Navy at NAS Kodiak in November 1942. It was operated by the Navy, probably as NC20620, but crashed in October 1943 before being retrospectively allocated a BuAer number (see Goose Production List).

MORSE AERO Inc, Utica, NY
1424, 32
Robert E Morse, President. The company was re-named Bob Morse Inc in 1977 with an address in Whitesboro, NY, but retaining Robert E Morse as President. (see also *Franklin-Morse Inc.*) The SCAN-30 was converted to Continental IO-520-E power (see Chapter 5).

MORSE, CR, Anchorage, AK
1450

MORSE, DW, Deer Park, WA
1359

MOTORCAR TRANSPORT Co,
Pontiac, MI
1086
On the Bill of Sale from the Atwood Vacuum Company the purchaser was given as the Motorcar Transport Company "and/or Contract Cartage Company".

MOUNT COOK AIRLINES,
Christchurch, NZ
1182, B-104, 1356, 1362, 1391, 1432, 1439, 1466
Mount Cook Airlines (MCA), part of the Mount Cook Group, can trace its origin back to 1906 when Rodolph L Wigley formed the Mount Cook Motor Company. Subsequently his son, Henry Wigley, pioneered scenic flights which included landings on glaciers in the southern Alps.

The Widgeons were acquired when MCA took over *New Zealand Tourist Air Travel* (NZTAT) in December 1967. When G-44 ZK-BAY (c/n 1362) was lost in an accident on Christmas Eve 1970 the MCA board decided that the replacement should be a G-21A because for a similar operating cost it would carry more payload. Accordingly G-21A ZK-DFC was delivered on 19th October 1972, becoming the first Goose on the New Zealand civil aircraft register. When a second G-21A crashed before delivery the strains on the amphibian services really began to show and when the only G-21A went in for a major overhaul, only four G-44s were left to provide services to the Hauraki Gulf from Auckland, and to the Southland, Stewart Island and Fjordland from Invercargill. In the years 1969 to 1973 the amphibians carried around 30,000 passengers a year, but after several loss-making years, the MCA board judged that the amphibian operations should be discontinued on 30th April 1976. In June that year, some ex-MCA amphibian pilots and engineering staff founded *Sea Bee Air*

G-21A N19DF (c/n B-104) ready for delivery to Mount Cook Airlines in 1972 when it became the first Goose on the New Zealand register. The photograph may have been taken during the east-bound delivery flight from Wichita, Kansas to New Zealand. (Jennifer Gradidge Collection)

As well as the two Goose aircraft, Mount Cook Airlines operated 6 Widgeons. Here G-44A Super Widgeon ZK-CFA (c/n 1439) is seen in the company colours at Paihia, Bay of Islands in April 1976. (Note the exhaust position at the top rear of the Continental IO-470-D engine nacelles).
(Neville Parnell via Jennifer Gradidge)

G-44 Widgeon ZK-CHG (c/n 1356) in the colours of Mount Cook Airlines (after conversion to Continental IO-470 power), water-taxying into Mechanics Bay, Auckland in March 1975. (John Wegg)

to take over the MCA amphibian operations, thus ensuring these vital services would continue until 1990.

[Note: In 1974 a second G-21A (c/n1182) was destined for Mount Cook Airlines, but after being prepared for the ferry flight from Wichita, KS, by *Aircraft Facilities International Inc*, the aircraft crashed after take-off on the 9th October 1974. The registration ZK-MCC had been reserved.]

MOUNTAIN PACIFIC PIPELINES,
Calgary, AB
1415

The MOWER LUMBER Co,
Charleston, WV
1463
The company bought the G-44A from Grumman after it had been used as a demonstrator.

MT HAWLEY AVIATION Co,
Peoria, IL
1239
The company owned by Les Jones operated the G-44 during the late 1940s.

MUHLER, Wayne C, Erie, CO
1429

MULTNOMAH Corp, The, Cincinnati, OH
1168

MUNN, Chas A, Amado, FL
1202

MUNSEY, Park, Kodiak, AK
1267

MURDOCK LUMBER Co,
Chicoutimi, QC
B-14, 15
John Murdock, President. Acquired the SCAN-30 in 1959 from *Lee Mansdorf (dba US Missiles Corp)*, in exchange for the G-21A.

The Mower Lumber Company's G-44A Widgeon NC86637 (c/n 1463) in 1949. Note the appropriate name "Splinter" on the bow, above the company name. The aircraft was converted with Continental O-470-B engines in 1955, and after many changes in ownership, is currently based in Alaska. (MAP)

MURFIN HEATING & COOLING Ltd,
Downsview, ON
1235, 1458
BF Murfin, President. Aircraft based at
Toronto.

MURPHEY, Beau, Inc, Atlanta, GA
1371
Beau Murphey, President

MURPHY, George W,
Corvallis, OR
and later at Springfield, OR
1328

MURPHY, Patrick M, Warsaw, KY
1394, 21
dba Patrick Murphy Aircraft Co, and acted
as sales agent for the G-44 twice, in 1985
and 1989.

MURPHY, William E, Coral Gables, FL
J-54

MURRAY, Leo J, Co, Norfolk, MA
1334
Leo J Murray, President, was apparently a
woollen rag merchant.

MURRELL, Harvey S, Chicago, IL
1364

**MUSÉE HISTORIQUE de
l'HYDRAVIATION**,
Biscarosse, France
1218, 1341
G-44 c/n 1341 which was originally going
to be used to provide parts for the
restoration of c/n 1218, was itself under
restoration at the French Air Force instructional school, Escadron Avion 21.317, at St
Agnant airfield, near Rochefort, in April
1997. The two aircraft have since been
rebuilt as one, which is displayed at the
museum in Biscarosse.

MUSEU do AR
- see *Portuguese Air Force Museum*

MUSEU de MARINHA
- see *Portuguese Naval Museum*

MUSEU AEROESPACIAL,
Rio de Janeiro, Brazil
1290

MUSEUM OF FLIGHT FOUNDATION,
Seattle, WA
B-32

NACA
- see *National Advisory Committee for
Aeronautics*

NAGASAKI AIRLINES,
Nagasaki, Japan
1153
Founded on 12th June 1961 and operated
services from Nagasaki to the island of
Fukue. It is not clear when the G-21A was
operated by Nagasaki Airlines but it
returned to the USA in March 1965. The
company was purchased by All Nippon
Airways on 1st December 1967.

NAKA NIHON KOKU
(Central Japan Airlines)
Nagoya, Japan
1153
The airline was founded on 4th May 1953.
The G-21A was modified with eight seats
in December 1960 and from 15th July
1962 it operated a scheduled route from
Nagoya to the resorts of Shima and
Kashimoto on the Kii Peninsula. The
company was purchased by All Nippon
Airways on 25th January 1965, but by then
the aircraft was with Nagasaki Airlines (see
above).

NAMIHAS, Dr Ivan,
Tustin, CA & Villa Park, CA
dba *Trans Catalina Airlines*.
J-18, J-19

NASHUA AVIATION & SUPPLY Co Inc,
Nashua, NH
1353

NASMYTH, John "Spike" H,
Kent, WA
J-5
The former USAF Major, who had been
shot down and imprisoned in Vietnam for
6½ years, owned the G-73 in 1991/1992
before selling it to *Tropical Sea Air* in
Bangkok, Thailand. See also *Spike Air Ltd*.

NASMYTH & PARTNERS,
("Spike" Nasmyth) J-54
- see above and *Spike Air Ltd*
The former USAF Major became a ferry
pilot, and later an author, writing of his
experiences in Vietnam and other flying
adventures. Nasmyth ferried the G-73 from
Costa Rica to Miami, FL before it went to
Waglisla Air in Canada in 1988.

NASSAU AVIATION Co,
Nassau, Bahamas dba *Skyways Ltd*.
1084, 1448

**NATIONAL ADVISORY COMMITTEE
FOR AERONAUTICS** – NACA
NACA's Langley Aeronautical Laboratory
at Langley Field, VA operated several
JRF-5 aircraft between July 1945 and
March 1960 in support and communica-
tions roles, as well as two heavily modified
Widgeons that were engaged in research
activities.

The Goose

Commencing in July 1945 the US Navy
had one JRF-5 on permanent loan to
NACA at Langley where it was used for
general communications work, a significant part of which was the shuttling of
personnel and stores to and from the
Pilotless Aircraft Research Station at the
nearby Wallops Island, VA facility. While
the early aircraft remained in regular US
Navy markings, NACA also used a local
system to identify their assets be they
permanent or on loan.

All aircraft received a unique sequential
number from the date of receipt but many
received additionally a NACA 'fleet
number' that was often worn on the
aircraft, a system that is still used today.
The fleet number was re-used as the aircraft
was replaced and for many years the
JRF-5s used '103'.

The aircraft were rotated back into
US Navy hands for servicing until
June 1948 after which one particular
Goose (BuAer 37778) was retained on
indefinite loan. On 26th August 1954 a
second aircraft was loaned to NACA but
this aircraft, 37816, was lost in a crash at
Wallops Island on 3rd November
1954. It was replaced on 24th February
1955 by 87748. Shortly after that, on
20th April 1955, 37778 was permanently transferred from the Navy to
NACA and it remained in use until July
1958 when it is assumed to have been
retired. 87748 was also eventually
transferred to NACA on 27th March 1957
and it remained in use until 23rd March
1960.

The National Aviation & Space
Administration's history of these aircraft,
written many years later and relying on
fragmentary data, provides only a
confusing account of the NACA fleet
numbers after 1954 but it appears that the
last two aircraft, 37778 and 87748, were
probably '103' and '202' respectively with
87748 becoming '103' after the withdrawal
of 37778 (the NASA version, without
dates, has 37816 becoming '103' with
87748 becoming '202' and then '103' but
does not properly explain 37778's ongoing
identity).

The JRF-5 fleet can be summarised
thus:

Receipt No.	BuAer Serial	Service Dates	Notes
248	34094	10Jul45-01Apr46	
	NACA 103		
271	34088	01Apr46-11Jun48	
	NACA 103		
289	37778	11Jun48-07Jul58	
	NACA 103		Stricken by USN to NACA 20Apr55
316	37816	26Aug54-03Nov54	Said to have been NACA 103 (written-off in crash at Wallops Island 03Nov54 when on USN charge)
318	87748	24Feb55-23Mar60	Said to have been NACA 202 and later 103 (stricken by USN to NACA 15Apr57)

Receipt No.	BuAer Serial	Service Dates	Notes
285	32972	Aug47-Jun51	Became XJ4F-2 31Oct49
287	32976	May48-Jun53	Became E-175 circa Dec52

The Widgeon

NACA's use of the Widgeon was, unlike that of the Goose, strictly for experimental purposes. 32972 was acquired by NACA Langley for project work in August 1947 by which time the US Navy had only one surviving Widgeon (32976) engaged in project work.

Thus 32972 was obtained from the US Coast Guard, but it was later returned to formal US Navy ownership in October 1949. It was 'owned' by the Bureau of Aeronautics Research and Development and Design and Engineering (RD&DE) while loaned to NACA but unfortunately little is known of its activities or the reason, significant or otherwise, for a renumbering as the XJ4F 2 in 1949. The aircraft's records suggest that it flew perhaps 25 hrs during its time at Langley. In June 1951 it moved to the Naval Air Test Center Patuxent River, where it continued to fly regularly until May 1953.

Langley's other Widgeon was the unique EDO-modified E-175. The *'Petulant Porpoise'* is more fully described in Chapter 5 and suffice to record here that it arrived in May 1948 and remained on NACA charge until May 1953 undertaking work on behalf of the BuAer's RD&DE.

**NATIONAL AIR &
SPACE MUSEUM,**
Washington, DC
1048
Situated in the centre of Washington, this museum houses part of the *Smithsonian Institution* collection. The current building was opened in 1976. Another hall, the Steven F Udar-Hazy Center, was opened near Washington Dulles Airport and the G-21A, which carries the false markings "NC702A", and is painted in the standard Grumman yellow and black scheme, is now displayed there.

NATIONAL AVIATION MUSEUM,
Ottawa, Canada
- see *Royal Canadian Mounted Police*
B-77

NATIONAL BANK OF ALASKA,
Anchorage, AK
4
The bank re-possessed the SCAN-30 and sold it to *James D Perry* in September 1982.

NATIONAL CITY BANK of DENVER,
Denver, CO
16
The bank repossessed the aircraft in November 1964 and sold it to *Graubart Aviation Inc* in March 1966.

**NATIONAL INSURANCE
UNDERWRITERS,**
St Louis, MO
1448
The underwriters bought the salvage rights to the remains of the G-44A from *Skyways Ltd* after its crash in the Bahamas and had the aircraft rebuilt by *Dean Franklin* in Miami.

NATIONAL MANAGEMENT Ltd,
Montreal, QC
1343
The company owned the Super Widgeon from March 1953 until August 1956.

**NATIONAL MUSEUM OF NAVAL
AVIATION,** Pensacola, FL
1086, 1260
Based at NAS Pensacola, the museum has been enlarged over the years so that over 100 aircraft can be displayed both inside, and, for the larger types, in the outside display area. The Goose and Widgeon are both displayed inside, and wear US Coast Guard paint schemes.

NATIONAL PARK SERVICE MUSEUM,
Floyd Bennett Field, NY
B-130
Naval Air Station New York at Floyd Bennett Field was deactivated in 1971 and most of the land, except that leased by Coast Guard Air Station (CGAS) Brooklyn, was transferred to the National Park Service as part of the Gateway National Recreation Area. In 1997 the G-21A was displayed at the Gateway of Flight Museum at Floyd Bennett Field. CGAS Brooklyn was decommissioned in 1998 but its facilities remained in use by the New York City Police Aviation Unit. The aircraft was re-painted in New York Police Department colours in 2004.

NATIONAL TRANSPORT MUSEUM,
Cali, Colombia
1084
In March 1998, the local Aero Club Pacifico, the antique and classic auto club of Colombia and a railway group collectively formed the National Transport Museum Foundation. Later the Colombian International Plastic Modellers Society joined the organisation and a building was erected near Cali airport. Naturally, reflecting the different member groups, railway engines, rolling stock and cars are displayed alongside the aircraft collection, which included the ex-*Aerolineas La Gaviota* G-21A. The aircraft has since been sold in the USA.

Above: *Former US Coast Guard JRF-3 (c/n 1086) is seen here displayed at the National Museum of Naval Aviation in Pensacola, Florida wearing the incorrect serial 'V190'. V190 was in fact c/n 1085, but the FAA has perpetuated an error that occurred on a Bill of Sale in 1948 (see aircraft histories).*
(Jennifer Gradidge)

Right: *The National Park Service's Goose N644R (c/n B-130) was donated to the Cradle of Aviation Museum at Floyd Bennett Field, New York in 1997. Seen here in July 1997, it has since been repainted in New York Police Department colours.* *(EW Priebe)*

NAVAL AVIATION MUSEUM,
Pensacola, FL
- see *National Museum of Naval Aviation*
above.

NEAL & Co Inc, Homer, AK
1213
Tony Neal, President. - see also *Fanda Corporation*.

NEDERLANDSCH NIEUW GUINEE PETROLEUM MAATSCHAPPIJ
(NNGPM)
- see *Dutch New Guinea Petroleum Co*

NEILL, JW, Los Angeles, CA
dba Murphy Motors.
1325

NELSON, Robert L, Portland, OR
1371
Later at Green Bay, WI and Brentwood, CA. On Nelson's death his heir, *Connie M Davis*, was granted ownership of the G-44.

NETHERLANDS NEW GUINEA PETROLEUM Co (NNGPM)
- see *Dutch New Guinea Petroleum Co*

NEUMEISTER, John T, Sussex, NJ
dba *Flying Sportsmen Inc.*
41
John Neumeister found his SCAN-30 in Kinshasa, Zaire in 1976 where it had been abandoned after allegedly taking part in a CIA mission. The aircraft was returned to New Jersey in June 1979 for complete restoration. (see SCAN-30 Production List).

NEVADA EXPLORATION
1020

NEW BEDFORD AVIATION Inc,
South Dartmouth, MA
1389
The company bought the J4F-2 from the War Assets Administration for $7,500 and sold it the same day for $7,501.

NEW BRUNSWICK HOLDING Co Ltd,
Fredricton, NB
J-13
JJ Fraser Winslow, President.

NEWELL ENTERPRISES Inc
- see below

NEWELL, Gordon J, Chadwicks, NY
1206, 16, 41
dba *Newell Enterprises Inc*. Newell was also owner and President of *Mohawk Ltd*, which operated SCAN-30 c/n 35. Newell also had an address in Utica, NY from where he applied for registration of the G-44 c/n 1206, but the Certificate of Registration carried a New Hartford, NY address!

NEW ENGLAND AIR MUSEUM,
Windsor Locks, CT
1178
The museum opened in May 1968 and is located at Bradley International Airport. On

PACE Gannet N4122A (c/n 41) the last airframe built by SCAN in France is seen here at Oshkosh on 4th August 1986 after rebuild by John Neumeister.   (Jennifer Gradidge)

A rare January 1939 shot of Nevada Exploration's Goose NC20650 (c/n 1020) at Oakland, California. The aircraft served with the Royal Canadian Air Force during WWII before going to Loftleidir in Iceland, before ending its days with Kodiak Airways Inc in Alaska, where it crashed on Christmas Eve 1961.   (via Jack McNulty)

Newfoundland Air Transport's G-44A Super Widgeon CF-KPT (c/n 1415) at Gander in 1969. Sold in the USA in 1987, it is currently owned and operated in Alaska.
                    (Dennis Goodwin via Jennifer Gradidge)

3rd October 1979 a tornado destroyed more than a dozen of the museum's aircraft and damaged many more. The JRF-5 was modified to produce the V/STOL Kaman K-16B (see Chapter 5 for details), and survived the storm.

NEWFOUNDLAND AIR TRANSPORT Ltd,
Corner Brook, NL
1415
The company was founded in 1961 to fly local charter services and later merged with *Labrador Airways* to become *Newfoundland & Labrador Air Transport Ltd* (see next entry).

NEWFOUNDLAND & LABRADOR AIR TRANSPORT Ltd, Corner Brook, NL
1415
Flew scheduled passenger, cargo and mail services between Deer Lake, Port au Choix, St Anthony and southern Labrador, with charter services serving eastern Canada.

NEWFOUNDLAND AIRWAYS Ltd,
St John's, NL
1230
In 1949 all aircraft on the Newfoundland register were transferred to the Canadian register and thus the G-44, which had been VO-ABU, became CF-GPJ. It was based at Gander and used for local services.

A rare picture of G-21A Goose NC1200V (c/n 1145) while operated by the New York Police Department. The former JRF-6B then saw service in Canada, the USA, New Zealand, Fiji, Australia and Thailand before being dismantled and shipped to Germany, for European Seaplane Services. It was last noted in 2011, stored at Landsberied, near Munich. *(via NGHC)*

NEW YORK DAILY NEWS,

New York, NY later dba *WPIX Inc*
J-22
The famous newspaper was founded by Joseph Patterson. The G-73 was purchased in May 1947 to add an aerial photography capability when covering news stories. Named "*Miss Daily News*", the aircraft had the cockpit side windows built lower than standard to facilitate photography.

NEW YORK POLICE DEPT,

New York, NY
1145, B-130, 1377
The G-21A, c/n 1145, was put to an unusual use in the late-1940s, when in an effort to fill the city's water reservoirs, it was used to "seed" the clouds in an attempt to produce rain. The second G-21A, c/n B-130, is displayed at the Gateway of Flight Museum at Floyd Bennett Field, NY and is said to have been used by the New York City Police Aviation Unit "after the Second World War".

NEW YORK STATE, Fisheries Dept,

Chautauqua Fish Hatchery, NY
1152
The G-21A was used at Chautauqua Lake, NY in a support role, which included putting young fish into the Chautauqua Lake from the air.

NEW YORK YANKEES Inc, The,

New York, NY
B-71, J-42
The famous baseball team, owned by *Daniel R Topping*, operated the G-21A from 1952 until up-grading to the G-73 in 1959. The G-21A was registered to Topping and *Del E Webb*, dba *New York Yankees*, from December 1953.

NEW ZEALAND TOURIST

AIR TRAVEL Ltd, (NZTAT), Auckland

1356, 1362, 1391, 1432, 1439, 1466
NZTAT was formed in 1954 after Harry English had resigned from the board of *Amphibian Airways* in order to start amphibian services in the Auckland area. Captain Fred Ladd, who had just resigned from Fiji Airways, was appointed chief pilot. The first G-44, ZK-BGQ (1391) had been bought in Tahiti, shipped to Auckland, and rebuilt by Tasman Empire Airways Ltd before entering service on 19th June 1955. Non-scheduled flights from Mechanics Bay, Auckland to Great Barrier Island began in October 1955. A second G-44 was added in January 1960 and in August 1961 NZTAT took over *Amphibian Airways*, thereby acquiring two more G-44s. One of these was retained at Invercargill to maintain services to Stewart Island while the other three aircraft operated out of Auckland. The aircraft were subsequently rotated between Auckland and Invercargill as required by seasonal variations in demand and by maintenance schedules. In July 1963 a fifth Widgeon was added and a year later, a sixth. Many ad hoc charters were flown, together with many ambulance

The New York State Fisheries Department's G-21A Goose NC606 (c/n 1152) adding to the fish stocks in a New York lake in the 1950s. The Goose later served in Polynesia before going to Antilles Air Boats in September 1968. *(New York State photo)*

The New York Yankees' Goose N30Y (c/n B-71) at an unknown location in the 1950s. The Goose was sold to McKinnon Enterprises Inc in 1960 and registered N152M. That registration was cancelled on 18th June 1965 after an accident, of which no details are known. *(R Stuckey via Art Krieger)*

Ranger-engined G-44A Widgeon ZK-BPX (c/n 1432) of NZ Tourist Air Travel, in 1960. Transferred to Mount Cook Airlines in December 1967, it crashed at Halfmoon Bay, Stewart Island after a gear-down water landing on New Year's Day 1974. There were no injuries, but the aircraft was written off during a salvage attempt. (JDR Rawlings)

G-44 Widgeon ZK-BGQ (c/n 1391) after being rebuilt in Auckland and put into service with NZ Tourist Air Travel Ltd. The aircraft had been prone to water-looping episodes, a tendency which would not be cured until keel modifications and installation of step vents had been carried out. (Jennifer Gradidge Collection)

and medevac flights to the islands of the Hauraki Gulf. Because a suitable replacement aircraft could not be found, NZTAT had all six Widgeons re-engined with 260hp Continental engines between 1964 and 1966. On 31st March 1967, Captain Fred Ladd resigned as Chief Pilot & General Manager of NZTAT, and celebrated by flying G-44, c/n 1391, under the Auckland Harbour bridge.

Mount Cook Airlines seized the opportunity to expand its operations in the Hauraki Gulf and took over NZTAT and all the G-44s in December 1967.

NICHOLS, Charles F & Judith A,
Trustee,
Baldwin Park, CA
dba *Yanks Air Museum*, Chino, CA.
B-140, 1299

NIEDNER, Paul F, Jr, St Charles, MO
B-35
Co-owned the Goose with *Tom Ahlers & William Sims*.

NISSEN, Clarence G,
Milwaukee, WI
1345, 1383
President of *Milwaukee Crane & Service Co.*

NITTO AIR LINES / JAPAN DOMESTIC AIRLINES

1430, J-6, J-38, J-40, J-52, J-56
Nitto Air Lines was founded in Osaka on 4th July 1952 by a small company named Tadashi Fujimoto, which was financially backed by Osaka's Sankei newspaper. Scheduled services from Osaka's Itami Airport to an anchorage at Shirahama on the Kii Peninsula began in December 1954. These holiday flights were extended to the Inland Sea in the late 1950s and in June 1960 the route was further extended to

serve Kushimoto and Shima, and eventually Nagoya. Nitto was merged into *Japan Domestic Airlines* (JDA) on 15th April 1964. G-73, c/n J-40, had been lost in a crash in February 1964, and by June 1966, the other four had been sold in the USA.

NNGPM –
Nederlandsch Nieuw Guinea
Petroleum Maatschappij
- see *Dutch New Guinea Petroleum Co.*

NOEL, James, Lafayette, LA
dba James Noel Flying Service Inc.
1464
Noel acted as sales agent for the Widgeon and only had it a week before selling it to *Dean Franklin*.

NOONAN, Thomas H, Cincinnati, OH
dba *Cincinnati Air Taxi Inc*, and also *Amphibious Sales Co.*
16

NORDAIR, Montreal, QC
J-34
Nordair was formed on 27th November 1956 when Boreal Airways was re-named. The G-73 was used for charters out of Montreal and also saw service with Nordair Arctic Ltd, a subsidiary set up in 1969 to fly short-haul routes out of Frobisher Bay and charters carrying government workers, students, hunters, mining equipment and tourists to Pangnurtung Eskimo settlement and Cape Dorset. During its time with Nordair, J-34 was converted to PT-6A-28 power by Frakes Aviation. The aircraft was leased to *Survair Ltd* in July 1976, and operated services from Frobisher Bay.

NORDGREN, Alfred, Troutdale, OR
1291
The G-44 was voted Best Amphibious Aircraft at Sun 'n Fun 1995.

NORSK TEKNISK MUSEUM
- see *Norwegian Technical Museum*

NORTH AMERICAN
RARE METALS Ltd, Toronto, ON
1324
Andrew Robertson, President. Operated the G-44 in 1957/58.

Nordair's G-73T Turbo Mallard CF-UOT (c/n J-34) at Montreal on 12th July 1973. After various owners in Canada, the aircraft was registered to Mallard Aviation Corporation in the Cayman Islands. It is currently in storage in the USA awaiting sale or long lease. (Tim Martin)

NORTH CAROLINA PULP Co,
Plymouth, NC
1160
HM Kieckhefer, President.
Also at Camden, NJ.
1408
The company manufactured bleached and unbleached sulphate pulps and speciality boards and paper, at their pulp mill in Plymouth, NC. The Certificate of Registration application for the G-21A was made by the North Carolina Pulp Company c/o Kieckhefer Container Corp, Camden, NJ.

NORTH COAST AERO LLC,
Port Townsend, WA
1129, B-142
Clifford Larrance, owner

NORTH COAST AIR SERVICES Ltd,
Prince Rupert, BC
1311, J-7, J-21, J-23
Formed in 1961 by WWII veteran and former Queen Charlotte Airlines pilot John N (Jack) Anderson to provide services from Seal Cove, Prince Rupert to the Queen Charlotte Islands and settlements on the north coast of British Columbia. The G-44 was operated from 1967 until going to Guatemala in the 1970s via Dean Franklin, from whom the G-73, J-23, was acquired in 1974 to replace J-7 which unfortunately crashed on 5th March 1974, killing the pilot (Anderson's son, Bob) and two passengers.

The G-73s were later used on the scheduled run to Ketchikan, AK and carried locals the twenty miles from Seal Cove to Simpson. J-21 was sold in 1984 for $125,000, and J-23 was gone by 1987.

NORTH COUNTRY AIRWAYS Inc,
Nashua, NH
29
Herbert F Goodwin, President. The company name changed to *North Country Management Corp* in February 1973 (see below).

NORTH COUNTRY MANAGEMENT Corp,
Silver Lake, NH
29
In December 1985 Goodwin transferred his company stock and the SCAN-30 to the HF Goodwin Revocable Trust. Herbert F Goodwin died on 11th June 1993 and William D Goodwin became Trustee. On 22nd November 1999 he resigned and all assets, including the SCAN-30, were transferred to successor Trustee, Susan Ann Goodwin. The aircraft was sold to *Telford Allen* on 16th December 2002.

NORTHEAST AVIATION Co,
Portland, ME
1375, 1411
Milton V Smith, President. Aircraft based at Portland Municipal Airport.

NORTHERN AIR CARGO,
Kodiak, AK
1164
Leased the G-21A to *Kodiak Western Alaska Airlines* in the late 1970s.

NORTHERN AIRCRAFT SALES Co Inc,
San Carlos, CA
1323

NORTHERN AIRCRAFT TRADERS Ltd,
Anchorage, AK
1451, 1471, 1474
The three G-44As were acquired from the *Bangladesh Flying Club* in exchange for two Piper Senecas. After restoration and conversion to Super Widgeon status by Hillard Aviation in Fort Worth, they were sold to separate owners in the early 1990s.

NORTHERN AIRWAYS Inc,
Burlington, VT
1410
Edward A Deeds, President. Later known as *Air North Inc*, the company was founded in 1956. The chain of events that led to the G-44A being owned by Northern Airways is detailed under *Baron Corporation*.

NORTHERN CONSOLIDATED AIRLINES, Anchorage, AK
1268, 1270, J-36, J-44
Ray Peterson started fixed-base operations from Bethel, AK in 1937. In November 1945 he persuaded six other small pioneer concerns to amalgamate under his presidency to form *Northern Consolidated Airlines* (NCA). This amalgamation obtained CAB approval on 1st December 1947 and G-44 c/n 1268 was bought in 1949. In 1955 NCA took over Bristol Bay Airlines and thereby its routes from Dillingham, and in April 1962 took over the Anchorage to King Salmon route from Pacific Northern Airlines.

Peterson pioneered the development of the Turbo Mallard when he had a Pratt & Whitney (Canada) PT-6 engine fitted to J-36, and carried out a 50-hour flight test programme (see Chapter 4).

In 1963 NCA was awarded the Anchorage-Iliama-Big Mountain-King Salmon-Dillingham-Bethel route. The rationalisation of routes within Alaska was taking place throughout the 1960s and in line with that process NCA was merged with *Wien Air Alaska*, to form *Wien Consolidated Airlines* in February 1968.

NORTHERN HELICOPTERS Ltd,
Richmond, BC
1423
PB Jones, President. The G-44A was registered nominally to this company on 10th August 1966, but a Bill of Sale dated 9th June 1966, transferred it to *Red Dodge*, Anchorage, AK for $18,000. It is therefore

The former North Coast Air Services' G-44 Super Widgeon CF-HEN (c/n 1311) with additional registration N62881 after sale to Dean Franklin was photographed at Opa Locka, Florida in August 1973. After twenty years on the Guatemalan register, it returned to the USA for restoration in 2003 and is currently flying with an owner in Nevada. *(Steve Krauss)*

Dean Franklin sold Mallard c/n J-23 to North Coast Air Services Ltd in 1974. It is seen here as C-GHDD, with the name "Patricia" still on the bow. The legend under the cockpit window is "Mallard". J-23 is now a G-73AT registered VH-PPI with Paspaley Pearling Company Pty Ltd. *(Fred J Knight Collection)*

doubtful that the aircraft was ever operated by Northern Helicopters Ltd, and it was cancelled from the CCAR on 17th August 1966.

NORTHERN MOUNTAIN AIRLINES Ltd,
Prince George, BC
1200
J Neilsen, President. Based at Fort St James, the G-21A was used in the late 1960s to haul 8ftx4ft sheets of plywood to the Pine Point Railway construction sites. This was achieved after a large cargo door was cut in the starboard side of the aircraft. The G-21A was sold in 1969 and in 1973 Northern Mountain Airlines was merged with Thunderbird Air to form Northern Thunderbird Air Ltd.

NORTH JERSEY SALES & CONSTRUCTION Co, Paterson, NJ
1355
Joseph A McBride, President. The company was a distributor of diesel engines, generator units, refrigeration and heating equipment and operated the G-44 during 1948/49.

NORTHLAND AIRLINES, Winnipeg, MB
1145, J-19, J-55
Peter M Lazarenko, President. Leased the G-21A from *BC Airlines*. Northland Airlines was bought by Midwest Aviation & became *Midwest Airlines*.

NORTHLAND FISHERIES Ltd,
Winnipeg, MB
J-19
Peter M Lazarenko, President. Lazarenko had previously operated the G-73 under the name of *Courier Trading & Enterprises Ltd*. See also *Northland Airlines* above.

NORTH MICHIGAN AIR SERVICE Inc,
Petoskey, MI
1345
HJ Templin, President.

NORTHWARD AVIATION,
Edmonton, AB
26
Operated the SCAN-30 for *Wright Industrial Equipment Ltd* from 1966 until 1971.

NORTHWEST AIRMOTIVE,
Anchorage, AK
1377
KD Oldham & BD Layman partners.

NORTH WEST AIR SERVICE Inc,
Seattle, WA
1061
The company was owned by Vance Roberts who was President of Vance International Airways at the same address on Boeing Field, Seattle.

NORTHWESTERN AERONAUTICAL Co,
St Paul, MN
1141
Converted the surplus JRF-6B to G-21A standard.

NORTHWESTERN FLYING SERVICES Ltd,
Nestor Falls, ON
J-19
AC Wensley, President. Operated the G-73 in the mid-1970s.

NORTHWEST INDUSTRIES Ltd,
Edmonton, AB
1077
Owned the G-21A briefly in 1966.

NORTHWEST WATERBIRD Inc,
Wilmington, DE
1410
Matthew Brady, President.

NORTON DRILLING Co,
New Orleans, LA
1448
CA Norton, President.

NORTON, Howard E, Berkeley, CA
1267, 1268
dba Norton Marine & Air Service. Norton bought the surplus former US Coast Guard J4F-1s for $5,000 each and within two months had sold both for a total of $16,500. The original Certificate of Airworthiness application gives the owners of c/n 1267 as Henry J Arnaudt and Jack H Tarman of Oakland, CA, and a mortgage document for c/n 1268 also notes Arnaudt and Tarman as owners. It must be assumed that the two were connected in some way to Norton Marine & Air Service, although nothing in the file gives a clue as to what that connection might have been.

NORWEGIAN TECHNICAL MUSEUM,
Oslo, Norway
1332
The museum is located in the northern suburbs of Oslo. The G-44 was displayed there as LN-HAL and was last noted in May 1995. In 2002 the aircraft was on loan at the Flyhistorik Museum Sola in Stavanger, but by May 2011 it was reported in storage somewhere in the Stavanger area

NUNALLY, Winship, Atlanta, GA
1219, 1418

NUNASI-CENTRAL AIRLINES Ltd,
Winnipeg, MB
B-55
Formerly *Ontario Central Airlines Ltd*.

NW FLYING SERVICE, Nestor Falls, ON
J-19

NW WATERBIRD Inc, Wilmington, DE
1324

NYHOLM, Paul,
Hempstead, Long Island, NY
1371
Nyholm was working as an aircraft mechanic for *Aero Trades Company* at Roosevelt Field, Mineola, on Long Island in October 1942. He was given the "hulk" of the Widgeon by the Royal Navy in October 1945, by which time he had his

own business. Later dba *Aeromobile Equipment Co* in partnership with Mildred Nyholm.

NZTAT
- see *New Zealand Tourist Air Travel*

OAKLEY AIR Ltd, Vancouver, BC
1045
Owner/pilot Cliff Oakley operated ad-hoc charters within coastal British Columbia. Because of a lack of work in BC, he operated whale-watching and sight-seeing flights at Half Moon Bay, CA in partnership with a local operator from February to May 1991. Oakley died when the G-21A crashed on 6th May 1991 during a positioning flight from Vancouver to Squamish, BC prior to an intended charter from Squamish to Thompson Sound, BC.

OAKSMITH, Stanley, Jr, Ketchikan, AK
1337
dba *Ketchikan Air Service* in partnership with *Martin R Hanson*.

OCEAN DRILLING & EXPLORATION Co,
New Orleans, LA
1420
Alden J Laborde, President.

O'CONNELL, HJ, Supplies, Ltd,
Montreal, QC
B-50, 1473
HJ O'Connell, President. The G-21A was operated from May 1956 until it crashed on 25th June 1958. The G-44A was owned for a year from April 1960.

OCTAL Inc, Mountain View, CA
1380
Ralph H Guditz, President. Octal moved to Bellevue, WA in 1990, and became known as *Fugu Ltd* in 1996.

ODYSSEY AIRCRAFT LEASING Inc,
Dania, FL
1445
Steve St Clair, President, who also presided over *Manatee Inc*.

OFFSHORE Co, The, Baton Rouge, LA
1463

OHIO AVIATION Co, Vandalia, OH
1213
Aircraft sales & service company specialising in the refurbishment of war-surplus machines.

OHIO VALLEY AVIATION Inc,
Wheeling, WV
16

OKEECHOBEE FARMS Co,
West Palm Beach, FL
1439
Owned by the *Sanchez* family that fled from Castro's Cuba to Miami in 1959. The G-44 was nominally sold by *Florentino Sequeiro* to Okeechobee Farms on 4th April 1961.

Ontario Central Airlines' Goose CF-IEC (c/n B-32) leased from Griffco Aviation from 1955 until 1959, was photographed at Seattle, Washington in 1956. The Goose was later operated by Pacific Western Airlines before being sold in the USA and is currently flying with an owner in Idaho.
(Douglas D Olson via Jennifer Gradidge)

OKLAHOMA STATE BUREAU OF NARCOTICS & DANGEROUS DRUGS CONTROL,
Oklahoma City, OK
31

OLD CROW LLC, Wilmington, DE
c/o Corporation Service Co
1389

OLDER, Lane E, Bellingham, WA
dba Old Aire
1325, 1385

OLDHAM, KD - see *Northwest Airmotive*

O'MEARA, Robert W, Chicago, IL
1448

OMNI AIRCRAFT SALES Inc,
Washington, DC
1370

OMNI ENTERPRISES Inc, Heron, MT
J-56

ON MARK AVIATION, Van Nuys, CA
1147
Owned by Hal Beale.

ONAL AIR TRANSPORT Corp,
New York, NY
1317
Thomas A Coffey, President.

ONTARIO CENTRAL AIRLINES Ltd
(OCA), Kenora, ON
Barney E Lamm, President
B-32, B-45, B-55, B-120
Lamm established his fly-in fishing lodge, Ball Lake Lodge, on the Wabigoon River in 1946. In 1947 he founded Ontario Central Airlines to operate charter services in northwest Ontario, from bases at Kenora, Ball Lake Lodge and Red Lake. The Kenora base was at the floatplane dock on Lake of the Woods in the centre of the town. Jack Howard flew B-120 and would often fly down to International Falls, MN to collect American fishermen who wanted to use Ball Lake Lodge. Occasionally the G-21As were used for fire-fighting duties and for supply flights to mineral mining interests around Hudson's Bay. In June 1955 OCA bought G-21A, c/n B-32, from *Griffco Aviation Company.* The two companies quickly decided that a lease arrangement would suit them better and the Goose was sold back to Griffco and leased to OCA. In 1965 OCA acquired Catalina CF-OWE which carried heavier cargo while the G-21As transported the personnel to these remote destinations. By 1968, the company address was Redditt, Ontario and by 1972 it was based on the shore of Lake Winnipeg in Gimli, Manitoba, by which time the amphibian operations out of Kenora had been sold to *Parsons Airways.* (Gimli was a former RCAF station used to train pilots under the British Commonwealth Air Training Plan.) OCA was bought by Austin Airways of Timmins, Ontario in 1979, although B-120 was still registered to OCA when sold to *The Air Ranger Ltd* in May 1980. (OCA was renamed *Nunasi-Central Airlines Ltd* after takeover by the Nunasi Corp in 1984.)

ONTARIO GOVERNMENT, Canada
Dept of Lands & Forests
28
Hydro-Electric Power Commission
J-33
The SCAN-30 was based at Sault Ste Marie.

ONTARIO PAPER Co, Thorold, ON
J-2
The company set up by *Colonel Robert McCormick* to provide newsprint for his newspaper, *The Chicago Tribune.* McCormick bought the G-73 from the Montreal Trust Company *(Holt)* in 1950, and also retained the services of its pilot, Fred Hotson.

ORANGE COUNTY AVIATION,
Santa Ana, CA
J-18

ORINOCO MINING Co (OMC),
Caracas, Venezuela
B-59
OMC, a subsidiary of the US Steel Corporation, opened up the Cerro Bolivar iron ore deposit in Venezuela in 1954. The Cerro Bolivar is situated to the west of the Caroni River and ore is transported by company-built railroad to Puerto Ordaz on the Orinoco. The Orinoco was dredged to establish the port which allowed shipment of the iron ore to the sea. By the end of 1956, OMC had invested $230 million in the Cerro Bolivar operation, which was supported by the G-21A between 1957 and 1967.

ORRELL, Capt Robert W,
Cardinal, VA
1437
Orrell bought the G-44A, new, from Grumman in February 1946.

OSBORN, WB, San Antonio, TX
J-19

OSPREY AVIATION Inc,
Perrysburg, OH
1454

OSTERMANS AERO AB,
Stockholm, Sweden
1367
A charter company that operated the G-44 during 1948 and Lockheed 18s in the 1950s. Later had a fleet of DC-7s and merged with Aero Nord in November 1965 to form Internord.

Mallard CF-BKE (c/n J-2) of the Ontario Paper Company at an unknown location. The aircraft was named "Celeste" and the company title was displayed on the tail-fin. The precise date of the photograph is unknown, but was during the 1960s. *(Fred J Knight Collection)*

Pacific Coastal's ill-fated G-21A C-FPCK (c/n 1187) on the ramp at the wartime RCAF hangar at Port Hardy, Vancouver Island in 1997. Note the Air BC maple-leaf motif on the tail. The former Cuban Navy JRF-5 was unfortunately destroyed in an accident on Thormanby Island, 40 miles NW of Vancouver, British Columbia, on 16th November 2008. (Karl Hayes)

OSWEGO FALLS Corp,
Fulton, NY
1314

OUT ISLAND AIRWAYS Ltd,
Nassau, Bahamas
1084, 1445
A subsidiary of *Island Flying Services of America Inc*. See also *Bahamasair*.

OVERTRADE Inc, Salem, OR
B-128
S Smith, President.

OY TAKUUVALMISTE AB,
Helsinki, Finland
1367

OZARK MANAGEMENT Inc,
Jefferson City, MO
B-8
William E "Wes" Stricker, President.

OZARKS AUTO SHOW Inc,
Hollister, MO
31
The SCAN-30 was displayed on the airshow circuit in the American Midwest. The company's Dealer's Aircraft Registration Certificate expired on 4th October 2007, and the current status of the aircraft is uncertain.

PACE
- see *Pacific Aircraft Engineering Corp* below

PACIFIC AIRCRAFT ENGINEERING Corp, (PACE),
Sun Valley, CA
11, 16, 25, 31, 32, J-6, J-40, J-56, J-57
Tom Katsuda, President. PACE was set up as a conversion company, with workshops at the Lockheed Air Terminal in Burbank, to re-engine SCAN-built Widgeons with Lycoming R-680-E3 nine-cylinder radials, and market them as PACE Gannets. (see Chapter 5).

PACIFIC AIRCRAFT SALVAGE Inc,
Vancouver, BC
B-145, 1235

PACIFIC COAST AIR MUSEUM,
Santa Rosa, CA
1214
Formed in 1990 by a group of aircraft owners headed by Lynn Hunt, who became President. The collection is housed at Sonoma County Airport, about five miles north of Santa Rosa. The museum boasts airworthy Grumman Albatross aircraft, but the G-44 was put into storage awaiting restoration.

PACIFIC COASTAL AIRLINES Ltd,
Vancouver, BC
1077, 1083, 1184, 1187, B-76, B-83, B-107, B-129
The company, founded in 1960 by Don McGillvray, operated scheduled services from Nanaimo-Cassidy Airport to Vancouver, and to points on Vancouver Island including Victoria, Duncan, Port Alberni, Qualicum, Comox and Port Hardy. The company was bought by *Air West Airlines* in February 1980. In June 1980 Air West became part of *Air BC* and in 1984 the Port Hardy, BC operations of Air BC were transferred to *Trans Provincial Airlines* (*TPA*). In 1986 Air BC sold TPA but retained the Port Hardy base, using the old RCAF hangar. By 1987, the Port Hardy operation had become known as *Pacific Coastal Airlines*, an Air BC subsidiary. In January 1988 Powell Air (Daryl Smith) bought 50% of the company from Air BC and later bought the remaining half from former Air BC executive, Iain J Harris. This all made for some confusing paperwork. In December 1987, 1077 and B-129 were leased by Pacific Coastal to Air BC Ltd dba Pacific Coastal Airlines (sic). This one year lease was extended to two years, after which Pacific Coastal sold the G-21As to *Greyvest Financial Services* but then immediately leased them back! Although the company was based in Vancouver, all Goose operations were from Port Hardy, BC. B-76 was added to the fleet in March 2007, but unfortunately crashed on 3rd August 2008, killing the pilot and four of the six passengers. In September 2012 Pacific Coastal Airlines announced that the Goose fleet was being withdrawn from service due to the lack of availability of certified spare parts.

PACIFIC COCONUT PROCESSING Corp
- see *Turnbull, Raymond C*

PACIFIC EXPLORATION Inc
1141
The G-21A, leased from the *Reconstruction Finance Corp*, was used for survey work in Costa Rica in 1947.

PACIFIC FLYING BOATS Inc, Bear, DE
J-54

PACIFIC LEASING Corp Ltd,
Vancouver, BC
B-142

PACIFIC NEW GUINEA LINES,
Rabaul, New Britain
1466
Peter Sharp bought the G-44A for his Pacific New Guinea Lines in March 1994 (still registered as VH-WET) but it was not delivered to Rabaul until 19th April 1994 and was not put into service. The aircraft was sold to *Massim Expeditions and Tours Pty Ltd* of Rabaul in April 1994. It was registered in Papua New Guinea as P2-WET but by December 1994 it was back in New Zealand.

PACIFIC NORTH AMERICAN DEVELOPMENT & FINANCIAL Corp,
Vancouver, BC
B-117
Christopher F Green, President.

PACIFIC NORTHERN AIRLINES
- see *Western Alaska Airlines Inc*

PACIFIC SAND & GRAVEL Co,
Centralia, WA
1383

PACIFIC WESTERN AIRLINES Ltd,
Vancouver, BC
1157, B-6, B-32, B-129, B-142, B-145, 1309, J-7, J-9, J-21, J-39
Founder: *Karl John Springer*. Pacific Western Airlines (PWA) was formed by the merger of *Central BC Airways* with Kamloops Air Service in 1950, Skeena Air Transport in 1951 and finally Associated Air Taxi in 1953. PWA operated coastal services throughout BC with the Widgeon from 1953, and added the G-73s, J-7 and J-9, in November 1954 to fly the scheduled Vancouver to Kitimat service. A third, J-39, was added in 1955 but was unfortunately lost in a crash in August of that year. J-9 provided transport for HRH Princess Margaret in July 1958 during the BC phase of her Canadian tour. Two G-73s, c/ns J-7 & J-9, were sold to BC Airlines in June 1960 along with four Norseman aircraft, equipment, spares, wharves and docks, and the transfer of ATB licences, for a total of $400,000.

In April 1966, PWA operated the following services by G-21A: Prince Rupert (Seal Cove and Digby Island) to Stewart via Alice Arm, and return, daily except Sundays. Flight number 291 out and 292 return (see timetable on next page).

Pacific Western Airlines' Mallard CF-HPU (c/n J-9) wearing the legend "Kitimat Princess" on the bow. After nearly 20,000 flying hours of service in Canada, the G-73 was sold to Chalk's International Airline in 1975, and was converted later to Turbo Mallard configuration for service with Virgin Islands Seaplane Shuttle. (Fred J Knight Collection)

PACIFIC WESTERN AIRLINES

DEP.	AR.	Meals	Flight	A/C Type	Stops	Remarks

PORT HARDY, B.C. — PDT — Tel. 949-6412

Campbell River — PDT		A				$14.25
1130	1230	S	106	DC3	-	Mo.We.Fr.
Comox — PDT		A				$18.10
1730	1825	S	102	DC6	-	Mo.We.Fr.
1730	1825	S	108	DC6	-	Tu.Th.Sa. Su.
Vancouver — PDT		A				$25.00
1130	1245	S	104	DC6	-	Tu.Th.Sa.
1130	1335	S	106	DC3	1	Mo.We.Fr
1600	1750		110	DC3	-	Mo.We.Fr.
1730	1915	S	102	DC6	-	Mo.We.Fr.
1730	1915	S	108	DC6	1	Tu.Th.Sa. Su.

POWELL RIVER, B.C. — PDT — Tel. 485-4261

Vancouver — PDT		A				$12.00
1615	1700		128	DC3	-	Daily
1830	1915		130	DC3	-	Th.Fr.Su.

PRINCE RUPERT, B.C. — PDT — Tel. 624-2313
(Seal Cove)

Alice Arm — PDT		A				$22.50
1015	1200		291	Goose	-	ex. Su.
Stewart — PDT		A				$25.00
1015	1235		291	Goose	2	ex. Su.

PRINCE RUPERT — PDT
(Digby Island)

Alice Arm — PDT		A				$22.50
1115	1200		291	Goose	-	ex. Su.
Stewart — PDT		A				$25.00
1115	1235		291	Goose	-	ex. Su.

STEWART, B.C. — PDT — Tel. 33-R

Alice Arm — PDT		A				$15.00
1245	F		292	Goose	-	ex. Su.
Prince Rupert — PDT		A				$25.00
(Seal Cove)						
1245	1405		292	Goose	1	ex. Su.

URANIUM CITY, SASK. — MST — Tel. 4121

Edmonton — MST		T				$40.00
1230	1610	L	184	DC6	2	Tu.Th.Sa.
(via Fort Smith)						
1550	2000	D	196/182	DC3/DC6	1	We.Fr.

URANIUM CITY, SASK. — MST — Tel. 4121

Fort Chipewyan — MST		T				$11.25
1230	1310	L	184	DC6	-	Tu.Th.Sa.
Fort McMurray — MST		T				$20.00
1230	1430	L	184	DC6	1	Tu.Th.Sa.
Fort Smith — MST		T				$11.00
1550	1650		196	DC3	-	We.Fr.

VANCOUVER, B.C. — PDT — Tel. 278-2151
Telex 045-463, Air Cargo 278-2448

Campbell River — PDT		A				$13.75
0830	0925		105	DC3	-	Mo.We.Fr.
0830	0925		125	DC3	-	Tu.Th.Sa.
1430	1530		131	DC3	-	Daily
1800	1900	S	133	DC3	-	Th.Fr.Su.
						last flt. Sept. 11
Comox — PDT		A				$10.75
0800	0915	CB	123	DC3	1	ex. Su.
1330	1410		107	DC6	-	Tu.Th.Sa.Su.
1330	1420		109	DC3	-	Mo.We.Fr.
*Hudson Hope — MST		A				$45.00
0730	1115	B	325	DC3	1	Mo.We.Fr.

*Service restricted to companies and their personnel designated by the B.C. Hydro and Power Authority for travel between Vancouver and Hudson Hope.

Port Hardy — PDT		A				$25.00
0730	0845	B	101	DC6	-	Mo.We.Fr.
0730	0845	B	103	DC6	-	Tu.Th.Sa.
0830	1035		105	DC3	1	Mo.We.Fr.
1330	1505		107	DC6	1	Tu.Th.Sa.Su.
1330	1530		109	DC3	1	Mo.We.Fr.
Powell River — PDT		A				$12.00
0800	0845	CB	123	DC3	-	ex. Su.
1515	1600		127	DC3	-	Daily
1730	1815		129	DC3	-	Th.Fr.Su.

WRIGLEY, N.W.T. — PDT

Edmonton — MST		T				$87.00
1520	0040	S	192/152	DC3/DC6	3	1 & 3 Sa.
Fort Simpson — PDT		T				$14.00
1520	1620		192	DC3	-	1 & 3 Sa.
Fort Smith — MST		T				$47.00
(via Yellowknife)						
1520	2215		192/152	DC3/DC6	2	1 & 3 Sa.
Yellowknife — MST		T				$31.00
1520	1650		192	DC3	1	1 & 3 Sa.

YELLOWKNIFE, N.W.T. — MST — Tel. 4481

Cambridge Bay — MST		A				$62.00
1015	1300	L	289	DC4	-	1-3-4 Sa.
Edmonton — MST		T				$56.00
1245	1615	L	182	DC6	1	Mo.Th.
1630	2000	D	182	DC6	1	We.Fr.
2115	0040	S	152	DC6	1	Tu.Sa.
1735	2055	D	290	DC4	-	1-3-4- Sa.
Fort Resolution — MST		T				$ 9.00
1045	1250		194	DC3	1	We.Fr.
Fort Simpson — PDT		T				$17.00
1300	1345		191	DC3	-	Sa.
Fort Smith — MST		T				$16.00
1045	1400		194	DC3	2	We.Fr.
1245	1345	L	182	DC6	-	Mo.Th.
1630	1730		182	DC6	-	We.Fr.
2115	2215		152	DC6	-	Tu.Sa.
Hay River — MST		T				$11.00
1045	1145		194	DC3	-	We.Fr.
Inuvik — PDT		T				$85.00
1240	1530	L	151	DC6	1	Tu.Sa.
Norman Wells — PDT		T				$51.00
1240	1340	L	151	DC6	-	Tu.Sa.
Wrigley — PDT		T				$31.00
1300	1505		191	DC3	1	1 & 3 Sa.

CHIEFTAIN AIRBUS
CALGARY—EDMONTON SERVICE

No reservations — no advance check-in — just be in time to catch your flight.

Pick up Boarding Pass on way through Terminal Building.

Carry your baggage to the Chieftain Aircraft and board immediately.

Ticketing enroute—Fare $12.00 one way.

Your baggage available as you deplane.

All times shown are local times
All schedules   1700 — 12 Noon
are quoted in the   1900 — 7 PM
24-hour clock.   2230 — 10.30 PM

B — Breakfast
CB — Continental Breakfast
L — Lunch
D — Dinner
S — Sandwich
A — First Class
T — Tourist/Coach/Economy

One-way fares are quoted.
Return fares are twice the one-way fare.

Above: *Pacific Western Airlines timetable dated April 1966.*

In September 1970, by which time RH Laidman was President, J-9 was leased back to Pacific Western but when *BC Airlines* was acquired by PWA in 1972, J-9 re-joined the PWA fleet, along with J-21. During the 1960s the coastal services were provided by the G-21As, including B-32 initially leased from *Griffco Aviation*, Seattle, WA. The remaining three G-21As were transferred to *Pacific Western Northern Service Ltd* at the end of July 1968 (on the Certificate of Registration for these three aircraft the company was listed as P.W. Northern Service Ltd) and then immediately sold to *Trans Provincial Air Carriers Ltd*. G-21A, c/n 1157, was owned during 1970-72, but may have been used for spares. G-73s J-9 and J-21 remained in service until April 1974 when they were sold to *West Coast Air Services*.

PACK RIVER Co, The,
Spokane, WA
1164
LV Brown, President.

PACKARD FLYING SERVICE Inc,
Ogalalla, NE
1364
Glenn D Packard, President.

PACKER PONTIAC Corp, Detroit, MI
1431, B-59, J-14
The company was incorporated on 1st November 1946 and bought the G-44A in August 1949, acquiring the G-21A by 1951 and the G-73 in 1955.

P A D AVIATION & NAVIGATION Co,
Chicago, IL
1146, 1148, 1165
C/ns 1146 & 1148 were sold to *Efferson & Associates* who sold them on to the Argentine Naval Commission, Washington, DC (see Military Operators section, Chapter 7). The third G-21A went to *Ellis Air Lines*.

PAGE, Paul E, Erie, CO
dba X'cellaero
B-104

PAGE AIRWAYS Inc, Rochester, NY
1377, 1445
An aircraft conversion and repair business, and broker, that also flew ad hoc charters.

PAGEBROOK HOLDINGS Inc,
Toronto, ON
1389
W Grenier, President

PAKISTAN GOVERNMENT,
Karachi, Pakistan
1476, 2
The G-44A was delivered in 1949 and crashed soon afterwards. The SCAN-30 was delivered in 1962 but details of the use of either aircraft are not known.

PALM BEACH YACHT SALES,
Palm Beach, FL
16
- see *Dexter D Coffin, Jr*

PALMER PONTIAC
1431

PALM SPRINGS AIR MUSEUM, CA
1161
The museum possesses one of the world's largest collections of WWII warplanes, which included the former JRF-6B displayed in a US Navy dark blue scheme with white undersides. In November 2011 the aircraft was offered for sale for $200,000 "as a project".

PAN AFRICAN AIRLINES (NIGERIA) Ltd,
Lagos-Ikeja, Nigeria
1381
A non-scheduled passenger and freight charter operator, which was also involved in support of oil exploration.

PAN-AIR Corp, New Orleans, LA
1054, 1130, 1133, B-139, B-140, J-38
Henry C Wallach, President. Pan-Air operated a charter and air taxi service from

The former Pan African Airlines' G-44 Widgeon N7256 (c/n 1381) converted to Continental power by McDermott. The aircraft is seen here at Shannon, Ireland on 13th October 1969, with floats removed for the ferry flight from Nigeria to the USA.   *(Malcolm Nason)*

New Orleans. All G-21As except c/n 1054 were also registered at various times to affiliated company *Comor Inc*. B-139 went to Canada in 1964, but the other three were still under mortgage by Pan-Air until at least January 1970. B-140 had retractable floats fitted under STC SA138-SW, and Pan Air also held STC SA551-SW to modify Beech 18 engine cowls to fit G-21As.

PAN AM AIR BRIDGE, Miami, FL
J-27, J-42

Pan American Airways was resurrected in 1996 by a consortium led by Charles Cobb. The consortium also bought *Chalk's International Airline* and set up Pan Am Air Bridge to operate G-73Ts on the Chalk's International routes, which they hoped would act as feeder routes for Pan Am's projected services from Miami.

In February 1998 the new Pan Am filed for Chapter 11 bankruptcy protection followed in January 1999 by the Chalk's subsidiary, *Flying Boat Inc*, which similarly filed for bankruptcy protection. In August 1999, *James Confalone* bought the assets of Flying Boat Inc from the court and on 17th December 1999 he changed the name of the operation to *Chalk's Ocean Airways*.

PAN AMERICAN WORLD AIRWAYS Inc,
New York, NY
1004, 1006, 1045, 1058, 1162, 1214, 1215, 1235, 1239, 1443

G-21A c/n 1004 flew scheduled services between Miami and Cat Cay in the Bahamas. C/ns 1006 and 1058 were operated by a subsidiary named *Pan American Airways – Africa Ltd* which was formed on 15th July 1941 to provide a transport service and route facilities in support of Lend-Lease deliveries on the southern Atlantic route to the Middle East via west Africa.

The G-44 Widgeons were specially modified (see Widgeon modifications, Chapter 5) as flight instrument trainers for flying boat crews. Painted all-yellow as befitted training aircraft, they served Pan Am from July 1941, operating from their North Beach HQ at La Guardia Field, NY.

During the war, the G-44s were still used by Pan American, but on behalf of the US Navy, as instrument and lead-in trainers for their larger equipment (also acquired by the US Navy and the USAAF) and the aircraft remained based at La Guardia where they were thus used in support of NATS operations. Although eventually purchased by the US Navy in 1943 as 'J4F-2's, the aircraft were not allocated BuAer serials until 1945, when they were belatedly numbered 99074 to 99077 and these numbers were therefore not worn (1235 was certainly 99077, but the other links are unknown). Throughout the war all FAA Form 337s continued to show Pan American as owner and, of course, quoted civil registrations. Pan American assigned the aircraft to their Atlantic Division in August 1944 when the US Navy leased them back to the airline. Aircraft 99074 to 99076 were eventually sold back to Pan American in August 1945 while 99077 remained with the USN until its disposal, with others, in February 1947. The assumption is that while the Goose 1004 was allocated a period BuAer serial (48229) in 1942 as part of a wider re-numbering of impressed Pan American aircraft, the Widgeons were simply overlooked.

Pan Am Air Bridge G-73T Turbo Mallard N2969 (c/n J-27) taxying ashore at North Bimini, Bahamas in June 1997. It was this aircraft that crashed in December 2005 while operating for Chalk's Ocean Airways, which led to the grounding of the Mallard fleet.

(Lothar Grim photo published as a postcard)

The Alaskan state flag is displayed on the bow of George Pappas' G-44 Widgeon N68102 (c/n 1351) visiting Oshkosh in July 1983. One of the G-44s still powered by Ranger engines, it is currently owned by Danny Abbott and based in Alaska. *(Jennifer Gradidge)*

Parsons Airways' G-21A Goose CF-HUY (c/n B-120) is seen here at Gimli, Ontario in July 1975. Note the much modified bow and the company logo on the tail-fin. The current status of the aircraft is unclear. *(John Wegg)*

PAN AVIATION, Miami, FL
B-76

PAN AVIATION, Dover, DE
J-54

PAN PACIFIC AERO Inc, Honolulu, HI
M Vitousek, President. Pan Pacific Aero were reported (Janes AWA 1969) to be operating scheduled services to Kaanapali (Maui) with Goose aircraft.

PANTECHNICON AVIATION Ltd,
Glenbrook, NV
J-5
The company moved to Ketchikan, AK in 1998, Portland, OR in 2000 and Minden, NV in 2004. The G-73 was operated for company use until grounded by the FAA following the Chalk's crash in December 2005. It was noted at Minden in June 2007 undergoing Airworthiness Directive work on the wing, and was flying again in April 2008.

PAPATHEODOROU, Christos A,
Long Beach, CA
1166

PAPPAS, George R, Anchorage, AK
1260, 1351

PAPUAN OIL DEVELOPMENT Pty,
Papua
1008
One of the original batch of G-21s, VH-AAY was used in support of oil exploration operations and also undertook mail flights from Port Moresby via Thursday Island to Darwin, Australia, to supplement the weekly de Havilland DH86B service operated by WR Carpenter. (see postal covers in Colour Gallery I).

PARADISE AIR SERVICES,
Palau, Philippines
1164
An air charter company owned by *Bob Keys* used the G-21A for ad-hoc charters supporting Palau's tourism trade, and even the occasional support flight for the Philippine military. Keys transferred the aircraft to the Australian register and based it in Noosa Heads, QLD in 1999. It was reported sold to the *Yaukuve Island Resort* in Fiji in 2005, but despite being painted as DQ-AYL, the aircraft remained in Australia and in 2009 another plan was put forward to provide services in the Solomon Islands. At the time of writing it is not clear whether these services were ever started.

Below: *Pastew Enterprises' G-44A Super Widgeon CF-IJO (c/n 1458) at Winnipeg, Manitoba on 25th September 1970. Sold in the USA in 1972, it is currently flying with an owner in Connecticut.* *(Tim Martin)*

PARKS, Colby R,
Anchorage, AK
1381

PARSONS AIRWAYS NORTHERN,
Flin Flon, MB
B-55
Founded 1953.

PARSONS AIRWAYS Ltd,
Kenora, ON
B-120
Founded by brothers Bud & Keith Parsons in 1946 and operated charters out of Kenora and Red Lake to north-western Ontario and northern USA, with Noorduyn Norseman aircraft.

When Barney Lamm moved his family and his *Ontario Central Airlines* from Kenora to Gimli, MB in 1972 he sold the Kenora floatplane operation to Rod Carey, the then owner of Parsons Airways. The G-21A was leased from May 1972, logging 1,054 flying hours until it crashed on 8th July 1976.

PASCO AVIATION Inc,
Zephyr Hills, FL
1340
ER Cantrell, President and was also President of *Angels Aviation* to whom the G-44 was transferred in January 1964.

PASPALEY PEARLING Pty Ltd,
Darwin, NT
J-22, J-23, J-26
The Paspaley Pearling Company use their G-73ATs to provide support to the pearl farms (which are actually vessels) by flying in supplies and rotating staff. Daily flights are made in the area to the west of Darwin along the coastline as far as Broome. Medevac flights are flown on demand. J-23 was acquired in 1990, with J-26 and J-22 arriving in 1994 and 1995 respectively. All three were rebuilt to G-73AT standard using several newly established Supplemental Type Certificates (see Chapter 5), and were certificated in Australia.

The G-73ATs, together with a Falcon 900C, are operated and maintained by Lloyd Aviation Jet Charter trading as *Pearl Air International*, under a separate Aircraft Operating Certificate and Certificate of Airworthiness.

PASTEW ENTERPRISES,
Calgary, AB
1458
Paul Boel, President. Aircraft based at Winnipeg, MB

This former US Navy J4F-2 was owned by Donald Paterson after conversion to Super Widgeon standard by McKinnon. It is seen here registered as CF-KKF (c/n 1312), at Winnipeg, Manitoba on 18th October 1958. The aircraft is currently preserved at the Alaska Aviation Heritage Museum on Lake Hood, Anchorage. *(via Ken Molson)*

PATERSON, Donald S, Winnipeg, MB
1298, 1312

PATIN, Leon H, Miami, FL
1371
There is no Bill of Sale to record from whom Patin bought the G-44 but a Certificate of Registration was issued in his name on 9th July 1963.

PATTERSON, George S
dba *G G Leasing Co* in partnership with *K Gene Zerkel*.
1206, 1324

PATTISON INDUSTRIES, Jim,
Richmond, BC
dba *Air BC*
1059, 1077, 1083, 1157, B-129, B-138, B-145
From 1979 until June 1980 Jim Pattison Investments bought out a number of British Columbia commuter airlines. These included *Airwest Airlines Ltd*, which had just acquired *Pacific Coastal Airlines*; *West Coast Air Services Ltd*; *Gulf Air*; *Island Airlines Ltd*; Haida Airlines; and *Trans Provincial Airlines*. The combined fleet was operated under the name Air BC except that the Trans Provincial Airlines aircraft continued in TPA colours. Another complication arose when Air BC Ltd sold G-21A, c/n 1077, to Pacific Coastal Airlines on 31st December 1987, then, on the same day, Air BC Ltd dba Pacific Coastal Airlines (sic) leased it back from Pacific Coastal Airlines (for 2 years).

PATTISON, PN, Grand Island, NY
dba *The Sportsman Air Service Inc* with *Max W Stell*
1451
In February 1949, Pattison became the sole owner of the G-44A and was described on a mortgage document as "owner and operator of a charter flying service".

PATTY, Ernest N, Jr, Seattle, WA
1440
Patty was President of *Alluvial Golds Inc*, a gold dredging operation based at Fairbanks, AK, with an office in Seattle. Because the company was mainly Canadian-owned, the G-44A was registered

in Patty's name. He was unfortunately killed when the aircraft crashed into a mountain on 25th October 1947.

PAULEY, Val R, Anchorage, AK
B-81

PAYLESS DRUGS Corp, Portland, OR
B-62
The chain of drug-stores was co-owned by *Peyton Hawes*, who bought the aircraft after it had been converted to a G-21G by McKinnon (see Chapter 5).

PAZSINT, Holly G, Wasilla, WA
1267

PEARL AIR INTERNATIONAL
- see *Paspaley Pearling Pty Ltd*

PECHULS, Rose, Los Angeles, CA
(co-owner)
dba *Los Angeles Air Service Inc*.
1138

PECK, Jack
- see *Alaska Aeronautical Industries*

PECK, Richard V, King Salmon, AK
1210
After the death of Richard V Peck the G-44 was sold by Rulon V Peck, administrator of the estate.

PEEKSKILL SEAPLANE BASE Inc,
Peekskill, NY
12

PEERLESS TOOL & ENGINEERING Co,
Chicago, IL
1416

PEIER, Heinz G, North Lima, OH
1153
dba Peier Inc, Waterloo, IA. Peier bought the G-21A in 1989 and spent three years on a restoration project. The aircraft, named "*Island Queen*" was based at Spruce Creek in Florida until the FAA revoked the Certificate of Registration and Peier sold it in Canada in 1998.

PEIRCE BROS OIL SERVICE Inc,
Waltham, MA
1213
Elisha Nye Peirce, President.

PELICAN AVIATION Corp,
New Iberia, LA
1441

PELICAN Corp, Fort Lauderdale, FL
1457

PELICAN SEAPLANES Inc,
Miami, FL
1409, J-13

PEMBERTON, Addison J & Wendra M,
Spokane, WA
1161

PENINSULAR AIRWAYS Inc, (PENAIR),
Pilot Point, AK
1140, B-86, B-97, B-115, B-122, B-138, B-139, B-140, 1220, 1239, 1378, 1430
Founded in 1955 by *Orin D Seybert* in Bristol Bay. In the mid-1960s the PenAir fleet also included Cessna 180s and 206s, along with a Piper PA-18 on floats. The company operated services from Cold Bay on behalf of *Reeve Aleutian Airways*, using Reeve flight numbers, to False Pass, Akutan and King Cove using G-21As, c/n 1140 & c/n B-86. By 1985 Piper PA-31s were being operated alongside the G-21As and when Pen Air bought-out *Air Transport*

G-21A Goose N741 (c/n B-97) in PenAir's smart blue, white and yellow livery awaits passengers on the small ramp at Akutan, Alaska in 1997. Pen Air was one of the few companies still flying the Goose on scheduled services when the aircraft crashed on 9th April 2008. The wreckage was sold to Samuel P Damico who planned to use the parts in the rebuild of c/n 1051. N741 was, however, still listed as current by the FAA in April 2013. *(Karl Hayes)*

Services of Kodiak in the 1990s, they acquired a base there from which they flew charters for the large Alitak cannery on the shore of Lazy Bay at the south end of Kodiak Island. G-21A c/n B-115 was appropriately named "*Spirit of Alitak*", and this cannery work continued until 2000. By 1981 the G-44s had gone, and by 2006 the remaining three G-21As were based at Dutch Harbor. PenAir acquired copies of the original Grumman drawings and specs and now manufacture their own parts to keep their Goose aircraft flying. In April 2008, c/n B-97 was involved in a crash leaving only c/ns B-122 and B-139 in the fleet of the largest commuter operator in Alaska, carrying people and mail to "any place there is human habitation" in the eastern Aleutian Islands. The most frequent service from Dutch Harbor was to the island of Akutan where the seafood plant employed some 800 people. Unfortunately, over the last weekend in October 2012, PenAir ended all Goose flights to Akutan because the concrete seaplane ramp there had been modified to accommodate a hovercraft, making it unusable for the Goose. Akutan was provided with a new airport but it is on Akun island, 6 miles away across the Bering Sea! The hovercraft service links the new airport with the village of Akutan. Since the summer of 2012 the Goose had been using the gravel beach alongside the ramp but this caused extreme wear and tear on the landing gear and was unable to continue without permanent damage to the Goose.

PEOPLES BREWING Co, Duluth, MN
1390

PEREZ, HR, Miami, FL
1380
Perez was President of LEBCA Internacional and planned to operate the G-44 in Venezuela in 1956. The plans fell through and the Widgeon returned to the US register, and was sold in July 1956.

PERFECT CIRCLE Co, Haggerstown, IN
J-19

PERFORMANCE AIRCRAFT Co Inc, Fort Lauderdale, FL
J-35
The G-73 was forfeited to the *US Customs Service* on 28th October 1991 (reason unknown).

Above: *G-44 Widgeon N141R (c/n 1378)was operated in Alaska by Peninsula Airways, for nearly 40 years. It was converted to McKinnon Super Widgeon configuration in 1970 and is now privately owned in Alaska.* (Guy Denton)

PERIMETER AVIATION Ltd, Winnipeg, MB
1458
Aircraft sales agent.

PERRY, Farwell W, Greenwich, CT
1236

PERRY, James D, Greenwich, CT
1233, 1239, 1266

PERRY, James D, Monroe, WA
1236, 4

PERRY, LJ, Schoolcraft, MI
and later at Kalamazoo, MI
1267, 1398
G-44 c/n 1267 was owned between 1950 and 1960. After Perry died, c/n 1398 was sold as part of his estate, which was administered by Hazel Perry.

PETERSON, Bertram, Miami, FL
(co-owner)
1388

PETERSON, Darrell M, Toledo, WA
1437

PETRICH, Keith Thomas, Seattle, WA
1063

PETROLEUM NAVIGATION Co, Seattle, WA
1351
E Lloyd Nelson, President.

PETRO STAR VALDEZ Inc, Anchorage, AK
1378

PHILLIPS PETROLEUM Co, Bartlesville, OK
29, 1430
The oil company has used many aircraft types for personnel transportation and oilfield support operations since the 1930s.

PHIPPS, John Schaffer, New York, NY
and later at Palm Beach, FL
1011
John Schaffer Phipps, lawyer, businessman and polo player, was heir to the family fortune amassed by his father, the Pittsburgh steel magnate, Henry Phipps. JS Phipps bought the eleventh G-21 in 1937, and later had it registered to his new address in Palm Beach, FL, where he had built a large mansion. In March 1948 he reported to the CAA that he had sold the aircraft to the US government "during WWII".

PIKE, William F, Los Angeles, CA
dba *West Coast Aircraft Ltd*.
1359, 1387

PILCHER, Matt V, Sarasota, FL
1323
Aircraft based at Sarasota-Bradenton Airport.

PINELLAS AVIATION SERVICE Inc, St Petersburg, FL
John Reid Topping, President
1389

Above: *Pinellas Aviation Service letterhead from March 1955.*

PIMA AIR & SPACE MUSEUM, Tucson, AZ
1330
The present 320-acre site was first used in 1976 when the museum was known as the Pima County Air Museum. The first indoor display was opened in March 1983 and the present name was adopted in 1991. The J4F-2 is the modified E-175, used by EDO Corporation to test the hull design for the XP5M-1, and named "*Petulant Porpoise*" (see Chapter 5).

PISSED AWAY N663G LLC, c/o Aero Law Group PLLC, Bellevue, WA
1429

PITCHER, Harold L, Fairbanks, AK
1233
The Bill of Sale from *Ross Aviation* gave the purchaser's name as Harold F Pitcher but the Certificate of Registration was issued to Harold L Pitcher in January 1962. The G-44 was re-possessed by the Indianapolis Morris Plan Corporation on 10th August 1962.

PLANECO Inc, Dover, DE
1389

PLANES Inc, Houston, TX
1328

PLETCHER, John W, III, Anchorage, AK
B-81
John Pletcher, an attorney, rescued the former US Navy JRF-6 from long-term open storage on the shore of Lake Spenard, AK and spent almost two years restoring it. Painted in wartime US Navy blue and grey, it won the Grand Champion Warbird award at the EAA's North West Regional Convention in July 1998.

PLUM ISLAND FLYING SERVICE Inc,
Newburyport, MA
1365
Owned by *Warren S & Viola M Frothingham*. When the Flying Service was incorporated in late 1947 the Bill of Sale showed VM Frothingham as co-owner along with the operation now known as Plum Island Flying Service Incorporated. The little-used J4F-2 was in fact in storage until September 1949 when it was sold to *William H Cook Jr* and by 1955 had yet to reach 1,000 hours of flying time.

PLUMMER, Warren C,
Winnipeg, MB
dba *Plummer Holdings*
1153, B-139
G-21A c/n B-139 was operated under lease by *Sioux Narrows Airways*. Plummer was also President of *Great Bear Lake Lodge Ltd*.

POELMAN AIRCRAFT Co Inc,
New Orleans, LA
1377

POLLACK, Frank V & Hazel M,
Troutdale, OR
1268
c/o Northwestern Aviation Sales Inc, Troutdale Airport, although the address given on the Certificate of Airworthiness application dated 24th May 1949 was in Spokane, WA.

POPE, Stephen,
Christchurch, NZ
1145
Pope used the G-21A for scenic tourist flights and the carriage of light freight.

POPSIE FISH Co, Homer, AK
1213
Gwen M Neal, President.
- see *Fanda Corporation*.

POPULAIR AVIATION SERVICES Inc,
Dorval, QC
1370
Marc Fortier, President. Leased the G-44 from *Gilles Tremblay Aviation*.

POPULAR MECHANICS, Chicago, IL
J-10
The publishers of the well-known monthly magazine owned the G-73 from November 1947 until December 1948.

PORTAGE BAY AIRCRAFT Ltd,
Seattle, WA
B-32
President: RE Richardson & later Dale E Kremer. The G-21A was owned during the 1980s.

PORTLAND AMPHIBIANS Inc,
Portland, OR
1452
President, *Thomas M Benedict*, who bought the G-44A in his own name in October 1969 before registering it in the company name in January 1970.

PORTUGUESE AIR FORCE MUSEUM,
Alverca, Portugal
1251
The Museu do Ar at Alverca, to the north of Lisbon, houses over 100 preserved and replica airframes. The G-44 is a former Força Aérea Portuguesa (Portuguese AF) machine and is preserved with its serial, 129.

PORTUGUESE NAVAL MUSEUM,
Lisbon
1242
The Museu de Marinha is next door to the St Jeremy monastery on the banks of the River Tagus, and possesses only three aircraft exhibits. The G-44, formerly CS-AHG, is preserved as '128', although it wore '120' when in Naval service.

POTTER AIRCRAFT Inc, George E,
New Orleans, LA
1266, 1420, 1424, 1435
George E Potter, President. Handled the re-sale of c/n 1420 twice. The second time, the G-44A was registered in the name of George E Potter Sr, Belle Chasse, LA. Potter seized c/n 1424 in October 1973 in lieu of unpaid maintenance bills. By 1984, George E Potter was dba *Aircraft Speciality Inc*.

POTTER, Melvin, Scarsdale, NY
1382

POWELL RIVER Co Ltd, Vancouver, BC
B-45, B-55, B-76, B-83, B-98
The Powell River Co Ltd (PRC) acquired two war-surplus JRF-5s, c/n B-45 (for $10,000) & c/n B-98 (for $15,000), in 1947/48 and began operations in the Queen Charlotte Islands. In 1949, c/n B-98 was used by BC Electric Company and Northern Construction Company in a joint venture with Powell River Company and *Malibu Seaero Ltd*. This arrangement was the forerunner of *B.N.P. Airways* which was formed in 1950.
  Between May 1952 and May 1955, during the time that Harold S Foley was company President, the B.N.P. G-21A (c/n B-76) was temporarily registered to PRC.
  In 1955, PRC purchased two low-time

former Royal Canadian Air Force Goose IIs (c/n B-55 & c/n B-83) and put them into storage along with the extensive spares inventory bought from the *War Assets Corporation* in 1948. The spares were owned by PRC, and separate from B.N.P. Airways. In 1960 PRC was merged with *MacMillan Bloedel*.

POWERS & GEORGE AIRCRAFT BROKERS, New York, NY
1334
Sold the G-44 on behalf of the *Leo J Murray Company* in 1949.

PRECISION VALVE Corp,
Yonkers & Bronxville, NY
1147, J-14, J-49
The Precision Valve Corp was set up by Robert Abplanalp to manufacture and market the plastic valve he had designed to fit spray cans. Abplanalp bought Walkers Cay in the Bahamas and developed it into a resort for fishermen and divers complete with an airline to get the customers there. The airline, *Walkers International*, was owned by the resort and was therefore a subsidiary of the Precision Valve Corp.
  The G-21D Hybrid was used alongside the G-73, J-14 under a Part 135 certificate from the late 1960s until 1980. In 1994 J-14 was replaced by the G-73T, J-49, but the operation was taken over by *Chalk's*.
  Ownership of Mallard J-49 was transferred to the Josephine Abplanalp Revocable Living Trust on 12th October 2012 and then to *Aviation Management International Inc* the same day.

PREMIUM SERVICE Corp,
Minneapolis, MN
J-32, J-58
The Premium Service Corporation, owned by the Carlson Companies group, sold Gold Bond trading stamps and had the G-73s registered appropriately, with 'GB' suffixes. J-58 crashed in May 1967 and was replaced by J-32.

PRESSED STEEL CAR Co Inc,
Chicago, IL
1168, 1438
John I Snyder Jr, President

Premium Service Corporation's G-73T Turbo Mallard N298GB (c/n J-32) at a snowy Toronto on 23rd March 1974. The Corporation, owned by the Carlson Companies group, sold Gold Bond trading stamps and had their G73s registered appropriately with 'GB' suffixes. (William Haines Collection)

Above: *Mallard CF-PQE (c/n J-55) operated by the Quebec Department of Transport & Communications, seen here at Ottawa, Ontario circa 1961. After a varied career in Canada, the UK and latterly with Virgin Islands Seaplane Shuttle, the aircraft was destroyed by Hurricane Hugo on 17th September 1989.* (Ken Molson)

PRICE AIR SERVICES Ltd, Toronto, ON
1311
Harry I Price, President. The G-44 was operated from its base at Malton, ON firstly under a private Certificate of Registration, then a commercial certificate from November 1960, before reverting back to private status in September 1962 until sold in 1965.

PRICE PIPER Inc, Spokane, WA
1292
Thomas J Price, President. The G-44 was registered on 17th April 1972, but was transferred to *Thomas J Price* on 26th April 1972.

PRICE, Thomas J, Spokane, WA
- *see above*
1292

PRIESTER, George J, Wheeling, IL
1357, 1385
Aircraft dealer with another address at Elmhurst, IL

PROBERT, Richard L, Long Beach, CA
dba *Aero Technology*
B-140
The G-21A was rebuilt in 2000 and is now displayed at the *Yanks Air Museum*, Chino, CA.

PROBERT, Wilton R, Oakland, OR
and at Long Beach, CA (co-owner)
1051, 1145, '1110' (1146), 1164
"Dick" Probert started the Probert School of Aeronautics at Van Nuys, CA in the 1930s, and flew C-87s to all parts of the Pacific war theatre during WWII. He formed *Avalon Air Transport* with Jean Chisholm as finance director in 1953. He bought c/n 1164 in 1979 but the FAA file confuses the story of precisely from whom it was purchased. An undated Bill of Sale transfers the G-21A from Robert Sholton to Fred Ball's *Island Hoppers Inc* in Kodiak but this is followed by another Bill of Sale, remarkably, from Sholton/Island Hoppers/Kodiak Western/Alaska Coastal and the BM Behrends Bank of Juneau to Wilton R Probert of Oakland, OR(sic) on 30th June

1979. Finally the file records, on 2nd October 1979, an undated Bill of Sale from Island Hoppers Inc to Probert, and he is issued a Certificate of Registration on 2nd October 1979. Wilton R Probert died in May 2008, aged 101 years.

PROCTER & GAMBLE TRADING Co, The,
Cebu City, Cebu, Philippine Islands
1456
Operated the G-44A with US marks until 1956.

PROGRESSIVE WELDER Co,
Detroit, MI
1329
Fred Johnson, President. Aircraft based at Detroit City Airport.

PROSPECT LEASING, Anchorage, AK
1464

PRUHS, J Dana, Anchorage, AK
1463

PRUYN, ML, Kisco, NY
1439

PT FREEPORT INDONESIA
- see *Freeport Sulfur Co*

PUETTER, Juergen, Calgary, AB
dba *147973 Canada Inc*.
B-117

PUGET UNITED TRANSPORTATION COMPANIES, San Francisco, CA
J-21
Sold the G-73 to *BC Air Lines* for US$75,000 in March 1960.

QNS PAPER Co Ltd, St Catherines, ON
J-2
John E Houghton, President. QNS bought the 90% share in the G-73 from the Ontario

Paper Co Ltd in May 1984. The aircraft was based at Toronto. In June 1987 the company became the Quebec & Ontario Paper Co Ltd and in December 1992 became *QUNO Corp*. In 1996, QUNO Corp merged with Donohue Acquisitions Inc to form *Donohue QUNO Inc*. In March 1997, Donohue QUNO became *Donohue Forest Products Inc*, and the following month bought the remaining 10% share of the G-73 from *Crown Cork & Seal* paving the way to selling the entire aircraft in the USA in October 1998.

QUEBEC CITY FLYING CLUB,
Quebec City, QC
14
Leased the SCAN-30 from *Garant Aviation Engineering* during the mid-1960s.

QUEBEC GOVERNMENT, Canada
Ministry of Colonisation
B-50, J-55
Department of Game & Fisheries
1240
Department of Transport & Communications
J-55
In 1960, the transport needs of the various government departments were rationalised and provided by the newly-formed Department of Transport & Communications, based at Ancienne Lorette, PQ.

QUEBEC SMELTING & REFINING Ltd,
Montreal, QC
1447

QUEST AVIATION
- see *Rivett, Ronald J*

QUNO Corp, St Catherines, ON
- see *QNS Paper*
J-2

RAA - see *Reeve Aleutian Airways*

RACE AVIATION Inc, Longmeadow, MA
John T Race Jr, President. - See below
1300

RACE FLYING BOATS Inc,
Newark, DE & Bear, DE
1300
After moving to Bear, DE in March 2001,
the company was re-named *Race Aviation
Inc* and the G-44 was re-registered in
October 2004.

RAI - see *Régie Aérienne Interinsulaire*

RAINBOW AIRCRAFT SALVAGE,
Seattle, WA
1059

RAINY LAKE AIRWAYS,
Fort Francis, ON
1153
Vernon J Jones, President. Charter services
were operated with the G-21A from 1965
until 1978.

RAINY PASS LODGE, Rainy Pass, AK
1270, 1301
The lodge was situated on a lake in Rainy
Pass, north of Anchorage. C/n 1301
crashed at Loon Lake in August 1953 and
was replaced by c/n 1270, which remained
in use until sold to *Northern Consolidated
Airlines* in 1962.

RAMSDELL, Henry W, Palm Beach, FL
1167
Ramsdell was President of *Suncoast
Airways Inc*.

RAMSTAD CONSTRUCTION Co,
Anchorage, AK
1378
JS Ramstad, President.

RANCHAIRE Inc, Aspen, CO
- see *Walter Scott*
J-52

RAND BROADCASTING Co, Miami, FL
J-28
Rex Rand, President.

RANFT, John J, Columbus, OH
1452

R & S AIRCRAFT SALES Inc,
Renton, WA
1323
Eugene Richards, President.

**RAPIDES PARISH CIVIL DEFENSE,
SHERIFF'S DEPARTMENT**,
Alexandria, LA
1303

RARITAN AVIATION Co,
New Brunswick, NJ
1168
Raritan operated the G-21A for Seward
Johnson of the *Johnson & Johnson
Company*.

RATLIFF, Marshal H, Battle Creek, MI
1398

RAUSCH, William L, Hackensack, NJ
1355
Rausch was President of *Rausch Flying
School & Service Inc*, a Cessna dealer
operating out of Teterboro, NJ, and briefly
owned the G-44 in 1949 before selling it to
Alaska Airlines.

RAUSE, George, Dillingham, AK
1232

RAWSON MOTORS Inc, Plainfield, NJ
1446

RBR AIRCRAFT Inc, Albuquerque, NM
J-14
Owned by *Roland La Font*.

RCMP - see *Royal Canadian Mounted
Police*

READING AVIATION SERVICE Inc,
Reading, PA
1452, 26
Acted as sales agent when the G-44A was
sold in 1960, and when the SCAN-30 was
sold in Canada in 1965.

READING EAGLE Co, Reading, PA
26
The Reading Eagle is the major daily
newspaper in Reading, PA and is family
owned. The SCAN-30 was operated in the
early 1960s.

REALITE Ltd, Vancouver, BC
1265, 1309, 1358
LJ Bennett, President. Although the
registration CF-GYZ was allotted (for c/n
1309) to *Associated Aero Services Ltd* on
28th March 1951, the Certificate of
Registration 10075 was issued to Realite
on 3rd April 1951. C/n 1309 was sold to
Pacific Western Airlines in July 1953, to be
replaced by c/n 1358 in 1956, while c/n
1265 was purchased in April 1958.

**REAM'S TRANS CARIBBEAN
AIR FREIGHT**, Riviera Beach, FL
1364
Conrad W Ream Jr, President.

**RECONSTRUCTION FINANCE
Corp** (RFC), Washington, DC
1109, 1114, 1141, 1157, 1205, 1206, 1218,
1230, 1232, 1233, 1300
The RFC was formed to dispose of US
government surplus materials at the end of
WWII. Although sales were made through
the RFC, approval for the sales was given
by the Munitions Assignment Board, which
was the final arbiter on Lend-Lease
allocations, and towards the end of World
War II this also covered sales to civilian
operators. This task was taken over by the
War Assets Administration in March 1946.
The RFC also operated the Seattle Loan
Agency, which provided finance for the
purchase of surplus government property.

*Rainy Lake Airways' Goose CF-SBS (c/n 1153) taking off for another wilderness fishing trip. The former JRF-6B was operated by various US owners,
including Catalina Seaplanes, but was eventually destroyed in an overnight hangar fire at Whitehorse, Yukon Territories on 18th/19th January 1999.
(Postcard published by Paul's Photos, Island Lake, IL)*

Red Fox Charters operated Mallard N22DF (c/n J-35) between May 1978 and April 1988. It is seen here at Boeing Field, Washington on 26th December 1979. The Mallard is currently being operated in Western Australia. *(Dennis Goodwin via Jennifer Gradidge)*

RED AIRCRAFT SERVICE Inc,
Fort Lauderdale, FL
1448
"Red" Gamber, owner.

RED CARPET HELICOPTERS Inc,
New Smyrna Beach, FL
31
Vaughn W Crile, President.

RED FOX CHARTERS Inc, Miami, FL
J-35
Owned by JA Belcher, Red Fox bought the G-73 from *Tyee Airlines Inc* in April 1978. During 1985 c/n J-35 was reportedly sold as a support aircraft for a hotel project in Palau, Philippines and did not return to the USA until October 1986. The FAA file has no details of this but shows a Special Certificate of Airworthiness being issued for a test flight, at 125% of gross take-off weight, from Honolulu, HI to Lakeport, CA on 24th March 1986. The aircraft was sold in 1988.

REDNER, Bob, Detroit, MI
1051
-see also *Killa Katchka*

RED S AIRCRAFT SALES, Leonard, OK
1085, B-73, 21, 31
Owned by *Harold D (Red) Stevenson.*

REEBAL FLYING SERVICE Inc
– see *Merrimac Aircraft Inc*

REED, JD Co, Inc, Houston, TX
1300

REEF WORLD AIRLINES,
Airlie Beach, QLD
J-22, J-23
The airline was originally known as *Air Whitsunday*, but due to declining business revenues the new name was tried as a marketing ploy by *Seair Pacific*, who had bought Air Whitsunday. It did not work, and the G-73s were sold in 1990 (c/n J-23) and 1995, both to *Paspaley Pearling Co*, who rebuilt them as G-73ATs.

REESE, Michael D, Portland, OR
1389
Also listed as Reese/McKinnon Air Park, Sandy, OR

REEVE ALEUTIAN AIRWAYS (RAA), Anchorage, AK
1140, B-86, B-103
Founded in 1932 as Reeve Airways. From 1946, the company operated scheduled and charter flights within Alaska, the Aleutian Islands and the Pribilof Islands with war-surplus DC-3s.
G-21A, c/n 1140, was added to the fleet in 1948, when "Aleutian" was added to the name to reflect the area served. Two Sikorsky S-43s were acquired in 1950 but these were superseded in 1957 when a second G-21A was added. Scheduled flights were flown on Mondays only, but this was extended as the network was built up along the chain of islands. C/n B-103 was written off at False Pass on 22nd June 1970, but was replaced by c/n B-86 in July 1972. The last RAA flight (by B-86) was on 14th December 1976.
In April 1977, the remaining two aircraft (c/ns 1140 & B-86) were delivered to

Bob Reeve poses in front of his Goose, N95468 (c/n 1140), in full Reeve Aleutian Airways colours, in the 1950s. The aircraft was reported derelict in 1976 but was sold to Peninsula Airways in April 1977. It was lost in an accident on 23rd January 1981, when it crashed into Driftwood Bay, near Dutch Harbor, Alaska and sank. *(Bob Reeve Collection)*

Peninsular Airways, who were then sub-contracted to operate from Cold Bay, using Reeve Aleutian flight numbers, to False Pass, Akutan and King Cove. The two aircraft were actually sold by RAA to *PenAir* by a Bill of Sale dated 16th December 1981.

REEVE-ELY LABORATORIES Inc,
New York, NY
1445
The company bought the G-44A in April 1947 and transferred ownership to the REEVE INSTRUMENT Corp in October 1947.

RÉGIE AÉRIENNE INTERINSULAIRE, (RAI),
Papeete, Tahiti
1391, J-29
In 1953, the struggling *Air Tahiti* was re-organised by the government of Oceania to form RAI. The G-44 was wrecked in a water-looping incident in 1953 and the wreckage sold to *New Zealand Tourist Air Transport*. Scheduled passenger services were flown by the G-73 and a Consolidated Catalina on the route Papeete, Bora Bora, Huahine and Raiatea (Utuora). Unscheduled flights were also made from the Society Islands to the Gambier Islands, the Tuamotus and the Australs. In 1954, TAI of France took a controlling interest in the company and on 1st January 1958, renamed it *Reseau Aérien Interinsulaire.* See also *Air Polynesie.*

REHBAUM, Robert W, Scotia, NY
35
Acquired the aircraft in 1971 and had many alterations/improvements incorporated over the following seven years (see SCAN-30 Production List). The aircraft was sold after Rehbaum's death in 1990.

REID, Ogden R, New York, NY
1474
Reid had the G-44A's main door altered to create an opening in the centre to facilitate in-flight photography.

**REINSURANCE & EXCESS
INSURANCE Co, The**, Vancouver, BC
1145
After a wheels-up landing in 1972, the insurers sold the *Air West Airlines* G-21A as salvage to *Wilton R Probert*.

REISER BURGAN Inc, Jacksonville, FL
1364
Grover Burgan, President.

REKOW, Lloyd A, Seattle, WA
dba *Foreign & Domestic Enterprises Inc*, which became well-known for Goose re-builds.
B-115

RELIABLE HOME EQUIPMENT Co Inc,
Richmond, VA
1345
HJ Bernstein, President.

REMMERT-WERNER Inc, Red Bank, NJ
& St Louis, MO - See below

REMMERT-WERNER of FLORIDA Inc,
Pompano Beach, FL
B-100, B-114, J-7, J-44
Large aircraft sales company that also carried out re-engineering, conversion and maintenance work on all types of executive aircraft, including G-21As. *Beldex Corp* was an affiliated company.

REPUBLIC AVIATION Corp,
Farmingdale, NY
1213
The Seversky Aircraft Corp was formed on 17th February 1931 and changed its name to Republic on 13th October 1939. The G-44 was operated for one year in 1943/4.

REPUBLIC of GUATEMALA,
Guatemala City, Guatemala
1153
The G-21A is believed to have been used by the President, Juan José Arévalo, and in 1947/48 was frequently to be seen moored at the presidential chalet at El Morlón on Lago Amatitlán, south of Guatemala City. Neither local serial nor operating unit is known, although the aircraft was doubtlessly based at Los Cipresales, Guatemala City.

REPUBLIC OIL REFINING Co,
Pittsburgh, PA
J-36
The company was known previously as Republic Oil Co, and used various executive aircraft. The G-73 was purchased new in April 1948 and sold in 1961, before being converted to turbine power for *Chalk's*.

RESEAU AÉRIEN INTERINSULARE
- see *Régie Aérienne Interinsulaire* above

RESORTS INTERNATIONAL Inc,
Miami, FL
B-141, J-10, J-27, J-36, J-42, J-44
Owned by *James Crosby*, Resorts International operated casinos in Nassau,

Bahamas and Atlantic City, NJ and purchased *Chalk's International Airline* in 1978. The aircraft were used to fly gamblers from Miami to Nassau. The G-21A was sold and the G-73s converted to turbine power. For full history see the *Chalk's Flying Service* entry.

REVERMAN, Henry J, Seattle, WA
1325, 1393
Appears to have acted as agent in 1955 in the sale of c/n 1325 from *Alaska Coastal Airlines* to *Sea Airmotive Inc*.

REYNOLDS, Richard J,
Winston-Salem, NC
1234
Reynolds was heir to the family tobacco fortune and undertook philanthropic work to help the under-priviledged.

RFC - see *Reconstruction Finance Corp*

RICE, Ned C, East Hartford, CT
RICE, Janet C, East Hartford, CT
3
Rice was an engineer with Pratt & Whitney. In 1990, in partnership with Widgeon owner *Dennis Burke*, he developed Supplemental Type Certificate SA 4774M to re-engine Widgeons with 350hp Lycoming engines, as used on the Piper Navajo Chieftain. After owning the SCAN-30 for 20 years Rice had it registered in the joint names in March 1985.

RICH, Willard, West Palm Beach, FL
1141

RICHARD PARIS INDUSTRIES Inc,
Fort Lauderdale, FL
1394
Richard Johnson, President.

RICHARDS, Fred C, San Francisco, CA
1317, 1338

RICHARDS, Fred R, Anchorage, AK
1213

RICHARDS, Jack, Aircraft Co Inc,
Oklahoma City, OK
J-5
A well-known aircraft dealer specialising in transport and executive aircraft.

RICHARDS, SA, Burlington, VT
1214

RICHARDSON, Richard, Clarcoma, FL
1354

RICHARDSON, Sid W, Fort Worth, TX
J-28

RICHLAND FLYING SERVICE,
Richmond, WA
1346
The service was owned by *RJ Wheat* and operated the G-44 from 1967-69.

RICHMOND, Albert I, New Bedford, MA
1389

**RICHMOND PULP & PAPER CO of
CANADA Ltd**, Montreal, QC
14
GH Kruger, President. The company traded-in a Cessna 180 in part exchange for the SCAN-30. It is reported that it was operated under US registry for circa 50 hours before taking up its Canadian marks. The company's pilot, Leo Dansereau, operated it out of Cartierville, QC during the early 1960s.

RICHMOR AVIATION, Hudson, NY
B-100
Richmor Aviation was based at Schenectady County Airport in Scotia, NY but the G-21A was based at Columbia County Airport in Hudson, NY.

RICK HELICOPTERS Inc,
Anchorage, AK
1388

RIGGS AIR SERVICE, Sitka, AK
1051
Operated the G-21A on services from Sitka from 1984 until 1987.

RIGGS, Eugene D, Sitka, AK
1387
The G-44 was later registered to Eugene D & J Ann Riggs, Wasilla, AK, and by 2003 at Big Lake, AK

RILEIK (CORPORATION) SA,
Panama City, Panama
J-21
Bought the G-73 from *North Coast Air Services* in 1984 for $125,000.

RIMOUSKI AIRLINE Ltd, Rimouski, QC
B-76
Elbert Dionne, President. Owned the G-21A for three months in 1947 before selling it to *Geo W Crothers Ltd*. It is therefore doubtful whether any services were flown. See also *Dionne Automobile Enrg.*

RITCHEY, Edw W, Fort Worth, TX
dba Ritchey Flying Service, operating out of Meacham Field, TX
1334

RIVER CONSTRUCTION Corp,
Fort Worth, TX
1300

**RIVERSIDE BUSINESS FLIGHT
SERVICE**, Riverside, CA
J-53

RIVERTON AIRWAYS Ltd,
Winnipeg, MB
14
WI Shuster, President. Leased the SCAN-30 from *Atlas Acceptance Corp* from July 1969 until December 1972. In August 1972 it was reported that "the aircraft requires a thorough inspection due to corrosion from 2 years outside storage". The file does not make clear how *Atlas Acceptance Corp* came into ownership of the SCAN-30, but in April 1973 it was sold by them to *Sam Allen Jr.*

Robson Leather's Goose CF-CNR (c/n 1136) at Oshawa, Ontario in June 1971, shortly before it crashed on take-off from that location on 25th June 1971. It was sold to an owner in Maine, but unfortunately crashed, again on take-off, on 30th July 1971 and was cancelled from the US register on 4th October 1971. *(Jack McNulty via Jennifer Gradidge)*

RIVETT, Ronald J, Aberdeen, SD
dba Quest Aviation.
B-70

RMIB Inc, Wilmington, DE
J-49

ROBERTS, Alfred R, Trappe, MD
1456
The address given on the Certificate of Registration application was "Belmont Farms".

ROBERTSON & O'CONNELL Ltd,
Montreal, QC
J-59

ROBERTSON, Andrew, Burlingame, CA
1430
Co-owned the G-44A with *Gerry Stroh* and *Paul Ennor.*

ROBERTSON, Dr Gordon, Bralorne, BC
1423

ROBINSON, David B, Miami Springs, FL
J-13

ROBINSON, James T
- see *Air Crane Inc* and *Island Flying Boats Inc*

ROBSON LEATHER Co Ltd, Oshawa, ON
1136
Ursula M Robson, President, Charles N Robson, Vice-President.

ROCHESTER AMPHIBIAN Inc,
Rochester, NY
1324, 1374, 36

ROCHESTER AMPHIBIAN AIRWAYS Inc, Rochester, NY
1444
President: *Eugene van Voorhis* until 1991, when Sandra L Rueckwald took the reins.

ROCHESTER ENTERPRISES Inc,
Rochester, VT
27
John Eaton, President.

ROCKEFELLER, Laurance S,
New York, NY
1049
Rockefeller had NC37000 assigned to Beaverbrook's G-21A but there is no evidence that the registration was actually applied to the aircraft.

ROCKWELL STANDARD Corp,
Aero Commander Division,
Bethany, OK
J-4
Purchased the G-73 from *Boris Sergievsky* in 1964 but only flew it for 41 hours before selling it to *Jack Adams Aircraft Sales* in December 1966.

ROD AERO AIRCRAFT BROKERAGE Inc,
Fort Lauderdale, FL
31
Rodney N Matthews, President. Bought the SCAN-30 from *Fred Garrison* in October 1991 and sold it back to him the following month!

RODAIR Inc, Montreal, QC
J-34
R Turcotte, President. Purchased the G-73 in August 1961 and based it at Cartierville, QC.

RODGERS, James L, Middlebury, IN
1292
Rodgers had owned the Super Widgeon, named "*Canadian Clipper*", since March 1974, but the Certificate of Registration expired on 30th June 2011 and therefore the ownership is now uncertain.

RODGERS, John D, Huntley, IL
dba *Stallion Aircraft Inc*, Bensenville, IL.
1013

RODGERS LOG Inc, Spruce Grove, AB
1184
Gail Rodgers, President. The G-21A was imported from the USA in 1998 with a view to restoring it. Stored at Edmonton, AB, it was not used, and was eventually sold to *Pacific Coastal Airlines* in 2005.

ROGER, Bruce A, Seattle, WA
1473

ROGERS, Charles, Vancouver, BC
J-23

ROGERS CONSTRUCTION Co,
Portland, OR
1218

ROHL, Shirley J, Anchorage, AK
1334
Co-owner with *David B Brown.*

ROSE, Howard J, Greenwich, CT
- see *Brandt Jordan Corp*
1353

ROSE, William R, South Barrington, IL
dba Rose Packing.
B-100

ROSKAY, Leland C, Niles, MI
1311

ROSS AVIATION Inc, Tulsa, OK
1233
JR Ross, President. The company was based at Riverside Airport, Tulsa, but a mortgage document dated 14th February 1961, noted that the G-44 was located at Cocoa Beach, FL.

ROSS ENTERPRISES, William,
Elk Grove Village, IL
B-55
and at Incline Village, NV
1129, B-142
Kathryn S Ross, President.

ROTH y Compañía Ltda, Chile
1004
Walter Roth, owner, was a business partner of *Federico Fuehrer K.*

ROUZIE, Richard L, Mercer Island, WA
1365
Rouzie owned a half-share in the G-44 between 1951 and 1971.

ROWAN DRILLING Co Inc,
Fort Worth, TX
1429

ROWATT, Paul, Chicago, IL
1413

ROYAL AMBASSADOR TRANSPORT Corp, Miami, FL
1468

ROYAL AVIATION, Unionville, MO
J-32

ROYAL BABY DUCK LLC,
Weatherford, TX
1454

ROYAL CANADIAN MOUNTED POLICE, Ottawa, ON
B-77
The Mounted Police Air Service was formed on 1st April 1937 as the "Air

The Royal Canadian Mounted Police Air Division's long-serving G-21A Goose CF-MPG (c/n B-77) in the early dark blue and yellow colour scheme carried in the 1950s. After almost fifty years' service with RCMP and flying more than 24,000 hours, the Goose was retired from service in January 1994 and is currently displayed in the National Aviation Museum, Rockcliffe, Ontario.   (RCMP photo)

Section" of the RCMP. The G-21A was bought from the War Assets Corporation for Can$50,000, and registered CF-MPG on 23rd April 1946. The aircraft provided transportation for personnel and prisoners alike and even, on 1st June 1962, carried HRH Prince Philip of the United Kingdom and his entourage to the Douglas Lake Ranch. Another facet of operations was demonstrated in May 1957 when the G-21A was despatched to the Queen Charlotte Islands, off the BC coast, with a bomb disposal crew who dealt with an un-exploded Japanese mine that had drifted across the Pacific. The aircraft was based at Pat Bay on Vancouver Island from 1952 until being moved north to Prince Rupert, BC in 1976 until retirement from service in late January 1994 after almost 48 years service, and over 24,000 flying hours. Fiscal restraints dictated that the RCMP would have to sell the aircraft (valued at $300,000), but a "Save the Goose" campaign was started by the Prince George Flying Club to purchase the aircraft and donate it to the nation. However, the federal and BC governments agreed to forego their respective shares of the proceeds of a sale and donated the G-21A to the National Aviation Museum at Rockcliffe, Ottawa, Ontario, where it was delivered 17th August 1995 and is now on display there.

ROYAL ISLAND AIRWAYS Inc,
New York, NY
1164
Richard L Dikovics, President.

RUAN EQUIPMENT Co, Des Moines, IA
J-38

RUBBER DEVELOPMENT Corp,
Washington, DC
1015, B-46
The Rubber Development Corporation played a very important role during World War II, operating many aircraft, including the two G-21As, in Brazil for the Amazon Rubber Program. This was of enormous help to the war effort in Europe and the USA. C/n 1015 was later operated by *British Guiana Airways Ltd*.

RUDE, Richard L, Spanaway, WA
1334
Rude was President of *Flying Fireman Ltd* and was also listed as dba *Misty Acres Inc*.

RUEBUSH, Lee Jr,
Carolina Flying Service, Tarboro, NC
1274

RUSHTON, Lawrence M, Goodrich, MI
and later at Vonore, TN
1386

RYAN, George F, Newport, RI
J-17

RYAN, Joseph James,
New York, NY & Arlington, VA
1014, 1411, J-12, J-39, J-43
Joseph James was the grandson of Thomas Fortune Ryan, one of the richest men in America at the time. He was a member of the Long Island Aviation Country Club (as was Leroy Grumman), and an aviation fanatic. Although he flew with a waiver from the CAA, despite his poor eyesight, he got a job at the Grumman flight test department and first owned the G-21A, which was requisitioned by the US Navy in 1942. In May 1945 he bought the G-44A, and finally, three G-73s! The third, c/n J-43, was named "*Huckleberry Duck*".

RYMER, Leroy Jr, Cleveland, TN
1454

SAATAS, Jakarta, Indonesia
B-54
Leased the G-21A to McDermott Inc for support of oil operations in the early 1980s.

SAATAS-EASTINDIO P T - see below

SAATAS EAST INDONESIA AIR TAXI,
Jakarta
B-54, B-119
Founded in 1971, and operated charters in West Irian and East Timor.

SAETA
- see *Sociedad Anónima de Explotación de Transporte Aereo*

SAFAIR FLYING SERVICE,
Teterboro, NJ
J-52
Safair was contracted to ferry the G-73 from Teterboro to west Africa for the President of Gabon. Unfortunately after landing in the Atlantic Ocean off Gabon, it was unable to take off again and was taken in tow by a ship. The aircraft was pulled underwater and sank.

SAFE FLIGHT INSTRUMENT Corp,
White Plains, NY
1230

SAFEWAY AIRWAYS, Anchorage, AK
1239, 1265, 1378, J-44
Founded by *Gentry Shuster* in 1947. After getting his commercial pilot's licence Shuster bought the Starr Airways facilities at Merrill Field, Anchorage, and also set up a Piper franchise there. In 1955 Shuster sold the business to United Airmotive. In the early 1960s mortgage documents were signed by Charles M Hallock (partner) on behalf of Safeway Airways. The G-73 was operated by *J Fred Frakes*, under the name of Safeway Airways during 1963, before being sold to *Northern Consolidated Airlines* in March 1964.

SAGGERS, Susan, UK
1411
After rebuild in the UK, the G-44A was reported to have been registered to Saggers, although operated from Biggin Hill as N444M by Michael Dunkerly, dba Shipping & Airlines Ltd.

JJ Ryan's much-travelled Mallard N3010 (c/n J-43) at San Francisco, California in 1951. The flags under the cockpit window indicate some of the places visited. The aircraft was painted overall red with black trim.   (WT Larkins)

After some years in Australia and Papua New Guinea, G-44A Widgeon ZK-AVM (c/n 1466) was back in New Zealand by 1995, and is seen here in 2000 in the white and red colours of Salt Air. It has since been restored and sold to a new owner in Auckland, New Zealand. (MAP)

SALLMON, Helga R, Missoula, MT
B-56

SALMON, Herman R, Van Nuys, CA
(co-owner)
1388

SALT AIR, Paihia, Auckland, NZ
1356, 1439, 1466
The later name for *Aquatic & Vintage Airways Ltd*, founded in 1992 by *Owen and Grant Harnish*. According to Owen Harnish the company name was changed (in 1996) to Salt Air because the former name "was a bit of a mouthful for the tourists". The company provided seaplane charter, scenic flights, photographic and freight charters throughout New Zealand. In 1999 Owen Harnish handed over the company to his son Grant. C/n 1439 was last flown in 1996. The two G-44As were in storage at Whitford near Auckland in 2007, with c/n 1356 being used for spares. C/n 1466 was sold in May 2012.

SANCHEZ, Rafael, Cuba
1439
A sugar cane and cattle farmer who used his G-44A for personal and business use from 1949 until he fled Cuba (in his Widgeon) in 1959, after Castro took power and confiscated the Sanchez farms. The aircraft was registered in the USA to his friend *Florentino Sequeiro*, who was an American citizen. Note: Mr Sanchez insists that the aircraft was registered as CU-<u>N</u>-346.

SANDERS, Robert P, Charlotte, NC
1386

SANDERS, Ruth, Jackson, CA
and Sutter Creek, CA
B-142

SANDERSON AIRCRAFT Ltd,
Malton, ON
1311
The company acted as broker for the sale of the G-44 to *Arthur Tateishi* in 1953.

SANSTAD, Mme Marie Therese
4
Wife of the *InterContinental Aviation* manager, Alan Sanstad.

SAPP, Darrell, Wauconda, WA
26
Sapp bought the remains of the SCAN-30 as salvage in 1972.

SAUNDERS, James C,
Miami, FL
1445
Saunders owned hardware stores in Miami, FL, and was President of *Island Charters Inc*, to whom the aircraft was registered in June 1978.

SAUNDERS-VIXEN AIRCRAFT Co Inc,
Eastsound, WA
1313
Richard Bach, President

SCAN
- see *Société des Constructions Aéro-navales du Port Neuf*

SCHACHLE, Charles,
Moses Lake, WA
1334
'Chuck' Schachle bought the G-44 from *Flying Fireman Ltd* when that company went into receivership in 1973. On the Certificate of Registration application form Schachle gave his address as c/o Flying Fireman Inc, Billings, MT but the Certificate was issued to Schachle as an individual at a Moses Lake, Washington address.

SCHADLE, Alvan G, Soldotna, AK
1267
Co-owner with *Elmer E Altschuler* in 2007 after the G-44 had been registered to *Alvan G & Linda A Schadle* in 1998, and Alvan G Schadle alone in 2006.

SCHADLE, Alvan G & Linda A,
Soldotna, AK
1267

SCHAFER BAKERY PRODUCTS Co,
Battle Creek, MI
1314

SCHEFF, Gilbert D and Brian L,
Anchorage, AK
dba *Records Management Inc*
1398

SCHENUIT, Frank G, Baltimore, MD
1233
dba, and President of, The Frank G Schenuit Rubber Co, he bought the surplus OA-14 in February 1945 for $11,500.

SCHLUETER, Donald H, Genesee, ID
1319

SCHOOL PROPERTIES Inc,
Minneapolis, M
J-4

SCHOONER ENTERPRISES Inc,
Miami, FL
1059
Jeanne Franklin, President. Another of the *Dean H Franklin* companies, with the same address as *Amphibians Inc*.

SCHULTZE, Arthur C, Matawan, NJ
(co-owner)
1378

SCHUSTER, Dr James E, Fond du Lac, WI
1265

SCHWAMM, John A & Linda E,
Anchorage, AK
1324, 1473, 1475
Schwamm, a real estate executive, bought the remains of 1324 from *Alaska Airlines*

John Schwamm's immaculate G-44 Widgeon N144GW (c/n 1324) rebuilt with a G-44A bow and 295hp Lycomings, is seen here at Oshkosh in July 1993. It is currently flying as N612GW with an owner in Rochester, New York. (Jennifer Gradidge)

pilot *David Strelinger* in 1991. With Strelinger's help the G-44 was rebuilt using a tail-fin from a Coast Guard J4F-1, a new set of wings, 295hp Lycomings (as fitted to the Helio Courier) driving 90-inch three-bladed Hartzell propellers; and a new set of instruments and avionics. The aircraft are used partly for business, but mainly for camping and fishing trips to all parts of Alaska.

SCHWARZ, Carl R, Kent, WA
36

SCHWITZER Corp, Indianapolis, IN
1409
which was previously:
SCHWITZER-CUMMINS Co,
Indianapolis, IN
1409
The Schwitzer company was founded in Indianapolis in 1918. It has produced turbochargers for diesel engines in varios types of vehicle since then and is now part of the multi-national BorgWarner group.

SCOTT FLYING SERVICE Inc,
New Orleans, LA
1398
Donald P Scott, President. Aircraft based at New Orleans Municipal Airport.

SCOTT, Walter, Aspen, CO
dba *Ranchaire Inc*
J-52

SCOTT, William Ben, Reno, NV
1429
President of Scott Motor Co.

SCRIBNER, RC, Pontiac, MI
1360
Possibly the same as below.

SCRIBNER, Richard, Pontiac, MI
1454
Possibly the same as above.

SEA-AIR Inc, Anchorage, AK
1313, 1355, 1387
Ward I Gay, President. *Sea Airmotive Inc* was temporarily operating under the name Sea-Air Inc during 1959. The company changed its name back to Sea Airmotive in April 1960. (See below).

SEA-AIR SHIPPING & SALVAGE Ltd,
Grand Turk, British West Indies
1274
According to a Bill of Sale dated 5th June 1979 the G-44 had been bought from *Coastal Air Inc*, of which *Dean Franklin* was President. The aircraft was cancelled belatedly from USCAR on 17th August 1981 as exported to the Turks & Caicos Islands. However a letter dated 21st May 1998 to the FAA from *Franklin* stated that the aircraft had "been stored at our facilities since March 1980 when it was sold to *Dean H Franklin*. It is now in our storage facilities at this time, and is in a state of rebuild." The G-44 was registered in June 2012 to an owner in Florida, but is still not airworthy.

SEA AIR SHUTTLE Corp, Carolina, PR
J-9, J-11, J-53

SEA AIRMOTIVE Inc, Anchorage, AK
1305, 1325, 1327, 1338, 1355, 1387
Ward I Gay, President. Sea Airmotive Inc, commenced operations in 1939 and was incorporated in 1951. By 1954 it was operating from Lake Hood Seaplane Base and also had a PA-18 and two PA-20s in the fleet. By April 1955 two G-44s were operated alongside two PA-18, two PA-20 and a Cessna 180, all on floats. C/n 1325 was acquired in April 1955 and registered in the name of *Alfred E Gay* (at the same address) from December 1955 until sold in September 1956 to *Cordova Airlines Inc*. C/n 1305 was bought in March 1957 (for spares?) and its registration (N79906) was transferred to c/n 1327. C/n 1355 was operated during the 1960s, until it was cancelled as "scrapped" in 1970. By 1978, Alfred E Gay had taken over as President, and the company had 38 aircraft. Sea Airmotive Inc reportedly became Seair in December 1977, but this may have been another temporary name change as a Bill of Sale dated 1979 states that the company is Sea Airmotive Inc (again). However, by 1985 the company was known as *Seair Alaska Airlines Inc*.

SEA BEE AIR,
Auckland, NZ
1145, B-62, B-104, 1391, 1439, 1466
Founded by the staff of *Mount Cook Airlines* when that company ceased amphibian services from Auckland in April 1976. Operations began on 22nd October 1976 with three Widgeons and one G-21A. In October 1977 a second G-21A (c/n 1145) was added and in 1981 the G-21E joined the fleet. Sea Bee Air's raison d'être was to provide amphibian services to the people of the Hauraki Gulf and the Bay of Islands, but this was supplemented by operations further afield. In 1979 Sea Bee Air based G-44A ZK-AVM (c/n 1466) in Suva, Fiji to provide non-scheduled and charter passenger and freight services within the Fiji Islands on behalf of Fiji Air. The Widgeon operated out of Lauthala Bay, Suva to Vinisea and Kaivala Bay on the island of Kandavu for two years before returning to New Zealand for an extensive refit.

Meanwhile, between March 1980 and September 1983, Sea Bee Air operated services on behalf of the Tuvaluan government. Based at Funafuti, the non-scheduled services linked the nine atolls of the Tuvalu group and provided charters to the Tokelau, Samoa, Kiribati, Nauru and

Sea Bee Air's G-21A Goose ZK-DFC (c/n B-104) taxying in Waitamata Harbour, Auckland circa 1985. Note only the "last three" of the registration are painted on the aircraft. This is allowed in New Zealand provided an aircraft is used only for internal flights. (Mark R Cranston)

G-21G Turbo Goose ZK-ERX (c/n B-62/1205) of Sea Bee Air Ltd at Nouméa-Magenta on 31st August 1981, while operating services on behalf of the Tuvaluan government. The services were discontinued in September 1983 due to lack of funding. The aircraft is currently operating as N77AQ with an owner in Oregon. (Roger Caratini)

Amphibian Airways' first Widgeon ZK-AVM (c/n 1466) here serving with Sea Bee Air, later went to Australia as VH-WET, and on 18th September 1994 survived the volcanic eruption in Rabaul, Papua New Guinea. It has since been restored and sold to a new owner in Auckland, New Zealand.
(Fred J Knight Collection)

AUCKLAND'S DOWNTOWN AIR SERVICE

SEA BEE AIR LIMITED

Mechanics Bay, Auckland — P.O. Box 1971
Phone 774-406   Telex SeaBee NZ 21253
       774-405
       774 404

PASSENGER TIMETABLE

FROM	TO	DEP.	ARR.	FLIGHT NO.	FARE
Mechanics Bay	Surfdale	8.00am	8.10am	CB510	25.00
''	''	8.45am	8.55am	CB512	25.00
''	''	12noon	12.10pm	CB514	25.00
''	''	4.30pm	4.40pm	CB518	25.00
''	''	5.00pm	5.10pm	CB520	25.00
				Return	40.00
Surfdale	Mechanics Bay	8.15am	8.25am	CB511	25.00
''	''	9.00am	9.10am	CB513	25.00
''	''	12.30pm	12.40pm	CB515	25.00
''	''	4.45pm	4.55pm	CB519	25.00
''	''	5.15pm	5.25pm	CB521	25.00
				Child Return	28.00
Mechanics Bay	Waiheke East & Pakatoa	12noon	12.15pm	CB514	60.00
				Return	110.00
Waiheke East & Pakatoa	Mechanics Bay	12.20pm	12.40pm	CB515	60.00
				Child Return	70.00
Mechanics Bay	Gt. Barrier	9.30am	9.55am	CB310	65.00
''	''	10.45am	11.10am	CB312	65.00
''	''	2.00pm	2.25pm	CB314	65.00
''	''	5.30pm	5.55pm	CB316	65.00
				Return	120.00
				Child	40.00
Gt. Barrier	Mechanics Bay	10.00am	10.25am	CB311	65.00
''	''	11.15am	11.40am	CB313	65.00
''	''	2.30pm	2.55pm	CB315	65.00
''	''	6.00pm	6.25pm	CB317	65.00
				Child Return	70.00
Mechanics Bay	Paihia (Bay of Is.)	8.45am	9.35am	CB846	120.00
		5.30pm	6.20pm	CB848	120.00
				Return	220.00
				Child	80.00
Paihia	Mechanics Bay	7.45am	8.35am	CB845	120.00
''		4.00pm	4.50pm	CB847	120.00
				Child Return	150.00

PLEASE NOTE: Final reporting time fifteen minutes prior to departure.

Charter flights available using helicopter, conventional aircraft and amphibian from downtown Auckland to any destination within New Zealand. — Please enquire.

SCENIC FLIGHTS

Amphibian			Helicopter		
	Adult child	minimun	Adult	Child	minimum
5min	$25 $15	2 adults	$25	$15	2 adults
10 min	$30 $18	4 pass.	$45	$25	4 pass.
15 min	$40 $25	4 pass.	$70	$35	4 pass.
20 min	$50 $30	4 pass.			

Prices subject to change without prior notice
Effective December 1985

Above: *Sea Bee Air timetable effective December 1985.*

Cook groups. G-44A, ZK-CFA (c/n 1439) was used until August 1981 when G-21G ZK-ERX (c/n B-62/1205) took over. In December 1982, 'ERX became the first aircraft to land at the newly-opened airport at Rakahanga in the Cook Islands. The British Overseas Development Agency withdrew funding for the Tuvalu service, and Sea Bee Air discontinued it in September 1983. The G-21G was returned to Auckland where it briefly provided services to the Hauraki Gulf, but was withdrawn from service by the end of 1983 and sold.

Sea Bee Air also provided a G-21A to operate on behalf of the Nadi-based, Sun Tours, Fiji. ZK-ENY (c/n 1145) was registered in Fiji as DQ-FDQ in October 1982 and carried Sun Tours titles on the forward fuselage, with Sea Bee's water-skiing bee on the tailfin. This operation involved non-scheduled flights linking Nadi with the island resorts of Mana, Malololailai, Treasure, Castaway and Beachcomber as well as services to other islands within the Fiji group, and to other South Pacific islands. The G-21A returned to Auckland for an extensive re-fit on 27th October 1984 and was returned to the New Zealand register as ZK-ENY in December 1984.

At this time Sea Bee Air was carrying more than 45,000 passengers annually and also providing up to 200 air ambulance flights for the St John's Ambulance Service. Early in 1987 fast boat services were introduced on routes out of Auckland at half the fare of the amphibian service with the result that from May 1987 Sea Bee Air's traffic share declined. This, to such an extent that by 1989 only the Great Barrier Island service remained, operated by Great Barrier Airlines, with Sea Bee as the holding company. On 26th August 1991 G-21A ZK-DFC was loaded aboard a boat bound for the USA and the era of regular amphibian services in New Zealand was at an end. The Widgeons were taken over by *Owen Harnish* who continued non-scheduled and charter operations for several years.

SEABOARD CONSTRUCTION Co,
Mt Kisco, NY
1419
Ben E Smith, President.

SEABREEZE MANUFACTURING Ltd,
Toronto, ON
1311
The G-44 was registered in the name of the company president, *Arthur Tateishi*.

SEACOAST AIRCRAFT,
Riviera Beach, FL
1364
LS Frisk, President.

SEAGULL AIR SERVICE,
Miami, FL (*PM Davis*)
J-13
Davis leased the much-travelled G-73 in 1973 before buying it in May 1975. It was sold in Canada in 1977.

SEAHORSE AIR SERVICE Inc,
Annapolis, MD
1411
Stanley Woodward Jr, President.

SEAIR - see *Sea Airmotive Inc*

SEAIR ALASKA AIRLINES Inc
- see *Sea Airmotive Inc*
By 1985, under *Alfred E Gay* as President, the Grummans had been sold and the company was operating DHC-2 Beavers, DHC-6 Twin Otters and Convair 580s.

SEAIR AIRWAYS Ltd, Kissimee, FL
30

SEAIR PACIFIC, Airlie Beach, QLD
J-22, J-23
Seair Pacific was an aviation promotion and sales company that purchased *Air Whitsunday* in June 1988. Because of a decline in business a name change to *Reef World Airlines* was tried as a marketing exercise, but with little success. The G-73s were sold to *Paspaley Pearling Co* in 1990 (c/n J-23) and 1995.

SEALRIGHT Co Inc, Fulton, NY
1314

SEAPLANE ADVENTURES LLC,
Greenwich, CT
J-27, J-30, J-36, J-42, J-44
C/ns J-27 & J-30 were operated by *Chalk's Ocean Airways* on schedules from Miami to the Bahamas, until all Mallards were grounded following the crash of c/n J-27 on 19th December 2005, killing all twenty on board.

SEAPLANE LEASING I LLC,
Coconut Grove, FL
J-27, J-30, J-36, J-40

SEAPLANE LEASING II LLC,
Fort Lauderdale, FL
J-42
The companies were owned by *James Confalone* and, although Seaplane Leasing was the registered owner of the G-73Ts, they were actually owned by the Ocean Bank, Miami, FL. The "permitted lessee" was, and they were operated by, *Flying Boat Inc, dba Chalk's Ocean Airways*, under a Part 121 Air Carrier certificate. The reference to Ocean in the title reflecting the ownership by the bank.

SEAPLANE PARTS LLC,
Gibsonville, NC
B-115

Boris Sergievsky's Mallard N2940 (c/n J-4) carries his WWI squadron crest on the forward hull. Note also the water rudder on the rear hull. After a varied career, the aircraft ended its days with Virgin Islands Seaplane Shuttle and was destroyed in an accident on 28th October 1986. The wreckage was sold for parts in May 1990. **(Ken Molson)**

SEAPLANE SERVICE Inc,
Opa Locka, FL
1214
Joseph Maugeri, President

**SEAPLANE SHUTTLE
TRANSPORT Inc**, New York, NY
aka *Cosmopolitan Broadcasting*
1110, 1132, 1153
Donald J Lewis, owner & President.
The G-21A c/n 1132 was granted an Experimental Certificate of Airworthiness "to show compliance with FARs" on 30th June 1980, but operations were limited to a radius of 25 miles from their base. In a letter to the FAA dated 21st August 1980 SST Inc requested to be allowed to conduct test-flights within a 50-mile radius of their Ridgefield Park, NJ base, in furtherance of their application for a Supplemental Type Certificate. The amended Experimental Certificate of Airworthiness was granted on 22nd August 1980 to expire on 30th December 1980. It is not known what the Supplemental Type Certificate was for, but as the aircraft was fitted with "*new left and right hand instrument panels of the same dimensions and thickness as previous panels. A second flight group was installed in R/H panel along with all new hoses*", the STC might have been issued to allow this modification. However, no record of such an STC has been found.

SEA SERVICE Inc, New Orleans, LA
1221, 1377

SEASPRAY AVIATION Corp,
George Town, Cayman Islands
J-34

SEATON, R, Bowmanville, ON
J-13
Seaton had the registration C-GRZI allotted to him in October 1977 because it was he who had prepared the aircraft for its Certificate of Airworthiness and did the certification paperwork. The G-73 was registered to the owner, *Dr Reginald Slade*, in June 1978.

SEATTLE LOAN AGENCY
- see *Reconstruction Finance Corp*

SEBAGO LAKE SHORES Inc,
South Casco, ME
4
JA Bowron, President.

SEE, Clarence, Jr, Syracuse, NY
dba *Land'N Sea Airways*, with partner *Maxwell Brace, Sr*
27

SEKIYA & Co Ltd, Tokyo, Japan
1153

**SENSITIVE RESEARCH
INSTRUMENT Corp**,
New Rochelle, NY
1378
An electrical instrument engineering company formed in 1919.

SEQUEIRO, Florentino, Miami, FL
1439
Rafael Sanchez registered the G-44A in his friend Sequeiro's name after fleeing Castro's Cuba in 1959, Sequeiro being an American citizen.

SERGIEVSKY, Captain Boris,
New York, NY
1006, J-4
Sergievsky was a test pilot for the *Sikorsky Aircraft Company* who set ten world records in the S-42 NC822M in 1934. He took delivery of the sixth G-21 off the production line in October 1937, named it "*Orel*", and used it as a personal aircraft and for high-society charter services until it was impressed by the USAAC in 1942. The charter services were continued with the G-73 from October 1946. Remembering his time as a Russian fighter pilot in WWI, Sergievsky had his old squadron badge painted on the nose of his aircraft. With his charter business expanding Sergievsky, with co-pilot Elmourza Natirboff, was one of the first to fly a G-73 over the northern (Greenland/Iceland) route to Europe. C/n J-4 was sold to *Aero Commander Division of Rockwell Standard Corp* in 1964, and Sergievsky ended his long flying career the following year, when he lost his licence due to medical reasons.

SERPASS, Harold, Dallas, TX
J-13

SEYAH Corp, New York, NY
1213
F William Zelcer, President. The corporation was originally the *Hayes Aircraft Accessories Corporation* but in 1942 the name was reversed to become Seyah. The G-44 was used by the Civil Air Patrol in 1942.

SEYBERT, Orin D, Pilot Point, AK
dba *Peninsular Airways.*
1378

SHACKELFORD, John S, Jr,
Roanoke, TX
1206
An airline pilot who based his G-44 at the Northwest Regional Airport in Roanoke.

SHANKS, James M, Juneau, AK
B-32

SHARP, John G, Mimico, ON
B-50
Sharp purchased the former RCAF Goose from the *War Assets Corporation* for $30,000 and within two months sold it to the *British American Oil Company* for $40,000.

SHARP, Peter
dba *Pacific New Guinea Lines*
1466

SHAW FLIGHT SERVICE Inc,
Anchorage, AK
B-126

SHAW, Joseph, Willowdale, ON
1235

SHELL COMPANY of ECUADOR Ltd,
Quito, Ecuador
1005, 1018, 1048, 1106, 1141, B-34
An affiliate of the *Shell Oil Company*, which had been granted a concession by the Ecuadorian government for oil exploration in 1937. An operating base, with a 750-yard long airstrip, was established on the banks of the Pastaza River in the Oriente region, in the foothills of the Andes, from where exploration teams and equipment were flown by a mixed fleet of Ford Tri-Motors, Budd Conestogas, DC-3s, Bristol 170s and G-21As. The base was some 3 miles from the village of Mera and soon became known as Shell Mera. In early 1947, when Airwork Ltd took over the flying operations, the runway was a 4,200-foot gravel strip and the operation boasted a large hangar and an engineering workshop. Despite Airwork managing the day-to-day operations, Shell retained ownership of the aircraft. Sir Richard Barlow, Airwork's South American manager, had just completed a survey of the task his company was to take on when he was killed in G-21A HC-SBL (c/n 1106) when it crashed into the Llanganate range at 14,000ft, on 3rd December 1946. The search for oil ceased at the end of 1949, with the Shell

Shell Ecuador's Goose Fleet Number 1, HC-AAM (c/n 1048) in the mud at Arajuno airfield on 19th February 1945, being pushed by labourers and pulled by the rope attached to the lorry. The rope had already snapped once, just before this picture was taken, but the Goose is now almost back on the runway. Note: the Arajuno strip was some 35 miles NE of the main Shell-Mera base. (See Photo Gallery for further photos). (RI Baker via HC Kavelaars Collection)

Shell Ecuador's Goose HC-SBA (c/n 1048) "Rio Napo", still designated with Fleet Number 1, on a beach in the Rio Aguarico in front of a seismic survey base camp in 1948. (P Hartmann via HC Kavelaars Collection)

team not having found economic amounts of crude, and all equipment (including aircraft) was removed. The last remaining Goose was withdrawn in September 1950.

The aircraft used at Shell Mera were allocated Fleet Numbers, as follows:

Fleet No	Registration
1	HC-AAM later HC-SBA
2	HC-SBB
2	HC-SBX
3	HC-SBT later HC-SBY
4?	HC-SBV
12	HC-SBL

SHELL OIL Co
- see *NNGPM, Shell Co of Ecuador, Shell Refining & Marketing Co, Shell Venezuela, Caribbean Petroleum Co.*

SHELL REFINING & MARKETING Co, London, UK
J-41
This name, rather than Royal Dutch Shell, was used for political expediency in order

that the G-73 could be flown from London to Indonesia on delivery to *NNGPM* in 1949, wearing UK registration G-ALLJ.

SHELL VENEZUELA,
Maracaibo, Venezuela
1048, B-34
Shell's affiliated company *Venezuelan Oil Development Corporation* operated a Fairchild F.24, several Lockheed 12As and a Vickers-Supermarine Sea Otter alongside the G-21As on supply missions to exploration crews on the Catatumbo and Escalante Rivers. C/n 1048, was registered YV-VOD-2 signifying that it was the second aircraft to carry that registration. In fact YV-VOD-1, a Lockheed 12A, was flying concurrently with the G-21A. Under an agreement signed in November 1941, c/n 1048 was transferred to Shell Ecuador, arriving at the Mera base on 14th April 1942. C/n B-34 was transferred from Ecuador to Venezuela in January 1949 and was re-registered as YV-P-AEP. *(See next page for photo of YV-VOD-2).*

SHELTAIR AVIATION CENTER LLC,
Miami, FL
J-30
Sheltair had the G-73 assigned to them on 5th August 2005, with *Seaplane Adventures* as debtor. The lien was released on 14th January 2008.

SHERIDAN EQUIPMENT Co Ltd,
Toronto, ON
1441 *(picture on page 276)*
WL Sheridan, President.

SHERMAN AIRCRAFT SALES,
West Palm Beach, FL
B-120, 1364
Dennis M Sherman, President

SHERMAN & MARQUETTE Inc,
New York, NY
J-51
This advertising company owned the G-73 from May 1953 until March 1954, when it was sold via *Atlantic Aviation* to *The Texas Company.*

SHERWOOD, George W, Detroit, MI
dba *Aero Quality Sales Co* and
Land-Sea-Airways
And later at Grosse Point Park, MI
J-34, J-45
In 1949, Sherwood became the pilot of Mallard J-45, which was owned by *Briggs Manufacturing Company*. After experiencing a serious electrical failure while landing the Mallard at Washington National Airport in 1954, Sherwood started experimenting with nickel-cadmium (ni-cad) batteries with a view to replacing the old lead-acid batteries in the Mallard. He eventually gained a Supplemental Type Certificate (STC) for the replacement installation and formed *Aero Quality Sales Company* to market the ni-cad batteries.

In 1956, Sherwood was given a Pilot Safety Award by the NBAA for having flown 1,182,060 miles without an accident, or injury to any passenger.

Another STC was granted to allow operation of the Mallard without wing floats and with a fairing on the hull behind the step. This increased the cruising speed

Above: *G-44A Widgeon CF-EHD (c/n 1441) of the Sheridan Equipment Company at Toronto-Malton, in April 1949. After a long career, mainly in Canada, during which it was converted to Link Super Widgeon standard, it now flies as N71Q with an owner in Illinois.* (Jack McNulty)

Above: *Goose (c/n 1048) wearing the appropriate registration YV-VOD-2 of the Venezuelan Oil Development Company. Purchased in December 1938, the aircraft was based in Maracaibo, Venezuela until transferred to Shell Ecuador's base at Mera, where it arrived on 14th April 1942.* (Carl F Lunghard via HC Kavelaars Collection)

from 180 to 204mph at 12,000 feet and had the unexpected benefit of a reduction in cabin noise.

When Briggs sold the Mallard to Evans Products, Sherwood went with it and became Chief Pilot for the new owner. When in 1963 Sherwood was instructed by Evans to sell the Mallard, he bought it himself! He formed Land-Sea-Airways and when business improved he bought the second Mallard, J-34.

By 1969, Sherwood was physically and mentally exhausted by the pressures of running the charter airline and the battery business, as well as caring for his sick wife. He sold both Mallards and having carried on the ni-cad battery business for another ten years, he sold it in April 1979 to the Lear Siegler Corporation.

SHERWOOD, Virginia Hall,
Boca Raton, FL
1380

SHIPPING & AIRLINES Ltd,
Biggin Hill, UK
1411
Operated the G-44A until 1996 after rebuild in 1985.

SHOLTON, Robert, Anchorage, AK
1164
Sholton was a founder of *Northern Air Cargo Inc*, which, having acquired the G-21A in October 1975, reportedly leased it to *Kodiak Western Alaska Airlines*. However the FAA file contains a Bill of Sale from Sholton to Kodiak Western dated 9th June 1977 (but no certificate of registration [CofR]), followed by another Bill of Sale that transfers the aircraft back to Sholton on 6th March 1978 with a CofR dated 16th May 1978. An undated Bill of Sale transfers the G-21A from Sholton to *Island Hoppers Inc* and this is followed by another Bill of Sale, remarkably, from Sholton/Island Hoppers/Kodiak Western/

Shipping & Airlines' G-44A Widgeon N444M (c/n 1411) fitted with 260hp Lycomings taken from Aero Commander G-ASJU. The aircraft is seen at Biggin Hill in the summer of 1986. The aircraft was delivered to the USA during June 1997 and is currently flying with an owner in Michigan. (Don Conway)

Alaska Coastal and the BM Behrends Bank of Juneau to Wilton R Probert of Oakland, OR on 30th June 1979. Finally on 2nd October 1979 the file records an undated Bill of Sale transferring ownership from Island Hoppers Inc to Probert and he was issued a CofR on 2nd October 1979.

SHORE, James Robert, Winnipeg, MB
As well as being president of *Marjim Corporation Ltd*, Shore was president of *Teal Air Ltd* and operated the G-44 from 1956 until 1961.

SHUSTER, Gentry W, Anchorage, AK
1239, 1265
Shuster obtained the G-44s on 31st March 1952 and operated them under the name of *Safeway Airways* from 1953. When his marriage was dissolved in 1955 he sold Safeway Airways to *United Airmotive*, selling c/n 1265 to *Mckinnon Enterprises*, but retaining c/n 1239. Thereafter Shuster operated as *Alcan Airways* and flew services for *Peninsular Airways* out of Nanek and King Salmon. C/n 1239 was mortgaged with the *First National Bank of Anchorage* who re-possessed the G-44

Don Simmonds' Mallard N611DS (c/n J-35) which was based in the Bahamas is seen here at an unknown location in 2000. The aircraft is currently being operated in Western Australia. *(MAP)*

when Shuster died in March 1967. C/n 1239 was named *"Little Lulu"* after Shuster's daughter.

SIERRA NEVADA CONTRACTORS Inc, Las Vegas, NV
1441

SIGGELKOW, Larry J, Las Vegas, NV
B-46

Gentry Shuster posing in front of his G-44 Widgeon N37189 (c/n 1239) for a Christmas card, circa 1954. The aircraft was named "Little Lulu" after his daughter. Seen here in the colours of Safeway Airways, Shuster later operated the Widgeon with Alcan Airways titles. *(via Bruce McClellan)*

SIKORSKY AIRCRAFT Co, Hartford, CT
- see also *Sergievsky, Boris*.
J-53

SILBERMAN, John P, Sherborn, MA
1364

SIMARD-BEAUDRY Inc, Montreal, QC
1315
Fridolin Simard, President. A nominal change after a company merger (see below). The G-44 was based at Montreal-Dorval.

SIMARD & FRERES, Cie Ltée, Montreal, QC
1315
Fridolin Simard, President.
Had the G-44 re-engined with Lycoming GO-480-B1D engines. During the winter of November 1960 until 20th January 1961 the aircraft was stored at Kingston Flying Club, ON. In 1965 the company became known as *Simard-Beaudry Inc* (see above), and in 1968 it became known as *Simco Ltée* (see below).

SIMCO Ltée, Ville d'Esteral, QC
1315
Fridolin Simard, President. Another change to the company's name, in 1968 (see above). The G-44 was based at Montreal-Dorval during 1968/69, and then at Ste Marguerite in 1970.

SIMMONDS, Don M,
Hopetown, Abaco, Bahamas
J-35

SIMPSON, R Scott, Manhattan Beach, CA
B-35

SIMS, William, St Charles, MO
B-35
Sims co-owned the G-21A with *Tom Ahlers & Paul F Niedner*.

SIMSBURY FLYING SERVICE Inc,
Simsbury, CT
1317
CB Baker, President.

SINCLAIR PANAMA OIL Corp,
New York, NY
1404
The Sinclair Oil & Refining Corp was formed on 1st May 1916 in New York City. By 1919, Sinclair had acquired concessions

to allow drilling for oil on thousands of acres of land in Central America and Mexico. The G-44A was based in the Panama Canal Zone in 1946/47.

SIOUX NARROWS AIRWAYS,
Sioux Narrows, ON
B-55, B-139
Operated services to hunting lodges owned by the Plummer group of companies. C/n B-139 was leased from *Great Bear Lake Lodge Ltd*, another of the companies controlled by *WC Plummer*, for the summer seasons of 1964 and 1965. Nominal ownership of the G-21A then passed to *Plummer Holdings*, who leased it to Sioux Narrows Airways again for the summer of 1966. Another nominal change allowed Great Bear Lake Lodge to lease the aircraft to Sioux Narrows Airways again in May 1968, for one year. In June 1969 the lease was extended to run for five years but in June 1970 the aircraft was sold to *Ilford-Riverton Airways*.

SIPLE, Wallace C,
Montreal, QC
1239
Bought the G-44 from *Pan American Airways* on 21st January 1947 and sold it the same day to *Hunter Moody/Decatur Aviation*.

SITKA SOUNDS SEAFOOD
– see *Edson & Associates*

SITTMAN, Donald B,
Miami, FL
1150
Sittman exchanged an AT-11 Beechcraft for the Bolivian Air Force JRF-6B in 1959 and had it converted to US civilian status (G-21A) in 1960. He was also Vice-President of *Africair Inc*.

SKAGIT AERO EDUCATIONAL MUSEUM, Monroe, WA
1393
Situated at Concrete Airport, WA, the museum was founded by Harold Hanson and operates from five hangars – two display hangars, one restoration hangar, one storage hangar and a small hangar which, in 2011, housed the G-44, awaiting restoration.

SKYWAYS (BAHAMAS) Ltd,
Nassau
1340, 1448, 1462, 1468
- see *Bahamas Airways Ltd*.

SKYWAYS BAHAMAS HOLDING Co Ltd
- see *Bahamas Airways Ltd*.

SKYWAYS Ltd - see *Nassau Aviation Co*

SLADE, Dr Reginald H, Burlington, ON
1306, J-13
Dr Slade based the G-44 at Mt Hope, ON from where it operated from 1971 until 1977, when it was replaced by the G-73. This was based at Hamilton, ON after

Dr Reginald Slade's immaculate McKinnon Super Widgeon CF-QPL (c/n 1306) at Mount Hope, Ontario on 26th June 1971. The aircraft was sold to Dean Franklin's Amphibian Parts Inc in 1978 and is currently flying with an owner in New Hampshire.   (Jack McNulty)

having skin corrosion treatment and re-painting in April/May 1978, but was then sold in the USA in November 1978 for US$199,999.

SLADE, Reginald, Reno, NV
dba Northern Air Inc
B-125

SLAGLE, 'Chuck'
- see *Aviation Associates Ltd & Westflight Aviation Inc*

SLATER, Victor L, Northville, MI
1375

SLIFKA, Jack, New York, NY
1415

SMALL, Gaston Elvin, III,
Elizabeth City, NC
1265

SMILAX Ltd, Nassau, Bahamas
J-5
Bought the G-73 in April 1985 and based it at Fort Lauderdale Executive Airport, FL from March 1986.

SMITH, Bernard E, New York, NY
1433, 1470, J-26
"Sell 'em Ben" Smith became a legend on Wall Street in the 1920s and 1930s because of his ability to make money despite the depressed state of the financial markets. Using this business acumen, he played his part in the birth of the G-21 (see Chapter 2). He subsequently owned two G-44As, delivered in May and June 1947, although he may have been only the purchasing agent, and it is believed that he was instrumental in procuring the two G-44As that went to the Israeli Air Force (see Chapter 7). The G-73 was delivered to him in August 1947 and Smith immediately flew the northern Atlantic route for a tour of Europe; the aircraft was noted at Haifa, Israel in May 1948. Named *"The Golden Jennababe"*, c/n J-26 was transferred in July 1948 to *Van Leer's Metal Products Inc*, which also had connections with Smith. In April 1950 the G-73 was sold to *Christian Dior Inc*.

SMITH, Charles B, Durham, NH
& later Rye, NH
B-49, 1372
Born in New Orleans, LA, Smith started flying charters and doing instruction on G-44s and G-21As, moving to Southern Airways as co-pilot on Martin 4-0-4s before eventually becoming a Lockheed 1011 Captain with Trans World Airlines. When McDermott Inc put all their prop-driven aircraft up for auction in 1985, Smith bought the G-44 and then spent three years re-building it. He bought the G-21A in September 1999, after selling the G-44, and in December 2000 registered it in the name of the "Charles B Smith Revocable Trust", of which he was the trustee. The G-21A was registered briefly to *Robert F Wood Jr* in April 2003 before returning to the Smith Trust. It was sold to *Joel Thompson* in March 2007.

SMITH EQUIPMENT Co, Columbia, SC
1306

SMITH, Gordon, & Co Inc, New York, NY
1168

SMITH, Hugh Z, & CURTIS, Robert E,
Anchorage, AK
dba *Goose Leasing*
B-115

SMITH KIRKPATRICK & Co,
New York, NY
1411, 1450, 1473
Sold the G-44As to the *Ministerio de Defensa Nacional*, Cuba in December 1952 for use by the Cuban Navy. Details can be found in the Military Operators section (Chapter 7).

SMITH, Lane W & Betsy F,
White Salmon, WA
1351

SMITH, Mearle AR, Bathurst, NB
1441

SMITH, Milton V, Portland, ME
1411
The Bill of Sale from Joseph J Ryan was witnessed in Zermatt, Switzerland on 26th

Above: *Thomas G Smith's little-used G-44A Widgeon CF-LGZ (c/n 1473) seen here at Toronto on 19th June 1969. After many years on the Canadian register, the aircraft was sold to an owner in Seattle, Washington in June 1986 and is currently flying from a new base in New Hampshire.*
(William Haines Collection)

Above: *Widgeon AN-BEC (c/n 1233) operated by SAETA in the 1960s. Seen here at Fort Lauderdale, Florida in January 1971, it was sold to an owner in Florida for $8,000 in October 1971. After serving with various owners within the USA, the FAA file notes that the Certificate of Registration, issued to Flying Barnyard Inc, expired on 31st December 2011.*
(Nigel P Chalcraft)

July 1949. Smith was President of *Atlantic Air Charter Service* and *Northeast Aviation Company*, and transferred ownership of the G-44A into the names of both companies.

SMITH, Ralph S, Charlotte, NC
1386

SMITH, Robert D
1473

SMITH, Thomas G, Guelph, ON
1473
Smith owned the G-44A from 1967 until 1977 but only flew it for some 400 hours.

SMITH, TW, Aircraft Inc, Cincinnati, OH
1324

SMITH, William D
- see Smith, William deVille

SMITH, William deVille, Dillingham, AK and later at Homer, AK
1351

SMITH, Wilton Lloyd,
New York, NY
(co-owner)
1001
Wilton Lloyd Smith headed the syndicate with *Marshall Field III* that placed the first orders for the G-21, thereby prompting Grumman to start a production line for the type.

SMITHSONIAN INSTITUTION, The,
Washington, DC
1048
The G-21A was transferred to the National Air & Space Museum, from the *National Museum of Naval Aviation* at Pensacola on 30th June 1983. After restoration by Buehler Aviation Research in Fort Lauderdale, FL it was displayed in the Hall of Air Transportation in Washington, DC in 1989. Following completion of the Steven F Udvar-Hazy Center near Dulles Airport, the aircraft was transferred for display there in December 2003 and remains on display there.

SNOW, William H, Princeton, NJ
1239
Snow owned the G-44 for two months in 1952.

SNOW GOOSE, Baltimore, MD
1083

SNOWDRAKE Ltd, Toronto, ON
1441
Robert M Smith, President. The G-44A was operated in the late 1960s out of Oshawa, ON.

SNOXALL, Belinda Jane, St Albans, UK
1317

SNYDER, John I, Jr, Scarsdale, NY
1168
Snyder was President of *US Industries Inc*.

SOARE, Malcolm A, Sidney, MT
B-63

SOBY, Peter A, Pinehurst, NC
& later Boulder, CO
1235

SOCIEDAD ANÓNIMA de EXPLOITACIÓN DE TRANSPORTE AEREO (SAETA),
Managua, Nicaragua 1233
José Ivan Alegrett Perez, President. SAETA operated the G-44 for three years from October 1968.

SOCIÉTÉ COMPAGNIE OCEANIENNE de TRANSPORT et TOURISME
- see *Air Tahiti*

SOCIÉTÉ des CONSTRUCTIONS AÉRONAVALES du PORT NEUF (SCAN),
La Rochelle, France
01, 1, 2, 3, 4, 5, 6, 7, 8, 19
The company was licensed by Grumman to build the G-44, which the French company designated the SCAN-30. With little flying-boat experience, SCAN

G-21A Goose DQ-AYL (c/n 1164) undergoing a rebuild for Solomon Islands Seaplanes at Wangaratta, Victoria, Australia in 2011. The projected services planned by Solomon Islands Seaplanes did not start due to financial problems. However, at the time of writing, an executive interior was being fitted and Bob Keys was planning to use the rebuilt Goose for services in Nauru.
(via Andrew Wade)

embarked on a production batch of forty aircraft, and the prototype flew in 1949. Sales were disappointing and perhaps thirty airframes were eventually sold, mostly via Canada, to the USA, where they were converted to "Super SCANs" or "PACE Gannets" (see Chapter 5).

SOCIÉTÉ TECHNICOPTERE, Paris
19
The SCAN-30 was based at Toussus-le-Noble.

SOLBERG, Lars, Bergen, Norway
1134

SOLBERG, Thor, Somerville, NJ
dba *Thor Solberg Flyveselskap*, Norway
1134
also dba *Thor Solberg Aviation Co*, Somerville, NJ
J-38
Solberg's father, born in Floro, Norway, flew from New York to Norway in a Loening amphibian in 1935 to emulate the journey made by Lief Erikson in the year 1000. Solberg Aviation bought the G-21A in 1947 and named it "*Lief Erikson II*". The G-73 was owned in 1951/52. Solberg Jr became a commercial airline pilot flying Boeings across the Atlantic. The company is now known as Solberg Aviation and operates as a FBO and Cessna Pilot Center from the Solberg Airport in Readington, NJ.

SOLOMON ISLANDS SEAPLANES Ltd
- see *Keys, Robert Harvey*

SOOKE FOREST PRODUCTS,
Victoria, BC
1045

SORENSEN, Clifford M, Detroit, MI
dba Continental Die Casting Corp
1404

SORREN, William C, Miami Beach, FL
1274

SOUCY AUTOMOBILE Inc,
Rimouski, QC
1315

SOUTH AMERICAN TRADING Corp,
New York, NY
1432
A company connected with the export of aircraft to Argentina and Venezuela in the early post-war years (eg FAMA).

SOUTH CENTRAL AIR TAXI Inc,
Kodiak, AK
1324
DW Henley, President. Henley bought the G-44 in September 1968 and was operating as *Henley's Air Service* until May 1969

when the company was re-named South Central Air Taxi Inc. The aircraft was written-off in a crash in October 1973.

SOUTHCENTRAL AVIATION Inc,
Anchorage, AK
1377
John L Griffis, President.

SOUTHEAST AIRLINES Inc, Miami, FL
and later at Dover, DE
1141, 1150
Irving L Jones, President; R Wettenhall, Chief Executive.
The airline operated scheduled services to Marathon and Key West with a mixed fleet including DC-3s, Martin 202As and Martin 404s.

SOUTHEAST LEASING Corp,
Falmouth, MA
1429

SOUTHEAST SKYWAYS Inc,
Juneau, AK
1051, 1110, B-32, 1346
Ronald L Warren, President. Formed in 1968, Southeast Skyways Inc provided support flights to scheduled and bush operators in south-eastern Alaska. It also flew charters for hunters and fishermen, and occasional services to Haynes, Skagway and Hoonah. Summer services were also flown to Angoon, Tenakee, Hawk Inlet, Excursion Inlet, Funter Bay, Elfin Cove, Chatham and Pelican. The G-21As were in service from 1974 until 1980.

SOUTHERN AERO Inc, Atlanta, GA
J-51
Aircraft sales agent.

Soucy Automobile's G-44 Widgeon CF-IHI (c/n 1315) on the Atlantic Aviation ramp at Teterboro, New Jersey on 5th September 1955, shortly after conversion to Lycoming power by Link Aeronautical Corporation.   *(Charles N Trask via Jennifer Gradidge)*

Southeast Airlines' G-21A Goose N703A (c/n 1141) at Miami, Florida in the mid-1960s. The aircraft was lost in a fatal crash in June 1971 while in service with Antilles Air Boats.   (Steve Krauss)

A rare 1949 photograph of South Seas Marine Products' Goose VQ-FAH (c/n 1126). The company failed about a year after the Goose was delivered and the aircraft was shipped back to the USA in September 1950. It was later operated by Bahamas Airways Ltd as VP-BAR. *(via RF Killick)*

Spartan Air Services' Mallard CF-HWG (c/n J-19) carried out an extensive photo-survey of the Seychelles island group in the Indian Ocean in 1960. The aircraft is seen staging through Prestwick, Scotland on 2nd May 1963. *(Bob Reid via Jennifer Gradidge)*

SOUTHERN INDEPENDENT ASSOCIATES Inc, Melrose, FL
1370

SOUTHERN PRODUCTION Co Inc,
Baton Rouge, LA
1463

SOUTH FLORIDA AVIATION INVESTMENTS, Opa Locka, FL
1215

SOUTH PACIFIC AIRLINES,
Sydney, NSW
J-4
South Pacific Airlines, owned by *Gregory Board*, operated freight and charter flights out of Sydney-Bankstown airport. The G-73 was registered to Board with a Miami, FL address in January 1976. It was exported to Australia and registered to SPA in August 1976, but was parked at Bankstown and did very little flying. It was used eventually for flying sequences for a TV series in Malaysia before being sold in the USA in 1977.

SOUTH SEAS MARINE PRODUCTS Ltd,
Suva, Fiji
1126
The Goose was owned during 1949 before the company failed and the aircraft had to be sold.

SOUTHWEST AVIATION Inc,
Fairacres, NM
31
Harold E Kading, President.

SPARROW DRILLING Ltd, Calgary, AB
1415

SPARTAN AIR SERVICES Ltd,
Ottawa, ON
J-19
This company, started in 1947, specialised in aerial mapping and photography. The G-73 was fitted with a watertight camera hatch in the hull, aft of the step on the centreline. So equipped, it was used in 1960 to carry out an extensive photo-survey of the Seychelles island group in the Indian Ocean, an operation which included a 23,000 mile return trip from Toronto to Mahé.

SPEARFISH AVIATION Inc,
Rapid City, SD and at Summerset, SD
1359, 29

SPENCER, John S, Indian, AK
14

SPERRY RAND Corp, New York, NY
1360

SPICER, EF, Stockbridge, MA
1213

SPICHER, SE, Concord, CA
1267, 1268
Spicher bought both aircraft from *Howard E Norton* in 1948.

SPIEDEL, Joe, III, Wheeling, WV
& Kendall, FL
B-100, 16

SPIEGEL, Frederick B, Washington DC
1419

SPIELMAN, JG, Sun Valley, CA
12, 16, 25
Ownership of the SCAN-30s was transferred from *Lee Mansdorf & Co* to Spielman with *Walter J Davidson*, *Charles H Harris* and *Tom Katsuda* at the same address as the *Pacific Aircraft Engineering Corp (PACE)* in January 1959 (c/ns 16 & 25 in March 1959). Ownership then passed from the four partners to *PACE* in February 1959 (c/n 16 in March 1959 and c/n 25 in April 1959).

SPIKE AIR Ltd, Richmond, BC
J-54
Set up by *Spike Nasmyth* to buy the G-73 from the Panamanian government in 1988. Nasmyth and his partner ferried the aircraft via Costa Rica, Belize, Key West and Miami to Victoria, BC where it was made airworthy and ready for sale.

SPORT AERO Co, Las Vegas, NV
B-100
Sport Aero operated the G-21A owned by *Collins Brothers Corporation* in the early 1980s.

SPORTSMAN AIR SERVICE Inc, The,
Grand Island, NY
1451
On a mortgage document dated 3rd July 1946 *PN Pattison* was described as the company's Business Manager and *Max W Stell* was described as Aviator.

SPORTSMEN AIRWAYS Inc, Duluth, MN
1390
Aircraft based at Skyharbor Seaplane Base, Duluth.

SPRINGER, Karl John, Toronto, ON
J-39
Springer was at various times the financial backer, President and Chairman of *Pacific Western Airlines*, and held title to some of PWA's aircraft, as security for some of the money he put into the company. The Mallard was based at Vancouver, BC.

SPROULE, JF
1462

SPRUNK, Marvin A, (*G G Leasing*)
1324

ST LAWRENCE AVIATION Co,
Wilmington, DE
J-23
President: *Gordon W Blair*.

ST LOUIS PARKS COLLEGE,
St Louis, MO
B-124

**ST VINCENT GOVERNMENT
AIR SERVICE**
-see *British West Indian Airways*

STADER, Richard E,
- see *Cater, Richard Eugene Stader*

STALDER, Fred N, Harrisonville, MO
1364

STALLION AIRCRAFT Inc,
Bensenville, IL
1013
The G-21E was operated by *John D
Rodgers* of Huntley, IL, who was President
of the company.

STANDARD AIRWAYS, Long Beach, CA
1030
This short-lived US supplemental airline
with a very mixed fleet of aircraft leased
the G-21A in 1963.

STANDARD BANK & TRUST Co,
Evergreen Park, IL
32

STANDARD OIL Co (New Jersey),
New York, NY
1018, B-141
- see also *Esso Shipping Co.*

STANDARD OIL DEVELOPMENT Co,
New York, NY
1018

STANDARD OIL Co of KANSAS,
Houston, TX
1055
Charles B Wrightsman, President. Became
the American Oil Co in 1948, but this was
after the G-21A had been sold to the British
American Ambulance Corps (in 1941).

**STANDELL MARINE SCIENCE &
RESEARCH**, Wilmington, DE
1429

STAPLES TOOL & ENGINEERING Co,
Cincinnati, OH
1402

STARFLITE Inc, Dillingham, AK
1340
Owned by *Michael U Harder* & dba
Manokotak Air.

STARFLITE Inc, White Plains, NY
1236
Started in 1957, the company operated a
large fleet of executive aircraft based at
Westchester County Airport, on lease or
charter to major corporations. The
Widgeon was operated in the early 1960s.

STARON FLIGHT Ltd, Vancouver, BC
1406
RL Cliff, President. The company was
granted an Experimental Flight Permit in
June 1966 to evaluate the installation of
Cessna 206 wingtips on the G-44A.

STATE AIRLINES, Charlotte, NC
J-3
The company had commenced irregular
air services in 1940 but was refused per-

mission for scheduled services in 1950.
Thereafter it became a leasing service and
dealer in spare parts, and bought the
remains of the Mallard from the insurance
company after a crash in 1950.

STATEN ISLAND AIRWAYS,
New York, NY
1459

STEELE, John R, Waukegan, IL
1328

STEIGERWALD, Paul H, Lancaster, PA
1319
Aircraft based at Garden Spot Airport,
Lancaster.

STEPHENS, Grant A,
Kodiak & Palmer, AK
1231, 1442
Both aircraft were wrecks when purchased
but are being rebuilt, in partnership with
Timothy R Martin of Anchorage, AK.

STEVENSON, Harold D "Red",
Leonard, OK
dba *Red S Aircraft Sales.*
1086, B-73, 21, 31

STEWART, BV, Reno, NV (co-owner)
1397

STEWART, D Murray, New York, NY
J-17

STEWART ISLAND AIR SERVICES Ltd,
Invercargill, NZ
1391, 1466
Stewart Island Air Services was formed on
1st May 1976 to continue the amphibian
service from Invercargill, at the southern tip
of New Zealand's south island, across the
Foveaux Strait to Stewart Island. The service
had been provided by *Mount Cook Airlines*
(MCA) since 1967, but in May 1976 MCA
leased a G-44A (c/n 1466) to Stewart Island
Air Services so that the service would
continue. However in October 1976, MCA
sold off their amphibian operations to *Sea
Bee Air* (SBA). Accordingly the leased
Widgeon was then owned by SBA, and in
November 1976, was returned to them off
lease. The service was continued, however,
by the lease of another SBA Widgeon (c/n
1391), which was operated until March
1977, when the Ryan's Creek airstrip opened
on Stewart Island and the G-44A was
replaced with a BN-2A Islander. The two G-
44As also provided tourist and emergency
flights throughout the Fjordland and
Southland regions of New Zealand's South
Island. The company was later incorporated
into Southern Air Ltd which by 1999 was
operating three Islanders.

STEWART, R, Victoria, BC
J-28, J-54

STEWART, SMITH (CANADA) Ltd,
North Bay, ON & Montreal, QC
B-50, B-76, 1235
Aircraft sales agent & insurance adjusters.

*"Red" Stevenson's SCAN-30 N7775C (c/n 21) re-engined with Lycoming R680E radials as a PACE
Gannet. Seen here at Oshkosh in July 1983 in pseudo early USAAC markings, shortly before crashing
into Lake Winnebago.*   *(Jennifer Gradidge)*

*Stewart Island Air Services operated G-44 Widgeon ZK-BGQ (c/n 1391) for four months from
November 1976, on lease from Sea Bee Air. Seen here in February 1977, wearing only the "last
three" of the registration, as allowed in New Zealand for aircraft used only on internal flights.*
(John Wegg)

STEINER, William, Downey, CA
B-14

STELL, Max W, Grand Island, NY
dba *The Sportsman Air Service Inc*
with *PN Pattison*
1451

STICK & RUDDER AVIATION Inc,
Middletown, DE
1084

STIFEL, Arthur C, III, Miami Beach, FL
1230
Stifel was president of *Aeromar Inc*. The
registrations on their Cessna 414 (N1AS)
and the G-44 (N5AS) were exchanged in
August 1975.

STINIS, Anthony, Fort Lauderdale, FL
1110, 1150
dba *Hill Air Co Inc,* see also below.

STINIS, Anthony, Jamaica Estates, NY
1233, 35, 36, 41
Stinis owned the G-44 from February 1953
until February 1961 and bought the three
SCAN-30s in partnership with *Olaf
Abrahamsen* for $11,700 from the *French
Ministry of Finance* on 14th August 1956.
They were delivered to Flushing Airport,
New York. See also above.

STOCKHOLM, Robert, Troy, NY
1356

STOCKHOLMS-TIDNINGEN,
Stockholm, Sweden
1332
A newspaper company.

**STONE MOUNTAIN AVIATION
MUSEUM**, Clarkston, GA
36
Milt Kimble, President. The SCAN-30 was
purchased from *Carl R Schwarz* on 28th
December 1987. Following a court case
against *Executive Dogs Inc*, Good Marketing Inc and Marvin Good, ownership of the
aircraft was awarded to *Mirabella Aviation
Inc*, Fort Pierce, FL in March 2007.

STONNELL, Walter A, Falls Church, VA
1153

STOREY, Gene Paul, Prince Rupert, BC
1059
Storey was President of *Trans Provincial
Airlines*.

STRANGE BIRD Inc,
c/o CT Corp System, Wilmington, DE
1471
and at West Palm Beach, FL
1061
Strange Bird Inc operates aircraft for
Jimmy Buffet, the entertainer and author.

STRATHCONA EQUIPMENT Co Ltd,
Montreal, QC
1334
W Howard Wert, President. Associate
company of the *Warnock Hersey* group.

*G-44 Widgeon SE-ARZ (c/n 1332) "Viking II" (on top of the tail-fin), was operated by the newspaper
group Stockholms-Tidningen AB, from April 1946 until June 1958, when it was sold in Norway. The
aircraft was donated to the Norwegian Technical Museum in Oslo in 1975 and was last reported in
storage in the Stavanger area.* (DM Hannah Collection)

STRELINGER, David P, Gig Harbor, WA
1324
An Alaskan Airlines pilot who bought the
salvaged wreck of the G-44 from an
insurance company after a crash which left
the aircraft with mangled wings and a
twisted aft fuselage. Strelinger sold the
wreck to *John Schwamm* and then helped
him rebuild it.

STROH, Gerry,
Burlingame, CA
1430
Stroh co-owned the G-44A with *Andrew
Robertson* and *Paul Ennor*.

STUDDERT, William P
- see *Tee Bar Three Ranch*

STURGES, Patrick Michael,
Hollywood, FL
1150, 1214, 1274

STURGES AIRCRAFT Inc,
Fort Lauderdale, FL
1462

SUGDEN, John F,
West Roxbury, MA
1353
Sugden bought the surplus J4F-2 for
$10,000 in 1946.

SUGDEN, Dr Richard G, Wilson, WY
J-50
Aircraft based at Driggs, ID.

SUITS, CG, c/o General Electric Co,
Schenectady, NY
1452
Dr Chauncey Guy Suits was a prominent
inventor and scientist who became Director
of Research of the General Electric
Company.

SULLIVAN, R Livingston,
Radnor, PA
1160, 1203

SUMRALL AIR SERVICE,
Melinda, Honduras
1408
Owned by *DA Sumrall* (see below).

SUMRALL, Donald A,
Hattiesburg, MS
1408, 32
G-44A c/n 1408 was registered to
Sumrall's Air Service, Hattiesburg, MS in
1969. The business was run by Donald
Arthur Sumrall and his wife Patsy Ruth
Sullivan Sumrall. By 1970 the G-44A was
painted white with orange and blue trim,
and operated alongside a Cessna 150. By
1971, Sumrall was registered as c/o
Antilles Air Boats, St Thomas, US Virgin
Islands, and applied for a Certificate of
Airworthiness for export, stating that the
aircraft was then located in Belize City,
British Honduras. The SCAN-30 was
acquired in 1982 when Sumrall's address
was Merritt Island, FL and the G-44A was
sold in 1984.

SUNCOAST AIRWAYS Inc,
Palm Beach, FL
B-19
Henry Ramsdell, President.

**SUNNY SOUTH AIRCRAFT
SERVICE Inc**,
Fort Lauderdale, FL
1424, 1445
The company signed a conditional sales
contract dated 21st May 1962 for the
transfer of ownership of c/n 1445 to
Gilbert A Hensler Jr. The aircraft was then
registered to Hensler on 15th June 1962.

SUN OIL Co,
Philadelphia, PA
1054, 1420
Sun Oil's Gulf Coast Division was based at
Beaumont, TX (see below) and also had an
operations base at Lafayette, LA. The
G-44A was converted to Lycoming power
in 1955.

SUN PIPELINE Co, Beaumont, TX
1167

SUN TOURS AIR, Fiji
- see *Sea Bee Air*

SUPER TEST PETROLEUM Inc,
Flushing, MI
1452

The Superior Oil Company's G-21A Goose NC28635 (c/n 1084) seen here in the 1940s. After service with Aerolineas La Gaviota, the Goose was displayed in the National Transport Museum in Cali, Colombia as HK-2058-P until 2007 when it was sold to a US-based owner.
(Fred J Knight Collection)

A rare photograph of Mallard NC2956 (c/n J-15) operated by Superior Oil Company. The legend under cockpit window reads "BATTA". The photograph was probably taken in 1949 shortly before the aircraft crashed at London-Heathrow during a take-off in the early hours of 28th October 1949.
(ASC Lumsden via Tom Singfield)

SUPERIOR AIRWAYS Ltd,
Thunder Bay,
Yukon Territory
1473
Leased the G-44A from *Westfort Leasing* for one year, 1965-66.

SUPERIOR OIL Co, The, Houston, TX
1084, B-120, 1221, 1300, 1428, 1444, 1446, 1473, J-15, J-23
The Superior Oil Company was incorporated in California on 31st October 1936 and has operated Grumman aircraft as executive transports and in support of oil exploration since 1940. Ex-Ferry Command pilot Charles Walling flew the G-21As after WWII, and later flew the G-73s. The principal base was Hangar #1 at Houston International Airport, while some G-44s were based at Lafayette, LA and the two G-73s were operated out of Cairo, Egypt to support oil operations along the River Nile.

SUPER TEST PETROLEUM Inc,
Flushing, NY
1452

SURVAIR Ltd, Ottawa, ON
J-34
The G-73 was leased from *Nordair* in the summer of 1976 to operate services out of Frobisher Bay.

SWANSON, NC,
Lander, WY
16

SWEDISH AIR FORCE MUSEUM,
Linköping, Sweden
B-63
The museum is located at the Malmslätt airfield, west of Linköping. The Flygvapen-museum is on the northern side of the airfield, with the stored aircraft including the JRF-5 on the military side of the field. The G-21A was acquired in 1985 in exchange for two Douglas Skyraiders from *Aces High Ltd* in the UK. It is painted as '81002' to indicate the second Goose (Tp81) in Swedish colours, although only one Goose (81001) ever saw service (see Chapter 7).

SWIFLITE Corp,
New York, NY
1235

SWIFT AIR SERVICE,
San Diego, CA
J-25
Owned by *JW Dowdle*. Operated services from San Diego to Santa Catalina Island and Las Vegas, NV with the G-73, under the name *Catalina-Vegas Airlines* from June 1962 until 22nd May 1967, when the aircraft crashed and sank.

TABOR, Edward Ware,
c/o FETTE Aircraft Service, Venice, FL
1381
Tabor also traded as Trans-Luxury Airlines in the immediate post-war period with Lockheed 18s and DC-3s.

TACA AIRWAYS AGENCY Inc,
New York, NY
1175
TACA, founded by Lowell Yerex and incorporated in New York on 5th June 1942, was at its peak in 1943 serving some 200 destinations in Central America, with cargo flights being the main source of revenue. The G-21A was purchased by TACA from the *Ford Motor Co* on 17th March 1944 and was registered to TACA Airways Agency Inc, New York, NY by April 1944. Transcontinental & Western Air (TWA) had bought a large interest in TACA on 5th October 1943 and one of the annual inspections on the G-21A was in fact carried out by TWA at La Guardia, NY. Whether the aircraft was used for TACA passenger or freight services is not known. On 30th March 1944 an application was made for permission for a survey flight from New York via Miami, through the Caribbean and South America as far as Asunción, and return by the 30th June 1944. The flight was not made and ownership of the G-21A was transferred, on 3rd April 1944 to *Charles E Matthews* of Tegucigalpa, Honduras, who made a similar request for permission to make the same flight in May 1944. Again, the flight was not made and the aircraft was sold to *The Texas Company* on 6th May 1944.

TAINTOR, Mark D & Diane Renee,
Carson City, NV
1371
The Taintors were Trustees of the Taintor 1996 Revocable Trust in whose name the G-44 was registered in 2001. Mark Taintor was a Hawaiian Airlines pilot with ratings on 14 types from the Shorts 330 to the Boeing 767.

TAIT, Marvin E, Port Huron, MI
21

TALBERT CONSTRUCTION EQUIPMENT Co, Lyons, IL
1368
Austin Talbert, President.

TALL TIMBER LODGE,
Lac du Bonnet, MB
1381
Founded by George Maryk in 1967 to operate flights to the Tall Timber Lodge on Lac du Bonnet. In 1976 the G-44 was registered to *Tall Timber Lodge Fly-in Service* which was owned by George and Anne Maryk and Arthur Gracow. The G-44 was based at Bird River, MB until sold in the USA in 1985.

TAMARACK AIR Ltd, Fairbanks, AK
(*William J Lentsch*)
1338

TANGLEFOOT WING & WHEEL Co,
Coolin, ID
B-32, B-56, J-2, J-57
Dr Loel Fenwick, President. The G-21A, c/n B-32, was used for camping trips to the rivers and lakes of British Columbia, while the G-73s were used for Fenwick family trips to any destination. J-2 had been purchased from *Donohue Forest Products Inc* in 1998 and was rebuilt to original specifications.

TANTOCO, Bert, Philippines
1456

TARYTA srl
- see *Taxi Aéreos Representación y Trabajos Aéreos, Srl*

TASMAN AIRLINES, Melbourne, VIC
B-54
Tasman Airlines was started by John Lyons in 1973 with the intention of operating tourist flights in the states of Victoria, South Australia and Tasmania. In June 1974 Tasman Airlines announced it would operate the G-21A from Hobart Airport to land on water at the West Point Casino and carry tourists between the casino and Port Arthur. It was also planned to have a G-44 as back-up aircraft. The G-21A was delivered from the USA via Alice Springs, NT, arriving on 20th October 1974. It was allocated the registration VH-CRC but this

was never carried on the aircraft which was parked at Sydney-Bankstown during October/November 1974 wearing "Tasman Airlines of Australia" titles. The Australian CAA was not in favour of the use of older aircraft for passenger services and the G-21A was never given an Australian Certificate of Airworthiness. By the time the aircraft was delivered it was clear that Tasman Airlines would not be allowed to use it as intended. It was advertised for sale on 13th November 1974 "for immediate delivery ex-Bankstown". It was flown to Melbourne-Essendon where it was parked for most of 1975 and into 1976. For unknown reasons, VH-CRL was used as a radio call-sign for the few flights the aircraft made in Australia, but N2721A was carried on the aircraft throughout.

TATEISHI, Arthur, Toronto, ON
1311
President of *Seabreeze Manufacturing Ltd* used the G-44 as personal transport from 1953 until selling it in 1960.

TAXI AÉREOS REPRESENTACIÓN y TRABAJOS AÉREOS Srl - *TARYTA Srl*,
San Carlos de Bariloche, Rio Negro, Argentina
1004
The TARYTA company was formed in 1947 by Camilo Pefaure and Leopoldo Baratta, two well-known citizens of

Bariloche. The Goose was acquired from the USA in 1947. Company literature noted that the Goose was captained by Camilo's brother, José Luis Pefaure, a legendary Argentine naval pilot of the 1930s and 1940s. The co-pilot/mechanic was Miguel Recalde, also ex-Argentine Navy.

After WWII ended tourism increased in the Bariloche area and the partners hoped to provide an air-taxi service to enhance the potential of that tourism boom. Authorisation for the airline was granted in April 1948, designating TARYTA a non-scheduled operator of air-taxi and tourism flights.

Bariloche was situated on Lake Nahuel Huapi and when a new town with a modern hotel was built on the other side of the lake tourists were soon asking for an air service to replace the 100km journey by gravel road. Very quickly the Hotel Correntoso became the main destination for the Goose and from there some tourists ventured across the Andes into Chile, flying to Puyehue, Puerto Varas and Osorno. Fares were:

> Bariloche - Hotel Correntoso: 33 pesos one way, 43 pesos return/person.
>
> Hotel Correntosos
> - Puyehue: 60 pesos
> - Puerto Varas: 112 pesos
> - Osorno: 134 pesos
>
> A scenic aerial flight from Hotel Correntoso - Isla Victoria – Hotel Llao Llao – Traful – Valle Encantado – Bariloche cost 90 pesos/ person or 630 pesos if you hired the Goose for seven persons.

By the end of 1950, with the worsening Argentine economy and the nationalisation of air services, the company ceased operations and the Goose was put up for sale.

TAXI PLANE CORP of AMERICA,
Miami, FL
1388

TAYLOR, Mark L, Riverdale, MI
4
Bought the SCAN-30 in 1992, and spent 8½ years restoring it and converting it to a Magnum Widgeon (see Chapter 5). The aircraft won the Grand Champion Lindy Award in the Seaplane Class at the AirVenture Oshkosh event in 2000. Taylor also assisted his son Steve to rebuild another SCAN-30 (see below).

TAYLOR, Richard R, Anchorage, AK
dba Prospect Leasing
and later at Gold Canyon, AZ
1453, 1464
Taylor applied for a Certificate of Registration for c/n 1464 on 3rd June 1983, but it was not issued until 31st January 1984 when it arrived with the wrong owner's name on it! Richard R Taylor wrote to the FAA requesting that the certificate be re-issued in his name, but there is nothing in the file to suggest that it was ever re-issued. He sold the aircraft in September 1984 and bought it back the following month!

Tasman Airlines' G-21A Goose N2721A (c/n B-54) in the company's blue and white colours in the mid-1970s. The aircraft was sold to SAATAS in Indonesia in September 1978 and was used by McDermott in support of oil exploration in the mid-1980s. *(Fred J Knight Collection)*

The former Pan American Airways Goose NC16913 (c/n 1004) at Morón Airfield after delivery from the USA in 1947. The aircraft was registered LV-AFP and used by TARYTA for services from San Carlos de Bariloche, Rio Negro. *(unknown via Álvaro Romero)*

TAYLOR, Steven M, Riverdale, MI
3
Son of Mark Taylor (see above). Using the experience gained in the rebuild of c/n 4, the father and son completed a similar conversion on this SCAN-30 in only 5½ years and won the Silver Lindy Award for seaplanes at Oshkosh, WI in 2009.

TEAL AIR Ltd, Winnipeg, MB
1389
JR Shore, President. Teal Air operated the G-44 from 1956 until 1961.

TEAL ASSOCIATION, Milwaukee, WI
1374
Aircraft based at General Mitchel Field, Milwaukee.

TEBO BROS ROCK PRODUCTS,
Battle Ground, WA
1437
Gerald L Tebo and Robert G Tebo, partners. After his brother and partner Gerald L Tebo died in 2003, Robert G Tebo transferred ownership of the G-44A to *Alaska Turbines STOL* of which he was manager.

TECON Corp, Dallas, TX
1356

TECUMSEH AVIATION, Tecumseh, MI
1240, 1398
Tecumseh Aviation was a Division of *Meyers Industries Inc* of which AH Meyers was President.

TEE BAR THREE RANCH,
Philipsburg, MT
1346
William P Studdert, owner of the ranch, made a conditional sales contract with *Alfred E Gay* on 14th February 1959. After payment had been received in full on 2nd October 1959, Gay was released from the contract and immediately sold the aircraft to *Cordova Airlines Inc.*

TEMPLIN, HJ, Petoskey, MI
dba *North Michigan Air Service*
1345

TENG, Paul, Long Beach, CA
1007

TENNESSEE GAS TRANSMISSION Co,
Houston, TX
1445

TERMINAL & SUPPLY Corp,
Des Moines, IA
J-38
An affiliate of *Ruan Equipment Co.*

TERRAVIA TRADING SERVICES Ltd,
Ascot, UK
J-55
Sales agent.

TERRI AVIATION Corp,
Fort Lauderdale, FL
1324

TERRYAIR
- see *Terry J Kohler*

TERRY, Ben, Miami, FL
(co-owner)
1388

TERRY MACHINERY Co,
St Laurent, QC
1213, 1473
WH Terry, President. Aircraft based at Cartierville, QC. The personal registration CF-WHT was issued out of sequence in August 1956 and applied to c/n 1213. When the G-44 was traded in for the G-44A in September 1956, the registration was retained. In August 1959 it was transferred to an Aero Commander 500 which had its registration (CF-LGZ) transferred to the G-44A.

TEUFEL NURSERY Inc, Portland, OR
B-123
Owned by Lawrence (Larry) Teufel. Registration of the Turbo Goose was transferred to *Teufel Holly Farms Inc* in February 2012. (see below)

TEUFEL HOLLY FARMS Inc,
Portland, OR
1061, B-123
Owned by Lawrence (Larry) Teufel.

TEXACO – The Texas Co, New York, NY
1018, 1054, 1175, 1236, 1454, J-11, J-30, J-50, J-51
The Texas Company was incorporated in Delaware on 24th January 1927. Later known as Texaco, it has used many Grumman aircraft for executive transportation and in support of oil exploration since

The Texas Company's Goose NC20648 (/n 1018) at the Aviation Country Club, Long Island, New York probably after overhaul in 1941. The company Fleet Number 'TEXACO 30' can just be discerned on the tailfin. The aircraft was sold to the US Navy in December 1941. *(Grumman photo 10140)*

The Texas Company's Goose NC3055 (c/n 1054) which served from June 1940 until November 1948 is seen here at an unknown location. The Fleet Number 'TEXACO-34' can be seen under the cockpit window. *(via TEXACO)*

Texaco's Mallard N1628 (c/n J-11) at Houma on 27th May 1963, in the company's later colour scheme. The aircraft was sold via Dean Franklin to Virgin Islands Seaplane Shuttle in 1984.
(via Art Krieger)

Texaco's Mallard N2948 (c/n J-11) with Fleet Number 64, is shown here in a Grumman publicity photo, before delivery. The G-73 was subsequently based at Houma, Louisiana in support of oil exploration and production. *(Harold G Martin)*

June 1938. Most of the amphibians were based at Houma, LA and used by the Domestic Producing Department in a support role, while G-21As, with the Texaco fleet numbers T-34 and T-41, were assigned primarily for the use of the Superintendent, New Iberia District, south-western Louisiana. The G-44, T-39, was purchased in anticipation of the requisitioning of G-21A, T-30, by the Civil Aeronautics Administration, prior to its sale to the RCAF, but the duties of T-30, were, in fact, assumed by G-21A, T-34, which was transferred to the Houma District, serving there until 1948.

The company became known as Texaco Inc, of Teterboro, NJ in 1959. The G-73Ts, J-30 & J-51, were exchanged for a Beech B.200 Kingair owned by Frakes Aviation in January 1986.

Texaco Fleet Numbers:
It is thought that these numbers were for aircraft identification in the maintenance shop, and were not necessarily carried externally on the aircraft:

T-30 c/n 1018	T-64 c/n J-11
T-34 c/n 1054	T-70 c/n 1454
T-39 c/n 1236	T-76 c/n J-51
T-41 c/n 1175	T-90 c/n J-50
T-61 c/n J-30	

TEXAS GULF SULFUR Co Inc,
Newgulf, TX
1424

TEXAS PETROLEUM Co,
Bogota, Colombia
1045

TEX-O-CAN FLOUR MILLS Inc,
Dallas, TX later known as *Burrus Mills*
J-18

THE CALIFORNIA Co, New Orleans, LA
1045
A Division of California Oil Co which later became The California division of *Chevron Oil Co*. The G-21A was operated from 1957 to 1974.

THE PRESSED STEEL Co,
Wilkes Barre, PA
1415

THE PURE OIL Co,
1221
It is assumed that this company owned the G-44 because it was assigned registration N456, which was a "fixed" registration used by the Pure Oil Company.

THOMAS, Lincoln G, Milwaukee, WI
1390
Previously co-owned the G-44 with *Francis Trecker*. The aircraft was based at General Mitchel Field, Milwaukee.

THOMASSON, Captain Edward A,
Picacho, AZ
1292
On the application for a Certificate of Airworthiness Thomasson gave his address as Wheeler Field, Oahu, HI, but the Certificate was issued with the Arizona address.

THOMPSON, Dennis E, Seward, AK
1355
Thompson owned the G-44 in 1953/4 before selling it to *Cordova Airlines Inc*.

THOMPSON FLYING SERVICE Inc,
Jackson, WY
1210
Carl Hellburg, President. A security agreement dated 1st December 1969 gives an address in Salt Lake City, UT

but this is not reflected in any registration documents in the file.

THOMPSON, Joel W, Mooresville, NC
B-49
Thompson bought the G-21A in 2007 and ferried it across the Atlantic to Europe en route to Australia, where it was last reported in 2009.

THOMPSON, William A, Joplin, MO
1340

THOMSON INDUSTRIES Inc,
Manhasset, NY
and later at Port Washington, NY
John B Thomson, President
1390
- see also *Ventura Air Services Inc*

THOMSON, AG, Jr, Miami Beach, FL
and later at South Miami, FL
1334

THOMSON, Peter Nesbitt
1334
Thomson was allotted the personalised registration CF-PNT but in the event the aircraft was registered to the *Warnock Hersey Company*.

THOR SOLBERG FLYVESELSKAP
- see *Solberg, Thor*

THOR SOLBERG AVIATON Co
- see *Solberg, Thor*

TIDEMARK Inc, Belle Chasse, LA
1420
- see *Ingram Contractors Inc*.

TILLINGHAST-STILES Co,
Providence, RI
1457

G-44 Super Widgeon CF-PNT (c/n 1334) of Timmins Aviation at Toronto-Malton in 1959. The aircraft was re-engined with Continental IO-470-Ds in 1980 and is currently flying with co-owners in Alaska.
(Jack McNulty)

TIMMINS AVIATION Ltd, Montreal, QC
1334, J-19
JA Timmins, President. Charter operator and sales agent.

TIRKKONEN, Aarne, Tampere, Finland
1367

TJONVEIT, Thor K,
- see *World Pacific Air Lease* and *Chalk's*

T O C OIL Co, Indianapolis, IN
1239
All paperwork associated with this company's ownership of the G-44 was signed by *Frederick T Holliday*, who was described as a "partner". When Holliday died on 15th July 1951 the aircraft was listed as an asset in his estate, with the Indiana Trust Company acting as executor. The G-44 was sold by them on 6th December 1951.

TODD, Van Winkle, Matawan, NJ
1378

TOIGO, Adolph J, New York, NY
dba *Ad Properties Inc*.
J-49

TONGASS HISTORICAL SOCIETY,
Ketchikan, AK
1157
The Tongass Historical Museum preserves the history of Ketchikan and Southeast Alaska. The G-21A was rebuilt using parts from c/n B-28, and is now displayed at the museum overlooking Ketchikan Creek.

Above: *Aarne Tirkkonen's G-44 Widgeon OH-GWA (c/n 1367) n winter configuration with floats removed and skis fitted. The aircraft is seen here taking off from Mänttä, Finland in February 1959.* *(Eino Ritaranta)*

TOPPING, Daniel R, & Webb, Del E,
New York, NY
dba *New York Yankees*
B-71, J-42
Topping was owner of the New York Yankees.

TOPPING, John R,
c/o Pinellas Aviation Service Inc,
St Petersburg, FL
1389
John Reid Topping was President of *Pinellas Aviation Service* which was

based at Pinellas International Airport, St Petersburg, Florida.

TORONTO GLOBE & MAIL,
Toronto, ON
J-5
The G-73 was registered to the *Globe Printing Company* and used from 1946 until 1953 in the corporate transport role, especially for company president George McCullagh; the aircraft was sold to *Canada Veneers Ltd* in 1953.

TOSCH AIRCRAFT INDUSTRIES
- see *Tosch, OW*

TOSCH FLYING SERVICE
- see *Tosch, OW*

TOSCH, OW, Nome, AK
1045, B-19
Tosch kept on the move with an address change to Seattle, WA in June 1954. By October 1955, he was doing business as Tosch Flying Service, New Orleans, LA. In August 1961 he signed a FAA Form 337 as Chief Inspector for Red Aircraft Service Inc in Fort Lauderdale, FL and by May 1964 he was in business as Tosch Aircraft, Fort Lauderdale, FL. In 1980, under the name of Tosch Aircraft Industries, he installed Continental IO-470-D engines in the G-44, c/n 1334.

TOURIST AIR TRAVEL,
Auckland, NZ
- see *New Zealand Tourist Air Travel*

TOWNSEND AIR SERVICES Ltd,
Gravenhurst, ON
1389

TOYO MENKA KAISHA Ltd,
Tokyo, Japan
J-6, J-38, J-40, J-52, J-56
The trading company which facilitated the purchase of the G-73s for *Nitto Air Lines*.

TRADE-AYER Inc, Linden, NJ
B-104, 1411, 1420, J-12, J-19
Frederick B Ayer, President. The aircraft dealership was founded by *Fred B Ayer* in 1946. *Ming-Ayer Inc* and *Welsch-Ayer Inc* were affiliates.

Mallard CF-EIZ (c/n J-5) owned by the Toronto Globe & Mail newspaper is seen here at Toronto-Malton, Ontario on 22nd April 1949, wearing the company logo on both tail-fin and bow. This much-travelled Mallard is currently flying with an owner in Nevada. *(Jack McNulty)*

The Grumman Widgeon gives executives and sportsmen more complete use of limited leisure.

Available for immediate delivery.

AIRCRAFT ENGINEERING CORPORATION, Bethpage, L. I., N. Y.

A contemporary advertisement for the Widgeon.

Above: *Widgeon, c/n 1228, N1340V, painted with its original identity as US Coast Guard J4F-1, V203. The aircraft is seen here at Oshkosh, Wisconsin, in August 1993.*   *(AJ Clarke)*

Left: *Chester Lawson's G-44A, N86638, c/n 1464, in the Florida sunshine in April 1992. The Widgeon is used to provide seaplane training from the Spruce Creek Airport, Florida.*
    (Austin J Brown)

Below: *The much-modified J4F-2, BuAer 32976, also wearing its later US Navy designation E-175, and the name "Petulant Porpoise", at Pima Air Museum, Arizona. Details of the EDO Corporation research project, involving this aircraft are given in Chapter 5.*
    (via Tom Singfield)

A poor but rare photo of G-44A, c/n 1439, CU-N346, owned by Raphael Sanchez, and seen here in Cuba in 1955. When Castro took power in Cuba in 1959, Sanchez fled the country, flying the Widgeon to Florida. *(RE Sanchez)*

Another picture of G-44A Widgeon, c/n 1439, this time in April 1962, as N9096R, owned by Miami Beach Realtor, Bill Danko. *(W Danko)*

By 1963, the G-44A, c/n 1439, had been shipped to New Zealand and had been re-engined with Continental IO-470-Ds. Seen here, as ZK-CFA with Sea Bee Air, climbing the ramp at Mechanics Bay, Auckland on Christmas Eve 1978. *(R Caratini)*

G-44A, c/n 1433, was registered as NC86607 to Ben E Smith in May 1947, and was in use by Léon Douzille at the SCAN factory at La Pallice by Spring 1948. Delivered to Israel on 26th June 1948 for Air Force use with A Squadron and given serial B-72, the aircraft later served with 103 Squadron with serial 1201. *(Grumman photo via Northrop Grumman History Center)*

G-44A, c/n 1466, which has spent most of its life south of the Equator, is seen here with Coral Wings titles, as VH-WET, at Cairns, Queensland, in November 1987.
(Tony Arbon)

Another picture of VH-WET, c/n 1466, with a "For Sale" notice in the cockpit window. This photo was taken at an unknown location, but possibly in 1994, before the Widgeon went to Papua New Guinea.
(Tony Arbon)

G-44A, c/n 1445, N86619, painted in the white, blue and yellow colours of Bahamasair, circa 1972. The Widgeon was used by the airline for only two years.
(via Paul W Wakefield)

THE smallest of the twin-engined Grumman flying-boats, the Widgeon was used as a submarine spotter by the Navy and Coastguard during World War II. Its two 200 hp in-line engines could take it to 165 mph, and maintain a cruising speed of 145 mph.

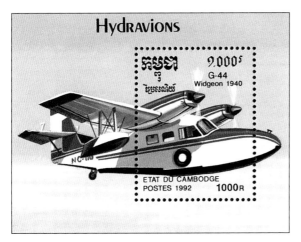

Above: *Matchbook covers issued by Grumman during WWII. The one on the left shows the JRF-6B Goose, while the other shows the J4F-1 Widgeon, and both depict the US Navy "E" Flag, for efficiency. The Grumman Corporation were allowed to fly this flag throughout the war, reflecting their huge contribution to the Navy's aircraft inventory.*

(Fred J Knight Collection)

Souvenir philatelic sheets
Right: *Issued by Trinidad & Tobago in remembrance of WWII, showing a JRF-6B Goose.* **Above:** *The Cambodian sheet, on the other hand, issued in 1992, and the attractive "Aircraft of the Forties" sheet from Bhutan (*Top*), both depict the Widgeon.*

(Fred J Knight Collection)

C/n 1362, ZK-BAY, at Paihia, Bay of Islands, North Island, New Zealand, circa 1969. The G-44 was by now with Mount Cook Airlines, and had been converted to Continental power. (Gladys M Goodall photo published as a postcard)

G-44A, c/n 1466, ZK-AVM, seen here (possibly at Ardmore, North Island, New Zealand) in 2000, in the colours of Salt Air, based at Paihia, Bay of Islands.
(Fred J Knight Collection)

G-44A, c/n 1445, N8H, seen here at Opa Locka, Florida, on 17th August 1977 awaiting delivery to James Saunders.   *(Fred J Knight Collection)*

A regular visitor to Oshkosh, Wisconsin, JL Rogers' Lycoming-powered Super Widgeon, c/n 1292, N62000, "Canadian Clipper", is seen there in July 1998.   *(Mike Moore)*

Another Lycoming-powered Super Widgeon visiting Oshkosh, Wisconsin, N4617N, c/n 1364, owned by Reiser Burgan Inc.   *(Mike Moore)*

Ex-Northcoast Air Services' Widgeon, c/n 1311, seen at Opa Locka, Florida, on 1st September 1973 with taped-on marks N62881, after sale to Dean Franklin. The tapes on the top of the tail-fin mask the aircraft's previous Canadian marks, CF-HEN.   *(PJ Marson)*

Widgeon, c/n 1346, C-FEHI, of United Engineering (1964) Ltd, in the hangar at Victoria Airport, British Columbia, in September 1979. The G-44 has now been rebuilt by Timothy R Martin in Anchorage, Alaska, and registered as N480AK.   *(Norman Thelwell)*

McDermott Widgeon, c/n 1317, 5N-AMD, at Shoreham, UK in September 1974, en route from Nigeria to the USA. In March 2013 the aircraft was with an owner in Florida.
(Peter J Bish)

Oren Hudson's long-serving G-44 Widgeon, c/n 1294, N302, at Big Lake, Alaska, on 4th July 1978. Note the Continental engines and Cessna droop wingtips. *(Fred Ball)*

The former Cuban Navy G-44A, c/n 1411, N444M, owned by Michael Dunkerly, and seen here over Holland in 1987. The Lycoming engines were taken from Aero Commander 520, G-ASJU, and fitted during the Widgeon's re-build in 1985. *(CJ Mak)*

Red Bull's SCAN-30 Widgeon, c/n 30, OE-FWS, seen here at Innsbrück in October 1988. After crashing in Lake Garda on 29th March 2005, the remains of the aircraft were purchased by Timothy R Martin, and taken to Anchorage, Alaska. *(Reimar Wendt)*

G-44A Widgeon, c/n 1454, N1629H, was operated by the Louisiana Wildlife & Fisheries Department, from 1954 until 1969. The aircraft is seen here, somewhere in Florida, in the mid-1980s.   *(Nigel P Chalcraft)*

G-44A, c/n 1429, N945JD, with Lucaya Air titles, at Fort Lauderdale, Florida, in January 1985. The aircraft carries the name "Magic Mistress". The Super Widgeon won the Paul E Garber Trophy at the Reno Air Race meeting in September 2010.   *(Fred J Knight Collection)*

Steven C Kreck's smart PACE Gannet (SCAN-30), c/n 31, N4453, at Watsonville, California, in June 1979. In March 2013 the aircraft was with an owner in Missouri, but with no Certificate of Registration.   *(Howard Valiant)*

Grumman

ANNOUNCES THE

Mallard

THE WORLD'S FINEST AMPHIBIAN

MODERN in design and performance

LUXURIOUS in appointment

SAFE . . . twin engines—tricycle landing gear. Licensed for 8 to 10 passengers by CAA in scheduled Air Transport category

For complete information write Sales Department,
Grumman Aircraft Engineering Corporation, Bethpage, Long Island, New York.

A contemporary magazine advertisement announcing the G-73 Mallard in 1946.

Mallard, c/n J-35, PK-AKD, at Bethpage, ready for delivery to Asiatic Petroleum Corporation, New York. The G-73 was ordered by Bataafsche Petroleum Maatschappij (BPM) of Batavia, Dutch East Indies, in September 1947. Delivered via the North Atlantic and Amsterdam, the aircraft arrived in Batavia on 8th July 1948.
                                                                                                                                        (Grumman)

California Amphibious Transport's Mallard, c/n J-18, N42DA, seen here in 1980. Note the legend "The Route of the Seagulls" on the rear hull.   (MAP)

Mallard, c/n J-22, CF-HUB, of West Coast Air Services Ltd, at Vancouver in 1978. This G-73 was later sold in Australia, and in 1998, was converted to G-73AT standard, for the Paspaley Pearling Company.
                                                                                                                                        (MAP)

Texaco's Turbo Mallard, c/n J-50, N1626, probably over Louisiana, circa 1983. After service in Indonesia with Freeport McMoran Inc, the G-73T returned to the USA, and private ownership, in 2001. (TEXACO)

Wien Air Alaska's Mallard, c/n J-44, N1208, "Katmai Queen", seen here somewhere in Alaska in 1976. The aircraft later saw service with Chalk's and Antilles Air Boats before being converted to G-73T standard in 1981. (CJ Mak)

The first of King Farouk's Mallards, c/n J-47, seen here during delivery with the serial wrongly applied (back to front) as "7F", rather than F7.
(via Tom Singfield)

Mallard, N7356, c/n J-56, in the early Chalk's colour scheme. "The Cat Cayer" is seen here at Miami, Florida in April 1970. In March 2013 the aircraft was registered to an owner in Texas.
(DM Hannah)

The much-travelled Mallard, N2442H, c/n J-13, in the later colours of Chalk's International, seen here at the Miami-Watson Island base, in June 1981.
(Fred J Knight Collection)

Also at Watson Island is the ill-fated Turbo Mallard, c/n J-27, N2969, in the colours of Pan Am Air Bridge. The G-73T was leased to Chalk's Ocean Airways in 2005, but was lost in the accident on 19th December 2005, that led to the grounding of virtually all remaining Mallards.
(Fred J Knight Collection)

Left: Chalk's 1993 invitation to "Fly a Legend", advertising scenic air tours of Miami in their Turbo Mallard aircraft.   (Fred J Knight Collection)

Above: Lothar Grim's classic image of N2969 "Sunset Express" in the airline's 75th anniversary colours, at North Bimini, Bahamas in July 1995, published as a postcard.   (Fred J Knight Collection)

*Below: Turbo Mallard, c/n J-42, painted to advertise Corona Extra beer, seen here at Fort Lauderdale International Airport, Florida, in April 1998.
        (Oscard via Fred J Knight)*

Mallard, c/n J-22, VH-LAW, of Seair Pacific at Airlie Beach, Queensland, in October 1989. The G-73 was originally operated by the New York Daily News, and still retains the lower cockpit window that was installed to facilitate aerial photography. (Tony Arbon)

After service in Canada and Dutch New Guinea, the much-travelled Mallard, c/n J-13, was owned by Trans Australia Airlines as VH-TGA and is seen here at Essendon Airport, Melbourne, Victoria in August 1963. (John Hopton)

Mallard P-2011, c/n J-35, was operated by the Indonesian Air & Water Police from 1963 until 1976. It is seen here at Paya Lebar on 5th August 1971. (Adrian M Balch Collection)

The former Pan American Airways training aircraft, by this time a Lycoming-powered G-44 Super Widgeon (c/n 1235), is seen here at Vancouver, British Columbia in July 1975 as C-FJXX with Tradewinds Aviation.   *(Neville Parnell via Jennifer Gradidge)*

TRADEWINDS AVIATION,
Vancouver, BC
1235

TRADITION AIR TRANSPORT,
Leucadia, CA
1145

TRANSAIR Inc, Linden, NJ
1408
Transair Inc started operations in January 1946 as a certificated passenger and cargo carrier. Operations were scaled down in the 1950s and the G-44A was acquired in 1969.

TRANSAIR Ltd, Winnipeg, MB
1200, B-98, J-55
The Grummans were acquired when Transair Ltd took over *Midwest Airlines* of Winnipeg in November 1969, although the aircraft continued to be operated by Midwest on services within Manitoba. The G-73 was sold in 1971 and the G-21As went to *West Coast Air Services* in 1973.

TRANS AIR Corp, New Orleans, LA
1213

TRANS AIRCRAFT Co, Hamilton, ON
1240

TRANS-AIRE Corp, New Orleans, LA
1438
John L Freiberg, President. Freiberg was also president of *Dynair Corp* and after transferring ownership of the G-44A from Trans-Aire to Dynair on 13th December 1965, immediately transferred ownership to his own name the same day. The aircraft was based at New Orleans-Lakefront Airport.

TRANS AMERICAN AIRWAYS Inc,
New York, NY
1106, B-59
The trading name of *Edgar J Wynn*. One of the many short-lived airlines set up in the immediate post-WWII period.

TRANS AMERICAN EXECUTIVE JET Inc, Fort Lauderdale, FL
J-5
Giovanni Borde, President.
The G-73 was based at International Wings Inc, Fort Lauderdale Executive Airport.

TRANS AUSTRALIA AIRLINES (TAA),
Melbourne, VIC
J-13
The Australian National Airlines Commission (Trans Australia Airlines) began negotiations on 19th July 1962 to purchase JZ-POB as a replacement for their Catalina VH-BRI which had sunk on 8th July 1962. After having bought the G-73 on 16th January 1963 with the aim of operating to the Barrier Reef, TAA overhauled it at their engineering base at Brisbane-Archerfield. It was proposed that the services from Mackay to several Barrier Reef islands would commence on 27th April 1963. At least four return trips were envisaged, to Brampton Island, Palm Bay, South Molle Island and Happy Bay each week, carrying up to twelve passengers. However, the work to achieve an Australian Certificate of Airworthiness was not completed until June 1963, when the re-furbished G-73 flew for the first time. Certificate of Registration No.3772 was issued and the aircraft re-registered as VH-TGA on 13th June 1963. The services to the Reef were never flown by the G-73, however, because after spending much time and money on the refurbishment, TAA decided that weather conditions would not be suitable for G-73 operations and a Twin Otter would be used instead. After performing demonstration flights to interested buyers at Cooma on 11th August 1963, the aircraft was flown to Melbourne-Essendon in full TAA Coral Air colour scheme, and later on to Brisbane for storage. The G-73 was sold to *Utah-Williamson-Burnett* in September 1963 to support the Manapouri Project in New Zealand.

TRANS-CARIBBEAN Corp of BROWARD Inc, Fort Lauderdale, FL
1364

TRANS CATALINA AIRLINES,
Long Beach, CA
J-18, J-19, J-42, J-58
Owned by *Dr Ivan Namihas* and *Dan Hill*, operations were managed by Frank Strobel (who later started *Catalina Flying Boats*).

Below: *Trans Catalina Airlines brochure, circa 1979.*

Long Beach Airport   (213) 420-2444
Pebbly Beach Terminal (213) 510-1000
Orange County Airport (714) 752-1600

TCA

Trans Catalina Airlines

Welcomes you aboard

Trans Catalina's Mallard N36DF (c/n J-18) "Spirit of Avalon" flew in a smart orange and white colour scheme and was rebuilt in 1984 by Andy Stinis in Fort Lauderdale, Florida. After the Mallard fleet was grounded in 2006, J-18 had a new wing spars fitted and is flying currently with an owner in New Jersey. Unusually, the registration is carried at the rear of the hull on the waterline!   *(Fred J Knight Collection)*

Three leased G-73s flew services to Santa Catalina Island from Long Beach-San Pedro and John Wayne Orange County Airport. Because of its size compared to the G-21A, the G-73 was advertised as 'wide-bodied'! J-18 was named "*Spirit of Avalon*"; J-19 was "*Catalina Clipper*"; and J-42 was "*Island Princess*". The fourth aircraft (J-58) was used for spares. By October 1979, however, the G-73s had been replaced by Cessna twins and the operation was entirely land-based.

TRANS-EASTERN AIRWAYS Inc,
St Petersburg, FL
c/n unknown
Operated air-taxi services from Pinellas International Airport, St Petersburg in mid-1956 with a G-44 and Cessna 195. By May 1957 the company was flying scheduled services from St Petersburg to Tampa, Lakeland, Anna Maria, Holmes Beach, Sebring, Avon Park, Venice, Fort Pierce, Pinta Gorda, Fort Lauderdale and Miami with G-44, Beech 18 and Cessna twins.

TRANS GASPESIAN AIRLINES Ltd,
Gaspe, QC
1240
Formed in 1952 and later re-named Air Gaspé, the company used the G-44 for charter flights in the St Lawrence area from June 1958 until the end of 1959 (although a survey in "*Flight*" magazine shows a Widgeon operated through to 1963). Air Gaspé merged with Regionair in 1982.

TRANS MOUNTAIN AIR SERVICES Ltd,
Campbell River, BC
1265
Donald E Braithwaite, President. Leased the G-44 from *Aquila Holdings* during 1975/6 and operated it out of Qualicum, BC. The lease paperwork is complicated by the fact that the original lease only involved Aquila's Cessna 172 CF-XNV. At an un-recorded date (circa June 1975) another

Cessna CF-GTK and the G-44 were added to the lease of CF-XNV and the period of lease was extended. The G-44 was returned to Aquila on 6th January 1977 and registered to them on 13th January 1977. Canadian records are complicated by the fact that Certificates of Registration are issued to the operator of the aircraft, not the owner.

TRANSOCEAN AIRLINES, Oakland, CA
1359
The company began operations from Oakland Municipal Airport, CA in March 1946 under the name of Orvis Nelson Air Transport (ONAT). The company was renamed Transocean Airlines (TALOA) on 1st June 1946 under the Chairmanship of Orvis Nelson. TALOA's G-44 was leased from *James S "Jim" Magoffin* from 1950-52 and used in support of the oil exploration work on Alaska's North Slope.

TRANSPORTATION LOCATORS Ltd,
Tulsa, OK
21
Bought the aircraft from *Airwing Inter-national Inc.*

TRANSPORTES AEREOS de CABO VERDE
1241, 1242, 1297
The company was formed in 1958 to operate services within the Cape Verde Islands. C/ns 1241 and 1242 arrived in 1958, with 1297 being purchased from Angola in 1960. The G-44s were operated alongside a DH Dragon Rapide and a Dove. C/n 1242 returned to Lisbon in 1960 for service with the Portuguese Government Survey Unit and although it is

Above: *A rare photograph of G-44 CR-CAI (c/n 1297). The Widgeon was operated by Transportes Aereos de Cabo Verde and is seen here at Mosteiros Airfield on Fogo Island, some time between June and November 1962.*
(José Francisco Duarte Ferreira via Luis Tavares)

Above: *The former Transocean Airlines' G-44 Widgeon N68395 (c/n 1359) is seen here upgraded to Lycoming power but without floats at Milwaukee, Wisconsin on 13th March 1956.*
(Leo J Kohn via Jennifer Gradidge)

known that c/n 1297 was in service in 1962, the fates of c/ns 1241 and 1297 are unknown.

TRANS PROVINCIAL
AIR CARRIERS Ltd, Terrace, BC
Formed in 1960 and changed name to *Trans Provincial Airlines Ltd* in August 1968.
- see next entry and also *Pacific Western Airlines*.

TRANS PROVINCIAL AIRLINES (TPA) Ltd,
Terrace, BC
1059, 1077, 1083, 1157, B-6, B-129, B-142, B-145
Known as *Trans Provincial Air Carriers Ltd* until 1968 when GE Reum was president, TPA operated scheduled and charter services from bases at Prince Rupert, Prince George, Ocean Falls, Smithers and Sandspit (on the Queen Charlotte Islands). When TPA became a division of *Air BC Ltd* in 1981 its main base was Seal Cove at Prince Rupert, but the company also operated out of Port Hardy.

Operating in Air BC colours but with TPA titles, the G-21As served the Queen Charlottes and northwestern British Columbia as far south as Ocean Falls. In October 1986 TPA was sold to an investment group headed by Gene Story, the former TPA chief pilot. The deal included all TPA assets except the Port Hardy base which would be operated by *Pacific Coastal Airlines*. In March 1993 *Coopers & Lybrand Ltd* was appointed Receiver for TPA, and in April 1993 B-145 was sold to *Hallmark Leasing Corporation*, Vancouver, BC.

Wearing the yellow colour scheme of Trans Provincial Airlines, G-21A CF-UMG (c/n B-145) and therefore the last Goose built, is seen here being worked on in August 1980. The aircraft later served with Waglisla Air in British Columbia, but crashed in December 1993. The wreckage was purchased from a salvage yard in Deer Park, Washington by Antilles Seaplanes and is now stored in Gibsonville, North Carolina. (Ingvar Klett)

TRECKER, Francis J,
Milwaukee, WI
1390
Trecker was President of the Trecker Aircraft Corporation, a division of the *Kearney & Trecker Corporation*, and co-owned the G-44 with *Lincoln G Thomas*. The aircraft was based at General Mitchel Field, Milwaukee, where the Trecker Aircraft Corporation set up an assembly facility for the licenced production of the Piaggio P.136 amphibian.

TREMBLAY AVIATION Inc,
Gilles, Richelieu, QC
1370
Gilles Tremblay, President. Leased the G-44 to *Populair Aviation Services Inc* from October 1977 until March 1978.

TRIBUNE Co, The,
Chicago, IL
1060
Registered name of "*The Chicago Tribune*" newspaper (see *Chicago Tribune*). The G-21A was purchased to replace c/n 1005 which suffered an accident in August 1939.

TRI-NEGRO OF ALASKA,
Anchorage, AK
1415
The company is owned by *Carter Garrett* who co-owns the G-44A with *Chaos Consulting Unlimited*.

TRIPLE A MACHINE SHOP Inc,
San Francisco, CA
1346

TRIPLE S AVIATION LLC,
Addison, TX
B-72
An aircraft service company, owned by Landon Studer, headquartered in Addison, TX and with a branch office in Dubai, offering business aircraft, helicopters and special use aircraft to the Middle East and south Asian markets. The G-21G was lost in a fatal accident at Al Ain Airport in the United Arab Emirates on 27th February 2011 in which Studer and three colleagues died.

G-21A Goose C-FEFN (c/n 1157) showing the outline of Trans Provincial Airlines' red colour scheme on 23rd August 1989 at Sandspit, Queen Charlotte Islands, British Columbia. After the Goose ground-looped at this same location on 28th February 1991, the wreckage was sold to the Tongass Historical Society in Ketchikan, Alaska. The Society rebuilt the aircraft and it is currently airworthy. (Ingvar Klett)

The Chicago Tribune's second G-21A Goose, NC2786 (c/n 1060), with the name "Tribune" displayed on the bow. The aircraft was acquired by the US Navy in 1942 as a JRF-4 and was struck off charge on 31st October 1944 and assumed scrapped. (via Art Krieger)

The former JRF-6B that served with the Bolivian Air Force during the 1950s is seen here in 1998 as G-21A Goose N5548A (c/n 1150) operated by Tropic Bird Holdings. It is currently flying for an owner in Florida.   *(MAP)*

Above: *Mallard HS-TPA (c/n J-54) in the all-yellow "Yellowbirds" colours of Tropical Sea Air, with company Goose HS-TOM in the background in 1992.*   *(MAP)*

Below: *Another picture of Mallard HS-TPA (c/n J-54) in the more conventional colour scheme of Tropical Sea Air in 1997, after it had been sold via John Schwamm to Victoria Air Maintenance Ltd, who overhauled it. Grounded in 2006 after the Chalk's crash, the Mallard is currently flying with an owner in Delaware.*   *(MAP)*

TROPIC BIRD HOLDINGS,
Boca Raton, FL
1150

TROPICAL SEA AIR Co Ltd,
Bangkok, Thailand
1145, J-5, J-54
The company gained a licence from the Thai government in January 1990 to operate services out of Don Muang and Phuket to Pattaya and Hua Hin. Operations did not begin until May 1991. J-54 was reported in service in November 1992

wearing small "Tropical Sea Air" titles on the nose under light blue cheat-lines. The G-21A was purchased in New Zealand, reportedly at an "outrageous price" and registered HS-TOM for use by the executives of the company, but had to be pressed into airline service when the engines on J-54, HS-TPA, were out of overhaul time. The aircraft were painted overall yellow and carried the logo "Yellowbirds" on the fuselage sides. Operations were halted in March 1993 and by April 1994 J-5 had been sold after a

court case to *James Confalone*. In fact, J-5, HS-TSB, had never left Florida. This was because J-54, HS-TSA, had been repaired by an Australian company during the ferry from the USA to Thailand, and HS-TSB was seized in lieu of unpaid bills for this work. By 1997, J-54 had been parked at the Thai Navy hangar at U-Tapao for some four years. It had gone there for re-skinning by the Royal Thai Navy, but the airline went out of business during the work. The G-73 was purchased by *Turbo North Aviation* and *John Schwamm* on 11th November 1997, and the next day a Bill of Sale was drawn up conferring ownership solely to Schwamm, who sold it the same day to *Victoria Air Maintenance Ltd.*

TRUMBULL, Thomas A, Toledo, OH
1398

TRUMP, Donald - see *Chalk's*

T U C O Co, Pahrump, NV
- see *IR3T Inc*
1086
Glen Hyde owner.

TULAKES AVIATION Inc, Bethany, OK
J-5, J-53
Aircraft based at Wiley Post Airport, Bethany.

TURBO NORTH AVIAITON
- see *Tropical Sea Air Co Ltd*

TURNBULL, Raymond C,
Beverly Hills, CA
dba *Pacific Coconut Processing Corp*
1434
The Certificate of Registration for the G-44A was revoked by the FAA on 25th January 1971 because Turnbull had failed to file an Aircraft Activity Report.

TURSAIR EXECUTIVE AIRCRAFT SERVICES Inc, Opa Locka, FL
3
Tursair were not the registered owner of the SCAN-30 but it is likely that they operated the aircraft for *Lehigh Acres Development Corp.*

TUTHILL Corp, Burr Ridge, IL
dba *Goose Lake Airways*
B-129
Chief Pilot Jim Burger, operating out of Chicago Midway Airport.

TWO JACKS Inc, Arlington, TN
and at Olive Branch, MO
1213, 4, J-53

TWO TAILS LLC, Las Vegas, NV
1372

TYEE AIRLINES Inc,
Ketchikan, AK
J-35
Michael W Woodson, President. Owned by Art Hack, Tyee operated the G-73 from March 1977 until April 1978 when it was sold to *Red Fox Charters* in Miami, FL.

U C LEASING Inc, Memphis, TN
1328

UDD, John Clarence, Brockville, ON
B-111, 1343
John Udd was a Montreal millionaire, President of *National Management Ltd*, which ran a number of large hotels in Canada. The G-44 was registered to National Management Ltd in 1953 and based at Montreal and Ottawa. When the Certificate of Registration was issued in Udd's name in 1956 the aircraft was based at Cartierville, QC, until sold in the USA in April 1958. The G-21A was sold after Udd's death to the *Corporation Archiepiscopale Catholique Romane de St Boniface*, which operated it in Peru.

UMPQUA RIVER NAVIGATION Co, Reedsport, OR
1427

UNILEASE Inc, Don Mills, ON
B-117
Unilease bought the G-21A from *Juergen Puetter* in 1991 and leased it back to him until 1993 when Puetter bought it back again!

UNION MINING Co, Pittsburgh, PA
1013

UNION NATIONAL BANK, Lowell, MA
1213

UNION OIL Co of CALIFORNIA,
Houston, TX
and Los Angeles, CA
1370, 1450, 1464, J-54
RN Taylor, President (in 1944). The company used the Grummans, based at Houma, LA, in support of exploration and development of oilfields in the Gulf Coast area.

UNION PRODUCING Co, Shreveport, LA
J-16, J-28, J-52
The exploration and production arm of the Union Oil Company. The company purchased J-16 from *McIntyre Porcupine Mines* for US$142,500 in 1951 and used the G-73s in support of oilfield operations.

UNITED AIRCRAFT Corp (UAC),
Stratford, CT
J-53
The G-73 was operated by the Sikorsky Division of UAC.

UNITED AIRCRAFT PRODUCTS Inc,
Dayton, OH
1429

UNITED AIRMOTIVE Inc,
Anchorage, AK
1215
Paul Kroenung, President. Aircraft based at Merrill Field, Anchorage.

UNITED CAPITAL Corp of ILLINOIS,
Wilmington, DE
J-28
Seth Atwood, President.

UNITED ENGINEERING (1964) Ltd,
Victoria, BC
1346
C Earl Hastings, President.

UNITED STATES
- see also under *US*

UNITED STATES MISSILES Corp,
Sun Valley, CA
B-14, 15, 32
Fred Mansdorf, President. A *Lee Mansdorf* company which traded SCAN-30 N60L to *Murdock Lumber Co* in exchange for the Goose.

**UNIVERSAL COMPAÑÍA
de SEGUROS, La**,
Buenos Aires, Argentina
1432
The fact that the G-44A went to this insurance company suggests that it may have been involved in an accident prior to April 1958.

UNIVERSAL TRADES Inc,
Green Cove Springs, FL
1356

UNIVERSAL TRADING Corp,
Panama City, Panama
B-54, 1411, 1430, 1450, 1473, J-6, J-38, J-52, J-56
Part of the *Frederick B Ayer* group of companies (for details see under *Ayer*). The three G-44As (c/ns 1411, 1450 and 1473) were purchased from the Cuban Navy in August 1956.

UNIVERSITY OF ILLINOIS BOARD OF TRUSTEES,
Urbana, IL
1385

UP OVER DOWN UNDER,
Brisbane, QLD
1164
One of *Bob Keys'* companies, which owned the G-21A from 1992.

URICHO, Robert, Jr,
Miami, FL
1375

URIEL, Bristol,
Miami, FL
B-63

US CUSTOMS SERVICE
- see *Mark IV Aviation, Performance Aircraft Co Inc* and *US Government*

US DISTRIBUTORS Inc,
Coconut Grove, FL
J-5, J-11, J-53
J-5 had been sold by the time all Mallards were grounded by the FAA in early 2006, following the Chalk's crash in December 2005.
J-11 was sold in April 2006, while J-53 was registered in October 2000 to the company at an address in Miami, FL and remained so until April 2008.

US GOVERNMENT, Dept of Interior,
Washington, DC
1129, B-6, B-22, B-24, B-28, B-47, B-56, B-72, B-81, B-97, B-102, B-115, B-122, B-123, B-130, B-137, B-138, B-142, B-144, 1260, 1266, 1281, 1294, 1299, 1313, 1319, 1320, 1327, 1341, 1360, 1373, J-24

Alaska Department of Public Safety
1129, B-28, B-47, B-97

Alaska Department of Fish & Game
1129, B-28, B-47, B-81, B-122, 1294

Alaska Fish & Wildlife Services
- see page 169

Bureau of Land Management (BLM)
B-115, B-123, B-130, B-137

Customs Service
J-35

Department of Commerce
B-97, 1303

Department of Justice, Washington, DC
1468

Department of Justice, US Border Patrol,
Miami, FL
1182

National Park Service
1299

The Alaska Railroad
B-97

US Fish & Wildlife Service
1147, B-6, B-47

War Department, Washington, DC
1206, 1233, 1461

The war-surplus aircraft were merely transferred from the military to the Department of the Interior at no charge. This was enabled under Public Law 247.

Although officially registered to the Department of the Interior in Washington, DC (the seat of government) most of the aircraft were operated in Alaska by the Fish & Wildlife Service (FWS) and the Bureau of Land Management (BLM), although some were used by the National Park Service, eg c/n 1299, which was based at Homestead, FL.

Above: *Fish & Wildlife Service badge.*

G-21A Goose N778 (c/n B-56) operated by the Alaska Fish & Wildlife Service is seen here at Anchorage on 6th August 1972.
(John P Stewart via PJ Marson)

G-21A Goose N749 (c/n B-6) operated by the Alaska Fish & Wildlife Service for waterfowl surveys is seen here flying over the snow-clad Northwest Territory.
(US Fish & Wildlife Service)

G-21A Goose N7251 (c/n B-28) operated by the State of Alaska, Department of Public Safety. The amphibian is seen here at Anchorage on 6th August 1972.
(John P Stewart via PJ Marson)

The Fish & Wildlife Service operated Goose NC709 (c/n 1147) in Alaska before it was converted to G-21C standard by McKinnon-Hickman. (MAP)

G-44 Widgeon N728 (c/n 1319) of the Alaska Fish & Wildlife Service, circa 1950. The aircraft was de-registered in 1953 after an accident, but was repaired and is now with a private owner in Idaho. (R Stuckey)

The BLM was also responsible for fire-fighting and modified some of the G-21As with "smoke-jumper" doors (see Chapter 5) to facilitate the delivery of fire-fighters close to the fire site.

Whilst the Fish & Wildlife Service of the Department of the Interior, Washington, DC had many Grummans based in Alaska, the G-21A, c/n B-47, was registered (locally) to the Alaska Department of Fish & Game in 1960, transferring to the Alaska Department of Public Safety in 1972.

The Fish & Wildlife Service in Alaska had their aircraft registered at the Office of Aircraft Services in Anchorage in the 1970s, and by 1990 most of the Department of the Interior's aircraft were registered to their offices in Anchorage, or Boise, ID.

G-21A B-72 was converted to Garrett turbo-prop power at the Fish & Wildlife Service hangar in Anchorage to provide a platform for marine mammal surveys over the Bering Sea.

The Department of Commerce was responsible for the Civil Aeronautics Administration (CAA). G-44 c/n 1303 was operated from Juneau, Alaska from 1949 until 1952, when it was transferred to the CAA Aeronautical Center in Oklahoma City. While in Alaska the aircraft was maintained in-house at Anchorage as well as by Alaska Coastal Airlines in Juneau. The Department of Commerce was also responsible for the National Marine Fisheries Service which operated G-21A (c/n B-97) from 1974 to 1976.

When the JRF-5, c/n 1182, was transferred to the Department of Justice in November 1954, the transfer document clearly stated that the aircraft was Navy serial 04355. However, the serial 37791 was added in a conspicuous position on the document and all future documents in the FAA file followed suit and quoted the wrong serial number, and therefore the wrong construction number. Even the weight and balance report dated 4th May 1955, originally quoting "JRF-5, serial 04355" had been altered to read "G-21A serial B-44", a mistake that was perpetuated until the aircraft crashed in 1974.

The G-44A (c/n 1461) was operated by the US Army, Corps of Engineers in the re-construction effort in Greece, post World War II.

In October 1991, the G-73, J-35, was forfeited by its owner (reason unknown) to the US Customs Service who then sold it in May 1992.

US INDUSTRIAL LEASING Corp,
New York, NY
1168

US INDUSTRIES Inc, New York, NY
1168
John I Snyder Jr, President.

US OIL of LOUISIANA Inc,
Houston, TX
1161, 1281, 9
John W Mecom, President. The G-44 was ferried to Nigeria in November 1965 for oil-field support operations. The SCAN-30 was destroyed in the Yemen in November 1962.

USHER, LE, Ipswich, UK
1218

USIBELLI COAL MINE Inc, Healy, AK
1298, 1346
C/n 1346 was purchased from Canada via Phoenix Aviation Ltd in Vancouver.

USIBELLI, Joseph E, Fairbanks, AK
- see above

US MISSILE CORP, Sun Valley, CA
B-14, 32
A *Lee Mansdorf* company.

**US PLYWOOD/
CHAMPION PAPERS Inc,**
Juneau, AK
B-125

**US SMALL BUSINESS
ADMINISTRATION** (USBA),
Anchorage, AK
1340
The USBA entered a financing agreement for the G-44 with *Michael Harder*. Harder broke the agreement and the Administration re-possessed the aircraft in July 1994.

UTAH, WILLIAMSON & BURNETT,
Invercargill, NZ
J-13
Affiliate of the world-wide conglomerate Utah Construction & Mining, San Francisco, CA. The G-73, purchased from *Trans Australia Airlines* in September 1963, was used as support aircraft for

Utah, Williamson & Burnett's Mallard ZK-CDV (c/n J-13) photographed at Christchurch, New Zealand, en route to Lake Manapouri in October 1963. The much-travelled Mallard is currently based in Nevada. (Fred J Knight Collection)

the Manapouri Power Project in New Zealand's South Island. Under the command of New Zealander Donald Nairn, who had flown Widgeons for the Fleet Air Arm in WWII, and with TAA's Captain A Kelly, the G-73, still registered VH-TGA, was delivered from Melbourne-Essendon on the 8th October 1963 to Tamworth and to Brisbane the next day, to install auxiliary fuel tanks for the Tasman crossing. The delivery continued via Coffs Island and Norfolk Island to Auckland, arriving on 13th October 1963. The next day the aircraft was flown to Wellington and then to Invercargill. VH-TGA then flew Invercargill to Christchurch on the 18th October 1963, where it went to NZNAC for overhaul and re-registration as ZK-CDV. After a check-flight on 23rd October the G-73 returned to Invercargill on 26th October, ready for service. Starting on 29th October 1963, Nairn flew the aircraft for the next five years taking supplies and personnel into and out of the Manapouri Project base at Deep Cove in the Fjordland region of New Zealand's South Island. Nairn flew 2,763 flights totalling 1,816:45 hours and carrying 13,526 passengers, 737 tons of freight and 287 ambulance cases. The G-73 was ferried to Christchurch in December 1968 for overhaul by NZNAC before being transferred to *Air Pacific* for services in Fiji. Nairn test flew the aircraft after overhaul and undertook several check rides with the Air Pacific pilot.

VACATION Inc, Hollywood, FL
21
Andrew Weisz, President in 1977, while Louise Weisz was President in 1981.

VALDEZ AERO SERVICES Inc,
Valdez, AK
1424
Charles F LaPage, President. Operated the G-44A in the mid-1980s.

VALENTINE, William W,
Los Angeles, CA
and later at Pasadena, CA
1133

VALLEY AIRCRAFT Inc, Oriskany, NY
27
John J Benton, President. Aircraft based at Oneida County Airport.

VALPEY, R Wesley, Jr,
Center Harbor, NH
and later at White Salmon, WA
21

VAN ARSDALE, Rickford, Salem, OR
1380

VAN BUSKIRK, LW, Inc, Easton, PA
1408
Owned the G-44A from 1947 until 1967.

VAN CAMP SEA FOOD Co Inc,
Terminal Island, CA
1338

VAN CLIEF, Daniel G, Charlottesville, VA
J-57

VANCOUVER AIRCRAFT SALES Ltd,
Vancouver, BC
1265, 1358
Acted as sales agent for c/n 1265 after McKinnon conversion to Lycoming GO-435-C2B engines.

VANDERBILT, GK, New York, NY
1218

VANDERBILT, Alfred Gwynne,
Long Island, NY
1434

VAN LEER'S METAL PRODUCTS Inc,
New York, NY
J-26
One of *Ben E Smith's* many commercial operations.

VAN WAGNEN, Brian J, Jackson, MI
1408

VAN WAGNEN, Brian J & Karen S,
Jackson, MI
1240

**VAUGHN MONROE
PRODUCTIONS Inc,**
Boston, MA
1210
Vaughn Monroe, President. Monroe was a trumpeter, singer and bandleader who had much success in the 1940s and 1950s.

VECTORED SOLUTIONS Inc,
Everett, WA
B-137
Doug de Vries, President.

**VENEZUELAN
OIL DEVELOPMENT Corp,**
Maracaibo, Venezuela - see *Shell Venezuela*
1048

VENTURA AIR SERVICES Inc,
Port Washington, NY
1390
John B Thomson Jr, President. Nick Tarascio, CEO. Ventura Air Services Inc was founded in 1955 to provide seaplane services from Manhasset Bay on Long Island to New York City. The company was purchased by John B Thomson Jr who was Chairman of *Thomson Industries Inc* in 1977. Since then the company has expanded to include helicopter and corporate jet charter and management.

VEST AIRCRAFT & FINANCE Co,
Denver, CO
1130, 1214, 1292, 1317, 1334, 1364
Don W Vest was owner and President of the aircraft dealership.

VICTORIA AIR MAINTENANCE Ltd,
Sidney, BC
J-54
Russ Popel, the company's owner, went to the U-Tapao Navy base in Thailand to make the G-73 flyable. In the event, J-54

was only flown two miles offshore from the port of Lom Chebang and craned from the water onto the bulk pulp carrier, "*Kite Arrow*", where it was secured to the deck for the two-week voyage to Hoquiam, WA.

VICTORIA FLYING SERVICES Ltd,
Sidney, BC
B-142

VICTORY AVIATION Corp,
Wilmington, DE
B-120
The G-21A was used by *Peter de Savary* as a support aircraft for his challenge for the 1983 America's Cup held at Newport, Rhode Island. His yacht was named "*Victory*", hence the name of the corporation to which it was registered. "*Victory*" did not live up to her name, however, finishing second to the Australians. See also *Blue Arrow Challenge Ltd*.

VIKING AIR Ltd, Sidney, BC
1129, 1157, B-52
Viking Air is one of the premier repair and refurbishment companies specialising in Grumman amphibians. The ex-*Pacific Western* G-21A, c/n 1157, was sold to *Alert Bay Air Services Ltd* in March 1973. In 1976 the registration C-GIGK was allocated to Viking Air to cover their projected work on the ex-*Alaska Airlines* Turbo-Goose B-52. In the event the registration was not used and the aircraft was re-built with piston engines and sold to *Channel Flying* in 1980. In June 1984 Viking Air bought the Type Certificate 4A24 for the McKinnon Turbo Goose conversions, but did not actually carry out any conversions. The ex-*Alaska Fish & Wildlife Services'* G-21A was overhauled by Viking in 1992, before being sold to *Ross Enterprises*.

VIKING AIRWAYS Inc, Petersburg, AK
1346

**VIRGIN ISLANDS SEAPLANE
SHUTTLE** (VISS),
Christiansted, US Virgin Islands
J-4, J-6, J-9, J-10, J-11, J-28, J-30, J-32, J-38, J-43, J-51, J-53, J-55
VISS was founded in 1981 by three New York investors led by Michael Braunstein, who became company president. Replacing

Above: *Virgin Island Seaplane Shuttle logo.*

Virgin Islands Seaplane Shuttle

tropicbird service

the ISLAND way to fly

unique . . . convenient . . .

downtown to downtown

serving

St. Thomas

Tortola

St. John

St. Croix

Virgin Islands Seaplane Shuttle
DAILY FLIGHT SCHEDULE
Effective October 8, 1984
Monday thru Saturday

St. Croix/St. Thomas		St. Thomas/St. Croix	
AM	PM	AM	PM
7:01	12:56	7:35	12:15
7:36	1:11 D	8:15*	1:30
7:51	1:26	8:25	1:45 D
8:11	2:06	8:45	2:00
9:01	2:21 D	9:15**	2:40
9:21	2:36	9:35	2:55
9:56**D	2:51 *	9:45*	3:10
10:11 D	3:16	9:55	4:05 D
10:31	3:31 D	10:30**D	4:20
11:06 D	3:46	10:45 D	5:00 *
11:21 D	4:26 *	11:05	5:15
11:41	4:41	11:40 D	5:30
	4:56	11:55 D	

D - Demand flights as needed *Tues/Thur **Mon/Wed/Fri

St. Croix to St. John	St. John to St. Croix
AM	AM
7:51 Sat	8:25 Sat
8:51 Tues/Thurs	9:25 Tues/Thurs 1 stop
PM	PM
2:51 Tues/Thurs 1 stop	3:50 Tues/Thurs
3:31 Sat	4:05 Sat
St. Thomas to St. John	**St. John to St. Thomas**
3:25 PM Tues/Thurs	9:25 AM Tues/Thurs

St. Croix to Tortola	Tortola to St. Croix
Mon/Wed/Fri	Mon/Wed/Fri
7:36 AM 1 stop	8:40 AM 1 stop
3:16 PM 1 stop	4:30 PM 1 stop
St. Thomas to Tortola	**Tortola to St. Thomas**
Mon/Wed/Fri	Mon/Wed/Fri
8:15 AM	8:40 AM
3:50 PM	4:30 PM

SUNDAY/HOLIDAY SCHEDULE

St. Croix/St. Thomas	St. Thomas/St. Croix
8:11 AM	8:45 AM
9:21	9:55
10:31	11:05
11:41	12:15 PM
1:26 PM	2:00
2:36	3:10
3:46	4:20
4:56	5:30

Please observe 20 minute check-in time

Passengers are permitted to carry 30 pounds of baggage - there is a charge of 30¢ per pound for any weight above 30 pounds. Carry-on baggage must be loaded in the rear baggage compartment of our aircraft. **Schedule subject to change**

Above: *Virgin Islands Seaplane Shuttle timetable dated 8th October 1984.*

Right: *Mallard N655SS (c/n J-55) in the white and blue colour scheme of Virgin Islands Seaplane Shuttle, in the Caribbean sunshine, circa 1986. The name "Tropic Bird" is carried on the bow, with small airline titles above the cheat-line on the rear fuselage. Unfortunately the aircraft was destroyed by Hurricane 'Hugo' on 17th September 1989.*
(Fred J Knight Collection)

Antilles Air Boats (AAB), VISS employed many of the AAB staff and two of the G-73s (J-4 & J-10), and commenced scheduled service between St Croix and St Thomas on 15th March 1982. More G-73s were purchased and some were converted to turbine power, all to provide inter-island services within the US and British Virgin Islands.

Late in 1987, VISS was planning an agreement with Trans World Airlines whereby VISS would provide feeder services from the Virgin Islands to connect with TWA services at San Juan, PR. Not having enough aircraft, VISS leased Twin Otters for the San Juan services but this only added to the airline's financial problems. By August 1988, VISS had gone bankrupt and been taken over by its main creditor, *Manufacturers Hanover Trust*, which continued the Mallard services, although J-51 had to be cannibalised to keep the others flying. VISS ceased operations in 1989 after Hurricane Hugo destroyed or damaged many of the ground installations and three of the Mallards, when it hit the islands on 17th September that year. The three remaining aircraft were used immediately after the debacle to ferry refugees out of, and relief workers into, the Virgin Islands; but the end was near. The remaining assets were assigned to the bank to be sold at bargain prices, the employees were laid off and the Twin Otters returned to the lessor. The G-73s were bought by *Caribbean Airline Services* in Puerto Rico.

VISAIR Ltd,
Nassau, Bahamas
J-5

VOLLUM, Dan, Hillsboro, OR
dba *AeroAir Inc*
B-62
The G-21G flew charters under the AeroAir banner. Vollum had bought the remains of *McKinnon Enterprises* and therefore the type certificates for the Turbo Goose. VL Manuel of *Antilles Seaplanes* purchased the McKinnon package from Vollum, thus giving Antilles the FAA approvals for all the Goose variants.

VOORHEES, Theodore G,
Delray Beach, FL
30

VOORHIS, Eugene van,
Rochester, NY
1444
Voorhis, President of *Rochester Amphibian Airways Inc* had the G-44A registered in his own name from 1970-72.

**VOWELL AIR SERVICES
(HELICOPTERS) Pty Ltd**, Tyabb, VIC
J-26
Later known as *Helicopter Resources Pty Ltd*, using the G-73 six days a week from 1985 until 1989 to ferry crews to and from oil rigs.

W A A - see *War Assets Administration*

Mallard N2954 (c/n J-14) "Walkers Cay Clipper", while owned by Walker's Cay Air Terminal Inc at Fort Lauderdale International, Florida in August 1981. This was the aircraft leased to Howard Hughes in 1955. It was allegedly stolen from Miami International Airport on 1st May 1955 and made a forced landing in the Everglades, west of Fort Lauderdale, with one main gear locked down.
(RH Milne)

WAGLISLA AIR,
Prince Rupert & Richmond, BC
B-145, J-23, J-54
Vivian Wilson, President. The company operated charter services out of Prince Rupert, BC. The G-21A was leased from *Hallmark Leasing Corp*, Vancouver, BC in June 1993 but crashed shortly after take-off from Prince Rupert on 4th December 1993.

WAGNER, John, Jr, La Guardia,
New York, NY
1233

WALE ENTERPRISES Inc,
Costa Mesa, CA
1153

WALKER, Peter, Sydney, NSW
1466

WALKER AIRWAYS Inc, Detroit, MI
1404

WALKER'S CAY AIR TERMINAL Inc,
Fort Lauderdale, FL
1147, J-14, J-49
dba *Walker's International*, a subsidiary of *Precision Valve Corp* owned by Robert Alplanalp. It operated under a Part 135 certificate to provide services from Miami to Walker's Cay, Bahamas. The services were taken over by *Chalk's* in 1994.

WALKER'S INTERNATIONAL
- see above

WALLACE AIRCRAFT Co, Sarasota, FL
1380

WALLACE, G, Fitchburg, MA
1452
dba *Alpine Airways Inc.*

**WALSTEN AIRCRAFT PARTS
& LEASING Ltd**, Richmond, BC
B-138

**WALTER FULLER AIRCRAFT
SALES Inc**, Richardson, TX
1213
Walter Fuller, President.

WALTERS, Charles E, Spokane, WA
dba The Walters Company
B-62, B-138, 1427
Walters sold the G-21A, c/n B-138, to *McKinnon Enterprises* in August 1967 and bought G-21A, c/n B-62, from them in (early?) 1968. He then sold it back to them on 20th September 1968. Walters personally carried a heavy mortgage on the aircraft which allowed McKinnon to convert the aircraft to turbine power (G-21G) at Walter's expense. However, McKinnon also owed money to other creditors, notably the First National Bank of Portland, who eventually seized G-21G, c/n B-62, and other McKinnon assets (see Chapter 5). The G-44A was owned from 1968 until 1971.

WAMSER, Carl H, Greendale, WI
1472

WAR ASSETS ADMINISTRATION
(WAA), Washington, DC
1063, 1085, 1106, 1132, 1133, 1138, 1160, 1164, 1165, 1167, 1170, 1266, 1323, 1324, 1329, 1346, 1350, 1378, 1387
The WAA was the US Government surplus disposal organisation which took over from the *Reconstruction Finance Corporation* in January 1946. It was also known briefly as the War Assets Corporation until 31st January 1946.

WAR ASSETS CORPORATION, Canada
1002, 1003, 1005, 1007, 1013, 1018, 1019, 1059, 1061, 1083, B-45, B-50, B-70, B-76, B-77, B-98, B-107
Set up by the Canadian Government to dispose of surplus materials at the end of WWII.

WARBIRDS WEST, Compton, CA
1048
Facilitated the transfer of the G-21A from *Air Catalina* to the *National Museum of Naval Aviation* at Pensacola in 1982 (see also *Dennis Buehn*).

WARD SALES Co Inc, Miami, FL
1384
Thomas H Ward Jr, President. Registration N9270H for the G-44 was revoked by the

FAA in December 1970 due to administrative failings on the part of the owner.

WARIS, Andrew, Clatskanie, OR
1338

WARNER, Fred, Fort Lauderdale, FL
1233

WARN INDUSTRIES Inc,
Milwaukee, OR
1059, 1129, B-142
Michael T Warn, President. Warn traded the G-21A (c/n 1059) to *Cessna Aircraft Co,* in exchange for a Cessna 208 Caravan in June 1997.

WARNOCK HERSEY, The, Co Ltd,
Montreal, QC
1334
The well-known engineering test laboratory with an address in Ville La Salle, QC, owned the G-44 in 1957. It passed to *Strathcona Equipment Co Ltd,* and in 1958 was registered to *Canadian Inspection & Testing Co* but these were probably Warnock Hersey associate companies or subsidiaries, as they all had W Howard Wert as president. See also *PN Thomson.*

WASHINGTON AIRCRAFT & TRANSPORT Corp, Seattle, WA
1323

WASHINGTON FISH & OYSTER Co,
Seattle, WA
1270
The war-surplus G-44 was purchased in 1946 for $10,000 to provide service to their canneries in Alaska.

WATER FOWL Inc, Fort Lauderdale, FL
1147
The G-21D was confiscated in Haiti in the 1990s and finally scrapped there.

WATERLINES Ltd,
Wilmington, DE
1054

WATSON, Joanne, Crescent City, FL
1160

WATSON, William, Miami, FL
dba *Anchor Air Inc.*
1160

WAYMAN, Ian A, Sebastopol, CA
and at Thornton, CO & Peyton, CO
1214

WAVE RUNNER AVIATION LLC,
Graham, NC
B-129

W C Inc, Portland, OR
1389

WEAKLAND, Patrick H,
Dumfries, VA and at
Tappahannock and Warsaw, VA
1419

WEBB, Del E, New York, NY
dba *New York Yankees*, in partnership with *Daniel R Topping.*
B-71, J-42

WEBB, Harry H, Shelburne, VT
1206
Aircraft based c/o Win Air Service Inc, Hancock Airport, Syracuse, NY.

WEBBER AIRLINES, Ketchikan, AK
aka *Webber Air Inc.*
1195, B-32, B-115

WEEKS, Kermit A, Miami, FL
1388
dba Weeks Air Museum Inc, Polk City, FL, where his collection of vintage aircraft are stored. The collection was re-named Fantasy of Flight in 2001 and later as the World's Greatest Aircraft Collection Inc.

WEESNER, R Paul, Miami, FL (co-owner)
1388

WEIR, Charles E, Anchorage, AK
1329

WELDWOOD CANADA Ltd,
Richmond, BC
B-117
Weldwood operated the G-21A from Campbell River, BC in the 1980s.

WELLS AIRCRAFT Inc, Hutchison, KS
4

WELLS, Ana Flora Alvarado de,
San José, Costa Rica
- *see below*
1233

WELLS, John M,
Mercedes, TX
1233
c/o Mercedes Flying Service. In a letter to the FAA dated 20th September 1964 from an address in San José, Costa Rica, Wells stated that the G-44 had been sold to Ana Flora Alvarado de Wells (at the same address) and requested cancellation of N37183.

WELLS, John Morris,
San Jose, Costa Rica and at
New Orleans, LA
dba *Heliteco.*
1277
A native of Arkansas, *Wells* was a former crop-duster who operated in Texas and Oklahoma. Heliteco was a helicopter charter service and aircraft maintenance facility at Pavas Airport, Costa Rica. In August 1975 the G-44 was in the process of a major overhaul and re-engine programme being carried out by Wells, with a view to using it for fishing charters to the lagoons on the Caribbean coast of Costa Rica and the islands of the Gulf of Nicoya. Whether the G-44 was so used is not known, but in February 1985 it was registered to Wells at a New Orleans address and was sold in November 1985.

William Watson's Goose N86640 (c/n 1160) at Opa Locka, Florida on 21st March 1979. After an extensive rebuild by Aero Technology in Long Beach, California the aircraft crashed during its first flight on 16th June 1990. The wreck was last reported stored at Sequoia, California.

(Peter Vercruijsse)

G-21A Goose N641 (c/n B-115) operated by Webber Airlines Inc out of Ketchikan, Alaska is seen here at Boeing Field, Seattle, Washington on 6th January 1979. The Goose was later operated by Peninsular Airways out of King Salmon, Alaska. *(Peter Kirkup via Jennifer Gradidge)*

WELLS FARGO BANK NORTHWEST NA TRUSTEE, Salt Lake City, UT
J-35

WELSCH, James C, Garden City, NY
1213, 1411, 1450, 1473
Aircraft sales agent dba Welsch Aviation Company who bought the G-44As in 1956 from the Cuban Navy via *Universal Trading Corporation* in Panama. The aircraft were still in Havana when he bought them and it was he who arranged the ferry flights into the USA. He later became President of *Welsch-Ayer Inc.*

WELSCH-AYER Inc, New York, NY
1213, 1411, 1450
JC Welsch, President. Affiliate of *Fred B Ayer & Associates*, the famous aircraft sales and leasing company.

WELSH, Robert J, Pasadena, CA
and later at La Mesa, CA
1467, 1475

WELTON, James F, Franklin, PA
1384
Aircraft dealer.

WENDT, Harmon Edgar,
Georgetown, British Guiana
1170
Captain Wendt was a pilot for *British Guiana Airways* and did much to develop air transport within the colony. This was recognised by the British Government when he and *Major Arthur Williams* were awarded medals for their pioneering work during the years 1934-47. In December 1957 Wendt was also awarded the Order of the British Empire (OBE), for his "exceptional flying and engineering skill".

WESTCHESTER AIRPLANE SALES Co
- see *J White*

WEST COAST AIRCRAFT Ltd,
Los Angeles, CA
1227, 1359, 1387
William F Pike, owner, bought the surplus J4F-2, c/n 1387, in June 1947 and operated it until March 1952.

WEST COAST AIR SERVICES Ltd,
Vancouver, BC
1200, B-98, J-9, J-10, J-21, J-22, J-26, J-53, J-54
West Coast Aircraft Services was the idea of brothers Al and Lloyd Michaud before WWII. It was revived in 1945 as a charter and flight training operation, and from 1956 it provided contract services for the forest industry from bases at Kamloops and Nelson. The two G-21As were acquired in 1973, and in April 1974 West Coast acquired two G-73s and the routes they served from *Pacific Western Airlines*. West Coast now had scheduled services to Bella Bella, Bella Coola and Namu, and later added schedules to the Gulf Islands. G-73s J-22, J-53 and J-54 were also added to the fleet in 1974 and G-73T J-22 joined in 1975. West Coast Air was merged into the *Air BC* group in 1980.

WEST COAST FLYING BOATS Inc,
Bear, DE
J-30

WEST COAST TRANSPORT Co Ltd
(WCT), Vancouver, BC
B-83, B-107
West Coast Transport was formed by Julius Bloedel, an American lawyer, so that he could register G-21A, B-107, in Canada as CF-IOL. In fact the Bill of Sale dated 8th September 1950 named Bruce McKenzie Farris, vice-president of WCT, as purchaser and the Certificate of Registration was issued to WCT, with Sidney Garfield Smith as president. Maintenance and hangar facilities were supplied under contract by *B.N.P. Airways*. When the Bloedel, Stuart & Welsh company merged with MacMillans to form *MacMillan Bloedel* in 1951, WCT still operated as the air transport arm of the conglomerate, flying customers and staff around British Columbia.

In the late 1950s pilot Dan McIvor developed water-bombing techniques by fitting removable external water tanks to G-21A, c/n B-107 (see Chapter 5). He also supplied ground personnel by both free-fall and parachuted air drops. McIvor left WCT in 1959 to form *Forest Industries Flying Tankers*.

In 1965 WCT absorbed the remains of *B.N.P. Airways* and took over their hangar, maintenance staff and the G-21A (B-83).

WCT remained a wholly-owned subsidiary of MacMillan Bloedel (MB) with Ernest G Shorter as president. Two-pilot crews were initiated in 1965 to facilitate operations from Vancouver Harbour, with docking facilities at the Kingcome Navigation wharf at the foot of Columbia Street in Gastown, Vancouver. In 1969, the G-21As were fitted with IFR avionics, the crews were upgraded to IFR standard and limited IFR operations commenced. The Vancouver Harbour operation was discontinued in 1969 due to the density of air and marine traffic and problems with heavy swells and driftwood. On 1st January 1980, WCT became a division of MB and was renamed MacMillan Bloedel Ltd Flight Operations. The G-21As were sold in October 1994 when helicopters took over.

WEST VIRGINIA PULP & PAPER Co,
New York, NY
1394
David L Luke Jr, President. Aircraft based at Canaan, CT.

WESTERNAIR,
Albuquerque, NM
J-5, J-54
Richard Durand, President. Dealer in secondhand aircraft.

WESTERN AIRCRAFT LEASING Co,
Claymont, DE
1213

Mallard C-GENT (c/n J-54) of West Coast Air Services at Vancouver, British Columbia in July 1975. This much-travelled aircraft is currently flying with an owner in Delaware.

(Neville Parnell via Jennifer Gradidge)

Goose CF-PVE (c/n 1200) of West Coast Air, seen here in June 1973. The aircraft was destroyed when it crashed into Nitinat Canyon at the foot of Mount Hooper, British Columbia on 9th September 1974.

(Steve Krauss)

Goose N2845D (c/n B-112) in Western Alaska Airlines colour scheme in the 1960s (note the 'WA' motif on the tail-fin). It was to have been used in the TV series "Tales of the Gold Monkey" but crashed on the way south from Alaska, near Cape Yakataga, on 20th February 1982.

(via Guy Denton)

WESTERN AIRMOTIVE Ltd,
Vancouver, BC
1265
Acted as sales agent for the G-44 in April 1958.

WESTERN ALASKA AIRLINES Inc,
Dillingham, AK Albert W Ball, President.
B-112, B-114, 1468
The airline had been operating bush services in the Bristol Bay area of Alaska since 1948 and in 1955 took over the bush operations of *Pacific Northern Airlines* (PNA). Scheduled services were started on the King Salmon-Dillingham-Togiak route on 20th February 1960 and from April that year services were flown throughout southwest Alaska including more of the former PNA routes to Levelok, Koggiung, Egegik, Pilot Point, Ugashik, Clarks Point, Ewol and Igingig. By November 1965, the Dillingham-King Salmon route was flown eleven times each week, and the routes from Dillingham, Manakotuk-Togiak and King Salmon-Ugashik were being served five times a week. The airline merged with *Kodiak Airways* to form *Kodiak Western Alaska Airlines* on 1st April 1973.

WESTERN CONTINENTAL AIRLINES,
Glendale, CA
1430

WESTERN ENTERPRISES Inc, (WEI),
Pittsburgh, PA
1153
WEI was a cover organisation created by the US Central Intelligence Agency (CIA) in 1951 to manage paramilitary operations against mainland China from the island of Taiwan (Formosa). Another such organisation is thought to have been the Air Carrier Service Corp, Washington, DC. Curiously, William W Brinkerhoff, President of Air Carrier Service Corp was granted power of attorney to register the G-21A on behalf of Western Enterprises Inc on 9th July 1952. A Certificate of Registration was not issued however, and it is thought that the G-21A was used in Taiwan by the CIA (see Chapter 7).

WESTERN NEWSPAPER UNION,
New York, NY
1013, 1236

WESTERN NEWSPAPERS UNITED Inc,
New York, NY
1362

WESTERN SKYWAYS SERVICE,
Troutdale, OR
1339

WESTFLIGHT AVIATION Inc,
Ketchikan, AK
1164
Charles F "Chuck" Slagle, President. The company operated services from Ketchikan Seaplane Base. See also *Aviation Associates Ltd*, dba Westflight Aviation. Slagle sold the G-21A to *Milne Bay Air*, Papua New Guinea in 1987 for $150,000.

WESTFORT LEASING, Fort William, ON
1473
G Dolcetti, President. Leased the G-44A to *Superior Airways Ltd* for one year, from November 1965.

WESTHOLM AVIATION Inc,
Crystal Bay, NV
and at Gardnerville & Minden, NV
1210, 1430, 1475
Joseph S Lodato, President. When the G-44 was purchased the buyer was described as "Westholm Aviation, Janet or Joseph Lodato". Joseph Lodato died in May 2000.

WEYERHAEUSER, Muriel H,
Chesterfield, MO
B-49
The Weyerhaeusers handled the sale of the G-21A from *ITT* to a Canadian buyer in 1982. Charles Weyerhaeuser was named as pilot on the ferry permit for the flight from St Paul, MN to the Canadian border at Noyes, MN, on delivery to *Air Park Aviation* in Winnipeg.

WHEAT, RJ
dba *Richland Flying Service Inc*,
Richland, WA
1346

WHITE, J
dba *Westchester Airplane Sales Co*,
New York, NY
1207

WHITE, James Robert, Stuart, FL
1370

WHITEHEAD'S Inc, Charlotte, NC
1374
Troy Whitehead, President. Based at Charlotte Municipal Airport, the company was later known as the Troy Whitehead Machinery Co Inc.

WHITNEY, Cornelius Vanderbilt,
Old Westbury, NY
1019
The banker who, in 1927, co-founded the Aviation Corporation of America with Juan Trippe and John A Hambleton, which later became *Pan American World Airways*. In 1931 Whitney bought the *Hudsons Bay Mining & Smelting Company*. The G-21A was a personal transport but was sold to the RCAF in 1941.

WHITNEY, John Hay & Betsey Cushing,
New York, NY
1371
The aircraft was based at MacArthur Airport, Ronkonkoma, Long Island, NY

WHITTEL, George, Lake Tahoe, NV
dba Thunderbird Lodge
1020

WHITTINGTON, Bill & Don,
Fort Lauderdale, FL - see *World Jet Inc*

WHYTE, Daniel D, New York, NY
1277

WICKWIRE SPENCER AVIATION Corp,
New York, NY
1407
EP Holder, President.

WIDGEON Inc, Crofton, MD
1274
Andy Michalak, President.

WIDGEON ENTERPRISES LLC,
Kent, WA
1375
The Widgeon was still operated in 2009 by *Fresh Water Adventures* out of Dillingham. - see also *Kerriston Ltd Partnership*

WIDGEON FRANKLIN Inc,
Columbus, OH
1313
Don M Casto III, President.

WIDGEON QUEST Inc, Reno, NV
1210
Ronald C Broyles, President.

WIEN AIR ALASKA - see below

WIEN AIR ALASKA Inc, Anchorage, AK
J-36, J-44
The company was founded in 1924 as Northern Air Transport and became Wien Air Alaska in 1936. It became *Wien*

Wien Air Alaska's Mallard N1208 (c/n J-44) in the airline's smart blue and yellow scheme. Note the water rudder at the aft end of the hull.   *(Peter A Kirkup via Jennifer Gradidge)*

Consolidated Airlines in February 1968 after the merger with *Northern Consolidated Airlines*, thus acquiring the G-73s. The company was renamed Wien Air Alaska again 21st March 1974 and disposed of the G-73s on 27th November 1979 and 18th April 1978 respectively. The company was also known as Wien Alaska Airlines at one time.

WIEN CONSOLIDATED AIRLINES Inc
(WCA), Fairbanks, AK
J-36, J-44
WCA was formed in February 1968 by the merger of *Northern Consolidated Airlines* with *Wien Air Alaska*. The CAB awarded the new operator the non-stop route from Anchorage to Fairbanks and WCA was responsible for all routes to the northwest of a line from Fairbanks to Anchorage. Became *Wien Air Alaska* again on 21st March 1974.

WIEN, Kurt M, Stratham, NH
and later at West Ossipee, NH
1228

WIEN, Noel Merrill, Anchorage, AK
1213, 1228
Noel Wien is the founder of *Wien Air Alaska*. G-44, c/n 1228, was transferred to Noel M Wien & Barbara M Wien at Kent, WA in March 1992 and then at Eastsound, WA in April 1998.

WIEN, Richard A, Fairbanks, AK
1334

WIGMA Corp, Royal Oak, MI
1463
C Gilbert Medley Jr, President.

WILCO Inc, Las Vegas, NV
1420
Will Roberts, President.

WILD, JR,
Port Moresby, Papua New Guinea
dba *Milne Bay Air*
1164
John Wild bought the G-21A from *Chuck Slagle's Aviation Associates* in 1987 for $150,000. A telex from the Civil Aviation Department in Port Moresby in August 1987 requesting urgent confirma-

tion that the aircraft had been cancelled from the US Civil Aircraft Register stated "aircraft required for SAR/Medevac standby".

WILDERNESS AIR CHARTER,
Minneapolis, MN
1083

WILHITE, Randy J, Jackson, MI
1343

WILLARD, Ronald Wayne,
Long Beach, CA
1371

WILLIAMS DRILLING Co,
Baton Rouge, LA
B-139

WILLIAMS, Douglas L, Anchorage, AK
1457

WILLIAMS, Major Arthur James,
New York, NY
1007
- see *British Guiana Airways*

WILLIAMS, Dr Richard E,
Myrtle Creek, OR
1371

WILLIAMS, Robert G, Billings, MT
B-56

WILLIAMSON, George F,
Sandy, OR
1083
Chief pilot for BC Hydro (formerly *B.N.P. Airways*) had flown Goose amphibians for the *Royal Canadian Air Force* and *Malibu*

Seaero. Williamson was responsible for providing a G-21A for the Duke of Westminster and to avoid restrictive export regulations Williamson registered the aircraft in his own name, but using *McKinnon's* address in Sandy, OR.

The aircraft was overhauled and refitted completely in Vancouver and then flown back to Oregon where McKinnon oversaw the export procedures to get the aircraft to the UK where it was operated by *Grosvenor Estates.*

WILLIS AIR SERVICES,
Teterboro, NJ
1165
This was one of the immediate post-WWII non-scheduled cargo charter operators, founded in October 1945, which also operated DC-3s.

WILLIS, Charles F, III, & Co Inc,
Seattle, WA
1051, 1110

WILLIS, Roger & Charlotte,
Ashland, AL
- and later at Miami, FL
1442

WINCAPAW, William H,
Tottenville, NY
1352

WINDHAUSEN, Matthew Thomas,
Eagle Bay, NY
dba *Adirondack Seaplane Service*
1206
"Bud" Windhausen also flew c/n 1306, with Dick Benson, for the *J P Lewis Paper Co* out of Beaver Falls, NY.

WINDJAMMER AIR TAXI Inc,
Miami Beach, FL
aka *Windjammer Flying Services Inc*
B-19, B-100
Michael Burke, President.

WINDJAMMER CAPITOL & LEASING,
Escondido, CA
1420
James Hoffman, President. The Certificate of Registration application gave an address in Lawton, OK. Ownership of the G-44A was then transferred to Hoffman whose address was also in Lawton, OK.

WINDLE, W W, Co, Millbury, MA
1299

Goose N3692 (c/n 1083) at Baltimore on 5th February 1958, while operated by Wilderness Air Charter of Minneapolis, Minnesota. Note the name 'Snow Goose' on the bow. This aircraft was owned later by Grosvenor Estates and was the only Goose converted to turbine power by Marshall of Cambridge Engineering.
(Carson Seeley via Jennifer Gradidge)

WINDY HILL WIDGEON WORKS LLC,
Boulder, CO, c/o Marilyn M Soby.
1235

WING, W Gordon, Houston, TX
1328

WINGS OVER MIAMI MUSEUM,
Tamiami, FL
1472
The G-44A was on loan from *Loughrea Maritime*.

WINN AIR SERVICE Co Inc,
Syracuse, NY
1266, 1303
This operator was based at Hancock Field in Syracuse. It is not certain whether or not the company owned c/n 1303, but a letter from Winn Air Service to the FAA dated 29th July 1974 stated that the aircraft, previously owned by *J Curtiss McKinney*, had been scrapped.

WINSHIP AIR SERVICE Inc,
Anchorage, AK
B 45
D Winship, President. Operated the G-21A from July 1975 until it was written off on 12th May 1978.

WOLAB Corp, Allan Tool Division,
Columbus, OH
1213, 1216
LL Leveque, President.

WOLD, William C, & Associates,
New York, NY
J-29
Aircraft sales agents with another facility at Greenwich, CT
J-49

WOLFE, Monroe J, New Orleans, LA
1377, 1380
Co-owner with *Mitchell Ashy*, and also see *A & W Inc*.

WOLFENDEN ENTERPRISE Inc
1210
Bought the G-44 from the St Lucie County Court, FL in April 2007, selling it a fortnight later.

WOOD, Garfield A, Detroit, MI
dba *Gar Wood Industries*
1012, 1017, 1220, 1407, J-14
Garfield Arthur Wood was born in 1880 and became famous as a powerboat racer, winning five consecutive Gold cup races, and was a millionaire by 1920. He won the English Harmsworth Trophy on eight consecutive occasions, allowing the cup to be kept permanently in the USA. His first G-21A was destroyed in a hangar fire at Miami in April 1938 but he immediately replaced it with c/n 1017. The second G-21A was impressed by the US Navy in 1942 but by then he had his first G-44, which he sold in 1946 to be replaced by the G-44A. The G-73 was delivered in February 1947. Wood leased the aircraft to *Howard Hughes* in 1955 just prior to selling it to *Packer Pontiac Corp*.

WOOD-MOSAIC Co
- see *Charles Stewart Maclean*

WOOD, Robert F, Jr, Driggs, ID
B-49

WOODRUFF, Mark A, Ossipee, NH
1359

WOODS, Warren W, Palmer, AK
dba *Woods Air Service* and aka *Woods Air Fuel Inc*
1232, 1377, 1380
Woods Air Service, founded in 1962, provided services out of Palmer Municipal Airport. The G-44, c/n 1380, was registered in the names of Warren W and Christine M Woods from 1973 to 1976. The G-44, acquired in April 1964, has probably not been flown since 1960 and maybe used for spares. Woods Air Fuel Inc (President, WG Woods) also operated two DC-3s and a DC-6B, and were still flying from Palmer in 2010.

WOODWARD, Stanley, Washington, DC
1411
Woodward based the G-44A at Palma-San Bonet, Majorca from 1972 until it crashed in February 1981. After rebuild, the G-44A was sold to *DHF Realty Inc* in Miami, FL.

WORLD JET Inc, Fort Lauderdale, FL
1147, 1215
The corporation was owned by Bill & Don Whittington. They bought the G-21D from Hal Beale of *On Mark Aviation* in March 1980.

WORLD PACIFIC AIR LEASE Inc
(WPAL), Irving, TX
J-27, J-30, J-32, J-42, J-44, + J-28 parts
One of the companies owned by Thor K Tjontveit, whose Air Alaska had purchased *Flying Boat Inc*. The five G-73Ts were registered to WPAL in January 1998, but on 11th January 1999 Flying Boat Inc filed for Chapter 11 bankruptcy protection. *James Confalone* bought the assets from the court in August 1999.

WORLD'S GREATEST AIRCRAFT COLLECTION Inc, Polk City, FL
1388
The re-named *Fantasy of Flight*.

WORLDWIDE AIR Inc, Miami Lakes, FL
J-21

WORLDWIDE AVIATION DISTRIBUTORS Inc, Miami, FL
1053, 1109, 1133, B-18, B-46, B-74, 1274, 10, 13
This company was incorporated by *James Confalone* on 28th October 1999 and although the company is not active Confalone represents them as their registered agent.

WPIX Inc, New York, NY
J-22
Previously known as the *New York Daily News*.

WRAY, Melvin C,
Assonet, MA dba Monument Manufacturing Co
1389

WRIGHT INDUSTRIAL EQUIPMENT Ltd, Edmonton, AB
26
James Wright, President. Leased the SCAN-30 to *Pacific Western Airlines* during the mid-1960s and to *Northward Aviation Ltd* in 1966.

WRIGHT, Alfred F & Jeanne S,
Fairbanks, AK
1300
dba Wright Air Service, flying the G-44 out of Fairbanks-East Ramp International Airport from 1978 until 1987.

WRIGHTSMAN, Charles B, Houston, TX
1055
and later at Palm Beach, FL
J-31
Wrightsman was the one time President of *Standard Oil Co of Kansas* and the G-73 was based at Houston for his use. In 1948 the G-73 was flown to the United Kingdom by pilots Al Franks and Pete de Rose at the start of a four month trip which included visits to Norway, Holland, France, Italy, Greece, Saudi Arabia and the Dutch East Indies. In December 1948, the G-73 was nominally registered to *International Air Service Inc*, but still operated by Wrightsman.

This former Cuban Navy G-44A Widgeon (c/n 1411), registered as N444M to Stanley Woodward, is seen here at Shannon, Ireland on 16th August 1972. It was rebuilt after a crash in February 1981 and is currently flying with an owner in Michigan.
(Malcolm Nason)

WRIGLEY, Philip K, Chicago, IL
1385

WUNDER MACHINE Co Ltd,
Kitchener, ON
1240

WYATT, Lynn W, Jr,
Anchorage, AK
1464
Wyatt had co-owned the Widgeon with *Ronald B Fowler* before becoming sole owner in February 1983.

WYLDE WOOD AVIATION Inc,
Portsmouth, NH
32
Richard W Skeffington Jr, President.

WYNN, Edgar J, New York, NY
dba *Trans American Airways Inc*
1106, B-59

YACHT WINGS INTERNATIONAL,
Vancouver, BC
1423
JC Hames, President. Operated the G-44A from November 1963 until August 1966, but only accumulated some 15 hours flight time!

YAKER, Marshall I, El Paso, TX
1214

YANKS AIR MUSEUM, Chino, CA
B-140, 1299
The G-21A was restored during 2000-10, while the G-44, still registered as N2PS, was noted dismantled and stored here in October 2007.

YAUKUVE ISLAND RESORT,
Fiji
1164
After overhaul at Bundaberg, QLD, the G-21A was ferried to Caboolture for repainting and was noted there on 10th March 2005. Seen at Archerfield on 7th August 2005, painted as DQ-AYL, awaiting delivery to Fiji, but the project was abandoned.

YELLOWBIRDS, Bangkok, Thailand
- see *Tropical Sea Air*
1145

YONGE, Laurie W, Jr, Oklawaha, FL
B-30

YOREO, SF de, Fort Worth, TX
25

YOUNG, B, Patterson Lakes, VIC
1145

YOUNG, Thomas Owen,
Lake Oswego, OR
1293
and later at Battle Ground, WA
1373

YOUNGHUSBAND, L
1413

YUILLE, Charles L, Hollywood, FL
co-owner with *JE Jacks*
1274
and at Miami, FL
1310

YUKON OFFICE SUPPLY Inc,
Anchorage, AK
1239
The G-44 was co-owned with *Bevan Investment Co*.

YUTE AIR ALASKA Inc, Dillingham, AK B-140, 1387
Philip L Bingman, President. Founded in 1963, the company owned the G-44 from 1979 until 1989 and also operated a Piper PA-31-350 Chieftain.

ZAP AIRWAYS Inc, Anchorage, AK
1206
K Gene Zerkel, President (see also below)

ZELCER, F William, New York, NY
1213
Zelcer was president of both the *Hayes Aircraft Accessories Corporation* and the *Seyah Corporation* (at the same address), and had the G-44 registered in his own

name in 1943, at which time it was used by the Civil Air Patrol.

ZERKEL, K Gene, Anchorage, AK
1206, 1324
dba *G G Leasing Co* in partnership with *George S Patterson*. Zerkel was also sometime President of *Alaska Aircraft Sales Inc, GEE BEE Inc* and *Zap Airways Inc*.

ZIESMER, Richard A, Puyallup, WA and later Spanaway, WA and University Place, WA
1431

ZIGLER FLYING SERVICE Inc,
Jennings, LA
1428

ZIMICKI, John L, Loudonville, NY
1420

ZUMA, Anthony, Houston, TX
1328

1147967 Alberta Ltd, Calgary, AB
1414

132802 CANADA Ltée, (Aero Taxi),
St Hubert, PQ
1414
Claude Michaud, President. Leased the G-44A from *Aviation 3C Inc* from October 1989 until September 1990. The company was re-incorporated as *157488 Canada Inc* by 1993 (see below).

147973 Canada Inc, Calgary, AB
B-117
Juergen Puetter, President. The G-21A was based at Montreal-Dorval until sold to *Unilease Inc* in 1991. Puetter then leased it back from Unilease, and moved to Senneville, QC in 1992 and Sidney, BC in 1993 when he purchased the aircraft from Unilease, operating it until 1998.

157488 Canada Inc (Aerotaxi),
St Hubert, PQ
1414
Claude Michaud, President. Previously known as *132802 Canada Ltée* (see above), and had leased the G-44A from *Aviation 3C Inc*, but purchased it from them in 1993.

20th CENTURY FOX FILM Corp,
Beverly Hills, CA aka 20th Century Fox Studio.
J-9

2bw, Newport Beach, CA
1130

241805 Alberta Ltd, Edmonton, AB
B-120
Operated the G-21A from July 1980 until November 1983.

343066 ALBERTA Ltd, Edmonton, AB
J-34
One of *Sandy Mactaggart's* companies

575L LLC, Fairbanks, AK
1463

The Wunder Machine Company's McKinnon Super Widgeon CF-BVN (c/n 1240) seen here at Mount Hope, Ontario in August 1967. It was the first Widgeon to be registered outside the USA and was so registered, to JP Bickell in December 1941, at a time when export approval would have been complicated. The aircraft is now powered by Lycoming GO-480-G1D6 engines and flies with co-owners in Michigan.
(Jack McNulty via Jennifer Gradidge)

The Gweduck during a test flight over the Seattle area on 30th September 2009. Note the tufts over the pilot's window and on the nacelle, to evaluate airflow in these areas. *(Jim Schoeggl)*

CHAPTER 9: THE FUTURE

ALTHOUGH THE ORIGINAL GRUMMAN PRODUCTION LINES IN BETHPAGE, NEW YORK are long gone, the Grumman amphibian legacy lives on in two projects geared toward manufacturing all-new versions of the legendary Goose and Widgeon. The Antilles "Super Goose" will be a 100% new production version of the turbine-powered McKinnon G-21G "Turbo Goose" first built in 1969 and which was itself a derivation of the Grumman G-21A. The Ellison-Mahon "Gweduck" is an all-composite, piston-powered amphibian flying boat that was originally based on the Grumman G-44A.

The Antilles "Super Goose"

Antilles Seaplanes LLC was created in 2000 as a simple plan to spice up the pending retirement of two friends. Founder VL Manuel, Jr, an entrepreneur and CPA, and his partner Tim Henderson, owner of a small aircraft accessory overhaul and manufacturing business, decided that they wanted a 'special' aeroplane project around which they could focus their eventual retirement. A seaplane exactly fitted the bill. After seeing an advertisement in Trade-a-Plane, they travelled to Miami to look at an old Goose and to talk to the seller, the legendary Dean Franklin.

Dean Franklin, former owner of Chalk's, the world's oldest scheduled airline and reputed to have been the instructor who taught Howard Hughes to fly seaplanes, spent three days enthralling the partners with tales of the Golden Age of flying boats and travel around the Caribbean and the world. At the ripe old age of 92, Mr Franklin was himself finally looking to retire and he had more than just an airplane to offer. For the paltry sum of one million dollars, the partners could buy the Goose, a

whole warehouse full of spare parts and a full set of technical and engineering drawings that Franklin had first obtained directly from Grumman after the company had decided to stop supporting their various seaplane lines in the 1960s.

Manuel and Henderson, who was a pilot and certified aircraft mechanic, reasoned that if they took Mr Franklin up on his offer, they could use the spare parts as necessary to restore their own Goose and then sell off the rest of the parts to cover all of their expenses. After making the deal, they trucked thirteen trailer loads of parts and one Goose hulk from Miami to the tiny old mill town of Gibsonville, North Carolina, just east of Greensboro, near the middle of the state. The Goose was ex-Antilles Air Boats' N1048V (c/n B-46), and the seaplane parts were stashed in renovated warehouse space inside the mill.

Two additional Goose wrecks were obtained from an aircraft salvage operation in Deer Park, Washington. The first was N66QA (c/n 1054), which was first operated by The Texas Company (TEXACO) as NC3055 in the early 1940s. In the 1950s, it went back to Grumman for several years and during that time its registration was changed to N704A. Grumman sold it to McKinnon Enterprises in April 1960 and it was modified to have retractable wingtip floats. Soon after, it was sold to the Sun Oil Company (aka Sunoco), and re-registered N33S. It was acquired eventually by Pan Air at New Orleans Lakefront airport. In 1979, N33S was sold to a two individuals in Florida, and in November 1982 it was seized by the government of Belize for drug-smuggling. Although purchased several months later by two "other" gentlemen from Florida, its subsequent service and history were not

well documented. In the mid-1990s, it ended up in the salvage yard in Washington state, where Manuel found it.

The third Goose they obtained had last been registered in Canada as C-FUMG (c/n B-145), and had crashed near Prince Rupert, British Columbia in December 1993, after experiencing engine problems. As a result of the crash, the pilot and the passenger in the co-pilot's seat were fatally injured, but the three other passengers seated in the main cabin, although also injured, survived. B-145 was notable as the very last Goose built by Grumman in 1945.

After obtaining the hoard of parts and the three salvaged airframes, the partners set up Antilles Seaplanes LLC as a formal company, named in tribute to Antilles Air Boats and the Caribbean legacy of the Goose. Very soon thereafter, people from all over the world started contacting them about buying the parts they needed to keep their own old Goose aircraft in the air. The volume of calls was sufficient to inspire the Antilles partners to consider manufacturing new parts as well. An engineering effort was undertaken to validate their legacy Grumman drawings and to prototype examples of the new parts, eventually leading to FAA-PMA certification for many new parts. Antilles also commissioned a new business plan, and carried out its own research from which it was calculated that a market for as many as 200 *new* Goose aircraft might exist.

By 2005, N1048V had been scrapped and the bare stripped-out fuselage had been sold to an individual in Pittsford, New York for use in rebuilding N327 (c/n 1051), which had crashed and burned near Penn Yan, New York in February that year. Antilles in the meantime had erected a new 20,000sq ft assembly plant in Gibsonville, North Carolina. They were also engaged in disassembling N641, c/n B-115, which they had bought in almost operational condition from Peninsular Airways (aka PenAir) of Anchorage, Alaska in 2001, and then re-building it completely from scratch with 100% new parts. That process, in which every part of the Goose was studied, documented and compared to the original Grumman blueprints, proved a very useful learning tool and served as an aid in the "reverse-engineering" of many parts and component assemblies of the Goose design.

After losing his original partner in December 2005 and investing some $7 million of his own, as well as borrowed money into the venture, Manuel received a boost when a North Carolina-based business syndicate invested "several million dollars" in Antilles Seaplanes, with a promise of even more to come if certain production and profit targets were met. That injection of financial capital enabled Antilles' parent company, Atlantic Coast Seaplanes LLC, to buy Type Certificate 4A24, all of the McKinnon Supplemental Type Certificates, and other engineering data for the G-21 series, from former owners Dan Vollum and Aero Planes LLC of Hillsboro, Oregon.

Manuel next enlisted the help of his brother Jeff, who had a background in automotive parts production and assembly lines through working for the multi-national corporation GKN. Jeff was also an experienced machinist who ran a commercial machine shop. Together they decided to build new "Super Gooses" based on the already approved and certified McKinnon model G-21G type design. Unlike McKinnon, who had originally just converted original Grumman G-21A airframes, they would do it from scratch, fabricating new parts with the aid of the Grumman and McKinnon engineering drawings. By installing modern avionics and using modern materials and finishes, they would produce a much improved version of the original Goose, which they calculated would turn a profit after only 16 new aircraft had been sold.

One of the targets set by the business syndicate was the roll-out of the first completely new Antilles G-21G "Super Goose" by the first quarter of 2009. However, the worldwide economic

recession hit both Antilles and its investor group, who were deeply involved in the declining real estate market, very hard. By March 2013, the roll-out of the first new airplane and the injection of additional funding had not happened.

In spite of the stagnant economy and being forced to temporarily lay-off almost all of its employees, Antilles Seaplanes remains dedicated to the G-21G project. A core team of managers who firmly believe in it and who share the original dream expressed by VL Manuel, continues to do what it can to search for new funding, plan for the time when they will be able to bring back the old employees and hire many new ones as well, and to start up production again. They also continue to provide technical support to the original McKinnon and Grumman G-21 aircraft still operating around the world.

Ellison-Mahon Gweduck

A project that began as an attempt to eliminate the corrosion problems associated with the Grumman Widgeon and other metal seaplane/amphibians, by building an aircraft using composite materials, developed over some five years into a complete re-design. The Gweduck, as the plane was named, is a completely new aircraft of modern composite construction, which nevertheless bears more than a passing resemblance to its Grumman ancestors.

It was designed by Ben Ellison, with the help and encouragement of Bryan Mahon, a seaplane enthusiast with much practical knowledge of seaplane operational issues. Unfortunately Bryan Mahon died in 2004 at the age of 92 and did not live to see the Gweduck fly, but his son Ross, who has contributed to the project since the beginning, continues to help with ongoing development.

The Gweduck is powered by two Lycoming IO-540 piston engines driving MT 3-blade constant speed propellers which can be feathered and reversed. With seating for two pilots and four passengers, the amphibian is projected to cruise at 135 knots on 60% power at 3,000 feet, with an 1,800 pound useful load.

The first aircraft, c/n 1, registered as

N204EM to Ellison-Mahon Aircraft Inc on 12th May 2006, made its first flight from Lake Washington in Washington State on 10th February 2008. Subsequent test flights with former Boeing test pilot "Buzz" Nelson, accompanied by Ross Mahon, demonstrated that the Gweduck's water handling was excellent and that the amphibian was very quickly up on the step and airborne, with no tendency to porpoise.

Runway trials, carried out at Renton Municipal Airport, Washington in May 2009, demonstrated what Ellison reported as "very good runway handling". Opposite rotation engines eliminate yaw torque and the aircraft tracks straight down the runway during take-off. Landings can be made either 3-point or main-wheel, again with docile handling characteristics.

Subsequent flight testing and flight operations, spanning much of North America, indicate considerable potential for this aircraft to service the recreational and utility markets. Water operations in particular have demonstrated easy to master flying qualities with excellent take-off performance even at high gross weights. Take-offs have been made in wind conditions of 25 knots and seas of 1.5 feet.

Downwind take-offs, both from land and water, have been demonstrated with 8 knots tailwind. Operations on the water have included driving the aircraft out of the water onto beaches and ramps, mooring to buoys and routine docking. With the retractable wing tip floats and reversing props, the Gweduck can be taxied conveniently up to a floating dock.

The Gweduck has been certificated in the Amateur Built category and will be marketed as a kit aircraft for amateur construction. By March 2013, Composite Creations Inc had been selected as the kit manufacturing partner to take the project forward. The first kit will be used for the FAA kit evaluation process, and for developing the builder documentation and fabrication of some incidental tooling and jigs. It could be a year before the first kit is complete, and a 'production' kit has been priced at $350,000 with an initial batch of five planned. Total cost to complete a Gweduck is estimated to be $700,000 or more, depending on the choice of avionics, interior and extra equipment.

The Gweduck takes on fuel at the dock in Eyak Lake, Cordova, Alaska on 30th April 2010. It drew the attention of several locals as well as the crew of a passing Blackhawk helicopter. The floats are retracted to allow the aircraft to tip and raise the shore-side wing to clear the dock. Ross Mahon can be seen with the fuel hose on top of the aircraft. (Jim Schoeggl)

C/n 1001, the first G-21, registered NC16910, looking as if some work has been done to the rear of the hull. This undated photo was taken at Ronkonkoma on Long Island (note the Aero Trades facility in the background). *(Grumman photo)*

APPENDIX 1:
G-21 GOOSE PRODUCTION LIST

In the following production list, all Bills of Sale to a new owner are from the previous noted owner,
unless otherwise stated, although some ownerships have been repeated to aid clarity.

Certificate of Registration validity data for aircraft on the US Civil Aircraft Register is correct to May 2013.

Canadian Certificates of Registration were issued with suffixes denoting whether for Private (P),
Commercial (C) or State (S) use.

In 1989 the requirement for renewing the Certificate of Airworthiness annually was dropped and instead
an annual statistical report was required on the aircraft's Due Date.

1001 Built as **G-21**. Experimental CofA applied for 29May37 and first flew same date from Bethpage on Long Island, NY. Registered as **NX16910** 02Jly37 at TFH:25hrs, and Transfer of Title (BoS) to Lloyd-Smith 03Jly37; delivered to co-owners, Wilton Lloyd-Smith and Marshall Field III, New York, NY on 16Jly37 by pilot, Steve Parkinson. The G-21 Approved Type Certificate, No.654 was awarded on 29Sep37 and thus the aircraft was re-registered as **NC16910** from that date, with Licence Authorisation to expire 10Mar38. This was renewed 28Feb38 to expire 04Feb39; uprated to **G-21A** standard during 1938 with CofR 01Jly39; TFH:672hrs a/o 14Jun39, and 982hrs a/o 14Jly40 when it was offered to the Royal Canadian Air Force. It was sold however by the estate of Lloyd-Smith to Aerovias Nacionales Puerto Rico, San Juan, Puerto Rico 19Sep40 for $40,000; CofR 29Oct40 to exp 15Jly41; cvtd from 8 to 10 place airplane 11Nov40 with CofA to exp 15Jly41; CofA and CofR renewed 16Jly41; authorization for a flight from San Juan, PR to Miami, FL for an engine change 29Oct42. BoS to Charles H Babb Co, New York, NY 30Jan43 at TFH:2,336hrs, when it was again offered to the RCAF and again refused. BoS to US Corps of Engineers, Edmonton, AB, Canada for work on the Canol ("Canadian Oil") project in Edmonton, AB, Canada 03Mar43 with CofR 04May43. The Goose was in fact purchased by the contractors on the project – WA Bechtel Company, HC Price Company and WE Callahan Construction Company- but all their purchases were re-imbursable by the US Government, so the Goose automatically became the property of the US War Department. A letter, dated 11May48, states that the Goose was transferred "to the HQ Alaskan Wing, Army Transport Command, Edmonton, AB, Canada for operation on the Canol Run". Fate uncertain but as far as can be ascertained when the project was completed all the surplus aircraft were buried on site.

1002 Built as **G-21** and registered **NC16911** to Henry Sturgis Morgan, New York, NY 25Aug37. Uprated to **G-21A** standard during 1938. Purchased by Dept of Munitions & Supply, Ottawa for the Royal Canadian Air Force 30Sep40, exported to Canada 16Oct40, wearing ferry markings **CF-BTF**, (the RCAF record card notes the seller to be 'JP Morgan'). Taken on RCAF strength at Rockcliffe with serial **940** 16Oct40 and known to the RCAF as **'Goose'** throughout its life; initially continued to wear its civilian registration letters; records state held as Stored Reserve at Rockcliffe 16Oct40 for one day until transferred to Western Air Command 17Oct40. After 1hour 5mins instruction on type (in CF-BTE c/n1005) followed by 15minutes solo in CF-BTE on 22Oct40, and 40minutes solo in CF-BTF on 23Oct40, F/O Archie Vanhee left Rockcliffe the following day, with LAC Smith as crew, to deliver CF-BTF to Vancouver. They reached Kenora, ON, via Kapuskasing, after 7hours 35minutes that day. The next day, 25Oct40, CF-BTF reached Lethbridge, AB via Regina, SK, after a further 6hours 10minutes flying time. On 28Oct40 Vanhee and Smith took CF-BTF from Lethbridge to Oliver, BC in 4hours 5minutes and arrived Vancouver (presumably Sea Island) 31Oct40 after a further 1hour 35minutes. Although RCAF serial 940 had been allocated, it is believed both civil and military markings were carried, ie. CF-BTF/940. Vanhee's log book shows CF-BTF delivered from Vancouver to No.13 (Operational Training) Sqn, Patricia Bay 04Nov40; coded 'AN-H' with No.3 (OT) Sqn by 14Mar41 when damaged in a heavy landing at Patricia Bay; taken to No.3 Repair Depot, Jericho Beach 29Apr41. Returned to service, date unknown, but presumably with No.13 (OT) Sqn as a further 350 flight hours recorded before going to Boeing Aircraft, Vancouver, BC (Sea Island) for overhaul 08Sep41. Off overhaul 22Jan42 and returned to WAC, Patricia Bay; with No.122 (Composite) Sqn, Patricia Bay by 27Feb42 when damaged at Ucluelet, BC (the lower hull was damaged when shear bolts on the main undercarriage failed. Aircraft was parked). Code 'AG-P' worn; used by No.166 (Communications) Sqn, Sea Island and transfer is assumed to have taken place circa 15Jly43 (No.122 (Comp) Sqn had a communications flight that deployed to Sea Island 15Mar43 and which was subsumed into the new No.166 (Comms) Sqn 15Jly43). The aircraft remained active within WAC, presumably with No.166 (Comms) Sqn although this detail does not appear on the record card, until at least Jun44; also reported to have seen some use with No.7 (Bomber Reconnaissance) Sqn (located at Prince Rupert until 23Apr44, then Alliford Bay); available for disposal within WAC 01Jun44. SOC 05Jan45 to War Assets Corporation (TFH:3,051hrs) with location stated as No.3 Repair Depot, Sea Island. WAC to Charles H Babb Co, Burbank, CA 22Jan45; registered as G-21A, NC16911 to Powel Crosley Jr, Cincinnati, OH 02Mar45. To Bahamas Airways, Nassau, Bahamas as VP-BAE, 16Dec46. To Pan American Airways Inc, New York, NY 03Jan47 as NC66020. Returned to Bahamas Airways Ltd 03Jan47 as VP-BAE. Written off in crash on Nassau South Shore 16Mar47 and cancelled from USCAR 25Mar47.

1003   Built as **G-21** and registered **NC16912** to E Roland Harriman, New York, NY 17Sep37. Uprated to **G-21A** standard during 1938. Purchased by the Royal Canadian Air Force in 1941; taken on RCAF strength at Rockcliffe with serial **942** 29Mar41 and known to the RCAF as **'Goose'** throughout its life; initially continued to wear its civilian registration NC16912. With No.12 (Communications) Sqn, Rockcliffe until assigned to Western Air Command 29Apr41 where further assigned to No.13 (Operational Training) Sqn, Patricia Bay. Coded 'MK-H' with No.13 (OT) Sqn by 03Oct41 when damaged at Patricia Bay (aircraft struck a corner of the seaplane hangar while taxying, damaging the port wing and propeller); to Boeing Aircraft, Vancouver, BC (Sea Island) for repairs and overhaul 08Oct41. Off repair 24Apr42 and returned to No.13 (OT) Sqn; later with No.122 (Composite) Sqn, Patricia Bay and then with No.166 (Communications) Sqn, Sea Island (transfer is assumed to have taken place circa 15Jly43 (No.122 (Comp) Sqn had a communications flight that deployed to Sea Island 15Mar43 and which was subsumed into the new No.166 (Comms) Sqn 15Jly43). The aircraft remained active within WAC, presumably with No.166 (Comms) Sqn, although this detail does not appear on the record card. By 24Jan44 with No.7 (Bomber Reconnaissance) Sqn, Prince Rupert, when involved in accident: while parked on the ramp at Prince Rupert, aircraft was struck by Canso 11107, also of No.7 (BR) Sqn, sustaining damage to the leading edge of the port wing. Repaired and available for disposal within WAC 08Nov44; SOC 09May45 to War Assets Corporation at TFH:2,260hrs with location stated as No.22 Repair Depot, Sea Island. Aircraft overhauled and engines rebuilt at Boeing Aircraft. CF-BHL allotted to Hamiltair Ltd, Princess Louise Inlet, BC on 24Apr45. BoS to Malibu Seaero Services Ltd 20Jun45 with CofR(C) 3181 for **CF-BHL** and CofA 728 05Jly45. BoS to B.N.P. Airways, Vancouver 06Nov50 with CofR(C) 9134 24Nov50. BoS to Central British Columbia Airways Ltd 22May52 with CofR(C) 10996 same date. Accident at 1515hrs on 27Jan53: aircraft crashed and sank near

Butedale, BC. The VFR flight left Port Hardy, BC at 1354 PST for Kemano, BC with five passengers, eta Kemano was 1545 PST. On passing Butedale at approximately 1510hrs and at about 800feet altitude over the Princess Royal Inlet, the pilot noticed a snow shower ahead and decided to make a precautionary landing straight ahead in the channel. During the approach to land the aircraft entered the snow shower, restricting the pilot's forward visibility. Just after touching the water, the aircraft was reported to have struck an object which tore a hole in the nose. The aircraft pitched into the water and turned over. The pilot and passengers donned life jackets but these were later removed and used as paddles to try and move the aircraft nearer to the shore. Only slow progress was made and with the approach of darkness, the cold weather, and the fear that the aircraft might suddenly sink, a vote was taken and they decided to attempt to swim ashore. The pilot was the only one to reach the shore, the five passengers perishing in the attempt. The pilot was found and rescued the following afternoon. The aircraft sank in deep water and was not recovered. Cancelled from CCAR 23Nov54.

1004   Built as a **G-21** and registered **NC16913** to Charles W Deeds (of United Aircraft), West Hartford, CT 28Sep37. Uprated to **G-21A** standard by 07Jan38. To Gillies Aviation Corp, Bethpage, Long Island, NY 21Jly41. To Pan American Airways Inc, New York, NY 21Jly41. Believed to have been acquired (or at least planned to have been acquired) by the US Navy in 1942 as a **'JRF-5'** and allocated BuAer serial **48229**. US Navy records do not record acceptance date or delivery date; location recorded as 'unknown' Aug44 to Feb45 (earlier records missing). SOC by BuAer 31Mar45; aircraft assumed to have remained with Pan American throughout this period and indeed on 1945 USCAR with Pan American A/W Inc, New York, NY and in active passenger use in early 1946. Cancelled from USCAR 22Aug47 to Argentina. Delivered to Morón Airfield, Argentina as NC16913. Registered **LV-AFP** by 18Aug47, to Carlos & Fernando Mihanovich, Buenos Aires, possibly acting as purchasing agents. To TARyTA, srl, San Carlos de Bariloche, Rio Negro 29Nov47. Sold to Federico Fuehrer, Buenos Aires (when TARyTA ceased operations) and reregd **LV-FDT** 18Jly51; TFH:6,202hrs a/o 02Oct51. To Hugo Gonzalez as **CC-CAO-0122** 31Oct51. To Walter Roth Minte 06Mar52 and transferred to Roth y Cia Ltda 05Aug52; CofR expired 31Aug54; TFH:7,850hrs a/o 19Jan61. Accident 22Jan62: crashed on take-off from the NW bank of O'Higgins Lake in southern Chile; two on board perished and a third died later in Santiago. The registration LV-FDT was finally cancelled when a special ruling, Disposición No. 172/96, was issued on 20Nov96.

      Note: *The aircraft marked as 'NC16913' on display at Garden City, NY is not c/n 1004.*

1005   Built as **G-21** and registered **NC16914** to The Chicago Tribune (Colonel Robert R McCormick), Chicago, IL 12Oct37. Uprated to **G-21A** standard during 1938. (Grumman photographs show this aircraft fitted with skis, but the author has found no evidence of use in this configuration. The photographs were possibly only for publicity purposes.) Accident Aug39: aircraft flipped over on landing; repaired; cancelled from USCAR 08Oct40 to Canada. Sold to the Royal Canadian Air Force and ferried to Canada as **CF-BTE**. Taken on RCAF strength at Rockcliffe with serial **939** 25Sep40 and known to the RCAF as **'Goose'** throughout its life. With No.12 (Communications) Sqn, Rockcliffe throughout its operational life. [Initially continued to wear its civilian registration letters. Last noted flight as CF-BTE 24Oct41 and first noted as 939 in end of month establishment 30Nov41 with first noted flight as 939 on 26Dec41.] To Canadian Car & Foundry, QC for major overhaul 21Oct43 ("time expired"); assumed to have come off overhaul 13Jun44 when available for disposal with No.3

C/n 1003, CF-BHL on the ramp at BNP Airways' hangar at Vancouver. This Goose crashed off the British Columbia coast on 27th January 1953, while on a flight from Port Hardy to Kemano, operated by Central British Columbia Airways.   *(via Ingvar Klett)*

C/n 1005, Shell Ecuador's Goose, Fleet Number 2, HC-SBB, moored to the floating landing stage in Rio Pastaza, near Macuma, Ecuador, circa 1945/46.   *(RI Baker via Kavelaars Collection)*

Training Command (No.12 (Comms) Sqn at Rockcliffe had been assigned to No.3 TC since 01Nov41); formally SOC to War Assets Corporation 04Oct44 (TFH:2,004:10hrs) with location stated as No.9 Repair Depot, St. Johns, QC. Already sold by WAC to Charles H Babb Co, Glendale, CA and then sold to Shell Ecuador as **HC-SBB** in Aug44; del to Ecuador Dec44. Based at Shell Mera in support of oil exploration, given Fleet No.2, and named *"Curaray"*. Overshot runway at Arajuno 06Feb45 but repaired. Propeller and one float damaged taxying off Rio Boco Villano 01Apr47. Repaired. Aircraft written off on 17Feb49, attempting a water landing on the Rio Curaray with one undercarriage leg down. The crew of two were slightly injured.

1006 Built as **G-21** and registered **NC16915** to Captain Boris Sergievsky, (chief pilot for the Sikorsky Aircraft Co), New York, NY 21Oct37; aircraft name: *"Orel"*. Uprated to **G-21A** standard during 1938. Offered for sale to the Royal Canadian Air Force in Aug41 at TFH:395hrs, but ntu and acquired by the USAAF and formally accepted 14Mar42. Designated **OA-13A** and allocated the serial **42-38215**. To Miami 31Jan43, presumably Pan American Field, and formally taken on charge by Pan American 27Apr43; transferred to their African-Middle East operations (ATC) 01May43 and to Central African Wing 29May43. SOC by ATC following an accident circa 1944, details unknown.

1007 Built as a **G-21** and registered **NC16916** to the President of Crosley Radio Corporation, Powel Crosley Jr, Sharonville, OH 02Nov37; aircraft name: *"Lesago"*. Uprated to **G-21A** standard during 1938, the aircraft was registered to Gillies Aviation, Long Island, NY sometime after 15Feb41 prior to sale to Royal Canadian Air Force. Taken on RCAF strength at Dartmouth with serial **943**; known to the RCAF as '**Goose**' throughout its life; initial allocation to Eastern Air Command at Dartmouth 25Aug41, where assigned to the Station Flight; No.12 (Communications) Sqn, Rockcliffe 01Nov41. Minor damage in storm at Rockcliffe 20Aug42 when thrown about in high winds, striking Goose 944, Electra Junior 7654 and Norseman 2477 (all of No.12 (Comms) Sqn). More seriously damaged in glassy water landing accident on Lake St Gabriel, QC, 12Aug43 when aircraft caught a float, overturned and sank; recovered to No.9 Repair Depot, Cap de La Madelaine. To Canadian Car & Foundry, Montreal, QC, 05Nov43 for overhaul; date of return to No.12 (Comms) Sqn (assuming it happened) not recorded, but made available for disposal by parent command, No.3 Training Command, 14Jly44. SOC to War Assets Corporation 22Nov44 (TFH:1,145hrs) with location stated as No.9 Repair Depot, Cap de la Madelaine. Registered **NC39084** to Major Arthur James

The remains of British Guiana Airways' Goose, VP-GAA, c/n 1007, after the crash on 2nd October 1952. After being rebuilt by Dean Franklin in Miami, the Goose served with Bahamas Airways, and later saw service on the run to Santa Catalina Island, becoming the longest surviving of the original G-21s. (John Havers Collection)

C/n 1007, the longest surviving of the original twelve G-21s, N10020, is seen here in the colours of Catalina-Channel Airlines, wearing Fleet Number: 3. (Jennifer Gradidge Collection)

Williams, New York, NY, founder of British Guiana Airways, 28Jly45. (Some confusion here, as British Commonwealth Office records show 39084 to be the American Certificate of Airworthiness number, although it does also quote "the same number appears on Aircraft Registration Certificate!"). A British Certificate of Airworthiness (No.7267) was issued 07Jly45 to allow the aircraft to be flown from Canada to British Guiana on 29Aug45. Accident 20Dec48: damaged when struck wharf on take-off at Georgetown, British Guiana; repaired; later as **N39084**; re-registered as **VP-GAA** to British Guiana Airways Ltd 15Sep50 and cancelled from USCAR 07Dec50. Accident 02Oct52: suffered severe damage to the bow landing on the Demerara River, at Georgetown. Further damage was inflicted during the salvage operation. Bahamas Airways bought the wreck as salvage for £2,000, intending to use it as spares. On further inspection, when the wreck arrived in Nassau, it was decided to send it to Dean H Franklin Aviation Enterprises in Miami for repair, at a cost of £10,600. VP-GAA was cancelled 11Dec53 and it entered service with Bahamas Airways Ltd as **VP-BAA**, named *"Andros"*, on 27Jan54. The aircraft suffered many unexplained and incurable vibrations and became unpopular with the Bahamas Airway's pilots. It was sold to Trade-Ayer Inc, NJ, 05Jly56, delivered 12Jly56 and regd **N10020**. Leased to Catalina Channel Airlines Inc, Long Beach, CA with FN:3 in 1959 and purchased by them 09Mar62. Registered to Paul Teng, Long Beach, CA 06Jan67. Accident at Catalina Island 07Mar69: substantial damage when hit submerged object on take-off. Returned to Pebbly Beach. Pilot + 6 uninjured. Re-regd as **N13CS** to Catalina Seaplanes Jun69. Accident 30Jly71: substantial damage when hit by landing N11CS (c/n 1166) in Avalon Bay. Pilot + 7 pax and 9 others in N11CS uninjured. During its time in California c/n 1007 was used on services from Long Beach to Santa Catalina Island. It was last noted derelict at Uplands, CA in 1978, then in a poor state at San Pedro, CA in 1980. The FAA cancelled the registration N13CS in Jan91. C/n 1007 was the longest surviving airframe of the original twelve G-21s.

1008 Built as a **G-21** and del to Asiatic Petroleum, New York, NY 25Oct37. (Asiatic Petroleum was the American purchasing arm of the Shell Oil Company). Crated and shipped to Sydney, Australia aboard *SS Port Darwin*, arr 26Dec37. Registered **VH-AAY** 10Jan38 and F/F Sydney-Rose Bay same date; flown to Papua for operation by Papuan Oil Development Pty Ltd. Arrived at Port Moresby 15Jan38. VH-AAY cancelled 20Jun39 and regd **PK-AES** 21Jun39. During 1939 the aircraft was used by Mijnbouw Maatschappij Nederlandsch Nieuw Guinea (MMNNG), the Dutch New Guinea Mining Company. The following year c/n 1008 was transferred to NV Bataafsche Petroleum Mij (BPM), the Batavia Petroleum Company. The Goose was ferried to Bandung, Java where Koninklijke Nederlandsch-Indische Luchtvaart Maatschappij (KNILM) the Royal Dutch Indies Airline Co overhauled the aircraft, and it was suitably re-registered **PK-BPM**. The delivery flight from Bandung to the NNGPM base at Babo was piloted by Captain Joop Vonk at the end of May 1939. Vonk and his maintenance chief, who was also on the flight, were very impressed by the fact that the G-21A lifted off the calm water in only 19 seconds – a great improvement over the Sikorsky S.38Bs which the Grumman replaced. Still on register 01Jan41. Fate uncertain but reported destroyed by enemy action at Koepang, Timor on 24Jan42.

C/n 1008 was the first Goose to be exported. It was shipped to Australia in late 1937 and registered as VH-AAY on 10th January 1938. After supporting oil exploration and mining activities in the Dutch East Indies, the aircraft is believed to have been destroyed by enemy action, as the Japanese advanced through Timor in 1942. (Grumman photo 6177)

1009 Built as a **G-21** and registered **G-AFCH** to Lord Beaverbrook, the British newspaper publisher, and delivered 26Oct37. It was delivered to Batavia, Dutch East Indies (wearing UK marks) for survey work with Koninklijke Nederlandsch-Indische Luchtvaart Maatschappij (KNILM) the Royal Dutch Indies Airline Co. Reregd **PK-AER** to Mijnbouw Maatschappij Nederlandsch Nieuw Guinea (MMNNG), the Dutch New Guinea Mining Company, Jly38. Believed destroyed by enemy action at Lake Tondano 26Dec41.

1010 Built as a **G-21** for Asiatic Petroleum, New York, NY with reg **VH-AAZ** reserved. Delivered to New York 17Nov37. Aircraft reregd as **PK-AKR** for NV Bataafsche Petroleum Mij (BPM) (the Batavia Petroleum Company), arriving by boat in Java (at Batavia?) in first half of 1938. With the Japanese advance in the area PK-AKR was evacuated from Borneo to Java 21Jan42, but despite this, was probably captured by the Japanese. Fate uncertain.

1011 Built as a **G-21** and ordered Aug37 by John Shaffer Phipps, New York, NY, with BoS 26Nov37. Regd to Phipps as **NC1294** 29Nov37 and uprated to **G-21A** standard in 1938. Reregd (address change) to John S Phipps, Palm Beach, FL 31Jan39; TFH:608hrs a/o 12Apr39; TFH:824hrs a/o 19Nov40 and TFH:1,089hrs a/o 18Nov41. Chief pilot for Phipps was Fred Gerald Powell of Mineola, NY. Allegedly gifted to the US Navy by the State of South Carolina although the contract number C97603 quoted on 07004's records suggests a purchase (perhaps funded by a retrospective donation) but circumstances of transfer from Phipps are nevertheless uncertain. Designated a **JRF-1** and allocated BuAer serial **07004** circa Dec41; accepted at NAS Anacostia 21Jan42; to NAS Norfolk 30Jan42 for major overhaul; issued (at least on paper) to MCAS Cherry Point 22Jly42 but no record of subsequent use and eventually SOC there 27Jly44. Phipps was reported on 08Mar48 as stating that the Goose was "sold to US government during WWII". NC1294 was cancelled 13Apr48. [The US Navy record card appears to incorrectly quote 07004's previous identity as 'NC1924']

1012 Built as **G-21** but converted to **G-21A** before delivery to Garfield A Wood, Detroit, MI, as **NC16917** on 09Dec37. Destroyed in a hangar fire in Miami, FL Apr38. Replaced by c/n 1017 (qv).

1013 Built as **G-21A**, 12May38. BoS Grumman Aircraft Engineering Corporation to John P Bickell 13May38 and US CofA for Export E-3838 issued 17May38; registered **CF-BKE** with CofR(P) 2261 and CofA 216 to JP Bickell, Toronto, ON, Canada 23May38. Mr Bickell, who was President of McIntyre Porcupine Mines, donated his Goose to the Royal Canadian Air Force shortly after the outbreak of war. Taken on RCAF strength 12Sep39, as CF-BKE at RCAF Stn Rockcliffe, Ottawa. Known to the RCAF as '**Goose**' throughout its life, the aircraft continued to wear its civilian registration letters above and below the wings; initially with No.12 (Communications) Flt, Rockcliffe (Ottawa) with whom it suffered minor damage 20Oct39. Serial **924** allotted to CF-BKE 26Oct39 and test flown same day wearing serial and registration. Temporary storage at Rockcliffe 06Jan40. No.12 (Comms) Flt, Rockcliffe 17Feb40. Assigned to Western Air Command 10Apr40; delivered to Vancouver, BC 17-19Apr40 and TOS 20Apr40. Initial use with Western Air Command appears to have been with No.120 (Bomber Reconnaissance) Sqn, Sea Island, with whom it suffered minor damage during a heavy landing on rough water in the Vancouver area 16May40; periodically loaned to No.6 (Bomber Reconnaissance) Sqn, Alliford Bay, BC circa Apr-Jly40; with No.111 (Coastal Artillery Co-operation) Sqn, Patricia Bay (still marked 924/CF-BKE) and on that unit's disbandment 01Feb41 to No.3 (Coastal Artillery Co-operation) Detachment; immediately assigned to Communications Flight, Western Air Command Headquarters, Victoria, although retained on No.3 Det strength; to Boeing Aircraft, Vancouver, for overhaul 26Sep41 (major overhaul, time expired) and while there believed transferred to No.122 (Composite) Sqn, replacing No.3 (CAC) Det 10Jan42; on return to WAC from Boeing 04Mar42 assigned to No.13 (Operational Training) Sqn, Patricia Bay and sometime coded 'MK-G'. To No.3 Training Command 03Oct42 and assigned to No.12 (Comms) Sqn, Rockcliffe; to Eastern Air Command 16Sep43 and believed assigned to No.167 (Communications) Sqn, Dartmouth; reassigned to No.3 Training Command 14Dec43, flying unit allocation uncertain but probably No.12 (Comms) Sqn, Rockcliffe. To No.3 Training Command (BCATP) 10May44; stored reserve No.3 Training Command 26May44 and approved for disposal 28Jly44 (2,159hrs). SOC to War Assets Corporation 01Jan45. BoS WAC (Montreal) to the broker Charles H Babb Co, New York, NY 22Jan45 with CofR **NC18175** 26Feb45; complete overhaul by Noorduyn Aviation Ltd, Montreal Jun45 with temporary CofA 18Jly45 for ferry, for which permission granted 21Jly45, to fly Cartierville-Montreal-Canadian border on delivery to Albany, NY via Burlington, VT; CofA issued 22Jly45. BoS to James C Marchant, Roslyn, Long Island, NY 24Jly45 with CofR 26Sep45. Accident 22Dec45 but aircraft rebuilt and repainted by Aero Trades, Roosevelt Field, Mineola, NY with CofA 12Oct46 and renewed 31Jan51 at TFH:1,132:10hrs. BoS to Western Newspaper Union, New York, NY 15May52 with CofR 21May52. BoS to Halliburton Oil Well Cementing Company, Duncan, OK 02Jun54 with CofR as **N121H** 16Jun54; CofA renewed 31Mar56 at TFH:2,566hrs. CofR revised for nominal change to Halliburton Company 08Aug60; retractable float kit per SA4-682 and gross wt. increase kit per SA4-1467 both installed Oct62. Cvtd to **McKinnon G-21E**, c/n **1211**, with 680hp PT6A-27 engines; CofA

issued 05May70 after 8hrs 15min of test flying, and CofR issued 03Aug71. Accident at 0800hrs on 02Sep71: struck dredging bucket during water landing at Westwego SPB, LA after a flight from Little Lake, LA; 2 crew and 4 pax uninjured; right wing and float damaged. BoS to American Aviation Inc, Brooksville, FL 22Nov91. BoS to Air Power Ltd, Hillsboro, OR 25Nov92 with CofR 10Dec92; address change to Medford, OR Mar93. BoS to Stallion Aircraft Inc, Bensenville, IL 01Jly94 with CofR 09Sep94. Accident 13Jun95: crashed on take-off at DuPage A/P, West Chicago, IL while being operated by John D Rodgers of Huntley, IL. Two fatalities, and report states that fire consumed aircraft. Reported to be with Air Classics Museum of Aviation, Aurora, IL in 2004 but still on USCAR registered to Stallion Aircraft. CofR expired 30Sep12 and cancelled from USCAR 30Jan13.

1014 Built as **G-21A** May38 and registered **NC20620** to Grumman Aircraft Engineering Corp. BoS to Joseph James Ryan, New York, NY 10Jun38. Pilot and right seat, and two chairs left side of cabin, equipped with back type parachutes; CofA 11Jun38. Accident 17Oct38: minor damage incurred at Glendale, CA. Ryan was later based at Juneau, AK and CofR and CofA were both issued 16Jun41 at TFH:825hrs "approx". BoS to Morrison Knudsen Company Inc, Anchorage, AK 25Jun42 with CofR 08Aug42. Letter from Morrison Knudsen to CAA 16May48 confirms "aircraft requisitioned by US Navy and sold to them at NAS Kodiak Nov42". Retrospectively allocated BuAer serial **99078** circa early 1945 with type reference **JRF-1**. Used in Alaska and based at NAS Kodiak; crashed while landing, wheels down, on a small lake at Narrow Cape, Kodiak 12Oct43 while operating from Kodiak, probably as NC20620 (the US Navy accident report identified the aircraft only as 'JRF-1 #1014'). The aircraft was badly damaged although technically repairable. SOC by US Navy at Kodiak 25Feb44 (the incomplete aircraft movement card for 99078 was raised some time after Aug44 as one of a batch of miscellaneous acquisitions and the records were not contemporaneously created). Still registered on 1945 USCAR as NC20620 to Morrison Knudsen Co Inc, but the 1948 correspondence also noted "later wrecked by them [US Navy] at Kodiak". Cancelled from USCAR 23Jun48.

1015 Built as **G-21A** and delivered to Lloyd Aereo Boliviano, La Paz, Bolivia 22Jun38, on Export CofA E-3963 dated 20Jly38. Aircraft regd as "*Moxos*". Allocated **CB-24** in May41, but probably not carried. Traded to US government 12Feb43 against $50,000 credit for purchase of Lockheed 18, c/n 2217, NC28357. To Rubber Development Corporation, Washington, DC and registered **NC30082** 23Feb43; based at Manaus, Brazil. To British Guiana Airways Ltd (BGA) and del to Georgetown Mar46. Reregd as **VP-GAD** 25Sep50 and NC30082 cancelled from USCAR 22Dec50. To Government of British Guiana 05Oct56, op by BGA. BGA became Guyana Airways Corporation on 01Sep63. New registration letters 8R-GAD allocated in 1966, but aircraft destroyed in a serious but non-fatal crash at Kamarang, Guyana 11Aug66, when still wearing registration VP-GAD. Remains taken to Timehri Airport, Georgetown where visible for some years.

1016 Built as **G-21A**. Purchased by on behalf of the Royal Canadian Air Force by the Canadian Govt from Gillies Aviation, NY; details of any temporary registrations unknown but ferried from Gillies to Fairchild Aviation Ltd, Longueuil, QC for modification to RCAF standards. Delivered to RCAF at Ottawa with serial **917** 26Jly38 and simply referred to as '**Goose**'; post-acceptance flights assigned 'B' Flt, No.7 (General Purpose) Sqn. Ottawa 02Aug38; undertook engine and airframe tests with the Test and Development Flight, Rockcliffe between 28Nov38 and 19Dec38, returning to No.7 (GP) Sqn. Damaged in cat 'C' accident at St Hubert 10May39; repaired and returned to No.7 (GP) Sqn 06Jly39; No.12 (Communications) Flt, Rockcliffe 19Sep39 [No.7 (GP) Sqn and the element known as the 'Communications Flight' was disbanded and replaced by No.12 (Comms) Flt 10Sep39 and Ottawa was re-named Rockcliffe]. Damaged while being moved at Rockcliffe 13Feb40 (port undercarriage collapsed and port wing struck the ground). Repaired but damaged again in wheels-up landing at Island Airport, Toronto, 17May40 when the undercarriage was forgotten during the landing checks; repaired and reassigned to Western Air Command 01Oct40 with No.13 (Operational Training) Sqn, Sea Island, moving to Patricia Bay 01Nov40; sometime code 'AN-S' applied. To Boeing Aircraft, Vancouver for overhaul 02Oct41; No. 122 (Composite) Sqn, Patricia Bay 23Mar42; damaged in wheels-up landing caused by mechanical failure at Sea Island 19Apr42; to Boeing Aircraft, Vancouver for repair 22Apr42; returned to No.122 (Comp) Sqn 07May42. Destroyed when aircraft flew into trees near Yakataga, AK 21Jly42. En route to Anchorage when flying from Yakutat to Cordova the crew encountered poor weather and descended to a low altitude to facilitate navigation. The aircraft crashed into trees on a mountainside killing one of the seven occupants (one of the survivors subsequently drowned while seeking help).

A memo, dated 13Aug42, from Flight Lieutenant GD Preston of No.122 (Composite) Squadron, Patricia Bay, BC reads:

"Search Party to Goose 917, American Civilian Members
1. When the occupants of Goose 917 had been located by the US Naval plane from Yakutat, and a note dropped at the emergency field at Yakataga, stating their position, four men set out in search of them. These men walked all that night, the next day and the next night, locating three men a short distance from where located by air, and guided them to the Yakataga Field.
2. On their return, we started to organize another party to proceed to the scene of the crash, where two other members of the crew of Goose 917 still remained. The four American men, tired as they were, were ready to start off again, but later we decided to spot the aircraft position first by air.
3. The next morning, these men accompanied me in aircraft Goose 940, to locate the position of aircraft 917. After locating the position of the crashed aircraft, we were able to land only a few miles from the scene of the crash. These men proceded up the mountain and brought out the remaining two survivors.
4. The help and experience of these men in the bush proved invaluable. I would like to recommend that these men be compensated in some way or other for their lost time and wonderful co-operation in the rescue of the survivors of 917.
5. These men have not asked for any re-imbursement, but it is felt that a gift of $40 or $50 to each man would create a feeling of goodwill towards RCAF personnel in Alaska."

The four men concerned were: Joe Meloy and BC Watson of Yakataga, AK and Don George and CAA Miller of Anchorage, AK. They each received $50 and a letter of thanks from AVM JA Sully.

The wreckage was recovered and reduced to spares at No.3 Repair Depot Jericho Beach, BC and SOC 23Oct42.

1017 Built as **G-21A** and registered **NC20643** to Garfield A Wood, Detroit, MI 08Jly38 as a replacement aircraft for c/n 1012. Acquired by the US Navy from Wood (trading as Aero Trades Co, Roosevelt Fld, NY) and accepted at NAS New York 20Jun42 as a **JRF-1**, BuAer **09782**; NAS Alameda 17Jly42 for dispatch to NAS Maui; NAS Maui 22Aug42; NAS Pearl Harbor (Pacific Fleet) date unk; A&R NAS Pearl Harbor 12Jly43; NAS Palmyra Island Nov43 and SOC there 31Jly44. Fate unknown.

1018 Built as **G-21A** and registered **NC20648** to The Texas Company Inc, New York, NY 30Jly38; FN:30, based at Houma, LA. Accident at 1330hrs on 20Jly39: left axle broke after striking end of amphibian ramp at Lafitte, LA. Accident at 1145hrs on 06Jly40: left wing hit oil derrick while taxying at Lake Pelto. Complete overhaul 14Apr41. Sold to US Government (US Navy) for $64,000, at TFH:1085hrs, 18Dec41, under Defense Requisition No.3634 dated 01Dec41. Overhauled at NAS San Diego and sold to Royal Canadian Air Force; taken on strength with serial **798** 17Apr42. Known to the RCAF as 'Goose' throughout its life; initial allocation to Western Air Command's No.122 (Composite) Sqn at Patricia Bay 17Apr42; used by No.166 (Communications) Sqn, Sea Island and transfer is assumed to have taken place circa 15Jly43 (No.122 (Comp) Sqn had a communications flight that deployed to Sea Island 15Mar43 and which was subsumed into the new No.166 (Comms) Sqn 15Jly43). To Canadian Pacific Airlines, Vancouver, BC 30Aug43 for overhaul; No.166 (Comms) Sqn, Patricia Bay 03Jan44; Canadian Pacific Airlines, Vancouver, BC 16Jun44 for overhaul; made available for disposal by parent command, WAC, 03Jly44 although location unclear. SOC to War Assets Corporation 05Jan45 (TFH:1,250hrs) with location stated as No.3 Repair Depot (Jericho Beach). Sold by to Charles H Babb Co, Glendale, CA, as **NC20648** on 22Jan45. Registered to Standard Oil Developing Co, New York, NY 21Feb45; R-985-AN-12B engines installed, camera and view finder, large emergency door on right side of hull, cargo sides and cargo floor in hull, all fitted Jly45. Foreign Flight Authorization approved 31Jly45 for delivery to Ecuador. Sold to Standard Oil Co (New Jersey), New York, NY 14Mar47 and aircraft operated in Colombia by 04Apr47; major overhaul 03Oct47. To RM Hollingshead Corp, New York, NY 18Jun48. To Asiatic Petroleum Corp, New York, NY. To Shell Company of Ecuador Ltd as **HC-SBV**, 23Mar49; N20648 cancelled from USCAR 14Apr49 as exported to Ecuador; Export CofA E-16672 28Apr49. Maybe Shell FN:4. Accident at 0800hrs on 28Apr49: crashed into Rio Pastaza, upstream from Shell Mera base, during a test-flight for single engined performance. Unfortunately the engine failed! Two crew, and one local on the ground, were killed. Aircraft written off and the wreck was removed by flood waters during the night of 12/13May49, leaving no trace.

1019 Built as **G-21A** and registered **NC2385** to Cornelius Vanderbilt Whitney, Old Westbury, NY Aug38. Also listed on 1939 and 1941 USCARs. Purchased by Royal Canadian Air Force (via Gillies Aviation) and taken on RCAF strength at Dartmouth with serial **944**; known to the

RCAF as '**Goose**' throughout its life. Initial allocation to the Station Communications Flight at Rockcliffe 30Sep41, but more formally to No.12 (Communications) Sqn, Rockcliffe 01Nov41; used between 02Nov41 and 15Nov41 to survey a winter route across the USA suitable for large flying boats, reaching El Paso, TX in process. Minor damage in storm at Rockcliffe 20Aug42 when thrown about in high winds striking Goose 943, Electra Junior 7654 and Norseman 2477 (all of No.12 (Comms) Sqn); made available for disposal by parent command, No.3 Training Command, 28Jly44. SOC to War Assets Corporation 01Jan45 (TFH:1,582hrs) with location confusingly stated as No.9 Repair Depot, St John's (No.9 RD was located at Cap de la Madeleine). Regd **NC2385** to Gulf Oil Company, Pittsburgh, PA 01Jan45. By 1966 N2385 was with Eichert Franklin Inc, Miami, FL and by 1973 with Chalk's Flying Service. Reregd as **N1621A**(2) in 1975. To Artco International Corp, Coral Gables, FL by Oct77. Sold to Aerolineas La Gaviota Ltda, San Andrés, cancelled from USCAR 28Oct77, and registered **HK-2059** Oct77. Noted on delivery through Opa Locka, FL 02Nov77; aircraft named *"San Andrés"*. Missing en route Isla de Providencia to Isla de San Andrés, with nine on board, 30Nov79. Aircraft written off and registration cancelled 06Apr81

1020 Built as **G-21A** and registered **NC20650** to Nevada Exploration, 18Aug38. To George Whittell/Thunderbird Lodge, Lake Tahoe, NV in 1939. USCAR 15Feb41 shows owner as Frank W Fuller Jr, San Francisco, CA. Sold to US government (US Navy). Overhauled at NAS San Diego and sold to Royal Canadian Air Force and taken on strength with serial **796**; known to the RCAF as '**Goose**' throughout its life; initial allocation to Eastern Air Command's No.145 (Bomber Reconnaissance) Sqn, Torbay 21Apr42. Severely damaged after ground-looping while attempting a landing in high cross-winds at Torbay 03Sep42; to Clarke Ruse Aircraft (location uncertain) for repair 20Oct42; returned to EAC 27Jan43, operating unit uncertain but with No.121 (Composite) Sqn, Dartmouth in early 1943 and later assigned to No.167 (Communications) Sqn, Dartmouth (the transfer is assumed to have taken place 15Jly43 when No.121 (Comp) Sqn's Communications Flight became No.167 (Comp) Sqn). To Canadian Car & Foundry for overhaul 08Feb44 where condition was found to be "poor"; allocated to No.9 Repair Depot, Cap de la Madelaine for write-off 07Jun44 and SOC 29Aug44. Registration **PP-XAN** allocated (probably Jly or Aug45) but not used. Aircraft ferried to Reykjavik, Iceland, arr 28Oct45. Registered **TF-RVA** to Loftleidir Icelandic Airlines 10Jan46. Cancelled 07Apr51 on sale to Cordova Air Services as **N1503V**. To Avalon Air Transport, in 1953 as FN:1. Sold to Kodiak Airways Inc, Kodiak, AK. CofA 19Aug56. Accident 24Dec61: crashed shortly after take-off from Old Harbor, Kodiak Island, AK. Aircraft destroyed by the impact and sank in 75feet of water. One passenger was drowned; pilot and three others rescued. TFH:8,694hrs.

G-21A, Goose, c/n 1020, NC20650, is seen in this undated photo prior to being sold to the Royal Canadian Air Force in 1942. The aircraft served post-WWII with Loftleidir in Iceland and ended its days with Kodiak Airways in Alaska, where it crashed and sank on Christmas Eve 1961.
(Peter M Bowers Collection)

1021 Built for US Navy as **XJ3F-1**, BuAer serial **1384**. NAS Anacostia for evaluation 09Sep38; NAS Norfolk 27Sep38; NAS Anacostia 04Oct38; INA Bethpage 02Nov38 and acc 04Nov38; NAS Anacostia 23Dec38; NAS Norfolk 21Feb41; NAS Lakehurst 22Jly41; A&R NAF Philadelphia 15Jly43; NAMC NAF Philadelphia 15Nov43; NAS Lakehurst by Aug44 and SOC there 31Oct45 as obsolete. Transferred to Department of Interior, Fish & Wildlife, Washington, DC Sep46 as **G-21A** with registration **NC727**; water rudder fitted. Sold to Catalina Channel Airlines, Long Beach, CA by Oct59 and re-registered **N2767A**. Accident 20Apr65: failed to maintain flying speed and stalled during climb-out after take-off from Pebbly Beach and crashed off Santa Catalina Island, CA. Two crew seriously injured but 7 pax uninjured. Aircraft substantially damaged, but still on USCAR 01Jan69. Not regd as of Jun82.

1022 Built for US Army Air Corps as **OA-9** with serial **38-556**. Acc 21Nov38 and del 26Nov38 to Wright Field where used by the Flying Branch. Suffered collapse of right landing-gear during landing at Cleveland MAP, OH 04Apr39 and taken to Fairfield Air Depot (Patterson Field) for evaluation and SOC 29Nov39 (TFH:69hrs).

1023 Built for US Army Air Corps as **OA-9** with serial **38-557**. Acc 10Mar39 and del to Chanute Field 14Mar39 where used by the Headquarters Sqn, Technical School; assigned 1st Air Force, Mitchel Field Jun41 and then to St John's, Newfoundland (the future Fort Pepperrell) 01Jly41 where used by 71st Base Headquarters Sqn. Destroyed in a fatal crash at White Hills, St John's 19Dec42 and SOC 02Jan43 (TFH:1,121hrs).

1024 Built for US Army Air Corps as **OA-9** with serial **38-558**. Acc and del to Langley Field 18Mar39 where probably used by the Base Headquarters and 1st Air Base Sqn. By sea to Hawaii 01Aug39 and taken on strength Hickam Field 17Oct39; 78th Pursuit Sqn, 18th Pursuit Grp, Wheeler Field Nov39. Wrecked in wheels-up landing at Wheeler 16Oct41 (by which time on strength of the Headquarters Sqn, 18th PG); to Hawaiian Air Depot (Luke Field, Ford Island) where initially thought repairable (Cat 3) but SOC 25May42 (TFH:692hrs).

1025 Built for US Army Air Corps as **OA-9** with serial **38-559**. Acc and del to Langley Field 27Mar39 where used by the 3rd Observation Sqn May-Jun40; Drew Field 04Jan41; MacDill Field circa Mar41; West Point Academy (loan) 18May42; Middletown Air Depot (Olmsted Field) 31Aug42; Bolling Field 01Oct42; West Point Academy 14Nov42; 320th BH&ABS Stewart Field 24Apr43. Ferried by ATC to Panama 02-17Mar44 via Newcastle, DE, Lake Charles, LA and Houston and Brownsville, TX; assigned 6th Air Force (Albrook Field, Panama) 17Mar44 and used by the Headquarters Flt. Destroyed in fatal ditching 4 miles NE of the Madden Dam, Panama 29Jun44 and SOC 19Jly44.

1026 Built for US Army Air Corps as **OA-9** with serial **38-560**. Acc and del to Mitchel Field 31Mar39 where used by the 97th Observation Sqn, IV Army Corps. Destroyed in a take-off accident at West Point Academy, NY 30Sep40 and SOC 06Feb41 (TFH:435hrs).

1027 Built for US Army Air Corps as **OA-9** with serial **38-561**. Acc 10Apr39 and del to Hamilton Field 14Apr39. By sea to the Philippines 25Jly39 and taken on strength by Philippines Air Depot, Nichols Field 07Nov39. Destroyed in a water landing accident Laguna de Bay, Rizal (adjacent to Nichols) 22Nov39 and SOC 22Mar40 (TFH:102hrs).

1028 Built for US Army Air Corps as **OA-9** with serial **38-562**. Acc 17Apr39 and del to Maxwell Field 20Apr39; Eglin Field 22Nov40 (although already on strength of 13th Air Base Sqn, Eglin by Jun40); Fairfield Air Depot 15Jan42; Bolling Field 24Feb42. Assigned 6th Air Force (Albrook Field, Panama) 12Mar42; detached to Brazil ('Military Intelligence') at Belem by 13Jun42 with formal transfer date 17Sep42; Panama 08Dec42; Brazil 22Jun43. Returned to US 14Sep43 and assigned to North Atlantic Wing, ATC 28Sep43; subsequent movements unrecorded but returned to US 22Apr44; assigned South Atlantic Wing ATC 01Jun44 and to the Caribbean Transport Wing 31Oct44; returned to US 18Nov44 to 4006th Base Unit, Miami (Miami Air Depot); 1103rd Base Unit, Morrison Field (Caribbean Division, ATC) 31Jan45. Damaged 02Jun45 when with the Air-Sea Rescue Sqn, ATC in water landing at Cat Cay, Bahamas; presumably repaired and SOC 02Nov45 to RFC, Bush Field, GA. Registered as **G-21A, NC86590**, with RFC, Washington, DC Nov45. Sold to Ellis Airlines, Juneau, AK Nov46, as FN:2. Accident 31May47 at Ketchikan. CofR as **N86590** issued 20Jun49. Cancelled from USCAR 30Sep50, reason unknown.

1029 Built for US Army Air Corps as **OA-9** with serial **38-563**. Acc and del to Bolling Field 24Apr39 where assigned to 2nd Staff Sqn. Wrecked in water landing accident 10May39, 3 miles NE of Point Lookout, Chesapeake Bay, MD; SOC 13Jly39 (TFH:22hrs).

1030 Built for US Army Air Corps as **OA-9** with serial **38-564**. Acc 01May39 and del to Gray Field, Fort Lewis 04May39 where assigned to 91st Observation Sqn (IX Corps); Savannah (Hunter Field) 08Dec40; West Point Academy, NY (loan) 18May42; Bolling Field 01Aug42; Middletown Air Depot (Olmsted Field) 21Aug42; Bolling Field 27Aug42; Middletown Air Depot 21Sep42; Bolling Field 01Oct42. To Military Attaché, Caracas, Venezuela 31Mar43; returned from Venezuela 04Aug44; 36th Street Apt (1105th AAFBU, Pan American Field, Miami, FL) 01Sep44 until departure from US to Panama 04Sep44; assigned 6th Air Force (Albrook Field, Panama) 15Sep44. Condemned in theatre by 6th Air Force 31Jan45 although circumstances unknown. Apparently returned to service by

G-21A Goose, c/n 1030, registered as CF-HFF, looking rather dull in this undated photo. It was probably taken in the mid-1950s when the aircraft was owned by Canadian Aircraft Renters Ltd. It was sold to Catalina Channel Airways, circa 1960 and was destroyed when it crashed on take-off from Avalon Bay, Santa Catalina Island, on 13th July 1964.
(Fred J Knight Collection)

Caribbean Air Command by 08Feb47 at Atkinson Field, Georgetown, British Guiana. Re-designated **ZA-9A** 01Jly48; 5918th Air Base Sqn, Atkinson AFB 25Jly48; 5920th Air Base Group, Waller AFB, Trinidad 01May49. Declared surplus 01Nov49 and SOC 22Nov49 to Foreign Liquidating Commission. BoS HQ Waller AFB, Trinidad to John B Bogart, Caracas, Venezuela 08Nov49, for $4,000. Registered as **G-21A, N51699**. BoS from Bogart to Canadian Aircraft Renters Ltd 18May53. Authority to ferry Miami, FL to Montreal, PQ 29Jun53. CF-HFF allotted to Canadian Aircraft Renters Ltd 30Jun53. US CofA for Export E-25663 issued 07Jly53. Registered **CF-HFF** with CoR(C) 12339 and CofA 4168 to Canadian Aircraft Renters Ltd, Toronto, ON 07Jly53; CofA renewed at TFH:2,551hrs valid until 07Jly55, and at TFH:3,051hrs valid until 16May58. Sold to Holladay Aviation Inc, Charlottesville, VA 17Oct57 and cancelled from CCAR 29Oct57. Sold to Catalina Channel Airways, Long Beach, CA as **N4221A**, FN:1, by Sep62. Leased to Standard Airways, Long Beach, CA 01Apr63. Accident 13Jly64: crashed on take-off from Pebbly Beach, Avalon Bay, Santa Catalina Island. Pilot + nine uninjured, but aircraft reported as "destroyed". Cancelled from USCAR 17Sep64.

1031 Built for US Army Air Corps as **OA-9** with serial **38-565**. Acc 05May39 and del to Pope Field 09May39 where presumably assigned to 92nd Air Base Sqn; Bolling Field 05Feb40 where assigned to 2nd Staff Sqn. Hull failed in water landing accident on the Anacostia River, DC 24Feb40 and SOC 13May40 (TFH:157hrs).

1032 Built for US Army Air Corps as **OA-9** with serial **38-566**. Acc 15May39 and del to Moffett Field 18May39 where assigned to 82nd Observation Sqn; the 82nd OS moved to Hamilton Field 12Sep40 (although base change is not recorded on record card). Aircraft damaged in landing accident at Hamilton 25Sep40 [record card shows 38-566 at Moffett until 18Jan42 and an unidentified OA-9 marked '10 9-AB' indicating the Moffett-based 9th Air Base Group was photographed at Moffett in Dec41]; Fairfield Air Depot (Patterson Field) 18Jan42; Bolling Field 12Feb42; assigned 6th Air Force (Albrook Field, Panama) 17Mar42 and to Albrook and then France Field/Panama Air Depot. Detached to Brazil ('Military Intelligence') by 17Sep42; Panama 08Dec42; to Brazil 05May43. Returned to US 14Sep43 and assigned to Caribbean Wing, ATC 16Oct43; subsequent movements unrecorded but returned to US 30Sep44; subsequent ATC movements unrecorded. Damaged (Cat 3, significant but normally repairable) in landing accident 24Apr46 10 miles west of New Amsterdam, British Guiana; presumably repaired as records show a return to the US 06May46 (to 1103rd AAFBU, Morrison Field, Miami) and a subsequent overseas departure 23May46; however then shown as condemned and salvaged 'overseas' by ATC 03Jun46.

1033 Built for US Army Air Corps as **OA-9** with serial **38-567**. Acc 22May39 and del to March Field 26May39; by sea to the Philippines 25Jly39 and taken on strength by Philippines Air Depot, Nichols Field 07Nov39; assigned to Nichols Field 29Nov39; assumed to have been the aircraft operated (dates uncertain) by the 2nd Observation Sqn at Clark Field until Nov40 and then at Nichols. Final flight appears to have taken place circa Nov41 (TFH:607hrs). Condemned and SOC at Philippines Air Depot 18Jan42 (formal strike action following Japanese capture of Philippines Air Depot).

1034 Built for US Army Air Corps as **OA-9** with serial **38-568**. Acc 01Jun39 and del to March Field 06Jun39; by sea to Hawaii 26Jly39 and taken on strength Hickam Field 17Oct39; Base HQ and 17th Air Base Sqn, Hickam by Jun40; briefly on charge Wheeler Field circa Dec39-Feb40.

Wrecked in forced landing at sea 300 yards offshore Kolo, Molokai, HI 16Jan41 when flown by 42nd Bomb Sqn pilot (assigned to 11th Bomb Group, Hickam) although aircraft by then on strength of 17th Air Base Group (TFH:135hrs).

1035 Built for US Army Air Corps as **OA-9** with serial **38-569**. Acc 05Jun39 and del to March Field 06Jun39; by sea to Hawaii 26Jly39 and taken on strength Hickam Field 17Oct39 [card date is 17Nov39 and is assumed to be in error]; 6th Pursuit Sqn, 18th Pursuit Grp, Wheeler Field circa Dec39; 78th Pursuit Sqn, 18th Pursuit Grp, Wheeler Field 20Jun40; to Hawaiian Air Depot (Luke Field, Ford Island) circa Mar42 where active until at least circa Nov42 by when TFH:642hrs. No more operational records until condemned and dropped from inventory at Hawaiian Air Depot by 7th Air Force (Oahu) 11Jun45, circumstances unknown.

1036 Built for US Army Air Corps as **OA-9** with serial **38-570**. Acc and del to Langley Field 12Jun39; to Puerto Rico 29Jun39 and in use with the Air Corps det, Borinquen Field when damaged in a forced-landing three miles south-east of Caguas, PR 05Mar40. To Middletown Air Depot, PA (Olmsted Field) for repairs 25Apr40 arriving circa Jun40; McChord Field 02Sep40; Hamilton Field 19Feb41 where assumed used by the 45th Air Base Grp; Bolling Field ('Military Intelligence') 01Sep42; detached to Brazil date unknown. Destroyed in non-fatal crash-landing at Boa Vista, Brazil 07Nov42, (pilot Arthur J Williams' assigned base was listed as Bolling Field); salvaged parts including wings to Atkinson Field, British Guiana; condemned and SOC 09Jan43.

Note: *Major Arthur James Williams was the founder of British Guiana Air Services.*

1037 Built for US Army Air Corps as **OA-9** with serial **38-571**. Acc and del to Langley Field 22Jun39; by sea to France Field, Panama 30Aug39, arriving Albrook Field circa Oct39; initially assigned to 15th Air Base Sqn, Albrook. Wrecked in non-fatal forced-landing at Rio Hato, Panama 31Jly40; local decision to write-off made 08Aug40 (TFH:175hrs). [see 38-572 below]

1038 Built for US Army Air Corps as **OA-9** with serial **38-572**. Acc and del to Langley Field 28Jun39; by sea to France Field, Panama 30Aug39, arriving Albrook Field circa Oct39; initially assigned to 15th Air Base Sqn, Albrook; assigned to 74th Attack Sqn, 16th Pursuit Grp (becoming 74th Bomb Sqn 01Nov39). Suffered minor damage in a forced-landing on Gatun Lake, Canal Zone 03Oct39 but then wrecked in a water landing accident at Tigre Island, San Blas, Canal Zone 12Dec39. SOC 16Feb40 (TFH:114hrs). [1st Lt Thomas C Darcy was the pilot of both 38-571 and 38-572 for their final landings. Clearly neither these nor other incidents were held against him and General Darcy's final flying command was that of the USAF Fighter School].

1039 Built for US Army Air Corps as **OA-9** with serial **38-573**. Acc 10Jly39 and del to Barksdale 14Jly39; to France Field, Panama 30Aug39; to 25th Bomb Sqn, 6th Composite Bomb Grp, France Field Sep39. Involved in a minor landing accident at Jaque, Panama 11Sep39; to 16th Air Base Sqn, France Field. Involved in a repairable water-landing accident at La Palma, Panama 04Dec39; assumed transferred to 26th Fighter Command when so formed at Albrook Field 06Mar42 and with the Headquarters Sqn, 26th FC when again damaged in a landing accident at Anachuona Bay, Panama 07Jly42. To Panama Air Depot (France Field) for Cat 3 repairs 11Aug42; with 6th Air Force as of 28Feb43 (Albrook Field); PAD work completed Mar43. No more operational records until condemned 29Jan44 (6th Air Force noted it to be at the Albrook depot as of that date in a state of decrepitude beyond economical repair and unsafe). Dropped from inventory by 6th Air Force 17Mar44.

1040 Built for US Army Air Corps as **OA-9** with serial **38-574**. Acc 14Jly39 and del to Barksdale 18Jly39; by sea to France Field, Panama 30Aug39; initially assigned to 16th Air Base Sqn, France Field; to Albrook Field circa Jun40. Wrecked in accident on Gatun Lake, Canal Zone 20Jan41 and SOC 03Jun41 (TFH:189hrs).

1041 Built for US Army Air Corps as **OA-9** with serial **38-575**. Acc and del to Mitchel Field 20Jly39; by sea to Hawaii 01Aug39 and taken on strength Hickam Field 17Oct39 [card date is 17Nov39 and is assumed to be in error]; to Wheeler Field Nov39 and with 19th Pursuit Sqn, 18th Pursuit Grp, Wheeler Field by Jun40; to Headquarters Sqn, 18th Pursuit Grp. Wrecked in rough sea landing accident, 300 yards offshore Bellows Field, HI (Waimanalo Bay) 17Nov41. Wreck taken to Depot (Luke Field?) but destroyed in depot shops during Japanese attack 07Dec41 (TFH:562hrs).

1042 Built for US Army Air Corps as **OA-9** with serial **38-576**. Acc and del to Bolling Field 08Aug39 and assigned to the 1st Staff Sqn by Jun40 when record card noted 'Special Eqpt – Chief of Staff' ; (on paper) at Middletown Air Depot (Olmsted Field) 27Dec41; assigned Atkinson Field, British Guiana 28Dec41 and received Feb42. Damaged in take-off accident at 'Georgetown' (assumed to be Atkinson Field) 06Jly43 when on the strength of the 347th Air Base Group; repaired and returned to the 347th ABG, Atkinson 24Aug43; to 347th Service Group, Atkinson 23Nov43. More seriously damaged in landing accident (cat 4 – normally a write-off) at Zandery Field, Surinam 04Mar44 when on strength of 551 Service Sqn, 347th Service Grp, Atkinson. No further records until condemned for parts salvage by 6th Air Force 09Mar47; administratively recorded as assigned to Caribbean Air Command 30Apr47 and finally SOC 10Jun47.

1043 Built for US Army Air Corps as **OA-9** with serial **38-577**. Acc 21Aug39 and del to Hamilton Field 27Aug39 and assigned to the 5th Air Base Sqn by Jun40; subsequently assigned to the 45th Air Base Sqn, Hamilton. Wrecked in a landing accident on Clear Lake, CA 09Dec40 (aircraft sank); SOC 18Mar41 (TFH:295hrs).

1044 Built for US Army Air Corps as **OA-9** with serial **38-578**. Acc and del to Langley Field 01Sep39 and assigned to the Air Base Flight Section, GHQ Air Force by Jun40; Middletown Air Depot (Olmsted Field) 02May42; Eglin Field 30May42; Bolling Field 04Aug42; detached to Peru ('Military Intelligence') 17Sep42; South Atlantic Wing, ATC 22Oct43. Subsequent movements not well recorded but returned to US from an overseas assignment 12Jun44; 1455th Base Unit, Gore Field 01Sep44; 1103rd Base Unit, Morrison Field, Miami, FL 26Oct44. Sustained moderate damage (cat 3) in a landing accident at Bom Fim Lake, Natal, Brazil 23Jun45 and condemned for salvage by South Atlantic Wing, ATC 06Sep45.

1045 Built for US Army Air Corps as **OA-9** with serial **38-579**. Acc 11Sep39 and del to Maxwell Field 12Sep39 where assigned to the 13th Air Base Sqn; Eglin Field 22Nov40; Maxwell Field 27Feb41; Orlando, FL (temporary loan) 07Apr41; Eglin Field 01Jly51 (probably assigned to 54th Bomb Sqn, 23rd Composite Grp); Wright Field 29Jly41; Eglin Field 30Sep41; West Point Academy, NY 25May42; Bolling Field 21Jly42; Middletown Air Depot (Olmsted Field) 25Jly42; Military Attaché, Tegucicalpa, Honduras ('Military Intelligence') by17Sep42; Panama Air Depot (France Field) for repairs 11May43 that were completed in May43; Stewart Field 03Jun43; to an unidentified overseas Service Command Unit/Military Mission 31Dec43, returning to US (but maybe only on paper) 15May44; to 6th Air Force (Albrook Field, Panama) 19Jun44 and SOC (condemned/surveyed) 17Jly44. BoS US War Dept, New Orleans, LA to Pan American World Airways Inc, New York, NY 18Sep44 for $7,500. BoS to Aerovias Nacionales de Colombia, Barranquilla, Colombia 25Sep44 for $7,500 at TFH:1,652hrs; a note on the BoS stated: "plane damaged beyond economical repair while in public service"; regd **C-99**. Application for ferry permit for Pan Am **NC1309** from Canal Zone Air Terminal, Balboa Heights to Barranquilla, Colombia 15Nov44. Application for CofR NC1309 by Pan Am 29Nov44. CofA issued 02Dec44 and ferry permit granted 03Dec44. BoS to Texas Petroleum Co, Bogota, Colombia 14May45 for $50,000. Application by Texas Petroleum Co for ferry permit from Barranquilla to Bethpage, NY was granted 30Oct45. Meanwhile BoS to Charles H Babb Co, New York, NY 03Jan46. BoS to Gulf Research & Development Corp, Pittsburgh, PA 07Jan46 with CofR **NX33178** 16Mar46, and CofA same date after inspection and repair by Grumman Aircraft Engineering Corp. CofA issued 23Apr46 "for operation of experimental equipment in connection with survey work for oil and other geophysical purposes"; renewed 27May47 and 26May48. NC1309 cancelled from USCAR 06Mar48. BoS to ML Hardy, Waynesboro, PA 24Mar50 with CofR NX33178 21Apr50. BoS to Genesee Airport Inc, Rochester, NY 12May50 with CofR 01Jun50. BoS to Stanley W Donogh, Bellevue, WA 17Apr51 with CofR 30Apr51; CofA 28May51 at TFH:1,519hrs (sic). BoS to OW Tosch, Nome, AK 02May52 with CofR 09May52; address change to Seattle, WA 15Jun54 and by Oct55 dba Tosch Flying Service, New Orleans, LA. Reregd **N60X** 11Oct55. BoS to The California Company, New Orleans, LA 30Apr57 with CofR 06Jun57; nominal change to The California Co, a division of California Oil Co, New Orleans, with CofR 07Apr61; and later The California Co Division of Chevron Oil Co. Increase in gross weight to 9,200lbs per STC SA4-1467 including installation of retractable wingtip floats per STC SA4-682, during major overhaul completed 18Dec61. Accident Jun63: aircraft damaged by windstorm at Leeville, LA; returned to New Orleans A/P on ferry permit dated 21Jun63 and repaired by 01Jly63. Accident 08Apr64: substantial damage when gear collapsed on landing Lafayette, LA. 2 crew uninjured. BoS Chevron Oil to McKinnon Coach Inc, Sandy, OR 03Jan74 with CofR 29Jan74. Letter to FAA from McKinnon 31Jan74 confirming sale to Sooke Forest Products; cancelled from USCAR 06Mar74 as exported to Canada. Registered **C-GHAV** with CofR(P) to Sooke Forest

Products, Victoria, BC, Canada 19Mar74. CofA lapsed 31Mar82. Offered for sale Sep85, at TFH:13,498hrs, for US$225,000 by Coopers & Lybrand Ltd, Vancouver who acted as trustees when Sooke Forest Products went bankrupt. Inspected Jan86 and CofA renewed valid until 08Jan87. CofR(P) to Coulson Helicopters Ltd, Port Alberni, BC Jan87. CofR(C) to Oakley Air Ltd, Vancouver, BC, Canada 22Feb88. Accident 06May91: crashed on approach to Squamish Airport, BC killing owner/pilot Cliff Oakley and his passenger. Aircraft burnt out and written off. Cancelled from CCAR 29May91.

1046   Built for US Army Air Corps as **OA-9** with serial **38-580**. Acc and del to West Point Academy, NY 21Sep39 and used by Army Air Corps det there until May44; assigned to 6th Air Force (Albrook Field, Panama) 18May44 and SOC (condemned/survey) 08Jun44.

1047   Built for US Army Air Corps as **OA-9** with serial **38-581**. Acc 02Oct39 and del to Wright Field 09Oct39 where used by the Flying Branch; assigned 1st Air Force (Mitchel Field) and briefly at Mitchel prior to permanent transfer to St John's, Newfoundland (the future Fort Pepperrell) 01Jly41; Middletown Air Depot (Olmsted Field) 18May42; Newfoundland 20Jly42. Subsequent records are confusing with apparent reference to an 'accident' 17Nov42 and then no further records until 1946 when shown as 'wash out' 16Mar46 (but entry made 14Oct47). Also shown as lost to inventory 01Jun46 in Newfoundland; administratively recorded as assigned to ATC Atlantic 30Apr47 and finally SOC 18May48. [This could conceivably be the aircraft involved in the 'Hap' Arnold incident mentioned on page 124]

1048   Built as **G-21A**. Purchased by Asiatic Petroleum Corporation, New York, NY and registered **YV-VOD-2** for Shell's affiliate, Venezuelan Oil Development Corporation, 09Dec38; Export CofA E-4587 dated 28Dec38. The aircraft was based at Maracaibo, Venezuela until 14Apr42 when it arrived at Shell Mera and ownership was transferred to Shell Ecuador. Reregd as **HC-AAM**, FN:1; returned to Grumman 23Jly42 for installation of camera hatch; returned to Grumman for overhaul 23Mar44-24Oct44 and by Aug45 reregd as **HC-SBA**, and named "*Rio Napo*". Damaged in accident Aug45 and returned to US (Mexican overflight permit 20Aug45) for repairs - i/s Dec45. Damaged in accident at Shell Mera 23Aug47. Cost of repair $8,000. Belly landed at Villano, Ecuador 02Aug49 "destroying fuselage". Aircraft returned to Grumman for rebuild. Between Dec38 and Apr50, 1048 flew 4,110hrs in Shell service. Registered **N702A** to Grumman Aircraft Engineering Corp 17May51. To Amphibious Airways Inc, Miami Beach, FL (Chalk's) 1954. Regd to Chalk's Airline by 1968, as FN:9 and named "*Blue Marlin*". Registered to Thomas A Nord, Pembina, ND in 1969, with CofR 30Sep71 as **N14CS** with Catalina Seaplanes Inc, San Pedro, CA; became Air Catalina in Sep74. To Warbirds West/ Dennis Buehn, Compton, CA Dec82, and via the Naval Aviation Museum, Pensacola was registered to the Smithsonian NASM, Washington, DC 30Jun83. Cancelled from USCAR Jun85. Restored by Buehler Aviation, Fort Lauderdale, FL and displayed in the NASM Hall of Transportation as "**NC702A**", from 1989. It was moved to the newly-opened Steven F Udvar-Hazy Center, near Washington's Dulles Airport in December 2003. Displayed in main hall in yellow/black colour scheme, and last noted May12.

G-21A Goose, c/n 1048, HC-AAM, was operated by Shell Ecuador in support of their oil exploration work in the Oriente region of Ecuador. It is seen here moored to the bank of the Rio Curaray, near the geological base camp at Lorocachi, in March or April 1943.
(JJ Dozy via HC Kavelaars Collection)

1049   Built as **G-21A** Dec38. Export CofA E-4555 dated 23Dec38; registered **G-AFKJ** for Lord Beaverbrook, Leatherhead, Surrey, UK 27Dec38; UK CofA dated 04Jan39. Beaverbrook used the aircraft on a hunting trip in Africa in 1939 and then had it shipped to USA for his use when on trips there. WWII started and the aircraft remained in storage except when used by the Inter-American Escadrille Inc. (IAE) for a Civil

Air Mission to South America; regd as **NC37000** to Laurance S Rockefeller. By Jan42, after much argument with the US authorities, Lord Beaverbrook had decided to hand over the Goose to the UK Air Ministry although by then he had created enough confusion to cause the Ministry of Aircraft Production to initially allocate the aircraft to the RCAF rather than the RAF (presumably because Beaverbrook was a Canadian). It was then taken on RAF charge 18Feb42 and overhauled at the Naval Aircraft Factory at Lakehurst, NJ using Lend-Lease funds. On 31Mar42 a cable stated that the Goose had been delayed because of trouble with the fuel tanks, but "should be ready for shipment to England by April 9th". While in transit to the UK it was allotted the RAF serial **MV993** 'for the Minister of Aircraft Production' (ie the ATA) 31Jly42 and the civil registration G-AFKJ was cancelled. It was TOC at Lockheeds, Speke 21Aug42 and served first with the ATA at White Waltham, and then 24 Sqn at Hendon, with name "*Thurso Castle*", being used for communications duties and as a VIP transport, from February 1943 until July 1944. Part of 24 Sqn became Metropolitan Communications Sqn on 08Apr44 and the Goose was transferred there on 26Jan45. Accident 02Sep45: strut collapsed and penetrated float which filled with water at Calshot and aircraft capsized. Fate unknown.

1050   Built as **G-21A** and delivered to Peruvian Air Corps at Bethpage 24Dec38 with serial **2TP-1H**. Export CofA E-4600 dated 05Jan39, but actual delivery date to Peru reported to have been 24Mar39. Initially operated by the Sección de Transporte, Escuadrón de Aviación No.2, at Las Palmas, Lima. Subsequent service use difficult to track and reader is referred to the Peru military narrative (page 111); by a process of elimination the aircraft is known to have been lost by April 1945 (either on 06Dec43 or 10Apr45). See also c/n 1052.

1051   Built as **G-21A** and delivered to Peruvian Air Corps 30Dec38 with serial **2TP-2H**. Export CofA E-4623 dated 10Jan39 and reported to have been delivered through Albrook Field, Panama 21Aug39. Initially operated by the Sección de Transporte, Escuadrón de Aviación No.2, at Las Palmas, Lima; early service use difficult to track and reader is referred to the Peru military narrative (page 111); assumed to have been assigned to the 61 Escuadrón Fotográfico at Las Palmas from at least Oct46 until at least Jun50. Re-serialled circa 1950 on creation of the Air Force becoming **323**; 31 Escuadrón de Información Estratégica, Piura by Jun54 until at least Jun58. Declared surplus and bids invited 15Jly58; BoS 29Sep58 for $8,500 (plus $1,000 for aircraft's overhaul by FAP) (or $8,600) to Elwood R Alexander of Dasatour Travel Agency, Lima. BoS to Avalon Air Transport, Long Beach, CA 08Oct58, for $8,600. Ferry permit from Lima to Long Beach 26Nov58. CofR **N327** 31Dec58; cvtd to civilian use and repainted Feb59 with CofA 20Mar59 at TFH:1,816hrs; FN:1, replacing c/n1020. CofA 24Jun60. Accident 08Oct61: crashed and sank Avalon Bay, Santa Catalina Island, CA. Cancelled from USCAR as destroyed 11Jun70. BoS to Golden West Airlines Inc 10May72. BoS to Carrier Aircraft, Long Beach, CA 15May72 for $500. BoS to Wilton R Probert, Long Beach, CA 19May72 for $550 with CofR N327 08Jun73. BoS to KC Aircraft Sheet Metal Inc, Long Beach, CA 24May74 for $500. BoS to Southeast Skyways Inc, Juneau, AK 25May74 with CofR 18Jun74. BoS to Charles F Willis III Co Inc 15Jun79. BoS to Robert L Hall, Kodiak, AK 20Jun79 with CofR 12Jly79; to be op by Kodiak Western Airlines. Flown at Honolulu, HI 1982, as "**NC327**" "*Cutter's Goose*" for the TV series "*Tales of the Gold Monkey*"; displayed at Universal Studios, Los Angeles by Feb83. Major overhaul 19Jly83 to 27Apr85 by Aeroservice, Arlington, WA. Incident reported at Sitka, AK 20Aug85. BoS Hall to Classic Restorations Inc, Wilmington, DE 14Sep88 with CofR 07Oct88; reported stored at Cradle of Aviation Museum, Garden City, Long Island, NY in 1992. BoS to James W Chrysler, Seattle, WA 18Mar94 with CofR 05Apr94. Accident at TFH:8,279hrs, on 22Jly94: substantial damage when left landing gear collapsed after landing at Bremerton, WA (pilot + 2 pax uninjured). BoS to

G-21A Goose, c/n 1051, NC327, at Honolulu, Hawaii, in December 1982, painted as "Cutter's Goose" for the television series "Tales of the Gold Monkey".
(John Wegg)

Cliff Larrance, dba North Coast Aero, Port Townsend, WA 14Jan97 with CofR 25Feb97. Incident at Bremerton, WA 09Aug98. BoS to Thomas McDonald, Whitehouse Station, NJ 19Aug98 with CofR 16Dec98; address change to Clermont, FL 29Oct99. BoS to Killa Katchka Inc, West Bloomfield, MI, 16May00 for $230,000, with CofR 31Aug00. BoS to Jetcraft Corp, Raleigh, NC 23Jly04 with CofR 30Jly04. Accident 15Feb05: crashed during training flight at Penn Yan, NY. The instructor reduced power to right engine, aircraft lost altitude, and crashed in flames; no fatalities. Wreckage sold by the insurance company to Samuel P Damico, Pittsford, NY 28Feb05 for rebuild (using parts from c/ns B-46 and B-97 and the wing centre section of B-145); CofR 02May05, and current May13, with CofR due to expire 30Jun14.

1052   Built as **G-21A** and delivered to Peruvian Air Corps at Bethpage 19Jan39 with serial **2TP-3H**. Export CofA E-4676 dated 27Jan39 but actual delivery date to Peru reported to have been 24Mar39. Initially operated by the Sección de Transporte, Escuadrón de Aviación No.2, at Las Palmas, Lima. Subsequent service use difficult to track and reader is referred to the Peru military narrative (page 111); by a process of elimination the aircraft is known to have been lost by April 1945 (either on 06Dec43 or 10Apr45). See also c/n 1050.

1053   Built as **G-21A** and delivered to Peruvian Air Corps 01Feb39 with serial **2TP-4H**. Export CofA E-4773 dated 17Feb39, but actual delivery date to Peru reported to have been 24Mar39. Initially operated by the Sección de Transporte, Escuadrón de Aviación No.2, at Las Palmas, Lima; early service use difficult to track and reader is referred to Peru military narrative (page 111); assumed to have been assigned to the 61 Escuadrón Fotográfico at Las Palmas from at least Oct46 until at least Jun50. Re-serialled circa 1950 on creation of the Air Force becoming **324**; 31 Escuadrón de Información Estratégica, Piura by Jun54 until at least Jun58; declared surplus and bids invited 15Jly58; BoS 29Sep58 for $8,600 (inc $1,000 for aircraft's overhaul by FAP) to Elwood R Alexander of Dasatour Travel Agency, Lima. BoS to Avalon Air Transport, Long Beach, CA 08Oct58 for $8,600. Regd as **N328**, FN:2, replacing c/n 1125. To Catalina Air Lines Inc, Long Beach, CA by 1964. Non-fatal accident 05Feb67: substantial damage at Long Beach, when blown over by prop wash from departing C-119. To Antilles Air Boats, Christiansted, US Virgin Islands by 1968. (Antilles ceased operations 1981.) (N328 used as ferry registration for delivery of B-46 (qv) from Guyana, Apr73). To Dean H Franklin Enterprises Inc, Miami, FL 16Mar92. To Worldwide Aviation Distributors Inc, Miami, FL with CofR 07Feb00. Current May13, but with no CofA and CofR due to expire 31Dec13.

1054   Built as **G-21A** and delivered to Gillies Aviation, Hicksville, Long Island, NY 17Feb39 as **NC3055**; CofA issued 18Feb39; used as a demonstrator. Permission granted 11Oct39 for a flight from New York to Cuba via Miami by Franklin T Kurt, to take Dr L Soro and three of his family members back to Havana. Offered for sale to RCAF 12Jan40 at TFH:275hrs for US$63,100, and although Kurt flew the aircraft to Canada 01Apr40, presumably for a demonstration, the offer was ntu. Sold to The Texas Company, New York, NY, 14Jun40 at TFH:320hrs and CofA issued 30Aug40; used by Texaco's Producing Department's Louisiana-Arkansas Division, initially at New Iberia, LA. CofA 02Apr41 at TFH:649hrs; tfd to Houma, LA (FN:34) early 1942, to replace c/n 1018. Major overhaul Mar43 by Southwest Airmotive Co, Dallas, TX. Sold to Malcolm L Hardy, Waynesboro, PA 23Nov48 for $28,500; tfd by BoS to Hardy Aviation Inc, Waynesboro, PA, 24May49. To Grumman Aircraft Engineering Corp, Bethpage, NY 25Jly49; reregd **N704A**, 01Aug49. Sold to McKinnon Enterprises Inc, Sandy, OR, 05Apr60; retractable floats fitted. Reregd **N33S** 31Mar61 and to Sun Oil Company, Philadelphia, PA, 29Apr61. BoS to Pan Air Corporation, New Orleans, LA, 05May66 for $62,552.92, with CofR 27Jly70. To Goose Transport Inc, Gainesville, FL, 17Aug79 and CofR issued 24Jan80. Reported "destroyed" by crashing Beech 18, N43L 10Sep80. Seized by Belize Government, 09Nov82, after alleged use for drug running, and ordered to be forfeited 24Mar83 after a court hearing. Sold by Belize Government for Blze$20,000 and del to purchasers Jeffrey E & Robert A Johnson of Fort White, FL, 11Jly83 at Sartenejo village in the Corozal District of Belize. To Jeffrey E Johnson (co-owner), Fort White, FL, with CofR 12Dec83. Re-registered as **N66QA**, 14Jan84 and placed on aircraft 18Jan84. To Waterlines Ltd, Wilmington, DE with CofR 11Mar85. Still "active" Jun97. Wreck found in Discount Aircraft Salvage yard in Deer Park, WA by staff from Antilles Seaplanes LLC. Purchased and taken to Gibsonville, NC where it is stored. Still (wrongly) listed May13 as owned by Waterlines, and airworthy, but CofR had expired 31Mar11.

1055   Built as **G-21A** Dec39. BoS Grumman Aircraft Engineering Corp to CB Wrightsman, Houston, TX 11Jan39 as **NC3022** with CofA 12Jan39. BoS to Standard Oil Co of Kansas, Houston, TX 19Jan39. CofA

31Dec40 at TFH:609hrs. BoS to British American Ambulance Corps Inc, New York, NY 28Apr41 with CofR 24Jun42 and marked with its titles. Sold, probably at nominal price, to the UK government 22Sep41 and cancelled from the USCAR 21Aug43. Allocated serial **HK822** by Air HQ Middle East circa Nov41; packed and shipped to 107 MU, RAF Kasfareet, Egypt and then flown to RAF Habbaniyah, Iraq for repainting matt black and application of serial and code letter 'N'. To the RAF's Desert Air Force's Sea Rescue Flight in North Africa 25Nov41 (on which date this highly mobile unit was headquartered at Burg El Arab near Alexandria, Egypt); transferred to No.1 Air Ambulance Unit, RAAF in late 1942 and accepted by the unit at Heliopolis on 01Dec42. Flt/Lt Bartle flew the Goose to Benina on the 3rd, and practised water landings on the 5th. On 9th December 1942 while doing more water landings and take-offs, while fully loaded, HK822 crashed into the sea on attempting to land and overturned 15 miles NNW of Benghazi. All seven on board escaped into a small rubber dinghy but although they paddled all night they made little headway against the wind and currents. At 0645hrs next morning a search was made for the Goose by DH-86A, A31-7, but nothing was found. At midday the passengers and crew were rescued by a Walrus from the Sea Rescue Flight, and taken to Berka West aerodrome. The Goose was never found.

1056   Built as **G-21A** and delivered to Asiatic Petroleum Corporation, New York, NY 31Jly39 as **PK-AKA**. Shipped to Dutch East Indies and re-assembled at the Dutch Navy yard at Sourabaya. Operated without wheels (to gain 300lbs useful load) from Shell Oil base at Babo 1939/40. Both c/n 1056 and c/n 1057 were landed on the river at Babo, taxied over the specially built cradle and then winched up a slipway to the top of the riverbank. Leased to KNILM Nov41. Broken up at Army request at Andir, 08Mar42 in advance of Japanese invasion.

G-21A Goose, c/n 1056, purchased by the Asiatic Petroleum Corporation, for NNGPM at Babo, Netherlands New Guinea, PK-AKA is seen here at the Aviation Country Club on Long Island, New York, in late 1939.
(Carl F Lunghard photo via HC Kavelaars Collection)

1057   Built as **G-21A** and delivered to Asiatic Petroleum Corporation, New York, NY 08Aug39 as **PK-AKB**. Delivered to Dutch East Indies and re-assembled at the Dutch Navy yard at Sourabaya. Operated without wheels (to gain 300lbs useful load) from Shell Oil base at Babo 1939/40 (see c/n 1056). Destroyed by enemy action at Dobu 02Feb42.

1058   Built as **G-21A** 12Sep39 with CofA 15Sep39, and delivered to James Paul Donahue, New York, NY 26Sep39, as **NC3021**. Permission was granted 17Feb40 for a proposed flight from Miami to Cuba, Haiti, Puerto Rico, Martinique, Trinidad, Venezuela, British Guiana, Surinam, French Guiana, Brazil, Paraguay, Uruguay, Argentina, Chile, Peru, Ecuador, Colombia, Panama, Canal Zone, Costa Rica, Nicaragua, Honduras, El Salvador, Guatemala, British Honduras, Mexico and return to Miami. Pilot Thomas T Reavey was to take passengers JP Donahue (owner) and Joseph Kupper, both from NYC, and Charles Munn Jr, of Palm Beach, FL. The flight was not made and was "postponed indefinitely" on 29Apr40. By 16Sep40 the aircraft had flown 408hrs, and enquiries were made about shipment to Hawaii. Following accidents at Miami 19Mar41 when Donahue landed his Goose without lowering the wheels, and at Mineola, NY 13Jly41 when pilot John L Okenfus again forgot to lower the landing gear, c/n 1058 was returned to Grumman for repair and fitment of a new keel, 23Jly41. A new CofR was issued 09Sep41. Sold to Gillies Aviation, Bethpage, NY 15Sep41. Sold to Pan American Airways - Africa Ltd, New York, NY 15Sep41. New Wasp Jr SB3 engines fitted 28Nov41 and CofR issued 13Dec41, but contractually acquired by the USAAF 29Nov41 (reportedly at Wright Field) and formally accepted 14Mar42 with cancellation from the USCAR 01Apr42. Designated **OA-13A** and allocated the serial **42-38214**. To Miami 31Jan43, presumably at Pan American Field, and formally taken on charge by Pan American 27Apr43; transferred to their African-Middle East operations, Egypt (ATC) 01May43 and to Central African Wing 29May43. Destroyed in a landing accident Monrovia, Liberia 14Sep44 (pilot Joseph E Miller of Pan American) and eventually condemned and SOC by ATC 12Jan45.

1059   Built as **G-21A** 21Oct39 and sold to Robert Lehman, Sands Point, Long Island, NY same day. Regd as **NC2788**, 26Oct39 and CofA issued to expire 20Jan40. Sold to US Government (US Navy) and cancelled from USCAR 06Jan42. Overhauled at NAF Philadelphia and sold to Dept of Munitions & Supply, Ottawa, Canada (23Aug41?). Taken on RCAF strength with serial **797**; known to the RCAF as '**Goose**' throughout its life; initial allocation to Eastern Air Command 08Jun42 but early squadron allocation uncertain; with No.121 (Composite) Sqn, Dartmouth by 12Feb43 when involved in a wheels-up landing at Dartmouth following engine failure. To Clarke Ruse Aircraft (location uncertain) for repair 10Mar43; returned to charge of No.3 Training Command 28Aug43 although squadron allocation unrecorded; to Canadian Car & Foundry, Cartierville, QC 01Oct43 for overhaul; returned to No.3 Training Command charge 04Nov43; reallocated to Eastern Air Command 10Dec43 and believed assigned to No.5 Communications Flight, Torbay; assigned to No.161 (BR) Squadron, Dartmouth circa 22Apr44. Made available for disposal by EAC 01Jun44; SOC 25Oct44 (TFH:887hrs) to War Assets Corporation with location stated as No.4 Repair Depot, Scoudouc. Registered **CF-BXR** to Laurentian Air Services Ltd, Ottawa, ON with CofR(C) 3131 for and CofA 627 both issued 19Dec44. Accident at 1123hrs on 09Sep49: Pilot swung the prop of Fleet 80, CF-DQG, by himself from the right behind the prop; the throttle had been left in the fully open position. On start-up the pilot attempted to hold the aircraft back but after at least seven tight circles the pilot was forced to release his hold. The Fleet then made for the Laurentian Air Services hangar. A large arc of ca. 125 yards radius was made, ending on the tarmac almost immediately in front of the DoT (Administration) hangar. At this point the aircraft became airborne, narrowly missing a TCA DC-3 which was loading, and flew into the Laurentian Air Services hangar at an altitude of ca. four feet. The left wing of the Fleet struck the left mainplane and wing tip float of Goose CF-BXR. After striking Seabee CF-DKH and causing superficial hull and mainplane damage, the Fleet came to rest with its nose against the east wall of the hangar. Damage to the Goose: "left wing and wing tip float right off, right elevator right off, right front side hull station 16 forward and inside formers right off, nose piece badly damaged".

Goose c/n 1059, CF-BXR, in a later colour scheme of Laurentian Air Services Ltd, seen here at Baltimore in June 1968. The airline titles, on the cheatline, are in both English and French
(David W Lucabaugh via Jennifer Gradidge)

Accident 25Sep72: Substantial damage (no injuries) on landing at Schefferville, QC. Reregd to Laurentian Air Services Ltd, Maniwaki, QC 13Jun74. Sold to Gene P Storey and leased to Trans Provincial Airlines (TPA) Ltd, Prince Rupert, BC with CofR(C) to them 26Mar75. BoS Gene P Storey to The Flight Department Inc 01Jun78. Cancelled from CCAR 14Jun78 and CofR for **N9642A** issued to The Flight Department Inc, San Francisco, CA 15Jun78. Repossessed Sep78, cancelled from USCAR 16Oct78 and reregd as **C-FBXR** with CofR(C) to Trans Provincial Airlines Ltd 15Dec78. Accident 08Oct79: after striking a log during take-off at Fern Passage, BC pilot beached aircraft to evacuate occupants. Pilot + 9 pax uninjured, but aircraft swept away by tidal current and sank. Salvaged and CofR(C) to Air BC Ltd, Richmond, BC 28Jan81 and nominal change to Jim Pattison Industries, Richmond, BC 17May83, repaired using parts from c/n 1157; CofR(C) to Trans Provincial Airlines, Prince Rupert, BC 02Jun88; TFH:19,746hrs a/o 31Jly90. Accident 31May92: capsized while moored at Rose Harbour, BC. Salvaged by Rainbow Aircraft Salvage, Seattle, WA. Cancelled from CCAR 08Oct92. BoS Rainbow to Schooner Enterprises 18Nov92. CofR **N67DF** issued 16Dec92 to Schooner Enterprises, Miami, FL. CofA 17May95. BoS to Michael T Warn, Milwaukie, OR 26May95 with CofR 12Jun95. **N63MW** applied for 21Jun95 and CofR issued 27Apr96. Reregd **N72179** 09May97 when 63MW transferred to Cessna 208 Caravan. BoS to Cessna Aircraft Co, Wichita, KS 12Jun97. BoS to Aero Air, Hillsboro, OR 12Jun97 with CofR 26Aug97. BoS to Devcon Construction Inc 19Mar98 with CofR 30Mar98 for Devcon Construction Inc, Tualatin, OR. **N39FG** requested

26Mar98, assigned 28Apr98 and placed on aircraft 17Jun98; at Vancouver for major corrosion repair, Feb05. To Diesel Acquisitions LLC, West Linn, OR with CofR 25Apr11. Current and airworthy May13, with CofR due to expire 30Apr14.

1060   Built as **G-21A** and registered **NC2786** to The Tribune Company, Chicago, IL 03Nov39 to replace c/n 1005. Still shown on USCAR 15Feb41 but acquired by the US Navy and accepted at NAS Glenview 04Mar42 as a **JRF-4**, BuAer **09767**. To NAF Annapolis 09Mar42; NAS Norfolk 24Mar42; NAS Corpus Christi Sep42; NATTC Ward Island (Corpus Christi) 26Feb43. Records unreadable/ missing until in with NATTC Corpus Christi Aug44 and SOC 31Oct44. No subsequent history and therefore assumed scrapped by US Navy at end of useful life.

1061   Built as **G-21A** 13Dec39. Allotted CF-BQE 14Nov39. BoS Grumman Aircraft Engineering Corp to JP Bickell, Toronto, ON 15Dec39; US CofA for Export E-5711 issued 04Jan40. Permission to fly Roosevelt Field, NY to Miami, FL 09Jan40, and return 12Jan40; delivered Roosevelt Field, NY to Canada via Buffalo, NY 15Jan40. Registered as **CF-BQE** with CofR(C) 2595 and CofA 422 to John Paris Bickell, Toronto, ON 29Jan40. Sold to the Royal Canadian Air Force in 1940; apparently taken on RCAF strength at Ottawa 01Nov40 with serial **941**; known to the RCAF as '**Goose**' throughout its life, the aircraft initially continued to wear its civilian registration letters. Suggestions that this aircraft initially served with No.12 (Communications) Sqn at Rockcliffe (Ottawa) may have arisen because the aircraft spent some time at Ottawa being prepared for its flight to Vancouver. Airframe and engine tests followed by a familiarisation flight were carried out on 05Nov40. Cloud flying practice on 06Nov40 was followed by another test on 13Nov40 before S/L Plant flew the aircraft from Ottawa on its delivery flight (via Winnipeg and Regina) on 14Nov40. The aircraft's record card shows an initial allocation to Western Air Command's No.13 (Operational Training) Sqn, Patricia Bay 01Nov40. [The aircraft actually arrived in the afternoon of 15Nov40.] No.3 Repair Depot, Jericho Bay 03Sep41; No.13 (OT) Sqn 01Oct41 and coded 'AN-J' (date uncertain); Boeing Aircraft, Vancouver, BC for overhaul 13Mar42 (major overhaul, time expired). Returned to WAC 29May42 unit uncertain but by 28Oct42 with No.122 (Composite) Sqn Patricia Bay; struck a dock and damaged 28Oct42 when water-taxiing at Nootka Bay, BC; Canadian Pacific Airlines, Vancouver, BC for overhaul 02Nov42. Returned to WAC, presumably to No.122 (Comp) Sqn, 11Nov42; used by No.166 (Communications) Sqn, Sea Island and transfer is assumed to have taken place circa 15Jly43 (No.122 (Comp) Sqn had a communications flight that deployed to Sea Island 15Mar43 and which was subsumed into the new No.166 (Comms) Sqn 15Jly43); still wearing old code 'AN-J' until at least 01Dec43 while in use by No.166 (Comms) Sqn; the aircraft remained active within WAC, presumably with No.166 (Comms) Sqn although this detail does not appear on the record card; available for disposal within WAC 15Jly44. SOC to War Assets Corporation 05Jan45 (TFH:2,363hrs) with location stated as No.3 Repair Depot (presumably at Sea Island). BoS WAC to Charles H Babb Co, Glendale, CA, 22Jan45 as **NC48550**. To North West Air Service, Seattle, WA Feb45. BoS Babb to Alaska Coastal Airlines, Juneau, AK, 05Feb45 and CofR issued 07Feb45; overhauled and water rudder installed Sep45; later as **N48550**; complete overhaul Jun52. Accident at 1500hrs on 14May57: substantial damage in crash at Wrangell, AK, while en route Juneau to Ketchikan with pilot and nine pax. No fatalities. Tfd by BoS to Alaska Coastal-Ellis Airlines, Juneau, AK, 18Sep62 and CofR issued 27Sep62 and CofA 15Oct62 at TFH:18,705hrs; nominal change to Alaska Coastal Airlines Inc, Juneau, AK, notified by BoS 16Jun66; TFH:22,447hrs a/o 05Feb68; merged into Alaska Airlines Inc, Seattle, WA, 27Mar68 and CofR issued 19Apr68. BoS Alaska A/L to Antilles Air Boats, St Thomas, US Virgin Islands, 19Sep69 with CofR 09Dec69; Beech C-18 engine cowls installed May75. Accident in US Virgin Islands 07Jun78, no details. Antilles AB ceased operations in 1981 and aircraft reported wfu Mar82. BoS to Amphibian Sales Inc (Dean Franklin), Miami, FL, undated, but recorded 25Jly88. BoS to Teufel Holly Farms Inc, Portland, OR, 01Jly88 with CofR 25Jly88. **N21LT** applied for 29Feb88, assigned but ntu; CofA 15May96. To Strange Bird Inc, West Palm Beach, FL with CofR **N48550** 14Sep99. CofR expired 30Sep12, but was re-issued 06Dec12 to expire 31Dec15. Current and airworthy May13.

1062   Built as **G-21A** and registered **NC3042** to Gulf Oil Corporation, Pittsburgh, PA 21Dec39. Purchased by USAAF Nov42 for $62,843.74 as an **OA-13A**, with serial **42-97055**. Acc Bolling Field 24Nov42 and cancelled from USCAR "to War Dept" 26Jan43; San Antonio Air Depot 08Dec42; 16th Photographic Sqn, 1st Photographic Charting Grp, Bolling Fld 29Jan43; 16th PRS detached to Talara, Peru 28Feb43 and aircraft appears to have been in Peru from 15Apr43 until 31Jly43 (paper dates); detached to Natal, Brazil 26Sep43 and from there to Recife 31Dec43;

C/n 1062, Gulf Oil Goose NC3042, which was purchased by the US Army Air Force in November 1942, and designated as an OA-13A. The aircraft is seen here at an unknown location, circa 1940.

(Peter M Bowers Collection)

returned to Bolling 30Aug44, departing once more (mapping) 14Nov44. SOC ('lost to inventory') 14Jun46. No subsequent history and therefore assumed scrapped at end of useful life.

1063   Built for US Coast Guard as **JRF-2**. Del to CGAS Brooklyn 07Dec39 as **V174**. In use by Senior CG Officer, 7th Naval District, NAS Charleston by Dec41; CGAS Biloxi by Feb43; CGAS Port Angeles by 19Aug44; detached to NAAS North Bend 13Jan45. To St Louis for flood protection duties 28Feb45; CGAS Port Angeles 08May45 to Dec45. SOC in 1946 and disposed of by WAA, (recorded in storage at Buchanan Fld, Concord, CA 21Jan47). Sold to Keith Thomas Petrich, Seattle, WA Jan47 and registered as **G-21A, NC68902**, but subsequent fate unknown.

1064   Built for US Coast Guard as **JRF-2**. Del to CGAS Brooklyn 07Oct39 as **V175**; CGAS Elizabeth City Aug40 until at least Jan42; CGAS Port Angeles, by Nov42 until 27Dec43 when to overhaul at NAS San Diego; subsequent history and fate not known.

1065   Built for US Coast Guard as **JRF-2**. Del to CGAS Brooklyn 12Oct39 as **V176**. CGAS San Francisco Oct39; CGAS Port Angeles by Dec41. Destroyed in fatal accident 06Apr43; while en route Port Angeles to NAS Seattle on a routine training exercise, the aircraft struck Blyn Mountain, WA in thick fog, killing all four crew.

1066   Built for US Navy as **JRF-1A**, BuAer serial **1671**. Acc and del NAS Anacostia 15Sep39; NAS Norfolk 09Oct39; VJ-1 *USS Rigel* (AD-13) 24Oct39; VJ-3 *USS Rigel* 30Sep40; VJ-1 *USS Rigel* date unk; VJ-3 (Base Force, Pacific Fleet) Pearl Harbor 10Mar41. Remained active with VJ-3 (moving to NAS Puunene circa Sep43) until Aug44 when SOC 31Aug44, circumstances unknown but assumed to have been considered obsolete. No subsequent history and therefore assumed scrapped by US Navy at end of useful life.

1067   Built for US Navy as **JRF-1A**, BuAer serial **1672**. Acc and del Anacostia 25Oct39; NAS San Diego (Base Force) 30Oct39; VJ-3 *USS Rigel* (AD-13) 03Nov39; NAS Pearl Harbor 05Sep40; VJ-3 *USS Rigel* 26Sep40; NAS Pearl Harbor 05Jun41; VJ-3 (Base Force, Pacific Fleet) Pearl Harbor 08Jly41; NAS Pearl Harbor 22Apr42; VJ-3 Pearl Harbor 12Aug42. Records missing but believed transferred to VJ-11 NAS Puunene Jly43, moving to Efate circa Oct43; confirmed with VJ-11 Efate Mar44; VJ-8 Efate Oct44. By 4Dec44 unserviceable ('awaiting action') Espiritu Santo Nov44 and SOC 31Dec44 as obsolete. No subsequent history and therefore assumed scrapped by US Navy at end of useful life.

1068   Built for US Navy as **JRF-1A**, BuAer serial **1673**. Acc and del dates unknown but shipped to VMS-3 (Fleet Marine Force) MCAS St Thomas 07Nov39 and received 30Nov39. Sustained repairable damage 14Mar42 after crash-landing at St Thomas and returned to service with VMS-3 by Dec42; believed temporarily relocated with VMS-3 to NAS San Juan Mar-Apr43; Hedron 3, 3rd MAW MCAS St Thomas Apr43; Hedron 9, 9th MAW MCAS St Thomas Apr44. To NAS Guantanamo Bay 19Jun44 and SOC 31Aug44. No subsequent history and therefore assumed scrapped by US Navy at end of useful life.

1069   Built for US Navy as **JRF-1**, BuAer serial **1674**. Acc 24Nov39 and del NAS Seattle 08Dec39; A&R at NAD Seattle 10Mar43 and assumed still present Nov43 when reported in non-operational pool. Records missing until with NAS Seattle by Aug44 and SOC 31Aug44, circumstances unknown but assumed to have been considered obsolete. No subsequent history and therefore assumed scrapped by US Navy at end of useful life.

1070   Built for US Navy as **JRF-1**, BuAer serial **1675**. Acc 28Nov39 and del NAS Norfolk 29Nov39; NAS Anacostia 02Feb40; INA Bethpage 21Feb40; NAS Anacostia 06Mar40; Naval Attaché Venezuela (Caracas) 16Apr40; NAS Coco Solo 25Sep40; Naval Attaché Venezuela 07Oct40; NAS Coco Solo 16May42; A&R NAS Coco Solo 20Apr43. Naval Attaché Venezuela 15Nov43 (although previously involved in minor accident 26Aug43 in river landing near Giradot, Colombia when on strength of the Naval Attaché, Bogota). Records missing until with NAS Trinidad by Aug44. Probably withdrawn 21Oct44 and SOC 31Oct44, circumstances unknown but assumed to have been considered obsolete. No subsequent history and therefore assumed scrapped by US Navy at end of useful life.

1071   Built for US Navy as **JRF-1**, BuAer serial **1676**. Acc and del to Naval Attaché, Cuba (Havana) 07Dec39; NAS Norfolk 05Aug42; Naval Attaché Cuba 08Oct42. Records missing but still with Naval Attaché Cuba by Aug44; NAS San Juan Sep44; Naval Attaché Cuba Oct44 but SOC 31Oct44, circumstances unknown but assumed to have been considered obsolete. No subsequent history and therefore assumed scrapped by US Navy at end of useful life.

1072   Built for US Navy as **JRF-1**, BuAer serial **1677**. Acc and del dates unknown but shipped to Naval Attaché Colombia (Bogota) 18Dec39. Severely damaged in a crash in Colombia 03May40 and considered beyond economic repair. Strike recommended 16May40 and SOC 31May40 (TFH:97hrs at time of accident).

1073   Built for US Navy as **JRF-1A**, BuAer serial **1678**. Acc and del dates unknown but shipped to NAS Coco Solo 02Jan40. Left wing badly damaged in accident 15Feb40 but assumed to have been repaired (recorded as entering a major overhaul 23Nov42) and still with NAS Coco Solo 01Mar43. Records missing but then listed at NAS Coco Solo 23Aug44 (possible withdrawal date). SOC 31Aug44, circumstances unknown but assumed to have been considered obsolete. No subsequent history and therefore assumed scrapped by US Navy at end of useful life.

1074   Built for US Navy as **JRF-1A**, BuAer serial **1679**. Acc and del dates unknown but crated and shipped to Wheeler Field, Pearl Harbor 29Jan40 and received there 12Mar40. Suffered damage to left wing, float, keel and undercarriage in what was presumably a landing accident at Pearl Harbor 25Apr40 and still at Pearl Harbor Dec41. Recorded as with Pacific Fleet, San Diego 28Aug42 and to NAS Alameda 29Aug42 for rework; NAS Pearl Harbor 29Mar43; NAD Palmyra 13Apr43. Following engine failure on take-off from a small lake on Washington Island (Terainia), Line Islands 27Oct43, the aircraft porpoised and flipped on its back; moderate damage to the hull was exacerbated by subsequent corrosion caused by seven days' immersion in stagnant water at this remote site ("the plane hull and wings could not be moved from the lake through the jungle due to physical restriction of the canal, railroad and ocean surf"). NAS Pearl Harbor 15Nov43 (presumably an administrative exercise) and SOC 08Dec43.

1075   Built for US Navy as **JRF-1**, BuAer serial **1680**. Acc 31Jan40 and del NAS San Diego 09Feb40; A&R San Diego 01Aug43; The record card simply states "misc" 15Nov43; NAS San Diego 29Jan44 and SOC 31Aug44, circumstances unknown but assumed to have been considered obsolete. No subsequent history and therefore assumed scrapped by US Navy at end of useful life.

1076   Built for US Coast Guard as **JRF-2**. Del to CGAS Elizabeth City 13Feb40 as **V184**; at Elizabeth City until at least early 1941; at CGAS Biloxi by Dec41 until at least Feb43; subsequent history and fate not known.

1077   Built for US Coast Guard as **JRF-2**. Del to CGAS Brooklyn 26Feb40 as **V185**; CGAS Elizabeth City by Aug40; CGAS Salem by Dec41 until at least early 1943; CGAS Miami date unk; subsequent US Coast Guard/US Navy history unknown. Sold surplus Nov46 and converted to **G-21A**. Regd to Harry Garland, dba Garland Aviation Co, Detroit, MI as **NC95400** Nov46. Later as **N95400** to Gilbert A Hensler Jr, Nassau, Bahamas; reregd to Bahamas Air Traders Ltd by Aug63 and to Island Flying Service Ltd, Bahamas by 1965. BoS Island Flying Service to Northwest Industries Ltd, Edmonton, AB 22Dec65. Cancelled from USCAR 07Mar66 and CF-UAZ allotted to Northwest Industries 14Mar66. Retractable wing-tip floats fitted in 1966, using McKinnon kit No.31. BoS Northwest to BC Air Lines, Vancouver, BC, Canada 02May66 with CofA10266 and CofR36157(C) for **CF-UAZ**, same date. CofA renewed at TFH:10,629hrs, valid until 02May69. BoS to Trans Provincial Airlines Ltd, Terrace, BC 01Apr69 with CofR(C) same date. CofA renewed at

TFH:11,423hrs, valid until 02May70; at TFH:21,500hrs, valid until 18Jun81. CofR re-issued as **C-FUAZ** 14Jan81 to Air BC Ltd, Richmond, BC. CofA renewed at TFH:23,297hrs, valid until 18Jun83. CofR(C) to Jim Pattison Industries Ltd, Richmond, BC 17May83 (nominal change) but operated as Trans Provincial Airlines in their c/s. CofA renewed at TFH:23,616hrs, valid until 11Aug84; at TFH:25,216hrs, valid until 25Aug87. BoS to Air BC Ltd 31Dec87. CofR(C) to Air BC Ltd (op as Trans Provincial Airlines) 11Feb87. CofA renewed at TFH:25,832hrs, valid until 25Aug88. BoS Air BC to Pacific Coastal Airlines Ltd 31Dec87 but leased back same date to Air BC for 2 years. CofR(C) to Air BC Ltd, Richmond, BC 31Dec87 but operated as Pacific Coastal Airlines. CofA renewed at TFH:25,994hrs, valid until 25Aug89. BoS Pacific Coastal to Greyvest Financial Services Ltd 26Apr89 but leased back to Pacific Coastal Airlines Ltd, Richmond, BC 01May89 for 83 months with CofR(C) to them 06Jun89. TFH:26,527hrs reported on Due Date of 25Aug89. Accident at 17.25hrs on 05Jun90: while taxiing after landing at Port Hardy, BC, right u/c collapsed during a right turn. Aircraft came to rest on keel and right wing struck the ground and was damaged. No injuries. TFH:26,968hrs, reported on Due Date of 25Aug90; TFH:28,733hrs reported on Due Date of 15Feb94. BoS to GE Capital Canada Leasing Services Inc 29Apr94. BoS to Pacific Coastal Airlines Ltd 16Nov94. TFH:29,775hrs reported on Due Date of 15Feb96. CofR(C) to Pacific Coastal Airlines Ltd, Richmond, BC 02Apr96. TFH:33,735hrs reported on Due Date of 15Feb03. CofR renewed 23Nov05 (address change). Withdrawn from service at Port Hardy, BC 24Sep12.

1078   Built for US Coast Guard as **JRF-2**. Del to CGAS Elizabeth City 02Mar40 as **V186** and at Elizabeth City until at least Feb43; subsequent US Coast Guard/US Navy history unknown and "out of inventory" by Aug46. Subsequent history and fate not known.

1079   Built for US Coast Guard as **JRF-2**. Del to CGAS Brooklyn 25Mar40 as **V187**. Senior CG Officer, 14th Naval District, NAS Honolulu by Dec41; subsequent history uncertain but aircraft is suspected to have been the US Navy JRF-2 with CASU-1 NAS Pearl Harbor by May43 and with CASU-4 NAS Puunene by Dec43 until circa Mar44 and again circa Jun44 until circa Oct44. Subsequent history and fate not known.

1080   Built as **G-21A** and del 09Mar40 to Koninklijke Nederlandsch-Indische Luchtvaart Maatschappij (KNILM) as **PK-AFR** on Export CofA E-5979 dated 28Mar40. Destroyed in Japanese air raid at Semplak Bogor, Java 20Feb42.

1081   Built as **G-21A** and had a 'NX' registration applied. Delivered to Koninklijke Nederlandsch-Indische Luchtvaart Maatschappij (KNILM) 13Mar40 in Dutch East Indies as **PK-AFS**, on Export CofA E-5977 dated 28Mar40. Shot down by Japanese military aircraft over Koepang, Timor 26Jan42.

1082   Built as **G-21A**, (Grumman records show it as G-21B but the Export CofA records it correctly as G-21A). Sold to Dept of Munitions & Supply, Ottawa for use by the Royal Canadian Air Force as **Goose** serial **925**. Ferried New York to Ottawa, as **NX925**, by pilot Romeo Vachon, 06Jly40, on Export CofA E-6300 dated 05Jly40. Acc by RCAF at Rockcliffe (Ottawa) 07Jly40 and assigned to the Communications Flt, Rockcliffe; unit re-titled No.12 (Comms) Unit 30Jly40 and finally No.12 (Communications) Sqn 30Aug40. Reassigned to the Eastern Air Command's Communications Flt, Halifax 28Apr41 becoming No.121 (Composite) Sqn 10Jan42 with code 'EN-B'. Went missing between Sydney, NS and Torbay, Nfld 07Nov42: aircraft crashed at sea near Horse Chops, Trinity Bay, Nfld with five fatalities; unable to complete the journey before dark, pilot attempted a forced landing in rough sea. Final write-off by RCAF at Gander, NL 15Jan43.

1083   Built as **G-21A**, (Grumman records show it as G-21B, but the Export CofA records it correctly as G-21A). Sold to Dept of Munitions & Supply, Ottawa for use by the Royal Canadian Air Force becoming **Goose** serial **926**. Ferried New York to Ottawa, as **NX926**, by pilot Romeo Vachon, 15Jly40, on Export CofA E-6328 dated 30Jly40. Acc by RCAF at Rockcliffe (Ottawa) 16Jly40 and assigned to the Communications Flt, Rockcliffe; unit re-titled No.12 (Comms) Unit 30Jly40 and finally No.12 (Communications) Sqn 30Aug40. Capsized at mooring on the St Lawrence River, near Quebec City 05Sep41 (recovery was complex and resulted in the award of the AFC to Wing Commander LE Wray who finally got a line attached); to Noorduyn Aircraft for overhaul and repairs 17Sep41 (duration eight months); to storage Reserve No.3 Training Command 28May42 (presumably at Rockcliffe) and off storage with No.3 TC, Rockcliffe 25Jun42, presumably assigned to No.12 (Comms) Sqn. Reassigned to the Eastern Air Command's No.121 (Composite) Sqn, Dartmouth 11Dec42; to Clarke Ruse Aircraft (presumably at Dartmouth)

for major overhaul 12Apr43 ("time expired"). Returned to EAC 01Oct43, presumably with No.121 (Composite) Sqn but not so stated on movement card; to Stored Reserve with EAC 23May44 pending further disposal instructions; with EAC and available for disposal 29Sep44. CF-BZY allotted to Canada Veneers Ltd 23Apr45. SOC to War Assets Corporation 25Jun45 (TFH:1,563hrs) with location stated as being No.4 Repair Depot, Scoudouc. Incident 12Dec45: on flight from Montreal, PQ to Toronto, ON ran out of fuel but landed safely on Stillwater Reservoir, near Watertown, NY. Registered with CoR(C) 3335and CofA 842 for **CF-BZY** to Canada Veneers Ltd, St John, NB 29Oct45; inspected and CofA renewed valid until 13Nov47. Accident at 1900hrs on 02Aug47 at Buctouche, NB: while taxying after landing after a flight from St John, NB, aircraft attempted to round a turn at a speed slightly greater than practical. The right wingtip float dug in too deep and sheared off. Power was applied to raise the wing and the aircraft was headed to soft mud flats where a stone pier made a slight crack in the hull. Authority to ferry Charlottetown, PEI to Bethpage, NY for repair by Grumman 09Aug47; authority to ferry back to Charlottetown, PEI 08Sep47; inspected and CofA renewed valid until 30Jun48. Aircraft offered to DoT for $32,000, 30Apr49 but ntu; CofA renewed at TFH:2,988hrs, valid until 07May52. Authority to ferry to Snow Goose, Baltimore, MD 25May51. **N3692** allocated but ntu. US CofR **N3692** issued 11Jun51. Cancelled from CCAR 10Aug51. To Wilderness Air Charter, Minneapolis, MN by Feb58. To GF Williamson, Sandy, OR Jly64. (George Williamson, chief pilot of B.N.P. Airways, BC was responsible for obtaining a Goose for Lord Robert Grosvenor, Duke of Westminster, while Sandy, OR was the address of McKinnon Enterprises.) Conversion work to prepare it for the trans-Atlantic ferry flight to England was done by B.N.P. Airways at Vancouver, BC. An auxiliary belly fuel tank was fitted and supplemented by four 45-gallon drums which were strapped down in the fuselage, near the centre of gravity. A pump was installed, to allow transfer of fuel from the drums to the main wing tanks, and to make room for all of this the carpet was rolled up and stowed at the rear of the fuselage with the seats and the life-raft! Test flights, still regd as N3692, were made on 27/28Sep64 and again on 30Sep64. Ken McCuaig flew the aircraft (with George Williamson) back to Sandy, OR on 03Oct64 to carry out tests on the fuel system. After some test flights (with Williamson and McKinnon on board), followed by a 20-minute test-flight for the FAA, including a water landing, a CofA was issued on 06Oct64. The BoS dated 06Oct64 noted that the aircraft was sold by Williamson to the Grosvenor Estate Trustees, with McKinnon acting as agent. On 08Oct64 the aircraft was regd as **G-ASXG** to George Kershaw Ridley, Trustee of the Assets of the Grosvenor Estate, Ecclestone, Cheshire. Piloted by Ken McCuaig, the Goose was ferried from Sandy, OR to Vancouver, BC via Seattle, WA at the start of its delivery flight. The delivery continued on 14Oct64 via Winnipeg, MB; Kapuskasing, ON; Mont Joli, PQ; Gander, NL; Torbay, NL; Lajes (Azores); to Lisbon, Portugal (26Oct64). The fuel drums were removed, the carpets replaced, and the radios repaired by engineers from TAP, the Portuguese national airline. On 28Oct64 McCuaig set course for England via Bordeaux, France and on 30Oct64 G-ASXG landed at Cambridge after a flight of 7,400 miles in 47hours 10minutes flying time. Marshall of Cambridge Ltd overhauled and prepared the aircraft and a British CofA was issued on 12Nov64. Cvtd to **G-21A Turbo** (using McKinnon STC turbine engine kit No:2) by Marshall of Cambridge Ltd between 12Feb68 and 15Jly68 at TFH:6,990hrs (see Chapter 6); FF Cambridge 28Jun68; CofA 19Jly68 and regd (wrongly) as a "G-21C Hybrid Turbo Goose" 26Jly68. Offered for sale Jly71 for US$275,000. **CF-AWH** allotted to Airwest Airlines Ltd, Vancouver, BC 28May73. Aircraft del Leavesden – Prestwick for overhaul 10Aug73. UK regn cancelled 06Sep73. Del to Canada ex Prestwick, via Stornaway, 17Sep73. CofR(C) as **C-FAWH** to Airwest Airlines Ltd, Vancouver, BC issued Apr74. Accident 01Jun74: substantial damage, but no injuries, in crash due to engine failure at Vancouver, BC. Accident 03Aug79: right main gear

C/n 1083, G-ASXG, of Grosvenor Estates, moored at Kylestrom, Scotland in February 1965. Converted to turbine power in 1968, the aircraft returned to Canada and was later converted back to piston power.
(Lady Mary Grosvenor via Ken McCuaig and Jerry Vernon)

failed on landing at Stewart, BC. Right wing tip and fuselage hit ground. Pilot minor injuries.; 4 pax uninjured. CofR to Airwest Operations Ltd (nominal) 29Aug79. Leased to Trans Provincial Airlines, Prince Rupert, BC with CofR(C) 13Sep79. Became Air BC Ltd on 31st October 1980. Accident 10Apr81: struck parked floatplane Beaver, N64395, while water taxying at Ketchikan, AK. CofA lapsed 27Apr81. Nominal change with CofR(C) to Jim Pattison Industries Ltd, Richmond, BC by Oct83, but still op by Air BC. Because of high maintenance/ overhaul costs for the PT-6A engines the Goose was converted back to piston power **(G-21A,** c/n 1083) by Air BC in 1985. Inspected Aug85 and CofA renewed valid until 20Aug86. CofR(C) to Air BC Ltd, Richmond, BC 31Dec87. Sold to Pacific Coastal Airlines, Port Hardy, BC. Accident 12May88: crashed on take-off Rivers Inlet, BC, believed due windshear. Pilot and four passengers uninjured; 2 passengers slightly injured. The wings were torn from the aircraft by the impact with the water. The aircraft was written off and cancelled from CCAR 20Nov89. Parts of the wreckage are still to be found in "the Goose graveyard" behind the Pacific Coastal hangar at Port Hardy, BC.

1084 Built as **G-21A** Aug40. BoS Grumman Aircraft Engineering Corp to Superior Oil Co., Houston, TX 14Aug40 with CofR **NC28635** 01Aug40 (sic). Test flown 16Aug40 by Franklin T Kurt and CofA issued 17Aug40. Aircraft based at Lake Charles, LA Jly41; wingtip floats removed 06Sep41. Accident at 1830hrs on 06Apr43: ground looped landing at Winslow, AZ in a strong crosswind. Both wingtips were damaged, right landing gear drag strut and right axle assembly broken. Repaired 01May43. Accident at 1830hrs on 02Jun43: After de-planing co-pilot and passengers at Wardwell Field, Casper, WY, a strong gust of wind lifted left wing, right wingtip hit ground, the tail lifted and another gust flipped aircraft onto its back. Substantial damage but no injuries. Repaired 17Sep43. Edo N-760 wingtip floats installed 28Sep45 with CofA 24Oct45. Letter 04Mar47 noting sale to Nassau Aviation Co Ltd, Nassau, Bahamas and cancelled from USCAR 20Mar47. Regd **VP-BAL** to Nassau Aviation Co Ltd 26Feb47. To Bahamas Airways Ltd, Nassau 30Oct47; aircraft name: *"Abaco"*. Renamed *"Bimini"* Aug51. Accident at 1735hrs on 25Oct53: damaged by striking a submerged object during take-off run at Deep Creek, Andros. Although the hull was damaged and leaking, pilot Joseph Hethel continued the take-off run, got airborne and completed the flight (Charter No.2019), landing at Oakes Field, Nassau at 1830hrs (local). Neither the pilot nor 2 pax were injured. Forced landing after double engine failure 07Dec59 in Monteque (?) Bay. Reregd **VP-BBI** after repair. Cancelled from Bahamian CAR 17Sep62. BoS Bahamas A/W to Gilbert Anderson Hensler Jr, dba Bahamas Air Traders, Nassau, Bahamas 08Oct62 with CofR **N86639** 21Feb63; CofA 20Jan66 at TFH:11,547hrs. BoS to Sherlock D Hackley, Nassau, Bahamas 17Aug67 with CofR 21Sep67 to Hackley at Oxford, MD. BoS to Island Flying Services of America, New York, NY 30Jun70 with CofR 30Aug72 at Miami, FL address. BoS to Gander Aircraft & Engineering Corp, Miami, FL 29Aug74 with CofR 16Oct74. BoS to Artco Intl Corp, Coral Gables, FL 22Jly77 with CofR 08Aug77. Regd **HK-2058** 05Oct77 with Aerolineas La Gaviota Ltda, San Andrés; aircraft name, *"Providencia"*. Cancelled from USCAR 28Oct77 as exported to Colombia and del through Opa Locka, FL 02Nov77. To Aerolineas del Llano Ltda, Villavicencio 1984; still named *"Providencia"*. To Moises Press Kleinberger, Cali, Colombia (date unknown). Cancelled from Colombian CAR 14Jly05 "due at least 3 years inactivity". Wfu and displayed as **HK-2058-P**, at National Transport Museum, Cali, Colombia, where it was noted in 2006. BoS Kleinberger to Air Mart Intl, Panama 20Sep07. BoS to Dinca Inc, Bear, DE 10Oct07 with CofR **N119AA** 06Dec07. Noted as such at Cali, Colombia 25Feb08. Ferried to USA, arriving Key West, FL 09Oct08 and noted parked at Opa Locka, FL 10Oct08. CofA issued 01Jun09 at TFH:16,330hrs. To Stick & Rudder Aviation Inc, Middletown, DE; CofR applied for 14Feb12 and issued 14Apr12. **N121SR** reserved 13Aug12 and CofR issued 11Sep12. Current and airworthy May13, with CofR due to expire 30Apr15.

1085 Built as **JRF-3** for US Coast Guard and delivered to NAS Anacostia 20Nov40 as **V190** (FAA files show V-191); CGAS Brooklyn by Apr41. Destroyed in fatal accident 16Apr42: aircraft was diverted from a local test flight from Brooklyn to confirm a reported submarine sighting southeast of Nantucket, MA. In conditions of darkness and rain the aircraft impacted cliffs on Block Island, off the coast of Rhode Island, killing all three crew. [The aircraft currently exhibited at the National Museum of Naval Aviation, Pensacola as 'V190' is the former V191, c/n 1086. The FAA files incorrectly show the c/n of V191 as 1085. The error appears to have resulted from confusion, in respect of the true c/n of NC5583N/N12CS, which was perpetrated from the beginning on the Bill of Sale from the War Assetts Administration in April 1948]

1086 Built as **JRF-3** for US Coast Guard and del to NAS Anacostia 19Oct40 as **V191**. Retnd to Grumman at Bethpage for completion of

C/n 1086, Catalina Airlines' Goose, N12CS, taxies in at Long Beach in 1974. The aircraft were painted in various colours, but with the same scheme, this aircraft being white and dark blue. (MAP)

installation of de-icing equipment 20Nov40; returned to CGAS Brooklyn in early 1941 and remained there until at least 28Jun43 when involved in a minor taxying accident. Subsequent US Coast Guard/US Navy history unknown but "out of inventory" by Aug46. Sold by War Assets Administration, 16Apr48, for $13,000 to Seth Atwood, Rockford, IL; CofR **NC5538N** (quoting c/n 1085) issued 20May48 to Atwood Vacuum Machine Co. Aircraft stripped and overhauled, hull re-sealed and repainted by Parks Aircraft Sales & Service Inc, Wheeling, IL, Jly48 to **G-21A**. BoS Atwood to Atwood Vacuum Machine Co, Rockford, IL 01Nov50. BoS to Motorcar Transport Co, and/or Contract Cartage Co, Pontiac, MI, 22Nov50, with CofR **N5538N** issued 22Jan51; CofA 18Sep52 at TFH:4,290hrs. BoS to Dean H Franklin, Miami, FL, 08Nov56, with CofR 05Dec56; tfd to Franklin Flying Service Inc, Miami, FL, 06Oct61, with CofR 28Oct61. Letter from DH Franklin 31Oct61 requesting Experimental CofA for 90 days for test flights to evaluate canted engine mounts and re-designed wingtips. Experimental CofA issued 07Nov61 allowing flights from Miami Intl A/P. CofA 07Feb62 at TFH:5,459hrs. Another request for Experimental CofA 15Feb62 and issued same date. "Acft modified per STC 17SO" 21Mar62 and CofA 22Mar62 at TFH:5,490hrs. Tfd to Gander Aircraft Corp, Miami, FL, 08Aug62 with CofR 21Aug62 (engines listed as R985-14B). Accident 11Jly66: substantial damage after landing in a tugboat wake off Catalina Island. Tail dipped into water and twisted. Pilot +3 pax uninjured. Reported (by NTSB) as operated by Catalina Seaplanes but FAA files show: BoS Gander Aircraft to Catalina Seaplanes Inc, San Pedro, CA, 27Mar67. **N12CS** applied to aircraft, 28Jun69; Accident 30Jan70: substantial damage in wheels-down landing at Pebbly Beach Seaplane Base on a flight from Long Beach to Avalon. Pilot + 3 pax uninjured. Accident at 1600hrs on 03Dec70: collision with Mooney 20C, N9232V, while taxying Long Beach, CA. The Mooney had landed after a flight from Van Nuys, CA. Ground Control instructed the Goose pilot to delay taxi for take-off in order to avoid a Cessna and the Mooney. The Goose pilot misunderstood the instruction, and avoided the Cessna but crashed into the Mooney. BoS to Catalina Airlines Inc, Gardena, CA, 29Dec76, with CofR 28Feb77; reported in poor state at San Pedro, CA 1980. Retractable floats installed per STC SA138SW by Dennis Buehn 09Apr80. BoS to Red Stevenson (dba Rcd "S" Aircraft Sales), Leonard, OK, 29Aug83, with CofR 13Dec83. Used at Universal Studios back-lot as a prop for the TV series, *"Tales of the Gold Monkey"*. BoS to Charles G Hyde (aka Glen Hyde), Roanoke, TX, 11Jly86, with CofR 13Aug86. Tfd to TUCO Co, Pahrump, NV, 15Oct86, with CofR 03Mar87, but TUCO was not in fact formed and therefore above sale was declared invalid 27Oct87. There is also a BoS 01Feb87 from Hyde to IR3T Inc, at same address as TUCO, with CofR issued 27Oct87; IR3T Inc changed address to Roanoke, TX in Apr89. FAA wrote to IR3T Inc, 03Sep93, requesting confirmation of sale to "Naval Aviation Museum". Cancelled from USCAR, as "expired", 21Jan11 (still quoting c/n as 1085).

Acquired by the then Naval Aviation Museum 20Mar89, and currently displayed by National Museum of Naval Aviation as "**V190**" (an incorrect serial, perhaps resulting from confusion over the true identity of N12CS).

1087 Built as **JRF-3** for US Coast Guard and del to NAS Anacostia 26Nov40 as **V192**. CGAS Brooklyn by 1941; detached to Traverse City, MI Apr41 and again circa Aug41. Reported to have made reconnaissance flights over the Great Lakes during ice-breaking operations in the first two weeks of April 1941; CGAS Salem by Feb43. Subsequent US Coast Guard/US Navy history unknown; "out of inventory" by Oct48. Subsequent history and fate not known.

1088 Built as **G-21B** for Aviação Naval Portuguesa (Portuguese Naval Aviation) with serial **97**. Test-flown with marks **NX97** and del 15Apr40. Delivered by sea to CAN Bom Sucesso, Lisbon and assumed to have been one of the first aircraft reassembled in Jun40; operating from CAN Aveiro in 1942. Prefix letter 'G' added to serial, application date uncertain; active at Bom Sucesso in 1950 and 1951. Transferred to the Força Aérea Portuguesa (Portuguese Air Force) May52 and moved to BA-6 Montijo where on strength Jun53; at BA-7 Aveiro in 1953, Apr-May55 and last noted active there Oct56. No subsequent commercial history, fate unknown.

1089　Built as **G-21B** for Aviação Naval Portuguesa (Portuguese Naval Aviation) with serial **98** and del 25Apr40. Delivered by sea to CAN Bom Sucesso, Lisbon and assumed to have been one of the first aircraft reassembled in Jun40; operating from CAN Aveiro in 1942. Prefix letter 'G' theoretically added to serial, application date uncertain. Subsequent history unknown but not on charge when fleet was transferred to the Força Aérea Portuguesa (Portuguese Air Force) in May52. Fate unknown.

1090　Built as **G-21B** for Aviação Naval Portuguesa (Portuguese Naval Aviation) with serial **99** and del 04May40. Delivered by sea to CAN Bom Sucesso, Lisbon for reassembly and active there in 1945. Prefix letter 'G' added to serial, application date uncertain; still at Bom Sucesso by 31Jan49 when TFH recorded as 928hrs. Transferred to the Força Aérea Portuguesa (Portuguese Air Force) May52 and moved to BA-6 Montijo; seen engine-less at Montijo Jun53 and although still on strength had effectively been retired. No known subsequent commercial history. Fate unknown.

1091　Built as **G-21B** for Aviação Naval Portuguesa (Portuguese Naval Aviation) with serial **100** and del 14May40. Delivered by sea to CAN Bom Sucesso, Lisbon for reassembly; to CAN Ponta Delgado, Azores Dec40. Destroyed in a storm at Ponta Delgada 03Nov41.

1092　Built as **G-21B** for Aviação Naval Portuguesa (Portuguese Naval Aviation) with serial **101** and del 20May40. Delivered by sea to CAN Bom Sucesso, Lisbon for reassembly; active at Bom Sucesso in 1940 and 1941; operating from CAN Aveiro in 1942. Prefix letter 'G' added to serial, application date uncertain; active at Bom Sucesso in 1945 and by 31Jan49 TFH recorded as 988hrs. Transferred to the Força Aérea Portuguesa (Portuguese Air Force) May52 and moved to BA-6 Montijo where on strength Jun53. Last recorded at BA-7 Aveiro in 1954. No subsequent commercial history. Fate unknown.

1093　Built as **G-21B** for Aviação Naval Portuguesa (Portuguese Naval Aviation) with serial **102** and del 27May40. Delivered by sea to CAN Bom Sucesso, Lisbon for reassembly; operating from CAN Aveiro in 1942; to CAN Ponta Delgada, Azores circa 1942 (replacing the lost 100) and active there in 1943 and 1944. Prefix letter 'G' added to serial, application date uncertain; returned to Bom Sucesso in 1945 prior to Ponta Delgada closure and by 31Jan49 TFH recorded as 452hrs; active Bom Sucesso 1949 to 1951. Transferred to the Força Aérea Portuguesa (Portuguese Air Force) May52 and moved to BA-6 Montijo where on strength Jun53 and last recorded. No subsequent commercial history. Fate unknown.

1094　Built as **G-21B** for Aviação Naval Portuguesa (Portuguese Naval Aviation) with serial **103** and del 04Jun40. Delivered by sea to CAN Bom Sucesso, Lisbon for reassembly; to CAN Ponta Delgada, Azores Dec40 and active there until 1944. Prefix letter 'G' added to serial, application date uncertain; returned to Bom Sucesso in 1945 prior to Ponta Delgada closure and by 31Jan49 TFH recorded as 513hrs; active Bom Sucesso in 1951. Transferred to the Força Aérea Portuguesa (Portuguese Air Force) May52 and moved to BA-6 Montijo where on strength Jun53; at BA-7 Aveiro in 1953, 1954 and 1955 and reportedly still active at Aveiro 13May59. No subsequent commercial history. Fate unknown.

1095　Built as **G-21B** for Aviação Naval Portuguesa (Portuguese Naval Aviation) with serial **104** and del 14Jun40. Delivered by sea to CAN Bom Sucesso, Lisbon for reassembly and active there until at least 1950. Prefix letter 'G' added to serial, application date uncertain; by 31Jan49 TFH recorded as 701hrs; transferred to the Força Aérea Portuguesa (Portuguese Air Force) May52 and moved to BA-6 Montijo where on strength Jun53 (under overhaul at OGMA, Alverca a/o 30Apr53 when TFH:940hrs); any further operational history unknown. No subsequent commercial history. Fate unknown.

1096　Built as **G-21B** for Aviação Naval Portuguesa (Portuguese Naval Aviation) with serial **105** and del 18Jun40. Delivered by sea to CAN Bom Sucesso, Lisbon for reassembly; to CAN Ponta Delgada, Azores Dec40 and active there until 1944. Prefix letter 'G' added to serial, application date uncertain; returned to Bom Sucesso in 1945 prior to Ponta Delgada closure and active there in 1946 and 1947; by 31Jan49 TFH recorded as 623hrs. Transferred to the Força Aérea Portuguesa (Portuguese Air Force) May52 and moved to BA-6 Montijo where on strength Jun53;

at BA-7 Aveiro in 1953 when last recorded with FAP. Registered to DGAC, Lisbon as **CS-AHF** in late 1956 but not apparently used (and register only recorded the identity as 'G-105'). Fate unknown.

1097　Built as **G-21B** for Aviação Naval Portuguesa (Portuguese Naval Aviation) with serial **106** and del 22Jun40. Delivered by sea to CAN Bom Sucesso, Lisbon for reassembly and active there in 1942. Prefix letter 'G' added to serial, application date uncertain; transferred to the Força Aérea Portuguesa (Portuguese Air Force) May52 and moved to BA-6 Montijo where notionally on strength Jun53; a/o 30Apr53 TFH:622hrs. Wfu at OGMA, Alverca, date unknown, with scrapped remains still visible Apr63.

1098　Built as **G-21B** for Aviação Naval Portuguesa (Portuguese Naval Aviation) with serial **107** and del 08Jly40. Delivered by sea to CAN Bom Sucesso, Lisbon for reassembly; CAN Aveiro in 1942. Prefix letter 'G' added to serial, application date uncertain; at Bom Sucesso in 1946 and 1947 (by 31Jan49 TFH recorded as 645hrs); active Bom Sucesso in 1951. Transferred to the Força Aérea Portuguesa (Portuguese Air Force) May52 and moved to BA-6 Montijo where on strength Jun53; at BA-7 Aveiro in 1954 and 1955. Reportedly scrapped at Aveiro (still without the 'G' prefix to serial), date uncertain.

1099　Built as **G-21B** for Aviação Naval Portuguesa (Portuguese Naval Aviation) with serial **108** and del 23Jly40. Delivered by sea to CAN Bom Sucesso, Lisbon for re-assembly; CAN Aveiro in 1942. Destroyed in take-off accident on River Tagus, Lisbon 31Aug43; aircraft sank, drowning the pilot although others survived. Remains recovered from river.

1100　Contract for US Navy as JRF-1, but completed as **JRF-4**, BuAer serial **3846**. Acc and del to NAS Anacostia 04Dec40; INA Bethpage 30Dec40; Hedron FMF, NAS San Diego 05Jan41 (used by Commanding General); Hedron 2nd MAW, NAS San Diego 14Sep42; NAS Alameda 31Jan43; Hedron 24, MAG-24 (Service Group, Marine Air Wings Pacific) MCAS Santa Barbara 10Feb43; A&R NAS Pearl Harbor 20Feb43 (month unreadable but off-strength MAG-24 in Feb43); Hedron 24, MAG-24 (4th Marine Base Air Defense Wing) Hawaii 10Jun43; Hedron 4, 4th MAW en route Tutuila 23Aug43, VMJ-353, 4th M(BD)AW Tutuila Dec43 and to Funafuti Jan44 and last reported with VMJ-353 April44; VS-51 Tutuila May44 until at least circa Aug44. Assumed to have been the JRF-4 assigned to COMAIRSOPAC Guadalcanal circa Oct-Dec44 but administratively on (aircraft history card) charge at station level at NAF Tutuila from at least Aug44 until SOC 31May45 (aircraft 'unreported' after Mar45).

1101　Contract for US Navy as JRF-1 but completed as **JRF-4**, BuAer serial **3847**. NAS Jacksonville 02Dec40; CINCLANT NAS Quonset Point 20May41; A&R NAS Norfolk 13Jan43; NAD Miami 25Mar43; NAS Norfolk (Atlantic Fleet)13Apr43; NAS Miami 20Apr43; COMNAVNAW 20Apr43. With Atlantic Fleet 12Jan44 but otherwise records missing until assigned Hedron 15, FAW-15 Port Lyautey by 21Jly44 when damaged beyond repair at Gibraltar: aircraft was caught by updraft during crosswind landing and subsequent heavy landing resulted in undercarriage collapse and substantial airframe damage. SOC 31Jly44.

1102　Contract for US Navy as JRF-1 but completed as **JRF-4**, BuAer serial **3848**. Acc and del dates unknown but shipped 23Dec40 to NAS Miami and received 26Dec40. Lost at sea 24Nov42 during rescue when aircraft capsized in heavy seas. The pilot made a sea landing 40 miles East of Fort Lauderdale, FL to rescue four survivors of a mid-air collision. Following their recovery, the sea state prevented a take-off and the aircraft was initially towed by a surface vessel although this was abandoned and the aircraft resumed its taxy. Five hours after the initial landing the starboard wing became heavy and submerged. Crew and survivors were transferred to a rescue vessel and the aircraft was abandoned. SOC Miami 22Dec42.

1103　Contract for US Navy as JRF-1 but completed as **JRF-4**, BuAer serial **3849**. Acc and del dates unknown but shipped 07Jan41 to NAS Pensacola and received 27Jan41. Destroyed 14May42 in fatal crash close to Tarkiln Field, FL (pilot was assigned to VM Unit, Pensacola): while deliberately flying at 1,000ft with power only on starboard engine, control was lost, aircraft crashed into woods and burned with two fatalities and one serious injury. SOC Pensacola 15May42.

1104　Contract for US Navy as JRF-1 but completed as **JRF-4**, BuAer serial **3850**. Acc 11Jan41 and del NAS Corpus Christi 12Jan41; NATTC Ward Island (Corpus Christi) 26Feb43. Records missing until with NATTC Corpus Christi by Aug44 and SOC there 31Jan45, reason unknown.

1105 Contract for US Navy as JRF-1 but completed as **JRF-4**, BuAer serial **3851**. Acc 03Feb41 and del NAS Norfolk 04Feb41; A&R NAD Norfolk 10Mar43. Aircraft destroyed in landing accident in Upper Hampton Roads Bay, VA 06Nov43. Pilot (from NAS Norfolk) was undertaking familiarisation flying and had made several earlier landings before misjudging his altitude and flying the aircraft into the water; no fatalities but only engines salvageable. SOC 15Nov43.

1106 Contract for US Navy as JRF-1 but completed as **JRF-4**, BuAer serial **3852**. Acc and del NAS Anacostia 11Feb41; NAD Annapolis 29Jun42. Apparently repaired following a serious landing accident on Annapolis Roads, 05Jun42 (overturned and submerged and was recommended for strike). NAS Norfolk 19Jly42; NAD San Juan 23Mar43 and still present Sep43 after which records are missing; NAS San Juan by Aug44; NAS Trinidad Sep45; Pool NAS San Juan Nov45 and SOC there 30Nov45 as obsolete and surplus, to War Assetts Administration. Cvtd to **G-21A** and regd **NC17083** to Edgar J Wynn, dba Trans American Airways, New York, NY 07Jun46. To Charles H Babb Co, New York, NY 15Jun46. To Asiatic Petroleum Corp, New York, NY 17Jun46. Sold to Shell Co of Ecuador, Quito, Ecuador 17Jun46, as **HC-SBL**, FN:12. Export CofA E-10386 dated 17Sep46. Accident 03Dec46: crashed into side of mountain in the Llanganates range in eastern Andes. The last radio contact with the aircraft was four minutes after take-off from Shell Mera base on a med-evac flight to Quito. The aircraft hit 300ft below the top of the 14,000ft peak while attempting to fly through Banos Pass in poor weather. Capt OE Gates, Shell's Chief Pilot in Ecuador; Sir Richard Barlow and a male nurse were all killed along with the two sick labourers who were being flown to hospital.

C/n 1106, Shell Ecuador's Goose HC-SBL, moored to a floating landing stage in the Rio Aguarico, circa October 1946, weeks before crashing in the Llanganates range in the eastern Andes.
(HR Sharman via Kavelaars Collection)

1107 Contract for US Navy as JRF-1 but completed as **JRF-4**, BuAer serial **3853**. Acc 03Mar41 and del NAS San Juan 12Mar41; A&R NAS Norfolk 23Mar43 (probably for repairs following a ground-loop on landing at San Juan 10Feb43); NAS Norfolk 10Apr43; NOP Hampton Roads (Norfolk) 23Mar44. Records missing until with A&R NAS Norfolk Aug44; NAS Miami 30Oct44; CQTU Glenview Dec44; 'awaiting action' at Glenview Oct45 and offered for sale by WAA by Mar46. SOC at Glenview 31Jly46, as obsolete and surplus. Converted to **G-21A**. **NC69208** assigned to Raymond Paul Hoover, Chambersburg, PA. Sold to Bataafsche Petroleum Maatschappij (Batavia Petroleum Co), Balikpapan, Dutch East Indies, and regd as **PK-AKA**(2) 17Oct46. Export CofA E-14961 issued to Asiatic Petroleum Corp, New York, NY 05Mar47. Wfu and reg cancelled 17Oct58. Transferred to the Tentara Nasional Indonesia – Angkatan Udara (TNI-AU) circa 1958. Received serial **PB-518** and operated by Skadron Udara 5 initially at Lanud Husein Sastranegara, Bandung then at Lanud Abdul Rahman Saleh, Malang. Returned to civil registration as **PK-RAM** with Merpati Nusantara Airlines, Jakarta in Dec77. Subsequent history not known.

1108 Contract for US Navy as JRF-1 but completed as **JRF-4**, BuAer serial **3854**. Acc 20Mar41 and del NAS Alameda 02Apr41; NAS San Diego 16Oct42 (probably as a result of serious damage incurred there during landing ground-loop on that day); NAS Alameda 24Nov42; NAD Alameda 15Jly43 and in NOP there 01Nov43. Records missing until with NAS Alameda Aug44 until Jun45; subsequent records confusing but thought to be at NAS Seattle by Jly45 awaiting re-work that eventually began 05Nov45; NAS Anacostia Dec45; Pool NAS Norfolk Dec47 until at least Aug48; records then missing until awaiting overhaul NAS Norfolk early 1950; NAS Quonset Point 25Jly50 for overhaul. Non-flyable and awaiting disposal 06Nov51. SOC at Quonset Point 08Feb52 for parts/scrap (TFH:1,545hrs).

1109 Contract for US Navy as JRF-1 but completed as **JRF-4**, BuAer serial **3855**. Acc and del NAS Anacostia 14Apr41; NAD Norfolk 15Jly43; NAS Patuxent River 20Jly43. Records missing until with Patuxent River Aug44 for radio test work and, from Jun45, electronics test work. SOC at Patuxent River 30Sep45 as obsolete. Sold by RFC, for $25,000, to Harrisville Combing Mills Inc, Harrisville, RI, 10Sep46. CofR as **G-21A**, **NC66102** issued 26Sep46; inspected and overhauled by A/T Maintenance Co, Army Hangar No.3, Miami, FL 04Oct46; nominal change to The Harrisville Co, 31Oct47. Sold to Bahamas Airways Ltd, Nassau, 26Jan48 and regd as **VP-BAM**, 14Feb48; aircraft name: *"Kingfish"* and later *"Andros"*. Accident 29Sep54: crashed attempting a take-off at Behring Point, Andros, for a flight to Oakes Field, Nassau with pilot + seven pax. The aircraft porpoised during the take-off run and after gaining an altitude of 20 or 30 feet crashed into the water and was wrecked, although there were no casualties. No definite cause could be found. Cancelled from Bahamas Register 29Sep54. Wreck sold to Dean H Franklin, Miami, FL, 28Oct54 for £85. **N3334F** and **N3332F** were requested for the rebuilt aircraft but neither available so FAA reserved **N3634F**, 21May56, but ntu. Regd **N332D**, 23Aug56. In response to a letter from FAA, 14Mar79, Franklin stated "aircraft undergoing complete overhaul", and on 12Jun91 requested FAA to allow regn to remain in effect although aircraft dismantled and stored. To Worldwide Aviation Distributors Inc, Miami, FL, with CofR 08Mar00. Not airworthy and CofR expired 31Mar11. Cancelled from USCAR 03Oct12.

1110 Built for US Navy as **JRF-5**, BuAer serial **6440**. Acc and del NAS Norfolk 23Jun41; Commander Support Force NAS Norfolk 24Apr41 and damaged in forced landing 30Apr42. Repaired, and to Commander Atlantic Fleet NAS Norfolk 24May42; NAS Seattle 02Aug42; NAS Kodiak Aug42; NAS Seattle 27Aug42. Records unreadable/missing although damaged at Otter Point, AK 29Sep43 when flown by a pilot based at NAS Dutch Harbor (a crewman retracted the undercarriage before airborne). A&R NAS Moffett Fld by Aug44 and under reconditioning there Dec44 until Aug45; Pool NAS Alameda Oct45; NAS Livermore Nov45; NAS Alameda Dec45 until at least Dec47. Records missing until to NavAirActSRC, NAF Annapolis by early 1950; NAF Annapolis 24Mar50. Slightly damaged in premature water take-off at Annapolis 04Apr51; NAS Quonset Point 22Aug51 for overhaul. Declared surplus 03Oct52 and SOC for transfer to the US Coast Guard 09Jan53 (TFH:2,078hrs); adopted designation **JRF-5G** with serial **6440**. USCG station allocation unconfirmed but believed to have been detached to (or at least visited) the CG Academy, New London CT in mid 'fifties. Disposal details unknown but reportedly to naval storage. Information provided by the USCG to the FAA in 1968 indicates that this aircraft was sold to Paraguay in 1958 (see page 107 for further details). Purchased by the Aviación Naval Paraguaya (ANP) in 1958 and overhauled at Atlanta, GA; allocated serial **T-001**. Lost on delivery flight 17Nov59: aircraft was ferried by an American pilot Miami-Nassau-San Juan but went missing between Nassau and San Juan; no trace found. [The G-21A N3282 registered with the quoted c/n 1110 is believed to be c/n 1146 qv].

1111 Built for US Navy as **JRF-5**, BuAer **6441**. Acc and del NAS Norfolk 05Aug41. Records missing but at NAS Argentia in 1941 (and assumed with Commander Patrol Wing 7 Dec41) until at least Apr43, although reported to have been in use with 745 Sqn, FAA, Yarmouth NS, dates unk; NAS Argentia by Aug44; Pool NAS Quonset Point Jan46; NAS Seattle Feb46 for reconditioning; Pool NAS Alameda Jly46; NAS Whidbey Island Sep46 until at least May47; Records missing, then to NavAirActSRC, NAF Annapolis by 20Jly49 when aircraft bounced on landing off Tolley Point, Chesapeake Bay, MD, buckling the skin. Repaired and on strength NavAirActSRC by Jan50 and organisationally moved to NAF Annapolis 24Mar50; NAS Quonset Point 14Jly50 for pre-disposal storage. Declared surplus 14May51 and SOC at Quonset Point 06Sep51, for parts/ scrap (TFH:2,009hrs).

1112 Built for US Navy as **JRF-5**, BuAer serial **6442**. Acc 12Aug41 and del NAS Jacksonville 13Aug41. Records unreadable/missing but at NAOT Jacksonville in 1943; Atlantic Fleet NAS Jacksonville Apr44; OTU VM Jacksonville by Aug44; NAS Seattle Oct45 for reconditioning; unreadable Aug46; NAS Alameda Sep46; NAF Adak 29Oct46. Badly damaged in landing accident at Tanaga, AK 22Mar47 when pilot landed fast in crosswind resulting in bounce, undercarriage collapse and ground-loop. Aircraft subsequently lost at sea 04Feb48, two miles west of Great Sitka, AK. Following a fuel flow problem, a safe emergency landing was made at sea and attempts made to resolve the problem. When these failed, a rescue vessel attempted to take the aircraft in tow. Fear of fire from float lights dropped by circling aircraft prevented crew from dumping fuel from wing tanks and this weight caused the right float to take on water. This, with ambient sea and weather state caused the abandonment of the tow and a failed attempt to hoist the aircraft aboard ship. The aircraft capsized and in deteriorating weather it was sunk by gunfire. SOC at Adak 30Apr48.

1113   Built for US Navy as **JRF-5**, BuAer serial **6443**. Acc and del Aug41; NAS Norfolk 02Sep41; NAS Trinidad 02Oct41. Seriously damaged in cross-wind landing accident (ground-looped), St Lucia, British West Indies 12Aug43 and SOC 14Aug43. [A hand-written notation on the accident card suggests that this decision was amended and that a repair (taking six months) would be undertaken. The movement card shows it going to the NOP NAS Norfolk 18Jan44 and to NOP NAS Trinidad 12Feb44 but these might be administrative entries and not necessarily indications of the aircraft's whereabouts. Nothing more reported]. No known subsequent history.

1114   Built for US Navy as **JRF-5**, BuAer serial **6444**. Acc and del Atlantic Fleet NAS Norfolk 12Sep41; unreadable; Commander Atlantic Fleet NAS Norfolk 15Jun42. Records missing, then to Hedron 16, FAW-16 NAF Recife by Aug44; Pool Hedron 2, FAW-5 NAS Norfolk Jun45; NAS Patuxent River Jly45 and SOC 31Aug45 as obsolete. To RFC Washington, DC Jly46. To Alaska Coastal Airlines, Juneau, AK by 1949, as **G-21A, NC88820**. Accident 02Dec49: crash-landed on beach at Farm Island, SE Alaska in snow. Total loss but salvaged and rebuilt. Later as **N88820**. Accident 08Sep53: badly damaged by "ground swell" alighting at Surprise Harbor, Tyee, AK after a flight from Juneau. Accident 15Aug54: damaged when hull struck runway at Skagway, AK. Pilot forgot to lower undercarriage but landed safely after go-around. Was on a flight from Juneau to Haines, AK. To Alaska Coastal Ellis Airlines 01Apr62; Accident 21Aug66: after an "uncontrolled descent", crashed into glacial crevasse near Juneau, AK. One crew and eight pax killed; aircraft written off; on scene investigation prevented by position of wreck.

1115   Built for US Navy as **JRF-5**, BuAer serial **6445**. Acc 24Sep41 and del NAS Norfolk 30Sep41 and to NAS Guantanamo Bay on same date. Records missing but on strength Guantanamo Bay by Aug44; NAS Jacksonville post-Apr46 and certainly on strength by Jun46 and SOC there 31Oct46 as obsolete and surplus. To Bataafsche Petroleum Maatschappij (Batavia Petroleum Co), Balikpapan as **G-21A, PK-AKB**(2) 17Oct46. Export CofA E-14997 issued to Asiatic Petroleum Corp, New York, NY 31Oct47. Wfu and regn cancelled 17Oct58. Transferred to the Tentara Nasional Indonesia – Angkatan Udara (TNI-AU) circa 1958; received serial **PB-521** and operated by Skadron Udara 5 initially at Lanud Husein Sastranegara, Bandung than at Lanud Abdul Rahman Saleh, Malang. Thought to have been used subsequently for ground instructional purposes, and by 1986 in such use/storage at Lanud Suryadarma, Kalijati as PB-521; still there in 2009.

1116   Built for US Navy as **JRF-5**, BuAer serial **6446**. Del NAS San Diego 08Oct41 (although actual receipt date probably 16Oct41); NAS Kaneohe Bay 19Mar42 (actual receipt 04Apr42). Aircraft lost at sea near Barking Sands, Kauai, HI near Kaneohe Bay 26Jan44; following a double-engine failure shortly after take-off (probably caused by a fractured fuel-line) the aircraft made a forced landing at sea and rapidly sank. Five of the six on board survived but the sixth man, a non-swimmer and unable to get his life-jacket on, drowned. (Pilot was assigned to NAS Kaneohe Bay). SOC 31Mar44.

1117   Built for US Navy as **JRF-5**, BuAer serial **6447**. Del NAS Seattle 11Oct41; NAS Sitka 12Nov41; NAS Seattle 08Oct42; NAS Sitka 31Dec42; reallocated Seattle but no evidence of delivery; to NAS Sitka 31Mar43. Damaged following a stall during a night cross-wind landing at Juneau Apt, AK 17Jun43. Repaired but subsequently lost 21Jly43 in fatal crash at Sukoi Inlet, Kruxof Island, AK. Aircraft was on authorised transport flight in poor weather from Juneau to Sitka when it crashed killing all six on board. SOC 23Jly43.

1118   Built for US Navy as **JRF-5**, BuAer serial **6448**. Acc and del NAS New York 16Oct41; NAS Seattle (no date); NAS Kodiak Nov41; NAS Sitka Sep43. Records unreadable/missing but thought to be the aircraft identified on accident card as "JRF-5 #8446" assigned to Sitka that ground-looped while taxying at Annette Island 17Sep43 (aircraft had landed with wet and defective brakes and control was lost while taxying in a confined area with a locked tail-wheel). The badly damaged aircraft required major overhaul; A&R NAS Moffett Fld by Aug44 until Sep45 then to NAS Moffett Fld; NAS Alameda 18Jly46 and to Pool Alameda Aug46; NAF Annapolis (Naval Academy) 13Sep47. Destroyed in crash and subsequent fire 18Sep47. Aircraft was being ferried from Alameda to Annapolis and was on final sector from Spartensberg, SC to Annapolis when port engine was shut down following a bad fuel leak. Aircraft was unable to sustain altitude over high ground on one engine and made a forced landing, wheels-up, on a cleared hill-top six miles south of Moneta, VA. The starboard engine caught fire and crew were unable to contain the fire which spread to the entire aircraft. SOC 30Nov47.

1119   Built for US Navy as **JRF-5**, BuAer serial **6449**. Acc 23Oct41 but first station allocation is recorded as NAS New York 31Aug42; Pacific Fleet NAS Seattle 07Sep42; NAD New York 02Jun43; NAF Kodiak 15Nov43. Records incomplete but at NAS Seattle in 1944; unreported in Aug-Sep44; NAS Moffett Fld Oct44; NAS Seattle 09Feb45 for reconditioning; NAS Moffett Fld 30Jun45; NAS Alameda Sep45. Made a forced landing at Alameda 28Nov45 following fuel exhaustion blamed on a combination of a clogged gauge and a failure to manually check fuel levels (no injuries); aircraft damaged beyond economic repair and SOC at Alameda 31Jan46.

1120   Built for US Navy as **JRF-5**, BuAer serial **6450**. Acc 31Oct41 and del NAS Quonset Point 15Nov41. Records incomplete but still at Quonset Point 23Feb42 (when damaged in hard landing at Bethpage), 23May42 (when again damaged in hard landing at Quonset Point) and in Aug44. Destroyed 06Jan45 when starboard engine failed in icing conditions; aircraft forced landed on Hayes River, Nova Scotia, coming to rest in trees (there were no injuries). SOC Quonset Point 31May45.

1121   Built for US Navy as **JRF-5**, BuAer serial **6451**. Acc 11Nov41 and del NAS Quonset Point 15Nov41. Records unreadable/incomplete but involved in repairable accident in Newfoundland 10Aug42 when with/attached to Task Force 24, presumably at NAF Argentia; with CASU-21 Norfolk by Aug44 (and probably from Jly43); NAS Seattle May45 for reconditioning; Pool NAS Norfolk Aug45; Hedron FAW-3, NAS Coco Solo Sep45 until at least Jly46. Records incomplete, then to FASRON-102, NAS Norfolk Jan47; BAR Bethpage Feb47; NAS San Diego Jun47 until at least Jly47. Records unreadable but thought to be at NAS Pearl Harbor by Feb48 and certainly so by Jan49; FASRON-11, NAS Pearl Harbor Feb49; FASRON-7, NAS San Diego Mar49 and to O&R San Diego Apr49. SOC San Diego 31Dec49 as obsolete. CofR N58981 applied for by Idaho State Educational Agency for Surplus Property (ISEASP), Boise, ID. Letter to CAA 17Apr50 from Chief, Surplus Property Utilization Program, Washington, DC requesting CAA return CofR application for JRF-5 from ISEASP. Also stating that the ISEASP would be advised that "the aircraft should be transferred to a more eligible institution where there is an existing educational requirement for such property". BoS US Government (through the Secretary of Health, Education & Welfare) to Alaska Coastal Airlines, Juneau, AK 01Apr54, for $15,000. CofR N58981 applied for 20Apr54; cancellation requested 22Apr54; CofR **N58981** issued 29Apr54. Cancelled from USCAR for salvage for parts 13May54.

1122   Built for US Navy as **JRF-5**, BuAer serial **6452**. Acc and del NAS New York 18Nov41; NAS Anacostia 24Nov41. Records unreadable but at Anacostia in Mar43 and from Aug44 until Mar45; NAS Seattle Apr45 for reconditioning; NAS Oakland Aug45; VN8D5 NAF Annapolis Aug46. Badly damaged in water-loop on Severn River 11Mar47 (pilot landed downwind and failed to take-off again once yaw had commenced); NAS Norfolk 21Mar47 until at least Aug48. Records missing and then to NAS Norfolk awaiting re-work by Jan50; Pool BAR Bethpage 30Jan50 for overhaul; NAF Annapolis 07Jly50. Damaged when right undercarriage collapsed on landing at NAAS Oceana 03Aug50 (repaired and remained active at Annapolis); NAS Quonset Point 27Dec51 for overhaul. Declared surplus 03Oct52 and SOC at Quonset Point 09Jan53 (TFH:1,907hrs). Circumstances of disposal strongly suggest that it was transferred to the US Coast Guard (in which case theoretically becoming a **JRF-5G** with serial **6452**), but no known service details and no evidence of subsequent disposal or later civilian use.

1123   Built for US Navy as **JRF-5**, BuAer serial **6453**. Acc and del NAS New York 26Nov41; NAS Anacostia (date unreadable); Roosevelt Base, CA Dec41. Damaged in heavy landing at NAS Terminal Island 16Dec41; records unreadable but at Roosevelt Base in 1943; NAS Terminal Island (date unreadable); A&R NAS Moffett Fld by Aug44; VJ-1 NAS Pearl Harbor Nov44; VJ-7 NAS Pearl Harbor Oct45; VJ-2 NAS Moffett Fld Jun46; VN8D5 NAF Annapolis Sep46; Pool BAR Bethpage Jly47 until 19Mar48. Records unreadable but aircraft unreported Apr-May48; FASRON-104 NAS Bermuda Jun48 until at least Aug48. Records missing but with FASRON-104 NAS Bermuda by 15Jly49 when involved in a minor accident at Kindley Fld, Bermuda (tail-wheel failed); NAS Norfolk 28Feb50 for overhaul; NAS Quonset Point 25Jly50 for overhaul. Declared surplus 14May51 and SOC for MDAP disposal to France 13Jly51 (TFH:1,905hrs). To France's Aéronautique Navale wearing abbreviated serial **453**; transit details unknown but by sea to Saigon, Vietnam and delivered to 8ème Escadrille de Servitude (8.S) at Cat Lai where accepted 06Mar52, coded 8.S-6. Damaged in an accident 18Mar53 and repaired; slightly damaged by small arms fire 18Feb54. Used by 8.S throughout Indo-China theatre until 1956, by which time based at Tan Son Nhut. Withdrawn from Vietnam (Saigon, Tan Son Nhut) in the *La Fayette* May56; arrival date in France unknown but circa Jun56 and to Saint-

Mandrier for intended 120-hour check. In operational use with 8.S at Algiers-Maison Blanche as 8.S-6 1956-1957; overhauled at Saint-Mandrier Dec56-Jan57; in work at Saint-Mandrier Jly57 (TFH:3,593hrs); returned to 8.S at Maison Blanche. At Saint-Mandrier Mar59 and SOC 20Jun59 although disposal circumstances unknown.

1124   Built for US Navy as **JRF-5**, BuAer serial **6454**. Acc and del NAS New York 02Dec41; NAS Corpus Christi (date unreadable); NAS Norfolk (Jan43 but date unreliable); NAC Hampton Roads (date unreadable); NAS Norfolk (date unreadable); NAC Hampton Roads (date unreadable). Records incomplete but at NAS Norfolk by Aug44; NAAS Chincoteague Jan46. Damaged when undercarriage collapsed on landing at Chincoteague 17Jly46; NAS Norfolk Aug46 for reconditioning; Pool BAR Bethpage Jan47; Pool FASRON-102 NAS Norfolk Jun47; NAS Norfolk Jly47; unreadable allocation to unknown NAS Aug47 until at least Aug48; records missing; NAS Norfolk by Jan50 awaiting overhaul; NAS Quonset Point 25Jly50 for overhaul. Declared surplus 14May51 and SOC for MDAP disposal to France 13Jly51 (TFH:1,490hrs); to France's Aéronautique Navale wearing abbreviated serial **454**; transit details unknown but by sea to Saigon, Vietnam and delivered to 8ème Escadrille de Servitude (8.S) at Cat Lai where accepted 06Mar52 and coded '8.S-7'. Lost in a water landing accident at Cantho, Mekong Delta 06Jly53 and SOC 29Oct53.

The manufacturer's numbers 1125 to 1174 were allocated to fifty G-38 model navigation trainer aircraft that were, after protracted contractual negations, eventually procured for the British Fleet Air Arm under Lend-Lease (and see 116 for details of this contract). The aircraft were known as Goose IA in British service and received the unique US Navy designation JRF-6B. No US Navy/BuAer serials were initially allocated to these aircraft although US records indicate that that the reference numbers '0181B' to '0230B' were allocated as a pre-delivery naval administrative identity but these numbers were not true BuAer/US Navy 'serials'. At an early stage of the procurement process it is believed that the British serials BW778 to BW827 were reserved for the intended acquisition but they were later cancelled and re-allocated to another unrelated and subsequently cancelled purchase.

As will be read below, six aircraft were diverted from this contract (LL-86447) by the US Government prior to delivery into British hands. At the close of the war all surviving aircraft were returned to the US Government and 36 JRF-6Bs were given new and 'real' BuAer identities in 1946. These serials, 66325 to 66359 and 89492 (randomly allocated), had previously been allocated to other US Navy aircraft on contracts that had been cancelled at the war's end.

In the following listing of these 50 aircraft the suggested 'BW' serials and the '0181B' etc numbers have been ignored as being, at best, irrelevant to their histories (although c/n 1146 is perhaps the exception that proves the rule!). In this context it should be noted that the US Army Air Force records raised in 1942 for the diverted aircraft 1155 to 1159 identify them by the manufacturer's number (eg 1155) and the intended British 'FP' serial and not by any US Navy identity.

1125   Built for Great Britain as **JRF-6B/Goose IA**, with serial **FP475**. First flight 08Jan42 and acc 10Jan42. TOC by 749 Sqn, FAA, Piarco, Trinidad 12Mar42 and coded 'W2A'. Returned to the US Govt in 1945 and taken on US Navy charge with new serial **66355**; Pool Hedron, FAW-11 (located at San Juan, PR and controlling US Navy ops in Trinidad) by Jan46; Pool NAS Jacksonville 14Feb46; NAS Seattle 21Feb46 but subsequently unreported until at NAS Miami where present by Apr46 until at least Jun46. Pool NAS Jacksonville date unknown and SOC 31Jly46 as obsolete and surplus and relocated to an unspecified WAA site in Georgia (Atlanta?). Ferried to Reykjavik with TF-RVG and RVI, via Mont Joli, PQ (overnight 02/03Nov46); Goose Bay, where delayed due to weather in Greenland; departed Goose Bay at 0736hrs 16Nov46, via Bluie West, and arrived Reykjavik 18Nov46, for Loftleidir hf. Regd as **G-21A, TF-RVJ,** 07Dec46. Dismantled and shipped to USA Mar53 and regn cancelled 10Apr53. Regd **N1583V** to Avalon Air Transport, with FN:2. To Kodiak Airways, Kodiak, AK 1956. Accident at 1050hrs on 24Dec61: crashed shortly after take-off from Old Harbor en route Kaguyak with five on board; one passenger killed. Repaired. Accident 11Dec74: lost en route Old Harbor to Kodiak, AK with five on board.

1126   Built for Great Britain as **JRF-6B/Goose IA**, with serial **FP476**. Acc Jan42 and TOC by 749 Sqn, FAA, Piarco, Trinidad 24Mar42, coded 'W2B'. Involved in forced landing following engine failure 01Dec42 and more seriously damaged 16Jan43 when the port oleo failed to lower for landing; repaired. Returned to the US Govt in 1945 and taken on US Navy charge with new serial **66334**. Pool NAS Miami by Jan46. NAS Seattle 19Mar46 and SOC there 31Aug46 as obsolete and surplus. Regd as **G-21A, NC68377** to William W Valentine, Pasadena, CA. Regd **VQ-FAH**

C/n 1126, of Bahamas Airways Ltd was registered VP-BAR, in October 1953. Named "Bahama", the Goose crashed on 31st October 1956, and the remains were sold, probably to Dean Franklin, for rebuild.
(Bahamas Airways via WH Llewellyn)

to South Seas Marine Products Ltd, Suva, Fiji 26Jan49. Company failed and aircraft shipped to USA 21Sep50. Fijian regn cancelled 07Oct50. Regd **N68377** to MacDonald Construction Co, Miami, FL 24Jan51 (acft painted yellow with red trim). Sold at TFH:1,469hrs for $43,000 to Bahamas Airways Ltd (BAL); insured to BAL 15Apr53, corrected to 22Apr53 and del to Miami, as N68377, 22Apr53. Regd **VP-BAR** Oct53 and aircraft named *"Bahama"*. N68377 cancelled from USCAR 07May54. Accident 31Oct56: overturned landing at Man o'War Cay, Bahamas, but was sold and rebuilt in Miami. Reregd as **N68377** believed to Dean Franklin. Fate unknown and regn not assigned 2008. According to the FAA, the records were destroyed in March 1979, but no reason was given.

1127   Built for Great Britain as **JRF-6B/Goose IA**, with serial **FP477**. Acc Jan42 and TOC by 749 Sqn, FAA, Piarco, Trinidad 12Mar42, coded 'W2C'. With 749 Sqn until at least Feb44 but no record of return to the US Govt or of subsequent sale to the commercial market. Fate uncertain

1128   Built for Great Britain as **JRF-6B/Goose IA**, with serial **FP478** and acc Feb42. Although recorded as TOC by 749 Sqn, FAA, Piarco, Trinidad (on 12Mar42), the aircraft was in fact destroyed at Piarco 24Feb42 prior to the allocation of any code letters and probably acceptance by the squadron. FP478 collided with Blackburn Shark K8455 of 750 Sqn, Piarco while on approach to Piarco following local exercises. The collision occurred at an altitude of 75ft, both pilots being unaware of the other and failing to see warning signals from the tower (the Shark struck the Goose amidships from above and behind). All four on board, including a US Navy instructor pilot, were killed.

1129   Built for Great Britain as **JRF-6B/Goose IA**, with serial **FP479**. Acc Feb42 and TOC by 749 Sqn, FAA, Piarco, Trinidad 24Mar42, coded 'W2D'. Returned to the US Govt in 1945 and taken on US Navy charge with new serial **66359**. NAS Miami by Feb46; NAS Seattle by Mar46 where SOC 30Sep46 as obsolete and surplus. To US Dept of Interior, Fish & Wildlife Service, Chicago, IL as **G-21A**, with CofR **NC710** 15Jan47. Tfd to Alaska Fish & Game Dept, Juneau, AK 05Apr60 with CofR for **N710SA** 11Aug60. Reregd **N7101** 01Jly63. BoS Fish & Game Dept to Dept of Public Safety, Anchorage 01Jly72 with CofR 13Sep72. Red/black painted hulk seen at Viking Air, BC Mar80. Sold to Viking Air Ltd, Sidney, BC 24Aug80 and cancelled from USCAR 08Oct80. BoS to W Ross Enterprises, Incline Village, NV 15Dec92. BoS to Larry Teufel 28Jun95 but Teufel was only the agent and in fact the sale was to Michael T Warn, Milwaukie, OR with CofR for **N9074U** 17Apr98. BoS Warn to North Coast Aero LLC, Port Townsend, WA, 22Feb99 with CofR 19Aug99. BoS to Amphib Inc, Lake Zurich, IL 29Mar05 with CofR 08Dec05; reported as a rebuild project at Kenosha, WI. Current but not airworthy May13, with CofR due to expire 29Feb16.

1130   Built for Great Britain as **JRF-6B/Goose IA**, with serial **FP480**. Acc Feb42 and TOC by 749 Sqn, FAA, Piarco, Trinidad 24Mar42, coded 'W2E'. Damaged in landing accident 04Feb43 attributed to binding brakes; repaired. Returned to the US Govt in 1945 and taken on US Navy charge with new serial **66339**; Pool Miami by Jan46 and SOC there as 30Jun46 obsolete and surplus (R-985-AN-6B engines). BoS WAA to Nelson A Miles, West Palm Beach, FL 10Dec46 for $15,000. **NC36808** allocated but ntu. CofR **NC9243H** issued 16Dec46. Overhauled and 5 seats installed Jan/Feb47 by Aero Trades Inc, Roosevelt Field, Mineola, NY with CofA 07Feb47; later as **N9243H**. Overhauled Feb51 with CofA 02May51; major overhaul Jly/Aug52 with CofA 20Aug52 at TFH:2,824:35hrs. BoS to Paul G Horvath, Miami Beach, FL 11Sep53 with CofR 21Sep53; CofA renewed 09Jan54 at TFH:3,372hrs; 06Jan55 at TFH:3,533hrs. BoS to Air-Sea Charters Inc, Miami Beach, FL 11Aug55 with CofA 14Aug55 at TFH:3,715hrs and CofR 07Sep55. BoS to Frank W

G-21A, c/n 1130, N93G of Catalina Air Lines Inc, waiting for passengers, at Gate 5 at Long Beach Airport, California, circa 1968.
(Clay Jansson via Jennifer Gradidge)

By 1976, Catalina Airlines Inc was operating G-21A, N93G, c/n 1130. The former Fleet Air Arm JRF-6B Goose was sold for scrap in 1981.   (MAP)

Cuttrelle, Miami, FL 30Mar57 with CofR 23Apr57. BoS to Comor Inc, New Orleans, LA 11Jun57 with CofR 14Jun57. BoS to GH McNew, South Miami, FL 01Jly57 with CofR 07Mar58. Reregd **N93G** 07May58. BoS to Pan Air Corp, New Orleans, LA 11Feb59. BoS to Vest Aircraft & Finance Co, Denver, CO 12Feb59. BoS to Paul D Choquette, dba Inlet Airways, Homer, AK 23Apr59 with CofR 27May59. BoS to Inlet Airlines Inc, Anchorage, AK 28Sep59 with CofR 16Dec59. Repaired Jun60 after landing accident but nfd. BoS Cable Airport Inc to Catalina Air Lines Inc, Long Beach, CA 03Mar67 (Cable Airport sold the aircraft to pay unpaid storage charges of $6,000); CofR to Catalina Air Lines 10Apr67; major overhaul Aug67. In 1968, Aero Commuter Inc merged with Catalina Air Lines. Cable Commuter and Skywark were added to the group which was then swallowed up by Golden West Airlines Inc. Tfd by BoS to Golden West Airlines Inc 01Dec69, with CofR 10Dec69 and aircraft wore "Catalina Golden West" titles. BoS to KC Sheet Metal Co, Long Beach, CA 16Nov73 with CofR 28Nov73. Featured in film *"Gone in 60 Seconds"* in 1974. CofR 10Jly74 for address change. BoS to Lew Mahieu, Long Beach, CA 28Feb75 with CofR 18Mar75. BoS to Catalina Airlines Inc, Gardena, CA 18Mar76 with CofR 29Mar76; aircraft name: *"John"*. Accident at 1532hrs on 28May76: left engine failed during initial climb after take-off and landed on grass Long Beach, CA with gear locked up due to malfunction; pilot + 8 pax uninjured. No Forms 337 after Sep76 and reported in poor state at San Pedro, CA in 1980. BoS to KC Sheetmetal Inc, Long Beach, CA 12Mar81 "for scrap", with CofR 16Jly81. BoS to 2BW, Newport Beach, CA 30Aug85 with CofR 10Apr86. CofR suspended after "undelivered Triennial" 21Feb90 (not known at last address for at least 2 years), and CofR expired 30Jun11. Registration still listed as assigned to 2BW a/o May13.

1131   Built for Great Britain as **JRF-6B/Goose IA**, with serial **FP481**. Acc Feb42 and TOC by 749 Sqn, FAA, Piarco, Trinidad 24Mar42, coded 'W2F'. Destroyed in fatal accident 17Aug45 when en route to Tobago. Pilot misjudged his altitude and struck sea, some ten miles west of Crown Point, Tobago, killing three of the six on board.

1132   Built for Great Britain as **JRF-6B/Goose IA**, with serial **FP482**. Acc Feb42 and TOC by 749 Sqn, FAA, Piarco, Trinidad 24Mar42, coded 'W2G'. Returned to the US Govt, presumably in late 1945, but not taken on US Navy charge until 31Dec46, possibly because of administrative oversight. Received new serial **89492** Dec46 by which time in Pool NAS Norfolk. Remained at Norfolk until at least May47 after which SOC. BoS WAA, Richmond, VA to Malcolm L Hardy, Waynesboro, PA, 26May47 for $380. CofR **NC69263** issued 22Jan48; tfd by BoS to Hardy Aviation Inc, Waynesboro, PA, 24May49 and CofR issued 31May49. Bought R-985-AN3-14B engine s/n 201243 and R-985-AN12B-14B s/n 13460 from Texas Co and had them overhauled by Southwest Airmotive, Dallas, TX.

Later as N69263. Surveyed by BOAC, May50, for possible use by Bahamas Airways. BoS to Hickory Spinners Inc, Hickory, NC, 03Apr51; test-flown 06May51, overhauled and CofA issued 12Jun51. CofR **N69263** issued 21Jun51. CofA issued 20Jun52 at TFH:376hrs, and 29Jun55 at TFH:1,435hrs. BoS to Leeward Aeronautical Sales Inc, Miami, FL, 06Feb60 and CofR issued 06Apr60. BoS to Edward N Moore/Joseph Q Adams/ Dean H Franklin, Miami, FL, 05Apr60 (sic). BoS to Kodiak Airways Inc, Kodiak, AK, 16Apr62, CofR issued 20Jun62 (with R-985-AN3 engines) and CofA 27Dec62 at TFH:2,990hrs; CofA renewed 22Jan64 at TFH:3,832hrs. Saved from the tidal wave of 27Mar64 by Al Cratty, who flew the aircraft from the seaplane base to the Kodiak Municipal airstrip as the wave approached. BoS to Kodiak Western Alaska Airlines Inc, Kodiak, AK, 14Apr75 with CofR 14May75. BoS to Amphibian Sales Inc, Miami, FL, 22Feb78 with CoR 14Aug78. Dep Miami 17Apr79 on del to New York; to Seaplane Shuttle Transport Inc, New York, NY, 04Jun79 with CofR 18Jun79; Experimental CofA issued 30Jun80, amended 22Aug80 and cancelled 30Dec80; Std CofA 20Mar81 at TFH:10,238hrs. BoS to Air Aquatic Inc, Weatherford, OK, 09Feb83, with CofR 19Apr83, and tfd by BoS to Shaun V Baldacchino / Jerry P McLean (same address) Weatherford, OK, 26May83 with CofR 05Aug83. Re-possessed by American Federal Savings & Loan Association (AFSLA), Mustang, OK 22Nov83 and CofR applied for 21Feb84, but then AFSLA disclaimed re-possession and allowed Baldacchino & McLean to sell aircraft to Bill Carroll / Gene N Hill/ Joe Abandonato, Huntington Beach, CA, recorded on BoS 12Jan84, with CofR 02May84. Operated by Catalina Flying Boats until sold to Bill A Moller, Rancho Palos Verdes, CA on BoS 23Apr87 with CofR issued 02Jun87. (The aircraft was noted at Long Beach, CA Aug88, still wearing Catalina Flying Boats colours). BoS to Amphibian Sales Inc, Miami, FL, 29Jan90. BoS to Baron Aviation Services Inc, Vichy, MO, 31Jan90 and CofR issued 02Mar90. Current and airworthy May13, with CofR due to expire 31Dec13.

1133   Built for Great Britain as **JRF-6B/Goose IA**, with serial **FP483**. Acc Mar42 and TOC by 749 Sqn, FAA, Piarco, Trinidad 24Mar42, coded 'W2H'. Returned to the US Govt in 1945 and taken on US Navy charge with new serial **66330**. Pool NAS Miami by Jan46; NAS Seattle 22Mar46 and SOC there 30Sep46 as obsolete and surplus. Sold by WAA to William W Valentine, Los Angeles, CA, 21Mar47 for $16,011. Regd as **G-21A, NC68376**, 06Jun47 and later as **N68376**. Sold to Pan Air Corp, New Orleans, LA, 09Feb52. BoS to A Brown Moore / Paul E Coguenhem, New Orleans, LA, 09Feb52; tfd to Comor Inc, New Orleans, LA, 10Feb52. Reregd **N93N** 27Feb52. CofA 05Mar56. To Pan Air Corp, New Orleans, LA, 24Jun63. BoS to Dean H Franklin, Miami, FL, 07Oct77 and reregd **N23DF**, 08Nov77 (placed on aircraft 08Dec77). Accident at 1315hrs on 13Dec77: struck buildings during forced landing Miami Lakes, near Opa Locka, FL. Both engines failed due to fuel mismanagement. NTSB stated that right tank contained 70gals whilst left tank was empty. One crew + one pax seriously injured and aircraft reported as "destroyed". Remains to Worldwide Aviation Distributors Inc, Miami, FL with CofR 27Mar00, which expired 31Mar11, but regn still assigned a/o May13.

1134   Built for Great Britain as **JRF-6B/Goose IA**, with serial **FP484**. Acc Mar42 and TOC by 749 Sqn, FAA, Piarco, Trinidad 24Mar42, coded 'W2J'. Damaged when taxiing 31Mar43 (aircraft struck hangar door) and repaired. Returned to the US Govt in 1945 and taken on US Navy charge with new serial **66340**. NAS Miami by Jan46; NAS Seattle by Mar46 and SOC there 31Aug46 as obsolete and surplus (TFH:720hrs). Reported regd as **NC9295H** and then reregd, as **G-21A, NC9293H**, to Thor Solberg Aviation Co, Somerville, NJ, inspected 20Jun47 and overhauled at Solberg Hunterdon A/P, NJ for ferry flight to Bergen, Norway Oct47. Tfd to Thor Solberg Flyveselskap, Bergen 14Oct47, named: *"Liev Eiriksson II"*. CofR No:205A for **LN-SAB** issued 15Nov47; to winter storage 30Dec47. Made ready for inspection 16Jun48 and inspected at Flatøy 29Jun48. BoS to Trygve Lunde, Bergen, Norway 04Apr48 with CofR 17Nov48. CofA expired 29Dec48. BoS to Lars Solberg, Bergen 17Mar50 with CofR 12May50. Last inspection in Norway at TFH:799hrs 13Jly50. Sold to the Svenska Flygvapnet (Royal Swedish Air Force) in 1951 although Norwegian registration not formally cancelled until 29Oct60. Given Flygvapnet designation **Tp81** and the serial **81001**; allocated to F21 Kallax 05Oct51 and accepted 09Nov51 and coded '31'; recoded '60' with F21 circa 1955. Crashed on take-off from Hemavan, Sweden 05Apr62, the crew suffering only minor injuries, and SOC by Flgvapnet 30Aug62 (TFH:2,795hrs).

1135   Built for Great Britain as **JRF-6B/Goose IA**, with serial **FP485**. Acc Mar42 and TOC by 749 Sqn, FAA, Piarco, Trinidad Apr42, coded 'W2K'. With 749 Sqn in 1942 but no further service record known and no record of return to the US Govt or of subsequent sale to the commercial market. [NB code 'W2K' was reallocated, date uncertain, to FP501 suggesting that FP485 was no longer in use by then.]

1136 Built for Great Britain as **JRF-6B/Goose IA**, with serial **FP486**. Acc Mar42 and TOC by 749 Sqn, FAA, Piarco, Trinidad, coded 'W2L'. Returned to the US Govt in 1945 and taken on US Navy charge with new serial **66356**. Pool Hedron, FAW-11 (located at San Juan, PR and controlling US Navy ops in Trinidad) by Jan46; Pool NAS Jacksonville 14Feb46; NAS Seattle 21Feb46 and SOC there 30Sep46 as obsolete and surplus. Regd as **G-21A, NC1080M** to Paul G Horvath, Miami, FL 17Apr47 and later as **N1080M**. ABC/Amphibian Bahamas Charter Service, Miami, FL by Dec62. **CF-CNR** allotted 18Jan65; authority to ferry Miami, FL to Oshawa, ON 22Jan65. BoS from ABC to Robson Leather 05Feb65; US CofA for export E-65041 dated 26Feb65; applied for CofR 22Mar65 but on inspection severe local corrosion was found in the bow compartment and its door, the cockpit floor and interior, the bottom cap of the wing front spar, et al. Repaired and inspected 09Aug66 at TFH:1,790hrs. CoR(P) 39060 and CofA 11881 issued to Robson Leather Co Ltd, Oshawa, ON 28Oct66. CofA renewed at TFH:2,053hrs, valid until 18Apr72. Accident at 1825hrs on 25Jun71: pilot Charles Robson; after receiving take-off clearance from Oshawa, ON, throttles were advanced but aircraft started to weather-cock into crosswind from left. The aircraft left the runway and power was cut. In order to avoid parked aircraft on side of taxi strip, right rudder and brakes were applied causing aircraft to turn sharply to the right, causing right wing to strike ground. N1080M cancelled from USCAR 14Jly71 and CF-CNR cancelled from CCAR 21Jly71 after sale to Lewis O Hilton, Greenville, ME 21Jly71. Reregd **N101LH** 20Jly71. Accident 30Jly71: crashed on take-off at Greenville, ME. Both engines failed due to lack of fuel. Aircraft had not been refuelled since purchase and had performed the ferry/delivery flight and had flown 45 mins local when it crashed. Pilot had only six hours on type. One pax fatal and pilot seriously injured, aircraft damaged by fire and cancelled from USCAR 04Oct71.

1137 Built for Great Britain as **JRF-6B/Goose IA**, with serial **FP487**. Acc Mar42 and reportedly delivered to Piarco, Trinidad 16May42 and TOC by 749 Sqn, FAA, coded 'W2M'. Returned to the US Govt in 1945 and taken on US Navy charge with new serial **66348**. NAS Miami by Jan46; NAS Seattle by Feb46 and SOC there 31Aug46 as obsolete and surplus. In open storage at Long Beach Airport, CA in 1947. Regd as **G-21A, NC68158** to Charles E Hunsinger, Long Beach, CA. Fate unknown.

1138 Built for Great Britain as **JRF-6B/Goose IA**, with serial **FP488**. Acc Mar42 but apparently not delivered to Piarco until 09Dec42. TOC by 749 Sqn, FAA, Piarco, Trinidad and coded 'W2AH' (previously code 'W2N' unconfirmed). With 749 Sqn until at least Jly43; to 111 OTU, Oakes Fld, Nassau 1943. Returned to US Navy and ferried Nassau to NAS Miami 26Nov43 and reportedly in storage at NAS Norfolk Jan44. Formally returned to the US Govt in 1945 and taken on US Navy charge with new serial **66325**. Pool NAS Miami by Jan46; NAS Seattle 21Mar46 and SOC there 30Sep46 as obsolete and surplus. BoS WAA to Charles E Hunsinger, Long Beach, CA, 21Mar47 for $15,557. CofR **NC68157** issued 22Apr47. Cvtd to **G-21A** and seats installed by Long Beach Airmotive, with CofA 07Jly47. Sold to Kenneth F Brown, Long Beach, CA, 04Apr47 and CofR for G-21A issued 01Jly47. Sold to Amphibian Air Transport (AAT), Long Beach, CA, 18Nov48 and to assignee of AAT, MW Engelman, on same date, with CofR issued 29Nov48; aircraft re-possessed by Bank of America National Trust & Savings Association 01Jun49. BoS Bank of America to Rose Pechuls / Kirk Kerkorian, dba Los Angeles Air Service, Los Angeles, CA, 12Jly49 and CofR issued 22Jly49. Sold to Alaska Coastal Airlines, Juneau, AK, 16Dec49 and CofR issued 18Jan50 as **N68157**. Tfd by BoS to Alaska Coastal-Ellis Airlines, Juneau, AK, 18Sep62 with CofR same date; CofA 15Oct62 at TFH:12,447hrs. Tfd by BoS to Alaska Coastal Airlines Inc, Juneau, AK, 16Jun66 with CofR applied for same date (no evidence that the CofR was issued); TFH:16,223hrs a/o 05Feb68. Merged into Alaska Airlines Inc, 27Mar68 with CofR 19Apr68. BoS Alaska A/L to Alaska Island Air, Petersburg, AK, 18Feb71 with CofR 24Mar71. Rebuilt by Viking Air at Sidney, BC, Canada and retnd to service 1976. BoS to Wilson C Edwards, Big Spring, TX, 09May89 with CofR 20Jun89. Current and airworthy May13, with CofR due to expire 31Jly14.

1139 Built for Great Britain as **JRF-6B/Goose IA**, with serial **FP489**. Acc Mar42 but apparently not delivered to Piarco until 09Dec42. TOC by 749 Sqn, FAA, Piarco, Trinidad, coded 'W2AH' (previously code 'W2N' unconfirmed). With 749 Sqn until at least Jly43; to 111 OTU, Oakes Fld, Nassau 1943. Returned to US Navy and ferried Nassau to NAS Miami 26Nov43 and reportedly in storage at NAS Norfolk Jan44. Formally returned to the US Govt in 1945 and taken on US Navy charge with new serial **66325**. Pool NAS Miami by Jan46; NAS Jacksonville May46. SOC there 30Jun46 as obsolete and surplus and relocated to an unspecified WAA site in Georgia (Atlanta?). Ferried to Reykjavik with TF-RVG and

RVJ, via Mont Joli, PQ (overnight 02/03Nov46); Goose Bay, where delayed due to weather in Greenland; departed Goose Bay at 0739hrs 16Nov46, via Bluie West, and arrived Reykjavik 18Nov46, for Loftleidir hf. Regd as **G-21A, TF-RVI** 07Dec46. Accident 13Mar47: crashed on take-off from water at Budardalur, western Iceland. Four killed and aircraft written off.

1140 Built for Great Britain as **JRF-6B/Goose IA**, with serial **FP490**. Acc Apr42 and TOC by 749 Sqn, FAA, Piarco, Trinidad 16May42, coded 'W2P'. Returned to the US Govt in 1945 and taken on US Navy charge with new serial **66353**; Pool Hedron, FAW-11 (located at San Juan, PR and controlling US Navy ops in Trinidad) by Jan46; Pool NAS Jacksonville 08Feb46; NAS Seattle 21Feb46 and SOC there 31Aug46 as obsolete and surplus. Regd as **G-21A, NC95468** to Amphibian Air Transport, Long Beach, CA in 1947. To Reeve Aleutian Airways, Anchorage, AK 1948. Later as **N95468**. Accident 05Jun53: u/c collapsed and belly landed at Cold Bay, AK. Accident 09Jun54: u/c collapsed landing at Anchorage, AK. Reported derelict 1976. Sold to Penair, King Salmon, AK Apr77. Accident 23Jan81: crashed into water and sank in Driftwood Bay, near Dutch Harbor, AK; the mail flight had departed Dutch Harbor for a round trip and the last en route stop had been made at Nikolski, AK. The nature of the accident is unknown; pilot and passenger died; wing float found in sea but aircraft not recovered, and cancelled from USCAR, date unknown.

1141 Built for Great Britain as **JRF-6B/Goose IA**, with serial **FP491**. Acc Apr42 and TOC by 749 Sqn, FAA, Piarco, Trinidad 16Jun42, coded 'W2Q'. Returned to the US Govt in 1945 and taken on US Navy charge with new serial **66354**. Pool Hedron, FAW-11 (located at San Juan, PR and controlling US Navy ops in Trinidad) by Jan46; NAS Miami Feb46; NAS Seattle Mar46 and SOC there 31Aug46 as obsolete and surplus. BoS WAA to Defense Plant Corp, Seattle, WA 14Oct46 for $25,000. **N1200N** applied for 25Jan47 but ntu. Overhauled and cvtd from JRF-6B to **G-21A** by Northwestern Aeronautical Co, St. Paul, MN Jan47 with CofA 17Feb47. CofR **NC9698H** issued to RFC, Seattle Loan Agency, Seattle, WA 27Feb47; op by Pacific Exploration Inc. Accident 06Mar47: aircraft submerged after being holed at Punta Arenas harbour, Costa Rica. BoS Pacific Exploration (on behalf of RFC) to Román Macaya Lahmann, San José, Costa Rica 26Jun47 for $250. BofS Román M Lahmann to Robert Macaya, Oakland, CA 15Mar48. CofA 23Mar48 after major repairs by TACA Airways, San José, Costa Rica; CofR 15Apr48. BoS to Dall L Christensen, Long Beach, CA 12Jly48. BoS to MP Efferson & Associates Inc, Washington, DC 13May49 with CofR N9698H 13Jun49. BoS to The Shell Company of Ecuador Ltd, Quito, Ecuador 08Aug49. Cancelled from USCAR 15Aug49 and Export CofA E-16693 issued to Asiatic Petroleum Corp, New York, NY 21Sep49. Regd **HC-SBX,** Aug49 to replace HC-SBB (c/n 1005) and given FN: 2. Wfu Mar50. BoS Shell to Grumman Aircraft Engineering Corp, Bethpage, NY 08Nov50 with CofR **N703A** 17May51 and CofA 21May51 after overhaul; CofA 26Jun56 at TFH:1,656hrs. BoS to Willard Rich, West Palm Beach, FL 11Mar60 with CofR 14Apr60. BoS to John Cassullo, Cove Neck, Long Island, NY 22Apr60 with CofR 10Jun60. BoS to Paul G Horvath, Miami Beach, FL 28Sep60 with CofR 21Oct60. BoS to Irving Leslie Jones Jr, Miami, FL 31Oct60. BoS to Cat Cay Airways Inc, Miami, FL 19Nov60 with CofR 09Jan61. Cargo door installed Jan63 per STC SA39SO. BoS to Southeast Airlines Inc, Miami, FL 25Apr63 with CofR 02Jun63. BoS to Exeter Inc, Miami, FL 27Feb64 with CofR 03Mar64. Returned to Southeast Airlines Inc, Dover, DE by BoS 29Apr64, with CofR 27Jly64. BoS to Caribbean Flying Boats, San Juan, PR 18Feb70 with CofR 20Nov70, op by Antilles Air Boats (AAB);

Goose, c/n 1141, HC-SBX, owned by Shell Ecuador, was by late-1949 operated for them by Airwork Ltd. It is seen here moored at the seismic party base camp at Lorocachi, unloading supplies. The bundles awaiting collection on the jetty are parachutes, dropped earlier by a Dakota.

(MNW Herfst via Kavelaars Collection)

address change to c/o AAB, St Thomas, US Virgin Islands by 1972. Accident 18Jun71: experienced engine failure on both engines on a flight from St Thomas, US Virgin Islands to Fajardo, PR. Made a forced landing in sea near Culebra Island, PR but wave caught float and aircraft sank. Two pax killed, 8 pax and pilot injured. Aircraft totally destroyed and cancelled from USCAR 24Aug71.

1142   Built for Great Britain as **JRF-6B/Goose IA**, with serial **FP492**. Acc Apr42 and TOC by 749 Sqn, FAA, Piarco, Trinidad 16Jun42, probably coded 'W2R'. Destroyed in a take-off accident at Piarco 02Sep42. The aircraft experienced engine trouble and spun-in from 500 feet killing all five crew and students. FP492 was burnt out in the ensuing fire.

1143   Built for Great Britain as **JRF-6B/Goose IA**, with serial **FP493**. Acc May42 and TOC by 749 Sqn, FAA, Piarco, Trinidad 16Jun42, coded 'W2S'. Returned to the US Govt in 1945 and taken on US Navy charge with new serial **66352**. Pool Hedron, FAW-11 (located at San Juan, PR and controlling US Navy ops in Trinidad) by Jan46; NAS Miami Feb46; NAS Seattle Apr46 and SOC there 30Sep46 as obsolete and surplus. Regd as **G-21A, NC95406** to Bay Valley Air Service Inc, Stockton, CA. Sold to Michael P Efferson, dba Efferson & Associates, Washington, DC 26May48. Sold to Argentine Naval Mission, Washington, DC 10Jun48 and cancelled from USCAR 18Feb49. Following overhaul by the Aircraft Service Co of El Monte, CA, flown to Argentina and delivered 19Nov48. Given Aviación Naval (COAN) serial **0293** and initially used by Prefectura General Maritima (PGM); coded 'PGM-P-4' and presumably based at Punta Indio within COAN's Escuadra Aeronaval No2. Assumed to have been recoded circa 1950 as '3-P-22' indicative of patrol use within the Escuadra Aeronaval No3 at Punta Indio but not so recorded (but maybe '2-P-22' at Espora). While en route to the Isla Martín Garcia, Buenos Aires 11Jly52 the aircraft landed fast and sank in the Río de la Plata; recovered and repaired. Transferred to the Escuadra Aeronaval No3, Punto Indio 01Jan53 and recoded '3-P-52'; reassigned to the Escuadrilla de Propósitos Generales, Punta Indio 21Nov58 and recoded '3-G-9'. Wfu 30Mar60 and sold as scrap 05Dec60.

1144   Built for Great Britain as **JRF-6B/Goose IA**, with serial **FP494**. Acc May42 but apparently not delivered to Piarco until 09Dec42. TOC by 749 Sqn, FAA, Piarco, Trinidad and coded 'W2T'. Slightly damaged 30Jun43 when tailwheel braking device failed. Returned to the US Govt in 1945 and taken on US Navy charge with new serial **66345**. NAS Miami by Jan46; Pool NAS Jacksonville 05Feb46; NAS Seattle 14Feb46 and SOC there 30Sep46 as obsolete and surplus. Regd as **G-21A, NC95429** to Bay Valley Air Service Inc, Stockton, CA. Sold to Michael P Efferson, dba Efferson & Associates, Washington, DC 26May48. Sold to Argentine Naval Mission, Washington, DC 10Jun48; following overhaul by the Aircraft Service Co. of El Monte, CA flown to Argentina and delivered 19Nov48; and cancelled from USCAR 18Feb49. Given Aviación Naval (COAN) serial **0294** and initially used by Prefectura General Maritima (PGM); coded 'PGM-P-5' and presumably based at Punta Indio within COAN's Escuadra Aeronaval No2. Recoded circa 1950 as '3-P-23' ('3-P-24' also reported) indicative of patrol use within the Escuadra Aeronaval No3 at Punta Indio; transferred to the Escuadra Aeronaval No3, Punto Indio 01Jan53 and recoded '3-P-53'. Used in the Antarctic in the summer of 1955/1956; reassigned to the Escuadrilla de Propósitos Generales, Punta Indio circa 1956 and recoded '3-G-8'. Transferred by COAN to the Prefectura Naval circa 1958 with the new PNA identity **PM-8** (but retaining the COAN serial 0294); assumed to have been returned to COAN, date unknown. Transferred to Argentina's Misión Naval (MNA) in Paraguay in 1963 gaining new code 'MNA-11' May64. Loaned to the Aviación Naval Paraguaya (ANP), Asunción circa Mar66 although first date of use by the ANP is uncertain and probably pre-dates this. Believed to have been renumbered **129** circa 1966 although questionable when or whether the serial was applied. Used by the Servicio Aeronaval (SAN) and based at Base Aeronaval de Sajonia, Asunción; reportedly in poor condition and little used by 1967. Wfu by 1968 and believed to have been acquired, with other ANP Gooses, by US citizen Walter B von Kleinsmid of Long Beach, CA. Post-1967 the history of this aircraft becomes very complicated. It was reportedly formally gifted by Argentina to the Aviación Naval Paraguaya (ANP), Asunción 13Sep68 and subsequently scrapped in Asunción but this transfer may in fact have been the precursor of (or confused with) a commercial sale dated 03Dec68 by the MNA on behalf of the COAN to US citizen Wilton R Probert (von Kleinsmid's business partner). In other words, although used by the ANP in Paraguay, it was not their property to sell, even in a non-airworthy condition and the Americans had to buy it from Argentina. Officially this aircraft ceased to exist circa 1970. However, on arrival in the USA, the aircraft registered in the USA as N3283 (c/n B-29 according to its FAA registration) was wearing 0294 on its tail and had all the physical appearances of being the former MNA-11/129. It is presumed therefore

G-21A, c/n 1144, N3283, formerly operated by Antilles Air Boats, is seen here withdrawn from use, at Opa Locka, Florida in December 1981, still wearing the company logo on the bow and the US Virgin Islands flag on the tail. *(Nigel P Chalcraft)*

that the new owners exchanged this aircraft for the previously registered N3283 without amending the aircraft's identity with the FAA. This history (of 1144) thus continues with the history attributed by the FAA to aircraft 'B-29' (N3283). BoS Paraguayan Navy to von Kleinsmid 02Oct68 with CofR for **G-21A, N3283**, 06Nov68 with CofA 19Jan70. BoS to Caribbean Flying Boats Inc, San Juan, PR with CofR 03Nov70 but address c/o Antilles Air Boats (AAB) Inc, Christiansted, US Virgin Islands; Beechcraft C-18 engine cowlings fitted Mar75 per STC SA551SW. BoS CFB (PR) Inc to Antilles Air Boats, Christiansted, US Virgin Islands 20Mar79. Beech cowlings removed and Grumman cowls replaced May80. Antilles Air Boats ceased operations and aircraft flown to Opa Locka, FL 1981. BoS AAB to Amphibian Sales Inc, Miami, FL 28Jan86 (date recorded); dep Opa Locka, FL on truck 20Oct83. BoS to Kane K Baker, New York, NY 23Dec85 with CofR 28Jan86. BoS to David Cushnir, New York, NY 12Dec87 with CofR 31Mar88; address change to Opa Locka, FL 31Mar88. Believed not airworthy due no Forms 337 since Dec85 and status uncertain 2010 due "undelivered Triennial". The CofR expired on 31Mar11. [See page 108 for summary of the ANP aircraft].

1145   Built for Great Britain as **JRF-6B/Goose IA**, with serial **FP495**. Acc May42 and TOC by 749 Sqn, FAA, Piarco, Trinidad, coded 'W2U'. Returned to the US Govt in 1945 and taken on US Navy charge with new serial **66351**. NAS Miami by Jan46; NAS Seattle Feb46 and SOC there 30Sep46 as obsolete and surplus. Regd as **G-21A, NC1200V** to Police Dept, New York City, NY Apr47 and later as **N1200V**. To Beldex Corp, St Louis, MO Nov55. BoS McKinnon Enterprises Inc, Sandy, OR to BC Air Lines Ltd 04Jan65 and **CF-RQI** allotted same day. Authority to ferry Pompano Beach, FL – Edmonton, AB 07Jan65 with US CofA for export E-65034, 14Jan65. CofR 32401(C) and CofA 10125 to BC Air Lines Ltd, Vancouver, BC 05Mar65 at TFH:3,876hrs. Cancelled from USCAR 21Jun65. Retractable wing-tip floats fitted in 1965, using McKinnon kit No.26. CofA renewed at TFH:4,687hrs, valid until 14Jan67; at TFH:6,431hrs, valid until 14Jan69. Lease to Northland Airlines Ltd, Winnipeg, MB, 16Aug68 for 2 months with CofR(C) 47536 same day. CofA renewed at TFH:7,121hrs, valid until 14Jan70. Became Midwest Airlines 1969. CofR(C) to Airwest Airlines Ltd, Vancouver, BC 29May69. Accident at 1200hrs on 03Jun69: left wing struck a boat while approaching the dock at Namu, BC due to gusty wind. BoS BC Air Lines to Airwest Airlines Ltd 27Jun69. CofA renewed at TFH:7,253hrs, valid until 25Jly70; at TFH:8,406hrs, valid until 19Jan73. Accident at 0730hrs on 29Sep72: overturned and sank when pilot, Peter Daniel Lauren, landed with wheels-down in Comox Harbour, BC. Pilot + 2 pax injured; 6 uninjured. BoS 29Nov72 Insurance to Catalina Seaplanes Inc, CA as salvage for $16,616. Cancelled from CCAR 19Dec72. (Another BoS The Reinsurance & Excess Insurance Co, Vancouver, BC to Wilton R Probert was issued 08Jan73 to satisfy FAA requirements.) Rebuilt and regd to Tradition Air Transport Leucadia, CA, as **N62121**, by 1975. To Sea Bee Air, Auckland, NZ as **ZK-ENY** Oct77. Dep Auckland for Fiji 26Sep82 and NZ regn cancelled 30Sep82. Regd **DQ-FDQ** 01Oct82 for Sea Bee Air operating for Sun Tours Ltd, Nadi, Fiji. Returned to Auckland 27Oct84 for major refit. Reregd **ZK-ENY** to Sea Bee Air, Auckland 19Dec84. To Stephen Pope, Auckland Jly88 and Canterbury Planes, Christchurch, NZ by the end of 1988. Reregd **VH-ENY** and arrived Sydney, 06Jan89 and thence to Casey Airfield, Victoria, Australia 07Jan89 for B Young, Patterson Lakes, Victoria 21Nov89. Cancelled from register 29Oct90 and to Yellowbirds, Bangkok, Thailand Oct90 as **HS-TOM**. To Tropical Sea Air Co Ltd, Bangkok 14Jan91. Sold by auction at Phuket, Thailand, to Klaus Dieter Martin, Munich, Germany. Dismantled and shipped via Singapore to Hamburg, Germany from where it was trucked to Landsberied, near Munich for European Seaplane Services, Oberpfaffenhofen, Germany in 1995. Noted 70% restored in Apr02, and similar in Oct06. Carries no markings but stored inside shed. The restoration was being done using c/ns 1149 and B-141 for parts/spares. Last noted, still stored inside, 26Jan11.

1146 Built for Great Britain as **JRF-6B/Goose IA**, with serial **FP496**. Acc May42 and TOC by 749 Sqn, FAA, Piarco, Trinidad, coded 'W2AA'. Returned to the US Govt in 1945 and taken on US Navy charge with new serial **66326**. Pool NAS Miami by Jan46 and SOC there 30Jun46 as obsolete and surplus. BoS WAA to PAD Aviation & Navigation Co, Chicago, IL 09Oct46, for $25,000, and CofR as **G-21A, NC74585** issued 07Nov46. BoS to Michael P Efferson, dba MP Efferson & Associates, Washington, DC 21Jan47 with CofR same date. BoS to Argentine Naval Commission, Washington, DC 30Jan47 and cancelled from USCAR 17Feb47 as sold abroad. Given Aviación Naval (COAN) serial **0186** and initially used by Prefectura General Maritima (PGM) with code 'PGM-3'; initially based at Punta Indio within COAN's Escuadra Aeronaval No2 and so assigned 12Jun47. Suffered significant damage in a landing accident at Morón 23Feb48 when it left the runway and collided with an earth bank; repaired and returned to service. Recoded circa 1950 as '2-P-21' indicative of patrol use within the Escuadra Aeronaval No2 at Espora and so used in the Antarctic summers of 1951/1952 and 1952/1953. Transferred to the Escuadra Aeronaval No3, Punto Indio 01Jan53 and recoded '3-P-51'; used in the Antarctic 1953/1954 (where it was rescued by ARA Chiriguano R-28 after an emergency landing 06Feb53); used again in Antarctica 1954/1955. Reorganised into the Escuadrilla de Propósitos Generales, Punta Indio circa 1955 and appropriately recoded '3-G-7'. Involved in a landing accident at Punta Indio 08Feb56 in which the undercarriage was wiped out; repaired and returned to service with the Escuadrilla de Propósitos Generales. Transferred by COAN to the Prefectura Naval circa 1958 with the new PNA identity **PM-7** (but retaining the COAN serial 0186); returned to COAN Jan62 with limited flying hours remaining. Transferred to Argentina's Misión Naval en Paraguay, date uncertain, gaining new COAN code 'MNA-12'. Formally gifted to the Aviación Naval Paraguaya (ANP), Asunción 28Mar66 with handover ceremony taking place 04May66; ANP serial **128** worn by the handover date although date of first use by the ANP and that of serial allocation is uncertain and might pre-date this; used by the Servicio Aeronaval (SAN) and based at Base Aeronaval de Sajonia, Asunción. Wfu by 1968 and acquired, with other ANP Gooses, by US citizen Walter B von Kleinsmid of Long Beach, CA. The purchase, registration and overhaul of these aircraft was a lengthy affair and either by accident or intent the true identities of the newly registered US aircraft became confused. In the case of aircraft 128, von Kleinsmid reserved the registration **N3282** 25Apr68 and purchased the aircraft from the ANP 27May68. It would appear that the ANP and von Kleinsmid were unable to give the FAA a manufacturer's number and so assistance was sought from Grumman Aircraft Engineering Corp (GAEC) to provide an acceptable identity. The COAN serial 0186, still presumably worn on the tail, was offered to GAEC, but they failed to recognise it for what it was and assumed that somehow this was the long-buried BuAer paper number '0186B' (of c/n 1130). Consequently the FAA was advised 27May68 that the identity of N3282 was c/n 1130. The FAA was aware that the true 1130 was currently registered as N93G and rejected the submission. Von Kleinsmid now turned to the US Coast Guard for help as GAEC had advised him they had been the supplier of three JRF-5s to the ANP in 1959 (and Von Kleinsmid was also buying three other aircraft, two of which had been acquired by the ANP from the USCG). The USCG presumably confirmed that c/ns B-29 and B-53 (two of his purchases) and 1110 had been the three deliveries in 1959. Whether or not von Kleinsmid and the USCG were aware that 1110 (USCG 6440) had been lost without trace on its 1959 delivery flight remains open to question but the convenient 1110 seemed acceptable enough and thus was offered to the FAA 26Jly68, and duly accepted. The correspondence also suggests that GAEC had lost track of the Argentine and Paraguayan aircraft. This history (of 1146) thus continues with the history attributed by the FAA to aircraft '1110' (N3282).

Co-owned by Wilton R Probert by 08Jan70 and CofA issued that date at TFH:3,038hrs; STC SA295AL for installation of pax seats had been incorporated. BoS von Kleinsmid to Southeast Skyways Inc, Juneau, AK, 08Jan70 with CofR 10Feb70. BoS to Charles F Willis & Co Inc, Seattle, WA, 13Jun79 (cf c/n 1051). BoS to Robert L Hall, Kodiak, AK, 20Jun79 to be operated by Kodiak Western Airlines; CofR ?Jun79. BoS Hall to Seaplane Shuttle Transport Inc, New York, NY, 29Oct80 with CofR 05Jan81. BoS to Anthony Stinis/ Hill Air Co Inc, Fort Lauderdale, FL, 15Oct84 with CofR 26Nov84. BoS to Wilson C Edwards, Big Spring, TX, 11Feb88 with CofR 27Apr88, which expired 30Jun11. [See page 108 for summary of the ANP aircraft].

1147 Built for Great Britain as **JRF-6B/Goose IA**, with serial **FP497**. Acc Jun42 and TOC by 749 Sqn, FAA, Piarco, Trinidad, coded 'W2AB'. Returned to the US Govt in 1945 and taken on US Navy charge with new serial **66357**. Location unreported Jan46; Hedron, FAW-11 (located at San Juan, PR and controlling US Navy ops in Trinidad) 05Feb46; Pool NAS Jacksonville 14Feb46; NAS Seattle 25Feb46 and SOC there 30Sep46 as obsolete and surplus. Regd **NC709** in 1946 to US Fish & Wildlife Service,

Anchorage, AK and later as N709; based Kodiak until accident in autumn 1956. Sold to McKinnon Jan57 and became the first McKinnon conversion to **G-21C**, with four Lycoming GSO-480-B2D6 air-cooled engines; FF 25Jan58. Reregd **N150M** with c/n **1201** to McKinnon Enterprises Inc, Sandy, OR. Cvtd to **G-21D "Hybrid"**, with two UAC PT6A-20 turboprops and c/n **1251**, and reregd as such Jun60. To Precision Valve Corp, Yonkers, NY Dec66; CofA issued 16Feb67. To Peyton Hawes, dba Payless Drug Stores, Portland, OR 1974. To On Mark Aviation, Van Nuys, CA Sep77. Re-engined with PT6A-60A with intakes above the nacelles. To World Jet Inc, Fort Lauderdale, FL Mar80. Non-fatal accident at Fort Lauderdale, FL 21Jun80. To Water Fowl Inc, Fort Lauderdale, FL, Jly82 with CofR 05Nov82. Confiscated in Haiti for alleged drug smuggling in 1990s, and, after several failed attempts to rescue the Goose, it was reduced to scrap. (Some reports say it was seized in Cuba).

1148 Built for Great Britain as **JRF-6B/Goose IA**, with serial **FP498**. Acc Jun42 but apparently not delivered to Piarco until 05Dec42. TOC by 749 Sqn, FAA, Piarco, Trinidad and coded 'W2AD'. Returned to the US Govt in 1945 and taken on US Navy charge with new serial **66346**. NAS Miami by Jan46 and SOC there 30Jun46 as obsolete and surplus. BoS WAA to PAD Aviation & Navigation Co, Chicago, IL 09Oct46 for $25,000; CofR **NC74587** issued 07Nov46. BoS to Michael P Efferson, dba MP Efferson & Associates, Washington, DC 21Jan47 with CofR same date. BoS to Argentine Naval Commission, Washington, DC 30Jan47 and cancelled from USCAR 17Feb47, as sold abroad. Given Aviación Naval (COAN) serial **0185** and initially used by Prefectura General Maritima (PGM) with code 'PGM-2'; initially based at Punta Indio within COAN's Escuadra Aeronaval No2 and so assigned 12Jun47. Wrecked at sea off Río Santa Cruz, Santa Cruz 14Sep48 with the loss of all five crew. [Argentina's Antarctic base 'Jubany' was later named to commemorate the pilot lost in this accident; Teniente de Fragata José Jubany].

1149 Built for Great Britain as **JRF-6B/Goose IA**, with serial **FP499**. Acc Jun42 but apparently not delivered to Piarco until 05Dec42. TOC by 749 Sqn, FAA, Piarco, Trinidad and coded 'W2AC'. Returned to the US Govt in 1945 and taken on US Navy charge with new serial **66347**. NAS Miami by Jan46 until at least Jun46; Pool NAS Jacksonville by Jly46 and SOC there 31Jly46 as obsolete and surplus. Regd to Alaska Coastal Airlines 08Oct46 as **G-21A, NC28369**, and later as **N28369**. Became Alaska Coastal-Ellis Airlines 01Apr62 (with CofA 11Oct62) and then Alaska Coastal Airlines Inc Jun66; TFH:19,454hrs a/o 05Feb68; merged into Alaska Airlines in 1968. Noted in ex-Alaska A/Ls colours at Van Nuys, CA 12Jly73. To Antilles Air Boats, Christiansted, US Virgin Islands by 1976; wfu 1979 St Croix-Hamilton A/P; Antilles ceased operations 1981. Aircraft derelict by 1985 and cancelled from USCAR Aug88. Reregd **N28369** to DH Franklin Enterprises Inc, Fort Lauderdale, FL 30Mar92, but stored derelict at St Croix, US Virgin Islands. Crated and shipped to Germany for European Coastal Airlines in 1999. Awaiting restoration at Landsberied, near Munich in 2002. Still stored dismantled in AAB colours and titles Oct06, parts reported being used in restoration of c/n 1145. Still registered to Franklin when CofR expired 31Mar11. Last reported, stored outside at Landsberied, 26Jan11.

1150 Built for Great Britain as **JRF-6B/Goose IA**, with serial **FP500**. Available Jly42 but diverted by US Govt for delivery to Bolivia. Delivered by air to Bolivia Jly42 probably initially for the use of the US Air Mission to Bolivia; subsequently served with the re-titled Fuerza Aérea Boliviano (FAB) [Bolivian Air Force]; initial Bolivian identity unknown but by Jly52 in use with Escuadrón de Entranamiento at the Base Aérea 3 at Santa Cruz and still on unit strength in late 1954. Latterly reported to be in use with the Bolivian military airline Transportes Aéreos Militares marked **TAM-15**. Tfd by FAB to Donald B Sittman, Miami, FL in exchange for Beech AT-11, N62497. FAB pilot flew the JRF-6B to Panama where exchange took place. BoS dated 24Mar59 from FAB confirmed exchange. CofR N5548A applied for by Sittman 14Apr59. BoS from Sittman to Irving L Jones/ DB Sittman, Miami, FL, 11Sep59 with CofR **N5548A**, issued to Jones & Sittman, 16Oct59. Cvtd from Bolivian military to US civil standard and given CofA 25Mar60 at TFH:2,139hrs. BoS Jones/Sittman to Cat Cay Airways Inc, Lubbock, TX (Irving L Jones, President) 25Oct60 with CofR 09Jan61. BoS to Southeast Airlines Inc, Miami, FL (Irving L Jones, President) 25Apr63 with CofR 11Jun63. BoS to Exeter Inc, Miami, FL, 27Feb64 with CofR 03Mar64. BoS for return to Southeast Airlines Inc, Dover, DE, 29Apr64, with CofR 27Jly64. BoS to Antilles Air Boats Inc, St Croix, US Virgin Islands, 23Jun65, with CofR 06Sep65. Accident 19Mar66: substantial damage when stalled on take-off from St Thomas Harbour, US Virgin Islands. Pilot + ten pax uninjured. BoS 28Dec76 records sale to KC Aircraft Sheet Metal, Long Beach, CA but letter same date to KC from Charles Blair says he wanted to use N5548A as a test-bed for the installation of two IO-720 engines in Beech cowlings. To be engineered at Long Beach A/P at earliest possible date

G-21A, c/n 1150, registered N5548A, the former Bolivian Air Force JRF-6B, is seen in this undated photo carrying Cat Cay Airways titles (under the cheat-line) and the company logo on the bow. (MAP)

(presumably by KC?). A CofR was issued to KC 02Feb77, but the sale to KC was rescinded by Blair 25Jly77, requesting that N5548A be added to Caribbean Flying Boats-VI Inc fleet. BoS for this change was dated 18Jly77, and CofR issued19Aug77. Tfd back to Antilles Air Boats Inc, Jun78 with CofR 08Jun78. Antilles ceased ops in 1981. BoS to Amphibian Sales Inc (Dean Franklin), Miami, FL, undated, but possibly Feb81, although not recorded by FAA until 11Feb84. Aircraft reported wfu Mar82. BoS Amphibian Sales to Anthony Stinis, Fort Lauderdale, FL, 28Dec83, with CofR, 11Feb84. Tfd to co-owners A Stinis/ Frank A Hill, 20Dec88 and sold by them to Douglas F Martin, Boca Raton, FL 12Dec88 (admin lapse!) with CofR 19Nov91. To Tropic Bird Holdings, Boca Raton, FL 28Aug98; aircraft named *"Pappy's Choice"*. Accident on 25Mar99 (at TFH:13,136hrs): crashed into a canal about 2 miles South of Fort Lauderdale, FL after a loss of power in left engine; one fatality. The aircraft wreckage was released to Marco Flite Services Inc, Margate, FL 03Apr99. To Patrick M Sturges, Hollywood, FL with CofR 01Mar07. Current and airworthy May13, with CofR due to expire 30Nov13.

1151   Built for Great Britain as **JRF-6B/Goose IA**, with serial **FP501**. Acc Oct42 and TOC by 749 Sqn, FAA, Piarco, Trinidad, coded 'W2K'. Returned to the US Govt in 1945 and taken on US Navy charge with new serial **66350**. NAS Miami by Jan46; Pool NAS Jacksonville 05Feb46; NAS Seattle 13Feb46 and SOC there 31Aug46 as obsolete and surplus. Regd as **G-21A, NC95471** to Grenold Collins Flying Services, AK. Accident 03Jun48: damaged in crash at Naknek, AK. Fate unknown.

1152   Built for Great Britain as **JRF-6B/Goose IA**, with serial **FP502**. Del 31Oct42 and TOC by 749 Sqn, FAA, Piarco, Trinidad, coded 'W2V'. Returned to the US Govt in 1945 and taken on US Navy charge with new serial **66358**. Location unreported Jan46; Hedron, FAW-11 (located at San Juan, PR and controlling US Navy ops in Trinidad) 05Feb46; Pool NAS Jacksonville 14Feb46; NAS Seattle 26Feb46 and SOC there 31Aug46 as obsolete and surplus. Regd as **G-21A, NC606** (probably in 1946) to State of New York and used by the Chautauqua Fish Hatchery. Reregd **N606F** to Serge J Laignelot, Denver, CO 07May57. Cancelled from USCAR 07Oct63 and regd **F-OBYU** 12Aug64 for Sté. Air Polynesie, Papeete. Taken over by Réseau Aérien Interinsulaire in 1965. Cancelled as sold abroad 05Dec67. To **N8777A** for Antilles Air Boats, Christiansted, US Virgin Islands 27Sep68. Accident 23May71: initiated a go-around while landing at Charlotte-Amalie after a flight from St Croix. Hit an unoccupied boat which sank with the aircraft. Pilot + six pax uninjured. Accident at

C/n 1152, the former JRF-6B is seen here as NC606, in a busy scene at the Chautauqua Fish Hatchery in New York State, in the 1950s.
(New York State)

1316hrs on 12Jan73: substantial damage in forced landing in rough sea, near Fredericksted, US Virgin Islands, after both engines failed; pilot + 4 pax uninjured. Accident 05Apr78: crashed into deep water, en route St John to St Croix, due to engine failure. Aircraft written off, both pilots missing, all pax OK. Still registered Jan81 but CofR revoked by 2008.

1153   Built for Great Britain as **JRF-6B/Goose IA**, with serial **FP503**. Del 16Nov42 and TOC by 749 Sqn, FAA, Piarco, Trinidad, coded 'W2W'. Returned to the US Govt in 1945 and taken on US Navy charge with new serial **66327**. NAS Miami by Jan46 and SOC there 30Jun46 as obsolete and surplus. Any immediate US civil registration unknown but sold to the Government of Guatemala, presumably in 1946, where it was used as a presidential aircraft; assumed to have been based at Los Cipresales, Guatemala City, the aircraft was locally known as an 'OA-9' (1947-48 Fuerza Aérea Guatemalteca (FAG) AOBs show one aircraft on strength). Local FAG serial not known; final AOB entry 05May48. BoS Guatemalan Government to Frank W Albert, Philipsburg, PA, 08May48, CofR **NC66327** issued 29Jly48. Reregd as **G-21A, NC1376V** 29Jly48, and NC66327 cancelled 02Feb49; CofA 24Aug50. BoS to Hardy Aviation Inc, Waynesboro, PA, 07Mar51 with CofR 17Apr51 as **N1376V**. Sold to Far Eastern Foundation Inc, San Francisco, CA, 15Nov51 with CofR 29Dec51. BoS to Air Carrier Service Corp, Washington, DC, 08Jly52. BoS to Western Enterprises Inc, Pittsburgh, PA, 10Jly52 for $45,000. [Western Enterprises Incorporated of Pittsburgh, PA (WEI) was a cover organisation created by the US Central Intelligence Agency (CIA) in 1951 to manage paramilitary operations against mainland China from the island of Taiwan (Formosa). N1376V is assumed to have been the Goose, marked as 'OA9-0002', that was used in support of these activities. See page 115] BoS to James Walker Lassiter (assumed to have been the same James Lassiter employed by WEI as an instructor-pilot in Taiwan and Japan in 1952), Falls Church, VA, 16May57. BoS to Walter A Stonnell, Falls Church, VA, 26Oct57 with CofR 31Dec57 and CofA 26May58 at TFH:872hrs. Sold back to Air Carrier Service Corp, Washington, DC, 05Jly60; overhauled and ferry tanks installed by Atchison Clements Inc, Wichita, KS Aug60 and exported to Japan, 13Sep60 with US Export CofA E-40278. BoS Air Carrier to Sekiya & Co Ltd, Tokyo. Regd **JA5063**. To Naka Nihon Koku, Nagoya. Modified to carry 8 pax Dec60. Operated scheduled services to Shima and Kashimoto from 15Jly62. TFH:510hrs a/o 10Dec62. Returned to USA ex Nagasaki Airlines to McKinnon Enterprises Inc, Sandy, OR, 11Mar65 for $40,000. JA- regn cancelled 24Mar65 and Japanese CofA A-136 for export issued 11Mar65. Regd as **N93010** 18Apr65. Authority to ferry Sandy, OR to Winnipeg, MB 29Apr65 and US CofA for export E-65595 issued 07May65. BoS McKinnon to Warren C Plummer, Winnipeg, MB, 10May65 for $35,000. BoS 19May65 to Rainy Lake Airways, Fort Francis, ON at TFH:1,685hrs and CofR(C) 34960 for **CF-SBS** issued to them same date [CF-SBS had been allotted as early as 14Jan65]. CofA 11037 issued 17Jun65, valid until 06May66. Cancelled from USCAR 23Jly65. CofA renewed at TFH:1,854hrs, valid until 30May67; at TFH:2,886hrs, valid until 20May73. Sold to Amphibian Parts Inc, Miami, FL, 27Jan78 and cancelled from CCAR 08Feb78. CofR **N143DF** issued 11May78. Tfd by BoS to Amphibian Sales Inc, Miami, FL, 30Sep78 with CofR 11Dec78. Dep Miami on del to New York 12Apr79; CofA 16Apr79 at TFH:3,887hrs. BoS to Don Lewis, dba Seaplane Shuttle Transport Inc and aka Cosmopolitan Broadcasting Corp, New York, NY, 04Jun79 with CofR 18Jun79. Electric aux landing gear retraction mechanism installed per STC SA2-603, 16Oct80; CofA 25Feb82 at TFH:4,002hrs. Sold to Phyllis Manley/ Roberta E Becker/ John A Becker, c/o Catalina Seaplanes, Long Beach, CA, 11Jun84 with CofR 19Jly84, leased to Catalina Airlines. (John & Roberta Becker had a vested interest in Catalina A/L but Phyllis Manley had actually paid for the G-21A, so when Catalina A/L went bankrupt, 3 months after the lease began, Manley filed a revised BoS (dated 15Jun84) listing her as sole owner. Therefore CofR N143DF issued 24Jun86 confirmed Phyllis M Manley, Downey, CA as owner. BoS Manley to Wale Enterprises Inc, Costa Mesa, CA, 23Oct86 with CofR 10Dec86. Sold to C Chase Hoffman, Tulare, CA, 01Nov88 with CofR 23May89. Sold to Heinz G Peier, North Lima, OH, 03Jan90 with CofR 22Feb90.

C/n 1153, the former Catalina Seaplanes' G-21A, N143DF, at Long Beach, California, circa 1986. (EW Priebe)

Reregd **N848HP**, 15Mar90 and tfd to Peier Inc, Waterloo, IA, 13Nov93 with CofR 18Jan94, but CofR revoked 27Jan94 because Peier was not a US citizen. Aircraft name *"Island Queen"*. BoS Peier to Almon Landair Ltd, Whitehorse, YT 18Apr98 and allotted **C-GDAO** 05May98. Cancelled from USCAR 22May98. CofR(C) issued 02May98. Accident 18/19Jan99: destroyed in overnight hangar fire at Whitehorse, YK. The fire destroyed a WWII hangar owned by Trans North Helicopters, who lost seven helicopters and an aircraft. Summit Air lost five aircraft, and three private aircraft in cold storage (Beaver, Fleet Canuck and Goose) were also lost. Cancelled from CCAR 14Apr00.

Note: N143DF featured in the 1985 film *"Commando"*, which also starred Arnold Schwarzenegger. During filming the Goose was flown initially by Herb Johnson (former Chief Pilot for *Catalina Airlines*) but Chuck Kirk took over as pilot for the later scenes.

1154 Built for Great Britain as **JRF-6B/Goose IA**, with serial **FP504**. Del 22Nov42 and TOC by 749 Sqn, FAA, Piarco, Trinidad, code unknown. Aircraft was lost 06May43 following engine failure and a ditching. The pilot, the only occupant, was successfully recovered.

1155 Built for Great Britain as **JRF-6B** with the intended serial **FP505**. Re-allocated to the US Army Air Force and re-designated as an **OA-9** with serial **42-106979**. Accepted at New York (Bethpage?) 30Nov42 for use by military attachés in the Caribbean theatre: Guatemala (6th AF) 01Apr43; British Guiana 03Nov43; returned USA 01May44; Venezuela 08Jun44; at Panama Air Depot, France Field as of 03Nov44 for radio equipment change. Condemned 6th AF (CAC) 09Feb47 and salvaged for parts 28May47.

1156 Built for Great Britain as **JRF-6B** with the intended serial **FP506**. Re-allocated to the US Army Air Force and re-designated as an **OA-9** with serial **42-106980**. Accepted at New York (Bethpage?) 12Dec42 for use by military attachés in the Caribbean theatre. Unit allocation unknown. Wrecked on Caqueta River, Bogota, Colombia 16Feb43. Following unspecified mechanical failure, the aircraft hit water at high-speed, breaking the fuselage at the passenger cabin and tearing off the right float. Aircraft sank rapidly and subsequent recovery attempt was abandoned.

1157 Built for Great Britain as **JRF-6B** with the intended serial **FP507**. Re-allocated to the USAAF and re-designated as an **OA-9** with serial **42-106981**. Del 15Dec42 and accepted at New York (Bethpage?) 17Dec42 for use by military attachés in the Caribbean theatre: Venezuela 31Mar43; returned to US 05Oct43 and to 4121st ABU Kelly 29Oct43; departed US 25Nov43 for unknown destination; (returned from?) Cuba 01Nov44; Guatemala 23Nov44; returned to US and to 4006th ABU Miami 12Jly45. To RFC at Bush Field, Augusta, GA 01Oct45-24Nov45 and declared surplus 10Nov45 for disposal to RFC, Washington, DC. CofR **NC88821** issued to RFC 28Nov45. Lsd to Ellis Air Lines, Ketchikan, AK; water rudder fitted (to OA-9) Apr46. BoS RFC to Ellis Air Lines, Ketchikan, AK 01Mar47; Ellis A/L Model C water rudder fitted and aircraft cvtd to **G-21A** Apr47. Overhaul and repaint Apr49 with CofR **N88821** 20Jun49; complete overhaul Feb53, including "installation of wings from Coast Guard B-86". Tfd by BoS to Alaska Coastal-Ellis Airlines, Juneau, AK, 01Oct62 with CofR 09Oct62 and CofA 15Oct62 at TFH:17,118hrs. Tfd by BoS to Alaska Coastal Airlines Inc 16Jun66; TFH:21,567hrs a/o 05Feb68. Merged into Alaska Airlines Inc, Seattle, WA 27Mar68 with CofR 19Apr68. BoS to GK Griffith, dba Griffco Aviation, Seattle, WA 26May69 with CofR 24Sep69. BoS to Pacific Western Airlines Ltd, Vancouver, BC dated 04Apr69 but executed 03Nov70. BoS to Viking Air Ltd, Sidney, BC 29Feb72. BoS to Alert Bay Air Services Ltd, Campbell River, BC 30Mar73. Cancelled from USCAR 18Dec73 and regd as **CF-EFN**, 11Jan74; leased to Gulf Air Aviation Ltd, Campbell River, BC and CofR(C) issued 12Apr79. To Trans Provincial Airlines Ltd (TPA), Terrace, BC 29Apr80. Became Air BC Ltd, Richmond, BC 31Oct80. Reregd **C-FEFN** by Apr81 and became Jim Pattison Industries, Richmond, BC 17May83, but operated in TPA c/s. Moved base to Prince Rupert, BC and regd there 31Aug84. BoS Pattison to Trans Provincial Airlines Ltd, Prince Rupert, BC 17Jly86 and CofR(C) issued 02Jun88. TFH:11,695hrs a/o 31Jly90; Accident 28Feb91: ground-looped landing at Sandspit A/P, Queen Charlotte Islands. Wreckage barged to Prince Rupert, BC and stripped of parts for rebuild of c/n 1059. Derelict at Seal Cove, Prince Rupert and cancelled from CCAR, on sale to USA 18Dec92. Remains sold to Tongass Historical Society, Ketchikan, AK 28Oct92 with CofR **N88821** 08Mar93; restored using parts from c/n B-28 (qv). Current and airworthy May13, with CofR due to expire 31Jan14.

1158 Built for Great Britain as **JRF-6B** with the intended serial **FP508**. Re-allocated to the USAAF and re-designated as an **OA-9** with serial **42-106982**; del 19Dec42 and accepted at New York (Bethpage?) 27Dec42 for use by military attachés in the Caribbean theatre: Cuba (Columbia Apt, Havana) 26Feb43. Destroyed in accident in Biscayne Bay, Miami 14Nov43 (crashed during water-landing but with no serious injuries). Formally SOC 05Feb45 as 'condemned' although contemporary records make it clear that aircraft was "wrecked" in the 1943 incident.

1159 Built for Great Britain as **JRF-6B** with the intended serial **FP509**. Re-allocated to the USAAF and re-designated as an **OA-9** with serial **42-106983**. Del and accepted at New York (Bethpage?) 27Nov42 for use by military attachés in the Caribbean theatre: Haiti 20Feb43; Military Attaché Bogota, Colombia 04May43; in work at the Panama Air Depot, France Field from unknown date until Sep43; returned to the US from Haiti 11Mar44; Peru 11Apr44; Cuba 30Jun44. Destroyed in hurricane 18Oct44 ("reduced to junk").

1160 Built for Great Britain as **JRF-6B/Goose IA**, with serial **FP510**. Del 30Dec42 and TOC by 749 Sqn, FAA, Piarco, Trinidad, coded 'W2N'. Returned to the US Govt in 1945 and taken on US Navy charge with new serial **66343**. NAS Miami by Jan46 and SOC there 30Jun46 as obsolete and surplus. Sold by WAA, Atlanta, GA for $20,000 to North Carolina Pulp Co, Plymouth, NC, 30Nov46. **NC86640** applied for 09Apr47 by North Carolina Pulp Co, c/o Kieckhefer Container Corp, Camden, NJ. Cvtd from JRF-6B to **G-21A** by Grumman, Bethpage 10Apr47 with CofA same date; CofR issued 02May47 and later as **N86640**. BoS to Consolidated Cosmetics Inc, Chicago, IL 19Apr54 with CofR 27May54. BoS to Lanolin-Plus Inc, (same address) Chicago, IL, 05Aug55 with CofR 29Aug55 and CofA 17Sep55. BoS to R Livingston Sullivan, Radnor, PA 23Jan58 with CofR 21Feb58. BoS to William W Watson, Miami, FL 10Dec69 with CofR 29Jan70. BoS to Anchor Air Inc, (WW Watson, President) Miami, FL, 16Mar70 with CofR 02Apr70. Accident at 1000hrs on 24Apr74: gear collapsed while taxying after landing Nassau Intl A/P, Bahamas; pilot + 6 pax uninjured but aircraft substantially damaged. CofR revoked by FAA a/o 17Nov77 but re-issued 13Feb78. Tfd back to William W Watson, Miami, FL, by BoS 16May78 with CofR 01Aug78. BoS to Atlantic Amphibian Inc, Highlands, NJ (undated) but CofR application 17Feb80 and issued 21May81. Tfd by BoS to Joanne Watson, Crescent City, FL, 04Dec86. BoS to Harold F Mitchell, Majuro, Marshall Islands (undated) but CofR application 30Jan88 and issued 19Jly88. BoS to Aero Technology, (RL Probert, President) Long Beach, CA 06Apr90 with CofR 30May90. Accident at 1330hrs on 16Jun90 at Long Beach, CA: the aircraft had been in rebuild from Jan89 and this was its first flight to leak-check the hull before painting. Several water landings were made but during the last an eye witness stated it "hit the water". The pilot stated that during return to Long Beach all elevator control was lost and he elected to land in the water but forgot that the wheels were down. The landing was made using power and elevator trim and the aircraft nosed over near the shoreline causing substantial damage, and serious injury to pilot. NTSB determined the cause as a corroded elevator control cable turnbuckle that had failed due to stress corrosion cracking caused by tensile overload. Sold to James B French, Bakersfield, CA, 13Feb91 with CofR 07Jun91. Wreck stored dismantled at Sequoia, CA and CofR expired 31Dec11.

1161 Built for Great Britain as **JRF-6B/Goose IA**, with serial **FP511**. Del 31Dec42 and TOC by 749 Sqn, FAA, Piarco, Trinidad, coded 'W2R'. Returned to the US Govt in 1945 and taken on US Navy charge with new serial **66331**. Pool NAS Miami by Jan46; NAS Seattle 22Mar46 and SOC there 30Sep46 as obsolete and surplus. Regd as **G-21A, NC95467** to Amphibian Air Transport, Long Beach, CA in 1947 and later as **N95467**. To Hardy Aviation Inc, Waynesboro, PA and being overhauled and for sale at $25,000 when inspected by BOAC at TFH:1,766hrs, in May50. Sold to Gulf Oil of Louisiana Inc, Houston, TX with CofA dated 25Mar56. To Irving L Jones, Miami, FL by Jun63. To Antilles Air Boats, Christiansted, US Virgin Islands after 01Jun64; aircraft name: *"Excalibur VI"*. Non-fatal accident, 27Aug65: pilot forgot to extend landing gear to taxi up the ramp at Christiansted, and hit the seawall. Pilot + ten pax uninjured, but aircraft substantially damaged. Accident 05Dec67: substantial damage when stalled on take-off at Tortola, British Virgin Islands. Pilot + ten pax uninjured. To KC Aircraft Sheet Metal, Long Beach, CA by 1978. To Air Pac, Seattle, WA 1978. Later operated out of Dutch Harbor, AK. Accident at 1345hrs on 11Nov78: struck shipping buoy during water take-off, Akutan Bay, AK for an intended flight to Dutch Harbor, AK; pilot + one pax uninjured but aircraft substantially damaged. To Air Metal Fabricators Inc, Arlington, WA with CofR 04Nov91. Trucked to Palm Springs Air Museum, CA in 1996 at TFH:8,565hrs. Assembled, and displayed without serial, in blue US Navy scheme and noted there Jly04. Registry status uncertain Sep11, due undelivered Triennial, but noted for sale "as a project" for $200,000 Nov11. To Addison J and Wendra M Pemberton, Spokane, WA with CofR 24Jan12. Current and airworthy May13, with CofR due to expire 31Jan15.

1162 Built for Great Britain as **JRF-6B/Goose IA**, with serial **FP512**. Del 24Jan43; TOC by 749 Sqn, FAA, Piarco, Trinidad, coded 'W2AL'. Returned to the US Govt in 1945 and taken on US Navy charge with new serial **66337**. NAS Puerto Rico Aug45; Pool NAS Miami by Jan46. Damaged when undercarriage collapsed on landing at NAS Miami 11Jun46 following a test flight; CNAAT Jacksonville Dec46 and SOC there 31Dec46 as obsolete and surplus to War Surplus Assets Commission Mar47 (aircraft may have remained at Miami). Cvtd to **G-21A** by General Aviation, Miami, FL 06Mar47. Reported to Pan American Airways, New York, NY as **NC1057M** but to Charles S Collar, dba Bahamas Airways Ltd, Nassau 06Mar47 and reregd **VP-BAH** 10Mar47 with CofA same date. Aircraft name: *"Dolphin"*. Renamed *"Abaco"* Aug57. Accident 03Jan58: damaged landing French Creek, Andros Island, Bahamas. Reregd **VP-BAC**(2) 22May58 and re-named *"Bimini"* (VP-BAH re-used on a DC-3 1958-59). Left undercarriage collapsed 02Dec59. Re-registered to Bahamas Airways Ltd 26Mar60 as **VP-BBJ**. To Franklin Aviation Enterprises, Miami, FL as **N5521A** 1960; stored and then rebuilt. To Chalk's Airline, Miami, FL by 1967, aircraft name: *"Bonefish"*. To Caribbean Flying Boats, Christiansted, US Virgin Islands 1972. To Antilles Air Boats (AAB), Christiansted, US Virgin Islands by 1973. Wfu by 1979; AAB ceased ops in 1981. Aircraft derelict at St Croix-Hamilton A/P 1985. Cancelled from USCAR Aug88.

1163 Built for Great Britain as **JRF-6B/Goose IA**, with serial **FP513**. Del 15Jan43 and TOC by 749 Sqn, FAA, Piarco, Trinidad, coded 'W2AM'. Returned to the US Govt in 1945 and taken on US Navy charge with new serial **66344**. Pool NAS Miami by Jan46; Pool NAS Jacksonville 05Feb46; NAS Seattle 13Feb46 and SOC there 30Sep46 as obsolete and surplus. To WAA although details of any subsequent US registration undiscovered. Acquired by Efferson & Associates, Washington, DC in Jan47. Sold to the Argentine Naval Commission, Washington, DC 30Jan47 and delivered by sea from Ontario, CA. Given Aviación Naval (COAN) serial **0184** and initially used by Prefectura General Maritima (PGM) with code 'PGM-1'; initially based at Punta Indio within COAN's Escuadra Aeronaval No2 and so assigned 12Jun47. Damaged in an accident Mar48 and repaired. Recoded circa 1950 as '2-P-20' indicative of patrol use within the Escuadra Aeronaval No2 at Espora and so used in the Antarctic summers of 1951/1952 and 1952/1953. Transferred to the Escuadra Aeronaval No3, Punto Indio 01Jan53 and recoded '3-P-50'. Used in the Antarctic 1953/1954 where damaged and returned to Argentina by sea for repair; used again in Antarctica 1954/1955. Reorganised into the Escuadrilla de Propósitos Generales, Punta Indio circa 1955 and recoded '3-G-6'. Wfu in 1956 and eventually sold for scrap 05Dec60.

1164 Built for Great Britain as **JRF-6B/Goose IA**, with serial **FP514**. Del 24Jan43 and TOC by 749 Sqn, FAA, Piarco, Trinidad, coded 'W2AN'. Returned to the US Govt in 1945 and taken on US Navy charge with new serial **66336**. Pool NAS Miami by Jan46; NAS Seattle Mar46 and SOC there 30Sep46, as obsolete and surplus, to War Assets Administration and seen, unconverted, at Concord, CA 09Jan47. To Bay Valley Air Service, San Francisco, CA 07May47 and regd as **G-21A, NC95431** 10Jun47. To Alaska Coastal Airlines Inc, Juneau, AK 27Mar48, and later as **N95431**. Became Alaska Coastal-Ellis Airlines, Juneau, AK, 01Apr62 with CofR 18Sep62. Cvtd to PT6A-6A power 23Jan66 at TFH:12,638hrs (see Chapter 5) and first flew 28Feb66. The conversion was carried out under an STC and was therefore not certificated as a new type, i.e. the aircraft remained as a G-21A but notated as "Turbo". Nominal change to Alaska Coastal Inc Jun66; TFH:13,705hrs a/o 05Feb68. Merged into Alaska Airlines Inc, Seattle, WA 01Apr68 with CofR 27Mar68. re-engined with PT-6A-20s 22Jun68. Accident 12Aug68: substantially damaged by wheels–down water landing at Juneau Seadrome, AK on a ferry flight. To Foreign & Domestic Enterprises Inc, Seattle, WA 05May72. Rebuilt and returned to R-985 power 04Aug73. To The Pack River Co, Spokane, WA 15Aug73 with CofR **N72PR** 03Dec73. To Robert G Sholton, dba Northern Air Cargo, Anchorage, AK 15Oct75 and leased to Kodiak Western Airlines, Kodiak, AK. Regd to Kodiak Western Airlines Inc, Kodiak, AK 09Jun77. Returned to Robert G Sholton, Anchorage, AK with CofR 06Mar78. To Island Hoppers Inc, Kodiak, AK 28Aug78. Accident 02Sep78: damaged after leaving the runway at Old Harbor on an aborted take-off, after an engine failure. To Wilton R Probert, Oakland, OR 30Jun79. To Royal Island Airways Inc, New York, NY 28Apr81. To Westflight Aviation Inc, Ketchikan, AK 09Oct81. Tfd to Aviation Associates Inc, dba West flight Aviation, Ketchikan, AK 17Aug82. Non-fatal crash at Long Island, AK 15Oct85. Cancelled from USCAR Aug87. Flown Ketchikan to Long Beach, CA and shipped to Brisbane, Australia aboard the *SS Elgarin*, arr 07May87. Re-assembled and flown off Brisbane River to Archerfield A/P, QLD 08May87 for overhaul, prior to dep for Papua New Guinea (PNG). Del Archerfield – Port Moresby, PNG 15-17May87. To JR Wild, dba Milne Bay Air, Port Moresby, PNG as **P2-JWB** 20May87. Cancelled from USCAR 12Aug87. Dep Port Moresby 12Aug89 on del to Palau. To Bob

G-21A, c/n 1164, N72PR, was owned by Royal Island Airways in 1981. It is seen here at an unknown location. By the end of that year it was operating in Alaska and is currently being rebuilt in Australia in preparation for work in Nauru, in the South Pacific.

(Jennifer Gradidge Collection)

Keys, dba Paradise Air Services, Palau, Philippines as **RP-C864** in Aug89. Sold to Filipino owner, Manila 1991. Regn cancelled on sale to Australia, Dec93, after the aircraft was repurchased by Keys in exchange for an Aero Commander. Goose grounded as unairworthy at Manila. Ferried from Manila via Cebu, Davao, Palau, Biak, Merauke, Horn Island to Cairns, QLD 26Jun92, and to Noosa, QLD 28Jun92, for Bob Keys, dba Up Over Down Under, Brisbane, QLD. Based at Archerfield, Brisbane 1993-97. Noted still RP-C regd at Bundaberg, QLD 23Oct99. To **VH-MBA**(2) with RH Keys, Noosa Heads, QLD 17Apr00. Featured in TV series *"South Pacific 2001"* (noted in blue c/s as **"USN 931-79"** at Cairns, QLD 30Jly00, for filming). Complete overhaul at Archerfield and repaint as DQ-AYL Mar05 at Caboolture, QLD. **DQ-AYL** reserved for Yaukuve Island Resort, Fiji Aug05..... (to be ferried to Fiji by Bob Keys). Still regd to Keys as **VH-MBA**, 02Mar06, but stored dismantled in Hangar 5 at Brisbane-Archerfield by late-2006. Wing centre section under rebuild Wangaratta, VIC 2007, for planned tourist services in the Solomon Islands by Solomon Islands Seaplanes Ltd. Project postponed due to financial restraints in 2011, and then cancelled due to bureaucratic delays with licencing. At the time of writing (Mar13) the Goose was at Wangaratta completing its rebuild to executive configuration by Precision Aerospace. It was then planned to base it in Noumea for charter work.

1165 Built for Great Britain as **JRF-6B/Goose IA**, with serial **FP515**. Del 30Jan43 and TOC by 749 Sqn, FAA, Piarco, Trinidad, coded 'W2AP'. Returned to the US Govt in 1945 and taken on US Navy charge with new serial **66332**. Pool NAS Miami by Jan46 and SOC there 30Jun46 as obsolete and surplus. Sold by WAA, Washington, DC for $25,000 to PAD Aviation & Navigation Co, Chicago, IL 09Oct46 with CofR **NC74588** 07Nov46. Cvtd to **G-21A** by Willis Air Service, Teterboro, NJ, 05Jly47 and CofA 21Jly47. BoS to Ellis Air Lines Inc, Ketchikan, AK for $29,000, 16Nov48 with CofR 12Jan49 and later as **N74588**. Featured in the 1954 film *"Cry Vengeance"*. CofA 17May55 at TFH:4,788hrs. Tfd by BoS to Alaska Coastal-Ellis Airlines, Juneau, AK, 01Oct62 with CofR 09Oct62 and CofA 15Oct62 at TFH:9,501hrs. Tfd by BoS to Alaska Coastal Airlines Inc, Juneau, AK, 16Jun66 and CofR applied for same date but no evidence that CofR was issued. Accident 30Aug67: substantially damaged when hit a submerged log during landing at Seal Cove, Prince Rupert, BC; Pilot + 8 pax uninjured. TFH:12,295hrs a/o 05Feb68. Alaska Coastal Airlines Inc merged into Alaska Airlines Inc, Seattle, WA, 27Mar68 with CofR 19Apr68. BoS to Antilles Air Boats (AAB), St Thomas, US Virgin Islands, 31Oct72 with CofR 18Jan73. Increase in gross wt to 8,750lbs Sep78 per STC SA3630WE and overhauled Nov78. Wfu derelict St Croix-Hamilton 1981; CofR revoked by FAA 21May82. BoS to David Ketchum, Reno, NV May83. BoS to Elmer L Cote/Robert A Frost/ Roland N Duke, Newport Beach, CA, 26May83; CofR applied for 09Jun83 but not issued? BoS Cote to RA Frost & RN Duke, Costa Mesa, CA, 01Dec83; CofR applied for 15Jan84 but not issued? BoS to David Bettencourt, Honolulu, HI, 24May84 with CofR issued 09Jly84. BoS to Roland N Duke & Robert A Frost, Costa Mesa, CA, 17Feb88 with CofR 24Mar88. BoS to Charles G Hyde, Roanoke, TX 15Aug89. FAA requested Hyde to submit an aircraft regn application on 15May90 and again on 08Nov91, but received no reply. CofR suspended. Regd to Flight Data Inc, Carson City, NV 02Sep99. To Brett R Mayes, Williams, CA with CofR 14Jly10. Current and airworthy May13, with CofR due to expire 31Oct14.

1166 Built for Great Britain as **JRF-6B/Goose IA**, with serial **FP516**. Del 31Jan43 and TOC by 749 Sqn, FAA, Piarco, Trinidad, coded 'W2AQ'. Returned to the US Govt in 1945 and taken on US Navy charge with new serial **66349**. NAS Miami by Jan46; NAS Seattle Feb46 and SOC there 30Sep46 as obsolete and surplus. BoS WAA to Harold M Gollance, Waban, MA 25Feb47. Cvtd to **G-21A** 22Mar47 and regd **NC95479** 26Mar47. Cancelled 14Jan49 due to accident. Rebuilt by Dean Franklin, Miami, FL using remains plus parts acquired from NAS Quonset, RI & Air Service Caravan, New Bedford, MA. CofR **N333F** issued 01Nov54. BoS Franklin to Amphibians Inc, Miami, FL Oct56 with CofR 19Oct56. Complete overhaul by Dean Franklin with square wingtips and oversize spinners – *"The Golden Super Goose"*, 02Dec57. Used by Isle Royale Airways, Houghton, MI circa 1963. BoS Amphibians Inc to Franklin Flying Service Inc, Miami, FL 28Jun63. BoS to Catalina Channel Airlines, Long Beach, CA 01Aug64 with CofR 24Sep64. Engines uprated to R-985-14B standard 27Apr65. BoS to Christos A Papatheodorou, Long Beach, CA 17Feb67 with CofR 24Feb67. BoS to Catalina Seaplanes Inc, San Pedro, CA 17Feb69 with CofR 18Mar69. Re-regd **N11CS** 14Jun69. Accident 30Jly71: Substantial damage after hitting c/n1007, N13CS, while landing at Avalon after a flight from Long Beach, CA. N13CS was taking off but was partially hidden by a large boat. Despite evasive action the two Gooses collided. N11CS lost the right float and rolled over. Pilot + 8 pax, and 8 others in N13CS uninjured. Accident 12Dec71: aircraft substantially damaged when right landing gear collapsed on landing at Long Beach after a flight from Avalon. Pilot + 3 pax uninjured. BoS to Catalina Airlines Inc, Gardena, CA 29Dec76 with CofR 25Feb77. Retractable floats installed 24May78. Accident 14Apr79: crashed when wingtip hit water, attempting a go-around to avoid a boat wake, landing at Pebbly Beach, Avalon Harbour, Santa Catalina Island. One fatal (pilot?) + ten uninjured. Reported as "destroyed/scrapped" 18May80 and cancelled from USCAR 11Jly80.

1167   Built for Great Britain as **JRF-6B/Goose IA**, with serial **FP517**. Del 16Feb43 and TOC by 749 Sqn, FAA, Piarco, Trinidad, coded 'W2AR'. Returned to the US Govt in 1945 and taken on US Navy charge with new serial **66328**. Pool NAS Miami by Jan46; NAS Seattle 20 Mar46 but in Pool NAS Miami Apr46 (suggesting that the move to Seattle did not take place) and SOC at Miami 30Jun46 as obsolete and surplus. Sold by WAA, Atlanta, GA for $25,000 to Nicholas Ludington, Philadelphia, PA, 16Aug46. Sold to Sun Pipe Line Co, Beaumont, TX, 17Oct46. Cvtd to **G-21A** by Grumman, Bethpage, with CofA 02Dec46, and CofR **NC74107** issued 03Dec46; to **N74107** 01Jan49. BoS Sun Pipeline to Bowater Paper Co Inc, New York, NY, 20Jun49 for $35,000, with CofR 11Jly49. Sold to Bowaters Newfoundland Pulp & Paper Mills Ltd 31Mar50. Allotted **CF-GSU** 17May50; US CofA for export E-20256 issued 25May50; CofR 8784 and CofA 3275 to Bowaters Newfoundland Pulp & Paper Mills Ltd, Corner Brook, NL 25May50. Cancelled from USCAR 01Jun50. Inspected and CofA renewed at TFH:1,839hrs, valid until 19Jan52; at TFH:2,403hrs, valid until 05Nov54. Accident 02/03Oct55: aircraft landed at Dorval at 1626hrs on 02Oct55 and parked in a no-parking area. Next day at 0915hrs, the pilot found the aircraft had been extensively damaged, perhaps by a larger aircraft running up its engines nearby. BoS Bowaters to Eveready Supply Co, Bridgeport, CT, 06Jly56. BoS to Henry W Ramsdell, Palm Beach, FL, 03Jly56 (sic) as **N2038A**. Authority to ferry St Johns, QC to US border 06Jly56, and cancelled from CCAR 03Aug56. CofA 17Aug56 at TFH:2,763hrs. BoS to Joe G Marrs, Opa Locka, FL, 17Sep56 with CofR 05Nov56; address change to Lake Placid, FL with CofR 21Sep70. Cancelled from USCAR 22May84 (no reason given). Re-instated (date unknown) and listed as current and airworthy until CofR expired 31Mar13.

1168   Built for Great Britain as **JRF-6B/Goose IA**, with serial **FP518**. Del 27Feb43 and TOC by 749 Sqn, FAA, Piarco, Trinidad, coded 'W2AJ'. Still with 749 Sqn Aug43 but by mid-Sep43 used by 738 Sqn, Lewiston, ME for aircrew ferry purposes (carrying crew to NAS Willow Grove to collect Martlett IVBs), duration of stay unknown, but in use by SBNO, Roosevelt Field, NY Feb-Apr44. On strength with 749 Sqn 31Jan45 when involved in minor incident at Piarco. Returned to the US Govt in 1945 and taken on US Navy charge with new serial **66341**. NAS Miami by Jan46 and SOC there 30Jun46 as obsolete and surplus and relocated to an unspecified WAA site in Georgia (Atlanta?). Ferried to Reykjavik with TF-RVI and -RVJ, via Mont Joli, PQ (overnight 02/03Nov46); Goose Bay, where delayed due to weather in Greenland; departed Goose Bay at 0733hrs 16Nov46, via Bluie West, and arrived Reykjavik 18Nov46, for Loftleidir hf. Regd as **G-21A, TF-RVJ** 31Mar47. Sold to The Babb Co Inc, New York, NY, 12Apr49 and TF- regn cancelled 09Jly49. Complete overhaul Dec50 by National Aircraft Maintenance Corp, Newark, NJ, and CofA issued 12Jan51. CofR **N74110** issued 22Jan51 and then cancelled from USCAR as exported to Brazil 29Jan51 and regd **PT-AFO** to Manoel M de Figueiredo Ferraz, Sao Paulo. BoS Ferraz to Gordon Smith & Co Inc, New York, NY 25Apr53, and PT- registration cancelled 27Jly53. BoS to Pressed Steel Car Co Inc, Chicago, IL, 12Jun53 with CofR **N79C**, 28Jly53. Major overhaul by Mallard Industries Inc, Stratford, CT Feb54 with CofA 06Mar54 at TFH:1,778hrs. CofR corrected 29Apr55 stating CofR N79C was issued 28Jly53 to US Industries Inc, New York, NY (perhaps Pressed

Steel Car Co was part of US Industries?). Tfd by BoS from US Industries to John I Snyder Jr (President, US Industries), Scarsdale, NY 20May55 with CofR 06Jun55; based at Stratford, CT. Reregd **N79U** 28Nov55. Tfd by BoS from Snyder back to US Industries Inc, White Plains, NY, 29May57 with CofR 04Jun57. BoS to The Mischianza Corp, St Charles, IL, 07Jun57 with CofR 14Jun57. Leased back to US Industries Inc from 01Dec57 until Dec62 for $142,792, paid by instalments. BoS Mischianza to The Multnomah Company, Cincinnati, OH, 15Mar63. BoS to US Industrial Leasing Corp, New York, NY, 20Jun63 for $20,000, and CofR issued 02Jly63. BoS to Gilbert A Hensler Jr, Nassau, Bahamas 24May65 with CofR 03Jun65. BoS to Sherlock D Hackley, Nassau, Bahamas 17Aug67 for $55,000; address on CofR application, 06Sep67, given as Oxford, MD with CofR 22Sep67. BoS to Island Flying Services of America Inc, (SD Hackley, President) New York, NY, 30Jun70 with CofR, 06Aug70; address change to Miami, FL with CofR 30Aug72; operated by Bahamasair, Nassau, Bahamas by 1974. Accident 10Feb75: substantially damaged when ground looped at Staniel Cay, Bahamas. BoS to Dean H Franklin Aviation Enterprises Inc, Miami, FL 10May77. BoS to Raritan Aviation Co, New Brunswick, NJ, 01Aug77 with CofR as **N401SJ** 31Aug77; regn placed on aircraft 06Mar78. BoS to Goose Aviation Co, New Brunswick, NJ, 16May79 (nominal change) with CofR 13Sep79; based Mercer County A/P, West Trenton, NJ; change of address to Dayton, NJ 20Nov85 and another to Princeton, NJ 18Dec89 with CofR 11Jan90. Temp CofA issued 22Apr10, but current and airworthy May13, with CofR due to expire 30Apr15.

1169   Built for Great Britain as **JRF-6B/Goose IA**, with serial **FP519**. Del 28Feb43 and TOC by 749 Sqn, FAA, Piarco, Trinidad by Apr43 although code unknown (conceivably 'W2AS'), but destroyed 15May43. Aircraft attempted to take-off prematurely, struck a sandbank and overturned (location unknown but assumed to be Trinidad).

1170   Built for Great Britain as **JRF-6B/Goose IA**, with serial **FP520**. Del 28Feb43 and TOC by 749 Sqn, FAA, Piarco, Trinidad, coded 'W2AT'. Returned to the US Govt in 1945 and taken on US Navy charge with new serial **66338**. Pool Hedron, FAW-11 (located at San Juan, PR and controlling US Navy ops in Trinidad) by Jan46; Pool NAS Jacksonville 08Feb46; NAS Seattle Feb46 and SOC there 31Aug46 as obsolete and surplus to War Assets Administration, Washington, DC. BoS WAA, Los Angeles, CA to Anaconda Mining 17Feb47 for $15,000. CofR for **G-21A, NC66338** (probably using BuAer serial in error) to Anaconda Copper Mining Co, New York, NY 13Mar47. CofR corrected to **NC95465** 25Mar47. Aux 60 gallon fuel tank installed in right front seat space and reregd as 7-seat aircraft 10Apr47. Cancelled from USCAR 01Jly47 and transferred to Anaconda Copper Mining Co. (ACMC), Rio de Janeiro, Brazil. **PP-DGI** allocated after request for regn by Joaquim Gomes de Noróes e Sousa 22Aug47, aircraft based Belem. Flown to Bethpage for overhaul Jan48. Cancelled from the Brazilian register 26Apr48 and returned to ACMC, New York as **NC95465** 29Apr48 and later as **N95465**. Sold to Donald B McLouth, Detroit, MI 21Nov50 for $30,000, with CofR 28Nov50. N95465 cancelled from USCAR 19Dec50. Aux fuel tank removed 09Feb51 and re-cvtd to 8-seat aircraft. Nominal change to McLouth Steel Corp, Detroit, MI 30Mar51 and reregd **N10M** 25Apr51; TFH:3,469hrs a/o 12Jan53. Reregd **N1007** 16Apr56 (N10M transferred to G-73 c/n J-18 qv); TFH:4,691hrs a/o 09Nov56. To Harmon Edgar Wendt, Georgetown, British Guiana 10Dec56 for $47,500. Cancelled from USCAR 12Mar57. Regd **VP-GAU** to Governor of British Guiana 19Nov56. Regd to, and operated by, British Guiana Airways by 1960. To The Guyana Airways Corporation, 10Dec56. Regn cancelled 09Jun65 and aircraft written-off 04Dec66.

1171   Built for Great Britain as **JRF-6B/Goose IA**, with serial **FP521**. Del 10Mar43 and TOC by 749 Sqn, FAA, Piarco, Trinidad, coded 'W2AE'. Returned to the US Govt in 1945 and taken on US Navy charge with new serial **66329**. Pool NAS Miami by Jan46 and SOC there 30Jun46 as obsolete and surplus. Regd as **G-21A, NC79565** to Lincoln Thomas Aviation, Milwaukee, WI. BoS to Ludlow Jute Co Ltd, Boston, MA. Export CofA E-16684 issued 06Jly49 for Ludlow Jute Co Ltd, Calcutta, India as **N79565**. The log book of Ronald Keith Cannon shows that he flew Goose N79565 at Dacca, East Pakistan, in Jan58, doing circuits, with Capt H Law. Cancelled from USCAR 21Aug62. McKinnon records show this as *"Calcutta Goose"* which was modified with a radar nose kit in 1968. The owner was listed as D Ghosh, and there is also mention of a company called Associated Airworks at Dum Dum Airport, Calcutta. Details of registration in India, and fate, unknown.

1172   Built for Great Britain as **JRF-6B/Goose IA**, with serial **FP522**. Del 18Mar43, but details of immediate use unknown but used by Senior British Naval Officer from NAS Norfolk from Oct43 (while HMS *Indomitable* was in repair). TOC by 749 Sqn, FAA, Piarco, Trinidad

27Dec43, code unknown. Returned to the US Govt in 1945 and taken on US Navy charge with new serial **66333**. Pool Hedron, FAW-11 (located at San Juan, PR and controlling US Navy ops in Trinidad) by Jan46; NAS Seattle Feb46 and SOC there 31Aug46 as obsolete and surplus. To Ellis Air Lines, Ketchikan, AK Jun47 as **G-21A, NC74676** and later as **N74676**. Became Alaska Coastal-Ellis Airlines 01Apr62 and nominal change to Alaska Coastal Airlines Inc Jun66; TFH:14,237hrs a/o 05Feb68. Merged into Alaska Airlines, Seattle, WA in 1968. With Antilles Air Boats, Christiansted, US Virgin Islands by 1978. Accident 05Nov78: crashed and sank in 10,000ft water after engine failure, whilst on FAA test flight. Three on board rescued. Still regd Jan81 but CofR revoked by 2008.

1173   Built for Great Britain as **JRF-6B/Goose IA**, with serial **FP523**. Del 26Mar43 and TOC by 749 Sqn, FAA, Piarco, Trinidad, coded 'W2AG'. Returned to the US Govt in 1945 and taken on US Navy charge with new serial **66335**. Pool Hedron, FAW-11 (located at San Juan, PR and controlling US Navy ops in Trinidad) by Jan46; Pool NAS Jacksonville 08Feb46; NAS Seattle Mar46 and SOC there 30Sep46 as obsolete and surplus. Regd as **G-21A, NC68174** to Harry K Coffey, Portland, OR. To Kodiak Airways Inc, Kodiak, AK 1958. Written off after damaged by a tidal wave which destroyed the Kodiak A/W hangar after the earthquake at Anchorage, AK 28Mar64. Cancelled from USCAR 23Jun70.

1174   Built for Great Britain as **JRF-6B/Goose IA**, with serial **FP524**. Del 31Mar43. Status with 749 Sqn, FAA, Piarco, Trinidad uncertain and may never have been on strength. Flown from NAS Quonset to Roosevelt Field 27May43 by Lt Grout, US Navy. Lt Ed Walthall was appointed SBNO at Roosevelt Field in 1943, to oversee acceptance of FAA aircraft. FP524 was allocated to Walthall who used it for transport to various locations for meetings, etc. Walthall's last logbook entry for FP524 notes a flight from Squantum to Roosevelt on 26Nov43. Involved in accident at Grumman facility, Roosevelt Field, NY (NAF Mineola) 18Feb44: ground-looped on landing in crosswind suffering heavy, but not terminal, damage (FAA Cat. 'Y1') although US Navy accident report describes damage as "Port wing and landing gear washed-out, fuselage damaged". No evidence of repair or return to service and not known to have been formally returned to the US Govt in 1945. No record of subsequent sale or use.

1175   Built as **G-21A**. BoS Grumman Aircraft Engineering Corp to Ford Motor Co, Dearborn, MI 08Dec41(address given as "Willow Run Bomber Plant"; and del to Ford Motor Co, 12Dec41 as **NC3500**. Reported impressed ex Ford Motors but BoS Ford Motors to TACA Airways Agency Inc, New York, NY 17Mar44, "for ops in Costa Rica". Form ACA-776-A Application for Foreign Aircraft Permit dated 30Mar44 for proposed trip from New York-La Guardia to South America and return leaving April 10th to 15th, 1944 and returning about June 10th, 1944. Purpose was to survey various company routes then in operation, and various proposed routes. Pilot was listed as George E Farnham (ATR #10656). Two passengers listed: Dr & Mrs Alberto P Savergnini (both were Argentine citizens). Application in the name of TACA Agency by Charles E Matthews, but CAA marked "Voided". Form ACA-776 Another application for Foreign Flight Authorization for proposed trip as above, but made in the name of Charles E Matthews rather than TACA. Pilot and passengers the same but Mrs Savergnini listed as an American citizen. Co-Pilot listed as Fred H Brohan (Comml. #11306) and a supplemental page gives routing as follows:

New York (LGA)-Raleigh-Miami-Ciudad Trujillo-Port of Spain-Paramaribo-Belem-Recife-Rio de Janeiro-Montevideo-Buenos Aires-Asuncion-Buenos Aires-Porto Alegre-Rio de Janeiro-Recife-Belem-Paramaribo-Port of Spain-Ciudad Trujillo-Miami. Departure date was between 10th and 15th April from LGA with return indicated 30th June, 1944.

BoS TACA to Charles E Matthews, Tegucigalpa, Honduras 03Apr44; application for CofA at TFH:822hrs 03Apr44 and application for CofR 04Apr44. BoS Matthews to The Texas Co, New York, NY (based New Iberia District, LA) 16May44 at TFH:833hrs; FN:41. Accident 30May44: landing gear collapsed landing at Mobile, AL. TFH:1,333hrs a/o 25Jly46. Accident 29Jly47: crashed into bayou south of Houma, LA. No injuries but the aircraft was written off. Texaco requested transfer of marks NC3500 to their new Grumman Mallard, 11Sep47.

1176   Built for US Navy as **JRF-5**, BuAer serial **04349**. Acc and del NAS New York 23Jly42; NAS Anacostia 29Jly42; Naval Attaché Guatemala, Guatemala City 01Aug42; NAS Coco Solo 25Jan43 (probably for repairs following damage caused by landing in rough water at Moneypenny Anchorage, Gulf of Fonseca 04Jan43); Naval Attaché Guatemala 15Nov43; ComFairWestCoast, NAS San Diego Mar44; NAS Seattle for reconditioning Mar45; ComFair Seattle Jun45; CASU-7 NAS Seattle Sep45; ComFair Seattle Nov45; CASU-7 NAS Seattle Jan46; CASU-7A NAS Seattle Apr46; Pool CASU-7 NAS Seattle 21Jun46; Pool

FASRON-9 NAS Seattle Sep46; VN8D5 NAF Annapolis 26Nov46; Pool BAR Bethpage Mar47; Pool A&T NAS Quonset Point Jly47; Pool NAS Trinidad Aug47; BAR Bethpage Sep48; records missing; NAS Norfolk by Jan50 awaiting overhaul; NAS Quonset Point 25Jly50 for overhaul. Declared surplus 14May51 and SOC for MDAP disposal to France 13Jly51 (TFH:1,477hrs). To France's Aéronautique Navale wearing abbreviated serial **349**; transit details unknown but by sea to Saigon, Vietnam where accepted 28Jan52; initially delivered to 9ème Escadrille de Servitude (9.S) at Cat Lai where coded '9.S-21' and earmarked for use by Amiral FMEO but transferred to 8ème Escadrille de Servitude (8.S) at Cat Lai Mar52 and recoded '8.S-3'. Damaged in unknown circumstances 24Sep53 and judged to be beyond repair with airframe distortion. Condemned and SOC 21Apr54.

1177   Built for US Navy as **JRF-5**, BuAer serial **04350**. Acc 29Jly42 and del NAS New York 30Jly42; Flag 30 ComEastSeaFron (New York) 4Aug42. Force-landed in field at Batavia, NY 08Sep45 following a double-engine failure resulting from water contamination of fuel. Damage described as "replacement of minor parts". With ComEastSeaFron until Oct45 and SOC at NAS New York 31Jan46 (disposal code indicates scrappage due to general deterioration, presumably linked to the earlier accident).

1178   Built for US Navy as **JRF-5**, BuAer serial **04351**. Acc and del to NAS New York 11Aug42; NAS Norfolk 23Aug42; Commander Task Force 24 NAF Argentia 24Aug42 until 30Dec43; records missing but with NAMU Johnsville by Apr44; NAF Argentia May45; Pool BAR Bethpage Aug47; NAS South Weymouth Jun48 (storage); MCAS Cherry Point Feb49 and in storage by Jan50; NAS Quonset Point 28Jun51 for modernisation; FASRON-101 NAS Quonset Point 04Jan52 for delivery; Naval Mission to Havana, Cuba 08Jan52; FASRON-109 NAS Jacksonville 26Aug52 for repair; NAF Annapolis 13Jan53; SF Litchfield Park 19Oct53 (storage). Leased by US Navy to Avalon Air Transport of Long Beach, CA 22Aug55 (TFH:1,473hrs) with whom registered **N1523V** and given Fleet No:4. As a **G-21A** N1523V remained in use with Avalon until at least late 1956 and probably into 1957 after which the US Navy terminated the lease, telling Avalon that the aircraft was needed for experimental purposes. Civil registration cancelled Jan58. 04351 was recorded as still being on loan 28Feb57 but was subsequently stricken by the US Navy 12Dec57. In Jun58 the US Navy formally amended a Feb56 contract (NOa(s) 56-549C) with Kaman Aircraft, Bloomfield, CT to authorise the use of a surplus JRF-5 as a flight research vehicle in the furtherance of a V/STOL research project. When completed the article was given the project reference **K-16B**. Kaman formally described the article (understood to have been 04351) as being 'a surplus JRF-5 fuselage' 'furnished by the Bureau' although they were not specific about the date or circumstances. N1523V's passage from Long Beach to Bloomfield has not been satisfactorily explained but may have been via Grumman who provided Kaman with full technical specifications and some assistance in respect of the JRF-5's structure and systems. The JRF-5 was subsequently grossly modified with YT58-GE6 engines and a tilt-wing at Bloomfield where eventually it was considered flight ready. Tethered flight, however, was not authorised until the satisfactory completion of wind tunnel testing at the NASA Ames Laboratory at Moffett Field, CA. The K-16B was disassembled and air-freighted to Moffett by C-133 on 26Sep60 (in fact the C-133 went tech en route and the K-16B and its support equipment were transhipped at Travis AFB, CA and continued their journey by C-124). Full-scale testing on the Ames thrust stand was undertaken between 25Jan62 and 20Aug62 and this was followed by tests in the 40'x 80' wind tunnel between 05Sep62 and 21Sep62. The tests showed that the K-16B would be unsafe for flight due to insufficient thrust for vertical flight at indicated gross weight, lateral and directional control power deficiency and the propensity for both wing and horizontal tail to stall. Although these problems could have been overcome, funds were diverted to other more advanced projects (principally the XC-142 and X-22) and the K-16B programme was terminated. The K-16B was returned to Bloomfield where it eventually passed into storage before being donated to the Connecticut Air Historical Association (Bradley Air Museum, Bradley, CT) in 1965. The transaction, with the approval of the Bureau of Naval Weapons, was instigated in Mar65 and formally concluded 12May65. The K-16B was physically transferred in late Jun65. The museum, now known as the New England Air Museum, currently displays this fascinating aircraft as "**04351/N1523V**", (probably as a result of correspondence with the authors!).

1179   Built for US Navy as **JRF-5**, BuAer serial **04352**. Acc 19Aug42 and del to NAS New York 21Aug42; NAS Anacostia 28Sep42; NAS Norfolk 18Oct42; Hedron 16, FAW-16, NAS Natal 30Jun43; Atlantic Fleet 01Nov43; CASU-22 NAS Quonset Point date unknown (probably to Jun44); Pool NAS Norfolk 22Sep44; Hedron 12, FAW-12, NAS San Julian

Oct44; Pool Hedron, FAW-5, NAS Norfolk Jun45; NAS Seattle Jly45 for reconditioning and to Pool Seattle 08Jan46; Pool NAS Norfolk Mar46; NAS Guantanamo Jun46. Sustained heavy damage after ground-looping on landing in cross-wind at Guantanamo Bay 12Dec46 and SOC 31Dec46.

1180   Built for US Navy as **JRF-5**, BuAer serial **04353**. Acc 22Aug42 and del to NAS New York 27Aug42; NAS Norfolk 17Sep42. Crashed at sea during rescue mission 21Mar43 and SOC at Norfolk 26Mar43 (aircraft hooked wing-tip float and capsized – no injuries).

1181   Built for US Navy as **JRF-5**, BuAer serial **04354**. Acc 03Sep42 and del to NAS New York 04Sep42; AOTC NAS Jacksonville 12Sep42; A&R NAS Jacksonville 07May43; NAOT NAS Jacksonville 27Nov43; OTU T5 NAS Jacksonville Aug44; A&R NAS Jacksonville 20Sep44; CQTU NAS Glenview Oct44; NAMU Johnsville Jan45; NAS Miami Apr45; NAS Seattle for reconditioning Feb46; NAS Kodiak 04Aug46; Pool FASRON-112 NAS Whidbey Island Apr48; Pool NAS San Diego May48; Pool NAS Norfolk Sep48; Pool BAR Bethpage Feb49. NavAirActSRC NAF Annapolis Jun49 until 12Sep49 when it was involved in a water landing accident at Greenbury Point on the Severn River near Annapolis; power was cut prematurely and aircraft landed heavily causing significant damage. SOC 30Sep49.

1182   Built for US Navy as **JRF-5**, BuAer serial **04355**. Acc and del to NAS Norfolk 23Sep42; NAS Squantum 01Nov42; NAS Seattle 01Apr45 for reconditioning; NAS Squantum 01Aug45; NAS Charleston Feb46; Pool NAS Norfolk 23Dec47 until at least Aug48; records missing; NavAirActSRC NAF Annapolis by Jan50; NAF Annapolis 24Mar50; NAS Quonset Point 31May51 for overhaul; FASRON-101 Quonset Point 28Mar52 (pool, awaiting issue); ZP-1 NAF Weeksville 10Dec52; NAF Annapolis 30Mar53; NAS Quonset Point 17Jly53 for disposal. SOC at Quonset Point 30Sep53 for ground training/instructional use (TFH:1,853hrs). Transfer from NAS Quonset Point to Department of Justice, Miami, FL 01Nov54 of "JRF-5 aircraft, Grumman Goose Twin engine plane No: 04355". Someone has added (in different typeface) "serial #37791". The application for registration 15Feb55 for Dept of Justice, Immigration and Naturalization Service, quotes serial number as 37791 with "Navy 04355" circled underneath. The certificate of registration **N75333**, 23Feb55, gives serial as 37791 to which has been added, in pen, "B-44". CofA 11May55 at TFH:1,925hrs; aircraft overhauled Dec58. Transferred to Dade County Board of Public Instruction, Aviation School, Miami, FL 22Jun60 "for instruction of civilian mechanics at FAA approved school #3460, and for creating live maintenance problems through actual flight". CofR issued 12Sep60 again wrongly quoting "Navy 37791, B-44". #3460 was the George T Baker Aviation School to which the aircraft was released without restrictions on 24Jly73. BoS Dade County Board of Public Instruction Aviation School to Dean H Franklin, Miami, FL 14Jan74 with CofR 03Sep74. BoS to Aircraft Facilities International Inc, Wichita, KS 12Sep74 with CofR recorded 07Oct74. Sold to Mount Cook Airlines in New Zealand in 1974; ferry tanks installed and aircraft certified structurally satisfactory for ferry flight operation at 11,500lbs Sep74, but the ferry permit limitations issued 07Oct74 stated max weight must not exceed 10,785lbs. A permit for the ferry flight from Wichita to Auckland, New Zealand via Portland, ME and the US border was issued 01Oct74. Accident 09Oct74: took off from Wichita, KS en route to Newton, KS on ferry flight to New Zealand. Collided with trees during forced landing off airport following loss of one engine due fuel selector mis-alignment. Reported as "demolished", and cancelled from USCAR 02Dec74. (**ZK-MCC** assigned for Mount Cook Airlines, but not used.)

1183   Built for US Navy as **JRF-5**, BuAer serial **04356**. Acc 30Sep42 and del to NAS New York 04Oct42; NAS Miami 15Dec42; NAOT (presumably at Miami) 15Nov43; records missing but at NAS Miami by Aug44 and awaiting reconditioning there in Dec44. Reconditioned by Embry-Riddle, Miami May45; recorded as in 'minimum repair' at NAS Miami Jun45 until Jan46; CGAS St Petersburg Feb46; CGAS Biloxi Apr46. SOC at Biloxi by the US Navy 31Jly46 when formally transferred to the US Coast Guard. Details of subsequent USCG history unknown and no record found of later civilian use.

1184   Built for US Navy as JRF-5, BuAer serial **04357**. Acc 30Sep42 and del to NAS New York 11Oct42; NAS Pensacola 20Oct42; US Naval Attaché Guatemala, Guatemala City 15Apr43; NAD Pensacola 09Jun43; NAIT Pensacola 15Nov43; VM Unit, NAS Pensacola Oct44; NATB (NAS) Pensacola Apr45; NAS Seattle May45 for reconditioning; Pool NAS Seattle 31Aug45; NAIT Corry Fld Oct45; VN8D8-B NAAS Bronson Fld Nov45; VN4D8-N NAAS Barin Fld Dec45; Pool NAS Pensacola 26Jly46; FASRON-102 NAS Norfolk for repairs Aug46; NAS San Juan Dec46; Pool NAS Jacksonville 28Jly47; FASRON-102 NAS Norfolk

G-21A, c/n 1184, N2751A, was operated by Coast Air out of Ketchikan, Alaska in the mid-1970s. It is seen here at Victoria, British Columbia, on 27th September 1975, shortly before its sale to Kenmore Air Harbour.
(Jack McNulty Collection)

Sep47; Pool NAS Norfolk Oct47; Pool BAR Bethpage Apr48 until at least Aug48; records missing; O&R MCAS Cherry Point and in storage by Jan50; NAS Quonset Point 19Nov52 for modernisation; NAF Annapolis 08Apr53. SF Litchfield Park 21May55 (storage) and retired 25Aug55; SOC 07May56 (TFH:1,796hrs) and regd to Ellis Air Lines, Ketchikan, AK as **G-21A, N2751A** in 1956. Became Alaska Coastal-Ellis Airlines, Juneau, AK 01Apr62; test-flew with a mock-up turbo-prop nacelle on the starboard side (see Chapter 5). Nominal change to Alaska Coastal Airlines Inc Jun66 before merging into Alaska Airlines Inc, Seattle, WA in 1968. To Coast Air, Ketchikan, AK in 1973. Reregd **N1257A** to Kenmore Air Harbour, Kenmore, WA by 1976. To Catalina Flying Boats, CA in 1984. To Bill A Moller, Rancho Palos Verdes, CA Jun87. To Harvey G Gibson, San Jose, Costa Rica 17Oct.90. Noted at Pavas, Costa Rica in Apr93. Featured in film "*The Endless Summer II*" in 1994. Accident 1995: badly damaged when ran onto river bank during take-off. Sold to Las Vegas Aircraft Sales & Leasing Inc, Henderson, NV as "accident damaged rebuild project" Nov96. BoS to Rodgers Log 14Apr98. N1257A cancelled from USCAR 21May98. Allotted **C-GDDJ** 28May98 and CofR(P) to Rodgers Log Inc, Spruce Grove, AB 10Jun98. CofR(P) cancelled 08Jly05 and reregd to Pacific Coastal Airlines Ltd, Richmond, BC 20Jly05 with CofR(C) dated 05Aug05. Reported being restored with parts from c/n 1086 ?? (qv). Current Mar13.

1185   Built for US Navy as **JRF-5**, BuAer serial **04358**. Acc and del to NAS New York 17Oct42; allocated/delivered to NAS Corpus Christi 17Oct42; records missing; NAIT Corpus Christi by Aug44; VM Unit NAS Corpus Christi Oct44; NAMU Johnsville Nov44; VM Unit Corpus Christi Mar45; NATB (NAS) Corpus Christi Apr45; NAS Corpus Christi Jly46; VM Unit Corpus Christi Aug46; Pool NAS Corpus Christi 16Aug46; VN8D5 NAF Annapolis 26Aug46. Suffered undercarriage collapse while taxying up ramp at Annapolis 09Mar47; Pool BAR Bethpage May47; NavAirActSRC NAF Annapolis Sept47 until at least Aug48; records missing; NAS Norfolk by Jan50 awaiting overhaul; NAS Quonset Point 25Aug50 for overhaul. Declared surplus 14May51 and SOC for MDAP disposal to France 13Jly51 (TFH:1,814hrs); to France's Aéronautique Navale wearing abbreviated serial **358**; transit details uncertain but assumed to have arrived by sea at Saigon, Vietnam Feb52; accepted 29Feb52 and delivered to 8ème Escadrille de Servitude (8.S) at Cat Lai and coded '8.S-1'. No specific service details recorded but active/in storage with 8.S throughout the years 1952 to 1956; by 1956 based at Tan Son Nhut, Saigon. Withdrawn from Vietnam (Saigon, Tan Son Nhut) in the *La Fayette* May56; arrival date in France unknown but circa Jun56 and to Saint-Mandrier before operational use with 8.S at Algiers-Maison Blanche as 8.S-1 1956-1957; at Saint-Mandrier Feb57; transferred to 27 Flottille at Ouakam, Dakar, Senegal as a reserve aircraft. SOC 05Dec61 and no subsequent civilian use reported.

1186   Built for the Cuban Navy as **JRF-5**, and supplied via Lend-Lease. BuAer serial **39747** allocated in Oct42. Cuban serial **56** allocated. Aircraft understood to have been lost in Cuban service, details unknown.

1187   Built for Cuban Navy as **JRF-5**, and supplied via Lend-Lease. BuAer serial **39748** allocated in Oct42. Cuban serial **57** allocated; personal aircraft of President, Fulgencio Batista. Retnd to USA on Import Certificate IMP-663 and regd as **G-21A, N2720A** (to unknown persons). US CofA for export E-27201 and authority to ferry USA to Toronto, ON issued May55. Allotted **CF-IFN** 13May55; CofR(P) 13479 and CofA 4550 to Lanson Holdings Ltd, Toronto, ON 30May55. CofR(P) 16394 to Advocate Mines Ltd, Toronto, ON 09Jly56 with issued 10Jly56; inspected

G-21A, c/n 1187, CF-IFN, location and date unknown.   (KM Molson)

and CofA renewed at TFH:1,713hrs, valid until 20May58; at TFH:1,936hrs, valid until 12Jun59. CoR19976(P) to MJ Boylen, Toronto, ON 30Oct58; inspected and CofA renewed at TFH:3,179hrs, valid until 09Jun65; at TFH:4,373hrs, valid until 06May70. (Believed cvtd by McKinnon during 1960s). Leased to Abitibi Aviation Ltd, Hamilton, ON and CofR(C) to them 24Jun69; CofA renewed at TFH:4,601hrs, valid until 06May71. Sold by estate of MJ Boylen to Caribbean Flying Boats Inc, St Thomas, US Virgin Islands 13Nov70 at TFH:4,611hrs; authority to ferry Toronto, ON to US Virgin Islands issued 23Nov70, and cancelled from CCAR 23Dec70. Regd to Antilles Air Boats, Christiansted, St Croix, US Virgin Islands as **N8229**. TFH:8,239hrs a/o 07Jan73. To Caribbean Flying Boats Inc, Christiansted, St Croix, US Virgin Islands by 20Jly74; TFH:8,714hrs a/o 28Apr75; 9,986hrs a/o 21May76; 11,975hrs a/o 05Aug90 and 11,995hrs a/o 20Jun91. To Robert J Holmsted, North Bend, OR May93. Allotted **C-FPCK** 25Apr96. BoS Walter William Blade Jr, Peggy A Holmstedt & James Holmstedt to Pacific Coastal Airlines Ltd 31May96. N8229 cancelled 02Jly96. Inspected 04Jly96 at TFH:11,999hrs and CofA issued 05Jly96. CofR(C) for C-FPCK issued to Pacific Coastal Airlines Ltd, Richmond, BC 15Aug96. TFH:12,243hrs reported on Due Date of 15Feb97. TFH:15,443hrs reported on Due Date of 15Feb03. Accident at circa1030hrs on 16Nov08: crashed into wooded terrain, east of Spyglass Hill, on Thormanby Island, 40 miles NW of Vancouver, BC en route Vancouver to Toba Inlet, BC. The chartered flight was taking Plutonic Power personnel to a hydro-electric project work camp at Toba Inlet. The pilot and six passengers died at the scene, and although the remaining passenger was seriously injured, he managed to walk to the shoreline where he was picked up by a Canadian Coast Guard Auxiliary vessel. The Goose was destroyed by post-impact fire. Cancelled from CCAR 10Sep09.

1188   Built as **G-21A** and sold by Grumman Aircraft Engineering Corp to Columbia University, Division of War Research, LaGuardia Field, NY with CofR **NC1604**, 04Sep42. Used by the University's Airborne Instrument Laboratory in magnetic anomaly detection projects (anti-submarine operations) conducted on behalf of the NRDC. The registration **NX1604** was applied for 30Sep42 in this connection. On conclusion of this work the Goose was transferred to US Navy ownership by Bill of Sale, in 1942, by Columbia University, NY initially as '**JRF-4**' and then formally corrected to **JRF-5**. Allocated BuAer serial **35921**. BuAer's re-use of this serial (it previously having been allocated to the last of a cancelled batch of PBN-1 Nomads) makes the precise date of transfer uncertain but aircraft unrecorded on aircraft movement card until Aug45 when (as JRF-5) "unreported" and NC1604 remained on USCAR in 1946. Used in experimental work NAS Lakehurst Sep45; Pool NAS Norfolk Feb48 until at least Aug48; records missing; 1st Naval District NAS Quonset Point by Jan50 and to overhaul there 01Mar51; FASRON-101 NAS Quonset Point 25Mar52 (pool, awaiting issue); NAF Annapolis 22Jan53; NAS Quonset Point 01Sep53 for overhaul and allocated to MDAP 31Mar54. SOC for MDAP disposal to Japan 13May54 (TFH:660hrs); shipped to Japan where de-preserved by the FASRON-11 detachment at NAF Oppama; used for crew training and working-up at NAF Oppama. Transferred to the JMSDF and given serial **9012**; formal handover to Second Kanoya Kokutai, Kanoya 18Oct55; relocated to Omura and thus to Omura Kokutai 01Dec56. Retired circa 1960 and returned to US charge although remaining at Omura; Sold by US Government ex Omura Air Station, Kyushu, Japan 20Dec63 to Catalina Airlines Inc, Long Beach, CA for $7,770. Sold to Tom Danaher Autos, Wichita Falls, TX, 03Feb64 with CofR as **G-21A, N291VW**, 14Apr64. Special CofAs issued 28Jun78, 11Jly79, 29Jly81 and 14Jly82 to allow one flight on each occasion for Airshow at Lake Wichita A/P; oddly TFH shows 2226.2 or 2227.2hrs on each one! Standard CofA 09May90 shows TFH:2238.5hrs. Featured in the 1997 film *"The Spanish Prisoner"*. CofR expired 30Jun11. Re-registered to Tom H Danaher 14Oct11 and current and airworthy May13, with CofR to expire 31Oct14.

1189   Built for US Navy as **JRF-5**, BuAer serial **34060**. Acc and del to (unreadable)19Apr43; NAS San Diego 23Apr43; Pacific Fleet (San Diego) 07May43; records unreadable but to FABU-1 Noumea 24May43; to ComAirSoPac, NAS Guadalacanal date uncertain. SOC 27Aug43 following a landing accident that day at Big Bay, Espiritu Santo. Following a stall at low altitude and a bounced landing, the right wing caught and the aircraft went onto its back and sank. All six on board, including the pilot assigned to the Staff of Commander Fleet Air, South Pacific, swam ashore and survived. The flight had been carrying a ferry target observation group.

1190   Built for US Navy as **JRF-5**, BuAer serial **34061**. Acc 23Apr43 and del 24Apr43; NAS San Diego 27Apr43; records missing but with ComAirSoPac, NAS Guadalacanal by Aug44; VJ-13 NAS Guadalcanal Apr45; Pool NAS Samar Nov45; in transit to Guam Dec45; Pool CASU-F12 NAS Orote Jan46; Pool NAS Pearl Harbor Apr46; NAS Alameda Sep46 for reconditioning; Pool NAS Alameda Jan47; BAR Bethpage 19Aug47; to storage at NAS South Weymouth Jly48 until at least Aug48; records missing; Pool BAR Bethpage by Jan50 (in overhaul); NavAirActSRC NAF Annapolis 07Mar50; NAF Annapolis 24Mar50. Force-landed in open country near Salisbury, MD 05Jan51 when on training flight from Annapolis (no serious injuries); fuel flow system malfunctioned due to failure to fully fuel aircraft resulting in a fuel line blockage and failure of both engines. Aircraft taken to NAS Chincoteague and SOC by Annapolis 19Jan51 (TFH:936hrs) for parts/scrap.

1191   Built for US Navy as **JRF-5**, BuAer serial **34062**. Acc and del Apr43; records missing but with NAS Norfolk by Aug44; NAS Seattle 30Mar45 for reconditioning; Pool NAS Seattle Jun45; NAS Patuxent River Jly45; Pool A&T NAS Quonset Point Dec47; Pool NAS Norfolk Jan48 until at least Aug48; records missing; NavAirActSRC NAF Annapolis by Jan50; NAF Annapolis 24Mar50; NAS Quonset Point 01Nov50 for overhaul; FASRON-102 NAS Norfolk 28Jun51 (ferry); FASRON-104 NAF Port Lyautey 23Aug51 (transit); Naval Attaché Oslo, Norway 12Sep51; FASRON-76, RAF Hendon, London 25May53; FASRON-102 NAS Norfolk 27Jly53 awaiting overhaul; NAS Quonset Point 02Sep53 pending decision on future. SF Litchfield Park 11Oct53 (storage) and SOC 15Aug56 (TFH:1,726hrs). Regd as **G-21A, N323** to Avalon Air Transport, Long Beach, CA 1956 with FN:7. To Catalina Airlines, Long Beach, CA 23Oct63. Non-fatal accident at Catalina Island 24May66: stalled on take-off due to porpoising in rough water. Substantial damage but pilot + eleven pax uninjured. Sold to Golden West Airlines Inc, Long Beach, CA 01Dec69. To Antilles Air Boats, Christiansted, US Virgin Islands 26Apr73; Accident 04Jun78: crashed into ocean off St Thomas, US Virgin Islands after in-flight engine failure. Stripped/derelict at St Croix-Hamilton by 1985. Revoked as unairworthy 27Jly09.

1192   Built for US Navy as **JRF-5**, BuAer serial **34063**. Acc 30Apr43 and del 07May43; records missing but with VJ-8 NAS Santa Ana by Aug44 (and probably from Sep43); VJ-11 NAS Santa Ana 19Sep44; NAS Seattle May45 for reconditioning; VJ-11 NAS Santa Ana 25Aug45; VJ-19 Nov45 (presumably at Santa Ana on unit's return from NAS Engebi); VJ-8 NAS Santa Ana Dec45; VU-8 NAS Santa Ana Nov46; FASRON-7 NAS San Diego Jan47; Pool BAR Bethpage June 47; NavAirActSRC NAF Annapolis Oct47 until at least Aug48; records missing; Pool BAR Bethpage by Jan50 (overhaul); NAS San Diego 04May50 (transit); FASRON-112 NAS Whidbey Island 26May50 (ferry); FASRON-114 NAS Kodiak 05Jun50; NAS San Diego 11Apr52 for intended overhaul. SF Litchfield Park 22May52 (storage); NAS Quonset Point 15May53 for MDAP disposal. Declared surplus 19May53 and SOC for MDAP disposal to France 22Jly53 (TFH:2,131hrs). To France's Aéronautique Navale wearing abbreviated serial **063**; transit details unknown but by sea to Saigon, Vietnam and delivered to 8ème Escadrille de Servitude (8.S) at Cat Lai where accepted 11Feb54 and coded 8.S-15. Few specific service details known but in use with 8.S until 1956 by when based at Tan Son Nhut. Withdrawn from Vietnam (Saigon, Tan Son Nhut) in the *La Fayette* May56; arrival date in France unknown but circa Jun56 and to Saint-Mandrier for 240-hour check before operational use with 8.S at Algiers-Maison Blanche as 8.S-15; overhauled at Saint-Mandrier Jly57; remained in use with 8.S in Algeria 1958-1959 until the unit was discontinued in Oct59. Transferred to 27 Flottille at Ouakam, Dakar, Senegal as a reserve aircraft. SOC 05Dec61 and no subsequent civilian use reported.

1193   Built for US Navy as **JRF-5**, BuAer serial **34064**. Acc 14May43 and del 15May43; records missing but with Hedron 15, FAW-15 NAS Port Lyautey by Sep44. US Navy records show this aircraft to have been stricken 28Feb45 at Port Lyautey as a 'diversion' using a disposal code sometimes used to show a transferred asset (albeit an obsolete asset). The assumption is that although USAAF correspondence dated 17Mar45 shows the identity of 45-49089 to be BuAer 37809 (also on the strength of FAW-15 at Port Lyautey in Feb45, but with an unbroken US Navy history.

See c/n B-62), the aircraft that became 45-49089 was actually 34064. Thus the history continues: transferred in-theatre to the USAAF (ATC in French Morocco) as **OA-13B** serial **45-49089** Mar45. Destroyed in a landing accident at Rabat Sale Apt, Morocco 29Aug45 while on US Army Air Force strength.

1194   Built for US Navy as **JRF-5**, BuAer serial **34065**. Acc and del 20May43; early records missing. Ground-looped 15Aug43 when with FAW-12 and (minimal) accident report notes "major overhaul (or strike)". Assigned Atlantic Fleet 25Sep43; Commander FAW-12, NAS Miami 03Nov43. Write-off decision "loss" apparently made 30Mar44 and SOC 11Apr44 (Atlantic Fleet).

1195   Built for US Navy as **JRF-5**, BuAer serial **34066**. Acc 25May43 and del 26May43; records missing but assigned to ComFAirshipWing by Aug44; Blimp Hedron 4, FAirshipWing-4 NAF Ipitanga Oct44; ComAirshipsLant NAS Norfolk Jly45. Awaiting reconditioning/repairs at NAS Norfolk Aug45 and SOC there 31Oct46 as obsolete and surplus. Regd as **G-21A, NC69264** to Vince Daly, Kodiak, AK; aircraft name: *"Anna M"*. To Hardy Aviation Inc, Waynesboro, PA by May50; offered for sale at $33,500; inspected by BOAC at TFH:1,570hrs, May50 for possible use in West Indies. Allotted **CF-OQA** 06Jun62. Authority to ferry Portland, OR to Vancouver, BC 16Jly62 on US CofA for Export E-46013. CofR(C) 30032 to BC Air Lines Ltd, Vancouver, BC as CF-OQA 02Aug62 with CofA 9507 07Aug62; CofA renewed at TFH:4,912hrs, valid until 29Jly64; at TFH:5,610hrs, valid until 29Jly65. Accident at 1305hrs on 10Dec64; on a flight from Klemtu, BC to Prince Rupert, BC, pilot Ronald Maurice Bell was following the shoreline on Tolmie Channel, BC in low ceiling and snow showers. He entered Cougar Bay in error and in attempting a precautionary landing ran up on rocks at the end of the bay. Cancelled from CCAR Apr65. To Webber Airlines, Ketchikan, AK as **N1045** in 1966. Accident 25Aug78: crashed into Sumner Strait, at Point Baker, AK. Eleven killed and aircraft written off.

1196   Built for US Navy as **JRF-5**, BuAer serial **34067**. Acc 29May43 and del 03June43; records missing but with Hedron MAG-12 (1st MAW) Emirau Island by Aug44; Hedron MBG-61 (1st MAW) Emirau Feb45 and SOC there 30Sep45 as obsolete. No evidence of an accident or of a subsequent use and aircraft is assumed to have been scrapped locally.

1197   Built for US Navy as **JRF-5**, BuAer serial **34068**. Acc and del 10Jun43; records missing but NAS Attu by Aug44; NAS Kodiak 31Mar46 (arrival date 04Apr46); NAS Alameda 20Jly46 for reconditioning; Pool NAS Alameda Jan47; Pool BAR Bethpage Jun47; NAS Patuxent River Dec47. Aircraft severely damaged in water landing at Patuxent River 09Sep48. Following a familiarisation flight, aircraft was landed normally in calm conditions but then nosed over and flipped on its back. Investigation suggested that tail wheel may have been in locked-down position and acted as an arrestor hook when aircraft met the water (this was the aircraft's first water landing for two months). No serious injuries and aircraft SOC 30Sep48.

1198   Built for US Navy as **JRF-5**, BuAer serial **34069**. Acc and del 15Jun43; records missing but with US Naval Mission to Brazil by Oct44 until at least Jun46; records unreadable but under repair with FASRON-102 NAS Norfolk by Nov46; BAR Bethpage 09Dec46; VN8D5 NAF Annapolis May47; NavAirActSRC NAF Annapolis Aug47 until at least Aug48. Records missing but still at Annapolis when lost in accident at NAAS Mustin Fld, 28Jun49: aircraft ground-looped and nosed-over on landing due pilot error, causing major damage; SOC 31Jly49.

1199   Built for US Navy as **JRF-5**, BuAer serial **34070**. Acc and del 19Jun43; Atlantic Fleet NAS Norfolk 21Jun43; Commander FAW-11 NAS San Juan 27Jun43; VS-63 (headquartered at) NAS San Juan 30Jun43. Aircraft dug in and capsized during landing on Essequibo River, British Guiana 07Jly43. FAW-11 pilot had landed with wheels in fully lowered position. SOC 08Jly43.

1200   Built for US Navy as **JRF-5**, BuAer serial **34071**. Acc 26Jun43 and del 27Jun43; records missing but at NAS Adak by Aug44; NAF Dutch Harbor Mar45; NAS Kodiak Oct45; NAS Seattle Mar46 for reconditioning; Pool NAS Seattle Nov46; Pool BAR Bethpage Feb47; NAAS Chincoteague Jun47; Pool NAS Norfolk Jan48; NAAS Chincoteague Feb48; NAS Norfolk Mar48; NAS Anacostia Apr48 until at least Aug48; records missing; Pool BAR Bethpage by Jan50 in overhaul; NAF Annapolis 10Aug50. Damaged at NAAS Mustin Fld 29Sep51 when undercarriage collapsed on landing (not properly locked by Annapolis crew); NAS Quonset Point 31Jan52 for overhaul and modification to **JRF-6** (to JRF-6X 05Jan53 and JRF-6 30Jun53); FASRON-102 NAS Norfolk 13Jly53 (delivery – by sea according to record card); NAS

Bermuda 29Aug53; FASRON-102 NAS Norfolk 11Aug54 (ferry); NAF Annapolis 02Sep54; NAS Anacostia 13Jan56 (transit). SF Litchfield Park 22Jan56 (storage) and SOC 11Sep56. Sold 01Oct56 (to whom?) and regd as **G-21A, N9547C**. The FAA file contains no registration information but from the 'Airworthiness' file it can be ascertained that the aircraft was re-registered **N27Q** to Coastal Aero, Houston, TX 04Feb57. CofA 25Mar57 at TFH:2,130hrs. To Gordon G Guiberson, Los Angeles, CA by Dec63 and CofR applied for 05Dec63 although not issued. Electric landing gear retract mechanism installed by McKinnon Dec63 per STC SA4-1551. **CF-PVE** allotted to Northern Mountain Airlines Ltd, Prince George, BC 06Mar64. Authority to ferry Sandy, OR to Vancouver, BC 06Mar64. BoS 24Mar64 Gordon G Guiberson, Los Angeles, CA to Northern Mountain for $40,377.36 at TFH:2,346hrs with aircraft noted as being at Sandy, OR. Aircraft overhauled and upgraded by McKinnon during Apr64, incl gross wt increase to 9,200lbs, installation of cargo door, removal of rear cabin bulkhead and installation of ten cabin seats. Authority to ferry Sandy, OR to Vancouver, BC 28Apr64 with US CofA for export E-46835 29Apr64. CofR(C) 33265 for CF-PVE 06May64 with CofA 9598, 20May64. Accident at 1035hrs on 26Jun64: pilot, Merv Hasse, landed on a sand strip at Pine Point, NT, left wheel hit a soft spot and gear collapsed. CofA renewed at TFH:2,705hrs, valid until 20May66. N27Q belatedly cancelled from USCAR 11Mar69. BoS to Midwest Airlines Ltd 17Jun69, traded for two Beech 18s. Aircraft modified with a large cargo door on starboard side (at unknown date). CofR(C) to Midwest Airlines Ltd, Winnipeg, MB 19Jun69. CofA renewed at TFH:4,311hrs, valid until 10Jly71. BoS 16Nov72 to West Coast Air Services Ltd, Vancouver, BC with CofR 03Apr73. CofA renewed at TFH:5,975hrs, valid until 27Jun75. Accident at 1215hrs on 09Sep74: while on a flight from Tofino, BC – Vancouver, BC crashed into Nitinat Canyon at the foot of Mt Hooper in low cloud and poor visibility. An explosion was heard as aircraft struck mountainside and burned. Evidence at the scene indicated that the wing struck a tree while turning. Pilot and ten passengers killed. Cancelled from CCAR 02Oct78 and wreck reported sold Oct79. (From accident report there could not have been much left!)

Because the G-44 Widgeon was by now in production using c/ns starting at 1201, the Goose line was continued using c/ns in a supplementary series, B-1 to B-156.

B-1   Built for US Navy as **JRF-5**, BuAer serial **34072**. Acc 30Jun43 and del to ADU New York 03Jly43; NAS Coco Solo 28Jly43; records missing but with FAW-3 NAS Coco Solo when involved in a fatal accident 02Jun44. Aircraft had been positioned to Puntarenas, Costa Rica to assist in search for the missing British vessel *Atako*. As search was ongoing, the aircraft returned to overnight at San Jose, Costa Rica but was unable to land due low cloud and fog. Pilot elected to return to the coast for a water-landing but ran low on fuel and crashed into jungle in north-western Costa Rica just short of the coast killing the pilot (the radioman successfully parachuted to safety shortly before the crash). SOC by Coco Solo 31Aug44.

B-2   Built for US Navy as **JRF-5**, BuAer serial **34073**. Acc 09Jly43 and del 10Jly43; records missing but with USCG operations at CGAS Miami by Aug44 and SOC there 30Sep45 due storm damage, presumably caused by the hurricane of 15Sep45.

B-3   Built for US Navy as **JRF-5**, BuAer serial **34074**. Acc 15Jly43 and del 17Jly43; Atlantic Fleet NAS Norfolk 21Jly43; 'Hdrn 5' 06Aug43 (in view of subsequent history assumed to be BlmpHedron 5, Trinidad); FLAG 78 09Aug43; BlmpHedron 5 Carlsen Fld, Trinidad 20Dec43. Aircraft damaged in heavy landing at sea, two miles offshore, Gulf of Paria, west of Carlsen Fld, 03Apr44 (pilot, from FAW-5, had been undertaking practice landings but had had difficulty getting airborne; aircraft apparently stalled after finally becoming airborne). On 01Jly44 FAW-5 crew (with the same pilot who had been involved in the earlier incident) became lost en route Trinidad to Seawell Fld, Barbados due to a combination of weather, radio failure and poor navigation. Following fuel exhaustion aircraft force-landed at sea to the west of St Lucia; all six on board were safely recovered but the aircraft was sunk by naval gunfire. SOC 14Jly44.

B-4   Built for US Navy as **JRF-5**, BuAer serial **34075**. Acc 19Jly43 and del 20Jly43; Pacific Fleet NAS San Diego 02Aug43; Pacific Fleet NAS Seattle 06Aug43; CGAS Port Angeles 15Nov43. Lost in fatal accident 19Nov43 while undertaking special patrol and logistics operations in Alaska. Following a departure from Port Heiden, AK for Kodiak in poor visibility and heavy icing conditions, the aircraft attempted to return but impacted a mountain slope killing the Coastguard crew of three and a passenger. Their remains were recovered in 1987. Formally SOC by US Navy 04Jan44.

B-5   Built for US Navy as **JRF-5**, BuAer serial **34076**. Acc and del 26Jly43; records missing until Aug44; location between Aug44 and Feb45 unreported. Stricken from BuAer records 31Mar45 but then reinstated Jly45 when at CGAS Miami. Finally SOC by US Navy at Miami 30Sep45 due storm damage, presumably caused by the hurricane of 15Sep45.

B-6   Built for US Navy as **JRF-5**, BuAer serial **34077**. Acc and del 31Jly43; records missing but with US Naval Attaché to Dominican Republic, Ciudad Trujillo (now Santo Domingo) by Aug44; Pool A&R NAS Norfolk 17Sep44; NAMU Johnsville Nov44; US Naval Attaché to Dominican Republic, Ciudad Trujillo Mar45; NAS Trinidad 15Dec45. Damaged in take-off water-loop at NAS Trinidad 05Apr46; Pool FASRON-101 NAS Quonset Point Apr47; Pool BAR Bethpage May47; unidentified FASRON Sep47; allocated to ALUSNA Sweden, Stockholm 30Oct47 and in transit and unreported until Jan48 when with US Naval Attaché to Sweden; at Stockholm until at least Aug48; records missing but still with Attaché Stockholm when damaged at Bordeaux, France 02Jly49 when undercarriage collapsed on landing and aircraft left the runway, damaging the hull. To Pool BAR Bethpage by Jan50 (in overhaul); NAS Anacostia 27Jun50; loaned to the US Dept of the Interior 08Jly50. Declared surplus by US Navy 25Nov53 but remained on loan to Dept of the Interior. SOC by US Navy 11Jly55 (TFH:1,218hrs) but probably remained with the Department of the Interior. Cvtd to **G-21A** for US Fish & Wildlife, Washington, DC and regd **N749** in 1956. Accident 05Aug65: substantial damage in hard landing at Hay River, BC, Canada. Pilot + 2 pax uninjured. Reregd **N7401** to Griffco Aviation Co, Seattle, WA. Allotted CF-UVJ 25May66 with authority to ferry Seattle to Vancouver, BC. Ferry authority issued again 15Jun66. US CofA for export E-67218 issued 04Aug66. BoS Griffco to Pacific Western Airlines, Vancouver, BC 05Aug66 for US$105,000 at TFH:4,709hrs. CofR(C) 38453 for **CF-UVJ** and CofA 12244 issued 12Aug66; CofA renewed at TFH:5,413hrs, valid until 03Aug68. Accident at 1920hrs on 18Jly67: while landing at Seal Cove, Prince Rupert, BC, aircraft hit a submerged log but managed to taxi up the ramp. CofA renewed at TFH:5,989hrs, valid until 03Aug69; CofR(P) 45421 issued to P. W. Northern Service Ltd, Vancouver, BC 02Aug68. CofR(C) 45430 issued to Trans Provincial Airlines Ltd, Terrace, BC, 05Aug68. Accident at 1445hrs on 09Sep68: while en route Stewart to Prince Rupert, BC aircraft landed on rough water at Breezy Point, Portland Canal, BC. Pontoon punctured wing and aircraft ran aground on rocky shoreline. CofA renewed at TFH:6,647hrs, valid until 16Jly70; at TFH:10,697hrs, valid until 29Aug75. CofR re-issued as **C-FUVJ** 14Feb75. CofA renewed at TFH:12,312hrs, valid until 29Aug77; at TFH:15,497hrs, valid until 29Aug80. Accident at 1800hrs on 30Aug79: crashed 1½ miles NE of Digby Island Airport, Prince Rupert, BC at the end of a flight from Kitsault, BC. Both engines cut out at 500ft on base leg of approach. Aircraft crashed into rolling ground. Fuel ran out due to the shut-off valve on the left fuel tank being left in the "off" position after maintenance. Pilot (Dennis (Denny) Charles Adams) + six pax fatal, 3 seriously injured. Aircraft DBF and cancelled from CCAR 14Nov80.

B-7   Built for US Navy as **JRF-5**, BuAer serial **34078**. Acc and del 06Aug43; records missing but with NAS Argentia by Aug44; NAS Seattle Jun45 for reconditioning; CASU-67 NAS Memphis 31Jan46; Pool Hedron 5 FAW-5, NAS Norfolk 27Jun46; Pool NAS Norfolk 26Jly46; NAF Bermuda Sep46; FASRON-104 NAF Bermuda Nov46; Pool NAS Norfolk Jly48 until at least Aug48; records missing; NAS Norfolk by Jan50 awaiting overhaul; Pool BAR Bethpage 9May50 for overhaul; NAS Quonset Point 25Oct50 (awaiting issue); FASRON-915 NAS Trinidad 17Nov50; FASRON-101 NAS Quonset Point 30Jan52 (awaiting issue); assigned and aboard *USS Currituck* (AV-7) 08Aug52; NAS Quonset Point 06Apr53 for overhaul. Identified for MDAP disposal 19May53. Declared surplus 20May53 and SOC at Quonset Point for MDAP disposal to France 22Jly53 (TFH:1,090hrs). To France's Aéronautique Navale wearing abbreviated serial **078**; transit details unknown but by sea to Saigon, Vietnam and delivered to 8ème Escadrille de Servitude (8.S) at Cat Lai where accepted 11Feb54 and coded 8.S-7. Few specific service details known and perhaps in early storage but in use with 8.S until 1956 by which time based at Tan Son Nhut. Withdrawn from Vietnam (Saigon, Tan Son Nhut) in the *La Fayette* May56; arrival date in France unknown but circa Jun56 and to Saint-Mandrier for 240-hour check before operational use with 8.S at Algiers-Maison Blanche as 8.S-15. Overhauled at Saint-Mandrier Jan58; remained in use with 8.S in Algeria 1958-1959 until the unit was discontinued in Oct59. Transferred to 27 Flotille at Bel Air and Ouakam, Dakar, Sénégal and re-coded 27.F-11. Used by 27.F until destroyed in a fatal crash at Tambacounda, Senegal 27Jan61; aircraft crashed on take-off killing the prominent Rear Admiral Pierre Ponchardier, his wife and four others. SOC 23Mar61.

B-8   Built for US Navy as **JRF-5**, BuAer serial **34079**. Acc 12Aug43 and del 16Aug43; NAD New York, 17Aug43. Formally transferred to the US Coast Guard wef 21Aug43 and given serial **V224** (SOC by US Navy

22Feb44). During course of US Coast Guard service serial modified to '**224**' (28Dec45) and designation **JRF-5G** adopted circa 1950. Returned to US Navy at SF Litchfield Park 20May54 for storage, awaiting disposal and SOC 07May56 (TFH:3,703hrs). BoS US NAS North Island, San Diego, CA to Ellis Air Lines, Ketchikan, AK 08May56 with CofR **N2752A** 02Jly56. Cvtd to **G-21A** but wheels removed 15Nov56 and cleared to operate at 8,800lbs MTOW with CofA 10Dec56 at TFH:3,717hrs. Tfd by BoS to Alaska Coastal-Ellis Airlines, Juneau, AK 01Oct62 with CofR 10Oct62. Reported wfu Nov64. Tfd by BoS to Alaska Coastal Airlines Inc, Juneau, AK 12Jly66; merged into Alaska Airlines Inc, Seattle, WA 27Mar68 with CofR 19Apr68. BoS to Foreign & Domestic Enterprises Inc, Seattle, WA 05May72 with CofR 27Jun75; complete overhaul Nov75. BoS to Channel Flying Inc, Juneau, AK 02Jan76 with CofR 22Jan76, and another CofR 27Nov82 for address change. BoS to Wilson C Edwards, Big Spring, TX 06Jly89 with CofR31Jly89. Stored dismantled Carson City, NV 1995 and noted there, dismantled, Aug95 marked as "C4" and "2752A". BoS to Ozark Management Inc, Jefferson City, MO 23Feb96 with CofR 22Apr05. **N339TH** applied for 27Apr98 but ntu. Reregd **N9KL** 22Apr05. Current and airworthy May13, with CofR due to expire 30Apr14.

B-9   Built for US Navy as **JRF-5**, BuAer serial **34080**. Acc 21Aug43 and del 23Aug43; records missing but at NAF Aratu by Aug44; ComAirLant NAS Norfolk 27Sep44; Hedron 16, FAW-16 NAF Recife Oct44; ComFAirShpsLant NAS Lakehurst Jly45 and SOC 30Sep45 due storm damage (date and circumstances unknown but conceivably in Brazil).

B-10   Built for US Navy as **JRF-5**, BuAer serial **34081**. Acc and del 26Aug43 ADU New York; NAD, NAS San Juan 29Sep43; non-operational Pool NAS San Juan 01Nov43; records missing but operational with NAS San Juan by Aug44. Destroyed in landing accident at Pointe-à-Pitre, Guadeloupe 14Nov44; fuselage broke in half at wheel wells after apparently normal landing and aircraft sank. SOC 30Nov44.

B-11   Built for US Navy as **JRF-5**, BuAer serial **34082**. Transferred to the US Coast Guard, pre-delivery, 21Aug43; acc and del 01Sep43; NAD New York 07Sep43; given US Coast Guard serial **V225**; ferried from CGAS New York (Floyd Bennett Field) to CGAS San Francisco 21Sep43 during which flight AP1 Carroll R Boyd fell from the aircraft and was killed near Kratzerville, PA. Records show aircraft as lost 23Oct43, details unknown. SOC by US Navy 19Nov43 with record showing location as NAS Alameda and aircraft assigned to CG Operations (the USN strike record refers to this aircraft as '34082' and not 'V225').

B-12   Built for US Navy as **JRF-5**, BuAer serial **34083**. Acc 08Sep43 and del 09Sep43; records missing but with VJ-7 by Aug44 (VJ-7 was located at NAF Majuro, Marshall Islands but moved to NAS Pearl Harbor in Aug44. When involved in a minor landing accident at Barber's Point 03Jly44 the pilot was from VJ-1, Pearl Harbor). To storage at NAS Barbers Point Oct45 and to NAS Pearl Harbor by Jun46 for shipment to NAS Alameda; NAS Alameda Sep46; AOG NAS Licthfield Park Aug47; Pool BAR Bethpage Nov47 until at least Aug48; NavAirActSRC NAF Annapolis by Jan50; NAF Annapolis 24Mar50; NAS Norfolk 03Apr50 awaiting overhaul; NAS Quonset Point 11May50 in overhaul; NAS San Diego 08Jan51 awaiting issue; FASRON-8 NAS Alameda 19Jan51 (transit): NAS Advanced Base Sangley Point 14Feb51 (NAVSTA Sangley Point from Nov51); FASRON-119 NAS Sangley Point 26Aug52 awaiting overhaul; FASRON-8 NAS Alameda 26Nov52 (transit); NAS San Diego 16Dec52 awaiting re-work; NAS Quonset Point 03Apr53 awaiting overhaul but retired 26Aug53 in non-flyable condition. SOC 02Nov53 for parts/scrap (TFH:2,665hrs).

B-13   Built for US Navy as **JRF-5**, BuAer serial **34084**. Acc 14Sep43 and del 15Sep43; non-operational pool at NAS Traverse City, 20Sep43. Destroyed in a ground collision 13Dec43 and SOC 15Dec43.

B-14   Built for US Navy as **JRF-5**, BuAer **34085**. Acc and del 20Sep43; records missing but with NATTC Corpus Christi by Aug44; to NAS Seattle for reconditioning May45; NATTC Corpus Christi 31Aug45; Pool NAS Pensacola Oct45; NABT NAAF Corry Fld Nov45; Pool NAS San Juan 30Jly46. Ground-looped after landing in cross-wind at NAS San Juan 08Oct46 (in repair Oct-Dec46); Pool FASRON-102 NAS Norfolk Aug47; Pool NAS Norfolk Oct47 until at least Aug48; records missing; NAS Anacostia by Jan50; NAS Quonset Point 06Aug51 for overhaul. Transferred to US Coast Guard and SOC by US Navy 13Oct52 (TFH:1,273hrs); designated **JRF-5G** with serial **4085**. USCG station allocation unconfirmed but subsequently disposed of at CGAF Barbers Point in 1954. BoS US Coast Guard, Honolulu, HI to Wm Steiner, Downey, CA 13Dec54 with CofR **N2819D** 29Jly55. Sold to RL Avey, Baie

D'Urfe, PQ. Authority to ferry Long Beach, CA to Quebec, PQ 23Oct56. Cancelled from USCAR 12Dec56 as exported to Canada on CofA E-28581. Sold to Murdock Lumber Co, Chicoutimi, PQ. CofA 6310 issued 18Nov56 and CofR(P) 17102 for **CF-JIF** issued 27Nov56. Authority to ferry Montreal to Roberval, PQ 14Dec56; authority to ferry Quebec to St Honore, PQ 27May58; authority to ferry St Honore to St Johns, PQ 27Jun58. CofR renewed at TFH:2,261hrs valid until 25Jly59. BoS to US Missiles Corp, Sun Valley, CA (traded for SCAN c/n 15, N60L) 28Aug59. N64LM applied for 25Nov59; CofA issued 18Dec59 at TFH:2,400hrs; letter from US Missile Corp 27Dec59 requesting N64L instead, but CofR **N64LM** issued 12Feb60, although a pencilled note states "records adjusted 1-6-60". Cancelled from CCAR 08Dec59. BoS for **N64L** US Missile Corp to Catalina Channel Airlines, Long Beach, CA 20Jun60 with CofR 29Aug60. BoS to William J de Creeft, Montclair, CA 09Sep60 with CofR 28Sep60; CofA renewed 13Jan61 at TFH:2,456hrs; Hayes wheels and brakes replaced by Goodyear wheels and brakes May61; Hamilton Standard constant speed propellers replaced by Hartzell HC-93Z30-2D propellers May62, per STC SA1-52; address change to Carpinteria, CA by Jan63. Cancelled from USCAR 07Feb63 after an accident, but no details known.

B-15   Built for US Navy as **JRF-5**, BuAer serial **34086**. Acc 28Sep43 and del 30Sep43; records missing but with Hedron 12 FAW-12, NAS San Julian by Aug44; NACTU Atlantic, presumably at NAS Boca Chica Jun45. SOC 31Jly45 following weather-related crash.

B-16   Built for US Navy as **JRF-5**, BuAer serial **34087**. Transferred to US Coast Guard, pre-delivery, 21Aug43; acc 04Oct43 and del 05Oct43; given US Coast Guard serial **V226** and administratively SOC by US Navy 22Feb44; CGAS Salem by 30Oct44 when involved in wheels-up landing accident at Logan Fld, Boston, MA incurring 'minor damage' albeit categorised at Cat C. During course of US Coast Guard service serial theoretically modified to '**226**' (28Dec45); reported to have been SOC Oct46 following a (presumably non-fatal) crash. [This might well be connected with a vague US Army Air Force accident report summary of a 'USN' JRF-5 stationed at NAS Mayport that crash-landed '30 miles south of Cross City, FL' (ie probably in the Gulf of Mexico) on 25Oct46. According to the USAAF there were no fatalities but the aircraft damage was categorised as '4' – completely destroyed. This incident has not otherwise been found in archived US Navy accident records.]

B-17   Built for US Navy as **JRF-5**, BuAer serial **34088**. Acc 06Oct43 and del 07Oct43; records missing but with NAS Clinton by Aug44; VPB-153 NAS Clinton 11Sep44 (strictly speaking VB-153 did not become VPB-153 until 01Oct44); NAS Clinton Oct44; NAS Houma Jan45; NAS Clinton Mar45; NAS Seattle Aug45 for reconditioning; Pool NAS Seattle 09Jan46. To NACA Langley Fld 23Mar46 where dual-identified as BuAer 34088 and NACA **103** (the second of five aircraft to use this serial); Pool NAS Norfolk Jun48 until at least Aug48; records missing; Pool BAR Bethpage by Jan50 for overhaul; NavAirActSRC Annapolis 28Feb50; NAF Annapolis 24Mar50. Collided with a buoy on take-off from Annapolis 14Apr51, swerved, struck wake of passing boat, nosed down and sank. SOC by Annapolis 04May51 (TFH:1,287hrs).

B-18   Built for US Navy as **JRF-5**, BuAer serial **34089**. Acc and del 18Oct43; records missing but with NAS Miami by 23Jly44 when involved in landing accident at NAS Vero Beach (undercarriage collapse); NAS Miami Aug44; NAS Fort Lauderdale Jan45 awaiting reconditioning; VTB OTU-1 NAS Fort Lauderdale Jan45; NAS Seattle May45 for reconditioning; VTB OTU-1 NAS Fort Lauderdale 10Sep45; NAS Jacksonville Oct45; VM Unit NAS Jacksonville Jan47; Pool NAS Norfolk Jan48 until at least Aug48; records missing; NavAirActSRC Annapolis by 21Jly49 when aircraft bounced on landing at Annapolis, buckling the skin; with NavAirActSRC Jan50 and administratively to NAF Annapolis 24Mar50; NAS Quonset Point 11Apr51 for overhaul. Transferred to US Coast Guard and SOC by US Navy 13Oct52 (TFH:1,368hrs); adopted US Coast Guard designation **JRF-5G** with serial **4089**. Returned to US Navy at SF Litchfield Park 19Jly54 for storage and allocated to MDAP 20May55. NAS Alameda 08Jly55 for preparation for delivery to an unconfirmed MAP recipient, believed to have been the JMSDF for spares' use. SOC 21Sep55 (TFH:1,907hrs). Stored until circa mid-1960s when returned to US hands and sold for $1,515 by US Army Depot Command, Japan with an address in San Francisco, CA to Allied Aircraft Sales, Phoenix, AZ 25Jly67. The FAA file records: "In testimony whereof the seller caused this instrument to be executed at: US Army Depot Command, Sagamihara City, Kangawa Prefecture, Japan". BoS Allied to Troy Hawkins, Wichita Falls, TX, 04Aug67 and CofR as **G-21A, N12681**, 14Sep67. BoS to Dean Franklin Enterprises, Miami, FL, 28May70; CofR

applied for 27Jly71 and issued 15Mar74? To Worldwide Aviation Distributors Inc, Miami, FL with CofR 22Jun00. Current, but non-airworthy Sep11. In fact the FAA file contains no Forms 337 so the aircraft may never have been airworthy since 1967. The CofR expired 31Dec11, although the regn remains assigned May13. Fate unknown.

B-19   Built for US Navy as **JRF-5**, BuAer serial **34090**. Transferred to US Coast Guard, pre-delivery, 21Aug43; acc and del 19Oct43; given US Coast Guard serial **V227** and formally SOC by US Navy 22Feb44. During course of US Coast Guard service serial modified to '**227**' (28Dec45) and designation **JRF-5G** adopted circa 1950. Wfu by US Coast Guard at CGAS Miami, and stored Elizabeth City, 17Aug53 at TFH:circa 4,062hrs. BoS US Coast Guard to Mackey Airlines Inc, Fort Lauderdale, FL 03Mar56 with CofR **N2578B** 20Sep56. BoS to Suncoast Airways Inc, Palm Beach, FL 01Mar57 with CofR 20Mar57. Reregd **N40R** 08May57; aircraft dis-assembled for overhaul. Cvtd to **G-21A**, seats installed in cabin per STC SA2-223, Jly57, with CofA 12Jly57 at TFH:4,062hrs. BoS to Windjammer Flying Service Inc, Miami Beach, FL 04Oct62 with CofR 23Oct62; new seats installed per STC SA2-223 and 3-place divan installed on right side of cabin per STC SA2-760 Mar63. BoS to OW Tosch, dba Tosch Aircraft, Fort Lauderdale, FL 14May64 with CofR 29Jly64. BoS to Antilles Air Boats Inc (AAB), St Croix, Christiansted, US Virgin Islands 10Nov64 with CofR 20Nov64. Accident 28Feb70: starboard engine failed on climb-out from St Croix. Aircraft hit water, nosed over and sank. Pilot + 5 pax uninjured but aircraft substantially damaged. Last FAA 337 15Jan70. Letter from AAB to FAA 09Jan81 requesting G-21A, B-19, "be de-registered as it had not been flown for the past ten years and it is our intent to eventually scrap it" Cancelled from USCAR, at owner's request, 02Feb81. AAB ceased ops in 1981.

B-20   Built for US Navy as **JRF-5**, BuAer serial **34091**. Acc and del 25Oct43; records missing but with Curtiss-Wright Corp, location uncertain but probably Buffalo, NY, by Aug44; CASU-F43, Guam Feb45; Commander Marianas (presumably at Agana, Guam) Jun45; CASU-F12, NAS Agana Sep45; in transit en route NAS Pearl Harbor Apr46. To NAS Alameda, Jun46 for repair/reconditioning, but SOC at Alameda 30Sep47.

B-21   Built for US Navy as **JRF-5**, BuAer serial **34092**. Acc and del 31Oct43; records missing but with NAS Seattle by Aug44; Pool BAR Bethpage Feb47; VN8D5 NAF Annapolis Jun47; NavAirActSRC NAF Annapolis Aug47. Transferred from the US Navy to the US Air Force (Air Materiel Command) 24Oct47 while aircraft was still at Annapolis (SOC by US Navy 30Nov47) for modification and trials of a hydro-ski concept (see Chapter 5); taken on USAF charge 09Nov47 by 4000th AF Base Unit, Wright Field. Designated **OA-9** with serial **48-128** (with buzz number 'OA-128'); bailed to EDO Aircraft, College Point, NY 04Dec47. Re-designated **ZA-9** (indicating obsolescence!) 01Jly48. On termination of the programme reassigned to the US Navy 21Apr49 and returned from College Point 26Apr49. Formally reinstated by US Navy 30Jun49. Records missing but operational in Flight Test, NATC Patuxent River by Jan50. Declared non-flyable and surplus 25Jan50 and SOC at Patuxent River for parts/scrap Mar50 (TFH:771hrs).

B-22   Built for US Navy as **JRF-5**, BuAer serial **34093**. Acc and del 09Nov43; records missing but with NAS New York by 03Jun44 when involved in landing accident at La Guardia Apt, NY suffering minor damage; NAS New York by Aug44; NAS Seattle Aug45 for reconditioning; NAS Miami 26Feb46; NAAS Corry Fld Nov46; VM Unit NAAS Corry Fld Feb47; VU Unit NAAS Corry Fld Sep47; (unreadable, probably NAS Pensacola) Nov47; Pool (unreadable) NAS Pensacola Jan48; Pool A+R NAS Pensacola, Mar48 and SOC 30Apr48 as obsolete and surplus. NC742 reserved 17May46 for Dept of the Interior, Fish & Wildlife Service, Washington, DC and regd **NC742** as **G-21A** 12Apr48, later becoming **N742**. Used by Fish & Wildlife Service out of Anchorage and Juneau, AK. Model 'C' water rudder installed 12Feb51 (see Chapter 5). Accident 01Sep54: crashed at Admiralty Island, AK. Five fatalities and noted as "washout". Cancelled from USCAR 28Sep54.

B-23   Built for US Navy as **JRF-5**, BuAer serial **34094**. Acc 15Nov43 and del 18Nov43; records missing but with Hedron 11, FAW-11 NAS San Juan by Aug44; CASU-21 NAS Norfolk Jun45. To NACA Langley Fld Jly45 where dual-identified as BuAer 34094 and NACA **103** (the first of five aircraft to use this serial); NAS Seattle Apr46 for reconditioning; NAS Alameda Sep46 still awaiting reconditioning; Pool NAS Alameda Jan47; Pool BAR Bethpage Jly47; NAS Whidbey Island May48 until at least Aug48; records missing; 13th Naval District NAS Whidbey Island by Jan50; NAS Norfolk 03Apr50 awaiting overhaul; NAS Quonset Point 02Jun50 for overhaul; NAF Annapolis 02Jly51. SOC at Annapolis 20Mar53 after local accident.

B-24   Built for US Navy as **JRF-5**, BuAer serial **37771**. Acc and del 29Nov43; records missing but with VJ-13 NAAS Shelton by 09Jly44 (and probably from circa Feb44) when involved in a landing accident at NAS Seattle and with VJ-13 Aug44; VJ-19 NAS Moffett Fld 12Sep44 moving to NAS Puunene Oct44; to unreadable CASU Oct45 (in Hawaiian area, CASU-31 NAS Hilo, a JRF-5 user, looks likely); NAS Pearl Harbor Dec45; NAS Alameda Sep46 for reconditioning; Pool NAS Alameda Jan47; Pool BAR Bethpage Jly47; NAS South Weymouth Feb48 until at least Aug48; records missing; MCAS Cherry Point storage by Jan50. To NAS Quonset Point 06Feb53 for modernisation and modification to **JRF-6** (to JRF-6X 07Feb53 and JRF-6 30Jun53); NAS San Diego 30Jly53 (transit); FASRON-110 NAS San Diego 11Aug53 (transit); FASRON-114 NAS Kodiak 07Oct53; FASRON-112 NAS Whidbey Island 10Feb55 (transit); NAF Annapolis 16Mar55. Surplus and SOC at Annapolis 02Jly56 (TFH:1,684hrs). Regd as **G-21A, N721** for US Wildlife Service, Washington, DC, probably in 1956, but certainly by Oct59. To State of Alaska, Anchorage as **N7211** by 1966. Hulk, carrying AK Fish & Game crest, seen at Viking Air, BC Mar80. CofR(P) for **C-GPIA** to Anglo-Canadian Aviation, Pitt Meadows, BC Oct84. CofR(P) to Norman Berard, Mission, BC 23Nov87. Cancelled from CCAR 29Jan88 and reregd **N7211** to Wilson C Edwards, Big Spring, TX 05Feb88 with CofA 19Feb88. Current and airworthy May13, with CofR due to expire 31Dec13.

B-25   Built for US Navy as **JRF-5**, BuAer serial **37772**. Transferred to US Coast Guard, pre-delivery, 21Aug43; acc 18Nov43 and del 19Nov43; given US Coast Guard serial **V228** and formally SOC by US Navy 22Feb44; during course of US Coast Guard service serial modified to '**228**' (28Dec45) and designation **JRF-5G** adopted circa 1950. Wfu by US Coast Guard and returned to US Navy at SF Litchfield Park 25May54 for storage and allocated to MDAP 20May55. NAS Alameda 27Jun55 for preparation for delivery to an unconfirmed MAP recipient believed to have been the JMSDF for spares' use; SOC 21Sep55 (TT=2,653hrs); not subsequently reported in military use; no known subsequent commercial use; fate unknown.

B-26   Built for US Navy as **JRF-5**, BuAer serial **37773**. Transferred to US Coast Guard, pre-delivery, 21Aug43; acc and del 24Nov43; given US Coast Guard serial **V229** and formally SOC by US Navy 22Feb44. During course of US Coast Guard service serial modified to '**229**' (28Dec45) and designation **JRF-5G** adopted circa 1950. Wfu by US Coast Guard and returned to US Navy at SF Litchfield Park 15May54 for storage and allocated to MDAP 20May55. NAS Alameda 23Jun55 for preparation for delivery to an unconfirmed MAP recipient believed to have been the JMSDF for spares' use; SOC 21Sep55 (TT=2,785hrs); not subsequently reported in military use; no known subsequent commercial use; fate unknown.

B-27   Built for US Navy as **JRF-5**, BuAer serial **37774**. Assumed to have been delivered in Nov43; movement record card does not survive but with Hedron 16, FAW-16 NAF Recife by 30May44 when damaged during a landing at Ibura Fld, Recife. Undercarriage collapsed during landing roll resulting from a combination of a design shortcoming and crew error. Understood to have been SOC 31Oct44, presumably as a result of this accident although damage was considered repairable.

B-28   Built for US Navy as **JRF-5**, BuAer serial **37775**. Acc 30Nov43 and del 13Dec43; records missing but with CGAS San Francisco by Aug44. Damaged at San Francisco MAP during scramble response to an emergency call 14Aug44 (aircraft ground-looped on take-off); NAS Seattle Aug45 for reconditioning; CGAS San Francisco 29Mar46. Formally transferred to the US Coast Guard and SOC by the US Navy 31Jly46. Subsequent US Coast Guard history and disposal details unknown but presumably made surplus in mid-1950s. Regd as **G-21A, N725** to Dept of the Interior, Washington, DC circa 1957 (replacing G-44, c/n 1327). Reregd **N725S** to Alaska Fish & Game, Juneau by Jun63. Reregd **N7251** to State of Alaska, Dept of Public Safety, Anchorage 13Sep72. Seen in blue/white/gold c/s in good condition at Viking Air, BC Mar80. Accident 11Oct94: crashed near Haines, AK. Two fatalities. Cancelled from USCAR 13Mar99 as "destroyed". Wreckage being used in restoration of c/n 1157(qv).

B-29   Built for US Navy as **JRF-5**, BuAer serial **37776**. Acc 30Nov43 and del 16Dec43; records missing but with CG det Traverse City by 27Apr44 when damaged in landing on Lake Erie, MI while involved in rescue mission following the collision of two ships; CGAS Brooklyn by Aug44; NAS Seattle Sep45 for reconditioning. To US Coast Guard 03May46 (station unrecorded on US Navy record card) and formally transferred to the US Coast Guard and SOC by the US Navy 31Jly46. Subsequent US Coast Guard history and disposal details unknown but in view of later history assumed to have adopted the **JRF-5G** designation

circa 1950 and used the revised serial **7776**. Wfu and stored. Purchased by the Aviación Naval Paraguaya (ANP) in 1958. Overhauled at Atlanta, GA and allocated serial **T-003**. Delivered ex-Miami 17Nov59 and ferried to Paraguay via Brazil using radio call sign ZP-TCI, passing through Salvador 24Nov59. Used by ANP at Sajonia, Asunción until early 1966 when the ANP created the Servicio Aeronaval (SAN) and the aircraft was utilised on regular internal air services. Allocated a new serial, believed to have been **127**, in early 1966, but probably never worn. Wfu, date uncertain, and sold to Walter B von Kleinsmid, Long Beach, CA 02Oct68, probably in non-airworthy condition. Overhauled at Asunción and registered as **G-21A, N3283** 06Nov68. Airframe believed to have subsequently been exchanged with that of c/n 1144 prior to the ferry to the USA although N3283 remained registered as c/n B-29 (see page 108 for explanation). Last reported at Asunción circa 1970 marked as 'N328' with fourth digit of previous registration deleted. [The post-1968 history of N3283, c/n 'B-29', recorded on FAA records will be found under its correct c/n, 1144].

B-30   Built for US Navy as **JRF-5**, BuAer serial **37777**. Acc and del 21Dec43; records missing but at NAS Seattle by Aug44. SOC at Seattle 31May46 following mechanical damage on the ground. Regd as **G-21A, NC1019N** to Ellis Air Lines, Ketchikan, AK Nov46 and later as **N1019N**. Became Alaska Coastal-Ellis Airlines, Juneau, AK 01Apr62, with CofA 15Oct62. Nominal change to Alaska Coastal Airlines Inc Jun66; TFH:15,518hrs a/o 05Feb68. Merged into Alaska Airlines Inc, Seattle, WA in 1968. At Viking Air, Victoria, BC in Alaska c/s, 23Jly74. Sold to Laurie W Yonge Jr, Oklawaha, FL with CofR 06Mar84. Current and airworthy May13, with CofR due to expire 28Feb14.

G-21A, c/n B-30, was registered as NC1019N in November 1946 and still carries the marks N1019N, today. It is owned by Laurie W Yonge Jr and is seen here at Tamiami, Florida in 2004.   *(AJ Clarke)*

B-31   Built for US Navy as **JRF-5**, BuAer serial **37778**. Acc 27Dec43 and del 28Dec43; records missing but at NAS Kaneohe Bay by Aug44; NAS Palmyra Island Jan45; NAS Pearl Harbor Oct46; Pool NAS Alameda Mar47; BAR Bethpage 30Jly47. To NACA Langley Fld 11Jun48, where dual-identified as BuAer 37778 and NACA **103** (the third of five aircraft to use this serial). Remained with NACA Langley until SOC by the US Navy 20Apr50 and formally transferred to National Advisory Committee for Aeronautics (TFH:1,401hrs). Subsequent markings uncertain and reportedly on strength until 07Jly58. Fate uncertain.

B-32   Built for US Navy as **JRF-5**, BuAer serial **37779**. Acc 29Dec43 and del 03Jan44; records missing but at NAS Trinidad by Aug44; NAS Seattle 10Dec45 for reconditioning and to NAS Seattle strength 28Jun46; Pool NAS Norfolk May48 until at least Aug48; records missing; NavAirActSRC NAF Annapolis by Jan50 and administratively to NAF Annapolis 24Mar50; NAS Quonset Point 13Aug51 for overhaul. Declared surplus at Quonset Point 03Oct52 and SOC 09Jan53 (TFH:2,234hrs). To US Coast Guard with adopted designation **JRF-5G** and serial **7779**; CGAS Port Angeles, dates uncertain, but assumed withdrawn in 1954. BoS US Coast Guard Port Angeles, WA to Griffco Aviation Co, Seattle, WA 25Jan55 for $8,650; CofR **N4945V** 07Feb55 and CofA for **G-21A** 08Jun55. BoS to Ontario Central Airlines Ltd 05Jun55 with CofA for export E-28421; authority to ferry Seattle, WA to Kenora, ON 06Jun55. BoS back to Griffco Aviation 15Jun55 and then leased to Ontario Central Airlines. CofA 5060 issued 09Jun55 and CofR 14216 as **CF-IEC** issued 17Jun55. Cancelled from USCAR 15Jly55; inspected and CofA renewed 04May57. **N2844D** applied for 25Apr56, CofR issued 18Aug58 and cancelled from CCAR 08Aug58. CofA 07Jly59 at TFH:1,208:30hrs (presumably since civilianisation). BoS Griffco to Pacific Western Airlines, Vancouver, BC 08Aug60. Allotted **CF-MSK** 15Aug60 with CofA for export E-43701 issued 18Aug60 at TFH:1,484hrs. Canadian CofA 7627 and CofR(C) 23493 issued 18Aug60 and N2844D cancelled from USCAR 16Nov60. Returned to **N2844D** with BoS Pacific Western

Airlines to Griffco 20Oct60 and cancelled from CCAR 26Oct60. Authority to ferry Seattle, WA to Vancouver, BC 23Mar61 with CofA for export E-43703 issued 24Mar61 at TFH:1,643hrs but CofR **N9750Z** issued 03Apr61. Canadian CofA 7666 issued 24Mar61. BoS Griffco to Pacific Western Airlines, Vancouver, BC 23Mar61 and CofR(C) 26618 for **CF-MSK** issued 06Apr61, and N9750Z cancelled from USCAR 24Apr61. CofA renewed at TFH:2,475hrs, valid until 24Apr64. Accident at 0900hrs on 29May63: substantial damage after hitting a wharf on take-off in Prince Rupert harbour, BC. Pilot, GA Kent, retracted the wing floats but then allowed the left wing-tip to drop and strike the water causing a swing to the left and the aircraft collided with the wharf. CofA renewed at TFH:3,503hrs, valid until 29Apr66. Accident at 1715hrs on 10Mar66: dep Stewart, BC 1554hrs on a direct flight to Prince Rupert, BC but landed at Maple Bay due to weather. Departed Maple Bay 1645hrs but encountered snow showers and tried to land at approx 1715hrs between mainland and a small island but undershot, hit overhead wires and crashed in Portland Canal. Six fatalities. Pilot taken to hospital with minor injuries. Aircraft reported by NTSB as "destroyed" but recovered from canal next day. BoS Pacific Western Airlines to Foreign & Domestic Enterprises Inc, Seattle, WA 22Nov66 with CofR **N9750Z** 31Aug67. Cancelled from CCAR 31Jly67. BoS to Webber Air Inc, Ketchikan, AK 30Dec68 with CofR 20Aug69. BoS to Southeast Skyways Inc, Juneau, AK 06Jan71 with CofR 14Jan71. BoS to James M Shanks, Juneau, AK 04Dec79 with CofR 23Jan80. Picture windows installed per McKinnon STC SA101WE, 18Mar80. Accident at 0810hrs on 20Jly80: substantial damage during attempted precautionary water landing in fog at Juneau, AK. Pilot continued a planned VFR flight to Hoonah, AK into adverse weather conditions, misjudged his altitude and made a hard landing; one pax seriously injured, pilot + seven pax minor injuries. BoS Shanks to Portage Bay Aircraft Ltd, Seattle, WA 21Aug80 with CofR 21May82. JRF-5 wing floats replaced by J2F Duck wing floats Jun81. BoS to Museum of Flight Foundation, Seattle, WA 05Mar91. BoS to Loel Fenwick, Cavanaugh Bay, ID 27Apr91 (date recorded) with CofR 02Apr91. Non-fatal crash at Spokane, WA, 17Apr91. Address change to Coolin, ID May00. CofR expired 30Jun11 and aircraft cancelled from USCAR 12Sep12. Restored to register 13Dec12 and was current and airworthy May13, with CofR to expire 31Dec15.

B-33   Built for US Navy as **JRF-5**, BuAer serial **37780**. Acc 31Dec43 and del 07Jan44; records incomplete but with Coastguard Operations at CGAS Miami when lost in a landing accident at Santa Lucia, Cuba 04Mar44. While attempting a routine full stall landing, the left landing-gear failed and the aircraft ground-looped resulting in substantial damage. SOC by US Navy at CGAS Miami 05Apr44.

B-34   Built for US Navy, as **JRF-5**, BuAer serial **37781** but diverted off contract to the British Air Commission, Washington, DC as **Goose II**, serial **FP470**, and delivered 19Jan44. To 111 OTU, Oakes Fld, Nassau date uncertain but certainly in use by Sep44; to 45 Group (HQ Dorval, Montreal) 29Nov45 although aircraft remained at Oakes Fld with 1318 (Communications) Flt that formed 15Jan46; coded 'GA' by early 1946. Returned to the US Govt and on US Navy charge by Feb46 with new BuAer serial **66360** (aircraft was initially misidentified by USN as surplus JRF-6B, hence the new serial). Ferried from Oakes Fld to NAS Miami 14Apr46 where awaiting reconditioning 30Apr46 and still present Jly46. Allocated to CNAAT Jacksonville but move unconfirmed and SOC 31Aug46 as obsolete and surplus. To The Babb Co Inc, New York, NY. Export CofA E-15340 issued 17Apr47 for export to Shell Co of Ecuador Ltd, Quito; regd as **G-21A, HC-SBT** Apr47, FN:3. Tfd to Shell Oil Co, Caracas, Venezuela as **YV-P-AEP** 05Jan49. Accident 26Aug49 when operated by Caribbean Petroleum Co: damaged by gear collapse during landing at Shell Mera, Ecuador, but returned to service Oct49. Regd to Asiatic Petroleum, New York, NY as **HC-SBY**, Oct49, and operated, with a large cargo door on the right side of aircraft, by Shell Ecuador from its Mera base; given FN:3. Wfu Mar50 and put up for sale. TFH:1,171hrs a/o May50. To Grumman Aircraft Engineering Corp, Bethpage, NY Nov50 for overhaul (although BOAC report May50 states aircraft already factory overhauled) and regd to GAEC as **N701A**. CF-OIA allotted to Carl Millard Ltd 28Mar62. Permits issued 28Mar62 and 04Apr62 for ferry flights from Williamsport, PA to Toronto, ON. CofA 9664 and CofR(P) 28186 for **CF-OIA** to Carl Millard Ltd, Toronto, ON 11Jun62. CofR amended to Commercial 19Oct62; CofA renewed at TFH:3,701hrs, valid until 04Apr64. Operated on temporary CofA by Great Bear Lake Lodge Ltd, Sioux Narrows, ON (lease?) from 26May64. Accident 28May64: Pilot (Plummer) lost control during take-off at Sioux Narrows A/P, ON. Applied brakes, aircraft nosed over. Pilot + one passenger escaped without injury, but aircraft DBF and written off. Cancelled from CCAR 26Jun64.

B-35   Built for US Navy as **JRF-5**, BuAer serial **37782**. Acc 31Dec43 and del 26Jan44; records missing but with CGAS Biloxi by Aug44; NAS Seattle Aug45 for reconditioning; CGAS San Francisco 07Jun46. Formally transferred to the US Coast Guard and SOC by the US Navy 31Jly46; circa

G-21A, c/n B-34, HC-SBT, moored on the landing stage at Tiputini on th Rio Napo, Ecuador. One of Shell's Dakotas (HC-SBS) is approaching to commence a parachute drop on the airstrip, which is under construction. The Goose will later return the parachutes to base for re-use.

(I Swemle via HC Kavelaars Collection)

1950 adopted the designation **JRF-5G** with serial **7782**; US Coast Guard withdrawal date uncertain but loaned to the US Navy circa 01Jan58 for long-term bailment to EDO Corporation, College Point, NY for modification and research into Gruenberg hydrofoil system (see Chapter 5). US Navy agencies using the aircraft during this period were BWR Elmshurst, NY Jan58; BWR Garden City, NY Aug60; BWR Bethpage, NY Apr61 and RDT&E Norfolk, VA Jan65 until 30Jun65 when programme was terminated. Aircraft located at College Point until 1963 and then at NATC Patuxent River until 1964 (in US Coast Guard markings at College Point and US Navy/NATC markings at Patuxent River). Thought to have been returned to US Coast Guard by US Navy circa 30Jun65. In US Navy storage at NAS Norfolk and reportedly sometime displayed at US Marine Corps museum, MCAS Quantico until exchanged for "like property" (an A6M2 "Zero") by Robert E Diemert, Carman, MB 08Oct76. **C-GOOS** provisionally allocated to RE Diemert, but ntu and cancelled 18May77. BoS Diemert to James C McKinney 12May77 with CofR **N64687** for ferry 31May77. BoS to Paul F Niedner Jr, Tom Ahlers & William Sims, St Charles, MO 04Jun77 with CofR 18May78. Reregd **N742PC** 31May78 with CofA 21Aug78 at TFH:4,875hrs. BoS to Donald E DeTemple, Woodland Hills, CA 11Jan80 with CofR 19Jun80. Tfd by BoS to Bonanza Airlines International Inc, c/o DeTemple, Woodland Hills, CA 20Jun80 with CofR 13Mar81. Re-possessed by Federal Deposit Insurance Corp, Costa Mesa, CA (as Liquidator for Bonanza) 15Nov83 with CofR 25Jan84. BoS Liquidator to R Scott Simpson, Manhattan Beach, CA 27Nov85 with CofR 16Jan86. Reported DBF in hangar at Long Beach, CA 28Aug87, but listed as current and airworthy May13, with CofR due to expire 30Sep13.

B-36 Built for US Navy as **JRF-5**, BuAer serial **37783**. Acc 29Jan44 and del 03Feb44; records missing but with CASU-32 NAS Kahului by Aug44; AROU-1 Los Negros, Admiralty Islands Feb45; Pool AROU-2 NOB Samar May45; NOB Samar Jun45; VJ-9 San Marcelino, Philippines Jly45; Pool NOB Samar Nov45; Pool CASU-F12 NAS Agana Jan46; NAS Pearl Harbor Apr46; NAS Alameda Sep46 for reconditioning; Pool NAS Alameda Jan47; Pool BAR Bethpage 09Jly47; Pool FASRON-102 NAS Norfolk Apr48 until at least Aug48; records missing; NavAirActSRC NAF Annapolis by Jan50; Pool BAR Bethpage 28Feb50 for overhaul; BAR RD&E College Point, NY 04Aug50 for bailment to and modification by the EDO Corporation to test single hydro-ski concept (see Chapter 5). To NATC NAS Patuxent River 11Sep51; retired circa 08May53 and to NAS Quonset Point 29Jun53 for overhaul. Declared surplus 16Jly53 and SOC 30Sep53 for parts/scrap (TFH:956hrs).

B-37 Built for US Navy as **JRF-5**, BuAer serial **37784**. Acc 30Jan44 and del 03Feb44; records missing but with NAS Traverse City by Aug44; TTF NAS Traverse City Sep44; NAS Traverse City Jun45; NAS Atlantic City Aug45; Pool NAS Seattle Nov45 for reconditioning; NAS Anacostia 15Jly46; Pool NAS Norfolk May48 until at least Aug48; records missing; 10th ND NAS Trinidad by Jan50; FASRON-102 NAS Norfolk 24Feb50 for issue; 4th ND NAS Atlantic City 09May50; NAS Quonset Point 27Sep50 for overhaul. Declared surplus 14May51 and SOC for MDAP disposal to France 13Jly51 (TFH:922hrs). To France's Aéronautique Navale wearing abbreviated serial **784**. Transit details uncertain but reportedly arrived by sea at Saigon, Vietnam on board *SS Eastern City* 28Feb52; accepted 29Feb52 and delivered to 8ème Escadrille de Servitude (8.S) at Cat Lai where coded 8.S-2. Damaged in accident Mar52 and repaired; few specific service details recorded but known to have been held in reserve by 8.S in 1953. Large red crosses applied circa May54 for medevac and armistice activities; by 1956 based at Tan Son Nhut, Saigon. Withdrawn from Vietnam (Saigon, Tan Son Nhut) in the *La Fayette* May56; arrival date in France unknown but circa Jun56 and to Saint-Mandrier before operational use with 8.S at Algiers-Maison Blanche as 8.S-2 1956-1957. Overhauled Saint-Mandrier, completion Dec56, and returned to Maison-Blanche; 8.S operational service in Algeria continued until Sep59 when transferred to Saint-Mandrier. SOC at Saint-Mandrier 24May60.

B-38 Built for US Navy as **JRF-5**, BuAer serial **37785**. Acc 03Feb44 and del 04Feb44; to Atlantic Fleet 16Feb44; records missing but with Hedron 15, FAW-15 NAS Port Lyautey by Aug44; NAS Port Lyautey Oct44. Lost 03Nov44 when en route Naples, Italy to Bizerte, Tunisia: starboard engine failed and propeller lost together with generator power; force-landed in rough seas approximately 60 miles from Stromboli and aircraft subsequently sank; crew of three were recovered five days later suffering from slight exposure. SOC 31Dec44.

B-39 Built for US Navy as **JRF-5**, BuAer serial **37786** but diverted off contract for sale to Royal Canadian Air Force. Del Feb44 and formally TOC 03Mar44; ferried ex USA 09Mar44 (TFH:29hrs) becoming **Goose II**, serial **382** with RCAF. Initial allocation to Eastern Air Command and

G-21A, c/n B-39, N60093, at an unknown location, possibly in the early 1950s. The Goose was exported to Guatemala in 1957.
(Peter M Bowers Collection)

assigned to No.167 (Communications) Sqn, Dartmouth 03Mar44; to EAC Storage Reserve No.6 Reserve Equipment Maintenance Unit, Mont Joli 15Sep45. Made available for disposal 15Jly46 by No.6 Repair Depot although location confusingly suggested as Picton (No.5 REMU Picton was absorbed by No.6 RD at Trenton in 1946). SOC 04Oct46 (with location stated as Mont Joli) to War Assets Corporation. Sold to WRG Holt, Montreal, QC. CF-ESZ allotted to Aircraft Industries of Canada Ltd 01Nov46; inspected 23Nov46 at TFH:639hrs; CofA 1662 and CofR(C) 5162 **CF-ESZ** issued to William Robert Grattan Holt, Montreal, QC 27Nov46. Following the death of WRG Holt, ownership passed to HP Holt; CofR(C) 6400 issued to Herbert P Holt, Montreal, QC 27Jan47. BoS dated 11Dec48 to Canada Coach Lines Ltd, Hamilton, ON for $20,000; CofR(P) 7684 issued 29Dec48; CofA renewed at TFH:814hrs, valid until 29Apr50. CofA renewed, valid until 06Jun51. BoS 21May51 to Cruises & Traffic Sales Ltd, Mount Hope, ON for $17,210.99 and 22May51 to The Diamond Match Co, New York, NY for $31,000. Cancelled from CCAR 13Jun51. Cvtd "from Canadian to US status" by Page Airways, Rochester, NY Jun51 at TFH:1,030hrs and regd **N60093** 27Dec51. CofA renewed 12Jun53 at TFH:1,934hrs. BoS Diamond Match to William J During, Fayetteville, NY 20Sep55 with CofR 02Mar56; inspected 29Aug57 at TFH:3,309hrs. Cancelled from USCAR 12Sep57 as exported to Guatemala, to be used there by Keystone Helicopter Corp, Philadelphia, PA. Fate unknown.

B-40 Built for US Navy as **JRF-5**, BuAer serial **37787**, but diverted off contract for sale to Royal Canadian Air Force. Del Feb44 and formally TOC 06Mar44 becoming **Goose II**, serial **383**. Initial allocation to No.3 Training Command and believed assigned to No.12 (Communications) Sqn, Rockcliffe 06Mar44; to Storage Reserve No.6 Repair Depot, Trenton 03May46; assigned to No.9 (Transport) Group, Rockcliffe 05Sep46 of which No.12 (Communications) Sqn was a component; assignment changed 01Apr48 when No.9(T) Grp became the Air Transport Command; No.12 (Comms) Sqn, Rockcliffe was renumbered No. 412 (Composite) Sqn 01Apr47 and No.412 (Transport) Sqn 01Apr49. Written-off following accident with No.412 (T) Sqn 25Aug51: aircraft swung to port, flipped over and sank when the nose dug in when landing in semi-glassy conditions on Weslemkoon Lake, ON. SOC by No.6 Repair Depot 05Sep51.

B-41 Built for US Navy as **JRF-5**, BuAer serial **37788**. Acc 16Feb44 and del 18Feb44; records missing but with CGAS St Petersburg by 29Apr44 and 19Jun44 when damaged in separate landing accidents at Albert Whitted Fld, St Petersburg; still on strength at St Petersburg Aug44; further minor damage in another landing accident at Peter O'Knight Fld, Tampa 29Jun45; NAS Seattle 28Oct45 for reconditioning. To US Coast Guard 28Jun46 (station unknown) and formally transferred to the US Coast Guard and SOC by US Navy 31Jly46; given the revised designation **JRF-5G** circa 1950. From CGAD Annette Island, AK to storage at Elizabeth City 24Nov53 at TFH:2,784hrs. Offered for sale ex Elizabeth City (as JRF-5G, 37788) 06Jan56. Regd as **G-21A, N1543V** to Avalon Air Transport, Long Beach, CA circa 1956, and given FN:5. Featured in TV series "*Sea Hunt*". Cancelled from USCAR 11Sep58. Seen at Long Beach, CA Jun61 wearing registration **PK-DBP**, although probably never registered as such. Scrapped at Long Beach circa 1962. The hulk remained there until 1967 when all remains were removed.

B-42 Built for US Navy as **JRF-5**, BuAer serial **37789**. Acc 22Feb44 and del 26Feb44; records missing but with MCAS Eagle Mountain Lake by Aug44; CGAS San Diego Sep45; Pool NAS Seattle Apr46, presumably for reconditioning. Allocated to US Coast Guard Headquarters Jly46 (station unrecorded on US Navy record card) and formally transferred to the US Coast Guard and SOC by the US Navy 31Jly46; adopted revised designation **JRF-5G** and modified serial **7789** circa 1950; station allocations unknown but ferried, purpose unknown, CGAS San Diego to

CGAS San Francisco 13Jun52. Wfu by US Coast Guard and returned to US Navy at SF Litchfield Park 08Dec54 for storage and allocated to MDAP 20May55. NAS Alameda 20Jun55 for preparation for delivery to an unconfirmed MAP recipient believed to have been the JMSDF for spares' use; SOC 21Sep55 (TT=3,104hrs); not subsequently reported in military use; no known subsequent commercial use; fate unknown.

B-43 Built for US Navy as **JRF-5**, BuAer serial **37790**. Acc and del 26Feb44; records missing but with VJ-3 NAS Puunene by Aug44; VJ-11 NAS Puunene Nov45; NAS Pearl Harbor 11Jun46; NAS Alameda Sep46 for reconditioning; Pool BAR Bethpage 31Dec46; Pool FASRON-102 NAS Norfolk Jun47; NAS Argentia Aug47 until at least Aug48; records missing; NavAirActSRC NAF Annapolis by Jan50. Damaged in taxiing incident 04Feb50 when pilot struck the ramp while taxiing at Annapolis (damage to keel, skin, landing gear, brakes and salt water immersion but repairable); administratively to NAF Annapolis 24Mar50; NAS Norfolk 17Apr50 for overhaul but never undertaken. SOC at Norfolk 25May51 (parts/scrap) as a consequence of the Annapolis accident (TFH:1,366hrs).

B-44 Built for US Navy as **JRF-5**, BuAer serial **37791**. Acc and del 06Mar44; records missing but with CASU-1 NAS Pearl Harbor by Aug44; NAS Pearl Harbor Dec45; NAS Alameda Sep46 for reconditioning; Pool BAR Bethpage Jun47; NavAirActSRC NAF Annapolis Nov47 until at least Aug48; records missing; NAS Norfolk by Jan50 awaiting overhaul; NAS Quonset Point 27Sep50 for overhaul. Declared surplus 14May51 and SOC for MDAP disposal to France 13Jly51 (TFH:1,780hrs). To France's Aéronautique Navale wearing abbreviated serial *791*; transit details uncertain but reportedly arrived by sea at Saigon, Vietnam Feb52. Accepted 29Feb52 and delivered to 8ème Escadrille de Servitude (8.S) at Cat Lai where coded 8.S-4; no specific service details recorded but aircraft survived and by 1956 was based at Tan Son Nhut, Saigon. Withdrawn from Vietnam (Saigon, Tan Son Nhut) as deck-cargo in the *Golo* May56 for intended use in Nouméa; redirected to France, arrival date unknown, but presumably delivered to Saint-Mandrier in 1956. In operational use with 8.S at Algiers-Maison Blanche as 8.S-4 and eventually returned to Saint-Mandrier for overhaul where it was SOC 25Aug59. Cannibalised for spares and scrapped. [Suggestions that this aircraft became N75333 are based on misinterpretation of FAA data, and the assumption that N75333's c/n was 'B-44'. For explanation see c/n 1182.]

B-45 Built for US Navy as **JRF-5**, BuAer **37792** but diverted off contract for sale to the Royal Canadian Air Force. Del Mar44 and formally TOC 24Mar44, becoming **Goose II**, serial **384** with RCAF. Initial allocation to Western Air Command 24Mar44 and believed assigned to No.122 (Composite) Sqn, Patricia Bay; to No.166 (Communications) Sqn, Sea Island by 02May45 when the landing gear collapsed on landing at Penticton Apt, BC; repair details unknown. To Storage Reserve No.7 Reserve Equipment Maintenance Unit, Abbotsford 13Apr46; approved for disposal at Abbotsford 02Apr47. BoS from WAC (Sales Order: HO16699) to Powell River Co Ltd 01Sep47 for $10,000. Authority to ferry Abbotsford, BC to Vancouver, BC 08Sep47 and formally SOC by RCAF to War Assets Corporation 25Sep47. Allotted CF-GEB 12Sep47. CofR(C) 6464 as **G-21A, CF-GEB,** with CofA 2537 issued 10Oct47; to Powell River Co, Vancouver, BC. Accident 25Nov47: after take-off from Aero Camp, west side of Cumsheua Inlet, and at circa 200ft, the aircraft was struck by a whirlwind. The aircraft climbed to 2,000ft where it was subjected to very turbulent air. The pilot, James HA Lougheed, landed at Skidegate Lake. The next day the pilot was asked by the US Coast Guard and the RCAF to fly to the scene of the Clarksdale Victory shipwreck to assist, if possible. The aircraft landed at the East end of Nestra Inlet and the pilot talked to the Coast Guard. After returning to Sandspit, an inspection found damage to the right stabilizer and the skin over the cockpit. Inspected and CofA renewed at TFH:1,512hrs, valid until 05Oct49; at TFH:1,957hrs, valid until 03Jly52. BoS Powell River to B.N.P. Airways Ltd, Vancouver, BC 30May52 for $48,000. Inspected and CofA renewed at TFH:2,199hrs, valid until 03Jly53; CofR(C) 11092 issued to B.N.P. Airways 31May52; inspected and CofA renewed at TFH:2,998hrs, valid until 11Jan56. CofR(C) 15170 issued to Ontario Central Airlines, Kenora, ON 08Jun56; inspected and CofA renewed at TFH:3,342hrs, valid until 12Apr58; at TFH:4,728hrs (now with –AN14B engines), valid until 03Jly61; at TFH:5,145hrs, valid until 18May65. CofR(P) 33284 to Dean Channel Forest Products, Nanaimo, BC 29May64; inspected and CofA renewed at TFH:6,263hrs, valid until 18May66. CofR(C) 32479 to BC Air Lines Ltd, Vancouver, BC 28Apr65. Accident at 0950hrs on 02Jan66: crashed at Vancouver, BC. Flight 235 dep Vancouver 0916hrs on a VFR flight plan to Tahsis, on Vancouver Island. After passing Nanaimo, on Vancouver Island, at 0935hrs, the pilot, Francis Emmitt McCarvill, advised that he was returning to the mainland due to heavy snow. At 0947hrs the flight was cleared for a straight-in approach to Runway 12 from present position. Landing clearance was given and

acknowledged but when the controller asked if the pilot had the runway in sight there was no reply. The aircraft crashed at approx 09.50 in a marshy area about 250ft from the airport seawall on the extended centreline of Runway 12, and about 2,000ft from the threshold. The aircraft was reported as "destroyed". The left wing was broken off outboard of the flap area and the left engine had separated from the wing. The nose section was crushed back into the cockpit area extensively damaging the pilot's controls. The hull was broken across the top behind the wing centre section and down through the main and emergency exit cut-outs. The tail section was relatively intact. The pilot and two passengers were killed, and the remaining six passengers were seriously injured. Cancelled from CCAR 01Apr66. BoS BC A/L to Griffco Aviation, Seattle, WA 07Feb66. BoS to Foreign & Domestic Enterprises Inc, Seattle, WA 19Aug66. CofR as **N1042** issued 24Aug67; complete overhaul Jly74 at TFH:6,967hrs and CofA issued 06Aug74. BoS to Winship Air Service, Anchorage, AK Jly75 and CofR issued 07Jly75. Accident at 1340hrs on 12May78: crashed on take-off run from the lagoon near Port Moller, AK for an intended flight to Cold Bay, AK, operated by Gifford Aviation. Left wingtip float remained in the water and aircraft did not get airborne. Pilot and 2 pax minor injuries but aircraft destroyed. BoS to KC Aircraft Sheet Metal Inc, Long Beach, CA 14Nov79 and CofR issued 04Feb80. Cancelled from USCAR as "destroyed" 23Apr83.

B-46 Built for US Navy as **JRF-5**, BuAer serial **37793** but diverted off contract to the British Air Commission, Washington, DC as **Goose II,** serial **FP471**, and delivered 06Mar44. Allocated to the BCATP (Canada) and delivered to No.3 Training Command of the Royal Canadian Air Force, Montreal 24Apr44; assigned to No.3 Communications and Ferry Flight, St Hubert. Damaged 04May44 during water landing practice on the Lake of Two Mountains, QC: aircraft struck a number of strong swells that buckled the nose; following accident to Canadian Car & Foundry for repairs 13May44. Post-repairs to Storage Reserve with No.3 TC 26Jun44 and after 15Jan45 with No.1 Air Command (location uncertain); released from Canadian charge and returned to BAC, Washington 05Mar45. Assumed to have been returned to US Government but any military identity untraced (BuAer 37793 was not re-used). Transferred to Rubber Development Corp, Washington, DC 30Mar45. Foreign flight approval from Miami, FL to Manaus, Brazil 23Apr45. Regd as **G-21A, NR46497** 05May45 "as cargo hauler in overload condition". Regd as **NC46497** 15May45. Sold to Arthur J Williams, dba British Guiana Airways Ltd, Georgetown, British Guiana (via Foreign Liquidation Commissioner, Rio de Janeiro) 26Mar46 for $3,000. Reregd **NC1048V** to British Guiana A/W Ltd. 26Aug48; complete overhaul Jly49. Reregd as **VP-GAC** 15Sep50 to British Guiana A/W Ltd and cancelled from USCAR 27Dec50. To Governor of British Guiana 14Dec55 (op by BGA Ltd). Became Guyana Airways Corp 01Sep63 and reregd **8R-GAC** 19Jly67. Used by the Governor of Guyana in 1969. Bought from Guyana Airways Corp by Antilles Air Boats (AAB), St Thomas, US Virgin Islands for US$92,500 27Mar73 and cancelled from Guyana register 02Apr73. Ferried from Timehri Airport to US Virgin Islands as "N328"; N328(2) allotted 13Apr73, but ntu and CofR for **N1048V** issued 04Apr73 and i/s with AAB 23May73. Accident at 1105hrs on 07May74: struck rocks after encountering a large swell while water taxiing on the step after landing St Thomas, US Virgin Islands after a flight from Fajardo, PR; pilot + eight pax uninjured but aircraft substantially damaged. No Forms 337 after 1979, AAB ceased ops in 1981. Reported wfu Mar82. BoS to Dean H Franklin, Miami, FL 07Oct83. Trucked away from Opa Locka, FL with wings removed 12Oct83. CofR to Dean H Franklin 30Jan84. BoS to Larry J Siggelkow, Las Vegas, NV 10Jun85 with CofR 02Oct86. BoS to Amphibians Inc, Miami, FL 17Sep91 with CofR 05Jun92. BoS to Worldwide Aviation Distributors Inc, Miami, FL 17Nov99 with CofR 01Feb00. BoS to Aero Accessories Inc, Gibsonville, NC 04Feb00 with CofR 10May00. Fuselage sold to Sam Damico, Pittsford, NY for use in rebuild of c/n 1051 (qv). Still wrongly listed by FAA to Aero Accessories, as valid, but not airworthy, May13, with CofR due to expire 31May14.

B-47 Built for US Navy as **JRF-5**, BuAer serial **37794**. Acc and del 22Mar44; records missing but with Hedron 2, FAW-5 NAS Norfolk Aug44; NAS Alameda Apr46 for reconditioning; Pool NAS Alameda Jan47; NavAirActSRC NAF Annapolis 25Aug47 until at least Aug48; records missing; NAS Norfolk by Jan50 awaiting overhaul; BAR Bethpage May50 for overhaul; NAF Annapolis 10Aug50; NAS Quonset Point 18Dec51 for overhaul. Declared surplus at Quonset Point 03Oct52 and SOC by US Navy 09Jan53 (TFH:1,877hrs). To US Coast Guard with adopted designation **JRF-5G** and serial **7794**; station allocation unknown. BoS US Coast Guard to US Fish & Wildlife Service, Dept of the Interior, Washington, DC 28Feb58 with CofR for **G-21A/JRF-5, N782** 13May58. Tfd to Dept of Fish & Game, Juneau, AK 05Apr60 and CofR **N782SA** issued 11Aug60. Reregd **N7821** Jly63 and reported in store Nov63. Reported as JRF-5G, s/n 794 in US Coast Guard c/s, Anchorage, AK in

1971. BoS Dept of Fish & Game to State of Alaska, Dept of Public Safety, Anchorage 01Jly72 with CofR 31Aug72. BoS to Roy W Mabee, Anchorage, AK 09Oct96 with CofR **N7821** issued 26Jun97. The FAA file on this aircraft contains no airworthiness data and therefore it might be assumed that it has not been operated since 1958, which would perhaps explain the sighting in 1971. Reported stored dismantled, unpainted, in hangar at Chino, CA in 2008 – used as parts source for N6DF, c/n B-128. The CofR expired 31Dec11.

B-48   Built for US Navy as **JRF-5**, BuAer serial **37795**. Acc 24Mar44 and del 25Mar44; records missing but with CGAS San Diego by Aug44. Destroyed 05Sep45 when aircraft struck high-tension wires in Mission Valley Gorge near the Mission Dam, San Diego, CA; aircraft was making a second (and unauthorised) low run through the gorge when it struck the wires and was thrown on its back causing it to crash nose down and inverted, killing both crew. SOC by US Navy 30Sep45.

B-49   Built for US Navy as **JRF-5**, BuAer serial **37796** but diverted off contract to the British Air Commission, Washington, DC as **Goose II** serial **FP472**, and delivered 01Apr44. Ferried from Roosevelt Field, NY to Nassau 30Apr44 for No:111 OTU, Oakes Field, Bahamas; to 45 Group, (HQ Dorval, Montreal) 29Nov45 although aircraft remained at Oakes Fld with 1318 (Communications) Flt that formed 15Jan46; reportedly coded 'GB' by early 1946. Returned to the US Government and on US Navy charge by Feb46, with new BuAer serial **66361** (aircraft was initially misidentified by US Navy as a surplus JRF-6B, hence the new serial). Ferried from Oakes Fld to NAS Miami 03Apr46 by 1318 (Comms) Flt pilot (UK records formally state 14Apr46) pending reconditioning and still present Jly46; allocated to CNAAT Jacksonville but move unconfirmed and SOC 31Aug46 as obsolete and surplus. Details of purchaser and any US civilian registration unknown but reportedly delivered to Aviación Militar Hondurena circa 1946; based at BA Toncontín, Tegucigalpa and given serial **110**. BoS Honduran AF to Marrs Aircraft, Hollywood, FL 18Jun51 with CofR as **G-21A, N3945C** 21Dec51 (actually issued as N3845C but corrected 07Jan52); major repair and overhaul by Rober Ortez, Tecucigalpa, Honduras Feb52; further repair and re-paint by Marrs May52 with CofA with R-985-AN1 engines at TFH:664hrs 21May52. BoS Marrs to DH Franklin, Miami, FL 23May52 with CofR 09Jun52; CofA renewed 07Jly55 at TFH:1,636hrs; (FAA file also contains a CofA for G-21A, N755G dated 01Sep55). Tfd by BoS to Franklin Flying Service Inc, Miami, FL 20Jun56 with CofR 06Jly56; major inspection and repair Nov57. Back to Dean H Franklin Aviation Enterprises Inc, Miami, FL by BoS 03Jly69, with CofR 01Oct69. Letter from Franklin to FAA 12May70 stating that N755G had been painted on aircraft; electric auxiliary gear retraction mechanism installed per STCs SA2-539 and SA2-603 and Hartzell HC-93Z30-2B props installed per STC SA1-52 Apr70. Cockpit cabin interior refurbished and aircraft re-painted in ITT c/s by Air International, Miami May70. CofR **N755G** issued 19May70. BoS to International Telephone & Telegraph Corp, New York, NY 25May70 with CofR 08Jun70. BoS to International Paper Co, New York, NY 26Sep80 with CofR 11Dec80. BoS to Muriel H Weyerhaeuser, Chesterfield, MO 15Mar82. De-registration requested 16Mar82 due export to Canada and cancelled from USCAR 22Mar82. Ferry permit issued 24Mar82 from St Paul, MN to Canadian border at Noyes, MN for pilot Charles Weyerhaeuser. Export CofA E-201465 at TFH:3,406hrs. CofR(C) for **C-GRCZ** May82 for Air Park Aviation Ltd, Lac du Bonnet, MB. CofR(C) to Green Airways Ltd 25May83. CofR(C) to Keyamawun Lodge Ltd, Red Lake, ON 19Jly83. Accident 17May85: substantial damage when right gear collapsed on landing at Red Lake A/P, ON. BoS Keyamawun Lodge to Charles Greenhill, Mettawa, IL 02Sep90 with CofR **N121GL** 17Sep90 and cancelled from CCAR 17Sep90. CofA 09Oct90 at TFH:4,959hrs; address change to Mettawa, IL and CofR 11Mar93. BoS to Inland Marine South Corp, Chattanooga, TN 05Mar94 with CofR 24May94. Attended the Ware Island (AL) Fly-in, flown by Jerry Holmes, Jun95. Operated by National Fisheries Science Center, Plymouth, ME. Tfd by BoS to Gerald Holmes & Associates, Chattanooga, TN 31Dec97 with CofR 18Mar98. BoS to SC Johnson & Son Inc, Racine, WI 22May98 with CofR 25Jun98. BoS to Charles B Smith, Rye, NH 30Sep99 with CofR 18Nov99; installation of auxiliary fuel tanks in outboard wing sections per STC SA4-683 23Feb00. Tfd by BoS to "Charles B Smith Revocable trust of 1999" 01Dec00 with CofR same date; re-issued 05Nov01 with caveat "Charles B Smith, Trustee". BoS to Robert F Wood Jr, Driggs, ID 01Apr03. Tfd back to Smith Revocable Trust of 1999 by BoS 25Apr03, with CofR 30Jun03. BoS to Joel W Thompson, Mooresville, NC 16Mar07 with Temporary CofR 03Oct07 to expire 02Nov07. Export CofA E-251704 issued 03Oct07 at TFH:5,881hrs; flown to England Oct07 via Reykjavik 19Oct07, Biggin Hill 19Oct07, arriving London-Gatwick 23Oct07. (FAA 337 notes damaged keel repaired 16Nov07 at Richmond, ME.) Dep North Weald, UK 09Jun08 and via Singapore-Seletar A/P, Aug08, en route to Australia, where it was noted at Darwin 27Oct08. Noted in hangar R36 at Sydney-

Bankstown 08Jly09 where it had been for "about six months". Aircraft leaning to starboard due to hydraulic problem. Cancelled from USCAR 23Oct12 as "exported to Australia" and registered **VH-GWH** 07Dec12 to Hunt Aerospace Pty Ltd, Howard Springs, NT (operated by Air Frontier Pty Ltd out of Darwin, NT).

B-50   Built for US Navy as **JRF-5**, BuAer serial **37797** but diverted off contract for sale to the Royal Canadian Air Force. Del 13Apr44 and formally TOC becoming **Goose II** serial **385** with RCAF; initial allocation to Eastern Air Command and No.3 Training Command 13Apr44 and assigned to No.5 Communications Flight, Torbay (also known as Torbay Station Flight); absorbed into No.1 Composite Detachment, Torbay 01Sep44. To Stored Reserve 22Aug45 location uncertain but with No.6 Reserve Equipment Maintenance Unit, Mont Joli by18Oct45; subsequent records confusing but indicate storage at or by No.6 Repair Depot (Trenton) at Reserve Equipment Maintenance Satellite, Mount Pleasant, PE and then (apparently) at Picton; approved for disposal at Picton 15Jly46. SOC to War Assets Corporation 04Oct46 with location stated as Mount Pleasant. Sales Order HO3682 dated 09Sep46 from WAC to John G Sharp, Mimico, ON for $30,000; application for regn by Sharp 31Oct46 but ntu. BoS 14Nov46 from Sharp to British American Oil Co Ltd for $40,000. Cvtd by Grumman from JRF-5 to **G-21A** 06Feb47; CofR(C) 5197 and CofA 1693 for **CF-EXA** to British American Oil Co, Toronto, ON both issued 14Mar47, but wef 31Oct46. Inspected and CofA renewed, valid until 02Oct48. Accident 26Oct48: crashed and sank at Memnin Bay (on Lake Meniwen) QC, Canada; after touchdown at 1715hrs, the aircraft started to swerve to the right and left wing pontoon was forced under the water and snapped off. When the aircraft stopped, the left wingtip was trailing in the water and the pilot, RJ McVicar, was unable to steer the aircraft to shore. The left wing continued to fill with water and while the aircraft was being towed it capsized. Sold to Stewart Smith (Canada) Ltd 22Nov48 and ferry Lake Meniwen to North Bay, ON authorised 25Nov48 after salvage. Sold to Ministry of Colonization, Quebec Government, QC 20Jan49 for $25,000. CofR(S) 7978 and CofA 3077 issued 22Apr49. CofA renewed at TFH:1,832hrs, valid until 24Apr52; at TFH:2,615hrs, valid until 14May54. CofR(P) 13948 to HJ O'Connell Supplies Ltd, Montreal, QC 18Apr56. CofA renewed at TFH:3,962hrs, valid until 28May58; at TFH:4,268hrs, valid until 28May59. Accident 25Jun58: after a flight from Mont Joli, QC, pilot started descent to Runway 10 at Montreal A/P. The throttles were advanced to check the rate of descent but there was no response and the aircraft hit the ground, coming to rest about ¾ mile from the threshold and was substantially damaged. Cancelled from CCAR 31Mar60.

B-51   Built for US Navy as **JRF-5**, BuAer serial **37798**. Acc and del 04Apr44; records missing but with CGAS Miami by 15May44 when the aircraft was damaged in a landing accident at San Julian Fld, Cuba (the undercarriage failed on landing due to a combination of a design short-coming and assumed crew error). Repaired and still on Miami strength Aug44. SOC at Miami by US Navy 30Sep45 with strike code indicating a fire on the ground, perhaps caused by the hurricane of 15Sep45.

B-52   Built for US Navy as **JRF-5**, BuAer serial **37799**. Acc and del 10Apr44; records missing but with Commander, All Forces, Aruba-Curacao, Curacao by Aug44; NAS San Julian Dec45; FASRON-102 NAS Norfolk Aug46 for repair; Pool BAR Bethpage 03Dec46; VN8D5 NAF Annapolis May47; NavAirActSRC NAF Annapolis Aug47 until at least 26Jly48 when aircraft was damaged on the seadrome at Annapolis: aircraft hit a channel buoy while attempting to take-off; records missing; NavAirActSRC NAF Annapolis by Jan50 and administratively to NAF Annapolis 24Mar50; NAS Quonset Point circa Sep50 for overhaul (which appears to have commenced Oct51); NARTU Lakehurst 03Mar52; NARTU Anacostia 15Dec52; SF Litchfield Park 07Jan54 awaiting disposal but recorded as a loaned aircraft 24Feb55. Leased from US Navy under contract NOaS55-211m 04Mar55 by Marine Airways and Alaska Air Transport dba Alaska Coastal Airlines, Ketchikan, AK and regd as (JRF-5) **N4773C** 10Mar55. Cvtd to **G-21A** by Long Beach Airmotive Inc, Long Beach, CA Apr55 and readied for delivery flight Long Beach to Alaska with CofA 12Apr55 at TFH:2,293hrs; further modified for Alaska Coastal Airlines operations, and water rudder installed (per Ellis Air Lines drawing No.B-9-8) with CofA 15May55 at TFH:2,312hrs. Administratively released from Litchfield Park 02Aug55. Cvtd to PT6A-20 power by Alaska Coastal 04Dec55. The conversion was carried out under an STC and was therefore not certificated as a new type, i.e. the aircraft remained as a G-21A, but annotated **Turbo** (see Chapter 5). Lease ended by BoS US Government (Navy Dept) to Alaska Coastal Airlines, Juneau, AK 15May58 (for $32,000), CofR for JRF-5 (G-21A) issued 12Jun58, and SOC by US Navy Dec58, quoting US Navy TFH:2,293hrs. Tfd by BoS to Alaska Coastal-Ellis Airlines, Juneau, AK 18Sep62 with CofR for G-21A 27Sep62; nominal change by BoS to Alaska Coastal Airlines Inc 16Jun66;

G-21A, c/n B-52, N37487, was rebuilt, over a period of five years, by Bill Dasilva and won the "Best Amphibian" award at EAA Oshkosh in 1993. It is seen here at Oshkosh, the following year. (MAP)

TFH:12,431hrs a/o 05Feb68; merged into Alaska Airlines Inc, Seattle, WA 27Mar68 with CofR 19Apr68. Accident at Sitka, AK 1968. Repaired. Accident 30Aug70: forced landing on water near Juneau, AK due prop blade breaking away in flight. BoS to Viking Air Ltd, Sidney, BC 05Nov73. Cancelled from USCAR 05Jun74 and in store at Viking Air, Victoria, BC by Jly74. Regn **C-GIGK** allotted to Viking Air 01Jun76 but ntu, and cancelled from CCAR 05Sep78. Rebuilt with R-985-AN3 piston engines by Viking Air by Jan80 when sold to Channel Flying Inc, Juneau, AK with CofR **N4773C** 26Mar80. Reregd **N37487** to Channel Flying Inc, Juneau, AK 06Sep83. Accident 01Jun86: crashed at Hobart Bay, AK (Pilot + 4 pax uninjured) after flight from Juneau. Sank in 300ft water after wheels-down water landing. Wreck seen at Arlington, WA Jly87. BoS Channel Flying to Carl Eurick, Seattle, WA 11Mar88. Parts bought from "Seattle salvage company" for rebuild by Bill Dasilva and BoS from Eurick to Urbano M and Virginia G Dasilva, Dexter, MI 12Apr88 with CofR 09May88; a water rudder was incorporated in the rebuild (see Chapter 5). After the 5-year rebuild project it won "Best Amphibian" award at EAA Oshkosh 1993 at TFH:19,800hrs. BoS to Charles Greenhill, Mettawa, IL 10Mar94 with CofR 06Apr94 with Experimental CofA 06May94, to show compliance with FAR. Regn **N42GL** issued 03Oct94 and placed on aircraft 17Mar95. Noted at Warbird Fly-in, Kalamazoo, MI Jly00. Nominal change with BoS to Amphib Inc, Lake Zurich, IL 21Aug02 with CofR 12Sep02. Current May13, but airworthiness still listed as "Experimental", and CofR due to expire 31Aug15.

B-53 Built for US Navy as **JRF-5**, BuAer serial **37800**. Acc and del 15Apr44; records missing but with CGAS San Francisco by Aug44; NAS Seattle Dec45 for reconditioning. Allocated to US Coast Guard Headquarters 25Jun46 (station unrecorded on US Navy record card) and formally transferred to the US Coast Guard and SOC by the US Navy 31Jly46; CGAS Brooklyn by Oct48; subsequent USCG history and disposal details unknown but in view of later history assumed to have adopted the **JRF-5G** designation circa 1950 and used the revised serial **7800**. Wfu and stored until purchased by the Aviación Naval Paraguaya (ANP) in 1958 and overhauled at Atlanta, GA. Allocated serial **T-002**; delivered ex-Miami 17Nov59 and ferried to Paraguay via Brazil. Used by ANP at Sajonia, Asunción until early 1966 when the ANP created the Servicio Aeronaval (SAN) and the aircraft was utilised on regular internal air services. Allocated a new serial, believed to have been **126**, in early 1966. Wfu, date uncertain. BoS Argentine Navy (signed by the Chief of la Misión Naval Argentina de Instruccion en el Paraguay) to Wilton R Probert, Long Beach, CA 03Dec68 for $24,000, although probably in non-airworthy condition. Overhauled at Asunción and CofR **G-21A, N3284** issued 09Oct69; (see page 108 for explanation of this purchase). Probert indicated to the FAA that he would ferry the aircraft from Buenos Aires to USA himself; special CofA to perform maintenance 18Sep70 and standard CofA 02Oct70 at TFH:4,736hrs. BoS Probert to Caribbean Flying Boats Inc, c/o Antilles Air Boats Inc, St Thomas, US Virgin Islands 02Oct70 with CofR 20Nov70; spray rails installed Oct70; Beechcraft C-18 engine cowlings fitted Dec74. Nominal change to Caribbean Flying Boats (VI) Inc by Sep78; op by Antilles Air Boats, Christiansted, US Virgin Islands; aircraft named "*Miss Mañana*". Tfd to Chalk's Intl Inc, Miami, FL 19Dec81. Reported wfu Mar82 and sale reported Apr82. No Forms 337 after Sep78 suggesting not flown since then, but still listed as airworthy May13, although with no CofR and status "pending cancellation" due sale reported.

B-54 Built for US Navy as **JRF-5**, BuAer serial **37801** but diverted off contract for sale to the Royal Canadian Air Force. Del 09May44 and formally TOC becoming **Goose II**, serial **387** with RCAF; initial allocation to Eastern Air Command and assigned to No.167 (Communications) Sqn, Dartmouth 09May44. Damaged at Moncton when the undercarriage

collapsed (due mechanical failure) 30Jun44; to No.21 Repair Depot, Moncton for repair 03Jly44. Returned to EAC and presumably No.167 (Comms) Sqn 09Sep44; to EAC Storage Reserve No.6 Reserve Equipment Maintenance Unit, Mont Joli 18Oct45; held by No.6 Repair Depot, presumably at Trenton, in long-term storage until made available for disposal 24Aug54. To Crown Assets Disposal Corporation and SOC 14Feb56 (although actual disposal thought to have occurred circa Dec54). Sold to Universal Trading Corp, Panama City, Panama as **G-21A, N2721A**. To Kiekhaefer Corp, Chicago, IL by 1962. To Franklin Flying Service, Miami, FL 1966, operated by Chalk's Flying Service, Miami, FL; aircraft named "*Bimini Bonefish*". Painted with "Tasman Airlines Australia" titles and noted as such Miami, FL 21Jly74. Del via Stornaway - Edinburgh - Southend, UK 16Aug74, arr Sydney, Australia 25Oct74. Regd to Tasman Airlines, Melbourne, VIC 28Aug74. Regn **VH-CRC** allocated 06Aug76, but ntu and aircraft carried **N2721A**. [The registration was widely wrongly reported to be VH-CRL.] CofA issued 15Jly78 and dep Adelaide on del to West Irian, Indonesia. Regd **PK-LEH** to SAATAS, Indonesia, 21Sep78 and leased to McDermott Inc by Apr84. To SAATAS East Indonesia Air Taxi by 1985. Wfu and registration cancelled 1990.

G-21A, c/n B-54, seen here at Jakarta, Indonesia, in June 1984, registered as PK-LEH to SAATAS, Indonesia. The Goose was on lease to McDermott Inc and carries their company logo on the bow. (S Wills via AJ Payne)

B-55 Built for US Navy as **JRF-5**, BuAer serial **37802** but diverted off contract for sale to the Royal Canadian Air Force. Del 09May44 and formally TOC becoming **Goose II**, serial **386** with RCAF; initial allocation to No.3 Training Command and believed assigned to No.12 (Communications) Sqn, Rockcliffe 09May44; to Storage Reserve No.6 Repair Depot, Trenton 01Feb46; assigned to No.9 (Transport) Group, Rockcliffe 24Apr47 of which No. 412 (Composite) Sqn was a component; assignment changed 01Apr48 when No.9(T) Grp became the Air Transport Command; to Storage Reserve No.6 Repair Depot, Trenton 06Jly49; No.412 (Transport) Sqn, Rockcliffe 11Jun52 (del 30Jun52); used radio c/s VC-AOQ 1952-53 with code 'AO-Q'; to Storage Reserve No.6 Repair Depot, Trenton and made available for disposal 20Sep54. To Crown Assets Disposal Corporation and SOC 12Jan55. Regd as **G-21A, CF-HUY** to Powell River Co Ltd, Vancouver, BC with CofR 15000 and CofA 5489, issued 12May55. CofR 18935 to Sioux Narrows Airways Ltd, Sioux Narrows, ON 05May59. Accident 13Jun70: substantial damage when nosed over after landing at Taltheilei, NT after a charter flight. No injuries. To Parsons Airways Northern, Flin Flan, MB, 23Jun72. Accident 10Sep73: substantial damage after wheels-down landing in Hatchet Lake, SK. Pilot uninjured. CofA lapsed 26May74. To Barney E Lamm, Gimli, MB as **C-FHUY**, 27Jun78. Inspected Jun78 and CofA renewed valid until 27Jun79. To Ontario Central Airlines, Gimli, MB 08May83. To Nunasi-Central Airlines Ltd, Winnipeg, MB 27Jun84. Cancelled from CCAR 23Jun87. To William Ross Enterprise, Elk Grove Village, IL as **N7F**, Jly87. To Philip L Bingman, Anchorage, AK Oct93. To Lester LR Bingman, dba Freshwater Adventures, Dillingham, AK 12Feb98. Reregd **N159F** 16Feb08 but not airworthy; CofR issued to Freshwater Adventures Inc, Dillingham, AK 19Jly10, but still not airworthy and CofR expired 31Mar12. CofR re-issued 21May12, valid until 31May15 but remained unairworthy a/o May13.

B-56 Built for US Navy as **JRF-5**, BuAer serial **37803**. Acc and del 02May44; records missing but with NAS Bermuda by Aug44 (NAF Bermuda wef 01Jly45); Pool FASRON-102 NAS Norfolk Jan47; Pool FASRON-201 NAS Norfolk Feb47; Pool BAR Bethpage May47; NavAirActSRC NAF Annapolis Oct47 until at least Aug48; records missing; NAS Norfolk by Jan50 awaiting overhaul; Pool BAR Bethpage 17Jan50 for overhaul; NART NAS New Orleans 26Jun50; NART NAS Minneapolis 01Dec51. To NAS Quonset Point, 29Feb52 for disposal in flying condition and SOC 11Sep52 (TFH:1,533hrs) with AN-12 engines. Transferred to US Dept of Interior, Fish & Wildlife Service, Washington, DC 28Oct52. Converted to **G-21A** status by Baltimore Aero Service, regn applied to aircraft and test flown 24Nov52; CofA in both the Standard (8,000lbs MGOW) and Restricted (above 8,000lbs MGOW) categories issued 26Nov52 at TFH:1,553hrs. CofR (as JRF-5) **N778** issued 05Dec52;

ferried to Alaska, where presumably placed in storage by the Fish & Wildlife Service, Lake Hood, Anchorage. Regd as G-21A, N778 to Fish & Wildlife Service, Anchorage with CofA 15Dec55 at TFH:2,350hrs (with AN-14B engines). Modifications made in Jan58 by Universal Aircraft Industries, Denver, CO included: installation of Franklin metal wing-covering kit, electric landing gear retraction motor, and Hartzell HC-93Z30-2C three-bladed full feathering props. A 42-gallon auxiliary fuel tank was installed on the floor of the fuselage compartment behind the pilot, and test-flown 29Apr60. AN-14B engines overhauled by Dallas Airmotive Inc, "test-run and preserved for long-term storage" Apr61, then fitted to aircraft 15May61. CofR to Office of Aircraft Maintenance, Anchorage, AK 08Feb74; address change to Dept of the Interior, Boise, ID 16Jan91 with CofR issued 31Jan91; listed as an "active aircraft" at Boise, ID Mar93. BoS to Tanglefoot Wing & Wheel Co, Coolin, ID 25Jan94. BoS to Helga R Sallmon, Missoula, MT 29Jun94 with CofR 09Aug94. BoS to Robert G Williams, Billings, MT, 28Sep99 with CofR 04Nov99. Current with Restricted CofA May13, with CofR due to expire 30Nov15.

B-57　　Built for US Navy as **JRF-5**, BuAer serial **37804**, acc and del 20May44; records missing but with CGAS Brooklyn by Aug44; NAS Seattle Dec45 for reconditioning. Allocated to US Coast Guard Headquarters 28Jun46 (station unrecorded on US Navy record card) and formally transferred to the US Coast Guard and SOC by the US Navy 31Jly46; known to have survived until at least Apr50 when with CGAS Miami, but subsequent history unknown. No known record of civilian use.

B-58　　Built for US Navy as **JRF-5**, BuAer serial **37805**. Acc 08May44 and del 09May44; FAW-5 NAS Norfolk; records missing but allocated to Hedron 7, FAW-7 Plymouth/NAF Dunkeswell 04Jly44 having been shipped to the UK as deck cargo in *USS Albemarle* (AV-5). Allocated to Commander, US Ports and Bases, France 12Aug44 (records show location a/o 31Aug44 as 'unknown'); Hedron 7, FAW-7 Plymouth/NAF Dunkeswell 30Sep44; ComNavEu RAF Hendon Jly45; ComNavEastLant RAF Hendon Mar47; Pool NAS Norfolk May47 until at least Aug48; records missing; NAS Norfolk by Jan50 (storage); Pool BAR Bethpage 11Apr50 for overhaul; NAF Annapolis 18Sep50. To BAR RD&DE College Point, NY 08Jun51 for bailment to and modification by the EDO Corporation to test twin hydro ski concept (see Chapter 5); to NATC NAS Patuxent River 11Jun53. Terminal damage in flying accident circa 24Oct55 and SOC at Patuxent River 25Oct55 for parts/scrap (TFH:880hrs).

B-59　　Built for US Navy as **JRF-5**, BuAer serial **37806** but diverted off contract to the British Air Commission, Washington, DC as **Goose II**, serial **FP473** and delivered 10May44. Allocated to the BCATP (Canada) and delivered to No.3 Training Command of the Royal Canadian Air Force, Montreal 29May44; operating unit unconfirmed but perhaps assigned (as was FP471) to No.3 Communications and Ferry Flight, St Hubert; to Storage Reserve with No3 TC 17Aug44 and after 15Jan45 with No.1 Air Command (location uncertain). Released from Canadian charge and returned to BAC, Washington 05Feb45; assumed to have been returned to US Govt with FP471 (B-34) in which case delivered to National Airport, Washington, DC. Regd **NR1800** to Foreign Economic Administration, Washington, DC 1945. Reregd as **G-21A, NC1800** to Edgar J Wynn, dba Trans American Airways, New York, NY Aug46. To International Holdings, NY 1947, but based in Ontario, Canada. To **N1800** for Packer Pontiac, Detroit, MI, by Oct51. Regd **YV-P-APZ** to Orinoco Mining Co, Caracas, Venezuela, with CofR and CofA 10Jan57; cancelled 02Jun67. To **N1133** for Catalina Airlines, Long Beach, CA 02Aug67. In 1968, Aero Commuter Inc merged with Catalina Air Lines. Cable Commuter and Skywark were added to the group which was then swallowed up by Golden West Airlines Inc. Non-fatal landing accident at Avalon, CA 30Aug69. To Golden West Airlines Inc, Long Beach, CA by 01Dec69. Accident at 0933hrs on 05Apr73: an unexpected gust from the left after landing caused the right float to dig into the water and aircraft veered into rocks at Avalon-Two Harbors, CA, after a flight from Long Beach, CA; pilot + six pax uninjured but aircraft substantially damaged. To Catalina Seaplanes, Long Beach, CA as **N18CS** by 1975. Accident 10Apr76: crashed after left engine lost power on a return flight from Camp Fox. Aircraft landed "across sea" off Avalon, took on water and sank. Cancelled from USCAR Jun95.

B-60　　Built for US Navy as **JRF-5**, BuAer serial **37807** but diverted off contract for sale to the Royal Canadian Air Force. Del 30May44 and formally taken on Canadian strength, becoming **Goose II** serial **388** with RCAF. Initial allocation to No.3 Training Command 30May44 but changed to Western Air Command 01Jun44 and believed assigned to No.122 (Composite) Sqn, Patricia Bay; to No.166 (Communications) Sqn, Sea Island by 11Mar45 when aircraft jumped the chocks at Sea Island: while conducting engine runs the chocks slipped and 388 ran over a 20ft

embankment and overturned into the water; recovered and inspected for possible repair but eventually SOC 13Apr45 and formally written-off by No.3 Repair Depot, Jericho Beach 19Jly45. Regd as **G-21A, NC4762** to Alaska Coastal Airlines, Juneau, AK Feb46; rebuilt by Alaska Coastal a/o 01Feb53, using parts bought from B.N.P. Airways, Vancouver, BC; Grumman Aircraft Engineering Corp, Bethpage, NY and Powell River Co, Vancoucer, BC. Refurbishment included installation of a water rudder per Ellis Air Lines drawings. CofR **N4762C** issued 18Feb53. Tfd by BoS to Alaska Coastal-Ellis Airlines, Juneau, AK 18Sep62 with CofR 27Sep62 and CofA 15Oct62 at TFH:6,804hrs; nominal change to Alaska Coastal Airlines Inc shown on BoS dated 16Jun66. Merged into Alaska Airlines Inc, Seattle, WA 27Mar68 with CofR 19Apr68. BoS to Antilles Air Boats Inc (AAB), St Thomas, US Virgin Islands 19Sep69 with CofR 09Dec69. AAB ceased ops 1981. Cancelled from USCAR 19Oct81 as scrapped.

B-61　　Built for US Navy as **JRF-5**, BuAer serial **37808** but diverted off contract for sale to the Royal Canadian Air Force. Del 07Jun44 and formally taken on Canadian strength becoming **Goose II** serial **389** with RCAF. Initial allocation to No.3 Training Command 07Jun44 but changed to Western Air Command 08Jun44 and believed assigned to No.166 (Communications) Sqn, Sea Island; with No.166 (Comms) Sqn when lost in accident at Bella Bella, BC 04Feb45: nose dug in on landing and the aircraft flipped onto its back; recovered and inspected for possible repair by No.3 Repair Depot, Jericho Beach 09Feb45 but eventually formally written-off 27Jly45.

B-62　　Built for US Navy as **JRF-5**, BuAer serial **37809**. Acc 31May44 and del 01June44; records missing but with Station Ops Dakar, FWA (modern Senegal) by Sep44; NAF Port Lyautey 07Nov44; Hedron 15, FAW-15 NAF Port Lyautey Jan45; Pool Hedron, FAW-5 NAS Norfolk Sep45. Hull badly damaged when undercarriage collapsed on landing at Norfolk 09Nov45; NAS Norfolk Dec45 for reconditioning; Pool NAS Norfolk Jan47 and SOC 28Feb47 as obsolete and surplus. Regd as **G-21A, NC5556N** (owner unknown). Regd **TF-ISR**(2) 15Sep47 for Flugfelag Islands hf, Reykjavik, Iceland; aircraft name: "*Snarfaxi*". Wfu 1956 and used as maintenance trainer. Cancelled 07Jly67 and sold to Harold J Hansen, American Aviation Inc, Seattle, WA 11Jly67 and regd **N5558**, (with c/n noted as B-1062 !). Sold to McKinnon Enterprises Inc, Portland, OR Oct67. Retractable wing-tip floats fitted 1968, using McKinnon kit No.34. Sold to Charles E Walters, Spokane, WA. Sold back to McKinnon 20Sep68 and cvtd to **McKinnon G-21G**, c/n **1205**. Re-possessed by First National Bank of Portland and regd to them. Bought at auction 17Jan72 by Peyton Hawes, Portland, OR. Sold to Sea Bee Air, Auckland, New Zealand Dec80 and regd **ZK-ERX**. Ferry tanks installed in the cabin and nose by Viking Air, Patricia Bay, BC. Routed Oakland, CA – Hawaii - Pago-Pago and Tonga to New Zealand. Unforecast headwinds caused the first two attempts to be abandoned! The third almost ended in tragedy when the Goose ran out of fuel before reaching Hawaii. After a landing in open ocean, about 30 miles from Hawaii, fuel was delivered by boat enabling the flight to continue to Honolulu. The ferry reportedly cost $50,000 and the aircraft finally arrived Auckland 03Mar81. In service 09Jly81 after overhaul by Air New Zealand. Aircraft used by Sea Bee Air for services in the central and south Pacific, including for the government of Tuvalu. Returned from Tuvalu to Auckland Sep83 for overhaul. Stored at Air New Zealand hangar until 30th October 1984, when it took part in a formation flight (with ZK-DFC and ZK-ENY) over Auckland. Shipped to USA 17Nov84, arriving Tacoma, WA 07Dec84 for Aero Quest Inc, Cleveland, OH; modified during 1985 with a large cargo door installed in the right side of the fuselage. Regd **N70AQ**. Transferred to Kalt Manufacturing Co, Cleveland, OH 10Dec84 and reregd **N77AQ**. Non-fatal accident at Elyria, OH 13Jun88. Offered for sale at $750,000 at TFH:2,700hrs. To Aero Air (Dan Vollum), Hillsboro, OR, Jly90. CofA 10Mar98. To Aero Planes LLC, Hillsboro, OR with CofR 28Jan00 as **G-21G** with PT6A-60A engines. Current and airworthy May13, with CofR due to expire 30Apr16.

B-63　　Built for US Navy as **JRF-5**, BuAer serial **37810**. Acc and del 08Jun44; records missing but with VJ-11 NAS Santa Ana by Aug44; VJ-10 NAAS Shelton Sep45; VJ-3 NAF Tinian Island Dec45; CASU-F12 NAS Orote Jly46; NAS Pearl Harbor 19Oct46 for reconditioning (via *USS Point Cruz* CVE-119, Oct46); Pool NAS Pearl Harbor Jan47; Pool NAS Alameda Mar47 where SOC 31Mar48 as obsolete and surplus. Regd as **G-21A, NC79901** to Ellis Air Lines, Ketchikan, AK Jun48. Became Alaska Coastal-Ellis Airlines, Juneau, AK 01Apr62 and nominal change to Alaska Coastal Airlines Inc Jun66; TFH:14,188hrs a/o 05Feb68; merged into Alaska Airlines Inc, Seattle, WA 1968. To Antilles Air Boats (AAB), Christiansted, US Virgin Islands 1969. Accident at Roadtown, Tortola, US Virgin Islands 02Sep78. AAB ceased ops 1981 and aircraft reported wfu Mar82. To Malcolm A Soare, Sidney, MT May85. To Bristol Uriel, Miami, FL Sep85. Cancelled from USCAR 12Nov85 as "sold to Sweden".
G-BMGS allocated to Aces High Ltd, Duxford, UK but ntu. Goose traded

to Swedish Air Force Museum (Flygvapenmuseum) in exchange for Douglas Skyraiders! Airfreighted to Sweden by Lockheed C-130, ex Burlington, VT Dec86. Aircraft painted as '81002' and stored on the military side of the airfield at Malmslätt, west of Linköping. Noted there in 1997, but in storage by 2006.

B-64 Built for US Navy as **JRF-5**, BuAer serial **37811**. Acc and del 14Jun44; records missing but with Pool NAS Pearl Harbor by Aug44; AR&OH-1 NAB Manus 19Sep44; ComAir 7th Fleet (HQ Brisbane, Australia but location of JRF not known) Oct44; ComPhilSeaFron (assumed at Tolosa, Leyte) by May45; Pool AROU-2 NOB Samar Aug45; Samoa (assumed at NS Tutuila) Oct45 awaiting minimum repairs; NAS San Diego Dec46 for repairs; Pool NAS San Diego Jan47 and SOC there 28Feb47 as obsolete. Regd **NC68190** to James Conroy. To Michael P Efferson & Associates, Washington, DC May48. Sold to Argentine Naval Mission, Washington, DC 10Jun48; following overhaul by Aeromotive of Long Beach, CA, flown to Argentina and delivered 19Nov48. Given Aviación Naval (COAN) serial **0295** and initially used by Prefectura General Maritima (PGM); coded 'PGM-P-6' presumably based at Punta Indio within COAN's Escuadra Aeronaval No2. Recoded circa 1950 as '3-P-25', presumably indicative of patrol use within the Escuadra Aeronaval No3 at Punta Indio. Used in the Antarctic in the summer of 1950/1951. Sank in heavy weather in Caleta Observatorio, Melchior Base, Antarctica 03Apr51; aircraft recovered by *ARA Bahía Buen Suceso* (B-6) but SOC in 1953.

B-65 Built for US Navy as **JRF-5**, BuAer serial **37812**. Acc 20Jun44 and del 26Jun44; records missing but with Pacific Fleet NAS Pearl Harbor by Aug44; CASU-31 NAS Hilo 29Sep44; NAS Honolulu Nov45; NAS Pearl Harbor Mar46; NAS Alameda Sep46 for reconditioning; Pool BAR Bethpage Jun47; NAS Lakehurst Dec47; NAES NAS Lakehurst Apr48; NAES Philadelphia (NAAS Mustin Fld) May48 until at least Aug48; records missing but badly damaged at Mustin Fld 29Dec48 when parked (struck by taxiing PB-1W 77258 causing cat B damage to left wing, hull and tail); Pool BAR Bethpage by Jan50 in overhaul; NavAirActSRC NAF Annapolis 07Mar50 and administratively to NAF Annapolis 24Mar50; NAS Quonset Point 10Jan51 for overhaul which did not commence until 05Jan53 when modernised and modified to **JRF-6** (to JRF-6X 05Jan53 and JRF-6 17Jun53); NAF Annapolis 07Jly53; due for re-work 29Feb56 but to SF Litchfield Park (at least on paper) 11Mar56 and SOC the same day (TFH:2,536hrs). Sold to Fuerza Aérea Hondurena (Honduran Air Force), based at BA Toncontín, Tegucigalpa and given serial **811**. Withdrawn from use by 1959. Del by Honduran AF to Miami, FL 13April59, under US Import License No: 2806, with BoS to Franklin, Adams & Moore, 14Apr59. Cvtd to G-21A standard by Gander Aircraft Corp, Miami, FL Jly/Aug59 with CofA 19Aug59 at TFH:2,585hrs. Regd as **G-21A, N8015E** to Dean H Franklin, Joseph Adams & Edward Moore, Miami, FL 19Nov59 and operated for MGM Studios in 1960. Accident 12Feb60: crashed into sea off Annotto Bay, Jamaica while en route Port Antonio-Montego Bay. By Jun70 the aircraft was owned solely by Franklin, and was stored / dismantled. Cancelled from USCAR 29Apr72 but fate unknown.

B-66 Built for US Navy as **JRF-5**, BuAer serial **37813**. Acc and del 24Jun44; records missing but with MCAS Parris Island by Aug44 until at least Apr46; NAS Alameda by Jly46 for reconditioning; Pool NAS Alameda Jan47; Pool BAR Bethpage Jun47; NavAirActSRC NAF Annapolis Nov47 until at least 30Mar49 when involved in landing accident at NAS Patuxent River: aircraft sustained moderate damage when right undercarriage leg collapsed during landing roll; records missing; in overhaul Pool BAR Bethpage by Jan50; NAS Norfolk 17Jan50 (transit); FASRON-102 NAS Norfolk for shipping 27Jan50; NAF Port Lyautey 11Apr50 (transit); Naval Attaché Oslo, Norway 13May50; FASRON-104 NAF Port Lyautey 12Sep51 for shipping; NAS Norfolk 06Nov51 en route overhaul; NAS Quonset Point 18Apr52 for overhaul which did not commence until 05Jan53 when modernised and modified to **JRF-6** (to JRF-6X 05Jan53 and JRF-6 30Jun53); FASRON-102 NAS Norfolk 14Jly53 for shipping; FASRON-115 NAS Trinidad 21Sep53; NAF Annapolis 03Dec53; SF Litchfield Park 20Jly56 (retired, awaiting strike) and SOC 11Sep56 (TFH:2,058hrs). BoS USN Air Station North Island, San Diego to Avalon Air Transport (as JRF-6) 29Oct56 for $18,571.40. Regd as **G-21A, N324**, to Avalon Air Transport, Long Beach, CA 15Nov56 with FN:8. Seven seats + jump seat installed Apr57; TFH:5,262hrs a/o 19Oct60; Accident 17Jly62: substantial damage after No.3 prop blade failed on take-off at Avalon Bay SPB, CA. Pilot + 6 pax uninjured. CofA issued 19Jly63 at TFH:6,005hrs. To Catalina Air Lines Inc, Long Beach, CA 30Oct63; aircraft named "*Michelle*". In 1968, Aero Commuter Inc merged with Catalina Air Lines. Cable Commuter and Skywark were added to the group which was then swallowed up by Golden West Airlines Inc. To Golden West Airlines Inc, Los Angeles, CA 01Dec69. BoS Golden

West to KC Aircraft Sheet Metal Co Inc, Long Beach, CA 16Nov73 and CofR issued 26Nov73. BoS to Lew Mahieu, Long Beach, CA 28Feb75 and CofR issued 24Mar75. BoS to Catalina Airlines Inc, Gardena, CA 18Mar76 and CofR issued 29Mar76. Reported donated to Naval Air Museum, Pensacola but noted in store at Santa Monica, CA 29Jun78. BoS to Golden West Aviation Ltd, Vancouver, BC 01Jly80. BoS to Dennis G Buehn, Compton, CA 02Jly80 and CofR issued 12Sep80; address change to Carson City, NV and CofR issued 06Mar90. BoS to Charles Glen Hyde, Roanoke, TX 15Mar90; CofR issued to Glen Hyde, Carson City, NV 02Aug93; tfd by BoS to Flight Data Inc, Carson City, NV, 06Jun99 and CofR issued 20Jly01. Current and airworthy Dec11, but CofR expired 31Mar12 and cancelled from USCAR 02Oct12.

B-67 Built for US Navy as **JRF-5**, BuAer serial **37814**. Acc 29Jun44 and del 06Jly44; records missing but collected by a Port Angeles US Coast Guard crew from CGAS Brooklyn 21Jly44 and delivered to Port Angeles 31Jly44 and in use there until at least 16Aug44; USN records indicate that the aircraft was at CGAS Elizabeth City at the end of Aug44 and still there end Sep44; unreported 31Oct44; CGAS Port Angeles by 30Nov44 until at least Jly46 and formally transferred to the US Coast Guard and SOC by US Navy 31Jly46 as obsolete. Details of subsequent USCG history unknown and no record of later civilian use.

B-68 Built for US Navy as **JRF-5**, BuAer serial **37815**. Acc 29Jun44 and del 06Jly44; records missing but en route NAF Manus Island 31Aug44; records show a transfer of charge to the *USS Casablanca* (CVE-55) 10Sep44 but the *Casablanca* had departed San Francisco for Manus Island 24Aug44 carrying aircraft and this transfer may indicate the date of an incident; AR&OH Unit1 NAF Manus Island 30Sep44; to CAC Manus Island Oct44 and SOC 31Oct44. Another reference suggests a strike date at Manus of 11Oct44, but this may be an alternative administrative date.

B-69 Built for US Navy as **JRF-5**, BuAer serial **37816**. Acc 13Jly44 and del 14Jly44; records missing but en route NAF Annapolis Aug44; VN8D5 NAF Annapolis Nov44. Received "major damage" in forced landing in field 13 miles north-east of Louisville, NC 27Dec44 after being forced down in poor weather (aircraft was enroute Annapolis to Chapel Hill, NC); Pool NAS Norfolk Jan45 (presumably not airworthy); NAF Philadelphia (Mustin Fld) Mar45 and reconditioned there Jly-Sep45; Pool NAAS Franklin Oct45; NAS Trinidad Dec45. Damaged in ground-loop at Atkinson AAF, British Guiana 16Dec46 after landing with wet brakes (aircraft had departed NAF Essequibo, British Guiana, twenty one minutes earlier). Further damaged in water-loop landing at Carenage Bay, NAS Trinidad 24Jun47; Pool BAR Bethpage Aug47; to storage NAS South Weymouth Jun48 until at least Aug48; records missing; in storage MCAS Cherry Point by Jan50; NAS Quonset Point 19Nov52 for modernisation; NAS Anacostia 08Apr53; SF Litchfield Park 13Aug53 (storage). Loaned to NACA Langley Fld, VA 26Aug54 where dual-identified as BuAer 37816 and NACA **103** (the fourth of five aircraft to use this serial). Destroyed in a crash at Wallops Island, VA 03Nov54 and SOC by US Navy 27Nov54 for parts/scrap (TFH:911hrs).

B-70 Built for US Navy as **JRF-5**, BuAer serial **37817**, but diverted off contract for sale to the Royal Canadian Air Force. Del 28Jly44 and formally taken on Canadian strength becoming **Goose II** serial **390** with RCAF. Initial allocation to No.3 Training Command and believed assigned to No.12 (Communications) Sqn, Rockcliffe 28Jly44; to Storage Reserve No.6 Repair Depot, Trenton 17Aug45; available for disposal at No.6 RD Trenton, 15Jly46 at TFH:138hrs; notice of sale to The T Eaton Co Ltd 31Jly46. SOC to War Assets Corporation 22Aug46. Regd as **G-21A, CF-ETJ**, with CofR 5106 and CofA 1608, 05Sep46 to The T Eaton Co

G-21A, c/n B-70, CF-ETJ, of Canadian Forest Products at Vancouver, British Columbia, in March 1965. The company operated the Goose from 1952 until 1982. (Ingvar Klett)

Ltd, Trenton, ON; inspected and CofA renewed 05Sep47. Accident 10Aug48: ground-looped after landing at Toronto; inspected and CofA renewed 07Oct48; inspected and CofA renewed 16Mar50. BoS from Eaton to Massey-Harris Co Ltd, Toronto, ON 27Mar50 with CofR 8661, 29Apr50; inspected and CofA renewed at TFH:554hrs, valid until 16Mar52; at TFH:735hrs, valid until 16Mar53. BoS to RL Avey, Dorval, QC 16May52 for $47,500. BoS to Can-Forest Products, Sproat Lake, BC 16May52 with CofR 11014 dated 11Jun52, wef 23May52; engines now AN-14B, inspected and CofA renewed at TFH:886hrs, valid until 16Mar54; at TFH:1,920hrs, valid until 02Apr64; at TFH:3,622hrs, valid until 11Apr74; certs re-issued as **C-FETJ** 30Mar76; inspected and CofA renewed at TFH:5,103hrs, valid until 12Jun83. BoS to AirPac Inc, Anchorage, AK 29Jly82. Cancelled from CCAR 08Aug82 and regd as **N2889J** 10Aug82; address change to Dutch Harbor, AK Mar83. To Ronald J Rivett, Aberdeen, SD with CofR 05Jan88. Reregd as **N888GG** Jly89, to Rivett dba Quest Aviation. Current, but not airworthy May13, with CofR due to expire 30Sep13.

B-71   Built for US Navy as **JRF-5**, BuAer serial **37818** but diverted off contract for delivery to Loftleidir, Reykjavik eventually becoming TF-RVK. Grumman photo shows the aircraft (as TF-RVK) fitted with an external fuel tank under the wing just outboard of the port engine. Dep Bethpage, Long Island 29Sep44 for ferry flight to Reykjavik (see Loftleidir in Civilian Operators section). In service 23Oct44, but not regd to Loftleidir hf, Reykjavik, Iceland, as **G-21A, TF-RVK**, until 08Mar45. Damaged in accident 15Sep45 when foundered after landing at Skeyafjord, Iceland. Aircraft returned to Grumman for rebuild and re-delivered by sea. BoS Loftleidir to Gordon Smith & Co Inc, New York, NY 08Sep52 at TFH:2,924hrs; CofR applied for 18Sep52. BoS to New York Yankees Inc, New York, NY 19Sep52, quoting regn as TF-RVK; ferried NYC to Atlanta, GA 21Sep52, as TF-RVK, for overhaul by Aero Corp. TF-RVK eventually cancelled 14Oct52. CofA and CofR **N1507V** issued 12Dec52. CofA renewed 10Nov53 at TFH:3,115hrs. Tfd by BoS to Daniel R Topping and Del E Webb, dba NY Yankees, New York, NY 10Dec53 with CofR 28Jan54; CofA renewed 09Jan56 at TFH:2,985hrs. Reregd **N30Y** 04Jan57 with CofA 08Jan57 at TFH:3,195hrs; and 07Jan59 at TFH:3,608hrs. BoS to Linden Flight Service Inc, Linden, NJ 18Jan60. BoS to McKinnon Enterprises Inc, Sandy, OR 08Feb60 with CofR **N152M** 13Oct60. N152M cancelled 18Jun65 after an accident but no details known.

B-72   Built for US Navy as **JRF-5**, BuAer **37819**. Acc and del 26Jly44; records missing but with NAS Whidbey Island by Aug44; NAS Alameda Aug46 for reconditioning; Pool BAR Bethpage Jun47; NAS Quonset Point Jan48 until at least 30Sep48; records missing but at NAS Quonset Point by 28Jly49 when tail-wheel collapsed on landing; records missing; in overhaul Pool BAR Bethpage by Jan50; 13th ND NAS Whidbey Island12Apr50; NAF Annapolis 12Aug50; NAS Quonset Point 27Dec51 for overhaul but available for disposal 12Aug52 and SOC 13Oct52 (TFH:1,420hrs). Regd as JRF-5, **N780**, to US Dept of Interior, Fish & Wildlife Service, Washington, DC 13Nov52 (transfer date was 28Oct52) and ferried to Alaska where immediately placed in storage by the Fish & Wildlife Service, Lake Hood, Anchorage. Remained in open storage until 1968 when cvtd to Garrett/AiResearch TPE-331 turbine power, in the US Fish & Wildlife Service hangar at Lake Hood, Anchorage; then referred to as **McKinnon G-21G, c/n 1240,** although this was not the officially recognised designation (see Chapter 5). Aircraft name: *"The Aleutian Goose"*. To Terry J Kohler, Sheboygan, WI Oct93 as **N92MT**. Cancelled from USCAR 15Sep94 and to **CC-CTG**, with TJ Kohler/Rio Puelo Lodge, Puerto Montt, Chile 14Sep94; aircraft name: *"Gran Ganso"*. Restored as **N92MT** to Terry J Kohler, Sheboygan, WI in 1995. Del to Viking Air, Victoria, BC 01May95 and auctioned 12May95. Cancelled from Chilean CAR 28Dec95 and reregd **N86MT** to TJ Kohler, Sheboygan, WI 12Jan96 with CofA issued 17May96; operated by Windway Aviation, Sheboygan, WI. To JRW Aviation, Dallas, TX 31Jly98. To Aircorp III Inc, Anchorage, AK 12Oct00. Reregd **N221AG** 19Jun01. To Triple S Aviation LLC, Addison, TX with CofR 17Dec09. Exhibited at Farnborough Airshow Jly10. Accident 27Feb11: crashed just after take-off from Al Ain Intl A/P, United Arab Emirates on an intended flight to the USA, via Saudi Arabia. Landon Studer, owner of Triple S Aviation, and three others on board, were all killed.

B-73   Built for US Navy as **JRF-5**, BuAer serial **37820**. Acc 28Jly44 and del 29Jly44; records missing but with Naval Attaché Venezuela (Caracas) by Sep44; CNRCForces (NAS Norfolk?) Feb46; Pool Hedron, FAW-5 NAS Norfolk Mar46, SOSU-2 NAS Norfolk 11Jly46; FASRON-201 NAS Norfolk Aug46; NAF Bermuda Feb47; NAS Bermuda Apr47; Pool FASRON-102 NAS Norfolk Aug47; Pool NAS Norfolk Oct47; Pool BAR Bethpage Mar48 until at least Aug48; records missing; in storage MCAS Cherry Point by Jan50; NAS Quonset Point 11Feb53 for modernisation and modification to **JRF-6** (to JRF-6X 11Feb53 and JRF-6

G-21A, N322, c/n B-73, the former US Navy JRF-6 Goose which had provided services to Santa Catalina Island with various operators since 1956. The aircraft is seen here with Catalina Airlines Inc as "Ricky", in the mid-1960s.   (Fred J Knight Collection)

30Jun53); FASRON-101 NAS Quonset Point 13Jlyy53 (for issue); *USS Currituck* (AV-7) aboard *Currituck* 21Jly53; *Currituck* at NAS Norfolk 01Feb55; declared surplus at NAS Norfolk 17Oct55. Sold to Avalon Air Transport, Long Beach, CA 26Apr56 and SOC by US Navy 11May56 (TFH:1,501hrs). Regd as **G-21A, N322**, 10May56, with FN:6. Re-named Catalina Amphibian Air Lines temporarily 23Oct63 and B-73 was painted with new titles, again with FN:6. Name reverted to Catalina Air Lines Inc, Gardena, CA 1963. Non-fatal landing accidents at Avalon, CA 10Aug69 and 18Aug69. In 1968, Aero Commuter Inc merged with Catalina Air Lines. Cable Commuter and Skywark were added to the group which was then swallowed up by Golden West Airlines Inc. To Golden West Airlines 01Dec69. To KC Aircraft Sheet Metal Co Inc, Long Beach, CA 16Nov73 and seen stored there awaiting new owner 30Dec73. To Lew Mahieu, Long Beach, CA 28Feb75. To Catalina Airlines Inc, Gardena, CA 18Mar76; aircraft name: *"Ricky"*. CofA 16Jly79. To Air Fast Freight, Long Beach, CA 1981. To Red Stevenson, dba Red 'S' Aircraft Sales, Leonard, OK 29Aug83. To Wilson C Edwards, Big Spring, TX 17Oct86 with CofR 28Nov86. Non-fatal accident 06Jly87: forced landing in a field and nosed over at Big Spring, TX due to blocked fuel system vent; TFH:18,870hrs. Repaired and was airworthy and current until CofR expired 31Mar13.

B-74   Built for US Navy as **JRF-5**, BuAer serial **37821**. Acc 31Jly44 and del 02Aug44; CGAS Elizabeth City Aug44. Damaged in landing accident at NAS Charleston 04Jan45 during familiarisation training (after which Elizabeth City ASR operations and training were transferred to Charleston AAF); CGAS Elizabeth City until at least Jly46 when formally transferred to the US Coast Guard and SOC by US Navy 31Jly46. Adopted the designation **JRF-5G** circa 1950, with serial **7821**; station allocation details unconfirmed but ex CGAD Annette Island to storage at Elizabeth City 15Oct53 at TFH:2,459hrs; storage at AR&SC Elizabeth City until sold to Mackey Airlines Inc, Miami, FL and regd as **G-21A, N2579B** 03Mar56, with CofA 02Jly56. To Bahamas Airways Ltd, Nassau 20Jan58 and regd as **VP-BAB** 26Feb58. Accident 10Mar58: made water landing with landing gear down and sank at Green Turtle Cay, and regn cancelled 27Mar58. Salvaged and sold for $1,100 for re-build by Dean Franklin Aviation Enterprises Inc, Miami, FL, 03Apr58. Transferred by Franklin to his own company, Coastal Air Inc, by BoS 17Nov58, with CofA 27Jan59 after rebuild and CofR **N5542A** 27Feb59 (with incorrect previous identity '37281' thought to have resulted from typo made by DCA Bahamas on previous correspondence). Leased to Bahamas Airways Ltd, Nassau (as N5542A) by 10Feb59. Reregd as **VP-BBK**, 27Jan60 to Bahamas Airways Ltd. To Dean H Franklin Aviation Enterprises Inc, Miami, FL 11Apr62, with CofR **N2579B**, 27Nov62. To Worldwide Aviation Distributors Inc, Miami, FL with CofR 27Mar00. Registration still assigned May13, but CofR had expired 31Mar11. Fate unknown.

B-75   Built for US Navy as **JRF-5**, BuAer serial **37822**. Acc 11Aug44 and del 12Aug44; Naval Attaché Cuba (Havana) and en route via NAS Miami Aug-Sep44 (in Havana by 30Sep44); NAS Alameda Sep46 for reconditioning; Pool BAR Bethpage 23Dec46; VN8D5 NAF Annapolis May47; NavAirActSRC NAF Annapolis aug47 until at least Aug48; records missing but with NAS Key West by 14Sep49 when involved in landing accident at Key West (undercarriage collapsed following flap-retraction during landing roll); with 6th ND NAS Key West by Jan50. Significantly damaged in water-loop on landing at Key West 26Apr50 requiring repairs to both wings, floats and fuselage; Pool NAS Key West 28Apr50 awaiting action; NAS Quonset Point 20Sep50 for overhaul which was eventually commenced 29Oct51 but identified for disposal in non-flyable condition 02Jly52. SOC NAS Quonset Point 13Oct52 for parts/scrap (TFH:1,516hrs and aircraft appears not to have flown following Apr50 accident).

B-76   Built for US Navy as **JRF-5**, BuAer serial **37823** but diverted off contract for sale to the Royal Canadian Air Force. Del 24Aug44 and formally taken on Canadian strength becoming **Goose II** serial **392** with RCAF. Initial allocation to No.3 Training Command 24Aug44 but changed to Western Air Command 30Sep44 and assigned to No.166 (Communications) Sqn, Sea Island from 16Oct44 until at least 1945; to Western Air Command Communications Flight, Sea Island 31Oct45; damaged at Sea Island 09May46 when the starboard landing gear collapsed on landing; to No.7 Reserve Equipment Maintenance Unit (Abbotsford) charge for repair 16May46. To War Assets Corporation and SOC 16Jan47 when still located at Sea Island (TFH:770hrs). War Assetts Corp sales order HO7897 to Kashower Air Service Ltd, Oshawa, ON 18Nov46. BoS to Dionne Automobile Enrg, Rimouski, QC 23May47. Tfd by BoS to Rimouski Airline Ltd, Rimouski, QC 20May47. Regd as **G-21A, CF-FEM**, to Rimouski A/L Ltd with CofR 5933 and CofA 2213, 25Jly47, both wef 27May47. Sold to Geo W Crothers Ltd, Leaside, ON 21Oct47 at TFH:1,261hrs; CofR 6427 issued 29Oct47; inspected and CofA renewed 08Mar48. Accident at 1849hrs on 03Apr48: while landing on Runway 29 at Toronto, the gear folded up and aircraft came to rest on the grass at the side of the runway. BoS DeHavilland Aircraft of Canada to British American Oil Co Ltd via loss adjusters, Stewart, Smith (Canada) Ltd, Montreal, QC 26Nov48. To British American Oil Co Ltd, Toronto, ON CofR 7605 14Dec48 and reregd **CF-BAE** (CofR 7605 again!) 14Dec48; inspected and CofA renewed 06May49. Accident at 1000hrs on 27Aug49: while landing at Lake of Bays, ON, and just as the aircraft was ready to fall off the step, a gust of wind from the left side raised that wing forcing the right wing to submerge, breaking off the float. Towed to shore without capsizing. Inspected and CofA renewed 14June50; CofR amended to Private 29Jun50; inspected and CofA renewed at TFH:1,910hrs, valid until 14Jun52. BoS British American Oil to B.N.P. Airways Ltd, Vancouver, BC 13Dec51; CofR 10645 issued 13Dec51. BoS to Powell River Co, Vancouver, BC 30May52; inspected and CofA renewed at TFH:2,266hrs, valid until 14Jun53; CofR(P) 11090 issued to Powell River Co 31May52; inspected and CofA renewed at TFH:2,622hrs, valid until 19Apr55; CofR amended to Commercial 21Apr54. CofR(P) 15003 issued 31May55 to B.N.P. Airways Ltd, Vancouver, BC. Accident at 2105hrs on 30Jly55: after a flight from Patricia Bay, BC and touchdown on Runway 07, at Vancouver, BC, the undercarriage folded. Suspected piece of driftwood wedged between hull and draglinks. Inspected and CofA renewed at TFH:3,407hrs, valid until 19Apr58; at TFH:4,214hrs, valid until 02Mar62; at TFH:4,795hrs, valid until 06May65; CofR(P) 33292 issued to Crown Zellerbach Canada Ltd, Vancouver, BC 26May64; inspected and CofA renewed at TFH:5,287hrs, valid until 06May67. Accident at 1200hrs on 27Mar67: during taxying for take-off at Northwest Bay, Vancouver Island, BC, for a flight to Vancouver, BC the hull was holed. Tail was damaged due to buffeting while being driven ashore in a sinking condition. Inspected and CofA renewed at TFH:5,557hrs, valid until 11May68; at TFH:6,971hrs, valid until 26Apr73; at TFH:7,965hrs, valid until 27May78. Certificates re-issued as **C-FBAE** 30May77; inspected and CofA renewed at TFH:8,203hrs, valid until 27May79; at TFH:9,962hrs, valid until 27May84; to Crown Forest Industries (nominal change) 30Dec83. Advertised for sale at TFH:10,500 hrs, Nov84, for $250,000. BoS to Pan Aviation Inc, Miami, FL, 17Jan85. Reregd as **N91GS** and cancelled from CCAR 22Jan85. To Amphibian Sales Inc, Miami, FL, Oct90. To William J Burdis/Classic Wings Inc, Coraopolis, PA, Apr91. Reregd **N93GS** to Thomas Friedrich/Caribbean Clipper Inc, Isle of Islay, Scotland, 29Sep93; aircraft name: *"Island Clipper"*. Undertook a flight from the West Indies to Africa in 1994, stopping at the Farnborough (UK) Airshow en route. Stored at Westcott Airfield, nr Aylesbury, UK. Accident Oct96: starboard undercarriage collapsed at Elstree, UK; still awaiting spares Feb97. Cancelled from USCAR 09Mar07 as exported to Canada. Regd **C-GPCD** to Pacific Coastal Airlines, Port Hardy, BC 04Apr07. Accident at 0725hrs on 03Aug08: crashed onto a mountainside near Kyuquot Inlet, BC on a flight from Port Hardy to Chamiss Bay, BC. The Goose had been chartered by Seaspan International Ltd, a marine transportation company based in Vancouver, to fly employees to a remote logging site to load barges. The aircraft caught fire on impact and suffered major damage. Five of the seven on board, including the pilot, were killed, but two survived. Transportation Safety Board of Canada investigators faced a huge challenge to remove the wreckage from the steep hillside.

B-77   Built for US Navy as **JRF-5**, BuAer **37824** but diverted off contract for sale to the Royal Canadian Air Force. First flight 14Aug44. Del USNAS Brooklyn, NY to Montreal 23Aug44 and Montreal to Ottawa 24Aug44, by ferry pilot Lt Holmes, USNR. Formally taken on Canadian strength becoming **Goose II** serial **391** with RCAF. Initial allocation to No.12 Communications Sqn within No.3 Training Command, Montreal; to Eastern Air Command Storage Reserve 30Sep44 initially with No.6 Reserve Equipment Maintenance Unit, Moncton, NB 06Dec44; transferred

to same unit at Mont Joli 27Jun45, but stored at No.603 Reserve Equipment Maintenance Satellite, Mount Pleasant; available for disposal at Mount Pleasant 02Jan46. SOC to War Assets Corporation 14Feb46. **CF-BFS** allocated but ntu 1946. Sold to Royal Canadian Mounted Police Air Service, Ottawa, ON for Can$50,000, 30Mar46, at TFH:26hrs [with official transfer dated 03Apr46]. Regd as **G-21A, CF-MPG** with CofA 1073 and CofR 3489, 23Apr46. CofR re-issued as **C-FMPG**, 1977. Retired from service in January 1994 at Prince George, BC after more than 24,000 flying hours. A successful *"Save the Goose"* campaign was set up on 17Aug95. The Goose was delivered to the National Aviation Museum, Rockcliffe, Ottawa in 2000, and has remained in store at Rockcliffe since then.

B-78   Built for US Navy as **JRF-5**, BuAer serial **37825**. Acc and del 28Aug44; NAS New York Aug44; Pool NAS Alameda, 04Sep44; CAC Manus Oct44; CNAB Manus Feb45; NAB Sangley Point Jly45; NAB Samar 01Jly46; (under repair Sep-Nov46); NAS San Diego Dec46 for repair; Pool NAS San Diego Jan47; Pool BAR Bethpage Apr47; NavAirActSRC NAF Annapolis Aug47 until at least Aug48; records missing; NavAirActSRC NAF Annapolis by Jan 50 and administratively transferred to NAF Annapolis 24Mar50. To NAS Quonset Point 22Jun51 for overhaul; ready for issue 19Jun52 but available for disposal 23Jun52 and SOC 13Oct52 (TFH:2,363hrs). Transferred to US Coast Guard with revised designation **JRF-5G** and serial **7825**; CGAF Barbers Point by Feb54; disposal details uncertain but assumed SOC locally. Regd as **G-21A, N5623V** to Dept of Public Instruction, Honolulu, HI. To Everbrite Electric Signs, Milwaukee, WI. To McKinnon Enterprises Inc, Sandy, OR with CofR 17Dec57 and cancelled 15Jan58. Cvtd to **G-21C**, c/n **1202**, with four Lycoming GSO-480-B2D6 engines by McKinnon in 1959 with Form 317 dated 06Aug59. CofR **N3459C** to Everbrite Electric Signs, Milwaukee, WI, presumably after conversion in 1959. Sold back to McKinnon 30Jan67. Cancelled from USCAR 19Sep67 to Government of East Pakistan, Dacca as **AP-AUY**, with CofA No:399. East Pakistan became Bangladesh in 1971. Cancelled from Pakistan register 13Feb74. To Government of Bangladesh, Dhaka as **S2-AAD**. Regn reported cancelled, although the fuselage (no wings, engines or tail) was still at Dhaka-Zia International Airport in February 2011. The aircraft was scrapped during 2011.

B-79   Built for US Navy as **JRF-5**, BuAer serial **37826**. Acc and del 30Aug44; NAS New York Aug44; NAS Pasco 12Sep44; NAS Astoria 14Sep44 until at least Apr46; records unreadable May46; VN8D5 NAF Annapolis Nov46; Pool BAR Bethpage Jan47; VN8D5 NAF Annapolis Jun47; NAS San Diego Jly47; FASRON-112 NAS Whidbey Island 07Feb48; NAS Kodiak May48 until at least Aug48; records missing; NAS Kodiak by Jan50; NAS San Diego 29May50 awaiting overhaul; NAS Quonset Point by Nov50 for overhaul. Declared surplus 14May51 and SOC for MDAP disposal to France 13Jly51 (TFH:1,065hrs). To France's Aéronautique Navale wearing abbreviated serial **826**; transit details uncertain but arrived by sea at Saigon, Vietnam Feb52; accepted 17Mar52 and delivered to 8ème Escadrille de Servitude (8.S) at Cat Lai where coded 8.S-12. Damaged beyond repair in landing accident at Phnom-Penh, Cambodia 06Mar54 when undertaking a medevac mission. SOC 11Aug54.

B-80   Built for US Navy as **JRF-5**, BuAer serial **37827**. Acc 31Aug44 and del 06Sep44; MCAS Mojave 19Sep44; NAS Lakehurst Aug45; VN8D5 NAF Annapolis Aug46. Damaged when undercarriage collapsed on landing at Beltsville, MD 25Sep46; NAS Norfolk 30Sep46; VN8D5 NAF Annapolis Nov46. Damaged at Annapolis 24Feb47 when taxying up ramp from water: junior pilot under instruction got into difficulties in cross-wind and senior pilot assisted but without full controls. In subsequent confusion a lack of co-ordination with brakes and engines resulted in aircraft nosing over in water with wing and engine damage; Pool NAS Norfolk Mar47 (presumably for repairs); Pool BAR Bethpage Jun47; NAS Alameda Jan48 until at least Aug48; records missing; 12th ND NAS Alameda by Jan50; NAS Norfolk 26Mar50 awaiting overhaul; NAS Quonset Point 22Jly50 for overhaul; NAF Annapolis 06Jly51; NAS Quonset Point 08Apr53 for intended overhaul. Identified for MDAP disposal 19May53, declared surplus 20May53 and SOC at Quonset Point for MDAP disposal to France 22Jly53 (TFH:1,441hrs). To France's Aéronautique Navale wearing abbreviated serial **827**; transit details unknown but by sea to Saigon, Vietnam; accepted 11Feb54 and delivered to 8ème Escadrille de Servitude (8.S) at Cat Lai where coded 8.S-14. Few specific service details known, but in use with 8.S until 1956 when based at Tan Son Nhut. Damaged in a ground handling incident involving the South Vietnamese AF at Tan Son Nhut 19May56 shortly before being withdrawn by sea from Vietnam (Saigon, Tan Son Nhut). Arrival date in France unknown but still awaiting repairs at Saint-Mandrier in Mar57; assumed to have been used from then until circa Oct59 by 8.S at Algiers-

Maison Blanche as 8.S-14. Transferred to 27 Flottille at Bel Air and Ouakam Dakar, Sénégal and re-coded 27.F-12. Used by 27.F until the loss of 078/27.F-11 and withdrawn from use 05Dec61. No known subsequent use.

B-81   Built for US Navy as **JRF-5**, BuAer serial **37828**. Acc 31Aug44 and del 12Sep44; MCAS Santa Barbara 23Sep44; ACORNTRADET Port Hueneme Mar46; NAS Alameda Jly46 for reconditioning; Pool NAS Alameda Jan47; Pool BAR Bethpage 29Jly47 for overhaul; Pool A&T NAS Quonset Point May48; NAS Norfolk Aug48; records missing; 5th ND NAS Norfolk by Jan50; NAS Norfolk 31Mar50 awaiting overhaul; NAS Quonset Point 02Jun50 for overhaul; allocated NAF Annapolis 11Mar51 but apparently not delivered until circa May51; NAS Quonset Point 04Dec52 for modernisation and modification to **JRF-6** (to JRF-6X 05Jan53 and JRF-6 15Jly53); NAF Annapolis 07Jly53. Declared surplus at Annapolis 29Feb56 and SOC 09Mar56 (TFH:2,635hrs). Regd as **G-21A, N703**, to US Dept of Interior, Washington, DC 1956 [This registration had previously been used by Widgeon c/n 1281]; operated by Alaska Fish & Wildlife Service. Last flight with the Fish & Wildlife Service, before 1994-96 restoration, was in Oct65. Regd to Norman E Brunquist, Anchorage, AK by 1977 and wfu derelict on east shore of Lake Spenard 1977-1994. To Val R Pauley, Anchorage, AK, Apr91. To John W Pletcher III, Anchorage, AK Jun94 with CofR 27Jly94. Totally restored at Goose Hangar, Lake Hood, AK Jun94 – Feb96. FF after restoration Aug95. Accident 06May96: crashed on landing at Anchorage, AK; rebuilt and painted in blue US Navy scheme as "**37828**". Attended EAA Fly-in, Arlington, WA 10Jun98 and 07Jly05. Experimental CofA 21May01 to show compliance with FAR. Attended the Alaska Grumman Fly-in at Marion Lake, near Anchorage Jly12. Current May13, with CofA still listed as Experimental and with CofR due to expire 31Oct14.

G-21A, c/n B-81, N703, served with the Alaska Fish & Wildlife Service between 1956 and 1965. It is seen here in open storage at Anchorage, Alaska, in August 1972.   *(John Stewart via PJ Marson)*

B-82   Built for US Navy as **JRF-5**, BuAer serial **37829**. Acc 22Sep44 and del 23Sep44; on delivery en route NAS Alameda 30Sep44; VJ-18 NAS Moffett Fld Oct44, enroute Ulithi Dec44-Mar45, Ulithi Mar-Jun45 and moved to NAF Eniwetok Jly45; CASU-35 NAF Eniwetok 13Oct45; unreported Oct-Dec45; Pool CASU-F12 NAS Orote by Jan46; NAS Pearl Harbor Nov46 for reconditioning (via *USS Point Cruz* CVE-119, 19Oct46); Pool NAS Pearl Harbor Jan47; Pool NAS Alameda Mar47 where SOC 31Aug47 as obsolete. No further records and assumed to have been scrapped.

B-83   Built for US Navy as **JRF-5**, BuAer serial **37830** but diverted off contract for sale to the Royal Canadian Air Force. Del 02Oct44 and formally taken on Canadian strength becoming **Goose II** serial **393** with RCAF. Initial allocation to No.3 Training Command and immediately to Storage Reserve at unknown location 02Oct44; still in storage when No.1 Air Command created out of No.3 TC 15Jan45; to Test and Development Establishment, Rockcliffe, 06Sep45 for "Goose performance reduction tests" with the last flight recorded on 03Oct47; to Storage Reserve No.6 Repair Depot, Trenton (although location listed as Picton) 23Oct47; remained in storage with No.6 RD until approved for disposal 24Aug54. To Crown Assets Disposal Corporation, but not administratively SOC until 14Feb56 although CF-HUZ allotted to Powell River Co 07Dec54 and BoS Crown Assets Disposal Corp (Sales Order 82862) 09Dec54 to Powell River Co, Vancouver, BC. Authority to ferry Picton, ON to Vancouver, BC 26Jan55. BoS to B.N.P. Airways Ltd, Vancouver, BC 03Aug55 and CofA 5510 and CofR(C) 15044 both issued for **G-21A, CF-HUZ** 13Sep55. Inspected and CofA renewed at TFH:654hrs, valid until 06May57; at TFH:1,815hrs, valid until 20Apr61; at TFH:2,587hrs, valid until 20Apr65. BoS to West Coast Transport Co Ltd, Vancouver, BC 01Jun64 and CofR(P) issued 02Jun64; inspected and CofA renewed at TFH:2,821hrs, valid until

20Apr66; at TFH:6,489hrs, valid until 04Jun72; at TFH:10,520hrs, valid until 04Jun77; CofR re-issued as **C-FHUZ** 22Apr77; inspected and CofA renewed at TFH:13,014hrs, valid until 04Jun80; CofR(P) issued to McMillan Bloedel Ltd, Richmond, BC 22Jan80 (nominal change). Aircraft name: "*Dryad II*". Inspected and CofA renewed at TFH:16,625hrs, valid until 04Jun86; at TFH:19,850.0hrs, valid until 04Jun91; at TFH:22,096hrs, valid until 04Jun95. BoS MacMillan Bloedel to Pacific Coastal Airlines Ltd, Port Hardy, BC 11Oct94 (sale included C-FIOL, c/n B-107) and CofR(C) issued 08Nov94; inspected and CofA renewed at TFH:22,483hrs, valid until 04Jun96; at TFH:25,118hrs, valid until 15Feb00; at TFH:27,766hrs, valid until 15Feb04. Withdrawn from service 24Sep12 due to the lack of availability of certified spare parts.

B-84   Built for US Navy as **JRF-5**, BuAer serial **37831**. Acc and del 25Sep44; on delivery en route NAS Alameda Sep44; ARU SOLS, Guadalcanal Nov44; VJ-8 Efate Dec44, to NAF Russell Islands (Reynard Fld) Jan45, to NAB Samar Jly45; Pool NAB Samar Nov46; NAS San Diego Dec46; Pool BAR Bethpage Jun47; NavAirActSRC NAF Annapolis Oct47 until at least Aug48; records missing; NAS Norfolk by Jan50 awaiting overhaul; Pool BAR Bethpage 15Mar50 for overhaul; NAF Annapolis 18Sep50; FASRON-102 NAS Norfolk (for issue) 21Jan52; *USS Currituck* (AV-7) 25Jan52 aboard *Currituck*; NAS Quonset Point 30Jun52 for intended overhaul and (on 05Jan53) identified for modification to JRF-6X standard, neither of which happened. Identified for MDAP disposal 19May53; declared surplus 20May53 and SOC at Quonset Point for MDAP disposal to France 22Jly53 (TFH:2,076hrs). To France's Aéronautique Navale wearing abbreviated serial **831**; transit details unknown but by sea to Saigon, Vietnam and delivered to 8ème Escadrille de Servitude (8.S) at Cat Lai; accepted 11Feb54 and coded '8.S-8'. Withdrawn from Vietnam (Saigon, Tan Son Nhut) on board the *La Fayette* May56; arrival date in France unknown but circa Jun56 and to Saint-Mandrier before operational use with 8.S at Algiers-Maison Blanche as '8.S-8'. Lost while on operations from Naval Air Station Lartigue, Algeria 04Oct56: while on a low-level over-water flight between Cape Carbon and Cape Tenes, the aircraft struck an off-shore rock at Cape Tenes, crashed and was destroyed by fire. One crew-member was killed on impact, the other four survived. Formally SOC 26Feb57.

B-85   Built for US Navy as **JRF-5**, BuAer serial **84790**. Acc 28Sep44 and del NAS New York 29Sep44; CGAS Elizabeth City Oct44 until at least Jly46 when formally transferred to the US Coast Guard and SOC by US Navy 31Jly46; CGAS Salem. Crashed 7 miles east of Harrisburg, PA 18Dec49 after fuel had been exhausted.

B-86   Built for US Navy as **JRF-5**, BuAer serial **84791**. Acc 29Sep44 and del NAS New York 30Sep44; CGAS Biloxi Nov44 until at least Jly46 when formally transferred to the US Coast Guard and SOC by the US Navy 31Jly46; CGAS Annette by Aug48. Collided with dock after landing at Annette 10Aug50, right float sheared and right wing damaged. Salvaged for parts and SOC 19Sep50. Up for auction 10Mar51 and Ellis Air Lines bid of $230 accepted 16Apr51. Towed from Tamgass Harbour, Annette Island to Ketchikan by Ellis crash boat "*Zoomie*", for a lengthy rebuild. Regd as **G-21A, N4763C** to Ellis Air Lines, Ketchikan, AK 03Feb53. CofA 01Jun54 at TFH:1,780hrs. Put into service as a flying boat, with wheels removed to increase payload, and remained a boat for entire Ellis service. Accident 24Oct61: hit a log landing at Whale Pass, AK in choppy seas and overturned. Pilot, Paul Mattle, dived back into the upturned cabin and rescued a female passenger from drowning. Aircraft salvaged, towed back to Ketchikan and placed into long-term storage. Some rebuild work including a replacement nose assembly. Never flew again with Ellis. BoS to Alaska Coastal-Ellis Airlines, Juneau, AK 01Apr62 (acft not airworthy); nominal change to Alaska Coastal Airlines Inc 12Jly66 before merging into Alaska Airlines Inc, Seattle, WA 1968. BoS to Foreign & Domestic Enterprises Inc, Seattle, WA 14Jly69, for rebuild back to amphibian configuration, and CofR issued 11Feb72. BoS to Reeve Aleutian Airways, Anchorage, AK Jly72 with CofR 03Jly72. Del to Peninsula Airways, Apr77 for ops in Alaska under a security agreement. Regd to Peninsula A/W, Pilot Point, AK 24May79 and BoS Reeve to PenAir dated 16Dec81; address change to King Salmon, AK 18Dec81. Completion of major overhaul and rebuild by Viking Air Ltd, Sidney, BC 26May82 and ferried back to Anchorage 04Jun82; aircraft based at Dutch Harbor, Aleutian Islands. Non-fatal crash at Togiak, AK 18May89. To Mike Cusack, Anchorage, AK 14Feb90. To Cormack Aircraft Service Ltd, England in 1992, but aircraft did not leave Alaska. To Flying Boat Co, Wilmington, DE Jun92. Non-fatal crash at Dillingham, AK 26Jly96. Regd N4763C to Phillip L Bingman, Dillingham, AK dba Freshwater Adventures, 05Nov96. Reregd **N985R**, after restoration by Dennis Buehn, Jun2002. To Tom Johnston, dba Florida Charters in 2003. To Dennis G Buehn, Carson City, NV, 17Mar04; for sale Oct07 by Hibbard Aviation at TFH:23,450hrs for $495,000 (P&W 985-AN-14B engines). Sale reported to Fowler & Penner

Aeroplane Menders LLC, Midway, UT 11Jan08. To Peninsula Airways Inc, Anchorage, AK with CofR 01Jly09. To Frank Dworak, Stow, MA with CofR 14Dec12. Current and airworthy Apr13, with CofR due to expire 31Dec15.

B-87　　Built for US Navy as **JRF-5**, BuAer serial **84792**. Acc 30Sep44 and dcl 04Oct44; CGAS St Petersburg Oct44 until at least Jly46 when formally transferred to the US Coast Guard and SOC by the US Navy 31Jly46. Adopted the new designation **JRF-5G** circa 1950, with serial **4792**; CGAS San Francisco by Feb51 until at least Apr52. Wfu by US Coast Guard, returned to US Navy at SF Litchfield Park 07Dec54 for storage and allocated to MDAP 20May55. NAS Alameda 27Jun55 for preparation for delivery to an unconfirmed MAP recipient believed to have been the JMSDF for spares' use; SOC 21Sep55 (TT=3,675hrs); not subsequently reported in military use; no known subsequent commercial use; fate unknown.

B-88　　Built for US Navy as **JRF-5**, BuAer serial **84793**. Acc 30Sep44 and del 10Oct44; CAC Manus Nov44; CNAB Manus Feb45; NAB Manus May45; CNAB Manus Jly45; NAB Manus Feb46 and awaiting shipment Mar-Nov46; FASRON-13 NAS Orote Dec46; Pool NAS Pearl Harbor Jan47; Pool A&T NAS Pearl Harbor Feb47; Pool NAS Alameda Mar47 and SOC there 31Mar48 as obsolete and surplus. Regd as **G-21A**, **N79914** to Ellis Air Lines, Ketchikan, AK Dec49. Became Alaska Coastal-Ellis Airlines, Juneau, AK 01Apr62. Accident 20Jan64: substantial damage after striking power lines at Petersburg, AK while doing a low pass. Pilot + one pax uninjured. Nominal change to Alaska Coastal Airlines Inc Jun66; TFH:12,694hrs a/o 05Feb68. Merged into Alaska Airlines Inc, Seattle, WA 1968. To Antilles Air Boats (AAB), Christiansted, US Virgin Islands 1971. AAB ceased ops in Jly81. Wfu derelict St Croix-Hamilton A/P 1985. To Dean H Franklin Enterprises Inc, Fort Lauderdale, FL with CofR 20Mar92, but stored derelict at St Croix, US Virgin Islands. Crated and shipped via Miami, FL and Bremerhafen to Landsberied, Germany for European Coastal Airlines in 1999. Still in open storage, dismantled, all silver, Oct06. Regn still assigned but CofR expired 31Mar11. Aircraft still at Landsberied Aug11.

B-89　　Built for US Navy as **JRF-5**, BuAer serial **84794**. Acc and del 16Oct44; en route NAS Alameda 31Oct44; Pool NAS Alameda Nov44; en route NAS Pearl Harbor Jan45; AR&OH Unit 1 (later AROU-1) NAB Manus Feb45; ARTU NAB Manus 26Apr45; AROU-1 NAB Manus 02May45 although assignment was for purposes of striking the aircraft. Damage described as caused by water landing, date unknown, following a failure of the right-hand engine and is assumed to have occurred prior to assignment to the AR&OH unit at Manus. SOC 31Oct45 at ARTU Manus following administrative confusion about fate!

B-90　　Built for US Navy as **JRF-5**, BuAer serial **84795**, but diverted off contract for sale to the Royal Canadian Air Force. Del 03Nov44 and formally taken on Canadian strength becoming **Goose II** serial **394** with RCAF. Initial allocation to No.3 Training Command and immediately to Storage Reserve at unknown location 03Nov44; still in storage when No.1 Air Command created out of No.3 TC 15Jan45; assigned to No.9 (Transport) Group, Rockcliffe 06Jly46. To Storage Reserve at No.6 Repair Depot, Trenton 14Nov47. Destroyed in hangar fire at Trenton during night of 31Dec51/01Jan52 and SOC 30Jan52.

B-91　　Built for US Navy as **JRF-5**, BuAer serial **84796**. Acc 27Oct44 and del NAS New York 28Oct44; Pool NAS Glenview Nov44; MCAS Cherry Point 22Dec44; MCAS Parris Island Jun45; NAS Norfolk May46; NAS Alameda 17Jun46 for reconditioning; Pool NAS Alameda Jan47; Pool BAR Bethpage Jun47. To storage NAS South Weymouth Jan48 until at least Aug48; records missing; in storage at MCAS Cherry Point by Jan50; NAS Quonset Point 05Jly51 for modernisation; 10th ND NAS Guantanamo Bay 11Jan52. Involved in flying accident while at Guantanamo Bay on or about 25Mar53; NAS Norfolk 22May53 awaiting re-work; NAS Quonset Point 30Jun53 for overhaul but SOC 18Sep53 for parts/scrap as a result of earlier accident (TFH:853hrs).

B-92　　Built for US Navy as **JRF-5**, BuAer serial **84797**. Acc 27Oct44 and del NAS New York 28Oct44; Hedron 7, FAW-7 Plymouth/NAF Dunkeswell Dec44; ComNavEu RAF Hendon Jly45; returned to the USA via *USS Adria* (AF-30) 27Dec46; unreported until Apr47 when with Pool BAR Bethpage; NAS Norfolk Jlyy47 until at least Aug48; records missing; awaiting overhaul NAS Norfolk by Jan50; NAS Quonset Point 22Jly50 for overhaul; 1st ND NAS Quonset Point 27Aug51; NAF Annapolis 10Mar53; NAS Quonset Point 07Jly53 for overhaul and allocated to MDAP 31Mar54. SOC for MDAP disposal to Japan 13May54 (TFH:1,359hrs). Shipped to Japan where de-preserved by the FASRON-11 detachment at NAF Oppama; used for crew training and working-up at NAF Oppama. Transferred to the JMSDF and given serial **9011**; formal handover to

Second Kanoya Kokutai, Kanoya 18Oct55; relocated to Omura and thus to Omura Kokutai 01Dec56; no known accidents and assumed retired circa 1960 and thus would have been returned to US charge. No known subsequent history and assumed to have been scrapped in Japan.

B-93　　Built for US Navy as **JRF-5**, BuAer serial **84798**. Acc 30Oct44 and del 09Nov44; Hedron 7, allocated to Commander, US Ports and Bases, France 22Dec44 and formally noted with FAW-7 Plymouth/NAF Dunkeswell 31Dec44; ComNavEu RAF Hendon Jly45. Returned to the USA via *USS Adria* (AF-30) 27Dec46; unreported until Apr47 with Pool BAR Bethpage; VN8D5 NAF Annapolis Jly47; NavAirActSRC NAF Annapolis Aug47 until at least Aug48; records missing; NavAirActSRC NAF Annapolis by Jan50 and administratively to NAF Annapolis 24Mar50; NAS Quonset Point 11Jun51 for overhaul; NAS San Diego 09Mar52 for issue; FASRON-114 NAS Kodiak 02Apr52 (to re-work 27Sep53); NAS San Diego 05Oct53 for disposal in flying condition. SF Litchfield Park, 29Jan54; leased (under contract NOas 55-210-m) to Marine Airways Inc and Alaska Air Transport Inc, dba Alaska Coastal Airlines, Ketchikan, AK 04Mar55, with CofR **N4774C**, 10Mar55. CofA after cvtd to **G-21A** by Long Beach Airmotive Inc, CA 22Apr55 at TFH:2,851hrs. BoS US Navy to Alaska Coastal A/L, Juneau, AK 15May58 for $32,000, with CofR 12Jun58. Formally retired by US Navy 31May58 and SOC 10Dec58. Normally used as a freighter only with bucket seats installed. Accident 20Aug58: hit glassy surface and sank landing in Lynn Channel, near Haines, AK, 65miles NNW of Juneau, AK. Capt Dawson + 5 pax injured, 2 uninjured, but one passenger later died. Aircraft sank in 150ft of water and salvage attempts were unsuccessful. Nominally regd to Alaska Coastal-Ellis Airlines, Juneau, AK 01Apr62. Noted as "no longer in use" Oct64 but nominal change of regn to Alaska Coastal Airlines in 1965. Cancelled from USCAR 23Jun70 as destroyed.

B-94　　Built for US Navy as **JRF-5**, BuAer serial **84799**. Acc 31Oct44 and del 02Nov44; NAS Coco Solo Nov44; NAS Alameda Jly46 for reconditioning; Pool NAS Alameda Jan47; Pool BAR Bethpage Jun47; AES-46 MCAS Cherry Point Nov47 until at least Aug48; records missing; awaiting overhaul NAS Norfolk by Jan50; NAS Quonset Point by Nov50 for intended overhaul but declared surplus 14May51 and SOC for MDAP disposal to France 13Jly51 (TFH:765hrs). To France's Aéronautique Navale wearing abbreviated serial **799**; transit details uncertain but reportedly arrived by sea at Saigon, Vietnam on board *SS Eastern City* 28Feb52. Accepted 29Feb52 and delivered to 8ème Escadrille de Servitude (8.S) at Cat Lai where coded 8.S-5; formally accepted 29Feb52; few specific service details recorded but active with 8.S in 1953 and 1954; by 1956 based at Tan Son Nhut, Saigon. Withdrawn from Vietnam (Saigon, Tan Son Nhut) aboard the *La Fayette* May56; arrival date in France unknown but circa Jun56 and to Saint-Mandrier for 240-hour check before operational use with 8.S at Algiers-Maison Blanche; overhauled Saint-Mandrier and flying in France by 11Sep56 when reported at Cuers. To 8.S at Algiers-Maison Blanche as 8.S-5 and in operational service in Algeria 1957-1958; transferred to 27 Flottille at Ouakam, Dakar, Sénégal as a reserve aircraft circa 1959. SOC 05Dec61; spares to be recovered 19Dec61 on behalf of SAMAN.

B-95　　Built for US Navy as **JRF-5**, BuAer serial **84800**. Acc 31Oct44 and del 02Nov44; NAS Miami Nov44; NATTC Corpus Christi Feb45; NAS New Orleans Jly45; NAS Glenview Aug45 (at NART Glenview Mar-May46); VN8D5 NAF Annapolis Sep46; Pool BAR Bethpage Aug47; Pool FASRON-102 NAS Norfolk Apr48 apparently until at least Jan49 although records are missing/vague and delivery to Oslo may have occurred in 1948; Naval Attaché Oslo, Norway by Jan50; NAF Port Lyautey 13May50 (transit en route overhaul); NAS Norfolk 16Aug50 awaiting overhaul; NAS Quonset Point for overhaul 24Oct50; FASRON-102 NAS Norfolk 20Mar52 (transit); FASRON-795 NAS Jacksonville 25Apr52 moving to NAS Bermuda Aug52; FASRON-111 NAS Bermuda 05Mar53 and by sea to Norfolk for repairs 17Aug53; FASRON-102 NAS Norfolk 17Nov53 for repairs; NAS Quonset Point 09Dec53 for overhaul and allocated to MDAP 31Mar54. SOC for MDAP disposal to Japan 13May54 (TFH:1,168hrs). Shipped to Japan where de-preserved by the FASRON-11 detachment at NAF Oppama; used for crew training and working-up at NAF Oppama. Transferred to the JMSDF and given serial **9014**; formal handover to Second Kanoya Kokutai, Kanoya 25Nov55; relocated to Omura and thus to Omura Kokutai 01Dec56. No known accidents and assumed retired circa 1960 and thus would have been returned to US charge; no known subsequent history and assumed to have been scrapped in Japan.

B-96　　Built for US Navy as **JRF-5**, BuAer serial **84801**. Acc 31Oct44 and del 09Nov44; NAS Richmond Nov44 where SOC 30Sep45 following storm damage. This is assumed to have been caused by the hurricane and fire that destroyed the base 15Sep45.

G-21A, c/n B-97, N741 of Pendir on the small ramp at Akutan, Alaska as passengers board and the aircraft is loaded. *(Eamon Power)*

C/n B-98, CF-GEC, of West Coast Air on the company ramp at Vancouver, British Columbia, in 1977. *(CJ Mak)*

B-97   Built for US Navy as **JRF-5**, BuAer serial **84802**. Acc 15Nov44 and del 18Nov44; NATTC Corpus Christi Nov44; NATTC Jacksonville Jly45; GCA School NATTC Banana River Dec45 and to NAS Banana River by Dec46; VM Unit NAS Corpus Christi Jan47; Pool NAS Corpus Christi Nov47 and SOC there 31Mar48 as obsolete and surplus. A letter dated 16Jan48 to Naval Commandant, Corpus Christi, TX to allow a Reeve Airways pilot to ferry the Goose from Corpus Christi to Anchorage, AK for The Alaskan Railroad, Dept of Interior, Anchorage. CofR as **G-21A, NC3903B** issued 18Mar48. Repaired at San Antonio, TX 19May48, after landing accident; later as **N3903B**. Tfd to Dept of Interior, Fish & Wildlife, Service, Juneau, AK Mar52 with CofR **N741** 24Sep52. Repaired minor damage after storage Oct52. CofA 17Apr57 at TFH:1,649hrs. Tfd to Department of Commerce, National Marine Fisheries Service, Juneau, AK with CofR 08Feb74; water rudder installed Jun74. Tfd to State of Alaska, Dept of Public Safety, Anchorage with CofR 07Jan76; to be used for SAR missions. Aircraft rebuilt Jun81 incorporating STCs SA4-1109, SA4-1467, SA96NW and SA1751WE. Accident circa 1115hrs on 21Mar94: crashed on Margerie Glacier at 9,650ft elevation on the Canadian side of Mt Fairweather, BC. The G-21A was on a VFR flight from Juneau to Anchorage and then on to Yakutat, AK. The pilot, Claude E Swackhammer, was the Deputy Commissioner of Public Safety for the State of Alaska who was taking the director of Alaska's Highway Safety Planning Department to Yakutat, and an Alaskan State Trooper Lieutenant to Anchorage. Eighteen boxes of evidence were also being delivered to Anchorage in conjunction with a criminal court case. The aircraft impacted the snowfield above the glacier in controlled flight, with wings level, in a climb. The pilot and a passenger in the rear cabin were uninjured, but the passenger in the co-pilot's seat received minor injuries. The aircraft sustained substantial damage and was further damaged during salvage. The NTSB determined that a major cause of the accident was the fact that the G-21A was 1,403lbs over max gross weight and had 80lbs of frozen water in the bilges. TFH:8,773hrs a/o 21Mar94. Major overhaul and repairs by Viking Air Jly95. BoS Alaska Dept of Public Safety to Peninsular Airways, Anchorage, AK 24Sep96 with CofR 12Dec96. Seating capacity increased to ten per STC SA02044AK-D Nov97. Accident at 1630hrs on 09Apr08: substantial damage after collision with a trailer van during final approach to Runway 30 at Unalaska Airport, AK. PenAir Flight 325 had originated at the Akutan Seaplane Base at circa 1615hrs and was carrying 8 passengers as well as the pilot. One passenger sustained serious injuries whilst the pilot and remaining pax suffered minor injuries. Wreck sold by PenAir to Samuel P Damico, Pittsford, NY on BoS 16Nov09 with CofR 07Jan10; used for parts in rebuild of c/n 1051 (qv). Still listed as current by FAA, May13, with CofR due to expire 30Sep13.

B-98   Built for US Navy as **JRF-5**, BuAer serial **84803** but diverted off contract for sale to the Royal Canadian Air Force. Del 05Dec44 and formally taken on Canadian strength becoming **Goose II** serial **395** with RCAF. Initial allocation to No.3 Training Command and immediately to Storage Reserve at unknown location 05Dec44; issued to an active Western Air Command unit assumed to have been No.166 (Communications) Sqn, Sea Island (with whom it certainly served) 08Feb45; No.166 (Comms) Sqn was replaced by the Western Air Command Communications Flight 31Oct45 and 395 may have moved accordingly although this is unconfirmed. To Storage Reserve at No.10 Repair Depot (Calgary) but located at Abbotsford 13Sep46; approved for disposal at No.10 RD, Abbotsford 23Apr47. SOC to War Assets Corp 25Sep47 and regd as **G-21A, N94750**. Canadian CofR (C) 7262 and CofA 2840 for **CF-GEC** issued to Powell River Co Ltd, Vancouver, BC 08Jun48. Tfd to B.N.P. Airways Ltd, Vancouver, BC with CofR(C) 9135, 24Nov50. CofR(S) to BC Hydro & Power Authority, Vancouver, BC 02May64. CofR to Courier Trading & Enterprises Ltd, Winnipeg, MB 04Jly69. CofR(C) to Midwest Airlines Ltd, Winnipeg, MB 08Sep69. [Midwest became part of Transair, Winnipeg, MB in Nov69, but this was not recorded on the CCAR.] CofR(C) to West Coast Air Service,

Richmond, BC 02May73. Accident 14Aug78: destroyed in crash at Westview A/P, Powell River, BC, attempting a downhill, downwind take-off to avoid weather at the other (uphill) end of the runway. Witnesses said that "the aircraft never got airborne. It veered off the runway, hit a bank and split in two". Of the prominent business executives on their annual fishing trip to the Dean River, near Bella Coola, 2 were seriously injured, pilot + 5 pax minor injuries, and 2 uninjured. Fuselage broke into three. Parts and pieces taken to Viking Air, Victoria, BC for possible rebuild! Wreckage noted at Patricia Bay A/P, Victoria, BC 29Apr79 and CofA lapsed 01Aug79. Still regd to West Coast Air Services 1982, but eventually cancelled from CCAR 14Jun85.

B-99   Built for US Navy as JRF-5, BuAer serial **84804** but diverted off contract for sale to the Royal Canadian Air Force. Del 16Dec44 and formally taken on Canadian strength becoming **Goose II** serial **396** with RCAF. Initial allocation to No.3 Training Command and immediately to Storage Reserve at unknown location 16Dec44; issued to an active Western Air Command unit assumed to have been No.166 (Communications) Sqn, Sea Island (with whom it certainly served) 20Apr45; damaged when port undercarriage collapsed on landing at Boundary Bay 21Aug45; repaired and returned to No.166 (Comms) Sqn; No.166 (Comms) Sqn was replaced at Sea Island by the Western Air Command Communications Flight 31Oct45 and 396 transferred accordingly. To Storage Reserve at No.10 Repair Depot (HQ Calgary) 13Jun46 but location not stated. Reduced to spares and produce and SOC by No.10 RD 13Jun46.

B-100   Built for US Navy as **JRF-5**, BuAer serial **84805**. Acc 25Nov44 and del NAS NewYork 28Nov44; NAS San Juan Dec44 until at least Mar47; FASRON-101 NAS Quonset Point May47; Pool BAR Bethpage Jun47. To storage NAS South Weymouth Jan48 until at least Aug48; records missing; in storage MCAS Cherry Point by Jan50; NAS Quonset Point 27Mar53 for modernisation and modification to **JRF-6** (to JRF-6X 27Mar53 and JRF-6 30Jun53); NAF Annapolis 17Jly53; scheduled for rework 02Apr56 but to SF Litchfield Pk, 20Apr56 for disposal and SOC 11Sep56 as salvage/scrap (TFH:2,192hrs). BoS US Navy, North Island, San Diego to Beldex Corp, St Louis, MO 29Oct56 for $22,222.22. CofR **N88U** issued 03Dec56 with CofA 04Mar57 at TFH:2,192hrs. BoS to Remmert-Werner of Florida Inc, Pompano Beach, FL 09Dec57 with CofR 20Dec57. BoS to Keystone Helicopter Corp, Philadelphia, PA 15Sep58. BoS to Joe Spiedel III, Wheeling, WV 16Sep58 with CofR 27Oct58. BoS to Fleet Rental Co, Clarksburg, WV 14Jly60 with CofR 13Aug60. BoS to American-Bahamian Air Service Inc, Lantana, FL 15Mar61 with CofR 21Jun61. BoS to AC Clewis Jr, Tampa, FL 25Nov61 with CofR 17Jan62. BoS to Warner H Kimball, Fort Lauderdale, FL 29Sep62 with CofR 02Nov62. BoS to Windjammer Air Taxi Inc, Miami Beach, FL 26Nov62 with CofR 10Dec62. BoS to Mercantile National Bank, Dallas, TX 23Oct64 with CofR 19Jan65. BoS to Dean H Franklin, Miami, FL 30Jan65 with CofR 09Feb65; op by Chalk's Airline, Miami, FL as FN:7 and named "*Giant Tuna*"; authorisation to ferry Miami – Sebring, FL 08Oct65 for engine change. BoS Franklin to Robert Hall, Kodiak, AK 31Mar70 for $60,000; another BoS from Hall and Franklin to Robert L Hall and Helen C Hall was dated 16Apr70 with CofR to co-owners Hall 01May70; electric gear retraction system fitted Mar72. BoS R&H Hall to Kodiak Western Alaska Airlines Inc, Kodiak, AK 28Dec73 with CofR 14Feb74; cargo door installed on right side of aircraft Jun75 per STC SAX-439, during major o/h and repaint. BoS to Foreign & Domestic Enterprises Inc, Seattle, WA 16Jan78 with CofR 17Jly79; complete overhaul Jan80. BoS to Collins Brothers Corp, Las Vegas, NV 13May80 with CofR 20Jun80. The following work carried out by Viking Air Ltd, Sidney, BC Jly80: picture window installed per McKinnon STC SA101WE, G-21A water rudder installed as per B.N.P. Airways Ltd drawing No. 1648 (approved 05Apr61) and two additional aft-facing seats installed. Operated by Sport Aero Co, Las Vegas; reregd **N600ZE** 02Aug80 and placed on aircraft 19Aug80. BoS Collins to Richmor Aviation Inc, Hudson, NY 31Jan86 with CofR

26Feb86; noted at Columbia County A/P, NY Apr86 with "*Kanaka Rapids Ranch*" titles; Form 337 dated 12Jun86 shows owner as Liberty Air, Hudson, NY. BoS to William R Rose, dba Rose Packing, South Barrington, IL 22Aug87 with CofR 18Sep87. Incident at Oshkosh, WI 30Jly91. Lake & Air Inc Amphibian Landing Gear Position Advisory System installed Oct07 per STC SA39CH. To Forest Hill Management LLC, Forest Hill, MD with CofR 16Jun10. Current and airworthy May13, with CofR due to expire 31Aug14.

B-101 Built for US Navy as **JRF-5**, BuAer serial **84806**. Acc 30Nov44 and del 11Dec44; Pool NAS Alameda Dec44; VJ-9 NAS San Diego Feb45; VJ-12 San Diego Apr45; VJ-7 NAS San Diego Nov45; VU-7 NAS San Diego Nov46. Badly damaged in taxying accident at NAS San Diego 14Feb47: the VU-7 pilot reported faulty brakes and returned to the parking area but after a lengthy taxy the brakes worked poorly and, in a congested area and strong wind, the aircraft struck Douglas JD-1 77166; the JD-1 suffered minor damage but the JRF-5 incurred significant damage to the left side of the aircraft. To Pool NAS San Diego Feb47 and SOC there 31Mar47 as obsolete. Regd as **G-21A, N62899** for James F Conroy, Long Beach, CA. To HF Keeler, Seattle, WA 1954. BoS to Forest Industries 10Mar67; authority to ferry Renton, WA to Vancouver, BC 16Mar67 and flown to B.N.P. Airways, Vancouver for overhaul. Cancelled from USCAR 16Mar67 with US CofA for export E-76690. CofR(C) 38681 for **CF-VFU**, and CofA 12321 issued 07Apr67 to Forest Industries Flying Tankers Ltd, Alberni, BC. Acted as "bird-dog" for the Martin Mars water bombers. CofA renewed at TFH:2,302hrs, valid until 15Mar69; at TFH:3,495hrs, valid until 05May73; cabin picture windows installed per STC SA101WE and CotA at TFH:3,889hrs, valid until 05May74; at TFH:4,913·0hrs, valid until 05May76. Accident at 1410hrs on 23Feb76: after a flight from Sproat Lake the right main undercarriage collapsed after landing at Victoria Intl A/P, BC (pilot: Peter Lauren). CofA renewed at TFH:5,429.hrs, valid until 05May77; at TFH:8,861hrs, valid until 05May84. CofR re-issued as **C-FVFU** 22Apr83; main fuel tank enlarged to 336 US gallons per STC SA1752WE, 19Apr84 and CofA renewed at TFH:9,081hrs, valid until 05May85; at TFH:10,918hrs, valid until 05May90; address change to Port Alberni, BC with CofR (C) 20Dec91. TFH:12,984hrs reported on Due Date 05May94; TFH:15,573.1hrs reported on Due Date 05May01. BoS to TFL Forest Ltd, Vancouver, BC 19Jly01; leased by TFL Forest Ltd to Flying Tankers Inc, Port Alberni, BC 19Jly01 (until 31Dec03) with CofR (C) 28Sep01. BoS TFL Forest Ltd to C-Tec Ltd 06Oct01. To Croatia for ops by European Coastal Airlines, Nov01. Long range tanks installed by Viking Air, Victoria, BC for ferry flight to Germany. Pilots K Dankl & B Varga left Victoria, BC 02Nov01 and flew via Brandon, MB - Thunder Bay, ON - La Grande Rivière, QC - Kuujjacq, QC - Sondre Stromfjord, Greenland - Reykjavik, Iceland (06Nov) - Wick, Scotland (07Nov) and Groningen-Eelde, Holland, arriving in Oberpfaffenhofen 09Nov01, after 48 hours flying. Re-painted in European Coastal Airlines c/s at Kopesvar, Hungary in early 2002. CofR(P) to C-Tec Ltd, St John, NB 06Feb02. Flown Sarmellek Balaton, Hungary to Salzburg, Austria 04Mar02. Left main wheel detached after landing. A/P closed for two hours but Goose later repaired at Red Bull hangar. Returned to Oberpfaffenhofen 09Apr02. Reported active in Croatia in May02, as C-FVFU, aircraft named "*Aline*", but ECA went out of business. Cancelled from CCAR 08Jly05 "to

Croatia". Stored Borovo, Croatia from 2005 with plans to resume passenger services in Jun08. Noted stored at Borovo Naselje, Vukovar, Croatia in Oct08, but no further reports.

B-102 Built for US Navy as **JRF-5**, BuAer serial **84807**. Acc 29Nov44 and del 07Dec44; 'in delivery' NAS Willow Grove Dec44-Jan45; NAS San Diego Feb45 (with NRSL San Diego Oct45); NRSL San Diego Jan46; NAAS San Clemente 06Jun46; NRSL San Diego 12Jly46; NAS Alameda Sep46 for reconditioning; aircraft was ferried by VRF-2 crew from Alameda to Bethpage and was flying between El Paso, TX and Grand Prairie, TX 21Apr47 when it ran out of fuel, the pilot having failed to refuel at El Paso. Aircraft made a forced landing in a field at Big Springs, TX and nosed over onto its back sustaining moderate damage. To AOG NAS Dallas Feb47; Pool BAR Bethpage Nov47; to storage NAS South Weymouth Jly48 until at least Aug48; records missing. In storage MCAS Cherry Point by Jan50; NAS Quonset Point 11Feb53 for modernisation and modification to **JRF-6** (to JRF-6X 11Feb53 and JRF-6 30Jun53); NART NAS Grosse Ile 23Jly53; to SF Litchfield Park 22Feb54 for storage, and for disposal 30Aug55. SOC 03Feb56 (TFH:529hrs). Regd as **G-21A, N789** to US Wildlife Service, Washington, DC by Apr59. To US Dept of Interior, AK. Non-fatal accident 27May66: substantial damage in wheels-up landing at Goose Bay A/P near Anchorage. 2 crew uninjured. Was active in Alaska for 40 years. To Alaskan Aviation Heritage Museum, Lake Hood, Anchorage with CofR 30Jly98. Painted in US Wildlife Service colours complete with titles. CofR expired 31Mar12, but was re-issued 09Jly12. Noted at the museum 12Sep12. Current but not airworthy May13, with CofR due to expire 31Jly15.

C/n B-102, N789, is seen here at Anchorage, Alaska in 1972. After many years' service with the Department of the Interior, the Goose was retired to the Alaska Aviation Heritage Museum, Lake Hood, Anchorage.
(John Stewart via PJ Marson)

B-103 Built for US Navy as **JRF-5**, BuAer serial **84808**. Acc 30Nov44 and del 05Dec44; Pool NAS Alameda Dec44; CASU-36 NAAS Arcata Jan45; CGAS San Francisco 01Mar45; CASU-36 NAAS Arcata Jly45; Pool CASU-6 NAS Alameda Jun46; VN8D5 NAF Annapolis 15Oct46; Pool BAR Bethpage 20Jun47; NAS Anacostia Dec47 until at least Aug48; records missing; in overhaul Pool BAR Bethpage by Jan50; 12th ND NAS Alameda 30Mar50; NAS Quonset Point 18Nov51 for overhaul and

C/n B-100, N88U, of Foreign & Domestic Enterprises, probably at Seattle, Washington, in 1978.　　　*(Jennifer Gradidge Collection)*

identified for disposal 24Jun52. SOC 13Oct52 (TFH:1,378hrs); transferred to US Coast Guard, presumably with revised designation **JRF-5G** and serial **4808**. Details of US Coast Guard service unknown but assumed to have been withdrawn, with others, circa 1955. Regd as **G-21A**, **N1513V** to Avalon Air Transport FN:3 circa 1955. To Reeve Aleutian Airways, Anchorage, AK 1957. Accident 22Jun70: crashed and sank in 110ft of water at False Pass, AK after a flight from Cold Bay. Pilot + 2 pax uninjured, but aircraft written-off.

B-104   Built for US Navy as **JRF-5**, BuAer serial **84809**. Acc 30Nov44 and del 11Dec44; en route NAS Alameda 31Dec44; Pool NAS Alameda Jan45; CASU-F13 Admiralty Islands (unit was a split force at Pityilu and Ponam and the JRF was not a normally assigned type) Mar45; Pool AROU-2 NAB Samar Apr45; ComAir 7th Fleet, NAB Samar May45; NAB Sangley Point June45; NAB Palawan Oct45; Pool NAB Samar Sep46; NAS San Diego Dec46 for repair; Pool NAS San Diego Jan47; AOG Dallas Apr47; Pool BAR Bethpage Jun47; NavAirActSRC NAF Annapolis Nov47. Moderate damage sustained during aborted take-off from seadrome, Annapolis 11Aug48; records missing; NavAirActSRC NAF Annapolis by Jan50 and administratively to NAF Annapolis 24Mar50; NAS Quonset Point 02Jly51 awaiting overhaul (commenced 12Dec52) and then modernisation and modification to **JRF-6** (to JRF-6X 09Feb53 and JRF-6 17Jun53); FASRON-102 NAS Norfolk 09Jly53 (initially in transit but then repairs from 13Aug53); NAF Annapolis 16Oct53; to SF Litchfield Park 10May56 for disposal and SOC 11Sep56 (TFH:2,827hrs). BoS NAS North Island, San Diego, CA to Ming-Ayer Inc, Linden, NJ 02Nov56 for $22,711.69. **N1621A** assigned 21Nov56 and CofR (as JRF-6) issued 02Jan57. Converted to G-21A status by Mattituck Airbase Corp, Linden, NJ Feb57, including fitting of two overhauled AN-14B engines, with CofA 14Feb57 at TFH:2,948hrs. Transferred by BoS Ming-Ayer to Trade-Ayer Inc, Linden, NJ 15Aug58 with CofR as **G-21A** 21Sep59. [On a mortgage document dated Apr59 the aircraft was noted as located at Trenton, NJ.] Transferred by BoS Trade-Ayer Inc to Frederick B Ayer & Associates Inc, New York, NY 22Aug61 with CofR28Sep61. BoS to Dean H Franklin Aviation Enterprises Inc, Miami, FL 21May62 with CofR 18Jun62; retractable float mechanism installed per STC SA138W and gross weight increased to 9,000lbs Dec63 (by Pan-Air). Modifications made in Dec66 included: original 2-piece cabin door replaced by one-piece fibre-glass door hinged from the top, one-piece bow hatch fitted and windows installed left and right side at Station 27A. Transferred by BoS to Franklin Flying Service Inc, Miami, FL (same address) 03Jly69 with CofR 01Oct69; operated by Chalk's Airline, Miami, FL by 1970, with aircraft name: "*Barracuda*" and FN:3. **N19DF** placed on aircraft 27Jly71, transferred back to Dean H Franklin Aviation Enterprises, Miami, FL 30Jly71 and CofR issued 01Sep71. BoS to Mount Cook Airlines, Christchurch, New Zealand 18Aug72; CofA, with AN-1 engines and Hartzell HC B3R30-2E props, 28Aug92 at TFH:17,094hrs. BoS

Mount Cook A/L to FLOAIR Inc, Wichita, KS 21Aug72 with CofR 14Sep72. Del via Canada, Iceland, England, Middle East as N19DF by FLOAIR pilot F Schlienz, arr Auckland 05Oct72. N19DF removed from aircraft on arrival in Auckland and cancelled from USCAR 26Feb73. Regd **ZK-DFC** for Mount Cook Airlines, Christchurch, New Zealand 06Oct72. To Sea Bee Air, Auckland, New Zealand Jun76. To Great Barrier Airlines Ltd, Auckland, New Zealand 18Oct89. Last flt from Ardmore-Mechanics Bay 26Aug91 to be loaded on a ship. NZ regn cancelled 02Sep91. BoS Great Barrier A/L to Paul E Page, Erie, CO 25Aug91 for $100,000, with CofR **N3116T** 13Sep91; CofA 28Aug92; BoS to Intercon Developments Ltd, Boca Raton, FL 01Sep92 with CofR 08Sep92. To Provo Air Charter; Temporary CofA 08Sep92. Accident 15Dec92: crashed during water landing off west coast Caicos Island. No fatalities but aircraft written off. Salvage rights bought by Klaus Dieter Martin, Munich, Germany in 1993, but a diving expedition failed to locate the wreck. Officially still "active" Sep98 with Intercon Developments, and listed as assigned May13, but CofR had expired 30Sep12.

B-105   Built for US Navy as **JRF-5**, BuAer serial **84810**. Acc 16Dec44 and del 18Dec44 NAS New York; Pool NAS Alameda Jan45; CASU-F13 Admiralty Islands (unit was a split force at Pityilu and Ponam and the JRF was not a normally assigned type) Mar45; ComAir 7th Fleet, NAB Samar May45; ComAirPhil NAB Samar Aug45; Pool NAB Samar Oct45; NAS San Diego Dec46 for reconditioning; AOG Dallas Apr47; Pool BAR Bethpage Jun47; NAAS Mustin Fld Oct47 until at least Aug48; records missing; NAS Norfolk by Jan50 awaiting overhaul; NAS Quonset Point 13Jun50 for overhaul; NAF Annapolis 22Jun51; NART NAS Willow Grove 28Oct52 (awaiting issue, perhaps indicative of an incident there); NAS Quonset Point 13Feb53 awaiting overhaul and then modernisation and modification to **JRF-6** (to JRF-6X 14Feb53 and JRF-6 19Aug53); NAF Annapolis 01Sep53. SOC May54 for parts/scrap after a flying training accident on or about 14May54 from Annapolis (TFH:1,469hrs).

B-106   Built for US Navy as **JRF-5**, BuAer serial **84811**. Acc 21Dec44 and del NAS New York 22Dec44; Pool NAS Alameda Jan45; CASU-F13 Admiralty Islands (unit was a split force at Pityilu and Ponam and the JRF was not a normally assigned type) Mar45; AROU-2 NAB Samar May45; ACORN-47 NAB Palawan Jun45. Lost at sea 25Jly45 after pilot lost contact with radio beam and became temporarily lost. Aircraft ran low on fuel on approach to field (Palawan?) and elected to make water landing but undercarriage was not retracted by the time it landed. The aircraft flipped onto its back and sank, the crew suffering only minor injuries. SOC by ACORN-47, 31Aug45.

B-107   Built for US Navy as **JRF-5**, BuAer serial **84812** but diverted off contract for sale to the Royal Canadian Air Force. Del 20Jan45 and formally taken on Canadian strength becoming **Goose II** serial **397** with

C/n B-107, the former Royal Canadian Air Force Goose II, seen here as C-FIOL, "Dryad", during a photo shoot for MacMillan Bloedel in British Columbia in August 1994.   *(Fred J Knight Collection)*

RCAF. Initial allocation to No.1 Air Command and immediately to Storage Reserve at unknown location 20Jan45; assigned to No.12 (Communications) Sqn, Rockcliffe 30Aug45 with annotation suggesting use by the AOC; to No.9 (Transport) Group, Rockcliffe 05Jly46 of which No. 412 (Composite) Sqn was a component wef 01Apr47 and to which 397 was sometime assigned; made available for disposal by No.9 (T) Grp 11Sep47. SOC at Rockcliffe to War Assets Corp 08Jan48 (TFH:201hrs). Sales Order HO18168 from WAC to Imperial Oil Ltd 19Dec47. CofA 2843 and CofR(C) 7265 for **G-21A, CF-IOL** to Imperial Oil Ltd, Toronto, ON both issued 05Feb48, although aircraft log book shows a test flight by Imperial Oil pilots 04Feb48 and a note that "wing floats removed for winter ops" 10Feb48. Sold to Imperial Oil Air Transport Ltd, Toronto, ON (nominal change) with CofR(P) 8275 04Mar49. CofA renewed at TFH:605hrs, valid until 14Mar50. BoS to Bruce McKenzie Farris 08Sep50 with CofR(P) 9045 to West Coast Transport Co Ltd, Vancouver, BC 26Sep50. CofA renewed at TFH:1,112hrs, valid until 24Apr52; at TFH:2,810hrs, valid until 09Mar58; at TFH:5,225hrs, valid until 28Mar63; at TFH:7,426hrs, valid until 11Jan68; at TFH:10,728hrs, valid until 24Apr73; at TFH:15,449hrs, valid until 10May79. Certs re-issued as **C-FIOL** in 1979. CofR(P) to MacMillan Bloedel Ltd, Richmond, BC 23Jan80, aircraft name: "*Dryad*". BoS to Pacific Coastal Airlines Ltd, Richmond, BC 11Oct94 with CofR(C) issued 08Nov94. Accident 05Feb01, repaired 09May01. TFH:30,587hrs reported on Due Date 15Feb02; TFH:31,097hrs reported on Due Date 15Feb03. Withdrawn from service 24Sep12 due to the lack of availability of certified spare parts.

B-108 Built for US Navy as **JRF-5**, BuAer serial **84813**. Acc 27Dec44 and del NAS New York 28Dec44; Pool NAS Alameda Jan45; CASU-F13 Admiralty Islands (unit was a split force at Pityilu and Ponam and the JRF was not a normally assigned type) Mar45; NAB Samar May45; CNAB Mactan Islands, NAB Cebu 23Aug45; NAB Mactan Apr46; Pool NAB Samar 23Jly46 (under repair Sep-Nov46); NAS San Diego Dec46 (under repair); Pool NAS San Diego Jan47; Pool BAR Bethpage 17Apr47; NavAirActSRC NAF Annapolis Oct47 until at least Aug48; records missing but with NAMC Mustin Fld by 20Jly49 when involved in landing accident there (port undercarriage collapsed after landing resulting in ground-loop and minor damage). To RD&DE NAAS Mustin Fld by Jan50; 5th ND NAS Norfolk 23Mar50. Damaged on ramp at Annapolis seadrome 23Sep50 when port undercarriage leg collapsed; NAS Quonset Point 12Jan51 for overhaul; NAS San Diego 31Mar52 awaiting issue; FASRON-895 NAS Seattle 09May52; FASRON-113 NAS Seattle Feb53; FASRON-113 NAS Whidbey Island Aug53; assigned *USS Curtis* (AV-4) at NAS San Diego 03Dec53; declared surplus at San Diego 25Aug54. To SF Litchfield Park 06Oct54 for storage and allocated to MDAP 20May55. NAS Alameda 11Jly55 for preparation for delivery to an unconfirmed MAP recipient believed to have been the JMSDF for spares' use; SOC 21Sep55 (TT=1,477hrs); not subsequently reported in military use; no known subsequent commercial use; fate unknown.

B-109 Built for US Navy as **JRF-5**, BuAer serial **84814**. Acc 30Dec44 and del 04Jan45; Pool NAS Alameda Jan45; CASU-F13 Admiralty Islands (unit was a split force at Pityilu and Ponam and the JRF was not a normally assigned type) Mar45; NAB Samar Apr45; CNAB Philippines NAB Samar Aug46; Pool NAB Samar 19Jly46; NAS Tanapag Mar47; Pool FASRON-13 NAS Orote Aug47; Pool aboard *USS Antietam* (CV-36) Sep47; Pool NAS San Diego Oct47; Pool NAS Norfolk May48 until at least Aug48; records missing but with NavAirActSRC NAF Annapolis by 18Jly49 when damaged in a heavy water landing off Tolley Point, Chesapeake Bay, MD; records missing; awaiting overhaul at NAS Norfolk by Jan50; Pool BAR Bethpage May50 for overhaul; NAF Annapolis 25Oct50; 6th ND NAS Sanford 15Jan52 (and to RD&DE project 16Jan52); RD&DE NATC Patuxent River Feb52. Destroyed in fatal crash 07Jly52 14 miles north-east of Kirtland AFB, NM while temporarily assigned to 'Project HAIR' and nominally based at NAS Sanford. SOC 22Jly52 from Patuxent River charge (TFH:1,549hrs).

B-110 Built for US Navy as **JRF-5**, BuAer serial **84815**. Acc 31Dec44 and del 11Jan45; BAR Goodyear, Akron Jan45; 'Project TED' Jun45; VN8D5 NAF Annapolis Nov45; NAS Alameda Jly46 for reconditioning; Pool NAS Alameda Jan47; Pool BAR Bethpage Jun47; NavAirActSRC NAF Annapolis Nov47 until at least Aug48; records missing; NAS Norfolk by Jan50 awaiting overhaul; NAS Quonset Point 04Aug50 for overhaul that did not commence until 23Oct51; awaiting final disposition at Quonset Point 08Feb52. Retired 22Dec52 and SOC 07Apr53 in flyable condition to a non-Navy user (TFH:1,259hrs). Regd as **G-21A, N103** to CAA, Washington, DC in 1951 for use in Alaskan region. Written off and cancelled from USCAR 03Jly52 following an accident in Alaska. (The US Navy record would appear to have been a retrospective adjustment – see also B-129 87735/N101 and B-133 87739/N102)

B-111 Built for US Navy as **JRF-5**, BuAer serial **84816**. Acc and del 10Jan45; CGAS Brooklyn Jan45; CGAS Salem Feb45 until at least Jly46 when formally transferred to the US Coast Guard and SOC by the US Navy 31Jly46. Adopted the new designation **JRF-5G** circa 1950, with serial **4816**; CGAS San Francisco by Aug50 until at least Feb51; interim US Coast Guard history unknown but ex CGAS St Petersburg to storage at AR & SC Elizabeth City 08Sep54 (TFH:2,927hrs). CF-UDD allotted to Lund Aviation (Canada) Ltd, Montreal, PQ 20Apr56 with authority to ferry Elizabeth City, NJ to Montreal, PQ. Authority to ferry Montreal – St Johns, PQ 15Aug56 for wing spar repair. Authority to ferry St Johns to Rochester, NY and Rochester to Montreal, PQ 13Sep56. US CofA for export E-27345. CofR(P) 17056 and CofA 4988 for **G-21A, CF-UDD**, to JC Udd, Brockville, ON 18Sep56. CofA renewed at TFH:3,127hrs, valid until 18Sep58; at TFH:4,212hrs, valid until 16Mar64. BoS Estate of JC Udd to Archiepiscopale Catholique Romaine de Saint Boniface for $35,500. CofR(P) 28979 to La Corporation Archiepicopale Catholique Romaine de Saint Boniface, MB 27May63. Cancelled from CCAR as sold in Peru 18Jun63. To **OB-AEX-702** for Vicaritario Aspostolico de San José del Amazonas, Iquitos, Peru 16Aug63. Reregd **OB-V-702**, Apr64. Peruvian CofA issued 23Mar66. Peruvian regn cancelled 22Oct66. CF-VIA allotted to La Corporation Archiepiscopale Catholique Romaine de Saint Boniface (CACRSB), MB 21Oct66 and authority to ferry Iquitos, Peru to Winnipeg, MB same date. BoS 17Jan67 CACRSB to Antilles Air Boats Inc for $45,000, but CofR(P) 39647 for **CF-VIA** and CofA 12122 issued belatedly to CACRSB 23Jan67 at TFH:5,872hrs. Cancelled from CCAR 03Mar67 to **N7777V**, Antilles Air Boats (AAB), Christiansted, US Virgin Islands, with CofR 21Mar67. Accident circa 1020hrs on 02Sep78: crashed into sea off St Thomas, US Virgin Islands after left engine failed, while operating Flight 941 from St Croix to St Thomas. Charles F Blair, AAB President and founder, and 3 pax were killed. Seven others survived. The captain's decision not to attempt an open sea emergency landing and fly instead in ground effect, coupled with the fact that the aircraft could not sustain single-engined flight due to drag induced by the loss of the left engine cowling and the improperly maintained right propeller, were determined as the probable causes. NTSB allegedly found evidence of forged maintenance logs and that aircraft had flown 22:05hrs beyond scheduled inspection time. The aircraft broke up on impact and sank in 85ft of water. Listed by FAA Oct10, as revoked.

B-112 Built for US Navy as **JRF-5**, BuAer serial **84817**. Acc 17Jan45 and del 19Mar45 (reason for delay unknown); VN8D5 NAF Annapolis Mar45; NAS Norfolk Jun45 for minimal repairs; VN8D5 NAF Annapolis Aug45; NAS Norfolk Oct46 for reconditioning; VN8D5 NAF Annapolis Dec46; Pool BAR Bethpage Aug47; Pool NAS San Diego May48; to storage NAS Litchfield Park Jly48 until at least Aug48; records missing; in storage MCAS Cherry Point by Jan50; NAS Quonset Point 28Nov52 for modernisation; NAF Annapolis 08Apr53; SF Litchfield Park 22May55 for storage and retired, awaiting strike, 25Aug55. SOC 08May56 (TFH:1,137hrs). BoS NAS North Island, San Diego, CA to Griffco Aviation, Seattle, WA 02May56 for $25,268 (wrongly quoted as c/n B122); CofA 21Jun56 at TFH:1,117hrs; CofR **N2845D** issued 22Jun56 again quoting c/n B122, but corrected to B-112 22May57. BoS to Western Alaska Airlines Inc, Dillingham, AK 23Dec59 with CofR 22Jan60. CofA 18Jan63 at TFH:2,726hrs. "Smoke-jumper" door installed per STC SA1-439 May69. Accident 15Jun70: substantially damaged by wheels-down water landing at New Stoyahok, AK on a flight from Dillingham to Koliganek, AK. Pilot +3 pax uninjured. Major overhaul and repair Mar74 including fitting of Hartzell 93Z30 three-bladed props per STC SA1-52. Transferred to Kodiak Western Alaska Airlines Inc (KWAA), Kodiak, AK with CofR 10Apr74. Reported leased (possibly to a TV production company) Feb81 and another CofR issued (to KWAA) 13Mar81. Was to be used in the TV series *"Tales of the Gold Monkey"* but crashed on the way

C/n B-112, N2845D, was the Goose originally chosen to star in the television series "Tales of the Gold Monkey", but it unfortunately crashed on the way south from Alaska to California in February 1982.

(Fred J Knight Collection)

south from Alaska 20Feb82 near Cape Yakataga. Lost power in both engines and ditched in rough seas. Both engines and one wing-float broke off in the rough landing but both pilots were rescued just as the plane sank. Replaced in the TV series by c/n 1051(qv). Remains obviously salvaged and transferred by BoS from Kodiak Western Alaska Airlines to Red Dodge, Anchorage, AK 16Feb82 (for spares?) with CofR 19Apr82. Status uncertain Oct10 – due "undelivered Triennial", but CofR expired 30Jun11, although the aircraft was listed as airworthy! Cancelled from USCAR 24Sep12.

B-113   Built for US Navy as **JRF-5**, BuAer serial **84818**. Acc 25Jan45 and del to NAS New York 27Jan45; Naval Attaché Guatemala, Guatemala City Feb45; FASRON-102 NAS Norfolk Sep46 for repair; Pool BAR Bethpage Jan47; VN8D5 NAF Annapolis May47; NavAirActSRC NAF Annapolis Aug47 until at least Aug48; records missing; NavAirActSRC NAF Annapolis by Jan50 and administratively to NAF Annapolis 24Mar50. To NAS Quonset Point 18Sep50 for intended overhaul but declared surplus 14May51 and SOC for MDAP disposal to France 13Jly51 (TFH:1,863hrs). To France's Aéronautique Navale wearing abbreviated serial **818**; transit details unknown but by sea to Saigon, Vietnam and delivered to 8ème Escadrille de Servitude (8.S) at Cat Lai 14Mar52; coded 8.S-11. Sank in the Dong Nai River near Cat Lai after a landing accident 25Apr53. SOC 23Aug53.

B-114   Built for US Navy as **JRF-5**, BuAer serial **87720**. Acc 30Jan45 and del 05Feb45; VN8D5 NAF Annapolis Feb45; NavAirActSRC NAF Annapolis Aug47; Pool BAR Bethpage 29Sep47 for major overhaul & acc 30Jun48. To storage NAS South Weymouth 29Jly48; to storage at A&T MCAS Cherry Point 14Jan49; NAS Quonset Point 10Feb53 (TFH:963hrs) for modernisation and modification to **JRF-6** (to JRF-6X 11Feb53 and JRF-6 30Jly53); NAF Annapolis 10Jly53; inspected and acc 31Dec54 (at TFH:1,584hrs). To SF Litchfield Park 14Apr56 for disposal and SOC 11Sep56 (TFH:2,154hrs) and sold surplus 01Oct56. Declared airworthy for ferry flight to Remmert-Werner, Red Bank, NJ (storage) 19Nov60. To Fred B Ayer & Associates, New York, NY by 1962 regd as **G-21A, N2021A**. Inspected 03Apr62 and deemed airworthy at TFH:2,179hrs; keel inspected 07Apr62 "after wheel failure on landing, but considered airworthy for flight to Seattle". To Western Alaska Airlines, Dillingham, AK Apr62. To Kodiak Western Alaska Airlines 1969. To Hal's Air Service Inc, Kodiak, AK by 1981. Accident 21Jly84: crashed and sank near Ouzinkie, off Spruce Island, 5 miles North of Kodiak, en route to Larsen Bay, while flying in dense fog. Harold W Dierich (owner/pilot) and three pax killed. TFH:6,129hrs. Fred Ball salvaged the many pieces of wreckage from 20ft of water 30Jly84. Cancelled from USCAR Dec85.

B-115   Built for US Navy as **JRF-5**, BuAer serial **87721**. Acc 30Jan45 and del 07Feb45; Pool NAS Alameda Feb45; CASU-64 NAAS Watsonville Apr45; CASU-54 NAAS Fallon Jan46; CASU-6 NAS Alameda Mar46; unreadable 26Jun46; VN8D5 NAF Annapolis Oct46; NavAirActSRC NAF Annapolis Aug47; Pool NAS Norfolk Oct47; Pool BAR Bethpage Mar48 until at least Aug48; records missing; RD&DE NAS Patuxent River by Jan50; NAS Quonset Point 18May50 for overhaul; FASRON-102 NAS Norfolk 21Apr51 for shipping; NAF Port Lyautey 21May51 (transit); Naval Attaché Athens, Greece 11Jly51. Damaged in landing accident at Muntadas Apt, Barcelona, Spain 15Jly51: aircraft was arriving from Port Lyautey [so probably not yet delivered to Athens], when crew failed to check that undercarriage was properly down and locked; landing was normal but starboard gear collapsed during roll. Aircraft was subsequently jacked and landing gear locked down for positioning flight back to Port Lyautey. To FASRON-104 NAF Port Lyautey 18Jly51 for repairs; Naval Attaché Athens, Greece 01Dec51; NAS Norfolk 09Jun54 for overhaul but to storage 15Jun54 and retired 24Jly55; SF Litchfield Park 09Aug55. SOC 16Sep55 (1,409hrs). Affidavit on file confirms transfer to Bureau of Land Management (BLM) same date. Regd as **N641**(2) to US Dept of Interior, BLM, Juneau, AK 12May61. "Smoke-Jumper" door fitted per STC SA1-439 24May61. Cvtd to **G-21A** and CofA 05Jly61 at "TT=124:45hrs" (sic); CofA 04May64 at TFH:2,587hrs; Accident 20May64: substantially damaged by ground loop after landing at Kenai, AK. Pilot + one pax uninjured. CofR to Alaska Office of Aircraft Services, Anchorage 27Jun74. Reported "destroyed/scrapped" 31Dec74 and cancelled from USCAR 09May75. BoS Alaska Aircraft Services to Lloyd A Rekow, Seattle, WA 08Oct75 with CofR 08Dec75. Noted at Boeing Field, Seattle, WA with no fuselage forward of the wings, Dec75. BoS to Foreign & Domestic Enterprises Inc, Seattle, WA 13Jan76 with CofR 30Jan76. BoS to Robert E Curtis and Hugh Z Smith dba Goose Leasing, Anchorage, AK 17Mar76 with CofR 19Apr78. The aircraft was seen painted in the colours of Webber Airlines Inc in January 1979 and therefore assumed operated by them. Later operated by Peninsula Airways, and transferred by BoS from Goose Leasing to Peninsular Airways, King Salmon, AK 01Feb82 with CofR 06Apr82; aircraft named: "Spirit of

Alitak". TFH:15,440hrs a/o 23May96. Ownership transferred to Seaplane Parts LLC, Gibsonville, NC 15Jan01. Regn pending in 2004 and 2008. According to David Marion of Antilles Seaplanes Inc this aircraft was "completely disassembled down to every single nut, bolt and rivet, in order to help us reverse engineer and double check all the legacy Grumman engineering drawings and blueprints from which we will be working to build new Gooses". The FAA lists the aircraft as airworthy May13, but with registration status "in question" due sale reported.

B-116   Built for US Navy as **JRF-5**, BuAer serial **87722**. Acc 27Feb45 and del NAS New York 28Feb45; CGAS Brooklyn Mar45; CGAS Miami Sep45 where it remained until at least Apr46. Damaged in landing accident at NAS Miami 16Apr46 (aircraft landed long and ground-looped); NAS Jacksonville by Jun46 and SOC by the US Navy 30Jun46 due to fire damage to the keelson and bottom skin resulting from the accident (aircraft was assigned to CGAS Miami at time of accident).

B-117   Built for US Navy as **JRF-5**, BuAer serial **87723**. Acc 17Feb45 and del NAS New York 19Feb45; Pool NAS Alameda Mar45; en route NAS Pearl Harbor Apr45; VJ-14 NAS Pearl Harbor May45; VJ-7 NAS Pearl Harbor Sep45. Suffered minor damage when undercarriage collapsed at Pearl Harbour 18Oct45 (VJ-14 pilot); VJ-1 NAS Pearl Harbor by 31Oct45; VJ-11 NAS Puunene 01Jun46; VU-6 NAS Puunene Nov46; NAS Pearl Harbor Dec46; FASRON-11 NAS Pearl Harbor Jly47; Pool NAS San Diego Aug47; Pool NAS Norfolk Oct47; Pool BAR Bethpage May48 until at least Aug48; records missing; Naval Attaché Athens, Greece by Jan50. Minor damage incurred in rough water during post-landing taxy at Mitilini Harbour, Lesbos, Greece 19Apr51. To FASRON-104 NAS Port Lyautey 11Jly51 awaiting overhaul and shipped 15Aug51; NAS Norfolk 04Sep51 awaiting overhaul and shipped 28Feb52; NAS Quonset Point 07Mar52 for overhaul and modification to **JRF-6** (to JRF-6X 05Jan53 and JRF-6 30Jly53); NAF Annapolis 10Jly53; NAS Anacostia 13Jan56; SF Litchfield Park awaiting strike 07Feb56 and SOC 11Sep56 (TFH:2,475hrs). BoS 29Oct56 US Naval Air Station North Island, San Diego, CA to Avalon Air Transport for $18,571.40. Regd as **G-21A, N325**(1) 15Nov56. BoS to Ada Oil Co, Houston, TX 28Dec56. N325 reserved for Avalon 24Jan57 for future use (see c/n B-127) and this aircraft reregd **N525** 31Jan57. BoS to Aviation Sales & Engineering, Houston, TX 10May57 with CofR 07Jun57. Major overhaul airframe and engines with CofA 16Jly57 at TFH:2,495hrs. Re-issued 29Jly58 at TFH:2,547hrs. BoS to Alley Lumber Co Inc, Medford, OR 29Sep58 with CofR 14Nov58 and CofA 02Feb59 at TFH:2,745hrs. BoS Alley Lumber to Alley Brothers, Medford, OR 30Apr60 with CofR 09Jun60. BoS to McKinnon Enterprises, Sandy, OR 12Jun61 with CofR 15Jun61. Aircraft modified for gross weight increase to 9,200lbs 10Jly61. CofA 02Mar62 at TFH:3,112hrs and 03May62 at TFH:3,152hrs. BoS to Peyton Hawes, Portland, OR 28Dec62. Tfd back to McKinnon by BoS 07Nov72, with CofR 22Nov72. BoS to Executive Seminars Inc, Lincoln, NB 05Apr73 with CofR 11Apr73. BoS to Land Management Corp of North America, Lincoln, NB 31May73 with CofR 22Jun73. **C-GYVG** allocated to Keewatin Arctic Camp Co 11Mar77. BoS Land Management to Keewatin Arctic Camp Co Ltd, Henik Lake, NT 14Apr78. N525 cancelled from USCAR 03Jly78. Leased to Calm Air International Ltd, Lynn Lake, MB 01May78 for one year. Inspected and CofA issued at TFH:6,350hrs, valid until 07Jly79. CofR(C) issued to Calm Air 07Jly78. Further lease from Keewatin to Calm Air 01May79. Inspected and CofA renewed at TFH:6,527hrs valid until 07Jly80. BoS Keewatin to Weldwood of Canada Ltd, Richmond, BC 11Feb80 with CofR(P) 26Feb80. Accident at 1215hrs on 15May80: after a flight from Powell River, BC, aircraft nosed over onto its back, landing at a logging strip at East Toba, BC, due to brake problem. 2 crew uninjured; pilot: William JT Cove. Inspected and CofA renewed at TFH:6,877hrs, valid until 01Dec81; at TFH:8,097hrs, valid until 01Dec86. BoS Weldwood to 147973 Canada Inc, Calgary, AB 27Dec85 with

C/n B-117, N525, at Vancouver, British Columbia, in May 1962, after it had been up-rated for a gross weight of 9,200lbs, by McKinnon Enterprises.   *(Ingvar Klett)*

CofR(P) 31Dec85. Inspected and CofA renewed at TFH:8,243hrs, valid until 01Dec87. TFH:8,536hrs reported on Due Date 09Mar91. BoS 147973 Canada Inc to Unilease Inc, Don Mills, ON 19Aug91. Leased to Juergen Puetter, Calgary, AB 20Aug91 for two years with CofR(P) to Puetter 20Aug91. TFH:8,585hrs reported on Due Date 09Mar92; CofR(P) to Juergen Puetter, Senneville, PQ (address change) 13Oct92. TFH:8,686hrs reported on Due Date 09Mar93. CofR(P) to Juergen Puetter, Sydney, BC (dba Hydroxyl Systems Inc) (address change) 01Apr93. BoS Unilease to Puetter 30Aug93. TFH:8,728hrs reported on Due Date 09Mar94 and TFH:8,855hrs reported on Due Date 09Mar98. BoS to Pacific North American Development & Financial Corp, Vancouver, BC 22May98 with CofR(P) 13Oct98. TFH:8,861hrs reported on Due Date 09Mar99. Noted at EAA Fly-in, Arlington, WA Jly00. TFH:8,978hrs reported on Due Date 09Mar03; CofR re-issued 04Jly07 on change of address to Victoria, BC. Current Mar13.

B-118   Built for US Navy as **JRF-5**, BuAer serial **87724**. Acc 24Feb45 and del NAS New York 27Feb45; NAS Anacostia Mar45. Damaged beyond repair 30Oct45 in misjudged water landing on Potomac River, six miles South of Anacostia; aircraft landed heavily after misjudgement of altitude in glassy conditions (no injuries). SOC 30Nov45.

B-119   Built for US Navy as **JRF-5**, BuAer serial **87725**. Acc 28Feb45 and del 09Mar45; Pool NAS Alameda Mar45; en route NAS Pearl Harbor Apr45; Pool NAS Pearl Harbor May45; MCAS Ewa Jun45; awaiting action NAS Pearl Harbor Mar46; CG det NAS Kaneohe Bay 30Apr46 until at least Jly46 when formally transferred to the US Coast Guard and SOC by US Navy 31Jly46. Noted at Grumman, Bethpage Oct47. Adopted the designation **JRF-5G** circa 1950, with serial **7725**; CGAS Salem by Jan51 until at least Oct51, and by Nov52 until at least Aug53. Used by US Coast Guard as a ground training aid at AR&SC Elizabeth City, date unknown. Sold to Avalon Air Transport Inc, Long Beach, CA 06Feb59 for $13,757 and regd as **N329**, 08Jly59 with FN:4. Overhauled and cvtd to **G-21A** with CofA issued 08Oct59 at TFH:1,883hrs. To Catalina Air Lines Inc, Long Beach, CA 28Oct63; CofA issued 21Dec63 at TFH:3,093hrs. Accident 02May64: substantial damage after water loop in rough water after landing in Avalon Bay, CA. Pilot + nine pax uninjured. In 1968, Aero Commuter Inc merged with Catalina Air Lines. Cable Commuter and Skywark were added to the group which was then swallowed up by Golden West Airlines Inc. Major overhaul and repaint Jun69. Tfd by BoS to Golden West Airlines Inc, Los Angeles, CA 01Dec69 with CofR 10Dec69. Accident 10Jan70: minor damage when hit a boat on landing at Pebbly Beach, CA. Pilot + 2 pax uninjured. BoS to KC Aircraft Sheet Metal Co Inc, Long Beach, CA 16Nov73 with CofR 26Nov73. BoS to Lew Mahieu, Long Beach, CA 28Feb75 with CofR 24Mar75. Tfd back to KC Aircraft Sheetmetal by BoS 04Apr75, with CofR 13May75. Repaint, new interior and avionics Aug76. BoS to PT Saatas, Jakarta, Indonesia 13Aug76 and cancelled from USCAR 16Aug76. Regd **PK-LEG** Aug76. Accident 25May78: damaged when ran off runway at Senipah. Wfu prior to 01Jan82 and regn cancelled 1990.

G-21A Goose, c/n B-119, N329, wearing Catalina Golden West titles, is seen here at Long Beach, California on 20th May 1972.

(John P Stewart via PJ Marson)

B-120   Built for US Navy as **JRF-5**, BuAer serial **87726** but diverted off contract and, following acceptance by US Navy 17Mar45. Transferred to US Army Air Force 19Mar45 as **OA-13B**, with serial **45-49088** and delivered to 4003rd AAFBU Newark, NJ 24Mar45 for overseas shipment by sea. Delivered to theatre 06Jun45 (assigned ATC North Africa). Condemned to salvage 08Sep45 but 'recovered' 01Apr46 (12th AF, French Morocco). Lost to inventory 01Jly46 (9th AF, Cairo). Regd as **G-21A, NC3096** to Superior Oil Co, Houston, TX 1947 and later **N3096**. Authority to ferry Houston to Kenora, ON 10Mar60. Cancelled from USCAR 10May60. CofR(C) 23672 and CofA 8406 issued 10May60 for **CF-IWW**

to Ontario Central Airlines, Kenora, ON; electric gear retraction mechanism fitted per SA2-603, inspected and CofA renewed at TFH:7,610hrs, valid until 04Apr62; Hartzell 3-bladed props installed 1962 per STC SA1-52; CofA renewed at TFH:9,102hrs, valid until 28May67. To Can Am Aircraft Ltd, Kenora, ON 30May66 with CofR(C) 38262; inspected and CofA renewed at TFH:9,828hrs, valid until 28May69. To Ontario Central Airlines, 28May68 now at Redditt, ON, with CofR(C) 41118; inspected and CofA renewed at TFH:10,892hrs, valid until 04Jun73. To Jack H Edwards, Kenora, ON (date not recorded). Leased to Parsons Airways Ltd, Kenora, ON with CofR(C) 07Jun72; inspected and CofA renewed at TFH:11,946hrs, valid until 02Jly77. Accident at circa 1440hrs on 08Jly76: substantial damage after forced landing in bush 3 miles South of Churchill, MB on flight from Red Lake to Churchill (Pilot: Jon Wilson). Left tank ran dry and engine would not restart when fuel switched to crossfeed. Aircraft would not maintain altitude on one engine and landed in trees short of runway 33. Pilot + 4 pax uninjured. Wreck bought from the insurers by Barney Lamm. Recovery of the wreck involved removing the wings and engines. Then the wreck was sling-loaded beneath a heavy-lift helicopter and taken to Churchill, MB. From there it undertook the long rail journey south to Winnipeg and then north to the Ontario Central Airlines base at Gimli, MB. Repairs took more than a year, including replacement (McKinnon) wings with retractable floats, and CofA renewed at TFH:11,952hrs, valid until 23Aug78. CofR(P) to Barney E Lamm, Gimli, MB 26Aug77 as **C-FIWW**. CofR(C) to Ontario Central Airlines Ltd, Gimli, MB 07Jun78; inspected and CofA renewed at TFH:11,970hrs, valid until 23Aug80. CofR(P) to The Air Ranger Ltd, Winnipeg, MB 29May80. CofR(P) to 241805 Alberta Ltd, Edmonton, AB 30Jly80. Inspected and CofA renewed at TFH:12,567hrs, valid until 23Aug84. BoS to Victory Aviation Corp, Wilmington, DE 01Nov83. New electric landing gear retraction mechanism installed per SA2-603. Cancelled from CCAR 02Dec83 at TFH:12,603hrs. CofR for **N4575C** 08Dec83 and CofA 12Dec83. BoS to American City Construction Co, New York, NY 21Dec83 with CofR 25Jan84. To Blue Arrow Challenge, New York, NY 21Jan88 with CofR 08Feb88. Aircraft dismantled and shipped to Leavesden, UK for rebuild Apr89. The restoration team was led by Doug Wyatt, who had been chief engineer for the Duke of Westminster's Goose, G-ASXG. The aircraft was not used as support for the 1992 Americas Cup challenge and was advertised for sale, in Dec91, before rebuild was complete. By the time of the first flight, on 06May93, the Goose had been fitted with two zero-timed engines and painted in the same scheme as the Duke's aircraft:- overall white with blue Goose motifs on the nose. Being registered in USA, the CofA had to be granted by the FAA. This was done after successful water handling tests on Bewl Bridge reservoir, in Kent, in late May93. BoS Blue Arrow to Sherman Aircraft Sales Inc, West Palm Beach, FL 06Dec94 with CofR 09Dec94. Ferry fuel system installed 14Dec94; flew Wick, Scotland – Reykjavik, Iceland 27Dec94, to Narsarssuak, Greenland (28Dec) en route to Sherman. Ferry fuel system removed 11Jan95. BoS to Aerofloat G21a Inc (Owner Trustee), Dover, DE 06May97 with CofR 13May97. Flew Godthab, Greenland – Reykjavik, Iceland 06Jun97 and Glasgow, Scotland 09Jun97 to be based at Weston, Ireland. Accident at 1408hrs on 26May02: crashed due to left gear collapse on landing in a 17kt cross wind, at Knock, Ireland after a flight from Weston, causing substantial damage but no injury. BoS Aerofloat G21a Inc (Owner Trustee) to Aerofloat G21a Inc (Owner Trustee), Wilmington, DE 04Oct02 (different address), with CofR 17Oct02; TFH:13,449hrs a/o 24Feb03. Noted at Weston Executive A/P, Ireland, Jun04 and "fully restored", Aug04. Last Form337 on file 13Sep06, but after a year based at Duxford it returned to Weston in Jan07, and flew regularly from there during 2007, operated by National Flight Centre. BoS to Senate Inc Trustee, Wilmington, DE 18Jun09. Sale reported Jly10, to Osmond J Kilkenny, Dublin, Ireland, but listed by FAA Oct10, as "certificate terminated". The CofR was cancelled 01Apr13, but the regn remained assigned.

B-121   Built for US Navy as **JRF-5**, BuAer serial **87727**. Acc and del 24Mar45; Pool NAS Alameda Mar45; CASU-63 NAAS Vernalis May45; CASU-36 NAAS Santa Rosa Dec45; Pool CASU-6 NAS Alameda May46 (reconditioning post-24Jun46); VN8D5 NAF Annapolis Aug46; NavAirActSRC NAF Annapolis Aug47; Pool NAS Norfolk Oct47 until at least Aug48; records missing; NavAirActSRC NAF Annapolis by Jan50 and administratively to NAF Annapolis 24Mar50. Significantly damaged in landing accident at Linden, NJ 18Jly50 when starboard undercarriage collapsed on landing (not properly locked in down position); NAS Quonset Point 19Jly50 where repairs commenced 07Mar51. Declared surplus 14May51 and SOC for MDAP disposal to France 13Jly51 (TFH:1,712hrs). To France's Aéronautique Navale wearing abbreviated serial **727**; transit details unknown but by sea to Saigon, Vietnam and delivered to 8ème Escadrille de Servitude (8.S) at Cat Lai 05Mar52. Accepted 06Mar52 and coded 8.S-8. Damaged in an accident 03Apr52: overturned on landing at Nha Trang, Vietnam 06Nov52 and SOC 09Jan53.

B-122 Built for US Navy as **JRF-5**, BuAer serial **87728**. Acc and del NAS New York 31Mar45; Pool NAS Alameda Apr45; CASU-37 NAAS Hollister May45; CASU-64 NAAS Watsonville Oct45; CASU-54 NAAS Fallon Jan46; Pool CASU-6 NAS Alameda Apr46 (reconditioning post-24Jun46); VN8D5 NAF Annapolis 09Sep46; Pool BAR Bethpage May47; NavAirActSRC NAF Annapolis Aug47 until at least Aug48; records missing; Pool BAR Bethpage in overhaul by Jan50; NAF Annapolis 05Apr50 (incurred damage to starboard wing float at Annapolis 15Aug51 and unclear if aircraft subsequently flown at Annapolis). To NAS Quonset Point 27Dec51 for overhaul where declared surplus 12Aug52 and SOC 13Oct52 (TFH:1,963hrs). Regd (probably as a JRF-5) **N781** to US Dept of Interior, Fish & Wildlife Service, Washington, DC, Nov52 and ferried to Alaska, where converted to **G-21A**. To Alaska Fish & Game, Juneau, AK as **N781S** by Jun62. Reregd **N7811** Jly64. To State of Alaska, Anchorage by 1966. Non-fatal crash at King Salmon, AK 29Jun90. Wfu Anchorage 1996 and offered for sale. To Peninsular Airways Inc, Anchorage, AK with CofR 12Dec96. Incident at Akhiok, AK 22May98. Restricted CofA 08Aug05. Accident 24Jun07: pilot had dropped off passengers at Dutch Harbor, AK and was taking off for return to base. A quartering gust of tailwind pushed the aircraft off the runway where the aircraft nosed over tearing off the right wing. 2 uninjured. TFH:13,121hrs. Current but with Restricted CofA, May13, with CofR due to expire 30Jun13.

B-123 Built for US Navy as **JRF-5**, BuAer serial **87729**. Acc 10Apr45 and del 13Apr45; Pool NAS Norfolk Apr45; CASU-21 NAS Norfolk May45; ComNav7 NAS Key West 29Sep45; NAS Key West Oct45; NAAS Mustin Fld 24Jun46; Pool BAR Bethpage Oct47 until at least Jly48; to RD&DE BAR Bethpage Aug48; records missing; Pool RD&DE BAR Bethpage (test work) by Jan50; NAS Quonset Point 22Jun50 for overhaul; NAS Anacostia 03Jly51. To NAS Quonset Point 08Apr53 awaiting overhaul but declared surplus 23Jly53 and SOC 30Sep53 (TFH:1,202hrs). Cvtd to **G-21A** at Fairbanks, AK and regd **N640** to US Dept of Interior, Bureau of Land Management (BLM), Anchorage, AK with CofR 19Apr54 and CofA 23Apr54 at TFH:1,236hrs; renewed 09May55 at TFH:1,521hrs. Major overhaul, including fitting R-985 AN-14B engines, by Transocean Airlines, Boeing Field, Seattle, WA Mar56 with CofA 03Apr56 at TFH:1,712hrs. Accident 31Aug66: heavy water landing at Alegnagik, AK. No fatalities but aircraft substantially damaged. ECofA 09Nov67 at TFH:5,884hrs, after conversion to **G-21A Turboprop**, retaining c/n B-123 (McKinnon G-21C c/n 1201 allocated but not used), with 2 UAC PT6A-20 engines, by McKinnon Enterprises, Sandy, OR. Accident 05Aug67: while evaluating prop surging at Sandy, OR, aircraft substantially damaged after colliding with "ditches". CofA 12Jan68 at TFH:5,932hrs. Nominal change to Office of Aircraft Services, Anchorage, AK with CofR 23Mar76. BoS Dept of Interior to State of Alaska, Dept of Public Safety, Anchorage, AK 14Dec84 with CofR 14Jan85. BoS State of Alaska to Teufel Holly Farms Inc, Portland, OR 03Oct96 with CofR 18Feb97; nominal change to Teufel Nursery Inc, Portland, OR 23Feb98 with CofR 15Apr98. Cancelled from USCAR 06Jly01 as "disassembled and scrapped". Cvtd to **G-21G** by Larry Teufel and regd (wrongly) as a **"Grumman/McKinnon G-21G", c/n 1201**, 10Jly01. CofA issued 10Oct05 and CofR to George R Teufel, Portland, OR 22Oct09. Tfd to Teufel Holly Farms Inc, Portland, OR with CofR 15Feb12. Current and airworthy May13, with CofR to expire 28Feb15.

B-124 Built for US Navy as **JRF-5**, BuAer serial **87730**. Acc 20Apr45 and del 24Apr45; CGAS Brooklyn Apr45; CGAS San Juan 30Jly45 until at least Jly46 when formally transferred to the US Coast Guard and SOC by the US Navy 31Jly46. Subsequent station allocation unknown but adopted revised designation **JRF-5G** and serial **7730** circa 1950. Wfu by US Coast Guard and returned to US Navy at SF Litchfield Park 18Jun54 and declared surplus 02Mar55. SOC 05Mar56 (TFH:2,609hrs). Regd as **G-21A, N6086V** to St Louis Parks College, St Louis, MO with CofA issued 24May57. Cancelled from USCAR 21May66. Fate unknown.

B-125 Built for US Navy as **JRF-5**, BuAer serial **87731**. Acc 27Apr45 and del NAS New York 28Apr45; Pool NAS Alameda May45; VJ-10 NAAS Shelton Jun45; VJ-2 NAAS Shelton Jly45; CASU-7 NAS Seattle Nov45; Pool CASU-7 NAS Seattle 21Jun46; VN8D5 NAF Annapolis Sep46; NavAirActSRC NAF Annapolis Aug47; Pool NAS Norfolk Oct47 until at least Aug48; records missing; NavAirActSRC NAF Annapolis by Jan50; NAS Anacostia 24Jan50 awaiting action; NAS Norfolk 09May50 (transit); NAF Port Lyautey May50 (transit). Loaned to US Dept of Interior, Greece 10May54. Returned to NAS Quonset Point 21Jly53 for overhaul and allocated to MDAP 31Mar54. SOC for MDAP disposal to Japan 13May54 (TFH:1,607hrs); shipped to Japan where de-preserved by the FASRON-11 detachment at NAF Oppama. Used for crew training and working-up at NAF Oppama. Transferred to the JMSDF and given serial **9013**; formal handover to Second Kanoya Kokutai, Kanoya 25Nov55; relocated to Omura and thus to Omura Kokutai 01Dec56. Retired circa

1960 and assumed to have returned to US charge; remained at JMSDF base Shimofusa in increasingly derelict condition until Sep68, when purchased surplus from the US Army Depot Command in (probably Sagamihara City) Japan by Tom Danaher, Wichita Falls, TX for $5,555.56, and regd as **G-21A, N60AL** 1968. Cvtd to **McKinnon G-21G**, c/n **1226**, with 2 UAC PT6A-27 by McKinnon Enterprises, Sandy, OR still regd N60AL. Reregd **N70AL** Oct69 with CofA 16Mar70. Sold to US Plywood/Champion Paper Inc, Juneau, AK 18Mar70 (later known as Champion International Corp). To Chevron Oil Co, California Division by 1983 and operated out of New Orleans-Lakefront A/P. To Reginald Slade/Northern Air Inc, Reno, NV 25Mar92. To Aeroplanes LLC, Hillsboro, OR 14Sep99. Noted at Sun 'n Fun, Lakeland, FL Apr01. To Killa Katchka Inc, West Bloomfield, MI, with CofR 02Jly04. Noted at Oshkosh, WI 2004 and 2005, and current and airworthy May13, with CofR due to expire 31Oct14.

B-126 Built for US Navy as **JRF-5**, BuAer serial **87732**. Acc 09May45 and del 10May45; Pool NAAS Franklin May45; CASU-24 NAS Wildwood Jun45; NAS Norfolk Oct45 for minor repairs and reconditioning; NAS Norfolk Dec45; Pool BAR Bethpage Jly47; Pool NAS San Diego Mar48; Pool NAS Norfolk Jun48. To storage NAS Litchfield Park Aug48; records missing; MCAS Cherry Point by Jan50 for storage; NAS Quonset Point 17Feb53 for overhaul and modification to **JRF-6** (to JRF-6X 17Feb53 and JRF-6 30Jun53); NAS Anacostia 28Jly53; NAF Annapolis 28May54. To SF Litchfield Park awaiting strike 08Jun56 and SOC 22Aug56 (TFH:1,477hrs). BoS NAS North Island, San Diego to Beldex Corp, St Louis, MO 29Oct56 (for $21,111.11) with CofR **N87U** 03Dec56 and CofA as **G-21A** 16Jan58. BoS Beldex to Schenley Industries Inc, New York, NY 23Oct58 with CofR 12Dec58; electrical gear retract system installed per STC SA2-603 Dec58. BoS Schenley to Shaw Flight Service Inc, Anchorage, AK 28May62 with CofR 21Jun62; Aircraft Rebuilders seats installed per STC SA46AL Nov62. CofA 21Oct64 at TFH:2,800hrs. BoS to Kodiak Airways Inc, Kodiak, AK 21Oct64 with CofR 16Nov64. Tfd to Kodiak Western Alaska Airlines Inc by BoS Apr75, with CofR 29Apr75. Accident at 1210hrs on 26Mar80: while step taxying after landing in Karluk Lagoon, Kodiak Island, aircraft swerved up onto beach; pilot + 3 pax uninjured but aircraft substially damaged. Rebuilt and reported leased (to whom?) Feb81. BoS to AMP Warehouse Agency Fund, Anchorage, AK with CofR 30Sep82. BoS to Foreign & Domestic Enterprises Inc, Seattle, WA 08Oct82; major overhaul Feb83 with CofR 13Jly83. BoS to Friedkin Investments Inc, Houston, TX 02Apr87 with CofR 23Apr87; nominal change to Thomas H Friedkin, dba Cinema Air Inc, Houston, TX 31Jly88 with CofR 22Aug88. Featured in the film *"Forever Young"*, in 1988, also starring Mel Gibson. BoS Cinema Air to Edmund Glen Johnson, Fort Worth, TX 26Feb93 with CofR 26Mar93. Tfd by BoS to Johnson, dba Blue Goose Enterprises Inc, Las Vegas, NV 28Apr93 with CofR 08Jun93. Painted in blue US Navy scheme as "**87732**". Used in Aug95, to celebrate the 50th Anniversary of VJ Day. The Goose took off from the aircraft carrier *USS Carl Vinson*, landed in Pearl Harbor and taxied up the ramp at Ford Island. After taking part in the NAS Barbers Point airshow, the aircraft returned to the mainland on the carrier. TFH:11,459hrs a/o Nov04. Current and airworthy May13, with CofR due to expire 31Aug14.

Goose, c/n B-126, registered as N87U, is seen here at Boeing Field, Seattle, Washington, on 14th August 1983, after undergoing a major overhaul by Foreign & Domestic Enterprises.

(Jennifer Gradidge Collection)

B-127 Built for US Navy as **JRF-5**, BuAer serial **87733**. Acc 23May45 and del 24May45; CGAS Brooklyn May45; CGAS San Francisco Jun45; CGAS Traverse City Dec45 until at least Jly46 when formally transferred to the US Coast Guard and SOC by the US Navy 31Jly46; CGAS Brooklyn by Oct48. Adopted the designation **JRF-5G** circa 1950, with serial **7733**; CGAS Salem by Dec51 until at least Mar53; disposal details unconfirmed but probably circa early 1957. N325 had been reserved for Avalon Air Transport 24Jan57 (see c/n B-117). Regd as **G-21A, N325**(2) and op by Avalon Air Transport, Long Beach, CA, with FN:9 circa 1957, although by

Apr 60 regd to Aircraft Lease Charter Inc, Oklahoma City, OK (but still in use with Avalon). To Catalina Channel Airlines, Long Beach, CA 1964; aircraft name: *"The Islander"*. To Catalina Seaplanes, San Pedro, CA 1965. Accident 29Sep68: crashed into sea and sank off Santa Catalina Island during ferry flight. Pilot killed and body not recovered. Aircraft listed by NTSB as "destroyed" and cancelled from USCAR 21Oct68.

B-128   Built for US Navy as **JRF-5**, BuAer serial **87734**. Acc and del NAS New York 30May45; Pool NAS South Weymouth Jun45; to storage NAS South Weymouth Jan46 until at least Aug48; records missing; in storage NAF Philadelphia by Jan50; NAS Quonset Point 01May51 for modernisation; NAF Annapolis 15Aug51. To NAS Quonset Point 18Jun53 for intended overhaul but to storage 31Mar55 and surplus awaiting disposal 11Aug55. Retired 11Aug56 and SOC at Quonset Point 23Nov56 (TFH:549hrs). Auctioned by US Navy and bought by Beldex Corp, St Louis, MO for $25,669.10. CofR for **N89U** issued 20Dec56. CF-HBC allotted to Hudson's Bay Co 03Mar61; authority to ferry Pompano Beach, FL to Winnipeg, MB 06Mar61; BoS Beldex to Hudson's Bay Co 10Mar61; US CofA for export E-45547 issued 10Mar61. CofR(P) 26261 as **G-21A, CF-HBC** issued to Hudson's Bay Co, Winnipeg, MB 22Mar61 and CofA 9218 issued 27Mar61. Cancelled from USCAR 18Apr61. CofA renewed at TFH:884hrs, valid until 28May63; at TFH:2,152hrs, valid until 09Apr69; at TFH:2,959hrs, valid until 24Apr74. Accident at 1700hrs on 14Jun73: ground looped while taxiing at Winnipeg, MB after a flight from Gods River, MB, due to unfavourable wind conditions. Substantially damaged but no injury to pilot (Alva R Snyder) or 3 pax. Accident at 1305hrs on 17Aug73: substantial damage again when ground looped while landing at Winnipeg, MB after a flight from Moosonee, ON. Applied brakes to attempt a quick turn off but left brake failed. No injury to pilot (Alva R Snyder) or 2 pax. Inspected and CofA renewed at TFH:3,114hrs, valid until 24Apr75. BoS Hudson's Bay Co to Arthur J Howser 26Apr74 for $112,000. Cancelled from CCAR 07Jun74 and CofR for **N88007** to Arthur J Howser, West Linn, OR 12Jun74. BoS to Peyton Hawes, Portland, OR 20Jan75 with CofR 20Feb75. CofA 28Oct77. BoS to McKinnon Coach Inc, Sandy, OR 15Jun78. BoS to Overtrade Inc, Salem, OR 16Jun78, with CofR 18Jly78. BoS to Air Pac Inc, Dutch Harbour, AK 10Mar80 with CofR 15Apr80. BoS to Amphibian Sales Inc, Miami, FL 04Jan90 with CofR 07Mar90. Regd **N6DF**, 05Mar91. BoS to Roy W Mabee, Anchorage, AK 03Jly91, with CofR 25Jly91. Stored Chino, CA a/o Oct07. Address change to Ketchikan, AK. Current and airworthy May13, with CofR due to expire 31Dec14.

Above: *C/n B-128, CF-HBC, of the Hudson Bay Company, at Vancouver, British Columbia, in May 1962, where B.N.P. Airways staff fitted new wing floats and repainted the aircraft.* *(Ingvar Klett)*

Below: *C/n B-129, C-FNIF, remained in yellow Trans Provincial colours when the company became part of Air BC. It is seen here at Vancouver, British Columbia, in July 1981.* *(Gary Vincent)*

B-129   Built for US Navy as **JRF-5**, BuAer serial **87735**. Acc 09Jun45 and del 12Jun45; Pool NAS South Weymouth Jun45. To storage NAS South Weymouth Jan46 until at least Aug48; records missing; in storage MCAS Cherry Point by Jan50; ready for issue 25Jun51 but undergoing repair 28Jun51; NAS Quonset Point 17Jly51 for modernisation and ready for issue 31Dec51. Awaiting final disposition at Quonset Point 25Jan52, retired 22Dec52 and SOC 07Apr53 in flyable condition to a non-Navy user (TFH:36hrs). [The US Navy record would appear to have been a retrospective adjustment – see also B-110 84815/N103 and B-133 87739/N102] Regd as **G-21A, N101** to CAA, Washington, DC in 1951 for use in Alaskan Region. Reregd **N121** 10Jun57. Tfd to FAA, Washington, DC 01Jan59. Reregd **N5096K** to Griffco Aviation, Seattle, WA 31May60. BoS to Pacific Western Airlines 13Apr61 and allotted CF-NIF same day. US CofA for export E.46084 and CofA 7685 both issued 17May61 at TFH:1,345hrs. N5096K cancelled from USCAR 17Jun61. CofR(C) 26663 issued for **CF-NIF** to Pacific Western Airlines Ltd, Vancouver, BC 19May61; inspected and CofA renewed at TFH:1,793hrs, valid until 16May63. Accident at 0005hrs on 27Sep62: after a flight from Fort Smith, NT, both engines failed due to fuel starvation, aircraft landed on soft ground, near Edmonton, AB, slid onto solid ground and overturned (pilot: Daryle Brown). Inspected and CofA renewed at TFH:2,137hrs, valid until 03Apr64. Accident at 2345hrs on 09May63: left engine failed circa 4 miles inland over Brodeur Peninsula, 20 miles West of Arctic Bay, en route to Spence Bay. Height could not be maintained on one engine and a return to Arctic Bay was made where a wheels-up landing was made on the ice. Authority to ferry Arctic Bay to Edmonton, AB 14May63; inspected and CofA renewed at TFH:2,491hrs, valid until 03Apr65; at TFH:4,954hrs, valid until 06Jun69. Tfd by BoS to P. W. Northern Services Ltd (nominal change) 25Jly68. BoS to Trans Provincial Air Carriers Ltd, Prince Rupert, BC 31Jly68. CofR(P) 45425 issued wrongly to P. W. Northern 02Aug68 and CofR(C) 45434 issued to Trans Provincial Airlines Ltd (TPA), Terrace, BC 05Aug68. Inspected and CofA renewed at TFH:5,651hrs, valid until 06Jun70; at TFH:9,600hrs, valid until 02Aug75. CofR re-issued as **C-FNIF** 23May75. Became Air BC Ltd, Richmond, BC 31Oct80. Inspected and CofA renewed at TFH:16,852hrs, valid until 20Aug83. CofR(C) issued to Jim Pattison Industries Ltd 17May83, nominal change and still op in TPA c/s. Inspected and CofA renewed at TFH:19,520hrs, valid until 20Aug87. BoS Jim Pattison Industries to Air BC Ltd 31Dec86 and CofR(C) issued 11Feb87; authority to ferry Vancouver to Port Hardy, BC 17Jun87. BoS to Pacific Coastal Airlines 31Dec87 but leased back to Air BC same date for one year, later extended to 31Dec89. Air BC operated the Goose in the colours of Pacific Coastal and a CofR(C) for this was also issued 31Dec87. Inspected and CofA renewed at TFH:20,434hrs, valid until 20Aug89. BoS Pacific Coastal to Greyvest Financial Services Ltd 26Apr89 (sale included C-FUAZ, c/n 1077). Lease by Greyvest to Pacific Coastal 01May89 for 83months and CofR(C) issued 06Jun89. Inspected and CofA renewed at TFH:23,549hrs reported on Due Date 15Feb94. Accident at 1335hrs on 07Jun94: after landing at Port Hardy, BC, the left brake failed, the aircraft ground-looped and ran off the right side of the runway. The fuselage and wing were substantially damaged. BoS Greyvest to GE Capital Canada Leasing Services Inc 10Nov94. BoS to Pacific Coastal Airlines 21Nov94. BoS to Hallmark Leasing Corp (still damaged) dated 15Aug94 and CofR(P) issued 25Nov94. TFH:23,717hrs reported 15Feb95. Repair in progress reported 15Feb97 at TFH:23,790hrs. [Note: If the reported flying hour totals are correct it might suggest that after the Jun94 accident, the aircraft was repaired by Feb95 and then suffered another (un-reported) accident prior to Feb97.] Inspected after repair 14Jly97 at TFH:23,811hrs. BoS to Tuthill Corp, Hinsdale, IL 20May98 and cancelled from CCAR 21May98. Regd **N453T** 22May98. Reregd as **N21A** with CofA 02Jly98. Accident 17Jun02: while on approach to Runway 22 at Northway, AK, after a flight from Whitehorse, AK, pilot

reported he encountered a strong crosswind. After touchdown, during the landing roll, a gust of wind lifted the right wing and the aircraft veered to the left, left the runway and rolled down an embankment into a wooded area. Substantial damage but no injury to three on board. To Wave Runner Aviation LLC, Graham, NC (Antilles Seaplanes) 11Jan08. Accident 29Jan08: pilot, David E Hamrick, was practising water take-offs and landings near Marathon, FL, after departing the Florida Keys Marathon Airport about 1645hrs. At about 1723hrs EST, during a water landing, the left wing contacted the water and the aircraft water-looped. Pilot and passenger, mechanic Don May, rescued by a nearby boat and taken to hospital, Hamrick with a severed artery in his arm and May with a broken leg. Aircraft substantially damaged but was recovered and taken to Homestead, FL. To Amphib Inc, Lake Zurich, IL with CofR 30Jun08. To DB Aero Inc, Wilmington, DE with CofR 13Apr11. Current and airworthy May13, with CofR due to expire 30Apr14.

B-130   Built for US Navy as **JRF-5**, BuAer serial **87736**. Acc and del 13Jun45; Pool NAS South Weymouth Jun45. To storage NAS South Weymouth Jan46 until at least Aug48; records missing; in storage NAF Philadelphia by Jan50; NAS Quonset Point 30Apr51 for modernisation; 12th ND NAS Alameda 18Nov51; NAF Annapolis 13Apr53; NAS Quonset Point 10Jly53 for overhaul but awaiting final disposition 28Jly53 and SOC 30Sep53 (TFH:473hrs). According to the Gateway of Flight Museum at Floyd Bennett Field the aircraft was used by New York City Police Aviation Unit "after the Second World War". Regd as **G-21A, N644** to US Dept of Interior, Bureau of Land Management, Anchorage, AK circa 1954, but certainly by 1958. Reregd **N644R** 23Mar76 with CofA same date. Del Anchorage-New York for the National Park Service Museum, Floyd Bennett Field, NY Feb97 and cancelled from USCAR 28Jly98. Repainted in 2004 as NY Police Dept aircraft.

B-131   Built for US Navy as **JRF-5**, BuAer serial **87737**. Acc 16Jun45 and del 18Jun45; Pool NAS South Weymouth Jun45. To storage NAS South Weymouth Jan46 until at least Aug48; records missing; in storage MCAS Cherry Point by Jan50; NAS Quonset Point 26Feb51 for modernisation; NAF Annapolis 31May51. To NAS Quonset Point 18May53 for overhaul, but awaiting final disposition 23Jly53 and SOC 30Sep53 (TFH:710hrs). Tfd to Dept of Interior, Washington, DC 1953, for ops in Alaska with Bureau of Land Management and regd as **N641**. Regd as **G-21A, N4772C** to Alaska Coastal Airlines, Juneau, AK 1953. To Alaska Coastal-Ellis Airlines, Juneau, AK 01Apr62; nominal change to Alaska Coastal Airlines Inc Jun66; TFH:12,094hrs a/o 05Feb68; merged into Alaska Airlines Inc, Seattle, WA Dec67. Accident 26Nov70: substantial damage when ground looped due to R/H brake seizure landing at Wrangell, AK, after a flight from Ketchikan. Pilot + 2 pax uninjured. To Antilles Air Boats, Christiansted, US Virgin Islands by 1978. Accident 21Feb78: crashed during forced landing in sea off St Croix, US Virgin Islands. Five killed, 1 crew uninjured. Cancelled from USCAR (date unknown).

B-132   Built for US Navy as **JRF-5**, BuAer serial **87738**. Acc and del 27Jun45; Pool NAS Quonset Point Jun45; Pool NAS South Weymouth Jly45. To storage NAS South Weymouth Jan46 until at least Aug48; records missing; in storage MCAS Cherry Point by Jan50 awaiting modification; NAS Quonset Point 05Feb51 for mods; NAF Annapolis 28May51. Minor damage at NAAS Webster Fld, VA 06Jly51 when aircraft departed the runway during landing roll (cockpit confusion when attempting to correct a minor problem caused aircraft to veer off runway); NAS Quonset Point 19Jan53 for overhaul. Identified for MDAP disposal 19May53; declared surplus 20May53 and SOC at Quonset Point for MDAP disposal to France 22Jly53 (TFH:595hrs). To France's Aéronautique Navale wearing abbreviated serial **738**; transit details unknown but by sea to Saigon, Vietnam and delivered to 8ème Escadrille de Servitude (8.S) at Cat Lai where accepted 10Feb54 and coded 8.S-11. Few specific service details known but slightly damaged by ground-fire 16Jun54; in use with 8.S until 1956 by when based at Tan Son Nhut. Withdrawn from Vietnam (Saigon, Tan Son Nhut) in May56 and shipped to France, details unknown but probably via Nouméa; arrival date in France unknown, but on 04Dec56 recorded as due for major check at Saint-Mandrier in 1957 and absent from 8.S operational records in Algeria in 1957; aircraft in work at Saint-Mandrier by Jly57 until at least 22Oct57 but there is also a reference to a ferry *to* Saint-Mandrier on 29Dec57. In operational use with 8.S at Algiers-Maison Blanche as 8.S-11 by 17Feb58. Transferred to Saint-Mandrier Sep58, but then noted as having suffered an accident on or by 07Nov58; accident was serious and airframe was heavily damaged resulting in it being SOC 26Jan59 at Saint-Mandrier. Authorised for cannibalisation 11Feb59.

B-133   Built for US Navy as **JRF-5**, BuAer serial **87739**. Acc 29Jun45 and del 02Jly45; Pool NAS South Weymouth Jly45. To storage NAS South Weymouth Jan46 until at least Aug48; records missing; in storage MCAS

Cherry Point by Jan50; NAS Quonset Point 02Jly51 for rework and ready for issue 22Jan52. Awaiting final disposition at Quonset Point 08Feb52, retired 22Dec52 and SOC 07Apr53 in flyable condition to a non-Navy user (TFH:54hrs). [The US Navy record would appear to have been a retrospective adjustment – see also B-110 84815/N103 and B-129 87735/N101]. Regd as **G-21A, N102** to CAA, Washington, DC in 1951 for use in Alaskan Region. Reregd **N122** 10Jun57. Transferred to FAA, Washington, DC 01Jan59, but reportedly written-off in Alaska at unknown date.

B-134   Built for US Navy as **JRF-5**, BuAer serial **87740** but diverted off contract for delivery from Grumman Aircraft Engineering Corp, Bethpage to Flugfelag Islands hf, Jly45. Del by sea and temporarily regd as **G-21A, TF-ISR**(1) for Flugfelag Islands hf, Reykjavik, Iceland 01Sep45; in service early Sep45, and officially regd 05Feb46. Accident 20Mar47: capsized landing at Nordfjordur, Iceland. No injuries but aircraft a total loss. Replaced by c/n B-62 (qv).

B-135   Built for US Navy as **JRF-5**, BuAer serial **87741**. Acc and del 18Jly45; BAR Bethpage Jly45; Pool BAR Bethpage Jan47 until at least Aug48; records missing; NavAirActSRC NAF Annapolis by Jan50 and administratively to NAF Annapolis 24Mar50. To NAS Quonset Point 05Sep50 for overhaul and declared surplus 14May51 and SOC for MDAP disposal to France 13Jly51 (TFH:1,201hrs). To France's Aéronautique Navale wearing abbreviated serial **741**; transit details unknown but by sea to Saigon, Vietnam and delivered to 8ème Escadrille de Servitude (8.S) at Cat Lai where accepted 17Mar52 and coded 8.S-9. Damaged in an accident at Soc Trang 11Sep52 and reported with 8.S awaiting repairs 15Sep52. Few specific service details known and perhaps in early storage but slightly damaged by small arms fire during support and evacuation operations in early 1954 when probably temporarily detached to Cat Bi. (Such incidents in the general area of Hanoi and Haiphong reported 08Apr54, 23Apr54, 03May54 and 16Jun54.) Damaged at Saigon, Tan Son Nhut 18Jun54 when undercarriage collapsed on landing; major repairs required lasting four months (TFH:1,608hrs at the time of the accident); life extended in major overhaul at Tan Son Nhut 09Feb55. During run-up to withdrawal from Indo-China decision taken to scrap aircraft locally but reconsidered and deemed serviceable for prolonged use (16Apr56); by now based at Tan Son Nhut. Withdrawn from Vietnam (Saigon, Tan Son Nhut) aboard the *La Fayette* May56; arrival date in France unknown but circa Jun56 and to Saint-Mandrier for 240-hour check before operational use with 8.S at Algiers-Maison Blanche; surveyed at Saint-Mandrier 15Oct56 and major overhaul under way by 01May57. By 22May57 in operational use with 8.S at Algiers-Maison Blanche as 8.S-9 and eventually returned to Saint-Mandrier for overhaul 12Nov57 (TFH: 2,767hrs). Under overhaul by 29Dec57 but structural damage discovered (so recorded 09May58); assumed not to have been repaired and SOC 25Aug59 due corrosion. Spares recovered as the airworthiness of the dwindling JRF-5 fleet became more difficult to maintain.

B-136   Built for US Navy as **JRF-5**, BuAer serial **87742**. Acc 27Jly45 and del NAS New York 30Jly45; VN8D5 NAF Annapolis Sep45 (minor repairs at NAS Willow Grove Oct45); NavAirActSRC NAF Annapolis Aug47; Pool NAS Norfolk Nov47; Pool BAR Bethpage May48 until at least Aug48; records missing; NavAirActSRC NAF Annapolis by Jan50 and administratively to NAF Annapolis 24Mar50. To NAS Quonset Point 05Sep50 for overhaul and declared surplus 14May51 and SOC for MDAP disposal to France 13Jly51 (TFH:996hrs). To France's Aéronautique Navale wearing abbreviated serial **742**; transit details unknown but by sea to Saigon, Vietnam and delivered to 8ème Escadrille de Servitude (8.S) at Cat Lai where accepted 17Mar52 and coded 8.S-10; few specific service details known and perhaps in early storage but slightly damaged by small arms fire during support and evacuation operations in early 1954 when probably temporarily detached to Haiphong. (Such incidents in northern Vietnam reported 15Mar54, 04Apr54 and 26Apr54.) Described as a reserve aircraft with 8S Sep54; by 19Jan56 in use as 8.S-10 on behalf of the SLS Indochine in the Saigon area by now based at Tan Son Nhut. Withdrawn from Vietnam (Saigon, Tan Son Nhut) in May56 and shipped to France, details unknown but probably via Nouméa; arrival date in France unknown but taken from storage at Saint-Mandrier 10Apr57. Photographic evidence shows that it served with 8.S at Algiers-Maison Blanche but specific details of operational service in Algeria unknown; transferred to 27 Flottille at Ouakam, Dakar, Sénégal as a reserve aircraft circa 1959. SOC at Saint-Mandrier 05Dec61 for spares recovery; some equipment recovered 19Dec61.

B-137   Built for US Navy as **JRF-5**, BuAer serial **87743**. Acc 30Jly45 and del NAS New York 31Jly45; Pool NAS Quonset Point Aug45; Pool NAS South Weymouth Dec45. To storage NAS South Weymouth Jan46 until at least Aug48; records missing; in storage NAF Philadelphia by

Jan50; NAS Quonset Point 01May51 for modernisation; 6th ND NAS Jacksonville 10Oct51; at NAS San Diego post May52 (circumstances unknown); NAF Annapolis 15Jly52. To NAS Quonset Point 11May53 for overhaul, but awaiting final disposition 23Jly53 and SOC 30Sep53 (TFH:338hrs). Letter from Dept of Navy 11Mar54 confirming transfer of 87743 to Dept of Interior for ops in Alaska. Cvtd to **G-21A** Apr54 with CofR **N642** to US Dept of Interior, Bureau of Land Management, Washington, DC 19Apr54 and CofA 29Apr54 at TFH:382hrs. Major overhaul by Long Beach Airmotive Inc, CA Mar55 with CofA 25Mar55 at TFH:656hrs; "Smoke-jumper" door installed Feb62 per STC SA1-439. Cvtd by McKinnon to **G-21C "Hybrid"**, c/n **1204**, with 2 UAC PT6A-20 engines with CofA 26Jly68 at TFH:5,746hrs. Transferrred to Office of Aircraft Services, State of Alaska, Anchorage with CofR 23Mar76. BoS Alaska Office of Aircraft Services to MA Inc, Oshkosh, WI 31Aug89 with CofR 06Feb90; extended dorsal fin installed 23Jun90 per STC SA4-681 and re-engined with PT6A-27s Nov91. Experimental CofA 24Nov92 at TFH:12,539hrs, to show compliance with FARs, after fitting of autopilot. Standard CofA 08Jan93. BoS to Vectored Solutions Inc, Everett, WA 26Mar10 with CofR 14Apr10. Current and airworthy May13, with CofR due to expire 30Apr14.

B-138   Built for US Navy as **JRF-5**, BuAer serial **87744**. Acc 31Jly45 and del 08Aug45; Pool NAS Quonset Point Aug45; Pool NAS South Weymouth Sep45; NAS Anacostia Oct45; NAS Quonset Point 01Jly46 and under repair Aug-Dec46; Pool NAS Quonset Point Jan47; Pool BAR Bethpage Apr47; NavAirActSRC NAF Annapolis Aug47. Damaged in terrestrial landing accident at NAS Patuxent River 28Jun48 after crew failed to ensure that undercarriage was down and locked (cat 'B' damage); Pool NAS Norfolk Jly48, presumably for repairs, and still there until at least Aug48; records missing; in overhaul Pool BAR Bethpage by Jan50; RD&DE NATC Patuxent River 18May50; NAS Quonset Point by May52 for overhaul. Declared surplus 12Aug52 for disposal in flying condition and SOC 13Oct52 (TFH:956hrs). Regd (probably as a JRF-5) **N779** to US Dept of Interior, Fish & Wildlife Service, Washington, DC Nov52, and ferried to Alaska, eventually gaining its CofA as **G-21A** (and in use as such with the Fish & Wildlife Service in May62). Wfs by FWS and reregd **N16484** 24Mar66 to Charles E Walters, Spokane, WA. Reregd as **N501M**, 05May66. Retractable wing-tip floats fitted 1967, using McKinnon kit No.33. Sold to McKinnon Enterprises Inc Sandy, OR 24Aug67. Cvtd to **G-21C Hybrid**, c/n **1203** with 2 UAC PT6A-20 engines by McKinnon, at TFH:3,928hrs 26Jun68. The registration N501M was cancelled from USCAR 02Feb68 (and transferred to G-44, c/n 1230). The G-21C was neither certified nor registered as such in the USA but sold directly to the Highways Dept, Government of BC, Canada 1968, with CofR(S) **CF-BCI** 03Apr69. Accident 24Jun71: substantial damage after overshooting landing at Victoria, BC; pilot seriously injured. CofR to Airwest Airlines, Vancouver, BC 19Jan73; CofR as **C-FBCI** to Airwest Operations Ltd 23Aug79. CofR(C) to Trans Provincial Airlines Ltd, Prince Rupert, BC in 1980. Accident 11Oct80: left brake failed and left main gear collapsed landing at Stewart, BC; (no injuries). CofA lapsed 02Aug81. CofR(C) to Air BC Ltd, Richmond, BC early 1981. CofR(C) to Jim Pattison Industries Ltd (owner of Air BC) 17May83. To Lindair Services Ltd, Richmond, BC Oct84 for major overhaul; engines replaced by PT6A-27 and (wrongly) re-designated **McKinnon G-21G** (see **Chapter 5**). Inspected Nov84 and CofA renewed valid until 02Nov85. CofR(P) to Crown Forest Industries Ltd, Richmond, BC 02Nov90. CofR(P) to Walsten Aircraft Parts & Leasing Ltd, Richmond, BC 26Jun91. Regd **N660PA** to Peninsular Airways Inc, Anchorage, AK 13Sep91 and cancelled from CCAR 18Sep91. Aircraft name: "*Spirit of Alaska*" and later "*Spirit of Akutan*". Accident 11Aug96: crashed near Dutch Harbor, AK during a flight from Anderson Bay. Aircraft "missing" with two presumed fatalities. TFH:13,381hrs. Part of main door and some smaller parts found washed up on a beach in spring 1998. Written off and cancelled from USCAR 10Jan98.

B-139   Built for US Navy as **JRF-5**, BuAer serial **87745**. Acc 14Aug45 and del NAS New York 05Oct45; Pool NAS Quonset Point Nov45. To storage NAS South Weymouth Feb46 until at least Aug48; records missing; in overhaul Pool BAR Bethpage by Jan50; NAS San Diego 04May50 awaiting issue; 17th ND NAS Kodiak 31May50; NAS San Diego 14May52 en route rework; NAS Quonset Point 16Jly52 for overhaul and modification to **JRF-6** (to JRF-6X 28Jly52 and JRF-6 28May53). To FASRON-102 NAS Norfolk 05Jun53 for sea freight to Oslo (but presumably via NAF Port Lyautey); Naval Attaché Oslo, Norway 26Jun53; FASRON-104 NAF Port Lyautey 20Jan54 ("inactive"); FASRON-102 NAS Norfolk 24May54 for repairs; NAS Quonset Point 13Sep54 for overhaul. To storage 31Mar55, retired 11Aug56 and SOC 23Nov56. For sale as JRF-6, Nov56, at TFH:581hrs. Condition described as "fair to poor. Both outboard wing panels and propellers available but not installed. Floats, ailerons, flaps, elevators and rudder missing….aircraft is

not considered flyable". BoS Nov56 US Navy to Pan Air Corp, New Orleans, LA for US$23,513:90 and CofR for **G-21A, N93E** 25Jan57. BoS to Comor Inc, New Orleans, LA 17Apr57 with CofR 30Apr57. Tfd back to Pan Air Corp, New Orleans, LA by BoS 24Jun63, with CofR 03Jly63. BoS to Williams Drilling Co, Baton Rouge, LA 27Nov63, with CofR 11Dec63. BoS to Pan Air Corp, New Orleans, LA 15Jun64. CF-WCP allotted to Great Bear Lake Lodge and authority to ferry New Orleans to Winnipeg, MB 15Jun64. BoS Pan Air to Great Bear Lake Lodge, Sioux Narrows, ON 17Jun64 for US$65,000. Lease from Great Bear Lake Lodge to Sioux Narrows Airways Ltd 20Jun64 until 10Sep64. US CofA for export E-40251 issued 21Jun64 at TFH:1,408hrs. CofR(P) 33785, for **CF-WCP**, issued 22Jun64 to Great Bear Lake Lodge Ltd and amended to Commercial 24Jun64. CofA 10032 issued 03Jly64 and N93E cancelled from USCAR 08Jly64. Inspected and CofA renewed at TFH:1,639hrs, valid until 20Jun66. Lease to Sioux Narrows Airways Ltd 15Jun65 until 10Sep65; inspected and CofA renewed at TFH:1,903hrs, valid until 20Jun67. BoS Great Bear Lake Lodge to Plummer Holdings Ltd, Winnipeg, MB 13Jun66 with CofR 38272(C) same date. Leased by Plummer to Sioux Narrows Airways Ltd 15Jun66 until 01Oct66. BoS Plummer to Great Bear Lake Lodge Ltd, Winnipeg, MB 17May67 and leased to Sioux Narrows Airways Ltd 18May67 for one year; inspected and CofA renewed at TFH:2,202hrs, valid until 20Jun68; CofR(P) 39876 issued to Great Bear Lake Lodge Ltd 17Jun67. Leased to Sioux Narrows Airways Ltd 18May68 for one year; inspected and CofA renewed at TFH:2,445hrs, valid until 20Jun69; CofR(C) 41074 issued 03Jun68. Leased to Sioux Narrows Airways Ltd 09Jun69 for 5 years; inspected and CofA renewed at TFH:2,699hrs, valid until 15Jun70 and CofR(C) to Sioux Narrows Airways Ltd issued 16Jun69. BoS Great Bear Lake Lodge to Plummer Holdings Ltd 02Jun70 and CofA renewed at TFH:2,837hrs, valid until 15Jun71. BoS to Ilford Riverton Airways Ltd, Winnipeg, MB 03Jun70 with CofR(C) 04Jun70; CofA renewed at TFH:4,060hrs, valid until 15Jun73. BoS to Dean H Franklin Aviation, Miami, FL 13Oct72 for US$72,500. Cancelled from CCAR 02Jan73 and regd **N90892** 06Feb73 but CF-WCP re-allotted 18Jan73 and cancelled from USCAR 09Mar73. CofA issued 13Mar73 at TFH:4,241hrs and CofR(C) issued to Island Airlines Ltd, Campbell River, BC as **C-FWCP** 14Mar73; CofA renewed at TFH:4,723hrs, valid until 11Mar75; at TFH:5,412hrs, valid until 11Mar79. Cancelled from CCAR 14Jly78. BoS to Catalina Airlines Inc, Gardena, CA 14Jly78 with CofA 17Jly78 at TFH:5,454hrs and CofR for **N22932** 25Jly78. Accident 17Sep79: crashed into sea off Pebbly Beach, East of Avalon, CA, when elevator cable separated from the yoke during take-off from Pebbly Beach; one fatality, but aircraft salvaged and sold to KC Aircraft Sheetmetal Inc, Long Beach, CA 12Mar81 with CofR 20Jly81. BoS to Air Transport Services Inc, Kodiak, AK 30Apr82, with CofR 21Jly82. BoS to Peninsular Airways Inc, Anchorage, AK 30Jan86 with CofR 17Sep86. Accident 07Jan93: badly damaged when wing dragged on water landing at Akutan, AK (eight uninjured) at TFH:12,054hrs. Major overhaul May95. Non-fatal crash at Dutch Harbour, AK 15Apr98. Aircraft name: "*Spirit of Unalaska*". Accident at 1715hrs on 04Apr04: PenAir's scheduled Flight 325 departed Akutan, AK at 1645hrs en route VFR to Unalaska. The landing was made in a near direct crosswind of 7 knots gusting to 14knots, causing the aircraft to ground loop to the right, and the left undercarriage collapsed; two pilots + 7 pax uninjured, but aircraft substantially damaged. TFH:16,220hrs. In for rebuild at Victoria Air Maintenance, Sidney, BC Aug/Oct04. Re-named "*The Spirit of Akutan II*". After PenAir ceased Goose operations to Akutan in Oct12, the aircraft was sold to Freshwater Adventures Inc, Dillingham, AK with CofR 30Jan13. Current and airworthy May13, with CofR due to expire 31Jan16.

B-140   Built for US Navy as **JRF-5**, BuAer serial **87746**. Acc 31Aug45 and del 11Sep45, but immediately released for transfer to Andian National Corporation Ltd, Toronto, Canada; USCofA for export E-9165 issued 01Oct45 and tfd to Andian National Corporation, Cartagena, Colombia 29Nov45 (via the RFC and approved by the Munitions Assignment Board). Regd in Colombia as **C-151**. Cancelled 23Oct47 and reregd **C-1530** until reregd **HK-1530E** 01Jan49. HK-1530E cancelled 07Feb55. BoS Andian to Bebco Inc, New Orleans, LA 21Mar55 with CofR for **N1530H** Apr55 and CofA 30Apr55 at TFH:5,887hrs and 14Mar56 at TFH:6,268hrs. BoS to Comor Inc, New Orleans, LA 06Jly56; Experimental CofA 07Mar62, at TFH:8,070hrs, for "modified extended wing tip, wing float and aileron configuration". Another Eexperimental CofA 12Jly62, at TFH:8,073hrs, "to test retractable wing floats". BoS to Pan-Air Corp, New Orleans, LA 24Jun63 with CofR 05Jly63. CofA issued 24Oct63 at TFH:8,091hrs; Experimental CofA 02Jun65 at TFH:8,779hrs and CofA 04Jun65 at TFH:8,783hrs. Reported operated by Katmai Air, Katmai National Park, AK, date unknown. BoS Pan Air to Peninsular Airways Inc, King Salmon, AK 04May81 with CofR 12Jun81. BoS to Yute Air Alaska Inc, Dillingham, AK Jly86 with CofR 21Jly86. BoS to Phillip L Bingman, Anchorage, AK 05Oct89 with CofR 08Dec89. Accident at 1600hrs on

13Aug93: aircraft collided with river bank during take-off from Togiak River, AK, for a flight to Dillingham, AK. Non-fatal, but half the left wing and the nose (as far back to the rudder pedals) were torn off. TFH:18,204hrs. BoS to Richard Probert, dba Aero Technology, Long Beach, CA 06Jun94 with CofR 23Jly94. CofR **N931RP** issued 10Jan97 but ntu and cancelled 15Oct99 (and tfd to Beech Duke ex JA5260). **N329**(2) reserved 15Oct99 and CofR issued 22Nov99. Seen under rebuild/restoration at Long Beach, CA, in 2000. Richard Probert was killed in a road accident in 2007, but restoration of the Goose was continued by Auggie Swanson at Warbird Connection in Chino, CA. To Charles F & Judith A Nichols Trustee, Baldwin Park, CA, dba Yanks Air Museum, Chino, CA, with CofR 20Jan10. Seen parked outside museum hangar, unpainted. Current and airworthy May13, with CofR due to expire 30Sep13.

B-141   Built for US Navy as **JRF-5**, BuAer serial **87747**. Acc 31Aug45 and del 11Sep45, but immediately released and returned to Grumman Aircraft Engineering Corp 11Sep45 for conversion to **G-21A**. BoS US Navy to Humble Oil & Refining Co, Houston, TX 06Sep45 for $79,243, with CofA and CofR for **NC41996** 01Nov45. BoS to Standard Oil Co (New Jersey), New York, NY 24Jun46 with CofR 29Jly46 and CofA same date at TFH:354hrs. BoS to Esso Shipping Co, (same address) New York, NY 29Dec49 with CofR 05Jan50. Operated from Corta, Colombia by the Andian National Corporation Ltd. Later as **N41996**; authorisation to ferry Cartagena, Colombia to Miami, FL 25Feb53 for airworthiness inspection at Aero Trades Inc, Ronkonkoma, NY. BoS Esso to Freeport Sulphur Co, New Orleans, LA 18Mar53 with CofR 23Mar53. CofA 14May53 at TFH:4,237hrs after o/h. CofA 05May54 at TFH:4,815hrs. Re-regd with CofR for **N200S** issued 13Jan56. Re-regd with CofR for **N2003** issued 08Oct59 and N200S tfd to Mallard J-27. BoS to Amphibian Parts Inc, Miami, FL 03May60 for $35,000 with CofR 14Jun60. BoS to Dean H Franklin, Miami, FL 29Nov65 with CofR 09Dec65. BoS to Antilles Air Boats (AAB), Christiansted, St Croix, US Virgin Islands 18Oct66 with CofR 19Dec66. Damaged making heavy landing "in West Indies" 13Aug68. Tfd to Resorts International 21Mar79. Wfu 1979 at St Croix-Hamilton A/P. AAB ceased ops Jly81. N2003 revoked by FAA 21May82. BoS AAB to Dean H Franklin Enterprises Inc, Fort Lauderdale, FL 01Oct83 with CofR N2003 20Mar92 (sic), but stored derelict at St Croix, US Virgin Islands. Crated and shipped to Germany for European Coastal Airlines 1999. CofR N2003 suspended in 2002. In open storage, dismantled, all silver at Landsberied, Bavaria a/o Oct06; parts reported being used in restoration of c/n 1145. Last reported still at Landsberied Aug11. CofR expired 31Mar11 and cancelled from USCAR 22Aug12.

B-142   Built for US Navy as **JRF-5**, BuAer serial **87748**. Acc 01Oct45 and del NAS New York 18Oct45; NAS Richmond Nov45; NAS Key West Dec45; ComAirLant NAS Norfolk 26Jun46; Pool NAS Norfolk Aug46; FASRON-102 NAS Norfolk Sep46 for repair. To Joint US-Brazilian Mission, Rio de Janeiro 25Oct46; NAS Trinidad Jly47. Damaged when undercarriage collapsed on landing at Waller Fld, Trinidad 26Aug47. To Pool FASRON-102 NAS Norfolk Dec47; Pool NAS Norfolk Feb48 until at least Aug48; records missing; NAS Argentia by Jan50; FASRON-102 NAS Norfolk 17May50 awaiting issue; NAF Annapolis 30Jun50; NAS Quonset Point 16May51 for overhaul; FASRON-102 NAS Norfolk 13Feb52 for sea-freighting; FASRON-104 NAF Port Lyautey 02Apr52; awaiting modifications at Port Lyautey 26Jun53; FASRON-102 NAS Norfolk 29Sep53 undergoing repairs; NAS Quonset Point 18May54 for overhaul. To SF Litchfield Park 06Jly54 for storage. Loaned to NACA, Langley Fld, VA 24Feb55. SOC by US Navy 27Mar57 (TFH:1,502hrs); remained with NACA initially as '**103**' and then '**202**' until 23Mar60 when sold. Regd as **G-21A, N704** to US Dept of Interior, Fish & Wildlife Service, Washington, DC by Nov62; (this is likely to be at least the second use of N704 although details of previous use are unknown). Reregd **N7041** 04Apr66 and cancelled from USCAR 06Oct66. To BC Airlines Ltd, Vancouver, BC as **CF-VAK** 15May67. CofR(P) 43734 and CofA 12536 to Pacific Leasing Corp Ltd, Vancouver, BC, 11Aug67. CofR(C) to Trans Provincial Airlines Ltd, Terrace, BC 02May69. CofR(C) to Victoria Flying Services Ltd, Sidney, BC 01Nov76. CofA lapsed 28Oct77. Seen in bare metal at Viking Air, Victoria, BC Mar80, and reported to be re-built by Viking Air, BC Nov80. Sale reported 27May82. Cancelled from CCAR on sale to USA 31May93. Regn **N9074N** reserved for Ross Enterprises, Incline Village, NV 07Aug95, but ntu. To Michael T Warn, Milwaukee, OR 17Apr98. To North Coast Aero LLC, Port Townsend, WA 27Apr99. To Charles Greenhill, Lake Zurich, IL in 2005. To Ruth Sanders, Jackson, CA with CofR 06Dec06. Under restoration, dismantled, at Lone Eagles Nest, CA in 2007. Address change to Sutter Creek, CA. Current, but not airworthy May13, with CofR due to expire 30Apr16.

B-143   Built for US Navy as **JRF-5**, BuAer serial **87749**. Acc 29Oct45 and del 05Nov45. To Naval Attaché to Sweden, Stockholm Dec45 (in

delivery Dec-Feb46) until 31Aug48; subsequent location unreported until SOC 30Nov48. Strike code indicative of routine 'obsolete and surplus' disposal status but 'cat III' suggests damage. No known subsequent history.

B-144   Built for US Navy as **JRF-5**, BuAer serial **87750**. Acc 30Oct45 and del NAS New York 02Nov45. To storage NAS South Weymouth Mar46 until at least Aug48; records missing; in storage MCAS Cherry Point by Jan50; NAS Quonset Point 25Jan51 for modernisation; NAF Annapolis 11Jun51; NAS Quonset Point 13Feb53 for overhaul and modification to **JRF-6** (to JRF-6X 14Feb53 and JRF-6 11Aug53). To BAR Buffalo, NY 20Aug53 (assumed to be associated with Bell Aircraft activity). To SF Litchfield Park 28Mar55 for storage, retired 30Aug55 and SOC 02Apr56 (TFH:731hrs). Regd as **G-21A, N720** to US Dept of Interior, Fish & Wildlife Service, Washington, DC. Accident 30Aug58 (25Aug also reported): crashed in Brooks Range, AK. Three fatalities, including pilot Clarence Rhode, Fish & Wildlife Service Director. Remains of aircraft not found until 1979.

B-145   Built for US Navy as **JRF-5**, BuAer serial **87751**. Acc 31Oct45 and del NAS New York 18Dec45. To storage NAS South Weymouth Mar46 until at least Aug48; records missing; in storage NAF Philadelphia by Jan50; NAS Quonset Point 01May51 for modernisation; NAF Annapolis 10Oct51. To NAS Quonset Point 11May53 for overhaul, but awaiting final disposition 23Jly53 and SOC 30Sep53 (TFH:338hrs). Transferred to Department of Interior, Washington, DC 1953 for ops in Alaska. Cvtd to **G-21A** and **N643** allocated but ntu? Reregd as **N643H** to Fleet Air Transport Inc, Anchorage, AK by Apr60. To Foreign & Domestic Enterprises, Seattle, WA by Apr66. To Griffco Aviation, Seattle, WA by Apr66. Allotted CF-UMG 01Apr66. US CofA for export E-67197 issued 28Apr66. CofR(C) 36714 and CofA 10999 issued for **CF-UMG** to Pacific Western Airlines Ltd, Vancouver, BC 03May66 at TFH:1,849hrs and cancelled from USCAR 08Jun66. Inspected and CofA renewed at TFH:3,126hrs, valid until 27Apr69. BoS to P. W. Northern Services Ltd, Vancouver, BC 25Jly68 and CofR(P) 45426 issued 02Aug68. BoS 31Jly68 to Trans Provincial Air Carriers, who then changed their name to Trans Provincial Airlines (TPA), Terrace, BC and CofR(C) 45435 issued to them 05Aug68. Inspected and CofA renewed at TFH:5,658hrs, valid until 17Jun72. Accident 22Sep71: on a flight from Stewart, BC to Terrace, BC, diverted to Kitsumkalum Lake, BC due to inadequate forward visibility at Terrace Airport due to atmospheric smoke. Landed on lake at 1250hrs in glassy water conditions and collided with an unknown object during run-out. When water seen entering cabin from forward floor area, passengers panicked and commenced leaving aircraft by door. Pilot unaware of situation until the third passenger left. Pilot beached aircraft and attempted to rescue passengers. Substantial damage but no injuries. Inspected and CofA renewed at TFH:6,030hrs, valid until 21Mar73. Accident at 1600hrs on 31Aug80: left main gear failed (due to damage caused by previous hard landings) on landing at Stewart, BC, after a flight from Prince Rupert. Five uninjured. Nominal change to Air BC Ltd, Richmond, BC 16Jan81 as **C-FUMG**. Inspected and CofA renewed at TFH:15,271hrs, valid until 13Sep83. Accident 11Dec82: after take-off from Prince Rupert, BC for a flight to Kitsault, BC, the right main wheel failed to retract. On returning and attempting to lower the gear, the left main failed to extend. Landed at 1215hrs on the runway with one wheel up and one wheel down. CofR(C) to Jim Pattison Industries Ltd, Richmond, BC 17May83, nominal change and still op in TPA c/s; inspected and CofA renewed at TFH:18,778hrs, valid until 13Sep87. CofR(C) to Trans Provincial Airlines Ltd, Prince Rupert, BC 02Jun88. TFH:19,204hrs reported on Due Date 13Sep89. Accident at 1445hrs on 05Mar90: after landing at Masset, BC, after a flight from Prince Rupert, BC, the aircraft was taxied through the channel towards the harbour and struck navigational lights with the right wing. TFH:22,115hrs reported on Due Date 15Oct92. Coopers & Lybrand appointed as Receiver for TPA Ltd 19Mar93. To Hallmark Leasing Corp, Vancouver, BC 12May93; leased to Waglisla Air, Richmond, BC 23Jun93 (until 30Jun96). CofR to Waglisla Air Inc, Richmond, BC 08Sep93. Accident 04Dec93: struck trees after take-off at 1225pm on a scheduled flight to Kincolith and crashed 10km North of Prince Rupert, BC due to engine problems. Pilot and 1 passenger killed, 3 injured. To Pacific Aircraft Salvage, Vancouver, BC 1994 and wreck stored at Vancouver A/P 1995. Aircraft written off and cancelled from CCAR 04Dec95. Note: the accident report suggests (from the lat/long co-ordinates) that the crash was south of Prince Rupert, but this cannot now be checked because the file was destroyed in 2005. Remains reported in Discount Aircraft Salvage junk yard in Deer Park, WA. Bought from there by Antilles Seaplanes LLC (together with c/n 1054) and now stored in Gibsonville, NC (see **Chapter 9**).

B-146 – B-156 BuAer 87752 – 87762 were cancelled on VJ Day, 1945 and not built.

The second G-44, c/n 1202, NC28664, was delivered to Chas A Munn on 27th February 1941. Acquired by the USAAF in 1942, as OA-14 with serial 42-38218, it was destroyed in a landing accident at American Falls, Idaho on 11th September 1944. *(Jennifer Gradidge Collection)*

APPENDIX 2:
G-44 PRODUCTION LIST

In the following production list, all Bills of Sale to a new owner are from the previous noted owner, unless otherwise stated, although some ownerships have been repeated to aid clarity. Certificate of Registration validity data for aircraft on the US Civil Aircraft Register is correct to May 2013.

Canadian Certificates of Registration were issued with suffixes denoting whether for Private (P) or Commercial (C) use.

Throughout the list, Canadian Airworthiness can be assumed to be continuous, unless otherwise stated. Airworthiness Certificates are only shown as renewed before and after either changes of ownership or accidents, and also to show total flying hours (TFH).

1201   Built as **XG-44** in 1940 and regd as a **G-44**, **NX28633** to Grumman Aircraft Engineering Corp, Bethpage, NY. First flew 28Jun40. Reregd **NC28633** on issue of Type Certificate No.734 on 05Apr41. Still regd to Grumman on 1947 USCAR. Reported crashed, but no details. Fate unknown.

1202   Built as **G-44** and regd **NC28664** to Chas A Munn, Amado, FL 27Feb41. Acquired by the USAAF and formally accepted 06Jly42. Designated as **OA-14** and allocated serial **42-38218**. With USAAF at Miami from at least 06Jly42 until at least 09Jan43; Stewart (West Point Academy) 29May43; to 2002nd BU Stewart circa spring 1944 and suffered Cat.3 damage in landing accident at West Point, NY 09Jly44; 265th BU, Pocatello 19Jly44; destroyed in Cat.5 fatal landing accident at American Falls Reservoir, American Falls, ID 11Sep44 when on strength of 265th BU. [Registration **NC5623V** has been reported for this Widgeon, but it was actually assigned to G-21A, c/n B-78, which became McKinnon G-21C, c/n **1202**.]

1203   Built as **G-44** and regd **NC28665** to R Livingston Sullivan, Radnor, PA Mar41. Acquired by USAAF and formally accepted 15Mar42. Designated as **OA-14** and allocated serial **42-43460**. Bolling Field

15Mar42; Fairfield Air Depot 25Apr42; Chicago, IL Jun42; Elmendorf 17Jly42 (11th Air Force assigned to 77th BS, 28th Comp Grp); destroyed in a Cat.5 fatal landing accident 21 miles east of Portage, AK 29Oct42 when on strength of 77th BS. SOC 24Nov42 at Elmendorf.

1204   Built as **G-44** and regd **NC28666** to George F Baker 3rd, New York, NY Apr41. Acquired by USAAF and formally accepted 20May42. Designated as **OA-14** and allocated serial **42-38355**. West Palm Beach, FL (Morrison Fld) 20May42 (ACFC); 320th HQ&ABS, Stewart (West Point Academy) 16Feb43; Cat.3 damage in landing accident at Stewart Fld 24Jun43 (when with 320th HQ&ABS) and repaired; 2124th BU Laguna Madre 13Aug44; 2123rd BU Harlingen 15Aug44 (Laguna Madre, TX was a Harlingen auxiliary field); 2117th BU Buckingham 23Sep44 and crash-landed six miles west of Lake Trafford, FL 28Feb45 suffering Cat.4 damage. Reclamation completed 04Apr45.

1205   Built as **G-44** and regd **NC777** to Archbold Expeditions, New York, NY Apr41. Acquired by USAAF and formally accepted 14Mar42. Designated as **OA-14** and allocated serial **42-38340**. Bolling Field 14Mar42; Guatemala (presumably Air Attaché, Guatemala City) 21May42; Bolling 21Aug42; Fairfield Air Depot (Patterson Fld) 25Aug42;

Great Falls 22Oct42; Ladd 29Nov42 (assigned 11th Air Force); Elmendorf 05Jly43; transferred to RFC at Adak, AK 08Aug45. Regd as **G-44, NC61900** to RF Thomas, Niles, MI by Jly46 and on 1947 USCAR. To **N61900** Gay Airways Inc, Anchorage, AK by Mar56. Cancelled from USCAR 13Nov63 but fate unknown.

1206 Built as **G-44**. BoS Grumman Aircraft Engineering Corp to Edwards Transportation Co, Houston, TX, 18Apr41, with CofR **NC28667** and CofA same date. BoS Edwards Transportation to Defense Supplies Corp, Washington, DC 12Feb42 with CofR 19Mar42. Acquired by USAAF and formally accepted 11Apr42 (covered by BoS Defense Supplies to War Dept, Washington DC dated 19Jun42. CofR cancelled 30Jun42). Designated **OA-14** and allocated the serial **42-38223**. Hensley 11Apr42 (ACFC); Drew 04Dec42; Columbia 15Mar43 where involved in a Cat.4 landing accident at Lake Murray, SC 23Mar43; condemned 12Apr43 but transferred to the Warner Robins Air Depot (via Cochran, GA 15Jun43); Warner Robins, GA 16Apr43 for repair; to Lake Charles date unknown and by Oct44 with the 332nd BU Lake Charles; ferried from Lake Charles to 215th BU, Pueblo 05Oct44; transferred to the RFC, location not stated, 17Aug45. BoS RFC to Hickory Spinners, Hickory, NC 18Aug45 with CofR **NC52742** 11Sep45. Acft disassembled and rebuilt by Grumman Aircraft Engineering Corp as **G-44**, with new log book and CofA 23Oct45. BoS Hickory Spinners to Hickory Spinners Inc, Hickory, NC 11Jun46 with CofR 18Jun46. Sensenich wooden props removed 13Aug47 and replaced with Koppers Aeromatic props at TFH:550hrs. Accident 15Aug48: "washout", and CofR cancelled 03Jun49. BoS Hickory to Link Aeronautical Corp, Binghampton, NY 03Jun49 with CofR 23Jun49; address change to Endicott, NY with CofR **N52742**. Cvtd to **Super Widgeon** with 270hp Lycoming GO-480-B1D engines May58 at TFH:700hrs; hull bottom modified to G-44A profile, STCs SA4-60, 4-61, 4-63 also applied and CofA issued 12May58. BoS to Matthew Thomas Windhausen, dba Adirondack Seaplane Service, Eagle Bay, NY 29Sep60. **N160W** reserved 16Mar61 with CofR 11May61. BoS to Harry H Webb, Shelburne, VT 12Apr63 with CofR 07May63; address change to c/o Win Air Service Inc, Hancock A/P, Syracuse, NY 21May63. BoS Estate of HH Webb to Gordon J Newell, Utica, NY 11Jun75 with CofR 09Oct75 at a New Hartford, NY address. BoS to Harold W Mansur, Fairbanks, AK 28Sep77 with CofR 15Nov77. BoS to GG Leasing Co, Anchorage, AK 15Jun79, with CofR 17Jly79. BoS GG Leasing to K Gene Zerkel, GS Patterson and GG Leasing Inc, dba Zap Airways Inc, Anchorage, AK 16Dec81 with CofR 10May82. BoS to Alaska Aircraft Sales Inc, Anchorage, AK 22May85 with CofR 20Jun85. **N7GZ** reserved 02Jly85 and placed on acft 16Aug85. **N6647K** issued 17Jan91, placed on acft 12Apr91 and CofR 13May91. BoS to Gee Bee Inc, Anchorage, AK 30Jun91, with CofR 31Jly91. BoS to Alaska Acft Sales Inc, Anchorage, AK 27Nov91 with CofR 24Dec91. BoS to Thomas E McGuire, Anchorage, AK 17Jun92 with CofR 24Aug92. BoS Estate of McGuire to John S Shackelford Jr, Roanoke, TX, 29Dec94 with CofR 10Mar95. Current and airworthy May13, with CofR due to expire 31Oct16.

1207 Built as **G-44** and regd **NC28668** to J White, dba Westchester Airplane Sales Co, New York, NY Apr41. Acquired by USAAF and formally accepted 14Mar42. Designated **OA-14** and allocated the serial **42-38216**. Bolling 14Mar42; Eglin 04Sep42; Bolling 15Sep42; Eglin 10Oct42; Stewart (West Point Academy) 16Jan43 and with 320th BH&ABS at Stewart by May43; to Foster and with 2539th BU Foster circa mid-1944 (dates unreadable) and SOC there in 1944 in unknown circumstances.

1208 Built as **G-44** and regd **NC28669** to Charles S Collar, Nassau, Bahamas, dba Bahamas Airways, 30Apr41. Purchased, date uncertain, by the Corps of Engineers and used at Borinquen Field, PR; purchased by the AAF from the Corps of Engineers Nov44, designated **OA-14** and assigned serial **44-52997**. Used by 6th AF (apparently still at Borinquen Fld in Mar45) and acquired artwork and name '*The Stud Duck*'; condemned and salvaged as obsolete in Caribbean theatre 27Aug46 (presumably at Borinquen Fld); made airworthy and ferried to Oakland MAP, CA where present in Jan48 intact (less the port propeller) and in full military markings. CofA as **G-44** 03Jun56, and regd **N1250N** to FK Brunton, Bellevue, WA probably in 1956, but certainly by Aug62. Sale reported 1975. To James J Campbell, Morton, WA by 1981. To Carroll J Campbell, Toomsuba, MS with CofR 31May92; address change to Wasilla, AK, but CofR expired 31Mar11, fate unknown.

1209 Built 06May41 as **G-44** and regd **NC28670** to F Dupont, Easton, MD May41. Acquired by USAAF and formally accepted 15Mar42. Designated **OA-14** and allocated the serial **42-38356**. To Bolling 15Mar42; assigned Ferry Command 27Mar42 at Presque Isle (and further assigned to the North Atlantic Wing 01May43); to Morrison (West Palm Beach and assigned to Caribbean Division, ATC) 21Aug43; reassigned to 1103rd BU Morrison 1944 and destroyed in a Cat.5 landing accident at Lake Worth Air Sea Rescue Unit, FL 04Sep44. Surveyed 29Nov44 and reclamation process formally completed 19Oct45.

1210 Built as **G-44**. BoS Grumman Aircraft Engineering Corp to Thomas C Eastman, Hicksville, NY, 08May41 with CofA and CofR **NC28671** same date. BoS to Jack & Heintz Inc, Bedford, OH 15Feb44 with CofR 05May44; Experimental CofA 06Jun45 for flight-testing an experimental auto-pilot and regd **NX28671**. Experimental CofA issued again 24Jan46 for more test flights by Grover Tyler, Chief Test Pilot, followed by a Standard CofA 15Aug46. BoS Jack & Heintz Precision Industries Inc to Henry A Canning, Cleveland, OH 07Jan47 for $10,000. CofR **N28671** issued 18Mar47. BoS to Collins Bros Inc, Mechanicville, NY 02Jun48 for $9,000, and CofR issued 18Jun48. BoS to Indamer Corp, New York, NY 05Nov51 with CofR 16Nov51; vented step installed Apr52. BoS to Vaughn Monroe Productions Inc, Boston, MA 11Jly52 with CofR 30Jly52; CofA 31Oct52 at TFH:1,945hrs. BoS to Georgia Longini, Barrington, IL 29May53 with CofR 09Jly53. BoS to S Stanley Griffin, West Palm Beach, FL 12May55 with CofR 26May55. BoS to Amphibian Parts Inc, Miami, FL 09Dec58 with CofR 11Feb59. Cvtd to Continental I0-470-D power Oct62 and Experimental CofA issued 05Nov62 for R&D; re-issued 06Feb63 and 18Jly63; cvtd to IO-470-E with Hartzell HC-82XF-2B props per STC SA81SO, with CofA dated 17Jan64 at TFH:2,812hrs. BoS to ABC Service, Miami, FL 27Apr64 with CofR 14May64. Reregd **N132X** 11Jun64. BoS to Manley Bros, Chesterton, IN 07Jly66 with CofR 09Aug66. Accident 31Jly66: acft "destroyed" after stalling after a bounced downwind landing at Kendallville Municipal A/P, IN. Pilot + 4 pax seriously injured. Returned to ABC Service/FW Cuttrelle on BoS 10Oct66 and CofR issued 15Nov66. BoS (undated, but possibly Dec69) Cuttrelle to Thompson Flying Service Inc, Jackson, WY. CofR applied for 09Dec69 and issued 11Feb70. CofR revoked by FAA 22Oct76, but re-issued to Richard V Peck, King Salmon, AK 20Jan77 after aircraft transferred to him on BoS dated 12Oct74. After Richard V Peck died, title to the aircraft was transferred by BoS from Rulon V Peck (Administrator of his estate) to "Westholm Aviation, Joseph or Janet Lodato", Gardnerville, NV 13Mar78. BoS Joseph S Lodato to Widgeon Quest Inc, Reno, NV 01Oct97. BoS (undated) to Executive Dogs Inc, Wilmington, DE with CofR 20Jly05. **N254Q** issued 29Aug05, placed on aircraft 22Sep05 and CofR issued 15Nov05. Major overhaul and rebuild by Mirabella Aviation Sep-Dec05 (Forms 337 show TFH:2,812hrs, cf 17Jan64 above!); 23-gallon auxiliary fuel tanks installed in each wing Dec05. Ownership was granted to Mirabella Aviation Inc, Fort Pierce, FL 08Mar07, after a court case against Executive Dogs Inc, Good Marketing Inc and Marvin Good individually. Offered for sale by auction, with Continental IO-520 engines, Apr07 at TFH:2,812hrs. Sold by the St Lucie County Court to Wolfenden Enterprise Inc 26Apr07. BoS to James Randall Baird, Naples, FL 07May07 with CofR 19Jly07. Cleveland wheels and brakes installed 12Nov07 per STC SA121EA, still quoting TFH:2,812hrs. McCauley props installed Apr09 per STC 00893CH. Current and airworthy May13, with CofR due to expire 30Apr15.

1211 Built 08May41 as **G-44** and regd **NC28672** to Gannett Publishing Co Inc, Portland, ME May41. Acquired by USAAF and formally accepted 14Mar42. Designated **OA-14** and allocated serial **42-38285**. Bolling 14Mar42; Hamilton 04Sep42 and to Class 26 (ground instructional use) at Hamilton 09Nov43.

1212 Built as **G-44** and regd **NC28673** to Edward O McDonnell, New York, NY May41. Reported scrapped but still on USCAR 1945/46/47. The aircraft's appearance at RAF Kasfareet, Egypt circa 25May42 has never been fully explained but it is widely assumed that the aircraft was acquired by or gifted to the British American Ambulance Corps while remaining on the USCAR until 1947. It would then have been presented to the RAF (as happened with other aircraft). There is photographic evidence of what is presumably this aircraft being packed for overseas shipping by Dade Brothers of NY. It can be seen to be wearing the titles '*British American Ambulance Corps*' and '*The Cape Codder*'. Its RAF career in Africa saw it at 107 MU, Kasfareet from 25May42 but subsequent movements, probably in West Africa, are unknown until reported with a detachment of 1314 Flight (Accra, Gold Coast) at Waterloo, Sierra Leone in 1945 – still marked as NC28673. Vaguely reported as wfu in 1945, its fate is unknown. The reason for its operation by the RAF wearing a civil registration is also unclear but it may well be that it did have a RAF serial, albeit unknown, allocated by 206 Group, RAF Middle East, Cairo. [A spurious RAF serial 'MV989' has been linked to this aircraft but is clearly incorrect. The true serial, assuming that it received one, is likely to be one of the unidentified aircraft in the range HK820 to HK999, allocated to 206 Group for their use in September 1941.]

1213 Built as **G-44** and regd **NC28674** to Grumman Aircraft Engineering Corp. BoS to Hayes Aircraft Accessories Corp, New York, NY 24May41 with CofA and CofR same date; nominal change to Seyah Corp with CofR 17Aug42; BoS Seyah to F William Zelcer (same address) 22Oct42 with CofR 11Jan43; used by Civil Air Patrol. BoS to Republic Aviation Corp, Farmingdale, NY 18Aug43 with CofR 19Aug43. BoS to Allan Tool & Manufacturing Division, Wolab Corp, Columbus, OH 01Sep44 with CofR 08Nov44. BoS to John W Galbreath, Columbus, OH 28Jan46 with CofR 17Jun46. BoS to Ohio Aviation Co, Vandalia, OH 25Sep50. BoS to Union National Bank, Lowell, MA 21Mar51. BoS to Merrimac Aircraft Inc, Dracut, MA 21Mar51 with CofR 11Apr51; used by Reebal Flying Service Inc, Dracut, MA. BoS to Peirce Bros Oil Service Inc, Waltham, MA 17Jly51 with CofR 17Aug51; CofA 26May52 at TFH:2,956hrs. BoS to EF Spicer, Stockbridge, MA 21May53 with CofA 13Jun53 at TFH:3,202hrs and CofR 07Jly53. BoS to Link Aeronautical Corp, Endicott, NY 11Jly55 with CofR 08Aug55. Cvtd to **Super Widgeon** with Lycoming GO-480-B1B by Link Aeronautical Corp, Endicott, NY 23Feb56 and CofA 17Jly56 at TFH:3,475hrs. CF-WHT allotted to Terry Machinery 20Aug56; authority to ferry Endicott, NY to Montreal. QC 21Aug56; US CofA for export E-27344 and CofA 4986 both issued 05Sep56. BoS Link Aeronautical Corp to Lund Aviation (Canada) Ltd, Montreal, QC 05Sep56 [The Canadian file has 10Sep56]. BoS to Terry Machinery Co, St Laurent, QC, 13Sep56 with CofR(P) 17052 as **CF-WHT**. Traded for G-44A, c/n 1473 on BoS to James C Welsch, Garden City, Long Island, NY 01Aug57 and cancelled from CCAR 17Sep57. Tfd by BoS to Welsch-Ayer Inc, New York, NY 22Jly57 (sic) and reregd **N5560A** with CofA 28Aug57 at TFH:4,087hrs and CofR 23Oct57. BoS to Trans-Aire Corp, New Orleans, LA 12Feb58 with CofR 06Mar58 Reregd **N199TA** with CofR 23Jun60. BoS to Little Rock Airmotive, Little Rock, AR 25Aug64. Reregd **N199T** with CofR 15Dec70; Experimental CofA 03Feb71 after major overhaul and CofA 10Feb71 at TFH:4,732hrs. BoS to Arkansas Aviation Sales Inc, Little Rock, AR 20Feb71. BoS to Two Jacks Inc, Arlington, TN 01Dec71. BoS to Walter Fuller Aircraft Sales Inc, Richardson, TX 07Jun72 with CofR 21Jun72. BoS to Western Aircraft Leasing Co, Claymont, DE 26Feb74 with CofR same date. Accident at 0930hrs on 27Jly74: ground-looped and gear collapsed on landing at Norwood, MA after a flight from Louisville, KY via Wilkes Barre, PA; pilot + 2 pax uninjured but aircraft substantially damaged. BoS to Harold Averbuck, Newton, MA Aug74 with CofR 23Aug74. BoS to James L and Janice O Faiks, Anchorage, AK 09Aug75 with CofR 29Aug75. BoS to Noel Merrill Wien, Anchorage, AK 03Oct75 with CofR 31Oct75. BoS to Fred R Richards, Anchorage, AK 10Mar76 with CofR 26Mar76. BoS to Fanda Corp, Homer, AK Apr77. BoS to Neal & Co Inc, Homer, AK 08Apr81 with CofR 20Jly81. BoS to Popsie Fish Co, Homer, AK 20Jly89 with CofR 05Oct89. To Alaska USA Federal Credit Union, Anchorage, AK with CofR 25May10. To Michael U Harder, Dillingham, AK with CofR 28Oct10. Current and airworthy May13, with CofR due to expire 31Oct13.

1214 Built as **G-44**. BoS Grumman Aircraft Engineering Corp to Pan American Airways Inc, New York, NY 28May41, with CofA and CofR **NC28675** same date. Conversion work for dual control instrument and flight trainer carried out by Aero Trades, Mineola, NY and Pan Am, La Guardia, completed 09Aug41 and approved 27Sep41. Purchased by the US Navy in 1942 for operations by the NATS under contract to Pan American at New York. Aircraft designated **J4F-2** and, circa early 1945, retrospectively allocated one of three BuAer serials, **99074, 99075** or **99076** (their subsequent recorded USN histories are identical but without previous identification details) which, by definition, is unlikely to have been worn at any time. US Navy records incomplete but with Pan American Atlantic Division by Aug44 until Jun45; transferred to Pan American Airways Jun45 and sold to them on Disposition contract NOA(s)7525 dated 31Aug45, and SOC by US Navy same date. Certificate of Ownership 19Dec45. Restored as **NC28675** to Pan American Airways Inc, New York, NY. BoS to Wallace C Siple, Montreal, QC 21Jan47. BoS to Hunter C Moody, Decatur, IL 21Jan47 with CofR 04Mar47. BoS to Decatur Aviation Co, Decatur, IL 24Jly47 with CofR 05Aug47. BoS to Mid-Hudson Flying Service Inc, Kingston, NY 02Aug47 with CofR 30Dec47. BoS to SA Richards, Burlington, VT 22Jun49 with CofR 18Jly49 as **N28675**. BoS to Samuel C Johnson, Racine, WI 25May50 with CofR 29Jun50. Tfd by BoS to Johnson Air Interests Inc, Racine, WI 07Dec51 with CofR 02Jan52; CofA 02May52 at TFH:3,350hrs. BoS to Vest Aircraft & Finance Co, Denver, CO 10Jan53. BoS to Fred O Lindsley Jr, Montclair, NJ 19Mar53; hull modified and step vent installed, major overhaul and repaint, with CofA 08Jly53 at TFH:820hrs (sic) there is no apparent reason for this change in aircraft flying time (compared with the previous year). BoS to LE Farley Inc, Houston, TX 25Feb54 with CofR 05Apr54; CofA 21Sep55 at TFH:1,329hrs. BoS to GH McNew, South Miami, FL 11Jan56 with CofR 03Feb56. BoS to Comor Inc, New Orleans, LA 26Dec56 with CofR 29Mar57. BoS to Frank W Cuttrelle, Miami, FL

06Feb58 with CofR for **N78Z** 28Feb58. BoS to ABC Services, Miami, FL 07Dec61 with CofR 23Jan62. BoS to Louis Demola, Red Bank, NJ 15Jun66, but not carried out and BoS ABC to Seaplane Service Inc, Opa Locka, FL 03May68 with CofR 09Sep68. BoS to Marshall I Yaker, El Paso, TX 17May84 with CofR 08Jun84. BoS to Robert J Iozia, Ruidoso, NM 24Mar87 with CofR 09Apr87. BoS to Lisa and Dorothy Krajcirik, Glenn, CA 09Jun87. BoS to Ian A Wayman, Sebastopol, CA 20Jan92 with CofR 04Jun92; address change to Thornton, CO 30Apr97 and to Peyton, CO 07Jan00. Stored at Pacific Coast Air Museum, Sontoma County A/P, Santa Rosa, CA. BoS Wayman to Lake Air Inc, Fort Lauderdale, FL 14Jun00 with CofR 27Jly00. BoS to Aviation Service Center Inc, Fort Lauderdale, FL 23Aug00. BoS to Executive Dogs Inc, Wilmington, DE 03May02. BoS to Patrick Michael Sturges, Hollywood, FL 07Jun02, with CofR 18Nov02. Current and airworthy May13, with CofR due to expire 30Nov15.

1215 Built as **G-44**. BoS Grumman Aircraft Engineering Corp to Pan American Airways Inc, New York, NY 06Jun41 with CofA and CofR **NC28676** same date. Conversion work, for dual control instrument and flight trainer, carried out by Aero Trades, Mineola, NY and Pan Am, La Guardia, completed Nov41. Purchased by the US Navy in 1942 for operations by the NATS under contract to Pan American at New York. Aircraft designated **J4F-2** and, circa early 1945, retrospectively allocated one of three BuAer serials, **99074, 99075** or **99076** (their subsequent recorded US Navy histories are identical but without previous identification details) which, by definition, is unlikely to have been worn at any time. US Navy records incomplete but with Pan American Atlantic Division by Aug44 until Jun45; transferred to Pan American Airways Jun45 and sold to them on Disposition Contract NOA(s)/525 dated 31Aug45, and SOC by US Navy same date. All auxiliary controls/equipment removed 17Dec45. Certificate of Ownership (Pan Am) 19Dec45. Restored as **NC28676** to Pan American Airways Inc, New York, NY. BoS to Elmer O Beardsley, Lilliwaup, WA 17Dec45 with CofR 18Mar46 and CofA 03May46 at TFH:4,043hrs. Later as **N28676**. BoS to Alaska Airlines Inc, Everett, WA 06Mar52 (sic) but BoS Alaska A/L to United Airmotive Inc, Anchorage, AK 23Jun51 with CofR 31Mar52. CofA 15Jly53 at TFH:5,020hrs. BoS United Airmotive to Herman L Martin, Walla Walla, WA 24Nov53 with CofR 30Dec53. CofA 28Feb61 at TFH:5,046hrs. BoS to Kodiak Airways Inc, Kodiak, AK 01Jun61 with CofR 17Jly61. CofA 27Dec62 at TFH:6,215hrs; 22Jan64 at TFH:6,810hrs. Survived the 1964 earthquake and tidal wave because Bob Leonard flew it from the seaplane base to the Kodiak Municipal strip before the wave arrived. Accident 02May69: substantially damage by forced landing when both engines failed on scheduled flight Larsen Bay – Kodiak. Unable to extend landing gear so landing was attempted at Kodiak NAS, seriously injuring the pilot. Cancelled from USCAR as "destroyed" 22Jun70. Re-built with Continental IO-470-E engines and restored as **N28676** in 1974. Reregd **N85U** 06Sep74 to Kodiak Western Alaska Airlines, Kodiak, AK. Crashed and sank in Kodiak Channel 1976. Cancelled again as "destroyed" 18Jly77 but re-instated 15Aug78. BoS to Green Valley Aviation Inc, Everett, WA Oct78. BoS to Amphibian Sales Inc, Miami, FL Oct78 with CofR 19Oct78. Reregd **N37DF** and CofR issued 13Dec80. BoS to Dudley Beek, Miami, FL 16Jly82. BoS to Albert C Harris, North Miami Beach, FL 15May86 with CofR 06Aug86. BoS to Miami Avionics Corp, Opa Locka, FL 12Mar90 with CofR 26Mar90. BoS to Island Flying Boats Inc, Opa Locka, FL 14Oct92. BoS to South Florida Aviation Investments Inc, Opa Locka, FL Mar93. BoS to World Jet Inc, Fort Lauderdale, FL Sep96 with CofR 05Nov96. BoS to Floridays Inc, Wilmington, DE, 05Dec97 with CofR 05Feb98. **N144SL** reserved 09Feb98 but ntu and cancelled 14Oct05. Hull bottom modified to G-44A lines 18Jun98, as per Grumman Report No.1709. An FAA 337 dated 20Mar99 documents installation of Hartzell HC-C2YF-2CUF/8468-3 propellers on the Teledyne Continental IO-550-E engines which had been fitted at an earlier (unrecorded) date under the Gander Aircraft Corp STC SA81SO. (N144SL listed as reserved again 09Sep09 and 24Sep10 by Brian Van Wagnen, Jackson, MI.) Still regd **N37DF** to Floridays Inc, May13, with CofR due to expire 31Dec13 and listed as airworthy with Ranger 6-440 series engines!

1216 Built 12Jun41 as **G-44** and regd **NC28677** to Country Club Flying Services Inc, Hicksville, NY. To Gillies Aviation, Hicksville, NY, Jun41. Believed to have been briefly loaned to the Royal Canadian Air Force for evaluation by No.12 (Communications) Squadron, Rockcliffe, ON while continuing to wear US civil registration NC28677. To Grumman Aircraft Engineering Corp, Bethpage, NY 1945. To Allen Tool & Manufacturing Division, Wolab Corp, Columbus, OH, with CofR 02Oct45. Cancelled from USCAR 13Jly48, reason unknown.

1217 Built as **G-44** and regd **NC28678** to Hickok Manufacturing, Rochester, NY Jun41. Not on USCAR 1945. Fate unknown.

G-44, c/n 1218, N3103Q, at Luqa, Malta, in February 1987 shortly before it was shipped to the England for an intended rebuild. It was not rebuilt in the UK and was sold to the Musée de l'Hydraviation in Biscarosse, France. Rebuilt with parts from c/n 1341, it is now displayed at the museum, as 'NC28679'. *(via Tom Singfield)*

1218 Built Jun41 as **G-44** and regd **NC28679** to GK Vanderbilt, New York, NY Jun41. Acquired by USAAF and formally accepted 20May42. Designated **OA-14** and allocated the serial **42-38217**. Morrison (West Palm Beach and eventually assigned to Caribbean Division, ATC) 20May42; Bahamas 07May43; Stewart (West Point Academy) 30Jun43 and with 320th BH&ABS when involved in Cat.3 damage landing accident at Stewart 21Jly43; to Foster (Matagorda Peninsula) date unknown and suffered Cat.3 damage in take-off accident Matagorda Island 22Dec43 while on strength of 857th SEFTS (based at Matagorda/Foster); 2541st BU Matagorda Island by 03Feb45 when transferred to 2539th BU, Foster; 571st BU Greensboro 09Apr45; 4020th BU Wright-Patterson 23Apr45; 571st BU Greensboro 30Apr45; 503rd BU Gravelly Point (Washington National Apt) 05May45 and to RFC same date. Regd as **G-44, NC58337** to Airtronics Development Corp, Dayton, OH 1945 and still on USCAR 1947 and later as **N58337**. To Rogers Construction Co, Portland, OR by Jun63. Reregd **N3103Q** to International Aviation Development Corp, Reno, NV, 1966. Acft name "*Arax*". Operated by Libyan Aviation Co (LAVCO), Malta, and based in Nigeria from Oct66. To ATC Inc, Reno, NV 1972, operated by ARAX Airlines, Nigeria and del ex Malta 1971. Stored Hal Far, Malta Apr77 (no regn). Under rebuild at Safi, Malta a/o 1982 and reported under repair at Luqa, Malta Sep83. Arr Felixstowe, Suffolk, UK by ship ex Malta 17Apr87 and by road to Ipswich, UK for rebuild 29Apr87. (N750M, c/n 1341 also imported for spares. Also included in the shipment were 2 sets of wings, 2 zero-hour engines, 4 props and 5 floats). Cancelled from USCAR 14Nov88 and regd **G-DUCK** to LE Usher, Ipswich, Suffolk, UK, 15Nov88. Sold incomplete to the Musée de l'Hydraviation, Biscarosse, France along with the remains of c/n 1341. Crated to Biscarosse ex Ipswich Oct92 and cancelled from UKCAR 24Mar93. One Widgeon has been assembled from the two and is now displayed at the museum. (The author noted an unmarked/unpainted Widgeon at Biscarosse Jun95 while another (or the same?) Widgeon was reported under restoration at St Agnant airfield, Rochefort in Apr97). Noted displayed at Biscarosse with Lycomings and 3-bladed props as "NC28679" in 2005 and still there in Aug12.

1219 Built 09Jly41 as **G-44** and regd **NC28680** to Winship Nunnally, Atlanta, GA, Jly41. Acquired by USAAF and formally accepted 12May42. Designated **OA-14** and allocated the serial **42-53003**. Bolling 12May42; assigned to 6th AF in Caribbean and to Trinidad (assumed to have been Waller Field) 21May42; Aruba 10Oct42; Curaçao 31Jly43 where used by 309th Services Grp and 24th Services Grp in 1943, precise dates uncertain. Condemned and SOC 30Apr45 by 6th AF, presumably following an earlier incident. Location not specified, Aruba implied. [Replaced for Nunnally by c/n 1418 (qv).]

1220 Built as **G-44** and regd **NC28681** to Garfield Wood, Detroit, MI, Aug41. To Katharine Gibbs Schools Inc, New York, NY by 01Aug46. Later regd as **N28681**. Converted to Lycoming power (installer unknown) prior to 1961, by which time it was reregd **N148M** to Binghampton Container Co, Binghampton, NY. Accident 08Sep64: substantially damaged when crashed on take-off from Terney Lake, Canada. Pilot + 4 pax minor injuries. To Peninsula Airways, King Salmon, AK by 1968. Accident 15Dec68: attempted take-off from a lagoon at low tide at Sanak Island, AK but failed to maintain flying speed. Hit a rock and the bank. Pilot + one pax seriously injured and 2 others injured. Aircraft destroyed and cancelled from USCAR 23Jun70.

G-44, c/n 1220, a Lycoming-powered Widgeon, registered N28681, of the Binghampton Container Company, at Ottawa, Ontario circa 1961. The aircraft later served with Peninsula Airways out of King Salmon, Alaska, but was destroyed in a crash on 15th December 1968. *(KM Molson)*

1221 Built Aug41 as **G-44** and regd **NC28682** to The Superior Oil Co, Houston, TX, Aug41 and still on USCAR 1947 (a circa 1947 photograph shows the aircraft wearing a prominent US Army Air Force 'star and bar' on the fuselage as well as registration NC28682 and Superior Oil logo). Reregd **N456**, probably with The Pure Oil Co. To **N45S** with Sea Service Inc, New Orleans, LA by 1962. To J Ray MacDermott, New Orleans, LA 1966. To HB Fowler & Co, Harvey, LA 1972. Tfd to MacDermott (Nigeria) Ltd, Ikeja, Nigeria as **5N-AMC**, Sep74. Written off at Warri, Nigeria, 29Nov76. N45S cancelled from USCAR Mar86.

1222 Built for US Coast Guard as **J4F-1**, serial **V197**. Del to USCG Jly41 and with CGAS Salem by Dec41 until at least Feb43; SOC Jan44 following what is assumed to have been a non-fatal crash.

1223 Built for US Coast Guard as **J4F-1**, serial **V198** Del to USCG Jly41 and with CGAS Brooklyn by Dec41 until at least Feb43; CGAS Biloxi by 10Jly44 when slightly damaged in landing accident at Biloxi Auxiliary Strip; left landing gear collapsed on touch-down but pilot took off immediately; landing gear was safely locked down during subsequent flight and aircraft made a safe landing on grass at Keesler Fld. MS; CGAS Biloxi by mid-1946; SOC Nov46 as surplus but no details known of any subsequent use.

1224 Built for US Coast Guard as **J4F-1**, serial **V199**. Del to USCG Aug41 and with CGAS Elizabeth City by Dec41; SOC Dec41 following what is assumed to have been a non-fatal crash.

1225 Built for US Coast Guard as **J4F-1**, serial **V200**. Del to USCG Aug41 and with CGAS St Petersburg by Dec41 until at least Feb43; no known subsequent service records, no records of a strike date and no known subsequent commercial history. Assumed to have been withdrawn and scrapped by USCG, date unknown.

1226 Built for US Coast Guard as **J4F-1**, serial **V201**. Del to USCG Aug41 and with CGAS San Francisco by Oct41 until at least Feb43. SOC and sold surplus and regd as **G-44, NC69082**, to Early J Moore, Belmont, CA Aug47. Fate unknown.

1227 Built for US Coast Guard 25Aug41, as **J4F-1**, serial **V202**. Del to USCG Aug41 and with CGAS Biloxi by Dec41 until at least mid-1946 (detached to Houma circa Jly42); SOC as surplus by Nov46. Regd as **G-44, NC68361**, to Wm F Pike, dba West Coast Aircraft Ltd, Los Angeles, CA Nov46. Cancelled 07Mar58. Reregd **N95Z** ? Fate unknown.

J4F-1, c/n 1226, serial V201, of the US Coast Guard, poses in the California sunshine in the early-1940s. It was sold surplus in 1947, but its subsequent history is unknown. *(William T Larkins)*

1228   Built for US Coast Guard as **J4F-1**, serial **V203**. Del to USCG Aug41 and with CGAS Port Angeles by Dec41 until at least Jan45 (off strength by Dec45); SOC as surplus by Nov46. BoS War Assets Administration to Sam W Canady, Lexington, NC 17Feb47 for $5,000. Cvtd to G-44 standard with CofA 06Sep47 at TFH:1,823hrs noting "aircraft last flown 29Jan47". The FAA file does not contain a CofR but the BoS dated 23May50 from Canady to Walter G Clark Co, Charleston, WV quotes **G-44, N1340V**. BoS 24May50 to Lambros Seaplane Base, Ridgefield Park, NJ. N1340V cancelled from USCAR 31May50, but restored as N1340V, 11Dec53; application by Lambros is undated, but CofR issued 15Jan54, with CofA 28May64. BoS to Noel M Wien, Anchorage, AK 07Oct82 with CofR 07Dec82. A great deal of overhaul and repair work was done during 1988 including the installation of dual modified Cessna 310Q control yokes. Address change to Kent, WA with CofR 21Dec88. Transferred by BoS to Noel M Wien & Barbara M Wien, Kent, WA 20Mar92 with CofR 17Apr92; address change to Eastsound, WA 16Apr98; transferred by BoS to Kurt M Wien, Stratham, NH 01Jly00 with CofR 26Jly00; address change to West Ossipee, NH with CofR 02May02. BoS to Garry Applebaum, Hopkins, MN 17 Sep02 with CofR 31Oct02, and later at Kenosha, WI. BoS to Claire Aviation, Wilmington, DE 04Dec06, with CofR 11May07 which expired 30Sep11. CofR re-issued to Claire Aviation 06Aug12. Current and airworthy May13, with CofR to expire 31Aug15.

1229   Built for US Coast Guard as **J4F-1**, serial **V204**. Del to USCG Aug41 and with CGAS Traverse City by Dec41; CGAS San Diego by Nov42. Damaged at San Diego 10May44 when aircraft became prematurely airborne during water take-off. Aircraft became airborne after catching the swell of a passing motor boat and, with inadequate flying speed, fell back on the water before becoming airborne a second time. With insufficient time to climb to safe height over a populated area the pilot elected to make a fully stalled water landing during which the left wing dropped, tearing off the wing-tip float. The right wing subsequently struck the mast of a small sloop. Damage was described as minor albeit categorised as 'C'. With no known further service details and no known subsequent civilian history it is possible that this proved to be a terminal accident.

1230   Built as **G-44** and regd **NC1700** to Roger Wolf Kahn, New York, NY Sep41. Acquired by USAAF and formally accepted 14Mar42. Designated **OA-14** and allocated the serial **42-38219**. Bolling 14Mar42; France Fld, Panama 21May42 (with visits to the Panama Air Depot); Bolling Jly42; Panama Air Depot Jly42; Albrook Fld Sep42; Panama Air Depot Oct42; Peru (presumably at Lima) Nov42; Panama Air Depot Nov42; Stewart (West Point) 14Jan43; to Tyndall, FL date unknown and with 2135th BU by 01Mar45. To RFC from 2135th BU Tyndall 03Apr45 and formally SOC 06Apr45. Regd as **G-44, NC54096** to Nathanial A Kalt, Dallas, TX 1945. To Johnson & Johnson, New Brunswick, NJ by Aug46. To Guest Enterprises Inc, New York, NY by 1947. To CJ Fisher, Presque Isle, ME by 1948. CofR(C) 22 and CofA Val.8 to Newfoundland Airways Ltd, as **VO-ABU**, 17Nov48. Newfoundland joined Canada 31Mar49 and aircraft reregd **CF-GPJ**, with CofR(C) 7989 and CofA 3084 both issued 12May49. BoS Newfoundland A/W to Associated Air Taxi 27Aug49 for $13,500; CofR 8224 issued to Associated Air Taxi Ltd, Vancouver, BC 31Aug49. Accident at 0900hrs on 26Dec49 near Goat Island, Ganges Harbour, Saltspring Island, BC: while taxiing to take-off position aircraft ran over a submerged reef and punctured hull. The aircraft was run up onto the reef so that it would not sink and at low tide the hull was patched and the aircraft floated off on 27Dec49 (pilot: JD Hannay). Inspected and CofA renewed at TFH:1,569hrs, valid until 12May51. Accident at 1255hrs on 30Aug52: after a flight from Esperanza, BC the aircraft was decelerating after landing in the inner harbour at Tahsis, BC when it hit a submerged "vertical deadhead". Authority to ferry Vancouver, BC - Patricia Bay, BC 03Dec53; CofA renewed, valid until 18Jan55 and 17Jan56. Accident at 1500hrs on 15Mar55: while being operated by the BC Dept of Public Works, student pilot made a hard landing resulting in severe porpoising (pilot: H Layton Bray, with student GF Gilbert, on locals at Patricia Bay, BC). CofR(S) 15022 to BC Government, Dept of Public Works, Sidney, BC, 27Jan55. Re-engined with Lycoming GO-480-C1D6, inspected and CofA renewed at TFH:4,025hrs, valid until 08Feb58. CofR(S) 16929 to BC Government, Dept of Highways, Victoria, BC, 11Jly57; inspected and CofA renewed at TFH:7,071hrs, valid until 23Jun67; BoS Her Majesty the Queen, in Right of the Province of British Columbia to McKinnon Enerprises, Sandy, OR 30Sep67 in exchange for Goose, c/n B-138, N501M. Cancelled from CCAR 18Mar68 and regd as **N501M**, 02Apr68. Cvtd to **Super Widgeon** with Lycoming GO-480-B1D engines, with CofA 13May68 at TFH:7,142hrs. BoS to Arthur C Stifel III, Miami Beach, FL 28Sep71 with CofR 14Dec71. BoS to Aeromar Inc, Miami Beach, FL (same address) 06Aug73. Reregd **N5AS** 18Jun74. Experimental CofA 17Jly74

G-44 Super Widgeon, c/n 1230, N1AS, the former USAAF OA-14, of Aeromar Inc, is seen here at Opa Locka, Florida in March 1983. The miniscule marks are just visible on the silver square on the tailfin.

(Nigel P Chalcraft)

at TFH:7,437hrs for VFR ops from Tamiami Airport with Lycoming GO-480-G2D6 with reversing props. Experimental CofA 19Feb75 at TFH:7,447hrs for VFR ops from Opa Locka Airport and Standard CofA issued 14May75 at TFH:7,475hrs. Reregd **N1AS** 11Aug75 (N1AS was on Cessna 414 and was exchanged with N5AS from the G-44). CofA 21Jan77 at TFH:7,674hrs. BoS Aeromar to Assets Protected – Trustee, Salt Lake City, UT 07Nov94. BoS Trustee to Aeromar 8 Inc, 12Jly96. BoS to Aero Holdings, Salt Lake City, UT 13Jly96. BoS to Gladen E Hamilton, Vashon, WA, 13Jly96 with CofR 25Jly96. BoS to Safe Flight Instrument Corp, White Plains, NY 20Feb98 with CofR 09May98. Accident 12May98: substantial damage after wheels-up landing at Cleveland, OH. Rebuilt by Ace Aviation Inc, San Rafael, CA. BoS to Beacon West LLC, c/o Robert G Williams, Coeur D'Alene, ID 17Oct01 with CofR 12Feb02. Address change to Hayden Lake, ID. Current and airworthy May13, with CofR due to expire 31Dec13.

1231   Built as **G-44** and regd **NC37181** to Grumman Aircraft Engineering Corp 1941. BoS to Chas W Deeds, Hartford, CT 22Sep41 with CofA and CofR **NC1055** same date. BoS to Chandler-Evans Corp, South Meriden, CT 02Feb42 with CofR 08Apr42. BoS to American Export Airlines Inc (AEA), New York, NY 24Aug42 with CofR 29Sep42; sold on by AEA to the US Government 25Aug42. Allocated BuAer identity **09789** (although the serial allocation dates from circa Feb42 and may therefore have anticipated future US Navy ownership); pre-Aug44 US Navy records missing but served with AEA, New York under NATS contract, notionally as a **J4F-2**, from at least Feb44 until transferred to NAS Glynco 07Feb45 (a CoA issued to AEA 27Sep44 showing TFH:1,981hrs refers to this aircraft only as c/n 1231 NC1055); NAS Seattle Oct45 for reconditioning and SOC at Seattle 31May46 as obsolete. BoS War Assets Administration to Rex Dyer, Compton, CA 09Dec46 for $7,500, (this BoS identifies c/n 1231 as 09789, the former NC1055). CofR **NC68335** issued 13Mar47, (but still shown on published 1947 USCAR as NC1055 with American Export Air Lines Inc, New York, NY). BoS Dyer to Lee Mansdorf, Los Angeles, CA 09Mar48 with CofR 18Mar48 and later as **N68335**. BoS to Bob Hall's Air Service, Kodiak, AK 25Jan51 with CofR 01Feb51. CofA 09May52 at TFH:2,815hrs. BoS to Kodiak Airways Inc, Kodiak, AK 20Jan53 with CofR 09Feb53. CofA 10Apr53 at TFH:3,312hrs; 25Jan54 at TFH:3,687hrs. Permission to operate at 5,200lbs gross wef 24Feb55; CofA 07Mar55 at TFH:4,307hrs; 24Nov62 at TFH:8,797hrs. Aircraft substantially damaged and pilot + 3 pax with minor injuries when gear collapsed after undershoot at Karluk, AK 21Jan64. All usable parts salvaged but the hull remained, until removed many years later. Cancelled from USCAR 23Jun70. Remains sold by Kodiak A/W to Grant A Stephens, Kodiak, AK 07Jly81 with CofR **N6833W** 08Jly81; address change to Palmer, AK Feb04; aircraft being restored using parts from c/n 1442. To Timothy R Martin, Anchorage, AK with CofR 11Mar13. Currently a rebuild project May13, with CofR due to expire 31Mar16.

1232   Built as **G-44** and sold by Grumman Aircraft Engineering Corp to J Gordon Gibbs, Marion, MA 26Sep41 with CofA and CofR **NC37182** same date. BoS Gibbs (now at a Park Avenue, New York address) to Defense Supplies Corp, Washington, DC 18Feb42 with CofR 19Mar42. BoS to US War Department, Washington, DC and formally accepted by USAAF 09May42. Designated **OA-14** and allocated the serial **42-38221**. Bolling 09Mar42 (probably with 1st Photographic Group); assigned Panama 20May42; Ponce Fld, PR Jun42; Panama AD Jun42; Bolling Jly42; assigned Puerto Rico 25Jly42 (presumably at Ponce Fld); West Palm Beach Jly42; Puerto Rico Jly42; Ponce Fld Sep42; San Juan, PR Sep42 (and then regular moves within Puerto Rico until at least Mar43); Laredo 26May43; Bolling 07Jun43; Atlanta 13Aug43 where recorded as assigned to 1st Photo Charting Group (HQ at Atlanta); from Atlanta to

Drew, date uncertain; 314th ABS, Drew by 12Nov43 when it suffered Cat.3 damage in a ground-loop landing accident at Lake Butler, FL; 215th BU Pueblo 05Sep44. To RFC 17Aug45. BoS RFC, Denver, CO to Fontana School of Aeronautics, Iron Mountain, MI, 02Aug45 for $14,666; CofA at TFH:561hrs and CofR as **G-44, NC37182** both issued 23Aug45; transferred by BoS to M & A Fontana at the same address 03Jan49 with CofR 27Jan49; hull vents installed, hull step shortened and hull keel re-inforcement installed May50. BoS to Guy W Gully, Farrell, PA 19Aug50 with CofR 25Aug50. CofA 26Dec56 at TFH:1,447hrs. BoS to Lindsley McChesney, Troy, NY 29Nov57 with CofR **N37182** 16Dec57. BoS to George Krause, Dillingham, AK 20Sep60 with CofR 31Oct60. BoS to Warren W Woods, dba Woods Air Service, Palmer, AK, 13Apr64 with CofR 21Apr64; transferred to Woods himself (at a different PO Box No.) by BoS 04Jan66 with CofR 13Jan66; transferred by BoS to Woods Air Fuel Inc, Palmer, AK 13Dec95 with CofR 17Jun96. The file contains no Forms 337 after Dec56, and CofR expired on 31Dec11. Fate unknown.

1233   Built as **G-44.** BoS Grumman Aircraft Engineering Corp to Hickok Manufacturing Co Inc, Rochester, NY 09Oct41 with CofA and CofR **NC37183** same date. BoS to Defense Supplies Corp, Washington, DC 23Feb42 for $23,319.50, with CofR 10Mar42. BoS to US War Department, Washington, DC 02May42 for $29,536.79; formally accepted by USAAF 14Mar42. Designated **OA-14** and allocated the serial **42-38339.** Bolling 14Mar42; assigned ARD at La Guardia, NY Mar42; Wright Fld (loan) 26May42; La Guardia 30May42; assigned 1st AF and to Mitchel 19Mar43; by Oct44 with 132nd BU Suffolk County (1st AF); Cat.3 damage in a taxying accident at Mitchel 19Oct44 (when on 132nd BU strength); 110th BU Mitchel 03Nov44. Formally to RFC 26Feb45 and SOC 23Apr45. BoS Defense Plant Corp, Washington, DC to Frank G Schenuit Rubber Co, Baltimore, MD 20Feb45 for $11,500. Temporary CofA and ferry permit issued 22Feb45 for 42-38339 for flight from Mitchel Field to Roosevelt Field, NY. Complete overhaul and re-paint by Aero Trades, Roosevelt Field Jun45 with CofA 08Jun45 at TFH:720hrs. CofR to Frank G Schenuit, dba Frank G Schenuit Rubber Co as **G-44, NC37183** 10Sep45. Tfd by BoS to The Frank G Schenuit Rubber Co 25Oct46 with CofR 23Oct47. BoS to Atlantic Creosoting Co Inc, New York, NY 20Jly48 with CofR 30Jly48. CofA 27May49 at TFH:938hrs. BoS to John Wagner Jr, La Guardia, NY 09May50 with CofR **N37183** 09Jun50. BoS to Anthony Stinis, Jamica Estates, NY 07Feb53 with CofR 12Feb53. CofA 08Aug55 at TFH:1,115hrs. BoS to Ross Aviation Inc, Tulsa, OK 02Feb61 with CofR 14Mar61. BoS to Harold F Pitcher, Fairbanks, AK 08Sep61 with CofA 19Dec61 at TFH:1,647hrs and CofR to Harold L Pitcher 02Jan62. Re-possessed by Indianapolis Morris Plan Corp 10Aug62. BoS to Charlene Adams, North Miami Beach, FL 05Mar63 with CofR 25Apr63. BoS to John M Wells, c/o Mercedes Flying Service, Mercedes, TX 16Mar64 with CofR 22May64. Tfd by BoS to Ana Flora Alvarado de Wells, San José, Costa Rica 25Sep64, and cancelled from USCAR 06Oct64. Reregd as **TI-1050L** to Flora de Wells 03May65. To **AN-BEC** with Sociedad Anónima de Explotación de Transporte Aereo (SAETA) circa Oct68; AN-BEC cancelled 18Oct71. BoS SAETA to Fred Warner, Fort Lauderdale, FL 20Oct71 for $8,000. BoS to Bill Brennand Aircraft Sales, Neenah, WI 29Feb72 for $13,000 with CofR **N6291** 14Mar72. BoS to Aircraft Sales Inc, Charlotte, NC 24Jly73. BoS to American Lease Plans Inc, Anderson, SC 30Jly73 with CofR 06Sep73; leased to Aircraft Sales Inc 02Oct73; BoS back to Aircraft Sales Inc 03Oct75 for $22,147.02. **N9AS** reserved 13Nov75, placed on acft 21Nov75 and CofR issued 28Nov75. BoS to Ron Gilmore 11Sep77 with CofR to Ronald J Gilmore, Sellersville, PA 27Feb78. CofR revoked 24Sep82 due failure to submit a Triennial Report. BoS to JD Perry, Greenwich, CT 19Oct80. BoS James Perry to The Flying Barnyard Inc, Greenwich, CT 17May88, with CofR N9AS re-instated 10Jun88. The FAA file contains no airworthiness information after Dec61 and the aircraft is listed (May13) as non-airworthy with CofR expired 31Dec11. Fate unknown.

1234   Built as **G-44**, regn **NC37184** allocated but ntu. Regd to Richard J Reynolds, Winston Salem, NC as **NC1920**, Oct41. Acquired by the USAAF and formally accepted 14Mar42. Designated **OA-14** and allocated the serial **42-38220.** Bolling 14Mar42; MacDill 06Nov42. Cat.4 damage in a taxying accident at MacDill 06Aug43 when with 28th Base HQ&ABS and then destroyed in a Cat.5 landing accident on Lake Butler, FL 27Feb44 (on strength of Base det MacDill at that time).

1235   Built as **G-44**, regn **NC37185** allocated but ntu. Regd as **NC1000** to Swiflite Corp, New York, NY, 22Oct41 and operated by Cities Service Corp. To Pan American Airways and cvtd to training aircraft circa early 1942. Purchased by the US Navy in 1942 for operations by the NATS under contract to Pan American at New York. Aircraft designated **J4F-2** and retrospectively allocated BuAer serial **99077** circa early 1945 and

therefore not worn until 1945 at earliest; records missing but served with PAA Atlantic Division, New York from at least Apr44 until May45; NAS Seattle May45 for reconditioning; Pool NAS Norfolk 08Oct45. SOC at Norfolk 28Feb47 as obsolete and surplus. Regd as **G-44, N9933H** to Aluminium Industries Inc, Cincinnati, OH by 1956. Cvtd to **Super Widgeon** by McKinnon. BoS Aluminium Industries Inc to Carl Millard Ltd, Toronto, ON 02Nov56. Allotted CF-JXX 14May57. Inspected 17Jun57 at TFH:3,113hrs and CofA 6007 issued. N9933H cancelled from USCAR 01Jly57 and CofR(P) 18384issued for **CF-JXX** to Carl Millard Ltd, 05Jly57; inspected and CofR renewed, valid until 15Jly59. BoS to Murfin Heating & Cooling Ltd, Downsview, ON, 20Nov58 CofR(P) 20679 issued 23Dec58; BoS to Blair Gordon, Montreal, QC 21Sep61 and CofR(P) 24482 issued 28Sep61. BoS 31Oct61 to Chamcook Airways Ltd for $45,000 and CofR(P) 24512 issued to Chamcook A/W, Montreal, QC 08Nov61; inspected at TFH:4,178hrs and CofA renewed, valid until 23Feb65. BoS 15Jun64 to Commander Aviation Ltd, Malton, ON. BoS 31Jly64 to Joseph Shaw, Willowdale, ON and CofR(P) 31967 issued 21Aug64. Accident at 1455hrs(GMT) on 03Oct64: after a flight from Temagami, ON, and while taxiing after landing at Toronto, the right undercarriage collapsed. Inspected and CofR renewed at TFH:4,220hrs, valid until 17Nov65. BoS 23Mar65 Shaw to Harrison Airways, Richmond, BC, for $48,500, and CofR(C) 34438 issued 01Apr65. Accident at 1330hrs on 15Mar66: on a flight from Vancouver to Warn Bay, BC the left engine failed 3 miles East of Alberni Inlet, BC. Pilot, Mervin McKerral, made a precautionary landing in rough water at Port Alberni substantially damaging the aircraft. BoS 30Jun67 to Industrial Wings Ltd, Vancouver, BC, at TFH:4,685hrs. BoS 30Jun67 to Industrial Acceptance Corp Ltd, Vancouver, BC, and CofR(P) 43700 issued 25Jly67. BoS to Harrison Airways Ltd, Richmond, BC, for $53,538 and CofR(C) 45420 issued 31Jly68. Accident at 0853hrs on 21Aug68: while both aircraft were taxiing towards Runway 12 at Vancouver Airport, BC the Widgeon's nose and right wing struck RCAF T-33, 21098, left wingtip tank, vertical fin and rudder, at intersection of Taxiways X and N. (Pilot: Mervin McKerral). Accident at 1415hrs on 08Oct71: after a flight from Port Alberni, BC while on approach to land in the mouth of the Franklin River, the aircraft struck cables at circa 20-50ft. (Pilot: Hugh Moffat Fraser). Accident 08Jan72: damaged by overnight windstorm while parked at Bella Coola, BC. Accident at 1830hrs on 10May72: on take-off from Vancouver for a flight to Victoria, BC the pilot, David Allen Potter, became aware of left main gear failure and landed on grass area, coming to rest on Runway 12. Inspected and CofA renewed at TFH:7,023hrs, valid until 05Nov75. BoS 19Jun75 Harrison A/W to Tradewinds Aviation, Vancouver, BC, to include CF-JXX, Cessna U206 CF-RQR, spare parts, lease of buildings and licences, for $130,000. CofR(C) issued to Tradewinds 20Jun75 and re-issued as **C-FJXX** 27Jun75. Accident at 1600hrs on 28Sep75: while landing on South arm of Fraser River, BC, aircraft struck a large swell, porpoised, nosed over and sank (pilot: Fred May). BoS 10Nov76 Stewart Smith (Canada) Ltd to Pacific Aircraft Salvage Inc, Vancouver, BC "as is". BoS to Green Valley Aviation Ltd, Everett, WA. Seen at Paine Field, Seattle, WA undergoing rebuild of forward fuselage 03Jan77. Cancelled from CCAR 27Oct78 and regd **N9015R** to Green Valley Aviation Inc, Granite Falls, WA, Nov78, with Experimental CofA 10Nov78 (after installation of Lycoming GO-480 engines?). Restored to **N9933H** with Island Chevron Service Inc, Kodiak, AK, 02Dec78. Accident at 1720hrs on 02Sep80: stalled and crashed into sea after water take-off from Kodiak, AK for a flight to Danger Bay, AK; pilot uninjured but aircraft substantially damaged. To Peter A Soby, Pinehurst, NC 30Jly84 and later at Boulder, CO. Sold to Windy Hill Widgeon Works LLC, c/o Marilyn M Soby, Boulder, CO with CofR 13Jly99. Current May13, but airworthiness still listed as Experimental, with CofR due to expire 31Oct14.

1236   Built as **G-44**. BoS Grumman Aircraft Engineering Corp to The Texas Co, New York, NY 29Oct41 for US$30,689.86, with CofA and CofR **NC37186** same date, with F/N:39. Repaired after accident 08Mar43 in Louisiana. BoS to Gannett Publishing Co Inc, Portland, ME, 24Aug44 for US$25,000, at TFH:458hrs, and CofR issued 05Sep44. Name change to Guy Gannett Publishing Co (same address) with amended CofR **N37186** 28Jly50. Cvtd to **Super Widgeon** with Lycoming GO-435-C2B engines with Hartzell HC-82-20-2 props using a McKinnon-Hickman kit; re-inforced hull and step vent kit installed, aircraft re-covered and re-painted by Aero Trades Inc Jun53, with CofA 11Jly53 at TFH:4,081hrs. BoS to Commandair Inc, White Plains, NY for $20,000 29Dec58 with CofR 03Feb59. BoS to Western Newspaper Union, New York, NY 30Jly59 with CofR 25Aug59. BoS to Farwell W Perry, Greenwich, CT 11Apr62 with CofR 11May62. CofA 09Jun56 at TFH:5,009hrs. Stored unpainted at Sultan, WA in 2002, and at Monroe, WA in 2005. BoS to James D Perry, Monroe, WA 08Nov04 with CofR 18May09. CofR expired 30Sep11 and cancelled from USCAR 09Nov12. Restored to register 04Jan13, with CofR to expire 31Jan16.

1237   Built as **G-44** and regd **NC37187** to Link Aeronautical Corp, Binghampton, NY, Nov41. To American Skyports Inc, New York, NY by Sep46. To Noel Gayler, Dept of Navy, Washington, DC as **N37187** by Oct62. Accident 21Feb64: wheels-up landing at Arlington, VA. To J Ray MacDermott, New Orleans, LA, Apr65. Accident at 1905hrs on 25Nov65: ditched in ocean near Lagos after loss of one engine during ferry to Nigeria. Pilot seriously injured and aircraft "destroyed".

1238   Built as **G-44** and regd **NC37188** to Island Airways, NY, Nov41. Acquired by US Army Air Force and formally accepted 14Mar42. Designated **OA-14** and allocated the serial **42-38222**. Bolling 14Mar42. Destroyed in a Cat.5 landing accident on Potomac River, one mile NW of Fort Washington, MD 25Mar42. Aircraft was on the strength of the Air Corps Ferrying Command (ACFC) at the time of the accident.

1239   Built as **G-44** and regd **NC37189** to Pan American Airways Inc, New York, NY, 21Nov41 with CofA same date and CofR 05Dec41; conversion work for student training completed 05Mar42. Purchased by US Navy in 1942 for operations by the NATS under contract to Pan American at New York. Aircraft designated **J4F-2** and, circa early 1945, retrospectively allocated one of three BuAer serials, **99074**, **99075** or **99076** (their subsequent recorded US Navy histories are identical but without previous identification details) which, by definition, is unlikely to have been worn at any time; US Navy records incomplete but with Pan American Atlantic Division by Aug44 until Jun45; transferred to Pan American Airways Jun45 and sold to them on Disposition Contract NOA(s)7525 dated 03Aug45, and SOC by US Navy as obsolete and surplus 31Oct45. Restored as **NC37189** to Pan American Airways Inc, New York, NY with CofA 17Jun46. BoS to Wallace C Siple, Montreal, PQ 21Jan47. BoS to Hunter C Moody, Decatur, IL 21Jan47 with CofR 24Feb47. BoS to Decatur Aviation Co, Decatur, IL 24Jly47 with CofR 05Aug47. BoS Decatur/Moody to Mount Hawley Aviation Co, Peoria, IL 17Nov47; CofA 24Nov47 and CofR 25Nov47; hull modified at step and vents installed, Jun50. BoS to TOC Oil Co/FT Holliday, Indianapolis, IN 15Jly50. CofR **N37189** issued 15Aug50. BoS Indiana Trust Co (Holliday Trustee) to William H Snow, Princeton, NJ 06Dec51 with CofR 20Feb52. BoS to Gentry W Shuster, Anchorage, AK, dba Safeway Airways with CofR 15Apr52; aircraft name: "*Little Lulu*". Cvtd to **Super Widgeon** with Lycoming GO-480-B1 power with retractable floats, May55 by McKinnon-Hickman; auxiliary fuel tanks installed in each wing and wings covered in 24ST Alclad in Mar57, both as per Mansdorf drawings; CofA 31May57; address change to Kingman, AZ 20Aug64. Accident 15Jly66: substantially damaged when pilot (uninjured) landed long at Igiugig A/P, Iliamna, AK to minimise taxi. But the brakes failed and he executed an intentional ground loop in soft sand. When Shuster died in 1967 the First National Bank of Anchorage re-possessed the aircraft and applied for a CofR 24Mar69. BoS 1st Natl Bank of Anchorage to Robert O Denny, Anchorage, AK 04Sep69 with CofR 20Oct69. BoS to Yukon Office Supply Inc/Bevan Investment Co 12Dec69 with CofR 06Feb70. BoS to Alfred E Gay, Gringo Pass, AZ 01Jun72; BoS to Gringo Pass Inc, Lukeville, AZ 15Dec72 (nominal change) with CofR 15Mar73. BoS to Peninsular Airways Inc, Pilot Point, AK 08Aug73 with CofR 28Jan74. Accident at 1200hrs on 14Feb78: right gear collapsed on take-off at Pilot Point, AK continuing a flight from Iliama, AK to Perryville, AK; one pax seriously injured + pilot uninjured, but aircraft substantially damaged. BoS to Green Valley Aviation, Granite Falls, WA 01Mar79. CofR 15Apr80. Sale reported Dec80 to JD Perry, Greenwich, CT. Cancelled from USCAR 20Sep12, due reported sale.

C/n 1239, the former Pan-American Airways' NC37189, is seen in this pre-1950 photo, possibly at Decatur, Illinois. The aircraft saw service in Alaska before and after being converted to Super Widgeon standard in May 1955. *(Jennifer Gradidge Collection)*

C/n 1240, was the first Widgeon to be exported. JP Bickell received the aircraft, as CF-BVN, in January 1942. Converted to Super Widgeon standard by McKinnon in 1954, it was sold to an owner in Michigan in 1967. Registered as N7491, it has remained in Michigan to this day. This undated photo was probably taken in the late 1960s showing the aircraft carrying the logo "Tecumseh MICHIGAN" forward of the Indian head on the bow. *(William Haines Collection)*

1240   Built as **G-44** and allotted **CF-BVN** to JP Bickell (Pres of McIntyre Porcupine Mines Ltd, 12Nov41. CofR(P) 2924 and CofA 553 to JP Bickell, Toronto, ON 08Jan42 (to replace Goose, CF-BKE, donated to RCAF); CF-BVN is believed to have been based at Malton, ON (the primary Victory Aircraft factory) from 1942 until 1945. CofR(C) 3242 to OH Barrett/ RC Berkinshaw, Toronto, ON, 05Oct45. CofR(P) 7602 to GH Godsall Equipment Ltd, Toronto, ON, 10Dec48. Accident at 1640hrs 10Oct49, on Lake Aylmer, 20 miles South of Thetford Mines, PQ: after a landing on glassy water and while taxying on the step, the left float hit an obstacle, forcing the left wing up and the right float into the water. The left float was torn off and the aircraft capsized. Towed to shore while inverted, dismantled and trucked to Malton, ON for repair. CofR(P) 8748 to Century Motor Sales Ltd, Toronto, ON, 31May50. Sold to Dept of Game & Fisheries, Quebec City, QC, 22Jun51. Cvtd to **Super Widgeon** with Lycoming GO-435-C2B2 engines 23Aug54 using McKinnon-Hickman Kit No.101270. To Trans Gaspesian Airlines Ltd, Gaspe, QC 11Jun57. To Trans Aircraft Co, Hamilton, ON, 09Jan59. To McAvoy Air Service Ltd, Yellowknife, NT, 19Jly63. To Wunder Machine Co Ltd, Kitchener, ON 31Dec64. Accident at 0735hrs on 17Jly66: en route Prince George, BC – Fort Nelson, BC at Mile 167 Alaska Highway, near Sikanni Chief, BC; 57.15N x 122.43W. Partial failure of left engine led to a precautionary landing on a small strip. During final approach the aircraft swung to the left edge of the runway and touchdown was made with the aircraft in a steep right bank. The right wing float touched first and then the hull and left undercarriage hit a pile of earth and debris. The left wing struck small trees, the aircraft slowed and then swung sharply to the right before stopping. BoS to Meyers Industries Inc, Tecumseh, MI 15Nov67 with CofR **N7491** 10Apr68. Cancelled from CCAR Dec67. Acft carried legend "*Tecumseh Michigan*" on bow. CofA 24Jun68 at TFH:3,260hrs. BoS to Raymond Betzoldt, Clinton, MI 23Feb72 with CofR 24Mar72. BoS to James N Merillat, Tecumseh, MI 03Mar75 with CofR 15Mar75. CofR revoked by FAA 11Nov77 due failure to submit an Aircraft Activity Report, but **N7491** re-issued 21Dec77. BoS to Brian J and Karen S VanWagnen, Jackson, MI 01Mar04 with CofR 30Mar04. Cvtd to Lycoming GO-480-G1D6 engines per STC SA380WE, and increase of gross weight to 5,500lbs, 13May05. Current and airworthy May13, with CofR due to expire 30Apr14.

In December 1941, following the Japanese attacks in the Pacific, the United States briefly suspended all exports of military aircraft pending decisions on possible diversions to the United States' armed forces. Although absolute documentary proof has not been found it is virtually certain that BuAer serials **09805** to **09816** were set aside in December 1941 for the potential acquisition of the twelve aircraft that were in production as the model G-44 for the Portuguese Navy. Clearly the decision reached was that these aircraft, **c/ns 1241 to 1252**, would not be taken by the US Navy and deliveries went ahead with little delay. Three were delivered in December 1941, seven in January 1942 and two in February 1942. This BuAer serial block, listed by US Naval historians as that of the J4F-2 model, was not re-used and has no linkage with any other aircraft, nor is it correct to describe it as the previous identity of the Portuguese aircraft.

1241   Built as **G-44** for the Aviação Naval Portuguesa (Portuguese Naval Aviation) with serial **119**; delivered 22Dec41; active at CAN Ponta Delgada, Azores in 1943 and 1944; prefix letter 'W' added to serial, application date uncertain; at CAN Bom Sucesso by 1946; land-based at CAN Portela by 1947; at Bom Sucesso by 31Jan49 (TFH:591hrs). Transferred to the Força Aérea Portuguesa (Portuguese Air Force) May52; with BA-6 Montijo in 1953 although at 30Apr53 still on TFH:591hrs at Portela, where said to be in overhaul. Regd **CS-AHE** to (Director General Civil Aviation) (DGAC), Lisbon 1957. Sold as **CR-CAF** 13Sep58 for Transportes Aéreos de Cabo Verde. Fate unknown.

1242   Built as **G-44** for the Aviação Naval Portuguesa (Portuguese Naval Aviation) with serial **120**; delivered 24Dec41; active at CAN Bom Sucesso until 1946; prefix letter 'W' added to serial, application date uncertain; land-based at CAN Portela by 1947. Transferred to the Força Aérea Portuguesa (Portuguese Air Force) May52; still based at Portela in 1953. Regd **CS-AHG** to (Director General Civil Aviation) (DGAC), Lisbon 20Nov56 with CofA No:164. Regd **CR-CAG** with Transportes Aéreos de Cabo Verde 1958. Ret to **CS-AHG** 1962 for the Portuguese Government Survey Unit. CofA inspection 28Nov69 at TFH:1,130hrs, valid until 28May70. Noted wfu at Lisbon Jan74. Acquired by the Museu de Marinha in Lisbon, where currently displayed as "**128**".

1243   Built as **G-44** for the Aviação Naval Portuguesa (Portuguese Naval Aviation) with serial **121**; delivered 30Dec41; reported active at CAN Bom Sucesso between 1943 and 1946; prefix letter 'W' theoretically added to serial, application date uncertain, nothing more known post-1946 and assumed wfu.

1244   Built as **G-44** for the Aviação Naval Portuguesa (Portuguese Naval Aviation) with serial **122**; delivered 05Jan42; active at CAN Ponta Delgada, Azores from Nov42 until 1944; prefix letter 'W' added to serial, application date uncertain. Transferred to the Força Aérea Portuguesa (Portuguese Air Force) May52; at BA-6 Montijo in 1953 and 1956; subsequent history unknown.

1245   Built as **G-44** for the Aviação Naval Portuguesa (Portuguese Naval Aviation) with serial **123**; delivered 08Jan42; active at CAN Bom Sucesso in 1944 and 1945; prefix letter 'W' added to serial, application date uncertain; at Bom Sucesso by 31Jan49 (TFH:271hrs). Transferred to the Força Aérea Portuguesa (Portuguese Air Force) May52 and by 1953 at BA-6 Montijo; active with the FAP in 1956; subsequent history unknown.

1246   Built as **G-44** for the Aviação Naval Portuguesa (Portuguese Naval Aviation) with serial **124**; delivered 14Jan42; active at CAN Ponta Delgada, Azores from 1942 until at least 1944; CAN Portela by Dec46 until at least Aug48; prefix letter 'W' added to serial, application date uncertain; at Bom Sucesso by 31Jan49 (TFH:373hrs). Transferred to the Força Aérea Portuguesa (Portuguese Air Force) May52; at Portela Aug53 until Jan54; at BA-7 Aveiro in 1954; subsequent history unknown.

1247   Built as **G-44** for the Aviação Naval Portuguesa (Portuguese Naval Aviation) with serial **125**; delivered 19Jan42; active at CAN Bom Sucesso in 1944 and 1945; prefix letter 'W' added to serial, application date uncertain; at Bom Sucesso by 31Jan49 (TFH:310hrs). Transferred to the Força Aérea Portuguesa (Portuguese Air Force) May52; at BA-6 Montijo 1953; at BA-7 Aveiro in 1954 and 1956; subsequent history unknown.

1248   Built as **G-44** for the Aviação Naval Portuguesa (Portuguese Naval Aviation) with serial **126**; delivered 21Jan42; active at CAN Ponta Delgada, Azores by Dec42 until at least Dec43; prefix letter 'W' added to serial, application date uncertain. Transferred to the Força Aérea Portuguesa (Portuguese Air Force) May52; at BA-6 Montijo in 1953; by 1956 believed to have been re-serialled **2401** and reportedly modified for photography purposes; subsequent service history unknown, but '2401' was displayed at Monsanto Park, Lisbon by 1968; fate unknown.

1249   Built as **G-44** for the Aviação Naval Portuguesa (Portuguese Naval Aviation) with serial **127**; delivered 26Jan42; active at CAN Ponta Delgada, Azores in 1943 and 1944; prefix letter 'W' added to serial, application date uncertain; at Bom Sucesso by 31Jan49 (TFH:664hrs). Transferred to the Força Aérea Portuguesa (Portuguese Air Force) May52; at Portela by 1956 until at least 1958; subsequent history unknown.

1250   Built as **G-44** for the Aviação Naval Portuguesa (Portuguese Naval Aviation) with serial **128**; delivered 31Jan42; active at CAN Bom Sucesso in 1944 and 1945; prefix letter 'W' added to serial, application date uncertain; at Bom Sucesso by 31Jan49 (TFH:539hrs). Transferred to the Força Aérea Portuguesa (Portuguese Air Force) May52; at BA-6 Montijo in 1953; subsequent history unknown. [The aircraft displayed as '128' in the Naval Museum, Lisbon is c/n 1242]

1251   Built as **G-44** for the Aviação Naval Portuguesa (Portuguese Naval Aviation) with serial **129**; delivered 08Feb42; active at CAN Ponta Delgada, Azores in 1943 and 1944; prefix letter 'W' added to serial,

application date uncertain; assigned to the Mozambique Hydrographic Mission from 1947 until 1952 and retained in Mozambique for the Governor's use. Presumably, at least notionally, transferred to the Força Aérea Portuguesa (Portuguese Air Force) May52 although apparently not on metropolitan Portugal's strength in 1953. Returned to Portugal on unknown date and currently preserved at the FAP Museu do Ar, Alverca as '129' with 'Mocambique' inscription and radio call-sign 'CT-ABK' visible in cockpit.

1252   Built as **G-44** for the Aviação Naval Portuguesa (Portuguese Naval Aviation) with serial **130**; delivered 18Feb42; active at CAN Bom Sucesso in 1945; assigned to the Hydrographic Mission at Cabo Verde in 1946 and 1947 and in Guinea from 1948 until 1952 (although apparently at Bom Sucesso circa 31Jan49 when TFH:361hrs); prefix letter 'W' added to serial, application date uncertain. Transferred to the Força Aérea Portuguesa (Portuguese Air Force) May52; at BA-6 Montijo in 1953; active with FAP in 1956; subsequent history unknown.

Following the USA's entry into the war in December 1941, production of aircraft for the commercial market ceased. Initially all new aircraft were delivered to the US Coast Guard, and then to friendly nations for military purposes, but by late 1942 all production was for the US Navy.

1253   Built for US Coast Guard as **J4F-1**, serial **V205**. Del to USCG 25Feb42; CGAS Brooklyn by Feb43 until at least May45; SOC Aug46 as surplus, but with no known subsequent civilian history.

1254   Built for US Coast Guard as **J4F-1**, serial **V206**. Del to USCG Feb42; CGAS Port Angeles by Feb43 until at least 09Feb45 when to CGAS San Francisco (status uncertain); no known subsequent service records, no records of a strike date and no known subsequent commercial history. Assumed to have been withdrawn and scrapped by USCG, date unknown.

1255   Built for US Coast Guard as **J4F-1**, serial **V207**. Del to USCG Feb42; CGAS Port Angeles by Feb43 until at least Dec45 (involved in a minor taxying accident with J2F-6 36967 at NAS Sand Point 14Jun45, but flying again by 02Aug45). No known subsequent service records, no records of a strike date and no known subsequent commercial history. Assumed to have been withdrawn and scrapped by USCG, date unknown.

1256   Built for US Coast Guard as **J4F-1**, serial **V208**. Del to USCG Mar42; CGAS Elizabeth City, NC by Feb43; CGAS Port Angeles by 20Dec44; no known subsequent service records, no records of a strike date and no known subsequent commercial history. Assumed to have been withdrawn and scrapped by USCG, date unknown.

1257   Built for US Coast Guard as **J4F-1**, serial **V209**. Del to USCG Mar42; to CGAS St Petersburg by Feb43; no known subsequent service records, no records of a strike date and no known subsequent commercial history. Assumed to have been withdrawn and scrapped by USCG, date unknown.

1258   Built for US Coast Guard as **J4F-1**, serial **V210**. Del to USCG Mar42; CGAS Brooklyn by Feb43 until at least Feb44; CGAS Biloxi by 29Jun45 when aircraft water-looped on landing at Biloxi during training flight. Aircraft landed slightly nose-low and cart-wheeled, pivoting about the nose and left wing-tip and sustaining extensive damage to the starboard wing, instruments and engine and coming to rest capsized (surprisingly only categorised as 'D' damage). SOC Nov46 as surplus, but with no known subsequent civilian history.

1259   Built for US Coast Guard as **J4F-1**, serial **V211**. Del to USCG Apr42; CGAS Biloxi by Jly42 (when detached to NAS Houma) until at least Feb43; SOC Apr48 as surplus, but with no known subsequent civilian history.

1260   Built for US Coast Guard as **J4F-1**, serial **V212**. Del to USCG Apr42 (manufactured 10Apr42); CGAS Biloxi by Jly42 (when detached to NAS Houma) until at least Feb43; while detached to Houma was credited with the destruction of the German submarine U-166 off the Louisiana coast 01Aug42. The discovery of the wreck of U-166 elsewhere in 2001 finally confirmed that the submarine in question was actually U-171 and that it had not been damaged in the attack (U-171 later succumbed to a mine off Lorient, France). SOC 24Feb48 as surplus and transferred to Dept of Interior, Fish & Wildlife Service, Washington, DC. Regd as **G-44, NC743** Apr48 and later as **N743**. To **N2770A** with Kodiak Airways, Kodiak, AK mid-1950s. Landed in Kodiak Channel with wheels down 1959 and sank. Rebuilt by George Pappas, Anchorage, AK with Continental engines by Jun60. CofA 09Jan64. To RJ Anderson Co, Anchorage, AK by 1966. Accident 18Jly66: substantial damage in wheels-up landing at Seldovia, AK. Pilot + 4 pax minor injuries. To Lawrence Aircraft Sales Inc, Homer, AK 1966, operated by Homer Air Services, Homer, AK. To Alaska Air Guides Inc, Anchorage, AK 1970. Reregd **N324BC** to William Cunningham, Anchorage, AK in 1973. Reregd **N212ST** to Steven T Hamilton, dba Hamilton Restoration Ltd, Reno, NV Jly80. Cancelled from USCAR 15Oct85. Acquired by the National Naval Aviation Museum, Pensacola, FL 04May84, and fully restored to USCG markings as V212. N212ST was reserved again 22Nov93, but ntu and cancelled by FAA 18May11. Aircraft currently displayed in Pensacola.

1261   Built for US Coast Guard as **J4F-1**, serial **V213**. Del to USCG May42; CGAS St Petersburg by Feb43. SOC Nov46 as surplus. Regd as **G-44, NC5508N** to Grumman Aircraft Engineering Corp in 1947, but noted as unassigned [ie no customer]. Fate unknown.

1262   Built for US Coast Guard as **J4F-1**, serial **V214**. Del to USCG May42; CGAS Biloxi by Jly42 (when detached to NAS Houma) until at least Feb43. SOC as surplus, date unknown. Regd as **G-44, N700A** (possibly to Grumman Aircraft Engineering Corp in 1949 ?). Fate unknown.

1263   Built for US Coast Guard as **J4F-1**, serial **V215**. Del to USCG May42; CGAS Brooklyn by Feb43; CGAS San Francisco by 12Oct44 when destroyed in landing accident at Mills Fld Seadrome, San Francisco. Pilot landed in haze and smoke and misjudged his height above the surface; aircraft landed nose-low and flipped on its back seriously injuring both crew; wreckage recovered to CGAS San Francisco and SOC.

1264   Built for US Coast Guard as **J4F-1**, serial **V216**. Del to USCG May42; CGAS St Petersburg by Feb43; no known subsequent service records, no records of a strike date and no known subsequent civilian history. Assumed to have been withdrawn and scrapped by USCG, date unknown.

1265   Built for US Coast Guard as **J4F-1**, serial **V217**. Del to USCG 30May42; CGAS Biloxi by Jly42 (when detached to NAS Houma) until at least Feb43. SOC as surplus, Mar47. Regd as **G-44, NC1234N** to FK Brunton, Bellevue, WA. Operated by Alaska Airlines in 1950. To Gentry W Shuster, Anchorage, AK by Apr52. Cvtd to **Super Widgeon** with Lycoming GO-435-C2B with Hartzell HC-83x20-2A props by McKinnon 19Jly55. Regn CF-IIQ allotted to Vancouver Aircraft Sales Ltd, Vancouver, BC 31Oct55; authority to ferry Portland, OR to Vancouver, BC 29Nov55; BoS McKinnon-Hickman Co, Portland, OR to Vancouver Aircraft Sales 30Nov55; US CofA for export E-27751 dated 30Nov55. BoS to Granby Mining 08Dec55 at TFH:5,795hrs. CofR(P) 15106 and CofA 5528 for **CF-IIQ** issued to The Granby Consolidated Mining, Smelting & Power Co Ltd, Vancouver, BC, 30Nov55. BoS to Western Airmotive Ltd, Vancouver, BC 01Apr58. BoS to Realite Ltd 01Apr58 with CofR(P) 18623 to Realite Ltd, Vancouver, BC 02Apr58. BoS to Imperial Airways 12Nov59; inspected and CofR renewed 26Nov59 and CofR(P) 23278 issued to Imperial Airways Ltd, Prince George, BC 27Nov59. Leased to Ben Ginter Construction Co Ltd for 6 months from 01Dec59. Cvtd to **Super Widgeon** with Lycoming GO-480-B1D with Hartzell HC-83x20-2B props by McKinnon 16Dec60; inspected at TFH:7,865hrs and CofA renewed, valid until 01Jly67. Accident at 1905hrs on 30Jly66: operated by Ginter Construction Ltd. On take-off from McConnell Lake, BC for a flight to Prince George, BC, the aircraft stalled and sank in deep water. Report concluded that the stall was possibly due to the amount of water in the rear fuselage causing the centre of gravity to exceed its maximum possible aft position. Aircraft salvaged from lake and trucked to Calgary, AB Sep66; inspected and CofA renewed at TFH:7,945hrs, valid until 27Aug69. Accident 02Jun71: on a flight from Prince George, BC to Middle River construction camp, located between Trembleur and Takla Lakes, pilot, Wm Hall, made a heavy landing on Middle River which damaged the horizontal stabiliser. Not noticed until after return to Prince George. Inspected and CofA renewed at TFH:8,054hrs, valid until 01Jun73. Leased to Aquila Holdings Ltd, Parksville, BC. Sub-lease by Aquila Holdings Ltd to Trans Mountain Air Services Ltd for 30 days, 01May75. BoS Imperial Airways to Canadian Flying Machines, Langley, BC 12Jun75. BoS to Aquila Holdings Ltd, Campbell River, BC 13Jun75. CofR(C) issued to Trans Mountain Air Services Ltd 19Dec76 (under lease from Aquila); inspected and CofA renewed at TFH:8,100hrs, valid until 31Jly77. CofR(P) to Aquila Holdings Ltd, Parksville, BC 13Jan77; BoS to Dewiley Holeman 27Jan77 and cancelled from CCAR 08Mar77. CofR **N99341** to Dewiley Holeman, King Cove, AK 20Apr77. CofA 18Mar77 with Lycoming GO-480-B1D engines. BoS to Kachemak Air Service Inc, Homer, AK 08Dec78 with CofR 07Feb79. Reregd **N99431** 17Feb79 and placed on acft 03Mar79. BoS to Dr James E Schuster, Fond du Lac, WI 03Nov81 with CofR 15Mar82. Accident 19Apr83: nosed over in water landing with gear down at Fond du Lac, WI. BoS to Janet Y Burns, Hampshire, IL

02Jun83 with CofR 30Aug83. BoS to Gaston Elvin Small III, Elizabeth City, NC 31Jly00 with CofR 15Jan04. No FAA repair Form 337s after Sep82, but listed as current and airworthy May13, with CofR due to expire 30Sep13.

1266   Built for US Coast Guard as **J4F-1**, serial **V218**. Del to USCG Jun42; CGAS Salem by Feb43. SOC as surplus, Apr48. Transferred from War Assets Administration to Dept of Interior, Fish & Wildlife Service, Washington, DC 24Feb48 with CofR **NC744** 31Mar48. Cvtd to **G-44** by Piedmont Aviation Inc, Winston Salem, NC May48 and CofA issued 14Jun48; cancelled from USCAR "at owners request" 17Jly50. BoS Dept of Interior to McKinnon Enterprises, Sandy, OR 15Jan57 with CofR **N151M** 27Feb57. BoS to Win Air Service Co Inc, Hancock Field, Syracuse, NY 08Jly57 with CofR 29Apr58. BoS to Ingram Contractors Inc, Harvey, LA 08Jan70 with CofR 17Apr70; regn revoked 15Nov72; BoS to George E Potter, New Orleans, LA 12Jun77. BoS to Green Valley Aviation, Everett, WA 07Feb78. BoS to JD Perry, Greenwich, CT 17May88 (but not recorded until 25May04!). BoS to The Flying Barnyard Inc, Greenwich, CT, 17May88 (but not recorded until 25May04!, when CofR was issued). There is no airworthiness data in the FAA file after CofA 14Jun48. CofR expired 30Sep11 and cancelled by FAA 13Dec12.

1267   Built for US Coast Guard as **J4F-1**, with serial **V219**. Del to USCG Jun42; CGAS San Diego by Nov42 until at least Feb43. SOC as surplus Dec46. BoS War Assets Administration, Concord, CA to Howard E Norton, Berkeley, CA 05Mar47 for $5,000, with CofR as **G-44, NC91040** 30Apr47. BoS to SE Spicher, Concord, CA 15May48 for $10,500 with CofR 13Aug48. BoS to G Oscar Fulweiler, Piedmont, CA 17Jan49 with CofR **N91040** 20Oct49. BoS to LJ Perry, Kalamazoo, MI 10Apr50 with 21Apr50. CofA 02Nov52 at TFH:1,992hrs. BoS to Jack Adams Aircraft Sales Inc, Walls, MS 30Sep60 with CofR 13Oct60. BoS to Airlease Corp, San Francisco, CA 22Nov60 with CofR 28Feb61. BoS to Jackson Adams, Phoenix, AZ 28Jly61. BoS to Bob's Auto Sales, Iron Mountain, MI 28Jly61 with CofR 20Oct61. BoS to Kodiak Airways Inc, Kodiak, AK 13May64, with CofR 21May64 and CofA 02Jun64 at TFH:2,600hrs. Cvtd to **Super Widgeon** with Continental IO-470-M engines and Hartzell HC-A2XF-2B props per Franklin STC SA152SO, Aug67. Accident 22Jly72: substantially damaged when hit rock after landing on Portage Lake after a flight from Kodiak, AK. Pilot + 5 pax uninjured. BoS to Park Munsey, Kodiak, AK 17Nov72 with CofR 08Jan73. BoS to Kodiak Western Alaska Airlines Inc, Kodiak, AK 15Mar74 with CofR 12Apr74. Major overhaul Nov75. BoS to Douglas O & Kathleen E Cooper, Anchorage, AK 02Sep80 with CofR 20Nov80 (at Willow, AK address). BoS to Donald A & Taeko W Coker, Anchorage, AK 12Mar82 with CofR 17Jly82. Aircraft completely disassembled for repair due excessive corrosion Apr85. Experimental CofA 04Jun85 to show compliance with FAR after conversion to IO-470-E engines and HC-82YF-2B props. CofA 09Jly85 at TFH:9,362hrs. Tfd to Coker Air Transport Ltd, Anchorage, AK by BoS 01Oct85 with CofR 07Nov85. Heavy duty main landing gear installed per STC SA380WE May87. Heavy duty floor boards installed in bow compartment per STC SA5-58 Dec92. BoS to Alvan G & Linda A Schadle, Soldotna, AK 15Apr98 with CofR 23Jun98. BoS to Holly G Pazsint, Wasilla, AK 10Jun00. BoS to Alvan G Schadle, Soldotna, AK 26May06 with CofR 31Aug06. Tfd to Schadle and Elmer E Altschuler, Soldotna, AK by BoS 10Apr07 with CofR 14May07. Attended the Alaska Grumman Fly-in at Marion Lake, near Anchorage Jly12. Current and airworthy May13, with CofR due to expire 30Apr14.

1268   Built for US Coast Guard as **J4F-1**, 18Jun42 with serial **V220**. Del to USCG Jun42; CGAS San Diego by Nov42 until at least Feb43. SOC Feb47. BoS War Assets Administration, Concord, CA to Howard E Norton, Berkeley, CA 05Mar47 for $5,000. CofR as **G-44, NC91039** issued 30Apr47. BoS to SE Spicher, Concord, CA for $6,000 24Feb48 with CofA 19Apr48 and CofR 20Apr48. BoS to Frank V & Hazel M Pollack, c/o Northwestern Aviation Sales Inc, Troutdale, OR 03Aug48 with CofR **N91039** 13Aug48. BoS to Northern Consolidated Airlines Inc, Anchorage, AK 24Jun49 with CofR 01Aug49. The FAA file contains no airworthiness information after Apr50. Sale reported 14Jan77 and remained so until cancelled from USCAR 19Nov12. Regn remained reserved a/o May13.

1269   Built for US Coast Guard as **J4F-1**, serial **V221**. Accepted, presumably by USCG, Jun42 but aircraft transferred to the US Navy Oct42 for use by the Naval Attaché, Trujillo City, Dominican Republic. BuAer serial **34585** allocated but presumably never worn. Destroyed in fatal crash at La Romana, Santo Domingo, Dominican Republic 24Oct42: stalled shortly after take-off when pilot attempted to turn while executing an excessively steep climb out; aircraft crashed 900 yards from the end of the runway and caught fire; only two of the five on board survived the crash and one of them subsequently died from burns and internal injuries; SOC by US Navy 31Oct42 (US Navy accident report only quotes serial 'V-221', aircraft movement record card explains 34585's PI as 'CG221'). [The US Coast Guard serial 221 was used a second time by a J4F, speculated to have been c/n 1273, formerly BuAer 33952]

1270   Contractually acquired by US Navy 10Jun42 as a new production **J4F-2**, BuAer serial **30151**, although acquisition circumstances unclear. Acc 10Jly42 and del 31Jly42; records missing but with BAR Bethpage by Aug44; NAS Seattle Jly45 for reconditioning; reconditioning completed 06Nov45 by A&R Seattle and aircraft passed to ADU (Pool) NAS Seattle 07Nov45 where it was flown once while awaiting disposal. Test-flown at Seattle 02May46 but after routine landing starboard undercarriage leg collapsed and aircraft swung to right, leaving the runway and incurring 'severe' damage to right wing, float, landing gear and hull; enquiry felt that there had been a faulty adjustment of the landing gear latch link during the earlier reconditioning; repaired and SOC 31Jly46 at Seattle as obsolete. Regd as **G-44, NC58832** to Washington Fish & Oyster Co, Seattle, WA Nov46. Foundered Shuyak Island, AK 19Jly47. Salvaged. To Gren Collins 27May48. To Alaska Airlines, Kodiak, AK 1952 as **N58832**. To Rainy Pass Lodge, Rainy Pass, AK circa 1954, as **N79905**(2), replacing c/n 1301. To Northern Consolidated Airlines, Anchorage, AK 1962 and reregd **N23456**, 07Jun63. To Kodiak Airways, Kodiak, AK 14Apr64; cvtd to Continental IO-470 engines with CofA 02Jun64. Accident 12Nov64: substantially damaged when left wingtip float hit submerged object during take-off from Alitak Harbour, AK on a scheduled flight. Pilot + 4 pax minor injuries. To Harold F Mitchell, Majuro, Marshall Islands 1978. Regd **N1270** to William R Brunton, Freeport, Bahamas, Feb87. Reported sold to Costa Rica Mar88, but no details known. Restored as **N23456** to Classic Wings Inc, Coraopolis, PA Nov91. To Kenny Ashby, Anchorage, AK, 03Dec92. Acft name: "*Sea Straight*". To Tod V Dickey, Phoenix, AZ 18Sep00. **N2345** reserved Sep00, but ntu. To Hangar One Inc, Wilmington, DE, with CofR **N23456** 29Oct07. Listed as airworthy May13, but CofR had expired 31Dec12.

1271   Built as **J4F-2** for Força Aérea Brasileira (Brazilian Air Force); accepted by FAB 15Jly42 and in flight test at Bethpage 03Aug42; subsequently received local serial **01**. At Galeão AFB in Oct42 and allocated to it on 06Nov42. Received new serial and local type designation **UC-4F2** 30Jly45, becoming **UC4F2 2667**; based at Galeão Jly45. Crashed Ponta Negra, near Rio 21Apr48 [Ponta Negra is a point on the coast to the east of Rio]. SOC 14Oct48.

1272   Built as **J4F-2** for Força Aérea Brasileira (Brazilian Air Force); accepted by FAB 23Jly42 at Bethpage; subsequently received local serial **02**. At Galeão AFB by Sep42 and allocated to it 06Nov42. Received new serial and local type designation **UC-4F2** 30Jly45, becoming **UC4F2 2668**; based at Galeão Jly45. To the Fábrica do Galeão for overhaul 02Oct47; reallocated to Belém AFB 13Jun50 and taken on charge 13Nov50. By Nov52 officially listed as **ZCA4F2**; to Santa Cruz AFB 01Feb54. Crashed shortly after take-off from Bauru, state of São Paulo 17Aug54 and written off. SOC at Santa Cruz 07Jun56.

1273   Built for the Aviación de Marina de Guerra (Cuban Navy) as **J4F-1** with delivery scheduled for Jly42 (and flown at Bethpage by a Brazilian crew 01Aug42); assumed delivered to Cuba at Bethpage as delivery stated to have been on schedule (in which case markings unknown) but rejected and returned to Grumman Aircraft Engineering Corp. Reallocated to the US Navy by 04Sep42 as **J4F-2** with BuAer serial **33952** assigned 09Sep42; del circa Sep42 (arguably therefore becoming the USN's first production J4F-2) but early records missing. Speculated as being the J4F-2 that replaced the ill-fated c/n 1269 with the US Coast Guard, becoming **221** by 28Feb43 at CGAS Port Angeles and remaining there until at least Sep45; (as 221) moderately damaged (Cat.C) in landing accident at Port Angeles 05Sep45 when aircraft water-looped after pilot misjudged his altitude over glassy sea. US Navy records resume in Aug44 when aircraft location shows as 'unknown'. Stricken by US Navy from unknown location 31Mar45; reinstated 31Oct45 in unknown circumstances; recorded on card with Pool NAS South Weymouth Oct45; unexplained reference to NAS Quonset Point Nov45; unreported Nov45 through Mar46 and SOC 30Apr46. No known subsequent history.

1274   Built for the Aviación de Marina de Guerra (Cuban Navy) as **J4F-1** with delivery scheduled for Jly42; assumed delivered to Cuba at Bethpage as delivery stated to have been on schedule (in which case markings unknown) but rejected and returned to Grumman Aircraft Engineering Corp. Reallocated to the US Navy by 04Sep42 as **J4F-2** with BuAer serial **33953** assigned 09Sep42; NAS New York 21Sep42 (possible del date); VS1D4 NAS Cape May 21Oct42 (assigned Eastern Sea Frontier); subsequent records missing but with Hedron 2, FAW-9 NAS Elizabeth City by Aug44; NAF Philadelphia (Mustin Fld) Jan45; Pool NAS Quonset Point 31May45; Pool NAS South Weymouth Sep45; Pool

NAS Quonset Point Nov45; NAS Key West Feb46 and SOC there 31Jly46 as obsolete and surplus. Temp CofA and ferry permit for 33953 for flight from Woodward Field, Camden, SC to Marrs field, Miami, FL 09Nov46. BoS War Assets Administration to Lee Ruebush Jr, Carolina Flying Service, Tarboro, NC 28Oct46 for $7,500. BoS to Charles L Yuille and JE Jacks, Hollywood, FL 08Feb47 with CofR as **G-44, NC1059M** 12Mar47, and marks placed on acft 29Mar47. Tfd by BoS to Charles L Yuille, Miami, FL 09Apr47 with CofA 17Apr47 and CofR 24Apr47. BoS to Arthur Burns Chalk, Miami, FL 15Sep49 with CofR as **N1059M** 26Sep49. Step re-inforcement and step vents installed Jan50. CofA 28Apr52 at TFH:1,633hrs. BoS to William S Sorren, Miami Beach, FL 01Jly65 with CofR 16Aug65. BoS to Dean H Franklin, North Bay Village, FL 20Aug65 with CofR 16Sep65. Cvtd to Continental IO-470 power. Tfd by BoS to Dean H Franklin Aviation Enterprises Inc, Miami, FL 01Oct76 and reregd **N67DF** 19Oct76. BoS to Widgeon Inc, Crofton, MD 15Jly77 with CofR 03Aug77. BoS to Coastal Air Inc, Miami, FL Nov78 with CofR 12Jan79. BoS to Sea-Air Shipping & Salvage Ltd, Grand Turk, British West Indies 05Jun79. Belatedly cancelled from USCAR 17Aug81 as exported to Turks & Caicos Islands. However, a letter from Franklin 21May98 (sic) stated that G-44, c/n1274, had "been stored at our facilities since March 1980 when it was sold to Dean H Franklin. It is now in our storage facilities at this time, and is in a state of rebuild." The file then contains a BoS from Sea-Air Shipping & Salvage Ltd to Dean H Franklin, Miami, FL dated 24Mar80! CofA 15Sep97. BoS to Dean H Franklin Enterprises Inc, North Miami Beach, FL 18May98 with CofR **N671DF** 09Jun98. BoS to Worldwide Aviation Distributors Inc, Miami, FL 17Nov99 with CofR 05Jan00. BoS to Aero Accessories Inc, Gibsonville, NC 04Feb00 with CofR 11May00. BoS to Patrick M Sturges, Hollywood, FL 25Oct01, with CofR 27Nov01. Current but not airworthy May13, with CofR due to expire 30Nov15.

1275   Built as **J4F-2** for Força Aérea Brasileira (Brazilian Air Force); accepted by FAB at Bethpage 11Aug42; subsequently received local serial **03**. At Belém AFB by Nov42 until at least Mar43 (but not casually reported after then). Received new serial and local type designation **UC-4F2** 30Jly45, becoming **UC4F2 2669**; based at Belém Jly45. Transferred to Afonsos Air Depot on 14Oct48 and SOC on the same date.

1276   Built as **J4F-2** for Força Aérea Brasileira (Brazilian Air Force); accepted by FAB at Bethpage 23Aug42; subsequently received local serial **04**. At Belém AFB Nov and Dec42. Received new serial and local type designation **UC-4F2** 30Jly45, becoming **UC4F2 2670**; based at Belém Jly45. Crashed Ananindeua, near Belém, Pará, 28Feb47. SOC from Belém AFB 28Aug47.

1277   Built for the Aviación de Marina de Guerra (Cuban Navy) as **J4F-1** with delivery scheduled for Aug42; perhaps delivered to Cuba at Bethpage as acceptance stated to have been on schedule (in which case markings unknown) but rejected and returned to Grumman Aircraft Engineering Corp; reallocated to the US Navy by 04Sep42 as **J4F-2** with BuAer serial **33954** assigned 09Sep42. NAS New York Aug42; VS1D4 NAS Cape May 21Oct42 (assigned Eastern Sea Frontier); subsequent records missing but with VS-36 NAS Cape May Aug44 [VS1D4 became VS-36 01Mar43]. Undercarriage collapsed on take-off at NAS Cape May 13Sep44 due to material failure causing Cat.C damage; NAF Philadelphia (Mustin Fld) Dec44 and under reconditioning there May-Jly45; Pool NAAS Franklin Jly45; Pool NAS Quonset Point Aug45; Pool NAS South Weymouth Sep45; CASU-26 NAAF Otis Fld Oct45. Damaged in forced-landing on Sebago Lake, North Windham, ME 20May46: following the failure of the starboard engine the pilot elected to make a water landing rather than make for nearby Brunswick; in the ensuing landing the aircraft crabbed and the port float dug in; pilot then over corrected and starboard float dug in and aircraft water-looped damaging the starboard float, strut and associated fittings. SOC at Brunswick 31Jly46, as obsolete and surplus. Regd as **G-44, NC69331** to Daniel D Whyte, New York, NY. To US Oil of Louisiana, Houston, TX by Sep62. Reported dbr (date and place unknown). Cancelled from USCAR 07Apr72 and to **HP-585** with Aeromar SA, 1972. Abandoned while in for repair. Re-possessed by Banco Nacional de Panama and sold to John Morris Wells, dba Heliteco, San José, Costa Rica 26Sep74 for $10,000. Regn **TI-AFU** had been allocated Dec64, but ntu. HP-585 cancelled 01Jly75. CofR **N144JW** to John M Wells, New Orleans, LA 13Feb85. BoS to Aircraft Specialties Inc, Bellechasse, LA 05Nov85. BoS to William C Latham, Manassas, VA 06Oct86 with CofR 02Apr87, **N54VT** reserved 09Dec87, CofR issued 15Jan88 and marks placed on acft 25Jan88. 5,500lbs gross weight landing gear per STC SA380WE, Whelen wing-tip strobe lights per SA800EA and emergency door kit per SA4-967 all installed Jan88. CofA 19Mar88 at TFH:2,583hrs quotes Lycoming GO-480-B1D engines. Accident 18Oct94: landed with gear up on a private grass strip at Haymarket, VA after a 15-minute flight from Manassas Airport. Owner/pilot uninjured but aircraft substantially damaged. TFH:3,684hrs. Listed as airworthy May13, but CofR had expired 30Jun11.

1278   Built for the Aviación de Marina de Guerra (Cuban Navy) as **J4F-1** with delivery scheduled for Aug42; perhaps delivered to Cuba at Bethpage as acceptance stated to have been on schedule (in which case markings unknown) but rejected and returned to Grumman Aircraft Engineering Corp. Reallocated to the US Navy by 04Sep42 as **J4F-2** with BuAer serial **33955** assigned 09Sep42. NAS New York 18Oct42 (possible del date); VS1D3 NAS New York 15Dec42 (assigned Eastern Sea Frontier); VS1D1 NAS Squantum 27Feb43; subsequent records missing but with Hedron-1, FAW-9 NAS Squantum by Aug44; CASU-28 NAS Groton Jan45; NAS Seattle 02Feb45 for reconditioning; Pool NAAS Franklin 31Jly45; Pool NAS Norfolk Nov45; Naval Attaché to Egypt (Cairo) 29Dec45 and SOC in Cairo 30Sep46 as obsolete and surplus. BoS US Central Field Commissioner to A/S Lufttransport, Ålesund, Norway 23Apr47. Temporarily regd **LN-HAW** in Cairo, Egypt 09May47; flown to Norway and regd as **G-44**, LN-HAW to Lufttransport 19Jun47. Accident 04Jly47: wheels-up landing at Oslo-Fornebu. Accident 09Jly47: take-off accident at Ålesund harbour. Accident 22Jly50: crashed and caught fire in bad weather at Vingrom, near Lillehammer, Norway. Three fatalities and aircraft written off. Regn cancelled 03Apr51.

1279   Built as **J4F-2** for Força Aérea Brasileira (Brazilian Air Force); accepted by FAB at Bethpage 29Sep42 and being flown there with FAB serial **05** 10Oct42; departed Bethpage on delivery 31Oct42. At Belém AFB between Nov42 and Jan43 but regularly reported at Galeão AFB between Jly43 and Dec44. Received new serial and local type designation **UC-4F2** 30Jly45, becoming **UC4F2 2671**; based at Galeão Jly45. No further details except wfu, date and circumstances unknown. SOC from Galeão AFB 17Sep47.

1280   Built as **J4F-2** for Força Aérea Brasileira (Brazilian Air Force); accepted by FAB at Bethpage 29Sep42 and being flown there with FAB serial **06** 11Oct42; departed Bethpage on delivery 31Oct42. Regularly reported at Galeão AFB between Feb43 and Jan44. Received new serial and local type designation **UC-4F2** 30Jly45, becoming **UC4F2 2672**; based at Galeão AFB Jly45. No further details except wfu, date and circumstances unknown. SOC from Galeão AFB 17Mar47.

1281   Built for the Aviación de Marina de Guerra (Cuban Navy) as **J4F-1** with delivery scheduled for Sep42 but rejected, presumably pre-delivery, and re-allocated to the US Navy by 04Sep42 as **J4F-2** with BuAer serial **33956** assigned 09Sep42. NAS New York 03Oct42 (possible del date); VS1D4 NAS Cape May 20Dec42 (assigned Eastern Sea Frontier); VS2D5 NAS Norfolk for operations at NAS Charleston & MCAS Cherry Point 27Feb43; subsequent records missing but with VS-38 NAS Norfolk by Aug44 [VS2D5 became VS-38 01Mar43]; CFASA NAS Lakehurst Oct44; NAS Seattle 06Feb45 for reconditioning; Pool NAS Seattle May45; Pool NAAS Franklin Jun45; CASU-67 NAS Edenton Jly45; CGAS Biloxi 07Jun46 until at least Jly46 when formally transferred to the US Coast Guard and SOC by the US Navy 31Jly46. In storage at AR&SC Elizabeth City by 25Sep46 when released for temporary use by USCG helicopter training operations. SOC by USCG, date unknown. (NC703 was reserved circa 17May46 for unknown type). Tfd from USCG Elizabeth City to US Dept of Interior, Washington, DC Nov48 for operation by Fish & Wildlife Service in Alaska with CofR as **G-44, N703** 18Nov48. Cvtd to civil status by Piedmont Aviation, Winston Salem, NC with CofA 21Mar49. Hull re-inforcement and step vents installed May53 with CofA 18May53 at TFH:1,700hrs. Offered for sale Mar56 and cancelled from USCAR 22Mar56. BoS to John W Mecom, Houston, TX 11May56 with CofR **N10610** 27Dec56. CofA 08May59 at TFH:2,043hrs. Cvtd to Continental IO-470-D engines and Hartzell HC-A2XF-2A props per McDermott STC SA2-13 Jun59. In Jly59, the following were installed: aux fuel tanks in both wings per McKinnon SA4-62, 2-place couch per SA2-632, gross weight increase to 5,500lbs, and aircraft cleaned and re-painted. CofA 02Sep59. Tfd by BoS to US Oil of Louisiana Inc, Houston, TX 01Mar60 with CofR 14May60. Temp fuel system installed 23Nov65 and ferry permit issued 24Nov65 for flight from Mount Pocono, PA to Boston and US/Canadian border en route Lagos, Nigeria, noting gross weight not to exceed 5,472lbs. Tfd by BoS to John W Mecom Co, Houston, TX 22Dec76 with CofR 03May77. BoS to Circle Bar Drilling Co, New Orleans, LA 09Jan79, with CofR 02Feb79. BoS to Dean H Franklin Aviation Enterprises Inc, Miami, FL 15Oct80 with CofR 02Dec80. No airworthiness data after 01Aug78. Sale reported 21Feb81 and remained so until CofR cancelled by FAA 29Jun11. Fate unknown.

1282   Built for the Aviación de Marina de Guerra (Cuban Navy) as **J4F-1** with delivery scheduled for Sep42 but rejected, presumably pre-delivery, and re-allocated to the US Navy by 04Sep42 as **J4F-2** with BuAer serial **33957** assigned 09Sep42. NAS New York 19Oct42 (possible del date) and assigned to Eastern Sea Frontier 03Nov42; subsequent records missing but with VS-34 NAS New York by Aug44 (and thus

assumed to have previously been with VS1D3 NAS New York that became VS-34 01Mar43); NAF Philadelphia (Mustin Fld) Dec44 and to reconditioning May45; Pool NAAS Franklin 22Aug45; Pool Hedron-5, FAW-5 NAS Norfolk Dec45; Pool CASU-67 NAS Edenton Jun46; FASRON-4 NAS Memphis Aug46 and SOC there 30Sep46 as obsolete and surplus. Regd as **G-44, NC9232H** to Lionel K Levy, New York, NY with CofR 20Nov46. Later as **N9232H** which was cancelled from USCAR 07Aug51. Fate unknown.

1283   Built as **J4F-2** for Força Aérea Brasileira (Brazilian Air Force); accepted by FAB at Bethpage 31Oct42 with FAB serial **07**. Assigned to Florianópolis AFB 17Dec42. Received new serial and local type designation **UC-4F2** 30Jly45, becoming **UC4F2 2673**; based at Florianópolis Jly45; transferred to Fábrica do Galeão for overhaul 02Oct47 when Florianópolis AFB was closed; assigned to Belém AFB 31May51; transferred to Santa Cruz AFB 20Feb52. Crashed Guanabara Bay, near Santos Dumont airport, Rio 29Apr52. SOC 20Aug52.

1284   Built as **J4F-2** for Força Aérea Brasileira (Brazilian Air Force); accepted by FAB at Bethpage 31Oct42 with FAB serial **08**; assigned to Florianópolis AFB 17Dec42. Received new serial and local type designation **UC-4F2** 30Jly45, becoming **UC4F2 2674**; based at Florianópolis AFB Jly45; transferred to Belém AFB 07Oct47 when Florianópolis AFB was closed; Crashed Belém 01Sep49. SOC from Belém AFB 13Jan50.

1285   Built as **J4F-2** for Força Aérea Brasileira (Brazilian Air Force); accepted by FAB at Bethpage 09Nov42 with FAB serial **09**; assigned to Belém AFB 17Dec42; at Belém Mar43. Received new serial and local type designation **UC-4F2** 30Jly45, becoming **UC4F2 2675**; based at Belém Jly45. Crashed Vigia, Pará 30Nov45. SOC from Belém AFB 06Apr48.

1286   Built as **J4F-2** for Força Aérea Brasileira (Brazilian Air Force); accepted by FAB at Bethpage 11Nov42 with FAB serial **10**; assigned to Belém AFB 17Dec42; at Belém Mar43. Received new serial and local type designation **UC-4F2** 30Jly45, becoming **UC4F2 2676**; based at Belém Jly45. Belly-landed Belém, 23May45, and DBR. SOC from Belém AFB 06Apr48.

1287   Built as **J4F-2** for Força Aérea Brasileira (Brazilian Air Force); accepted by FAB at Bethpage 18Nov42 with FAB serial **11**; noted at the Afonsos Air Depot in Jun and Sep43. Received new serial and local type designation **UC-4F2** 30Jly45, becoming **UC4F2 2677**; assigned to 1o Grupo de Transporte, Calabouço Jly45. Transferred posthumously 07Oct47 to Belém AFB, though it had crashed between Bocaina de Minas and Alagoas, state of Minas Gerais, 18Sep47. Site of accident also referred to as Pedra Negra. SOC from Belém AFB 27Jan48.

1288   Built as **J4F-2** for Força Aérea Brasileira (Brazilian Air Force); accepted by FAB at Bethpage 24Nov42 with FAB serial **12**; departed Bethpage on delivery 03Jan43; noted at Belém in Jan43 and at Santa Cruz between May43 and Oct44. Received new serial and local type designation **UC-4F2** 30Jly45, becoming **UC4F2 2678**; based at Santa Cruz Jly45. Transferred posthumously 07Oct47 to Belém AFB, though it had crashed Guanabara Bay, Rio 19Aug47. SOC from Belém AFB 09Dec47.

1289   Built as **J4F-2** for Força Aérea Brasileira (Brazilian Air Force); accepted by FAB at Bethpage 29Nov42 with FAB serial **13**; reported at Florianópolis in Sep43 and at Afonsos Air Depot in Jly44 and May45. Received new serial and local type designation **UC-4F2** 30Jly45, becoming **UC4F2 2679**; assigned to 1o Grupo de Transporte, Calabouço Jly45. Transferred to Belém Air Depot 11Apr47; to Belém AFB. SOC from Belém AFB as damaged beyond economical repair, 21Dec50.

1290   Built as **J4F-2** for Força Aérea Brasileira (Brazilian Air Force); accepted by FAB at Bethpage 30Nov42 with FAB serial **14**; assigned to the Seção de Aviões de Comando, Galeão 11Mar43; to Santa Cruz AFB 15Dec43. Received new serial and local type designation **UC-4F2** 30Jly45, becoming **UC4F2 2680**; based at Santa Cruz Jly45; to Fábrica do Galeão for overhaul 02Oct47; to Belém AFB 08Jan51; to Santa Cruz 20Feb52. By Nov52 officially listed as **VZCAF2**; to the Departamento de Aeronáutica Civil (DAC) as **VZCAF2 2680**; carried name 'Baluba Beech' prior to 1963. [A complex FAB 'in-joke'. 'Baluba Bear' was a dumb, comic-strip bear and the Beech reference was to the FAB's C-45s. The former senior officer who provided this 2010-vintage explanation also commented that the aircraft had once sunk in Sepetiba Bay, Rio and had been rebuilt]. DAC reserved the registration **PP-GQV** but this was ntu; wfu and apparently in open storage with Aero Clube de Nova Iguaçu, Rio when damaged by hail 01Feb63. Reregd **PP-HPU** 27Feb63 for the Aero Clube de Caxias do Sul. On 24Jly63 the DAC enquired of the club whether the aircraft was still wanted (reply untraced). The DAC (the Civil Aeronautics Department) was a branch of the Ministry of Aeronautics in charge of civil aviation that distributed government-owned aircraft to the flying clubs. The Aero Clube de Caxias do Sul had been allocated the aircraft but it was not interested in its acquisition and thus it remained in open storage at Nova Iguaçu. When seen derelict without engines or rudder in Oct65 the serial could be read as **C4F2 2680**. Formally SOC by DAC 29Nov65 but remained at Nova Iguaçu until eventually rescued and acquired by the Museu Aeroespacial (Aerospace Museum), Campo dos Afonsos, Rio de Janeiro in 1977. Currently displayed as **14** in original colour scheme. [Throughout its life and notwithstanding two attempts at civil registration the aircraft has remained government property].

1291   Built as **J4F-2** for US Navy, BuAer serial **32937**. Acc 23Dec42; NAS New York 28Dec42; NAS San Diego 20Jan43; NAS Alameda 10Feb43; NAS Pearl Harbor 05Mar43; Hedron, FAW-2 NAS Kaneohe Bay 07Mar43; records missing but with Hedron-2, FAW-2 NAS Kaneohe Bay by Aug44 until at least Apr46 and SOC there 30Jun46 as obsolete. First CofA issued 11Apr49 and regd as **G-44, NC69058** to Early J Moore, San Carlos, CA. To Lana R Kurtzer, Seattle, WA, by 1955, as **N69058**, with CofA 13Oct55. Noted hangared at Seattle Harbor 04Jan77, with Kurtzer Air Service. Not on USCAR 1978 but reregd to Lana R Kurtzer, Seattle, WA 1984. To Edson & Associates, Sitka, AK Jan88 and operated by Sitka Sounds Seafood. To Alfred Nordgren, Forest Grove, OR, Aug92. To Ag Northwest Inc, Hermiston, OR with CofR 15May96. Accident at Hermiston, OR 28Dec00: precautionary landing on grass after landing gear problems. Gear collapsed and left wing contacted ground damaging the wing spar. To Eugene F and Alice Maahs, Hermiston, OR, with CofR 04Jun02. Current and airworthy May13, with CofR due to expire 31Jly14.

G-44, c/n 1291, N69058, operated by Sitka Sounds Seafood, is seen here at Arlington, Washington, in August 1991.   *(AJ Payne)*

1292   Built for US Navy as **J4F-2**, BuAer serial **32938**. Acc 29Dec42; NAS New York 29Dec42; NAS San Diego 20Jan43; NAS Alameda 14Feb43; NAS Pearl Harbor 01Mar43; Hedron, CASU-1 NAS Pearl Harbor 09Mar43; records missing but with CASU-38 NAS Kaneohe Bay by Aug44; NAS Pearl Harbor Mar45 and reconditioned Apr45 and SOC there 31Jly45 as obsolete (but possibly following an incident 20Jly45). BoS RFC Honolulu to K-T Flying Service Ltd, Honolulu, HI, 01Oct45 for $5,100, with CofR as **G-44, NC62000** 10Jun46. BoS to Captain Edward A Thomasson, Picacho, AZ 09Jan50 for $4,500, with CofR **N62000** 13Feb50. BoS to Vest Aircraft & Finance Co, Denver, CO 01Sep50. BoS to Dwight L Calkins, Spokane, WA 02Oct50 with CofR 10Oct50. CofA 22Jly52 at TFH:749hrs. In Mar55 the aircraft was cvtd to **Super Widgeon** by McKinnon-Hickman, with Lycoming GO-480-B1 engines and Hartzell HC83X20-2A props, the keel was re-inforced and step vents installed, and the aircraft re-painted. CofA 25Mar55 at TFH:772hrs. Tfd by BoS to Calkins Manufacturing Co, Spokane, WA 10Apr56 with CofR 17Apr56. BoS to Price Piper Inc, Spokane, WA 14Mar72 with CofR 17Apr72. Tfd by BoS to Thomas J Price Jr, Spokane, WA 21Mar72 with CofR 26Apr72. BoS to James L Rodgers, Middlebury, IN 20Mar74 with CofR 10Apr74. Acft name: "*Frankly My Dear*" and later "*Canadian Clipper*". Address change, with amended CofR, 06May04. CofR expired 30Jun11, fate unknown.

1293   Built for US Navy as **J4F-2**, BuAer serial **32939**. Acc 31Dec42; NAS New York 07Jan43; NAS Norfolk 10Jan43; records missing but with Naval Attaché to Haiti by Oct44; NAS Guantanamo Bay Dec45 and SOC there 31Aug46 as obsolete and surplus. Regd as **G-44, NC1068M** to HL Brundage, Miami, FL 31Mar47; later as **N1068M**. Sold to General Leopoldo Vivas Gonzalez, date unknown. Sold to Abelardo Hernandez B, Caracas, Venezuela, date unknown. Sold to Silvio F DeYoreo, Rochelle Park, NJ 19Aug57. Reregd **YV-T-CTX** to De Yoreo 30Oct57 with CofA same date, but cancelled 31Dec57, as sold to USA. Remained the property of De Yoreo and CofA issued 03Mar58. Re-regd **N4147A** 23Jly58; address change to Bedford, TX by 1975. To James Barnett Driscoll, Wasilla, AK, Apr88. To Thomas O Young, Lake Oswego, OR with CofR 10Oct97; address change to Battle Ground, WA. Cancelled from USCAR 25Apr12 as exported to Canada.

1294   Built for US Navy as **J4F-2**, BuAer serial **32940**. Acc 11Jan43; NAS New York 11Jan43; Naval Attaché to Dominican Republic (handwritten records barely legible) 14Jan43; records missing but with Hedron-1, FAW-5 NAS Norfolk (aircraft assumed based at NAAS Harvey Point) by Aug44; NAF Philadelphia (Mustin Fld) Dec44 for reconditioning; Hedron, FAW-5 nominally at NAS Norfolk Jun45 (two aircraft on FAW-5 strength 30Jun45 based at NAAS Harvey Point and NAS Boca Chica but one only – presumably this aircraft – on strength 31Jly45 at Harvey Point); NAAS North Bend Aug45; Hedron, FAW-5 NAS Norfolk Sep45; SOSU-2 NAS New York Oct45; CGAS Salem 06Jun46 until at least Jly46 when formally transferred to the US Coast Guard and SOC by the US Navy 31Jly46. SOC by USCG circa 1949. Regd circa 1949 as **G-44, NC722** to Department of Interior, Washington, DC for use by Alaska Fish & Game, Juneau, AK, and later as **N722**, until 07Jun56. Reregd **N302** to Oren B Hudson, Iliamma, AK 08Jun56. CofA 09Sep58. Nominal change to O Hudson (dba Hudson Air Service), Anchorage, AK by 1978. To Oren B and Ruth G Hudson Trustee, Anchorage, AK with CofR 16Apr01. CofR expired 30Jun11, fate unknown.

G-44 Widgeon, c/n 1294, N302, owned by Oren Hudson, on the Nuyakuk River, Alaska in 1983, while on charter to the US Fish & Game Service. Note the down-turned Cessna wingtips.   *(Oren Hudson)*

1295   Built for US Navy as **J4F-2**, BuAer serial **32941**. Acc 30Jan43; NAS New York 09Feb43; NAS San Diego 15Feb43; NAS Pearl Harbor 09Mar43; records missing but with NAS Barbers Point by Aug44; Pool NAS Pearl Harbor May45; NAS Johnston Island 24May45; NAS Astoria Aug45; NAS Johnston Island Sep45 and SOC there 31Oct46 as obsolete. Regd as **G-44, NC69077** to Early J Moore, Belmont, CA. Fate unknown.

1296   Built for US Navy as **J4F-2**, BuAer serial **32942**. Acc 30Jan43; NAS New York 09Feb43; NAS San Diego 16Feb43; NAS Seattle 02Mar43; Commander Alaskan Sector, NAS Kodiak 07Mar43. Records missing but badly damaged at NAS Sitka 16May44: during a cross-wind water landing in the channel adjacent to Sitka the right wing was allowed to hit the water causing the aircraft to turn on its back and partly submerge in salt water. Although salvaged, the aircraft was badly damaged and was shipped to Seattle for major overhaul; awaiting reconditioning at NAS Moffett Fld by Oct44; NAS Seattle 09Feb45 for reconditioning; Pool NAS Alameda Aug45 and SOC there 31Mar46 as obsolete and surplus. Regd as **G-44, NC58521** to Milton Box Company Inc, Pendleton, OR, in 1947. Fate unknown.

1297   Built for US Navy as **J4F-2**, BuAer serial **32943**. Acc 31Jan43; records missing but with Hedron-15, FAW-15 NAS Port Lyautey by Aug44; NAS Port Lyautey 04Jly45; Naval Attaché to Egypt (at Cairo) Sep45 and SOC there 31Mar46 as obsolete and surplus. Regd as **G-44 NC79801** to Wallace Clair, New York, NY in 1946 but noted at Croydon, UK 20Oct46 still in full US Navy markings. Evaluated by the Centre d'Essais en Vol (CEV), Istres, France in early 1947 and known to have been flown from the Étang de Berre by a naval pilot between 05Feb47 and 11Feb47. Registration details for these trials recorded by pilot as 'Widgeon G44A 1297'. Damaged in France (perhaps at Istres/Berre) and abandoned by owner. Sold by Wallace to SCAN, La Pallice 15Jly47 and cancelled from USCAR 17Nov47. Rebuilt with CofA dated 15Mar48, and regd **F-BDAE** 16Mar48. When inspected by BV at La Pallice 20Mar48 the TFH were stated as 828hrs of which 50 were since re-build. Sold by SCAN to Société Helicop Azur/Air Monaco 08Mar48, with transfer paperwork noting its identity as 'Widgeon G-44 SCAN no 101'. The registration **F-BENK** was reportedly allocated to this aircraft post Mar48 in unknown circumstances, but was never used. Sold to the Office des Bois de l'Afrique Equatoriale Française, Libreville (the Forestry Commission, French Equatorial Africa, in modern Gabon) 28Apr49, and regd 18May49. Sold to the Sta Angolana de Levantamentos Aereos, Luanda (Angolan Aerial Surveys) as **CR-LCP** in 1952 quoting c/n as '1297' (officially exported from France Apr53). Sold to Transportes Aéreos de Cabo Verde as **CR-CAI** in 1960. Still in service in 1962, but ultimate fate unknown.

1298 Built for US Navy as **J4F-2**, BuAer serial **32944**. Acc 27Feb43; NAS Norfolk 12Mar43; NAS Anacostia 15Mar43; records missing but with MCAS Ewa by Aug44; Pool NAS Pearl Harbor Jly45 and SOC there 31Aug45 as obsolete and surplus (possibly following an accident 04Aug45). Regd as **G-44, NC62002** to K-T Flying Service Ltd, Honolulu, HI Aug46. Reregd **N353CW** and was the first conversion to **Super Widgeon**, with 270hp Lycoming GO-480-B1D engines, by McKinnon. Authority to ferry Portland, OR to Brandon, MB on US CofA for export E-46003 17Mar61. CofR(P) 26292 and CofA 9236 for **CF-NHG** to Donald S Paterson, Winnipeg, MB 20Apr61; inspected and CofA renewed at TFH:2,332hrs, valid until 05Apr63; at TFH:4,090hrs, valid until 03Aug77. BoS to Usibelli Coal Mine Inc 07Oct83 for US$100,000. Cancelled from CCAR 17Oct83 and regd **N4492N** to Usibelli Coal Mine Inc, Healy, AK with CofR 19Oct83. CofA 27Mar84 at TFH:4,477hrs, Tfd by BoS to Joseph E Usibelli, Fairbanks, AK 09Dec86. BoS to Joseph Emil Usibelli Trustee, Fairbanks, AK 27Nov99 with CofR 22Dec00. Current and airworthy Mar13, with CofR due to expire 29Feb16.

C/n 1298, the first G-44 converted to Super Widgeon standard by McKinnon, is seen here, as CF-NHG, at Winnipeg, Manitoba in the 1960s, when owned by Donald Paterson. (Fred J Knight Collection)

1299 Built for US Navy as **J4F-2**, BuAer serial **32945**. Acc 27Feb43; NAS Norfolk 14Mar43; ZP-51 05Apr43 (ZP-51 was a component of FAW-30, assigned to Airship Group 2 which, in Apr43, operated from Richmond, Trinidad, San Juan and Guantanamo Bay. This aircraft's base is not specified). Records missing but with A&R NAS Norfolk by Aug44; NAOTC NAS Jacksonville Dec44; NAS Miami Feb45 for repairs and reconditioning; Pool NAS Daytona Beach Feb46; NAS Banana River Mar46 and SOC there 30Jun46 as obsolete and surplus. Regd as **G-44, NC69168** to WW Windle Company, Millbury, MA and later as **N69168**. To Groveton Papers Co, Groveton, NH by Jun63. To McKinnon Enterprises, Sandy, OR 1969. To Peyton Hawes, Portland, OR 1970 and reregd **N2PS** 1973. Accident at 1315hrs on 11Nov73: crashed after take-off for a flight to Miami, FL and came to rest in water at Dry Tortugas-Garden Key, FL; pilot + 2 pax uninjured, but aircraft substantially damaged. NTSB found a broken elevator cable to be the cause. To Dept of Interior, National Park Service, Homestead, FL by 1977. N2PS cancelled from USCAR 24Sep84. BoS Amphibian Sales Inc, Miami, FL to Aero Sales & Leasing 06Nov92 as parts. Allotted C-GWJA 17Nov92. CofR(P) to Aero Sales & Leasing Ltd, Campbell River, BC, as **C-GWJA** 04May93; address change to Merville, BC 18Jun96. Reported as restoration project 01Jan99 to 31Jan03. Cancelled from CCAR 12Sep05 to USA and regd **N299CN** 18Nov05 to Charles F and Judith A Nichols Trustee, Baldwin Park, CA on Temporary CofA No:T057534. Stored, dismantled, at Yanks Air Museum, Chino, CA (still marked as N2PS) a/o Oct07. N299CN listed as current, but not airworthy May13, with CofR due to expire 31Oct15. [Note: *N2PS is currently carried by a Cessna 206H operated by the Department of the Interior out of Boise, ID.*]

1300 Built for US Navy as **J4F-2**, BuAer serial **32946**. Acc 22Mar43; NAS San Diego 10Apr43; records missing but with CASU-31 NAS Hilo by Aug44; Pool NAS Pearl Harbor Feb45 and SOC there 31Jly45 as obsolete but possibly following an incident/accident 20Jly45. BoS RFC

Honolulu to K-T Flying Service Ltd, Honolulu, HI 01Oct45 for $8,000; wing tip floats, anchor and ropes removed Nov45 to give 74lbs increase in useful load. CofA and CofR as **G-44, NC62003** issued 03Dec45. BoS to Early J Moore, Belmont, CA 01Dec47 with CofR 27Apr48; re-possessed by Bank of America National Trust & Savings Association 03May49, then as **N62003**; repaired May50 after landing accident. BoS Bank of America to Aircraft Sales & Brokerage Co, Long Beach, CA 28Aug50. BoS to WJ Holliday, Indianapolis, IN 29Aug50 with CofR 06Oct50. BoS to F Kirk Johnson, Fort Worth, TX 18Jun51 with CofR 02Aug51. BoS to River Construction Corp, Fort Worth, TX 31Aug51; major overhaul and keel modification with CofA 19Mar52 and CofR 27Mar52. Cvtd to **Super Widgeon** with Lycoming GO-435-C2Bs, per STC SA4-64, by Lockheed Acft Service Inc, Burbank, CA Mar53 with CofA 14Apr53 at TFH:1,253hrs. BoS to JD Reed Co Inc, Houston, TX 07Jly55 with CofR 01Aug55. BoS to The Superior Oil Co., Lafayette, LA 18Oct55 with CofR 25Oct55, and CofA dated 16Feb56 at TFH:2,505hrs; cvtd to 24volt system Nov57. Aircraft rebuilt Mar59 (after accident?); address change to Houston, TX 19Mar59. Reregd **N403E** 03Jun63; horizontal stabiliser modified per McDermott STC SA61SW, May65. BoS to Houston-Beechcraft Inc, Houston, TX 03Aug66 and sold same day to John W Ingle, Naples, NY, with CofR 01Sep66; aux fuel tanks installed per McKinnon STC SA4-958, Sep70; "extensive repairs" Jly74 after wind damage. BoS to Alfred F & Jeanne S Wright, (dba Wright Air Service), Fairbanks, AK 31Jan77 with CofR 02Mar78; modified for 5,500lbs gross weight (water) per STC SA380WE and escape hatch installed per SA4-967, Apr78. BoS to Kenneth Larson, Anchorage, AK 01Aug87 with CofR 26Aug87. BoS to H&H Aero Inc, Wilmington, DE 26Jun89 with CofR 27Jly89. BoS to Jord Corp, Wilmington, DE 30Sep91 with CofR 13Jun92. Regn **N60JK** issued 04Aug92 but ntu and cancelled 09Sep93. BoS to John H Callanan, Clifton Park, NY 21May93 with CofR 09Sep93 as **N403E**. BoS to Race Flying Boats Inc, Newark, DE 21May99 with CofR 23Jun99; address change to Bear, DE with CofR 23Mar01. Tfd by BoS to Race Aviation Inc, Longmeadow, MA with 01Oct04 for $210,000, with CofR 09Dec04. Although there are no airworthiness Forms 337 in the file after May86, the aircraft was listed as current and airworthy May13, with CofR due to expire 31Jan16.

1301 Built for US Navy as **J4F-2**, BuAer serial **32947**. Acc 22Mar43; NAS San Diego 11Apr43; NAS Seattle 13Apr43; records missing but with NAS Kodiak by Aug44. Badly damaged in water-loop at Woman's Bay, Kodiak 30Sep45; aircraft swung to the left after normal evening landing and then to the right as pilot attempted to correct the swing; right float torn off and with other damage (Cat B) a major overhaul was recommended. Investigation concluded that the swing had probably been caused by left wheel falling slightly out of its wheel well, but noted that pilot should have elected to land on the prepared strip rather than water. Active Apr46 but SOC at Kodiak 30Sep46, as obsolete and surplus. Regd as **G-44, NC79905** to EG Branha, Anchorage, AK. To Rainy Pass Lodge, Rainy Pass, AK as **N79905**. Damaged at Loon Lake, AK 18Aug53. Cancelled from USCAR 08Oct53 and replaced by c/n 1270 (qv).

1302 Built for US Navy as **J4F-2**, BuAer serial **32948**. Acc 26Mar43; NAS Norfolk 08Apr43; Hedron-12, FAW-12 NAS Key West 20Apr43; records missing but with FAW-12 NAS Key West by Aug44. Destroyed on Sacramento River, near Red Bluff, CA 26Feb45 when being ferried by a VRF-1 crew based at NAS Seattle, destination unknown (but perhaps Seattle). Pilot undertook simulated emergency landing at too low an altitude and struck the water, submerging the bow followed by the aircraft reversing direction and coming to rest in three feet of water in a "demolished" condition. On inspection the right landing gear was found to be extended; the crew suffered minor injuries and the accident was 100% blamed on the pilot; SOC 28Feb45. [VRF-1 is said to have been the largest squadron in the US Navy].

1303 Built for US Navy as **J4F-2**, BuAer serial **32949**. Acc 31Mar43 and del 01Apr43; NAS Norfolk 05Apr43; Hedron-3, FAW-3 NAS Coco Solo 07Apr43; records missing but with FAW-3 NAS Coco Solo by Aug44; NAS Seattle Mar45 for reconditioning; Pool NAAS Franklin Jly45; NAS Richmond Oct45; NAS Key West Dec45; CGAS St Petersburg 03Jun46 until at least Jly46 when formally transferred to the US Coast Guard and SOC by the US Navy 31Jly46. SOC by US Coast Guard circa 1948. **NC99** (previously assigned to Norseman c/n 211) reserved 18Oct48. Tfd to the CAA for assignment to the Alaskan Region for logistical support activities. CofA 28Jan49. CofR as **G-44, N99** to US Department of Commerce, Civil Aeronautics Administration, Washington, DC issued 05Apr49. Complete overhaul (inc new water rudder) and painted in CAA colour scheme, with CofA 03Jan50. Re-assigned by CAA to Aeronautical Center, Oklahoma City 04Jun52 for seaplane training. Hull modified and step vents installed Jly52 at Oklahoma City. CofA 03Sep52 at TT:2,007hrs. CAA request to cancel CofR N99, 11Aug54, due wfs for dead storage.

Declared surplus and tfd to Louisiana Property Agency, Baton Rouge, LA Jun58, and CofR cancelled again 18Aug58. BoS US Department of Commerce to State of Louisiana Civil Defense Agency, Baton Rouge, LA 22May58, "to be used for aerial reconnaissance for Civil Defense use in disaster". CofR as **N4990N** applied for 22May58, but not issued. BoS State of Lousiana Civil Defense Agency to Rapides Parish Civil Defense, Sheriff's Department, Alexandria, LA 02Jun58 with CofR **N4990N** 17Sep58. CofA 05May59 at TT:2,254hrs. BoS to J Curtiss McKinney, Titusville, PA 21Nov61 with CofR 08Feb62. A letter from FAA dated 22Jan71, to Winn Air Service, Syracuse, NY, stated that the FAA had reason to believe that a change of ownership had taken place. A reply from Winn Air Service to FAA, 29Jul74, noted that the aircraft had been scrapped. Cancelled from USCAR 02Aug74.

1304   Built for US Navy as **J4F-2**, BuAer serial **32950**. Acc 31Mar43; NAS San Diego 20Apr43; assigned to Pacific Fleet, NAS San Diego 24Apr43; NAS Dutch Harbor 10May43. Destroyed with four fatalities on 23Apr44 when aircraft flew in level flight into Mount Idak, Unmak Island, AK in poor visibility. SOC 27Apr44.

1305   Built for US Navy as **J4F-2**, BuAer serial **32951**. Acc 16Apr43 and del 18Apr43; NAS San Diego 24Apr43; records missing but with NAS Adak by Aug44 until at least Apr46; records unreadable but with NAS Kodiak by Aug46 where SOC 30Sep46 as obsolete and surplus. BoS War Assets Administration to Patrick R Arnold, Anchorage, AK 09Jun47, for $4,000. BoS to Hakon Christensen, Anchorage, AK 11Aug47 with CofR for **G-44, NC79906** 14Oct47. BoS Estate of Hakon Christensen to Sea Airmotive Inc, Anchorage, AK 15Mar57, as **N79906**. Cancelled from USCAR Mar57 and regn transferred to c/n 1327 (qv).

1306   Built for US Navy as **J4F-2**, BuAer serial **32952**. Acc and del 25Apr43; NAS Norfolk 30Apr43; records missing but with ZP-23, FAirShipWing-2 Chorrera Fld, Panama by Aug44; BlimpHedron-2 Chorrera Fld Sep44. Damaged during water landing in San Blas Gulf, Panama 15Sep44 when aircraft hit an unseen obstruction and took on water (pilot immediately took-off, minimising damage, but Cat C repairs necessary). NAMU Johnsville 01Nov44; NAF Philadelphia (Mustin Fld) Jan45 and under reconditioning May-Jly45; Pool NAS Quonset Point 21Jly45 and in minimal repair Feb-Apr46. SOC at Quonset Point 31Aug46 as obsolete and surplus. Regd as **G-44, NC66273** to Smith Equipment Company, Columbia, SC, and later as **N66273**. To Amphibious Charters Inc, Beaver Falls, NY as **N273L** in May62. To J Curtiss McKinney, Titusville, PA as **N278L**, 23Mar64. To Endicott P Davison, New Canaan, CT 1969. Cvtd to **Super Widgeon** with Lycoming GO-435-C2B2 engines (date unknown). CF-QPL allotted to Dr Slade, Burlington, ON 27May71. Authority to ferry Linden, NJ to Hamilton, ON 27May71 with US CofA for export E-96948 04Jun71. BoS Davison to Slade 10Jun71. Inspected and cancelled from USCAR 16Jun71 at TFH:5,609hrs with CofA 17Jun71. CofR(P) for **CF-QPL** to Reginald H Slade, Burlington, ON, 25Jun71; CofA renewed at TFH:5,942hrs, valid until 28Jun76. Reverted by BoS to James C McKinney, Titusville, PA 19May76 for $57,000. BoS Estate of McKinney to Amphibian Parts Inc, Miami, FL 1978 and cancelled from CCAR 20Mar78. To **N25DF** for Richard Hough, Morristown, NJ, Jan78. To Richard R Hough, dba Fisher Forestry & Realty Co, Concord, NH, Nov90. To Robert M Hough, Derry, NH, with CofR 28Aug92; uprated to Lycoming GO-480-G1D6 engines; address change to Windham, NH. Current but not airworthy May13, with CofR due to expire 31Jan15.

1307   Built for US Navy as **J4F-2**, BuAer serial **32953**. Acc 30Apr43 and del 02May43; records missing but with Hedron-11, FAW-11 by Aug44 (FAW-11 was headquartered at NAS San Juan but its two J4F-2s were based at NAS Trinidad and NAS Guantanamo Bay, thus location uncertain – see 32957); CASU-21 NAS Norfolk 14Jun45; NAS Seattle 21Jly45 for reconditioning; CASU-67 NAS Memphis 27Dec45; FASRON-4 NAS Memphis Aug46 and SOC there 30Sep46 as obsolete and surplus. Regd as **G-44, NC9211H** to Benjamin L Churuton(?), c/o Frost Box Company, Pawtucket, RI. To Inlet Airlines Inc, Anchorage, AK May58 as **N9211H**. Cancelled from USCAR 03Sep71. Fate unknown.

1308   Built for US Navy as **J4F-2**, BuAer serial **32954**. Acc 30Apr43; NAS Tillamook date unknown. Following an engine problem while holding for a conventional landing at Tillamook on 16Sep43, pilot elected to undertake a precautionary water landing in Tillamook Bay. Landing in ideal conditions the starboard wing was allowed to drop allowing the float to dig in and the aircraft water-loop. The badly damaged aircraft became inverted and sank and, although recovered and initially identified for major overhaul, was subsequently SOC 30Oct43.

1309   Built for US Navy as **J4F-2**, BuAer serial **32955**. Acc 17May43 and del 18May43; records missing but with VJ-15 NAS Brunswick by Sep44; ComDesLant NAS Brunswick Oct44; VJ-15 NAS Brunswick

Oct45; ComDesLant NAS Brunswick Nov45; VJ-15 NAS Brunswick May46; NAS Brunswick Jly46 and SOC there 30Sep46 as obsolete and surplus. Regd as **G-44, NC9863H** to Atwood Vacuum Machine Co, Rockford, IL by 17Dec46; and by 03Jul47 to Seth G Atwood, Rockford, IL as **N9863H**; by 14Oct49 to Atwood Vacuum Machine Co, Rockford, IL. Regn CF-GYZ allotted to Associated Aero Services Ltd, Vancouver, BC 28Mar51. BoS Seth G Atwood/ Atwood Vacuum Machine Co to Realite Ltd and USCofA for export E-19460 both dated 03Apr51. CofR(C) 10075 and CofA 3462 for **CF-GYZ** issued 03Apr51, to Realite Ltd, Vancouver, BC. Leased to Associated Air Taxi Ltd 12Apr51 for one year. CofA renewed at TFH:1,089hrs, valid until 03Apr53, and at TFH:1,525hrs, valid until 12Feb54. BoS Realite Ltd to Pacific Western Airlines Ltd, Vancouver, BC 16Jun53 for $14,500; CofR(C) 12126 issued 16Jun53. CofA renewed at TFH:2,444hrs, valid until 25Nov55. On 22May56 'YZ took off at circa 1040hrs for a non-scheduled flight from Kemano, BC to Kittimat, BC with the pilot and two pax. Before take-off from Kemano the pilot had been requested to look out for a missing man who might have been on a beach between Dorothy Island and Hopkins Point. At circa 1130hrs the aircraft was seen in the vicinity of Dorothy Island apparently making the search as requested, and when last seen was heading North over Hopkins Point. When the aircraft failed to arrive at Kittimat a search was begun at 1215hrs. At 2020hrs the aircraft was found submerged in 35 feet of water, about 100yds from the West shore of Eagle Bay, BC. The pilot and both pax were dead and the aircraft destroyed. The wreckage was salvaged but the starboard wing and engine were not found. Both the rudder trim tab indicator and the trim tab were set for full left rudder perhaps indicating a loss of power on the starboard engine. The undercarriage was locked down, but no evidence of malfunction could be found in the aircraft and engine controls. Cancelled from CCAR 18Jun56.

1310   Built for US Navy as **J4F-2**, BuAer serial **32956**. Acc 22May43 and immediately transferred to the UK (BPC) as **JS996**; 111 OTU Oakes Fld, Nassau, presumably from May43 and certainly by Aug43; remained at Oakes Fld for ASR purposes, eventually being returned from 111 OTU to 45 Group 15Dec45. Subsequent military history vague but briefly on strength of 1318 (Communications) Flight at Nassau in early 1946 where probably used for 'diplomatic' purposes *(see logbook entry on the next page)*. Flown Nassau-Miami 26Feb46 and noted on UK records as recaptured by the Foreign Liquidation Commission Miami 28Feb46. Regd as **G-44, NC66197** to Charles L Yuille, Miami, FL. To Astron Corp, Houston, TX 1963. Cancelled from USCAR 12Jun65. Fate unknown.

1311   Built for US Navy as **J4F-2**, BuAer serial **32957**. Acc 22May43 and del 28May43; records missing but with Hedron-11, FAW-11 by Aug44 (FAW-11 was headquartered at NAS San Juan but its two J4F-2s were based at NAS Trinidad and NAS Guantanamo Bay, thus location uncertain – see 32953); Pool NAS Seattle Jly45 and reconditioned Aug-Dec45; Pool CASU-67 NAS Memphis 24Jan46; FASRON-4 NAS Memphis Aug46 and SOC there 30Sep46 as obsolete and surplus. Regd as **G-44, NC9591H** to Detroit School of Aviation Inc, Royal Oak, MI. To Leland C Roskay, Niles, MI, as **N9591H**. CF-HEN allotted to Sanderson Aircraft Ltd, Malton, ON 17Jun53; authority to ferry Niles, MI to Toronto, ON 18Jun53. BoS Leland Roskay to Sanderson Aircraft and US CofA for export E-24501 both dated 17Jly53; BoS to Tateishi 21Jly53; CofR 12227 and CofA 4126 both issued for **CF-HEN** to Arthur Tateishi, Toronto, ON 17Jly53 (Tateishi was President of Seabreeze Manufacturing, Toronto, ON). Inspected and CofA renewed at TFH:962hrs, valid until 07Jly55. Cvtd to Lycoming GO-480-B1B power 02Apr56; inspected and CofA renewed at TFH:1,318hrs, valid until 07Jly57. BoS to Price Air Services 27Jun60; CofR(P) 25082 to Price Air Services Ltd, Toronto, ON issued 03Aug60; CofR amended to Commercial 17Nov60; inspected and CofA renewed at TFH:2,175hrs, valid until 09Apr62. CofR amended to Private 10Sep62. BoS to Carl Millard Ltd 23Apr65. BoS to Boothe Leasing 23Apr65; CofR(P) 34538 to Boothe Leasing of Canada Ltd, Toronto, ON 23Apr65; inspected and CofA renewed at TFH:2,392hrs, valid until 01Jun66; nominal change to Greyhound Leasing & Financial of Canada Ltd, Toronto, ON 17Oct66 with CofR(P) 34538. BoS Greyhound Leasing to North Coast Air Services Ltd 28Feb67 (covering CF-HEN and Cessna 180 CF-IRQ). CofA renewed at TFH:2,882hrs, valid until 01Jun68. CofR(C) 43643 issued to North Coast Air Services Ltd, Prince Rupert, BC 02Jun67; inspected at TFH:3,407hrs and CofA renewed, valid until 03Nov72. BoS to Dean Franklin Aviation Enterprises, Miami, FL 19Jly73 and cancelled from CCAR 20Jly73. Seen at Opa Locka, FL 01Sep73, with North Coast titles, wearing CF-HEN and N62881. To Antonio Bascaro, Ciudad Guatemala, Guatemala as **N62881**, in 1973. Reported regd to JJ Campbell, Woodinville, WA by 1975, but regd **TG-BIZ** to Richard Eugene Stader Cater, Guatemala City, Guatemala, with CofR 10Dec82. Aircraft colour scheme described as white, orange and blue. BoS Richard E Stader to Michael L Cozad, Las Vegas, NV 26Jun02. TG-BIZ cancelled 23Jly03, aircraft returned to USA for restoration and stored at Chandler, AZ. CofR

YEAR 1946		AIRCRAFT		PILOT, OR 1ST PILOT	2ND PILOT, PUPIL OR PASSENGER	DUTY (INCLUDING RESULTS AND REMARKS)
MONTH	DATE	Type	No.			
—	—	—	—	—	—	—— TOTALS BROUGHT FORWARD
Feb.	21	Widgeon	JS996	F/L Brown	Self.	NASSAU. Air Test.
"	..	LIN		Self.		NASSAU. True Fade - synergy range. & let-down.
"	26	Widgeon	JS996	F/L Brown	Self. w/o Lawrence	NASSAU - MIAMI Delivery flight navigation duties carried out.
"	..	Dakota	KN673	F/L Rees.	c/c Roberts Self.	MIAMI - NASSAU. Return flight.
March 1st 1946.					O.C. 1318 Comm: Flt.	

GRAND TOTAL [Cols. (1) to (10)]

J4F-2, c/n 1310: Eddie Miles' logbook showing, delivery flight of Widgeon, JS996, from 1318 Communications Flight, Nassau to Miami, Florida, on 26th February 1946. *(courtesy Eddie Miles)*

N744MC issued 05Dec03 to Cozad, with Temporary CofA T036205 which expired 04Jan04. Standard CofA 26Aug10, at TFH:4,725hrs, with Lycoming GO-480-B1D engines and Hartzell HC-83X20-2C1 props. Current and airworthy May13, with CofR due to expire 30Jun13.

1312   Built for US Navy as **J4F-2**, BuAer serial **32958**. Acc 19May43 and del 30May43; records missing but with NAS Guantanamo Bay by Aug44 and SOC there 31Aug46 as obsolete and surplus. Regd as **G-44**, **NC1069M** to HL Brundage, Miami, FL 31Mar47 and later **N1069M**. Reregd **N69T** 06Apr53 and **N86T** 24Jan57, before going to Canada as a **Super Widgeon** (Lycoming GO-480-B1B). Regn CF-KKF allotted to Carl Millard Ltd 06Jan58 and CofA 6721 issued 22Jan58, but CofR(P) 19463 issued for **CF-KKF** to Donald S Paterson, Winnipeg, MB 29Jan58. CofR renewed at TFH:2,126hrs, valid until 29Jan60. CofR(P) 24415 to G Blair Gordon, Montreal, PQ, 07Jly61; CofR renewed at TFH:2,596hrs, valid until 31Mar63. CofR(P) 31963 to Commander Aviation Ltd, Malton, ON 18Aug64. CofR(P) 34083 to Boothe Leasing of Canada Ltd, Toronto, ON 05Oct64. CofR(P) 36797 to Acceptance Mortgage Corp, Vancouver, BC 30Jun66. BoS 23Mar67 to McKinnon Enterprises Inc, Sandy, OR for $52,750 and cancelled from CCAR 02May67. Regd as **N13122** as **Super**

Widgeon with 295hp Lycoming GO-480 engines, with CofA 02Oct67. To James Magoffin, Fairbanks, AK Jan70 and to co-owner James S Magoffin Snr, Fairbanks, AK, 09Dec97. Preserved at Alaska Aviation Heritage Museum, Lake Hood, Anchorage and regd to them 09Apr02. Current and airworthy May13, with CofR due to expire 28Feb14.

1313   Built for US Navy as **J4F-2**, BuAer serial **32959**. Acc and del 17Jun43; records missing but with NAS Whidbey Island by Aug44; NAS Seattle May45 for reconditioning; NAS Whidbey Island 04Jly45; CGAS Port Angeles 10Jun46 until at least Jly46 when formally transferred to the US Coast Guard and SOC by the US Navy 31Jly46; eventually to USCG storage at AR&SC Elizabeth City. SOC by USCG circa 1949. Tfd from CGAS Elizabeth City to US Department of Interior, Fish & Wildlife Service, Washington, DC 28Jun50 with CofR for J4F-2, **N708**, 01Aug50. Cvtd "from Coast Guard to civil status" by Baltimore Aero Service, MD with CofA 05Aug50 at TFH:1,022hrs. Re-engined with 260hp Lycoming GO-435-C2B, 20May53 as **Super Widgeon** by McKinnon-Hickman Co, Portland, OR with CofA same date at TFH:1,736hrs. Retractable water rudder installed Apr55 with CofA 28Apr55; CofA 17Apr56 at TFH:2,470hrs; wfu in Alaska by Aug58. BoS to LE Flahart, Anchorage, AK 07Aug58 with CofR for **G-44**, **N708C**, 14Nov58. BoS to Sea-Air Inc, Anchorage, AK 04Sep59 with CofR 06Oct59. BoS to Interior Airways Inc, Fairbanks, AK 06Jun60 with CofR 06Aug60. BoS to James S Magoffin, Fairbanks, AK 23Feb72 with CofR 20Mar72. Accident at 1030hrs on

16Jly74: wheels-up landing at McKinnon A/P, Sandy, OR after local test flight. Pilot uninjured but aircraft substantially damaged. Acft acquired by McKinnon Coach Inc, Sandy, OR in lieu of unpaid bills by Magoffin, with "BoS" dated 03Feb75 and CofR 01Mar75. BoS to Widgeon Franklin Inc, Columbus, OH, 19Apr76 with CofR 29Apr76. Regn **N5SW** reserved 22Sep77, but ntu, and confirmed as **N708C** 17Jan79. BoS to Saunders-Vixen Aircraft Co Inc, Eastsound, WA 09Apr02 with CofR 29May02. Re-engined with Lycoming GO-480-B1D by Aug05. Current and airworthy May13, with CofR due to expire 31Aug14.

1314   Built for US Navy as **J4F-2**, BuAer serial **32960**. Acc 29Jun43 and del 01Jly43; records missing but with Commander, All Forces, Aruba-Curacao, Curacao by Aug44; NAS Key West Sep44; NAS Boca Chica Oct44; NAS Key West Mar45; NAS Seattle Aug45 for reconditioning; Pool NAS Seattle Mar46; and SOC there 31Jly46 as obsolete and surplus. Regd as **G-44, NC70060** to Schafer Bakery Products Co, Battle Creek, MI, and later as **N70060**. Operated by Great Lakes Charters, Camden, NY a/o Nov54. Reregd **N128A** to Oswego Falls Corp, Fulton, NY 11Mar59. To Sealright Co Inc, Fulton, NY 1966. To J Curtiss McKinney, Titusville, PA 1969. Accident at 1537hrs on 13Sep69: struck trees in forced landing at Halifax, NS after both engines failed. The G-44 ran out of fuel at the end of a flight from Gander, NL; pilot + 4 pax uninjured but aircraft substantially damaged. Cancelled from USCAR 05Jun70.

1315   Built for US Navy 15Jun43 as **J4F-2**, BuAer serial **32961**. Acc 21Jun43 and del 22Jun43; NAS San Diego 08Jly43; NAS Alameda 11Jly43; NAS Pearl Harbor 20Jly43. Aircraft lost following minor damage 20Sep43 at NAS Hilo: CASU-31 pilot was undertaking a local test-hop when the aircraft was water-looped, damaging both port and starboard floats and wing-tips; the aircraft was towed to the nearby dock for recovery but salt water was allowed to enter the aircraft via the cockpit hatch (a crane should have been used to lift the aircraft). Although initially identified for major overhaul with Cat 'B' damage it was subsequently SOC 09May44. A letter from Link Aeronautical Corporation to CAA, dated 03Nov54, stated that Link had bought the hull and centre section of the aircraft bearing s/n 1315 in October 1946, with a long-term view of rebuilding it with parts of other aircraft; also requesting to reserve registration N77L. CofR as **G-44, N76K** issued to Link Aeronautical 15Nov54. Cvtd to **Super Widgeon** with Lycoming GO-435-C2B power by Link Aeronautical Jun55 per Lockheed conversion kit and Lockheed master drawing #SPD-712-116. Authority to ferry Endicott, NY to Rimouski, QC 14Jun55. Cancelled from USCAR 23Jly55. BoS Link to Soucy Automobile 27Jun55, exported on CofA E-26402 and cancelled from USCAR 28Jly55. CofR(C) 13807 issued for **CF-IHI** to Soucy Automobile Inc, Rimouski, QC, 27Jun55; CofA 4870 issued 05Aug55. Accident at 1435hrs on 21Jan56: after an instrument let down into Mont Joli Airport, QC, and with the windshield covered with ice, the pilot, JA Henri Rouselle, forgot to lower the undercarriage. CofA renewed, valid until 27Mar57; CofR amended to Private 27Jun56; CofA renewed at TFH:406hrs, valid until 10Apr58; authority to ferry Montreal, QC to Canada/US border (en route to Linden, NJ) 13Aug58; CF-IHI cancelled 18Aug58 and CF-HPD allotted to Simard & Frères; authority to ferry US/Canada border to Montreal, QC 27Aug58. Inspected at TFH:418hrs and CofR 20141(P) for **CF-HPD** and CofA 7307 issued to Simard & Frères, Cie Ltée, Montreal, QC 05Sep58; inspected and CofA renewed at TFH:783hrs, valid until 18Sep60 [now with Lycoming GO-480-B1D engines]. CofA renewed at TFH:1,107hrs, valid until 18Sep61. Placed in storage with Kingston Flying Club, ON for the winter Nov60; authority to ferry Montreal, QC to Linden, NJ 09May62 and return 08Jun62. Tfd by BoS to Simard-Beaudry Inc 21Jan65; inspected and CofA renewed at TFH:1,331hrs, valid until 04Jun66. CofR(P) 33119 issued to Simard-Beaudry Inc, Montreal, QC 09Jun65. Accident at 1545hrs on 02Jly67: due to bad weather, on a flight from Baie Comeau, QC to Quebec City, the pilot, Bruce Hikky, elected to land at Montmagny. The aircraft landed on soft ground on the side of the runway and overturned. CofA renewed at TFH:1,583hrs, valid until 25Mar69. BoS to Simco Ltée 17Jun68; CofR(P) 42501 issued to Simco Ltée, Ville d'Esteral, QC 21Jun68. BoS to Bradley Air Services Ltd 22Sep70 for $20,000; CofR(C) to Bradley A/S Ltd, Carp, ON 23Sep70; CofA renewed at TFH:1,772hrs, valid until 11Aug73. BoS to Aircraft Sales Inc 01Mar74 and cancelled from CCAR 22Apr74. To **N8AS** with Aircraft Sales Inc, Charlotte, NC 1974; CofA 04Jun76 at TFH:1,807hrs, now with Lycoming GO-480-B1D engines; transferred by undated BoS to Donald Anklin, Charlotte, NC with CofR 18Jun76. BoS to Lake New England Inc, Laconia, NH 26Aug76. BoS to Michael B Braunstein, Weirs Beach, NH 05Aug78 with CofR 30Aug78. Experimental CofA 23Jly82 to test a wing-mounted radar pod, on Copake Lake, NY; Standard CofA 30Jly82 after testing completed; another Experimental CofA issued 16Aug82 and Standard CofA re-issued 18Aug82 after another 3½hours' testing. By Oct82 Braunstein had an address in New York City. Both engines removed Apr95 and modified to

295hp Go-480-G1D6 standard per Lycoming instructions and had Hartzell HC A3V20-2 props by Jun00. In Feb06 Braunstein advised the FAA of address change to Craryville, NY with new CofR issued 21Mar06. Current and airworthy Apr13, with CofR due to expire 31Jan15. Accident 02May13: the aircraft crashed into the Hudson River, near Germantown, NY, killing the owner. The aircraft was destroyed, initial reports describing a fire on the surface of the river.

1316   Built for US Navy as **J4F-2**, BuAer serial **32962**. Acc 23Jun43 and del 24Jun43; records missing but with NAS Great Exuma Island by Aug44; NAS Norfolk 06Nov44 for reconditioning; Pool NAS Norfolk Jly45 and SOC there 31Oct45. Strike code unspecific but aircraft clearly lost as a result of incident/accident.

1317   Built for US Navy as **J4F-2**, BuAer serial **32963**. Acc and del 31Jly43; records missing but with NAS Hilo by Aug44; NAS Barbers Point Mar46; NAS Ford Island Apr46; NAS Pearl Harbor 11Jun46 and SOC there 30Jun46 as obsolete and surplus. BoS War Assets Administration to JK Mardick, Honolulu, HI 22Jan47, for $2,500. BoS to Fred C Richards, San Francisco, CA 26Feb47, for $3,400. BoS to RV Hedin, South Minneapolis, MN 07Apr47, for $3,900, with CofR **NC67867** 18Apr47 and CofA 05May47. BoS to Arrowhead Skyhaven, Inc, Isabella, MN 12Sept47, for $12,000, with CofR 30Sep47. BoS to Albert G Lary & Co, Los Angeles, CA 06Jlyy48, with CofR 29Jly48. BoS to Vest Aircraft & Finance Co, Denver, CO 15Oct48. BoS to Thomas A Coffey, American Express Co, New York, NY 26Apr50 with CofR **N67867** same date. BoS to Onal Air Transport Corp, New York, NY 23May50 with CofR 25May50. BoS to Simsbury Flying Service Inc, Simsbury, CT 14Nov52; CofA 26Jan53 at TFH:1,071hrs and CofR 28Sep53. BoS to The HB Davis Co, Baltimore, MD 07Dec53 with CofR 15Dec53; CofA 01Dec55 at TFH:1,645hrs. BoS to Charles Stuart MacLean, dba Wood-Mosaic Co, Louisville, KY 03Dec55 with CofR 14Dec55. MacLean died 07Jlyy61 and his daughter, as Trustee was awarded ownership of the G-44 under the terms of MacLean's will. A BoS dated 31May67 effects the transfer to Kathleen MacLean Gowell, Louisville, KY and CofR issued 29Jun67. BoS to J Ray McDermott & Co Inc, Harvey, LA 14Jun68 with CofR 05Jly68. Re-engined with 260hp Continental IO-470-D with Hartzell HCA2XF 2A propellers per STC SA2-13, during major overhaul Apr70. Main fuel tanks capacity increased to 176gal total and one 34gal fuel tank installed in each outer wing panel per STC SA4-958 Feb71. Increase in gross weight to 5,400lbs by installation of McKinnon floatation and landing gear kits per STC SA380WE and SA2-284 Apr71. Ferry fuel system installed 17Jun71 and Special Flight Permit issued 18Jun71 for ferry from Newton, KS via Portland, ME to Lagos, Nigeria. Reregd **5N-AMD** by J Ray McDermott Ltd, Ikeja, Nigeria, Jan72, and N67867 cancelled 06Mar72. Began return to New Orleans via Shoreham and Glasgow, UK during Sep74 and in store Glasgow from Oct74. 5N-AMD cancelled 08Oct74. Restored as **N67867** 07Aug75 (to McDermott, New Orleans, LA) and painted as such in Glasgow, UK and arrived USA 19Sep75. CofA 29Feb76 after overhaul at TFH:7,181hrs. Shipped back to Nigeria after Oct76, regd **5N-AMG** and N67867 cancelled from USCAR again 08Feb77. By 1986 aircraft was stored intact at Warri, Nigeria but unflyable due to CofA lapse. BoS McDermott (Nigeria) Ltd to Walter Bueker, Warri, Nigeria 21Sep88. Nigerian regn cancelled by Apr91. Imported to UK via Germany by Tony Allen and restored to flying condition by Mark Hales. **G-BTKJ** allocated 14May91 for Belinda Jane Snoxall, St Albans, Herts. Wfu 1991 and stored Brooklands, UK until 1994. BoS Mark Hales (as owner) to Warren F Chmura, Norwich, UK 14Aug94. BoS Chmura to Warren F Chmura (Trustee), Norwich, UK, 19Mar95 and restored as **N67867** with CofR 21Jly95 and CofA 19Nov95. UK regn cancelled 20Jly95; Chmura

C/n 1317 during restoration at Spanhoe Lodge, Northamptonshire, in 1994. The aircraft eventually had its original US registration, N67867, restored and it is currently flying with an owner in Florida.   (AJ Clarke)

informed FAA 13Nov95 that his address had changed and he was dba Southern Trust, St Just, Cornwall, UK, work had finished on the acft and it was ready to fly. CofA issued 19Nov95 at TFH:11,175hrs; test-flown at Spanhoe Lodge, UK 09Dec95 and stored at Little Staughton, UK 1995-96. Visited PFA Rally, Cranfield, UK, Jly97. BoS Chmura Trustee to JMQ Inc, Gulf Breeze, FL 12Nov97 with CofR 14Nov97. Prepared for transatlantic ferry by Eastern Air Executive Co at Sturgate, near Gainsborough, UK and routed via Wick-Vagar-Rekyavik 22Nov97 and KUS 28Nov97 en route to Florida. Three-blade McCauley propellers installed per STC SA00893CH, 23Jan01. Current and airworthy May13, with CofR due to expire 31Dec15.

1318 Built for US Navy as **J4F-2**, BuAer serial **32964**. Acc 16Jly43 and del 17Jly43; records missing but with NAS Trinidad by Sep44; NAS Norfolk Nov44 for reconditioning; Pool NAS Norfolk Jly45 and SOC there 31Oct45. Strike code indicates a crash due pilot error while on a training flight.

1319 Built for US Navy as **J4F-2**, BuAer serial **32965**. Acc 20Jly43 and del 21Jly43; records missing but with NAS Atlantic City by Aug44; NAS Seattle by May45 for reconditioning; Pool NAAS Franklin 30Jun45; NAS Atlantic City Aug45; CGAS Brooklyn 06Jun46 until at least Jly46 when formally transferred to the US Coast Guard and SOC by the US Navy 31Jly46. Active with CGAS Brooklyn until at least Oct48; overhauled at USCG Acft Repair & Supply Base Elizabeth City May49 and tfd to US Dept of Interior, Fish & Wildlife Service, Washington, DC 01Jun49, with CofR **NC728** 10Jun49. Cvtd from J4F-2 to **G-44** Jun49 with CofA 01Jly49 at TFH:1,140hrs. Hull modification kit installed Dec50; 30gal auxiliary fuel tank installed Mar51 at TFH:1,642hrs; TFH:2,021hrs a/o 24Apr52. DBR and cancelled from USCAR 24Jun53. BoS to Howard Hanifl, Robbinsdale, MN 01May54. BoS to George Lambros Jr, Ridgefield Pk, NJ 05May54 with CofR **N1595V** 10May54; major overhaul and repaint Oct56, with CofA 18Oct56. Tfd by BoS to Lambros Seaplane Base, Ridgefield, NJ 24Apr57 with CofR 14May57. BoS to Paul H Steigerwald, Lancaster, PA 05Apr63 with CofR 29Apr63. Accident at 2045hrs on 30Aug69: porpoised and sank during night landing on river at Wrightsville, PA; pilot + 2 pax uninjured but aircraft substantially damaged. BoS to Gladen R Hamilton Jr, Edgewater, MD 28Oct75 with CofR 12Nov75; address change to Vashon, WA 22Sep86. BoS to Donald H Schlueter, Genesee, ID 17Jun96 with CofR 11Feb97. Current and airworthy May13, with CofR due to expire 31Dec13.

1320 Built for US Navy as **J4F-2**, BuAer serial **32966**. Acc and del 27Jly43; records missing but with NAS Brunswick by Aug44; NAS Seattle by 30Jun45 for reconditioning which presumably did not happen; NAS Brunswick Jly45; NAS Seattle Aug45 for reconditioning; NAS Brunswick 16Oct45; CGAS Salem 06Jun46 until at least Jly46 when formally transferred to the US Coast Guard and SOC 31Jly46 by US Navy. SOC by USCG to War Assets Administration, probably in 1947. Tfd to Dept of Interior, Fish & Wildlife, Chicago, IL 24Feb48 and regd to them as **NC702**, 31Mar48 (replacing c/n 1350 qv). Cvtd and reconditioned to **G-44** status, repaired and inspected at Winston Salem, NC, 14Sep48. CofAs issued 28Oct48, 30Jly49, 05May50 and 07Dec50. DBR at San José, Costa Rica 19Jan51 and cancelled from USCAR 14Aug51.

C/n 1320, NC702, smartly painted for the US Department of the Interior, circa 1948. The aircraft was damaged beyond repair, while working for the Department in San José, Costa Rica, on 19th January 1951. *(MAP)*

1321 Built for US Navy as **J4F-2**, BuAer serial **32967**. Acc 27Jly43 and del 28Jly43 to ADU at NAS New York; NAF Annapolis 29Jly43; records missing but with NAF Annapolis by 06Mar44 when involved in forced landing due icing at Towanda, PA (minor damage) and in Aug44. SOC 31Dec44 following an accident but presumably reassessed and repaired as reinstated at NAAS Charlestown 31Mar45; Pool NAS Quonset Point Jun45 where minimally repaired Aug-Sep45; NAS Seattle Oct45 for reconditioning; Pool NAS Seattle Jan46 and SOC there 30Apr46 as obsolete. Regd as **G-44, NC67794** to Alaska Coastal Airlines, Juneau, AK, later **N67794**. Accident 04Nov54: crashed while operating ACA Flt No.60

C/n 1321, NC67794, of Alaska Coastal Airlines, at an unknown location circa 1947. The aircraft carries the (partly unreadable) legend, ??? Air Service, on the bow. *(Jack McNulty)*

from Sitka to Juneau. The flight was to be via Pelican City, Chickagof Island, AK and Hoonah but a few minutes after leaving Pelican City at 1305hrs with 2 pax, the aircraft crashed in a mountain pass en route to Hoonah. The pilot was fatally injured but the passengers survived the crash, which destroyed the aircraft.

1322 Built for US Navy as **J4F-2**, BuAer serial **32968**. Acc and del 31Jly43; Atlantic Fleet, NAS Norfolk 13Aug43. Aircraft lost 20Sep43 adjacent to Chambers Fld, NAS Norfolk in Willoughby Bay, Hampton Roads, VA; crewed by a Hedron-5, FAW-5 NAS Norfolk pilot based at NAAS Harvey Point, the aircraft became prematurely airborne during the water take-off and subsequently dropped back to the water, the nose dug in and the aircraft flipped on its back injuring the four occupants. SOC 07Oct43.

1323 Built for US Navy as **J4F-2**, BuAer serial **32969**. Acc and del 10Aug43; records missing but with CQTU NAS Glenview when involved in accident 25Aug43: while undertaking touch and-go landings on Fox Lake, IL, the cross-wind current was misjudged and the left wing float caught, causing the aircraft to water-loop and sink inverted into seven feet of water. Recovered and repaired; records missing but with CQTU NAS Glenview by Aug44; Pool NAS Sanford Jan45; NAS Seattle Jun45 for reconditioning; NAAS Mayport 14Nov45; Pool NAS Banana River Dec45; CNAAT NAS Jacksonville Oct46 and SOC (presumably at Jacksonville) 31Oct46 as obsolete and surplus. BoS War Assets Administration to Matt V Pilcher, Saratoga, FL 20Nov46 with CofR **NC66432** 06Dec46; CofA after cvtd to **G-44**, 01Mar47 at TFH:200hrs. BoS to Richard D McNally, Miami, FL 15May47 with CofR 23Jun47; cvtd to dual control Jun47. BoS to Island Airways Inc, Miami, FL 10Oct49 with CofR 18Oct49 as **N66432**. BoS to John C Monte Jr, East Aurora, NY 16May50 with CofR 15Jun50. BoS to Washington Aircraft & Transport Corp, Seattle, WA 23Jan52 with CofR 09Apr52 and CofA 08May52 at TFH:1047hrs. BoS to Bellingham Canning Co, Bellingham, WA 31Mar53. BoS to Kodiak Airways Inc, Kodiak, AK 30Mar53 (sic) with CofR 13May53 and CofA 22May53 at TFH:1,271hrs and 07Feb55 at TFH:2,107hrs. Shipped to International Aircraft Service, Sun Valley, CA Apr56 for re-engining with Lycoming R-680-E3A radials. The bow was also uprated to G-44A standard; CofA renewed 15May56 at TFH:3,485hrs. Badly damaged in glassy water landing but rebuilt at Kenmore, WA Apr57 with CofA 28May57 at TFH:2,660hrs; CofA renewed 25Apr58 at TFH:2,811hrs; 17Dec60 at TFH:3,422hrs with note that aircraft flew zero hrs in last 12 months. BoS to R & S Aircraft Sales Inc, Renton, WA 31Dec60 with CofR 31Mar61. BoS to Dr Robert H Chandler, Downers Grove, IL 25Apr61 with CofR 17May61. BoS to Northern Aircraft Sales Co Inc, San Carlos, CA 29Sep61. BoS to Robert L Dukes and John H Flynn Jr, Seattle, WA 29Sep61 with CofR 23Oct61. Still regd Jly64 but reported crashed on Oregon coast. Cancelled from USCAR 25May65, reason not given but maybe due to reported crash.

1324 Built for US Navy as **J4F-2**, BuAer serial **32970**. Acc 17Aug43 and del 19Aug43; records missing but with NAS Edenton by Aug44; NAS Seattle Jun45 for reconditioning; NAS Norfolk 27Aug45; NAS Edenton Nov45; Pool NAS Norfolk Jun46; and SOC there 28Feb47 as obsolete and surplus. BoS War Assets Administration, Washington, DC for $8,388 to Fontana School of Aeronautics, Iron Mountain, MI, 30Jan47. CofR **NC5555N** as **G-44**, 21Mar47. BoS to Aeromarine Skyways, Bayfield, WI, 09May47 with CofR 22May47 and CofA 30May47. BoS to Dickrell & Schraufnagel, Mason, WI, 23Apr48 with CofR 06May48. BoS to EJ Duval, New Auburn, WI, 17May49 with CofR 27May49 as **N5555N**, and CofA 18Jly53 at TFH:731hrs. Cvtd to **Super Widgeon** with Lycoming GO-480-B1B engines by McKinnon-Hickman. CF-IKH allotted to Carl Millard Ltd, Toronto, ON, 09Nov55. Cancelled from USCAR with CofA for export E-30475 20Jly56. CofA 4779 issued 11Jly56 and CofR(P)

16413 issued for **CF-IKH** (to Millard) 19Jly56. CofR(P) 18474 to North American Rare Metals Ltd, Toronto, ON 28Mar57; inspected and CofR renewed at TFH:898hrs, valid until 12Jly58. CofR(P) 19992 to Irving Oil Transport Ltd, St John, NB 06Nov58; CofA renewed at TFH:1,323hrs, valid until 22Mar62. BoS to Madden & Smith Aircraft Corp, Miami, FL, 21Nov62. and Regd **N176MS** 21Dec62 and cancelled from CCAR 13Dec62. CofA 16Jan63 at TFH:1576hrs. BoS to Terri Aviation Corp, Fort Lauderdale, FL, 24Apr63 with CofR 13May63. BoS to TW Smith Aircraft Inc, Cincinnati, OH, 27May63. BoS to James W Harvey, dba Harvey Flying Service, Kodiak, AK, 12Jun63 with CofR 21Jun63. BoS to David W Henley, dba Henley's Air Service, Kodiak, AK, 26Sep68; nominal change to South Central Air Taxi Inc, Kodiak, AK, 10May69 with CofR 16Jun69. Accident 30Mar70: substantial damage after aborted take-off at Kodiak prior to a flight to Discovery Bay, AK. Left prop feathered when prop governor control arm disconnected and acft veered off runway. Pilot + 3 pax minor injuries. Accident at 0705hrs on 06Oct73: crashed after stalling on take-off at Kodiak, AK. Cancelled from USCAR at owners request 07May74, but salvaged and sold to Baxter E Mitchell, Anchorage, AK, 15May74. Restored as **N176MS** 06Jun74 with CofR 07Jun74. BoS to G & G Leasing Co, Anchorage, AK, 10Aug79 with CofR 12Feb80. BoS to The Bergt Corp, Anchorage, AK, 06Jan81 with CofR 18Feb81. Landing gear uprated to 5,000lbs gross wt, Dec81. Accident at 1045hrs on 20Jun85: crashed landing on glassy water, in moderate rain, at the inlet of Nerka Lake, Dillingham, AK, after departing Anchorage at 0830hrs. Aircraft subsequently sank and came to rest inverted in clear water in Wood River, with the gear retracted and flaps extended; pilot + 2 pax minor injuries. Accident at 0900hrs on 30Jun87: stalled and crashed after water take-off at Wood River/Lake Nerka, AK for a flight to Togiak, AK; pilot + 2 pax uninjured but aircraft substantially damaged. Salvaged and sold by insurance company to David P Strelinger, Gig Harbor, WA, 30Oct87 with CofR 29Jan88. Reregd **N144GW** 19Jun91. BoS to John Schwamm, Anchorage, AK, 18Aug91. Rebuilt with a vertical tail-fin from a Coast Guard J4F-1, new wings, 295hp Lycoming GO-480 engines and new avionics, and CofR issued 25Oct91. Displayed at EAA Oshkosh, WI, 1992. To NW Waterbird Inc, Wilmington, DE, 05Apr96. To Commonwealth Aviation Corp, Port Orange, FL 15Mar04. To Loughrea Maritime II LLC, Charlotte, NC with CofR 10Jly07, later at Aiken, NC. To Rochester Amphibian Inc, Rochester, NY with CofR **N612GW** issued 28Sep11. Current and airworthy May13, with CofR due to expire 30Sep14.

1325   Built for US Navy as **J4F-2**, BuAer serial **32971**. Acc and del 24Aug43; records missing but with NAAS San Clemente by Aug44; NAS Seattle Jun45 for reconditioning; NAAS San Clemente 30Aug45. Damaged during landing roll at San Clemente 21Feb46: after rolling through 300 feet the port landing gear collapsed, resulting in minor damage to the port wing-tip float. SOC at San Clemente 31Jan47 as obsolete and surplus. BoS War Assets Administration to CD McKee, c/o Nelson-Kelley Co, San Diego, CA 29Jan47, for $3,501. BoS to JW Neill, dba Murphy Motors, Los Angeles, CA 31Mar47, with CofA 10Apr47 and CofR as **G-44, NC67646** 22Apr47. BoS to Alaska Island Airlines Inc, Petersburg, AK 13May47 with CofR 20May47; water rudder installed May49; CofA 18Dec51 after complete overhaul; false step removed and keel re-inforced at step Jly52; CofA 22Feb55 at TFH:3,872hrs. BoS to Alaska Coastal Airlines Inc, Juneau, AK with CofR **N67646** 28Feb55. BoS to Henry J Reverman, Seattle, WA 09Mar55. BoS to Sea Airmotive Inc, Anchorage, AK 08Apr55 with CofR 20May55. BoS to Alfred E Gay, Anchorage, AK 29Nov55 with CofR 14Dec55. CofA 27Apr56 at TFH:4,703hrs. BoS to Cordova Airlines Inc, Anchorage, AK, 07Sep56 with CofR 01Oct56. Returned to Alfred E Gay on BoS 22Oct59 with CofR 17Nov59. Tfd by BoS to Gay Airways Inc, Anchorage, AK 01Jan60 with CofR 01Apr60. BoS to LE Flahart, Anchorage, AK 10Feb60 with CofR 23May60. BoS to John R Logan & Martin K Lilleburg, Mercer Island, WA 19Oct65 with CofR 01Nov65. Tfd by BoS to John R Logan, Mercer Island, WA 02Feb67 with CofR 09Mar67. BoS to Lane E Older, Bellingham, WA 06Oct68 with CofR 13Dec68. BoS to Charles R Gundlach, Toledo, OH 24Jun75 with CofR 12Jly75, which was revoked by the FAA 22Oct76 for failure to return an Aircraft Activity Report. BoS to Executive Air Service Inc, Bellingham, WA 31Mar78, with CofR 01May78, which was revoked by the FAA 24Sep82 due to undelivered Triennial. BoS to Robert E McCormick, Renton, WA 19May82 with CofR 27Feb87; address change to Selah, WA. TFH:6,371hrs a/o 01May91 and had not flown by 30Aug03, despite many repairs. Current and airworthy May13, with CofR due to expire 31Dec13.

1326   Built for US Navy as **J4F-2**, BuAer serial **32972**. Acc and del 28Aug43; records missing but with OTU VB2-1 NAS Beaufort by Oct44; NAS Beaufort Jan45; OTU VB2-1 NAS Beaufort Apr45; NAS Seattle Jun45 for reconditioning; OTU VB2-1 NAS Beaufort 17Aug45; NAAS Mayport Nov45; NAS Banana River Apr46. CGAS St Petersburg Jly46 when formally transferred to the US Coast Guard and SOC by the US Navy

31Jly46; transferred, presumably from USCG, to NACA, Langley Fld Aug47; records missing; returned to the US Navy 31Oct49 as **XJ4F-2** and to O&R at MS NAS Norfolk; records missing; with RD&E NACA, Langley Fld by Jan50 until Jun51; NATC Patuxent River 18Jly51; nominally Pool NAF Philadelphia 08May53 awaiting disposal. Retired 31Aug54 and SOC 11Oct54 at Patuxent River for spares/scrap (TFH:822hrs).

1327   Built for US Navy as **J4F-2**, BuAer serial **32973**. Acc 31Aug43 and del 01Sep43; records missing but with BAR General Motors Eastern Aircraft Division, Linden Fld, NJ by Aug44; NAS Seattle Jun45 for reconditioning; NAS Seattle 10Oct45. CGAS Port Angeles 10Jun46 until at least Jly46 when formally transferred to the US Coast Guard and SOC by the US Navy 31Jly46. SOC by US Coast Guard circa 1950. Del from CGAS Brooklyn and cvtd to **G-44** by Baltimore Aero Service 20Jly50 with CofA same date at TFH:1,165hrs. CofR **N725** to Department of Interior, Fish & Wildlife Service, Washington, DC 21Jly50. BoS to Sea Airmotive Inc, Anchorage, AK 21Jan57 with CofR for **N79906** 12Apr57 (regn transferred from c/n 1305, qv). Cvtd to **Super Widgeon** with Lycoming GO-480-B1D engines, picture windows and escape hatch 12Apr57 with CofA at TFH:1,479hrs. BoS to Baker & Ford Co, Bellingham, WA 09Aug57 with CofR 03Sep57. BoS to Cordova Airlines Inc, Anchorage, AK 18Aug59 with CofR 27Jan61. CofA 01Dec62 at TFH:5,110hrs; bow compartment cvtd to a 200lbs luggage compartment 02Jly63. CofA 11Oct63 at TFH:5,684hrs. BoS to Don Johnson, dba Kenai Float Plane Service Inc, Kenai, AK 12Jan68 with CofR 07Feb68. Accident 16Jun69: substantially damaged after hitting a submerged rock on landing run at Mekoryuk, AK. Pilot + 2 pax minor injuries. BoS to Lew Mahieu, Willow, AK 01Sep85. BoS to Alaska Juneau Aeronautics Inc, Juneau, AK 17Oct88. BoS to Michael D Mills, Gustavus, AK 25Nov88 with CofA 30Dec88 at TFH:7,316hrs and CofR 28Mar89. BoS to Lori Egge, Wasilla, AK 28May97 with CofR 19Aug97; nominal change to Lori L Michels 26Nov99. BoS Lori L Michels to CF-BGS Inc, Oakville, ON 11Apr03. **C-FBCP** allotted to CF-BGS Inc, 16Apr03 and N79906 cancelled from USCAR 27May03. Authority to ferry Wolf Lake, AL to Centralia, ON 28May03. Inspected and CofA and CofR issued 07Jly03. Current Mar13.

1328   Built for US Navy as **J4F-2**, BuAer serial **32974**. Acc 12Sep43 and del 13Sep43; records missing but with NAAS Harvey Point by Aug44; NAS Seattle Jun45 for reconditioning; Pool NAS Seattle Sep45; Pool NAS Norfolk Nov45; Pool CASU-67 NAS Memphis 03Jun46; FASRON-4 NAS Memphis Aug46 and SOC there 30Sep46 as obsolete and surplus. BoS War Assets Administration to John R Steele, Waukegan, IL 29Nov46 with CofR as **NC9900H** 20Dec46, and CofA as **G-44**, 04Jan47. BoS to Currey Flying Service, Galesburg, IL 06Oct48 with CofR 10Nov48. BoS to Robert J Ferguson, Lincoln, NE 02Aug50 with CofR **N9900H** 25Sep50. BoS to Electroanalysis Co, Victoria, TX 06Aug51 with CofR 17Aug51. BoS to DH Braman, Victoria, TX 26Sep52 with CofR 09Oct52. Experimental CofA 11Feb53 after cvtd to **Super Widgeon** with 260hp Lycoming GO-435-C2 engines, at TFH:113hrs (since civil?). BoS to Howard Aero Service Inc, San Antonio, TX 11Jly55 with CofR 05Aug55. BoS to Anthony Zuma, Houston, TX 30Nov55. BoS to Continental Oil Co, Houston, TX 30Nov55 with CofR 15Dec55. CofA 25Jan56 at TFH:415hrs, with permanent CofA 31Jly56; engines changed to GO-435-C2B Dec56. BoS to W Gordon Wing, Houston, TX 17May57 with CofR 12Jun57. BoS to Planes Inc, Houston, TX 25Aug58 with CofR 05Dec58. BoS to Airmarine Leasing Corp, Gainesville, FL 08Sep59 with CofR 06Oct59. BoS to George W Murphy, Corvallis, OR 22Jun62 with CofR 16Jly62; address change to Springfield, OR with CofR 05Jan71. BoS to Incon Corp, Roseburg, OR 23May73 for $20,000, with CofR 24Jly73. BoS to UC Leasing Inc, Memphis, TN 23Oct73 with CofR 16Nov73. BoS UC Leasing to John Gifford, dba Gifford Rentals, Anchorage, AK 27Sep77. BoS Gifford to William G Joplin Leasing Co, Monroe, WA 11Apr78 with CofR 09May78. Major alterations Aug78: hull rebuilt to **G-44A** profile; heavy gear landing truss members installed to allow gross wt increase to 5,500lbs (for land only). Cleveland wheels and brakes installed; right hand auxiliary door installed per STC SA4-63; McKinnon exhaust and exhaust augmentors installed per STC SA 662NW; auxiliary fuel system, inc 25 gallon wing float tanks, installed. BoS to James L Dodson, Fairbanks, AK 22Dec82 with CofR 18Aug83. Accident at 1400hrs on 28Jly84: aircraft encountered severe wind shear shortly after take-off from Shanin Lake, AK. Pilot, Dodson, lost directional control and hit a mudbank. Four uninjured, but aircraft substantially damaged; TFH:2,300hrs. Acft re-possessed by Key Bank of Alaska 14Dec95 with CofR 26Feb96. BoS Key Bank to James E Carner, Fairbanks, AK 14Jly97 with CofR 26Sep97. BoS to E Geneva Inc, Incline Village, NV 04Jan01, with CofR 08Jun01. Current and airworthy May13, with CofR due to expire 31Oct14.

1329   Built for US Navy as **J4F-2**, BuAer serial **32975**. Acc 15Sep43 and del 16Sep43; records missing but with NAS Trinidad by Aug44; NAS Seattle 25Sep45 for reconditioning; Pool NAS Seattle Jan46 and SOC there 31Mar46 as obsolete. Regd as **NC66645** 28Jun46. BoS War Assets Administration to Gunner K Johansen, Ferndale, MI 18Jly46. Cvtd from J4F-2 to **G-44** by Aviation Maintenance Corp, Van Nuys, CA with CofA 23Jly46; dual control columns fitted Aug46. Accident 09Oct46 and repaired Nov46. BoS to Progressive Welder Co, Detroit, MI 18Nov46 with CofR 11Mar47. BoS to Modern Die & Tool Co, Detroit, MI 30Dec46 with CofR 09Apr47. BoS to Commonwealth Petroleum Co, Chicago, IL 29Mar48 with CofR 05Apr48. BoS to Industrial Engineering & Manufacturing Co Inc, Brimfield, IN 08Apr50 with CofR **N66645** 17May50. BoS to Glaser Construction Co, Lafayette, LA 26May51 with CofR 25Jun51; CofA renewed 28Feb53 at TFH:1,549hrs. BoS to Link Aeronautical Corp, Endicott, NY 14Jun56 with CofR 25Jan56. CofA 15Feb60 with Ranger 6-440 engines. CofR 14Jly61 to Kail Aeronautical Corp, Endicott, NY. BoS Kail to Iris K Morgan, Binghampton, NY 11Feb63 with CofR 29Mar63. BoS to Leon D Cool, Rockville, MD 27Jly64 with CofR 10Oct64. BoS to J Curtiss McKinney, Titusville, PA 25Apr67 with CofR 19May67. BoS to Charles E Weir, Anchorage, AK 06Aug73 with CofR 28Nov73. Loaned for display at the Alaska Aviation Heritage Museum, Lake Hood 1988-90. BoS to A Douglas Hulen, Anchorage, AK 06Nov92 with CofR 09Dec92; returned to Alaska Aviation Heritage Museum, Lake Hood, Anchorage, 1992 and until 1999. Tfd by BoS to Hulen and James R Branham, Anchorage, AK, 10Aug94 with CofR 09Dec94. Tfd by BoS to AD Hulen and Helen M Hulen, Anchorage, AK 21Jan97 with CofR 14Mar97. **N645DH** issued 01Aug00 and placed on acft 17Aug00. BoS (un-dated) Helen M Hulen deceased to AD Hulen, but CofR issued 15Mar01; noted at the museum at Lake Hood Dec05. Current and airworthy May13, with CofR due to expire 31Oct13.

1330   Built for US Navy as **J4F-2**, BuAer serial **32976**. Acc 20Sep43 and del 21Sep43; records missing but with Hedron-2, FAW-5 NAS Norfolk by Aug44; Hedron-1, FAW-5 NAS Boca Chica Apr45; NACTULANT NAAS Martha's Vineyard Jun45; Pool NAS Seattle Jly45 (under reconditioning Aug-Nov45); CASU-67 NAS Memphis 27Dec45; Pool FASRON-4 NAS Memphis Aug46; BAR Bethpage 13Aug46. Allocated to EDO Aircraft Corp, College Point, NY Jan47 (Pool BAR New York Feb48 and Pool BAR EDO by Jun47 until May48); grossly modified by EDO to incorporate half-scale replica of the Martin XP5M-1 hull and subsequently other hull designs (the last of which was retained throughout its life). To NACA Langley Fld May48 and formally loaned to NACA from 28Feb50 until 08Jun53. While on loan, trialled at NATC Patuxent River circa May52 and to Torpedo Unit, NAS Quonset Point 15Dec52; all US Navy records refer to this aircraft as **E-175** (and not J4F-2) wef 15Dec52; NATC Patuxent River 08Jun53 [The aircraft's history recorded on the movement card is confusing and contradictory, but other official US Navy data indicates that the E-175 was on the strength of the Torpedo Unit, Quonset Point until May53 when it moved to Patuxent River and remained there until eventual retirement. The record card nevertheless shows a period of bailment to BAR College Point (EDO) circa Nov53]. To storage (non-flyable) at Patuxent River 12Oct55 wearing name "*Petulant Porpoise*"; NAS Norfolk 07Feb56 and SOC (as E-175) 08Feb56 (TFH:975hrs). Remained in storage at Norfolk until eventually acquired by the National Air Museum (NAM) collection; del to NAM at Silver Hill, Washington, DC 15Sep60 and formally accessioned by NAM 14Mar61. Remained in storage at Silver Hill until 15Dec76 when the National Air & Space Museum (NASM, so renamed in 1966) agreed to exchange it, together with F8F-1D BuAer 90446, for the modified F8F-2 N1111L which was subsequently displayed at the NASM. The exchange was agreed with the Fighter Aircraft Museum, Inc of Mission Hills, CA and N1111L 'Conquest II' had been owned by Darryl Greenamayer. Following formal 'de-accessioning' by the NASM 19Jan77, 32976 was collected from Silver Hill by Greenamayer's truck 14Feb77 for transportation to Mission Hills. Remained in storage at Mission Hills until loaned in 1987 to the Pima County Air Museum, Tucson, AZ (now the Pima Air & Space Museum) where still displayed in 2010.

1331   Built for US Navy as **J4F-2**, BuAer serial **32977**. Acc 25Sep43 and del 28Sep43; records missing but at NAF Trenton by Aug44; NAS Seattle Aug45 for reconditioning; NAS Terminal Island Apr46; CGAS San Diego 11Jun46. Formally transferred to the US Coast Guard and SOC by the US Navy 31Jly46. Destroyed 02Jan48, while being ferried from San Diego to an east coast station (Elizabeth City?). Following a fuel stop at NAS Memphis and en route Chattanooga, TN, the aircraft struck trees and crashed and burned on Signal Mountain, a few miles north of Chattanooga. The accident happened at night and killed both crew members.

1332   Built for US Navy as **J4F-2**, BuAer serial **32978**. Acc 28Sep43 and del 30Sep43; NAS Argentia by 18Oct43; transferred from NAS Argentia to the UK (FAA) 27Mar44 as **FP474** with US Navy strike date of 30Mar44, apparently as short-notice replacement for FP461/37728 returned to the US Navy in early-mid 1944. Subsequent British use

uncertain, with suggestions that it was used by the British Air Commission itself. Returned to the US authorities, presumably in 1945, for disposal although not used by the US Navy. Regd as **G-44, SE-ARZ** to Stockholms-tidningen (newspaper), Sweden, 03Apr46, named "*Viking II*". To D Hareide, Åalesund, Norway, 12Jun58. Swedish regn cancelled 12Jun58 and reregd **LN-HAL** 03Jly58. Accident 23Aug59: non-fatal taxying accident in Åalesund harbour. To Moerefly A/S, Åalesund 11Oct60. Accident 22Mar69: crash-landing in Åalesund Harbour. CofA expired 31Dec70. Donated to Norsk Teknisk Museum (Norwegian Technical Museum) (NTM), Oslo 1975. Regn cancelled 30Jun78. Noted (as LN-HAL) at Flyhistorisk Museum Sola, Stavanger, Norway 10Nov02, whilst on loan from the NTM. Reported in store in the Stavanger area in May 2011.

1333   Built for US Navy as **J4F-2**, BuAer serial **32979**. Acc 06Oct43 and del 07Oct43; records missing but with NAS Kahului by Aug44; NAS Pearl Harbor May46 and SOC 31Jly46 obsolete and surplus. Regd as **G-44, NC69078** (to unknown owner). Fate unknown.

1334   Built for US Navy as **J4F-2**, BuAer serial **32980**. Acc 13Oct43 and del 17Oct43; records missing but with CASU-24 NAS Wildwood by Aug44; Pool NAS Seattle Jly45 and under reconditioning Aug-Oct45; CASU-24 NAS Wildwood Dec45; CASU-27 NAS Chincoteague Jan46; NAS Atlantic City May46 and SOC 31Jly46 as obsolete and surplus. BoS War Assets Administration, Atlanta, GA to Jordan Fletcher, Norfolk, MA 25Nov46, for $10,000. BoS to Leo J Murray Co, Norfolk, MA 14Dec46 with CofR **NC9212H** 16Dec46 giving address as Franklin, MA. Cvtd to **G-44** by Fletcher Aviation at Franklin-Norfolk A/P, MA with CofA 28Jan47 [Aircraft painted silver with vermilion trim and black below the water-line]. BoS to Marine Aircraft Corp, New York, NY (through Powers & George Aircraft Brokers) 19Jly49, with CofR **N9212H** 28Jly49. BoS to Hessler Inc, Wilmington, DE 10Dec49 with CofR 31Jan50. BoS to Edw W Ritchey (dba Ritchey Flying Service), Fort Worth, TX 29Mar50. BoS to Vest Aircraft & Finance Co, Denver, CO 31Mar50. BoS to AG Thomson Jr, Miami Beach, FL 29Jly50 with CofR 13Oct50. False step removed, keel re-inforcing kit installed from Station 13 to 15A and step vent kit installed between Stations 16 and 17, per Grumman blueprints 17407 and 17188, 27Oct50. Address change to South Miami was recorded on CofR 14Oct52. BoS to Karl Knight, Miami, FL 22Oct52 with CofR 24Nov52 at TFH:1,395hrs. BoS to Joe Marrs, Hollywood, FL 25May54 with CofR 27Jan55. BoS to Perry Boswell Jr, Delray Beach, FL 09Feb55 with CofR 11Mar55. BoS to Feadship Inc, Fort Lauderdale, FL 09Mar56, with CofR 16Mar56 and CofA 01Jun56 at TFH:1,648hrs. CF-PNT allotted to Peter Nesbitt Thomson 05Feb57. BoS Feadship Inc to Hersey (sic) Corp Ltd 11Feb57, with US CofA for export E-31912 12Feb57 at TFH:1,804hrs. CofR(P) 17128 and CofA 6319 for **CF-PNT** to The Warnock Hersey Co Ltd, Montreal, QC 12Feb57. Cvtd to Continental O-470-M power 30Jun57. CofR(P) 17238 to Strathcona Equipment Co Ltd, Montreal, QC 05Jly57. CofA renewed at TFH:1,932hrs, valid until 12Feb59. BoS to Canadian Inspection & Testing Co Ltd, Montreal, QC 01Mar58 with CofR(P) 17375 12Mar58. Accident 08Nov58: wheels-up landing at St John A/P, PQ when pilot forgot to lower the landing gear. BoS to Timmins Aviation Ltd, Montreal, QC 15Dec58 with CofR(P) 20216, 16Jan59. BoS to Belle Construction Ltd, Ville d'Alma, QC 08Oct59 with CofR(P) 20439, 13Oct59; CofA renewed at TFH:2,249hrs, valid until 13May61. BoS to Chibougamau Express Ltée, St Felicien, QC, 06Oct61, with CofR(P) 24505 02Nov61; CofA renewed at TFH:2,698hrs, valid until 01Jun64. Accident 24Jly63: pilot, Benoit Gobeil, belly-landed the aircraft on a flight from Lac Norrie to St Felicien. Repaired by 28Mar64, inspected and CofA renewed at TFH:2,889hrs, valid until 01Jun65; and at TFH:4,347hrs, valid until 09May69. BoS to Field Aviation Co Ltd, Malton, ON with CofR(P) 48138, 31Dec68. BoS to Canada Kelp Co Ltd, Vancouver, BC, 27Dec68 with CofR(P) 46717, 28Jan69. CofA renewed at TFH:4,642hrs, valid until 05Jun70. BoS Robert D Young (Receiver and manager of Canada Kelp Co) to Flying Fireman Ltd, Victoria, BC 30Dec70 for $14,000. CofA renewed at TFH:4,647hrs, valid until 22Apr72. CofR(C) to Flying Fireman Ltd 06May71; CofA renewed at TFH:4,864hrs, valid until 18May74. BoS to Charles Schachle, Moses Lake, WA 10Oct73, and cancelled from CCAR 24May74. [The application for CofR was by Schacle, c/o Flying Fireman Inc, Billings, MT but amended to the individual, at Moses Lake, WA on the CofR **N90727** dated 04Apr75]. BoS to Richard L Rude, dba Misty Acres Inc, Spanaway, WA 31Jan77. CofR applied for 04Feb77 but not issued? Cvtd to Continental IO-470-D engines with Hartzell HC-A2VF-2 props by Tosch Aircraft Industries, flight tested 07Apr80 and CofA issued 06Jun80 at TFH:4,910hrs. BoS to Richard A Wien, Fairbanks, AK 06Jun80 with CofR 09Jly80. Rudder re-covered with Ceconite 101 material per STC SA4-755 Jun 91. Address change within Fairbanks recorded on CofR 09Oct93. Hartzell props replaced by McCauley model 3AF32C528 3-bladed props per STC SA00893CH, Apr99 at TFH:6,169hrs. Elevators and ailerons re-covered with Ceconite 101 material per STC SA1351WE, 24May02. BoS to Shirley J Rohl and David B Brown, Anchorage, AK 13Oct06, with CofR 19Dec06. Attended the Alaska Grumman Fly-in at Marion Lake, near Anchorage Jly12. Current and airworthy May13, with CofR due to expire 30Apr16.

1335   Built for US Navy as **J4F-2**, BuAer serial **32981**. Acc and del 20Oct43; records missing but with CFASA NAS Lakehurst by Aug44; BlimpHedron-2, FAW-2 Chorrera Fld Oct44 moving to NAS Richmond Nov44. Destroyed in conventional landing accident at Richmond 27Jan45: aircraft experienced wind-shear at 100 feet, stalled and heavy-landed when undertaking a practice landing. SOC 31Mar45.

1336   Built for US Navy as **J4F-2**, BuAer serial **32982** but diverted off contract to the British Air Commission, Washington, DC with serial **FP455** for use by the Fleet Air Arm. Del 27Oct43. On 04Dec43, SBNO Lt Ed Walthall flew FP455 from Roosevelt Field to Willow Grove and back, twice. Used by 738 Sqn, NAAF Lewiston; reported in use Jly44 but no record found of formal return to the US Government or US Navy [The lack of a surviving US Navy record strongly suggests that the aircraft was not returned to the US Navy for its own use but that this does not preclude the possibility that the aircraft was returned to the US authorities for disposal. However the lack of any subsequent history hints at an accident or withdrawal while in British hands].

1337   Built for US Navy as **J4F-2**, BuAer serial **32983**. Acc 28Oct43 and del 08Nov43; records missing but with NAPT NAS New Orleans by Aug44; NAS New Orleans Oct44; NAPT NAS New Orleans Jan45; NAS New Orleans Feb45; NAS Seattle 04Sep45 and SOC there 31Mar46 as obsolete. BoS War Assets Administration to Clackamas Logging Co, Portland, OR 10Dec46 for $7,500. Cvtd to **G-44** with CofA 31Dec46 and CofR for **NC58837** 10Jan47. BoS to Stanley Oaksmith Jr and Martin R Hanson, dba Ketchikan Air Service, Ketchikan, AK 14May49 with CofR 26Jly49 as **N58837**. Accident at Mirror Lake 27Jly49: details not known but props replaced and left wing float repaired. Water rudder installed per Alaska Island Airlines' drawings 21Oct49. Accident at Annette Island airfield 13Jun50. Repaired and CofA renewed 02Jun52 at TFH:1,594hrs; 09Jun53 at TFH:1,868hrs. BoS Ketchikan Air Service to Kodiak Airways Inc, Kodiak, AK 02Mar56 with CofR 11May56. Regn cancelled at owners request 10Dec59 for "salvage for parts". BoS RL Hall to Fred Carlson, Sun Valley, CA 01May93. BoS to Edwin E Forsberg, Salem, OR 02Mar93 (sic) with CofR19Apr93. Address change to Elk Grove, CA. The registration remains assigned but the CofR expired 30Jun11. Aircraft in process of restoration Aug12.

1338   Built for US Navy as **J4F-2**, BuAer serial **32984**. Acc 31Oct43 and del 07Nov43; records missing but with NAS Puunene Aug44; NAS Honolulu Dec45; Pool NAS Pearl Harbor Feb46 and SOC there 30Jun46 as obsolete and surplus. BoS War Assets Administration Honolulu to JK Mardick, Honolulu, HI 22Jan47, for $2,500. BoS to Fred C Richards, San Francisco, CA 26Feb47 for $3,600. CofR as **G-44, NC69067** issued 06May47. BoS to Early J Moore, Belmont, CA 01Nov47. BoS to Van Camp Sea Food Co Inc, Terminal Island, CA 03Nov47 with CofR 20Nov47. BoS to Andrew Waris, Clatskanie, OR 01Aug50 with CofR **N69067** 28Sep50; BoS to Alaska Airlines, Anchorage, AK 21May51 with CofR 06Jun51. BoS to Collins Air Service, Anchorage, AK 28Apr52 for $10,000, with CofR 28May52. A conditional sales contract for $10,000 from Collins to Paul B Hansen, Pacific Palisades, CA was dated 07May52. A CofR was issued to Hansen 12Sep52 and, with the contract fully paid, the title was transferred to Hansen 05Jly54; hull vented and keel re-inforced Jan53 per Grumman Service Bulletin prints #17402, 17189 and 17407; CofA 02May53 at TFH:1,227hrs. Operated by Hansen for Kadiak(sic) Fisheries, Port Bailey, AK. Converted to **Super Widgeon** May58 per installation of Lycoming GO-480-B1D engines with Hartzell HC83x20-2C props, installation of auxiliary fuel tanks (STC SA4-2) and main gear modification (STC SA4-60). Hansen registered an address change to Chugiak, AK 09Feb62. BoS to James W Harvey, dba Harvey's Flying Service, Kodiak, AK 08Apr63 with CofR 21May63. BoS to Sea Airmotive Inc, Anchorage, AK 24Sep66 with CofR 17Oct66. BoS to James S Magoffin, Fairbanks, AK 12Dec66 with CofR 06Mar67; on another BoS Magoffin transfers title to himself 12Jan70 with another CofR 27Jan70, perhaps to reflect operation by Interior Airways Inc, Fairbanks, AK in 1970. BoS Magoffin to James P Haggland, College, AK 09Jan75 with CofR 23Jan75. BoS to William J Lentsch, dba Tamarack Air Ltd, Fairbanks, AK 20Nov83 with CofR 20Jan84; ownership transferred back to Haggland, Fairbanks, AK by BoS 23May86 with CofR 11Jly86. No Forms 337 since Jan87, but listed as current and airworthy May13, with CofR due to expire 28Feb15. [The accuracy of the listing is doubtful, however, as the aircraft is still listed with Ranger engines!]

1339   Built for US Navy as **J4F-2**, BuAer serial **32985**. Acc 08Nov43 and del 09Nov43; records missing but with CASU-22 NAS Quonset Point by Sept44; NAS Seattle Aug45 for reconditioning (completed 21Feb46) and SOC there 31Jly46 as obsolete and surplus. Regd as **G-44, NC58847** to Western Skyways Service, Troutdale, OR. To Kodiak Airways, Kodiak, AK 05Apr50; acft name: *"Helen"*. Accident 16Jan56: engine failure en route to Chignik Bay, AK and crashed into Hook Bay. No fatalities but aircraft destroyed by surf. Cancelled from USCAR 21May65.

1340   Built for US Navy as **J4F-2**, BuAer serial **32986** but diverted off contract to the British Air Commission, Washington, DC with serial **FP456** for use by the Fleet Air Arm. Del 17Nov43 and used by the Senior British Naval Officer (SBNO), Roosevelt Field 20Dec43 for a flight to Squantum and return. To SBNO, NAS Brunswick and remained at Brunswick and used by 1835 Sqn Jan-Feb45, still at Brunswick May45. Returned to the US authorities and recorded at Westchester County A/P, NY Aug45 awaiting disposal by the War Assets Administration. BoS Reconstruction Finance Corp to RE Dowling Realty Corp, New York, NY 25Oct45; permit issued 25Oct45 to ferry FP456 from White Plains, NY to Grumman factory at Bethpage. Cvtd from J4F-2 to **G-44** and CofR **NC41826** issued 31Oct45 with CofA 11Dec45. Accident 28Nov46: no details, but acft overhauled and certified airworthy 22Jan47. CofA 05Feb53 at TFH:2,023hrs and 11Jan55 at TFH:2,317hrs. BoS to Skyways Nassau Ltd 06Dec55. Cancelled from USCAR 12Dec55 and regd as **VP-BAK**(2), 02Feb56. Lsd to Bahamas Airways Ltd, 01Nov58. BoS Skyways (Bahamas) Ltd to Coastal Air Inc, Miami, FL 03Oct59. Cancelled from Bahamian CAR 14Oct59. Experimental CofA issued 25Oct60 for research and development. CofR **N9311R** issued 12Dec60. Cvtd to **Super Widgeon** per STC SA2-937, with Continental O-470-B engines and Hartzell HC82XF-2B propellers 18Jan61. Experimental CofA issued 19Jan61 at TFH:4,130hrs with Std CofA 20Mar61. BoS to Graubart Aviation Inc, Valparaiso, IN 01Oct61. BoS to Hart & Bledsoe Investment Co, Jasper, TX 06Oct61 with CofR 13Oct61. Tfd back to Graubart Aviation Inc, Valparaiso, IN on BoS 12Apr62. BoS to Angels Inc, Tampa, FL 13Sep62 with CofR 24Sep62. Tfd by BoS to Angels Aviation Inc, Tampa, FL 09Jan63 with CofR 01Feb63. BoS to Pasco Aviation Inc, Zephyr Hills, FL 01Nov63 with CofR 07Nov63. Tfd back to Angels Aviation Inc, Zephyr Hills, FL on BoS 20Jan64. Aircraft re-possessed by Appliance Buyers Credit Corp, St Joseph, MI 24Aug64 and CofR issued to them 08Sep64. BoS Appliance Buyers Credit Corp to Amphibian Parts Inc, Miami, FL 01Feb65 with CofR 17Feb65. BoS to Kodiak Airways Inc, Kodiak, AK 12Apr65. Acft disassembled for repair/rebuild; CofA 10May65 at TFH:4311hrs, with CofR 25May65. Accident 20Nov67: substantial damage due bounced landing into Sharatin Bay, AK, in bad (IFR) weather. Precautionary landing because pilot not instrument rated. 2 crew uninjured. BoS to Martin Aviation Co, Walla Walla, WA 09Feb68 with CofR 26Aug69 and CofA 08Apr70. BoS to Alvin Celcer and William E Hamilton, Casa Grande, AZ 20May75 with CofR 11Jun75. Aircraft re-possessed and assigned to William A Thompson, Joplin, MO 10Nov78 with CofR 30Nov78. BoS to James B Burr, dba Rocky Mountain Helicopters Inc, Provo, UT 04Aug82 with CofR 28Oct82. BoS to Grand Touring Cars Inc, Scottsdale, AZ, 11May84 with CofR 13Aug84. BoS to B A Leasing Corp, San Francisco, CA 02Aug85. Leased to International American Advertising Corp, dba American Graphics & Chromeprint, San Rafael, CA, with CofR 09Sep85. Re-possessed by B A Leasing 31Oct85 and sold to Starflite Inc, Dillingham, AK 07May86 with CofR 02Jun86; CofR for Starflite, dba Manokotak Air 10Jun88; another CofR for Starflite Inc 01Oct92. Temporarily re-possessed by US Small Business Association, Anchorage, AK 25Jly94, but then returned to Starflite Inc with CofR 19Oct94. BoS to Michael U Harder, Dillingham, AK 26Oct07, with CofR 21Dec07. Current and airworthy May13, with CofR due to expire 30Jun13.

C/n 1340: this undated photo shows the Continental-powered G-44, N9311R, converted by Dean Franklin Aviation Enterprises in 1961.

(Jennifer Gradidge)

1341 Built for US Navy as **J4F-2**, BuAer serial **37711**. Acc 27Nov43 and del 29Nov43; records missing but with NAS Seattle by Aug44 (reconditioned Aug-26Nov45). CGAS Port Angeles 10Jun46 until at least Jly46 when formally transferred to the US Coast Guard and SOC by the US Navy 31Jly46. SOC by US Coast Guard circa 1950. Del from CGAS St Petersburg, FL Jly50 and regd as **G-44, N750** to US Department of Interior, Washington, DC 28Aug50. Cvtd "from Coast Guard to civil status" by Baltimore Aero Service, MD with CofA 01Sep50 at TFH:2,152hrs; operated in Alaska by Fish & Wildlife Service. CofA 09May53 as **Super Widgeon**, after McKinnon-Hickman conversion with Lycoming GO-435-C2B engines at TFH:2,888hrs. Retractable water rudder installed per Alaska Island Airlines drawings Mar54. BoS to Interior Enterprises Inc, Fairbanks, AK 04Apr58 with CofR **N750M** 08May58. CofA 27May58. Tfd by BoS to Interior Airways Inc, Fairbanks, AK 05Jan60 with CofR 22Jan60. BoS to International Aviation Development Corp, Danville, CA 09Dec70; address change to Reno, NV and CofR issued 25Jan71. Ferry tanks installed 30Sep71, for flight from Wichita, KS to Malta, via Portland, ME, at max weight of 6,875lbs; Special Flight Permit issued 04Oct71. BoS to ATC Inc, Reno, NV, 25Feb72; address change to Santa Rosa, CA and CofR issued 14Apr72. Overhauled at Malta-Hal Far 1972 and operated by Arax Airlines, Nigeria and del ex Malta Aug72. Seen derelict at Hal Far, Malta, Apr77 and Feb87. Declared unairworthy by FAA 31Mar87. Shipped to UK and arrived Ipswich, Suffolk by road 29Apr87 for use as spares in rebuild of c/n 1218 (qv). Hulk crated to France Oct92. To Musée Historique de l'Hydraviation, Biscarosse and seen under restoration at St Agnant airfield, Rochefort in April 1997. Registration remains assigned to ATC Inc a/o May13, but CofR expired 30Jun11.

1342 Built for US Navy as **J4F-2**, BuAer serial **37712**. Acc 24Nov43 and del to NAS New York 25Nov43; precise records missing but diverted to Uruguayan Navy in 1943 with initial serial **SG-1** (incomplete US Navy aircraft history card suggests a strike date of 16Jly44). At Base Aeronaval No.1, La Isla Libertad until circa 1947 when relocated to BA No.2, Laguna del Sauce. Re-numbered **A-751** in 1948. Sold to Washington Martinez Cobas 1960s; **CX-BDG** reserved for Cobas/dba Aero Punta 05Apr79. To E Frois/Aero Punta, Montevideo (with Aero Punta titles but no CofA). Sold by Cobas to John Thomas Hewitt, Montevideo 13Sep83, for US$5,000 and regd CX-BDG. Cancelled from Uruguay CAR 07Jan85 and regd as **"J-4-F", N1944W** to John T Hewitt, El Segundo, CA, 11Jan85. Stored/under restoration at Paysandu, Uruguay with plan to ferry back to USA in Dec85. Hewitt address change to Rancho Palos Verdes, CA Jan88 and to Huntington Beach, CA Feb88; painted as N1944W in 2000. Current (as J4F-2), but not airworthy, May13, with CofR due to expire 30Sep13.

1343 Built for US Navy as **J4F-2**, BuAer serial **37713**. Acc 29Nov43 and del 30Nov43; records missing but with NAS Tillamook by Aug44; NAS Seattle Aug45 for reconditioning; NAAS Arlington 07Dec45; NAS Astoria 15Feb46 until at least 30Apr46; NAS Tillamook by Jun46 where SOC 31Jly46 as obsolete and surplus. Regd as **G-44, NC58828** to Angus Gerald McKinnon, Sandy, OR. Re-engined with Lycoming GO-435-C2B by McKinnon as **Super Widgeon N58828**. CF-HAC allotted to National Management Ltd 18Mar53 with authority to ferry Portland, OR to Montreal, PQ same date. US CofA for export E-19289 issued 25Mar53, and cancelled from USCAR 24Apr53. BoS AG McKinnon to National Management Ltd, Montreal, QC, 25Mar53; authority to ferry Montreal to Ottawa, ON 09Apr53. CofR(P) 11875 and CofA 3959 for **CF-HAC** both issued 25Mar53. CofA renewed at TFH:1,135hrs, valid until 11Feb55. Renewed at 21Feb55 and 15Mar56. CofR(P) 17020 issued to John Clarence Udd, Brockville, ON, 18Aug56, but aircraft based Cartierville, PQ. CofA renewed at TFH:1,984hrs, valid until 22Aug58. BoS to Burns Bros Plumbers Inc, Syracuse, NY 29Apr58 and cancelled from CCAR 30Apr58. To **N137B** with Fly By Lease, Oswego, NY by May62. Reregd **N77BD** to Fly By Lease Corp, Syracuse, NY 09Jun71. To Bresee Chevrolet Co Inc, Liverpool, NY, 12Feb85. CofA 29Nov88; advertised for sale Jly95 at TFH:4,800hrs. To Randy J Wilhite, Jackson, MI with CofR 14Sep99. Current and airworthy May13, with CofR due to expire 30Apr15.

1344 Built for US Navy as **J4F-2**, BuAer serial **37714** but diverted off contract to the British Air Commission, Washington, DC with serial **FP457** for use by the Fleet Air Arm. Del 29Nov43 for SBNO, Roosevelt Field. Used at NAS Squantum where damaged May44 while on charge of 857 Sqn; later at NAS Brunswick and used by 1835 Sqn Jan-Feb45. Sank in Long Island Sound with four 1835 Sqn fatalities 17Feb45, following engine failure while en route NAS New York (Floyd Bennett Fld) to Brunswick.

1345 Built for US Navy as **J4F-2**, BuAer serial **37715**. Acc 30Nov43 and del 08Dec43; records missing but with Hedron-12, FAW-12 headquartered at NAS Key West by Aug44 (in Aug44 FAW-12 had two aircraft on strength, one at NAS Boca Chica and the other at NAF San Julian but only one at Boca Chica by Mar45 – individual aircraft not identified); NAS Edenton Jun45; NAS Norfolk, Jly45 and SOC there 31Oct46 as obsolete and surplus. BoS War Assets Administration to Reliable Home Equipment Co Inc, Richmond, VA for $1,200, 06Dec46. BoS to EJ Conklin Aviation Corp, Richmond, VA for $1,200, 09Jan47. BoS to North Michigan Air Service Inc, Petoskey, MI 12Apr47 with CofR **NC1173V** 13Aug47. BoS to Thomas R Metzger and Hugh A Boss, Greenville, MI 05Jun48, with CofR 09Jly48. BoS to Milwaukee Crane & Service Co, Cudahy, WI 12Sep52, with CofR 03Oct52, as **N1173V**. CofA renewed 23Apr53 at TFH:800hrs. BoS to Clarence G Nissen, Milwaukee, WI 17Apr56 with CofR 30Apr56. CofA 16Jan57 at TFH:371hrs (sic) after conversion to **Super Widgeon** with Lycoming GO-480-B1D engines installed 11Dec56; CofA 09Jan64 at TFH:1,701hrs; 10Mar66 at TFH:1,985hrs. Accident 14Oct66: crashed on take-off from Lakehead A/P, Fort William, ON. One pax seriously injured; pilot + one pax minor injuries. Aircraft reported by NTSB as "destroyed". Cancelled from USCAR 03Mar67 and N1173V tfd to c/n 1383 (qv).

1346 Built for US Navy as **J4F-2**, BuAer serial **37716**. Acc 12Dec43 and del 16Dec43; records missing but with Hedron-16, FAW-16 headquartered at NAF Recife by Aug44 (in Sep44 FAW-16 had two aircraft on strength, one at NAF Rio de Janeiro and the other at NOF Belem and by Feb45 two more at Recife and NAF Aratu – location of this individual aircraft therefore not identified); CASU-21 NAS Norfolk 12Jun45; CASU-22 NAS Quonset Point 12Jly45; ComFAir Quonset 26Jly45; NAS Seattle Sep45 for reconditioning and SOC there 31May46 as obsolete. BoS War Assets Administration to Hamilton Aero Ltd, Beverly Hills, CA 04Nov46 for $10,000; CofA 09Apr47 and CoR as **J4F-2, NC67586** 12Feb48. BoS to A Paul Mantz, dba Paul Mantz Air Services, Burbank, CA 15Mar50 with CofR as **G-44, N67586**. BoS to WH Coffin, dba WH Coffin Air Service, Los Angeles, CA 20Sep50 with CofR 10Oct50; CofA 05Mar54 at TFH:1,614hrs. BoS to Triple "A" Machine Shop Inc, San Francisco, CA 16Oct54 with CofR 28Oct54. Cvtd to **Super Widgeon** by McKinnon-Hickman with Lycoming GO-480-B1 engines and Hartzell HC 83x20-2A props; keel re-inforcement and hull vents installed Feb55; CofA 25Apr55 at TFH:1,751hrs. BoS to William P Kruse, San Francisco, CA 01Nov55 with CofR 18Nov55. Returned to McKinnon-Hickman Co, Portland, OR by BoS 24Feb56 with CofR 07Mar56. BoS to T Bar Three Ranch, Philipsburg, MT 18Apr56. Gross weight increase to 5,500lbs (land and sea) per STCs SA4-60 and SA4-61 Jan58; Cessna wing tips installed Feb58, and CofR issued 31Jly59. BoS to Alfred E Gay, dba Gay Airways, Anchorage, AK 06Oct59 with CofR 30Oct59. BoS to Cordova Airlines Inc, Anchorage, AK 22Oct59 with CofR as **Super Widgeon** 29Dec59. Emergency escape hatch installed Mar60; major repairs Aug61 after accident on a beach on Hichinbrook Island; CofA 01Dec62 at TFH:4,363hrs. Bow compartment cvtd to 200lbs baggage compartment per STC SA5-58, Aug63. Accident 17Jly64: substantially damage in wheels-up landing at Cordova Municipal A/P, AK. Pilot + seven pax minor injuries. BoS to RJ Wheat, dba Richland Flying Service Inc, Richland, WA 23Aug67; tfd by BoS to Richland Flying Service Inc 16Aug67 with CofR 05Sep67. BoS to American Aviation Inc, Renton, WA 19May69 and sold by them to Interior Airways Inc, Fairbanks, AK 03Jun69 with CofR 09Jun69. BoS by JS Magoffin (President of Interior A/W) to Southeast Skyways Inc, Juneau, AK 16Oct69. BoS to Viking Airways Inc, Petersburg, AK 15Nov69 with CofR 11Feb70 (as G-44A!). BoS to United Engineering (1964) Ltd, Victoria, BC 10Oct72 and cancelled from USCAR 05Nov73. **CF-EHI** allotted to C Earl Hastings, Victoria, BC 24May73; inspected 15Oct73 at TFH:6,697hrs; CofA issued 21Oct73; CofR(P) for United Engineering (1964) Ltd, Victoria, BC, 07Nov73. CofA renewed at TFH:7,182hrs, valid until 21Oct75; and at TFH:8,731hrs, valid until 21Oct80. Cancelled from CCAR 26May80, after sale to Usibelli Coal Mine Inc, Healy, AK, 12May80. CofR **N3767Z** issued 12Jun80 and CofA 20Jun80 at TFH:8,924hrs. Accident 02Jly83: fuselage split open and acft sank in 200ft of water after a hard landing in Walker Lake, AK. Salvaged and sold to Timothy R Martin, Anchorage, AK 21Sep89 with CofR 27Oct89. Rebuilt using parts from SCAN-30 c/n 30, G-44 c/n 1347 and G-44A c/n 1442. Re-regd **N480AK** 13Oct09 with CofA 06Nov09 at TFH:9,000hrs. Current and airworthy May13, with CofR due to expire 31Jan16.

1347 Built for US Navy as **J4F-2**, BuAer serial **37717**. Acc and del 28Dec43; records missing but with NAAS Quillayute by 14Jun44 when damaged at NAS Seattle (keel damaged when undercarriage collapsed). On charge NAAS Quillayute Aug44; NAAS Arlington Sep45; Pool NAS Astoria Jan46 until at least Apr46; NAS Tillamook by Jun46 and SOC there 31Jly46 as obsolete and surplus. Regd as **G-44, NC67805** to John Spoor Broome, Oxnard, CA. Cancelled from USCAR 04Apr48, reason unknown, but parts used by Timothy R Martin in rebuild of c/n 1346 (qv above).

1348   Built for US Navy as **J4F-2**, BuAer serial **37718**. Acc 29Dec43 and del 01Jan44; allocated to Atlantic Fleet NAS Norfolk 01Jan44. Suffered undercarriage collapse on landing at NAS New York 14Jun44 after pilot (from CASU-23, MCAS Quantico) failed to properly check that it was locked down; categorised as having repairable Cat C damage. Ferried from New York to Quantico but then struck while parked by taxying CASU-22 F6F-5N 20Jun44; cat B damage sustained to port wing and engine cowl; A&R Norfolk Aug-Sep44 and SOC there 31Oct44.

1349   Built for US Navy as **J4F-2**, BuAer serial **37719**. Acc 31Dec43 and del 17Jan44; records missing but with NAS Pearl Harbor by Aug44 and SOC there 30Jun46 as obsolete. BoS War Assets Administration to Hugh A MacDonald, Honolulu, HI 30Dec46 for $5,379. Cvtd to **G-44** (inc removal of bomb racks) 22Jan47 with CofR for **NC62095** 24Jan47 and CofA 03Feb47. BoS to Edwin C Jameson Jr, New York, NY 04Feb47 with CofR 25Aug47, and later as **N62095**; CofA renewed 16Jan53 at TFH:184hrs (SMOH); 18Feb54 at TFH:329hrs; 20Jan55 at TFH:441hrs; 30Dec55 at TFH:524hrs. CofR revoked 10Jly81 after last flew in 1967. BoS Estate of Jameson to Dennis K Burke, Pembroke, MA, 08Jun03 with CofR 26Jun03. Re-assembled by North River Aviation Inc, Halifax, MA and "ready for flight" Jun03. Address change to Vero Beach, FL. Current, but not airworthy May13, with CofR due to expire 31Jan15.

1350   Built for US Navy as **J4F-2**, BuAer serial **37720**. Acc 12Jan44 and del 13Jan44; records missing but with NAS Brunswick by Aug44; NAS Seattle Oct45 for reconditioning; Pool NAS Seattle Jan46; NAS Brunswick Mar46; NAS Seattle, Apr46 and SOC there 31May46 as obsolete. Tfd by War Assets Administration, Washington, DC to Department of Interior, Fish & Wildlife Service, Chicago, IL, 16Sep46. Regn **NC770** applied for 25Sep46, but ntu. Regd **NC702** to Dept of Interior, Washington, DC 10Oct46. CofA issued 25Oct46. Destroyed in landing accident at Lake Mead, AZ, 31Oct46. Replaced by c/n 1320 (qv), and cancelled from USCAR 31Mar48.

1351   Built for US Navy as **J4F-2**, BuAer serial **37721**. Acc 19Jan44 and del 22Jan44; records missing but with NAS Astoria by Aug44; NAS Seattle May45 and SOC there 31Jly46 as obsolete and surplus. BoS War Assets Administration to Lee Mansdorf, Los Angeles, CA for $7,500 06Nov46. BoS L Mansdorf to Harry Mansdorf, Los Angeles, CA 21Nov46 with CofR as **G-44, NC68102** same date. Cvtd to G-44 and CofA issued 27Dec46. BoS to General Construction Co, Seattle, WA 29Mar47 with CofR 30Apr47. BoS to Petroleum Navigation Co, Seattle, WA 04Jun48 with CofR 11Jun48; dual control yoke installed on CofA 18Mar49. BoS to William deVille Smith, Dillingham, AK for $9,000, 21Dec50, with CofR **N68102** 04Jan51. CofA 02Jun52 at TFH:1,641hrs; hull vents and keel re-inforcement installed and false step cut off as per Grumman instructions and kit Jun55 and CofA issued at TFH:2,340hrs; address change to Homer, AK 14Aug56. BoS to Alaska Aeronautical Industries, Spenard, AK, 01Jly60. BoS transferring title back to Smith, 07Jly60, for $16,000, with CofR 08Sep60. Another BoS 01Feb62 transferred title back to Alaska Aeronautical Industries, Anchorage, AK with CofR 16Feb62; this transaction showed Jack Peck as "partner" and is followed by another BoS 30Jly64 transferring title from Alaska Aeronautical Industries to Alaska Aeronautical Industries showing Jack Peck as "owner", with CofR 25Aug64. A 'conditional' BoS 10Jun66 from Jack Peck to George R Pappas, Anchorage, AK for $20,351 with CofR 28Jun66. Aircraft named "Cindi Ann"; (the FAA file also contains another 'conditional' BoS from Peck to Pappas dated 18Aug67); escape hatch per SA4-63 (with deviations per SA64AL), enlarged windows per SA5-51, single-piece windshield per SA4-2 and Cessna droop wingtips per SA366AL all installed by Pappas, and CofA issued 22May70. BoS to Lane W & Betsy F Smith, White Salmon, WA 27Jly94 with CofR 01Aug94. BoS to Danny Abbott, Salem, WI 17Aug07 with CofR 11Oct07. Current and airworthy May13, with CofR due to expire 30Sep15.

1352   Built for US Navy as **J4F-2**, BuAer serial **37722** but diverted off contract to the British Air Commission, Washington, DC with serial **FP458** for use by the British in Canada. Del 26Jan44, but no specific details of British use known other than documentation suggesting use in Canada prior to Sep44 and therefore perhaps by British Commonwealth Air Training Plan. Returned to the US authorities and recorded at Westchester County AP, NY Aug45 awaiting disposal by the War Assets Administration (WAA). BoS WAA to Arne A Maki, Long Island City, NY 07Jun46, for $14,000. BoS to William H Wincapaw, Tottenville, NY 01Aug46 with CofR **NC94527** and CofA 09Aug46 at TFH:92hrs. BoS to General Industries Inc, Melbourne, FL 23Nov46 with CofR 21Jly47. BoS to Adolph Duchini, New York, NY 15Nov48 with CofA 04Jan49 (noting last flight on 08Jun47), and CofR 07Feb49. Cancelled from USCAR 14Apr50 after "washout" accident 20Dec49. Wreckage to

Aero Trades Inc, Mineola, NY by BoS 03Apr50 and restored as **N94527** with CofR 29May50. Cancelled from USCAR as salvage for parts 22Dec59.

1353   Built for US Navy as **J4F-2**, BuAer serial **37723** but diverted off contract to the British Air Commission, Washington, DC with serial **FP459** for use by the Fleet Air Arm. Acc 30Jan44 and del 05Feb44 but no specific details of British use in 1944 known; assigned to the US Navy's NATC at NAS Patuxent River Mar-Nov45 and returned to US Navy charge by Dec45; Pool NAS Norfolk Dec45; Pool CASU-67 NAS Memphis Jun46; FASRON-4 NAS Memphis Aug46 and SOC there 30Sep46 as obsolete and surplus. BoS War Assets Administration to John F Sugden, West Roxbury, MA 06Nov46 with CofR as **G-44, NC9207H** 03Dec46 and CofA 16Dec46. BoS to The International Paper Box Machine Co, Nashua, NH 11Jan49 with CofR **N9207H** 07Jly49; CofA 30Apr55 at TFH:1,271hrs. BoS to Raymond A Labombarde, Nashua, NH 14Jun55 with CofR 11Jly55. Returned to The International Paper Box Machine Co by BoS 20Jly56 with CofR 22Aug56. BoS to Atlantic Aviation Corp, Teterboro, NJ 24Oct63. BoS to Nashua Aviation & Supply Co Inc, Nashua, NH 29Nov63. BoS to Brandt Jordan Corp of New Bedford, New Bedford, MA 06Dec63, with CofR 17Jan64 but FAA Form 337s 15Jan64 through to 08Jan66 give owner as Howard J Rose, Greenwich, CT. Hartzell HC-D2X20-3/8833 props installed Mar67 and Experimental CofA issued 03Mar67 to show compliance with FAR at TT:2,594hrs; Standard CofA 23Mar67. Accident 25Jly67: substantially damaged when both engines failed on take-off from East Freetown, MA and hit trees when force-landing off airport. Pilot seriously injured. Sale reported Jan77, but in the "Suspense" file, a letter from the FAA, dated 23Oct03, to William Klaila, Brandt Jordan Corp, South Middleboro, MA requesting clarification of the aircraft's status, was returned by Katherine Klaila (for William Klaila, deceased) stating that aircraft was destroyed in a crash at Carver, MA in 1967. Despite this the FAA still has the registration assigned to Brandt Jordan Corp, May13, with a valid CoR which is due to expire 30Sep13.

1354   Built for US Navy as **J4F-2**, BuAer serial **37724**. Acc and del 17Feb44; records missing but with NAS Quonset Point by Aug44 and SOC there 31Jly46 as obsolete and surplus. Regd as **G-44, NC66550** to Richard Richardson, Clarcoma, FL. Reregd **N144TA** to CC Montag, Portland, OR 26Feb58. Cancelled from USCAR 10Jan64. To East Pakistan Flying Club, Dacca, East Pakistan as **AP-AOQ** Nov63, with CofA No: 343. Written off 24Jan67 at unknown location and cancelled from register 23May67.

1355   Built for US Navy as **J4F-2**, BuAer serial **37725**. Acc 18Feb44 and del 02Mar44; records missing but with NAAS Chincoteague by Aug44; NAS Norfolk, Sep45 for reconditioning and SOC there 28Feb47 as obsolete and surplus. Sold by War Assets Administration to NA Kalt, Dallas, TX 11Feb47, for $5,626 and regd as **G-44, NC1188V**. BoS 25Jan47(sic) Kalt to North Jersey Sales & Construction Co, Paterson, NJ for $8,826. CofA after overhaul and re-paint 09Aug47 at TFH:627hrs. TFH:1,200hrs at 18Aug48 and CofA renewed 07Sep48. BoS to William L Rausch, Hackensack, NJ 01Mar49 for $6,500, and CofR 30Jun49. BoS to Alaska Airlines Inc, Anchorage, AK 14Jly49 and CofR 09Nov49 as **N1188V**. CofA renewed 24Feb50. TFH:1,249hrs at 03Apr51. CofA renewed 26Feb52. BoS to Dennis E Thompson, Seward, AK 27Apr53 and CofR 20May53. CofA renewed 04May53 at TFH:1,685hrs. BoS to Cordova Airlines Inc, Anchorage, AK 12Nov54 and CofR 23Nov54. CofA renewed 03May55 at TFH:1,913hrs after major overhaul and re-paint; and 15Jan59 at TFH:3,338hrs. BoS to Sea-Air Inc, Anchorage, AK 18Aug59 and CofR 07Oct59. Cancelled from USCAR 15Apr70 as "scrapped".

1356   Built for US Navy as **J4F-2**, BuAer serial **37726**. Acc 18Feb44 and del 03Mar44; records missing but with NAS Norfolk Aug44; NAAS Manteo, Oct44; NAAS Chincoteague, Jan46; Pool NAS Norfolk Jly46 and SOC there 28Feb47 as obsolete and surplus. Regd as **G-44, NC97102** to

G-44 Widgeon, c/n 1356, ZK-CHG, of NZ Tourist Air Travel Ltd, at Mechanics Bay, Auckland in September 1964. The aircraft was re-engined with Continental IO-470-Ds and later served with Mount Cook Airlines.
(Jennifer Gradidge Collection)

Albert J Koerts. BoS to J Gordon McDonald, Ann Arbor, MI 15Oct47. To **N97102**. BoS to Fliteways Inc, Milwaukee, WI 20Sep51. BoS to Tecon Corp, Dallas, TX 04Jun52. BoS to Universal Trades Inc, Green Cove Springs, FL 07May53. To Robert Stockholm, Troy, NY by Aug62. Cancelled from USCAR 29Apr64. To Tourist Air Travel, Auckland, New Zealand, May64, and regd **ZK-CHG** 06Jly64. Re-engined with 260hp Continental IO-470-Ds as **Super Widgeon**. To Mount Cook Airlines, Christchurch, New Zealand, 01Jan68. Accident 07Mar69: damaged in water landing at Mechanics Bay, Auckland. Wfu 16May75; storm damage at Christchurch 01Aug75 and used for spares. To Sea Bee Air Ltd, Auckland Oct76; noted derelict/stripped Mechanics Bay 1985. To Owen Harnish, Auckland 10Jly90 and stored. ZK regn cancelled 31Jly98 as wfu. Stored dismantled at Ardmore a/o Nov12.

1357   Built for US Navy as **J4F-2**, BuAer serial **37727** but diverted off contract to the British Air Commission, Washington, DC with serial **FP460** for use by the Fleet Air Arm. Acc 29Feb44 and del 08Mar44 to Roosevelt Field for SBNO. He flew from Roosevelt Field to Anacostia 03Apr44 and returned next day. Returned to US Navy charge by Oct45; Pool NAS Norfolk Oct45 until at least Apr46; Pool CASU-67 NAS Memphis by Jun46; FASRON-4 NAS Memphis Aug46 and SOC there 30Sep46 as obsolete and surplus. BoS War Assets Administration to Vernie L Johnson, dba Adirondack Aero Sevice, Warrensburg, NY 08Nov46 with CofR **NC60080** 25Nov46. Cvtd to **G-44** with CofA 10Apr47. BoS to George J Priester, Oak Park, IL 02Feb49 with CofR 10Feb49 as **N60080**; address change to Elmhurst, IL 21Aug51; CofA renewed 01Jly54 at TFH:1,813hrs; 02Jly55 at TFH:1,873hrs; address change to Wheeling, IL 04Nov55; CofA renewed 09Jly56 at TFH:1,942hrs; 03Jly59 at TFH:2,182hrs. Crashed at Chicago 25Sep59. Cancelled from USCAR 02Sep70 as "damaged/not flyable/ salvage".

1358   Built for US Navy as **J4F-2**, BuAer serial **37728** but diverted off contract to the British Air Commission, Washington, DC with serial **FP461** for use by the Fleet Air Arm. Acc 15Mar44 and del 16Mar44. Returned to the US Navy in exchange for BuAer 32978/FP474 early-mid 1944, although circumstances not understood. US Navy records missing but with BAR Convair at Allentown, PA by Aug44; NAS Glynco Aug45 (under repair at NAS Jacksonville Apr46) and SOC at Glynco 31Jly46 as obsolete and surplus. Regd as **G-44, NC4614N** to Bill W Bonebrake Inc, El Reno, OK. Accident 25Aug55: minor damage in forced landing Lake Michigan, MI. CF-IIR allotted to Vancouver Aircraft Sales Ltd, Vancouver, BC 31Oct55; US CofA for export E-28354; CofR(P) 15108 for **CF-IIR** and CofA 5530 both issued 10Nov55 to Realite Ltd, Vancouver, BC. Aircraft loaned (not leased) to Bennett & White Construction Co Ltd. Accident at 0915hrs on 11Jly56: engine failed, crashed into a mountain and caught fire, on south side of Lee Creek Canyon, 15miles NE of Kamloops, BC. Pilot Carl John Baxter and 3 pax killed. Aircraft written off and cancelled from CCAR.

1359   Built for US Navy as **J4F-2**, BuAer serial **37729**. Acc and del 22Mar44; records missing but with NAS Wildwood by Aug44; BAR Beech Aircraft, Wichita, KS 08Jan46 and SOC there 30Jun47 as obsolete and surplus. Regd as **G-44, NC68395** to West Coast Aircraft Inc, Los Angeles, CA. To James Magoffin, Fairbanks, AK and leased to Transocean Airlines, Oakland, CA by 1950. CofA 10Oct55 as **Super Widgeon** with Lycoming GO-435 engines. To Green Bay Paper & Box Co, Green Bay, WI by Jun56. Reregd **N95J** to Ted T Anderson, North Miami, FL 07Mar58. To Debian Aviation Inc, Miami, FL by Jly64. Accident 12Apr65: substantial damage after loss of one engine and wheels-up landing at Nassau, Bahamas. Pilot + 6 pax minor injuries. To Debian Aviation, Miami, FL 1966. To Michael D Bentley, Nassau, Bahamas 1970-72. Restored to USCAR 1975 as N95J. To Frank Hill, Fort Lauderdale, FL 1976. To Amphibian Sales Inc, Miami, FL Aug86. To Aviacorp of Florida Inc, Miami, FL Feb88; reported resident at Larnaca, Cyprus, Dec89; based in France 1990/91; at aircraft auction Wroughton, UK, at TFH:3,482hrs 29Apr91. Accident 27Mar92: damaged in forced landing at Blackbushe, UK and noted dismantled on a truck through Lincolnshire, UK 11May92. To DW Morse, Deer Park, WA, Nov92. To Spearfish Aviation Inc, Rapid City, SD, with CofR 13Aug97. CofR expired 30Jun12 and cancelled from USCAR 11Oct12. Restored to register 18Mar13. To Mark A Woodruff, Ossipee, NH with CofR 08Apr13, to expire 30Apr16.

1360   Built for US Navy as **J4F-2**, BuAer serial **37730**. Acc 29Mar44 and del 01Apr44; records missing but with Hedron-16, FAW-16 headquartered at NAF Recife by Oct44 CASU-27 NAS Chincoteague 12Jun45; CASU-21 NAS Norfolk May46. CGAS Brooklyn 05Jun46 until at least Jly46 when formally transferred to the US Coast Guard and SOC by the US Navy 31Jly46. SOC by US Coast Guard circa 1950 and del from CGAS Port Angeles, Jly50. Regd as **G-44, NC744**(2) to US Dept of Interior, Washington, DC 1950 to replace c/n 1266. Cvtd to McKinnon

Super Widgeon in 1953. To **N5531A** for Sperry Rand Corp, New York, NY by May62. To **PT-DGY** for Jari Industria & Comercio SA, Belem, Brazil 01Mar70. Donated to Inst. Linguistico de Verão, Brasilia /JAARS Aviation for missionary work 1972. Brazilian regn cancelled 12Feb74. Regd **N17481** to RC Scribner, Pontiac, MI with CofA 21Jun74. To Charles S Harvey, Kodiak, AK, with CofR 27Apr81; named "Steve Harvey" and operated for Bob Stanford as Island Air Service Inc from Apr81. Leased to PenAir 1985 and flown for them by Steve Harvey until 1998. Accident 31Jly95: ground-looped during take-off roll at Kodiak, AK, due to broken left wheel rim. Ferried to Bremerton, WA for repair, and cvtd to Lycoming GO-480 power by Avian Aeronautics Aug95. Nominal change to Harvey Flying Service, Kodiak, AK in 2000. Current and airworthy May13, with CofR to expire 28Feb14.

1361   Built for US Navy as **J4F-2**, BuAer serial **37731**. Acc 31Mar44 and del 10Apr44; records missing but with BAR Wright- Patterson Fld by Aug44; CASU-26 NAAS Otis Oct44 and SOC there 31Jly46 as obsolete and surplus. Regd as **G-44, NC75222** to Louisiana Department of Wildlife & Fisheries, New Orleans, LA. Reregd **N111W**(2) to Circle Inc, Harvey, LA 21Feb57. To Ingram Contractors Inc, Harvey, LA by Jly64. To Diamond Drilling Co, New Orleans, LA. Accident 27Dec68: pilot (uninjured) was talking to passengers and crashed into the Mississippi near Lutcher, LA; 3 pax seriously injured; aircraft sank and has never been found (although NTSB report states "substantial damage"). Cancelled from USCAR 08May69.

1362   Built for US Navy as **J4F-2**, BuAer serial **37732** but diverted off contract to the British Air Commission, Washington, DC with serial **FP462** for use by the Fleet Air Arm. Acc and del 17Apr44; used by Senior British Naval Officer at NAS Pensacola Aug-Sep44 (and there was still a Widgeon on charge there, for his use, Apr45) but no other specific details of British use in 1944 or 1945 known. Returned to US Navy charge by Oct45; Pool NAS Norfolk Oct45 until at least Apr46; Pool CASU-67 NAS Memphis by Jun46; FASRON-4 NAS Memphis Aug46 and SOC 31Oct46 as obsolete and surplus. Regd as **G-44, NC9236H** to unknown owner, Syosset, Long Island, NY. To Western Newspapers United Inc, New York, NY. To Amphibian Airways, Invercargill, New Zealand 22Sep52 as **ZK-BAY**. Badly damaged when capsized on landing Queenstown 30Dec52. Rebuilt. To Tourist Air Travel, Auckland, New Zealand 04Aug61. Cvtd to **Super Widgeon**, with Continentals, by Tasman Empire Airlines at Auckland, with FF 14Oct63 at Auckland-Mangere. Accident 29Jan65: substantial damage on landing at Pakatoa Island, Hauraki Gulf. To Mount Cook Airlines, Christchurch, New Zealand, 01Jan68. Accident 24Dec70: crashed off Browns Island, Auckland while on charter to New Zealand Television News. While filming a vessel that was on fire in Auckland's Waitemata Harbour, the G-44 dived into the water, killing all four on board.

1363   Built for US Navy as **J4F-2**, BuAer serial **37733** but diverted off contract to the British Air Commission, Washington, DC with serial **FP463** for use by the Fleet Air Arm. Del 26Apr44, but no specific details of British use known. Returned to the US authorities, presumably in 1945, for disposal although not used by the US Navy. Regd as **G-44, NC60824** to Nelson A Miles, Mineola, NY, Sep46. Fate unknown.

1364   Built for US Navy as **J4F-2**, BuAer serial **37734**. Acc 29Apr44 and del 02May44; records missing but with NAPT, NAS Glenview by Aug44 and SOC there 31Jly46 as obsolete and surplus. BoS War Assets Administration to Norman Blake, Oklahoma City, OK, for $10,000, 29Oct46. BoS to Harvey S Murrell, Chicago, IL 21Nov46 with CofR **NC4617N** 23Dec46. Cvtd from "Navy cargo to NC status" (**G-44**) by Southwest Aviation Service Inc, Oklahoma City, OK with CofA 21Feb47; overhauled and repainted with CofA 24Sep48; "2 foot of keel" installed in front of the first step Oct49. BoS to Vest Aircraft & Finance Co, Denver, CO 14Feb51. BoS to Gussie R Jamison, Chickasha, OK 23Feb51 with CofR **N4617N** 06Mar51; new-type vented step and factory kit re-inforcement plate in keel at Station 15 installed Jly51 by Link Aeronautical Corp; McCauley props replaced by Curtiss Reed metal props Jly51. BoS back to Vest Aircraft & Finance 15Aug51. BoS to Englewood Airport, Englewood, CO 23Aug51 with CofR 10Sep51. Experimental CofA issued 16Apr54 for test flying Lycoming GO-435-C2 engines, reissued 29Sep54, 11Jan57 for Lycoming GO-435-C2B engines, again on 26Jun58 (TFH:535hrs), and finally on 27Jun59 (TFH:539hrs); STCs SA4-621, SA4-849, SA4-850, SA4-954 and SA2-952 all installed Sep59 with Standard CofA 21Oct59 at TFH:545hrs, as **Super Widgeon** with Lycoming GO-435-C2B engines. BoS 27Feb61 transferred title to Anderson Manufacturing Co, Englewood, CO (Russell Anderson being president of both companies) with CofR 13Mar61; address change to Denver, CO with CofR 23Jun62. Accident 01Sep71: substantial damage in hard water landing on Lake McConaughty, Ogallala, NE. Right wing float separated and aircraft capsized. Pilot (uninjured) had not made a water landing for two years. BoS Anderson Co to Packard Flying Service Inc, Ogalalla, NE 11Sep71 with CofR 12Nov71. BoS to Dexter Aircraft Sales Inc, Pebble Beach, CA 19Apr73. BoS to Dennis M Sherman dba Sherman Aircraft Sales, West Palm Beach, FL 27Apr73. BoS to Aircraft Sales Inc, Charlotte, NC undated but recorded 14Jun73. Regn **N9DA** requested 14Jun73 and placed on aircraft 20Aug73. BoS to John P Silberman, Sherborn, MA 19Nov73 with CofR 04Dec73. BoS to Robert C Moran, Key West, FL 26Mar75 with CofR 12Apr75. BoS to Aircraft Sales Inc, Charlotte, NC 22Aug77. Regn **N4617N** reserved 10Nov77 and placed on aircraft 14Nov77. BoS to Fred N Stalder, Harrisonville, MO 19Dec77 with CofR 12Jan78. BoS to Ream's Trans Caribbean Air Freight, Riviera Beach, FL 25Aug78 with CofR 19Sep78. BoS to Morgan-Rourke Aircraft Sales, Bartlesville, OK 01Jun79. BoS to Donald J Anklin, Mooresville, NC (undated but recorded 17Mar80). BoS recording nominal change, Anklin to Aircraft Sales Inc, Mooresville, NC 11Aug80. BoS to M&F Fish Farms, Del Ray Beach, FL 14Aug80 with CofR 26Sep80, but another BoS dated 16Sep80 (sic) transferred the title from M&F back to Anklin dba Aircraft Ltd, Mooresville, NC. BoS Aircraft Ltd to Seacoast Aircraft, Riviera Beach, FL 07Jly81, with CofR 24Jun83 (sic). BoS to Trans-Caribbean Corp of Broward Inc, Fort Lauderdale, FL 07Feb84 with CofR 08May84. BoS to James P Hollingsworth, South Miami, FL, 06Jly84. BoS to Robert L Montgomery, Hollidaysburg, PA 20Sep89 with CofR 28Sep89. BoS to American Aviation Inc, Brooksville, FL 19Sep90. BoS to ISRMS Inc, Land-o-Lakes, FL 09Oct90 with CofR 10Dec90. BoS to Reiser Burgan Inc, Jacksonville, FL 03Jun97 with CofR 28Aug97. Current and airworthy May13, with CofR due to expire 30Apr15.

1365   Built for US Navy as **J4F-2**, BuAer serial **37735**. Acc 29Apr44 and del 13May44; records missing but with NAPT, NAS Grosse Ile by Aug44; NAF Middle River Apr45; NAAS Harvey Point Jun45; NAAS Chincoteague Sep45; Pool NAS Norfolk, 02Jly46 and SOC there 28Feb47 as obsolete and surplus. BoS War Assets Administration to Plum Island Flying Service, Newburyport, MA for $7,685.99 14Jan47, with CofR for **G-44 NC9218H** 11Mar47. Another BoS transfers title from VM Frotheringham (as co-owner of Plum Island Flying Service) to Plum Island Flying Service Inc, Newburyport, MA 31Dec47 with CofR 04Feb48; The aircraft was stored ex War Assets Administration, until Sep49, when a BoS from Plum Island F/S Inc tfd title to William H Cook Jr, Mercer Island, WA 17Sep49, with CofR 25Oct49 as **N9218H**. BoS for half share from Cook to Richard L Rouzie, Mercer Island, WA 13Apr51 with CofR 30Apr51; CofA 01May54 at TFH:920hrs; and 24Jun57 at TFH:1,196hrs. BoS Cook & Rouzie to William H Cook Jr, Bellevue, WA 19Mar71 with CofR 20May71; CofA 15Apr82 at TFH:3,050hrs. Reported "destroyed/ scrapped" 31Jan91 and cancelled from USCAR 01Apr91, at request of owner.

C/n 1365, in a pleasant white and blue colour scheme and registered N9218H, is seen here at Renton, Washington on 17th April 1981, when owned by William H Cook Jr.   *(Peter Kirkup)*

1366   Built for US Navy as **J4F-2**, BuAer serial **37736**. Acc and del 22May44; records missing but with NAMU Johnsville by Aug44; NAMU Philadelphia (Mustin Fld) Jun45 until at least 30Apr46. Used by NAMU in experiment to have aircraft towed into the air from water (the J4F-2 had previously been successfully towed into the air from the runway). The first attempt was made at Johnsville 23Apr46 but ended in disaster with the death of the pilot and the loss of the aircraft. Aircraft crashed, stunning the pilot who was unable to escape from the submerged aircraft and then drowned; two other occupants escaped with minor injuries. The accident board blamed overconfidence and a lack of careful planning for the accident. SOC at Philadelphia 31May46.

Widgeon, c/n 1367, OH-GWA, on skis, with an interested crowd looking on, at Mänttä, Finland, on 8th February 1959. The aircraft was destroyed in a fatal crash on 28th June 1968, while attempting a take-off in gusty wind conditions at Malmi.   *(Eino Ritaranta)*

1367   Built for US Navy as **J4F-2**, BuAer serial **37737** but diverted off contract to the British Air Commission, Washington, DC with serial **FP464** for use by the Fleet Air Arm. Del 27May44; in use at NAS Brunswick Apr-May45 but otherwise no specific details of British use known. Returned to the US authorities, presumably in 1945, for disposal although not used by the US Navy. Export CofA E-9322 dated 25Jan46. To AB Aero Service, Stockholm, Sweden 06Apr46 as **G-44, SE-APO**. To Ostermans Aero AB, Stockholm 10Oct47. To Dagens Nyheters AB, Stockholm 17May49. To **OH-GWA** for Aarne Tirkkonen, Tampere, Finland 17Jly58; operated on skis with floats removed, during winter. To Oy Takuuvalmiste AB, Helsinki, Finland 02Oct65 and based at Malmi. Accident 28Jun68: crashed on take-off in gusty wind at Malmi. Two killed. Found to be overloaded with the centre of gravity too far aft. Regn cancelled 18Nov68.

1368   Built for US Navy as **J4F-2**, BuAer serial **37738** but diverted off contract to the British Air Commission, Washington, DC with serial **FP465** for use by the Fleet Air Arm. Del 28May44; in use at NAS Brunswick Apr45 but otherwise no specific details of British use known. Returned to the US authorities, presumably in 1945, for disposal although not used by the US Navy. Sold by War Assets Administration to Mercury Aviation Service, Detroit, MI 16May46. Ferry permit issued to Douglas T Bell 16May46 to fly acft (with Army identification No. "US1801") from Woodward Field, Camden, SC to Detroit. (Note: The 1947 USCAR shows this G-44 as **NC1801** with the US Government, Foreign Economic Administration, Washington, DC. The FAA file, however, makes no mention of this.) Regd as **G-44, NC40011**. BoS Mercury A/S to Jerry Crandall, Detroit, MI 23May46 with CofR 11Jun46 and CofA 22Jun46. BoS to TB Gibbs, Delavan, WI 11Nov46 with CofR 27Dec46. BoS to Talbert Construction Equipment Co, Lyons, IL 07Jun48 with CofR 29Jun48. BoS to Genesee Airport Inc, Rochester, NY 31May49 with CofR 04Aug49 as **N40011**; CofA 21Sep49 at TFH:473hrs. BoS to Malcolm L Hardy, Waynesboro, PA 27Feb50 with CofR 07Mar50. BoS to Hylan Flying Service, Rochester, NY 01May50 with CofR 05Jun50. CofA issued 04Nov53 at TFH:1,652hrs. Cvtd to **Super Widgeon** with Lycoming GO435-C2B engines, auxilliary fuel tanks and exhaust silencers installed by Link Aeronautical Corp Apr55. CofA issued 21Apr55 at TFH:1825hrs; 22Apr56 at TFH:2,074hrs. Accident 30Jun70: substantial damage when lost power on port engine on take-off from Chibougamau, QC, Canada. Forced landed in construction area on airport and gear collapsed. NTSB reported aircraft was circa 1,000lbs over max gross weight. Pilot + 4 pax minor injuries. Cancelled from USCAR 26May71, as dismantled.

1369   Built for US Navy as **J4F-2**, BuAer serial **37739**. Acc 31May44 and del 01Jun44; records missing but by Aug44 assigned and en route to BAR General Motors Eastern Aircraft Division, Trenton, NJ and in place by 31Oct44; NAS Norfolk Sep45; NAS Edenton Dec 45; NAS Norfolk Feb46 for minor repairs; Pool NAS Norfolk Jun46 and SOC there 28Feb47 as obsolete and surplus. Regd as **G-44, N9929H** to Cordova Airlines Inc, Anchorage, AK by Dec62. Accident 23Jly63: aircraft "destroyed" after overshoot on downwind landing at Seldovia, AK. Aircraft ran down embankment but the two crew suffered only minor injuries; pilot was on a route check. Later bought back from insurers by Cordova A/L for scrap or spares. Cancelled from USCAR 22Sep63. Reported "sold" Sep65 but fate unknown.

1370   Built for US Navy as **J4F-2**, BuAer serial **37740** but diverted off contract and sold to Union Oil of California, Los Angeles, CA for $39,275.49. Del ex Bethpage 17Jun44 with CofR for **G-44, NC1004**

15Jly44 and CofA 19Jly44. BoS to Butcher-Arthur Inc, Houston, TX 07May48 with CofR 12May48 and later as **N1004**. BoS to Commercial Petroleum & Transport Co, Houston, TX (nominal change) 13Dec50, with CofR 11Jan51. CofA renewed 16Jly52 at TFH:2,289hrs. BoS to Commercial Barge Lines Inc, Houston, TX 01Jan53 with CofR 14Jan53. Cvtd to **Super Widgeon** with Lycoming GO-435-C2Bs 20May53. CofA renewed 11Jun53 at TFH:2,372hrs, and 24May55 at TFH:2,763hrs. BoS to Commercial Transport Corp, Houston, TX 22Feb56. BoS to Brown & Root Inc, Houston, TX 23Feb56 with CofR 28Mar56. CofA renewed 14Mar56 at TFH:2,821hrs. Reregd as **N70U** 04Jan57. Cvtd to Lycoming GO-480-B1D engines 09Dec63. Experimental CofA 11May67 after changing the angle of the horizontal stabiliser and cvtd to Lycoming GO-480-G1D6 engines. Standard CofA renewed 18May67 at TFH: 8,324hrs. Accident 01Nov68: substantially damaged by wheels-down water landing at Belle Chasse, LA (NAS New Orleans). Pilot uninjured. Piper PA23-250 exhaust assembly installed on each engine with exhaust on lower side of nacelle. Test flown 30Sep75 by Pan Air Corp, New Orleans, LA. BoS Brown & Root to Omni Aircraft Sales Inc, Washington, DC 16May77. BoS to Amphibian Parts Inc, Miami, FL 16May77. Reregd **N70DF** 15Jly77 (and N70U transferred to Cessna 500). Authority to ferry Miami, FL to Montreal, PQ 30Aug77. Emergency exit fitted on right side of acft 13Sep77. BoS to Gilles Tremblay Aviation Inc, Montreal, QC 15Sep77 with US CofA for export E-165247 issued 22Sep77, and cancelled from USCAR 23Sep77. Application for regn by Gilles Tremblay Aviation Inc and CofA issued 07Oct77 at TFH:11,947hrs. Lease by Tremblay Aviation to Populair Aviation Service Inc 11Oct77 for one year. CofR(C) for **C-GVGQ** issued to Populair Aviation Service Inc, Dorval, PQ 12Oct77. BoS Gilles Tremblay to Lumanair Inc, Aurora, IL 31Mar78 with CofR 08Jun78. Cancelled from CCAR 02May78. Transport CofA issued 30Aug78 at TFH:11,967hrs. BoS to Donald J Anklin, Davidson, NC 11Sep78. Tfd by BoS to Aircraft Sales Inc, Mooresville, NC 19Jan79. BoS to Paul S Array, Delray, FL 19Jan79 with CofR for **N68PA** 25Aug79. Reregd **N68BA** 11Apr81. BoS to Southern Independent Associates Inc, Melrose, FL 04Mar81, with CofR 08Jly81. CofA renewed 03May85 at TFH:15,000hrs. BoS to James Robert White, Stuart, FL 20Apr86 with CofR 14May86 and reregd **N901JW**, 20Apr87. CofR expired 30Sep11. Fate unknown.

1371 Built for US Navy as **J4F-2**, BuAer serial **37741** but diverted off contract to the British Air Commission, Washington, DC with serial **FP466** for use by the Fleet Air Arm. Del 23Jun44 to SBNO Roosevelt Field, who flew it to Floyd Bennett Field 20Jly44, where the undercarriage collapsed. Repaired and in use at NAS Brunswick with 738 Sqn by Mar45. Nosed over on landing 27Mar45, location uncertain, and declared beyond economical repair. Letter from SBNO, NAF Roosevelt Fld, Mineola, NY 08Oct45 certified that "the hulk of Widgeon aircraft No:1371, being of no further use to the Royal Navy, has been handed over to Paul Nyholm for disposal." Regd as **G-44, NC60886** to Paul Nyholm, Hempstead, Long Island, NY 11Jly46. BoS to Aeromobile Equipment Co, Hempstead, NY 22Aug47 with CofR 28Aug47; major overhaul by Aero Trades Inc, Roosevelt Field, Mineola with CofA 19Jly48. BoS to John Hay Whitney and Betsey Cushing Whitney, New York, NY 22Apr49 with CofR N60886 17May49. Wooden props replaced with Curtiss metal props Mar51. BoS to City Electric of Anchorage Inc, Anchorage, AK 21Mar52 with CofR 28Mar52; CofA 29Apr53 at TFH:429hrs. Curtiss props replaced with Hartzell HC-12X20-9 props Nov53 and reregd **N47CE** 05Apr56. Lycoming R680E-3B engines, with Hartzell HC-93Z20-2C props, installed by International Aircraft Service Inc, Sun Valley, CA with CofA 16Jly56 at TFH:981hrs. BoS to Associated Services Inc, Anchorage, AK (with same address as vendor) 26Oct56, with CofR 06Nov56. BoS to American Aircraft Sales Inc, Renton, WA 19Jan62. BoS to Florida Airmotive Sales Inc, Fort Lauderdale, FL 24Feb62 with CofR 10Apr62 (listed on application as "Super Scan Widgeon 30 G-44"). Reregd **N47C** 11Apr62 and sold to Flying "W" Inc, Medford, NJ 28Mar63 with CofR 09Apr63. BoS back to Florida Airmotive 12Apr63. Presumably Florida Airmotive sold the aircraft because the CofR dated 09Jly63 was issued to Leon H Patin, Miami, FL. The next BoS transfers title from Patin to Beau Murphey Inc, Atlanta, GA 20Apr64 with CofR 20May64. BoS to Dean H Franklin, Miami, FL 14Jun66 with CofR 15Sep66. BoS to JW Dowdle, Chula Vista, CA 11Jly67 with CofR 07Sep67. BoS to Ronald Wayne Willard, Long Beach, CA 02Nov67 with CofR 16Nov67. BoS to Commute Air Inc, Kalispell, MT 04Jun68 with CofR 11Jun68. Aircraft re-possessed by Robert F Goldsworthy, Rosalia, WA 07Jly69 with CofR 18Sep69. BoS Goldsworthy to Dr Richard E Williams, Myrtle Creek, OR 10Nov69 with CofR 26Jan70. BoS to Robert L Nelson, Portland, OR undated but recorded 06Jun75; CofA 06Nov75 at TFH:2,178hrs. Accident 10Nov75: nosed over and sank during water take-off at Collinsville, CA; two occupants swam to safety and the aircraft was recovered. CofR issued for address change to Green Bay, WI 26Oct77. Converted to **Super Widgeon** with Lycoming GO-480-G1D6 engines, with Hartzell HC-83X20-

2C/9333-CH3 props, installed Aug81 per STC SA4-111. Address change to Brentwood, CA 03Jun96. BoS Manuel C Rose (Administrator) to Connie M Davis (heir), Knightsen, CA 15Jun00. (Davis was Nelson's girlfriend, and although his family contested the will, she was awarded ownership of the aircraft after the matter was referred to the Probate Court.)

The aircraft was found by Mark Taintor, in pieces, at The Funny Farm airport, near Byron, CA. He takes up the story:

"The parts were scattered in several farm buildings. Bob (Nelson) collected aircraft parts from various types of aircraft, as well as many military surplus pallets and boxes of stuff not associated with aviation. These buildings were filled with junk which made finding the Widgeon parts a treasure hunt. I believe that the spirit of Bob helped me find all the parts. One time, I was walking into one of the buildings to do some sheet metal work on a shear. As I walked in a voice in my head said 'Turn right, go into that storage room. Look in the garbage can, open the small cardboard box and find the cigarette pack'. Inside that cigarette pack was the jack screw for the elevator trim tab! This type of thing happened many times during the assembly. We found every part for the aircraft except one 2¼ control cable pulley.

"We re-assembled her at The Funny Farm. It took about 30 days spread over 2 or 3 months. We flew her out, on a ferry permit, to Columbia Airport in the foothills of the Sierra Nevada, in central California. It was about a 30-minute flight (gear down), not having done any work on the gear system at this point. We registered the aircraft in Nevada for tax reasons – my sister-in-law lived in Carson City. We then worked on the aircraft some more, rebuilding the gear system and some electrical work. I then moved her to Las Vegas (Boulder City Airport) and rebuilt the props and gearboxes. Then flew her to Tacoma Narrows Airport in Washington. We sold the old girl and she went to Alaska."

BoS to Mark D and Diane Renee Taintor, Carson City, NV 18Oct99(sic) with CofR 22Feb01. After being ferried to Gig Harbor, WA it was placed in storage in a hangar for 2 years and then in open storage until sold. BoS to Lewis M Erhart, Anchorage, AK 20Apr09, with CofR 29Sep09. Although file contains no FAA Form 337s since 1981, aircraft is current and airworthy May13, with CofR due to expire 31May15.

G-44 Super Widgeon c/n 1371, registered N47C, at Tacoma Narrows Airport, Washington, after rebuild by Mark Taintor. (Mark Taintor)

1372 Built for US Navy as **J4F-2**, BuAer serial **37742**. Acc 29Jun44 and del 01Jly44; records missing but to NAF Newport News 23Nov44. Sustained moderate damage in water-loop in Narragansett Bay, Rhode Island, in vicinity of Could Island 02Jly45: inexperienced pilot lost control on the landing run and aircraft sustained moderate damage to left wing, float and struts. SOC at Newport News 31Oct46 as obsolete and surplus. BoS War Assets Administration to Memphis Flying Service Inc, Germantown, TN for $10,000 07Nov46 with CofR **NC65992** 02Dec46. Cvtd to **G-44** and painted silver with blue trim, with CofA 04Jan47. BoS to CG Gilley, Lafayette, LA for $9,000 28Jun50 with CofR as N65992 18Jly50; CofA 23Jun53 at TFH:403hrs. BoS to Loffland Bros Co, Tulsa, OK 28May55 with CofR 21Jun55. Experimental CofA 20Sep55 at TFH:2,021hrs after fitting Continental O-470-B engines with Hartzell HC82XF-2B props with Standard CofA 21Nov55; another Experimental CofA 23Jan57 with Continental O-470-M engines installed by McDermott and Standard CofA issued 30Jan57 at TFH:2,705hrs. Reregd **N92L** with address change to New Iberia, LA 19Aug57; another address change back to Tulsa, OK 13Sep58 with CofR 13Oct58. Flotation compartments installed per STC SA4-61 Aug59; Continental IO-470-D engines, with HC A2X-2 props, installed per STC SA2-13 Sep59 and gross weight increase to 5,400lbs Dec59. BoS Loffland Bros to J Ray McDermott & Co Inc, Harvey, LA for $35,000, 29Oct65 with CofR 29Nov65. Two 55-gallon and two 30-gallon fuel drums installed in cabin for delivery flight from Fort Lauderdale, FL via Boston, MA - St Johns, NF - Santa Maria, Azores - Las Palmas, Canaries - Dakar, Senegal - Roberts Field, Liberia and finally (after 51 hours) Lagos, for operations in Nigeria (del 20Feb–07Mar66). Reported to have flown 5–8 hours a day in Nigeria, retnd from Lagos to

USA during 16 days in Jly71 via Roberts Field, Liberia - Ville Los Lisantos, Liberia – Seville – Shannon – Reykjavik – Greenland - Goose Bay - St Johns and Baltimore to Monroeville, LA, logging 74.8 flight hours. Disassembled in 1973 at Eunice, LA and used for spares; nominal change to McDermott Inc, New Orleans, LA Dec82 with CofR 08Mar83. BoS to Halter Yachts Inc, New Orleans, LA 11Dec85. BoS to Aircraft Speciality Inc, Belle Chase, LA 09Sep86. BoS to Robert H Miller Jr, Eunice, LA 12Oct86. BoS to Charles B Smith, Durham, NH 05Dec87 with CofR 07Nov87. Rebuilt at Gulfport, MS, with 260hp Continental IO-270 engines, and FF in 1991. Empennage assembly modified per SA61SW, Cessna wingtips installed per STC SA366AL, and one-piece windshield installed per STC SA4-2 Jun91. Based at Sanford, MA from 1994; attended Sun'n Fun 1995, at which time it was named: "*Scotty Ann*". Address change to Rye, NH 16Apr97 with CofR 21Jly97. BoS to John M Huft, Pagosa Springs, CO 09Sep99 with CofR 01Nov99. BoS to Jerry T Gonsoulin, Houma, LA 27Aug03 with CofR 29Oct03. Address change to Pensacola, FL 18May04. Installation of Shadin fuel flow management system per STC SE552GL Jun06; for sale for $345,000 Jan08 at TFH:11,837hrs. BoS to Two Tails LLC, Las Vegas, NV 04Jan10, with CofR 15Jan10. Current and airworthy May13, with CofR due to expire 30Sep13.

1373   Built for US Navy as **J4F-2**, BuAer serial **37743**. Acc 30Jun44 and del 21Jly44; records missing but with NAF Annapolis by Aug44; VN8D5, NAF Annapolis Nov44 until 08Jly46 when transferred to an unknown location and SOC there 31Jly46 as obsolete and surplus. Transferred from War Assets Administration to Department of Interior, Fish & Wildlife Service, Washington, DC 05Sep46 with CofR **NC701** issued 27Sep46 to Fish & Wildlife Service, Chicago, IL. Cvtd from J4F-2 to **G-44** by Southern Airways Company, Birmingham, AL Nov46 with CofA 09Dec46; renewed 06Jun52 at TFH:2,319hrs. Lycoming GO-435-C2-B engines with Hartzell HC-82X20-2A/9333C-3 props installed and approved for 5,000lbs gross weight by McKinnon-Hickman Co per STC SA380WE Oct54. CofR cancelled at owner's request 04Sep58. BoS to Alaska Aeromarine, King Salmon, AK 05Jan59 with CofR **N701J** 04Mar59 and CofA 24Mar59 at TFH:3,264hrs; (owner of Alaska Aeromarine was Richard H Jensen). BoS RH Jensen to Richard LE Jensen, Fairbanks, AK 01Apr71 with CofR 22Apr71. CofR revoked by FAA 14Nov73. BoS RLE Jensen back to Richard H Jensen, Girdwood, AK 12Jun76 with CofR 11Jly77. CofR revoked again 21May82 (non-return of Triennial report) and **N701J** re-issued again 10Aug82 to RH Jensen at a King Salmon, AK address. BoS The estate of RH Jensen to Thomas Owen Young, Lake Oswego, OR 29May03 with CofR 06Aug03; address change to Battle Ground, WA with CofR 19Sep06. Lycoming GO-480-B1D engines with Hartzell HCA3V20-2C/V9333C-3 props installed with associated changes May09. Current but not airworthy May13, with CofR due to expire 31Jan15.

G-44 Super Widgeon, c/n 1373, N701J, owned by Richard H Jensen, visiting Oshkosh on 31st July 1977. Note the Alaskan flag on the tailfin.
(Peter Kirkup)

1374   Built for US Navy as **J4F-2**, BuAer serial **37744**. Acc 21Jly44 and del 22Jly44; records missing but with NAAS Martha's Vineyard by Aug44 until at least 30Apr46; NAS Quonset Point by Jun46 and SOC there 31Jly46 as obsolete and surplus. BoS War Assets Administration to Nathan Lease, Dublin, GA for $7,500 28Oct46. BoS to Whitehead's Inc, Charlotte, NC 28Oct46 with CofR **NC52833** 27Jan47. Cvtd to **G-44** and CofA issued 18Mar47; nominal change to Troy Whitehead Machinery Co Inc, Charlotte, NC by BoS 31Dec47 with CofR 11Mar48. BoS to JL Kipnis, Jacksonville, FL 12Mar48 with CofR 02Apr48. BoS to The Carl Miller Co, Milwaukee, WI 04Oct49 with CofR **N52833**, 18Oct49. BoS to Fliteways Inc, Milwaukee, WI 19Dec50. BoS to Teal Association, Milwaukee, WI 05Mar51 with CofR 29Mar51. BoS to WR Eldridge, Austin, TX 10Aug51 with CofR 31Aug51; CofA 26May52 at TFH:1,002hrs. BoS to George W Devine, Corpus Christi, TX (for $15,000) 12Aug52 with CofR 21Aug52. BoS to TL James & Co Inc, Ruston, LA 15Feb54 with CofR 05Apr54. Cvtd to **Super Widgeon** with Lycoming GO-480-B1 engines and Hartzell

HC83X20-2A props installed by McKinnon-Hickman Co, Portland, OR, and CofA issued 07Jan55 at TFH:1,281hrs. BoS to Kerr-McGee Oil Industries Inc, Oklahoma City, OK 12Dec55 with CofA 11Jan56 at TFH:1,510hrs and CofR 14Feb56. No Forms 337 after this. Accident 08Nov57 and cancelled from USCAR 02Jly58. The aircraft was presumably repaired at unknown date, after the accident. Ownership was granted to Mirabella Aviation, Fort Pierce, FL 08Mar07, after a court case against Executive Dogs Inc, Good Marketing Inc and Marvin Good. BoS Mirabella to Aircraft Specialties Inc, Fort Pierce, FL 15Jun07 with CofR 27Feb08. To Rochester Amphibian Inc, Rochester, NY, with CofR 18Jan11. Current but not airworthy May13, with CofR due to expire 31Jan14.

1375   Built for US Navy as **J4F-2**, BuAer serial **37745** but diverted off contract to the British Air Commission, Washington, DC with serial **FP467** for use by the Fleet Air Arm. Acc 31Jly44 and del 07Aug44; no specific details of British use in 1944 or 1945 known. Returned to US Navy charge by Oct45; Pool NAS Norfolk Oct45 until at least Apr46; Pool CASU-67 NAS Memphis by Jun46; FASRON-4 NAS Memphis Aug46 and SOC there 30Sep46 as obsolete and surplus. BoS War Assets Administration to Nathaniel A Kalt, Dallas, TX 04Nov46 (for $7,500) with CofR **NC74630**, as J4F-2, 21Nov46. BoS to Charles B Dickson, Cincinnati, OH 12Dec46 with CofA 18Dec46 and CofR, as **G-44**, 10Jan47. BoS to Robert Uricho Jr, Miami, FL 11Mar49. Dual control column installed 10May49; CofR N76430 23Jun49; ferry permit granted 12Jly51 to "return aircraft to home base for repairs" (Fort Lauderdale to Miami). Wing floats removed 12Jly51, right float repaired and four feet of forward fuselage keel replaced Dec51. BoS to George C Hall Jr, Fort Lauderdale, FL 13Feb52 with CofR 03Mar52. BoS Hall (then listed as Crystal Transit Co, Buffalo, NY) to Northeast Aviation Co, Portland, ME 11Nov52 with CofA 16Nov52 at TFH:934hrs; CofR 16Feb53. BoS to Victor L Slater, Northville, MI 17Apr54 with CofR 28Apr54. BoS to Carolina Paper Box Co Inc, Burlington, NC 05May55 with CofR 12Jly55. Reported crashed at Ciego de Avila, Cuba 22Jan58 and cancelled from USCAR 19Feb58 due "total accident". Despite this a BoS transfers title to Fred W Fenn, Ojus, FL 27May58 with CofR 29Oct59. Rebuilt and repaired by Fenn Aircraft Service, North Perry A/P, Hollywood, FL Feb60. BoS to Bud Branham and Joe Savage Jr, Rainy Pass Lodge, Anchorage, AK 02Apr61 with CofR 24May61. BoS to John O and Ruth Gorman, Carmichael, CA 15Jun62 with CofR 27Jly62. BoS to David S Garber, Menlo Park, CA 18Nov63 with CofR 29Nov63. BoS to Henry Ober Moffett, Kent, Barbados, West Indies 24Oct64 with CofR 19Nov64. BoS to Dean H Franklin, Miami, FL 14Oct65 with CofR 01Nov65. **N1035L** was assigned to Franklin 11May66 and placed on acft 18May66. Converted to **Super Widgeon** with Continental IO-470-M engines installed per STCs SE152SO and SA81SO and gross weight increased to 5,400lbs per STC SA2-284 Jun66. BoS to A Clinton Lindburg, St Louis, MO 10Jun66 with CofR applied for same date. BoS to Kenneth H Bunch, Glenallen, AK 22Mar74 with CofR applied for same date and CofA 06Apr74; emergency exit installed per STC SA4-63 Jly75. **N101KB** assigned to Bunch (dba Gulkana Air Service) 11Sep82 and placed on acft 18Sep82. BoS Evelyn M Bunch (for estate of KH Bunch) to AvAmerica Inc, Anchorage, AK 30Mar92. BoS to Philip Bingman dba Freshwater Adventures Inc, Anchorage, AK 30Mar92 with CofR 27Apr92, 200lb baggage compartment installed in acft bow per STC SA5-58, Jun94 (per Strato Engineering Co Report K-1 and Kodiak Airways Report No: 102, dated 02Oct61). **N139F** assigned 04Apr95, placed on acft 20Apr95 and CofR issued 19May95. Accident 10Jun95: ran out of fuel and crashed during forced landing. Nominal change by BoS Philip Bingman to Lester R Bingman, Dillingham, AK dba Fresh Water Adventures Inc, 20May97 with CofR 12Feb98. Accident 02Sep98: substantially damaged in crash near Dillingham, AK, operated by Fresh Water Adventures. After departure from Dillingham en route to a remote lake, some 100miles to the north, the acft was in a narrow pass when the pilot realised that the prevailing weather conditions would not allow a safe transit. While attempting a 180° turn to exit the pass, acft hit the ground. Pilot + 2 pax uninjured. BoS Bingman to Kerriston Ltd Partnership, Kent, WA 01Oct98 with CofR 20May99. McCauley 3AF32C528/82NEA-4 props installed per STC SA00879CH (although G-44 not included in STC!) Jun00; Cessna-type wing tips installed per STC SA366AL Jly00. BoS to Widgeon Enterprises LLC, (same address) Kent, WA 30Apr09, with CofR 03Jun10. Accident circa 1645hrs, 07Oct12: aircraft crashed during landing and sank in Tikchik Lake, about 50 miles north-northeast of Aleknagik, AK. The aircraft, operated by Freshwater Adventures, departed Dillingham about 1600hrs for a positioning flight to pick up a hunting guide and his client from an island in the lake for the return trip to Dillingham. The pilot, the sole occupant, sustained fatal injuries and the aircraft, after coming to rest partially submerged with its wings level with the surface of the water, sank after about ten minutes. The wreckage was located on the bottom of the lake in about 40 feet of water on 09Oct12. Cancelled from USCAR 30Jan13, but regn reserved for Widgeon Enterprises LLC same date.

1376   Built for US Navy as **J4F-2**, BuAer serial **37746** but diverted off contract to the British Air Commission, Washington, DC with serial **FP468** for use by the Fleet Air Arm. Acc 31Jly44 and del 12Aug44; in use with FAA at NAS Bunker Hill by Sep44. Used by SBNO at NAS St Louis from Sep44 until Oct45. Returned to US Navy charge by Dec45; Pool NAS Norfolk Dec45 until at least Apr46; Pool CASU-67 NAS Memphis by Jun46; FASRON-4 NAS Memphis Aug46. Lost 24Sep46 in accident on Mississippi River, WNW of NAS Memphis: aircraft was flying from Memphis at 2,000ft when starboard engine cut and altitude could not be maintained; pilot felt unable to reach NAS Memphis and elected to make a river landing in calm conditions; pilot misjudged his altitude and landed slightly nose-low resulting in the nose digging in and the aircraft flipping onto its back. The pilot (the only occupant), escaped but the aircraft sank and could not be found by recovery crews. SOC at Memphis 30Sep46.

1377   Built for US Navy as **J4F-2**, BuAer serial **37747** but diverted off contract to the British Air Commission, Washington, DC with serial **FP469** for use by the Fleet Air Arm. Acc 19Aug44 and del 21Aug44; no specific details of British use in 1944 or 1945 known although believed to have been in use at Dartmouth, NS in May 1945. Returned to US Navy charge by Oct45; Norfolk, Oct45 and SOC there 31Oct46 as obsolete and surplus. BoS War Assets Administration to Police Department, New York, NY 29Nov46. Cvtd to **G-44** 14Jan47 and CofR **NC9233H** issued 27Jan47; and later as **N9233H**. BoS to Page Airways Inc, Rochester, NY 29Nov55 with CofR 22Dec55. BoS to Mitchell Ashy and Monroe J Wolfe, New Orleans, LA 23Jun56 with CofR 15Nov56. CofA 26Aug57 at TFH:1,336hrs. BoS to Louisiana Aircraft, Baton Rouge, LA 07Jan57 with CofR 01Feb57. BoS to Donald D Brignac, Houma, LA 11Jly57 with CofR 26Jly57. Reregd as **N133H** Aug57 with CofA 26Aug57. BoS to Poelman Aircraft Co Inc, New Orleans, LA 07Jan59. BoS to Sea Service Inc, New Orleans, LA 07Jan59 with CofR 09Feb59. BoS to Perry Boswell Jr, Delray Beach, FL 16Aug60 with CofR 16Sep60. BoS to Jack Adams Aircraft Sales Inc, Walls, MS 30Dec60. BoS to Gulf South Aviation Inc, Shreveport, LA 27Jan61 with CofR 27Mar61. Tfd back to Jack Adams by BoS 03May61. BoS to Executive Business Transportation Inc, Anchorage, AK 28Apr61. BoS to BD Layman, ER Layman and KD Oldham, Anchorage, AK 29May61 with CofR 30Aug61. BoS to Northwest Airmotive, Anchorage, AK 11Jun62 (nominal change). BoS to James W Harvey, Kodiak, AK 15Jan63 with CofR 23Jan63. McKinnon escape hatch fitted 04Feb63. BoS to Aircraft Sales Co, Anchorage, AK 08Jan64. BoS to Alaska Air Guides Inc, Spenard, AK 08Jan64 with CofR 27Apr64. Cvtd to 260hp Continental IO-470-M engines 19Jun66. Accident 01Aug66: substantially damaged when right engine failed and pilot aborted take-off from Merrill Field, Anchorage. Pilot + 2 pax minor injuries. BoS to Warren W Woods, Palmer, AK 28Sep71 with CofR 20Oct71. BoS to Randall D and Kathleen M Frank, Palmer, AK 05Mar73 with CofR 25Jun73. BoS to Southcentral Aviation Inc, Anchorage, AK 24Oct75 with CofR 14Nov75. BoS to Jack L Griffis, Orange, CA 02Feb77. BoS to Kenai Air Alaska Inc, Kenai, AK 06Jly78 with CofR 05Dec78. Reregd **N700BL** 16Dec78. BoS to Vernon L Lofstedt, Kenai, AK 13Jan86 with CofR 07Feb86. BoS to Aqua Air LLC, Wilmington, DE 25Feb02 with CofR and Temporary CofA both issued 01May02; operated by Patrick J Coyle, Orange Park, FL. Accident 16May02 at TFH:3,810hrs: loss of engine power shortly after take-off from Boise, ID and crashed into a house. According to a statement, given to the NTSB by the pilot, he was on the third day of the delivery flight of the aircraft which he had recently purchased. Leaving Kenai, AK on 14May02 the route was to Sitka via Yakutat. Next day the G-44 was flown from Sitka, AK to Prince Rupert, BC, then to Port Hardy on Vancouver Island and on to Bellingham, WA. Coyle and his pilot-rated passenger had departed Bellingham, WA on the day of the crash and arrived at Boise, ID after a flight of 3.4hrs and had planned to fly on to Kemmerer, WY. The wreckage was taken to Western Aircraft, Boise, ID and released to the owner's representative on 05Jun02. CofR expired 30Sep11. Fate unknown, but presumed scrapped.

1378   Built for US Navy as **J4F-2**, BuAer serial **37748**. Acc and del 28Aug44; NAAS Mustin Fld 05Sep44 until at least Apr46; records unreadable but SOC there 31Aug46 as obsolete. BoS War Assets Administration, Atlanta, GA to Conn-Air Inc, Danbury, CT, 15Nov46, for $10,000, with CofR as **G-44, NC60379,** 21Nov46 and CofA 17Dec46. BoS to Van Winkle Todd, Matawan, NJ, 03Jan49 with CofR 17Jan49 as **N60379.** Tfd by BoS to Van Winkle Todd and Arthur C Schultze, Matawan, NJ, 09Feb49 with CofR 17Feb49. Engines cvtd from 6-440C-2 to C-5 standard 20Jun49. Tfd back to Van Winkle Todd, Matawan, NJ by BoS 13Mar52 with CofR 20Mar52. CofA 05Apr55 at TFH:1,467hrs. BoS to Sensitive Research Instrument Corp, New Rochelle, NY, 25Apr58 with CofR 03Jun58. Reregd **N199VC** 10Jly58. BoS to Atlantic Aviation Corp, Teterboro, NJ 09Oct58. BoS to Lambros Inc, Ridgefield Park, NJ, 11Oct58. BoS to Safeway Airways, Anchorage, AK, 11Oct58. CofR applied for 27Oct58 but apparently not issued. Conditional BoS to James

W Harvey, Kodiak, AK, 10(sic)Oct58 for $14,900 with CofR 08Dec58. BoS to Ramstad Construction Co, Anchorage, AK, 13Jly59. BoS to Red Dodge, Anchorage, AK, 04Oct60 with CofR 08Jun61. Enlarged cabin windows per STC SA5-51 and one-piece windshield per SA4-2, all installed Sep61. Because of the larger windows it was not possible to fit the five-digit registration on the fuselage per requirements of CAR1.102. Therefore a smaller registration number was requested and **N141R** was issued 30Aug61. Returned to Safeway Airways, Anchorage, AK by BoS 13Oct61, and then to James W Harvey, Kodiak, AK on the same day, for $24,000, with CofR 31Oct61. BoS to Orin D Seybert, Pilot Point, AK (dba Peninsula Airways) 05Apr63, with CofR 01May63. Emergency escape hatch installed per SA4-63 and SA64AL, May63. Tfd to Peninsular Airways Inc, Pilot Point, AK by BoS 03May66. Aircraft named "*Spirit of Pilot Point*". Cvtd to McKinnon **Super Widgeon**, with aux fuel tanks, per SA4-958 and overhauled and re-painted by Winn Air Service Co Inc, Syracuse, NY Jun70. CofR revoked by FAA 02Oct74 but re-instated to Peninsula A/W Inc, Anchorage, AK 12Nov74. TFH:10,599hrs a/o May95. To Petro Star Valdez Inc, Anchorage, AK, 01Sep00. To Alaska Grummans LLC, Anchorage, AK, 25Mar04. To Walt Fricke, dba Cat Island Air Tour & Trading Co LLC, Golden Valley, MN Oct04. To Steven J and Karen M Compton, Anchorage, AK, with CofR 31Oct05. Accident 26May06: substantial damage after take-off from Willow, AK and landing on a nearby lake with the wheels down causing the aircraft to nose over. Repaired at Victoria, BC and returned to Alaska 19Feb09 in full Royal Navy c/s and noted at Merrill Field, Anchorage Jly10. Attended the Alaska Grumman Fly-in at Marion Lake, near Anchorage Jly12. Listed as current and airworthy May13 (with Ranger 6-440 engines!), with CofR due to expire 31Jly15.

1379   Built for US Navy as **J4F-2**, BuAer serial **37749**. Acc 31Aug44 and del 01Sep44; Pool NAS Jacksonville 08Sep44; NAS St Simons Oct44; NAS Banana River Oct45; Pool NAS Jacksonville Apr46 and SOC there 30Apr46 following an accident.

1380   Built for US Navy as **J4F-2**, BuAer serial **37750**. Acc 31Aug44 and del 26Sep44; in delivery NAS New York 30Sep44; NAS Jacksonville Oct44; VPB2 OTU-4 NAS Jacksonville Oct44; NAS Jacksonville Dec44; OTU VFN-1 NAS Vero Beach Jan45; VF-OTU-6 NAS Sanford Mar46; VPB-2 ATU-3 NAS Banana River Apr46; NAS Banana River by Jun46; CNAAT NAS Jacksonville Aug46 and SOC there 31Aug46 as obsolete and surplus. BoS War Assets Administration to David S Harter, Camden, SC for $7,500, 28Oct46. BoS to Wallace Aircraft Company, Sarasota, FL for $10,000, 29Oct46. Cvtd from J4F-2 to **G-44**, overhauled and repainted, with CofR **NC66435** 29Nov46 and CofA 25Feb47. BoS to Virginia Hall Sherwood, Boca Raton, FL 02Jan47 with CofR 28Feb47. BoS to Nelson A Miles, Lake Success, NY 19Sep47 with CofR 08Oct47; major overhaul with CofA issued 21Jly50. BoS to Silvio Gargiulo, New York, NY 28Feb51 with CofR **N66435** 27Aug53 (sic); CofA 15Sep53 at TFH:1,447hrs. BoS to NA Miles dba Midet Aviation Corp, West Palm Beach, FL 24Oct53 with CofR 07Jly54. BoS to HR Perez, Miami, FL 10Jun55. Perez was President of LEBCA Internacional and the CofR was cancelled 04Apr56 as exported to Venezuela, but the purchase in Venezuela was not completed and the CofR re-instated 21Jun56. BoS Perez to A & W Inc, Eunice, LA 16Jly56 with CofR 31Jly56 and CofA 10Aug56 at TFH:1,896hrs. BoS to Monroe J Wolfe, New Orleans LA 19Oct56 with CofR **N111W**(2) 15Nov56. BoS to McKinnon Enterprises, Sandy, OR 14Feb57 with CofR **N75222**(2) 25Feb57. Cvtd to **Super Widgeon** with Lycoming GO-480-B1D engines, escape hatch and upgrade to 4,700lbs gross weight Jly57. BoS to Peyton Hawes, Portland, OR 21Aug57 with CofR 10Sep57; upgrade to 5,500lbs gross weight land and water Sep57; outer wing panels exchanged for ones rebuilt to STCs SA4-928 (retractable floats), SA4-958 (aux fuel tanks), SA4-964 (landing lights) and SA4-1031 (metallised wings), Jly60. BoS Hawes back to McKinnon 28Dec62 with CofR 03Jan63. BoS to Atlas Leasing Co., Portland, OR 10Jly63 with CofR 19Jly63. BoS to JC McKinney, Titusville, PA 27Aug68 with CofR 05Nov68. BoS to Warren W & Christine M Woods, Palmer, AK 10Aug73 with CofR 05Sep73. BoS to Charles P Allen, Anchorage, AK, 16Nov76 with CofR **N45CA** 31Jan77, and placed on aircraft 01Feb77. Charles P Allen was dba Charlie Allen Flying Service by 1984; nominal change to CP Allen & Marlyn A Allen, Anchorage, AK by BoS 21Dec86. BoS to Octal Inc, Mountain View, CA, confusingly dated 31Jly86; address change to Bellevue, WA with CofR 07Feb90. Octal became Fugu Ltd, Bellevue, WA, with CofR 15Oct96. BoS to Rickford van Arsdale, Salem, OR 17Mar05 with CofR 21Apr05. **N45PV** issued 21Apr05, placed on aircraft 20May05 and CofR issued 18Jun05. Current and airworthy May13, with CofR due to expire 31Jly14.

1381   Built for US Navy as **J4F-2**, BuAer serial **37751**. Acc 09Sep44 and del 11Sep44; BAR Nash-Kelvinator Co, Kenosha, WI 09Sep44; ComAirLant NAS Norfolk 21Oct45; Pool NAAS Franklin Nov45; Pool

G-44, c/n 1381, N65956, "Vamp II", seen here at Spanish Wells, Bahamas, circa 1960. (NA3T Transport Photos)

Hedron, FAW-5 NAS Norfolk Jan46; Pool CASU-67 NAS Memphis Apr46; FASRON-4, NAS Memphis Aug46 and SOC there 30Sep46 as obsolete and surplus. Regd as **G-44, NC65956** to Edward W Tabor, c/o Fette Aircraft Service, Venice, FL. To Peter J Lloyd, Nassau, Bahamas by May62; aircraft named: "*Vamp II*", later **N65956**. To Oscar A Clot, Miami, FL by Jly64. Cvtd to Franklin **Super Widgeon** with Continental IO-470-M engines (date unknown). Cancelled from USCAR 22Oct65. Ferry fuel system installed for delivery flight to Nigeria. Reregd **5N-AFS** to Pan African Airlines (Nigeria) Ltd, Lagos, Nigeria, Nov65. Nigerian regn cancelled 15Nov68. BoS from Lion Enterprises Etablisment to Aviation Facilities Inc, Miami, FL 15Jan69 and CofR **N7256** issued 27Jan69. Ferry fuel system re-installed 18Feb69 and ferry permit issued 24Feb69 for delivery flight from Lagos, Nigeria to Miami, FL. [Note: A suggested route was via Monrovia, Dakar, Santa Maria and Gander but another via Shannon & Bahamas was noted as best route.] Del Nigeria to USA via Shannon, Eire 13Oct69. CofR revoked 24Nov71. BoS to Africair Inc, Miami, FL 20Nov74 and CofR re-instated 04Dec74 (operated without floats). C-GTTL allotted to Tall Timber Lodge, Lac du Bonnet, MB 11Jly75. BoS from Africair to Dean H Franklin Aviation Enterprises Inc, Miami, FL 24Jly75. Authority to ferry Miami, FL to Winnipeg, MB 28Jly75. CofA issued 12Aug75 at TFH:3,721hrs and CofR 13Aug75, but cancelled 18Aug75 as exported to Canada. CofR(P) for **C-GTTL** to George Maryk, Lac du Bonnet, MB 21Aug75; CofR(C) to Tall Timber Lodge, Lac du Bonnet, MB (nominal) 26May76; CofA renewed at TFH:4,441hrs, valid until 12Aug85. BoS Tall Timber Lodge Fly-in Service to Colby R Parks, Anchorage, AK, 21Aug85 for US$76,000. Cancelled from CCAR 30Aug85 and restored as **N7256** 06Sep85 with CofA 11Sep85 at TFH:4,457hrs. CofR renewed 17Jun12. Current and airworthy May13, with CofR due to expire 30Jun15.

1382 Built for US Navy as **J4F-2**, BuAer serial **37752**. Acc 25Sep44 and del 26Sep44; NAS New York, 24Sep44 to at least 30Jun46; SOC 31Jly46, location uncertain, as obsolete and surplus. Regd as **G-44, NC60081** to Melvin Potter, Scarsdale, NY and later as **N60081**. To Salvatore Maugeri, Miami, FL by Jly62; to same owner at Safford, AZ, Jun63. To Donald L Shepherd, Boynton Beach, FL 1966. To Henry O Moffett and Vincent Bilzi, Centerport, NY, 03Aug67. CofR revoked after Jan77. Fate unknown.

1383 Built for US Navy as **J4F-2**, BuAer serial **37753**. Acc 30Sep44 and del 04Oct44; NAAS San Nicolas Sep44 until at least 30Sep45; NAAS Ream Fld by Nov45; NAAS San Clemente Mar46; NAAS Ream Fld Apr46 and SOC there 31Aug46 as obsolete and surplus. Regd as **G-44, NC67460** to Frank A Gallison, Merced, CA. To RK Dent, Seattle, WA, by May63. To Pacific Sand & Gravel Co, Centralia, WA by Jly64. Reregd **N1173V**(2) to Crane Engineering Corp, Greendale, WI 03Mar67 (see c/n 1345). N67460 cancelled from USCAR 15Mar67. To Clarence C Nissen, Milwaukee, WI by 1987. Accident at 1030hrs on 01Oct87: crashed on take-off from asphalt strip at Delavan, WI for a flight to Milwaukee, WI. Loss of control due to strong cross-wind, ran off runway to the left, struck a tree and overturned. Pilot suffered minor injuries but aircraft substantially damaged. N1173V cancelled from USCAR Mar88.

1384 Built for US Navy as **J4F-2**, BuAer serial **37754**. Acc 30Sep44 and del 04Oct44; MCAS Cherry Point Oct44; NAS Houma May45; MCAS Eagle Mountain Lake Aug45; ComNABases 8th Naval District (assumed to be at) NAS New Orleans Mar46 until at least 30Jun46; SOC, location unknown, 31Aug46 as obsolete and surplus and sold by War Assets Administration 28Oct46 to George J McCray, Jamestown, NY for $7,500. Tfd to Neil R McCray, Jamestown, NY 19Nov46 and regd as **G-44, NC9270H** 25Nov46, with CofA issued 13May47 at TFH:270hrs. BoS to James F Welton, Franklin, PA 27Jun47. BoS to RD Frawley, Dravosburg, PA 15Oct47; CofA issued 19Feb48, with comment "aircraft

last flown 30Oct47", and regd to Frawley 29Mar48; CofA issued 24Mar49 with comment "aircraft last flown 30Jly48". Later as **N9270H**. BoS to Dean H Franklin, Miami, FL 07Sep51; CofA issued 08Sep51 again with comment "aircraft last flown 30Jly48", and regd to Franklin 14Sep51. BoS to Joe G Marrs, Hollywood, FL 23May52 with CofR 24Jly52. BoS for $12,500 to Ward Sales Co Inc, Miami, FL 23Dec52 with CofR 08Jan53. CofR revoked by FAA 18Dec70, reason unknown. Fate unknown.

1385 Built for US Navy as **J4F-2**, BuAer serial **37755**. Acc 20Oct44 and del 23Oct44; MCAS Quantico Oct44. Involved in taxying collision with F4U-1 13817 at Quantico 29Mar45 (the right wing tip was smashed and damage was categorised as 'C'). Undercarriage collapsed while taxying at Washington National A/P, DC 22Aug45 (Cat C damage). SOC at Quantico 30Sep46 as obsolete and surplus. BoS War Assets Administration, Atlanta, GA to Dealers Transport Co, Chicago, IL for $10,000, 04Nov46 with CofR as **G-44, NC65914** 20Nov46. Cvtd from J4F-2 to **G-44**, overhauled and repainted 29Nov46 by Aero Corp, Atlanta, GA. BoS to George J Priester, Elmhurst, IL 29Dec51 with CofR **N65914** 17Jan52. BoS to Philip K Wrigley, Chicago, IL 12Jun53 with CofR 23Jun53; CofA 23Jun57 at TFH:1,231hrs. BoS to Illinois University Board of Trustees, Urbana, IL 18Jly60 with CofR 29Aug60. BoS to Executive Aircraft Co, Kansas City, MO 01Jly63 with CofR 19Jly63. BoS to JS Lodato, San Jose, CA 20Nov63 with CofR 11Dec63. BoS to Edwards Engineering Co, South San Francisco, CA 19Jly66, for $21,000, with CofR 29Jly66. BoS to Lane E Older, Bellingham, WA 01Aug71 with CofR 29Sep71. Accident 02Apr04 Lake Whatcom, WA: after experiencing a rough-running left engine the pilot tried to land in a nearby bay adjoining the airport. Unfortunately the tide was out and the water was only six inches deep. The right wing float dug into the sub-surface terrain damaging the right aileron and four wing ribs. Repaired, and airworthy May13, with CofR due to expire 30Apr15.

1386 Built for US Navy as **J4F-2**, BuAer serial **37756**. Acc 28Oct44 and del 30Oct44; NAS Miami Oct44; NAS Daytona Beach Feb46; NAS Banana River Mar46; CNAAT NAS Jacksonville Aug46 and SOC there 31Aug46 as obsolete and surplus. BoS War Assets Administration to Robert P Sanders, Charlotte, NC, for $10,000, 28Oct46. BoS to Ralph S Smith, Charlotte, NC 03Dec46. Cvtd to **G-44** by Whiteheads Inc, Charlotte, NC with CofA 14Dec46 and CofR **NC52945** 30Dec46. BoS to Earl J Grippen, Endicott, NY 01Apr48; CofR issued as NC52946 in error 09Apr48 but corrected 27Apr48 at owner's request; CofA 06Apr49 at TFH:427hrs. BoS to G Philip Ellsworth, Poughkeepsie, NY dba Poughkeepsie Aviation Services 28Sep53 with CofR **N52945**, 06Oct53. Main step vents installed on hull and step extension removed and keel re-inforcement installed from Station 15 to 15a, per Grumman drawing #17407, with CofA 16Apr54 at TFH:1,506hrs. Reregd **N101PE** to G Philip Ellsworth, Wappinger Falls, NY 07Mar58. Cvtd to **Super Widgeon** with Lycoming GO-480-B1D engines, with Hartzell HC83X20-2C props, installed by Link Aeronautical Corp Mar61, per Lockheed drawing SPD 712116 (previously approved on G-44A, c/n 1419, N41988, 22Sep55) and 2x 22gallon aux fuel tanks installed by Link Aeronautical Corp Mar61, per ACA Form 337 dated 03Mar55 on G-44A, c/n 1438, N77K. CofR revoked 23Nov70 due failure to return AC Form 8050-73. BoS Hazel W Ellsworth (for the estate of GP Ellsworth) to Ruth Ilardi, Victor, NY 18Oct79 and N101PE restored on CofR 23May88 (sic). BoS to Lawrence M Rushton, Goodrich, MI 04May94 with CofR 08Sep94; address change to Vonore, TN 13Apr04. Current, but not airworthy May13, with CofR due to expire 30Jun15.

1387 Built for US Navy as **J4F-2**, BuAer serial **37757**. Acc 31Oct44 and del 02Nov44; Pool NAS San Diego Nov44; record card suggests a subsequent allocation to NAS New York but aircraft unreported 31Dec44; NAAS Ventura County Jan45; NAS Terminal Island Nov45; NAS San Diego Aug46. Damaged in water-loop at San Diego 20Feb47 after sound landing: while undertaking touch and goes power was applied for take-off but right engine stopped abruptly due to a vapour lock and the right wing dug in; right wing and sundry components badly damaged. SOC at San Diego 31Jly47 as obsolete. BoS War Assets Administration to West Coast Aircraft Ltd, Los Angeles, CA 18Jun47 for $5,750, with CofR as **G-44 NC63350** 05Jan48 and CofA 19Jly49 after wing repairs. West Coast Aircraft was owned by Wm F Pike and on 20Oct49 ownership was tfd to him, with CofR 25Oct49. Engines changed from Ranger 6-440-C2 (175hp) to 6-440-C5 (200hp) by Fresno Airmotive, CA Mar50. BoS to Ward I Gay, Anchorage, AK 29Mar52 with CofA 20May52 at TFH:596hrs, and CofR **N63350** 28May52. BoS to Sea Airmotive Inc, Anchorage, AK 21Feb53 with CofR 31Mar53; Grumman Aircraft Engineering Corp vented step kit installed with CofA 17Apr53 at TFH:647hrs. Cvtd to **Super Widgeon** May58 with Lycoming GO-480-B1D engines with McKinnon kit per STC SA4-65; and installed cargo door on right side, same date. A nominal change by BoS 10Aug59 to Sea-Air Inc, Anchorage, AK, with CofR

14Oct59; then ownership reversed to Sea Airmotive Inc (at same address) by BoS 20Apr60. Accident at 1030hrs on 08Sep73: substantially damaged when aircraft porpoised after aborted take-off from Post Lake, near Farewell, AK; pilot + 2 pax uninjured. Company reportedly re-named Seair, Dec77, but BoS Sea Airmotive to Yute Air Alaska Inc, Dillingham, AK 14May79 with CofR 15Jun79. BoS to Eugene D and J Ann Riggs, Sitka, AK 06Mar89 with CofR 31Mar89; modified for 5,500lbs gross weight (land & sea) and hull modified to meet buoyancy requirements Jun91. Accident at 1445hrs on 07Sep91: nosed over landing on strip at Metaline Falls, WA due to parking brake being engaged; pilot uninjured but aircraft substantially damaged; underwent a 13-month rebuild by Riggs. Address change to Wasilla, AK with CofR 16Nov98, and to Big Lake, AK with CofR 10Sep03. Tfd to sole ownership by Eugene D Riggs with CofR issued 31May11. Current and airworthy May13, with CofR due to expire 31May14.

1388   Built for US Navy as **J4F-2**, BuAer serial **37758**. Acc and del 22Nov44; in process of delivery NAS New York 30Nov44; NAS Alameda Dec44 and SOC there 30Sep46 as obsolete and surplus. BoS War Assets Administration to Harry Garland, Detroit, MI 13Nov46 for $7,500, with CofR as **NC9600H** 10Jan47 and CofA 07Feb47. BoS to George J Healey, Detroit, MI 29Jan48 with CofR 11Feb48 after cvtd to **G-44** by Servair Inc, Detroit, MI. CofA renewed 02Feb48. Returned to Harry Garland by BoS 28Jun48, with CofR 02Jly48. CofA renewed 02Feb49. Tfd by BoS to Garland Manufacturing Co, Detroit, MI 08Sep49 with CofR 16Sep49 as **N9600H**. CofA renewed 08Feb50. BoS to R Paul Weesner and George Lewis, Miami, FL 05Oct50 with CofR 25Oct50. Tfd by BoS from Weesner & Lewis to Weesner alone, 05Feb51, with CofR 21Feb51. BoS to Ben Terry and Bertram Peterson, Miami, FL 27Apr51. BoS to Taxi Plane Corp of America, Miami, FL 27Apr51 with CofR 21May51. Badly damaged on take-off from Port Antonio, Jamaica, and submerged 03May51. BoS to Lee Mansdorf, Los Angeles, CA 20Dec51. Cvtd to Lycoming R-680-E3 radial engines and CofR 04Mar54. BoS Mansdorf to Mansdorf and James F Conroy, Long Beach, CA 09Jly54 with CofR 04Aug54. BoS to Rick Helicopters Inc, Anchorage, AK 12Mar58 with CofR 17Apr58. BoS to John Conroy, Kenneth W Healy and Herman R Salmon, Van Nuys, CA 06Dec61 with CofR 18Dec61. Reregd **N404Q** 01Mar67. BoS to Aerodyne Enterprises Inc, Goleta, CA 03Dec74. BoS to John M Conroy, Goleta, CA 21Jan75. BoS to Lew Mahieu, Long Beach, CA 23Jan75. BoS to Dennis Buehn, Compton, CA 29Oct76 with CofR 15Nov76. BoS to James E Landry, Seattle, WA 29May77 with CofR 11Jly77. BoS to James W and Linda M Dreewes, Snohomish, WA 01Aug84 with CofR 09May85. BoS to Weeks Air Museum Inc, Miami, FL 19Jly98 (as a gift) with CofR 02Nov98; address change to Fantasy of Flight, Polk City, FL Dec01. Not airworthy, but regd to World's Greatest Aircraft Collection Inc, Polk City, FL by Apr12, with CofR renewed Jan13, to expire 31Jan16.

1389   Built for US Navy as **J4F-2**, BuAer serial **37759**. Acc 29Nov44 and del 02Dec44; Pool NAAS Franklin Dec44; Hedron, FAW-16 NAF Recife Jan45 (in Jan45 FAW-16 had four aircraft on strength, two at Recife, one at NAF Rio de Janeiro and the other at NOF Belem – location of this individual aircraft therefore not identified – see c/n 1392). Minor damage incurred 21Feb45 when port undercarriage collapsed on landing at NAF Igarape Assu. To NAS Norfolk 29May45; CASU-27 NAS Chincoteague Jun45; NAS Quonset Point Jly45 for minimal repairs and SOC there 30Nov46, as obsolete and surplus. BoS War Assets Administration to New Bedford Aviation Inc, South Dartmouth, MA 13Nov46, for $7,500. BoS to Albert I Richmond, New Bedford, MA 13Nov46 for $7,501. Cvtd to **G-44** and repainted silver with green trim by East Coast Aviation Corp, State Airport, Hillsgrove, Rhode Island, with CofR **NC9208H** 04Dec46 and CofA 09Dec46. To Grumman Aircraft Engineering Corp 18Jly47 for repair to right wing and fuselage side (after accident?). BoS to Melvin C Wray, dba Monument Munufacturing Co, Assonet, MA 10Oct47 for $12,750, with CofR 31Oct47; CofA 04May52 at TFH:628hrs. BoS to Kenneth Forester, Oradell, NJ Apr54. BoS to John R Topping, c/o Pinellas Aviation Service Inc, St Petersburg, FL 02Mar55 with CofR **N68T** 04May55. Major overhaul including removal of keel extension and installation of step vents with CofA 09May55 at TFH:657hrs. Reregd **N63T** (at unknown date) and sold to Graubart Aviation Inc, Chicago, IL 25May56. BoS to Carl Millard Ltd, Toronto, ON 02Jun56. Allotted **CF-JFV** 11Jly56. US CofA for export E-30497 and CofA 4791 issued 30Jly56. CofR(P) 16445 for James R Shore, Winnipeg, MB 02Aug56. N63T cancelled from USCAR 06Aug56. CofR(P) 15797 to Teal Air Ltd, Winnipeg, MB 30Jan57; inspected and CofA renewed at TFH:1,079hrs, valid until 30Jly58. CofR(P) 21941 to James Robert Shore, Winnipeg, MB 06Jan60; CofA renewed at TFH:1,408hrs, valid until 28Apr62. CofR(P) 27152 to Field Lumber Co (1956) Ltd, Sturgeon Falls, ON 30Jun61; cvtd to Continental IO-470-D engines; inspected and CofA renewed at TFH:1,714hrs, valid until 15Aug65, based at Field, ON. CofA renewed at TFH:2,304hrs, valid until 05Jun71, based at Guelph, ON; at

TFH:2,457hrs, valid until 05Jun72. CofR(P) to Field Lumber (1956) Ltd, Field, ON (nominal change) 09May72; CofA renewed at TFH:2,507hrs, valid until 05Jun73, based at Guelph, ON; at TFH:2,521hrs, valid until 05Jun76, based at Stoney Creek. In storage 1979-83. CofA renewed at TFH:2,561hrs, valid until 05Aug84. CofR re-issued as **C-FJFV** 24Aug83. Sold to Townsend Air Services Ltd, Gravenhurst, ON 08Sep83, and then to Pagebrook Holdings Inc, Toronto, ON 19Sep83 with CofR(P) 13Jly84. CofA renewed at TFH:2,693hrs, valid until 20Apr90. Cvtd to Continental IO-520-E engines, imported under E-261970 and E-261984 dated 28 and 29Sep89 respectively. TFH:2,854hrs reported on inspection of 20Jun94. BoS Pagebrook Inc to Planeco Inc, Dover, DE 05Jly96. **N44PB** reserved 10Jly96 and CofR issued 30Aug96. Cancelled from CCAR 29Aug96. Wheels and brakes cvtd per SA121EA and landing gear uprated per SA4-60 by Aerotech Consultants, Victoria, BC Sep96. Continental IO-520E-2B engines with Hartzell PHC-3CYF-2UF props installed by Aerotech, BC Dec96 with CofA 14Jan97 at TFH:2,938hrs. BoS to WC Inc, Portland, OR 07Jun97. BoS to Michael D Reese, Portland, OR, 07Jun97 with CofR 23Mar98. Reregd to him as **N135MR** 05May99 with nominal change to Michael Reese/McKinnon Air Park, Sandy, OR same date. Attended EAA Fly-in, Arlington, WA, 12Jly03. BoS Reese to Old Crow LLC, c/o Corporation Service Co, Wilmington, DE 23Jan07 with CofR 27Feb07. **N135MG** issued 02Mar07, placed on aircraft 31Oct07 and CofR issued 12Dec07. Current and airworthy May13, with CofR due to expire 31Dec13.

1390   Built for US Navy as **J4F-2**, BuAer serial **37760**. Acc 30Nov44 and del 07Dec44; NAS San Diego Dec44; NAAS Salton Sea Apr45; NAAS San Clemente Jun45. Damaged during landing roll at San Clemente Island 16Jan46: weakened retaining latch on starboard landing gear failed when aircraft hit a rough patch on the runway and the gear retracted, causing significant damage to the right wing and float. SOC at San Clemente 31Mar46 as obsolete. BoS War Assets Administration to Edward R Conry, Minneapolis, MN, for $8,000 12Aug46, with CofR as **G-44, NC67271** 02Oct46. BoS to Sportsmen Airways Inc, Duluth, MN 19Mar47. BoS to Peoples Brewing Co, Duluth, MN 15May47 with CofR as **N67271**, 18Feb49. BoS to Gopher Aviation Inc, Rochester, MN 24Apr51. BoS to Lincoln Thomas and Francis Trecker (co-owners), Milwaukee, WI 24Aug51 with CofR 18Oct51; CofA 27Jun52 at TFH:496hrs; keel modification and step vents installed Jly52. Tfd to Lincoln G Thomas, Milwaukee, WI as sole owner by BoS 21Apr55, with CofR 03May55 and CofA issued 21Oct55 at TFH:608hrs. BoS to James C Welsch, Garden City, Long Island, NY 20Apr56 with CofR 03May56. BoS to Thomson Industries Inc, Manhasset, Long Island, NY 20Apr56 with CofR 15May56. Lycoming GO-480-B1D engines, with Hartzell HC83X20-2A props, installed per STC SA4-65 by Mattituck Airbase Corp, Linden, NJ with CofA 25Feb60. Accident 18Mar66: substantially damaged after water loop on take-off from Sands Point, Manhasset Bay, NY. Pilot + 1 pax minor injuries. Address change to Port Washington, NY Jly92. BoS to Ventura Air Services Inc, Port Washington, NY Oct02 with CofR 03Feb03. The Widgeon is actually owned by the owner of Ventura Helicopter Inc. It is maintained in pristine condition and kept at Sands Point SPB in Port Washington, NY. It has not flown for several years but was current and airworthy May13, with CofR due to expire 31Dec13.

1391   Built for US Navy as **J4F-2**, BuAer serial **37761**. Acc 19Dec44 and del 20Dec44; in process of delivery NAS New York 31Dec44; NAS San Diego Jan45; NAF Thermal Apr45; NAS Los Alamitos Oct45 until at least Jun46; location Jly-Oct46 uncertain (unreadable) but SOC 31Oct46 as obsolete and surplus. Regd as **G-44, NC67193** to RE Lenox, Forest Grove, OR. Reregd **F-OAGX** 24Oct51 to Air Tahiti, Papeete, which became RAI, in 1953. Damaged, believed by water-looping, (but no further details) in 1953. Wreckage sold to Tourist Air Travel, Auckland, New Zealand for £6,000. Rebuilt/overhauled by Tasman Empire Airlines at Auckland in late 1954; first test-flight (pilot: Capt J McGraine) as **ZK-BGQ** 03May55. Continued problems with water-looping until

G-44 Widgeon, c/n 1391, ZK-BGQ, in the blue/white colours of Mount Cook Airlines, after re-engining with Continental IO-470s. Note the "Beware of Propeller" warning on the under-wing float.

(Neville Parnell via Jennifer Gradidge)

G-44 Widgeon, c/n 1391, ZK-BGQ, operated by Sea Bee Air from Auckland, New Zealand, after conversion to Continental power, and with prominent step vent installed. (Note only the "last three" of the registration are carried on the aircraft, which is allowed in New Zealand provided an aircraft is used only for internal flights).   (Fred J Knight Collection)

G-44 Super Widgeon, c/n 1394, N91080, formerly owned by West Virginia Pulp & Paper Company, at Brookhaven, New York on 6th July 1968, after being sold to Richard C Jackson.   (Jennifer Gradidge Collection)

modified with a shorter step and step vents. Cvtd to **Super Widgeon** with Continental IO-470-D engines 1962. Suffered minor damage at Auckland 11Nov63. To Mount Cook Airlines, Christchurch, Dec67. (Belatedly the French registration was cancelled, as "destroyed", 15Nov71.) To SeaBee Air, Auckland Oct76. Leased to Stewart Island Air Services, Invercargill for four months, Nov76 and returned to SeaBee Air Mar77. Leased again to Stewart Island A/S a/o Jan78. Returned to Sea Bee Air. Accident 21Jan80: crashed and written off on landing at Kaipara Harbour, Auckland. Two fatalities.

1392   Built for US Navy as **J4F-2**, BuAer serial **37762**. Acc 21Dec44 and del 22Dec44; Pool NAS Norfolk Dec44; Hedron, FAW-16 NAF Recife Jan45 (in Jan45 FAW-16 had four aircraft on strength, two at Recife, one at NAF Rio de Janeiro and the other at NOF Belem – location of this individual aircraft therefore not identified – see c/n 1388); suffered minor damage 15Mar45 when landing at NAF Ipitanga; flight had originated at NAF Aratu and water landing was normal until the starboard float struck a submerged water fillable bomb that had drifted in from bombing area. To CASU-21 NAS Norfolk 12Jun45; FAETULANT NAS Norfolk Aug45; Pool Hedron-5, FAW-5 NAS Norfolk Mar46; FAETULANT NAS Norfolk May46; Pool CASU-67 NAS Memphis Jun46; FASRON-4 NAS Memphis Aug46 and SOC 30Sep46 as obsolete and surplus. Regd as **G-44**, **NC52409** to Fuller Longley, Chattanooga, TN. Cancelled from USCAR 28Feb52, reason unknown.

1393   Built for US Navy as **J4F-2**, BuAer serial **37763**. Acc and del 30Dec44; in process of delivery NAS New York Dec44; Pool NAS San Diego Jan45; Pool AROU-2 NAB Samar Jly45; Pool NAB Samar Oct45; en route Guam 31Dec45; Pool CASU-F12 NAS Orote Jan46; Pool NAS Pearl Harbor Apr46. Wfu at Pearl Harbor 13Jun46 and SOC there 30Jun46 as obsolete and surplus. BoS War Assets Administration (Honolulu) to Malvern O May, Pearl Harbor 21Jan47, for $5,015, with CofR **NC62096** 05Feb47. Cvtd to **G-44** at Oahu, HI, with CofA 14Feb47. BoS to Carl Brandenfels Enterprises, St Helens, OR 14Mar49 with CofR 25Mar49. Step extension removed, step re-inforcement and step vents installed Mar50, with CofA 01Apr50. BoS to Pacific Sand & Gravel Co, Centralia, WA 19Nov51 with CofR **N62096** 07Dec51. BoS to Henry J Reverman, Seattle, WA 12Apr54 with CofR 21Apr54. BoS to HD McDonald, Seattle, WA 05Jan55 with CofR 31Jan55. CofA 30Mar56 at TFH:1,932hrs. BoS to Walter H Keilt, Seattle, WA 01Mar58 with CofR 19Mar58; address change to Alderwood, WA 15Jly70. BoS to Skagit Aero Educational Museum, Monroe, WA 10Nov07 with CofR 10Jun09. Current Jan13, with CofR due to expire 31Dec14. There is nothing in the FAA Airworthiness file after the CofA in Mar56, and therefore it is likely that it has not flown since circa 1960.

1394   Built for US Navy as **J4F-2**, BuAer serial **37764**. Acc 06Jan45 and del 09Jan45; Pool NAS San Diego Jan45; en route Guam 31Jly45; Pool CASU-F12 NAS Orote 05Aug45; CASU-F58 NAS Sangley Point 20Aug45 until at least 30Sep46. SOC 31Oct46, presumably at Sangley Point, as obsolete and surplus. BoS Foreign Liquidation Commission to Ensign Alan R Cotariu, MAB Guam, Marianas Islands for $5,250 22Apr47. CofR **NC91080** to Cotariu, Los Angeles, CA 16May47. Crated to Gibbs Field, San Diego, CA; overhauled, wings re-covered and painted by Gibbs Flying Service Jly47 with CofA 08Jly47. BoS to West Virginia Pulp & Paper Co, New York, NY 17Nov47 with CofR 10Dec47, later **N91080**. Cvtd to **Super Widgeon** with Lycoming GO-435-C2B engines, and Hartzell HC-82X20-2/9333C props, by McKinnon-Hickman Co with CofA 28Nov53 at TFH:4,317hrs (sic) but possibly 3,417hrs as CofA 16Nov54 quotes TFH:3,839hrs (with 422hrs on the new engines). BoS to

Richard C Jackson, Somersworth, NH 19Jan68 with CofR 02Apr68; address change to Rochester, NH with CofR 02May78. BoS to Basic Bible Church of America, Deatsville, AL 25Feb80 with CofR 29Apr80. BoS to Patrick M Murphy, dba Patrick Murphy Aircraft Co, Warsaw, KY 10Jun85. BoS to Richard Paris Industries Inc, Fort Lauderdale, FL 10Sep85 with CofR 29Jan88. **N78RJ** issued 26Feb88, confirmed painted on acft 20Feb89, but BoS Richard Paris Industries to Patrick M Murphy 03May89 quotes regn as N91080. BoS Murphy to Charles Greenhill, Northbrook, IL 04May89 with CofR N78RJ 08Jun89. **N744G** issued 15Sep89, painted on acft 01Oct89 and CofR 14Nov89; address change to Mettawa, IL 31Dec92, with CofR 15Jan93. BoS to Frank M Marzich, Rockford, IL 13May97, with CofR 18Feb98. Current and airworthy May13, with CofR due to expire 31Dec13.

1395   Built for US Navy as **J4F-2**, BuAer serial **37765**. Acc 26Jan45 and del 27Jan45; in process of delivery NAS New York 31Jan45; NACTULANT NAAF Martha's Vineyard Feb45. Starboard wing burnt during refuelling accident at Newark, NJ 12Aug45. To Pool CASU-67 NAS Memphis Apr46; CGAS Biloxi 07Jun46 until at least Jly46 when formally transferred to the US Coast Guard and SOC by the US Navy 31Jly46. Last known operating location CGAS Biloxi in mid 1946 but no further details known (Biloxi ceased to operate the J4F in June 1947). No records of a strike date and no known subsequent civilian history.

1396   Built for US Navy as **J4F-2**, BuAer serial **37766**. Acc 30Jan45 and del 03Feb45; Pool NAS Alameda Feb45; CFAS Pacific NAS Moffett Fld Apr45; ZP-31 NAS Santa Ana Dec45 until 17Jly46. SOC 31Jly46, presumably at Santa Ana, as obsolete and surplus. Regd as **G-44**, **NC58514** to Herman L Martin, Walla Walla, WA. Accident 13Feb50: crashed at Las Flores Canyon, Malibu, CA. No further reports, so assumed acft written off in crash.

1397   Built for US Navy as **J4F-2**, BuAer serial **37767**. Acc 31Jan45 and del 05Feb45; Pool NAS Alameda Feb45; CASU-36, NAAS Santa Rosa Apr45. Water-looped at Clear Lake, CA 26Apr45 with serious (Cat B) damage to left wing and both floats. Junior CASU-36 pilot dug in the nose on first familiarisation flight. To CASU-6 NAS Alameda Apr45; NAS Alameda 24Jun46 and SOC there 31Jly46 as obsolete and surplus. Regd as **G-44**, **NC56198** to Herbert W George and BV Stewart, Reno, NV. To Kodiak Airways, Kodiak, AK early 1950s. Accident 31Mar61: crashed at 3,800ft on Crown Mountain, near Kodiak, AK. Cancelled from USCAR 13Apr62. Wreckage left to the elements but salvaged years later.

G-44 Widgeon, c/n 1397, N56198, Kodiak Airways' third of the type, is seen here at Kodiak in the 1950s. Note the "Fly Kodiak Airways" legend on the forward hull.   (via Guy Denton)

1398   Built for US Navy as **J4F-2**, BuAer serial **37768**. Acc 10Feb45 and del 12Feb45; CASU-28, NAAF Groton Feb45; (unit moved to NAS Charleston Feb46) until at least 11Jly46. SOC 31Jly46, presumably at Charleston, as obsolete and surplus. BoS War Assets Administration to Charles E Compton, Chicago, IL 28Oct46 for $7,500, with CofR as **G-44, NC9870H** 04Dec46. BoS to Lambros Seaplane Base, Ridgefield, NJ 07Nov52 with CofR **N9870H** 18Nov52. BoS to Island Airways of Fort Lauderdale Inc, Fort Lauderdale, FL 17Feb54 with CofR 26Feb54; CofA 14Sep55 at TFH:1,264hrs. BoS to OH Cheer Jr, New Orleans, LA 07Mar58 for $13,500, with CofR 13Mar58. BoS to Scott Flying Service Inc, New Orleans, LA 26Mar59 with CofR 19Oct59. BoS to LJ Perry, Schoolcraft, MI 02Feb62, with CofR 12Mar62. BoS Estate of LJ Perry to Marshall H Ratliff, Battle Creek, MI 09Jly63, with CofR 02Aug63. BoS to Tecumseh Aviation, Division of Myers Industries Inc, Tecumseh, MI 29Nov67, with CofR 10Jan68. BoS to Thomas A Trumbull, Toledo, OH 08Aug74, with CofR 29Aug74. **N33Q** placed on aircraft 09Jan75 and CofR issued 14Jan75. BoS to Raymond J Jones Jr, Pontiac, MI 03Jly75, with CofR 23Jly75. BoS to Magnolia Corp, Cypress, TX 23Oct75, with CofR 11Nov75. BoS to Gilbert D and Brian L Scheff, dba Records Management Inc, Anchorage, AK 26Aug83, with CofR 09May84. BoS to

Roy W Mabee, Anchorage, AK 16May88, with CofR 14Jun88. Stored Chino, CA a/o Oct07. Current and airworthy May13, with CofR due to expire 30Nov14.

1399   Built for US Navy as **J4F-2**, BuAer serial **37769**. Acc 20Feb45 and del 21Feb45; in process of delivery at NAS Lakehurst 28Feb45; Pool NAS Alameda Mar45; Pool AROU-2 NAB Samar Jly45; NAB Samar Sep45; en route Guam 31Dec45; Pool CASU-F12 NAS Orote Jan46; Pool NAS Pearl Harbor Apr46. Wfu at Pearl Harbor 14Jun46 and SOC there 30Jun46 as obsolete and surplus. Regd as **G-44, NC68242** to Interior Enterprises Inc, Fairbanks, AK, and later as **N68242**. Accident 29Jun56: total loss when crashed and caught fire "in Alaska", with two fatalities. Photographs show the wreckage "near Tern Mountain, in the Bethel area".

1400   Built for US Navy as **J4F-2**, BuAer serial **37770**. Acc 26Feb45 and del 28Feb45; in process of delivery at NAS New York 28Feb45; NAS Lakehurst Mar45. Water-looped on landing on Barnegat Bay, NJ 19May45: pilot allowed bow to dig in and aircraft sheared to starboard; following probable over-correction the aircraft then looped violently to the left, capsized and sank. Crew escaped uninjured, the aircraft was seriously damaged and was SOC at Lakehurst 30Jun45.

G-44A Production List

1401   Built as **XG-44A** and regd **NX41818** to Grumman Aircraft Engineering Corp. First flight 08Aug44. Later regd as **G-44A**, **NC41818**, under the G-44 ATC 734, and used as demonstrator and company hack, but still as NX41818 on the 1947 USCAR. Fate unknown.

1402   Built as **G-44A** and regd **NC41971** to Staples Tool & Engineering Co, Cincinnati, OH Feb45; later as **N41971**. To Spain as **EC-AJU** 14Jly54. Regd to José López de Carrizosa y Martel, dba Aerotecnica SA 14May55; to Ricardo Carrasco Flandes 25May62. Aircraft name: "*Gavina I*". Wfu, and noted derelict at Barcelona-Sabadell, May70. Broken up at Sabadell in 1977.

1403   Built as **G-44A** and regd **NC41972** to Edwards Transportation Co, Houston, TX Mar45, and still regd 1947. Delivered to the Civil Aviation School, Bangkok, with no known serial, but possibly **B.S6-4/94** after transfer to the 7 Wing, Royal Thai Air Force 12Jly51. Wfs circa 1956.

1404   Built as **G-44A** and regd **NC41973** to Grumman Aircraft Engineering Corp 12Mar45. To Clifford M Sorensen, dba Continental Die Casting Co, Detroit, MI, 16Mar45. To Walker Airways Inc, Detroit, MI 19Jly46. To Sinclair Panama Oil Corp, New York, NY 23Oct46 (based Canal Zone). To Gillies Aviation Corp, Hicksville, Long Island, NY 30Jun47. To J William Ellworth, Greenport, Long Island, NY. To Gillies Aviation Corp, Hicksville, Long Island, NY 12Apr48. To Doubleday & Co Inc, Garden City, Long Island, NY 19Apr48. To Link Aeronautical Corp, Bing-hampton, NY 02Feb49, later **N41973**. Wfs prior to Jly54 and hull and tail group used in rebuild of c/n 1438 (N77K). Cancelled from USCAR 10Oct55.

1405   Built as **G-44A** and regd **NC41974** to Southern Aircraft Corp, Garland, TX, Mar45, and still regd 1947. Fate unknown.

1406   Built as **G-44A** and regd **NC41975** to Grumman Aircraft Engineering Corp, Apr45. Used as demonstrator. Later as **N41975**. To The Kay Evelyn Co, Houston, TX, Oct62. Cvtd to Continental IO-470-D power, date unknown. CF-SHO allotted to Staron Flight Ltd 08Mar65. Authority to ferry Portland, OR to Vancouver, BC 20Apr65 on US CofA for export E-65768. CofR(C) 33579 and CofA10879 for **CF-SHO** to Staron Flight Ltd, Vancouver, BC 28May65. CofA renewed at TFH: 4,225hrs, valid until 26Jan67. Experimental flight permit 13Jun66 to evaluate installation of Cessna 206 wingtips. CofA renewed at TFH: 4,835hrs, valid until 04Nov69. CofR 45655(P) to Norman Manning Ltd, Vancouver, BC 19Feb69. Leased to North Coast Air Services Ltd, Prince Rupert, BC with CofR(C) 11Jly69. Accident 1969 and cancelled from CCAR 13Jan70. [A memo, dated 18Dec69, in the file notes: "*has been officially destroyed and written-off; certs also destroyed*." Sounds like an accident but could be interpreted as being broken-up.]

1407   Built as **G-44A** and regd **NC41976** to Grumman Aircraft Engineering Corp 06Apr45 with CofA same date. BoS to Wickwire Spencer Aviation Corp, New York, NY, 07Apr45 with CofR 21Apr45.

BoS to Gar Wood, Detroit, MI 11Oct45 with CofA 20Apr46 and CofR 02Jun46. BoS to Harry Garland, Detroit, MI 29Jly47 with CofR 14Aug47. BoS to McLouth Steel Corp, Detroit, MI 20Jan48 with CofR 28Jan48. BoS to Estate of William G Helis, New Orleans, LA 31May51 with CofR 06Aug51 as **N41976**. CofA renewed 24Jun53 at TFH:1,680hrs. Cvtd to Lycoming GO-480-B1 engines by Pan Air Corp with CofA 20Jly55 at TFH:2,047hrs; CofA renewed 07Jun56 at TFH:2,169hrs. Overhauled and re-skinned with increase in gross wt to 5,500lbs 23Jun61 and re-engined with Lycoming GO 480-B1D 12Apr89. Cancelled from USCAR 13Jun12, but regn reserved same date for Estate of William G Helis.

1408   Built as **G-44A** and regd **NC41977** to Grumman Aircraft Engineering Corp (GAEC) 12Apr45 with CofA same date. BoS to North Carolina Pulp Co, Camden, NJ, 16Apr45 with CofR 02Jun45; TFH:216hrs a/o 07Nov45. Hull modified & step vent installed by GAEC Jly46. BoS to LW VanBuskirk Inc, Easton, PA 18Aug47 for $16,750, with CofR 11Sep47, and later as **N41977**. Overhauled by Aero Trades Inc, Ronkonkoma, Long Island, NY, with CofA 04Feb54 at TFH:1,770hrs. Reregd **N77V** 04Dec50. Cvtd to **Super Widgeon** per McKinnon kit, with Lycoming GO-480-B1D engines, by Mattituck Airbase Corp, Linden, NJ Jun57 and spray rails fitted on both chines per STC SA4-65, Feb58. BoS to Transair Inc, Linden, NJ 17Oct67 with CofR 27Oct67. BoS to Jack Adams Aircraft Sales Inc, Walls, MS 22Aug69. BoS to Donald A Sumrall, dba Sumrall's Air Service, Hattiesburg, MS 24Oct69 with CofR 19Dec69; address change to c/o Antilles Air Boats, St Thomas, US Virgin Islands by 1971. Export CofA applied for stating that acft was then located in Belize, British Honduras and E-105250 issued 30Oct71 to Donald A Sumrall, St Thomas, US Virgin Islands for transfer to British Honduras registration. **VP-HBW** allocated Nov71 to Sumrall Air Service, Melinda, Honduras, but regn ntu. Address change to Miami, FL 13Apr74. CofR N77V revoked 31Oct75 due failure to return an Aircraft Activity Report. CofR re-issued 19Nov75 but revoked again 12Feb82 due failure to return a Triennial Registration Report. BoS to Aircraft Speciality Inc, Belle Chasse, LA 06Dec84, and sold on by them to Brian J van Wagnen, Jackson, MI, 19Aug86 with CofR **N77V**, 19May87. Regn **N44VW** issued 09Apr96, CofR issued 10Apr96, and placed on acft 11Apr96. Current, but not airworthy May13, with CofR due to expire 30Apr14.

1409   Built as **G-44A** and regd **NC41978** to Schwitzer Cummins, Indianapolis, IN, Apr45. Reregd **NC1591** to Schwitzer-Cummins Company, Indianapolis, IN by Dec45. Reregd **N3377** to Schwitzer Corp, Indianapolis, IN 27Dec51(?). Cvtd to Lycoming GO-480 power. To James Geier, Cincinnati, OH 1966. To Thomas B Bender, Mobile, AL in 1969. Accident 09May70: substantial damage to hull when landed in rough water near New Orleans while en route Mobile, AL to Chandeleur Island, LA. Pilot + 4 pax uninjured. To Marine Investments Inc, Mobile, AL 1972. To Pelican Seaplanes Inc, Miami, FL, 06Sep73. Reported damaged and used for spares. Seen damaged at St Lucia-Vigie 11Mar77. CofR revoked by 2008.

1410   Built as **G-44A** and regd **NC41979** to Grumman Aircraft Engineering Corp 18Apr45. BoS to Charles W Deeds, South Meriden, CT, 21Apr45 with CofR 28Apr45; CofA 08May46 at TFH:165hrs; address change to Farmington, CT 01Aug47, and later as **N41979**. CofA 02May52 at TFH:754hrs. Cvtd to **Super Widgeon** Jun53, with Lycoming GO-435-C2B engines and Hartzell HC 82x20-2 props (using a Lockheed Air Services kit) by Pratt & Whitney, East Hartford, CT. Hull modified and hull vents installed same date, leading to CofA 14Jun53 at TFH:1,094hrs. Major overhaul by Mattituck Airbase Corp, Linden, NJ including installation of aux fuel tanks (STC SA4-62), emergency exit (SA4-63), McKinnon un-feathering system (SA4-64) and hull spray rails (SA4-64). The acft was also re-covered and re-painted. BoS CW Deeds to Edward A Deeds, Chester Springs, PA 26Aug60 with CofR 15Sep60. BoS to Baron Corporation, New York, NY 01Aug64 with CofR 25Sep64. The FAA file then becomes confusing by including a Form 337, dated Mar65, stating that Federal Airlines Inc, Park Avenue, New York, NY owned the aircraft. The confusion is compounded by a mortgage document, dated 07Dec65, including N41979 as a Federal A/L aircraft. This is followed by a CofR for Federal A/L dated 26Apr65, and by Jan66, documents showing the airline's address as Burlington Municpal Airport, VT. There then follows a CofR, dated 30Aug67, for Northern Airways Inc, Burlington, VT, with Edward A Deeds as President. A nominal change, by BoS, to Air North Inc, Burlington, VT 01Jan70 with CofR 10Nov70. BoS Air North to Edward A Deeds II, Charlotte, VT 01Oct72 with CofR 16Mar73. BoS to Birgit N Deeds, Charlotte, VT 02Jan82 with CofR 03May82. Acft tfd back to Edward A Deeds, Charlotte, VT by BoS 08Nov90, with CofR 06Dec90. Cvtd to **Magnum Widgeon** by Peter Annis, Halifax, MA Dec91, with Lycoming TIO-540-J2BD & LTIO-540-J2BD engines and Hartzell HC-C3YR-2UF & HC-C3YR-2LUF props per STC SA4774M. Tfd to Air North, dba Northern Airways, Burlington, VT by Nov01. Advertised for sale Jan05: "one family ownership since new; lowest time Magnum conversion on market". BoS Deeds to Northwest Waterbird Inc, Wilmington, DE 02Nov06 with CofR 14Dec06. **N440GW** issued 22Feb07, placed on acft 09Nov09 and CofR issued 20Nov09. Current and airworthy May13, with CofR due to expire 30Apr16.

1411   Built as **G-44A** and regd **NC41980** to Grumman Aircraft Engineering Corp, Bethpage, Long Island, NY 18Apr45 with CofA same date. BoS to Joseph James Ryan, Alaska Airlines, Anchorage, AK 19May45, with CofR 25Jun45 and CofA 13May46. BoS to Milton V Smith, Portland, ME 11Jly49. BoS to Atlantic Air Charter Service, Portland, ME 18Jly49, with CofR **N41980** issued 16Aug49. BoS to Northeast Aviation Co, Portland, ME 27Mar50, with CofR 04Apr50. BoS to Smith, Kirkpatrick & Co, New York, NY 03Nov52. BoS to Ministerio de Defensa Nacional – Marina de Guerra, Havana, Cuba 15Dec52. Exported to Cuba ex Miami 28Dec52 for Cuban Navy, with serial **81**, **82** or **83**. BoS Cuban Navy to Universal Trading Corp, Panama City, Panama 27Aug56. BoS to JC Welsch, Garden City, NY 11Sep56 with CofR **N444M** 16Jan57. Tfd to Welsch-Ayer Inc, New York, NY by BoS 16Sep57 with CofR 01Oct57. BoS to Trade-Ayer Inc, Linden, NJ 15Aug58 with CofR 21Sep59. BoS to Lehigh Valley Oil Co, Allentown, PA 12Sep60 with CofR 05Oct60 and CofA 07Nov60. BoS to Seahorse Air Service Inc, Annapolis, MD 12Jun69 with CofR 19Dec69. BoS to Stanley Woodward, Washington, DC 17Dec69 with CofR 06Feb70. Cvtd to **Super Widgeon** 06Nov71, with Lycoming engines per McKinnon STC SA4-65 and wing fuel tanks per STC SA4-958. Address change to Palma-San Bonet, Majorca and del there Aug72. Accident 24Feb81: crashed and sank in Bough Beech Reservoir, near Sevenoaks, Kent, UK while en route Gatwick–Biggin Hill. Pilot was attempting a precautionary landing due to engine problems. Pilot + 2 pax suffered minor injuries. Wreck salvaged and taken to Biggin Hill for rebuild by JR Froud of Edenbridge. N444M

G-44A Widgeon, c/n 1411, formerly Cuban Navy, seen here as N444M, while with Trade-Ayer, at Linden, New Jersey, on 12th July 1958.
(Charles N Trask via Jennifer Gradidge)

cancelled 03Aug84 as "destroyed". Aero Commander 520 G-ASJU was purchased for its 260hp Lycoming engines. These were removed and fitted to N444M. (The remainder of 'SJU was donated to the Biggin Hill fire dump); FF after rebuild Oct85 although FAA 337 for repair approval was dated 16Apr86. Reported reregd N444M to Susan Saggers in Oct85. Operated by Michael Dunkerly, dba Shipping & Airlines Ltd, Biggin Hill, Kent, UK. BoS Woodward to DHF Realty Inc, Miami, FL 11May87 with CofR 08Jly87, but operated by Shipping & Airlines Ltd. Address change to DHF Realty Inc, Chicago, IL 25Jan88. BoS DHF Realty Inc, FL to DHF Realty Inc, Chicago, IL 16Nov94 with CofR 14Apr95. Del via Wick-Vagar-Reykjavik to USA 30Jun97. To Randy J Wilhite, Jackson, MI with CofR 23Aug10. Current and airworthy May13, with CofR due to expire 30Apr15.

1412   Built as **G-44A** and regd **NC41981** to RM Hollingshead Corp, Camden, NJ Apr45. Fate unknown.

1413   Built as **G-44A** and regd **NC41982** to L Younghusband in May45. To Paul Rowatt, Chicago, IL in 1945. To J Ray MacDermott & Co, Harvey, LA in 1950 as **N41982**; Accident 24May68: aircraft encountered severe turbulence and high winds after take-off due to thunderstorms in area. Crashed into water off Lafitte, LA. Pilot killed and aircraft destroyed. Cancelled from USCAR 06Aug68.

1414   Built as **G-44A** and regd **NC41983** to Chas B Knox Gelatine Co, Johnstown, NY May45. Flew from Key West, FL to Havana, Cuba 28Mar50 piloted by John Knox and 3 crew. Cvtd to **Super Widgeon** with Lycoming GO-235s by McKinnon-Hickman Co, Sandy, OR 22Mar54 and reregd as such as **N41983**. TFH:2,239hrs a/o 04May60. Regd **N213K** to John Knox, Lake Pleasant, NY 28Mar62 and to Knox Gelatine Co, Johnstown, NY 11Mar64. Accident 05Nov68: substantial damage to bow due hard landing at Knox Bay SPB on Lake Piseco, NY. Pilot + one pax minor injuries. Flown very little (due out of use between September and April most years) between 12May70 at TFH:3,557hrs until 30Apr89 at TFH:4,238hrs. BoS John Knox to Aviation 3C Inc 10Oct89 (although US BoS was to Aerotaxi). Cancelled from USCAR Oct89. Leased by Aviation 3C Inc to 132802 (Aerotaxi) 10Oct89 until 27Jly90. CofR(C) for **C-FNOX** to 132802 Canada Ltée, (Aero Taxi) St Hubert, QC, 26Oct89. BoS Aviation 3C Inc to 157488 Canada Inc (Aerotaxi) 31Jan93. CofR(C) issued to 157488 Canada Inc (Aerotaxi), St Hubert, PQ 24Feb93. CofR(P) issued to 157488 Canada Inc, St Hubert, PQ (nominal change) 25Feb98; TFH:4,727hrs a/o 17Aug98, with CofA valid until 17Feb99. BoS 157488 Canada Inc to Air Quasar Ltée (Aerotaxi), St Hubert, PQ 09Nov99 with CofR(P) 10Dec99; TFH:4,781hrs a/o 20May02, with CofA valid until 17Feb03. To 1147967 Alberta Ltd, Calgary, AB 30Apr07. Advertised for sale by Prairie Aircraft Sales Ltd, Calgary, AB at TFH:4,947hrs (engines noted as Lycoming GO-435-C2B). Current Mar13.

McKinnon Super Widgeon, c/n 1414, N41983, of Knox Gelatine, at Oakland, California in 1955. Careful study of the photo shows the legend "Knox Gelatine" under the cockpit window and a very faint registration mark on the top of the tailfin.   *(Jennifer Gradidge Collection)*

1415   Built as **G-44A** and regd **NC41984** to The Pressed Steel Co, Wilkes Barre, PA, May45. To Jack Slifka, New York, NY by 1947, and later as **N41984**. Cvtd to **Super Widgeon** 1958 with 270hp Lycoming GO-480-B1D engines, by McKinnon. Authority to ferry 13Jun58; CofR(P) 17827 and CofA 5385 for **CF-KPT** to Peter Bawden Drilling Ltd, Calgary, AB 25Jun58. CofR 32119 to Sparrow Drilling Ltd, Calgary, AB 26Apr64 and CofR 32119 to Peter Bawden Drilling (1964) Ltd, South Edmonton, AB 14Aug64 (nominal change). CofR 36175 to Mountain Pacific Pipelines, Calgary, AB 10May66. CofR(C) 37184 to Newfoundland Air Transport, Corner Brook, NL 06Jly66; CofR(C) to Newfoundland and Labrador Air Transport Ltd, Corner Brook, NL 1971. Leased to Labrador Airways, Goose Bay, Labrador 28Jly77 as **C-FKPT**; CofR to Labrador

Airways Ltd 28Jly77. Four TECO Model TE-432 seats installed under exclusive STC SA4-467. CofR (C) to Newfoundland & Labrador Air Transport Ltd, Corner Brook, NL 27Mar79 (nominal change). Cancelled from CCAR 30Oct87. To David S Garber, Leesburg, FL as **N58DG** Oct87, with CofA 19Nov87. To DS Garber (Trustee), Leesburg, FL 30Jly93. Accident 17Dec93: crashed landing on glassy water on Lake Griffin, Leesburg, FL after a flight from Leesburg Municipal A/P. Aircraft substantially damaged when it flipped tail over nose but remained afloat. Pilot minor injuries. Tail broke away during salvage by helicopter. TFH:8,801hrs. To Garrett Carter, dba Tri-Negro Alaska, and Chaos Consulting Unlimited, Anchorage, AK (co-owners) with CofR 07Feb2005. **N269AK** reserved 13Mar09 and CofR issued 14Apr09. Current and airworthy May13, with CofR due to expire 31Dec13.

1416 Built as **G-44A** and regd **NC41985** to Peerless Tool & Engineering Co, Chicago, IL, May45. Still regd 1947, and reregd **N41985** in 1949, but fate unknown.

1417 Built as **G-44A** 14May45 and regd **NC41986** with CofA 23May45; BoS to Fuller Brush Co, Hartford, CT 25May45, with CofR 09Jun45. Gross weight increased from 4,500lbs to 4,525lbs 28Dec45; TFH:530hrs a/o 17Jly46. Became **N41986** 01Jan49; TFH:2,598hrs a/o 30Jan53. Cvtd to **Super Widgeon** with Lycoming GO-435-C2B engines 21Jly53; TFH:4,386hrs a/o 07Feb56. BoS to Perry Boswell Jr, Delray Beach, FL 03May56 with CofR 13Jun56. Gross weight increased to 5,500lbs 25Aug56. BoS to Island Airways of Fort Lauderdale Inc, 01Feb57 with CofR 18Mar57. Accident 10Jan58 and cancelled from USCAR 03Apr58. BoS to Gander Aircraft Corp, Miami, FL Jan59 with CofR 03Nov59. No FAA 337s 1960-70; cancelled from USCAR Oct70.

1418 Built as **G-44A** and regd **NC41987** to Winship Nunnally, Atlanta, GA Jun45 as a replacement for c/n 1219 (qv). Still regd 1947, but fate unknown.

1419 Built as **G-44A** and regd **NC41988** to Grumman Aircraft Engineering Corp, 31May45 with CofA same date. BoS to Seaboard Construction Co, Mt Kisco, NY 06Jun45 with CofR 13Sep45. CofA renewed 03Jun46 at TFH:373hrs. BoS to Link Aeronautical Corp, Binghampton, NY 22Jly46 with CofR 10Sep46 and later as **N41988**. CofA renewed 25Jun54 at TFH:2,016hrs. Cvtd to **Super Widgeon** with 280hp Lycoming GO-480-B engines and Hartzell HC-83-20-2B props Sept55, with CofA 01Oct55. Ferry permit issued 12Jly58 to allow flight from City Island SPB, NY to Tri-City A/P, Binghampton, NY for repairs to left wing after accident. CofR revised 14Jly61 to Kail Aeronautical Corp, Endicott, NY. BoS Kail to Edwin A Link, Binghampton, NY 17Jly62 with CofR 02Aug62. Accident 03Sep67: substantially damaged when aircraft landed too close to an anchored fishing boat, porpoised several times and then hit the boat. Boat owner killed; pilot + 2 pax minor injuries. BoS to Florida Institute of Technology, Melbourne, FL 02May72 with CofR 11Dec72. BoS to Frederick B Spiegel, Washington, DC 30May80 with CofR 06May81. BoS to Aerex Inc, Wilmington, DE 15Oct88 with CofR 07Nov88. BoS to Patrick H Weakland, Dumfries, VA, 14Jan92 with CofR 30Mar92; address change to Tappahannock, VA 04Feb99, and to Warsaw, VA 11Jan00. Current and airworthy May13, with CofR due to expire 31Dec13.

1420 Built as **G-44A** and CofR **NC41989** issued to Grumman Aircraft Engineering Corp, 09Jun45. BoS to Management Associates, Boston, MA 13Jun45 with CofR 27Jun47(sic). BoS to John Zimicki, Loudonville, NY 01Dec53 with CofR **N41989** 11Dec53. Cvtd to **Super Widgeon** with Lycoming GO-480-B1B engines, landing lights and hull spray rail installed Jlyy54. BoS to Trade-Ayer Inc, Linden, NJ 20Aug55 with CofR 01Sep55. BoS to Sun Oil Co, Philadelphia, PA 06Sep55 with CofR 07Oct55. Reregd **N33S** to Sun Oil 02Dec55; CofA 12Dec55 at TFH:1,346hrs. Reregd **N338S** 31Mar61. BoS to Lamb Rental Tools Inc, Lafayette, LA 25Jly61 with CofR 01Sep61. BoS to Bailey Leasing Corp, Fort Wayne, IN 16Feb63 with CofR 28Feb63. BoS to Ocean Drilling & Exploration Co, New Orleans, LA 08Dec64 with CofR 18Jan65. BoS to George A Potter Aircraft Inc, New Orleans, LA (undated) with CofR 10Jly68. BoS to Ingram Contractors Inc, Harvey, LA 14Jan69 with CofR 19Feb69. Retractable wingtip floats installed Jan69 per STC SA4-928. 5,500lb gross weight landing gear installed using McKinnon kit per STC SA4-60 and re-engined with Lycoming GO-480-G1D6 and Hartzell HC83X20-2A/8433-0 propellers per STC SA4-111 Jun69. Reregd **N111W**(3) to Ingram Contractors 30Mar70 (but already painted on aircraft 16Mar70). Installation of 3" diameter tube vertically below right cockpit window to facilitate drop testing of smoke bombs Aug70 and Restricted CofA issued 19Aug70. BoS Ingram to Tidemark Inc, Belle Chasse, LA Apr72 with CofR 03Jun72. BoS to Diamond Services WHT Corp, Morgan City, LA 22May73 with CofR 23Aug73. BoS to Wilco Inc, Las Vegas, NV

21Oct77 with CofR 01Mar79. BoS to Windjammer Capitol & Leasing, Escondido, CA 01Nov81. Tfd by BoS to James Hoffman (President of Windjammer), Lawton, OK 10Jly82 with CofR 13Aug82. Aircraft wrecked circa 1983, and salvaged by a yard in Oceanside, CA. BoS Hoffman to George E Potter Sr (dealer), Bellechasse, LA 16Nov84 with CofR 19Dec84. BoS to Steven T Hamilton, Reno, NV 13May85 with CofR 03Jan86; address change to Carson City, NV and CofR re-issued 12Sep88. BoS to Erikson Group Ltd, Vancouver, WA, 01Nov92 with CofR 01Dec92. Returned to Steven T Hamilton, Reno, NV by BoS 26Jan93 with CofR 23Jun93; aircraft based at Carson City, NV. Current and airworthy May13, with CofR due to expire 31Oct14.

1421 Built as **G-44A** and regd **NC41990** to Grumman Aircraft Engineering Corp 09Jun45. BoS to Deere & Co, Moline, IL 22Jun45 with CofR 04Sep45. BoS to WS Good Jr, New Orleans, LA for$16,200 29May51 with CofR as **N41990** to William S Good Jr 06Jun51. BoS to J Ray McDermott & Co Inc, Harvey, LA 02Jun51 with CofR 18Jun51; address change to New Orleans, LA with CofR 11Feb59. McDermott conversion to Continental O-470-B engines and HC82XF-2A props by ME Bordes Jly55; changed again for O-470-M engines Jly57. Major overhaul including increase in gross weight to 5,000lbs per SA2-284 and engine change to IO-470-D with HCA2XF-2A props, with CofA 11Feb63 at TFH:6,826hrs. Another major overhaul Oct66, and increase in gross weight to 5,400lbs per McKinnon STC SA380WE and Mansdorf STC SA2-284 May75. Name change to McDermott Inc Dec82, with CofR 03Feb83. BoS to Halter Yachts Inc, New Orleans, LA, 11Dec85. BoS to John M Fuller Jr, Nashua, NH 24Dec85 with CofR 18Apr86; address change to Allied Bendix Aerospace, Arlington, VA with CofR 24Jly86. BoS John M Fuller Jr to Baron Aviation Services Inc, Vichy, MO, 08Aug90 with CofR 27Aug90. Tfd by BoS to company president CE Schmidt Jr 20Jly04 with CofR 28Oct04. BoS to Dixie Air Leasing LLC, Vichy, MO 17Nov06 with CofR 12Feb07. Current and airworthy May13, with CofR due to expire 31Dec13.

C/n 1421 is a McDermott conversion with Continental IO-470-D engines. It is seen here visiting Oshkosh, Wisconsin, in August 1991, still carrying its original N-number, N41990. (AJ Clarke)

1422 Built as **G-44A** and regd **NC41991** to E Anthony & Sons Inc, New Bedford, MA, Jun45 with CofR 23Aug45. Cancelled from USCAR 12May55 but fate unknown.

1423 Built as **G-44A** and regd **NC41992** to BFD Co, New York, NY, Jun45 and as **N41992** with CS MacLean by 1952. Allotment of **CF-FCH** to Millard Auto Aero Marine Ltd, Toronto, ON 15Apr52; BoS from CS MacLean to Millard 16Apr52; authority to ferry Detroit, MI to Toronto, ON 17Apr52. US CofA for export E-18017 issued 01May52. BoS Carl Millard Ltd to Amtor Corp Ltd 07May52. Accident 09May52: after a flight from Toronto Island, ON to Pigeon Lake, near Peterborough, ON the aircraft overturned after the left wing tip float submerged. Pilot + 4 pax uninjured. CofR(P) 10967 and CofA 3676 issued to Amtor Corp Ltd, Toronto, ON 01May52. Sold to Field Aviation Co Ltd, Oshawa, ON in damaged condition, for rebuild Sep52. Authority to Carl Millard to ferry Orillia, ON to Toronto, ON 03Nov54; inspected and CofA renewed, valid until 09Nov55, and CofR(P) 13249 to Carl Millard Ltd, Toronto, ON 16Nov54. CofR(P) 13303 to J Cooke (Concrete Blocks) Ltd, Aldershot, ON 27Jan55. Accident at 1500hrs on 09Oct55 at Cookstown, ON: on a flight from Muskoka, ON to Hamilton, ON left engine failed. Altered course for Lake Simcoe but was losing altitude slowly so decided to make a wheels-up landing in a field when it was impossible to reach water. During forced-landing the left float was severed (Pilot: William Sumner). Inspected and CofA renewed at TFH:110hrs, valid until 11Jan58. Accident at 1400hrs on 29Sep57 (pilot: William Sumner) at Kapuskasing A/P after a flight from Brunswick Lake: pilot forgot to lower undercarriage before landing. Inspected and CofA renewed at TFH:158hrs, valid until 13May59. CofR(P) 28273 to Dr Gordon Robertson, Bralorne, BC, 18Jly62. CofR(P)

30335 to Yacht Wings International Ltd, Vancouver, BC, 22Nov63. CofA renewed at TFH:425hrs, valid until 26Aug65. Accident at 0943hrs on 06Sep64 at Vancouver Intl A/P during local flying: pilot Richard John Racey landed on the river but the right float was torn away. One pilot and one passenger climbed onto the wing to prevent the aircraft capsizing. The aircraft was taxied up a ramp but just past the top of the ramp the left float struck a steel post and both persons fell from the wing onto the concrete taxiway. CofA renewed at TFH:431hrs, valid until 26Aug66. CofR(P) 38449 to Northern Helicopters Ltd, Richmond, BC 10Aug66. BoS dated 09Jun66 (sic) Northern Helicopters to Red Dodge Aviation Inc, Anchorage, AK for $18,000. Cancelled from CCAR 17Aug66 and regd **N1423** in 1967. Accident at 1000hrs on 27May68: left float and right forward hull damaged landing on lake near Anchorage, but landed safely at Anchorage, AK; 2 crew + 2 pax uninjured; TFH:1,200hrs at time of accident. Accident at 1600hrs on 30Jly83: crashed in woods at Big Lake, AK. A short time before the crash the aircraft was reported flying abrupt manoeuvres and "buzzing" boats. The initial impact with trees occurred circa 40ft above ground level. Both wing tips and a portion of the left stabiliser and elevator were found at the base of the trees that were first hit. From that first impact point the wreckage was scattered over an area 30ft wide and 140ft long. Pilot seriously injured and pax killed. Aircraft written off and cancelled from USCAR 20Jly05.

1424   Built as **G-44A** and regd **NC41993** to Grumman Aircraft Engineering Corp 29Jun45, with CofA same date. BoS to Grimes Manufacturing Co, Urbana, OH, 05Jly45 with CofR 05Nov45. After an accident in Aug48 the aircraft was disassembled, cleaned, resealed and instruments and radio equipment, engines and propellers all replaced, and tail number changed to **N41993**, Jan49. BoS to Texas Gulf Sulphur Co Inc, Newgulf, TX 15Sep52 with CofA 01Aug52 at TFH:872hrs and CofR 01Oct52. Cvtd to **Super Widgeon** with Lycoming GO-435-C2B engines, with CofA 16May53 at TFH:954hrs (inc 6 hrs test run). Spray guards fitted Aug53, as approved by CAA 11Dec51. CofA renewed 30Apr54 at TFH:1,159hrs. Experimental CofA for flight testing metalised flaps, 13Feb58 at TFH:1,654hrs; Standard CofA issued 20Feb58 at TFH:1,655hrs. BoS to Sunny South Aircraft Service Inc, Fort Lauderdale, FL 06Mar61. BoS to Gilbert A Hensler Jr, dba Bahamas Air Traders, Nassau, Bahamas 15Apr61 for $38,500, with CofR 18May61. BoS to AVEMCO Finance Corp, Silver Spring, MD 21May62, but CofR to Hensler 06Jun62. BoS Hensler to Sherlock D Hackley, Nassau, Bahamas 17Aug67 with CofR 21Sep67. BoS to Island Flying Services of America Inc, Miami, FL 30Jun70 with CofR 06Aug70. Operated by Out Island Airways and address change to Nassau, Bahamas by Dec71. Aircraft seized by George A Potter Aircraft, New Orleans, LA Oct73 in lieu of unpaid maintenance bills, and sold to Morse Aero Inc, Utica, NY on BoS 10Oct73, with CofR 11Jan74. BoS to Michael A & Adrienne J Maxwell, dba DeBarr Dental Center, Anchorage, AK 30Dec74 with CofR 09Jan75. Complete keel replacement, installation of picture window and escape hatch, May76 (per McKinnon drawings dated 14Oct59). **N644M** assigned 22Jun83, and placed on aircraft Jly83; "Lee Mansdorf & Co" main cargo door installed Sep84, per STC SA603WE (then held by Dean H Franklin). BoS Maxwell to Valdez Aero Services Inc, Valdez, AK, 26Dec84 with CofR 26Feb85. **N41993** assigned 11Mar85 and placed on aircraft 30Jly85. BoS to Big Red's Flying Service Inc, Anchorage, AK 01Jun87 with CofR 23Jly87. BoS to Ronald L & Jennifer J Fitzgerald, Hemet, CA, 25Apr89 with CofR Feb90. Special flight permit issued 02May91 for ferry Renton, WA to Bayview-Burlington, WA (out of CofA). BoS to Kids Investment, a California Limited Partnership, San Luis Obispo, CA 31Jan92. BoS to William & Joan C Hately, Anchorage, AK, for $72,000, Jly92 with CofR 20Aug92. Current and airworthy May13, with CofR due to expire 28Feb15.

1425   Built as **G-44A** and regd **NC41994** to Grumman Aircraft Engineering Corp Apr45. To Hickok Manufacturing Co Inc, Rochester, NY Jly45. Fate unknown.

1426   Built as **G-44A** and regd **NC41995** to Grumman Aircraft Engineering Corp Jly45. Used as demonstrator and company hack. Believed to be a replacement for NC86644, c/n 1470, which was destined for Israel, but had crashed in Spain 24Apr48. Delivered to Israel Jun48 for Air Force use with A Squadron (immediately becoming 1 Squadron) and given serial **B-73**; serial **1202** was allocated soon afterwards but had not been applied before subsequent accident. While undertaking practice water landings, the aircraft crashed into Lake Kineret (Sea of Galilee) 07Dec48 killing all four occupants; TFH:486hrs.

1427   Built as **G-44A** and regd **NC86601** to Grumman Aircraft Engineering Corp 27Nov45 with CofA same date. BoS to Endicott-Johnson Corp, Endicott, NY, 05Dec45 with CofR 21Dec45, and later as **N86601**. Repaired by Link Aero Corp Jly46, after accident. Tfd from

Endicott-Johnson to J Fred Frakes, Anchorage, AK for $33,000, on a conditional sales contract dated 22Apr54, "to be paid in instalments, including $30 per flying hour flown by the buyer in pursuit of his business". CofR issued to Frakes, College Place, WA 29Apr54; CofA 03May56 at TFH:4,257hrs. Cvtd to **Super Widgeon** by McKinnon with 270hp Lycoming GO-480-B1D engines and gross weight increase to 4,700lbs (water). BoS Frakes back to Endicott-Johnson Corp 19Mar62 with CofR 09Apr62; based at Tri-Cities A/P, Endicott, NY 18Mar62 until 01Jun62. Tfd to McKinnon Enterprises Inc, Sandy, OR for $46,811.67, on a conditional sales contract 22Jun62 with CofR 16Jly62. Overhauled and gross weight increased to 5,500lbs per STC SA380WE, large cabin windows installed per SA4-928, Aug65. Reregd **N414U** 13Aug65. BoS McKinnon to Umpqua River Navigation Co, Reedsport, OR, 14Aug65 with CofR 30Sep65. BoS to Chas E Walters, dba the Walters Co, Spokane, WA for $70,000 14Mar68 with CofR 01Apr68. BoS to Calkins Manufacturing Co, Spokane, WA 05Apr71 with CofR 28Apr71. BoS to William B Barratt, Spokane, WA 20Jly94 with CofR 27Dec94. Tfd by BoS from WB Barratt to William Scott Barratt and Jeneen Dee Barratt, Spokane, WA 05Feb01 followed by a BoS next day, to Beacon West LLC, Billings, MT with CofR 07Aug01 (still quoted as Ranger engined). Current and airworthy May13, with CofR due to expire 28Feb15.

1428   Built as **G-44A** and regd **NC86602** to Grumman Aircraft Engineering Corp with CofR and CofA 07Dec45. BoS to The Superior Oil Co, Houston, TX, 12Dec45. Sensenich wooden propellers replaced by Curtiss metal propellers (by Grumman) 12Dec45 and CofR issued 23May46; address change to Lafayette, LA 05Jan48 and CofR renewed 10Jan48. BoS to American Exploration Co, Lafayette, LA 09Jun48. BoS to Zigler Flying Service Inc, Jennings, LA 02Sep48 with CofR 14Sep48; CofA renewed 29Dec48. Accident 23Feb49 and noted as "washout" when cancelled from USCAR 16Jun49.

1429   Built as **G-44A** and regd **NC86603** to Grumman Aircraft Engineering Corp with CofR and CofA 14Dec45. BoS to United Aircraft Products Corp, Dayton, OH, 21Dec45 with CofR 13Mar46. BoS to Everbrite Electric Signs Inc, Milwaukee, WI 08Jun46 with CofR 01Jly46. BoS to Aero Trades Inc, Mineola, Long Island, NY 07Oct46 with CofR 01Mar48. BoS to Inter-Island Air Inc, New York, NY 16Jun48, with CofR 23Mar49 as **N86603**. BoS to Rowan Drilling Co Inc, Fort Worth, TX 16Mar51 with CofR 29Mar51. CofA 04Sep52 at TFH:1,129hrs. Re-engined with Lycoming GO-480-B1 and Hartzell HC-83X 20-20 propellers and CofA Oct55 as **Super Widgeon** at TFH:3,026hrs; major overhaul Jly59. BoS to Pegasus Flying Service Inc, New Orleans, LA 01Sep70 with CofR 09Sep70. BoS to Mohawk Communications Inc, Chadwicks, NY 10Jly72 with CofR 29Aug72. **N2GN** reserved 16Apr74 and placed on aircraft 10May74. BoS to Southeastern Leasing Corp, Falmouth, MA 31Oct74 with CofR 21Nov74. McKinnon outer wing tanks installed per STC SA4-958 Jly78. BoS to Maitland Bros Co, Littlestown, PA 20Jly79, but another BoS 12Sep79 gives address as Maitland Co, Las Vegas, NV with CofR 12Sep79. BoS Maitland Co to Veigh Cummings, Murray, UT 21Aug79, but CofR 03Jun80 gives address as Boulder City A/P, NV. BoS to Standell Marine Science & Research Ltd, Wilmington, DE, 19Apr84 with CofR 31May84. **N945JD** issued 15Jun84 and placed on aircraft 07Jly84, named "*Magic Mistress*". BoS to Lucaya Air Inc, Opa Locka, FL 21Mar86 with CofR 15Jly86 (but noted with Lucaya Air titles at Fort Lauderdale already in Jan85). Tfd by BoS to Lucaya Enterprises Inc, Fort Lauderdale, FL 21Feb89 with CofR 22May89. BoS to Florida Airmotive Inc, Lantana, FL, 25Jan90 with CofR 04Dec90. BoS to Wayne C Mulher, dba Muhl-Air, Erie, CO, 26Jun91 with CofR 30Jly91. BoS to Wm Ben Scott, Reno, NV 09Feb05 with CofR 17Mar05. **N663G** issued 09Nov05 and placed on aircraft 16Nov05. Won the Paul E Garber Trophy

Lycoming-powered G-44A Super Widgeon, c/n 1429, N945JD, "Magic Mistress", owned by Standell Marine, is seen here on 10th October 1984 in the Florida sunshine.   *(via Rafael E Sanchez)*

at the Reno Air Race meeting in September 2010. To Pissed Away N663G LLC, c/o Aero Law Group PLLC, Bellevue, WA with CofR 27Oct11. To Greatest Generation Naval Museum, San Diego, CA with CofR 24Jan13. Current and airworthy May13, with CofR due to expire 31Jan16.

1430   Built as **G-44A** and regd **NC86604** to Grumman Aircraft Engineering Corp 21Dec45 with CofA same date. BoS to Lt Cdr William Candy, US Naval Air Station Glenview, IL 14Jan46. BoS to Western Continental Air Lines Inc, Glendale, CA 05Mar46 with CofR 03Apr46. Accident 15Jun46: aircraft wrecked and declared a total loss; Pacific Finance Corp of California retained salvage rights for aircraft. BoS Pacific Finance to James F Conroy, dba Long Beach Airmotive, CA 22Jun46 and cancelled from USCAR 25Mar49. BoS to Gerry Stroh, Andrew Robertson & Paul Ennor, Burlingame, CA 22Oct51 with CofR 25Feb52 as **N86604**; CofA after overhaul 25Jly52 at TFH:360hrs. BoS to McKinnon-Hickman Company, Portland, OR 29Apr53 with CofR 13May53. Cvtd to **Super Widgeon** with Lycoming GO-435-C2B and over-wing exhaust system fitted 14Aug53 with CofA 20Nov53 at TFH:395hrs. BoS to Phillips Petroleum Co, Bartlesville, OK 02Jun54 with CofR 06Jly54 and CofA 21Feb55 at TFH:848hrs. Tfd back to McKinnon Enterprises, Sandy, OR by BoS 27Nov56, with CofR 21Dec56. Uprated for 5,500lbs land and water ops per STCs SA4-60 and -61; auxiliary fuel tanks installed per SA4-62 and auxiliary escape hatch installed per SA4-63, all Mar57. BoS to CJ Montag & Sons Inc, Portland, OR 12Mar57 with CofR 10Apr57. Re-engined (by McKinnon Enterprises) with Lycoming GO-480-B1D per STC SA4-111 Jun58; nominal change by BoS to CJ Montag & Sons 27May60 with CofR 05Jly60. Aircraft inspected, then disassembled and treated for 45 days shipment in hold, and CofA for export E-46001 issued 15Feb61 at TFH:2,800hrs. BoS to Toyo Menka Kaisha Ltd, Osaka, Japan 21Feb61 and cancelled from USCAR 18May61. Operated by Nitto Air Line, Osaka as **JA5081**. Later with Japan Domestic Air Lines Co Ltd. BoS JDA to Universal Trading Corp, Panama, Republic of Panama 09May66 and Japanese regn cancelled 10May66. BoS to Fred B Ayer & Associates Inc, New York, NY 16May66 with CofR **N317RA** 29Jun66; CofA 01Jun67 at TFH:3,793hrs. BoS to Peninsular Airways Inc, King Salmon, AK 14Mar69 with CofR 26Mar69. Regn revoked 02Oct74. BoS to Westholm Aviation, Gardnerville, NV 06Jan78 and sale reported 29Apr78. Cancelled from USCAR 06Sep12.

C/n 1430, the former Western Continental Airlines' G-44A Widgeon, N86604, is seen here in 1952. (Chalmers Johnson via Jennifer Gradidge)

1431   Built as **G-44A** with CofA 02Jan45. BoS Grumman Aircraft Engineering Corp to Draper Motors Corp, Detroit, MI, 08Jan46 with CofR **NC86605** 30Jan46. Dual control column installed Apr46. BoS to Packer Pontiac Co, Detroit, MI 03Aug49 for $10,000, with CofR 23Aug49. BoS to Bresee Chevrolet Company Inc, Syracuse, NY 25Sep50 with CofR 02Oct50 as **N86605**. CofA 21Jun51 at TFH:528hrs. Cvtd to **McKinnon Super Widgeon** by Winn Air Service Co, Syracuse, NY with GO-480-B1D engines and HC83X20-2C props Aug56. Authority to ferry Syracuse, NY to Montreal, QC 18May61. US CofA for export E-48545 at TFH:1,430hrs 26May61. BoS to Diamond Construction (1955) Ltd 26May61. Authority to ferry Montreal to Cartierville, QC 29May61; CofR(P) 24364 and CofA 9060 for **CF-NNH** to Diamond Construction (1955) Ltd, Fredericton, NB 02Jun61. CofR renewed at TFH:1,667hrs, valid until 26May63. CofR(P) 30532 to Commander Aviation Ltd, Toronto, ON 09Apr63. CofA renewed at TFH:1,751hrs, valid until 13Jun64. BoS 03Jly63 to Harrison Airways Ltd, Vancouver, BC, with CofR(C) 30247 09Jly63. CofA renewed at TFH:2,095hrs, valid until 15Jun65; at TFH:3,494hrs (with Lycoming GO-480-B1B engines), valid until 25Jly69; at TFH:5,028hrs, valid until 06Feb73. Accident 10Jly72 at 16.30hrs: just after touchdown in Vancouver Harbour after a flight from Rivers Inlet, BC the aircraft struck a heavy swell. Pilot, David Allen Potter, applied power to abort the landing but the aircraft veered to the right suddenly and struck the water broadside; aircraft capsized and sank while being towed to shore. Sold by Brouwer & Co to Aircraft Salvage & Rebuild, Omak, WA (as is/where is) 06Oct72 as salvage, and cancelled

from CCAR 01Nov72. Salvage BoS to Mr Dick Ziesmer for $9,875 05Oct72. CofR **N94388** to Richard A Ziesmer, Puyallup, WA 24Sep81; address change to Spanaway, WA 28Apr94. Although the FAA file contains no airworthiness data after Jly72, the aircraft was listed as current until the CofR expired 30Sep12. To Richard A Ziesmer, University Place, WA with CofR re-issued 07Feb13, to expire 29Feb16.

1432   Built as **G-44A** and regd **NC86606** to South American Trading Corp, New York, NY 12Jan46. To Alberto A Dodero, Corrientes, Argentina as **LV-NCG**, 12Jly46. To La Universal Cia de Seguros, Buenos Aires, Argentina 10Apr58. Cancelled from Argentine CAR 24Apr59. Reregd **N4262A**, Jly58 (to Trade-Ayer?). LV-NCG cancelled 24Apr59. Stored at Linden, NJ; one test flight on 15Nov59 the only flying time between 13Jly58 and Jan60. To **ZK-BPX** for Tourist Air Travel, Auckland, NZ, 06Jan60 and cancelled from USCAR 15Jan60. Accident 15Jan64: major damage on water landing with wheels down and capsized at St Pegasus, Stewart Island. To Mount Cook Airlines, Christchurch, NZ, Dec67. Accident 01Jan74: crashed at Halfmoon Bay, Stewart Island, after a gear-down water landing. No injuries but aircraft written off during salvage attempt. Part of aircraft displayed at the Museum of Transport & Technology, Auckland. Later used for spares by Sea Bee Air, after which stored in Auckland area. Some parts bought by Owen Harnish, dba Salt Air – only small pieces remained by Mar07.

1433   Built as **G-44A** and regd **NC86607** to Ben E Smith, New York, NY, 06May47. In use by Léon Douzille at the SCAN factory at La Pallice by spring 1948. Delivered to Israel 26Jun48 for Air force use with A Squadron (immediately becoming 1 Squadron) and given serial **B-72** with serial **1201** allocated soon afterwards; believed to have subsequently served with 103 Squadron, Ramat David, but out of inventory by late 1949. Reportedly sold to USA, although no subsequent civil registration has been found.

1434   Built as **G-44A** with CofA 18Jan46. This was the first aircraft to incorporate the hull changes necessary to be structurally eligible for an increase in gross weight to 4,700lbs. Regd **NC86608** to Grumman Aircraft Engineering Corp 24Jan46. BoS to Thomas C Eastman, Monkton, MD 04Feb46 with CofR 05Feb46. CofA 27May49 at TFH:943hrs; 18Jun52 at TFH:1,828hrs. Cvtd to **Super Widgeon** with Lycoming GO-435-C2B engines Aug54; two-bladed Hartzell propellers replaced by three-bladed Hartzell HC 83X20-2B 01Sep54; CofA 28Jun56 at TFH:2,593hrs. BoS to Holladay-Aero Inc, Arlington, VA 26Aug60. BoS to Alfred Gwynne Vanderbilt, Oyster Bay, Long Island, NY 27Aug60 and CofR as **N86608** applied for 03Sep60. McKinnon auxiliary fuel tanks installed per STC SA4-958 27Dec60; re-engined with Lycoming GO-480-B, using McKinnon conversion kit 26May61, and Lee Mansdorf heavy landing gear installed same date to bring gross weight up to 5,500lbs per STC SA4-60. TFH:3,293hrs a/o 19Sep61. BoS to Raymond C Turnbull, c/o Pacific Coconut Processing Corp, Beverly Hills, CA 24May63 with CofR 10Jun63. CofR revoked by FAA 25Jan71 and eventually cancelled from USCAR 20Sep12. Fate unknown.

1435   Built as **G-44A** with Ranger 6-440C-5 engines and Sensenich 82RS72 props. Regd **NC86609** to Grumman Aircraft Engineering Corp, Bethpage, NY, with CofR and CofA 25Jan46. BoS to Link Aeronautical Corp, Binghampton, NY 25Jan46 with CofR 23May46. CofA 25Jan47 at TFH:269hrs. Hartzell HC12x20/8428 props fitted 28Aug47. CofA 07Jan49 at TFH:806hrs and 24Mar55 at TFH:2,287hrs. BoS to J Ray McDermott & Co Inc, Harvey, LA 12Jly55 with CofR as **N86609** 29Jly55. Continental O-470-B engines and Hartzell HC82XF-2B/8433 props fitted per McDermott drawings Sep55 with CofA 30Sep55. Continental O-470-M engines fitted with CofA 29Jan57 at TFH:3,041hrs. Major overhaul and Continental IO-470-D engines fitted Feb65. Accident 23Jun75: crashed and sank in Lake Borgne, near New Orleans, LA, 23Jun75. Salvaged and sold to George E Potter and Nicholas N Caridas, New Orleans, LA 25Aug75 with CofR 23Apr76 after repairs. Tfd to Potter Industries Inc, New Orleans, LA 08Nov78 and sold same date to Dr Perry D Melvin, Warner Robins, GA, with CofR 21Dec78. Address change within Warner Robins recorded on CofR 23Sep82. Tfd by BoS to Susan G Melvin at same address 15Dec83, with CofR 07Mar84. Underwent a nine-year restoration project until 1994 during which it was tfd back to Dr Melvin by BoS 21Jun89 with CofR 21Jly89. Exhaust gas temperature system installed per STC SA522SW May90. TFH:10,125hrs a/o 30Jun92. Address change to Salt Springs, FL recorded on CofR 01Feb07. Won "Best All-Metal Amphibian" at Sun 'n Fun 2008. CofR renewed 01Nov11. Current and airworthy May13, with CofR due to expire 30Nov14.

1436   Built as **G-44A** Jan46 and regd **NC86610** to Grumman Aircraft Engineering Corp 01Feb46 with CofA same date. BoS to The Kawneer Co, Niles, MI 18Apr46 with CofR 14May46. BoS to Leon E Barnum, dba

Thunder Bay Flying Service, Alpena, MI 16Aug48 with CofR 14Oct48; and later as **N86610**. N86610 was revoked by FAA 09Sep71, due failure to return an Aircraft Activity Report. Eventually cancelled from USCAR 10Sep12.

1437   Built as **G-44A** and regd **NC86611** to Grumman Aircraft Engineering Corp, Bethpage, NY, with CofR and CofA 06Feb46. BoS to Capt Robert W Orrell, Cardinal, VA 11Feb46, with CofR 13May46. Repair to keel (after accident?) 15May47, with CofA same date. Sensenich wooden props replaced by Curtiss metal props 03Aug48 and Hartzell HC12X20-3A hydro-selective reversible props installed 14Jun49. BoS to Gulf Refining Co, Houston, TX for $21,150 20Nov51 with CofR as **N86611** 29Dec51. CofA 02Jan53 at TFH:827hrs and 17Jan55 at TFH:1,821hrs. Rangers removed and Continental O-470-B engines with Hartzell HC82XF-2B props installed May56 at TFH:2,286hrs. CofA 22Jun56 at TFH:2,332hrs. Tfd to Gulf Oil Corp, Houston, TX by BoS 31Dec56 for $27,686, with CofR 20Mar57. Re-engined with Continental IO-470-D with HCA2XF-2A props per STC SA2-13 and CofA 02Sep59 at TFH:3,567hrs. Major overhaul and re-skinning Feb62 which included installations per STCs SA2-13, SA2-284, SA2-1065, SA4-60 and outer wing panel modifications per Lee Mansdorf Drawing No.1201. Dual control wheel fitted Jly62. Address change to Dravosburg, PA Nov62. Overhauled Jan/Feb71. Beech Aircraft Corp control wheel fitted Dec74. One-piece windshield, per STC SA4-2, also installed Dec74. Flaps metallised per STC SA4-960 Sep76. In Oct78 work was carried out per STCs SA4-928, SA4-964 and SA4-1031. To Chevron USA Inc, New Orleans, LA, with CofR 28Aug85. BoS to Donna Macphee, Palm Springs, CA 23Mar90 with CofR 08May90. BoS to Tebo Bros Rock Products, Battle Ground, WA 08Jly91 with CofR 06May92. Address change to Oregon City, OR 10Jan94. After death of Gerald L Tebo tfd to Alaska Turbines STOL LLC, Battle Ground, WA by BoS 06Nov03 with CofR 02Jan04. To Darrell M Peterson, Toledo, WA with CofR 13Jun12. Current and airworthy May13, with CofR due to expire 30Jun15.

1438   Built as **G-44A** and regd **NC86612** to Grumman Aircraft Engineering Corp, Bethpage, NY 13Feb46 with CofA same date. BoS to American Skyports Inc, New York, NY 10Jun46, with CofR 21Jun46. Sensenich wooden props replaced by Curtiss metal props 25Jun46. Hull and wings repaired (after accident?) Feb47. Repaired again 11Apr47, after accident. BoS to Gray Dictating Machine Corp, New York, NY 19Aug48, with CofR 26Aug48. Tfd to Gray Audograph Corp, (same address) New York, NY 31Dec48, with CofR 05Jan49. BoS to Pressed Steel Car Co Inc, Chicago, IL 16Mar50 for $15,000. CofR **N86612** issued 29Mar50. Overhauled and re-painted Mar51. Reregd **N77K** 15Mar51. CofA 22Oct52 at TFH:1,108hrs. Cvtd to **Super Widgeon** by Lockheed Aircraft Service Inc, Bubank, CA, with Lycoming GO-435-C2B 260hp engines with Hartzell HC82X20-2 props, 04Feb53. Experimental CofA 16Feb53 for flight testing and Standard CofA issued 02Mar53. Accident 27Mar53: crashed near Candle Lake, CT. BoS to Link Aeronautical Corp, Endicott, NY 22Apr53, with CofR 18Dec53. Aircraft rebuilt using hull and tail group from c/n 1404 (N41973) Jly54. Two-bladed Hartzell props removed and replaced by three-bladed Hartzell HC83X20-2A/8433 props Oct54. Auxilliary fuel tanks installed in engine nacelles Feb55. CofA 02May55 at TFH:273hrs since rebuild. Lycoming GO-480-B engines with HC83X20-2B props installed by Link Aeronautical, per Lockheed drawings, Sep55. BoS to Glaser Construction Co Inc, Lafayette, LA 14Jan56, with CofR 02Feb56. CofA 14Apr56 at TFH:501hrs. BoS to Trans Air Corp, New Orleans, LA 06Jan59, with CofR 25Feb59. The GO-480-B engines were replaced by Lycoming GO-480-B1Ds Jly59. Tfd by BoS to Dynair Corp, New Orleans, LA 13Dec65 and to John L Freiberg, (same address), New Orleans, LA 13Dec65, with CofR 05Apr67. BoS to Arkansas Aviation Sales Inc, Little Rock, AR 17May71, with CofR 25May71. BoS to William E Gilbert, Christiansted, US Virgin Islands 23Jly71, with CofR 09Sep71. Address change to Gibson Island, MD and CofR amended 20Sep72. BoS to Aircraft Slaes Inc, Charlotte, NC 24Aug73. BoS to American National Bank & Trust of NJ, Morristown, NJ 15Aug74, with CofR 03Sep74. BoS to Stuart M Lamb Jr, Marblehead, MA 23Sep74, with CofR 06Dec74. Elevators re-covered with Ceconite, per STC SA4-755, Nov74. Accident at 1200hrs on 09Nov75: crashed during water landing on glassy water at Haverhill, MA after a flight from Beverly, MA. Pilot and pax seriously injured and aircraft substantially damaged, but salvaged. Cancelled from USCAR 07Jan76, as damaged/destroyed. BoS to Dennis K Burke, Chelsea, MA 28Nov94, with CofR 27Feb95. Reregd **N8076D** (date not recorded). BoS to Ace Aviation Inc, San Rafael, CA 12Sep97, with CofR 30Mar99. Address change to Sausalito, CA Mar03. CofR renewed 31Jan11, but listed as not airworthy May13, with CofR due to expire 31Jan14.

1439   Built as **G-44A** and regd **NC86613** to Grumman Aircraft Engineering Corp, Bethpage, NY. To ML Pruyn, Kisco, NY 12Apr46. To Rafael Sanchez, Cuba in 1948 and regd as **CU-N346** Jun49. Reregd

G-44A Super Widgeon, c/n 1439, ZK-CFA, in the red and white colours of NZ Tourist Air Travel Ltd, at Auckland in April 1968, after being re-engined with Continental IO-470s.   (Mervyn Prime via Jennifer Gradidge)

N9096R to Florentino Sequeiro, Miami, FL in 1959. Nominal change to Okeechobee Farms Co, West Palm Beach, FL Apr61. To Bill Danko, Opa Locka, FL, 05Apr62. To Tourist Air Travel, Auckland, NZ; arr Auckland aboard *MV Ashbank* 23Jun63 and regd as **ZK-CFA**, 26Jly63. Cvtd by Tasman Empire Airlines to **Super Widgeon** with Continental IO-470-D engines in 1963. To Mount Cook Airlines, Christchurch, NZ Dec67. Accident 29Feb72: overturned and badly damaged at Catherine Bay, Great Barrier Island. Wreck shipped to Auckland, arriving at Air New Zealand hangar at Auckland A/P 02Mar72 for inspection and then trucked to Hamilton 15Mar72 for repair. To Sea Bee Air, Auckland, NZ, 22Oct76. Flew services on behalf of the Tuvaluan Government from Mar80-Aug81 (see page 272). Incident 22Oct84: substantially damaged after heavy impact with sea during take-off in bad weather at Great Barrier Island. Flight continued to Ardmore, but out of service for 9 months for repairs at Hamilton. To Owen Harnish, Whitford, Auckland, New Zealand 1987; dba Aquatic & Vintage Airways Ltd 1992 and then name changed to Salt Air 1996. Last flown 1996 but still airworthy in 1999. Stored complete at owner's airstrip at Whitford, near Auckland and still there in May12.

1440   Built as **G-44A** and regd **NC86614** to Grumman Aircraft Engineering Corp, Bethpage, NY with CofR and CofA 25Feb46. BoS to Ernest N Patty Jr, Seattle, WA 07May46; letter from Patty stating that aircraft was actually purchased by Alluvial Golds Inc of which he was President. [Because less than 75% of the company stock was owned by US citizens, the aircraft was registered in his name.] A BoS dated 11May46 transferred ownership from Patty to Alluvial Golds Inc but the CofR was issued to Patty, 16May46. Letter to CAA 10Dec47 from Ernest N Patty Sr, stating that: "this aircraft, piloted by my son, Ernest N Patty Jr, crashed into a mountain during a severe storm on October 25th (assumed 1947, author) and was totally destroyed, and that my son and his passengers were instantly killed. The wreck was examined by your inspector at Fairbanks, Alaska." Cancelled from USCAR, as destroyed, 10Dec47.

1441   Built as **G-44A** and regd **NC86615** to Grumman Aircraft Engineering Corp, Bethpage, NY. Allotment of regn **CF-EHD** to Algoma Steel, Sault Sainte Marie, ON, Canada 01Aug46. BoS to Algoma Steel for $31,291.50 dated 12Aug46; USCofA for export E-10282 21Aug46. CofR(C) 5126 and CofA 11627 to Algoma Steel Corp Ltd, Sault Ste Marie, ON both issued 23Jly46. Aircraft inactive Jly47 to Aug48 when CofA renewed at TFH:73hrs, valid until 30Aug49. BoS to WL Sheridan 13Oct48; CofR(P) 7518 to Sheridan Equipment Ltd, Toronto, ON 29Oct48; CofA renewed at TFH:266hrs, valid until 30Oct51. BoS to R Daniel, Toronto, ON 20Apr51. BoS to Mearle Smith 20Apr51 with CofR(P) 10083 to MAR Smith, Bathurst, NB 28Apr51. Accident 09Jly51: after a flight from Bathurst, NB pilot, Mearle Smith, landed on the very rough Mullins Stream Lake at 18.35hrs. Shortly after touching down the pilot noticed a large wave; the aircraft bounced about six feet and on coming down the pilot hit his head on the bulkhead behind him. He came to and found the nose of the aircraft submerged and the cockpit full of water. The pilot and passengers had time to escape before the aircraft sank. Salvaged. BoS Smith to Dr John A Lockhart, Bath, NB 04Sep51. BoS to Edwin A Link, Gananoque, ON 09Oct51. Complete rebuild by Link Aeronautical Corp, Binghampton, NY 14Jly52 and cvtd to **Super Widgeon** with Lycoming GO-435-C2Bs. BoS to Carl Millard 16Jly52. BoS to HJ McFarland Construction Co Ltd, Picton, ON 21Jly52 with CofR(P) 11217 issued 22Aug52. Tfd back to Carl Millard by BoS 26Mar53; authority to ferry Malton, ON to Houston, TX 30Mar53. Reregd **N75071** for Brown & Root Oil Co, Houston, TX and reregd **N71Q** by Jun57. Accident 19Jun57: severely damaged making a forced landing at Houston International A/P. Repaired and back i/s by mid-Sep57. To Pelican

Aviation Corp, New Iberia, LA by Jun63. To Sierra Nevada Contractors Inc, Las Vegas, NV 1963. Allotted CF-WFM 24Mar64, cancelled from USCAR 25Mar64 and authority to ferry Los Angeles, CA to Oshawa, ON 26Mar64. CofR(P) 31737 and CofA 10619 for **CF-WFM** to William F Marshall, Oshawa, ON both issued 26May64; aircraft name: "*Kiska VII*". CofA renewed at TFH:5,078hrs, valid until 09Sep67. CofR(P) 43148 to Snowdrake Ltd, Toronto, ON 22Jun67 at TFH:5,108hrs; CofA renewed at TFH:5,323hrs, valid until 19Jly69. BoS Snowdrake to Richard Owen Burns, Hinsdale, IL 29Jan69. Cancelled from CCAR 05Feb69 and regd to Burns as **N4018**, with CofA 17Jun69. Restored as **N71Q** to RO Burns Jr, Chicago, IL by 1975. To Richard O Burns, Hinsdale, IL with CofR 30Dec75; address change to Downers Grove, IL. CofR applied for by Richard O Burns III, Lake Bluff, IL 08Apr13 and status in question May13 pending this application.

*C/n 1441, with an unmistakeable registration mark. Richard Burns' N4018 is seen here at Ottumwa, Iowa, in August 1969. Note the name "*Kiska VII*" on the bow, which along with the flag on the tailfin, is a remnant from its previous service in Canada.* (*William Haines Collection*)

1442 Built as **G-44A** and regd **NC86616** to Grumman Aircraft Engineering Corp 01Mar46, with CofA 07Mar46. BoS to E Roland Harriman, New York, NY, 09May46, with CofR 16May46. The Sensenich wooden propellers were replaced by Curtiss metal propellers 20Jun46. CofA renewed 02Apr47. According to an annual inspection report, dated 01Oct49, the aircraft was based at Grumman Airport, Bethpage, Long Island and had last flown on 10Sep49. Aircraft overhauled and overhauled Ranger engines installed during 800-hoiur inspection by Aero Trades Inc, Mineola, NY Dec50. CofA renewed 11Dec52 at TFH:1,942hrs. Cvtd to **Super Widgeon** with Lycoming GO-435-C2B engines (using McKinnon-Hickman Kit #101270) by Mattituck Airbase Corp, Linden, NJ Oct53, with CofA 03Nov53 at TFH:2,355hrs. The CAA wrote to Harriman on 04Oct54 to enquire as to whether he still owned the aircraft. A duplicate CofR, as **N86616**, was issued 22Dec54. Aircraft dismantled, cleaned/repaired as necessary and rebuilt with re-manufactured GO-435-C2B engines. The work, by Mattituck Airbase Corp, Linden, NJ was completed and a CofA issued on 02Jan55 at TFH:2,702hrs. CofA renewed 23Dec55 at TFH:3,054hrs. Goodrich wheels and brakes replaced by Cleveland wheels and brakes per STC SA121-EA, 29Dec64. BoS Harriman to Dean Franklin Aviation Enterprises Inc 21Jun72 with CofR 14Jly72. Tfd to Gander Aircraft Corp, Miami, FL by undated BoS, but recorded by FAA on 19Oct72, on which date the CofR was issued. BoS to Kodiak Airways Inc, Kodiak, AK 28Mar73. Existing wingtips replaced by Cessna Droop tips 09May73 (stating Kodiak Western Alaska Airlines as owner).Application for CofR by Kodiak Western Alaska Airlines Inc (KWAA), Kodiak, AK 25May73 and CofR issued to them 12Jun73. A belated BoS from Kodiak Airways to KWAA was dated 25Jan74 with another application for CofR, which was issued 08Feb74. Emergency exit door (recovered from an unidentified wrecked aircraft) fitted per STC SA4-63, 22Jun74. Wrecked at Karluk, AK pre Dec77, salvaged and stored in Palmer, AK (no NTSB report). BoS to Green Valley Aviation, Everett, WA 02Dec77. BoS to Roger and Charlotte Willis, Ashland, AL 07Feb78 with CofR 27Mar78. By Oct78, a Chattel Mortgage document gave their address as Miami, FL. BoS to Charles D Hagen, Edina, MN, 08Nov85 with CofR 16Jan86. BoS to Grant A Stephens, Anchorage, AK, 28Sep92, with CofR 26Jan93. Address change to Palmer, AK 26Jan96 and another change, although still in Palmer, 06Feb04. Not airworthy, and some parts used in rebuilds of c/ns 1231 and 1346. To Timothy R Martin, Anchorage, AK with CofR 11Mar13. Currently a rebuild project, with CofR due to expire 31Mar16.

1443 Built as **G-44A** and regd **NC86617** to Pan American World Airways, New York, NY, Jly46. Probably the Pan American G-44A that landed in the sea with one wheel down off Hopetown, Bahamas 20Jly46, causing substantial damage. Crashed 05Mar48, no further details known.

1444 Built as **G-44A** 13Mar46 and regd to Grumman Aircraft Engineering Corp with CofA and CofR for **NC86618** 15Mar46. BoS to Long Island Airlines Inc, Southampton, NY, 29Jly46, with CofR 14Aug46. BoS to Lambros Seaplane Base, Ridgefield Park, NJ 27Sep49, with CofR 04Oct49 as **N86618**; CofA 27Dec49 noted that last flight had been in Aug48. BoS to Superior Oil Co, Houston, TX, 13Apr51, with CofR 07May51. Experimental CofA issued after cvtd to **Super Widgeon** with Lycoming GO-435-C2 engines 10Apr52. Standard CofA renewed 23Jly52 after flight testing of above, and 25Jly53 at TFH:863hrs. Engines replaced by GO-435-C2B 11Mar54 and CofA 28Jly54 at TFH:1,197hrs; and 13Aug55 at TFH:1,614hrs. Reregd **N402E** to Superior Oil Co 20Aug59. BoS to Hylan Flying Service, Rochester, NY 15Feb68 with CofR 23May68. BoS to Eugene van Voorhis, Rochester, NY 08Aug70 with CofR 04Sep70. BoS to Rochester Amphibian Airways Inc, Rochester, NY 27Jly72 with CofR 15Aug72; CofR for address change 17May91. BoS to Lost In Time LLC, Rochester, NY 29Sep00 with CofR 18Jan01. Current, but not airworthy Mar13, with CofR due to expire 30Sep13.

1445 Built as **G-44A** and regd **NC86619** to Grumman Aircraft Engineering Corp, Bethpage, NY 20Mar46. BoS to McKay Products Corp, New York, NY 21Jun46, with CofR 17Jly46. BoS to Page Airways Inc, Rochester, NY 10Apr47 with CofR 23Apr47. BoS to Reeve-Ely Laboratories Inc, New York, NY 30Apr47 for $21,250, with CofR 28May47; tfd by BoS to Reeve Instruments Corp, New York, NY 10Oct47 with CofR 17Oct47, and later as **N86619**. BoS to Tennessee Gas Transmission Co, Houston, TX 25Sep51 with CofR 24Oct51. Cvtd to **Super Widgeon** with Lycoming GO-435-C2 engines with CofA 31Jly52 at TFH:1,434hrs; re-engined with Lycoming GO-435-C2Bs with Hartzell HC 82x20-2A props and landing gear upgrade Jun54, with CofA 13Jly54 at TFH:2,105hrs; and 09Apr56 at TFH:2,662hrs. Reregd **N505T** 28Mar57, but restored as **N86619** 10Feb59. BoS to Intracoastal Terminal Inc, Harvey, LA 01Jly59 with CofR 11Aug59. BoS to Louisiana Wildlife & Fisheries Commission, New Orleans, LA 20Apr60 with CofR 09Jun60. BoS to Flying W Inc, Medford, NJ 21Dec61 with CofR 19Jan62. BoS to Sunny South Aircraft Service Inc, Fort Lauderdale, FL 20May62. The following day, 21May62, they signed a conditional sales contract with Gilbert A Hensler Jr, Nassau, Bahamas; CofR issued to Hensler 15Jun62. BoS Hensler to Sherlock D Hackley, Nassau, Bahamas 17Aug67, for $48,514.92, with CofR 23Sep67 to Hackley, Oxford, MD. BoS to Island Flying Services of America, New York, NY 30Jun70 with CofR 06Aug70. Address change to Miami, FL 30Aug72 and operated by Out Island Airways, Nassau. BoS Hackley to Gander Aircraft & Engineering Corp, Miami, FL 09May75, for $25,000. BoS to John G Jackson, Christiansted, St Croix, US Virgin Islands 09May75, with CofR 22May75. Regn **N8H** issued 27May75, placed on acft 29May75 and CofR issued 06Jun75; address change to La Luz, NM 29Mar76. BoS to James C Saunders, Miami, FL 27Sep77 with CofR 14Oct77; tfd by BoS to Island Charters Inc, Miami, FL 15May78 with CofR 08Jun78. BoS to Manatee Inc, Fort Lauderdale, FL 04Mar82, and sold back to Island Charters Inc 10Mar82. BoS to Odyssey Aircraft Leasing Inc, Dania, FL 13May82 with CofR applied for 29Oct83. BoS to F Wyatt Cook, Wilson, WY, 24May93 with CofR as **N8HV** 14Sep93. BoS to Patrick J Coyle, Clymont, DE 08Oct01. BoS to Executive Dogs Inc, Wilmington, DE, 04Oct02 with CofR 21Jan03. No Forms 337 after Apr79, but current and airworthy May13 with CofR due to expire 30Sep13.

1446 Built as **G-44A** and regd **NC86620** to Superior Oil Co, Houston, TX, Feb46. To Rawson Motors Inc, Plainfield, NJ by Oct51. Regd as **CC-ETA-0233** to the Chilean Government, Dirección General de Tierras y Colonizacion (Dept of Lands & Colonisation) 04Jan52. Accident 14Jan61: made an emergency landing at Llanquihue Lake en route from Puerto Montt to Santiago when the right engine failed. While taxiing, the hull was damaged by rocks. Later that day, personnel from the Chilean Air Force arrived by helicopter and moved the G-44A to a sandy beach, further damaging the hull. After getting the landing gear down, the aircraft was parked but several days later it was discovered that it was badly damaged following a storm. With TFH:1,140hrs, cancellation was requested on 08Nov63 and the wreck was stored at Puerto Montt to be cancelled 25Nov63.

1447 Built as **G-44A** and regd **NC86621** to Grumman Aircraft Engineering Corp, Bethpage, NY. To George F Baker Jr, New York, NY May46. Accident Mar47: crashed in Trinity Bay, Newfoundland, but details unknown. CF-IJC allotted to Carl Millard Ltd, Toronto, ON 10Aug55. US CofA for export E-26488. Canadian CofA 4880 issued 25Aug55. CofR(P) 13830 for **CF-IJC** issued 26Aug55 to Chelsea Holdings Ltd / Quebec Smelting & Refining Ltd, Montreal, QC. Cvtd to **Super Widgeon** by Link Aeronautical Corp with Lycoming GO-480-B1B. CofR(P) 17040 to Chelsea Holdings/Lura Corp Ltd, Montreal, QC 09Jan56. Accident 05Oct56 at Montreal: pilot, L Gerald Benson, taxied the

G-44A behind Trans-Canada Air Lines Super Constellation, CF-TGH, whose prop-wash caught the left wing, lifting it up and causing damage to the right wing tip and float. Authority to ferry Montreal to St Johns, QC 11Oct56. Inspected and CofR renewed at TFH:1,386hrs, valid until 22Feb58. Accident 14Jly57 at Lac Dore, Chibougamau, QC: the G-44A sank at its mooring after a very heavy rainstorm in the early morning. Authority to ferry Chibougamau to Montreal 17Jly57. CofR(P) 17378 to Lura Corp/RP Mills & Co Ltd, Montreal, QC 29Jan58; CofA renewed at TFH:1,540hrs, valid until 03Apr60. Accident at 0935hrs on 14Jun59: pilot, SB McPhee, was performing practice water take-offs and landings at Lake of Two Mountains, QC. During an attempted take-off in adverse weather conditions the aircraft stalled and nosed over. No record of use Jun59-30Jun66. CofA renewed at TFH:1,589hrs, valid until 29Jun67. CofR(P) 39408 issued 03Apr67 to Carl Millard Ltd, Malton, ON, leased to Millardair Ltd Apr67; inspected and CofA renewed at TFH:1,605hrs, valid until 05Apr68. Lease/Purchase 07Apr67 from Carl Millard to Air Transit Ltd, St John's, NL for five years; CofR amended to Commercial 12Apr67. Accident 29Nov67: aircraft missing on flight from St John's, NL to St Anthony, NL (pilot, Douglas Wilfred Moore + 2pax). Some wreckage and clothing recovered on the shore at Trinity Bay, NL. Cancelled from CCAR 30Apr68.

1448   Built as **G-44A** and regd **NC86622** to Grumman Aircraft Engineering Corp, Bethpage, NY 18Apr46. To Nassau Aviation Co Ltd, Bahamas, 02Dec46 on US CofA for export E-11319, and cancelled from USCAR 27Jan47. Reregd **VP-BAC** 02Dec46 to Nassau Aviation. To Skyways Ltd, Nassau, Bahamas 29Nov49. To Bahamas Airways, Nassau, Bahamas 01May51; aircraft name: *"Exuma"*. Returned to Skyways Ltd, Nassau, Bahamas 15Oct53. Accident 28Dec54: crashed and badly damaged at Fresh Creek, Andros, Bahamas. Remains purchased by National Insurance Underwriters, Clayton, MO 24Jan55. Rebuilt at Miami by Dean Franklin Aviation, with zero-time Ranger engines, and CofA issued 30Aug55 at TFH:1,200hrs. Reregd **N20Z**, with CofR 20Sep55. BoS from Natl Insurance Underwriters to Red Aircraft Service Inc, Fort Lauderdale, FL 02Apr56, with CofR 11Apr56. CofA issued 14May57 after major overhaul at TFH:1,257hrs. BoS to Norton Drilling Co, New Orleans, LA 22Jly57 for $13,000, and CofR 05Aug57 at TFH:1,261hrs. BoS to Robert W O'Meara, Chicago, IL 30Sep58 with CofR 08Dec58. CofA issued 20Apr60 at TFH:1,741hrs. BoS to Joseph W Maugeri, Miami, FL 13Dec60, with CofA 21Sep61 at TFH:1,744hrs and CofR 25Sep61. BoS to Ted T Anderson, North Miami, FL 07Dec61 with CofR 08Jan62 and CofA issued 27Sep62 at TFH:1,782hrs. BoS to Cherokee Airways Inc, St Paul, MN 28Sep62 with CofR 18Jly63. Cancelled from USCAR 22Jly70 after accident in Sep63. No NTSB report found, and details unknown.

1449   Built 11Apr45 as **G-44A** and regd **NC86623**. Special seating installed in cabin and third window fitted on starboard side; CofA 17Apr46. Sold by Grumman Aircraft Engineering Corp to Long Island Airlines Inc, Southampton, NY, 12Jly46 with CofR 05Aug46. BoS to Lambros Seaplane Base, Ridgefield, NJ 27Sep49, with CofR as **N86623** 04Oct56. To Royal Thai Navy circa 1950. Although not cancelled from USCAR until 20Feb56 by CAA, due "no reply to audit questionnaire". Tfd to 7 Wing, Royal Thai Air Force as **B.S6-2/94** 12Jly51. Wfs circa 1956. Preserved at Thai AF Museum, Don-Muang AB, Bangkok by May86. Reported displayed with "Rescue" titles and only identity "4", May86 and Jan97, and still there Mar12 with "Rescue" titles but no serial.

1450   Built as **G-44A** 15Apr46 and regd **NC86624** to Grumman Aircraft Engineering Corp 24Apr46 with CofA same date. BoS to Long Island Airlines Inc, c/o Royce Grimm, Southampton, NY 27Jun46, with CofR 18Jul46. CofA after overhaul by Embry-Riddle Corp, Miami, FL 16Jun47. BoS to Lambros Seaplane Base Inc, Ridgefield Park, NJ 25Oct48 with CofR 28Oct48, and as **N86624** in 1949. BoS to Smith, Kirkpatrick & Co Inc, New York, NY 23Oct52. BoS to Ministerio de Defensa Nacional-Marina de Guerra, Havana, Cuba 11Dec52; del to Cuban Navy ex Miami, FL 28Dec52, with serial **81**, **82** or **83**. Cancelled from USCAR 11Feb53. BoS Cuban Navy to Universal Trading Corp, Panama, Republic of Panama, 27Aug56. BoS to JC Welsch, dba Welsch Aviation Co, Garden City, NY 11Sep56 with CofR **N444W** 16Jan57. Tfd to Welsch-Ayer Inc, New York, NY by BoS 16Sep57, with CofR 10Oct57 and CofA 24Oct57 at TFH:530hrs. BoS to Union Oil of California, Houston, TX 25Oct57 with CofR 07Nov57. Re-engined with Continental O-470-M and Hartzell HC82XF-2C props per STC SA2-13 Dec57 and operated out of Houma, LA. CofA 17Nov58 at TFH:1,251hrs. BoS to AiResearch Aviation Co, Los Angeles, CA 08Apr74. BoS to Dean Franklin Aviation Enterprises Inc, Miami, FL 01Jun74 with CofR 16Sep74. BoS to CR Morse, Anchorage, AK 17Jun75, with CofR 08Jly75. Accident 31Oct78: suffered uncontrolled descent and crashed after take-off from Cordova, AK on a flight to

Juneau, AK. The NTSB determined that the aircraft took off in adverse weather conditions (low ceiling, fog, snow and icing conditions) and continued VFR flight into adverse weather conditions. Pilot + 2 pax killed and aircraft written off. Wreckage recovered 21May79. CofR revoked by FAA 21May82 due unreturned Triennial Report and finally cancelled from USCAR 09Jly12.

1451   Built as **G-44A** with Ranger 6-440C-5 engines and Sensenich 82RS72 props and regd **NC86625** to Grumman Aircraft Engineering Corp, Bethpage, NY with CofR and CofA 24Apr46. BoS to PN Pattison and Max W Stell dba The Sportsman Air Service Inc, Grand Island, NY 03Jly46, with CofR 22Jly46. Curtiss-Reed metal props fitted 14Aug46. Acft was damaged in landing 29Jun47 but repaired. CofA 11May48 at TFH:409hrs. Tfd by BoS to PN Pattison as sole owner 02Feb49 for $11,400, with CofR 15Jun49, and later as **N86625**. CofA 05Jly50 noting last operated 19Sep49 and 14Aug51 noting last operated 25Oct50 at TFH:1,039hrs. BoS to MM Ispahani Ltd, Dacca, East Pakistan 24Aug51, exported on US CofA E-20465 and cancelled from USCAR 07Sep51. Regd as **AP-AFJ**, with CofA No: 137. Reregd as **S2-AAB**, 1972. Cancelled from Pakistan register 13Feb74. To Government Aircraft Workshop, Dhaka, Bangladesh. Reregd **S2-AAU** to Bangladesh Flying Club Ltd, Dhaka, Bangladesh 1979. Wfu and regn cancelled 11Mar81. Stored at Dhaka and seen in poor state 12Feb89. BoS (undated but recorded 09Aug94) Bangladesh Flying Club to Northern Aircraft Traders Ltd, Anchorage, AK exchanging Widgeons c/ns 1451, 1471 and 1474 for two Piper Senecas. BoS (undated) to Charles Stuart, Fort Worth, TX, but correction dated 01Nov90 states that purchaser was Charlie R Hillard, Fort Worth, TX and BoS dated 11Nov90 confirms Hillard as new owner. CofR **N6987U** issued 09Aug94. Reported to have been converted to **Super Widgeon** but the file contains no FAA 337s after 1951. BoS to James B Hanson dba Hanson Aero, Daytona Beach, FL undated but recorded 01Mar96, with CofR issued same date. BoS to Herbert E Andrus Jr, Granby, CT 26Apr96, with CofR 15Jun96. CofR renewed 27Jly11. Current but not airworthy May13, with CofR due to expire 31Jly14.

1452   Built as **G-44A** 08Jun46, and regd **NC86626** to Grumman Aircraft Engineering Corp, Bethpage, NY 10Jun46, with CofA same date. BoS to Alpine Airways Inc, Fitchburg, MA 19Jun46 with CofR 09Jun47, and later as **N86626**. CofA 26Jly52 at TFH:1,851hrs. McKinnon kit for conversion to **Super Widgeon** with Lycoming GO-480-B1B engines and Hartzell HC-83x20-2A props, installed Feb55 by Mattituck Airbase Corp, Linden, NJ and CofA issued 23Feb55 at TFH:2,586hrs. Reregd **N808W** 28Jan57; increased gross weight to 5,500lbs per STCs SA4-60 (land) and SA4-61 (water), and aux fuel tanks installed per SA4-62, Feb57 and CofA issued 20Feb57; emergency exit installed on right side per STC SA4-63, Mar58. BoS Alpine Airways to Reading Aviation Service Inc, Reading, PA 21Jan60, for $42,000, with CofR 04May60. BoS to Richard K Benson, Beaver Falls, NY 21May60, and sold same day to Anthony B Farrell, Northville, NY with CofR 27Jun60; tfd by BoS to Farrell, dba Akwissasne Flying Service, Northville, NY 21Jun61 with CofR 12Jly61. BoS to CG Suits, c/o General Electric Co, Schenectady, NY 20Oct65 with CofR 22Dec65. BoS to Super Test Petroleum Inc, Flushing, MI 29May68 with CofR 05Aug68. BoS to Thomas M Benedict, Portland, OR 02Oct69 with CofR 05Nov69; tfd by BoS to Portland Amphibians Inc, Portland, OR 20Dec69 with CofR 30Jan70. BoS to John J Ranft, Columbus, OH 06Apr73. Regn **N1SW** reserved 17Jan77, placed on acft 12Sep77 and CofR issued 21Sep77; repair to right wing and float Jan78 (after accident?). BoS to JP Air Inc, Cleveland, OH, 20Mar90 with CofR 06Apr90 (at TFH:6,951hrs). For sale on eBay Aug07 for $325,000 at TFH:7,493hrs with 270hp Lycoming GO-480-B1D engines. No Forms 337 after 24Feb02, but current and airworthy with JP Air Inc, May13, with CofR due to expire 31Jan14.

1453   Built as **G-44A** Jun46 and regd **NC86627** to Grumman Aircraft Engineering Corp, Bethpage, NY 14Aug46 with CofA 15Aug46. BoS to J Ray MacDermott & Co Inc, Harvey, LA, 03Dec47 with CofR 10Dec47 and later as **N86627**. Cvtd to Continental O-470-B engines with Hartzell HC 82F-2 propellers, with CofA 26Jly54 at TFH:3,300hrs; change to Continental O-470-M engines Jan57. Major overhaul May61 including installation of Grimes rotating beacon per STC SA2-1065; horizontal stabilizer leading edge raised 5/8th inch per STC SA2-13 May63; airframe overhaul and repaint Jly68; increase in gross weight to 5,400lbs per STC SA380WE Jun76. Nominal change to McDermott Inc, New Orleans, LA with CofR 03Feb83. BoS to Halter Yachts Inc, New Orleans, LA 11Dec85. BoS to Marjon Realty Inc, San Carlos, CA 24Dec85 with CofR 31Mar86. BoS to Dudley H Mead, dba Wingmead Aviation, San Francisco, CA, 01Oct89 with CofR 30Oct89. BoS to Richard R Taylor, Anchorage, AK 23Apr02 with CofR 04Jun02; address change to Gold Canyon, AZ (date not recorded). Current and airworthy May13, with CofR due to expire 31Jly14.

1454 Built as **G-44A** and regd NC86628 to Grumman Aircraft Engineering Corp, Bethpage, NY. To Kearney & Trecker Corp, Milwaukee, WI, Jly46 and still regd 1947. To WS Good Jr, New Orleans, LA (date unknown). Sold to Texas Co, Houma, LA, 09Mar51 for $19,380 and reregd **N1629**. Assigned to the Domestic Producing Dept at Houma, and flown by pilot MA Fuori, logging 559:45hrs in Texaco service. Reregd **N1629H** on 15Apr54 and sold to State of Louisiana 01Jun54, for $25,000. Cvtd to **Super Widgeon** (by Link Aeronautical Corp?) with Lycoming GO-480 engines, with CofA 01Jly56. Operated by Wildlife & Fisheries Dept, New Orleans, LA until sold to Leroy Rymer Jr, Cleveland, TN in 1969. To Richard Scribner, Pontiac, MI by 1977. Accident at 1910hrs on 10Aug77: crashed during take-off from lake at Cassopolis, MI. The aircraft was on a flight from Michigan City, IN to Battle Creek, MI when the pilot made a precautionary landing on the lake. During attempted take-off to continue flight, one engine failed and aircraft crashed into water. Pilot uninjured but aircraft substantially damaged. To Osprey Aviation Inc, Perrysburg, OH, Jan83. To Kenn-Air Leasing Corp, Gainesville, FL, Jly86. TFH:5,335hrs a/o Aug86. Accident at 1643hrs on 26Aug86: pilot stated that on touchdown on lake at Hawthorne, FL the aircraft felt strange. He added full power and took off again but just after take-off the aircraft rolled to the right and nose-dived. He removed power, and with the controls full back, the aircraft hit the water with no lateral control. NTSB examined aircraft and found large amounts of silicone in right main fuel tank and both fuel filters. Pilot + 3 pax received minor injuries. Reregd **N44CH** to Charlie R Hillard, Fort Worth, TX, 01May89. Painted as **"FP469"** in Fleet Air Arm c/s. To Royal Baby Duck LLC, Weatherford, TX with CofR 07Jan13. Current and airworthy May13, with CofR due to expire 31Jan16.

1455 Built as **G-44A** and regd NC86629 to Grumman Aircraft Engineering Corp, Bethpage, NY. To Joe R Dockery, Cleveland, MS Jun46. To Miller Brewing, Milwaukee, WI by Sep54. To Gilbert A Hensler, Nassau, Bahamas, as **N86629** by Jun63. To Sherlock D Hackley, Oxford, MD by 1969. To Crescent Holdings Inc, Harvey, LA 1972. Accident 31Mar74: crashed during forced landing in swamp at Falmouth, Jamaica and aircraft reported destroyed by fire.

1456 Built as **G-44A** 23Jun46 with CofR NC86630 to Grumman Aircraft Engineering Corp 23Jly46 and CofA 24Jly46. BoS to Alfred R Roberts, Trappe, MD 31Jly46 with CofR 15Aug46. BoS to The Proctor & Gamble Trading Co, Cebu City, Cebu, Philippine Islands 10May49 with CofR 31May49. Still owned by them in 1955 but memo dated 01Aug56, from CAA Chief Advisor, Manila to Pacific Area Supervisor, states that G-44A "now has Philippine registration and that US registration should be cancelled". Cancelled from USCAR 16Aug56. Sold to Blaine Gardner, Manila, Philippines as **PI-C277** Jly63. To Bert Tantoco, Philippines. Reported crashed Mindanao, Philippines and no longer regd after Oct65. Fate unknown.

1457 Built as **G-44A** and regd NC86631 to Grumman Aircraft Engineering Corp 27Aug46 with CofA same date. BoS to The Tillinghast-Stiles Co, Providence, RI 31Oct46 with CofR 27Dec46. BoS to J Ray McDermott & Co Inc, Harvey, LA 30Jun49 with CofR 03Aug49 as **N86631**. CofA 02Oct53 at TFH:2,476hrs and renewed 26Sep54. BoS to Link Aeronautical Corp, Endicott, NY 15Jly55 with CofR 10Aug55. CofR tfd to Kail Aeronautical Corp, Endicott, NY 17Apr61. BoS Kail Aeronautical to Iris K Morgan, Binghampton, NY 11Feb63 with CofR 29Mar63; address change to Montrose, PA 1970. CofR revoked by FAA 08Mar72 due unreturned Aircraft Registration Activity Report. BoS to Antique Aviation Sales Corp, Colonia, NJ 26Apr83 with CofR 07Dec83. BoS to Richard L Day & Rocio C Day, Colonia, NJ 26Aug85 with CofR 30Sep85. Returned to Antique Aviation Sales Corp, Colonia, NJ on BoS 20Jun90, with CofR 29Jun90. BoS to Intercon Developments Ltd, Boca Raton, FL, 25Jly91 with CofR 04Feb92. BoS to Pelican Corp, Fort Lauderdale, FL, 09Mar93 with CofR 16Mar93. BoS to Crosslands Inc, Wilmington, DE, 29Sep93 with CofR 20Oct93. BoS to Don L Aircraft Inc, Delray Beach, FL, 30Nov94 with CofR 08Feb95. BoS to Douglas L Williams, Anchorage, AK, 31Jly95 with CofR 03Jan96. Current and airworthy May13, with CofR due to expire 30Sep13.

1458 Built as **G-44A** and regd NC86632 to Grumman Aircraft Engineering Corp, Bethpage, NY. To Clark Auto, (at unknown address) Sep46, and later as **N86632**. Allotted CF-IJO 20Sep55. US CofA for export E-27221 issued 18Oct55. CofA 4631 issued 18Oct55 and CofR(P) 16071 for **CF-IJO** issued 21Oct55 to Carl Millard Ltd, Malton, ON. Inspected and CofR renewed at TFH:1,355hrs, valid until 14Jan58. CofR(P) 19963 issued 24Oct58 to Murfin Heating & Cooling Ltd, Downsview, ON. CofR(P) 20633 issued 27Nov58 to Carl Millard Ltd, Malton, ON. Cvtd to **Super Widgeon** (by Link Aeronautical Corp?) with Lycoming GO-480-B1D; inspected and CofA renewed at TFH:1,411hrs, valid until 17Jun61; CofR amended to Commercial 22Jun60. BoS Carl Millard Ltd to Marjim Corp Ltd, Winnipeg, MB, 03Feb62; inspected and CofA renewed at TFH:1,510hrs, valid until 02Mar63. CofR(P) 27699 issued 03Apr62 to Marjim Corp; inspected and CofA renewed at TFH:2,265hrs, valid until 22May68. Accident at 1830hrs on 09Jun67: on a flight from Winnipeg, MB to Gods Lake, MB aircraft bounced on landing and crashed into the water in a nose-down attitude. Pilot, James Robert Shore, and the 2 pax started to swim ashore but lost their lives, and the aircraft inverted and sank. Authority to ferry from Gods Lake, MB to Calgary, AB 06Oct67. Inspected and CofR renewed at TFH:2,274hrs, valid until 05Jun70. BoS to Pastew Enterprises, Calgary, AB 16Jly69 for $40,000 and CofR(P) issued 21Jly69; inspected and CofA renewed at TFH:2,436hrs, valid until 10Oct73. BoS to Perimeter Aviation Ltd, Winnipeg, MB 16Oct72 and sold same day to EM Boyle & AH Burchfield, Pittsburgh, PA and cancelled from CCAR 26Oct72. CofA 21Nov72 and reregd **N9GW** to Edward M Boyle, Pittsburgh, PA in 1973. Co-owners: EM Boyle, Albert H Burchfield

C/n 1455, a rare picture of the ill-fated G-44A, N86629, at an unknown date and location. *(Air-Britain)*

III & Janice K Burchfield, Pittsburgh, PA by Nov90. To Charlie R Hillard, Fort Worth, TX, Mar93. To James B Hanson, dba Hanson Aero, Daytona, FL with CofR 12Jan96. To Herbert E Andrus Jr, Granby, CT, with CofR 15Jun96. Current and airworthy May13, with CofR due to expire 31Jly14.

1459   Built as **G-44A** and regd **NC86633** to Staten Island Airways, NY Jly46. Long Island Airlines Inc, Southampton, NY 1947. Crashed at Bimini, Bahamas 10Mar47. Barged to Miami but destroyed in hangar fire during rebuild, at Miami, FL circa 1948.

1460   Built as **G-44A** and regd **NC86634** to Grumman Aircraft Engineering Corp, Bethpage, NY 11Sep46 with CofA same date. BoS to Everbrite Electric Signs Inc, Milwaukee, WI, 11Oct46 with CofR 17Feb48; later as **N86634**, and CofA renewed 04Sep52 at TFH:1,016hrs. Accident 21Jly53. Written off and cancelled from USCAR 07Oct53.

1461   Built as **G-44A** and regd **NC86635** to Grumman Aircraft Engineering Corp, Bethpage, NY 11Sep46 with CofA same date. CofA renewed 25Nov47; Sensenich wooden propellers removed and Curtiss 55518-10 metal propellers installed 19Mar48. BoS to Corps of Engineers, Dept of Army, District Engineer, Grecian District, Athens, Greece 08Apr48 with CofR 13May48. CAA memo dated 01Dec56 from Chief Advisor, Paris to European Area Supervisor noted that G-44A had not been re-certificated for two years prior to 1955 and enquiring as to its whereabouts. Cancelled from USCAR 20Feb56, due "no reply to audit questionnaire". Fate unknown.

1462   Built as **G-44A** and regd **NC86636** to Grumman Aircraft Engineering Corp, Bethpage, NY. To Four Winds Air Association Inc, (unknown address) 30Sep46. To Carstairs Enterprises Inc 25Aug48. To JF Sproule 17Nov50. To Bahamas Air Traders Ltd, Nassau 20Jan51 as **VP-BAT**. To Skyways (Bahamas) Ltd, Nassau 04Nov53. Leased to Bahamas Airways Ltd 01Nov58. Cancelled from Bahamian CAR 14Oct59. To Gilbert A Hensler Jr, NJ 14Oct59. Reregd **N9309R** to DH Franklin Aviation Enterprises Inc, Miami, FL 21Oct59; CofA 05Nov59 with Ranger engines. To Harris Aircraft Sales, Grafton, WI with CofR 26Jly60. Fitted with Continental engines by 1963. To Fort Dodge Airways, Moorland, IA, 21Feb64. To James AD Geier, Cincinnati, OH 09Jan66. To Florida Seaplanes Inc, Opa Locka, FL, 27Feb70. Wfu at Opa Locka 1977 and dismantled there by 1992. To Sturges Aircraft Inc, Fort Lauderdale, FL 31Jan02. To Executive Dogs Inc, Wilmington, DE 24May04. CofR expired 30Sep11. Fate unknown, but probably scrapped.

1463   Built as **G-44A** and regd **NC86637** to Grumman Aircraft Engineering Corp, Bethpage, NY 13Sep46, with CofA same date. BoS to Mower Lumber Co, Charleston, WV 08Apr48 with CofR 14Apr48. Aircraft name: "*Splinter*". CofA as **N86637** 22Apr52. CofA 02Apr53 at

TFH:565hrs. BoS to Southern Production Co Inc, Baton Rouge, LA 05Dec52 with CofR 16Dec52. BoS to The Offshore Co, Baton Rouge, LA 31Dec54 with CofR 15Feb55. Continental O-470-B engines installed per McDermott drawings Apr55, with CofA 12May55 at TFH:1,089hrs, and renewed 17May56. Landing gear (per Mansdorf STC SA4-60), modified hull compartment (per Mansdorf STC SA4-61) and gross weight increased to 5,400lbs for land and sea ops (per STC SA2-284) all installed in Dec60. BoS to Graubart Aviation Inc, Valparaiso, IN 19Oct62. BoS to Aero Plan Leasing Inc, Dayton, OH 05Feb63, with CofR for **N575L** 08Apr63. McKinnon retractable wing floats (per STC SA4-928), emergency exit on right side of fuselage (per STC SA4-967), one picture window on each side of cabin (per STC SA4-987) and Cleveland wheels and brakes (per Carl Millard STC SA-121EA) all installed in May63. Nominal change to Aeroplan Executive Fleet Inc, Dayton, OH Mar70, and address change to Delray Beach, FL Apr75. BoS Aeroplan to Wigma Corp, Royal Oak, MI 17Apr75 with CofR 05May75. BoS to Alaska Airco Inc, Fairbanks, AK 22Jly76 with CofR 03Aug76. BoS to John Hajdukovich, dba Frontier Flying Service, Fairbanks, AK 22Jly77 with CofR 11Aug77. BoS to J Dana Pruhs, Anchorage, AK 24Jan85 with CofR 21Feb85. Returned to J Hajdukovich, Fairbanks, AK on BoS 25Jly89, with CofR 27Nov89. Amphibian Landing Gear Position Advisory System installed Jly94 per Lake & Air Inc STC SA39CH. Tfd by BoS from Hajdukovich to Frontier Flying Service Inc, Fairbanks, AK 29May03 with CofR 14Jly03. To Icecap LLC Trustee, Anchorage, AK with CofR 13Mar09. Noted parked at Fairbanks, AK Jly10. Status in question May12 due regn pending after application by JMH Leasing LLC, Fairbanks, AK 24Dec11. CofR (N575L) issued to JMH Leasing 25Jun12. CofR issued to 575L LLC, Fairbanks, AK 07Nov12 (nominal change?). Current and airworthy May13, with CofR due to expire 30Nov15.

1464   Built as **G-44A** 07Jun46 and regd **NC86638** to Grumman Aircraft Engineering Corp 11Sep46, with CofA same date. On the CofA renewal, dated 08Dec47, it was noted that "the aircraft had been in dead storage since Jan47". Curtiss metal props replaced with Koppers Aeromatic props 12May48. BoS to Union Oil Co of California, Houston, TX, 12May48 with CofR 25May48. CofA 24Mar52 after all surfaces had been re-covered in Grade 'A' fabric and re-doped. CofA 28Feb53 at TFH:1,970hrs. Cvtd to 230hp Continental O-470-B power, with Hartzell HC82XF2B/8433 props, by McDermott 12May55. CofA 23May56 at TFH:2,809hrs (with engine hours at 155hrs). CofR re-issued as **N86638**, 22Aug56 on change of address in Houston, TX. Modifications for gross weight increase to 4,700lbs (water) and 5,400lbs (land), per STCs SA2-13 and SA2-284, carried out Sep61. Hayes brake and wheel assembly replaced by Cleveland wheels with disc brakes, per STC SA121EA, Feb71. BoS to James Noel Flying Service Inc, Lafayette, LA 01Dec75. BoS to Dean Franklin Aviation Inc, Miami, FL 09Dec75. BoS to Michael A and Adrienne Maxwell, Anchorage, AK 15Jly76 with CofR

C/n 1464, N86638, is a McDermott conversion with Continental O-470-B engines. Owned by Chester Lawson, it is seen here visiting Oshkosh, Wisconsin, in July 1993.   *(AJ Clarke)*

04Aug76. BoS to Lynn W Wyatt Jr and Ronald B Fowler, Anchorage, AK, 29Sep82 with CofR 13Dec82. Tfd by BoS to Lynn W Wyatt Jr as sole owner 10Feb83, with CofR 25Apr83. BoS to Robert R Taylor, dba Prospect Leasing, Anchorage, AK, 02Jun83. CofR applied for 03Jun83 but not issued until 31Jan84 when it arrived with the wrong owner's name on it! Richard R Taylor wrote to the FAA requesting that it be re-issued in his name but there is nothing in the file to indicate that it was re-issued. BoS to Cynthia A Capper, Anchorage, AK, 07Sep84 with CofR 11Oct84. Tfd back to Robert R Taylor, Anchorage, AK by BoS 15Oct84 with CofR 08Dec84. BoS to Leiann Denny, Anchorage, AK, 01Sep99 with CofR 17Nov88. Wings re-covered with Ceconite 101 material, per STC SA1351WE, Jun90. BoS to Chester M Lawson, Ponce Inlet, FL, 16Aug90 with CofR 12Sep90. Change of address to Port Orange, FL 20Sep91 and another to Daytona Beach, FL, with CofR 23Jly93. Rudder re-covered with Stits polyfibre P99, per STC SA1008WE, Apr99. CofR re-issued with another change of address to Port Orange, FL 18Aug12. Current and airworthy May13, with CofR due to expire 30Sep15.

1465   Built as **G-44A** and regd **NC86639** to Grumman Aircraft Engineering Corp, Bethpage, NY in 1948. Used as demonstrator and company hack. Accident 16Aug50: destroyed in aborted take-off at NAAS Mustin Field. Pilot, William J Cochrane of GAEC and civilian passengers, John Rowley and Roy Seligman. Aircraft took-off downwind and swerved off runway. Take-off was aborted but aircraft struck a runway light and became airborne. At about 30ft pilot decided that he was not going to clear wires and telegraph poles, and throttles were chopped. Pilot unsuccessfully attempted to ground-loop and aircraft continued on, hitting obstructions before coming to rest inverted on a rail-road embankment. Injuries but no fatalities.

1466   Built as **G-44A** 08Nov46 and regn **NC86640** allocated but ntu. Regd as **VH-AZO** to Australian Petroleum Co (Pty) Ltd, Sydney, Australia 08Oct46 for ops in New Guinea. FF 12Nov46 (as VH-AZO ?) with further test flights on 14 and 21Nov46. Shipped to Australia, at TFH:3hrs 35min, with Export CofA E-11202 13Dec46 and assembled at Rose Bay with CofA 29Apr47. Based Port Moresby, Papua New Guinea and operated by Qantas Empire Airways crews. Accident 09Aug47: damaged landing at Kariava, PNG. To Amphibian Airways, Invercargill, NZ 03Oct50. Accident 02Nov50: hull damaged when undercarriage collapsed landing at Sydney-Bankstown, NSW. Shipped as deck cargo on *"Aorangi"*, dep Sydney 07Dec50, arr Auckland, NZ 11Dec50. Assembled at Auckland-Mangere A/P and regd as **ZK-AVM** Dec50. Inaugurated services from Invercargill to Stewart Island on 20Mar51. Accident 24Dec52: overturned landing on Lake Wakatipu. To Tourist Air Travel Ltd, Auckland, NZ, 04Aug61. Cvtd by Tasman Empire Airlines, Auckland to **Super Widgeon** with 260hp Continental IO-470-D engines in 1962. Major damage at Auckland 24Oct63 in unknown circumstances. Accident 21Jun65: capsized and badly damaged landing at Mechanics Bay, Auckland. To Mount Cook Airlines, Christchurch, NZ Dec67. Accident 24Oct68: non-fatal crash landing with wheels down in Half Moon Bay, Stewart Island. Leased to Stewart Island Air Services Ltd, Invercargill, NZ, 01May76. Sold to Sea Bee Air, Auckland, NZ, Nov76. Shipped to Australia Jan79 for Peter Walker, Sydney, NSW. To comply with Australian Maritime Regulations the G-44A was registered as a power-boat with **AT373N** being applied to the bow of the aircraft. Loaned back to Sea Bee Air, Aug79, for services in the Fiji Islands, on behalf of Fiji Air, and based at Suva. Aircraft wore dual marks **ZK-AVM/ AT373N**. Shipped back to NZ, Jly81, wfu and stored dismantled at Mechanics Bay, Auckland pending a refit. Dep Auckland on del to Australia 25May87, arr Brisbane, QLD as ZK-AVM 26May87. To J Jones/Coral Wings, Cairns, QLD as **VH-WET**, 07Jly87. To Peter Sharp/Pacific New Guinea Lines, Rabaul, New Britain Mar94; and del Cairns-Rabaul 19Apr94. Australian regn cancelled 22Apr94 on sale to Massim Expeditions & Tours, Rabaul, PNG as **P2-WET**. Escaped the volcanic eruption in Rabaul 18Sep94 and del via Cairns 07Dec94 to New Zealand as **ZK-AVM**, to join ZK-CFA, c/n 1439 (qv), with Aquatic & Vintage Airways, Paihia Beach. To Owen Harnish, Auckland 01Jly96. To Grant Harnish, dba Salt Air, Paihia Beach in 1999; aircraft name: *"Snafu"*. To Owen Harnish, Auckland 25Jan01; noted hangared and partially dismantled at Auckland-Ardmore, Jan03. Under restoration at Whitford, near Auckland a/o Mar07. Sold to Warren Denholm, Auckland, NZ May12 and departed Whitford by road to Ardmore 11May12.

1467   Built as **G-44A** 21Jan47, with CofA 23Apr48 and regd **NC86641** to Grumman Aircraft Engineering Corp, Bethpage, NY 11May48. BoS to Leo M Biggs Inc, Detroit, MI, 30Jun48 with CofR 14Jly48, and later as **N86641**; CofA 16May53 at TFH:696hrs. Accident 19May53: crashed into Lake St Clair, MI. The aircraft had taken off from Detroit and the pilot, Lenis Hansen, was practising water landings. Hansen was killed, but the 2 pax escaped with minor injuries before the aircraft sank, a mile off the Canadian lakeshore, east of Windsor, ON. The wreck

was salvaged. The FAA file contains a spurious BoS from a J Perry to Virginia & Urbano DaSilva, Dexter, MI for $27,500. This was dated 17Apr85 and is followed by another BoS from Biggs to Urbano M & Virginia G DaSilva dated 29Apr87. This is followed by a CofR as **N86649**(2), 30Jly87. BoS DaSilva to Robert J Welsh, Pasadena, CA 18Feb88 with CofR 09May88; address change to La Mesa, CA 16Nov94 with CofR 07Feb97. In Oct98 the acft was completely overhauled and cvtd to **Super Widgeon** by Blue Max Aviation Service, San Diego, CA, with 295hp Lycoming GO-480-G1D6 engines and Hartzell HC-83x20-2C props. The following were also installed: auxilliary fuel tanks in wings per STC SA4-958, McKinnon spray rails per SA380WE, left and right rear picture windows per SA4-967 using drawing MPD-5042 in conjunction with Report MC-8, McKinnon landing light assemblies per SA4-964, metallised wing flaps per SA4-960 using McKinnon drawing MPD-2070, and McKinnon assembly parts for metallising wings aft of the spar per SA4-1031 using drawing MPD-2075. A Lee Mansdorf one-piece windshield was installed per SA4-2; a Whelen Engineering Co anti-collision strobe light system installation package per SA800EA, SA6NE & SA21NE; an Alcor exhaust gas temperature kit per SA522SW; the rudder, ailerons and elevator were re-covered with Ceconite 101 per SA1351WE and the elevator trim tab setting was changed per SA4-287 and McKinnon drawing MPD-8000. CofA 16Oct98 at TFH:696hrs. BoS Welsh to John T Benson, Naples, FL 27Sep99 with CofR 04Nov99. Current and airworthy May13, with CofR due to expire 31Jan16.

1468   Built as **G-44A** and regd **NC86642** to Grumman Aircraft Engineering Corp, Bethpage, NY. To US Dept of Justice, Washington, DC, Aug48, and later as **N86642** with DH Franklin Aviation Enterprises Inc, Miami, FL. To Skyways (Bahamas) Ltd, Nassau, Bahamas as **VP-BAX**, 14Oct58. Lsd to Bahamas Airways Ltd, Nassau, Bahamas 01Nov58. Cancelled from Bahamian CAR 07Oct59. To DH Franklin Aviation Enterprises as **N9312R**, 07Oct59. To Royal Ambassador Transport Corp, Miami, FL 04Nov59. To Dean H Franklin, Miami, FL 30Jan64. To Western Alaska Airlines Inc, Dillingham, AK 10May65. Cvtd to Continental IO-470 power with CofA 24May65. Sale reported 14Jan77 and cancelled from USCAR 08Mar78. Regn reserved for unknown owner 19Nov12.

1469   Built as **G-44A** and regd **NC86643** to Grumman Aircraft Engineering Corp, Bethpage, NY. To W Helis, New Orleans, LA May49. **N86648**(2) applied for by George Lambros Jr, Jupiter, FL 13Mar92. Unbelievably, that application was still pending in Jun12; aircraft non-airworthy and status uncertain. Cancelled from USCAR 14Aug12.

1470   Built as **G-44A**. BoS Grumman Aircraft Engineering Corp to Ben Smith, New York, NY, 27Jun47 with CofA same date and CofR **NC86644** 15Jly47. Believed to be acquired for use by the Israeli Air Force. Accident on 24Apr48: destroyed in a high-ground crash in Spain while en route Lisbon, Portugal to La Rochelle, France, sadly killing Leon Douzille (the manager of SCAN) and two others. Smith reported aircraft wfs 17Mar49 and cancelled from USCAR 24Mar49. (See also c/n 1426)

1471   Built as **G-44A** and reg **NC86645** allocated but ntu. Exported to Pakistan with Export CofA E-16086. To Government of East Pakistan as **AP-ADV**, Jan49 with CofA No 99. To Government of Bangladesh as **S2-ACB**, 1972 and cancelled from Pakistan register 13Feb74. Seen stored at Dhaka, 12Feb89. Regn cancelled 31Aug89. BoS (undated) Bangladesh Flying Club to Northern Aircraft Traders, Anchorage, AK (see also c/ns 1451 and 1474). Under restoration to **Super Widgeon** from Sep89 – Aug92 at Hillard Aviation, Fort Worth, TX. This included work under STCs SA4-60, SA4-61, SA4-65 (conversion to 270hp Lycoming GO-480-B1D engines), SA4-928, SA4-958, SA4-960, SA4-961, SA4-964, SA4-967, SA4-1001, SA4-1031 and SA121EA; a water rudder was also installed per Thurston Aeromarine Corp drawings, all of which allowed a CofA 01Aug92. BoS Northern Aircraft Traders to David H Lindow, Steamboat Springs, CO 10Jly92 with CofR **N888DL** 06Aug92. BoS to J Mesinger Corporate Jet Sales Inc, Santa Fe, NM 28Oct92. BoS to Strange Bird Inc, c/o CT Corp System, Wilmington, DE, 28Oct92. **N1471N** reserved 19Nov92, issued 04Dec92 and placed on aircraft 02Jan93. Accident at 1520hrs on 25Aug94: aircraft nosed over after being caught by a swell while on the step during take-off from water in Madaket Harbor, Nantucket, MA. Pilot, Jimmy Buffett, slightly injured and aircraft substantially damaged. TFH:6,176hrs. BoS to Dennis K Burke, Chelsea, MA, 18Nov94 with CofR 14Nov95. 350hp Lycoming TIO-540-J2BD and LTIO-540-J2BD with Hartzell HC-C3YR-2UF (-2LUF) props installed per STC SA4774NM, Nov02; auxiliary 21gallon fuel tanks installed per STC SA00182BO, Nov03. Regd **N3N**(2) (transferred from SCAN-30 c/n16) to Dennis K Burke, Vero Beach, FL 06Jun06, and placed on aircraft 26Jun06. Current and airworthy May13, with CofR due to expire 30Nov15.

1472   Built as **G-44A** and regd **NC86646** to Lloyd Alan Laflin, Castle Hot Springs, AZ Jun47. To Everbrite Electric Signs Inc, Milwaukee, WI as **N86646** with CofA 20Mar56. Cvtd to **Super Widgeon** with Lycoming GO-435 engines. To Carl H Wamser, Greendale, WI by Jan75. To John J Mark, Dunedin, FL by 1981. To MA Inc, Oshkosh, WI, 09Feb81. To Loughrea Maritime Inc, Charlotte, NC 23Mar00; on loan to Wings Over Miami Museum, Tamiami, FL 2004. To Executive Dogs Inc, Wilmington, DE with CofR 07Feb05. **N354Q** reserved 26Oct05 but ntu. Ownership was granted to Mirabella Aviation Inc, Fort Pierce, FL Jan07, after a court case against Executive Dogs Inc, Good Marketing Inc and Marvin Good. Offered for sale at auction by Mirabella at TFH:7,016hrs Apr07. Rebuild 50% complete Aug08, but still regd **N86646** to Executive Dogs, and status uncertain May13, due "undelivered Triennial". CofR due to expire 31Dec13.

1473   Built as **G-44A** and regd **NC86647** to Superior Oil Co, Houston, TX, Jun47. To Smith, Kirkpatrick & Co Inc, New York, NY. Sold to Ministerio de Defensa Nacional –Marina de Guerra, Havana, Cuba and del to Cuban Navy ex Miami, FL 28Dec52; allocated serial **81**, **82** or **83**. BoS Cuban Navy to Universal Trading Corp, Panama, Republic of Panama, 26Aug56. To JC Welsch, dba Welsch Aviation Co, Garden City, NY Aug56, with CofR **N4444W** Sep56. CF-WHT(2) allotted to Terry Machinery Co 17Sep56; authority to ferry Linden, NJ to Montreal, QC 19Sep57 and again 01Nov57. CofR(P) 17315 and CofA 6411 issued 07Nov57 for **CF-WHT**(2) to Terry Machinery Co, St Laurent, QC, replacing c/n 1213 (qv). N4444W cancelled from USCAR 06Dec57. Inspected and CofA renewed at TFH:3,415hrs, valid until 07Nov59. Reregd **CF-LGZ** 27Aug59. CofR(P) 20437 and CofA 7401 issued 08Oct59 to Commander Aviation Ltd, Montreal, QC. CofR(P) 20564 issued to HJ O'Connell Supplies, Dorval, QC 25Apr60; inspected and CofA renewed at TFH:4,102hrs, valid until 02May62. BoS O'Connell to Westfort Leasing Ltd, Fort William, ON, 16May61 and CofR(P) 26337 issued 18May61; inspected and CofA renewed at TFH:4,321hrs, valid until 02May63; at TFH:4,767hrs, valid until 01Jun66. Leased by Westfort to Superior Airways Ltd, Thunder Bay, Yukon Territory 09Nov65 for one year and CofR amended to Commercial 22Nov65. Inspected and CofA renewed at TFH:4,913hrs, valid until 13Jun68. BoS Westfort to Thomas G Smith, Guelph, ON, 16Aug67 and CofR(P) 43421 issued 30Aug67; inspected and CofA renewed at TFH:5,437hrs, valid until 13Jun77. BoS to Tim Donut Ltd, Oakville, ON, 04Apr77 and CofR(P) issued 14Apr77; inspected and CofA renewed at TFH:5,469hrs, valid until 13Jun78. Accident 15Aug77 at Lormer Lake, ON: on landing, after a flight from Kitchener, ON, aircraft started to porpoise and the right float dug in. Authority to ferry Lormer Lake to Toronto 01Sep77; inspected and CofA renewed at TFH:5,720hrs, valid until 19May86. BoS to BA Roger 17May86 and cancelled from CCAR 22May86. Reregd **N244BR** to Bruce A Roger, Seattle, WA, 09Jun86 with CofA 11Jly86. Reregd **N244GW** to John A & Linda E Schwamm, Anchorage, AK (to replace c/n 1475, qv) on Temporary CofR, T962336, 22May96 to expire 21Jun96. At EAA Fly-in, Arlington, WA, Jly02 and 12Jly03. Listed as "reserved" for Robert D Smith, 11Sep03, but still regd to John A & Linda E Schwamm Jan12. To Excalibur Air Service, Windham, NH with CofR 27Feb12. Current and airworthy May13, with CofR due to expire 28Feb15.

1474   Built as **G-44A** and regd **NC86648**. BoS Grumman Aircraft Engineering Corp to Ogden R Reid, New York, NY 06Apr48 with CofR 13Apr48; main cabin door re-worked, May48, to have opening in centre to permit in-flight photography. Cancelled from USCAR 11May50 as exported to Pakistan on CofA E-20244. To Government of East Pakistan, Dacca as **AP-AEA** Jan49 with CofA No: 103. To Government Aircraft Workshop, Dhaka, Bangladesh as **S2-AAA,** 1972 (although Bangladesh CAA stated that it was never regd, so maybe allocated but ntu?) and cancelled from Pakistan register 13Feb74. Stored at Bangladesh Flying Club, Tejgaon A/P, Dhaka from 1981 until Aug89; noted at Dhaka, in poor condition, 12Feb89. The Bangladesh Flying Club exchanged three Widgeons (c/ns 1451, 1471 and 1474) for two Piper Senecas with Northern Aircraft Traders Ltd, Anchorage, AK. Shipped from Bangladesh to Seattle, WA. Hillard Aviation collected aircraft from Seattle in Jan90 and transported it to their workshop at Meacham Field, Fort Worth, TX for restoration. BoS Northern Aircraft Traders to Aviation Rehab Inc, Euless, TX 06Dec93. Cvtd to **Super Widgeon** with Lycoming GO-480-B1D engines per STC SA4-65; other STCs used in refurbishment by Hillard Aviation were SA4-61, SA4-958, SA4-960, SA4-961, SA4-964, SA4-967, SA4-1001, SA4-1031 and SA121EA, culminating in CofR **N474JH** 17Mar94, with CofA 31Mar94 at TFH:5,231hrs. BoS to Latshaw Drilling & Exploration Co, Broken Arrow, OK, 25Mar97 with CofR 15May97. Noted at CAF Airshow, Midland, TX, Oct02. Current and airworthy May13, with an address in Tulsa, OK and CofR due to expire 31Jly14.

1475   Built as **G-44A** and regd **NC86649,** Sep48. BoS Grumman Aircraft Engineering Corp to Edwards Transportation Co, Houston, TX 02Feb49, with CofR 08Feb49, and later as **N86649**; CofA renewed 31Jan53 at TFH:1,114hrs; 22Feb56 at TFH:1,984hrs. Cvtd to **Super Widgeon** with Lycoming GO-480-C1D6 per McKinnon STC SA4-11, and landing lights installed per McKinnon STC SA4-964, Jun60. BoS to Joseph & Carol Lodato, San Jose, CA, dba Westholm Aviation, Crystal Bay, NV 08Apr71 with CofR 14Jly71. **N32BB** reserved 21Jun74 and placed on aircraft 29Jun74. Control surfaces re-covered per STCs SA2-16 and SA10008WE, and auxiliary fuel tanks installed per STC SA4-62, Jun76. BoS 01Jly76 transferred ownership to Joseph S Lodato, dba Westholm Aviation, Gardnerville, NV, with CofR 03Nov76. Cancelled from USCAR 13Mar81 as "destroyed/scrapped". Re-instated 21Aug82 to Westholm Aviation Inc, Gardnerville, NV. BoS Lodato to John A Schwamm, Anchorage, AK 13May84 with CofR 11Jan85. Accident 12Apr87: crashed into Santa Barbara Channel, at Ventura, CA. Aircraft stalled when pilot attempted low level pass over sailboat race, to take pictures. At circa 200ft, the pilot made a descending right turn and then levelled off. The aircraft stalled and although the pilot lowered the nose and added power, the engines did not respond in time to regain altitude and/or airspeed. The aircraft hit the water left wing first, caught fire and sank. The aircraft was not recovered. Two seriously injured; one uninjured. Cancelled from USCAR 06Apr88.

1476   Built as **G-44A** and regn **NC86650** allocated but ntu. To Government of Pakistan (East Bengal) as **AP-ADW**, Jan49, with Export CofA E-16087. Local CofA No: 100. Accident 19Sep49: sank after landing at Madaripur, E Pakistan. Written off and cancelled from register 04May50.

SCAN-30 Production List

01   Built as **SCAN-30** prototype with Salmson 8 AS-00 engines and regd **F-WFDM**, with FF Jan49. Accident 11Jly49: crashed into the River Seine at Les Mureaux, near Paris, injuring Jacqueline Auriol and others. Aircraft written off.

1   Built as **SCAN-30** and regd **F-WFHA** in 1949. FF believed 30Jly49. Fate unknown.

2   Built as **SCAN-30** Apr49 and prepared for storage; regd **F-WFHB** in 1949. Reregd **F-BFHB** (date unknown). To Alan H Sanstad, dba Intercontinental Aviation, 04Oct52. To Conair Corp, Montreal, QC by mid-1950s. Reregd **N63LM** to Lee Mansdorf & Co, Sun Valley, CA. Cvtd to **Gannet Super Widgeon** with Lycoming R-680E radials. Reregd **N63L** by 1960, and sold to Government of Pakistan as **AP-AMW**, Feb62 for use by the United Nations, with CofA No: 299. Cancelled from USCAR 06Dec62. Cancelled from Pakistan register 09May66. Fate unknown.

The second production SCAN-30, c/n 2, F-WFHB, pictured in 1949 shortly after completion. Note the type and manufacturer's construction number on the tailfin – a typical feature of French-built aircraft.

(PJ Marson Collection)

3 Built as **SCAN-30** Apr49 and prepared for storage. Regd **F-WFHC** 1949 and regn **F-BFHC** allocated but ntu. To Alan H Sanstad, dba Intercontinental Aviation, 04Oct52. To Conair Corp, Montreal, QC by 1954. BoS Conair to Lee Mansdorf & Company, Compton, CA 26Oct54. Cvtd to **Gannet Super Widgeon** with Lycoming R-680 engines. [On the application for CofA dated 20Oct59 the engines were described as R-680-E 3A, whilst on the Statement of Conformity dated, 13Nov59, they were R-680-13 with Hartzell HC-93Z20-2D1 props.] CofR **N62L** issued to Lee Mansdorf & Co 29Sep59. [Registrations N59LM to N65LM inclusive had been reserved for Mansdorf 27Oct55. The 'M' is omitted on all documents in the FAA file!] The Standard CofA was issued 13Nov59 quoting TFH: 0hrs. BoS to United States Missiles Corp, Sun Valley, CA 28Apr60, with CofR 25May60. BoS to Aircraft Leasing Corp, Chicago, IL 01Jun60, with CofR 27Jun60. BoS to Lee County Land & Title Co, Miami Beach, FL 30Nov62, with CofR 11Dec62. Aircraft name: "*Lucky Lee Jr*". To Lehigh Acres Development Corp, Miami Beach, FL 27Dec63, with CofR 06Jan64. [On an FAA Form 337, dated 30Mar64, the owner is noted as Tursair Executive Aircraft Services Inc of Opa Locka, FL. It is therefore likely that Tursair operated the aircraft for Lehigh Acres Development Corp.] BoS to Ned C Rice, East Hartford, CT 05Jun65, with CofR 28Jun65. Tfd by BoS to Ned C Rice and Janet C Rice (at same address) 18Dec84, with CofR 28Mar85. BoS to Steven M Taylor, Riverdale, MI 22Oct02, with CofR 03Dec02. Cvtd to 350hp Lycoming TIO-540-J2BD and LIO-540-J2BD engines as **Magnum Widgeon** in August 1991 (per STC SA4774NM) during 5½ year rebuild. **N540GW** reserved 08Dec08 (but CofR date is given as 03Dec02). Won the Silver Lindy Award at Oshkosh 2009. Current and airworthy May13, with CofR due to expire 31Jan16.

4 Built as **SCAN-30** Apr49 and prepared for storage. Regd **F-BFHD** to Société de Constructions AéroNavales du Port Neuf (SCAN) and CofA issued 21Jly50. Carried out a 20,000km sales tour of west Africa Nov/Dec50. To Alan H Sanstad, dba Intercontinental Aviation, 04Oct52. Equipped with 260hp Lycoming GO-435 engines it was re-designated **SCAN-30L** and test flown by Paul Mingam at La Rochelle during March 1954. Transferred to Mme Marie Therese Sanstad, Garches (wife of Intercontinental's Manager) 10Apr54, and registered to her, as F-BFHD, 17May54. Based at Toussus le Noble. Demonstrated by Alan Sanstad to Farner SA, Granges, Switzerland Feb55. Accident in Bieler See, Switzerland, 28May55: Sanstad and Willi Farner were practising water landings when the aircraft crashed and sank in about 25metres of water near Bienne. Sanstad was killed and Farner injured. It is not known whether the aircraft was recovered.

According to FAA files, however, the aircraft with c/n 4 was owned by Conair Corp, Montreal, QC by Oct54. Reregd **N4732V**, 07Oct54 with CofA same date. BoS Conair Corp, Montreal, QC to Lee Mansdorf, Compton, CA 26Oct54. In complete contradiction of the aircraft's French history, in a letter to the CAA, dated 09Feb55, Mansdorf stated that "*the aircraft was never registered in any foreign country, as it had never been completely assembled. I imported it incomplete without engines.*" Assembled with 300hp Lycoming R-680 engines as **PACE Gannet** with Experimental CofA 08Nov54. Lee Mansdorf request to FAA for reservation of N57LM to aircraft bearing N4732V, 09Dec54. Experimental CofA 16Mar55 at TFH:45hrs, and CofR for **N57LM** 25Jly55. BoS to Georgia Y Longini, dba Boats Inc, Chicago, IL 07Oct55, with CofR 16Nov55. CofA 07Oct55 claims "new aircraft with TFH:0hrs". BoS to Bestone Inc, Chardon, OH 21Jan57 with CofR 07May57. Reregd **N115WB** 12Feb58. New spray rails and nose bumper installed Jun59. BoS to Shebago Lake Shores Inc, South Casco, ME 30Jun69. BoS to Leisure Living Communities Inc, South Casco, ME (May70?). BoS to Arkansas Aviation Sales Inc, Little Rock, AR 05Feb71. BoS to Air Journeys Inc, Little Rock, AR 22Mar71 with CofR 06May71. BoS to Two Jacks Inc, Arlington, TN 19Oct72. BoS to Wells Aircraft Inc, Hutchison, KS 19Oct72 with CofR 27Nov72. BoS to Incon Corp, Roseburg, OR 20Apr73 with CofR 30Apr73. BoS Viking Air Ltd to Stanley C Hewitt, Ketchikan, AK 02Sep75 and BoS Incon Corp to Stanley C Hewitt 02Mar76 with CofR 25May76; address change to Wrangell, AK 19Jan81. Aircraft re-possessed by National Bank of Alaska 19Sep82 and sold to James D Perry, Kent, WA on BoS 19Sep82. BoS to Alan W Lyons, Sedro Woolley, WA, 03Sep83 with CofR 06Aug91. BoS to Mark L Taylor, Riverdale, MI, 18Jan92 with CofR 25Feb92. Re-engined with 350hp Lycoming TIO-540-J2BD and LIO-540-J2BD (per STC SA4774NM) as **Magnum Widgeon** 11Jun97. Reregd **N350GW** 29Nov99 and placed on aircraft 10Dec99 (but CofR issue date is 25Feb92). Won the Grand Champion Lindy Award at Oshkosh 2000. Current and airworthy May13, with CofR due to expire 31Dec13.

5 Built as **SCAN-30** and CofA issued 05Oct50. Regd to Société de Constructions AéroNavales du Port Neuf (SCAN) as **F-BFHE** 23Oct50. Delivered to Saigon, French Indo-China for use by the Escadrille du Haut-Commissariat, and operated on its behalf by the Armée de l'Air communications flight ELA 00.052 at Tan Son Nhut. Damaged in accident at Cao Lanh, southwest of Saigon, 29Dec51, and registration cancelled 24Apr54.

6 Built as **SCAN-30** and CofA issued 17Oct50. Regd to Société de Constructions AéroNavales du Port Neuf (SCAN) as **F-BFHF** 25Oct50. Delivered to Saigon, French Indo-China, for lease use by the Service de Santé, and operated on its behalf by the Armée de l'Air communications flight ELA 00.052 at Tan Son Nhut. Damaged in accident 25Jly51 off Cap Saint Jacques, near Saigon. Aircraft written-off and cancelled as destroyed 23Sep54.

7 Built as **SCAN-30** and CofA issued 13Jan51. Regd to Société de Constructions AéroNavales du Port Neuf (SCAN) as **F-BFHG** 05Mar51. Exported to Saigon, French Indo-China and operated by Mr Boyeaux (probably for the Emperor Bao-Dai). Damaged by fire in 1954 and aircraft wreck still at Tan Son Nhut A/P, Vietnam Aug57. Cancelled as destroyed 19Dec57.

8 Built as **SCAN-30** and regn **F-BFHH** reserved. Fate unknown.

9 Built as **SCAN-30** Jun49 and prepared for storage. To Alan H Sanstad, dba Intercontinental Aviation, 04Oct52. To Conair Corp, Montreal, QC by mid-1950s. BoS Conair to Lee Mansdorf & Co, Compton, CA 26Oct54. Overhauled Lycoming R680-13 engines fitted May56. **N59LM** requested 15Jun56, but **N62G** requested 22Jun56 and that N59LM should be reserved for future use. Aircraft modified per STC SA4-2 Jly56. CofA and CofR N62G issued 27Jly56 at TFH:5:45hrs. BoS to Ernest C Cockrell Jr, Houston, TX 28Jly56 with CofR 03Aug56. Aircraft inspected 05Nov58 at TFH:458hrs and 13Jan61 at TFH:822hrs. BoS to US Oil of Louisiana Inc, Houston, TX 21Feb61 with CofR 09Mar61. Reported at Aden 22Nov61 operated by The John Mecom Oil Co, Salif, Yemen. Aircraft "completely destroyed" at Taiz, Yemen 06Nov62 and cancelled from USCAR 01Mar63.

10 Built as **SCAN-30** Jun49 and prepared for storage. To Conair Corp, Montreal, QC by 1954. BoS to Lee Mansdorf & Co, Compton, CA 26Oct54. BoS to Franklin-Morse Aircraft Corp, Miami, FL 17Mar67 with CofR **N3923** issued 21Apr69 to Franklin-Morse at Utica, NY. BoS to Dean H Franklin Aviation Enterprises, Miami, FL 03Dec67. In response to an enquiry by the FAA, the company, now known as Morse Aero Inc, reported, on 25Oct71, that "N3923 is an uncompleted Grumman Widgeon hull". Cancelled from USCAR 02Jun75. Restored as **N3923** to Dean H Franklin Aviation Enterprises Inc, Miami, FL 11Jly98. BoS to Worldwide Aviation Distributors Inc, Miami, FL 17Nov99 with CofR 05Jan00. Current but not airworthy May13, with CofR due to expire 30Sep13.

11 Built as **SCAN-30** Jun49 and prepared for storage. To Conair Corp, Montreal, QC by mid-1950s. Letter from Canadian DoT 12Mar59 confirmed that c/n 11 had never been entered on the CCAR. Cvtd to **PACE Gannet**. BoS Tom Katsuda & J G Spielman to Charles M Kirk, El Rio, CA 13Sep62. CofR **N7918C** applied for 13Sep62 but not issued because not accompanied by relevant Bills of Sale, etc. Cancelled from USCAR 12Jan71 as "never registered", which begs the question as to why it was cancelled. The FAA file contains no airworthiness data.

12 Built as **SCAN-30** Jun49 and prepared for storage. To Conair Corp, Montreal, QC by mid-1950s. BoS to Lee Mansdorf & Co, Compton, CA 26Oct54. An affidavit, signed by Lee Mansdorf, certified that the aircraft was completed 07Jan59, and that "the aircraft has never been registered in a foreign country and has never been completely assembled until now." BoS to Walter J Davidson, J G Spielman, Charles H Harris and Tom Katsuda, Sun Valley, CA 07Jan59. BoS to Pacific Aircraft Engineering Corp, Sun Valley, CA 11Feb59. Cvtd to **PACE Gannet** with Lycoming R-680-E3 engines. An Experimental CofA was issued 13Feb59 to allow flight testing before certification, with CofR **N7911C** issued 18Mar59. Another Experimental CofA was issued 23Apr59 at TFH:35hrs, for "photography work", and Standard CofA issued 11May59. BoS to Peekskill Seaplane Base Inc, Peekskill, NY 02Jun61. BoS to James M W Martin, Greenwich, CT 23Jun61 with CofR 24Jly61. BoS Estate of J M W Martin to Airborne Attitude LLC, 09Nov06. BoS to Alpine Aviation LLC, Alpine, WY 20Nov06 with CofR 10Apr07. Reported non-airworthy a/o Feb11 and CofR expired 30Jun11. Fate unknown.

13 Built as **SCAN-30** Jun49 and prepared for storage. To Conair Corp, Montreal, QC by 1954. BoS to Lee Mansdorf & Co, Compton, CA 26Oct54. BoS to Franklin-Morse Aircraft Corp, Miami, FL 17Mar67 with CofR **N3924** issued 21Apr69. BoS to Dean H Franklin Aviation Enterprises Inc, Miami, FL 03Dec67. Cancelled from USCAR 13Oct93 as "destroyed/scrapped". Reregd **N672DF**, to Franklin 24Jun98. BoS to Worldwide Aviation Distributors Inc, Miami, FL, 17Nov99 with CofR 02Feb00. Current but not airworthy May13, with CofR due to expire 31Dec13.

14   Built as **SCAN-30** Jly49 and prepared for storage. Exported to USA and regd **N58LM** to Lee Mansdorf, Compton, CA 01Feb55. Cvtd to **PACE Gannet** with Lycoming R-680E-13 engines 1958. BoS to Richmond Pulp & Paper Co of Canada 15Dec58. Allocation of regn CF-LFQ to Richmond Pulp & Paper 09Jan59. US CofA for export E-37348 issued 05May59 at TFH:327hrs. CofR(P) 20319 and CofA 7361 issued to Richmond Pulp & Paper Co of Canada, Montreal, QC 08May59 for **CF-LFQ**. Authority to ferry St Johns, QC to Sun Valley, CA for repairs by Lee Mansdorf & Co 02Dec59. Inspected and CofA renewed at TFH:748hrs, valid until 05May61 and at TFH:2,262hrs, valid until 09May65. BoS to Garant Aviation Enrg 30Mar65. CofR(P) 33020 issued to Irenée Garant, Jean Marie Garant, Oscar Garant, Marcel Garant & Daniel Garant, St Francois, QC 09Apr65. Inspected and CofA renewed at TFH:2,703hrs, valid until 28Sep66. Leased by Garant to Quebec City Flying Club Inc Aug66. CofR amended to Commercial 26Aug66. Tfd by BoS from the Garant family to Garant Inc 12Dec66 and CofR(P) 37355 issued 30Dec66. Inspected and CofA renewed at TFH:2,760hrs, valid until 19Apr68. BoS to Marine Industries Ltd, Sorrel, QC, 23May67 and CofR(P) 42084 issued 25May67. Authority to ferry Quebec to Montreal, QC 07Jun68. Inspected and CofA renewed at TFH:2,781hrs, valid until 27Jun70. Leased by Atlas Acceptance Corp to Riverton Airways Ltd 10Jly69. BoS Marine Industries to Atlas Acceptance Corp 15Jly69. CofR(C) to Ilford Riverton Airways Ltd, Winnipeg, MB 14Aug69. Inspected and CofA renewed at TFH:3,208hrs, valid until 06Aug73. Reported Aug72 that "aircraft requires a thorough inspection due to corrosion from 2 years of outside storage". BoS Atlas Acceptance to Sam Allen Jr, Fort Frances, ON 24Apr73. Inspected 12Sep74 at TFH:3,330hrs but no CofA issued. Cancelled from CCAR 24Apr75. Reregd **N48011** to Sam Allen Jr, dba Frontier Enterprises Inc, Alexandria, MN, 30Jly75 with CofA same date. To John S Spencer, Indian, AK, with CofR 04Nov88, and reregd **N701Q** Jan91. Accident at 1520hrs on 09Oct04: substantial damage to both wings and the fuselage after forced landing in trees at Point MacKenzie, near Anchorage, AK, due to instrument panel fire. The pilot was heading for a dirt strip but was forced to land in trees due to the fire and smoke. TFH:4,100hrs. The pilot told the NTSB that he would leave the wreckage in situ until winter and use a sled to remove it once the ground was frozen. The aircraft was recovered and rebuilt and was sold to Wayne Alsworth, Port Alsworth, AK with CofR 08Apr13, due to expire 30Apr16.

15   Built as **SCAN-30** Jly49 and prepared for storage. To Conair Corp, Montreal, QC by mid-1950s. Exported to USA and regd **N60LM** to Lee Mansdorf, Sherman Oaks, CA in 1955. Cvtd to **PACE Gannet** with Lycoming R-680E-13 engines in 1959. Murdock Lumber traded their G-21A CF-JIF to United States Missiles Corp, Sun Valley, CA (Lee Mansdorf) for SCAN Widgeon N60L by BoS dated 08Aug59. CF-MLC allotted to Murdock Lumber Co 24Aug59 and authority to ferry Albany, NY to Montreal, QC 02Sep59. CofR(P) 20419 and CofA 7398 for **CF-MLC** to Murdock Lumber Co, Chicoutimi, QC 10Sep59. CofA renewed at TFH:219hrs, valid until 04Sep61 and at TFH:742hrs, valid until 05Dec64. CofR(C) 32747 to Airexec Services Ltd, Fort St John, BC 05Jun64. Accident at 1000hrs on 16Sep64: pilot, James W Burroughs, was attempting a take-off from Wasi Lake, BC, 165miles West of Fort St John, when engine failed and aircraft struck shore. Cancelled from CCAR 08Dec66. Retnd to USA as **N7913L** but fate unknown. CofR listed as revoked and registration assigned to a Beech A23-19.

16   Built as **SCAN-30** Jly49 and prepared for storage. To Conair Corp, Montreal, QC by 1954. BoS to Lee Mansdorf & Co, Compton, CA 26Oct54. BoS to J G Spielman, Tom Katsuda, Charles Harris & W J Davidson, Sun Valley, CA 16Mar59. Tfd by BoS to Pacific Aircraft Engineering Corp (same address), Sun Valley, CA 23Mar59, with CofR **N7912C** 20Apr59. BoS Katsuda & Spielman to Charles M Kirk, El Rio, CA 13Sep62. Aircraft repossessed by the Bank of America National Trust & Savings Association, Los Angeles, CA 03Jun63 and sold to Armette Ltd, Sun Valley, CA 08Aug63. BoS to Executive Aircraft Co, Broomfield, CO 13Aug63. CofR applied for by N C Swanson, Lander, WY 16Aug63 and issued 11Oct63, but, BoS Executive Aircraft Co to Executive Aviation Co, Broomfield, CO 08Oct63. Executive Aviation Co had financed the aircraft purchase and assigned it to The National City Bank of Denver. Experimental CofA issued 23Dec63 for "production flight testing" after conversion to **PACE Gannet** by Lee Mansdorf, with Lycoming R-680-E3 engines. CofA issued 04Feb64 at TFH:0hrs. CofR applied for by National City Bank of Denver 27Nov64 and issued 10Dec64. BoS National City Bank of Denver to Graubart Aviation Inc, Valparaiso, IN 10Mar66. BoS to

MG Christianson, Minneapolis, MN 14Mar66. BoS to Ohio Valley Aviation Inc, Wheeling, WV 25Apr66. BoS to Joe Speidel III, Kendall, FL 03Sep67. BoS to Dexter D Coffin Jr, dba Palm Beach Yacht Sales, Palm Beach, FL 05Sep67 with CofR 28Sep67. BoS to Carolina Aircraft Corp, Fort Lauderdale, FL 28Dec67. BoS to Stan Burnstein, dba Continental Aviation Co, Tulsa, OK 08Jan68 with CofR 02Feb68. BoS to Newell Enterprises Inc, Chadwicks, NY 01Mar68 with CofR 01Apr68. BoS to Cincinnati Air Taxi Inc, Cincinnati, OH 22Jly69 with CofR 10Sep69. BoS to Thomas H Noonan, dba Amphibious Sales Co, Cincinnati, OH 30Jly70. BoS to Maureen C Burke, Pembroke, MA, 30Jly70 with CofR 31Aug70. Plane Booster Inc droop wingtips installed Nov74 (as on Cessna 180/185, per STC SA957SW). Complete new avionics package installed Aug80. BoS Burke to Antique Aircraft Inc, Chelsea, MA 30Oct82 with CofR 10May83. CofR for **N3N** issued 21Feb86 and placed on aircraft 24Feb86. Experimental CofA 20Oct88 for flight testing after installation of 350hp Avco Lycoming TIO-540 engines, at TFH:1,730hrs. Another Experimental CofA issued 13Sep89 at TFH:1,774hrs. New TI-540-J2BD and LTI-540-J2BD engines fitted Oct89, with CofA 19Oct89 at TFH:1,780hrs as **Magnum Widgeon**. BoS to Dennis K Burke, Vero Beach, FL, 15Sep93 with CofR 14Oct93. **N3ND** assigned 14Feb06 and placed on aircraft 22Feb06. (N3N tfd to c/n 1471 qv). BoS to Tod V Dickey, Phoenix, AZ 25May06 with CofR 23Jun06. **N3TD** assigned 23Jun06, and placed on aircraft 23Jly06. Current and airworthy May13, with CofR due to expire 30Sep14.

17   Built as **SCAN-30** but no records found. (see below).

18   Built as **SCAN-30**. No records found but, with c/n 17, could be the "two flying boats" auctioned for scrap by Société de Constructions AéroNavales du Port Neuf (SCAN) in 1976.

19   Built as **SCAN-30** and regd **F-BGTD** in 1949. Cvtd to **SCAN-30G** by Paul Aubert & Legastellois at Buc. FF on 14May53. CofA issued 23Jun53. To Aero Club de France, Buc 01Jly53. Flight tested in UK by de Havilland (at Hatfield). To Charlotte Coulon, Pantin 23Mar55. To Soc Technicoptère, Paris, based at Toussus le Noble, 11Jly55. To Lake Air Charters Ltd, Mwanza, Tanganika as **VP-KNV** in 1956. To Irish Helicopters Ltd, (address unknown) as **EI-ALE**, 30Sep59. To Bruce Campbell Ltd, Hamble, UK as **G-ARIX**, 01Feb60. CofA issued at Biggin Hill 11May61 and aircraft del to Southampton 18May61. Accident 19May61: crashed landing off Calshot, Southampton Water. Aircraft overturned and partly submerged, beached at Hamble and written off. French regn cancelled, as scrapped, 16Nov71.

20   Built 20Jun49 as **SCAN-30** and prepared for storage. Reported regd **N7917C** to Intercontinental Aviation, Feb52 but BoS to Intercontinental is dated 04Oct52. To Conair Corp, Montreal, QC by 1954. Reregd as **N68596** to Lee Mansdorf & Company, Sun Valley, CA circa Jun57. Cancelled from USCAR 12Jan71. Fate unknown.

21   Built as **SCAN-30** Sep49 and prepared for storage. Reported regd **N7775C** to Intercontinental Aviation, Feb52 but BoS to Intercontinental is dated 04Oct52. To Conair Corp, Montreal, QC by 1954. BoS to Lee Mansdorf & Co, Compton, CA 26Oct54 with CofR 27Mar54 (sic). Cvtd to **PACE Gannet** with Lycoming R-680-E3 engines and Experimental CofA issued 11Mar64 for "production flight testing". Address change to Sun Valley, CA, by Mar64 and standard CofA issued 19Mar64 at TFH:0hrs. Accident 03Jly66: substantially damaged when struck submerged object on take-off at Lake Havasu, AZ. 2 crew received minor injuries. BoS to Executive Aero Inc, Eden Prairie, MN 29Mar68. BoS to Marvin E Tait, Port Huron, MI 15May69 with CofR 12Jan70. BoS to John R Gibbs, Rochester, MI 09Jly74, with CofR 24Jly74. BoS to Vacation Inc, Hollywood, FL 19May77 with CofR 22Jun77. Accident 04Jun77: damaged in water landing in Lake Okeechobee, FL, with right gear down. BoS to Airwing International Inc, Fort Lauderdale, FL 05Oct81 with CofR 14Dec81. Aircraft re-possessed by Vacation Inc 22Jun82 (with "BoS" dated 16Aug82) and CofR 21Aug82. However, another BoS, dated 24Aug82, transfers ownership from Airwing Intl Inc to Transportation Locators Ltd, Tulsa, OK with CofR 14Oct82. A BoS from Transportation Locators to Red Stevenson and an application for CofR, both dated 02May83, were not recorded by the FAA until 13Aug83. Meanwhile an accident occurred at 0837hrs on 05Aug83: crashed into Lake Winnebago near Oshkosh, WI during practice landings. A broken gear part caused right wheel to lower just before touchdown. Aircraft slewed to right violently and entire wing detached. Aircraft sank and written off. Three crew escaped injury. The NTSB report does not indicate the aircraft owner/operator at the time of the accident. CofR issued to Red Stevenson (dba Red S Aircraft Sales), Leonard, OK, 13Aug83. BoS to William E Harrison, dba Condor Aviation, Tulsa, OK dated 01Jly07(sic), but 1983 more likely. BoS to M & K Aviation Inc, Jeffersonville, IN 27Oct83. BoS to Patrick Murphy Aircraft Co, Warsaw, KY 17Apr86. BoS to R Wesley Valpey Jr, Center Harbor, NH 18Apr89; address change to White Salmon, WA with CofR 09Jan08. Current and airworthy May13, with CofR due to expire 30Sep13.

22　　Built as **SCAN-30** Sep49 and prepared for storage. To Alan H Sanstad, dba Intercontinental Aviation, 04Oct52. Reported exported to USA but owned by Conair Corp, Montreal, QC by mid-1950s. Fate unknown.

23　　Built as **SCAN-30** Sep49 and prepared for storage. To Alan H Sanstad, dba Intercontinental Aviation, 04Oct52. Reported exported to USA but owned by Conair Corp, Montreal, QC by mid-1950s. Fate unknown.

24　　Built as **SCAN-30**. To Alan H Sanstad, dba Intercontinental Aviation, 04Oct52. Reported exported to USA but owned by Conair Corp, Montreal, QC by mid-1950s. Fate unknown.

25　　Built as **SCAN-30** Oct49 and prepared for storage. To Alan H Sanstad, dba Intercontinental Aviation, 04Oct52. Reported exported to USA but owned by Conair Corp, Montreal, QC by 1954. BoS to Lee Mansdorf & Co, Compton, CA 26Oct54. Letter from the Canadian DoT 12Mar59 stated that the aircraft had not been registered in Canada. BoS to J G Spielman, Tom Katsuda, Charles Harris & W J Davidson, Sun Valley, CA 16Mar59. BoS to Pacific Aircraft Engineering Corp, at same address, Sun Valley, CA 28Apr59. Regd **N7913C** with Fairchild 6-440 engines, 29Jun59. The SCAN 30 was mortgaged to the Bank of America National Trust & Savings Association, and the Bank re-possessed the aircraft on 03Jun63 for breach of that finance agreement. Therefore the Bank was recorded as owner on the Bill of Sale dated 29Jan64 when ownership was transferred to S F de Yoreo, Fort Worth, TX. A CofR was issued 03Mar64. Address change to Bedford, TX 19Nov70. A Triennial Aircraft Registration Report was returned as not deliverable in Jly81, and the CofR was revoked by the FAA 12Feb82. Still listed as such until Aug12, but finally cancelled by FAA 10Sep12.

26　　Built as **SCAN-30**. BoS Centravia SA, Paris, France to McKinnon-Hickman Co, Portland, OR 28Sep55 with CofR **N2810D** 30Nov55 as **Super Widgeon** with Lycoming GO-480-B1B engines. To Reading Eagle Co, Reading, PA, by Jun63. To Reading Aviation Service Inc, Reading, PA. CF-SPA allotted to Wright Industrial Equipment 14May65 and authority to ferry Reading, PA to Edmonton, AB same date. BoS Reading Aviation to Wright with US CofA for export E-48742 17May65, and cancelled from USCAR 21Jun65. Lease from Wright to Pacific Western Airlines Ltd for 6 months 25May65. CofR(P) 32532 and CofA 10156 for **CF-SPA** to Wright Industrial Equipment Ltd, Edmonton, AB 28May65. CofR amended to Commercial 02Jun65. TFH:758hrs a/o 17Jun65. Leased to Pacific Western for a further 6 months, 26Nov65. CofA renewed at TFH:1,053hrs, valid until 17May67. Lease to Northward Aviation May66. Accident at 1610hrs on 24Jun66: veered off runway during take-off at Coppermine, NWT and hit sandbar. Aircraft substantially damaged but no injuries. CofA renewed at TFH:1,224hrs, valid until 12May72. BoS Wright to Raymond A Conant, Whitehorse, YK 25May71 (for $35,000) with CofR(P) 05Jly71. Accident at 1730hrs on 30Jly71: landed in glassy water conditions at Tin Cup Lake after a flight from Whitehorse. Aircraft started to porpoise then dived in and sank in several hundred feet of water. Wreck sold by British Acceptance Corp to Darrell Sapp, Wauconda, WA as salvage (sic), and cancelled from CCAR 28Mar72. Reregd **N7137N** to Clifford E Larrance, Port Townsend, WA, 29May90. Not airworthy and CofR expired 30Sep11. To Danae A Larrance, Port Ludlow, WA with CofR 22Mar12. Current but not airworthy May13, with CofR due to expire 31Mar15.

27　　Built as **SCAN-30**. BoS Centravia SA, Paris, France to McKinnon-Hickman Co, Portland, OR 28Sep55 with CofR **N2811D** 30Nov55. BoS to George M Brewster & Sons Inc, Bogota, NJ 20Apr56. Complete overhaul and cvtd to Lycoming GO-480-B1B power with CofA 01May56, and CofR **N50G** 24May56. BoS to Atlantic Aviation Corp, Teterboro, NJ 15Apr57. BoS to Maxwell Brace & Clarence See Jr, c/o Win Air Service, Syracuse, NY 15Apr57 with CofR **N58Q** 02May57. BoS to Land "N" Sea Airways, Syracuse, NY 18Jun57, with CofR 10Jly57. BoS to Rochester Enterprises Inc, Rochester, VT 15Jun61 with CofR 19Sep61. BoS to Eaton Lumber Co, Rochester, VT 31Aug66 (after the two companies merged) with CofR 27Mar68. BoS to Valley Aircraft Inc, Oriskany, NY 28Oct68 with CofR 19Feb69. Accident 13Jly69: aircraft porpoised and sank in Elusive Lake, Barrow, AK, after a flight from Sagwon, AK, operated by Interior Airways. Two fatalities and aircraft reported "destroyed" by NTSB. No Form 337s after 26May69, and cancelled from USCAR 24Jun76 for "admin reasons".

28　　Built as **SCAN-30**. BoS Centravia SA, Paris, France to McKinnon-Hickman Co, Portland, OR 28Sep55 and regd **N2812D**. Cvtd to **Super Widgeon** with Lycoming GO-480-B2B power with US CofA for export E-27755 and Canadian CofA 4778 both issued 27Jun56. BoS to Carl Millard Ltd, Toronto, ON 27Jun56. BoS to Department of Lands & Forests, Toronto, ON 12Jly56 at TFH:12hrs. CofR(S) 16412 as **CF-ODR** issued 17Jly56. CofA renewed at TFH:235hrs, valid until 27Jun58 and at TFH:514hrs (with Lycoming GO-480-B1B), valid until 04Sep59. CofA renewed at TFH:2,653hrs, valid until 03Aug69. BoS to Lorne Francis Corley, Islington, ON 19Mar69 with CofR(P) 46867 issued 27Mar69. TFH:4,402hrs reported on Due Date 03Mar01. BoS to Canadian Warplane Heritage, Mount Hope, ON 26Apr01 with CofR(P) 08May01. Noted displayed at Mount Hope Sep06. For sale at TFH:4,405hrs, Oct11, noting not flown since 2008. Still listed on CCAR Mar13.

29　　Built as **SCAN-30**. BoS Centravia SA, Paris, France to McKinnon Hickman Co, Portland, OR 28Sep55 with CofR **N2813D** 30Nov55. Cvtd to **Super Widgeon** with Lycoming GO-480 power Nov56, with CofA 28Nov56 at TFH:0hrs. BoS to Phillips Petroleum Co, Bartlesville, OK 21Jan57 with CofR 15Feb57. BoS to Jack Adams Aircraft Sales Inc, Walls, MS 03Dec62 with CofR 31Jan63. BoS to Graubart Aviation Inc, Valparaiso, IN 10Dec62. Re-possessed by Appliance Buyers Credit Corp 11Jly64, regd to them 28Jly64 and sold to North Country Airways Inc, Nashua, NH, 07Dec64 with CofR 29Dec64. Nominal change to North Country Management Corp, Silver Lake, NH, with CofR 15Mar73. Experimental CofA dated 13Jly76 for flight testing after cvtd to Lycoming GO-480-B1D power at TFH:2,588hrs. CofA issued 24Sep76 at TFH:2,600hrs. Aircraft dismantled by Nov99. BoS North Country Management to Susan Ann Goodwin, Trustee, Chelmsford, MA 22Nov99. BoS to Telford M Allen, Rockwood, ME 16Dec02. BoS to Oscar A Fontaine, Westport, MA 12May03, with CofR 03Dec03. Current and airworthy Jun12, with CofR due to expire 30Jun13. Regn application by Spearfish Aviation Inc, Summerset, SD 15Jun12. CofR issued to them 01Feb13 to expire 29Feb16.

30　　Built as **SCAN-30**. BoS Centravia SA, Paris, France to McKinnon-Hickman Co, Portland, OR 28Sep55. Cvtd to **Super Widgeon** and regd **N2814D**. To Louisiana Dept of Wildlife & Fisheries, New Orleans, LA in 1956. To Theodore G Voorhees, Delray Beach, FL, Jan77. To Seair Airways Ltd, Kissimmee, FL, Dec83. Reregd **N151SA**, Mar84 to Seair Airways Ltd, Nashua, WA. Cancelled from USCAR Nov86. To Aircraft Innsbruck Luftfahrt GmbH, Innsbruck, Austria as **OE-FWS**, Jan87. Overhaul by Dornier 1988 and flying as "308" at Innsbruck Oct90. Operated by Red Bull Enterprises, Salzburg, Austria from 1998 and on static display at ILA, Berlin, May02. Accident 29Mar05: crashed and sank north of Sirmione on Lake Garda, north Italy, after a flight from Salzburg, Austria, with 2 crew on board. No fatalities and aircraft salvaged and sold to Timothy R Martin, Anchorage, AK. Parts used in rebuild of c/n 1346. Remains to Edwin E Forsberg, Salem, OR 2008. Aircraft trucked from Alaska to California circa 01Jun12 for rebuild.

31　　Built as **SCAN-30** Nov49 and prepared for storage. To Alan H Sanstad, dba Intercontinental Aviation 04Oct52. Reported exported to USA but owned by Conair Corp, Montreal, QC 1954. BoS to Lee Mansdorf & Co, Compton, CA 26Oct54. Address change to Sherman Oaks, CA with CofR **N4453** 08Sep67. Cvtd to 300hp Lycoming R-680-E2 power, as **PACE Gannet**, with Experimental CofA 21Jun67 and Standard CofA 07Aug67. BoS to Executive Aero Inc, Eden Prairie, MN 29Mar68 with CofR 27Aug69. BoS to Business Aviation Services Corp, Spring Park, MN 15Jun70 with CofR 21Jly70. **YV-T-YTT** allocated Mar71 but ntu and cancelled Apr71. BoS to Aircraft Sales Inc, Charlotte, NC 02Jun72. BoS to Richard Bach, Long Beach, CA 18Jly72 with CofR **N4453**, 21Nov72. BoS to Creature Enterprises Inc, Bridgehampton, NY 10Jan73 with CofR 26Feb73. Used in TV series "*Fantasy Island*". BoS to Aztec Aircraft Inc, Long Beach, CA 04Nov74. BoS to James N Langley, Ashland, OR 04Nov74 with CofR 02Apr75. Address change to Redondo Beach, CA with CofR 24Mar78. BoS to Steven C Kreck, Carson City, NV 25May78 with CofR 06Jly78. BoS to Henry T Bermingham, New Orleans, LA 08Jun83 with CofR 23Aug83. Address change to Slidell, LA with CofR 07Dec83. BoS to Oklahoma State Bureau of Narcotics & Dangerous Drugs Control, Oklahoma City, OK 08Dec87 with CofR 25Feb88. BoS to Red Stevenson, Haskell, OK 23Jun88. BoS to Southwest Aviation Inc, Fairacres, NM 23Jun88 with CofR 01Aug88. BoS to Red Carpet Helicopters Inc, New Smyrna Beach, FL, 21Oct88. BoS to Vaughn W Crile, Washington, PA 21Oct88. BoS to Fred R Garrison, Needville, TX 08Jly89 with CofR 24Aug89. (TT=750hrs a/o 10Jly89 and operated by Rodney N Matthews.) BoS to Rod Aero Aircraft Brokerage Inc, Fort Lauderdale, FL, 21Oct91 with CofR 13Nov91. Returned to Fred R Garrison, Needville, TX by BoS 25Nov91 with CofR 16Dec91. BoS to ACE Aviation Inc, San Rafael, CA 24Jly98 with CofR 02Feb99. BoS (undated) to Leon C Felton, Sausalito, CA. BoS to Hudson Flight Ltd, Pampa, TX, 23Feb01 with CofR 19Jun02. BoS to Ozarks Auto Show Inc, Hollister, MO 12Nov02. Aircraft hangared at M Graham Clark Taney Airport, near Branson, MO. Dealer's Aircraft Registration Certificate expired 04Oct07. In May13, the registration assignment was listed as valid but with no CofR.

32 Built as **SCAN-30** Nov49 and prepared for storage. To Alan H Sanstad, dba Intercontinental Aviation 04Oct52. BoS Conair Corp, Montreal, QC to Lee Mansdorf & Co, Compton, CA 26Oct54. Cvtd to Lycoming R680-E3A power by Mansdorf & CofA issued 06Dec60 at TFH:0hrs. BoS to Tom Katsuda, dba Gannet Corp 22Dec60, with CofR **N7916C** 30Dec60. Experimental CofA 24Apr61 after cvtd to **PACE Gannet** with Lycoming R680-13 engines. CofA 31Jly61 at TFH:22hrs. BoS to Charles M Kirk, El Rio, CA 20Aug62 with CofR 06Sep62. BoS to Honorbuilt Trailer Manufacturing Co, Lakeview, CA 25Aug62 with CofR 14Sep62. BoS to Flightcraft Inc, Portland, OR 23Feb64. BoS to Arthur Eisele, Carson City, NV, 26Mar64 with CofR 15Apr64. Accident 25Aug64: aircraft "destroyed" after both engines failed, forced landed at Fairfield A/P, IA and gear collapsed. Pilot + 5 pax minor injuries. BoS to Mansdorf / US Missile Corp, Sun Valley, CA 27Apr65. BoS to Franklin-Morse Aircraft Corp, Miami, FL 17Mar67. Tfd by BoS to Morse Aero Inc, Utica, NY 12Jun68 with CofR 01Jly68; Experimental CofA 05May69 after cvtd to Continental IO520-E at TFH:62hrs; Experimental CofA 02Sep70 at TFH:72hrs and also 31Mar71. Accident at Chalk's Seaplane Base, Miami 05Aug71: pilot allowed nose to pitch down during take-off run on a test flight for engine approval. Aircraft nosed over with flaps full down. 2 crew uninjured, but aircraft substantially damaged. CofR revoked 24Nov71. Repossessed by Standard Bank & Trust Co, Evergreen Park, IL 01Feb72, with CofR 18Nov72. Reported "destroyed/scrapped" Dec73 and cancelled from USCAR 07Apr75. BoS Standard Bank to Morse Aero Inc, Utica, NY 23Mar75 and restored as **N7916C**, with CofR 05Apr75. Tfd by BoS from Morse Aero to Bob Morse Inc, Whitesboro, NY 01Jan77 with CofR 08Jly77. BoS to Donald J Anklin, Davidson, NC 27Apr78. Offered for sale by Aircraft Ltd in Jly78 at TFH:100hrs, fitted with 300hp Continental IO-520E engines, reversible propellers and retractable floats. BoS to Amphibians Mods Inc, Mooresville, NC 03Feb81. **N68PA**(2) applied for 03Mar81 but ntu and CofR for **N7916C** issued 04Jun81. BoS to Donald A Sumrall, Merritt Island, FL Jun82 with CofR 12Oct82. Reregd as **N78X** with special category CofR 18Dec82. BoS to Air Crane Inc, Pembroke Pines, FL Jan88 with CofR 15Jan88. BoS to Air Gold Coast Pty, Australia 25Apr88 and to Karl C Airlines undated. Both above sales declared null and void by Air Crane 24Jan91, and aircraft actually sold to Coral Sea Airways Pty Ltd, Mena, AR 25Sep90. Aircraft overhauled, fitted with Continental IO-470-UCM engines and gross weight increased to 4,860lbs with CofA 05Nov90 at TFH:2,387hrs. BoS to Dennis Michael Egelston, Mena, AR 16Oct91, with CofR same date. BoS to Wylde Wood Aviation Inc, Portsmouth, NH 20Jly92 with CofR 11Sep92. Experimental CofA 23Jun93 and annually until standard CofA 13Jan05 at TFH:2,645hrs (sic!). Current and airworthy Aug12, but CofR expired 30Sep12. Fate unknown.

33 Built as **SCAN-30** Dec49 and prepared for storage. To Alan H Sanstad, dba Intercontinental Aviation, 04Oct52. Reported exported to USA but owned by Conair Corp, Montreal, QC by 1954. BoS to Lee Mansdorf & Co, Compton, CA 26Oct54. Cvtd to **PACE Gannet** with Lycoming R680-E3 engines, with Experimental CofA 08Aug67 to show compliance with FAR. Production test completed 22Aug67 and Standard CofA issued 25Aug67 at TFH:4:44hrs, and regd **N4451** 08Sep67 as SCAN Type 30. BoS to Executive Aero Inc, Eden Prairie, MN 29Mar68. BoS to Great Circle Corp, Bellevue, WA 15May68 with CofR 17Jun68. BoS to Steve W & Mickie B Jones, Emmonak, AK 01Apr74 with CofR 30Apr74. BoS to John D H Johnston, Lake Stevens, WA 06Feb78 with CofR

17Mar78. Accident 27May79: on a flight from Wenatchee, WA to Lake Stevens, WA, pilot continued VFR flight into adverse weather conditions. The crash near Skynomish, WA killed the pilot & three passengers, and destroyed the aircraft. The wreck was recovered from a mountain slope 20Jly79. Cancelled from USCAR 30Aug82.

34 Built as **SCAN-30** Dec49 and prepared for storage. To Alan H Sanstad, dba Intercontinental Aviation, 04Oct52. Reported exported to USA but owned by Conair Corp, Montreal, QC by mid-1950s. BoS to Lee Mansdorf & Co, Compton, CA 26Oct54. CofR **N4452** to Lee Mansdorf & Co, Sherman Oaks, CA 08Sep67. Modified by Mansdorf & Co per STCs SA4-2, 4-53, 4-60, 4-61, 4-62, 4-63, 4-773, 4-774 and SA603WE. Lycoming R680-E3 engines fitted Sep67 to become a **PACE Gannet** with Experimental CofA, for test flying, issued 11Sep67, with Standard CofA 29Sep67 at TFH:6:50hrs. BoS to Executive Aero Inc, Eden Prairie, MN 29Mar68 with CofR 27Aug69. BoS to Lagoon Aviation Inc, Majuro, Marshall Islands, Micronesia 15Jun70. Auxilliary fuel tanks fitted Oct70 by Air Capital Intl Inc of Newton, KS, to allow ferry to Majuro via Honolulu, HI 28Oct70. Special flight permit allowed MTOW of 7,300lbs and max cruise of 140mph. Leased to Joseph Kramer, Majuro, Marshall Islands 12Jan71 with CofR 21Jan71. Accident at 0730hrs on 22Jan71: aircraft substantially damaged after pilot aborted take-off from Buckholz Army Field, at Ebeye, Marshall Islands, due to restricted elevator control; repaired Feb71. Accident at 1845hrs on 04Apr71: after a flight from Arno Atoll, aircraft landed at Majuro, Marshall Islands, taxied into a hangar and shut down engines. While the props were still wind-milling a person emerged from a door at rear of hangar and was hit by prop. Accident at 0845hrs on 01Aug73: after a flight from Majuro, Marshall Islands the aircraft landed on Arno Atoll lagoon and came to rest. The hull bow skin had separated during the landing and the aircraft sank and was not recovered. Pilot and three pax uninjured. Cancelled from USCAR 01Oct73.

35 Built as **SCAN-30**, but never completely assembled at the factory. Inspected by Bureau Veritas Dec49 and "prepared for long storage". An affidavit dated 15Sep56 confirmed "aircraft never registered in France or any other country". BoS French Ministry of Finance to Anthony Stinis & Olaf Abrahamsen, Jamaica Estates, NY 14Aug56 with CofR **N4120A** 25Sep56. BoS to Robert W Rehbaum, Scotia, NY 28Jan71 with CofR 18Mar71. Reregd **N10BR** 19Apr71. By Sep74 the following alterations had been made, per STCs: SA4-958 fuel capacity increased to 176 gallons total, SA4-53 allowable gross weight (land and sea) increased to 5,500lbs, SA2-559 emergency escape hatch fitted in right side of hull, SA121EA Cleveland wheels and brakes fitted and SA603WE entrance door enlarged (per Mansdorf drawings). Also both pilots seats and both middle seats replaced by adjustable pilots seats from a Cessna 337 and both rear seats replaced by pilot seats from Cessna Cardinal. The control wheel was replaced by one from a Cessna 337 Apr75. Ranger engines removed and replaced by Continental IO-470M Feb76. Cvtd to 300hp Continental IO-520E engines May78. BoS Estate of Rehbaum to Mohawk Ltd, Chadwicks, NY 15Oct90 with CofR 17Jun91. **N2GN**(2) assigned 19Jun91, placed on aircraft 01Jly91 and CofR issued 11Jly91. Experimental CofA 12Aug91; another 23Oct91 at TFH:14hrs and another 12Mar92 at TFH:25hrs. Cessna control wheel removed and original replaced May92. Further Experimental CofAs issued 29Sep92 at TFH:56hrs, 14Jan93 at TFH:76hrs, 14Jly93 at TFH:106hrs, 11May94 at TFH:109hrs and 09Nov94 at TFH:128hrs. Hartzell 3-bladed PHC-A3VF-2B/V7636N propellers fitted 01Dec94 per STC SA00268NY and a Standard CofA was eventually issued 20Dec94 at TFH:138hrs. BoS Mohawk to Albert H Burchfield, Pittsburgh, PA, 02Jan98 with Temporary CofR 05Mar98 to expire 04Apr98. PHC-A3VF props replaced with PHC-C3YF/FC8468-6R props and spinners Mar98. **N18GW** assigned

SCAN-30, c/n 33, N4451, re-engined with 300hp Lycoming R-680E radials, and re-designated PACE Gannet in August 1967. (via AJ Clarke)

SCAN-30, c/n 35, N18GW, owned by Albert H Burchfield, after suffering an accident is seen here at Muskoka, Ontario, Canada on 2nd November 2011. The aircraft's Certificate of Registration expired on 31st March 2011 and the aircraft was presumably scrapped. (Mike Ody)

SCAN-30, c/n 41, N4122A, after conversion to PACE Gannet, re-fuelling at Redhill, UK on 26th May 1979, en route from Zaire to the USA.
(Don Conway)

04Apr98, placed on aircraft 23Apr98, and CofR issued 24Apr98. Noted badly damaged at Muskoka, ON on 02Nov10. CofR expired 31Mar11 and presumed scrapped.

36   Built as **SCAN-30** in 1950. Cvtd to **SCAN-30G** and CofA issued 27Oct55. Regd to Commissariat Général à la Productivité, Cayenne, French Guiana, as **F-OARB**, 27Oct55. Advertised for sale by Aéronautique Legastelois, Paris, at TFH:20hrs, Jly56. Regn cancelled 23Aug56, on sale to USA. BoS French Ministry of Finance to Anthony Stinis & Olaf Abrahamsen, Jamaica Estates, NY 27Aug56 with CofR **N4121A** 25Sep56. Cvtd to Lycoming R-680E power. BoS to Agnes Ilardi, Rochester, NY 20Sep66 with CofR 30Jun67. BoS to Joseph P Ilardi, Rochester, NY 07Jly70 with CofR 14Sep70. BoS to Carl R Schwarz, Kent, WA 20Nov81. Reregd **N2701D** 16Feb82. **N890** assigned 20Mar82 with CofR 18Jan83. BoS to Stone Mountain Aviation Museum Inc, Clarkston, GA 28Dec87 with CofR 03Jun88. A spurious BoS transfers ownership from Mirabella Aviation Inc to Aircraft Specialities Inc, Fort Pierce, FL 15Jun07. Non-airworthy, and status uncertain a/o Aug08, due "undelivered Triennial". To Rochester Amphibian Inc, Rochester, NY, with CofR 19Apr11. Current but not airworthy May13, with CofR due to expire 30Apr14.

37   Built as **SCAN-30** Dec49 and prepared for storage. To Alan H Sanstad, dba Intercontinental Aviation, 04Oct52. Reported exported to USA but owned by Conair Corp, Montreal, QC by mid-1950s. **N4122A** allocated, but ntu (see c/n 41 below). Although not registered, ownership was granted to Mirabella Aviation Inc, Fort Pierce, FL Jan07, after a court case against Executive Dogs Inc, Good Marketing Inc and Marvin Good. BoS Mirabella Aviation Inc to Aircraft Specialities Inc, Fort Pierce, FL 15Jun07. Probably never registered and fate unknown.

38   Built as **SCAN-30A** in 1949, fitted with Salmson 8 AS-00 engines and CofA issued 03Oct52. To Dept de la Guyane, Cayenne-Rochambeau, as **F-OALL**, 20Jun53. Regn cancelled 19Oct60 as withdrawn from use. Fate unknown.

39   Built as **SCAN-30A** in 1949, fitted with Salmson 8 AS-00 engines and CofA issued 02Sep52. To Dept de la Guyane, Cayenne-Rochambeau, as **F-OALM**, 20Jun53. Regn cancelled 19Oct60 as withdrawn from use. Fate unknown.

40   Built as **SCAN-30A** in 1949, fitted with Salmson 8 AS-00 engines and CofA issued 01Oct52. To Dept de la Guyane, Cayenne-Rochambeau, as **F-OALN**, 20Jun53. Regn cancelled 19Oct60 as withdrawn from use. Fate unknown.

41   Built as **SCAN-30**, but never completely assembled at the factory. Inspected by Bureau Veritas Dec49 and "prepared for long storage". An affidavit dated 15Sep56 confirmed "aircraft never registered in France or any other country". BoS French Ministry of Finance to Anthony Stinis &

Olaf Abrahamsen, Jamaica Estates, NY 14Aug56 with CofR **N4122A**(2) 25Sep56, as a **Widgeon**. Cvtd to **PACE Gannet** with Lycoming R-680E engines, 1956. BoS to Marvin Dodge Baumgardner Inc, Bennington, VT 06Oct60 with CofR 12Jan61. Cvtd to Lycoming R-680-13 engines, by Lee Mansdorf Jan-Apr63, with CofA 09Apr63 at TFH:21hrs. BoS to Gayle Aviation Inc, Locust Valley, NY 14Nov64 with CofR 17Dec64. BoS to Lambros Seaplane Base, Ridgefield Park, NJ 12May66 with CofR 21Jly66. BoS to Gordon J Newell, Chadwicks, NY 04May67 with CofR 06Jun67. BoS to Modern Furniture Company of Greeneville Inc, Greeneville, TN 20Jly68 with CofR 29Oct68. BoS to Isabella Anderson Johnstone, Kinshasa, Republic du Congo 23Oct69. Noted on del to Zaire via Shannon, Ireland 19Oct69. Johnstone had married Barnes in Jan69, but died in May70. Gay George Barnes, Miami, FL thus inherited the SCAN in May70. On 08Mar72 the FAA revoked the CofR in the name of Modern Furniture Co of Greeneville Inc due to failure to sign FAA Activity Reports commencing Jly70. In the spring of 1976 John Neumeister from Sussex, NJ found N4122A at Kinshasa A/P, Zaire where it had been languishing for six years. Tracing the ownership of the Widgeon proved difficult but eventually it transpired that it was owned by a George Barnes who had allegedly flown the aircraft to Zaire on a CIA mission. Neumeister paid a mechanic to look after the SCAN by running the engines occasionally. The FAA file contains a BoS, dated 14Sep76, transferring ownership from the Modern Furniture Co of Greeneville Inc to the Modern Furniture Co of Elizabethon Inc, Elizabethon, TN. Another BoS, same date, transfers ownership from Modern Furniture Co of Elizabethon to Flying Sportsmen Inc, Sussex, NJ with CofR 20Dec76. Bizarrely the next BoS is from Flying Sportsmen to Gay G Barnes, Miami, FL 29Mar77 with CofR 01Jun77 and then, BoS dated 08May78, reverses the ownership to Flying Sportsmen Inc, with CofR 20Jun78. Later that year Neumeister flew to Zaire, with a friend, to ferry the aircraft back to the USA. They paid for the necessary permits to land in, or cross, all the countries in Africa on their route to England, where they planned to change the engines. That was the plan, but they blew an engine while crossing Sierra Leone and landed on the island of Sherbro, 75 miles south of Freetown. They were ferried out to Liberia in a Cessna 180, and returned to the USA. A year later Neumeister returned with engine parts but soon realised that the engine was beyond repair. Back in the USA he bought an engine for $6,000 and airfreighted it to Africa aboard the Pan Am flight that took them back yet again. Having fitted the new engine, they flew the Widgeon to Liberia, where Neumeister removed the propellers and again returned home, where he bought another engine for $6,000 and had the props overhauled for $3,000. Back in Liberia, the right engine was replaced and the props re-mounted. Neumeister and his brother Dave took off for the USA in May79. Routing was via Mauritania; Agadir, Morocco; Bordeaux, France (22May79); Heathrow-Redhill-Coventry and Prestwick, UK; (27May79) Reykjavik, Iceland; and Greenland arriving at Sussex A/P, NJ on 11Jun79. Neumeister cleaned the exterior back to bare metal and removed the interior in preparation for a complete restoration. To Carl H Ludwig, Irvington, NY, with CofR 06Nov96. Under restoration at Montgomery, Orange County, NY a/o Jly98. Current and airworthy May13, with CofR due to expire 31Oct15.

A formation of Mallards over an Idaho forest, led by N168WS (c/n J-5), with N730RS (c/n J-50) to starboard, NC2950 (c/n J-13) to port and with N7356 (c/n J-56) bringing up the rear. *(via Steve Hamilton)*

APPENDIX 3: G-73 MALLARD PRODUCTION LIST

In the following production list, all Bills of Sale to a new owner are from the previous noted owner, unless otherwise stated, although some ownerships have been repeated to aid clarity.
Certificate of Registration validity data for aircraft on the US Civil Aircraft Register is correct to May 2013.

Canadian Certificates of Registration were issued with suffixes denoting whether for Private (P) or Commercial (C) use.

Throughout the list, Canadian Airworthiness can be assumed to be continuous, unless otherwise stated. Airworthiness Certificates are only shown as renewed before and after either changes of ownership or accidents, and also to show total flying hours (TFH).

J-1   Built as **G-73** prototype, regd **NX41824** to Grumman Aircraft Engineering Corp, Bethpage, NY and FF 30Apr46. Approved Type Certificate No.783 was issued 08Sep46, aircraft reregd **NC41824** and used as demonstrator. Sold to Avalon Industries Ltd, (KC Irving), St John's, NL and exported with US CofA for export E-16666 dated 23Mar49. Regd **VO-ACC**, with CofR 35 dated 19Mar49 and CofA Val11. Reregd **CF-GPA** with CofR 7987 and CofA 3082 to Avalon 26Apr49. Inspected and CofA renewed at TFH:1,411hrs valid until 05Nov50 and at TFH:1,780hrs valid until 02Jan52. Accident at 0845hrs on 04Dec51: shortly after take-off from Millidgeville A/P, St John, NB on a flight to Quebec, QC the right engine caught fire. The pilot was unable to maintain direction with full power applied to the left engine, necessitating a reduction in power which, in turn, resulted in the aircraft losing height and striking trees which sheared off the left wing. No injuries but aircraft destroyed by fire. Cancelled from CCAR 09Jan52.

J-2   Built as **G-73**. CofA 1806 and CofR(P) 5324 issued for **CF-BKE** to McIntyre-Porcupine Mines (J P Bickle), Toronto, ON 28Sep46. CofR(P) 6916 to Maj Andrew P Holt, Montreal, QC 16Apr48. CofR(P) 9185 to Terence F Flahiff (attorney for Ontario Paper Co), Thorold, ON 19Dec50. CofR 19904 to Ontario Paper Co Ltd, Thorold, ON 30Sep58. Aircraft named: "*Celeste*". TFH:6,500hrs a/o 01Jan67. Inspected and CofA renewed at TFH:8,365hrs, valid until 02Oct71. BoS of 10% share from Ontario Paper to Continental Can Co 25May73. CofR(P) to Ontario Paper/Continental Can Co of Canada Ltd, Thorold, ON 06Jun73. Inspected and CofA renewed at TFH:8,989hrs, valid until 02Oct74. Nominal change 29Dec76: Continental Can Co became Continental Group of Canada Ltd. Inspected and CofA renewed at TFH:9,945hrs, valid until 16Dec78. Nominal change: Continental Group became Continental Can Canada Inc in 1983. Inspected and CofA renewed at TFH:11,289hrs, valid until 27May84. BoS for 90% from Ontario Paper to QNS Paper Co 24Jan84.

Inspected and CofA renewed at TFH:11,525hrs, valid until 27May85. CofR(P) to QNS Paper Co Ltd, St Catherines, ON 15May84. Inspected and CofA renewed at 12,556hrs, valid until 27May88. Nominal change: QNS became Quebec & Ontario Paper 12Jun87. CofR(P) issued 17Mar88. TFH:14,181hrs reported on Due Date of 27May93. Nominal change: Quebec & Ontario Paper became QUNO Corp 03Dec92. TFH:14,548hrs reported on Due Date of 27May95. Aircraft damaged (but no details known) and repaired 22Aug95. QUNO Corp amalgamated with Donohue Acquisitions Inc to form Donohue QUNO Inc 01Mar96 and another nominal change saw Continental Can Canada become Crown Cork & Seal Canada Inc, also in 1996. TFH:14,721hrs reported on Due Date of 27May96. CofR(P) to Donohue QUNO Inc (90%), Crown Cork & Seal Canada Inc (10%), Montreal, QC 31Dec96. Merger of Donohue QUNO with Donohue Forest Products to form Donohue Forest Products Inc 01Mar97. BoS (of the 10%) Crown Cork & Seal to Donohue Inc 08Apr97. TFH:14,841hrs reported on Due Date of 27May97. CofR(P) to Donohue Forest Products Inc, Montreal, QC 03Feb98. TFH:14,841hrs reported on Due Date of 27May98. BoS to Tanglefoot Wing & Wheel Co, Coolin, ID 06Oct98. Cancelled from CCAR on export to USA 22Oct98. Aircraft restored to original condition by Tanglefoot and regd **N12YZ** 23May00 and Transport CofA issued 03Jly03. Grounded by FAA after Chalk's crash in Dec05, but current and airworthy May13, with CofR due to expire 30Apr14.

J-3   Built as **G-73** and regd **NC2941** to Forstmann Woolens Co, Passiac, NJ 18Oct46. To Dearborn Motors Co, Detroit, MI 30Jun49, with CofA issued 08Sep49. Crashed on landing at Charlotte, NC and DBR 24May50, one killed and five pax injured. Remains sold by insurance company for $500 to State Airlines, Charlotte, NC. To Amphibian Parts Inc, (Dean Franklin) Miami, FL 20May59. Reregd **N2943**, 27Sep73. To Coastal Air Inc (Dean Franklin), Miami, FL, as **N41DF**, 18Jun80. Does not exist as a complete aircraft but could be rebuilt. "Grounded" by FAA after Chalk's crash in Dec05, and CofR expired 31Dec11, and presumed used for parts. Cancelled from USCAR 19Nov12.

J-4   Built as G-73 and regd **NC2940** to Capt Boris Sergievsky, New York, NY 18Oct46 and later as **N2940**. CofA issued 13Aug55. To Aero Commander Division of Rockwell-Standard Corp, Bethany, OK 21Dec64 at TFH:3,700hrs. Accident 12Feb65: substantially damaged by heavy landing on Lake Hefner, OK. ATR pilot taking rating test at controls. 3 crew + one pax uninjured. To Aircraftsman Inc, Oklahoma City, OK 14Dec66. To Jack Adams Aircraft Sales, Walls, MS 16Dec66 at TFH:3,741hrs. To Hart Stud Mill, Jasper, TX 28Aug67 at TFH:3,750hrs. Accident 12Jan69: substantially damaged when stalled during water take-off at Jasper, TX for what the NTSB reported as a "search and rescue" flight. Pilot + 2 uninjured. Reregd **N121SP** 25Apr69. To Dean Franklin Aviation Enterprises, Miami, FL 29Jun75 at TFH:4,741hrs. To Gregory R Board, Miami, FL, 16Jan76. Arrived Sydney-Bankstown, Australia as N121SP, 05May76. Reregd **VH-SPL** to South Pacific Airlines, Sydney, NSW 27May76 and cancelled from USCAR 16Jun76. Australian regn cancelled 23May77 and regd **N83781** to Mark R Board, Miami, FL, 20May77. Ferried to US from Singapore via France, UK (Jersey-Bournemouth-Hatfield 27Jan78; Kidlington 30Jan78 for radio checks and Prestwick 01Mar78) and Iceland 04Mar78. Aircraft named: "*Tropicbird*". To Jerry Harvey, Minneapolis, MN 10Mar78. To School Properties Inc, Minneapolis, MN 01May78. To ANTL Inc, and leased to Antilles Air Boats Inc (AAB), Christiansted, US Virgin Islands 11Dec78. Wfu by AAB, at TFH:7,000hrs, 11Sep81. To Chalk's International Airline, Miami, FL 24Sep81. To Virgin Island Seaplane Shuttle (VISS), Christiansted, US Virgin Islands 03Mar82 and in service 15Mar82. Reregd **N604SS** 20Apr82. TFH:9,515hrs a/o 20Mar85. Accident 28Oct86: crashed just after take-off from St Croix, US Virgin Islands, due to loss of aileron control. 1 fatal, 5 seriously injured and 9 with minor injuries. TFH:10,932hrs. Wreckage sold to Caribbean Airline Service for parts, May90. CofR expired 30Jun11.

J-5   Built as **G-73** Oct46 with FF 04Nov46 and CofA 05Nov46. **CF-GAM** applied for but ntu and **CF-EIZ** allotted to Toronto Globe & Mail, Toronto, ON 21Aug46. BoS from Grumman Aircraft Engineering Corp to The Globe & Mail 08Nov46. US CofA for export E-14650 assigned by the Washington office during the transition period when the preparation of Export Certificates was turned over to the Regional Offices. E-11228 issued 06Jan47 and cancellation of E-14650 was requested. CofR(P) 5887 and CofA 2190 both issued 12Nov46 to Globe Printing Co, Toronto, ON. CofA renewed at TFH:263hrs, valid until 12Nov48 and at TFH:1,309hrs, valid until 02Dec53. BoS to Canada Veneers Ltd, St John, NB 04Aug53 for $95,000 with CofR(P) 12236 06Aug53. Inspected and CofA renewed at TFH:1,322hrs, valid until 05Aug54. CofA renewed at TFH:2,729hrs, valid until 20Dec57. CofR(P) 15210 to Irving Oil Transport Ltd, St John, NB, 02Jan57 (replacing J-1, qv). CofA renewed at TFH:3,475hrs, valid

Mallard, c/n J-5, C6-BDW, in the early 1980s, when operated by Visair. The much-travelled aircraft is currently with an owner in Nevada. (MAP)

until 20Dec60. Cancelled from CCAR 21Jun62. BoS to Madden & Smith Aircraft Corp, Miami, FL, 16May62 with CofA 02Aug62 at TFH:3,501hrs and CofR **N74842** 22Aug62. Cancelled from USCAR 14Feb63 as exported to Panama. To Club de Pesca de Panama SA, Bay of Pinas, Panama and regd **HP-383** in 1964. BoS Club de Pesca de Panama SA to Club de Pesca de Panama, a division of Chemical Express Inc, Dallas, TX dated 03Apr64 but not signed until 01Sep66. BoS Chemical Express Inc to Jack Richards Aircraft Co Inc, Oklahoma City, OK 11Jly66 as **N74842**. BoS to Tulakes Aviation Inc, Bethany, OK, 15Jly66 and cancelled from HP- register 19Aug66. Regd **N168W** 07Nov66 and max allowable gross weight decreased to 12,500lbs 10Nov66 with CofA 18May67 at TFH:5,001hrs. BoS to Basler Flight Service Inc, Oshkosh, WI 28Sep67 with CofR 17Oct67. BoS to Business Aircraft Inc, Green Bay, WI 17Nov67 with CofR 20Dec67. BoS to Jack Richards Aircraft Co Inc, Oklahoma City, OK 09Feb70 with CofR 16Feb70. CofA suspended 09Oct70 and re-instated 27Nov70. BoS to Westernair of Albuquerque, Albuquerque, AZ 08Jan71 with CofR 26Jan71. BoS to Combs Aircraft Inc, Denver, CO 31Mar71. BoS to Edward F Dixon, Mt Carmel, PA 05Jun71 with CofR 30Jun71. Revoked 15Nov72 but re-issued 10May73. BoS to International Aircraft Fuel Ltd, Nassau, Bahamas 14Jun78 and cancelled from USCAR 03Jly78. Regd **C6-BDW** to Visair Ltd, Nassau, Bahamas in 1978. BoS to Smilax Ltd, Nassau, Bahamas 22Apr85. Aircraft based at Fort Lauderdale Executive A/P, FL after circa Mar86. CofA 23Jan87 at TFH:7,073hrs. Cancelled from Bahamian register 23Mar87. Reported regd **N15WJ** (not in FAA file) and offered for sale at Fort Lauderdale, FL in 1987 at TFH:7,073hrs. BoS to Trans American Executive Jet Inc, Fort Lauderdale, FL 14Jly89 with CofR as **N168WA** 01Sep89. BoS to John H Naysmith, Kent, WA 23Jly91 with CofR 17Sep91. BoS to Tropical Sea Air Co Ltd, Bangkok, Thailand 10Aug92. Cancelled from USCAR 27Aug92 and regd **HS-TPB** 31Aug92. Prepared for ferry flight in Canada and Camarillo, CA but never reached Thailand due to oil/fuel leaks preventing ferry flight. Noted stored engineless at Chalk's, Fort Lauderdale in Jly93. Thai regn cancelled Mar94. Bought at auction 05Apr94, by James Confalone, after Tropical Sea Air had been taken to court. BoS Chalk's to US Distributors Inc, Miami, FL 05Apr94 with CofR as **N168WA** 28Sep94 and reregd **N168TM** 30Sep94. Still at Fort Lauderdale, as HS-TPB, May96. BoS to Pantechnicon Aviation Ltd, Glenbrook, NV 19Nov96 with CofR 26Apr97. N168SW had been requested 26Mar97 and issued 05May97 but cancelled 25Jun97. Reregd as **N168WS** 25Jun97. Temporary CofA T97495 issued 05Sep97, with Transport CofA 08Sep97 at TFH:7,144hrs. Incident 01Oct97 at TFH:7,145hrs: nose gear collapsed during landing roll (circa 40knots) at Fort Lauderdale-Hollywood A/P, FL. Minor damage and no injuries. Address change to Ketchikan, AK 07Jan98 and to Portland, OR 06Sep00. Major overhaul at Victoria Air Maintenance, Sidney, BC Sep03. Pantechnicon address change to Minden, NV 26Aug04. Grounded by FAA after Chalk's crash in Dec05. Undergoing wing spar checks/repairs at Minden, NV Jun07. TFH:7,448hrs a/o Jly07. Cleared to fly by FAA 27Mar08 on a Temporary CofA, and FF after grounding, 09Apr08. Transport CofA issued (date not recorded) but current and airworthy May13, with CofR due to expire 31Jan14.

J-6   Built as **G-73** and regd **NC2943** to The Fuller Brush Co, Hartford, CT 27Nov46 and later as **N2943**. To Pacific Airmotive Corp, Burbank, CA 13May61. Arrived Tokyo-Haneda, Japan 12Jun61 and cancelled from USCAR 13Jun61. Regd **JA5090** to Toyo Menka Kaisha Ltd, Osaka, Japan in Jun61. To NITTO Aviation/ Toa Domestic Airways in Jun61. TFH:8,709hrs a/o Oct64. JA- regn cancelled 22Sep66. Regd **N7306** to Universal Trading Co (FB Ayer), Panama 13Sep66 and tfd to Frederick B Ayer & Associates Inc, New York, NY 13Sep66. Transport CofA issued 14Aug68. To Aircraft Holding Inc, Washington, DC 07Nov69. To Dean Franklin Aviation Enterprises, Miami, FL 02Apr70. To Chalk's International Airline, Miami, FL 28Aug72. Aircraft named: "*Island of*

Cat Cay". TFH:11,886hrs a/o Jan75. Wfu and stored at Fort Lauderdale, FL in 1983. To Virgin Island Seaplane Shuttle, Christiansted, US Virgin Islands in May84. Aircraft dismantled early 1985. To Dean H Franklin Enterprises, Fort Lauderdale, FL, with CofR 07Jan92. "Grounded" by FAA after Chalk's crash in Dec05 and remained in storage a/o Jan06. Listed as current and airworthy May13, with CofR due to expire 30Sep13.

J-7   Built 29Nov46 as **G-73**, CofA issued 19Dec46 and sold to Powel Crosley Jr, Cincinnati, OH 20Dec46. Regd **NC2944** and CofR issued 10Jan47. Radio equipment installed, and right wing repaired (reason unknown) 10Feb47. Address change to Crosley A/P, Sharonville, OH Oct47. Later as **N2944**. Authority to ferry St Louis, MO to Montreal, QC 18May54 and exported to Canada under export CofA E-20104 dated 20May54 via sales agent Remmert-Werner Inc, St Louis, MO and purchasing agents Babb Co Ltd, St John's, QC. Cancelled from USCAR 28May54. CofR(C) 13608 and CofA 4803 for **CF-HPA** both issued to Pacific Western Airlines, Vancouver, BC wef 21May54. Inspected and CofA renewed at TFH:2,520hrs, valid until 20May56 and at TFH:6,156hrs, valid until 06Apr60. Aircraft named: "*Kitimat Prince*". CofR(C) 18959 issued to BC Airlines Ltd, Vancouver, BC 15Jun59. Inspected and CofA renewed at TFH:11,120hrs, valid until 06Apr65 and at TFH:18,064hrs, valid until 14May71. BoS BC Air Lines to Abitibi Paper Co Ltd, Toronto, ON 20May70 for $75,000 with CofR(P) issued 24Jun70. Inspected and CofA renewed at TFH:18,275hrs, valid until 04Jly73. BoS to Dean Franklin, Miami, FL 08Mar73, for $85,000. Cancelled from CCAR 12Mar73. Regd **N17552** to Dean Franklin Aviation Enterprises Inc, Miami, FL 23Mar73 with US CofA dated 30Mar73. Regn **CF-HPA** allotted to North Coast Air Services Ltd 20Jun73. US CofA for export E-111236 issued 16Jly73 and authority to ferry Miami, FL to Vancouver, BC 19Jly73. BoS Franklin to North Coast Air Services 24Jly73. Inspected 30Jly73 at TFH:18,298hrs and cancelled from USCAR 09Aug73. CofR(C) issued to North Coast A/S, Prince Rupert, BC 11Oct73. Accident at 1630hrs on 05Mar74: on a flight from Seal Cove, Prince Rupert to Marsett, BC the aircraft became airborne after a longer than normal run (allegedly due to being overloaded). It then veered slightly to the left and then started a turn to the right. The turn continued for about 180° after which the wings levelled, but the aircraft was then heading towards steeply rising ground. It began to hit the trees at circa 425 feet above sea level and came to rest against a tree in a steep nose-down attitude, 2 miles SE of Seal Cove, BC. 3 killed (including pilot, Robert Norman Anderson, son of the company President) and 7 injured. Cancelled from CCAR 02Oct78.

J-8   Built as **G-73** and regd **NC2945** to Frank W Fuller, dba W P Fuller Paint Co, Hillsborough, CA 07Dec46 and later as **N2945**. CofA issued 27Oct55. TFH:4,221hrs a/o 15Jan67. To Reid W Dennis, Woodside,

CA 22Aug74 at TFH:5,260hrs. TFH:5,755hrs a/o 12Sep84. Grounded by FAA after Chalk's crash in Dec05. Current and airworthy May13, with CofR due to expire 28Feb15.

J-9   Built as **G-73**, regd **NC2946** 18Nov46, to Grumman Aircraft Engineering Corp, Bethpage, NY, and used as a demonstrator, including a trip to Tel Aviv, Israel, in 1947. To 20th Century Fox Film Corp, Beverly Hills, CA 23Nov48 and later as **N2946**. Featured in 1953 film "*Slattery's Hurricane*", which also starred Richard Widmark. Authority to ferry Los Angeles, CA to Vancouver, BC 21Sep54. BoS to Pacific Western Airlines Ltd 21Sep54. US CofA for export E-27625. CofA 5436 issued 23Sep54. CofR(C) 14895 issued for **CF-HPU** to Pacific Western Airlines, Vancouver, BC 28Sep54. Aircraft named: "*Kitimat Princess*". Accident at 1000hrs on 22Dec54: after a flight from Terrace, BC, the aircraft was approaching the ramp at Kitimat, BC when a gust of wind swung it off line. In attempting to line up again the nose-wheel struck the side of the ramp, causing considerable damage. Further damage was averted by pushing off into deep water and taxying back in on the centre of the ramp (pilot: LG Fraser). Inspected and CofA renewed at TFH:4,231hrs, valid until 22Sep56 and at TFH:6,684hrs, valid until 22Sep59. Accident at 1905hrs on 19Sep58: prior to take-off from Tofino, BC for a flight to Vancouver, BC the hydraulic pressure was normal but immediately fell to zero when gear up was selected after leaving the runway. The pilot, TM Kellough, made an immediate return to Tofino where an (unauthorized) repair was made. On arrival over Vancouver the undercarriage was selected down but

One of Grumman's G-73 demonstrator aircraft, c/n J-9, NC2946, visiting Tel Aviv, Israel in 1947. None of the type was sold in Israel, but two G-44As were supplied to the Israeli military in 1948.

(Guy Gudenkauf via NA3T Transport Photos)

C/n J-9, BC Airlines' Mallard, CF-HPU, seen in this pleasing shot in flight over British Columbia.   *(via H Scanlan)*

showed as "unlocked". A wheels-up landing was made on the grass but the aircraft ran further than expected and crossed the runway, damaging the keel. Inspected and CofA renewed at TFH:7,180hrs, valid until 20Apr60. BoS to BC Air Lines Ltd 25May59 included sale of 2 Mallards, 4 Norseman, equipment, wharves and docks plus transfer of ATB licences, for $400,000. CofR(C) 18960 issued to BC A/L, Vancouver, BC, 15Jun59, FN:101. Inspected and CofA renewed at TFH:8,194hrs, valid until 20Apr61, at TFH:12,815hrs, valid until 20Apr66 and again at TFH:18,587hrs, valid until 21Mar71. Permanent CofA granted. Lease to Pacific Western Airlines Ltd 01Sep70, with CofR(C) issued 24Sep70. TFH:19,949hrs a/o Jun71. BoS (for Mallards CF-HPU and CF-MHG) from BC Air Lines to Pacific Western Airlines 31Dec72. TFH:22,149hrs a/o Aug73. BoS to West Coast Air Services Ltd, Vancouver, BC 28Dec73 (Mallards CF-HPU and CF-MHG), but leased back to Pacific Western with CofR(C) issued 13Feb74. Inspected and CofA renewed at TFH:23,008hrs, valid until 15May75. CofR(C) issued to West Coast Air Services Ltd, Vancouver, BC 16May74. Sold to Gander Aircraft & Engineering Corp, Miami, FL 08Jan75 and cancelled from CCAR 28Jan75. Regd **N123DF** to Chalk's Flying Service (Dean Franklin), Miami, FL Jun75, at TFH:24,000hrs. Aircraft named: "*City of Nassau*" and renamed "*Island of Cat Cay*", Nov79. Cvtd to **G-73T** with UAC PT6A-34 engines and regd **N609SS** to Frakes Aviation, Cleburne, TX Nov84. FF after conversion 21Nov84 and Transport CofA issued 10Dec84. Del Cleburne-Houma-Fort Lauderdale-Caicos-St Croix for Virgin Island Seaplane Shuttle, 12Dec84. Roll-out after painting and final outfitting 26Dec84. Flew to San Juan for FAA inspection 02Jan85 and returned to Frakes, via Caicos-Miami-Fort Lauderdale-Gainesville (FL)-Alexandra (LA)-Cleburne, 18Jan85. FF after rework 29Apr85 and del Cleburne-Houma-Fort Lauderdale-Grand Turk-Caicos-St Croix 01May85. TT=33,340hrs a/o Apr88. Wfu at San Juan, PR Oct89, after damage by Hurricane Hugo 17Sep89. To Caribbean Airline Services Inc, Carolina, PR, May90 at TFH:35,000hrs. Leased to Sea Air Shuttle Inc, San Juan, PR Jan92. Returned to Caribbean Airline Services Inc, Carolina, PR 01Aug93. DBR when blown ashore while anchored off Venezuela in 1994. Aircraft dismantled and reported to have been taken to a "military airport". Presumed rebuilt and still listed as airworthy, but CofR expired 30Jun12. Cancelled from USCAR 11Oct12.

J-10   Built as **G-73**, regd as **NC2947** to Grumman Aircraft Engineering Corp, Bethpage, NY Dec46 and used as demonstrator. Hull damaged, and repaired Jly47. To Popular Mechanics (magazine), Chicago, IL 04Nov47, as **N2947**. Aircraft named: "*Apache III*". To Meurer Co Inc, New York, NY 10Dec48. To Bower Roller Bearing Co, Detroit, MI 13Dec48. Reregd **N294Z** to Federal Mogul Bower Bearings (nominal change) 29Jly55. TFH:3,770hrs at 28Sep55. To Federal-Mogul-Bower Bearings Inc (nominal change) 17Mar61. Accident 26Feb64: substantially damaged when gear collapsed landing at Clinton County A/P, Frankfort, IN. 2 crew + 3 pax uninjured. To Frakes Aviation, Angwin, CA 09Aug72 and restored as **N2947**. Allotted C-GHLA 31Oct74. BoS to West Coast Air Services, Vancouver, BC 18Nov74 with US CofA for export E-102219 and CofA issued 27Nov74. TFH:12,962hrs a/o 13Dec74. CofR(C) for **C-GHLA** issued to West Coast A/S 16Dec74. CofA renewed at TFH:15,343hrs, valid until 27Nov78. BoS to Amphibian Sales Inc (Dean Franklin), Miami, FL 26May78. Cancelled from CCAR 02Aug78 and regd **N26DF**. TFH:15,680hrs a/o 27Sep78. To Antilles Air Boats (AAB) Inc, Christiansted, US Virgin Islands 26Oct78. To ANTL Inc/Resorts Intl, North Miami, FL 27Oct78, at TFH:15,700hrs, and leased to AAB. Transport CofA issued 29Mar79. Wfu at TFH:17,721hrs, 11Sep81, and stored at St Croix. To Virgin Island Seaplane Shuttle, St Croix, US Virgin Islands and in service 15Mar82. Wfu due to severe wing damage during maintenance 03Apr84. Dismantled and shipped to Frakes for turboprop conversion, Jly84. To Associated Consultants Intl 28Dec84. Reregd **N610SS** in 1985, but not cvtd to G-73T. Sold to Frakes Aviation, Cleburne, TX, with CofR 24Sep91. Grounded by FAA after Chalk's crash in Dec05. Current and airworthy Aug12, but CofR expired 30Sep12. Regn still assigned to Frakes but cancelled from USCAR 11Mar13.

J-11   Built as **G-73** and FF 31Dec46. Regd **NC2948** to Grumman Aircraft Engineering Corp, Bethpage, NY and used as demonstrator. To Air Commuting Inc, New York, NY 09Jun47 and in service 25Sep47, at TFH:182hrs. Sold to Texas Co Inc, New York, NY for $80,000, 30Jun48 at TFH:240hrs. Ferried NY-Winston Salem-Houma, LA 05Jly48 and allocated FN:64. Later as **N2948** and CofA issued 06Apr56. Communications and radio navigation equipment modernised and weather radar installed at cost of $31,000 in Jan61. Reregd **N1628** by Jun63. TFH:6,985hrs a/o 17Dec66 and 10,243hrs a/o 18Jan75. Regd **N76DF** on sale to Dean Franklin, Miami, FL 20Sep83. To Virgin Island Seaplane Shuttle, St Croix, US Virgin Islands in 1984. Reregd **N611SS** and in service 21Mar85. Aircraft named: "*Tropic Bird*". TFH:14,175hrs at 26Mar85 and 16,886hrs a/o Apr88. To Caribbean Airline Services Inc, Carolina, PR May90. To Salvatore J Labate (trustee), Malvern, PA Jun91.

Leased to Sea Air Shuttle Inc, Carolina, PR Dec91. Re-possessed by Salvatore J Labate, Malvern, PA Sep93. To US Distributors Inc, Miami, FL 10May00. Severely damaged by Hurricane *Wilma* at Watson Island, FL Oct05. Grounded by FAA after Chalk's crash in Dec05. Offered for sale, "hurricane damaged, as is", for $125,000 Mar06. To Lake Air Inc, Fort Lauderdale, FL with CofR 18Apr06, but CofR expired 30Jun11. Regn still assigned to Lake Air Inc, May13, but fate unknown.

J-12   Built as **G-73** Jan47 with -S3H1 engines. Allocated for Air Commuting Inc, New York, NY with CofA 04Mar47, but not delivered. BoS Grumman Aircraft Engineering Corp to Joseph James Ryan, Arlington, VA 27Jun47, with CofR **NC2949** 08Jly47. Wing tip float fuel tanks installed Jly47, reinforced landing gear drag links installed to accommodate increase in gross weight to 12,750lbs, and CofA issued 04Aug47. BoS to General Tire & Rubber Co, Akron, OH 28Sep50. Engines overhauled and cvtd to -S1H1 standard by Pratt & Whitney with CofR **N2949** 31Oct50. CofA issued 05Jun51. Believed to be the General Tire & Rubber Grumman that crashed into Lake Erie off Ashtabula, OH 29Jun51, killing one of three on board. However, BoS to Malcolm A Miller, Akron, OH, 16Jun55 with CofR 05Aug55. BoS to Trade-Ayer Inc, Linden, NJ 30Jan56 with CofR 03Feb56. Cancelled from USCAR by FAA, 30Jan72. N2949 re-assigned to Malcolm A Miller, Akron, OH 29Jan96 and CofR re-issued 31Mar00 (for address change). Grounded by FAA after Chalk's crash in Dec05, presumed scrapped and CofR expired 31Mar11.

Mallard, c/n J-12, NC2949, was owned by JJ Ryan after the Air Commuting project failed.   (MAP)

J-13   Built as **G-73**. Regn **CF-FFG** allotted to Lord Beaverbrook 20Dec46. US CofA for export E-11301 issued 24Jan47. Tfd by BoS from Beaverbrook to Canprint Securities Ltd Mar47 and CofR 5638(P) and CofA 2043 issued to Canprint Securities Ltd, Montreal, QC (Beaverbrook) wef 25Jan47. BoS to New Brunswick Holding Co Ltd, Fredrickton, NB 30Oct47 with CofR 6518(P) issued 01Nov47. BoS to Herbert P Holt, Montreal, QC 09Jun48 for $125,000, with CofR(C) 7178 14Jun48. Inspected and CofA renewed at TFH:612hrs, valid until 08Sep51. BoS to Asiatic Petroleum Corp, New York, NY 02Apr51 and cancelled from CCAR 23Apr51. JZ-POA allocated Apr51, but ntu. Regd **PK-AKG** to Nederlandsch Nieuw Guinea Petroleum Maatschappij (Dutch New Guinea Petroleum Co - NNGPM), Babo, Dutch New Guinea, Apr51. Reregd **JZ-POB**, 15Jan55. Damaged in landing accident (location unknown) 28Sep56. Leased to de Kroonduif, Biak, Dutch New Guinea 25Oct59 until 31Aug60. Nose-gear collapsed landing at Mokmer 02Feb60. Operated by de Kroonduif for NV Ost-Borneo Mij Mar60, then wfu and abandoned at Biak, New Guinea 1960-62. To Peter Ahrens/East Coast Airlines, Brisbane, QLD 1962. Regn **VH-KWB** allocated Jun62 for East Coast Airlines, but ntu and operated by them as JZ-POB. Accident 16Jly62: an undercarriage failure, due to a broken hydraulic line, while trying to land at Brisbane-Archerfield after a flight from Redland Bay. Pilot, Peter Ahrens, returned to Redland Bay and made an emergency water landing with the port undercarriage down. To Trans Australia Airlines, Melbourne, VIC 16Jan62 and FF after overhaul Jun63. Reregd **VH-TGA** (CofR 3772) 13Jun63. To Utah Construction & Mining Co, Invercargill, NZ 02Sep63 and regd as **ZK-CDV**, 11Sep63 at TFH:2,300hrs. Del ex Melbourne 08Oct63 and arr Invercargill 17Oct63. TFH:4,031hrs a/o 11Jan66. NZ regn cancelled 21Feb69. Sold to Air Pacific Ltd, Suva, Fiji and regd **VQ-FBC**, 25Feb69. Aircraft named: "*Na Secala*". Regd **N2442H** on sale to Crow Inc, Toledo, OH 14Apr71 and dep Fiji same date. To Pelican Seaplanes Inc, Fort Lauderdale, FL, 15Dec73. To Barnett Leasing Co, Fort Lauderdale, FL 19Dec73 and leased to Seagull Air Service. To P M Davis, dba Seagull Air Service, Miami, FL, 09May75. BoS to R Slade 06Oct77. Authority to ferry Kalispell, MT to Hamilton, ON Oct77. Regn C-GRZI allotted to R Seaton, Bowmanville, ON 11Oct77. Authority to ferry Mt Hope, ON to Goderich, ON and return 07Apr78 (for painting and skin corrosion treatment). CofA and CofR(P) for **C-GRZI** issued to Reginald Slade, Burlington, ON 26Jun78 at TFH:5,295hrs. BoS Slade to Harold

Above: *NNGPM's second Mallard, c/n J-13, JZ-POB, mired in the mud at Sarmi airstrip on the north coast of Dutch New Guinea, some 160 miles west-northwest of Hollandia, after a night of heavy rain in 1958.* (Ch B Bär via HC Kavelaars)

Above: *C/n J-13 pilot JJ van der Plassche makes a low pass in JZ-POB to thank residents of Sarmi village for assistance in freeing the Mallard from the mud.* (Ch B Bär via HC Kavelaars)

Above: *Mallard, c/n J-13, C-GRZI, owned by RH Slade, at Mount Hope, Ontario, in June 1978. The G-73 was later operated by Chalk's, and Antilles Air Boats.* (Jack McNulty via Jennifer Gradidge)

Above: *C/n J-13, N2442H, while leased to Antilles Air Boats, leaving from Gate 1, Christiansted, St Croix, US Virgin Islands, on 7th February 1980. The member of the ground crew in the foreground appears to be holding the tail strut, while his colleagues have wheeled away the steps.* (Peter Vercruijsse)

Serpass, Dallas, TX 17Nov78, for US$199,999. Cancelled from CCAR 24Nov78 and reregd **N2442H**. To Chalk's International Airline Inc, Miami, FL 25Oct79. Leased to Antilles Air Boats (AAB), Christiansted, US Virgin Islands 1980. TFH:6,068hrs a/o Jun80. Returned to Chalk's when AAB ceased ops Sep81. For sale in Florida at TFH:7,125hrs in 1983. To Champlain Enterprises Inc, Miami, FL Oct83. To Kermit A Weeks, Tamiami, FL 01Aug84. To David B Robinson, Miami, FL Aug84. To Brinson Air Inc, Miami, FL Oct84. To Airport Facilities Inc, Miami Springs, FL Nov85. Sold back to David B Robinson, Miami Springs, FL Jan87. Noted derelict at Miami 26Jly87, but repaired and Transport CofA issued 30May90. To Amphibian Parts Inc, Miami, FL Oct90. To Steven T Hamilton, Carson City, NV Nov92. To Erickson Group Ltd, Vancouver, WA Dec92, but ntu. Restored to Steven T Hamilton, Reno, NV 17Jun93. Reregd **N2950** Mar98, but carries NC2950. Rebuilt to original specification by Victoria Air Maintenance, Victoria, BC in 2000. Only G-73 allowed to fly when the type was grounded by the FAA in 2006. Aircraft based at Minden, NV. Current and airworthy May13, with CofR due to expire 31Oct14.

J-14 Built as **G-73** and regd **NC2954** to Gar Wood Industries, Detroit, MI 15Feb47, and later as **N2954**. Leased to Howard Hughes and based Miami Intl A/P in 1955. Allegedly stolen from Miami Intl A/P on 01May55 and made forced landing in Everglades, west of Fort Lauderdale, with one main gear locked down. Aircraft trucked out for rebuild and CofA issued 29Dec55. Regd to Packer Pontiac, Detroit, MI 30Dec55. Accident 20Mar64: substantially damaged when gear collapsed on landing West Palm Beach, FL. Pilot + 3 pax uninjured. To Precision Valve Co, Yonkers, NY 23Dec66. To Walker's Cay Air Terminal Inc, Fort Lauderdale, FL 23Sep80. Aircraft named: *"Walker's Cay Clipper"*, and TFH:10,282hrs by 02Oct84. Sold to Roland Lafont, Albuquerque, NM 1993. Aircraft completely refurbished and repainted. To RBR Aircraft Inc, Albuquerque, NM May94. To Canyon de Chelly Motel Inc, Albuquerque, NM Oct94. Sold back to RBR Aircraft Inc, Albuquerque, NM 04Nov99. Grounded by FAA after Chalk's crash in Dec05. TFH:11,200hrs a/o 01Jan06. To Roland Lafont, Albuquerque, NM 08Mar07. Donated to Kalamazoo Air Zoo Museum, Portage, MI, with CofR 30Nov07. CofR expired 31Mar13. Displayed on museum's main campus.

Mallard, c/n J-14, N2954, owned by the Precision Valve Company, is seen here in Florida carrying the name "Walkers Cay Clipper". (MAP)

J-15 Built as **G-73** 07Feb47 and regd **NC2956** to Superior Oil Co, Houston, TX 08Feb47, with CofA issued 26Feb47. Wing float fuel tanks removed (land use only) 13Jun47 and long-range fuel system installed in cabin 21Oct47. Reregd **NX2956** and ferry permit issued 12Nov47 for delivery flight (pilot William C Seeger) via Gander-Shannon-Paris and Rome to Cairo, Egypt. Aircraft operated out of Cairo in support of oil exploration. Tanks removed in London, UK and reverted to NC2956 (05Jan48?). De-icing, radio and extra tank equipment installed at Dallas, TX 21Dec48. Aircraft named: *"Batta"*. Accident at 0100hrs on 28Oct49: after a night take-off from London-Heathrow, the aircraft reached a height of between 30 and 50 feet and then swerved to port approx 40° to the line of take-off. Height was lost and the undercarriage wheels struck the grass surface of the airfield some 150 yards from the edge of the runway. The aircraft continued across the airfield a few feet above the ground for a further 450 yards, and then crashed and burst into flames. Two crew and four pax killed; engineer, Mr OE Sivage, was injured. The Accident Investigation Report concluded that one cause of the accident was the fact that the aircraft was "grossly overloaded". Cancelled from USCAR 30Dec49 at TFH:1,200hrs.

J-16 Built as **G-73** Jan47 and allocated **NC2965**, for a US customer, but ntu. BoS Grumman Aircraft Engineering Corp to Algoma Steel Corp Ltd 14Mar47. US CofA for export E-14975 issued 19Mar47. CofR(P) 5398 and CofA 1863 for **CF-FOD** to Algoma Steel, Sault Ste Marie, ON both issued 24Mar47. CofA renewed at TFH:506hrs, valid until 09May51.

CofR 9287 issued to McIntyre Porcupine Mines Ltd, Toronto, ON 02Feb51. CofA renewed at TFH:589hrs, 09May52. BoS to Union Producing Co, Shreveport, LA 05Apr51, for US$142,500. Authority to ferry Toronto to Canadian/US border 05Apr51 and cancelled from CCAR 06Apr51. Regd as **N4949N** to Union Producing Co, Shreveport, LA in 1951. Accident at circa 1750hrs on 10Jan54: crashed near Wallace Lake, 10 miles South of Shreveport, after taking off from a duck hunting camp on Lower Mud Lake, LA, some 190 miles SSE of Shreveport. All 12 on board, including Tom Braniff, President of Braniff Airlines, were killed. The aircraft was destroyed by impact and subsequent fire. TFH:1,730hrs. Weather at the time was sleet and the probable cause of the crash was "rapid accumulation of wing icing to such a degree that the aircraft could no longer maintain altitude." It was also adjudged that the pilot, WC Huddleston, had not taken sufficient account of the weather conditions and forecasts.

J-17 Built as **G-73**, regd **NC2957** 28Feb47 and believed used by Grumman as demonstrator. Sold to George F Ryan, Newport, Rhode Island 04Mar47 and CofR issued 26Mar47. Wing-tip float tanks installed a/o 30Jly47. Ferry permit issued 15Oct47 for flight from Montreal, QC to Grumman, Bethpage for repairs (reason unknown). To D Murray Stewart (agent), New York, NY 31Dec47. To Grumman Aircraft Engineering Corp, Bethpage, NY 31Dec47, with CofR issued 29Jan48. Major repairs to wing and centre section stripped and completely rebuilt, and general overhaul 21Jun48. Wing and tail de-icing system installed 28Jan50. Sold to Bendix Aviation Corp, Detroit, MI 05May50, at TFH:1,500hrs. Reregd **N586** 08Jun50 and new radio equipment installed 22Jan51. Sold to Asiatic Petroleum Corp, New York, NY 10Jan52. Cancelled from USCAR 23Jan52. Fully overhauled, de-icing removed and auto pilot installed at Grand Rapids, MI 31Mar52. Regd **PK-AKH** to Nederlandsch Nieuw Guinea Petroleum Maatschappij (Dutch New Guinea Petroleum Co - NNGPM), Jakarta, Indonesia, Jun52 and ferried to New Guinea arriving 15Oct52. Wfu at TFH:5,623hrs circa 1959 and offered for sale through Shackleton Aviation in London. Also reported sold to Frederick B Ayer & Associates, New York in 1962. To Indonesian Air & Water Police Force 09Nov63, and given serial **PK-212** (see also J-35). Test-flown at Kemayoran (Jakarta) 18Mar64. Later re-serialled **P-2012**, but allegedly DBR 18May70. Fate unknown.

Mallard, c/n J-17, PK-AKH, of Shell's Jakarta administration, being pushed into the Hong Kong Aircraft Engineering Co (HAECO) hangar for overhaul in 1957. (JA Fierant via HC Kavelaars)

J-18 Built as **G-73** and regd **NC2958** to Tex-O-Kan Flour Mills Inc, Dallas, TX 08Apr47 and later as **N2958**. To Burrus Mills, Inc, Dallas, TX (nominal change) 24Feb52. Aircraft named: *"Milling Around"* and was operated at intervals by Ben Bransom Charter Service. To McLouth Steel

Mallard, c/n J-18, N98BS, owned by Jack Bart is seen here in 1999, looking immaculate and carrying the name "Tiloup du Lac". (MAP)

Corp, Detroit, MI 20Mar56, at TFH:2,744hrs. Reregd **N10M**, 29Mar56 and CofA issued 19May56. TFH:6,283hrs a/o 01Dec66. Reregd **N1002** at TFH:8,900hrs, 01Oct76. To Dean Franklin, Miami, FL 29Mar77 and reregd **N36DF**, 07Apr77. To Orange County Aviation, Santa Ana, CA 10Nov77. To Dr Ivan Namihas, Tustin, CA 23Dec77. Leased to All Seasons Air Pacific dba California Amphibious Transport or Trans Catalina Airlines, Dec77. Aircraft named: "*Spirit of Avalon*" and first service flown 15Feb78. Ops ceased Oct79. Reregd **N42DA**, 25Apr80 and aircraft named: "*Jonathon Livingston*". Stored at Merritt Island, FL from 1981. To Andy Stinis, Fort Lauderdale, FL for rebuild, Nov84. Regd **N98BS** to LAC Management (Jack Bart), Spotswood, NJ 26Oct90. Aircraft named: "*Tiloup du Lac*". Grounded by FAA after Chalk's crash in Dec05, but underwent wing re-sparring and FF after repairs 13Apr09. Current and airworthy May13, with CofR due to expire 31Jly15.

J-19   Built as G-73 and regd **NC2959** to Howes Bros Leather Co, Boston, MA 10Apr47. Nominal change to Howes Leather Co, Boston, MA 14Aug47 and later as **N2959**. Reregd **N123W** to Perfect Circle Co, Haggerstown, IN 03Dec51. Aircraft named: "*Magic Carpet*". To Trade Ayer Corp, Linden, NJ 04Apr51. To WB Osborn, San Antonio, TX 04Apr51 and reregd **N50Q** 25Apr51. Ferry regn **CF-KQZ** issued 17Apr58 for Carl Millard Ltd, Toronto, ON (agent). US CofA for export E-3668 and Canadian CofA 6778 both issued 29Apr58. Sold 12May58 to George W Crothers Ltd, Toronto, ON, and reregd **CF-JFC** with CofR(P) 19601 dated 05May58. CofA renewed at TFH:4,717hrs, valid until 29Apr60. CofR(P) 20513 and CofA 7423 issued for **CF-HWG** to Timmins Aviation, Montreal, QC 03Feb60. Leased to Spartan Air Services Ltd, Ottawa, ON 06Apr60. Cvtd to photo-survey aircraft and CofA renewed at TFH:4,871hrs, valid until 29Apr61. Carried out survey work in Seychelles. Sold by Timmins to Spartan Air Services Ltd 08Feb61, for $115,000. Sold by Spartan to Bristol Aero-Industries Ltd, Winnipeg, MB 08Feb61. CofR(P) 26473 issued 17Aug61 and CofA renewed at TFH:5,345hrs, valid until 09Aug62. Sold to Great Lakes Paper Co, Fort William, ON for $85,000 and CofR(P) 27290 issued 30Aug61. Cvtd from photo-survey back to standard configuration 29Sep61. CofA renewed at TFH:5,894hrs, valid until 07Feb66. Authority to ferry Long Island, NY to Fort William, ON 26Jan66. CofA renewed at TFH:6,454hrs, valid until 12Mar70. BoS to Northland Airlines Ltd, Winnipeg, MB 29Apr69. BoS to Midwest Airlines Ltd, Winnipeg, MB with CofR(C) 08May69. BoS to Courier Trading & Enterprises Ltd, Winnipeg, MB 06Aug69, with CofR(P) 19Aug69. CofA renewed at TFH:6,677hrs, valid until 08Jun71. BoS to Northland Fisheries Ltd, Winnipeg, MB 02Apr71, with CofR(P) 23Apr71 and CofA renewed at TFH:6,678hrs, valid until 08Jun72. To Edward F Dixon, Mount Carmel, PA as **N176W** 19Oct71 and cancelled from CCAR 25Oct71. Seized by Inland Revenue Service at Watson Island, Miami 29Nov72. To Dean Franklin, Miami, FL 26Feb73. C-GEFE allotted to Northwestern Flying Services Ltd, Nestor Falls, ON 29Apr75. Authority to ferry Miami, FL to Nestor Falls, ON 30Apr75. To James F Kayfes, Prescott, WI 01May75. BoS Franklin to Northwestern Flying Service (Kayfes) 01May75 with US CofA for export E-129933 issued 07May75. TFH:6,736hrs a/o 22May75. CofR(C) for **C-GEFE** issued 30May75. CofA renewed at TFH:7,179hrs, valid until 07Jun78. Returned to Dean Franklin, Miami, FL as **N95DF** Dec77, although a Canadian BoS, dated 05Jan78, transfers title from Northwestern Flying Service to Dr Ivan C Namihas, Villa Park, CA, dba Trans Catalina Airlines. Aircraft named: "*Catalina Clipper*" and Transport CofA issued 27Jan78. Cancelled from CCAR 30Jan78. Crashed 14Jan79 at Santa Catalina Island, CA and wfu at Long Beach, CA. To Dixon-Hill Aircraft Leasing Co, Santa Ana, CA 15Aug79. To Chalk's International Airline Inc, Miami, FL for spares 27May80. Fuselage and centre section to Frakes Aviation Inc, Cleburne, TX 01Feb83. Still regd Apr08, but status uncertain May13, due undelivered Triennial, although listed as airworthy, with CofR due to expire 31Dec13.

Mallard, c/n J-19, CF-HWG, of Spartan Air Services Ltd at Prestwick, Scotland in 1960, when the aircraft was used for a photo-survey contract in the Seychelles.					*(MAP)*

J-20   Built as **G-73** Mar47. Regn **CF-FLC** allotted to Hudson's Bay Air Transport 19Feb47. Authority to ferry from US/Canada border to Winnipeg, MB 03Apr47. BoS Grumman Aircraft Engineering Corp to Hudson's Bay Mining & Smelting, Winnipeg, MB 04Apr47 with US CofA for export E-15454 same date. Inspected 10Apr47 at TFH:21hrs. Tfd by BoS to Hudson's Bay Air Transport Ltd 10Apr47. CofA(R) 5697 and CofA 2095 both issued 11Apr47. CofA renewed at TFH:309hrs, valid until 20May49, at TFH:1,484hrs, valid until 07Apr54, at TFH:2,249hrs, valid until 15May59 and at TFH:2,657hrs, valid until 04Jun63. Destroyed by fire of unknown origin, in company hangar at Flin Flon, MB 04Apr63 (Otters CF-JOR and CF-KTI also destroyed). Cancelled from CCAR 11Jun63.

J-21   Built as **G-73** and regd **NC2961** to William E Boeing, Seattle, WA 22Apr47 and later as **N2961**. Aircraft named: "*Rover*". To Crowley Launch & Barge Corp, dba Puget United Transportation Companies, San Francisco, CA in 1960. BoS to BC Air Lines 14Mar60, for US$75,000. US CofA for export E-35647. CofA 7585 issued 29Mar60 and CofR(C) 23387 for **CF-MHG** to BC Air Lines Ltd, Vancouver, BC 19Apr60. Inspected and CofA renewed at TFH:1,928hrs, valid until 28Mar62 and at TFH:6,243hrs, valid until 28Mar66. Permanent CofA granted to Pacific Western Airlines 03Mar70 at TFH:12,656hrs while under lease. CofR(C) issued 24Sep70 to Pacific Western Airlines (under lease from BC A/L). FN:102. To West Coast Air Services Ltd, Vancouver, BC 31Dec73 and CofR(C) issued to Pacific Western 13Feb74 (under lease from West Coast A/S). CofA renewed at TFH:16,955hrs, valid until 16May75 and CofR(C) issued to West Coast A/S 16May74. CofA renewed at TFH:17,822hrs, valid until 15May76. CofR re-issued as **C-FMHG** 16May75. CofA renewed at TFH:20,087hrs, valid until 15May79. BoS JN Anderson to North Coast Air Services Ltd, Prince Rupert, BC 25Jun78 and CofR(C) issued 28Jly78. Inspected and CofA renewed at TFH:21,536hrs, valid until 02Sep83. BoS to Rileik (Corporation) SA, Panama City, Panama 02May84, for $125,000, and cancelled from CCAR 30Jly84. Reported regd **HH-RLA** in Haiti 1985 (for CIA ops). Regd **N775WA** to Worldwide Air Inc, Miami Lakes, FL Apr86 and CofA issued 20Jun86. TFH:22,114hrs a/o 20Aug86. To Wilson C Edwards, Big Springs, TX with CofR 17Jun87. Grounded by FAA after Chalk's crash in Dec05. Current and airworthy May13, with CofR due to expire 31Jly14.

J-22   Built as **G-73** (with R-1340-S3H1 engines). FF 18Apr47 and regd **NC2962** to New York Daily News, New York, NY 01May47. Later as **N2962** and dba WPIX Inc with aircraft named: "*Miss Daily News*". To Dean Franklin, Miami, FL in 1973, at TFH:4,422hrs. Allotted CF-HUB and authority to ferry Miami, FL to Vancouver, BC 07Dec73. US CofA for export E-111175 dated 19Dec73. BoS Franklin to West Coast Air Services Ltd, Vancouver, BC 31Dec73. Inspected 22Mar74 at TFH:4,479hrs and CofA issued. CofR(C) issued for **CF-HUB** 25Mar74, replacing J-7 (qv). Inspected and CofA renewed at TFH:5,792hrs (now with S1H1 engines), valid until 22Mar76. Certificates re-issued as **C-FHUB** 10May78. CofR issued to Air BC Ltd, Richmond, BC 28Jan81 (nominal change) and CofA renewed at TFH:11,020hrs, valid until 10May83. BoS to Kevin W Bowe, Santa Paula, CA 07Mar83, and cancelled from CCAR 10Mar83. To Air Whitsunday, Airlie Beach, QLD Mar83. Regd **N2416X** for ferry from Canada to Australia at TFH:11,286hrs. Departed Vancouver 09Mar83 (with J-26) and arrived Brisbane 12Apr83. Regd **VH-LAW** to Air Whitsunday, Airlie Beach, QLD 06May83. Aircraft named: "*Tropic Bird*". TFH:11,905hrs a/o Dec84. To Seair Pacific Pty Ltd, Airlie Beach, QLD (nominal change), dba Reef World Airlines, 1987. Arrived Darwin, NT 06Apr90 for Paspaley Pearling Co. Reregd **VH-PPE** to Paspaley Pearling Co Pty Ltd, Darwin, NT 06Nov95. Cvtd to **G-73AT** with CofA Feb98 (**see page xx**). From Mar06 operated for Paspaley by Lloyd Aviation Jet Charter Pty Ltd. Current Mar13 with TFH:23,767hrs.

J-23   Built as **G-73** Apr47 and regd **NC2964**. BoS Grumman Aircraft Engineering Corp to Superior Oil Co, Houston, TX 12May47, with CofA same date and CofR 21May47. Later as **N2964**. CofA renewed 14Jun52 at TFH:2,743hrs. Spray rails fitted 17Jan57, at TFH:4,680hrs. BoS to Lincoln 1st Federal Savings & Loan Association, Spokane, WA 28Nov62, at TFH:7,131hrs, with CofR 09Jan63. P&W R-1340-S1H1 engines installed Oct64. BoS to St Lawrence Aviation Co, Wilmington, DE 25Mar66, with CofR 06Apr66. Accident 11Apr67: substantial damage to flaps on landing in Hudson River, at Ossining, NY. Aircraft landed nose high into gusty headwind and 2ft waves. 2 crew uninjured. BoS to Gordon W Blair, Huntington Valley, PA 16Apr69, with CofR 19May69. Aircraft named: "*Patricia*". BoS to Dean H Franklin Aviation Enterprises Inc, Miami, FL 26Apr74. Cancelled from USCAR 07May74. Sold to North Coast Air Services Ltd, Prince Rupert, BC and CofR(C) as **C-GHDD** 15May74. CofA lapsed 28Jun83. To Waglisla Air, Richmond, BC by 1987. CofR(P) to Charles Rogers, Vancouver, BC 18Apr88. Cancelled from CCAR 09May89 and aircraft arrived Brisbane, QLD 10May89, still as C-GHDD.

Regd **VH-OAW**, 12May89 to Seair Pacific, Airlie Beach, QLD. Arr Darwin, NT 11Mar90 for Pearl Aviation, operated by Paspaley Pearling Co Pty Ltd. Reregd **VH-PPI** 28Feb02. Cvtd to **G-73AT** with CofA May05. (see page 46). From Mar06 operated for Paspaley by Lloyd Aviation Jet Charter Pty Ltd. Current Mar13 with TFH:22,900hrs.

J-24   Built as **G-73** and regd **NC2965**(2) to US Army Corps of Engineers, Vicksburg, MS 23Apr47. Aircraft named: "*Black Mallard*", later **N2965**. TFH:6,921hrs a/o 01Dec66. Tfd to Mississippi River Commission 01May70. To Dept of Interior, State of Alaska, Anchorage, AK 28Nov73, with CofR 07Dec73. Tfd to Office of Aircraft Services, AK 06Jan74. Restricted CofA issued for over-water and long-range survey flights at 1000lbs above normal gross weight, 09Sep74. Disappeared over Pacific Ocean en route Anchorage to Kodiak, AK 30Sep74; four on board missing. Presumed not recovered and cancelled from USCAR 18May76.

J-25   Built as **G-73** and regd **NC2968** to Chatham Manufacturing Co, Elkin, NC 09May47, and later as **N2968**. CofA issued 01May56. To J W Dowdle (Swift Air Service), San Diego, CA Jun62, and operated as Catalina-Vegas Airlines. TFH:9,745hrs a/o 11Nov66. Accident 27May67: crashed on take-off and sank off Avalon, Santa Catalina Island after porpoising in powerboat wake, and stalling on attempted go-around. Pilot killed; one crew + 2 pax seriously injured. Aircraft "destroyed". Salvaged and regd to Amphibian Sales Inc (Dean Franklin), Miami, FL, with CofR 05Jan88. "Grounded" by FAA after Chalk's crash in Dec05. Still regd Apr08, but status uncertain Feb13, due undelivered Triennial, with CofR due to expire 30Sep13.

J-26   Built as **G-73** and FF 23Aug47. Regd **NC2966** to Ben E Smith, New York, NY 27Aug47. Tfd to Ben E Smith/American Cosmopolitan Development Co, New York, NY 14May48. Aircraft named: "*The Golden Jennababe*". Tfd to Ben E Smith/Van Leer's Metal Products Inc, New York, NY 07Jly48. To Christian Dior New York Inc, New York, NY 28Apr50 as **N2966**, but based at Toussus-le-Noble, near Paris, and operated by Marcel Boussac, using the early post-war US radio call-sign "*WMHEZ*". Also allegedly operated by Bata Shoe Co, Bekcamp, MD in 1950s. TFH:556hrs a/o 16May57 and 1,659hrs by 1964. To GEMO Inc, 11Mar66, and dep Toussus-le-Noble 24Mar66 to USA, via Prestwick, 25Mar66. To Boyne Mountain Lodge Inc, Boyne Falls, MI 22Mar66. Cvtd to **G-73T** with PT-6A-34 turboprops by Frakes, with FF 29Jun72 at TFH:2,650hrs. BoS B & B Aviation Inc to West Coast Air Services Ltd, Vancouver, BC 19May75. US CofA for export E-102220 and CofA issued 02Jun75 with authority to ferry Cleburne, TX to Vancouver, BC 03Jun75. Arr Vancouver, BC 06Jun75 on delivery. TFH:3,148hrs a/o 26Jun75. CofR(C) for **C-GHUM** issued 27Jun75. CofA renewed at TFH:4,294hrs, valid until 02Jun77 and at TFH:9,398hrs, valid until 02Jun81. CofR(C) to Air BC Ltd, Richmond, BC 28Jan81 (nominal change). CofA renewed at TFH:11,776hrs, valid until 02Jun83. BoS to Kevin W Bowe, Santa Paula, CA 07Mar83 and cancelled from CCAR 10Mar83. Regd **N2419X** for ferry flight from Canada to Australia, and dep Vancouver (with J-22) 09Mar83 at TFH:12,508hrs. Regd **VH-JAW** to Air Whitsunday, Airlie Beach, QLD 13May83. Aircraft named: "*Frigate Bird*". TFH:13,427hrs a/o Dec84. To Vowell Air Services (Helicopters) Pty Ltd, Tyabb, VIC 28Jun85. To Helicopter Resources Pty Ltd, Tyabb, VIC (nominal change) 1987. Aircraft based Karratha, WA 1986-89, still named "*Frigate Bird*". Damaged in forced landing in Indian Ocean off Varanus Island, WA 25Aug88. Port wing torn away but repaired and back in service at Karratha Jan89. Del to Tyabb, VIC for storage Nov89. Regd **N73AH** to Aircraft Holdings Inc/Lloyd Helicopters, Miami, FL 04May90 and del ex Tyabb, VIC to Miami Jun90. Modified with front starboard entrance door and put up for sale. To Lloyd Helicopters (Singapore) Pte in 1992. Regn cancelled 16Jun94. Del Noumea-Cairns, QLD 04Jun94 and to Darwin, NT 05Jun94. Reregd **VH-JAW** to Paspaley Pearling Company Pty Ltd, Darwin, NT

24Jun94. Cvtd to **G-73AT** (see page 46) and reregd **VH-PPT** 09Apr01. CofA as G-73AT Jly01. Operated for Paspaley from Mar06 by Lloyd Aviation Jet Charter Pty Ltd. Current Mar13 with TFH:26,720hrs.

J-27   Built as **G-73** and regd **NC2969** to Vincent Astor, New York, NY 12May47, and later as **N2969**. Aircraft named: "*Flying Neurmahal*". CofA issued 17Jly56. To Freeport Sulfur Co, New Orleans, LA 30Apr59. Reregd **N200S** 08Oct59. TFH:3,450hrs a/o Jun63 and 4,695hrs a/o 11Feb67. Nominal change to Freeport Minerals Co 27Aug71. TFH:6,500hrs a/o 01Jly75. To Frakes Aviation, Cleburne, TX 26Jly76, for **G-73T** conversion per STCs SA2323WE and SA4410SW. Reregd **N2969** 12Apr80 and in service with Chalk's International Airline, Miami, FL 09Jly80. TFH:10,992hrs a/o 16May84. Aircraft named: "*Sunset Express*". To Flying Boat Inc, Fort Lauderdale, FL, Jan91. To Pan Am Air Bridge, Miami, FL 01Mar96. **N120PA** reserved Sep98, but ntu. World Pacific Air Lease Inc, Irving, TX 11Aug98 and leased to Chalk's. To Seaplane Leasing LLC, Coconut Grove, FL 08Dec99. To Seaplane Adventures LLC, Greenwich, CT 22Mar05 and leased to Chalk's Ocean Airways. TFH:31,219hrs a/o 05Dec05. Accident circa 1439hrs on 19Dec05: crashed into Biscayne Bay one minute after take-off from Watson Island, FL on flight CHK101 to Bimini. The right wing detached from the aircraft in flight, a fire started and the aircraft crashed into the water near a rock jetty. Two crew and 18 pax fatal, and aircraft destroyed. Preliminary cause due to metal fatigue cracking in wing spar. As a result the FAA issued Emergency Airworthiness Directive 2006-01-51 requiring detailed inspections of the wings of all G-73 aircraft, and the fleet was grounded (see **Chapter 5**). Scrapped at Atlanta, and cancelled from USCAR 10Jan11.

J-28   Built as **G-73**. BoS Grumman Aircraft Engineering Corp to Sid W Richardson, Fort Worth, TX 19Aug47, with CofA 19Aug47 and CofR **NC2970** 26Aug47. Two parachute flares removed (46lbs weight) 07Jan48. Later **N2970**. CofA 23Apr52 at TFH:1,662hrs. BoS to Union Producing Co, Shreveport, LA 05Mar54 with CofR 09Mar54. Major overhaul Mar/Apr54 with CofA 06Apr54 at TFH:1,777hrs. BoS to Coastal Aviation Co Inc, West Trenton, NJ, 22Mar65 with CofR 21Apr65. CofR 21Sep67 to Coastal Airlines Inc, Orlando, FL (nominal change). Accident 20Oct67: substantially damaged when left main gear collapsed on landing at Freeport, Bahamas. 2 crew + eleven pax uninjured; repaired Nov67. Re-possessed by Community National Bank (CNB), Rutherford, NJ 25Sep69. BoS CNB to Rand Broadcasting Co, Miami, FL 05Nov69, with CofR 30Jan70. BoS to Chalk's International Airline, Miami, FL 30Sep72, with CofR 20Oct72. TFH:7,700hrs a/o Jan74. Wfs 27Sep80 for major overhaul. BoS to Virgin Islands Seaplane Shuttle (VISS), St Croix, US Virgin Islands 01Aug84, with CofR 17Sep84. In service 24Mar85 and reregd **N628SS** 16Apr85. TFH:16,112hrs a/o 26Mar85 and 17,298hrs a/o Apr88. Wfu and parked at St Croix 1988. Substantially damaged by Hurricane Hugo, 17Sep89 and remains sold as scrap. Assets of VISS abandoned to Manufacturers Hanover Trust Co / CIT Corp and aircraft re-possessed 14Dec89 and sold to Caribbean Airline Services Inc (CAS), Carolina, PR 27Jly90. BoS to CAS Inc and Labate Aviation Inc (co-owners), Carolina, PR 15Nov90, with CofR 12Jly91. BoS to Flying Boat Inc, Fort Lauderdale, FL 30Jun92, with CofR 15Jly92. Mortgaged to United Capital Corp of Illinois 11Jan96. BoS to Air Alaska Commuter Holdings Inc, Hurst, TX 06Aug98. BoS to World Pacific Air Lease Inc, Irving, TX 06Aug98, with CofR 10Aug98. BoS Jeffrey H Mims, Chapter 7 Bankruptcy Trustee for World Pacific Air Lease to United Capital Corp of Illinois, Wilmington, DE 15Mar00, with CofR 04May00. BoS to Reg Stewart, Victoria, BC 28Mar06. Exists as parts only, but cancelled from USCAR 13Jun07 on export to Canada. Fate unknown.

Mallard, c/n J-26, N2966, owned by Christian Dior, visiting Cambridge, UK, on 31st May 1951. The aircraft was based at Toussus-le-Noble in France and used the early post-war US radio call-sign "WMHEZ" until at least the mid-1960s.   *(AJ Clarke)*

Mallard, c/n J-28, N2970, of Chalk's International Airline, looking the worse for wear at Miami-Watson Island, in March 1979. The Mallard was withdrawn from service in September 1980 for a major overhaul.

(Peter Vercruijsse)

J-29 Built as **G-73** and regd **NC2971** to Ford Motor Co, Detroit, MI 11Sep47 and later as **N2971**. Reregd **N304K**, Oct50. Sold to Ministère de la France Outre Mer Etablissements Français de l'Oceanie (French Government) 28Feb51 at TFH:1,200hrs. Regd as **F-OAII** 23Aug51 and operated by Air Tahiti. Aircraft named: *"Ciel de Polynesie"*. Badly damaged when struck buoy on take-off 18Mar53. Repaired. Accident 23Jly54: suffered an engine fire on the water at Bora Bora (replaced in service by Catalina F-OAVV). Eventually repaired, and test flown in October 1955. French registration cancelled 19Jan56, sold to William C Wold & Associates, New York, NY and returned to USA early 1956. **N10400** allocated but ntu (?). Aircraft offered for sale (at TFH:2,300hrs) from Jun56-Mar57. May have been scrapped or sold in South America. Fate unknown.

J-30 Built as **G-73** 16Sep47. BoS Grumman Aircraft Engineering Corp to The Texas Co, New York, NY 01Oct47, with CofR **NC3500** 09Oct47. In service 09Oct47 as FN:61, based at Houma, LA. Reregd **N1627** 17Mar52, with CofA 27Oct52 at TFH:2,234hrs. Major overhaul Aug/Sep55 and CofA 20Sep55 at TFH:3,564hrs. Name change to Texaco Inc, Teterboro, NJ 09Jly59. Radio communications and navigation equipment modernised and weather mapping radar installed, Feb61. TFH:7,623hrs a/o 17Dec66. Accident 23Jly68: substantially damaged due water loop after left wing float hit water during landing in shallow water at Grand Isle SPB, LA. 2 crew + one pax uninjured. TFH:11,159hrs a/o 31May77. Cvtd to **G-73T** with PT-6A-34 engines by Frakes Aviation, Cleburne, TX. Experimental CofA issued 04Aug80 at TFH:12,716hrs for test flights "to show compliance with FAR", and Transport CofA issued 15Aug80 at TFH:12,719hrs. TFH:14,334hrs a/o 01Oct84. Mallards J-30 and J-51 were "sold" to Frakes in exchange for a Beech B200 on BoS dated 07Jan86. Another BoS Frakes to Virgin Island Seaplane Shuttle, St Croix, US Virgin Islands, also dated 07Jan86 with CofR 13Mar86. Reregd **N630SS** 17Mar86 and placed on aircraft 21May86. BoS to Associated Consultants International, St Croix, US Virgin Islands 31Mar86, with CofR 25Sep86. Cvtd to airline configuration during 1990 for Flying Boat Inc, Fort Lauderdale, FL and operated by Chalk's. Re-possessed by Manufacturers Hanover Trust Co / CIT Group and sold to Frakes 11Sep91. BoS to Flying Boat Inc, Fort Lauderdale, FL 23Sep91, with CofR 24Sep91. Reregd **N130FB** 25Sep91 and placed on aircraft 29Apr92. Aircraft named: *"The Paradise Islander"*. Cvtd to 17 pax configuration with emergency exits per STC 4410SW, and bow hatch modified per STC SA4562SW, Jly92. BoS to Air Alaska Commuter Holdings Inc, Hurst, TX 06Aug98. BoS to World Pacific Air Lease, Hurst, TX 06Aug98, with CofR 06Aug98. Leased from World Pacific Air Lease to Air Alaska Commuter Holdings Inc 31Jly98 and sub-leased from them to Flying Boat Inc, dba Pan Am Air Bridge, 31Jly98. **N135PA** reserved 02Sep98, but ntu. BoS World Pacific Air Lease to Caribbean Airline Services Inc, San Juan, PR 11Sep98, with CofR **N130FB** same date. Re-possessed 05Aug99 by Jeffrey H Mims, Chapter 11 bankruptcy Trustee and sold to James Confalone. BoS Caribbean Airline Services to Seaplane Leasing I, Coconut Grove, FL 28Oct99, with CofR 02Dec99. Assigned to Ocean Bank, Miami, FL 28Oct99 with Flying Boat Inc as "permitted lessee" and leased to them same date. BoS Seaplane Leasing I to Seaplane Adventures LLC, Greenwich, CT 07Feb05, with CofR 23Mar05, but still leased to Flying Boat Inc, dba Chalk's Ocean Airways. TFH:27,182hrs a/o 05Dec05. Grounded by FAA after Chalk's crash in Dec05. Forfeited to K & J Aircraft Parts, in lieu of unpaid bills and lease to Flying Boat Inc terminated 17Jan08. Still regd Apr08. Reported by a Chalk's spokesman to be in the hangar at Fort Lauderdale Feb09, with wings removed to facilitate work on centre section. To West Coast Flying Boats Inc, Bear, DE with CofR 15Apr10. Current and airworthy May13, with CofR due to expire 31Jly14.

J-31 Built as **G-73** and regd **NC2992** to Charles B Wrightsman, Palm Beach, FL 20Jun47. To International Air Service Inc, West Palm Beach, FL 31Dec48 (still operated by Wrightsman) and later as **N2992**. To Lyon Inc, Detroit, MI 19Feb55. To J Curtis McKinney, Titusville, PA at TFH:4,300hrs, 06Mar61. To Kearney & Trecker Corp, Milwaukee, WI at TFH:4,500hrs, 11Feb64. Reregd **N1898T** 11Mar64. TFH:5,635hrs a/o 30Sep66. Reregd **N1888T** to John J Mark, Hales Corners, WI 31Dec73. To MA Inc, Oshkosh, WI 05Feb81. Transport CofA issued 27Apr88. Grounded by FAA after Chalk's crash in Dec05, but still regd Aug10. FAA reported "Certificate terminated", and registration pending following an application on 08Sep10, by Basler Turbo Conversions LLC, Oshkosh, WI. CofR issued to Basler 04Aug11. Current and airworthy Jun12, with CofR due to expire 31Aug14. CofR terminated due regn application 18Jun12 by Good Aviation LLC (at same address as Basler). CofR issued to Good Aviation 15Aug12. Current and airworthy May13, with CofR due to expire 31Aug15.

J-32 Built as **G-73** and regd **NC2972** to Burlington Mills Corp, Greensboro, NC 26Nov47, and later as **N2972**. To Beldex Corp, St Louis, MO 13Jly53. To Joyce Lumber Co (Beatrice Joyce Kean), Chicago, IL

28Aug53. TFH:3,888hrs a/o Jan55. CofA issued 09Jan56. Tfd to Beatrice J Kean, Grand Rapids, MI (nominal) by Jun63. To Flight Lease Inc, Columbus, OH 28May65 and leased to Crow Inc, Toledo, OH. Reregd **N298GB**(2) to Premium Service Corp (Carlson Companies), Minneapolis, MN 16Aug67. Cvtd to **G-73T** with PT-6A-27 engines at TFH:7,600hrs, 01Feb75. Re-engined with PT-6A-34 engines 24Mar75. Accident 11Jly77: crashed at Great Bear Lake, NWT. Seven on board safe, aircraft salvaged and rebuilt by Waco Airmotive, Waco, TX circa 1978. Regd to Royal Aviation, Unionville, MO 01Feb79. To Frakes Aviation, Cleburne, TX 27Feb84 for conversion to airline configuration for Virgin Islands Seaplane Shuttle (VISS), Christiansted, US Virgin Islands. Tfd to Associated Consultants International (VISS) 27Aug84 FF post conversion 24Mar85 and reregd **N632SS** same date. Ferried "green" Cleburne-Houma-Fort Lauderdale-Caicos-St Croix, 04Apr85 at TFH:8,171hrs. FF after painting 19Apr85 and in service to St Thomas 26Apr85. First service St Thomas-San Juan, 01May85. TFH:12,510hrs a/o Apr88. Substantially damaged by Hurricane *Hugo*, 16Sep89. To Caribbean Airline Services Inc, Carolina, PR Jly91. To Flying Boat Inc, Fort Lauderdale, FL Jly92. To Caribbean Airline Services Inc, Carolina, PR 30Jun98. To World Pacific Air Lease Inc, Irving, TX 11Aug98 and leased to Chalk's. To James Confalone Jr, Rye Beach, NH, with CofR 30Nov05. Grounded by FAA after Chalk's crash in Dec05. The aircraft was listed as current and airworthy until the CofR expired 31Mar13.

J-33 Built as **G-73** 18Dec47. Allotted CF-GEU 31Oct47. BoS Grumman Aircraft Engineering Corp to Ontario Hydro-Electric Power Commission, Toronto, ON 22Dec47, for $115,000. US CofA for export E-16037 issued 09Jan48. CofR(C) 6710 as **CF-GEU** and CofA 2656, both issued 24Dec47. CofA renewed at TFH:868hrs, valid until 28Jan51. CofR amended to Private 23Jan51. CofA renewed at TFH:2,417hrs, valid until 07Feb55. Accident 14Jan55: whilst en route from Windsor A/P, ON to Toronto, experienced heavy icing and attempted a precautionary landing at London (Crumlin) A/P, but lowering the undercarriage imposed additional drag. The aircraft stalled in close proximity to the ground and crashed at midnight at West Nissouri, ON, due North of the airport and 4,800ft from the East-West runway. The severe impact was with left wing down and slightly nose down. Robert Saunders, Chairman of Ontario Hydro died of his injuries, and aircraft was written off. TFH:2,595hrs. Cancelled from CCAR 28Sep55.

Mallard, c/n J-33, CF-GEU, operated by the Ontario Hydro-Electric Power Commission, is seen here at an unknown location, circa 1950.
(Ken Molson via Jennifer Gradidge)

J-34 Built as **G-73** and sold to Canadian Breweries Ltd, Toronto, ON 09Jan48. CofA 2661 and CofR(P) 6734 for **CF-GEV**, both issued 13Jan48. BoS to Rodair Inc, Montreal, QC 19Aug61 with CofR(P) 24480issued 21Aug61. CofA renewed at TFH:5,460hrs, valid until 24Dec62. CofR amended to Commercial 06Mar64. CofA renewed at TFH:5,888hrs, valid until 21Mar67. BoS to George W Sherwood, dba Aero Quality Sales Co, Detroit, MI 24Mar66. Aero Quality Sales given authority to ferry Montreal, QC to Detroit, MI 25Mar66, and cancelled from CCAR same date. CofR **N2977**(2) to George W Sherwood 26Mar66. Allotted CF-UOT 19Jly66. CofR(P) 37198 and CofA 11594 for **CF-UOT** to Canadair Ltd, Montreal, QC, 21Jly66. TFH:6,073hrs a/o 02Dec66. CofR(C) to Nordair Ltd, Montreal, QC, 08Jly71. Cvtd to **G-73T** by Frakes, with PT6A-28 turbines, by Jly73. Inspected and CofA renewed at TFH:7,760hrs, valid until 18Sep76. Leased to Survair Ltd, Ottawa, ON 15Jly76 for summer services out of Frobisher Bay. CofA renewed at TFH:7,936hrs, valid until 18Sep77. CofR(P) to Business Air Services Ltd, Goderich, ON, 25May77. CofA renewed at TFH:8,282hrs, valid until 18Sep80. Certificates re-issued as **C-FUOT** 30May80. CofA renewed at TFH:8,566hrs, valid until 18Sep82. Leased to Canadair Ltd, Montreal, QC and CofR(P) issued 23Sep81. Sold to Canadair Ltd, Montreal, QC and CofR(P) issued 04Aug82. CofA renewed at TFH:8,812hrs, valid until 18Sep84. BoS to Bannock Aerospace Ltd, Toronto, ON 11Jly84. BoS to

Mallard, c/n J-34, CF-GEV, operated by Rodair Inc and seen here at Ottawa, Ontario, circa 1961. *(Ken Molson)*

Gold Bar Developments Ltd, Edmonton, AB 11Jly84, with CofR(P) 20Aug84. CofA renewed at TFH:9,463hrs, valid until 21Nov87. BoS to 343066 Alberta Ltd, Edmonton, AB 28Nov86 with CofR(P) 23Dec86. CofA renewed 10Jun89 at TFH:9,973hrs, after conversion to PT6A-34 engines. Inspected 13Nov96 at TFH:10,998hrs. Tfd back to Gold Bar Developments by BoS 18Nov97. BoS to Seaspray Aviation Corp, Georgetown, Cayman Islands 19Nov97 and cancelled from CCAR on export to Cayman Islands, 15Dec97. Regd VP-CLK to Clayton Lewis, dba Mallard Aviation Corp, George Town, Grand Cayman, Cayman Islands 20Nov98. Advertised for sale/long lease from the company's Seattle, WA office Jan12, at TFH:11,817hrs, noting that the aircraft was "in storage in the USA".

J-35 Built as **G-73** and regd **PK-AKD** to Asiatic Petroleum Corp, New York, NY 11Mar48 for ops in Indonesia and arrived Batavia, 08Jly48. Wfu and offered for sale through Shackleton Aviation, London at TFH:4,310hrs, May62. To **P-211** with Indonesian Air & Water Police Force 09Nov63. Re-serialled as **P-2011** by Aug71. Cancelled 26Jun76 on export from Indonesia to Dean Franklin, Miami, FL who got it in exchange for a new Cessna 206s on a US BoS dated 26Jun76. Del via Luqa, Malta 10Jly76, Shannon, Eire and Reykjavik, Iceland 11Jly76. Aircraft named: "*Lady Luck*". CofR **N22DF** issued 16Sep76 and Transport CofA 26Nov76 at TFH:5,540hrs. BoS to Tyee Airlines Inc, Ketchikan, AK 23Mar77, with CofR 30Mar77. BoS to Red Fox Charters Inc, Miami, FL Apr78, with CofR 24May78. Reported sold in Palau 1985, for a hotel project, but not continued with. Special CofA 24Mar86 for flight from Honolulu, HI to Lakeport, CA, via Oakland Intl A/P, at 125% gross weight at take-off, with auxiliary oil and fuel tanks fitted. Returned to USA Oct86 at TFH:6,532hrs. BoS Red Fox to Performance Aircraft Co Inc, Fort Lauderdale, FL 18Apr88, with CofR 16May88. Aircraft forfeited to US Government 28Oct91. BoS US Customs Service to Mark IV Aviation, Fort Lauderdale, FL 20May92, with CofR 05Aug92. BoS to Mallard Aircraft Corp, Wilmington, DE 10Mar93, with CofR 31Mar93. Reregd **N100BR** to Mallard Aircraft Corp, Barrington, IL 08May93 and placed on aircraft 19May93. BoS to CAV Air Inc, Fort Lauderdale, FL 24Jly98. BoS to Don M Simmonds, Hopetown, Abaco, Bahamas 27Jly98, with CofR 04Aug98. Reregd **N611DS** 15Oct98 and placed on aircraft 22Oct98. Grounded by FAA after Chalk's crash in Dec05. For sale at Trade-A-Plane for $1.1million in Oct07, from Sandpoint, ID. Status uncertain as last Form 337 dated 09Jun99. To Wells Fargo Bank Northwest NA Trustee, Salt Lake City, UT with CofR 08Sep11. Ferry fuel system consisting of three 200-

Mallard, c/n J-35, N22DF, formerly of the Indonesian Police, is seen here on 23rd October 1977 at Seattle, Washington, when operated by Tyee Airlines Inc out of Ketchikan, Alaska. *(via PJ Marson)*

gallon fuel tanks were installed in the main cabin 18Jly12 for delivery flight to Australia. [The third fuel tank would only be used to carry a maximum of 140-gallons.] The Mallard left Hollister, CA for Christmas Island on 27Jly12, Pago Pago on 28th, Norfolk Island on 29th arriving at Coolangatta and Archerfield on 30Jly12. Details of operations in Australia not known. Current and airworthy May13, with CofR due to expire 30Sep14.

J-36 Built as **G-73** and regd **NC2974** to Republic Oil Refining Co, Pittsburgh, PA 17Apr48, and later as **N2974**. TFH:7,903hrs a/o 02Dec61.To J Fred Frakes, Anchorage, AK 14Apr62 at TFH:8,102hrs. Operated under charter to Red Dodge Aviation, Anchorage, AK, in 1962. To Northern Consolidated Airlines, Anchorage, AK, 01Mar64. Cvtd to one PT-6A-6 engine on starboard side for 50hrs of flight testing and then converted back to standard. TFH:9,353hrs a/o 26May66. Northern Consolidated became Wien Consolidated Airlines Inc, Fairbanks, AK Feb68. To J Fred Frakes, Angwin, CA 01Apr68. Cvtd to **G-73T** with PT-6A-27 engines and FF 05Sep69. CofA issued 30Mar72. TFH:13,000hrs a/o 13Jan75. Re-engined with PT-6A-34 engines, 24Oct75. Leased to Chalk's International Airline, Miami, FL, 27Nov79 for G-73T evaluation and sold to them 12Oct81. Aircraft named: "*Spirit of Miami*". TFH:15,553hrs a/o 16May84. Leased to Virgin Islands Seaplane Shuttle Inc 12Jun85, at TFH:16,541hrs. Returned to Chalk's 12Sep85, at TFH:16,917hrs. To Flying Boat Inc, Fort Lauderdale, FL Jan91. To Seaplane Leasing, Coconut Grove, FL 08Dec99. To Seaplane Adventures LLC, Greenwich, CT 22Mar05 (operated by Chalk's). Grounded by FAA after Chalk's crash in Dec05. Still regd Apr08 but believed only as parts. Reported by a Chalk's spokesman Feb09, to be in the hangar at Fort Lauderdale, with wings removed to facilitate work on centre section, but cancelled from USCAR 29Apr10.

J-37 Built as **G-73** and regd **PK-AKU** to Asiatic Petroleum Corp, New York, NY 02Jun48 for ops by Nederlandsch Nieuw Guinea Petroleum Maatschappij [(NNGPM) Dutch New Guinea Petroleum Co] in Indonesia, and arrived Batavia 08Jly48. Reregd **JZ-POC** in Dutch New Guinea, 15Jan55. PK-AKU was allocated for transfer back to Indonesian regn. Ferried to Singapore 04Apr58, but delivery refused due to poor condition of aircraft. Offered for sale via W S Shackleton Ltd, for £15,000, but wfu at Singapore in 1959. Used for fire practice at Paya Lebar Airport, between 01May60 and 09Jly60, and scrapped there by Sep60.

Mallard, c/n J-37, PK-AKU, at Grumman's Bethpage plant in 1948, awaiting delivery to NNGPM in Sorong, Dutch New Guinea. J-37 arrived in Batavia with J-35 on 8th July 1948, after a delivery flight across the north Atlantic, and via Amsterdam. *(Grumman photo via HC Kavelaars)*

J-38 Built as **G-73** and regd **NC2973** to Thomas S Lee Enterprises, 19May48 and later as **N2973**. To William Goetz, c/o Universal International Pictures, Universal City, CA 30Mar50. To Terminal & Supply Corp/Ruan Equipment Co, Des Moines, IA 20Oct50. To Thor Solberg Aviation Co, Summerville, NJ 07Nov51. To Esso Shipping Co (Standard Oil of New Jersey) 10Oct52; operated in Peru by subsidiary International Petroleum Co. To Butterworth System Inc (Standard Oil of New Jersey), Bayonne, NJ 16Jun58. Tfd to Esso Tankers Inc (Standard Oil of New Jersey), New York, NY 01Jan60. To Pan Air Corp, New Orleans, LA 28Dec61. To Toyo Menka Kaisha, Tokyo, Japan 10Jan62 and regd **JA5106** to Nitto Aviation/ Japan Domestic Airways, Osaka, 23Feb62. TFH:9,351hrs a/o Oct64. JA- regn cancelled, 25May66. Regd **N7338** to Universal Trading Co (F B Ayer), Panama 01May66 and tfd to Frederick B Ayer & Associates, New York, NY 01May66. To Dean Franklin, Miami, FL 19Oct67 for Chalk's International Airline. Transport CofA issued 09Feb68. Aircraft named: "*City of Miami*" and may have been "*Bimini Gal*". Wfu Sep73. TFH:11,000hrs a/o Jan74. Leased to Antilles Air Boats (AAB), Christiansted, US Virgin Islands, Mar74. To Caribbean Flying Boats Inc, US Virgin Islands 19Aug74 and continued lease to AAB.

TFH:14,085hrs a/o Jun80. AAB ceased ops Sep81. Flown to Frakes, Cleburne, TX and stored. To Associated Consultants International (Virgin Islands Seaplane Shuttle), St Croix, US Virgin Islands, 17Apr84. Reregd **N638SS** 06Dec85. To Frakes Aviation, Cleburne, TX 24Sept91, but not cvtd to G-73T and stored as parts at Cleburne. "Grounded" by FAA after Chalk's crash in Dec05. Regn still assigned and listed as airworthy May13, but CofR had expired 30Sep12.

J-39   Built as **G-73** and regd **NC2975** to JJ Ryan, Arlington, VA Jly48. Damaged in water landing at Ste Jovite, QC, Canada and returned to Grumman for rebuild. BoS Grumman Aircraft Engineering Corp to Imperial Oil Ltd 03Oct49 with US CofA for export E-16695 issued 04Oct49. Tfd by BoS to Imperial Oil Air Transport Ltd, Toronto, ON 31Oct49. CofA 3206 and CofR(P) 8443for **CF-IOA**, both issued 05Oct49. CofA renewed at TFH:951hrs, valid until 13Oct51 and at TFH:2,625hrs, valid until 13Oct55. BoS to K J Springer, Toronto, ON 13Apr55 with CofR(C) 13405 issued 14Apr55. Leased to Pacific Western Airlines, Vancouver, BC. Accident at 1525hrs on 27May55: while flying at 3,500 feet en route Vancouver to Kitimat, BC, the right wing was hit by an eagle causing considerable damage to wingtip and slot. Accident 03Aug55: disappeared en route Kemano-Kitimat, BC, whilst operating Flt No:63 from Vancouver to Kitimat with 2 crew and 3 pax. The aircraft was seen to fly up the Kemano River valley towards Kemano Camp 5. The pilot reported that he was taking the transmission line route, as his passengers wished to see it. The aircraft was last seen at Camp 11 flying at an estimated altitude of 500ft over the mountains in fog and low cloud. An extensive search was made by the RCAF between the 3rd and 24th August 1955, but nothing was found. Wreckage sighted 23Jly58 by MR McGowan of Okanagan Helicopters Ltd, after a record mild summer in BC had melted the ice-caps on the mountains causing a slide which carried the wreckage down from 5,000ft to a lower level. Investigation showed that the G-73 had hit the mountain with great force, at the 5,000ft level, and exploded and burned. Cancelled from CCAR Jan56.

J-40   Built as **G-73** and regd **NC2996** to Grumman Aircraft Engineering Corp, Bethpage, NY. Reregd **N5110** to General Motors Corp, Detroit, MI 10Dec48. Reregd **N5110** to Pacific Airmotive Corp, Burbank, CA, May60 at TFH:6,912hrs. To Toyo Menka Kaisha, Tokyo and regd **JA5067** to Nitto Aviation/ Japan Domestic Airways, Osaka, Japan 05Jly60. Accident 18Feb64: crashed in a rice field at Ninotsubo, near Osaka A/P after engine trouble and icing. Stewardess and one passenger killed, Capt T Sekiguchi, one crew and 6 pax all seriously injured.

J-41   Built as **G-73 and** regd **PK-AKE** to Asiatic Petroleum Co, New York, NY, 22Dec48; ferried to Amsterdam and reregd **G-ALLJ** to Shell Refining & Marketing Co, London, UK, 05Mar49, for political reasons, to allow onward ferry flight to Indonesia. Reregd **PK-AKE** to Nederlandsch Nieuw Guinee Petroleum Maatschappij (NNGPM) on arrival in Batavia 25Apr49. During maintenance at Jakarta on 27Jan51, aircraft was hosed down with gasoline, caught fire and DBR. Scrapped.

J-42   Built as **G-73** and regd **NC2976** to Grumman Aircraft Engineering Corp, Bethpage, NY in 1948. Sold to C F Kettering Inc (General Motors Corp), Dayton, OH, with CofR **N5115** 20Jan49; aircraft named: "*The Blue Tail Fly*". Reregd **N51151** 10Mar59. To Kiekhaefer Corp, Fond du Lac, WI, 10Jly59. To Daniel R Topping and Del E Webb, New York, NY 23Oct59; tfd to The NY Yankees, New York, NY (nominal change), 02Nov64 at TFH:4,770hrs. To Crow Inc, Toledo, OH, 17Dec65 at TFH:5,959hrs. TFH:8,754hrs a/o 21Jun75. To Beaver Aviation Service Inc, Grove City, PA 20Dec76. To Leon "Tony" Barnum, Whitehouse, OH

C/n J-42, Crow Inc's Mallard, N51151, was a visitor to Oshkosh in August 1977. The aircraft was later operated by Chalk's, both before and after being converted to G-73T standard by Frakes Aviation in 1981.

(Jennifer Gradidge)

28Dec76. To H Dan Hill and David G Dixon, Santa Ana, CA 15May78; tfd to Dixon/Hill Aircraft Leasing Co, Santa Ana, CA (nominal change) 25Jan79. Leased to Trans Catalina Airlines, Long Beach, CA; aircraft named: "*Island Princess*". To Chalk's International Airline Inc, Miami, FL 14Jun79; leased to Antilles Air Boats; TFH:10,842hrs a/o Jun80; ret to Chalk's for turbo conversion by Frakes, 11Sep81. TFH:13,842hrs in 1985. To Flying Boat Inc, Fort Lauderdale, FL, as **G-73T** Jan91 with CofA 27Jun91; aircraft renamed "*The Keys Explorer*". Reregd **N142PA** for Pan Am Air Bridge, 29Jan98 but op by Chalk's. To World Pacific Air Lease Inc, Irving, TX 11Aug98 and leased to Chalk's. Regd to Seaplane Leasing II LLC, Fort Lauderdale, FL but operated by Flying Boat Inc, dba Chalk's International Airlines. Incident 22May01 at TFH:29,548hrs: while taxiing to the Fort Lauderdale terminal after a 50-minute flight from Paradise Island, Bahamas (Flt:512) the right main gear collapsed. Minor damage and no injuries to two crew and 17 pax. To Seaplane Adventures LLC, Greenwich, CT 31Mar05 (op by Chalk's); TFH:34,787hrs a/o 05Dec05. Grounded by FAA after Chalk's crash in Dec05. Noted stored, with parts missing, at Fort Lauderdale, FL Oct07, but still regd Apr08. Reported by a Chalk's spokesman Feb09, to be stored on the ramp at Fort Lauderdale, essentially complete, but then wfu and cancelled from USCAR 25Mar10.

J-43   Built as **G-73** and regd **NC3010** to JJ Ryan, Arlington, VA 15Mar49, replacing J-39 (qv), and later as **N3010**. CofA issued 15Mar56. To Coastal Aviation Co, West Trenton, NJ in 1963. Operated out of Orlando, FL and aircraft named: "*Huckleberry Duck*". TFH:4,500hrs a/o Oct66. Tfd to Coastal Airlines Inc, Orlando, FL (nominal change) 08Jan69. Tfd to Robert J Anderson (Coastal A/L) 17Nov69. To Dean Franklin, Miami, FL and operated by Chalk's International Airline Inc, 05Dec69. Aircraft named: "*City of Bimini*". Hijacked to Havana, Cuba 07Mar72: two armed men entered the Mallard, which was about to depart for Bimini, Bahamas with five passengers, and demanded to be flown to Cuba. Pilot, James Cothron, shut down the engines, but was shot three times and thrown off the aircraft. Co-pilot Robert Wallis decided that it might be better to accede to the gunmen's wishes, and flew the Mallard to Cuba. The Mallard returned to Miami next morning with five relieved passengers, and a few bullet holes in the cabin! To Chalk's International Airline Inc, Miami, FL 28Aug72. Reported wfu Sep73. TFH:8,200hrs a/o Jan74 and 8,607hrs a/o 31Jan75. Wfu and stored at Fort Lauderdale, FL in 1983, for parts. Projected sale to Virgin Islands Seaplane Shuttle May84, was not proceeded with. Aircraft dismantled in early 1985. Regd to Dean Franklin Aviation Enterprises Inc, Fort Lauderdale, FL 07Jan92. Grounded by FAA after Chalk's crash in Dec05. Listed as current and airworthy May13, with CofR due to expire 30Sep13.

J-44   Built as **G-73** and regd **NC2977** to RM Hollingshead Co, Camden, NJ 13Apr49, and later as **N2977**. TFH:1,850hrs a/o Jun53. To Remmert-Werner Co, St Louis, MO 23Feb54. Tfd to Beldex Corp, St Louis, MO (Remmert-Werner affiliate) 01Mar54. Reregd **N1208** to Freuhauf Trailer Corp, Detroit, MI 15May54 at TFH:1,934hrs. To J Fred Frakes, Anchorage, AK 15Jan53. Tfd to Safeway Airways, Anchorage, AK (Frakes) 21Jan63. To Northern Consolidated Airlines, Anchorage, AK 17Mar64, with CofA issued 05Jun64 at TFH:3,981hrs. Accident 04Dec64: minor damage when gear collapsed landing at Bethel, AK. Pilot + 3 uninjured. Accident 20Dec65: substantially damaged when stalled after take-off at Bethel, AK. Pilot + seven minor injuries. TFH:4,880hrs a/o 25May66. To Wien Consolidated Airlines, 01Aug68; became Wien Air Alaska, 21Mar74. To Crow Inc, Toledo, OH, 18Apr78. To ANTL, Inc (Chalk's), Miami, FL 21Nov78. Aircraft named: "*Pride of Bimini*". Leased to Antilles Air Boats, Christiansted, US Virgin Islands. TFH:8,663hrs a/o 06Jun80. Wfu and returned to Chalk's for **G-73T** conversion, 11Sep81. TFH:12,108hrs a/o 16May84. Painted in Merv Griffin's Paradise Island c/s in 1989. To Flying Boat Inc, Fort Lauderdale, FL, Jan91. To World Pacific Air Lease Inc, Irving, TX 11Aug98 and leased to Chalk's. To Seaplane Leasing V LLC, Coconut Grove, FL 08Dec99 and wfu for parts. To Seaplane Adventures LLC, Greenwich, CT 23Mar05. Grounded by FAA after Chalk's crash in Dec05 and stored minus wings/tail at Fort Lauderdale, FL. Cancelled from USCAR 29Apr10.

J-45   Built as **G-73** with CofA 03May49. BoS Grumman Aircraft Engineering Corp to Briggs Manufacturing Co, Detroit, MI 04May49 with CofR **N2978**, 13May49. Engines changed from S3H1 to S1H1, with Hamilton Standard 23D40-51 props, May52. CofA 13Mar53 at TFH:2,025hrs. Original S3H1 engines overhauled and converted to S1H1, then re-installed on aircraft Jun53. Wing floats removed for winter operations Nov53. De-icing system installed Dec53. CofA 08Mar54 at TFH:2,672hrs. The S1H1 engines installed in May52 and removed in Jun53, were overhauled and installed again in Feb55, with CofA at TFH:3,124hrs. The interchange of the two sets of engines was repeated again in Jly56 and Feb57. Battery installation per STCs SA3-194 and SA3-263, Jun58. BoS to Evans Products Co, Plymouth, MI 27Oct59 with

CofR 17Nov59 at TFH:6,064hrs. Hull repaired 29Oct59 after accident. Work per STC SA89CE, Jly63. BoS to George W Sherwood, dba Aero Quality Sales Co, Detroit, MI 01Aug63 with CofR 09Aug63. CofA renewal 04Jan67 noted use as "Air Taxi" and aircraft had been flown 452hrs in previous 12 months. Tfd by BoS to Aero Quality Sales Co Inc, Detroit, MI 17May67 with CofR 10Jly67. CofA renewal 05Apr68 noted use as "Business Transportation" and aircraft had been flown 544hrs in previous 12 months. Similarly, on 01Apr69 aircraft had been flown 579hrs in previous 12 months. Tfd back to George W Sherwood, Grosse Park, MI 25Apr69 and tfd by BoS same date to Land-Sea-Airways Inc, Detroit, MI with CofR 02May69. Possibly used by Isle Royale Airways. DBF on ground near Ida, MI Oct70. Remains purchased by Crow Inc and Frakes. CofR was revoked by FAA 27Aug71 for failure to submit an Aircraft Activity Report. CofR revoked but regn still assigned to Land-Sea-Airways, May13.

J-46　Built as **G-73** and regd **NC74044** to John W Galbreath & Co, Columbus, OH 26May49. Crashed and DBF at Darby Dan Farm (aircraft base field) 30Sep50. Pilot killed and three pax injured. Cancelled from USCAR 31Oct50.

J-47　Built as **G-73** 30Mar49 and del to 3 Sqn, Royal Egyptian AF, Royal Flight, as **F-7**, via London, UK, 16Sep49 by Gp Capt Hassan Aqif of Royal Flight. To No.11 Comms Sqn by Jan56. The Mallards were re-numbered after Farouk's departure, gaining regular three-digit Air Force serials, one of which was 763 (see page 96). Noted wfu at Cairo in 1966 at TFH:3,360hrs. Fate unknown but presumed scrapped.

J-48　Built as **G-73** 30Aug49 and del to 3 Sqn, Royal Egyptian AF, Royal Flight, as **F-8**, Jan/Feb50 by Britavia of London, UK. Ferry flight from NY to UK was by Capt John W Hackett with navigator Mr M V Cole. F-8 was then flown from UK to Egypt by Gp Capt Hassan Aqif of Royal Flight. The Mallards were re-numbered after Farouk's departure, gaining regular three-digit Air Force serials, one of which was 763 (see page 96). Wfu and cannibalised to support J-47. TFH:1,960hrs a/o 1965. Reported wfu at Almaza, Cairo 1966. Fate unknown but presumed scrapped.

J-49　Built as **G-73** with Statement of Conformity and CofA 10Nov49. BoS to General Foods Corp, New York, NY 10Nov49 with CofR **N2979** 17Nov49. Engines changed from P&W S3H1 to S1H1 with Hamilton Standard 23D40-51 props 26Jan51. CofA renewed 06May52 at TFH:1,533hrs. BoS to P Lorrilard Co, New York, NY 17Mar52 with CofR 27Mar52. BoS to Ad Properties Inc, New York, NY 01Dec54 with CofR 16Dec54. Tfd by BoS to Adolph J Toigo (same address as Ad Properties) 11Jan56 with CofR 19Jan56. BoS to William C Wold Associates, Greenwich, CT 20Jan56 with CofR 26Jan56. BoS to Freeport Sulphur Co, New Orleans, LA 27Feb56 with CofR 05Mar56. CofA issued 15Mar56. Reregd **N300S** 20Jun56. CofA renewed 03Mar57 at TFH:2,732hrs. CofR re-issued for address change within New Orleans 18Dec57. Fuel tank type floats removed and plain type floats installed May60. Wing centre section and both outer wing panels removed for corrosion inspection and repair as necessary, Aug64. Left and right main fuel tanks modified to 190-gallon integral, Aug64. Nominal change to Freeport Minerals Co CofR applied for 27Aug71. Cvtd to **G-73T**, by Frakes Aviation, with Pratt & Whitney Aircraft of Canada PT6A-34 engines and Hartzell HC83TN-3DY/T10178B-5 props, per STC SA2323WE, 30Apr76 at TFH:8,833hrs. New nose wheel assembly installed Mar77 per STC SA1862SW. TFH:12,642hrs a/o 02Oct84. Tfd by BoS to Freeport-McMoRan Resource Partners, Ltd Partnership 27Jun86 with CofR 11Aug86. This was deemed a "prohibited conveyance" and was rescinded 01May89 and a CofR was issued to Freeport Minerals Co 12Sep89. **N685FM** was assigned to Freeport McMoran Inc, New Orleans, LA 27Jly90; CofR application was

G-73T Turbo Mallard, c/n J-49, N777PV, of the Precision Valve Corporation, undergoing maintenance in 2000.　　　　　　　　*(MAP)*

made on 07Sep90 and CofR issued 20Sep90. Cleveland wheel and brake conversion kit installed Jun92 per STC SA651GL. BoS to RMIB Inc, Wilmington, DE 23May94 with another BoS from RMIB to Precision Valve Corp, Bronxville, NY same date, with CofR 24May94. Walker's International, Fort Lauderdale, FL had reserved N777PV in May94 but instructed the FAA to re-assign it to their parent company, Precision Valve Corp, for J-49. It was so assigned and J-49 was reregd **N777PV**, on Temporary CofA T942335, 24May94 and placed on aircraft 22Jun94. TFH:18,400hrs a/o Jan06. Grounded by FAA after Chalk's crash in Dec05. Address change to Yonkers, NY 13Dec10. CofR renewed Oct11, but aircraft not airworthy Oct12 and CofR due to expire 31Oct14. BoS to Josephine Abplanalp Revocable Living Trust (same address), Yonkers, NY (for \$175,000) 12Oct12. BoS to Aviation Management International Inc, Fort Lauderdale, FL 12Oct12. In Nov12, the regn N777PV was assigned to Aviation Management International. To Centerline Holdings Inc, Camden, DE with CofR 28Feb13, to expire 29Feb16.

J-50　Built as **G-73** and regd **N2980** to Grumman Aircraft Engineering Corp, Bethpage, NY Mar50; used as demonstrator and company hack. Reregd **N1626** (FN:90) to Texaco Inc, Houma, LA 07Dec64 at TFH:3,131hrs. TFH:3,752hrs a/o 17Dec66. Cvtd to **G-73T**, with PT6A-34 engines, by Frakes Aviation, Cleburne, TX Jan81. TFH:10,408hrs a/o 2Oct84. Reregd **N686FM** to Freeport McMoran Inc, New Orleans, LA Nov91. Tfd to Indonesia to support copper mining survey work, and ferried Reykjavik, Iceland-Glasgow, UK-Lyon, France, 05-08Apr94. Reregd **PK-OCM** and operated by Airfast, Jakarta. To Dr Richard Sugden, Wilson, WY with CofR **N730RS** 26Apr01 and Transport CofA dated 01May01. Grounded by FAA after Chalk's crash in Dec05. CofR renewed Jan11. Current and airworthy May13, with CofR due to expire 31Jan14.

J-51　Built as **G-73**, 09Jan50 with Experimental CofA 13Apr50 due to -S1H1 engines. Regd **N2981** to Grumman Aircraft Engineering Corp 18Apr50 and Standard CofA 27Apr50 after CAA acceptance tests; used as demonstrator based at Bethpage. BoS to Fort Sumter Chevrolet Co Inc, Charleston, SC 30Aug50, with CofR 06Sep50. CofA 01Aug52 at TFH:810hrs. BoS to Southern Aero Inc, Atlanta, GA 10Feb53 with CofA 29Aug53 at TFH:1,180hrs. BoS to Sherman & Marquette, New York, NY 25May53 and reregd **N99V** 11Jun53. CofA 29Jan54 at TFH:1,317hrs. BoS to Atlantic Aviation Co, Teterboro, NJ (sales agents) 15Mar54 with CofR 16Mar54. BoS to Texaco Inc, Teterboro, NJ 15Mar54 for \$97,500 at TFH:1,326hrs, with CofR 16Mar54. Based at Houma, LA and reregd **N1629** 10Aug54 with FN:76. Engines changed to -S3H1 with CofA 26Jan55 at TFH:1,597hrs. TFH:5,658hrs a/o 17Dec66 and 7,699hrs a/o May77. Cvtd to **G-73T** with PT-6A-34 engines, by Frakes Aviation, Cleburne, TX Jan81 per Frake's STC 2323WE. TFH:12,815hrs a/o 02Oct84. Texaco exchanged J-51 and J-30, for a Beech B200 King Air owned by Frakes recorded on BoS to Frakes Aviation, Cleburne, TX 07Jan86. BoS to Virgin Islands Seaplane Shuttle (VISS), Christiansted, US Virgin Islands, 07Jan86 with CofR 20Mar86. Reregd **N651SS** 21Mar86 and placed on aircraft 21May86. Tfd by BoS to Associated Consultants International (VISS), St Croix, US Virgin Islands 31Mar86 with CofR 25Sep86. Cvtd to 17 pax airline configuration with emergency exits per STC SA4410SW and bow hatch modified per STC SA2323WE, Nov86. In service with VISS 21Dec86 at TFH:13,279hrs; TFH:15,240hrs a/o Apr88. Wfs and used for spares; substantially damaged by Hurricane *Hugo*, 16Sep89. Abandoned to Manufacturers Hanover Trust Co / CIT Group 14Dec89. BoS to Caribbean Airline Services (CAS) Inc, Carolina, PR, 27Jly90. BoS CAS to Caribbean Airline Services / Labate Aviation Inc (co-owners), Carolina, PR 15Nov90 with CofR 10Oct91. BoS CAS / Labate to Flying Boat Inc, Fort Lauderdale, FL 30Jun92 with CofR and CofA issued 15Jly92 and operated by Chalk's. Reregd **N150FB** 23Jly92 and placed on aircraft 11Jun93. Accident 18Mar94: crashed and sank after water take-off from Key West Harbor, FL. Chalk's Chief Pilot, John Alberto and co-pilot Alan Turner were both killed. It was Chalk's first fatal accident in 75yrs of operations. Cause probably due to failure to pump bilges free of water before take-off leaving "a lot of water" in rear of aircraft. Aircraft recovered from sea-bed 20Mar94 and released to Chalk's insurers, except the engines which were released to Atlanta Air Salvage, 17May94. Cancelled from USCAR 09Sep96 as "destroyed/scrapped".

J-52　Built as **G-73** and regd **N2982** to Admiral Corp, Chicago, IL, 01Jun50. Aircraft named: "*Admiral Flagship*". Reregd **N66A** 30Nov50. To Union Producing Co, Shreveport, LA 09Feb55. To Pan Air Corp, New Orleans, LA 21Nov62. Reregd **JA5117** to Nitto Aviation/ Japan Domestic Airways, Osaka, 26Dec62. TFH:3,933hrs a/o Oct64. JA- regn cancelled, 30Jun66. To Universal Trading Co (F B Ayer), Panama 31May66. Reregd **N7352** to Frederick B Ayer & Associates, New York, NY 31May66. To Commercial Centers Inc, Los Angeles, CA 04Jan68. TFH:4,697hrs a/o 07Jan69. To Ranchaire Inc, Aspen, CO (Walter Scott) 06Aug69. To Dean Franklin, Miami, FL 03Apr74. Reregd **TR-LSW** to Safair Flying Service,

Mallard, c/n J-52, was operated for the President of Gabon as TR-LSW, by Safair Flying Service, and is seen here at Teterboro, New Jersey, in 1974. The G-73 was lost when it sank in the Atlantic Ocean, off Gabon, in June 1975.   *(RH Milne)*

Mallard, c/n J-54, N27DF, of William Murphy, at Titusville, Florida, in February 1983, before reportedly being used by General Noriega in Panama.   *(Dennis Goodwin via Jennifer Gradidge)*

Teterboro, NJ 24May74 and ferried to Gabon. Used by the President of Gabon, West Africa from Jly74. Written off after landing in Atlantic Ocean, off Gabon, to pick up passengers from a ship. The G-73 was unable to take off and was taken in tow by the ship from the bow, but aircraft was pulled underwater and sank, Jun75.

J-53   Built as **G-73** and regd **N2983** to Copano Oil Co, Victoria, TX, 30Jun50. To D H Braman, Victoria, TX 17Dec58. To United Aircraft Corp (Sikorsky Div), Stratford, CT at TFH: circa 1,200hrs, 26Mar60. To Humble Oil & Refining Co, Houston, TX 28May60. To Chicago Steel Service Co, dba House of Stainless, Chicago, IL 13Feb63. To Riverside Business Flight Service, Riverside, IL 21Feb64. To K C Machine & Tool Co, Detroit, MI 21Mar67. TFH:2,545hrs a/o 31Mar68. To Tulakes Aviation Inc, Oklahoma City, OK 28Feb73. To Two Jacks Inc, Olive Branch, MO 18Sep73. Authority to ferry Portland, OR to Vancouver, BC 01Mar74. US CofA for export E-116674 issued 08May74 at TFH:3,504hrs. CofA issued 08May74. CofR(C) for **C-GIRL** to West Coast Air Services, Vancouver, BC 09May74. CofA renewed at TFH:4,561hrs, valid until 08May76 and at TFH:8,941hrs, valid until 15Jun81. CofR(C) to Air BC Ltd, Richmond, BC, 16Jan81 (nominal change). CofR(C) to Jim Pattison Industries Ltd (operating as Trans-Provincial Airlines), Richmond, BC (nominal change) 17May85. CofA renewed at TFH:10,784hrs, valid until 15Jun85. BoS J Pattison (dba Air BC) to Frakes 31Aug84 and cancelled from CCAR 04Sep84. Reregd **N2983** to Frakes Aviation Inc, Cleburne, TX "for mods". To Virgin Islands Seaplane Shuttle, Christiansted, US Virgin Islands, 12Apr85. Reregd **N653SS** May85, with Transport CofA 21Jun85. TFH:13,177hrs a/o Apr88. Substantially damaged by Hurricane *Hugo*, 16Sep89. To Caribbean Airline Services Inc, San Juan, PR, May90. Leased to Sea Air Shuttle Corp, Carolina, PR, 1992 and returned to lessor 1993. To Carolina Airline Services Inc, Carolina, PR 20Jan94. To US Distributors Inc, (James Confalone), Miami, FL with CofR 10May00. Grounded by FAA after Chalk's crash in Dec05. Noted derelict in Puerto Rico Feb08. CofR expired 30Sep11 and was revoked.

J-54   Built as **G-73** and regd **N2984** to Grumman Aircraft Engineering Corp, Bethpage, NY Nov50; used as demonstrator and company hack. To Union Oil Co, Los Angeles, CA at TFH:800hrs, 08Jan54. Reregd **N76U** 25Oct54. TFH:7,400hrs a/o 06Dec66. Reregd **N76UL** to AiResearch Aviation Co, Los Angeles, CA 01Apr64. Allotted C-GENT 10Jly74. To Dean H Franklin Aviation Enterprises Ltd, Miami, FL at TFH:9,500hrs, 20Aug74. BoS to West Coast Air Services Ltd 27Jly74. US CofA for export E-119797 issued 13Aug74 and N76UL cancelled from USCAR 20Aug74, at TFH:9,552hrs. CofR(C) for **C-GENT** to West Coast Air Services, Vancouver, BC 21Aug74. CofA renewed at TFH:10,244hrs, valid until 13Aug76 and at TFH:12,526hrs, valid until 13Aug79. BoS to Amphibian Sales Inc, Miami, FL 16Jan79, cancelled from CCAR 24Jan79 and reregd **N27DF**. To Pan Aviation, Dover, DE 30Jan79. To William E Murphy, Coral Gables, FL 13Feb80. Reported used by General Noriega in Panama. Impounded in Panama for drug smuggling in 1985. To William E Murphy, Coral Gables, FL, Nov85. To Nasmyth & Partners in 1987. Moved from Panama to San José, Costa Rica for overhaul. Test flown by Spike Nasmyth at Pavas A/P, Costa Rica, Sep88, then del via Belize and Key West to Miami to Amphibian Sales Inc (Dean Franklin), Miami, FL. Reregd **C-FWAF** to Waglisla Air Inc, Richmond, BC, with CofR(C) 16Nov88. Cancelled from CCAR 23Mar89 and reregd **N6DF** (assumed) to Dean Franklin, Miami, FL, Mar89. Cancelled from USCAR 28Mar89 and reregd **HP-1035** to P Janson (address unknown), Mar89. Reregd **C-FWAF** again with CofR(P) 03Apr89. CofR(P) to Spike Air Ltd, Richmond, BC 26Jan90. Ferry flight from California to Don Muang, Thailand via Honolulu and Australia as C-FWAF Mar91. Cancelled from CCAR again

Mallard, c/n J-54, N54GZ, of Pacific Flying Boats Inc, is seen here at Victoria, British Columbia on 30th August 2010, four days after the issue of its Transport Certificate of Airworthiness after a long-term overhaul by Victoria Air Maintenance.   *(Tim Martin)*

11Apr91 and aircraft regd **HS-TPA** to Tropical Sea Air, Bangkok, Thailand, 17Apr91. Noted at Phuket in full c/s 09Mar93. CofA issued 04Oct93 but reported in open storage at U-Tapao Navy base by Sep93 until 1997. BoS 11Nov97 Tropical Sea Air to Turbo North Aviation and John Schwamm. Tfd by BoS to John Schwamm, Anchorage, AK (as sole owner) 12Nov97. BoS to Victoria Air Maintenance Ltd, Sidney, BC 12Nov97. HS-TPA de-registered 14Nov97. Allotted C-GBQN 19Nov97. CofR(P) for **C-GBQN** to Victoria Air Maintenance Ltd, Sidney, BC 18Dec97. Authority to ferry U-Tapao, Thailand to Sydney, Australia 13Jan98. Shipped from Koh Sichang to Gray's Harbor, WA on board "*Kite Arrow*". Authority to ferry Hoquiam, WA to Victoria, BC 04Aug98. BoS to Philip Bingman, Lester Bingman Partners, Anchorage, AK 04May99, and cancelled from CCAR 06May99. Reregd **N7777Q** 27May99. To Westernair Inc, Albuquerque, NM 10Feb03 and CofA issued 04Oct03. Cancelled from USCAR 15Nov05, and regd as **C-GGMZ** to R Stewart, Victoria, BC 05Dec05. Grounded by FAA after Chalk's crash in Dec05. Cancelled from CCAR 05Feb10 to Pacific Flying Boats Inc, Bear, DE with CofR **N54GZ** 18Feb10 and Transport CofA 26Aug10. Current and airworthy May13, with CofR due to expire 31Dec13.

J-55   Built as **G-73** 18Nov50. Sold to John W Galbreath & Co, Columbus, OH 07Dec50, as replacement for J-46 (qv), and regd **N2986**. CofR issued 28Jan51. TFH:660hrs a/o Dec52. Allotted CF-HAV 07Apr53. Authority to ferry Columbus, OH to Montreal, QC 07Apr53 and US CofA for export E-24437 08Apr53. CofR(P) 11818 and CofA 3943 for **CF-HAV** to Miron & Frères Ltée, Montreal, QC issued 08Apr53. CofA renewed at TFH:1,014hrs, valid until 24Apr55. Authority to ferry Montreal, QC to Prestwick, UK (reason unknown) 08Jly54. Cancelled from USCAR 13May55 and CofR(S) 13771 issued 08Jun55 to Quebec Department of Colonisation. CofA renewed at TFH:2,057hrs, valid until 12Apr58 and at TFH:2,595hrs, valid until 11Mar60. Tfd to Quebec Department of Transport & Communication, Ancienne Lorette, QC 05Feb60 and CofA renewed at TFH:2,992hrs, valid until 11Mar61. CF HAV cancelled and reregd **CF-PQE** 04Mar60 with CofR(S) 20531 and CofA 7428. CofA renewed at TFH:3,573hrs, valid until 11Mar63. Sold for $70,000 to Dennis Ferranti Meters Ltd, Bangor, Wales, at TFH:3,595hrs, and cancelled from CCAR 03Aug62. Reregd **G-ASCS** 07Aug62 and arrived Speke, UK for service by Starways Ltd, 07Sep62. Tfd to Dennis Ferranti Co Ltd, Oldham, UK 12Sep62 with CofR R.7633/2 13Sep62. Oddly, in both above cases Ferranti is noted as "charterer" rather than owner and the charter is recorded as terminated on 31Jly67. Sold to Francois Maurice Lawreys, London, UK, 01Nov67 and with CofR R.7633/3 02Nov67. Sold to J A Goldschmidt Ltd, London, UK, 26Apr68 with CofR R.7633/4 08May68 and used by Grosvenor Estates Ltd, UK during Jun68. Aircraft stored at Cambridge, UK from Jly68. Sold for £17,000 by Terravia Trading Services Ltd, Ascot, UK to Northland Airlines Ltd, Winnipeg, MB 21Feb69. UK regn cancelled 13Apr69. Allotted CF-YQC 14Apr69. Sold to Midwest Airlines, Winnipeg, MB, 04May69. CofA issued at TFH:4,911hrs 17Jly69, and CofR(C) for CF-YQC issued 30Jly69. Midwest merged with Transair, Nov69. CofA renewed at TFH:4,913hrs, valid until 27Sep72. Sold for $68,000 to Chalk's Flying Service, Miami, FL, 28Sep71. Cancelled from CCAR 23Mar72 and reregd N73556 in Mar72. Aircraft named: "City of Miami". Transport CofA issued 17Apr72. TFH:6,200hrs a/o Jan74, and painted in bicentennial c/s 1976. To Virgin Islands Seaplane Shuttle, Christiansted, US Virgin Islands in 1982. Reregd N655SS, repainted and FF with new regn 01Mar85. TFH:17,600hrs a/o Apr88 and wfs. Destroyed by Hurricane Hugo 17Sep89 and sold for parts to Caribbean Airline Services Inc, San Juan, PR May90. To Flying Boat Inc, Fort Lauderdale, FL, 15Jly92, as parts. CofR expired 31Mar12 and cancelled from USCAR 06May13, but regn reserved same date.

J-56 Built as **G-73** and regd **N5118** to General Motors Corp, Detroit, MI 28Dec50. Reregd **N51181** 20Oct59 and to Pacific Airmotive Corp, Burbank, CA at TFH:5,010hrs, 02Nov59. To Toyo Menka Kaisha Ltd, Tokyo, Japan 09Nov59. Reregd **JA5057** to Nitto Aviation/ Japan Domestic Airways, Osaka 12Dec59. TFH:9,571hrs a/o Oct64. To Universal Trading Co (F B Ayer), Panama 31May66 and reregd **N7356**. To Frederick B Ayer & Associates, New York, NY, 31May66 and JA- regn cancelled 03Jun66. To Amphibious Airways Inc (Chalk's), Miami, FL 04Sep68 and aircraft named: "The Cat Cayer". Transport CofA issued 23Dec68. Tfd to Chalk's International Airline Inc (nominal change) 28Aug72 but wfu Sep73 at TFH:11,500hrs. To Antilles Air Boats, Christiansted, US Virgin Islands, 18Mar74. Reregd **N65CC** to Crown Controls, New Bremen, OH (via Dean Franklin?) 09May83. Flown to Wapakoneta, OH at TFH:15,808hrs, 10May83 for restoration and refurbishment. Reregd **N465CC,** Mar97, to Crown Credit Co Ltd, New Knoxville, OH. Reregd **N7356** to Omni Enterprises Inc, Heron, MT 13Jun00. To Ernest Martin, Kalispell, MT with CofR 25Sep00. Grounded by FAA after Chalk's crash in Dec05. For sale

at Trade-A-Plane for $1.65million in Oct07 from Sandpoint, ID. To John Mayes, Austin, TX with CofR 30Jly12. Current and airworthy May13, with CofR due to expire 31Jly15.

J-57 Built as **G-73** and regd **N2990** to American Cyanamid Corp, New York, NY, 29Jan51. CofA issued 03Jan56. To Pacific Aero Engineering Corp, Santa Monica, CA 29Nov57. To Daniel G van Clief, Charlottesville, VA 10Dec57. Aircraft named: "Jemima Puddle Duck". To California Oil Co, (Division of Standard Oil), New Orleans, LA 03May62 at TFH:3,312hrs. Nominal change to Chevron Oil Co 01Jly65 and another nominal change to Chevron USA Inc 01Jan77. TFH:10,800hrs a/o Apr82. To Melvin L Arthur, Phoenix, AZ, 27May82. Reregd **N188AC** 28Aug82 and nominal change to Arthur Corp, Phoenix, AZ 14Oct82. To American Aircraft Management, Scottsdale, AZ, Nov90. To Tanglefoot Wing & Wheel Co, Cavanaugh Bay, ID with CofR 21Nov91. Address change to Coolin, ID (undated). Grounded by FAA after Chalk's crash in Dec05, stored at Carson City, NV 2007. Current and airworthy May13, with CofR due to expire 31Oct15.

J-58 Built as **G-73** and regd **N2989** to General Foods Corp, New York, NY 15Mar51 (may have been **N289D** at some time). Reregd **N298GB** to Premium Service Corp, (Carlson Companies), Minneapolis, MN Jun62 at TFH:4,125hrs. TFH:5,075hrs a/o Mar67. Accident 03May67: crashed (due icing) on take-off from WW Hawes Municipal A/P, Huron, SD. Early morning (0502hrs) take-off with heavy accumulation of frost on wings. Pilot + one pax seriously injured. Aircraft remains sold to Crow Inc, and later resold to Trans Catalina Airlines and Frakes. Cancelled from USCAR (date unknown).

J-59 Last **G-73** built. Regd **N2993** to Grumman Aircraft Engineering Corp, Bethpage, NY 04May51 and used as demonstrator and company hack. Modified with slot-less wing (for test flights?), but then converted to original specification. TFH:643hrs a/o 11Mar54. Authority to ferry Bethpage, NY to Montreal, QC 27Jly54 with US CofA for export E-20976. CofA 4815 and CofR(P) 13649 issued for **CF-HPN** to Robertson & O'Connell Ltd, Montreal, QC 04Aug54, and cancelled from USCAR 09Aug54. Aircraft destroyed when hangar of Aircraft Industries of Canada Ltd burned at St John's, QC 08Dec54. Cancelled from CCAR 03Jan55.

Right: Mallard, c/n J-56, N7356, awaiting sale at Opa Locka, Florida, on 8th February 1983. The aircraft was purchased by Crown Controls three months later and flown to Ohio for restoration and refurbishment.
(Jennifer Gradidge Collection)

Left: Mallard, c/n J-57, N188AC, owned by the Arthur Corporation, is seen here at Oshkosh, Wisconsin, in the 1980s.
(Jennifer Gradidge)

G-21A Goose, c/n B-140, wearing the 1948-vintage Colombian registration C-1530.   *(Air-Britain photo)*

APPENDIX 4: REGISTRATION – C/N CROSS REFERENCE

Note: The left hand column gives the aircraft registration, the right hand column, the construction number.

Construction numbers are as follows:

Goose: 1001 to 1200 and B-1 to B-145

NB: McKinnon conversions will be found under their Grumman c/ns, as built.

Widgeon: 01 to 41 (SCAN) and 1201 to 1476

Mallard: J-1 to J-59

Hence, AN-BEC has c/n 1233 and is a Widgeon.

AN-	**Nicaragua**	**CB-**	**Bolivia**	BKE(2)	J-2	GAM	J-5	HUY	B-55
				BQE	1061	GEB	B-45	HUZ	B-83
BEC	1233	24	1045	BTE	1005	GEC	B-98	HWG	J-19
				BTF	1002	GEU	J-33	IEC	B-32
AP-	**Pakistan**	**CC-**	**Chile**	BVN	1240	GEV	J-34	IFN	1187
				BXR	1059	GPA	J-1	IHI	1315
ADV	1471			BZY	1083	GPJ	1230	IIQ	1265
ADW	1476	CAO	1004	CNR	1136	GSU	1167	IIR	1358
AEA	1474	CTG	B-72	EHD	1441	GYZ	1309	IJC	1447
AFJ	1451	ETA	1446	EHI	1346	HAC	1343	IJO	1458
AMW	2			EIZ	J-5	HAV	J-55	IKH	1324
AOQ	1354	**CF-**	**Canada**	ESZ	B-39	HBC	B-128	IOA	J-39
AUY	B-78	**C-F**		ETJ	B-70	HEN	1311	IOL	B-107
		C-G		EXA	B-50	HFF	1030	IWW	B-120
C-	**Colombia**			FCH	1423	HPA	J-7	JFC	J-19
		BAE	B-76	FEM	B-76	HPD	1315	JFV	1389
99	1045	BCI	B-138	FFG	J-13	HPN	J-59	JIF	B-14
151	B-140	BFS	B-77	FLC	J-20	HPU	J-9	JXX	1235
1530	B-140	BHL	1003	FOD	J-16	HUB	J-22	KKF	1312
(see also HK-)		BKE	1013						

Reg	C/N
KPT	1415
KQZ	J-19
LFQ	14
LGZ	1473
MHG	J-21
MLC	15
MPG	B-77
MSK	B-32
NHG	1298
NIF	B-129
NNH	1431
ODR	28
OIA	B-34
OQA	1195
PNT	1334
PQE	J-55
PVE	1200
QPL	1306
RQI	1145
SBS	1153
SHO	1406
SPA	26
UAZ	1077
UDD	B-111
UMG	B-145
UOT	J-34
UVJ	B-6
VAK	B-142
VFU	B-101
VIA	B-111
WAF	J-54
WCP	B-139
WFM	1441
WHT	1213
WHT(2)	1473
YQC	J-55
C-FAWH	1083
C-FBAE	B-76
C-FBCI	B-138
C-FBCP	1326
C-FBKE	J-2
C-FBXR	1059
C-FEFN	1157
C-FETJ	B-70
C-FHUZ	B-83
C-FIOL	B-107
C-FIWW	B-120
C-FJFV	1389
C-FJXX	1235
C-FKPT	1415
C-FMHG	J-21
C-FNIF	B-129
C-FNOX	1414
C-FPCK	1187
C-FUAZ	1077
C-FUMG	B-145
C-FUOT	J-34
C-FUVJ	B-6
C-FVFU	B-101
C-FWAF	J-54
C-FWCP	B-139
C-GBQN	J-54
C-GDAO	1153
C-GDDJ	1184
C-GEFE	J-19
C-GENT	J-54
C-GGMZ	J-54
C-GHAV	1045
C-GHDD	J-23
C-GHLA	J-10

Reg	C/N
C-GHUM	J-26
C-GIGK	B-52
C-GIRL	J-53
C-GOOS	B-35
C-GPCD	B-76
C-GPIA	B-24
C-GRCZ	B-49
C-GRZI	J-13
C-GTTL	1381
C-GVGQ	1370
C-GWJA	1299
C-GYVG	B-117

CR-C Cape Verde Islands

CAF	1241
CAG	1242
CAI	1297

CR-L Angola

LCP	1297

CS- Portugal

AHE	1241
AHF	1096
AHG	1242

CU- Cuba

N-346	1439

CX- Uruguay

BDG	1342

C6- Bahamas

BDW	J-5

(see also VP-B-)

DQ- Fiji

AYL	1164
FDQ	1145

(see also VQ-F)

EC- Spain

AJU	1402

EI- Eire

ALE	19

F- France

BDAE	1297
BENK	1297
BFAA	?

Reg	C/N
BFHB	2
BFHC	3
BFHD	4
BFHE	5
BFHF	6
BFHG	7
BFHH	8
BGTD	19
WFDM	01
WFHA	1
WFHB	2
WFHC	3

F-O French Overseas Colonies

OAGX	1391
OAII	J-29
OALL	38
OALM	39
OALN	40
OARB	36
OBYU	1152

G- Gt Britain

AFCH	1009
AFKJ	1049
ALLJ	J-41
ARIX	19
ASCS	J-55
ASXG	1083
BMGS	B-63
BTKJ	1317
DUCK	1218

HC- Ecuador

AAM	1048
SBA	1048
SBB	1005
SBL	1106
SBT	B-34
SBV	1018
SBX	1141
SBY	B-34

HH- Haiti

RLA	J-21

HK- Colombia

1530E	B-140
2058	1084
2058-P	1084
2059	1019

(see also C-)

HP- Panama

383	J-5
585	1277
1035	J-54

HS- Thailand

TOM	1145
TPA	J-54
TPB	J-5

JA- Japan

5057	J-56
5063	1153
5067	J-40
5081	1430
5090	J-6
5106	J-38
5117	J-52

JZ- Netherlands New Guinea

POA	J-13
POB	J-13
POC	J-37

LN- Norway

HAL	1332
HAW	1278
SAB	1134

LV- Argentina

APF	1004
FDT	1004
NCG	1432

N- United States of America (inc. NC/NL/ NR/NX)

1AS	1230
1SW	1452
10BR	35
10M	1170
10M(2)	J-18
100BR	J-35
101	B-129
101KB	1375
101LH	1136
101PE	1386
102	B-133
103	B-110
1000	1235
1002	J-18
1004	1370
1007	1170
1019N	B-30
1035L	1375
1042	B-45
1045	1195
1048V	B-46
1055	1231
1057M	1162
1059M	1274
1068M	1293
1069M	1312
1080M	1136
1096M	??
10020	1007
10400	J-29
10610	1281
11CS	1166
111W	1361

Reg	C/N
111W(2)	1380
111W(3)	1420
115WB	4
119AA	1084
1133	B-59
1173V	1345
1173V(2)	1383
1188V	1355
12CS	1086
12YZ	J-2
120PA	J-27
121	B-129
121GL	B-49
121H	1013
121SP	J-4
121SR	1084
122	B-133
123DF	J-9
123W	J-19
128A	1314
1200V	1145
1208	J-44
1234N	1265
1250N	1208
1257A	1184
1270	1270
1294	1011
12681	B-18
13CS	1007
130FB	J-30
132X	1210
133H	1377
135MG	1389
135MR	1389
135PA	J-30
137B	1343
139F	1375
1309	1045
1340V	1228
1376V	1153
13122	1312
14CS	1048
141R	1378
142PA	J-42
143DF	1153
144GW	1324
144JW	1277
144SL	1215
144TA	1354
148M	1220
1423	1423
1471N	1471
150FB	J-51
150M	1147
151M	1266
151SA	30
152M	B-71
159F	B-55
1503V	1020
1504	1147
1507V	B-71
1513V	B-103
1523V	1178
1530H	B-140
1543V	B-41
1583V	1125
1591	1409
1595V	1319

G-21A Goose, c/n B-50, wearing the Canadian registration CF-EXA, when based in Toronto, Ontario, with the British American Oil Company.
(Ken Molson)

G-73 Mallard, c/n J-55, the second of the type to wear UK marks, and registered G-ASCS. The photo was taken in 1963.   *(A Pearcy via MAP)*

G-21A Goose, c/n 1019, wearing contemporary Colombian marks, HK-2059, in November 1977, while operated by Aerolineas La Gaviota.
(Fred J Knight Collection)

160W	1206	244BR	1473	2946	J-9	328(2)	B-46	41974	1405		
168SW	J-5	244GW	1473	2947	J-10	329	B-119	41975	1406		
168TM	J-5	2416X	J-22	2948	J-11	329(2)	B-140	41976	1407		
168W	J-5	2419X	J-26	2949	J-12	3282	1110	41977	1408		
168WA	J-5	2442H	J-13	2950	J-13	3283	B-29	41978	1409		
168WS	J-5			2954	J-14	3284	B-53	41979	1410		
1604	1188	25DF	1306	2956	J-15			41980	1411		
1621A	B-104	254Q	1210	2957	J-17	33Q	1398	41981	1412		
1621A(2)	1019	2578B	B-19	2958	J-18	33S	1054	41982	1413		
1626	J-50	2579B	B-74	2959	J-19	33S(2)	1420	41983	1414		
1627	J-30			2961	J-21	332D	1109	41984	1415		
1628	J-11	26DF	J-10	2962	J-22	333F	1166	41985	1416		
1629	1454	269AK	1415	2964	J-23	338S	1420	41986	1417		
1629(2)	J-51			2965	J-16	339TH	B-8	41987	1418		
1629H	1454	27DF	J-54	2965(2)	J-24	3377	1409	41988	1419		
16484	B-138	27Q	1200	2966	J-26	33178	1045	41989	1420		
16910	1001	273L	1306	2968	J-25			41990	1421		
16911	1002	278L	1306	2969	J-27	3459C	B-78	41991	1422		
16912	1003	2701D	36	2970	J-28			41992	1423		
16913	1004	2720A	1187	2971	J-29	350GW	4	41993	1424		
16914	1005	2721A	B-54	2972	J-32	353CW	1298	41994	1425		
16915	1006	2751A	1184	2973	J-38	354Q	1472	41995	1426		
16916	1007	2752A	B-8	2974	J-36	3500	1175	41996	B-141		
16917	1012	2767A	1021	2975	J-39	3500(2)	J-30				
		2770A	1260	2976	J-42			42DA	J-18		
176W	J-19	2786	1060	2977	J-44	36DF	J-18	42GL	B-52		
176MS	1324	2788	1059	2977(2)	J-34	3692	1083	4221A	1030		
1700	1230			2978	J-45	36808	1130	4262A	1432		
17083	1106	289D	J-58	2979	J-49	36992	1083				
17481	1360	2810D	26	2980	J-50			44CH	1454		
17552	J-7	2811D	27	2981	J-51	37DF	1215	44PB	1389		
		2812D	28	2982	J-52	3767Z	1346	44VW	1408		
18CS	B-59	2813D	29	2983	J-53	37000	1049	440GW	1410		
18GW	35	2814D	30	2984	J-54	37181	1231	444M	1411		
188AC	J-57	2819D	B-14	2986	J-55	37182	1232	444W	1450		
1800	B-59	2844D	B-32	2989	J-58	37183	1233	4444W	1473		
1801	1368	2845D	B-112	2990	J-57	37184	1234	4451	33		
1888T	J-31	2889J	B-70	2992	J-31	37185	1235	4452	34		
1898T	J-31	28369	1149	2993	J-59	37186	1236	4453	31		
		28633	1201	2996	J-40	37187	1237	4492N	1298		
19DF	B-104	28635	1084			37188	1238				
199T	1213	28664	1202	3N	16	37189	1239	45CA	1380		
199TA	1213	28665	1203	3N(2)	1471	37487	B-52	45PV	1380		
199VC	1378	28666	1204	3ND	16			45S	1221		
1920	1234	28667	1206	3TD	16	39FG	1059	453T	B-129		
1944W	1342	28668	1207	30Y	B-71	3903B	B-97	456	1221		
		28669	1208	300S	J-49	3923	10	4575C	B-120		
2GN	1429	28670	1209	302	1294	3924	13				
2GN(2)	35	28671	1210	304K	J-29	3945C	B-49	465CC	J-56		
2PS	1299	28672	1211	3010	J-43	39084	1007	4614N	1358		
20Z	1448	28673	1212	3021	1058			4617N	1364		
200S	B-141	28674	1213	3022	1055	40R	B-19	46497	B-46		
200S	J-27	28675	1214	3042	1062	401SJ	1168				
2003	B-141	28676	1215	3055	1054	402E	1444	47C	1371		
2021A	B-114	28677	1216	3082	1055	403E	1300	47CE	1371		
2038A	1167	28678	1217	3096	B-120	404Q	1388	474JH	1474		
20620	1014	28679	1218	30082	1015	4018	1441	4732V	4		
20643	1017	28680	1219			40011	1368	4762	B-60		
20648	1018	28681	1220	311MC	174			4762C	B-60		
20650	1020	28682	1221	317RA	1430	41DF	J-3	4763C	B-86		
				3103Q	1218	414U	1427	4763V	B-86		
21A	B-129	291VW	1188	3116T	B-104	4120A	35	4772C	B-131		
212ST	1260	294Z	J-10			4121A	36	4773C	B-52		
		298GB	J-58	32BB	1475	4122A	37	4774C	B-93		
22DF	J-35	298GB(2)	J-32	322	B-73	4122A(2)	41				
221AG	B-72	299CN	1299	323	1191	4147A	1293	48011	14		
22932	B-139	2940	J-4	324	B-66	41818	1401	48550	1061		
		2941	J-3	324BC	1260	41824	J-1				
23DF	1133	2943	J-6	325	B-117	41826	1340	4945V	B-32		
2345	1270	2943(2)	J-3	325(2)	B-127	41971	1402	4949N	J-16		
2385	1019	2944	J-7	327	1051	41972	1403	4990N	1303		
23456	1270	2945	J-8	328	1059	41973	1404				

5AS	1230	60080	1357	66550	1354	709	1147	777PV	J-49
5SW	1313	60081	1382	66645	1329	7041	B-142	778	B-56
50G	27	60093	B-39	67DF	1274	70060	1314	779	B-138
50Q	J-19	60379	1378	67DF(2)	1059			7775C	21
501M	B-138	60824	1363	671DF	1274	71Q	1441	7777Q	J-54
501M(2)	1230	60886	1371	672DF	13	710	1129	7777V	B-111
505T	1445			67193	1391	710SA	1129		
5096K	B-129	610SS	J-10	67271	1390	7101	1129	78RJ	1394
		611DS	J-35	67460	1383	7137N	26	78X	32
5110	J-40	611SS	J-11	67586	1346			78Z	1214
5115	J-42	612GW	1324	67646	1325	72PR	1164	780	B-72
5118	J-56	61900	1205	67794	1321	720	B-144	781	B-122
51100	J-40			67805	1347	721	B-24	781S	B-122
51151	J-42	62G	9	67867	1317	722	1294	782	B-47
51181	J-56	62L	3			725	B-28	782S	B-47
51699	1030	62LM	3	68BA	1370	725(2)	1327	789	B-102
		628SS	J-28	68PA	1370	725S	B-28	7811	B-122
525	B-117	6291	1233	68PA(2)	32	727	1021	7821	B-47
52409	1392	62000	1292	68T	1389	728	1319		
52742	1206	62002	1298	685FM	J-49	7211	B-24	79C	1168
52833	1374	62003	1300	686FM	J-50	7251	B-28	79U	1168
52945	1386	62095	1349	688A	1370	7256	1381	7911C	12
		62096	1393	6833W	1231	72179	1059	7912C	16
54GZ	J-54	62121	1145	68102	1351			7913C	25
54VT	1277	62881	1311	68157	1138	73AH	J-26	7913L	15
540GW	3	62899	B-101	68158	1137	730RS	J-50	7916C	32
54096	1230			68174	1173	7306	J-6	7917C	20
		63L	2	68190	B-64	7338	J-38	7918C	11
5508N	1261	63LM	2	68242	1399	7352	J-52	7921C	31
5521A	1162	63MW	1059	68335	1231	7356	J-56	79565	1171
5531A	1360	63T	1389	68361	1227	73556	J-55	79801	1297
5538N	1086	630SS	J-30	68376	1133			79901	B-63
5542A	B-74	632SS	J-32	68377	1126	741	B-97	79905	1301
5548A	1150	638SS	J-38	68395	1359	742	B-22	79905(2)	1270
5555N	1324	63350	1387	68596	20	742PC	B-35	79906	1305
5556N	B-62			68902	1063	743	1260	79906	1327
5560A	1213	64L	B-14			744	1266	79914	B-88
5558	B-62	640	B-123	69T	1312	744(2)	1360		
		641	B-131	6987U	1451	744G	1394	8AS	1315
5623V	B-78	641(2)	B-115	69058	1291	744MC	1311	8H	1445
56198	1397	642	B-137	69067	1338	749	B-6	8HV	1445
		643	B-145	69077	1295	7401	B-6	808W	1452
57LM	4	643H	B-145	69078	1333	7491	1240	8015E	B-65
575L	1463	644	B-130	69082	1226	74044	J-46	8076D	1438
		644M	1424	69168	1299	74107	1167		
58DG	1415	644R	B-130	69208	1107	74110	1168	8229	1187
58LM	14	645DH	1329	69263	1132	74585	1146		
58Q	27	64687	B-35	69264	1195	74587	1148	83781	J-4
586	J-17			69331	1277	74588	1165		
58337	1218	65CC	J-56			74630	1375	848HP	1153
58514	1396	651SS	J-51	7F	B-55	74676	1172		
58521	1296	653SS	J-53	7GZ	1206	74842	J-5	85U	1215
58828	1343	655SS	J-55	70AL	B-125				
58832	1270	65914	1385	70AQ	B-62	750	1341	86590	1028
58837	1337	65956	1381	70DF	1370	750M	1341	86601	1427
58847	1339	65992	1372	70U	1370	75071	1441	86602	1428
58981	1121			700A	1262	75222	1361	86603	1429
		66A	J-52	700BL	1377	75222	1380	86604	1430
6DF	J-54	66QA	1054	701	1373	75333	1182	86605	1431
6DF(2)	B-128	660PA	B-138	701A	B-34			86606	1432
60AL	B-125	663G	1429	701J	1373	76DF	J-11	86607	1433
60JK	1300	6647K	1206	701Q	14	76K	1315	86608	1434
60LM	15	66020	1002	702	1350	76U	J-54	86609	1435
60X	1045	66102	1109	702	1320	76UL	J-54	86610	1436
600ZE	B-100	66197	1310	702A	1048			86611	1437
604SS	J-4	66273	1306	703	B-81	77AQ	B-62	86612	1438
606	1152	66327	1153	703	1281	77BD	1343	86613	1439
606F	1152	66330	1133	703A	1141	77K	1438	86614	1440
609SS	J-9	66338	1170	704	B-142	77V	1408	86615	1441
6086V	B-124	66340	1134	704A	1054	770	1350	86616	1442
		66432	1323	708C	1313	775WA	J-21	86617	1443
		66435	1380	708L	1313	777	1205	86618	1444

G-21A Goose, c/n 1008, wearing registration PK-AES, while operating in the Netherlands East Indies during the early 1940s.
(M Neuvenhelm via HC Kavelaars Collection)

G-44 Widgeon, c/n 1367, was registered as SE-APO, when owned by the Swedish newspaper publisher, Dagens Nyheter, in the early 1950s.
(Fred J Knight Collection)

G-44A Super Widgeon, c/n 1466, was delivered to Australia in 1946. Sold in New Zealand in 1950, it returned to the Australian register, as VH-WET, in July 1987.
(JH Mounce Collection)

86619	1445	926	1083		
86620	1446	9207H	1353		
86621	1447	9208H	1389		
86622	1448	9211H	1307		
86623	1449	9212H	1334		
86624	1450	9218H	1365		
86625	1451	9232H	1282		
86626	1452	9233H	1377		
86627	1453	9236H	1362		
86628	1454	9243H	1130		
86629	1455	9270H	1384		
86630	1456	9293H	1134		
86631	1457	9295H	1134		
86632	1458				
86633	1459	93E	B-139		
86634	1460	93G	1130		
86635	1461	93GS	B-76		
86636	1462	93N	1133		
86637	1463	931RP	B-140		
86638	1464	9309R	1462		
86639	1084	9311R	1340		
86639(2)	1465	9312R	1468		
86640	1160	93010	1153		
86640(2)	1466				
86641	1467	945JD	1429		
86642	1468	94388	1431		
86643	1469	94527	1352		
86644	1470	94750	B-98		
86645	1471				
86646	1472	95J	1359		
86647	1473	95DF	J-19		
86648(2)	1469	9547C	1200		
86618	1474	9591H	1311		
86649	1467	95400	1077		
86649	1475	95406	1143		
86650	1476	95429	1144		
		95431	1164		
87U	B-126	95465	1170		
8777A	1152	95467	1161		
		95468	1140		
88U	B-100	95471	1151		
888DL	1471	95479	1166		
888GG	B-70				
88007	B-128	9600H	1388		
88820	1114	9642A	1059		
88821	1157	9698H	1141		
89T	1312	97	1088		
89U	B-128	9750Z	B-32		
890	36	97102	1356		
9AS	1233	98BS	J-18		
9DA	1364	985R	B-86		
9GW	1458	9863H	1309		
9KL	B-8	9870H	1398		
901JW	1370				
9015R	1235	99	1303		
9074N	B-142	99V	J-51		
9074U	1129	9900H	1328		
9096R	1439	9929H	1369		
90140	1267	9933H	1235		
90727	1334	99341	1265		
90892	B-139	99431	1265		
917	1016				
91039	1268	**OB-**	**Peru**		
91040	1267				
91080	1394	AEX-702	B-111		
		V-702	B-111		
92L	1372				
92MT	B-72	**OE-**	**Austria**		
925	1082	FWS	30		

OH-   Finland

GWA	1367

PI-   Philippines

C277	1436

(see also RP-C)

PK-   Netherlands East Indies

AER	1009
AES	1008
AFR	1080
AFS	1081
AKA	1056
AKA(2)	1107
AKB	1057
AKB(2)	1115
AKD	J-35
AKE	J-41
AKG	J-13
AKH	J-17
AKR	1010
AKU	J-37
BPM	1008
DBP	B-41
LEG	B-119
LEH	B-54
OCM	J-50
RAM	1107
211	J-35
212	J-17

The latter two Mallards were operated by the Indonesian Air & Water Police and were later re-serialled as P-2011 and P-2012 respectively.

PP-   Brazil

DGI	1170
GQV	1290
HPU	1290
XAN	1020

PT-   Brazil

AFO	1168
DGY	1360

P2-   Papua New Guinea

JWB	1164
WET	1466

RP-   Philippines

C864	1164

(see also PI- above)

SE-   Sweden

APO	1367
ARZ	1332

S2-   Bangladesh

AAA	1474
AAB	1451
AAD	B-78
AAU	1451
ACB	1471

TF-   Iceland

ISR	B-134
ISR(2)	B-62
RVA	1020
RVG	1168
RVI	1139
RVJ	1125
RVK	B-71

TG-   Guatemala

BIZ	1311

TI-   Costa Rica

AFU	1277
1050L	1233

TR-   Gabon

LSW	J-52

VH-   Australia

AAY	1008
AAZ	1010
AZO	1466
CRL	B-54
ENY	1145
GWH	B-49
JAW	J-26
KWB	J-13
LAW	J-22
MBA	1164
OAW	J-23
PPE	J-22
PPI	J-23
PPT	J-26
SPL	J-4
TGA	J-13
WET	1466

VO-   Newfoundland

ABU	1230
ACC	J-1

VP-   British
VQ-   Possessions

VP-B   Bahamas

BAA	1007
BAB	B-74
BAC	1448
BAC(2)	1162
BAE	1002
BAH	1162
BAK	1340
BAL	1084
BAM	1109
BAR	1126
BAT	1462
BAX	1468
BBI	1084
BBJ	1162
BBK	B-74

VP-C   Cayman Islands

CLK	J-34

VP-G   British Guiana

GAA	1007
GAC	B-46
GAD	1015
GAU	1170

VP-H   British Honduras

HBW	1408

VP-K   Kenya & Tanganika

KNV	19

VQ-F   Fiji

FAH	1126
FBC	J-13

YV-   Venezuela

P-AEP	B-34
P-APZ	B-59
T-CTX	1293
T-YTT	31
VOD-2	1048

ZK-   New Zealand

AVM	1466
BAY	1362
BGQ	1391
BPX	1432
CDV	J-13
CFA	1439
CHG	1356
DFC	B-104
ENY	1145
ERX	B-62
MCC	1182

5N-   Nigeria

AFS	1381
AMC	1221
AMD	1317
AMG	1317

8R-   Guyana

GAC	B-46

(see also VP-G above)

The former Air Pacific Mallard, VQ-FBC, c/n J-13, running-up the port engine at Suva, Fiji, the day after the Crow team arrived, in October 1971, to make the Mallard airworthy. Note the Fijian registration and the aircraft name "Na Secala".
(Bill Rimer)

APPENDIX 5:
AIRCRAFT NAMES

Name	Reg'n	C/n
Abaco	VP-BAH	1162
Abaco	VP-BAL	1084
Admiral Flagship	N2982	J-52
Aline	C-FVFU	B-101
Andros	VP-BAM	1109
Andros	VP-BAA	1007
Anna M	N69264	1195
Apache III	N2947	J-10
Bahama	VP-BAR	1126
Bahamas Clipper	N2969	J-27
Barracuda	N1621A	B-104
Batta	N2956	J-15
Bimini	VP-BAC	1162
Bimini	VP-BAL	1084
Bimini Bonefish	N2721A	B-54
Bimini Gal	N7338	J-38
Black Mallard	N2965	J-24
Blue Marlin	N702A	1048
Bonefish	N5521A	1162
Calcutta Goose	N79565	1171
Canadian Clipper	N62000	1292
Caribbean Clipper	N93GS	B-76
Catalina Clipper	N95DF	J-19
Celeste	CF-BKE	J-2
Ciel de Polynesie	F-OAII	J-29
Cindi Ann	N68102	1351
City of Bimini	N3010	J-43
City of Miami	N7338	J-38
City of Miami	N7355	J-55
City of Nassau	N123DF	J-9
Cuba Libre	N130FB	J-30
Curaray	HC-SBB	1005
Cutter's Goose	N327	1051
Dolphin	VP-BBJ	1162
Dryad	CF-IOL	B-107
Dryad II	CF-HUZ	B-83
Excalibur VI	N95467	1161
Exuma	VP-BAC	1448
Frankly My Dear	N62000	1292
Frigate Bird	VH-JAW	J-26
Flying Neurmahal	N2969	J-27
Gavina I	EC-AJU	1402
Giant Tuna	N88U	B-100
Gran Ganso	CC-CTG	B-72
Hamel	CF-PNT	1334
Helen	N58847	1339
Huckleberry Duck	N3010	J-43
Island Clipper	N93GS	B-76
Island of Cat Cay	N7306	J-6
Island of Cat Cay	N123DF	J-9

Island Queen	N848HP	1153		Snarfaxi	TF-ISR	B-62
Island Princess	N51151	J-42		Spirit of Akutan	N660PA	B-138
Jemima Puddle Duck	N2990	J-57		Spirit of Alaska	N660PA	B-138
John	N93G	1130		Spirit of Alitak	N641	B-115
Johnathon Livingston	N42DA	J-18		Spirit of Avalon	N36DF	J-18
Katmai Queen	N1208	J-44		Spirit of Miami	N2974	J-36
Key West Clipper	N51151	J-42		Spirit of Pilot Point	N141R	1378
Kingfish	VP-BAM	1109		Spirit of Unalaska	N22932	B-139
Kiska VII	CF-WFM	1441		Splinter	N86637	1463
Kitimat Prince	CF-HPA	J-7		Steve Harvey	N17481	1360
Kitimat Princess	CF-HPU	J-9		Sunset Express	N2969	J-27
Lady Luck	N22DF	J-35		Tecumseh Michigan	N7491	1240
Lesago	NC16916	1007		Te Manu Nui o Nukuhiva	F-OAII	J-29
Liev Eiriksson II	LN-SAB	1134		The Aleutian Goose	N780	B-72
Little Lulu	N37189	1239		The Aleutian Goose	N642	B-137
Lucky Lee Jr	N62L	3		The Blue Tail Fly	N5115	J-42
Magic Carpet	N123W	J-19		The Cat Cayer	N7356	J-56
Magic Mistress	N945JD	1429		The Golden Jennababe	N2966	J-26
Michelle	N324	B-66		The Keys Explorer	N51151	J-42
Milling Around	N2958	J-18		The Paradise Islander	N130FB	J-30
Miss Daily News	N2962	J-22		The Route of the Seagulls	N42DA	J-18
Miss Manana	N3284	B-53		The Spirit of Akutan II	N22932	B-139
Moxos (in lieu of regn)	–	1015		The Stud Duck	44-52997	1208
Na Secala	VQ-FBC	J-13		Thurso Castle	MV993	1049
Orel	NC16915	1006		Tiloup du Lac	N98BS	J-18
Pappy's Choice	N5548A	1150		Tropicbird	N87381	J-4
Patricia	N2964	J-23		Tropic Bird	N611SS	J-11
Petulant Porpoise	32976	1330		Tropic Bird	VH-LAW	J-22
Pride of Bimini	N1208	J-44		Vamp II	N65956	1381
Providencia	HK-2058	1084		Viking II	SE-ARZ	1332
Ricky	N322	B-73		Walker's Cay Clipper	N2954	J-14
Rio Napo	HC-SBA	1048				
Rover	N2961	J-21				
San Andres	HK-2059	1019				
Sea Straight	N23456	1270				
Snafu	ZK-AVM	1466				

Note: C/ns 01 and 1 to 41 are SCAN Widgeon
1001 to 1200 and B-1 to B-145 are Goose
1201 to 1476 are Widgeon
J-1 to J-59 are Mallard

Above: *A close-up of the centre of the fuselage of G-21A Goose, c/n 1153, N848HP, showing the name "Island Queen", carried while owned by Heinz Peier, in the early 1990s.*   *(Jennifer Gradidge)*

Left: *A close-up of G-73 Mallard, c/n J-57, N2990, owned by Daniel G van Clief, is seen here at Paris-LeBourget in June 1961, showing the name "Jemima Puddle Duck".*   *(Jennifer Gradidge)*

APPENDIX 6: PERFORMANCE DATA

	Span ft in	Length ft in	Height ft in	Wing Area sq ft	Gross Weight lbs	Empty Weight lbs
G-21	49 0	38 3	12 2	375	7,500	5,320
G-21A	49 0	38 3	12 2	375	8,000	5,320
G-21B	49 0	38 3	12 2	375		
G-21C (1)	53 0	40 4	14 6		12,499	9,000
G-21C (2)	50 10	39 7	15 0	377.6	12,200	8,200
G-21D	50 10	43 4	14 6	377.6	12,499	9,000
G-21E					10,500	7,000
G-21G	50 10	39 7	15 0	377.6	12,500	6,700
G-44	40 0	31 1	11 5	245	4,500	3,050
G-44A	40 0	31 1	11 5	245	4,525	3,240
SCAN 30A	43 1	31 2	12 4	240	5,170	3,520
McKinnon Super Widgeon	40 0	31 0	11 5	245	5,500	4,425
PACE Gannet	43 1	31 2	12 4	240	5,490	3,800
G-73	66 8	48 4	18 9	444	12,750	8,870
G-73T	66 8	48 4	18 9	444	13,500	8,500
G-73AT	66 8	48 4	18 9	444	13,500	8,500
G-122	46 3	39 0	11 0	284	6,350	4,420

	Engine Rating hp	Max Speed mph	Cruise Speed mph	Climb Rate ft/min	Service Ceiling ft	Normal Range miles
G-21	400	195	175	1,490	24,000	795
G-21A	450	195	175	1,490	24,000	795
G-21B	450				22,000	
G-21C (1)	340	264	210	2,500	28,000	1,500
G-21C (2)	550	236	210	2,000	1,200	
G-21D	579	264	210	1,600	20,000	1,200
G-21E	550	236	175			
G-21G	680	236	175	2,000	20,000	1,600
G-44	200	164	138	1,000	14,600	800
G-44A	200	164	138	1,000	14,600	800
SCAN 30	various					
McKinnon Super Widgeon	260	185	164	1,750	18,000	1,000
PACE Gannet	300	190	167	1,850	18,000	990
G-73	600	215	180	1,200	23,000	1,200
G-73T	620	240	215	1,350	24,500	1,065
G-73AT	680	205	184	1,500	12,000	918
G-122 *	275	197	177	1,570	19,800	640
* = projected						

APPENDIX 7:
AIRCRAFT ENGINES

Goose

The Goose was powered by two Pratt and Whitney Wasp Junior radial engines with a displacement of 985 cubic inches resulting in its military identity of R-985. The engine variants fitted as original equipment were as follows:

Wasp Junior SB	G-21 aircraft 1001-1011
Wasp Junior SB-2	G-21A, G-21B, JRF-2 and JRF-3 aircraft 1012-1020, 1048-1065 and 1076-1099
Wasp Junior SB-3	G-21A aircraft 1175 and 1188
R-985-17	OA-9 aircraft 1022-1047
R-985-48	XJ3F-1 and JRF-1/1A aircraft 1021 and 1066-1075
R-985-50	JRF-4 aircraft 1100-1109
R-985-AN-6	JRF-5 aircraft 1110-1124, 1176-1187, 1189-1200 and B-1 to B-145 (except B-39, B-40, B-45 and B-50 for RCAF*)
R-985-AN-6B	JRF-6B 1125-1174 and JRF-5 B-39, B-40, B-45 and B-50*

*RCAF records show these aircraft (serials 382 to 385) to have R-985-AN-6B engines.

Note: As the R-985 was developed and improved, the Goose was fitted with the AN-12 and AN-14B versions of the engine. The AN-14B features the modification to the crankshaft that allows for the feathering feature of the Hartzell propeller.

Details of aircraft with modified engine installations are given in **Chapter 5**.

Widgeon

The Widgeon was powered by two Fairchild Ranger 6-440-C-5 inline engines. Although this commercial designation encompassed four separate military versions (L-440-2, -3, -5 & -7) all G-44 and G-44A production aircraft, including all US Navy aircraft, were fitted with the 6-440-C-5 model. However at least one US Army Air Force aircraft (c/n 1238, 42-38222) had, by the time of its demise in March 1942, apparently acquired new military-specification L-440-5 engines.

Details of aircraft with modified engine installations are given in **Chapter 5**.

Mallard

The Mallard was powered by two 600hp Pratt & Whitney R-1340-S3H1 Wasp engines.

One aircraft, J-51, had R-1340-S1H1 engines fitted.

Details of aircraft with modified engine installations are given in **Chapter 4**.

Type	Engine Manufacturer	Hp	Engine Model	Military Equivalent
G-21	P&W	400	R-985-SB Wasp Jr	
G-21A	P&W	450	R-985-SB-2 Wasp Jr	R-985-AN6
G-21B	P&W	450	R-985-SB-2 Wasp Jr	
G-21C (1)	Lycoming	340	GSO-480-B2D6	
(2)	P&W / UAC	550	PT6A-20	
G-21D	P&W / UAC	550	PT6A-20	
G-21E	P&W / UAC	550	PT6A-20	
G-21G	P&W / UAC Garrett/AiResearch	680 715	PT6A-27 TPE331-2UA-203D	
OA-9	P&W	450	Wasp Jr	R-985-17
XJ3F-1	P&W	450	Wasp Jr	R-985-48
JRF-1 / 1A	P&W	450	Wasp Jr	R-985-AN6
JRF-2	P&W	450	Wasp Jr	R-985-AN6
JRF-3	P&W	450	Wasp Jr	R-985-AN6
JRF-4	P&W	450	Wasp Jr	R-985-50
JRF-5	P&W	450	Wasp Jr	R-985-AN12
JRF-6B	P&W	450	Wasp Jr	R-985-AN6B
G-44	Ranger	200	6-440C-5	
G-44A	Ranger	200	6-440C-5	
J4F-1/J4F-2	Ranger	200	6-440C-5 *	
SCAN 30A	Salmson	240	8-AS-00	
30G	deHavilland	200	Gipsy Queen II	
30L	Lycoming	260	GO-435-C2	
McKinnon Super Widgeon	Lycoming	260 270	GO-435-C2B or GO-480-B1D	
McDermott Super Widgeon	Continental	240 260	O-470-B IO-470-D	
PACE Gannet	Lycoming	300	R-680E	
G-73	P&W	600	Wasp R-1340-S3H1	
G-73T	P&W / UAC	620	PT6A-27 & later -34	
G-73AT	P&W / UAC	680	PT6A-34	
G-122	Lycoming	275	GO-480-D1A	
* see notes above				

APPENDIX 8: APPROVED TYPE & SUPPLEMENTAL TYPE CERTIFICATES

Goose

Approved Type Certificate (ATC) 654 was issued for the G-21A Goose on 29th September 1937. The McKinnon Goose aircraft were certificated under Approved Type Certificate 4A24 which was approved for the G-21C on 7th November 1958, for the G-21D on 29th June 1960, for the G-21E on 17th July 1969 and for the G-21G on 29th August 1969. McKinnon transferred 4A24 to Viking Air Ltd on 6th June 1984. Viking Air Ltd transferred 4A24 to Aero Planes Inc on 4th September 1998 and TC 4A24

was re-issued to Aero Planes LLC on 5th May 2000. Subsequent modifications and improvements to the aircraft required a Supplementary Type Certificate (STC) to be issued by the FAA. In March 2008, most STCs were acquired by Atlantic Coast Seaplanes LLC (see Antilles Seaplanes in Chapter 9). More recent STCs covering installation of modern avionics are not included here. Details of these may be found on the Federal Aviation Administration website.

STCs for many of the Goose modifications are listed below:

STC No:	Description	Owner
SA1-3	Replacement of wing panel fabric with 025 Aluminium 24ST "Alclad"	
SA1-52	Installation of Hartzell three bladed propellers	
SA1-439	Installation of "Smoke-Jumper" door	
SA2-223	Installation of seats in cabin	
SA2-603	Installation of electric gear retraction mechanism	Dean H Franklin
SA2-760	Installation of 3-place divan in cabin	
SA2-952	Installation of fibreglass covering	Razorback Fabrics Inc
SA4-591	Increase maximum weight capacity of bow compartment	Alaska Coastal Airlines
SA4-677	Installation of picture window	AeroPlanes LLC.
SA4-678	Installation of radar nose 15½" extension kit	AeroPlanes LLC
SA4-680	Installation of wrap-around windshield per McKinnon drawings	McKinnonEnterprises
SA4-681	Installation of dorsal fin	AeroPlanes LLC
SA4-682	Installation of retractable float	Aero Planes LLC
SA4-683	Installation of auxiliary fuel tanks in outboard wing sections	AeroPlanes LLC
SA4-1109	Metalised wings	
SA4-1467	Installation of retractable wing floats	Aero Planes LLC
SA4-1550	Installation of leading-edge landing lights	McKinnon Enterprises
SA4-1551	Installation of electric gear retraction motor	Aero Planes LLC
SA39SO	Installation of cargo door (on c/n 1141 only)	
SA46AL	Installation of Aircraft Rebuilders seats	
SA59WE	Installation of electric fuel boost pump	McKinnon Enterprises
SA96NW	Installation of Sorm Industries horizontal stabiliser forward support fitting	Sorm Industries
SA99GL	Installation of Cleveland main wheels and brakes	Parker Hannifin Corp
SA101WE	Installation of picture window	Aero Planes LLC
SA108WE	Removal of rear cabin bulkhead	McKinnon Enterprises
SA138SW	Installation of retractable float	
SA295AL	Installation of passenger seats	Alaska Airlines Inc.
SA514AL	Installation of new hydraulic system	Fish & Wildlife Service
SA551SW	Modification of Beech C.18 cowl to fit G-21A	Pan Air Corp
SA585WE	Installation of cargo door	McKinnon Enterprises
SA585WE	Installation of ten cabin seats	McKinnon Enterprises
SA696WE	Aluminium skin on elevator control surface	Lancer Engineering
SA1320WE (1)	Re-engine with UAC PT6A-20 engines (G-21C)	Aero Planes LLC
SA1320WE (2)	Re-engine with UAC PT6A-20 engines and fit Alvarez-Calderon flaps, and related changes	Aero Planes LLC
SA1351WE	Replace existing fabric with Ceconite 101 material	Ceconite Inc
SA1589WE	Re-engine with UAC PT6A-20 engines	Aero Planes LLC
SA1751WE	Increase in main fuel tank capacity to 336gallons (G-21C)	Aero Planes LLC
SA02044AK-D	Increase in seating capacity to ten	
SA2809WE	Re-engine with AiResearch TPE331-2UA-203D engines, and increase in fuselage length (G-21G).	McKinnon Enterprises

Widgeon

Approved Type Certificate (ATC) 734 was issued for the G-44 Widgeon on 5th April 1941. The G-44A and French-built SCAN-30 Widgeons were also covered by this certificate.

STCs for many of the Widgeon modifications are listed below. Some of these were acquired by Seaplane Works Inc of Rochester, NY on 4th August 2010. More recent STCs covering installation of modern avionics are not included here. Details of these may be found on the Federal Aviation Administration website.

STC No:	Description	Owner
SA1-283	Installation of Stewart-Warner 940 series heater	Link Aeronautical Corp
SA1-566	Installation of Stewart-Warner 940F-12 or 940F-24 heater in front Compartment between Stations 4 and 5.	Link Aeronautical Corp
SA2-13 (1)	Installation of Continental O-470-B engines with Hartzell HC-82XF-2C propellers	JR McDermott Inc
SA2-13 (2)	Installation of Continental IO-470-D engines with Hartzell HC-A2MVF-2B propellers	JR McDermott Inc
SA2-16	Re-cover aft portion of wing with metal	
SA2-132	Modification of fuel tanks	Aircraft Tank Service
SA2-284	Increase gross weight to 5,400lbs	JR McDermott Inc
SA2-342	Conversion to 24volt electrical system	Allied Instrument Labs
SA2-632	Installation of two-place couch	United Airmotive Inc
SA2-396	Installation of Southwind heater Model 940	
SA2-937	Installation of Continental O-470-B engines	DH Franklin
SA2-1065	Installation of Grimes rotating beacon	Loffland Bros Co
SA4-2	Installation of Lycoming R680-E engines with Hartzell HC-93Z20-2D1 propellers (& inc one-piece windshield)	Gander Aircraft Corp
SA4-53	Hull compartment modification	Gander Aircraft Corp
SA4-60	Installation of up-rated landing gear	Lee Mansdorf & Co
SA4-61	Modification to hull compartment to meet buoyancy requirements of CAR 4a.490(a). 5,500lbs auw land & water.	Lee Mansdorf & Co
SA4-62	Installation of auxilliary wing fuel tanks	Pacific Aircraft Eng
SA4-63	Installation of emergency exit in right-hand side of hull	Charles M Kirk
SA4-64	Installation of Lycoming GO-435-C2B engines with Hartzell HC-A2X20-2 propellers per McKinnon drawings	A.C.E. Aviation Inc
SA4-65	Installation of Lycoming GO-480-B1D engines with Hartzell HC-83X20-2A propellers per McKinnon drawings	A.C.E. Aviation Inc
SA4-67	Installation of picture window in right-hand side of hull per McKinnon drawings	A.C.E. Aviation Inc
SA4-85	Installation of manually-operated landing gear locks	FK Brunton
SA4-111	Installation of Lycoming GO-480-C1D6 engines with Hartzell HC-83X20-2C propellers per Mckinnon-Hickman drawings	A.C.E. Aviation Inc
SA4-284	Elevator trim tab limits 15° up and 25° down	
SA4-287	Change of elevator trim tab setting per drawing MPD-8000	McKinnon Enterprises
SA4-467	Installation of four TECO Model TE-432 seats per McKinnon drawings and Strato Engineering Report No: MC-7. Limited to G-44A, c/n 1415 only. Issued in 1958, and re-issued 29th January 2004 to	A.C.E. Aviation Inc
SA4-621	Installation of water-tight compartments (5,500lbs)	
SA4-755	Re-cover surfaces with Ceconite 101	Cooper Engineering Co
SA4-773	Metal skin aft of rear spar and fuel tank access door	Pacific Aircraft Eng Co
SA4-774	Metal skin on flaps	Pacific Aircraft Eng Co
SA4-849	Installation of dual control yoke	
SA4-850	Installation of 100watt landing light in wing leading edges	
SA4-928	Installation of electrically retractable wing floats	McKinnon Enterprises
SA4-954	Installation of engine and propeller modification	
SA4-958	Increase capacity of each main fuel tank from 54 to 88gallons per McKinnon-Hickman drawings	A.C.E. Aviation Inc
SA4-960	Metallised flaps per Drawing MPD-2070	McKinnon Enterprises
SA4-961	Installation of all-metal entry door	McKinnon Enterprises
SA4-964	Installation of leading edge landing lights	McKinnon Enterprises
SA4-967	Installation of picture window, and emergency exit on right-hand side of fuselage per McKinnon drawing MPD-5042 and Strato Engineering Report No: MC-8	A.C.E. Aviation Inc

SA4-970	Installation of TECO Model TE-432 seats per McKinnon drawings and Strato Engineering Co Report No: MC-7	A.C.E. Aviation Inc
SA4-987	Installation of picture windows in cabin	
SA4-1001	Installation of spray rails	A.C.E. Aviation Inc
SA4-1031	Metalised wing aft of spar (Drawing MPD-2075)	McKinnon Enterprises
SA5-51	Installation of picture windows	Aircraft Rebuilders
SA5-58	Installation of 200lb baggage compartment in bow	
SA6NE	see SA800EA below	
SA21NE	see SA800EA below	
SA39CH	Installation of Amphibian Landing Gear Position Advisory System	Lake & Air Inc
SA61SW	Modify empennage assembly	McDermott
SA81SO	Installation of Continental IO-470-M engines	Gander Aircraft Corp
SA121EA	Installation of Cleveland main wheels and brakes (Parker-Hanifin)	Carl Millard
SA152SO	Installation of Continental IO-470-M engines	Gander Aircraft Corp
SA182BO	Installation of auxiliary fuel tanks on G-44A, c/n 1471 only. Issued 21st November 2003 to	Peter Annis
SA334SW	Installation of Inter-Av Inc Alternator system	
SA366AL	Installation of Cessna-type wing-tips	Aircraft Rebuilders
SA380WE	Specified allowable gross weights after incorporating engine changes under SA4-64, 65 and 111, per McKinnon technical data	A.C.E. Aviation Inc
SA522SW	Installation of Alcor exhaust temperature systems	Alcor Aviation Inc
SA603WE	Installation of large entrance door	Gander Aircraft Corp
SA800EA	Installation of anti-collision strobe light system package also covered by SA6NE and SA21NE	Whelen Engineering Co
SA835SO	Installation of Lycoming GO-480-G2D6 engines with Hartzell HCA3VF-5R reversing propellers	Aeromar Inc
SA00893CH	Install McCauley 3-bladed 3AF32C528 props	
SA1008WE	Re-cover elevators, ailerons & rudder per Stits Polyfibre Manual	
SA1103WE	Installation of Stewart Warner cabin heater per McKinnon drawings. Limited to G-44A, c/n 1427 only. Issued on 8th November 1965 and re-issued 10th May 2004 to	A.C.E. Aviation Inc
SA1351WE	Re-cover elevators, ailerons & rudder with Ceconite 101	Ceconite Inc
SA1904WE	Installation of Vibration Insulation Products engine mount	Vibration Insulation Products Corp
SA01933LA	Installation of Garmin Model 400W/500W series GPS-WAAS Navigation System.	Garmin AT Inc
SA02869CH	Installation of Lycoming GO-480-B1-D engines and associated changes to N701J, c/n 1373	B van Wagnen
SA4503NM	Recover surfaces with Ceconite 101	
SA4774NM	Re-engine with one Avco-Lycoming TIO-540-J2BD and one LTIO-540-J2BD engine, with corresponding Hartzell HC-C3YR-2UF and HC-C3YR-2LUF propellers, per McKinnon-Hickman drawings	A.C.E. Aviation Inc
SE552GL	Installation of Shadin fuel flow management system	

Mallard

Approved Type Certificate 783 was issued for the G-73 Mallard on 8th September 1946.

STCs for Mallard improvements are listed below.

More recent STCs covering installation of modern avionics are not included here. Details of these may be found on the Federal Aviation Administration website.

STC No:	Description	Owner
SA3-194	Sonotone sintered-plate alkaline NiCad battery installation	G W Sherwood
SA3-232	Sonotone CA6 or CA7 battery installation	G W Sherwood
SA1351WE	Replace existing fabric with Ceconite 101 material	Ceconite Inc
SA165AT	Thirteen-passenger interior arrangement	Hill Air Co
SA635SO	Reduction in max take-off weight from 12,750 to 12,500lbs	Dean H Franklin
SA651GL	Installation of Cleveland wheel and brake conversion kit	
SA2323WE	Installation of P&W PT6A-27 engines with Hartzell HC-83TN-3DY propellers	Frakes Aviation
SA4410SW	Installation of 17 passenger seats, emergency exit and floor modification	Frakes Aviation

APPENDIX 9:
GRUMMAN DESIGN NUMBERS

The Grumman Aircraft Engineering Corporation allocated sequential numbers to their aircraft projects. Those allocated to twin-engined amphibian projects are listed below. It should be noted, however, that only when a design was adopted for production was the prefix 'G-' added. For example, design number 3, the proposed Coast Guard aircraft was not built, and therefore it remained as Design No.3, and there was no G-3.

No.	Project
3	Proposed twin-engined amphibian for US Coast Guard
G-21	Goose
G-26	XJ3F-1 c/n 1021
27	Proposed twin-engined two-seat amphibian for US Navy
G-31	OA-9
G-38	JRF-1 / -1A / -4 / -5 / -6
G-39	JRF-2 / -3
G-44	Widgeon
47	Proposed patrol version of JRF
48	Proposed patrol amphibian (twin-engined)
G-73	Mallard
74	Proposed development of Widgeon
108	Amphibian study for US Air Force (twin-engined?)
122	Commercial twin-engined amphibian study

Design 122

The Design 122 was for an improved version of the Widgeon, as shown in the drawings on page 437. The dimensions and projected performance figures are given below:

Length overall	39' 0"
Height overall	11' 0"
Wing span	46' 3"
Wing area	284 sq ft
Tail span	15' 0"
Take-Off Gross Weight	6,350lbs
Empty weight	4,420lbs
Useful load	1,931lbs (including pilot, 4 passengers, 200lbs baggage, fuel, oil and first aid kit)
Engines	2 x 275hp Lycoming GO-480-D1A driving 88" Hartzell constant speed, full feathering, 3-bladed metal propellers.
Cruising speed	177mph at 60% power
Maximum speed	197mph at sea level
Landing speed	65mph at Take-Off Gross Weight

Above: *An early OA-9 Goose of the United States Army Air Corps. The stencil with the designation and serial number can just be made out half-way down the hull underneath the leading edge of the port side cockpit window, but unfortunately cannot be enciphered in this case.*

(Grumman via DM Hannah Collection)

Left: *Further illustrating the problems involved in identifying early Grumman military aircraft is this photo of another OA-9 Goose of the United States Army Air Corps. The stencil with the data on the aircraft is carried only on the port side of the aircraft. On this photo, however, we have the tail-fin markings "10 9-AB" to help. "9-AB" shows that the aircraft was operated by the 9th Air Base group at Moffett Field, California, while the "10" denotes the individual aircraft – in this case the 10th – of the Group. Research suggests that this aircraft is probably serial number 38-566 (c/n 1032) and the photo dates from December 1941.*

(Negative no.A.4407 via Fred J Knight Collection)

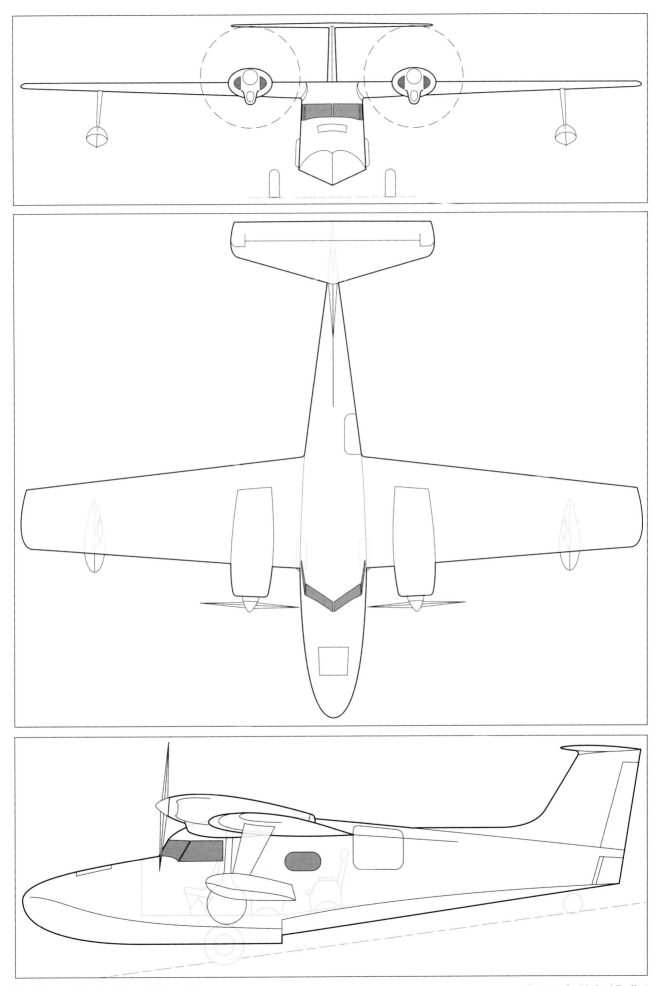

The Grumman Design 122 amphibian study. (Drawing by Michael Zoeller)

APPENDIX 10: BIBLIOGRAPHY

Doublet, Olivier & Morisseau, Jean-Francois	*Les Hydroavions de Port Neuf*	Paroles de Rochelais 2002
Francillion, René J	*Grumman Aircraft Since 1929*	Putnam/Conway Maritime Press 1989
Ginter, Steve	*Grumman Goose (Naval Fighters #63)*	Steve Ginter 2004
de Goutiere, Justin	*The Pathless Way*	J J Douglas Ltd 1972
Hotson, Fred/Rodina, Matt Jr	*The Grumman Mallard*	Robin Brass Studio Inc 2006
Janes All the World's Aircraft – various years		
Johnston, David L	*The Knights of Avalon*	Horizon Line Press 2004
Kurt, Franklin T	*Water Flying*	Macmillan 1974
Ladd, Capt Fred with Annabell, Ross	*A Shower of Spray & We're Away*	A H & A W Reed 1971
Larkins, William T	*USMC Aircraft 1914-59*	
Larkins, William T	*USN Aircraft 1921-41*	
Llewellyn, W H	*Pigs & Wings & Other Things*	W H Llewellyn 1989
Mayborn, Mitch, et al	*The Grumman Guidebook Vol.I*	Flying Enterprise Publications 1976
Nairn, Don	*Gold Wings & Webbed Feet*	Craig Printing Co Ltd 1996
Scanlan, Hugh	*Winged Shell*	Alison Hodge 1987
Sherman, Faith	*Goodbye Goose*	Faith Sherman 1981
Szura, Arue	*Folded Wings*	Pictorial Histories Publishing Co 1989
Thruelson, Richard	*The Grumman Story*	Praeger Publishers Inc 1976

The following publications have also proved invaluable over the years:

AAHS Journal,	Airways,	BARG,	Flight International,	Shell Aviation News,
Air Pictorial,	AMCAR,	CAHS Journal,	FlyPast,	SPA Journal,
Air-Britain publications,	Aviation Letter,	Esso Air World,	Propliner,	"Water Flying"

APPENDIX 11: ABBREVIATIONS

AB	Air Base	Cat	Category (military accident)	FAA	Federal Aeronautical
acc	accepted	CEPE	Central Experimental &		Administration/Federal
acft	aircraft		Proving Establishment		Aviation Agency (US use)
AF	AirForce		(RCAF)	F/C	Flying Club
aka	also known as	CFTSD	Canadian Forces Technical	FF	First flight
A/L	Air Line(s)/Airline(s)		Services Detachment	f/l	forced landing
a/o	as of (date of sighting, etc)	Cie	Compagnie	Fld	Field
a/p	Airport	c/n	constructor's number	flt(s)	flight(s)
approx	approximately	Co	Company (or County)	FN	Fleet Number (airlines, etc)
arr	arrived	CofA	Certificate of Airworthiness	F/S	Flying Service(s)
AR&SC	Aircraft Repair &	CofR	Certificate of Registration	ft	foot/feet
	Supply Center (USCG)	Cond	Condemned	GAC	Grumman Aircraft
A/S	Air Service(s)	config	configuration		Corporation
ASH	Air/Surface Model H (radar)	contd	continued	GAEC	Grumman Aircraft
	(Royal Navy)	conv	conversion		Engineering Corporation
asl	above sea level	Corp	Corporation	GAV	Aviation Group (Brazil)
ASR	Air Sea Rescue	cr	crashed	GC	Gliding Club
A/T	Air Transport	c/s	colour scheme	GCA	Ground Controlled Approach
ATC	Air Transport Command	csg	call-sign	gen	general
	(USAF/RCAF)	cvtd	converted (to/as)	GmbH	Gesellschaft mit beschränkter
AUW	All-up weight	dam	damaged		Haftung
Avn	Aviation	dba	doing business as	Govt	Government
A/W	Airways	DBF	Destroyed by fire	Gp	Group
BAFL	Base Aérea de Florianópolis	DBR	Damaged beyond repair	HM	His/Her Majesty('s)
	(Brazil)	Decomm	decommissioned (USCG)	h/o	handed over
BASP	Base Aérea de São Paulo	del	delivered/delivery	hp	horse power
	(Brazil)	dep	departed	HQ	Headquarters
BCATP	British Commonwealth Air	Det	Detachment or detached (to)	HRH	His/Her Royal Highness
	Training Plan (RCAF)	dism	dismantled	hrs	hours
BER	Beyond economical repair	Divn	Division	IFR	Instrument Flight Rules
blt	built	divtd	diverted (to)	ILS	Instrument Landing System
BoS	Bill of sale	E- (+ number)	US Export Certificate	Inc	Incorporated
Bt	bought	ECofA	(i) Experimental Certificate	incl	including
b/u	broken up		of Airworthiness;	Inst	Instructional
C	Centigrade		(ii) Export Certificate of	Intl	International
CADC	Crown Assets Disposal		Airworthiness	IR	Inactive Reserve (RCAF)
	Corporation (RCAF)	exp	expire(d)	i/s	in service
Cand	Candidate (for registration)	F	Fahrenheit	I/T	Inclusive Tour
Canx	Cancelled	FAA	Fleet Air Arm (British use)	Kg(s)	Kilogram(s)

Km(s)	Kilometre(s)	RTP	reduced to produce	SA	South Australia
KU	Composite Unit (RCAF)	rts	returned to service	TAS	Tasmania
kts	knots	RTS	Reduced to spares	VIC	Victoria
LAD	Last activity date	RU	Rescue Unit (RCAF)	WA	Western Australia
lb(s)	pound(s)	SA	Societa Anonima/		
ldg	landing		Sociedad Anonima	**Canadian States/Provinces**	
LG	Landing Ground	s/a	sold abroad		
LLC	Limited Liability Company	SAC	Strategic Air Command	The Canadian states listing shows the current	
lsd	leased		(USAF)	abbreviation (first and previous usages in	
lse	lease	SAMAN	Service d'approvisionnement	brackets).	
lsg	leasing		du materiel de l'Aéronautique		
Ltd	Limited		navale	AB (Alta)	Alberta
Ltda	Limitada	SAR	Search & Rescue	BC	British Columbia
m(s)	metre(s)	sched	scheduled	MB (Man)	Manitoba
MAC	Maritime Air Command	scr	scrapped	NB	New Brunswick
	(RCAF)	SEA	Section d'entretien aéronefs	NL (Nfld)	Newfoundland (& Labrador)
MAC	Military Airlift Command		(technical branch)	NS	Nova Scotia
	(USAF)	shp	shaft horse power	NT (NWT)	Northwest Territories
Mk(s)	Mark(s)	SLS Indochine	Section de liaison et de	NU	Nunavut
ml(s)	mile(s)		servitudes Indochine	ON (Ont)	Ontario
mod	modified	s/n	serial number	PE (PEI)	Prince Edward Island
Mods	Modifications	SOC	Struck off charge (US use)	QC (Que/PQ)	Quebec
MoS	Ministry of Supply	SOS	Struck off strength (RCAF)	SK (Sask)	Saskatchewan
MTOW	Maximum Take-off Weight	SPB	Seaplane base	YK (Yuk)	Yukon Territory
MU	Maintenance Unit	Sqn	Squadron		
NACA	National Advisory Council	SR	Sale reported		
	on Aeronautics	SS	Sold as scrap	**United States States and Territories**	
Natl	National	stbd	starboard		
nav	navigation(al)	Sté	Société	AK	Alaska
nfd	no further details	st.m	statute miles	AL	Alabama
NGHC	Northrop Grumman	sub-lsd	sub-leased	AR	Arkansas
	History Center	SURMAR	Maritime surveillance	AZ	Arizona
NLR	No longer registered		operations in Algeria	CA	California
nm	nautical miles	Svce(s)	Service(s)	CO	Colorado
No.	number	t/a	trading as	CT	Connecticut
nr	near	T&R	Transport & Rescue (RCAF)	DC	District of Columbia
ntu	not taken up	TCDS	Type Certificate Data Sheet	DE	Delaware
		TCofA	Temporary Certificate of	FL	Florida
o/b	on board		Airworthiness	GA	Georgia
o/h	overhaul(ed)	temp	temporarily	HI	Hawaii
o/o	on order	tf(d)	transfer(red) to	IA	Iowa
op	operated (by/as)	TFH	Total flying hours	ID	Idaho
ops	operations		(on sale/transfer, etc)	IL	Illinois
PAMA SP	Parque de Material	T/L	Total loss	IN	Indiana
	Aeronáutica de São Paulo,	t/o	take-off/taking off	KS	Kansas
	originally PASP (Brazil)	TOC	Taken on charge (US use)	KY	Kentucky
pax	passengers	TOS	Taken on strength (RCAF)	LA	Louisiana
p/i	previous identity	Trng	Training	MA	Massachusetts
plc	public limited company	TSU	Technical Services Unit	MD	Maryland
Ptnr(s)	Partner(s)		(RCAF)	ME	Maine
PtoF	Permit to Fly	u/c	undercarriage	MI	Michigan
Pty	Proprietary	UFS	Used for spares	MN	Minnesota
Pvt	Private	UK	United Kingdom	MO	Missouri
PWFU	Permanently withdrawn	unkn	unknown	MS	Mississippi
	from use	unregd	unregistered	MT	Montana
qv	(which) see	US	United States of America	ND	North Dakota
RAF	Royal Air Force	u/s	unserviceable	NE	Nebraska
RCofA	Restricted Certificate of	V	Validation (of foreign CofA)	NH	New Hampshire
	Airworthiness	VFR	Visual Flight Rules	NM	New Mexico
reblt	rebuilt	VIP	Very important person	NJ	New Jersey
recvd	received	WAA	War Assets Administration	NV	Nevada
reclm	reclaimed		(USA)	NY	New York
recond	reconditioned	WAC	War Assets Corporation	OH	Ohio
redel	redelivered		(Canada)	OK	Oklahoma
redes	redesignated	wef	With effect from	OR	Oregon
regd	registered	wfs	Withdrawn from service	PA	Pennsylvania
REMU	Reserve Equipment	wfu	Withdrawn from use	PR	Puerto Rico
	Maintenance Unit (RCAF)	Wg	Wing	RI	Rhode Island
REMS	Reserve Equipment	WHO	Western Hemisphere	SC	South Carolina
	Maintenance Satellite		Operational Zone (RCAF)	SD	South Dakota
	(RCAF)	w/o	written off	TN	Tennessee
repos	repossessed	WR	Workshop Reserve (RCAF)	TX	Texas
res	reserved			UT	Utah
retnd	returned			VA	Virginia
RFC	Reconstruction Finance			VI	Virgin Islands
	Corporation	**Australian States**		VT	Vermont
RMA	Royal Mail Airliner/Aircraft			WA	Washington
RN	Royal Navy	ACT	Australian Capital Territory	WI	Wisconsin
r/o	roll(ed) out	NSW	New South Wales	WV	West Virginia
rs	reserialled	NT	Northern Territory	WY	Wyoming
		QLD	Queensland		

The registration N10M was carried by two Grumman amphibians. On the left the former JRF-6B (c/n 1170), a G-21A Goose owned by McLouth Steel Corporation, was photographed at an unknown location in the early 1950s, while on the right G-73 Mallard c/n J-18 was operated by the same owner from 1956 to 1976 and is seen at another unknown location in 1972. (Goose: William Haines Collection; Mallard: PJ Marson Collection)

G-21A CF-IWW (c/n B-120) of Ontario Central Airlines, photographed at Winnipeg, Manitoba on 25th May 1961. (J McNulty)

G-21G CC-CTG (c/n B-72/1240) appropriately named "Gran Ganso" (Great Goose) taken in 1995. The long dorsal fairing held the control cables to allow an extra fuel tank to be fitted under the cabin floor. (MAP)

The former Paraguayan Navy G-21A (c/n B-53), registered N3284 on its return to the USA in 1969, is seen here in service with Antilles Air Boats in the U S Virgin Islands in the 1970s.   *(Stephen Piercey Collection)*

The Laurentian Air Services Ltd Goose CF-BXR (c/n 1059) in one of the colour-schemes carried. In this scheme the airline titling is carried on the cheat-line in both English and French – Services Aériens Laurentien Limitée – in addition to the attractive "LAS" logo on the fin.   *(Air-Britain)*

Goose G-21A (c/n B-59), a former Royal Canadian Air Force Goose II, spent ten years in Venezuela as YV-P-APZ with the Orinoco Mining Company. The photo was taken somewhere in Bolivar State in the late 1950s.   *(via Eric Bittner)*

Two of the colour-schemes carried by Bahamas Airways' G-21A Goose VP-BAH (c/n 1162). The earlier scheme on the left was probably mainly dark blue, whereas the later scheme on the right was predominantly white. The earlier scheme dates from the late 1940s, while the later scheme dates from the early 1950s.   *(both DM Hannah Collection)*

Reeve Aleutian's G-21A Goose N1513V (c/n B-103) served the airline from 1957 until 1970 and was photographed at Anchorage on 25th September 1968.
(JP Stewart)

The former US Coast Guard JRF-5 N725 (c/n B-28) was also photographed at Anchorage on 25th September 1968 and judging by its all silver scheme (except for the former Coast Guard band round the rear fuselage) it would appear not to have been used by the Alaska Fish & Game Department. Officially it had been re-registered as N725S five years previously!
(JP Stewart)

The Lambros Seaplane Base's Ranger-powered G-44 N1340V (c/n 1228) was photographed tied down at Essex County Airport in New Jersey on 15th July 1980. *(R Parmerter via William Haines Collection)*

Grumman demonstrator G-44A NC86639 (c/n 1465) was photographed on a sortie from Bethpage, probably in 1948. Note the Grumman emblem on the fin. *(Harold G Martin)*

Bahamas Airways Limited's G-44A VP-BAC (c/n 1448) was photographed at Nassau on 27th September 1952 and illustrates a variation on the airline's colour-scheme, compared with the photo on page 178. Here, the BOAC influence is marked by the "Speedbird" on both the nose and the fin, with Bahamas Airways' own winged emblem superimposed. *(PR Keating)*

SCAN-30 CF-LFQ (c/n 14) was modified as a PACE Gannet and was photographed in the early 1970s at an unknown location. (PJ Marson Collection)

SCAN-30 N4453 (c/n 31) was also modified as a PACE Gannet and was photographed when owned by James Langley at the US Navy Open House at Moffett Field, California in July 1975.
(C Anderson)

G-44 Widgeon (c/n 1371) in its earlier guise (compared with the photo on page 385). Here, N47C is powered unusually by two Lycoming R680E radial engines, as used in the PACE Gannet conversions of the SCAN-30. The aircraft was photographed at Medford, Oregon on 4th August 1972.
(JP Stewart)

The prototype Grumman G-73 Mallard NC41824 (c/n J-1) photographed from an unusual perspective, probably taken from another Grumman amphibian in late 1946 or early 1947.   *(Harold G Martin)*

Another fine Harold G Martin shot, taken when he was chief photographer for Grumman. The aircraft illustrated is G-73 Mallard N3010 (c/n J-43) prior to delivery to J J Ryan in 1949. The colours are brilliant red and black, outlined in silver.   *(Harold G Martin)*

Another variation on the Chalk's colour-schemes (see pages 191-194) is seen on G-73 Mallard N7306 (c/n J-6) freshly painted, this time with the titles on the rear fuselage. The photo was taken in the early 1970s, prior to the aircraft being named. (PJ Marson Collection)

Formerly operated by Japan Domestic Airways, G-73 Mallard N7352 (c/n J-52) still carries the Japanese cheat-line and the remains of the JDA emblem on the fin in this shot at Long Beach, California in February 1969. (JP Stewart)

G-73 Mallard (c/n J-7) carrying its short-lived US registration N17552. The aircraft was photographed at Opa Locka, Florida on 6th April 1973. (JP Stewart)

*G-73 Mallard N83781 (c/n J-4) of Antilles Air Boats entering the water down the slipway at St Thomas, US Virgin Islands, still on its land undercarriage
The photo was taken in October 1979.* (Stephen Piercey Collection)

Turbo-Mallard VH-JAW (c/n J-26) in the colours of Air Whitsunday, anchored in Sydney harbour, New South Wales, Australia on 21st August 1983.
(NM Parnell via ED Daw)

*Chalk's Turbo-Mallard N2969 (c/n J-27) taxying down the slipway at downtown Miami, Florida with its bigger brother, G-111 Albatross N112FB in the
background. This nostalgic photograph was taken on 23rd February 1983. It is hoped to cover the Albatross in detail in a few years' time.*
(Stephen Piercey)

ADVENTURES WITH SHELL OIL IN ECUADOR!

Taken at the runway at Arajuno on 19th February 1945, the photo shows circa 30 labourers trying to remove Goose HC-AAM (c/n 1048) from the spot near the bush where the aircraft came to a standstill after the pilot allowed the keel of the aircraft to hit the runway in an attempt to apply braking power after the normal wheel brakes failed due to water in the casing after a previous take-off from water.   *(RI Baker via HC Kavelaars Collection)*

After the failure of manpower to shift the Goose HC-AAM (c/n 1048), a truck was used to give additional help in removing the aircraft from the edge of the bush.   *(RI Baker via HC Kavelaars Collection)*

On a later occasion, the same Goose, now registered HC-SBA (c/n 1048) ran onto a mud bank landing on the Rio Napo near Tiputini in 1947. Labourers eventually managed to shift the aircraft by pulling and rocking it. Note the Shell emblem on the nose and the appropriate name "Rio Napo". This aircraft was active until 1982 and is now safely installed in the NASM in Washington, DC.   *(I Swemle via HC Kavelaars Collection)*